QUINLAN'S
ILLUSTRATED
DIRECTORY OF
FILM STARS

DAVID QUINLAN

Hippocrene Books, Inc.
New York

ISBN 0–87052–346–5

Printed in Great Britain

FOREWORD

This is, in every sense, a *new* illustrated directory of film stars. Each of the entries carried over from the first edition of this book has been checked and, where necessary, revised. But, more importantly, the transference of some actors and actresses to our companion volume, *The Illustrated Directory of Film Character Actors*, has created valuable space for the insertion of more than 300 players new to the book.

These have been culled principally from the 1930s and the present day, two eras perhaps under-stocked in our previous edition. With up-and-coming stars of the 1980s, the choice has been particularly difficult. In some cases I have had to take the plunge and hope that popular young faces will not burn themselves out within a few films. In others, apologies to fans of such as Tom Hanks, Tom Cruise, Michael J. Fox, Robert Hays, Amy Irving, Diane Lane, Ralph Macchio and other budding luminaries; they must await a further edition.

At all events, the book undoubtedly now represents a wider spectrum of above-the-title stars from British and American films, both major and minor. The 'continental' list, too, has been expanded; those whose names are likely to be most familiar to English-speaking audiences have been especially borne in mind.

In the biographical details, Academy Award nominations have been added to actual Oscars won. If there are any omissions, I should be most grateful to hear of anyone who has had their Oscar 'nod' left out.

Otherwise, the ground rules are the same, although dates of films continue to be a contentious issue. These are still intended to be those shown as the copyright dates on the credit titles of the film – but even the most reliable sources are on occasions proved fallible, and sometimes the only true guide is a look at the movie itself.

As to the filmographies that follow the biographical details, these should contain all the subject's feature film appearances to the end of 1985, plus all the shorts, TV movies, voice-over narrations, documentaries, guest appearances and films as director that the author could find. The number of title changes from country to country has also been significantly increased. Entries for 1986 films should be regarded as a bonus rather than as part of a complete list. Deaths, however, are complete to 1 June 1986.

In addition to actors who have checked their own filmographies and those thanked in acknowledgements, I should like to doff my cap to all those writers, known and unknown, whose work has been scoured over the past years in search of facts and figures.

Alphabetical order in the entries is again strictly kept by succession of letters; thus the appearance of Del Rio after Delon, but before De Marney. There has been some criticism of the splitting up of 'Mac' and 'Mc' names into two sections, but I have deemed it best not to change horses in midstream on this issue.

I hope that the pages that follow contain good browsing, good research material and good reading!   D.Q.

Addington, 1986

NOTE An asterisk (*) in a filmography designates a 'short film' – that is, one of three reels (about 35 minutes) or less.

ACKNOWLEDGEMENTS

Many readers have written in since the first edition of this book. Their comments, additions and suggestions have all been eagerly digested and will continue to be so. My thanks to Jim Allison, Bill Ayres, Arnold Black, John Brooker, D. P. Brummell, James Cameron-Wilson, Allan Dace, Patrick Doran, Earnest J. Farman, Brother Michael Fava, Alan Frank, Chris Hardstaff, Robert Harvey, David R. Head, Donna Heasley, Mitchel Henderson, R. H. Hersham, Alun L. Jones, F. H. Loxley, John Marven, Gerry McArdle, Steve Moore, P. Moulds, Lionel Perry, M. Ramsden, Seamus Roney, A. R. Taylor, Kenneth Thompson, Chris Watmore, Glan Williams, and Kevin Wilson for information and ideas gladly received. Gratitude also to the staffs of the British Film Institute's information and stills departments for their patient help and to Timothy Auger and all at Batsford for their continuing tolerance and support.

Almost all of the photographs in this book were originally issued to publicize or promote films or TV material made or distributed by the following companies, to whom I gratefully offer acknowledgement: Allied Artists, American-International, Anglo-Amalgamated, Artificial Eye, Associated British-Pathe, ATP, ATV, Avco-Embassy, BIP, Brent-Walker, British and Dominions, British United Artists, Cannon-Classic, Cinerama, Columbia, Walt Disney/Buena Vista/Touchstone Films, Eagle-Lion, Ealing Studios, EMI, Enterprise, Entertainment, Filmakers Associates, First Artists, First National, Gainsborough, Gala, Gaumont/Gaumont-British, Goldwyn, Granada TV, Grand National, Hammer, Hemdale, Lippert, London Films, London Weekend TV, Lorimar, Metro-Goldwyn-Mayer, Miracle, Monogram, New World, Orion, Palace Pictures, Paramount, PRC, The Rank Organization, Rediffusion, Republic, RKO/RKO Radio, Hal Roach, Selznick, 20th Century-Fox, UIP, United Artists, Universal/Universal-International, Virgin Films, Warner Brothers and Yorkshire TV.

BIBLIOGRAPHY

I have used the complete oeuvres, more or less, of the following magazines and periodicals:

Cahiers du Cinéma, Cinéma Français, Ciné Magazine, Cinématograph Française, Ciné Revue, Close Up – Cinema, Ecran, Film, Film Comment, Film Facts, Film in Review, Film Fan Monthly, Film Pictorial, Film Review, Film and Filming, Films Fortnightly, Films in London, Films Illustrated, Film Dope, Film Weekly, Focus on Film, Hollywood Reporter, Kinematograph Weekly/Cinema TV Today/Screen International, Kino, Le Film Français, Monthly Film Bulletin, The Movie, Movie Magazine, Midi-Minuit Fantastique, New York Times, New York Daily News, Picturegoer, Picture Show, Sight and Sound and *Variety*.

These span roughly the years 1912–1986, as do year books. I have examined year books of the following countries: Argentina, Australia, Austria, Canada, Czechoslovakia, Denmark, France, Germany (West Germany from 1946), Great Britain, Hungary, India, Italy, Mexico, Poland, Spain, Sweden, United States of America and Yugoslavia.

Books on individual actors and actresses are far too numerous to list here, but have been consulted wherever possible. The following more general volumes have been consulted on more than one occasion, and any cast lists they have provided studied in detail.

AARONSON, Charles S. (and others, eds). *International Motion Picture Almanac, 1933–1985*. Quigley Publications, dates as given.

ADAMS, Les, and RAINEY, Buck. *Shoot-em-Ups*. Arlington House, 1980.

ARMES, Roy. *A Critical History of British Cinema*. Secker and Warburg, 1978.

BARBOUR, Alan G. *Cliffhanger, a Pictorial History of the Motion Picture Serial*. A & W Publishers/BCW Publishing, 1977.

BAWDEN, Liz-Anne (ed). *The Oxford Companion to Film*. Oxford University Press, 1976.

BAXTER, John. *Hollywood in the Thirties*. Tantivy Press, 1968.

BAXTER, John. *Hollywood in the Sixties*. Tantivy Press, 1972.

BAXTER, John. *The Hollywood Exiles*. MacDonald and Jane's, 1976.

BERMINGHAM, C. O. *Stars of the Screen 1931–34* (four editions). Herbert Joseph, dates as given.

BLUM, Daniel. *A Pictorial History of the Silent Screen*. Spring Books, 1953.

BLUM, Daniel. *A Pictorial History of the Talkies*. Spring Books, 1958. (Revised) Grosset and Dunlap, 1970.

BODEEN, DeWitt. *From Hollywood*. Barnes, 1976.

BODEEN, DeWitt. *More from Hollywood*. Barnes/Tantivy, 1977.

BROWNLOW, Kevin. *The Parade's Gone By*. Alfred A. Knopf, 1968.

BROWNLOW, Kevin. *The War, the West and the Wilderness*. Secker and Warburg, 1978.

BROZ, Jaroslav and FRIDA, Myrtil. *Historie Československeho Filmu* (two vols) 1898–1930. Orbis Books, 1959. 1930–1945, Orbis Books, 1966.

CAMERON, Ian and Elisabeth. *Heavies*. Studio Vista, 1967.

CAMERON, Ian and Elisabeth. *Broads*. Studio Vista, 1969.

CLARENS, Carlos. *Crime Movies*. Secker and Warburg, 1980.

COPYRIGHT ENTRIES, 1912–1960. Washington DC: Copyright Office of the Library of Congress.

CORNEAU, Ernest N. *The Hall of Fame of Western Film Stars*. Christopher Publishing, 1969.

COWIE, Peter, ed. *International Film Guide*, 1948 through 1985. Tantivy Press, dates as given.

DIMMITT, Richard Bertrand. *A Title Guide to the Talkies* (two vols). The Scarecrow Press, 1965.

DIMMITT, Richard Bertrand. *An Actor Guide to the Talkies* (two vols). The Scarecrow Press, 1968.

EISNER, Lotte. *Fritz Lang*. Secker and Warburg. 1976.

EVERSON, William K. *The Bad Guys*. Citadel, 1964.

EYLES, Allen. *The Western*. Barnes/Tantivy, 1975.

FENIN, George N. and EVERSON, William K. *The Western*. Penguin Books, 1962, 1973.

FILMLEXICON *degli autori e delle opera* (six vols). Bianco e Nero, 1958, 1962.

FITZGERALD, Michael V. *Universal Pictures*. Arlington House, 1977.

FRANK, Alan. *The Horror Film Handbook*. B. T. Batsford, 1981.

FRANK, Alan. *The Science Fiction and Fantasy Film Handbook*. B. T. Batsford, 1982.

GIFFORD, Denis. *Catalogue of British Films, 1895–1970*. David and Charles, 1971.

GIFFORD, Denis. *The Illustrated Who's Who in British Films*. B. T. Batsford, 1978.

HALLIWELL, Leslie. *The Filmgoer's Companion* (eight editions). MacGibbon and Kee/Hart-Davis-MacGibbon/Granada Publishing. Dates various, 1965–1984.

HERBERT, Ian (and others, eds). *Who's Who in the Theatre* (17 editions). Pitman Publishing, dates various: 1929–1984.

HIGHAM, Charles, and GREENBERG, Joel. *Hollywood in the Forties*. Tantivy Press, 1968.

HOULE, Michael, and JULIEN, Alain. *Dictionnaire du Cinéma Québécois*. Fides, 1978.

JACKSON, Arthur. *The Book of Musicals*. Mitchell Beazley, 1977.

JEAVONS, Clyde. *A Pictorial History of War Films*. Hamlyn, 1974.

JONES, Ken D., McCLURE, Arthur F. and TWOMEY, Alfred E. *Character People*. Citadel Press, 1976.

KATZ, Ephraim. *The International Film Encyclopedia*. Macmillan, 1980.

KULIK, Karol. *Alexander Korda*. W. H. Allen, 1975.

LAMPARSKI, Richard. *Whatever Became Of . . .?* (nine volumes). Crown Publishing, various dates, 1967 through 1985.

LAMPRECHT, Gerhardt. *Deutsche Stummfilm* (nine volumes). Deutsche Kinemathek, 1967.

LEAB, Daniel J. *From Sambo to Superspade*. Secker and Warburg, 1973.

LOW, Rachael. *The History of the British Film* (seven volumes to date: Vol 1 written with Roger MANVELL). Unwin Brothers/George Allen and Unwin. Dates various, 1948–1985.

MALTIN, Leonard, and others. *The Real Stars* (two volumes). Signet Books, 1969 and 1972.

MALTIN, Leonard and BANN, Richard W. *Our Gang*. Crown Publishing, 1977.

MARILL, Alvin H. *Motion Pictures Made for Television 1964–1979*. BCW Publishing, 1980.

McCLURE, Arthur F. and JONES, Ken D. *Heroes, Heavies and Sagebrush*. Barnes, 1972.

McLELLAND, Doug. *The Golden Age of 'B' Movies*. Charter House, 1978.

MERCER, Jane. *Great Lovers of the Movies*. Hamlyn, 1975.

BIBLIOGRAPHY

MICHAEL, Paul, ed. *Movie Greats*. Garland Books, 1969.

MORELLA, Joe and EPSTEIN, Edward Z. *Rebels*. Citadel Press, 1971.

NOBLE, Peter, ed. *International Film and TV Yearbook*. 1946 through 1985. British and American Film Press/ Holdings Ltd/Screen International. Dates as given.

PALMER, Scott. *A Who's Who of British Film Actors*. The Scarecrow Press, 1981.

PARISH, James Robert. *Actors' Television Credits 1950–1972*. The Scarecrow Press, 1973.

PARISH, James Robert. *Film Actors Guide: Western Europe*. The Scarecrow Press, 1977.

PARISH, James Robert. *Great Western Stars*. Ace Books, 1976.

PARISH, James Robert. *Hollywood Character Actors*. Arlington House, 1978.

PARISH, James Robert. *Hollywood's Great Love Teams*. Arlington House, 1974.

PARISH, James Robert. *The Paramount Pretties*. Castle Books, 1972.

PARISH, James Robert. *The RKO Gals*. Ian Allan, 1974.

PARISH, James Robert, and BOWERS, Ronald L. *The MGM Stock Company*. Ian Allan, 1973.

PARISH, James Robert, and DeCARL, Lennard. *Hollywood Players: the Forties*. Arlington House, 1976.

PARISH, James Robert, and LEONARD, William T. *Hollywood Players – the Thirties*. Arlington House, 1976.

PERRY, George. *Forever Ealing*. Pavilion/Michael Joseph, 1981.

PICKARD, Roy. *The Oscar Movies* (two editions). Muller, 1977 and 1982.

PICKARD, Roy. *A Companion to the Movies*. Muller, 1977.

PICKARD, Roy. *The Hollywood Studios*. Muller, 1978.

PICKARD, Roy. *Who Played Who in the Movies*. Muller, 1979.

PICTURE SHOW *Who's Who on the Screen*. The Amalgamated Press, 1956.

PICTUREGOER *British Film and TV Who's Who*. Published with magazine. Odhams Press, 1953.

PICTUREGOER *Hollywood Who's Who*. Published with magazine. Odhams Press, 1953.

QUINLAN, David. *British Sound Films: The Studio Years 1928– 1959*. B. T. Batsford, 1984.

RAGAN, David. *Who's Who in Hollywood 1900–1976*. Arlington House, 1976.

READE, Eric. *The Australian Screen*. Lansdowne Press/ BCW Publishing, 1975.

RHODE, Eric. *A History of the Cinema*. Penguin, 1976.

ROBINSON, David. *Hollywood in the Twenties*. Tantivy Press, 1968.

ROTHEL, David. *The Singing Cowboys*. Barnes, 1978.

ROUD, Richard, ed. *Cinema: a Critical Dictionary* (two volumes). Secker and Warburg, 1980.

SCHEUER, Steven H. *Movies on TV*. Various editions, 1973– 1982. Bantam Books. Dates as given.

SHIPMAN, David. *The Great Movie Stars: the Golden Years*. Angus and Robertson, 1970, 1979.

SHIPMAN, Davis. *The Great Movie Stars: the International Years*. Angus and Robertson, 1972, 1980.

SILVER, Alain, and WARD, Elizabeth, eds. *Film Noir*. Secker and Warburg, 1980.

SKVORECKY, Josef. *All the Bright Young Men and Women*. Peter Martin Associates, 1971.

SPEED, F. Maurice. *Film Review*. Various editions, 1947–1985. MacDonald and Co/W. H. Allen.

STUART, Ray. *Immortals of the Screen*. Spring Books, 1965.

THOMAS, Tony. *Cads and Cavaliers*. Barnes, 1973.

THOMAS, Tony. *The Films of the Forties*. Citadel Press, 1975.

THOMSON, David. *A Biographical Dictionary of the Cinema*. Secker and Warburg, 1975.

TRUITT, Evelyn Mack. *Who Was Who on Screen* (three editions). R. R. Bowker Co, 1973, 1977 and 1984.

TV Feature Film *Source Book*, 1985 edition. Broadcast Information Bureau, 1985.

TWOMEY, Alfred E., and McCLURE, Arthur F. *The Versatiles*. Barnes, 1969.

VERMILYE, Jerry. *The Great British Films*. Citadel Press, 1978.

WEAVER, John T. *Forty Years of Screen Credits* (two volumes). The Scarecrow Press, 1970.

WEAVER, John T. and JOHNSON, A. Collins. *Twenty Years of Silents*. The Scarecrow Press, 1971.

WILLIAMS, Mark. *Road Movies*. Proteus, 1978.

WILLIS, John. *Screen World* (33 editions, to 1985). Muller.

WINQUIST, Sven G., and JUNGSTEDT, Torsten. *Svenskt Filmskadespelar Lexicon*. Forum, 1973.

WOLF, William. *Landmark Films*. Paddington Press, 1979.

WRIGHT, Basil. *The Long View*. Secker and Warburg, 1974.

ZIEROLD, Norman J. *The Child Stars*. MacDonald, 1965.

ZIEROLD, Norman J. *Sex Goddesses of the Silent Screen*. Regnery, 1973.

Anguish for As. Pier Angeli learns that Richard Attenborough has been sent to Coventry by his workmates in *The Angry Silence* (1960).

Big box-office Bs Lauren Bacall and
Humphrey Bogart contemplate his 'new' face
in 1947's *Dark Passage*.

Cs on top of the world. But Sean Connery
and Michael Caine are destined for disaster
in *The Man Who Would Be King* (1975).

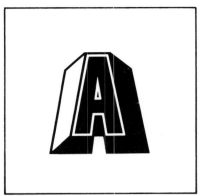

ABBOTT AND COSTELLO
ABBOTT, Bud (top)
(William Abbott) 1895–1974
COSTELLO, Lou
(Louis Cristillo) 1906–1959
Vaudeville comedians whose brash humour and slick cross-talk attracted immense audiences in the forties. Despite great personal friction (Costello demanded, and got, 60% of the take), they stayed together until 1957. Costello died from a heart attack two years later, and a comeback by Abbott with a new partner was not successful. Abbott, a lifetime epileptic, died of cancer after two strokes. Costello was a stunt man on several films of the late twenties, including *Bardelys the Magnificent* (1926), *Taxi Dancer* (1927) and *The Trail of '98* (1928).
1940: *Caribbean Holiday. One Night in the Tropics. Buck Privates (GB: Rookies). In the Navy. 1941: Hold That Ghost. Keep 'Em Flying. *Meet the Stars No. 4. 1942: Ride 'Em Cowboy. Rio Rita. Pardon My Sarong. Who Done It? 1943: It Ain't Hay (GB: Money for Jam). Hit the Ice. 1944: Lost in a Harem. In Society. 1945: Here Come the Co-Eds. The Naughty Nineties. Bud Abbott and Lou Costello in Hollywood. 1946: Little Giant (GB: On the Carpet). The Time of Their Lives. 1947: Buck Privates Come Home (GB: Rookies Come Home). The Wistful Widow of Wagon Gap (GB: The Wistful Widow). 1948: The Noose Hangs High. Abbott and Costello Meet Frankenstein (GB: Abbott and Costello Meet the Ghosts). 1949: Mexican Hayride. Africa Screams. Abbott and Costello Meet the Killer, Boris Karloff. 1950: Abbott and Costello in the* Foreign Legion. 1951: Abbott and Costello Meet the Invisible Man. Comin' Round the Mountain. 1952: Jack and the Beanstalk. Lost in Alaska. 1953: Abbott and Costello Meet Captain Kidd. Abbott and Costello Go to Mars. Abbott and Costello Meet Dr Jekyll and Mr Hyde. 1954: *Screen Snapshots No. 225. 1955: Abbott and Costello Meet the Keystone Kops. Abbott and Costello Meet the Mummy. 1956: Dance with Me, Henry. Costello alone: 1959: The 30 Foot Bride of Candy Rock. Abbott alone: 1946: The Ghost Steps Out. 1950: The Real McCoy.*

ADAMS, Brooke 1949–
Small, dark, chipper American actress, an on-stage performer at six and on TV at 16. Although given some useful-looking leading roles during a rather spasmodic career (she did best in the 1978 version of *Invasion of the Body Snatchers*), she has never quite become a reason for going to see a film and now looks set for a future increasingly on TV.
1965: OK Crackerby (TV). 1970: Shock Waves/Death Corps (GB: Almost Human. Released 1975). 1974: F Scott Fitzgerald and 'The Last of the Belles' (TV). The Great Gatsby. 1975: Murder on Flight 502 (TV). Who is the Black Dahlia? (TV). The Daughters of Joshua Cabe Return (TV). 1976: James Dean: Portrait of a Friend (TV). †Car Wash. 1977: Nero Wolfe (TV). *Minestrone. 1978: Invasion of the Body Snatchers. Days of Heaven. 1979: Cuba. A Man, a Woman and a Bank/A Very Big Withdrawal. 1980: Tell Me a Riddle. 1981: Utilities (released 1983). 1983: Innocents Abroad (TV). The Dead Zone. 1984: Haunted (TV). Special People (TV). Almost You. 1985: Key Exchange.*

† *Scene deleted from final release print*

ADAMS, Jill 1931–
Pretty, glossily groomed second-line British star with large brown eyes and full lips, born in England but raised in New Zealand. She was not quite enough of a pin-up or an actress to establish herself in the public eye in the 1950s, although she did perform serviceably and sparkily as heroine of some B features. Married to newscaster Peter Haigh from 1958 to 1976.
1953: The Case of the Bogus Count. 1954: The Young Lovers (US: Chance Meeting). The Love Match. 1955: One Jump Ahead. The Con-*

stant Husband. Doctor at Sea. Value for Money. One Way Out. Count of Twelve. 1956: Private's Progress. The Green Man. Brothers in Law. 1957: The Scamp. Death Over My Shoulder. 1958: Dust in the Sun. 1959: Carry On Nurse. 1960: Carry On Constable. 1961: Crosstrap. 1963: Doctor in Distress. The Yellow Teddybears. The Comedy Man. 1965: Promise Her Anything.

ADAMS, Julie (Betty May Adams) 1926–
Striking, jut-jawed brunette whose Hollywood career languished in minor westerns until Universal signed her up and changed her name to Julia (the Julie came later). She remained a reliable, faintly aristocratic leading lady (though with warmth to spare) for them for nine years and married another Universal player, Ray Danton (qv). Now best remembered as the girl carried off by the creature from the Black Lagoon.
1949: †Red Hot and Blue. †Hostile Country. †The Dalton Gang. 1950: †Colorado Ranger. †Crooked River. †Marshal of Heldorado. †For Heaven's Sake. †Fast on the Draw (later Sudden Death). †West of the Brazos. ‡Hollywood Story. ‡Bright Victory (GB: Lights Out). 1951: ‡Finders Keepers. ‡The Treasure of Lost Canyon. 1952: ‡Bend of the River (GB: Where the River Bends). ‡Horizons West. ‡The Lawless Breed. 1953: ‡Mississippi Gambler. ‡The Man from the Alamo. ‡Wings of the Hawk. 1954: ‡The Stand at Apache River. Francis Joins the WACs. The Creature from the Black Lagoon. 1955: Six Bridges to Cross. The Looters. One Desire. 1956: The Private War of Major Benson. Away All Boats. 1957: Slaugh-*

ter on 10th Avenue. Four Girls in Town. 1958: Slim Carter. The Dungeon (TV), Tarawa Beachhead. 1959: Gunfight at Dodge City. 1960: Raymie. 1962: The Underwater City. 1965: Tickle Me. 1967: Valley of Mystery. 1971: The Trackers (TV). The Last Movie. 1973: Go Ask Alice (TV). 1974: McQ. 1975: The Killer Inside Me. The Wild McCulloughs. Psychic Killer. 1977: Goodbye, Franklin High (released 1980). 1980: The Fifth Floor.

† As Betty Adams
‡ As Julia Adams

ADAMS, Maud (M. Wikstrum) 1945–
Tall, shapely, tawny-haired Swedish-born international model who attracted some showy big-budget leading roles without quite having the acting talent to match her ambitions. Producers seemed more interested in getting her clothes off, probably the reason she returned to modelling from time to time in between films. Best known for her decorative roles in two James Bond films.
1970: The Christian Licorice Store. The Plastic Dome of Norma Jean/Mahoney's Estate. 1971: U-Turn. 1974. Rollerball. The Man with the Golden Gun. The Girl in Blue. 1975: The Diamond Mercenaries (US: Killer Force). 1977: L'uomo senza pieta (US: The Merciless Man). 1978: Big Bob Johnson and His Fantastic Speed Circus (TV). 1979: Laura – Shades of Summer (released 1982. GB: Laura). The Hostage Tower/Alistair MacLean's The Hostage Tower. 1980: Playing for Time (TV). Tattoo. 1982: Target Eagle. 1983: Octopussy. 1984: Nairobi Affair (TV). 1985: Blacke's Magic (TV). 1986: Hell Hunters.

ADAMS, Nick (Nicholas Adamschock) 1931–1968
Stocky, fair-haired American leading man, often cast as harebrained, easily led or other kinds of tearaway. He enjoyed a good period of popularity from 1959 to 1963 in the TV series The Rebel and Saints and Sinners (as crusading gunfighter and crusading reporter respectively), but never quite made it to the top in the cinema. Ended by making movies in far-flung places and was found dead in 1968 from a drug overdose. Oscar nominee for Twilight of Honor.
1952: Somebody Loves Me. 1955: Mister Roberts. Strange Lady in Town. I Died a Thousand Times. Rebel Without a Cause. Picnic.

1956: The Last Wagon. Strange Adventure. Our Miss Brooks. 1957: Sing, Boy, Sing. Fury at Showdown. The Troublemakers (TV). 1958: The FBI Story. No Time for Sergeants. Teacher's Pet. 1959: Pillow Talk. 1962: The Interns. Hell is for Heroes! 1963: The Young Lovers. Twilight of Honor (GB: The Charge is Murder). The Hook. A Girl Named Tamiko. 1965: Young Dillinger. Frankenstein Conquers the World. Kaiju daisenso (US: Monster Zero). 1966: Die, Monster, Die (GB: Monster of Terror). Don't Worry, We'll Think of a Title. Willie and the Yank (TV. GB: cinemas, as Mosby's Marauders). 1967: Frankenstein Meets the Giant Devil Fish. Fever Heat. Zettai zetsumei (US: The Killing Bottle). 1968: Mission Mars.

ADAMS, Tom 1938–
Tall, dark, saturnine British leading man who starred in a series of James Bond spoofs in the 1960s. The budgets of the films were too low for any large-scale cinema success, and Adams's personality perhaps too inflexible for starring roles in bigger movies. Since 1972 he has played 'second lead' roles in TV dramas, soap operas and serials and cropped up as an enthusiastic 'salesman' in commercials.
1963: The Great Escape. This is My Street. 1964: *The Peaches. 1965: Licensed to Kill (US: The Second Best Secret Agent in the Whole Wide World). 1966: Where the Bullets Fly. The Fighting Prince of Donegal. 1967: Somebody's Stolen Our Russian Spy. Fathom. 1968: Subterfuge. Journey into Midnight (TV). 1970: The House That Dripped Blood. 1971: Von Richthofen and Brown (GB: The

Red Baron). 1972: Madigan: the Lisbon Beat (TV). The Fast Kill.

ADDAMS, Dawn 1930–1985
British-born glamour girl who appeared in some Hollywood films of the 1950s. She was screen-tested for National Velvet in 1944, but lost to Elizabeth Taylor, with whom she shared dark hair, dark eyes and a stormy and well-publicized love life which settled down when she married her second husband, a retired businessman. Lived in Malta in the 1970s, in America from 1982. Died from cancer.
1951: Night into Morning. The Unknown Man. 1952: The Hour of 13. Singin' in the Rain. Plymouth Adventure. 1953: The Robe. Young Bess. The Moon is Blue (and German version). Riders to the Stars. Secrets d'alcove (GB and US: The Bed). 1954: The Viscount of Bragelonne (US: Last of the Musketeers). Return to Treasure Island. Khyber Patrol. Mizar (GB: Frogman Spy). 1956: Rommel's Treasure. London Calling North Pole/House of Intrigue. 1957: Four in a Thunderjet. A King in New York. 1958: The Silent Enemy. Il mistero della Pensione Edelweiss. Sursis pour les vivants. The Volga Boatman (GB: The Boatmen. US: Prisoners of the Volga). L'île au bout du monde (GB: Temptation Island). 1959: Secret Professional. Voulez-vous danser avec moi? (GB and US: Come Dance With Me). The Treasure of San Teresa (US: Long Distance). The Scarlet Baroness. Geheimaktion schwartze Kapelle (US: Black Chapel). 1960: Die zornigen jungen Männer. The 1,000 Eyes of Dr Mabuse. The Two Faces of Dr Jekyll (US: House of Fright). 1961: Follow That Man. Les menteurs (GB: House of Sin). 1962: L'education sentimentale (GB: Lessons in Love). Come Fly with Me. The £20,000 Kiss. 1963: The Black Tulip. 1964: Ballad in Blue (US: Blues for Lovers). 1966: Where the Bullets Fly. 1969: Zeta One. The Vampire Lovers. Sappho/Sapho. 1973: Vault of Horror.

ADJANI, Isabelle 1955–
Wide-eyed, dark-haired, brittle French actress, at her bewitching best in shallow or sombre roles. Born in Paris to an Algerian father and German mother, she made her film debut during her school holidays and came into demand for international assignments after her Academy Award nomination for The

Story of Adèle H. She has continued to show up best, however, in home-grown movie produce.

1969: Le petit bougnat. 1971: Faustine et le bel été (GB: Faustine. US: Growing Up/Faustine and the Beautiful Summer). 1974: La gifle (GB and US: The Slap). 1975: The Story of Adèle H. 1976: The Tenant. Barocco. Violette et François. 1978: The Driver (GB: Driver). The Brontë Sisters. 1979: Nosferatu: Phantom der Nacht (GB and US: Nosferatu the Vampyre). 1980: Possession. Clara et les chic types. 1981: Quartet. L'année prochaine si tout va bien. 1982: Tout feu, tout flamme (US: All Fired Up). Antonietta. 1983: L'été meurtrier (GB and US: One Deadly Summer). Mortelle rondonée (US: Deadly Circuit). 1985: Subway. Camille Claudel. 1986: Maladie d'amour. Ishtar.

ADORÉE, Renée (Jeanne de la Fonte) 1898–1933

Tiny, brunette French star of Hollywood silent films. Born in a circus tent, she became a Folies Bergères dancer. Found her way (via Australia, and a film debut) to Hollywood by 1920. Big, expressive eyes contributed to her success in silents but ill-health and the advent of the talkies combined to wreck her career. Died from tuberculosis.

1918: £500 Reward. 1920: The Strongest. 1921: Made in Heaven: 1922: Honor First. Daydreams. The Law Bringers. Monte Cristo. A Self-Made Man. West of Chicago. Mixed Faces. 1923: The Eternal Struggle. Six Fifty. 1924: Women Who Give Up. A Man's Mate. The Bandolero. 1925: Exchange of Wives.

Excuse Me. Man and Maid. The Big Parade. Parisian Nights. 1926: The Black Bird. Blarney. La Bohème. The Exquisite Sinner. Tin Gods. 1927: Back to God's Country. Heaven on Earth. Flaming Forest. Mr Wu. On Ze Boulevard. The Show. 1928: A Certain Young Man. The Cossacks. Forbidden Hours. The Mating Call. The Michigan Kid. The Spieler (GB: The Spellbinder). 1929: The Pagan. Hollywood Revue of 1929. Tide of Empire. 1930: Redemption. Call of the Flesh. Singer of Seville.

AGAR, John 1921–

Tall, sturdy, fair-haired ex-US Army sergeant who drifted into films after marrying Shirley Temple (qv) in 1945 (they divorced in 1949). Lacked the mobility for major films, but sustained his leading man status in co-feature westerns and horrors until the early 1960s. Now plays bit parts and describes himself as 'poor but happy'.

1948: Fort Apache. 1949: Adventure in Baltimore (GB: Bachelor Bait). I Married a Communist (GB: The Woman on Pier 13). Sands of Iwo Jima. She Wore a Yellow Ribbon. 1950: Breakthrough. 1951: Along the Great Divide. The Magic Carpet. 1952: Woman of the North Country. 1953: Man of Conflict. 1954: The Rocket Man. The Golden Mistress. Bait. Shield for Murder. 1955: Revenge of the Creature. The Lonesome Trail. Tarantula. 1956: The Flesh and the Spur. Star in the Dust. Hold Back Tomorrow. The Mole People. 1957: Joe Butterfly. Ride a Violent Mile. The Brain from Planet Arous. Daughter of Dr Jekyll. Cavalry Command (released 1965). 1958: Attack of the Puppet People (GB: Six Inches Tall). Frontier Gun. Jet Attack (GB: Through Hell to Glory). 1959: Invisible Invaders. 1960: Raymie. 1961: Lisette. The Hand of Death. Journey to the 7th Planet. 1962: The Young and the Brave. 1963: Of Love and Desire. Law of the Lawless. 1964: Young Fury. 1965: Stage to Thunder Rock. Johnny Reno. Women of the Prehistoric Planet. 1966: The St Valentine's Day Massacre. Waco. Zontar, the Thing from Venus. 1967: The Curse of the Swamp Creature. 1968: Hell Raisers. 1969: The Undefeated. 1971: Chisum. 1972: Big Jake. 1976: King Kong. 1977: How's Your Love Life?

AGUTTER, Jenny 1952–

Tall, demure-looking, blonde British leading lady, in show business from childhood, from

the same ballet school (and mould) as Hayley Mills and Pamela Franklin (both qv). Film career faltered after some big hits in the early 1970s when she projected innocence more convincingly than most, but accelerated again following her British Academy Award for *Equus*. But she seemed to tire of playing roles that required her to be put-on and take her clothes off, and has spent most of the 1980s on stage and TV.

*1964: East of Sudan. 1965: Ballerina. 1966: A Man Could Get Killed. 1968: The Gates of Paradise. Star! 1969: I Start Counting. 1970: The Railway Children. Walkabout. 1971: The Snow Goose (TV). 1972: A War of Children (TV). 1976: Logan's Run. The Eagle Has Landed. The Man in the Iron Mask (TV). 1977: Equus. 1978: China 9, Liberty 37/Gunfighters (US: Clayton and Catherine). Dominique. The Riddle of the Sands. 1979: Mayflower: the Pilgrims' Adventure (TV). Sweet William. 1981: The Survivor. Amy. An American Werewolf in London. *Late Flowering Love. 1984: Secret Places.*

AHERNE, Brian 1902–1986

Matinée idol of the British stage in the twenties. He went to Hollywood in 1933, where his Englishness and lack of dynamism confined him to an interesting variety of lesser roles. A good foil for some powerful American leading ladies of the time. Married to Joan Fontaine, 1939–43. Oscar nomination for *Juarez*. Died from heart failure.

1924: The Eleventh Commandment. 1925: King of the Castle. The Squire of Long Hadley. 1926: Safety First. 1927: A Woman Redeemed. 1928: Shooting Stars. 1929: Underground.

1930: The 'W' Plan. 1931: Madame Guillotine. 1933: I Was a Spy. Song of Songs. The Constant Nymph. 1934: What Every Woman Knows. The Fountain. 1935: Sylvia Scarlett. I Live My Life. 1936: Beloved Enemy. 1937: The Great Garrick. 1938: Merrily We Live. 1939: Captain Fury. Juarez. 1940: The Lady in Question. Hired Wife. My Son, My Son. 1941: The Man Who Lost Himself. Skylark. Smilin' Through. 1942: My Sister Eileen. A Night to Remember. 1943: Forever and a Day. First Comes Courage. What a Woman! (GB: The Beautiful Cheat). 1946: The Locket. 1948: Smart Woman. Angel on the Amazon (GB: Drums Along the Amazon). 1952: I Confess. 1953: Titanic. 1954: Prince Valiant. A Bullet is Waiting. 1956: The Swan. 1959: The Best of Everything. 1961: Susan Slade. 1963: Lancelot and Guinevere. The Waltz King. 1965: The Cavern. 1967: Rosie!

AIMÉE, Anouk (Françoise Sorya) 1932–
Elegant brunette French actress who made her first films billed simply as Anouk. An elfin leading lady of both British and French films while still in her teens, she became a star all over again in her thirties with the international hit *Un homme et une femme*, which won her an Oscar nomination. Married (fourth of five) to Albert Finney from 1970 to 1978.
*1947: †La maison sous la mer. †La fleur de l'âge. 1948: †Les amants de Verone. 1949: †Golden Salamander. 1951: †Le rideau cramoisi/The Crimson Curtain. †*Conquêtes du froid. †Noche de tormenta. 1952: †La bergère et le ramoneur (voice only). †Nuit d'orage. †The Man Who Watched Trains Go By (US: Paris Express). 1954: Les mauvaises rencontres. Nina. †Forever My Heart. 1955: †Contraband Spain. Ich suche Dich. Stresemann. 1956: Pot bouille (GB: The House of Lovers). 1957: Montparnasse 19 (GB: The Lovers of Montparnasse. Modigliani of Montparnasse). Tous peuvent me tuer (GB: Anyone Can Kill Me). 1958: Carve Her Name with Pride. La tête contre les murs (GB: The Keepers). The Journey. 1959: Las dragueurs (GB: The Young Have No Morals. US: The Chasers). 1960: Le farçeur. Le dolce vita. Le temps d'un reflet. 1961: Lola. Quai notre Dame. L'imprévisto. Il giudizio universale (US: The Last Judgment). 1962: Eight and a Half/Otto e mezzo. (The Last Days of) Sodom and Gomorrah. Les*

grands chemins (GB and US: Of Flesh and Blood). 1963: Il successo. Il terrorista. Liola. I giorno più corto (US: The Shortest Day). 1964: Le voci bianche (GB: The Undercover Rogue. US: White Voices). 1965: La fuga. Il morbidone. 1966: Lo scandalo. Le stagioni del nostro amore (GB: A Very Handy Man). Un homme et une femme (GB and US: A Man and a Woman). 1968: Un soir, un train. The Appointment. 1969: Model Shop. Justine. 1976: The Mandarins. 1977: So c'était à refaire (GB: Second Chance). 1978: Non premier amour. Les petits matins. 1980: Salto nel vuoto (US: A Leap in the Dark). 1981: Tragedia di un uomo ridicolo. 1982: Qu'est-ce qui fait courir David? 1983: Il generale dell'armata morta. 1984: Vive la vie. Success is the Best Revenge. 1985: Flagrant Desire. 1986: Un homme et une femme: 20 ans déjà.

† As Anouk

ALBERGHETTI, Anna Maria 1936–
Dark-haired, Italian-born operatic singer with a sweet, wistful image, who made a big hit in 1953 in *The Stars Are Singing*. Suitable subsequent roles, however, in a Hollywood no longer orientated to musicals, proved difficult to find and she swiftly drifted away from the cinema, appearing on Broadway and in television until the late 1960s.
1950: The Medium. 1951: Here Comes the Groom. 1953: The Stars Are Singing. 1955: The Last Command. 1957: 10,000 Bedrooms. Duel at Apache Wells. 1960: Cinderfella.

ALBERT, Eddie (E. A. Heimberger) 1908–
Big, gruff, friendly American leading man who started in show business as a radio singer. He was mainly seen as hero's friend or comedy

relief until the 1950s but after his Oscar nomination for *Roman Holiday* he began to attempt a wider range of roles. Continuing to offer solid, thoughtful performances, even in forgettable films, he was further nominated for an Oscar in *The Heartbreak Kid*. The actor Edward Albert is his son.
1938: Brother Rat. 1939: On Your Toes. Four Wives. 1940: Brother Rat and a Baby (GB: Baby Be Good). An Angel from Texas. My Love Came Back. A Dispatch from Reuter's (GB: This Man Reuter). 1941: Four Mothers. The Wagons Roll at Night. Thieves Fall Out. Out of the Fog. The Great Mr Nobody. 1942: Treat 'Em Rough. Eagle Squadron. 1943: Ladies' Day. Lady Bodyguard. Bombardier. 1945: Strange Voyage. 1946: Rendezvous with Annie. The Perfect Marriage. 1947: Smash-Up (GB: A Woman Destroyed). Time Out of Mind. Hit Parade of 1947. 1948: Every Girl Should Be Married. The Dude Goes West. You Gotta Stay Happy. 1950: The Fuller Brush Girl (GB: The Affairs of Sally). USS Teakettle (later and GB: You're in the Navy Now). 1951: Meet Me After the Show. 1952: Actors and Sin. Carrie. 1953: Roman Holiday. 1955: The Girl Rush. Oklahoma! I'll Cry Tomorrow. 1956: Attack! The Teahouse of the August Moon. 1957: The Sun Also Rises. The Joker is Wild. 1958: The Gun Runners. The Roots of Heaven. Orders to Kill. 1959: Beloved Infidel. The Dingaling Girl (TV). 1961: The Young Doctors. The Two Little Bears. 1962: Madison Avenue. The Longest Day. Who's Got the Action? The Party's Over. Miracle of the White Stallions (GB: Flight of the White Stallions). 1963: Captain Newman MD. 1965: Seven Women. 1971: See the Man Run (TV). 1972: Fireball Forward (TV). The Heartbreak Kid. 1974: The Take. McQ. The Borrowers (TV). The Longest Yard (GB: The Mean Machine). Escape to Witch Mountain. 1975: The Devil's Rain. Hustle. Promise Him Anything (TV). Whiffs (GB: C.A.S.H.). 1976: Birch Interval. 1977: Moving Violation. 1978: Crash (TV). Foolin' Around (released 1980). 1979: Yesterday. The Concorde ... Airport '79 (GB: Airport '80 ... the Concorde). 1980: The Fall Guy (TV). How to Beat the High Cost of Living. Scoring. The Border. 1981: Take This Job and Shove It. The Oklahoma City Dolls (TV). 1982: Yes, Giorgio. Trouble in the High Timber Country (TV). 1983: The Demon Murder Case (TV). The Act. Dreamscape. 1984: Burning Rage (TV). 1985: In Like Flynn (TV). Head Office. Stitches. 1986: Turnaround.

ALBRIGHT, Lola 1925–
Blonde ex-typist and telephonist who broke into films in 1948, and was winning leading roles two years later. But she seldom got the parts that her talent and smouldering personality seemed to warrant, and was lost to TV for long periods, first in *Peter Gunn*, then in *Peyton Place*. Married to Jack Carson (*qv*) 1952–58.
1948: The Pirate. Easter Parade. 1949: The Girl from Jones Beach. Tulsa. Champion. 1950: Bodyhold. Beauty on Parade. When You're Smiling. The Good Humor Man. The Killer

That Stalked New York (GB: The Frightened City). Sierra Passage. 1952: Arctic Flight. 1953: The Silver Whip. 1954: The Treasure of Ruby Hills. 1955: The Tender Trap. The Magnificent Matador (GB: The Brave and the Beautiful). 1957: The Monolith Monsters. Pawnee (GB: Pale Arrow). Oregon Passage. 1958: Seven Guns to Mesa. 1961: A Cold Wind in August. 1962: Kid Galahad. 1964: Les félins (GB: The Love Cage. US: The Joyhouse). 1966: Lord Love a Duck. 1967: The Way West. The Helicopter Spies (TV. GB: cinemas). How I Spent My Summer Vacation (TV. GB: cinemas as Deadly Roulette). 1968: Where Were You When the Lights Went Out? The Impossible Years. The Money Jungle. 1973: My Secret Mother (TV). 1975: The Nurse Killer (TV). 1977: Delta Country USA. Terraces (TV).

ALBRIGHT, Hardie (Hardy Albrecht) 1903–1975
Tall, fair, beefily handsome American leading man, built vaguely along Nelson Eddy lines, and at his most popular in the early 1930s, when he successfully tackled several juicy roles. After 1934 the quality of his roles diminished, and he went back to the theatre, later returning to supporting parts in wartime Hollywood films, even appearing in a sex-instruction film. Wrote books on acting and direction. Died from congestive heart failure induced by pneumonia.
1931: Young Sinners. Hush Money. Heartbreak. Skyline. 1932: A Successful Calamity. So Big. The Crash. Jewel Robbery. The Purchase Price. Three on a Match. This Sporting Age. Cabin in the Cotton. The Match King.

1933: Song of Songs. The Working Man. Three-Cornered Moon. The House on 56th Street. 1934: Nana. Crimson Romance. The Scarlet Letter. White Heat. Beggar's Holiday. Two Heads on a Pillow. Silver Streak. Sing Sing Nights (GB: Reprieved). 1935: Ladies Love Danger. Women Must Dress. Red Salute (GB: Arms and the Girl). Champagne for Breakfast. Calm Yourself. 1940: Granny Get Your Gun. Ski Patrol. Carolina Moon. Flight from Destiny. 1941: Men of the Timberland. Bachelor Daddy. Marry the Boss's Daughter. The Loves of Edgar Allan Poe. 1942: Pride of the Yankees. Lady in a Jam. 1944: Army Wives. Mom and Dad (GB: A Family Story. Released 1957). 1945: Captain Tugboat Annie. The Jade Mask. Sunset in El Dorado. 1946: Angel on My Shoulder.

ALDA, Alan 1936–
American actor with quiet, wry personality, the son of Robert Alda (see following entry). He started on the stage in 1953, but his enigmatic portrayals have limited his film roles, and he has been seen mostly on TV, where he seems to find it easier to impose his personality on a show. In 1974 Alda won an Emmy as best actor in a comedy series for the top-rating *M*A*S*H*, in which he starred for several seasons.
1963: Gone Are the Days. 1968: The Extraordinary Seaman. Paper Lion. 1970: Catch 22. The Moonshine War. Jenny. 1971: The Mephisto Waltz. To Kill a Clown. 1972: The Glass House (TV. GB: cinemas). Playmates (TV). 1973: Isn't It Shocking? (TV). 1977: The Caryl Chessman Story/Kill Me If You Can (TV). 1978: California Suite. Same Time, Next Year. 1979: The Seduction of Joe Tynan. 1980: †The Four Seasons. 1986: †Sweet Liberty.

†*Also directed*

ALDA, Robert (Alphonso d'Abruzzo) 1914–1986
Hopeful-looking, dark-haired, occasionally moustachioed leading man who started at the top with his portrait of George Gershwin in *Rhapsody in Blue*. A good singer who became a rather stiff actor, he was offered few musical roles except on stage. Later made several films abroad, but never regained his star status in

the cinema. Father of Alan Alda (see preceding entry).
1945: Rhapsody in Blue. 1946: Cinderella Jones. Cloak and Dagger. The Beast with Five Fingers. The Man I Love. 1947: Nora Prentiss. 1948: April Showers. 1949: Homicide. 1950: Hollywood Varieties. Tarzan and the Slave Girl. 1951: Mr Universe. Two Gals and a Guy. 1955: La donna più bella del mondo/Beautiful But Dangerous. Assignment Abroad (TV. GB: cinemas). Secret File (TV. GB: cinemas). 1958: Gentleman from Second Avenue (TV). 1959: Imitation of Life. Un militaro e mezzo. A che sorvonno questi. 1960: Sepulchre dei rei (US: Cleopatra's Daughter). Musketeers of the Sea. 1961: Force of Impulse. 1962: The Devil's Hand. Tote e Peppino, divisi a Berlino. 1963: Revenge of the Barbarians. 1968: The Girl Who Knew Too Much. 1973: Seven Steps from Murder. The Serpent. 1974: Cagliostro. 1975: Off Shore. Last Hours Before Morning (TV). Won Ton Ton, The Dog Who Saved Hollywood. House of Exorcism. I Will, I Will ... for Now. 1976: Bittersweet Love. 1977: Perfect Gentlemen (TV). 1978: River of Promises (TV). Spider Man Strikes Back (TV. GB: cinemas). The Big Rip-Off/The Rip-Off (US: The Squeeze). Every Girl Should Have One. 1979: Supertrain (TV. Later: Express to Terror).

ALDON, Mari (Mary Aldon) 1929–
Blonde Canadian, British-educated actress, a former ballerina and singer, whose sweet personality made a brief impact at Warners in the early 1950s. Within a few years she descended to supporting roles, then retired after marrying director Tay Garnett. They later divorced.

1946: The Locket. 1951: Distant Drums. The Tanks Are Coming. 1952: This Woman is Dangerous. Tangier Incident. 1954: Mask of Dust (US: A Race for Life). 1955: The Barefoot Contessa. Summer Madness (US: Summertime). 1972: The Mad Trapper.

ALEXANDER, Jane (J. Quigley) 1939–
Anyone who can be good in such a film as The Betsy certainly deserves a place in this book, and this dark-haired, businesslike, un-pretty American actress of warm and individual personality is almost always good, as her record – four Oscar nominations (for The Great White Hope, All the President's Men, Kramer vs Kramer and Testament) to date and several acclaimed leading roles in TV movies – testifies. In acting since childhood, although I have not been able to ascertain whether she is the child Janie Alexander who appears in The Naked City (1948).
1970: The Great White Hope. A Gunfight. 1971: Welcome Home, Johnny Bristol (TV). 1972: The New Centurions (GB: Precinct 45, Los Angeles Police). 1973: Miracle on 34th Street (TV). 1974: This is the West That Was (TV). 1976: Death Be Not Proud (TV). All the President's Men. Eleanor and Franklin (TV). 1977: Eleanor and Franklin: The White House Years (TV). A Circle of Children (TV). 1978: The Betsy. A Question of Love (TV). Lovey – A Circle of Children Part II (TV). 1979: Kramer vs Kramer. 1980: Brubaker. Playing for Time (TV). 1981: Wind to the West. 1982: Night Crossing. In the Custody of Strangers (TV). 1983: Testament. 1984: When She Says No (TV). City Heat. Calamity Jane (TV). 1985: Sweet Country. Malice in Wonderland (TV). 1986: Square Dance. Jaguar.

ALEXANDER, Ross 1907–1937
Tall, dark, liquid-lipped, soulful-looking, rather gangling American leading man. On stage from 16, the loose-limbed Alexander was one of Warners' foremost lighter leading men in the mid-1930s, especially in college-style comedies opposite fluffy leading ladies such as Anita Louise (qv), but probably now best remembered as Demetrius in the 1935 A Midsummer Night's Dream. Plagued with worries that his career was slipping, Alexander shot himself at 29. He was married to actress Anne Nagel (also qv).

1932: The Wiser Sex. 1933: Crashing Society. 1934: Flirtation Walk. Gentlemen Are Born. Loudspeaker Lowdown. Social Register. 1935: A Midsummer Night's Dream. Captain Blood. We're in the Money. Shipmates Forever. Apple Sauce. Going Highbrow. Maybe It's Love. 1936: Brides Are Like That. I Married a Doctor. Boulder Dam. China Clipper. Hot Money. Here Comes Carter (GB: The Voice of Scandal). 1937: Ready, Willing and Able.

ALLAN, Elizabeth 1908–
Gracious, genteel, dark-haired English leading lady, adept at frightened misses early in her career when, for a while, she was under contract to M-G-M in Hollywood where she played well-bred heroines, often in period dramas. Returning to Britain in 1938, she appeared as upper-class wives in largely undistinguished films, but became popular in TV panel games.
1931: Alibi. Rodney Steps In. The Rosary. Black Coffee. Chin Chin Chinaman (US: Boat from Shanghai). Many Waters. Service for Ladies (US: Reserved for Ladies). 1932: The Chinese Puzzle. Michael and Mary. Nine Till Six. Down Our Street. Insult. The Lodger (US: The Phantom Fiend). 1933: The Shadow. The Lost Chord. Ace of Aces. The Solitaire Man. Looking Forward (GB: Service). No Marriage Ties. 1934: Java Head. David Copperfield. The Mystery of Mr X. Outcast Lady (GB: A Woman of the World). Men in White. 1935: Mark of the Vampire. 1936: A Woman Rebels. A Tale of Two Cities. Camille. *The Story of Papworth. 1937: The Soldier and the Lady (GB: Michael Strogoff). Slave

Ship. 1938: Dangerous Medicine. 1939: The Girl Who Forgot. Inquest. 1940: Saloon Bar. 1942: The Great Mr Handel. Went the Day Well? (US: 48 Hours). 1944: He Snoops to Conquer. 1949: That Dangerous Age (US: If This Be Sin). 1951: No Highway (US: No Highway in the Sky). 1952: Folly to be Wise. 1953: Twice Upon a Time. The Heart of the Matter. Front Page Story. 1955: The Brain Machine. Born for Trouble. 1958: Grip of the Strangler (US: The Haunted Strangler).

ALLBRITTON, Louise 1920–1979
Aristocratic, but peppy American of forties films. Despite often being cast as the other woman, she was poised, witty and had a great sense of comic timing. Her talents looked best in screwball comedy, but she did not pursue a career with the same singlemindedness after marriage to news commentator Charles Collingwood in 1946. Died from cancer.
1942: Parachute Nurse. Danger in the Pacific. Not a Ladies' Man. Who Done It? Pittsburgh. 1943: It Comes Up Love. Good Morning, Judge. Fired Wife. Son of Dracula. 1944: Follow the Boys. This is the Life. Her Primitive Man. San Diego, I Love You. Bowery to Broadway. 1945: The Men in Her Diary. That Night with You. 1946: Tangier. 1947: The Egg and I. 1948: Sitting Pretty. Walk a Crooked Mile. 1949: Don't Trust Your Husband. The Doolins of Oklahoma (GB: The Great Manhunt). 1964: Felicia.

ALLEN, Gracie 1902–1964
Uniquely scatterbrained brunette American comedienne, usually seen in films with hus-

band George Burns (*qv*), but most successful on stage and later on TV. Died from a heart attack.

1929: *Lamb Chops. 1930: *Fit To Be Tied. *Pulling a Bone. 1931: *The Antique Shop. *Once Over Light. *One Hundred Percent Service. 1932: The Big Broadcast. *Oh My Operation. *The Babbling Book. 1933: International House. College Humor. *Hollywood on Parade. *Let's Dance. *Walking the Baby. 1934: We're Not Dressing. Six of a Kind. Many Happy Returns. 1935: Love in Bloom. Here Comes Cookie. The Big Broadcast of 1936. 1936: College Holiday. The Big Broadcast of 1937. 1937: A Damsel in Distress. 1938: College Swing. (GB: Swing, Teacher Swing). 1939: The Gracie Allen Murder Case. Honolulu. 1941: Mr and Mrs North. 1944: Two Girls and a Sailor. 1954: *Screen Snapshots No. 224.

ALLEN, Karen 1951–
Personable little blue-eyed Hollywood brunette seen almost exclusively in 'nice-girl' roles. She landed the leading role in the blockbuster *Raiders of the Lost Ark* at the age of 30, then surprised many by declining to star in the sequel. She did well to start an acting career after an attack of kerato conjunctivitis which left her temporarily blind, but now looks too mature, with too few films behind her, to become a major star.

1976: The Whidjitmaker. 1977: *The Aftermath. 1978: Lovey: A Circle of Children Part II (TV). National Lampoon's Animal House. 1979: Manhattan. The Wanderers. 1980: A Small Circle of Friends. Cruising. 1981: Raiders of the Lost Ark. Shoot the Moon. 1982: Split Image/Captured! 1983: Until September. 1984: Starman. 1985: Animal Behavior.

ALLEN, Nancy 1954–
Plump-cheeked, sassy-looking, light-haired American actress who usually plays independent types. Her appearances in films by her husband, director Brian de Palma (married 1979), have been in sexy and outspoken roles, but she remains abrasively personable in anything and also has a talent for comedy. Her output, though, is pitifully small – on average only one film a year.

1973: The Last Detail. 1976: Carrie. 1978: I Wanna Hold Your Hand. 1979: 1941. 1980: Home Movies. Dressed to Kill. 1981: Blow-Out. 1983: The Buddy System. Strange

Invaders. 1984: The Philadelphia Experiment. Terror in the Aisles. Not for Publication. 1986: The Gladiator (TV). Sweet Revenge.

ALLEN, Woody (Allen Konigsberg) 1935–
Bespectacled, diminutive American writer-director-comedian with a small amount of scruffy hair. He brought the paradoxical combination of shyness, ineptness and obsession with sex to the screen and made it an international hit. Writes and directs most of his own material, which has lately shown a tendency to 'go serious' although mercifully shafts of the lunatic Allen humour keep breaking through. His scant regard for the Establishment was demonstrated when he failed to show up to accept his Oscar for Best Director (on *Annie Hall*) in 1978. The same film also brought him an acting nomination.

1965: What's New Pussycat? 1966: What's Up Tiger Lily? 1967: Casino Royale. 1969: †Take the Money and Run. 1971: †Bananas. 1972: †Everything You Always Wanted to Know About Sex* *But Were Afraid to Ask. 1973: Play It Again Sam. 1974: †Sleeper. 1975: †Love and Death. 1976: The Front. 1977: †Annie Hall. 1978: †Manhattan. 1980: †Stardust Memories. To Woody Allen, from Europe with Love. 1982: †A Midsummer Night's Sex Comedy. 1983: †Zelig. 1984: †Broadway Danny Rose. 1986: †Hannah and Her Sisters.

†And directed

Also as director:
1978: Interiors. 1985: The Purple Rose of Cairo.

ALLYSON, June (Ella Geisman) 1917–
Petite, husky-voiced blonde American actress, singer and dancer – everyone's idea of the girl next door in the forties, everyone's idea of the dutiful wife in the fifties. A sometimes stormy marriage to Dick Powell survived 18 years until his death in 1963. Overcame severe injuries sustained in a childhood fall.

1937: *Swing for Sale. *Pixilated. *Dime a Dance. 1938: *Dates and Nuts. *The Prisoner of Swing. †Sing for Sweetie. 1939: *Rollin' in Rhythm. 1943: Best Foot Forward. Girl Crazy. Thousands Cheer. 1944: Two Girls and a Sailor. Meet the People. 1945: Her Highness and the Bellboy. The Sailor Takes a Wife. Music for Millions. 1946: Two Sisters from Boston. Till the Clouds Roll By. The Secret Heart. 1947: High Barbaree. Good News. 1948: The Bride Goes Wild. The Three Musketeers. Words and Music. 1949: Little Women. The Stratton Story. The Reformer and the Redhead. 1950: Right Cross. 1951: Too Young to Kiss. 1952: The Girl in White (GB: So Bright the Flame). 1953: Battle Circus. Remains to be Seen. The Glenn Miller Story. 1954: Executive Suite. Woman's World. 1955: Strategic Air Command. The McConnell Story (GB: Tiger in the Sky). The Shrike. 1956: The Opposite Sex. You Can't Run Away from It. 1957: Interlude. My Man Godfrey. 1959: Stranger in My Arms. 1971: See the Man Run (TV). 1972: They Only Kill Their Masters. 1973: Letters from Three Lovers (TV). 1977: Curse of the Black Widow (TV). 1978: Vegas (TV). Blackout. 1979: Three on a Date (TV).

AMECHE, Don (Dominic Amici) 1908–
Benign, elegant, likeable American leading man with pencil moustache and almost an embarrassment of dark hair. He hung on to Hollywood stardom over a surprisingly long period, although he was too seldom seen in the comedy roles which enabled him to use the offhand sarcasm which he tempered with charm. Now plays the occasional leading character role which he evidently enjoys. He won an Academy Award for *Cocoon*.

1933: *Beauty at the World's Fair. 1935: Clive of India. Dante's Inferno. 1936: Sins of Man. Ramona. Ladies in Love. One in a Million. 1937: Love is News. Fifty Roads to Town. You Can't Have Everything. Love under Fire. 1938: In Old Chicago. Happy Landing. Josette. Alexander's Ragtime Band. Gateway. 1939: The

*Three Musketeers (GB: The Singing Musketeer). Midnight. The Story of Alexander Graham Bell (GB: The Modern Miracle). Hollywood Cavalcade. Swanee River. 1940: Lillian Russell. Four Sons. Down Argentine Way. 1941: That Night in Rio. Moon over Miami. Kiss the Boys Goodbye. The Feminine Touch. 1942: Confirm or Deny. The Magnificent Dope. Girl Trouble. 1943: Heaven Can Wait. Happy Land. Something to Shout About. 1944: Wing and a Prayer. Greenwich Village. It's in the Bag! (GB: The Fifth Chair). 1945: Guest Wife. 1946: So Goes My Love (GB: A Genius in the Family). 1947: That's My Man (GB: Will Tomorrow Ever Come?). 1948: Sleep My Love. 1949: Slightly French. 1952: *Hollywood Night at 21 Club. 1954: Phantom Caravan. Fire One. 1961: A Fever in the Blood. 1966: Rings around the World. Picture Mommy Dead. 1968: Shadow over Elveron (TV). 1970: Suppose They Gave a War and Nobody Came. The Boatniks. 1971: Gidget Gets Married (TV). 1975: Won Ton Ton, The Dog Who Saved Hollywood. 1983: Trading Places. 1985: Cocoon. 1986: A Masterpiece of Murder (TV).*

ANDERS, Merry (M. Anderson) 1932–
Blonde American actress, trained (and wasted) by 20th Century-Fox, with pleasant, slow-burning appeal reminiscent of Lola Albright (*qv*). Career-wise, she proved extremely tenacious despite an unassertive talent, continuing to star in 'B' features (some of them quite interesting) right up until the genre vanished.

1952: Belles on Their Toes. Wait 'til the Sun Shines, Nellie. Les Miserables. 1953: Titanic. The Farmer Takes a Wife. How to Marry a Millionaire. 1954: Princess of the Nile. Phffft!

Three Coins in the Fountain. 1955: All That Heaven Allows. 1956: The Night Runner. Desk Set (GB: His Other Woman). 1957: The Dalton Girls. Teenage Delinquents. Calypso Heatwave. Hear Me Good. Escape from San Quentin. 1958: Death in Small Doses. No Time to be Young. Violent Road. 1959: Five Bold Women. 1960: The Police Dog Story. The Walking Target. The Hypnotic Eye. Young Jesse James. Spring Affair. 1961: 20,000 Eyes. The Gambler Wore a Gun. When the Clock Strikes. The Secret of Deep Harbor. 1962: Air Patrol. Beauty and the Beast. The Case of Patty Smith (GB: The Shame of Patty Smith). FBI Code 98. 1963: House of the Damned. Police Nurse. A Tiger Walks. 1964: The Quick Gun. Raiders from Beneath the Sea. The Time Travelers. Young Fury. 1965: Tickle Me. Women of the Prehistoric Planet. 1967: Flight of the Cougar. 1969: Airport. 1971: Legacy of Blood.

ANDERSON, Rona 1926–
Scottish-born actress, on stage at 16. Came to films at 22 and was often seen as shy or helpless females. Her film career petered out with the demise of the British second-feature, a field in which she had been a regular participant, but she remained active on stage. Married to actor Gordon Jackson (*qv*) since 1951.

1948: Sleeping Car to Trieste. 1949: Floodtide. Poets' Pub. Torment (US: Paper Gallows). The Twenty Questions Murder Mystery. 1950: Her Favourite Husband (US: The Taming of Dorothy). 1951: Home to Danger. Whispering Smith Hits London (US: Whispering Smith versus Scotland Yard). Scrooge. 1952: Circumstantial Evidence. 1953: Noose for a Lady. Black 13. 1954: Double Exposure. The Black Rider. Shadow of a Man. Little Red Monkey (US: The Case of the Little Red Monkey). 1955: The Flaw. A Time to Kill. Stock Car. 1956: Soho Incident (US: Spin a Dark Web). The Hide-Out. 1958: The Solitary Child. Man with a Gun. 1963: The Bay of St Michel (US: Pattern for Plunder). 1964: Devils of Darkness. 1967: River Rivals (serial). 1968: Interlude. The Prime of Miss Jean Brodie.

ANDERSSON, Bibi (Birgitta Andersson) 1935–
Blonde Swedish actress with sensitive features, whose best work was all for Ingmar Bergman. Her forays towards international stardom did not pan out well, and she has remained largely in Scandinavian films.

1953: Dum-Bom. 1954: En Natt pu Glimminghaus. Herr Arnes Penngar (GB and US: Sir Arne's Treasure). 1955: Sommarnattens Leende (GB and US: Smiles of a Summer Night). Flickan i Regnet. 1956: Sister Paret Ut. Egen Ingang. 1957: Det Sjunde Inseglet (GB and US: The Seventh Seal). Sommarnoje Sokes. Smultronstället (GB and US: Wild Strawberries). Nära Livet (GB: So Close to Life. US: Brink of Life). 1958: Du är mitt äventyr. Ansiktet (GB and US: The Face). 1959: Den Kära Leken. 1960: Bröllopsdagen. 1961: Djävulens Oga (GB and US: The Devil's Eye). Karneval. Nasilje na Trgu (US: Square of Violence). Lustgarden. 1962: Alskarinnen (GB: The Mistress: Kort är Sommaren). 1964: Now about These Women ... (US: Not to Mention These Women). On. 1965: Duel at Diablo. Juninatt. 1966: Syskonbädd 1782 (GB: My Sister My Love). Persona. Scusi, lei a Favorevole o Contrario? 1967: Le Viol (GB: A Question of Rape). 1968: Svarta Palmkronor (US: Black Palm Trees). Flickorna (GB and US: The Girls). 1969: Taenk pa et Tal. Storia di una Donna (GB: The Story of a Woman). Una Estate in Quattro. En Passion (GB: A Passion. US: The Passion of Anna). The Kremlin Letter. 1971: The Touch. 1972: Mannen fran Andra Sidan. 1973: Scenes from a Marriage. 1974: The Hour of Parting. 1975: It is Raining on Santiago. Blondy (US: Vortex). 1976: Mon mari, sa maitresse et moi. 1977: I Never Promised You a Rose Garden. 1978: An Enemy of the People. Justices. Quintet. 1979: L'amour en question. The Concorde – Airport '79 (GB: Airport '80 ... the Concorde). Twee Vrouwen. 1980: Barnfoerbjudet/The Elephant Man. Prosperous Times. The Marmalade Revolution. 1981: Jag Rodnar. 1982: Black Crows/Svarte Fugler. 1983: Exposed. 1984: Berget på Mänens Baksida (US: The Hill on the Other Side of the Moon). 1986: Husmenna. Poor Butterfly.

ANDERSSON, Harriet 1932–
Dark-haired Swedish actress, principally in gloomy, sensual roles in Ingmar Bergman films, the nude scenes in one of which, *Summer with Monica*, quickly brought her into the international limelight. She was whisked from the chorus line into the cinema at 18 and, with her thick lips, soulful eyes and intense style, enjoyed 20 years of great popularity, especially in Scandinavia; international ventures were few and less successful.

1950: *Medan staden sover* (US: *While the City Sleeps*). *Två trappor över gården. Anderssonskans Kalle. Motorkavaljerer.* 1951: *Biffen och bananen. Puck hete jag. Frånskild. Dårskapens hus* (US: *House of Folly*). 1952: *Sabotage. U-boat 39. Trots* (GB and US: *Defiance*). *Sommaren med Monika* (GB: *Summer with Monica*. US: *Monika*). 1953: *Gycklarnas afton* (GB and US: *Sawdust and Tinsel*). 1954: *En lekyion i kärlek* (GB and US: *A Lesson in Love*). 1955: *Hoppsan! Kvinnodröm* (GB: *Journey into Autumn*. US: *Dreams*). *Sommarnattens leende* (GB and US: *Smiles of a Summer Night*). 1956: *Sista paret ut. Nattbarn* (GB: *Children of the Night*). 1957: *Synnöve solbakken.* 1958: *Kvinna i leopard. Flottans överman.* 1959: *Brott i Paradiset* (GB: *Crime in Paradise*). *Noc pòslubna.* 1961: *Barbara. Såsom i en spegel* (GB and US: *Through a Glass Darkly*). 1962: *Siska.* 1963: *Lyckodrömmen* (GB: *Dreams of Happiness*). *En Söndag i september* (GB: *One Sunday in September.* US: *A Sunday in September*). 1964: *För att inte tala om alla dessa kvinnor* (GB: *Now About These Women.* US: *Not to Mention These Women/All These Women*). *Att älska* (GB and US: *To Love*). *Loving Couples.* 1965: *För vanskaps skull. Lianbron. Här börjar äventyret.* 1966: *The Deadly Affair. Ormen* (GB and US: *The Serpent*). 1967: *Stimulantia. People Meet and Sweet Music Fills the Heart* (GB: *People Meet*). *Jag älskar, du älskar* (GB: *I Love, You Love*). *Flickorna* (GB and US: *The Girls*). *The Struggle for Rome.* 1969: *The Struggle for Rome II.* 1970: *Anna.* 1971: *I harsbandet.* 1972: *Cries and Whispers.* 1975: *Den vita väggen* (GB: *The White Wall*). 1977: *Hempas bar* (US: *Cry of Triumph '57*). 1979: *The Sabina. Linus eller tegelhusets hemlighet.* 1982: *Fanny and Alexander.*

ANDES, Keith 1920–

Tall, fair-haired, mild-mannered American actor who came to films (from the stage) too late to make much of an impact. A Universal-International contract from 1955 to 1958 brought him a second-grade stardom, but he lacked the distinctive personality that might have taken him further. Co-starred with Glynis Johns in the TV series *Glynis* but later played bit parts.
1944: *Winged Victory.* 1947: *The Farmer's*

Daughter. 1949: *Project X.* 1951: *Clash by Night.* 1952: *Blackbeard the Pirate. Split Second.* 1954: *The Key Man.* 1955: *The Second Greatest Sex. A Life at Stake.* 1956: *Away All Boats. Back from Eternity. Pillars of the Sky* (GB: *The Tomahawk and the Cross*). 1957: *Interlude. Homeward Borne* (TV). 1958: *The Girl Most Likely. Damn Citizen!* 1959: *Model for Murder. Surrender Hell!* 1964: *The Tattooed Police Horse.* 1968: *Hell's Bloody Devils.* 1969: *Smashing the Crime Syndicate.* 1970: *Tora! Tora! Tora!* 1974: *Ordeal* (TV). 1979: *The Ultimate Imposter* (TV).... *And Justice for All.*

ANDRESS, Ursula 1936–

Tigerish Swiss-born blonde star who, after a late introduction to international stardom in *Dr No*, enjoyed 10 years as a top film glamour girl, before her career seemed to submerge beneath her private love life. But she stepped up her work schedule again in the late 1970s, apparently ageless and as sexy as ever. Married to John Derek (*qv*) from 1957 to 1966. Later there was a lengthy liaison with the French star Jean-Paul Belmondo (also *qv*).
1954: *Le avventure di Giacomo Casanova* (GB: *The Loves of Casanova.* US: *Sins of Casanova*). *Un Americano a Roma/An American in Rome.* 1955: *La tempesta e passata/The Tempest Has Gone. La cantena dell'odio.* 1957: *Anyone Can Play.* 1962: *Dr No.* 1963: *Four for Texas. Nightmare in the Sun. Fun in Acapulco.* 1964: *Toys for Christmas.* 1965: *She. What's New, Pussycat? La decima vittima/The 10th Victim. Les tribulations d'un Chicois en Chine* (GB: *Up to His Ears.* US: *Chinese Adventures*

in China). 1966: *Once Before I Die. The Blue Max.* 1967: *Casino Royale. Le dolci signore.* 1968: *The Southern Star.* 1970: *Perfect Friday.* 1971: *Red Sun.* 1972: *Five Against Capricorn.* 1973: *The Last Chance* (US: *Stateline Motel*). 1974: *Colpo in canna* (GB: *Stick 'Em Up, Darlings!*). 1975: *Loaded Guns. L'infermiera* (GB: *I Will If You Will*). 1976: *40 grada sotto le lenzuola. Africa Express. Scaramouche/The Loves and Times of Scaramouche.* 1977: *The Fifth Musketeer. Double Murders. Casanova and Co* (GB: *The Rise and Rise of Casanova*). *Love in Four Easy Lessons.* 1978: *The Mountain in the Jungle* (GB: *Prisoner of the Cannibal God.* US: *Primitive Desires*). 1979: *Four Tigers in Lipstick/Letti selvaggi* (released 1985). *Una strana coppio di gangsters.* 1980: *Nobody's Perfect. Grip.* 1981: *Clash of the Titans. Chanel solitaire.* 1982: *Mexico in Flames/Red Bells.* 1985: *Liberté, égalité, choucroute.*

ANDREWS, Anthony 1948–

Fair-haired, blue-eyed, boyish-looking British actor of guileless appearance. His career progressed only slowly until he made an enormous hit in two television series, *Danger UXB* and *Brideshead Revisited.* Subsequently proved the most beautifully cast Sir Percy Blakeney in *The Scarlet Pimpernel* since Leslie Howard 50 years earlier, but found it less easy to make an individual impact in a wider variety of roles. Would also make a good *Raffles.*
1972: *A War of Children* (TV). 1973: *Take Me High* (US: *Hot Property*). 1974: *Percy's Progress* (US: *It's Not the Size That Counts*). *QB VII* (TV). 1975: *Operation Daybreak.* 1981: *Mistress of Paradise* (TV). 1982: *Ivanhoe* (TV). 1983: *The Scarlet Pimpernel* (TV). *Sparkling Cyanide/Agatha Christie's Sparkling Cyanide* (TV). 1984: *Under the Volcano. Notes from Under the Volcano. Observations Under the Volcano.* 1985: *The Holcroft Covenant.* 1986: *The Second Victory.*

ANDREWS, Dana (Carver D. Andrews) 1909–

Crackly-voiced Hollywood star, especially prominent in realist thrillers of the late forties. A leading man until the late sixties, he overcame personal problems to return in later years as a character player. Brother of Steve Forrest (*qv*).
1939: *Lucky Cisco Kid.* 1940: *The Westerner.*

Sailor's Lady. Kit Carson. 1941: Tobacco Road. Belle Starr. Swamp Water (GB: The Man Who Came Back). Ball of Fire. 1942: Berlin Correspondent. The Ox-Bow Incident (GB: Strange Incident). 1943: December Seventh. Crash Dive. North Star. 1944: The Purple Heart. Wing and a Prayer. Up in Arms. Laura. 1945: State Fair. Fallen Angel. A Walk in the Sun. Know Your Enemy: Japan (narrator). 1946: Canyon Passage. The Best Years of Our Lives. 1947: Boomerang. Night Song. Daisy Kenyon. 1948: The Iron Curtain. Deep Waters. No Minor Vices. 1949: Britannia Mews (US: Forbidden Street). Sword in the Desert. 1950: My Foolish Heart. Where the Sidewalk Ends. Edge of Doom (GB: Stronger Than Fear). 1951: The Frogmen. Sealed Cargo. I Want You. 1952: Assignment – Paris! 1953: Elephant Walk. 1954: Duel in the Jungle. Three Hours to Kill. 1955: Smoke Signal. Strange Lady in Town. While the City Sleeps. 1956: Comanche. *Hollywood Goes a-Fishing. Beyond a Reasonable Doubt. 1957: Night of the Demon (US: Curse of the Demon). Spring Reunion. Zero Hour. 1958: The Fearmakers. Enchanted Island. The Right Hand Man (TV). 1960: The Crowded Sky. Alas, Babylon (TV). 1961: Madison Avenue. 1964: The Satan Bug. 1965: Crack in the World. Brainstorm. The Woman Who Wouldn't Die. In Harm's Way. Town Tamer. The Loved One. Battle of the Bulge. Spy in Your Eye/Berlin, appuntamento per le spie. 1966: Johnny Reno. Supercolpo da 7 miliardi (GB: The 1,000 Carat Diamond. US: Ten Million Dollar Grab). 1967: Hot Rods to Hell. The Frozen Dead. The Cobra. I diamenti che nassuno voleva rubare (US: No Diamonds for Ursula). 1968: The Devil's Brigade. 1971: The Failing of Raymond (TV). 1972: Innocent Bystanders. 1974: Airport 1975. 1975: The First 36 Hours of Dr Durant (TV). Take a Hard Ride. Shadow in the Streets. 1976: The Last Tycoon. 1977: Good Guys Wear Black. 1978: Born Again. The Last Hurrah (TV). 1979: The Pilot. 1984: Prince Jack.

ANDREWS, Julie (Julia Wells) 1935–
British singer and actress with fresh, healthy looks, on radio as a child. Following stage hits with The Boy Friend and My Fair Lady, she briefly gained enormous popularity in the cinema of the 1960s; but her antiseptic air soon proved less popular at the box-office despite strenuous and praiseworthy (if sometimes a

trifle desperate) efforts to widen her range. Married to director Blake Edwards (second of two) since 1968, she is frequently seen in his films. Also writes children's stories. An Oscar-winner for Mary Poppins, she has also been nominated for The Sound of Music and Victor/Victoria.
1952: Rose of Baghdad (voice only). 1964: Mary Poppins. The Americanization of Emily. 1965: The Sound of Music. 1966: Torn Curtain. Hawaii. 1967: The Singing Princess (voice only). Thoroughly Modern Millie. 1968: Star! 1969: Darling Lili. 1974: The Tamarind Seed. 1979: '10'. Little Miss Marker. 1981: S.O.B. 1982: Victor/Victoria. 1983: The Man Who Loved Women. 1986: Crisis. Gift of the Heart.

ANGEL, Heather 1909–
After rave reviews in British films, this diffident English actress with clipped tones (her father was an Oxford don) went to Hollywood in 1932, where her best-remembered role proved to be in John Ford's The Informer. Later films were less remarkable (although she had a good run as the heroine of Paramount's Bulldog Drummond films), with leads in 'B' films mingling with supporting roles in bigger movies. Married to actor Ralph Forbes (1902–1951) – first of her three husbands – from 1934 to 1942.
1930: City of Song (US: Farewell to Love). 1931: A Night in Montmartre. Sooky. 1932: The Hound of the Baskervilles. Self-Made Lady. Mr Bill the Conqueror (US: The Man Who Won). Pilgrimage. Men of Steel. After Office Hours. Early to Bed. 1933: Berkeley Square. Frail Women. Charlie Chan's Greatest

Case. Orient Express. 1934: Murder in Trinidad. Springtime for Henry. Romance in the Rain. 1935: The Three Musketeers. The Headline Woman (GB: A Woman in the Case). The Informer. The Perfect Gentleman (GB: The Imperfect Lady). The Mystery of Edwin Drood. It Happened in New York. 1936: The Last of the Mohicans. Daniel Boone. 1937: Bulldog Drummond Escapes. Portia on Trial (GB: The Trial of Portia Merriman). The Duke Comes Back (GB: The Call of the Ring). The Bold Caballero (GB: The Bold Cavalier). Western Gold (GB: The Mysterious Stranger). 1938: Bulldog Drummond in Africa. Army Girl (GB: The Last of the Cavalry). Arrest Bulldog Drummond! 1939: Undercover Doctor. Bulldog Drummond's Bride. Pride and Prejudice. Bulldog Drummond's Secret Police. 1940: Kitty Foyle. Shadows on the Stairs. Half a Sinner. 1941: That Hamilton Woman (GB: Lady Hamilton). Suspicion. Singapore Woman. 1942: Time to Kill. The Undying Monster (GB: The Hammond Mystery). 1943: Lifeboat. Cry Havoc. *Three Sisters of the Moors. 1944: In the Meantime, Darling. 1948: The Saxon Charm. 1950: Alice in Wonderland (voice only). 1953: Peter Pan (voice only). 1962: The Premature Burial.

ANGELI, Pier (Anne Maria Pierangeli) 1932–1971
Tragic, dark-haired, dark-eyed Italian actress in Hollywood films. Initially very popular in M-G-M films, but her fiery emotional entanglements betrayed her gentle screen image and eventually sucked the life out of her career. She ended in sexploitation pictures and committed suicide. Married to singer and sometime film star Vic Damone (Vito Farinola 1928–), first of two husbands, from 1954 to 1958. A passionate affair with James Dean (qv) before her marriages ended with his premature death.
1950: †Domani è troppo tardi (GB: Tomorrow is Too Late). 1951: †Domani è un altro giorno (GB: Tomorrow is Another Day). Teresa. The Light Touch. 1952: The Devil makes Three. 1953: Mam'zelle Nitouche (GB: Oh No, Mam'zelle). The Story of Three Loves. Sombrero. 1954: The Flame and the Flesh. The Silver Chalice. 1955: Santarellina. 1956: Somebody Up There Likes Me. Port Afrique. 1957: The Vintage. 1958: Merry Andrew. Bernadette (TV). 1959: The Moon and Six-

pence (TV). 1960: The Angry Silence. SOS Pacific. Musketeers of the Sea. 1962: White Slave Ship. (The Last Days of) Sodom and Gomorrah. 1964: †Banco à Bangkok pour OSS 117 (GB: Shadow of Evil). 1965: Battle of the Bulge. †Spy in Your Eye/Berlin, appuntamento per le spie. †MMM 83 (GB: Mission Bloody Mary). 1966: †Per mille dollari al giorno. 1967: †Rose rosse per il Fuhrer (US: Code Name Red Roses). One Step to Hell (US: King of Africa). 1969: †Vive America. †Addio, Alexandra (GB: Love Me, Love My Wife). 1970: †Les enemoniades. Every Bastard a King. 1971: †Nelle pieghe della carne. Octaman.

† as Anna Maria Pierangeli

ANKERS, Evelyn 1918–1985
Fair-haired, Chilean-born actress and dancer who, after a beginning in British films, proved one of Hollywood's most effective screamers through a slew of low-budget horror films in the forties. Married to Richard Denning (qv) from 1942 to her death from cancer.
1936: The Bells of St Mary's. Land Without Music. Rembrandt. 1937: Fire Over England. Knight Without Armour. Wings of the Morning. Over the Moon (released 1939). 1938: The Claydon Treasure Mystery. Murder in the Family. The Villiers Diamond. Second Thoughts. Coming of Age. 1940: Burma Convoy. 1941: Hold That Ghost. Hit the Road. Bachelor Daddy. The Wolf Man. 1942: The Ghost of Frankenstein. Eagle Squadron. The Great Impersonation. Sherlock Holmes and the Voice of Terror. North to the Klondike. Pierre of the Plains. 1943: Captive Wild Woman. You're a Lucky Fellow, Mr Smith. Hers to Hold. All by Myself. His Butler's Sister. Son of Dracula. Keep 'Em Slugging. The Mad Ghoul. 1944: Ladies Courageous. Jungle Woman. Follow the Boys. The Invisible Man's Revenge. Pardon My Rhythm. Pearl of Death. Bowery to Broadway. Weird Woman. 1945: The Fatal Witness. The Frozen Ghost. 1946: Black Beauty. The French Key. Queen of Burlesque. Flight to Nowhere. 1947: Last of the Redmen (GB: Last of the Mohicans). The Lone Wolf in London. Spoilers of the North. 1949: Parole Inc. Tarzan's Magic Fountain. 1950: The Texan Meets Calamity Jane. 1956: The Empty Room (TV. GB: Cinemas). 1957: Clipper Ship (TV). 1960: No Greater Love.

ANNABELLA (Suzanne Charpentier) 1909–
Blonde French star of the twenties and thirties in girl-next-door roles, a favourite of director René Clair, and soon in English-speaking films. Married (second) Tyrone Power in 1939, which fatally interrupted her career. When the marriage ended in divorce in 1948, she returned to France.
1926: Napoléon. 1927: Maldone. 1928: Soir de femme. Barcarole d'amour. 1929: Romance à l'inconnue. Deux fois vingt ans. Trois jeunes filles nues. 1930: La maison de la flèche. Sous les toits de Paris. 1931: Le million. Soir de rafle. Gardez la sourire. Autour d'une enquête. Son altesse d'amour. 1932: un fils d'Amerique. Paris Mediterranée. Marie, legende Hongroise. Mademoiselle Josette, ma femme. Le quatorze Juillet. 1933: La bataille. Sonnenstrahl. 1934: Caravan. Variétés. La Bandera. 1935: Nuits Moscovites. L'équipage/Flight into Darkness. Veille d'armes. 1936: Anne Marie. 1937: La citadelle du silence. Hôtel du nord. Under the Red Robe. Dinner at the Ritz. Wings of the Morning. 1938: Suez. The Baroness and the Butler. 1939: Escape from Yesterday. Bridal Suite. 1943: Tonight We Raid Calais. *Screen Snapshots No. 8. Bombers' Moon. 1946: 13 Rue Madeleine. 1947: Eternal conflict. 1948: Dernier amour. 1949: L'homme qui revient de loin. 1950: *Désordre. Quema el Suelo. 1952: Le plus bel amour de Don Juan.

ANN-MARGRET (Ann Margaret Olsson) 1941–
Red-haired, feline, Swedish-born singer and dancer who started her Hollywood career in quiet roles. But her extravagant figure soon typecast her as a singing sexpot. Fought back to stardom in the 1970s after a bad accident nearly ended her career and showed improved warmth in her performances, being nominated for an Oscar twice, in Carnal Knowledge and Tommy.
1961: Pocketful of Miracles. 1962: State Fair. *The Ann-Margret Story. 1963: Bye Bye Birdie. 1964: Viva Las Vegas (GB: Love in Las Vegas). Kitten with a Whip. 1965: Bus Riley's Back in Town. The Pleasure Seekers. Once a Thief. 1966: The Cincinnati Kid. Made in Paris. The Swinger. Stagecoach. Murderers' Row. 1967: Il tigre (GB and US: The Tiger and the Pussycat). 1968: Maggie. Sette uomini e un cervello. Rebus. Il profeta (GB and US: Mr Kinky). Il rubamento. 1970: CC and Company. RPM. 1971: Carnal Knowledge. 1972: Un homme est mort (GB and US: The Outside Man). 1973: The Train Robbers. 1975: Tommy. 1976: Joseph Andrews. Folies bourgeoises/The Twist. 1977: The Last Remake of Beau Geste. 1978: Magic. The Cheap Detective. 1979: The Villain (GB: Cactus Jack). Ken Murray Shooting Stars. Middle Age Crazy. 1980: Lookin' to Get Out. 1982: The Return of the Soldier. I Ought to Be in Pictures. 1983: Who Will Love My Children? (TV. GB: cinemas). 1984: A Streetcar Named Desire (TV). 1985: Twice in a Lifetime. 1986: 52 Pick-Up.

ANNIS, Francesca 1944–
Sharp-faced, dark-haired, incisive British actress of pin-up proportions whose tremendous success in television drama series of the 1970s (especially Lillie) must have made up for getting into the wrong kind of films to become an international star. In films (from an acting family) as a child, she was later the first nude Lady Macbeth.
1959: The Cat Gang. 1960: His and Hers. The Young Jacobites (serial). No Kidding (US: Beware of Children). 1963: Cleopatra. West 11. The Eyes of Annie Jones. Crooks in Cloisters. Saturday Night Out. 1964: Murder Most Foul. Flipper and the Pirates. 1965: The Pleasure Girls. 1966: Run with the Wind. 1970: The Walking Stick. The Sky Pirates. 1971: Macbeth. 1973: Penny Gold. 1980: Short Cut to Haifa. 1983: Krull. 1984: Coming Out of the Ice. 1986: The Golden River. Under the Cherry Moon.

ANOUK. See Aimée, Anouk

ANSPACH, Susan 1939–
Silky American blonde actress with a penchant for offbeat roles. An under-used talent (also an interesting singer), she has played opposite most of the major male stars of the period in her strangely unfulfilled career. Her first major New York theatre company included Jon Voight, Dustin Hoffman and Robert Duvall; she worked at the Actors' Studio with Al Pacino and Rip Torn and co-starred in films with Jack Nicholson, Woody Allen, Elliott Gould, Richard Dreyfuss, Gene Hackman, Donald Sutherland and Keith Carradine. All this and comparatively little known? Someone missed out somewhere, for her performance in Makaveyev's *Montenegro* was quite remarkable.
1970: The Landlord. Five Easy Pieces. 1972: Play It Again Sam. 1973: Blume in Love. 1975: Nashville. 1976: I Want to Keep My Baby (TV). The Secret Life of John Chapman (TV). 1977: Rosetti and Ryan: Men Who Love Women (TV). Mad Bull (TV). 1978: Blue Collar. Journal (TV). The Big Fix. 1979: The Last Giraffe/Raising Daisy Rothschild (TV). He Wants Her Back. Running. 1980: The Devil and Max Devlin. Gas. Montenegro, or: Pigs and Pearls. 1982: Deadly Encounter (TV). 1983: Misunderstood.

ARBUCKLE, Roscoe (Fatty) 1887–1933
Popular plump comedian of the silent days whose attempts at pathos were also more skilful than most. Career was ruined in 1921 by a scandal, and ensuing court case, over one of Arbuckle's orgiastic parties in which a girl died in unpleasant circumstances. He later directed a few films under the name William Goodrich, but a heart attack claimed his life at 46.
*1910: The Sanitarium/The Clinic. 1913: The Gangsters. Passions. He Had Three. Help! Help! Hydrophobia! The Waiters' Picnic. A Bandit. For the Love of Mabel. The Tell Tale Light. A Noise from the Deep. Love and Courage. The Riot. Mabel's New Hero. Fatty's Day Off. Mabel's Dramatic Debut. The Gypsy Queen. Mother's Boy. The Faithful Taxicab. A Quiet Little Wedding. Fatty at San Diego. Fatty Joins the Force. The Woman Haters. Fatty's Flirtations. He Would a Hunting Go. 1914: A Misplaced Foot. The Under Sheriff. A Flirt's Mistake. In the Clutches of a Gang. Rebecca's Wedding Day. A Film Johnnie. Tango Tangler. A Rival Demon. His Favourite Pastime. Barnyard Flirtations. Chicken Chaser. A Suspended Ordeal. The Water Dog. The Alarm. The Knockout. Fatty and Minnie-Hee-Haw. Our Country Cousin. Fatty and the Heiress. Fatty's Finish. The Sky Pirate. Caught in a Flue. The Baggage Smasher. Those Happy Days. That Minstrel Man. Those Country Kids. Fatty's Gift. The Masquerade. A Brand New Hero. The Rounders. Fatty's Debut. Fatty Again. Tillie's Punctured Romance. Killing Horace. Their Ups and Downs. Zip The Dodger. An Incompetent Hero. Lovers' Post Office. The Sea Nymphs. Fatty's Jonah Day. Fatty's Wine Party. 1915: Leading Lizzie Astray. Among the Mourners. Shotguns That Kick. Fatty's Magic Party. Mabel and Fatty's Wash Day. Rum and Wallpaper. Fatty and Mabel's Simple Life. Fatty and Mabel at the San Diego Exposition. Mabel, Fatty and the Law. Fatty's New Role. Colored Villainy. Fatty and Mabel's Married Life. Fatty's Reckless Fling. Fatty's Chance Acquaintance. Love in Armour. Fatty's Faithful Fido. That Little Band of Gold. When Love Took Wings. Mabel and Fatty Viewing the World's Fair at San Francisco. Miss Fatty's Seaside Lovers. The Little Teacher. Fatty's Plucky Pup. Fatty's Tin Type Tangle. Fickle Fatty's Fall. 1916: The Village Scandal. Fatty and the Broadway Stars. Fatty and Mabel Adrift. He Did and He Didn't. The Bright Lights. The Other Man. His Wife's Mistakes. The Waiters' Ball. A Creampuff Romance. Rebecca's Wedding Day. 1917: The Butcher Boy. Rough House. His Wedding Night. Fatty at Coney Island. Oh! Doctor. Out West. 1918: The Bell Boy. Goodnight Nurse. Moonshine. The Cook. 1919: A Desert Hero. Backstage. A Country Hero. The Garage. 1920: Life of the Party. The Round-Up. Out West. The Traveling Salesman. Brewster's Millions. Crazy to Marry. 1921: Gasoline Gus. The Dollar a Year Man. The Fast Freight. 1922: Leap Year/Skirt Shy. 1923: *Hollywood. 1925: *Go West. 1932: Hey Pop. 1933: How've You Bean? Buzzin' Around. Close Relations. Tomallio. In the Dough.*
As director: *1925: The Tourist. The Movies. 1926: Cleaning Up. The Fighting Dude. Home Cured. My Stars. His Private Life. Fool's Luck. One Sunday Morning. 1927: Peaceful Oscar. *The Red Mill. *Special Delivery.*

1930: Won By a Neck. Three Hollywood Girls. Si Si Senor. Up a Tree. 1931: Crashing Hollywood. The Lure of Hollywood. Windy Riley Goes Hollywood. Queenie of Hollywood. Honeymoon Trio. Ex-Plumber. Pete and Repeat. Marriage Rows. The Back Page. That's My Line. Up Pops the Duke. Beach Pajamas. Take 'Em and Shake 'Em. That's My Meat. One Quiet Night. Once a Hero. The Tamale Vendor. Smart Work. Idle Roomers. 1932: Hollywood Luck. Anybody's Goat. Moonlight and Cactus. Keep Laughing. Bridge Wives. Mother's Holiday. Niagara Falls. Hollywood Lights. Gigolettes. It's a Cinch.

All shorts except (*) features

ARCHER, Anne. See Archer, John

ARCHER, John (Ralph Bowman) 1915–
Big, squarely built American actor with crinkly, reddish hair and crooked grin, who came to Hollywood at 22 after winning a talent contest. Played a few leading roles in his thirties, but his features thickened rather quickly, and the impetus of his career was also somewhat disrupted by war service. Married/divorced actress Marjorie Lord (1922–); the actress Anne Archer (1945–) is their daughter.
*1938: †Overland Stage Raiders. †Flaming Frontier (serial). The Last Gangster. Letter of Introduction. 1939: Career. 1940: Barnyard Follies. Scattergood Baines. Curtain Call. 1941: King of the Zombies. Gangs Inc. City of Missing Girls. Mountain Moonlight (GB: Moving in Society). *Sucker List. Cheers for Miss Bishop. Paper Bullets. 1942: Scattergood Survives a Murder. Bowery at Midnight. Police Bullets. The Moon is Down. Mrs Wiggs of the Cabbage Patch. Hi Neighbor. 1943: Crash Dive. Hello Frisco Hello. The Purple V. Sherlock Holmes in Washington. Shantytown. Guadalcanal Diary. 1944: Roger Touhy — Gangster (GB: The Last Gangster). The Eve of St Mark. 1947: The Lost Moment. 1948: After Nightfall. 1949: White Heat. Colorado Territory. 1950: The Great Jewel Robber. Destination Moon. High Lonesome. 1951: Santa Fé. Best of the Badmen. My Favorite Spy. 1952: The Big Trees. Sea Tiger. Sound Off. A Yank in Indo-China (GB: Hidden Secret). Rodeo. 1953: The Stars Are Singing. 1954: Dragon's Gold. 1955: No Man's Woman. 1956: Rock Around the Clock. 1957: Ten Thousand*

Bedrooms. Affair in Reno. Decision at Sundown. The She-Devil. 1959: Emergency Hospital. City of Fear. 1961: Blue Hawaii. 1964: Apache Rifles. 1965: I Saw What You Did. 1971: How to Frame a Figg. 1974: Thursday's Game (TV). 1976: Amelia Earhart (TV).

† As Ralph Bowman

ARKIN, Alan 1934–
Black-haired, Greek-looking American actor, equally at home with comic or serious characters. Briefly popular in the late 1960s, he proved an insubstantial performer in box-office terms and was later seen in co-starring or guest-starring roles; leading parts continued to be commercially unrewarding. Twice nominated for an Academy Award, in The Russians Are Coming, the Russians Are Coming and The Heart is a Lonely Hunter. Also directs. 1962: *That's Me. 1963: *The Last Mohican. 1966: The Russians Are Coming, the Russians Are Coming. 1967: Wait Until Dark. Woman Times Seven. 1968: The Heart is a Lonely Hunter. Inspector Clouseau. 1969: Popi. The Monitors. 1970: Catch 22. 1971: Little Murders. 1972: Last of the Red Hot Lovers. Deadhead Miles. 1974: Freebie and the Bean. 1975: Hearts of the West (GB: Hollywood Cowboy). Rafferty and the Gold Dust Twins. 1976: The Defection of Simas Kudirka (TV). The Seven Per Cent Solution. 1977: Fire Sale. 1978: The Other Side of Hell (TV). 1979: The In-Laws. The Magician of Lublin. Improper Channels. 1980: Simon. 1981: The Last Unicorn (voice only). Chu Chu and the Philly Flash. 1982: The Return of Captain Invincible. 1984: Big Trouble. 1985: Joshua Then and Now. Bad Medicine. 1986: A Deadly Business (TV).

ARLEN, Richard (Cornelius R. Van Mattimore) 1899–1976
Hefty, aggressive, ebullient American star who entered films as an extra in 1920. Distinguished by ruddy cheeks, and the just off-centre parting in his dark hair, Arlen remained a second-league star from 1925 until 1946, when he moved into supporting roles, apart from a few leads in minor British films of the 1950s. Married to actress Jobyna Ralston (second of three) from 1927 to 1945. Died from lung congestion.
1921: †Ladies Must Live. 1922: †The Green Temptation. 1923: Vengeance of the Deep.

†The Fighting Coward. †Quicksands. 1924: Sally. 1925: ‡Coast of Folly. Behind the Front. In the Name of Love. The Enchanted Hill. 1926: Volcano. Padlocked. Old Ironsides. 1927: Figures Don't Lie. Wings. The Blood Ship. Sally in Our Alley. She's a Sheik. Rolled Stockings. Beggars of Life. 1928: Feel My Pulse. Ladies of the Mob. Manhattan Cocktail. The Four Feathers. Under the Tonto Rim. 1929: The Man I Love. Dangerous Curves. Thunderbolt. The Virginian. 1930: Light of Western Stars. *Voice of Hollywood No 2. Burning Up. Paramount on Parade. Dangerous Paradise. The Sea God. The Border Legion. Santa Fé Trail (GB: The Law Rides West). Only Saps Work. 1931: The Conquering Horde. Gun Smoke. The Secret Call. Caught. The Lawyer's Secret. Touchdown (GB: Playing the Game). 1932: Wayward. Sky Bride. Guilty As Hell (GB: Guilty As Charged). Tiger Shark. The All American (GB: Sport of a Nation). Island of Lost Souls. *Hollywood on Parade No 4. 1933: Song of the Eagle. College Humor. Three-Cornered Moon. Golden Harvest. Alice in Wonderland. Hell and High Water (GB: Cap'n Jericho). Come on Marines. 1934: She Made Her Bed. Ready for Love. 1935: Helldorado. Let 'Em Have It (GB: False Faces). Three Live Ghosts. 1936: The Calling of Dan Matthews. The Mine with the Iron Door. 1937: Artists and Models. Secret Valley (GB: The Gangster's Bride). The Great Barrier (US: Silent Barriers). Murder in Greenwich Village. 1938: No Time to Marry. Call of the Yukon. Straight, Place and Show (GB: They're Off!). 1939: Missing Daughters. Mutiny on the Blackhawk. Tropic Fury. Legion of Lost Flyers. 1940: The Man from Montreal. Danger on Wheels. Hot Steel. The Leather Pushers. Black Diamonds. The Devil's Pipeline. 1941: A Dangerous Game. Lucky Devils. Mutiny in the Arctic. Men of the Timberland. Raiders of the Desert. Forced Landing. Power Dive. Flying Blind. 1942: Torpedo Boat. *A Letter from Bataan. Wrecking Crew. Wildcat. 1943: Alaska Highway. Aerial Gunner. Minesweeper. Submarine Alert. 1944: Timber Queen. Storm over Lisbon. The Lady and the Monster (GB: Donovan's Brain). That's My Baby! 1945: Identity Unknown. The Big Bonanza. The Phantom Speaks. 1946: The French Key. Accomplice. 1947: Buffalo Bill Rides Again. 1948: When My Baby Smiles at Me. Speed to Spare. Return of Wildfire (GB: Black Stal-

lion). 1949: Grand Canyon. 1950: Kansas Raiders. 1951: Flaming Feather. Silver City (GB: High Vermilion). 1952: Hurricane Smith. The Blazing Forest. 1953: Saber Jet. 1954: Devil's Point (US: Devil's Harbor). 1955: Stolen Time (US: Blonde Blackmailer). 1956: Hidden Guns. The Mountain. 1957: Cavalry Command (released 1965). Child of Trouble (TV). 1959: Warlock. 1960: Raymie. 1961: The Last Time I Saw Archie. 1963: The Young and the Brave. The Crawling Hand. Thunder Mountain (GB: Shepherd of the Hills). Law of the Lawless. 1964: The Best Man. Young Fury. 1965: Black Spurs. The Bounty Killer. Town Tamer. The Human Duplicators. 1966: Apache Uprising. Johnny Reno. Road to Nashville. To the Shores of Hell. Waco. 1967: Red Tomahawk. Fort Utah. Huntsville/Hostile Guns. 1968: Rogue's Gallery. Buckskin. The Frontiersman. 1970: Sex and the College Girl. 1975: Won Ton Ton, the Dog Who Saved Hollywood. 1976: A Whale of a Tale.

† As Van Mattimore
‡ Scenes deleted from final release print

ARLISS, George (G. Andrews) 1868–1946
Dominant, upper-class English stage actor who became a big star on both sides of the Atlantic. His presence and immaculate diction ensured him employment in a series of portraits of famous men. Won an Academy Award for his second film portrayal of Disraeli. Died from a bronchial ailment. Received additional Academy Award nominations for The Green Goddess (1930 version). 1921: The Devil. Disraeli. 1923: The Green Goddess. The Ruling Passion. 1929: Disraeli. 1930: Old English. The Green Goddess. 1931: Millionaire. Alexander Hamilton. 1932: The Man Who Played God (GB: The Silent Voice). Successful Calamity. 1933: The King's Vacation. The Working Man. Voltaire. 1934: The House of Rothschild. The Last Gentleman. 1935: Cardinal Richelieu. The Iron Duke. The Tunnel (US: Transatlantic Tunnel). 1936: The Guvnor (US: Mr Hobo). East Meets West. 1937: His Lordships (US: Man of Affairs, Dr Syn).

ARMENDARIZ, Pedro 1912–1963
Swarthy, flashing-eyed, moustachioed Mexican actor with a memorable smile. After years

in Mexican films, he went to Hollywood but failed to win a wide variety of roles, spending the greater part of his career as Mexican bandits. Learning that he had terminal cancer, Armendariz shot himself.

1934: *Maria Elena*. 1935: *Rosario. Bordertown*. 1937: *Las Cuatro Milpas. Amapola del Camino. Jalisca nunca Pierde. La Adelita. Mi Candidato*. 1938: *Los Millones de Chafian. La Dama del Rio. El Indio. Canto a Mi Tierra. La China Hilario. Una Luz en mi Camino*. 1939: *Con los Dorados de Villa. Borrasca Humana*. 1940: *Los Olvidados de Diaz. El Charro Negro. Pobre Diablo. Mala Yerba. El Jefe Maximo. El Zorro de Jalisco. El Secreto del Sacerdote*. 1941: *Ni Sangre ni Arena. La Epapaya del Camino. Simón Bolivar. Del Rancho a la Capital. Alía en el Bajia. La Isla de la Pasión*. 1942: *Soy Puro Mexicano. Tierra de Pasiónes*. 1943: *Las Calaveras del Terror. Flor Silvestre. Kangaroja. Guadalajara. Distinto Amanecer. Maria Candelaria. La Guerra de los Pasteles*. 1944: *El Corsario Negro. Alma de Bronco. La Campana de mi Pueblo. Las Abandonadas. El Capitan Malacara. Entre Hermanos. Bugambilla*. 1945: *Rayando El Sol. La Perla (GB and US: The Pearl)*. 1946: *Enamorada*. 1947: *Albur de Amor. La Casa Colorada. Juan Charrasqueado. The Fugitive*. 1948: *Maclovia. Al Caer la Tarde. En la Hacienda de la Flor. Fort Apache. Three Godfathers*. 1949: *Tulsa. La Malquerida. We Were Strangers. The Outlaw and the Lady. Pancho Villa. El Abandonado. Bodas de Fuego*. 1950: *Rosauro Castro. Tierra Baja. La Loca de la Casa. Por la Puerta Falsa. Camino de Infierno. Nos Veremos en el Cielo. Del Odio Nace el Amor (GB: Bandit General. US: The Torch)*. 1951: *Por Querer a una Mujer. Ella y Yo. La Noche Avanza*. 1952: *Carne de Presidio. El Rebozo de la Soledad. El Bruto. Les Amants de Tolède (GB: Lovers of Toledo. US: Tyrant of Toledo)*. 1953: *Lucretia Borgia. Reportaje. Mate a la Vida. Mulata*. 1954: *Dos Mundos y Un Amor. La Rebelion de los Colgados. Border River. El Diablo del Desierto (Borderia)*. 1955: *Les Amants du Tage. Tam Tam Mayumba (US: Native Drums. GB: Tom Toms of Mayumba). El Pequeno Proscrito. La Escondida (GB: The Hidden Woman)*. 1956: *The Conqueror. Diane. The Littlest Outlaw. Men and Wolves. Canasta de Cuentos Mexicanos. La Major que no Tuvo Infancia. El Impostor. Viva Revolución*. 1957: *Flor de Mayo*

(*GB: A Mexican Affair. US: Beyond All Limits). The Big Boodle. Ando volando Bajo. La Pandilla del Soborno. El Zarco (GB: El Zarco – the Bandit). Asi Era Pancho Villa. Affair in Havana. Manuela (US: Stowaway Girl)*. 1958: *Pancho Villa y la Valentina. Cuando Viva Villa es La Muerte. Café Colón. Spoilers of the Sea. Las Senoritas Vivanco. Los Desarraigados. La Cucaracha (GB: The Bandit). Sed de Amor*. 1959: *Yo Pecador. El Hombre Nuestro de Cada Día. Calibre 44. The Wonderful Country. El Pequeno Salvaje*. 1960: *La Cárcel de Cananca. El Induito. 800 Leguas por el Amazona. Dos Hijos Desobedientes*. 1961: *Los Hermanos del Hierro (US: My Son, the Hero). Los Valientes no Mueren. El Rejedor de Milagros. Francis of Assisi. Arrivani i Titani (GB: Sons of Thunder. US: The Titans)*. 1962: *La Bandida*. 1963: *Captain Sinbad. From Russia with Love*.

ARMSTRONG, Louis 1900–1971
Enormously popular and beloved, flat-faced, brow-mopping, beaming black American trumpeter whose relatively few film appearances still managed to convey the obvious pleasure he gained both from playing music and clowning around. There were also memorable vocal duets with such Hollywood stars as Bing Crosby and Danny Kaye. Known world-wide as Satchmo (Satchel-mouth). Died from heart failure.

1930: *Ex-Flame*. 1936: *Pennies from Heaven*. 1937: *Every Day's a Holiday*. 1938: *Dr Rhythm. Artists and Models*. 1939: *Going Places*. 1941: *The Birth of the Blues*. 1943: *Cabin in the Sky. *Show Business at War*. 1944: *Jam Session. Hollywood Canteen. Atlantic City*. 1945: *Pillow to Post*. 1947: *New Orleans*. 1948: *A Song is Born*. 1950: *Botta e risposta*. 1951: *The Strip. Here Comes the Groom*. 1952: *Glory Alley. La route de bonheur*. 1953: *Jazz Parade. The Glenn Miller Story*. 1956: *High Society*. 1957: *Satchmo the Great*. 1959: *The Five Pennies. The Beat Generation*. 1960: *Jazz on a Summer's Day*. 1961: *Paris Blues*. 1965: *When the Boys Meet the Girls*. 1966: *A Man Called Adam*. 1968: *Jazz: The Intimate Art (TV. GB: cinemas)*. 1969: *Hello, Dolly!* 1981: *Bix (voice only)*.

ARMSTRONG, Robert (Donald R. Smith) 1890–1973
Burly, dark-faced American character star and sometime leading man with rough-and-ready

tones and aggressive style. Remembered by most filmgoers for his Denham in the *King Kong* films, but often seen as fast-talking men on the make, or crooked politicians. Died from cancer.

1915: *The Silent Voice*. 1917: *War and the Woman*. 1921: *Boys Will Be Boys. Honey Girl. Shavings. Sure Fire*. 1924: *The Man Who Came Back*. 1925: *New Brooms. Judy*. 1927: *Is Zat So? The Main Event. The Leopard Lady. A Girl in Every Port*. 1928: *Square Crooks. The Cop. Celebrity. The Baby Cyclone. Show Folks. Shady Lady*. 1929: *The Leatherneck. Ned McCobb's Daughter. The Woman from Hell. Big News. Oh Yeah! (GB: No Brakes). The Racketeer (GB: Love's Conquest)*. 1930: *Big Money. Be Yourself. Danger Lights. Dumbbells in Ermine. Paid (GB: Within the Law)*. 1931: *Easy Money. The Tip-Off (GB: Looking for Trouble). Suicide Fleet. Iron Man. Ex-Bad Boy*. 1932: *Panama Flo. The Lost Squadron. Is My Face Red. Hold 'em Jail. The Most Dangerous Game (GB: The Hounds of Zaroff). The Penguin Pool Murder (GB: The Penguin Pool Mystery). Radio Patrol*. 1933: *Blind Adventure. The Billion Dollar Scandal. King Kong. I Love That Man. Fast Workers. Above the Clouds (GB: Winged Devils). Son of Kong*. 1934: *Search for Beauty. Palooka. The Great Schnozzle). The Hell Cat. She Made Her Bed. Manhattan Love Song. Kansas City Princess. Flirting with Danger*. 1935: *The Mystery Man. Sweet Music. G Men. Gigolette (GB: Night Club). Remember Last Night? Little Big Shot*. 1936: *Dangerous Waters. The Ex-Mrs Bradford. Public Enemy's Wife (GB: G-Man's Wife). All American Chump (GB: Country Bumpkin). Without Orders. *Pirate Party on Catalina Isle*. 1937: *The Three Legionnaires. It Can't Last Forever. Nobody's Baby. The Girl Said No*. 1938: *She Loved a Fireman. There Goes My Heart. The Night Hawk*. 1939: *The Flying Irishman. Unmarried (GB: Night Club Hostess). Man of Conquest. Winter Carnival. Flight at Midnight. Call a Messenger*. 1940: *Framed. Forgotten Girls. Enemy Agent (GB: Secret Enemy). San Francisco Docks. Behind the News*. 1941: *Mr Dynamite. Citadel of Crime. Dive Bomber. The Bride Wore Crutches. Sky Raiders (serial). My Favorite Spy*. 1942: *Baby Face Morgan. Let's Get Tough. It Happened in Flatbush. Gang Busters (serial)*. 1943: *Around the World. The Kansan*

(GB: Wagon Wheels). Adventures of the Flying Cadets (serial). The Mad Ghoul. 1944: The Navy Way. Action in Arabia. Mr Winkle Goes to War (GB: Arms and the Woman). Belle of the Yukon. 1945: Gangs of the Waterfront. Blood on the Sun. The Falcon in San Francisco. The Royal Mounted Rides Again (serial). Arson Squad. 1946: Gay Blades. Criminal Court. GI War Brides. Blonde Alibi. Decoy. 1947: The Fall Guy. The Fugitive. Exposed. 1948: Return of the Bad Men. The Sea of Grass. The Paleface. 1949: The Lucky Stiff. Crime Doctor's Diary. The Streets of San Francisco. Mighty Joe Young. Captain China. Sons of New Mexico (GB: The Brat). 1950: Destination Big House. 1952: The Pace That Thrills. 1955: Las Vegas Shakedown. 1956: The Peacemaker. 1957: The Crooked Circle. 1963: Johnny Cool. 1964: For Those Who Think Young.

ARNALL, Julia 1931–
Ash-blonde, Austrian-born actress-model of cool and detached personality, who came to Britain in 1950. Her vulnerable, but limited, appeal soon faded after a few star roles, and her Rank contract was terminated in 1957. Later did small parts and appeared in TV commercials – the medium in which she was first noticed.
1953: Knights of the Round Table. 1954: Man of the Moment. 1955: I Am a Camera. Value for Money. Simon and Laura. Lost (US: Tears for Simon). 1956: House of Secrets. 1957: The Man without a Body. Mark of the Phoenix. 1959: Model for Murder. 1960: The Trunk (filmed 1957). 1961: Carry on Regardless. 1966: The Quiller Memorandum. 1967: The Double Man.

ARNESS, James (J. Aurness) 1923–
Husky 6ft 8in American leading man with fair curly hair. With his bear-like build he found difficulty getting a range of roles, but then landed in television's *Gunsmoke* (GB: *Gun Law*) as Marshal Matt Dillon, a series that lasted 20 years. Since it ended in 1972, his giant frame, easy-going drawl and rather strained smile have proved just as difficult to cast as before.
1947: †The Farmer's Daughter. †Roses Are Red. 1948: †The Man from Texas. 1949: †Battleground. 1950: †Sierra. †Two Lost Worlds. †Wyoming Mail. †Wagonmaster.

†Double Crossbones. Stars in My Crown. 1951: Cavalry Scout. Belle le Grand. Iron Man. The People Against O'Hara. The Girl in White (GB: So Bright the Flame). The Thing from Another World. 1952: Carbine Williams. Horizons West. Big Jim McLain. Hellgate. 1953: Lone Hand. Ride the Man Down. The Veils of Bagdad. Island in the Sky. 1954: Hondo. Her Twelve Men. Them! 1955: Many Rivers to Cross. The Sea Chase. Flame of the Islands. 1956: The First Traveling Saleslady. Gun the Man Down/Arizona Mission. 1975: The MacAhans: How the West Was Won (TV).

† As James Aurness

ARNOLD, Edward (Gunther E. A. Schneider) 1890–1956
Portly, expansive leading American character actor. Became famous as Diamond Jim (and the detective Nero Wolfe) and later specialized in corrupt politicians and businessmen, remaining a top featured player until his death. Died of a cerebral haemorrhage.
1916: When the Man Speaks. The Primitive Strain. 1917: The Slacker's Heart/The Slacker. The Wrong Way. 1919: Phil-for-Short. A Broadway Saint. 1920: The Cost. 1927: Sunrise. 1932: Men of the Nile. Rasputin and the Empress. Okay America! (GB: Penalty of Fame). Three on a Match. Afraid to Talk. 1933: Whistling in the Dark. The White Sister. The Barbarian (GB: A Night in Cairo). Her Bodyguard. Jennie Gerhardt. I'm No Angel. Roman Scandals. Secret of the Blue Room. 1934: Sadie McKee. Madame Spy. Thirty Day Princess. Unknown Blonde. Hide-Out. Million Dollar Ransom. Wednesday's Child. 1935: The President Vanishes (GB: Strange Conspiracy).

*Biography of a Bachelor Girl. Cardinal Richelieu. The Glass Key. Diamond Jim. Remember Last Night? Crime and Punishment. 1936: Sutter's Gold. Meet Nero Wolfe. Come and Get It. 1937: John Meade's Woman. Easy Living. The Toast of New York. Blossoms on Broadway. 1938: The Crowd Roars. You Can't Take It with You. Let Freedom Ring. 1939: Idiot's Delight. Man about Town. Mr Smith Goes to Washington. 1940: The Earl of Chicago. Slightly Honorable. Johnny Apollo. Lillian Russell. 1941: The Penalty. The Lady from Cheyenne. Meet John Doe. Nothing But the Truth. Unholy Partners. Design for Scandal. Johnny Eager. All That Money Can Buy. 1942: Eyes in the Night. The War against Mrs Hadley. 1943: The Youngest Profession. 1944: Ziegfeld Follies (released 1946). Janie. Kismet. Mrs Parkington. Standing Room Only. Main Street After Dark. 1945: Weekend at the Waldorf. The Hidden Eye. 1946: Janie Gets Married. Three Wise Fools. No Leave, No Love. The Mighty McGurk. My Brother Talks to Horses. 1947: Dear Ruth. The Hucksters. 1948: Three Daring Daughters. Big City. Wallflower. Command Decision. 1949: John Loves Mary. Take Me Out to the Ball Game (GB: Everybody's Cheering). Big Jack. Dear Wife. 1950: The Yellow Cab Man. Annie Get Your Gun. *The Screen Actor. The Skipper Surprised His Wife. 1951: Dear Brat. 1952: Belles on Their Toes. 1953: City That Never Sleeps. Man of Conflict. 1954: Living It Up. 1956: The Houston Story. The Ambassador's Daughter. Miami Exposé.*

ARQUETTE, Rosanna 1959–
With her tawny hair, curvy figure, petite stature, real-life salty language and talent for wildcat comedy, this third-generation Hollywood performer could be the natural successor to Carole Lombard, enjoying a film freedom in which Lombard would have revelled. Like Lombard she can also be effective in more subdued roles. Granddaughter of comedy character actor Cliff Arquette, she broke through to stardom in *Desperately Seeking Susan* and now looks set for a run at the top.
1977: Having Babies II (TV). 1978: Zuma Beach (TV). The Dark Secret of Harvest Home (TV). 1979: More American Graffiti/The Party's Over/Purple Haze. 1980: Gorp. 1981: SOB. A Long Way Home (TV). The

Wall (TV). 1982: The Executioner's Song. Baby It's You. Johnny Belinda (TV). 1983: Off the Wall. One Cooks, the Other Doesn't (TV). 1984: Hit Parade (TV). The Aviator. 1985: Survival Guides (TV). Silverado. Desperately Seeking Susan. After Hours. 1986: 8 Million Ways to Die. Nobody's Fool.

ARTHUR, Jean (Gladys Greene) 1905–
Fluffily blonde, croaky-voiced (but with piquant sex appeal) American leading actress who started in low-budget westerns, then spent 20 years as a star. She really came into her own in 1930s' comedies and Frank Capra films, which allowed her warm and perky personality full play. Nominated for an Academy Award in *The More the Merrier*.
*1923: *Somebody Lied. Cameo Kirby. 1924: *Spring Fever. *Case Dismissed. *The Powerful Eye. The Temple of Venus. Fast and Fearless. Biff Bang Buddy. Bringin' Home the Bacon. Travelin' Fast. Thundering Romance. 1925: The Fighting Smile. Seven Chances. The Drug Store Cowboy. A Man of Nerve. Tearin' Loose. 1926: *Hello Lafayette. Thundering Through. Born to Battle. *Eight Cylinder Bull. The Hurricane Horseman. The Cowboy Cop. Twisted Triggers. Roaring Rider. The Fighting Cheat. Riding Rivals. The College Boob. Lightning Bill. Double Daring. Under Fire. *The Mad Racer. 1927: The Block Signal. Husband Hunters. The Broken Gate. Horseshoes. *Bigger and Better Blondes. Winners of the Wilderness. The Poor Nut. Flying Luck. The Masked Menace (serial). 1928: Wallflowers. Easy Come, Easy Go. Warming Up. Brotherly Love. Sins of the Fathers. 1929: The Canary Murder Case. The Mysterious Dr Fu Manchu. The Saturday Night Kid. The Greene Murder Case. Halfway to Heaven. Stairs of Sand. 1930: Street of Chance. The Record Run. Young Eagles. Paramount on Parade. The Return of Dr Fu Manchu. Danger Lights. The Silver Horde. 1931: The Gang Buster. The Lawyer's Secret. Virtuous Husband (GB: What Wives Don't Want). Ex-Bad Boy. 1933: Get That Venus. The Past of Mary Holmes. 1934: Whirlpool. The Defense Rests. The Most Precious Thing in Life. The Whole Town's Talking (GB: Passport to Fame). 1935: Public Hero Number One. Party Wire. Diamond Jim. The Public Menace. If You Could Only Cook. 1936: Mr Deeds Goes to Town. The Ex-Mrs Bradford. Adventure in Manhattan (GB: Manhattan Madness). The*

Plainsman. More Than a Secretary. 1937: History is Made at Night. Easy Living. 1938: You Can't Take It with You. 1939: Only Angels Have Wings. Mr Smith Goes to Washington. 1940: Too Many Husbands (GB: My Two Husbands). Arizona. 1941: The Devil and Miss Jones. 1942: The Talk of the Town. 1943: The More the Merrier. A Lady Takes a Chance. 1944: The Impatient Years. 1948: A Foreign Affair. 1953: Shane.

ASHCROFT, Dame Peggy 1907–
Britain's most distinguished living actress, a diminutive light-haired lady with something of a Margaret Sullavan (qv) appeal in her early days, has appeared only very rarely in films, confining her career almost entirely to stage – where she became a delicate and distinctive interpreter of Shakespeare – and radio. But her warmth and talent were evident even in unworthy cinematic roles, and she won an Academy Award for her performance in *A Passage to India* at 77. Made Dame Peggy in 1956, she is three times married and divorced.
*1933: The Wandering Jew. 1935: The 39 Steps. 1936: Rhodes of Africa (US: Rhodes). 1940: *Channel Incident. 1941: Quiet Wedding. 1958: The Nun's Story. 1967: Tell Me Lies. October Revolution (narrator only). 1968: Secret Ceremony. 1969: Three into Two Won't Go. 1971: Sunday, Bloody Sunday. 1973: Der Fussgänger/Le piéton/The Pedestrian. 1976: Joseph Andrews. 1984: A Passage to India. 1986: When the Wind Blows (voice only).*

ASHER, Jane 1946–
Red-haired, delicate-looking, slightly built British actress, a former child player who

flowered briefly in elfin and usually sensitive adult roles. Mostly on stage after 1970, she married the artist and cartoonist Gerald Scarfe and later became a published expert on cookery and cake-icing.
1952: Mandy (US: Crash of Silence). 1953: Third Party Risk. 1954: Dance Little Lady. Adventure in the Hopfields. 1955: The Quatermass Experiment (US: The Creeping Unknown). 1956: Charley Moon. 1961: The Greengage Summer (US: Loss of Innocence). 1962: The Prince and the Pauper. 1963: Girl in the Headlines (US: The Model Murder Case). 1964: The Masque of the Red Death. 1966: Alfie. 1968: The Winter's Tale. 1970: The Buttercup Chain. Deep End. 1972: Henry VIII and His Six Wives. 1984: Success is the Best Revenge.

ASHERSON, Renee (R. Ascherson) 1920–
Brown-haired, large-eyed, London-born actress who became a specialist in waiting women and diffident damsels. Her rather distant and indefinite personality was not entirely suited to the screen, and she returned to the stage in the mid-1950s after some disappointing film roles. Widow of Robert Donat (qv); married in 1953, they were separated at the time of his death five years later.
1944: †The Way Ahead (US: Immortal Battalion). Henry V. 1945: Caesar and Cleopatra. The Way to the Stars (US: Johnny in the Clouds). 1948: Once a Jolly Swagman (US: Maniacs on Wheels). The Small Back Room (US: Hour of Glory). 1949: The Cure for Love. 1950: Pool of London. 1951: The Magic Box. 1953: Malta Story. 1954: Time is My Enemy. The Red Dress. 1961: The Day the Earth Caught Fire. 1965: Rasputin the Mad Monk. 1969: The Smashing Bird I Used to Know. 1973: Theatre of Blood. 1979: A Man Called Intrepid (TV). 1985: Romance on the Orient Express (TV).

† As Renée Ascherson

ASHLEY, Elizabeth (E. Cole) 1939–
Brunette, sharp-featured American actress of somewhat tart personality, good at vixens and hard-shelled heroines. Mainly on stage (from the late 1950s), she was unlucky not to be a success at her first try in Hollywood, but picked up some good roles on TV in the 1970s. Married/divorced actors James Farentino and George Peppard (qv), 1962–1966 and 1966–1972, first and second of three. Her auto-

biography, *Actress – Postcards from the Road*, revealed a traumatic personal life.
1963: *The Carpetbaggers*. 1965: *Ship of Fools*. *The Third Day*. 1971: *The Face of Fear (TV)*. *Second Chance (TV)*. *The Marriage of a Young Stockbroker*. *Harpy (TV)*. 1972: *Your Money or Your Wife (TV)*. *When Michael Calls (TV)*. 1973: *The Magician (TV)*. *The Heist (TV. GB: Suspected Person)*. 1974: *Golden Needles*. *Paperback Hero*. *Rancho de Luxe*. 1975: *One of My Wives is Missing (TV)*. *92 in the Shade*. 1976: *The Great Scout and Cathouse Thursday*. 1977: *The War Between the Tates (TV)*. *Coma*. 1978: *A Fire in the Sky (TV)*. 1979: *Corky*. 1980: *Windows*. 1981: *Paternity*. 1982: *Captured!/Split Image*. 1983: *Svengali (TV)*. 1986: *Stagecoach (TV)*.

ASKEY, Arthur 1900–1982
Diminutive, much-loved, dark-haired, bespectacled English music-hall comedian ('Big-Hearted Arthur'), who delighted audiences with 'silly little songs' and won enormous success on radio in *Band Waggon*, Britain's first comedy series. His films have not worn too well, but the best are still sporadically funny. Catch-phrases: 'I thank you', 'Before your very eyes' and 'Hello, playmates'. Died from gangrene after having both legs removed.
1937: **Pathe Pictorial No 115 (The Bee)*. *Calling All Stars*. 1939: *Band Waggon*. 1940: *Charley's (Big-Hearted) Aunt*. 1941: *The Ghost Train*. *I Thank You*. 1942: *Back Room Boy*. **The Nose Has It*. *King Arthur Was a Gentleman*. 1943: *Miss London Ltd*. 1944: *Bees in Paradise*. 1954: *The Love Match*. 1955:

Ramsbottom Rides Again. 1956: **Skilful Soccer*. 1958: *Make Mine a Million*. 1959: *Friends and Neighbours*. 1972: *The Alf Garnett Saga*. 1977: **End of Term*. 1978: *Rosie Dixon – Night Nurse*. 1982: *The Pantomime Dame*.

ASKWITH, Robin 1950–
Perky, wide-smiling British actor who, after an uninteresting apprenticeship, proved extremely popular in the leading role of the 'Confessions' sex comedies of the 1970s. When the market for these subsided, he moved into similar sort of stuff (still vulgar but slightly laundered) in television comedy series.
1968: *Otley*. *If …* 1969: *Alfred the Great*. 1970: *Cool It Carol!* *Scramble*. †*Bartleby*. 1971: *Nicholas and Alexandra*. †*The Canterbury Tales*. *All Coppers Are …* 1972: *Tower of Evil (US: Horror of Snape Island)*. *The Flesh and Blood Show*. *The Four Dimensions of Greta*. *Bless This House*. *Hide and Seek*. 1973: *Carry On Girls*. *No Sex Please – We're British*. *Horror Hospital*. 1974: *Confessions of a Window Cleaner*. 1975: *The Hostages*. *Confessions of a Pop Performer*. 1976: *Confessions of a Driving Instructor*. *Stand Up Virgin Soldiers*. 1977: *Closed Up Tight*. *Queen Kong*. *Confessions from a Holiday Camp*. *Let's Get Laid*. 1982: *Britannia Hospital*.

† *As Robin Asquith*

ASTAIRE, Fred (F. Austerlitz) 1899–
Pencil-slim, hard-working innovative dancing star who made the grinding discipline of constant rehearsal come to the screen as pure

poetry. A hit on stage with his sister Adele, then on film with Ginger Rogers. Special Academy Award 1949. Won an Emmy in 1979 for *A Family Upside Down*. Nominated for an Oscar in *The Towering Inferno*.
1932: **Municipal Bandwagon*. 1933: *Dancing Lady*. *Flying Down to Rio*. 1934: *The Gay Divorcee (GB: The Gay Divorce)*. 1935: *Roberta*. *Top Hat*. 1936: *Follow the Fleet*. *Swing Time*. 1937: *Shall We Dance? A Damsel in Distress*. 1938: *Carefree*. 1939: *The Story of Vernon and Irene Castle*. 1940: *Broadway Melody of 1940*. *Second Chorus*. 1941: *You'll Never Get Rich*. 1942: *Holiday Inn*. *You Were Never Lovelier*. 1943: *The Sky's the Limit*. 1944: *Ziegfeld Follies (released 1946)*. 1945: *Yolanda and the Thief*. 1946: *Blue Skies*. 1948: *Easter Parade*. 1949: *The Barkleys of Broadway*. 1950: *Three Little Words*. *Let's Dance*. *Royal Wedding (GB: Wedding Bells)*. 1951: *The Belle of New York*. 1953: *The Band Wagon*. 1954: *Deep in My Heart*. 1955: *Daddy Long-Legs*. 1956: *Funny Face*. 1957: *Silk Stockings*. 1959: *On the Beach*. 1961: *The Pleasure of His Company*. 1962: *The Notorious Landlady*. 1964: *Paris When It Sizzles (voice)*. 1968: *Finian's Rainbow*. 1969: *Midas Run (GB: A Run on Gold)*. 1971: *The Over-the-Hill Gang Rides Again (TV)*. 1973: *Imagine*. 1974: *The Towering Inferno*. *That's Entertainment!* 1976: *That's Entertainment Part Two*. 1977: *Taxi Mauve (US: Purple Taxi)*. *The Amazing Dobermans*. 1979: *A Family Upside Down (TV)*. 1980: *The Man in the Santa Claus Suit (TV)*. 1981: *Ghost Story*.

ASTHER, Nils 1897–1981
Suave, charismatic and faintly mysterious Danish-born leading man. During spells in German films, Hollywood (twice) and Britain, he found himself cast as every nationality but his own. Best remembered as the Chinese warlord in *The Bitter Tea of General Yen*, Asther eventually returned to his native country, where he was regarded as something of a father-figure in the Danish cinema.
1916: *Vingarne*. 1917: *Hittebarnet*. 1918: *Himmelskibet*. *De mystiske Fodspar*. *Solen der draepte*. 1920: *Gyurkovicsarna*. 1922: *Vem dömer*. 1923: *Das Geheimnis der Herzogen*. *Norrtullsligan*. 1924: *The Courier of Carl XII*. *Wienerbarnet*. 1925: *Briefe, die ihn nicht erreichten*. *Finale der Liebe*. *Sveket nej Volontar*.

*Der Mann seiner Frau. 1926: Die drei Kuck-
ucksuhren. Der goldene Schmetterling. Das süsse
Mädel. Die versunkene Flotte. 1927: Gauner
im Frack. Budden Geheimnisse. Hotelratten.
Wiener Herzen. Der mann mit der falschen
Banknote. Topsy and Eva. Sorrell and Son.
1928: Hollywood Review. When Fleet Meets
Fleet. The Blue Danube. Adventure Mad.
Laugh Clown Laugh. The Cossacks. Adrienne
Lecouvreur. Loves of an Actress. The Card-
board Lover. Our Dancing Daughters. 1929:
Dream of Love. Wild Orchids. Hollywood
Revue of 1929. The Single Standard. 1930:
The Wrath of the Seas. King of Jazz. The Sea
Bat. 1931: But the Flesh is Weak. 1932: Letty
Lynton. The Washington Masquerade (GB:
Mad Masquerade). 1933: If I Were Free (GB:
Behold We Live). The Bitter Tea of General
Yen. Storm at Daybreak. The Right to
Romance. 1934: By Candlelight. Madame Spy.
The Crime Doctor. The Love Captive. 1935:
Abdul the Damned. 1936: The Marriage of
Corbal (US: Prisoner of Corbal). Guilty
Melody. 1937: Make Up. 1938: Tea Leaves in
the Wind. 1940: The Man Who Lost Himself.
1941: Forced Landing. Flying Blind. Dr Kil-
dare's Wedding Day (GB: Mary Names the
Day). The Night before the Divorce. The Night
of January 16th. 1942: Sweater Girl. Night
Monster (GB: The Hammond Mystery). 1943:
Submarine Alert. Mystery Broadcast. 1944:
Alaska. The Hour Before Dawn. The Man
in Half Moon Street. 1945: Bluebeard. Love,
Honor and Goodbye. Son of Lassie. Jealousy.
1948: The Feathered Serpent. 1953: That Man
from Tangier. 1960: När mörket faller. Svenska
Floyd. 1962: Vita frun. 1963: Gudrun.*

ASTOR, Mary (Lucile Langhanke) 1906–
Wanly beautiful, dark-haired American leading lady, capable of great depths. Despite a
quite inflammatory private life, she maintained her star status for more than 20 years.
Her best role, in *The Maltese Falcon*, came
too late to enable her to become the dominant
star she might have been, and she drifted into
'mother' roles. Won an Academy Award in
1941 for *The Great Lie.*
*1921:   †Sentimental   Journey/Sentimental
Tommy. *The Beggar Maid. *Bullets or
Ballots. *Brother of the Bear. *My Lady o' the
Pines. *The Bashful Suitor. 1922: *The Young
Painter. Hope. The Angelus. The Man Who
Played God. John Smith. 1923: Second Fiddle.*

*Success. The Scarecrow. The Bright Shawl.
Puritan Passions. To the Ladies. The Rapids.
The Marriage Maker. Hollywood. Woman
Proof. 1924: Beau Brummell. The Fighting
Coward. Unguarded Woman. Inez from Hol-
lywood (GB: The Good Bad Girl). The Fight-
ing American. The Price of a Party. 1925: Oh,
Doctor. Enticement. Playing with Souls. Don
Q, Son of Zorro. The Pace that Thrills. The
Scarlet Saint. 1926: Don Juan. The Wise Guy.
Forever After. High Steppers. 1927: The Rough
Riders (GB: The Trumpet Calls). The Sea
Tiger. Sunset Derby. Rose of the Golden West.
Two Arabian Knights. No Place to Go. 1928:
Heart to Heart. Sailors' Wives. Dressed to Kill.
Three-Ring Marriage. Dry Martini. 1929:
Romance of the Underworld. New Year's Eve.
Woman from Hell. Ladies Love Brutes. 1930:
The Runaway Bride. Holiday. The Lash (GB:
Adios). The Royal Bed (GB: The Queen's
Husband). 1931: Behind Office Doors. Sin
Ship. Other Men's Women. White Shoulders.
Smart Woman. 1932: Men of Chance. The Lost
Squadron. A Successful Calamity. Those We
Love. Red Dust. 1933: The Little Giant. Jennie
Gerhardt. The World Changes. Convention
City. The Kennel Murder Case. 1934: Easy
to Love. Upperworld. *The Hollywood Gad-
About. The Man with Two Faces. Return of the
Terror. The Case of the Howling Dog. 1935: I
Am a Thief. Straight from the Heart. Dinky.
Page Miss Glory. Red Hot Tires (GB: Racing
Luck). Man of Iron. 1936: The Murder of
Dr Harrigan. And So They Were Married.
Trapped by Television (GB: Caught by Tele-
vision). Dodsworth. 1937: The Lady from
Nowhere. The Prisoner of Zenda. The Hurri-
cane. 1938: Paradise for Three (GB: Romance
for Three). No Time to Marry. There's Always
a Woman. Woman Against Woman. Listen,
Darling. 1939: Midnight. 1940: Turnabout.
Brigham Young – Frontiersman (GB: Brigham
Young). 1941: The Maltese Falcon. The Great
Lie. 1942: In This Our Life. Across the Pacific.
The Palm Beach Story. 1943: Young Ideas.
Thousands Cheer. 1944: Meet Me in St Louis.
Blonde Fever. 1946: Claudia and David. Cyn-
thia (GB: The Rich, Full Life). 1947: Fiesta.
Desert Fury. Cass Timberlane. 1948: Act of
Violence. 1949: Little Women. Any Number
Can Play. 1956: A Kiss Before Dying. The
Power and the Prize. 1957: The Devil's
Hairpin. Mr and Mrs McAdam (TV). The
Troublemakers (TV). 1958: This Happy Feel-
ing. The Return of Ansel Gibbs (TV). 1959:
Stranger in My Arms. Diary of a Nurse (TV).
1960: Journey to the Day (TV). 1961: Return
to Peyton Place. 1964: Youngblood Hawke.
Hush ... Hush, Sweet Charlotte.*

† *Scenes deleted from final release print*

ATTENBOROUGH, Sir Richard 1923–
Stocky, buoyant, boyish British actor whose
film career has divided itself into four phases:
as weak and blustering youths (1942–1953); a
genial, faintly roguish leading man (1953–
1960); a versatile character star (1961–1970);
a workmanlike and occasionally inspired
director of daunting prestige subjects.
Knighted in 1975. Married to Sheila Sim (*qv*)

since 1945. Won the best director Oscar in
1983 for *Gandhi*. A stout campaigner and
fighter for the British film industry, he
proved its guiding light in the mid-1980s.
*1942: In Which We Serve. 1943: Schweik's
New   Adventures.   The   Hundred-Pound
Window. 1945: Journey Together. A Matter of
Life and Death (US: Stairway to Heaven).
1946: School for Secrets (US: Secret Flight).
1947: The Man Within (US: The Smugglers).
Dancing With Crime. Brighton Rock (US:
Young Scarface). 1948: London Belongs to Me
(US: Dulcimer Street). The Guinea Pig. 1949:
The Lost People. Boys in Brown. 1950: Morn-
ing Departure (US: Operation Disaster).
1951: Hell is Sold Out. The Magic Box. 1952:
*Sports Page No 6 – Football. Gift Horse (US:
Glory at Sea). Father's Doing Fine. 1953:
Eight O'Clock Walk. 1955: The Ship That
Died of Shame (US: PT Raiders). Private's
Progress. 1956: The Baby and the Battleship.
1957: Brothers-in-Law. The Scamp. 1958:
Dunkirk. Sea of Sand (US: Desert Patrol).
The Man Upstairs. 1959: Danger Within (US:
Breakout). I'm All Right Jack. Jet Storm. SOS
Pacific. 1960: The Angry Silence. The League
of Gentlemen. 1961: Only Two Can Play. 1962:
All Night Long. The Dock Brief (US: Trial
and Error). 1963: The Great Escape. Seance
on a Wet Afternoon. 1964: The Third Secret.
*A Boy's Day (narrator). Guns at Batasi.
1965: The Flight of the Phoenix. 1966: The
Sand Pebbles. 1968: Dr Dolittle. Only When I
Larf. The Bliss of Mrs Blossom. 1969: David
Copperfield (TV. GB: cinemas). The Magic
Christian. 1970: The Last Grenade (US:
Grigsby). A Severed Head. Loot. *Don't Make
Me Laugh (narrator). 10 Rillington Place.
1971: Cup Glory (narrator only). 1974: Death
in Persepolis. Rosebud. And Then There Were
None. 1975: Brannigan. 1976: Conduct Unbe-
coming. The Voyage. 1977: The Chess Players.
1979: The Human Factor.*

As director:
*1969: Oh! What a Lovely War. 1971: Young
Winston. 1977: A Bridge Too Far. 1978:
Magic. 1982: Gandhi. 1985: A Chorus Line.*

AUBREY, Anne 1937–
Voluptuous, tawny-haired English leading
lady, a victim both of poor casting and an
acrimonious running battle with her long-
time husband, actor Derren Nesbit (*qv*). Gen-

erally had rather more acting talent than her brief film career would indicate.

1957: High Flight. 1958: The Man Inside. No Time to Die! (US: Tank Force). The Secret Man. 1959: The Bandit of Zhobe. Idle on Parade (US: Idol on Parade). Killers of Kilimanjaro. Jazzboat. In the Nick. 1960: Carolina. Let's Get Married. 1961: The Hellions.

AUMONT, Jean-Pierre
(J-P Salomons) 1909–
Sandy-haired, wry-looking romantic French leading man who never quite realized his potential as an international star. In Hollywood from 1942 to 1948 after distinguished war service. Married (second) to Maria Montez (*qv*) from 1943 to her death in 1951. In 1956 he married actress Marisa Pavan (1932–) and they have since divorced and remarried. Aumont has also written plays and continues, in his seventies, to make international films.

1931: Echec et mat. 1932: Faut-il les marier? Jean de la Lune. Eve cherche un père. 1933: Dans les rues. La merveilleuse tragédie de Lourdes. Le voleur. Un jour viendra. 1935: Les yeux noirs. Les beaux jours. Maria Chapdelaine. 1936: Lac aux Dames. La porte du Large. Taras Bulba. L'équipage (US: Flight into Darkness). 1937: Cargaison blanche. Drôle de drame (US: Bizarre Bizarre). Le messager. Cheri-Bibi. Maman Colibri. 1938: La femme du bout du monde. Le paradis du Satan. Hôtel du nord. La belle étoile. 1939: Le deserteur (GB: SOS Sahara. US: Three Hours). Songs of the Street. 1943: Assignment in Brittany. 1944:

The Cross of Lorraine. 1946: Heartbeat. 1947: Song of Scheherezade. 1948: Siren of Atlantis. The First Gentleman (US: Affairs of a Rogue). Hans le marin (GB: The Wicked City). 1949: Golden Arrow/Three Men and a Girl (US: The Gay Adventure. Released 1952). 1950: La vie commence demain. L'homme de joie. L'amant de paille. 1951: La vendetta del corsaro. Ultimo incontro. Les loups chassent la nuit. 1952: Lili. 1953: Königsmark. Moineaux de Paris. 1954: Si Versailles m'était conté (GB: Versailles. US: Royal Affairs in Versailles). 18 heures d'escale. Charge of the Lancers. 1955: Napoléon. Mademoiselle de Paris. 1956: Hilda Crane. 1957: The Seventh Sin. 1958: Word from a Sealed-Off Box (TV). 1959: John Paul Jones. 1960: Una domenica d'estate. The Enemy General. 1961: The Devil at Four O'Clock. Carnival of Crime. 1962: The Blonde of Buenos Aires. Les sept péchés capitaux (GB: The Seven Deadly Sins. US: Seven Capital Sins). Five Miles to Midnight. 1963: The Horse without a Head. Always on Sunday (US: A Summer Sunday). 1964: Vacances portugaises. 1967: Cauldron of Blood (US: Blind Man's Bluff). 1969: Castle Keep. 1972: L'homme au cerveau greffé. 1973: La nuit americaine (GB and US: Day for Night). 1974: Porgi l'altra guancia (US: Turn the Other Cheek). 1975: The Happy Hooker. Mahogany. Catherine and Co. 1976: The Man in the Iron Mask. Des journées entières dans les arbres (GB: Entire Days Among the Trees). 1977: Le chat et le souris (GB: Seven Suspects for Murder. US: Cat and Mouse). 1978: Deux solitudes. Blackout. 1979: Something Short of Paradise. 1980: The Memory of Eva Ryker (TV). 1982: Difendimi dalle notte. The Evil Touch. Nana. 1983: Le sang des autres. 1985: Sweet Country.

AUSTIN, Charlotte 1933–
Pretty, perky, chestnut-haired, petite American singer and dancer (named after her birthplace – Charlotte, North Carolina). On stage as a child, she starred in her first film, a Columbia musical. 20th Century-Fox then picked up, but she was perhaps a little too much like their own Mitzi Gaynor, and they did very little with her. After a series of very minor roles for them, and leads in a couple of B-grade horror films, she retired from movies.

1952: Rainbow 'Round My Shoulder. 1953: The Farmer Takes a Wife. 1954: How to Marry a Millionaire. Desiree. Gorilla at Large. 1955:

Daddy Long Legs. How to Be Very, Very Popular. 1957: The Man Who Turned to Stone. 1958: Frankenstein 1970. The Bride and the Beast.

AUTRY, Gene (Orvon Autry) 1907–
Genial, stocky cowboy star who turned out second-feature westerns for 20 years. As with Roy Rogers, his films mixed action with song and he was one of the top moneymakers in Hollywood films in the early war years. Usually seen with horse Champion, he became a wealthy businessman in later times. Once said: 'I'm no great actor and I'm no great rider and I'm no great singer. But whatever it is I'm doing, they like it.'

1934: In Old Santa Fé. Mystery Mountain (serial). 1935: The Phantom Empire (serial). Tumbling Tumbleweeds. Melody Trail. Sagebrush Troubador. The Singing Vagabond. 1936: Red River Valley. Comin' round the Mountain. The Singing Cowboy. Guns and Guitars. Oh, Susanna! Ride, Ranger, Ride. The Old Corral. 1937: Round-Up Time in Texas. Git Along, Little Dogies (GB: Serenade of the West). Rootin' Tootin' Rhythm (GB: Rhythm on the Ranch). Yodelin' Kid from Pine Ridge (GB: The Hero of Pine Ridge). Public Cowboy No 1. Boots and Saddles. Manhattan Merry-Go-Round (GB: Manhattan Music Box). Springtime in the Rockies. 1938: The Old Barn Dance. Gold Mine in the Sky. Man from Music Mountain. Prairie Moon. Rhythm of the Saddle. Western Jamboree. 1939: Home on the Prairie. Mexicali Rose. Blue Montana Skies. Mountain Rhythm. Colorado Sunset. In Old Monterey. Rovin' Tumbleweeds. South of the Border. 1940: Rancho Grande. Shooting High. Gaucho Serenade. Carolina Moon. *Rodeo Dough. Ride, Tenderfoot, Ride. Melody Ranch. 1941: *Meet Roy Rogers. Ridin' on a Rainbow. Back in the Saddle. The Singing Hills. Sunset in Wyoming. Under Fiesta Stars. Down Mexico Way. Sierra Sue. 1942: Cowboy Serenade (GB: Serenade of the West). Heart of the Rio Grande. Home in Wyomin'. Stardust on the Sage. Call of the Canyon. Bells of Capistrano. *Screen Snapshots No 108. 1946: Sioux City Sue. 1947: Trail to San Antone. Twilight on the Rio Grande. Saddle Pals. Robin Hood of Texas. The Last Round-Up. 1948: The Strawberry Roan (GB: Fools Awake). 1949: Loaded Pistols. The Big Sombrero. Riders of the Whistling Pines. Rim of the Canyon. *Screen Snap-

shots No 179. The Cowboy and the Indians. Riders in the Sky. Sons of New Mexico (GB: The Brat). 1950: Mule Train. Beyond the Purple Hills. Cow Town (GB: Barbed Wire). Indian Territory. The Blazing Sun. 1951: Gene Autry and the Mounties. Texans Never Cry. Whirlwind. Silver Canyon. Hills of Utah. Valley of Fire. 1952: The Old West. Night Stage to Galveston. Apache Country. Wagon Team. Blue Canadian Rockies. Barbed Wire (GB: False News). 1953: Winning of the West. On Top of Old Smoky. Goldtown Ghost Riders. Pack Train. *Memories in Uniform. Saginaw Trail. Last of the Pony Riders. 1954: Hollywood Cowboy Stars. 1959: Alias Jesse James. 1968: Silent Treatment.

Alamo. 1961: Alakazam the Great (voice only). Sail a Crooked Ship. 1962: The Castilian. Panic in Year Zero. Voyage to the Bottom of the Sea. 1963: Operation Bikini. Drums of Africa. Beach Party. 1964: Bikini Beach. Pajama Party. Muscle Beach Party. 1965: Dr Goldfoot and the Bikini Machine (GB: Dr G. and the Bikini Machine). Beach Blanket Bingo (GB: Malibu Beach). Ski Party. How to Stuff a Wild Bikini. Sergeant Deadhead. I'll Take Sweden. Survival. 1966: Fireball 500. Pajama Party in a Haunted House. 1967: The Jet Set. Sumuru (GB: The Million Eyes of Sumuru). 1968: Skidoo. 1969: Ski Fever. The Haunted House of Horror. 1974: The Take. The Hunters (TV). 1978: Grease.

AYKROYD, Dan (Daniel Agraluscarsacra) 1951–

Slack-jawed, laconic-looking Canadian comic actor with dark hair flopping forward. He came to films with his TV partner John Belushi (after a minor debut in his native country), providing the same kind of wildly anarchic, scatological comedy the pair had pioneered on TV's *Saturday Night Live*. After Belushi's death, Aykroyd paused, then continued making comedy films with other partners (Bill Murray, Eddie Murphy, Chevy Chase), sometimes in projects that had originally been planned for Belushi. Aykroyd has said in recent times: 'I have yet to perform a solo role that works.' He's right.

1975: Love at First Sight. 1979: Mr Mike's Mondo Video. 1941. 1980: The Blues Brothers. 1981: Neighbors. 1982: It Came from Hollywood (video). 1983: Doctor Detroit. Trading Places. The Twilight Zone (GB: Twilight Zone the Movie). 1984: Ghost Busters. Indiana Jones and the Temple of Doom. Nothing Lasts Forever. 1985: Into the Night. Spies Like Us. 1986: Dragnet.

AVALON, Frankie (Francis Avallone) 1939–

Bright, slight, bouncy American actor-singer with dark, curly hair, whose boyish looks and cheerful personality kept him popular with the teenage audience until the late sixties. More recently reappeared in *Grease*, looking a little more serious, but otherwise just the same as ever.

1957: Jamboree (GB: Disc Jockey Jamboree). 1959: Guns of the Timberland. 1960: The

AYRES, Agnes (A. Hinkle) 1896–1940
Petite, dark-haired American leading lady of silent days, whose little-girl-lost, black-eyed appeal kept the men watching while their girlfriends had eyes only for her two-time co-star Rudolph Valentino. Her career was virtually ended by the coming of sound which found her the right age for character roles but unable to mature into them. She died tragically from a cerebral haemorrhage at 44.
1915: *† His New Job. 1917: Richard the Brazen. The Defeat of the City. The Girl and the Graft. The Purple Dress. The Enchanted Profile. 1918: The Bottom of the Well. $1,000. 1919: The Sacred Silence. Forbidden Fruit. 1920: Held by the Enemy. A Modern Salome. Go and Get It. The Inner Voice. 1921: The Affairs of Anatol (GB: A Prodigal Knight). The Sheik. Cappy Ricks. The Love Special. Too Much Speed. 1922: Clarence. The Ordeal.

The Lane That Had No Turning. Bought and Paid For. Borderland. A Daughter of Luxury. 1923: The Ten Commandments. Tess of the Storm Country. Racing Hearts. Hollywood. The Marriage Maker. The Heart Raider. 1924: The Story without a Name. When a Girl Loves. Bluff. Don't Call It Love. The Guilty One. Worldly Goods. 1925: Tomorrow's Love. Morals for Men. The Awful Truth. 1926: Her Market Value/Her Net Value. Son of the Sheik. 1927: *Eve's Love Letters. 1928: The Lady of Victory. Napoleon and Josephine. Into the Night. 1929: Bye, Bye, Buddy. The Donovan Affair. Broken Hearted. 1937: *Morning, Judge. Souls at Sea. Maid of Salem.

† As Agnes Ayars

AYRES, Lew (Lewis Ayer) 1908–
Softly spoken, diffident American leading man who, after beginning his career as a danceband musician, became famous both as the young soldier in *All Quiet on the Western Front* and in the *Dr Kildare* series. Career effectively spoiled when he declared himself a conscientious objector during World War II. Married to Lola Lane (Dorothy Mullican 1909–) from 1931 to 1933 and to Ginger Rogers (qv) from 1934 to 1941, first and second of three wives. Oscar nominee for *Johnny Belinda*.
1929: The Sophomore. Big News. The Shakedown. The Kiss. 1930: Compromised. All Quiet on the Western Front. Common Clay. The Doorway to Hell (GB: A Handful of Clouds). East is West. 1931: Iron Man. Up for Murder. Many a Slip. Spirit of Notre Dame (GB: Vigour of Youth). Heaven on Earth. 1932: The Impatient Maiden. Night World. Okay America! (GB: Penalty of Fame). The Cohens and Kellys in Hollywood. 1933: State Fair. Don't Bet on Love. My Weakness. 1934: Cross Country Cruise. She Learned About Sailors. Let's Be Ritzy (GB: Millionaire for a Day). 1935: Servants' Entrance. Lottery Lover. Silk Hat Kid. 1936: The Leathernecks Have Landed (GB: The Marines Have Landed). Panic on the Air. Shakedown. Murder with Pictures. 1937: Lady Be Careful. The Crime Nobody Saw. Last Train from Madrid. Hold 'Em Navy. 1938: Scandal Street. Holiday (GB: Free to Live/Unconventional Linda). King of the Newsboys. Rich Man – Poor Girl. Young Dr Kildare. Spring Madness. 1939: Ice Follies of

1939. Broadway Serenade. Calling Dr Kildare. These Glamour Girls. Remember? Secret of Dr Kildare. 1940: Dr Kildare's Strange Case. The Golden Fleecing. Dr Kildare's Crisis. Dr Kildare Goes Home. 1941: Maisie Was a Lady. The People versus Dr Kildare (GB: My Life is Yours). 1942: Dr Kildare's Wedding Day (GB: Mary Names the Day). Dr Kildare's Victory (GB: The Doctor and the Debutante). Fingers at the Window. 1946: The Dark Mirror. 1947: The Unfaithful. 1948: Johnny Belinda. 1950: The Capture. 1951: New Mexico. 1953: No Escape. Donovan's Brain. 1956: The Family Nobody Wanted (TV). 1961: Advise and Consent. 1963: The Carpetbaggers. 1971: Earth II (TV). The Man. The Last Generation. She Waits (TV). 1972: The Stranger (TV). The Biscuit Eater. 1973: Battle for the Planet of the Apes. The Questor Tapes (TV). 1974: Heatwave (TV). 1977: End of the World. Francis Gary Powers – The True Story of the U2 Incident (TV). 1978: Damien – Omen II. Suddenly Love (TV). Battlestar Galactica (TV. GB: cinemas). 1979: Letters from Frank. 1981: Of Mice and Men (TV). 1986: Under Siege (TV).

As director:
1936: Hearts in Bondage. The Leathernecks Have Landed (GB: The Marines Have Landed).

AYRES, Robert 1914–1968

Lean, dark, forceful American-born actor, of handsome if slightly sinister aspect. Brought up in England and Canada, he fought with the Royal Canadian Air Force in World War II and remained in Britain after the war. His career in the British cinema deserved more than entrenchment in second-features, but the bigger breaks somehow evaded him and by the late 1950s he was playing smaller roles. Died from a heart attack.
1948: They Were Not Divided. 1949: Scrapbook for 1933 (voice only). 1950: State Secret (US: The Great Manhunt). 1951: To Have

and to Hold. Night without Stars. Black Widow. 1952: 13 East Street. 24 Hours of a Woman's Life (US: Affair in Monte Carlo). Cosh Boy (US: The Slasher). 1953: The Wedding of Lilli Marlene. *The Mask. River Beat. 1954: Delayed Action. 1955: A Prize of Gold. Triple Blackmail. Contraband Spain. 1956: Dollars for Sale. It's Never Too Late. The Baby and the Battleship. Operation Murder. 1957: Time Lock. The Story of Esther Costello (US: The Golden Virgin). The Depraved. Cat Girl. 1958: A Night to Remember. First Man into Space. 1959: A Woman's Temptation. John Paul Jones. 1960: Date at Midnight. 1961: Transatlantic. Two and Two Make Six. 1962: The Road to Hong Kong. 1964: The Sicilians. 1965: The Heroes of Telemark. 1967: Battle Beneath the Earth. 1968: Isadora (US: The Loves of Isadora).

AZNAVOUR, Charles (Shahnour Aznavurjan) 1924–

Tiny, dark-eyed French actor-singer-composer of Armenian origin, self-described as 'a small man with a nose like a can-opener', but the romantic idol of millions, especially singing equally romantic songs. Aznavour, who started out in show business as a dancer,

has only toyed with films, but sometimes in unusual and rewarding roles.
1938: Les disparus de Saint-Agil (US: Boys' School). La guerre des gosses. 1956: Une gosse sans cesse. 1957: Paris Music-Hall. C'est arrivé à 36 chandelles. 1958: Les dragueurs (GB: The Young Have No Morals. US: The Chasers). Le tête contre les murs. 1959: La testament d'Orphée. 1960: Tirez sur le pianiste (GB: Shoot the Pianist! US: Shoot the Piano Player). La passage du Rhin (GB: Tomorrow is My Turn). Taxi for Tobruk. 1961: Les petits matins. Horace '62. 1962: Le rat d'Amérique. Les vierges. Tempo di Roma. Les quatres verités (GB and US: Three Fables of Love). Pourquoi Paris? The Devil and the 10 Commandments. 1964: Alta infidelità (GB and US: High Infidelity). Cherchez l'idole (GB: The Chase). 1965: Le metamorphose des Cloportes. Paris in August. 1966: Le facteur s'en v'a-t-en guerre. 1967: Caroline Chérie. 1968: Candy. The Games. 1969: Le temps des loups. 1970: The Adventurers. Un beau monstre. 1971: Les intrus. La part des lions. 1973: The Blockhouse. 1974: And Then There Were None. 1976: Folies bougeoises/The Twist. Sky Riders. 1979: The Tin Drum. 1981: Les fantômes du chapelier. 1982: Qu'est-ce qui fait courir David? Der Zauberberg (US: The Magic Mountain). 1983: Édith et Marcel. 1984: Viva la vie. 1986: Yiddish Connection.

1914: Symphony of Love and Death. 1915: The Wanderer beyond the Grave. 1916: He Who Gets Slapped. 1917: The Flowers Are Late. 1927: The Dove. 1928: The Street of Sin. Forgotten Faces. The Docks of New York. Avalanche. Three Sinners. The Man Who Laughs. 1929: A Dangerous Woman. The Wolf of Wall Street. The Man I Love. 1930: Are You There? Cheer Up and Smile. 1931: The Great Lover. *Screen Snapshots No 4. 1932: Freaks. Downstairs. 1933: The Billion Dollar Scandal. 1935: *Broadway Brevities. *The Telephone Blues. 1936: *The Double Crossky. 1943: Claudia.

BACALL, Lauren (Betty Perske) 1924–
Slinky, blonde, feline, husky-voiced American leading lady, dubbed 'The Look' who, at 20, co-starred with Humphrey Bogart (qv) in her first film, and was married to him from 1945 until his death in 1957. Married to Jason Robards Jnr (also qv) from 1961 to 1973. Has made too few films, especially in the late 1940s period when she was at her best.
1944: To Have and Have Not. 1945: Confidential Agent. 1946: Two Guys from Milwaukee (GB: Royal Flush). The Big Sleep. 1947: Dark Passage. 1948: Key Largo. 1949: Young Man with a Horn (GB: Young Man of Music). 1950: Bright Leaf. 1953: How to Marry a Millionaire. 1954: Woman's World. 1955: The Cobweb. *Salute to the Theatres. Blood Alley. 1956: Written on the Wind. 1957: Designing Woman. 1958: The Gift of Love. 1959: Northwest Frontier (US: Flame over India). 1964: Shock Treatment. Sex and the Single Girl. 1966: Harper (GB: The Moving Target). 1974: Murder on the Orient Express. 1976: The Shootist. 1977: Perfect Gentlemen (TV). 1979: Health. 1981: The Fan.

BACLANOVA, Olga 1899–1974
Fierce, intense, dark-haired Russian actress (a former ballet dancer) whose Hollywood career as a star was brief, but contained two performances still remembered today – in Josef Von Sternberg's *Docks of New York* and Tod Browning's *Freaks*. She came to America at 24 and stayed for many years (her heavy and inimitable tones hosting radio programmes in the 1930s) before eventually retiring to Switzerland. Sometimes blonde.

BAKER, Carroll 1931–
Blonde American actress, mainly in 'bitchy' roles. She moved easily from teenage nymphets to faintly overblown blondes with the passing of the years. Something of a sensation in her first major role, as the thumb-sucking Baby Doll, a part that won her an Oscar nomination, she subsequently proved difficult to cast to box-office profitability, sometimes turning to continental sexploitation films to keep her career ticking over.
1953: Easy to Love. 1956: Baby Doll. Giant. 1958: The Big Country. 1959: The Miracle. But Not for Me. 1961: Something Wild. Bridge to the Sun. 1962: How the West Was Won. 1963: Station Six Sahara. The Carpetbaggers. 1964: Cheyenne Autumn. 1965: Sylvia. The Greatest Story Ever Told. Mr Moses. Harlow. 1967: The Harem (US: Her Harem). Jack of Diamonds. 1968: Orgasmo (GB: Paranoia). Paranoia (GB: A Quiet Place to Kill). The Sweet Body of Deborah. 1969: Cosi dolce ... cosi perversa/So Sweet ... So Perverse. 1970:

The Spider. 1971: At the Bottom of the Pool. Captain Apache. The Fourth Mrs Anderson. 1972: The Devil Has Seven Faces. Behind the Silence. Bloody Mary. 1973: Baba Yaga – Devil Witch. The Flower with the Deadly Sting. Il coltello di ghiaccio. The Madness of Love. 1974: Take This My Body. 1975: James Dean – The First American Teenager. The Private Lesson. The Lure. The Sky is Falling. La moglie vergine (GB and US: Virgin Wife). 1976: Il corpo (US: The Body). La moglie di mio padre (GB: Confessions of a Frustrated Housewife). Zerschossene Träume. Bad/Andy Warhol's Bad. 1977: Cyclone. 1978: Ab Morgen sind wir reich und ehrlich (US: Rich and Respectable). 1979: The World is Full of Married Men. 1981: The Watcher in the Woods. 1983: Red Monarch (TV). The Secret Diary of Sigmund Freud. Star 80. 1985: Hitler's SS: Portrait in Evil (TV. GB: cinemas). What Mad Pursuit? (TV). 1986: Native Son.

BAKER, Diane 1938–
Demure, sensitive, pretty, dark-haired American actress, capable of projecting great warmth, but not progressing beyond ingenue roles in films. She was often successful, strangely, as outwardly calm characters capable of great spite, as in Hitchcock's *Marnie*. Nice to see her so busy in TV movies in the 1970s, but, in 1980, she became a producer.
1958: The Diary of Anne Frank. 1959: The Best of Everything. Journey to the Center of the Earth. Della (TV). 1960: Tess of the Storm Country. 1961: The Wizard of Baghdad. 1962: Hemingway's Adventures of a Young Man (GB: Adventures of a Young Man). The 300 Spartans. Nine Hours to Rama. 1963: Stolen Hours. 1964: Straitjacket. The Prize. Marnie. 1965: Mirage. 1966: Sands of Beersheba. The Dangerous Days of Kiowa Jones (TV. GB: cinemas). 1968: The Horse in the Gray Flannel Suit. Krakatoa, East of Java. 1969: Trial Run (TV). The DA: Murder One (TV). 1970: Do You Take This Stranger? (TV). The Old Man Who Cried Wolf (TV). Wheeler and Murdoch (TV). 1971: The Badge or the Cross (TV). Killer by Night (TV). Congratulations It's a Boy (TV). A Little Game (TV). 1972: The Sagittarius Mine. 1973: Police Story (TV. GB: cinemas). 1974: Half-Way to Danger. A Tree Grows in Brooklyn (TV). Can I Save My Children? (TV). 1975: The Dream Makers (TV). The Last Survivors (TV). 1976: Bak-

er's Hawk. Stigma (TV). Summer of 69 (TV).
1979: The Pilot. 1980: Fugitive Family (TV).

BAKER, George 1929–
Quiet, dark, very tall British leading man
(born in Bulgaria of Irish parents), popular
for a few years in the late fifties in a good
variety of roles. Later played senior civil servants, tried a comedy series on TV and made
a series of mystery films for TV in New Zealand.
1953: The Intruder. 1955: The Dam Busters.
The Ship That Died of Shame (US: PT Raiders). The Woman for Joe. 1956: The Feminine
Touch (US: The Gentle Touch). The Extra
Day. A Hill in Korea (US: Hell in Korea).
1957: These Dangerous Years (US: Dangerous
Youth). No Time for Tears. 1958: The Moonraker. Tread Softly, Stranger. 1963: Lancelot
and Guinevere (US: Sword of Lancelot). 1964:
The Finest Hours (voice only). The Curse of
the Fly. 1967: Mister Ten Per Cent. 1969:
Goodbye Mr Chips. Justine. On Her Majesty's
Secret Service. 1970: The Executioner. 1972:
A Warm December. The Rape. 1973: *The
Laughing Girl Murder. 1974: The Firefighters.
Three for All. 1975: The Twelve Tasks of
Asterix (English-language version, voice only).
1976: Intimate Games. 1977: The Spy Who
Loved Me. 1978: Died in the Wool (TV).
Colour Scheme (TV). Vintage Murder (TV).
Opening Night (TV). The Thirty Nine Steps.
1979: North Sea Hijack (US: ffolkes). 1980:
The Biggest Bank Robbery (TV). Hopscotch.

BAKER, Joe Don 1943–
Burly, surly, giant-sized American actor with
a habit of crashing his way through tough

thrillers. More successful in America than
internationally, where his films were less commercial after 1975 and his expanding girth
made him ever more fearsome, perhaps more
suited to villainy than heroism. His future,
however, may lie as a prominent television
grim-faced leading man in the style of Raymond Burr (qv).
1967: Cool Hand Luke. 1969: Guns of the
Magnificent Seven. 1970: Adam at 6 a.m.
1971: Mongo's Back in Town (TV). 1972:
Junior Bonner. Wild Rovers. Charley Varrick.
Walking Tall. Welcome Home, Soldier Boys.
That Certain Summer (TV). 1973: The Outfit.
1974: Golden Needles. 1975: Framed. Mitchell.
1976: Crash. 1977: The Pack (GB: The Long
Hard Night). The Shadow of Chikara/
Wishbone Cutter. Speedtrap. 1978: To Kill a
Cop (TV). Streets of Fear (TV). 1979: Power
(TV). 1982: Wacko. 1983: Joysticks. 1984:
The Natural. The Maltese Connection/Final
Justice. 1985: Fletch. 1986: Hostage Dallas.

BAKER, Sir Stanley 1927–1976
Forceful Welsh-born actor (knighted in 1976),
whose career progressed predictably from vil-
lains-you-love-to-hate to tough and sometimes crooked central characters. His hard,
uncompromising crime films of the early sixties pioneered the way for a new realism –
especially in terms of dialogue – in British
films of the genre. His star faded in the seventies, and he died from pneumonia after an
operation.
1943: Undercover (US: Underground Guer-
illas). 1948: All Over the Town. 1949:
Obsession (US: The Hidden Room). 1950:
Your Witness (US: Eye Witness). Lilli
Marlene. 1951: The Rossiter Case. Captain
Horatio Hornblower RN. Home to Danger.
Cloudburst. Whispering Smith Hits London
(US: Whispering Smith versus Scotland
Yard). 1953: The Cruel Sea. The Red Beret.
(US: Paratrooper). *The Tell Tale Heart.
Hell Below Zero. 1954: The Good Die Young.
Knights of the Round Table. Beautiful Stranger
(US: Twist of Fate). Helen of Troy. 1955:
Richard III. 1956: Child in the House. Alex-
ander the Great. A Hill in Korea (US: Hell
in Korea). Checkpoint. 1957: Hell Drivers.
Campbell's Kingdom. Violent Playground.
1958: Sea Fury. 1959: The Angry Hills. Blind
Date. Jet Storm. Yesterday's Enemy. 1960:

Hell is a City. The Criminal (US: The Con-
crete Jungle). 1961: The Guns of Navarone.
1962: A Prize of Arms. The Last Days of
Sodom and Gomorrah. The Man Who Finally
Died. In the French Style. Eva. 1963: Zulu.
1965: Dingaka. *One of Them is Brett (nar-
rator only). Sands of the Kalahari. Who Has
Seen the Wind? (TV). 1967: Accident.
Robbery. Code Name Heraclitus (TV). 1969:
La ragazza con la pistola (US: Girl with a
Pistol). Where's Jack? The Games. 1970: Per-
fect Friday. Popsy Pop (GB: The 21 Carat
Snatch). The Last Grenade. 1971: A Lizard
in a Woman's Skin (US: Schizoid). 1972:
Innocent Bystanders. 1975: Zorro. Pepita Jimi-
nez/Bride To Be.

BALFOUR, Betty 1903–
With blue eyes, a mass of golden curls and
great long pencilled eyebrows, Betty Balfour
was Britain's answer to Mary Pickford, and
that country's most popular star of the twenties by a wide margin, as her fey, elfin charms
and impish humour endeared her to millions.
With sound, she slipped into working-class
character roles, including a reprise of her
biggest twenties' hit, as the cockney flower-
girl Squibs.
1920: Nothing Else Matters. 1921: Mary Find-
the-Gold. Squibs. Mord Em'ly (US: Me and
My Girl). 1922: The Wee MacGregor's Sweetheart. Squibs Wins the Calcutta Sweep. 1923:
Love, Life and Laughter. Squibs MP. Squibs'
Honeymoon. 1924: Reveille. 1925: Satan's Sister. Somebody's Darling. The Sea Urchin.
1926: Blinkeyes. Cinders. 1927: Little Devil
May Care. Monkey Nuts. Die Sieben Töchter
der Frau Gyurkovics. 1928: A Little Bit of
Fluff (US: Skirts). Champagne. Paradise. Die
Regimentstochter (GB: Daughter of the Regi-
ment). 1929: The Vagabond Queen. Bright
Eyes. 1930: Raise the Roof. The Nipper (later
The Brat). 1933: Paddy the Next Best Thing.
1934: Evergreen. My Old Dutch. 1935: Brown
on Resolution (later For Ever England. US:
Born for Glory). Squibs. 1936: Eliza Comes to
Stay. 1945: 29 Acacia Avenue (US: The Facts
of Love).

BALL, Lucille 1911–
Red-haired, wide-mouthed, effervescent
American comedienne with inimitable, duck-
like voice. A former Ziegfeld girl, she survived
some striking pieces of miscasting and dozens

BANCROFT, Anne (Anna Maria Italiano) 1931–

Black-haired, dark-eyed American actress, adept at portraying great depths of passion, hatred or tragedy. Also has a goofy sense of comedy which has seldom been exploited. Acting until 1952 as Anne Marno, she made her Hollywood breakthrough via stage success after years in co-features. Won an Oscar for *The Miracle Worker* and a British Oscar for *The Pumpkin Eater*. Married to director/comedian Mel Brooks (*qv*). Additional Academy Award nominations for *The Pumpkin Eater*, *The Graduate* and *The Turning Point*.

of indifferent supporting roles to become TV's most popular funny lady in the 1950s, and one of its most powerful producers. Married from 1940 to 1960 to her TV co-star, Cuban-born bandleader Desi Arnaz (1917–). Lucie (1951–) and Desi Arnaz Jr (1953–) are their children.
*1929: Bulldog Drummond. 1933: Broadway Thru a Keyhole. Blood Money. Roman Scandals. 1934: Moulin Rouge. Nana. Bottoms Up. Hold That Girl. Bulldog Drummond Strikes Back. The Affairs of Cellini. Kid Millions. Broadway Bill (GB: Strictly Confidential). Jealousy. Men of the Night. Fugitive Lady. The Whole Town's Talking (GB: Passport to Fame). *Perfectly Mismated. *Three Little Pigskins. 1935: Carnival. Roberta. Old Man Rhythm. Top Hat. The Three Musketeers. I Dream Too Much. *A Night at the Biltmore Bowl. 1936: *Dummy Ache. *One Live Ghost. *Swing It. Chatterbox. Follow the Fleet. The Farmer in the Dell. Bunker Bean (GB: His Majesty Bunker Bean). That Girl from Paris. Winterset. 1937: Don't Tell the Wife. Stage Door. 1938: Joy of Living. Go Chase Yourself. Having Wonderful Time. The Affairs of Annabel. Room Service. The Next Time I Marry. 1939: Annabel Takes a Tour. Beauty for the Asking. Twelve Crowded Hours. Panama Lady. Five Came Back. That's Right, You're Wrong. 1940: The Marines Fly High. You Can't Fool Your Wife. Dance, Girl, Dance. Too Many Girls. 1941: A Girl, a Guy and a Gob (GB: The Navy Steps Out). Look Who's Laughing. 1942: Valley of the Sun. The Big Street. Seven's Days' Leave. 1943: Dubarry Was a Lady. Best Foot Forward. Thousands Cheer. 1944: Meet the People. Ziegfeld Follies (released 1946). 1945: Without Love. Bud Abbott and Lou Costello in Hollywood. 1946: The Dark Corner. Easy to Wed. Two Smart People. Lover Come Back. 1947: Lured (GB: Personal Column). Her Husband's Affairs. 1949: Sorrowful Jones. Easy Living. Miss Grant Takes Richmond (GB: Innocence is Bliss). 1950: A Woman of Distinction. Fancy Pants. The Fuller Brush Girl (GB: The Affairs of Sally). 1951: The Magic Carpet. 1954: The Long, Long Trailer. 1956: Forever, Darling. 1960: The Facts of Life. 1963: Critic's Choice. 1967: A Guide for the Married Man. 1968: Yours, Mine and Ours. 1973: Mame. 1985: Stone Pillow (TV).*

1952: Don't Bother to Knock. Tonight We Sing. 1953: The Robe. The Treasure of the Golden Condor. The Kid from Left Field. 1954: Demetrius and the Gladiators. The Raid. Gorilla at Large. 1955: A Life in the Balance. New York. Confidential. The Naked Street. The Last Frontier. 1956: Walk the Proud Land. Nightfall. 1957: The Restless Breed. Invitation to a Gunfighter (TV). The Girl in Black Stockings. So Soon to Die (TV). 1962: The Miracle Worker. 1963: The Girl of the Via Flaminia. 1964: The Pumpkin Eater. 1965: The Slender Thread. Seven Women. 1967: The Graduate. 1970: Arthur Penn, 1922: Themes and Variants. 1971: Young Winston. 1974: The Prisoner of Second Avenue. 1976: Silent Movie. Jesus of Nazareth (TV). The Hindenburg. Lipstick. 1977: The Turning Point. 1979: †Fatso. 1980: The Elephant Man. 1983: To Be or Not to Be. 1984: Garbo Talks! 1985: Agnes of God. 1986: Night, Mother.

† *And directed*

BANCROFT, George 1882–1956

My favourite American heavy from the days of early sound, Bancroft was also capable of projecting tough, dominant masculinity, notably in his four films for Josef von Sternberg, *Underworld*, *The Docks of New York*, *The Dragnet* and *Thunderbolt*. Now perhaps best remembered as the stage driver in Ford's *Stagecoach*, one of many supporting roles he later played. Received an Oscar nomination for *Thunderbolt*.
1921: The Journey's End. 1922: Driven. The Prodigal Judge. 1924: The Deadwood Coach. Teeth. 1925: Pony Express. Code of the West. The Rainbow Trail. The Splendid Road. 1926:

Old Ironsides (GB: Sons of the Sea). The Enchanted Hill. The Runaway. Sea Horses. 1927: Underworld (GB: Paying the Penalty). White Gold. The Rough Riders (GB: The Trumpet Calls). Too Many Crooks. Tell it to Sweeney. 1928: The Docks of New York. The Dragnet. The Showdown. The Mighty. 1929: Thunderbolt. The Wolf of Wall Street. 1930: Paramount on Parade. Derelict. Ladies Love Brutes. Rich Man's Folly. 1931: The World and the Flesh. Scandal Sheet. 1932: Lady and Gent. 1933: Blood Money. 1934: Elmer and Elsie. 1936: Mr Deeds Goes to Town. Hell-Ship Morgan. Wedding Present. 1937: A Doctor's Diary. John Meade's Woman. Racketeers in Exile. Angels with Dirty Faces. Submarine Patrol. Stagecoach. Each Dawn I Die. Rulers of the Sea. Espionage Agent. 1940: Little Men. Northwest Mounted Police. When the Daltons Rode. Green Hell. 1941: Young Tom Edison. Texas. The Bugle Sounds. 1942: Syncopation. Whistling in Dixie.

BANKHEAD, Tallulah 1902–1968

Drawling, extravagant American leading lady, excelling in bitchy roles. Films could rarely find the right material – or directors – for her and, when not making cutting remarks at Hollywood parties, she was seen chiefly on stage. She died from complications after an attack of Asian 'flu.
*1918: When Men Betray. Thirty a Week. 1919: The Trap. 1928: A Woman's Law. His House in Order. 1929: *Her Cardboard Lover. 1931: Tarnished Lady. My Sin. The Cheat. 1932: Thunder Below. The Devil and the Deep. Faithless. Make Me a Star. 1943: Stage Door Canteen. Lifeboat. 1945: A Royal Scandal*

(GB: Czarina). 1953: Main Street to Broadway. 1964: Fanatic (US: Die! Die! My Darling). 1966: The Daydreamer (voice).

BANKS, Leslie 1890–1952
Taciturn, solid British actor with a distinctive voice, rarely flamboyant but always reliable. Badly wounded in World War I (facial disfigurment converted classic good looks into rugged ones). Banks unexpectedly found himself a star of the British cinema in middle age, after a film debut in Hollywood. In private life a talented painter, he died from a stroke that followed a long illness.
1932: The Most Dangerous Game (GB: The Hounds of Zaroff). Strange Evidence. 1933: The Fire Raisers. 1934: The Night of the Party. Red Ensign. I am Suzanne! The Man Who Knew Too Much. 1935: Sanders of the River. The Tunnel (US: Transatlantic Tunnel). 1936: Debt of Honour. The Three Maxims (US: The Show Goes On). Fire Over England. 1937: Wings of the Morning. Farewell Again (US: Troopship). 21 Days (US: 21 Days Together). 1938: *Guide Dogs for the Blind. 1939: Jamaica Inn. Dead Man's Shoes. The Arsenal Stadium Mystery. Sons of the Sea. 1940. The Door with Seven Locks (US: Chamber of Horrors). Busman's Honeymoon (US: Haunted Honeymoon). Neutral Port. 1941: *Give Us More Ships. Cottage to Let (US: Bombsite Stolen). Ships with Wings. The Big Blockade. 1942: Went the Day Well? (US: 48 Hours). 1944: Henry V. 1947: Mrs Fitzherbert. 1948: The Small Back Room. 1950: Your Witness (US: Eye Witness). Madeleine.

BANKY, Vilma (V. Konsics) 1898–
Blonde, Budapest-born silent star, publicized as 'The Hungarian Rhapsody'. She made a few films in Hungary and Austria before being 'discovered' by Sam Goldwyn while he was on a European holiday. Had great success in Hollywood, but sound would probably have killed her career: by this time she was more interested in her marriage to fellow star Rod La Rocque (qv), which lasted until his death in 1969. A golf fanatic, still playing in her eighties.
1919: Im letzten Augenblick. 1920: Galathea. 1921: Tavasni Szerelem. Veszélyben a Pokol. 1922: Das Auge des Toten. Kauft Mariett-Aktien. Schattenkinder des Glücks. 1923: Die letzte Stunde. 1924: Das schöne Abenteuer

(US: The Lady from Paris). Hotel Potemkin. Das verbotene Land. Klown aus Liebe. 1925: Soll man heiraten? L'image. The Dark Angel. The Eagle. 1926: Son of the Sheik. The Winning of Barbara Worth. 1927: The Night of Love. The Magic Flame. 1928: Two Lovers. The Awakening. 1929: This is Heaven. 1930: A Lady to Love (and German version). 1932: The Rebel.

BANNEN, Ian 1928–
Black-haired Scottish actor who began his career in gentle roles, largely in comedy, but developed in the mid-1960s into an abrasive character star, fiercely portraying a series of single-minded and even psychotic men. Since that time, he has been less effective in straight leading roles, but has continued to impress when asked to express sourness and cynicism. Oscar nominee for *The Flight of the Phoenix.*
1956: Private's Progress. The Long Arm (US: The Third Key). 1957: Yangtse Incident (US: Battle Hell). Miracle in Soho. The Birthday Present. 1958: A Tale of Two Cities. She Didn't Say No! Behind the Mask. Carlton-Browne of the FO (US: Man in a Cocked Hat). 1960: On Friday at 11. A French Mistress. Suspect (US: The Risk). 1961: Macbeth. 1962: Station Six – Sahara. 1963: Psyche 59. 1964: Mister Moses. 1965: The Hill. Rotten to the Core. The Flight of the Phoenix. 1966: Penelope. 1967: Sailor from Gibraltar. 1969: Too Late the Hero. Lock Up Your Daughters! 1970: Jane Eyre. The Deserter. 1971: Fright. 1972: Doomwatch. The Offence. 1973: The Mackintosh Man. From Beyond the Grave. 1974: Il viaggio (US: The Voyage). Iden-

tikit/The Driver's Seat. 1975: Bite the Bullet. 1976: Sweeney! 1978: The Inglorious Bastards. 1979: Ring of Darkness. 1980: The Watcher in the Woods (shown in revised version 1982). Dr Jekyll and Mr Hyde (TV). 1981: Eye of the Needle. 1982: Night Crossing. 1982: Gandhi. 1983: The Prodigal. Gorky Park. 1985: Defence of the Realm. Lamb.

BANNON, Jim 1911–
Lanky, likeable, red-headed American actor who spent 10 years on radio before coming to Hollywood to play Red Ryder and other 'B' feature western heroes. Rather surprisingly, he did not mature into a familiar character actor and was not much seen after the low-budget cowboys ceased to ride the range. Actor Jack Bannon is his son.
1943: Riders of the Deadline. 1944: The Soul of a Monster. Sergeant Mike. The Missing Juror. Tonight and Every Night. 1945: I Love a Mystery. The Gay Senorita. Out of the Depths. 1946: Renegades. The Devil's Mask. The Unknown. 1947: Johnny O'Clock. Framed (GB: Paula). The Corpse Came COD. The Thirteenth Hour. T-Men. 1948: Miraculous Journey. Dangers of the Canadian Mounted (serial). The Man from Colorado. Frontier Revenge. Trail to Laredo (GB: Sign of the Dagger). 1949: Daughter of the Jungle. Ride, Ryder, Ride. The Fighting Redhead. Roll, Thunder, Roll. 1950: Kill the Umpire! The Cowboy and the Prizefighter. Jiggs and Maggie Out West. 1951: Riding the Outlaw Trail. Sierra Passage. Canyon Raiders. Nevada Badmen. Lawless Cowboys. Stagecoach Driver. Unknown World. Wanted Dead or Alive. 1952: Rodeo. 1953: Jack Slade (GB: Slade). The Great Jesse James Raid. War Arrow. 1957: Chicago Confidential. 1959: They Came to Cordura. Inside the Mafia. 1962: 40 Pounds of Trouble. 1963: A Gathering of Eagles. Man's Favorite Sport? 1964: Good Neighbor Sam. 1966: Madame X.

BARA, Theda (Theodosia Goodman) 1890–1955
The screen's first vamp, usually heavy on the stare and eye make-up and extravagantly costumed. Found enormous success in the early silent days, but it came and went all in a few years. Died from cancer after a long illness.
1914: A Fool There Was. 1915: The Clemenceau Case. The Devil's Daughter. The

Kreutzer Sonata (GB: Sonata). Lord Audley's Secret. The Two Orphans. Sin. The Galley Slave. Destruction. Carmen. The Stain. 1916: The Serpent. Gold and the Woman. The Eternal Sappho. East Lynne. Her Double Life. Romeo and Juliet. Under Two Flags. Fires of Hate. The Vixen. The Tiger Woman. Darling of Paris. The Light. 1917: Cleopatra. Camille. Madame Dubarry. Her Greatest Love. Heart and Soul. The Rose of Blood. The Soul of Buddha. 1918: Salome. Under the Yoke. The Forbidden Path. When a Woman Sins. The She Devil. The Message of the Lilies. La Belle Russe. 1919: Siren's Song. When Men Desire. A Woman There Was. Lure of Ambition. Kathleen Mavourneen. 1921: The Price of Silence. Her Greatest Love. 1923: The Hunchback of Notre Dame. 1925: The Unchastened Woman. *Madame Mystery. 1926: The Dancer of Paris. *45 Minutes from Hollywood.

BARDOT, Brigitte 1934–
Baby-faced blonde French sex symbol with a figure in a million. Publicized as the 'sex kitten', her steamy pot-boilers of the fifties set innumerable male temperatures rising all over Europe. Responsible almost single-handed for the breakthrough of the continental X film into the international market.
1952: Le trou normand (US: Crazy for Love). Manina (GB: The Lighthouse Keeper's Daughter. US: The Girl in the Bikini). Les dents longues. 1953: Le portrait de son père. Act of Love. St Versailles m'était conté (GB: Versailles. US: Royal Affairs at Versailles). 1954: Tradita (US: Night of Love). Helen of Troy. Le fils de Caroline Chérie. 1955: Futures vedettes (GB: Sweet Sixteen). Doctor at Sea.

Les grandes manoeuvres (GB and US: Summer Manoeuvres). La lumière d'en face (GB and US: The Light Across the Street). Cette sacrée gamine (GB and US: Mam'zelle Pigalle). 1956: Mio figlio nerone (GB: Nero's Weekend). En effeuillant la Marguerite (GB: Mam'selle Striptease. US: Please, Mr Balzac). Et Dieu créa la femme (GB: And Woman … Was Created. US: And God Created Woman). La mariée est trop belle (GB and US: The Bride is Too Beautiful). 1957: Une Parisienne (GB and US: Parisienne). Les bijoutiers du clair de lune (GB: Heaven Fell That Night. US: The Night Heaven Fell). 1958: En cas de malheur (GB and US: Love Is My Profession). La femme et le pantin (GB: A Woman Like Satan). 1959: Babette Goes to War. Le testament d'Orphée. Voulez-vous danser avec moi? (GB and US: Come Dance With Me). 1960: L'affaire d'une nuit (GB: It Happened at Night). La vérité (GB and US: The Truth) 1961: La bride sur le cou (GB: Please, Not Now!). Les amours célèbres. Vie privée (GB and US: A Very Private Affair). 1962: Le repos du guerrier (GB: Warrior's Rest. US: Love on a Pillow). 1963: Le mépris (GB and US: Contempt). Paparazzi. Tentazione proibite. Une ravissante idiote (GB: A Ravishing Idiot. US: Adorable Idiot). 1964: Marie Soleil. 1965: Dear Brigitte… Viva Maria. 1966: Masculin-Féminin. Two Weeks in September. 1967: Histoires extraordinaires (GB: Tales of Mystery. US: Spirits of the Dead). 1968: Shalako. 1969: Les femmes. 1970: L'ours et la poupée. Les novices. Boulevard du rhum (GB: Rum Runner). 1971: Les pétroleuses (GB: The Legend of Frenchie King). 1973: Don Juan 1973 ou Et si Don Juan était une femme (GB: Don Juan, or If Don Juan Were a Woman). Colinot Trousse-Chemise.

BARI, Lynn (Marjorie Fisher) 1913–
Dark-haired, cool-looking American leading lady who emerged from the chorus but never quite made it to the top, although she became deliciously known as 'the Paulette Goddard of the B feature'. Leading roles in bigger films proved too routine to break the image, and she continued as wordly-wise bad girls and 'other women'. Still active, mainly on stage.
1933: Dancing Lady. Meet the Baron. 1934: Bottoms Up. Coming Out Party. Stand Up and Cheer. Search for Beauty. Caravan. 1935:

George White's Scandals. Show Them No Mercy (GB: Tainted Money). Spring Tonic. The Great Hotel Murder. The Man Who Broke the Bank at Monte Carlo. Redheads on Parade. Thanks a Million. Music is Magic. My Marriage. 1936: Everybody's Old Man. Girls' Dormitory. The Song and Dance Man. Ladies in Love. Crack-Up. Pigskin Parade (GB: The Harmony Parade). Sing, Baby, Sing. 36 Hours to Kill. 1937: Wee Willie Winkie. Sing and Be Happy. 48 Fathers. This is My Affair (GB: His Affair). Lancer Spy. Love is News. Wife, Doctor and Nurse. Fair Warning. On the Avenue. I'll Give a Million. Life Begins in College (GB: The Joy Parade). You Can't Have Everything. 1938: Josette. Rebecca of Sunnybrook Farm. Speed to Burn. The Baroness and the Butler. Walking Down Broadway. Mr Moto's Gamble. City Girl. Battle of Broadway. Always Goodbye. Meet the Girls. Sharpshooters. 1939: Return of the Cisco Kid. Chasing Danger. News is Made at Night. Pack Up Your Troubles (GB: We're in the Army Now). Hotel for Women/Elsa Maxwell's Hotel for Women. Charlie Chan in City of Darkness (GB: City of Darkness). Hollywood Cavalcade. Pardon Our Nerve. 1940: Free, Blonde and 21. City of Chance. Lillian Russell. Earthbound. Pier 13. Kit Carson. 1941: Charter Pilot. Blood and Sand. Sleepers West. We Go Fast. Moon over Her Shoulder. Sun Valley Serenade. The Perfect Snob. 1942: Secret Agent of Japan. The Night before the Divorce. The Falcon Takes Over. The Magnificent Dope. Orchestra Wives. China Girl. 1943: Hello, Frisco, Hello. 1944: The Bridge of San Luis Rey. Tampico. Sweet and Lowdown. 1945: Captain Eddie. 1946: Shock. Home Sweet Homicide. Margie. Nocturne. 1948: The Man from Texas. The Amazing Mr X/The Spiritualist. 1949: The Kid from Cleveland. 1951: I'd Climb the Highest Mountain. On the Loose. 1952: Sunny Side of the Street. Has Anybody Seen My Gal? 1953: I Dream of Jeanie. 1954: Francis Joins the WACs. 1955: Abbott and Costello Meet the Keystone Kops. 1956: Women of Pitcairn Island. All's Fair in Love (TV. GB: cinemas). Trauma. 1958: Damn Citizen! 1962: Six-Gun Law. 1968: The Young Runaways.

BARKER, Lex (Alexander Barker)
1919–1973
Tall, blond and rather stolid American leading man of somewhat cool personality. Picked to

take over from Johnny Weissmuller as Tarzan, he quit after five films because of paucity of dialogue, but never rose above action movies. Two of his five marriages were to Arlene Dahl (1951–1952) and Lana Turner (1953–1957). Died of a heart attack.

1946: Doll Face (GB: Come Back to Me). Do You Love Me? Two Guys from Milwaukee (GB: Royal Flush). 1947: The Farmer's Daughter. Dick Tracy Meets Gruesome. Crossfire. Under the Tonto Rim, Unconquered. 1948: Mr Blandings Builds His Dream House. Return of the Bad Men. The Velvet Touch. 1949: Tarzan's Magic Fountain, 1950: Tarzan and the Slave Girl. 1951: Tarzan's Peril (GB: Tarzan and the Jungle Queen). 1952: Tarzan's Savage Fury. Battles of Chief Pontiac. 1953: Tarzan and the She-Devil. 1954: Thunder Over the Plains. The Yellow Mountain. Vendetta dei Thugs. 1955: The Man from Bitter Ridge. Duel on the Mississippi. Mystery of the Black Jungle (GB: Black Devils of Kali). 1956: The Price of Fear. Away All Boats. 1957: The Girl in the Kremlin. War Drums. Jungle Heat. The Deerslayer. The Girl in Black Stockings. 1958: Strange Awakening (GB: Female Fiends). The Son of the Red Pirate. Killers of the East. 1959: Mission in Morocco. La scimitarra di Saraceno. Terror of the Red Mask. Captain Falcon (GB: Robin Hood). The Pirate and the Slave Girl. La dolce vita. 1960: Le secret des hommes bleus. Pirates of the Coast (GB: Pirates of the Barbary Coast). Caravan to Zagota. Il cavalieré dai cento volti (GB: Knight of a Hundred Faces). Robin Hood and the Pirates. 1961: Secret of the Black Falcon. Marco Polo. Le trésor des hommes bleus. The Return of Dr Mabuse. 1962: Frauenarzt Dr Sibelius. Treasure of Silver Lake. The Invisible Dr Mabuse. 1963: Breakfast in Bed. The Mystery of the Indian Temple. Das Todesauge von Ceylon (GB: Storm over Ceylon). The Black Buccaneer. Winnetou I (GB: Winnetou the Warrior. US: Apache Gold). Hangman of Venice (GB: Blood of the Executioner). Kali-Yug, Goddess of Vengeance. 1964: Old Shatterhand (GB: Apaches' Last Battle). Code 7, Victim 5 (GB: Victim Five). $5,000 für den Kopf von Jonny R. 1965: Die Pyramid des Sonnengottes. Winnetou II (GB: Last of the Renegades). Die Hölle von Manitoba (US: The Desperate Trail). Der Schatz der Azteken. Attack of the Kurds (GB: Wild Kurdistan). Im Reiche des silbernen Löwen. 1966: Winnetou III. 24 Hours to Kill. Mister Dynamite (GB: Die Slowly, You'll Enjoy It More). Requiem for a Secret Agent. Dynamite al Pentagono. A Place Called Glory. The Shoot. 1967: Woman Times Seven. Winnetou und das Halbblut Apanatschi. Die Schlangengrube und das Pendel (GB and US: The Blood Demon). 1968: Devil May Care. The Longest Day in Kansas City. Winnetou und Shatterhand im Tal der Toten. 1969: L'uomo dal lungo facile. 1970: Wenn du bei mir bist.

BARNES, Barry K. (Nelson Barnes) 1906–1965
Tall, dark, lean-faced, saturnine British leading man in the John Justin/Michael Rennie mould. Very popular in the late 1930s,

especially in *Thin Man*-style comedy-thrillers, he picked up a mysterious bug in the mid-1940s (probably on war service), which baffled specialists and effectively ended his career, depriving him of 'all power and confidence'. Married to Diana Churchill (*qv*), who looked after him devotedly until his death.

1936: Dodging the Dole. 1937: The Return of the Scarlet Pimpernel. 1938: Who Goes Next? This Man is News. You're the Doctor. Prison without Bars. The Ware Case. 1939: Spies of the Air. This Man in Paris. The Midas Touch. 1940: Two for Danger. Law and Disorder. The Girl in the News. 1946: Bedelia. 1947: Dancing with Crime.

BARNES, Binnie (Gitelle Barnes) 1905–
Sophisticated blonde British-born actress with pencil-line eyebrows, often cast as the 'other woman'. Started in two-reel comedies, but made over 20 British features, before going to Hollywood in 1934. Married to producer Mike Frankovich since 1940.

1931: A Night in Montmartre. Love Lies. Dr Josser KC. Out of the Blue. 1932: Murder at Covent Garden. Partners Please. The Innocents of Chicago (GB: Why Saps Leave Home). Down Our Street. Strip, Strip, Hooray! The Last Coupon. Old Spanish Customers. 1933: Taxi to Paradise. Counsel's Opinion. Their Night Out. Heads We Go (US: The Charming Deceiver). The Private Life of Henry VIII. The Silver Spoon. The Lady is Willing. 1934: Nine Forty-Five. No Escape. The Private Life of Don Juan. Forbidden Territory. Gift of Gab. There's Always Tomorrow. One Exciting Adventure. 1935: Diamond Jim. Rendezvous.

La Fiesta de Santa Barbara. 1936: Sutter's Gold. Small Town Girl. The Last of the Mohicans. The Magnificent Brute. 1937: Three Smart Girls. Breezing Home. Broadway Melody of 1938. 1938: The First Hundred Years. The Adventures of Marco Polo. Holiday (later Unconventional Linda. GB: Free to Live). Getaway. Tropic Holiday. Three Blind Mice. The Divorce of Lady X. Thanks for Everything. Always Goodbye. 1939: Wife, Husband and Friend. The Three Musketeers. Frontier Marshal. Daytime Wife. 1940: 'Til We Meet Again. 1941: New Wine. This Thing Called Love (GB: Married But Single). Angels with Broken Wings. Tight Shoes. Skylark. Three Girls about Town. 1942: Call Out the Marines. I Married an Angel. In Old California. 1943: The Man from Down Under. 1944: Up in Mabel's Room. The Hour Before the Dawn. It's in the Bag (GB: The Fifth Chair). 1945: Barbary Coast Gent. The Spanish Main. Getting Gertie's Garter. 1946: The Time of Their Lives. 1948: The Dude Goes West. If Winter Comes. My Own True Love. 1949: The Pirates of Capri (GB: The Masked Pirate). 1950: Shadow of the Eagle. 1951: Fugitive Lady. 1952: Decameron Nights. 1954: Malaga (US: Fire Over Africa). 1966: The Trouble with Angels. 1968: Where Angels Go – Trouble Follows. 1973: Forty Carats.

BARR, Patrick 1908–1985
Affable, square-built British actor (born in India) who, after more than 20 years of solid supporting reliability as policemen, servicemen, doctors and best friends, suddenly became extremely popular on British television in the mid-fifties. This belated success led to a few leading roles in films, and a deservedly higher rating as an actor. Away on active service from 1940 to 1946.

1932: Men of Tomorrow. The Merry Men of Sherwood. 1933: Meet My Sister. 1934: Irish Hearts (US: Norah O'Neale). 1935: Gay Old Dog. 1936: Wednesday's Luck. East Meets West. Things to Come. Midnight at Madam Tussaud's (US: Midnight at the Wax Museum). 1937: The Cavalier of the Streets. The Show Goes On. The Return of the Scarlet Pimpernel. Incident in Shanghai. 1938: Sailing Along. Star of the Circus (US: Hidden Menace). Meet Mr Penny. Marigold. The Gaunt Stranger (US: The Phantom Strikes). Yellow Sands. 1939: Let's Be Famous. 1940:

Contraband (US: Blackout). The Case of the Frightened Lady (US: The Frightened Lady.) 1949: Man on the Run, Adam and Evelyne. The Blue Lagoon. Golden Arrow (US: Three Men and a Girl). 1951: To Have and to Hold. The Lavender Hill Mob. Death of an Angel. 1952: The Story of Robin Hood and His Merrie Men. King of the Underworld. I vinti. You're Only Young Twice! 1953: Murder at Scotland Yard. *Ghost for Sale. Black Orchid. *Murder at the Grange. Single-Handed (US: Sailor of the King). The Intruder. Black 13. Gilbert Harding Speaking of Murder. Escape by Night. 1954: Duel in the Jungle. Seagulls over Sorrento (US: Crest of the Wave). Time is My Enemy. The Brain Machine. The Dam Busters. 1955: *All Living Things. Room in the House. 1956: It's Never Too Late. 1957: At the Stroke of Nine. Saint Joan. Lady of Vengeance. 1958: Next to No Time! 1960: Urge to Kill. 1961: The Valiant. *Dam the Delta (narrator only). 1962: The Longest Day. *Jam Session. 1963: On the Run. Billy Liar! Ring of Spies. 1968: The Great Pony Raid. 1969: Guns in the Heather. 1972: The Flesh and Blood Show. 1973: The Satanic Rites of Dracula. (US: Dracula and his Vampire Bride). 1974: House of Whipcord. The Black Windmill. 1978: The First Great Train Robbery. Home Before Midnight. 1979: The Godsend. 1983: Octopussy.

BARRETT, Ray 1926–
Fair-haired Australian leading man with distinctive rugged, pock-marked, scowling features, especially effective in roles calling for cynicism and disillusion. Coming to England in the early 1960s, he played a few leads in minor crime dramas, and enjoyed great success in the television series The Troubleshooters. In the mid-1970s, he returned to Australia, subsequently playing a few leading character roles in films there.
1960: The Sundowners. 1962: Time to Remember. Jigsaw. *Moment of Decision. Touch of Death. 1963: 80,000 Suspects. To Have and Hold. 1964: Valley of the Kings (serial). 1965: The Reptile. 1966: Just Like a Woman. Thunderbirds Are Go (voice only). 1971: Revenge. 1974: The Amorous Milkman. 1975: The Hostages. 1976: Let the Balloon Go. Don's Party. 1977: The Chant of Jimmie Blacksmith. 1981: A Burning Man. 1984: Where the Green Ants Dream. 1985: Relatives. The Empty Beach. Rebel. 1986: Frenchman's Farm.

BARRIE, Wendy (Margaret Jenkins) 1912–1978
British blonde socialite leading lady, born in Hong Kong, who, after playing Jane Seymour to Charles Laughton's Henry VIII, went to Hollywood and enjoyed a colourful career, including once being engaged to a famous gangster. Later found renewed success as a popular radio and TV hostess of chat shows.
1931: Collision. 1932: Threads. The Call Box Mystery. Wedding Rehearsal. Where is the Lady?. The Barton Mystery. 1933: Cash (US: For Love or Money). It's a Boy. The Private Life of Henry VIII. This Acting Business. The House of Trent. 1934: Murder at the Inn. Without You. The Man I Want. Freedom of the Seas. There Goes Susie (US: Scandals of Paris). Give Her a Ring. 1935: It's a Small World. College Scandal (GB: The Clock Strikes Eight). The Big Broadcast of 1936. A Feather in Her Hat. Millions in the Air. 1936: Love on a Bet. Speed. Ticket to Paradise. Under Your Spell. 1937: Breezing Home. What Price Vengeance? (GB: Vengeance). Wings over Honolulu. Dead End. A Girl with Ideas. Prescription for Romance. 1938: I Am the Law. Pacific Liner. 1939: Newsboys' Home. The Saint Strikes Back. The Hound of the Baskervilles. Five Came Back. The Witness Vanishes. Day-Time Wife. 1940: The Saint Takes Over. Women in War. Cross-Country Romance. Men Against the Sky. Who Killed Aunt Maggie? 1941: Repent at Leisure. The Saint in Palm Springs. The Gay Falcon. Public Enemies. A Date with the Falcon. Eyes of the Underworld. 1943: Forever and a Day. Follies Girl. Submarine Alert. 1954: It Should Happen to You. 1963: The Moving Finger.

BARRY, Don 'Red' (D.B. Da Acosta) 1912–1980
Busy, forceful, intent-looking star of dozens of second-feature westerns in the 1930s and 1940s, including the Red Ryder serial that gave him his nickname – even though he didn't have red hair. After finishing with Ryder, Barry tried to widen his range, but the move was not popular with the public. In 1950, he moved into TV, and returned to the cinema four years later as a character actor, often in quite small roles. In August 1980, he shot himself.
1933: This Day and Age. 1934: *Movie Usher. 1936: Night Waitress. Beloved Enemy. 1937:

Navy Blue and Gold. The Last Gangster. The Woman I Love. Born Reckless. Dead End. 1938: Duke of West Point. *Think It Over. There's That Woman Again (GB: What a Woman). Letter of Introduction. Sinners in Paradise. The Crowd Roars. Young Dr Kildare. 1939: Wyoming Outlaw. Saga of Death Valley. Days of Jesse James. SOS Tidal Wave (GB: Tidal Wave). Only Angels Have Wings. Calling Dr Kildare. Panama Patrol. The Secret of Dr Kildare. Calling All Marines. 1940: Sailor's Lady. *Jackpot. Frontier Vengeance. The Tulsa Kid. Ghost Valley Raiders. One Man's Law. Texas Terrors. The Adventures of Red Ryder (serial). 1941: A Missouri Outlaw. Desert Bandit. Death Valley Outlaws. The Apache Kid. Phantom Cowboy. Wyoming Wildcat. Two-Gun Sheriff. Kansas Cyclone. 1942: The Cyclone Kid. Red-Headed Justice. Arizona Terrors. Outlaws of Pine Ridge. The Sombrero Kid. The Traitor Within. Remember Pearl Harbor. Stagecoach Express. Jesse James Junior. 1943: The Sundown Kid. Days of Old Cheyenne. Carson City Cyclone. Black Hills Express. Canyon City. Man from Rio Grande. Fugitive from Sonora. Dead Man's Gulch. The Westside Kid. 1944: The Purple Heart. California Joe. My Buddy. Outlaws of Santa Fé. 1945: Bells of Rosarita. The Chicago Kid. 1946: The Plainsman and the Lady. The Last Crooked Mile. Out California Way. 1947: That's My Gal. 1948: Madonna of the Desert. Train to Alcatraz. Lightnin' in the Forest. Tough Assignment. Slippy McGee. 1949: Red Desert. The Dalton Gang. Square Dance Jubilee. Ringside. Headin' for Trouble. 1950: Train to Tombstone. Border Rangers. I Shot Billy the Kid. Gunfire (GB: Frank James Rides Again). 1954: Untamed Heiress. Jesse James' Women. 1955: The Twinkle in God's Eye. I'll Cry Tomorrow. 1956: Seven Men from Now. 1957: Gun Duel in Durango. 1958: China Doll. Andy Hardy Comes Home. Frankenstein 1970. 1959: The Big Operator. The Last Mile. Warlock. Born Reckless. 1960: Walk Like a Dragon. Ocean's Eleven. 1961: The Errand Boy. 1962: A Walk on the Wild Side. Birdman of Alcatraz. Buffalo Gun. 1963: Twilight of Honor (GB: The Charge is Murder). Law of the Lawless. The Carpetbaggers. 1965: Town Tamer. Fort Courageous. Convict Stage. Iron Angel. 1966: Alvarez Kelly. Apache Uprising. War Party. 1967: Red Tomahawk. Fort Utah. Hostile Guns. 1968: Shalako. Bandolero! The Shakiest

Gun in the West. 1969: The Cockeyed Cowboys of Calico County (GB TV: A Woman for Charlie). 1970: Hunters Are for Killing (TV). Rio Lobo. Dirty Dingus Magee. 1971: Incident on a Dark Street (TV). Owen Marshall, Counsellor at Law (TV). The Gatling Gun. One More Train to Rob. Johnny Got His Gun. 1972: Junior Bonner. The Eyes of Charles Sand (TV). 1973: Partners in Crime (TV). Showdown. 1974: Big Rose (TV). Punch and Jody (TV). Boss Nigger (GB: The Black Bounty Killer). 1975: Hustle. From Noon Till Three. Whiffs (GB: C.A.S.H.). 1976: Blazing Stewardesses. 1977: Orca, Killer Whale. 1978: Seabo. The Swarm. The Crash of Flight 401/Crash (TV). Kate Bliss and the Tickertape Kid (TV). Buckstone County Prison. 1979: Goldie and the Boxer (TV). 1981: Back Roads.

As director:
1954: Jesse James' Women.

BARRY, Gene (Eugene Klass) 1921–
Smooth, black-haired American leading man, good at handsome villains when given the chance. In routine leading roles in the fifties, then had enormous personal success in the TV series Burke's Law. Afterwards, his film roles were, if anything, worse than before, and he returned to television.
1952: The Atomic City. The War of the Worlds. 1953: The Girls of Pleasure Island. Those Redheads from Seattle. 1954: Alaska Seas. Red Garters. Naked Alibi. 1955: Soldier of Fortune. The Purple Mask. 1956: The Houston Story. Back from Eternity. 1957: The 27th Day. Ain't No Time for Glory (TV). China Gate. Forty Guns. 1958: Hong Kong Confidential. Thunder Road. 1967: Prescription Murder (TV). Maroc 7. 1968: Istanbul Express (TV. GB: cinemas). 1969: Subterfuge. 1970: Do You Take This Stranger? (TV). 1971: The Devil and Miss Sarah (TV). A Capitol Affair (TV). The Showdown (TV). 1974: The Second Coming of Suzanne. 1977: Ransom for Alice (TV). 1979: Guyana: the Crime of the Century. 1980: A Cry for Love (TV). 1983: The Girl, the Gold Watch and Dynamite (TV). The Adventures of Nellie Bly (TV).

BARRYMORE, Ethel (E. Blythe) 1879–1956
American leading lady, sister of John and Lionel who, after a few rather too regal star-

ring roles in silent films, returned to the stage. In the forties she came back to Hollywood in triumph, winning an Oscar for None But the Lonely Heart and bringing great presence to a series of dowager roles. Died from a heart attack. Received additional Oscar nominations for The Spiral Staircase, The Paradine Case and Pinky.
1915: The Nightingale. The Final Judgment. 1916: The Kiss of Hate. The Awakening of Helen Richie. 1917: The White Raven. The Lifted Veil. The Eternal Mother. An American Widow. The Call of Her People. Life's Whirlpool. 1918: Our Mrs McChesney. 1919: Test of Honor. The Divorcee. The Spender. 1932: Rasputin and the Empress (GB: Rasputin the Mad Monk). 1933: *All at Sea. 1943: *Show Business at War. 1944: None But the Lonely Heart. 1945: The Spiral Staircase. 1947: The Farmer's Daughter. Moss Rose. Night Song. 1948: The Paradine Case. Moonrise. Portrait of Jennie (GB: Jennie). 1949: The Great Sinner. That Midnight Kiss. The Red Danube. Pinky. 1951: The Secret of Convict Lake. Kind Lady. 1952: It's a Big Country. Deadline, USA (GB: Deadline). Just for You. 1953: The Story of Three Loves. Main Street to Broadway. 1954: Young at Heart. 1956: Eloise (TV). 1957: Johnny Trouble.

BARRYMORE, John (J. Blythe) 1882–1942
Dominant American actor of stern but handsome looks (known as 'The Great Profile'), resonant voice and great presence, the brother of Ethel and Lionel Barrymore. A matinee idol in the 1920s, he had a few striking roles

at the beginning of sound, but his career was eventually overtaken by alcohol and high living, and he ended his days in unworthy, self-mocking roles. Married (third of four) to Dolores Costello (qv) from 1928 to 1935. Died from pneumonia after collapsing during rehearsal for a radio show.
1914: An American Citizen. The Man from Mexico. 1915: The Dictator. Are You a Mason? The Incorrigible Dukane. 1916: Nearly a King. The Lost Bridegroom. The Red Widow. 1917: Raffles the Amateur Cracksman. 1918: On the Quiet. Here Comes the Bride. 1919: The Test of Honor. 1920: Dr Jekyll and Mr Hyde. 1921: The Lotus Eater. 1922: Sherlock Holmes (GB: Moriarty). 1924: Beau Brummell. 1926: The Sea Beast. 1927: *Life in Hollywood No 4. *Twenty Minutes at Warner Brothers' Studios. When a Man Loves (GB: His Lady). The Beloved Rogue. 1928: Tempest. 1929: Eternal Love. Show of Shows. General Crack. 1930: The Man from Blankley's. Moby Dick. 1931: Svengali. The Mad Genius. 1932: Arsene Lupin. Grand Hotel. A Bill of Divorcement. State's Attorney (GB: Cardigan's Last Case). 1933: Rasputin and the Empress (GB: Rasputin the Mad Monk). Topaze. Reunion in Vienna. Dinner at Eight. Night Flight. Scarlet River. 1934: Counsellor-at-Law. Long Lost Father. Twentieth Century. 1936: Romeo and Juliet. 1937: Maytime. Bulldog Drummond Comes Back. Night Club Scandal. True Confession. Bulldog Drummond's Revenge. 1938: Bulldog Drummond's Peril. Romance in the Dark. Spawn of the North. Marie Antoinette. Hold That Co-Ed (GB: Hold That Gal). The Great Man Votes. 1939: Midnight. 1940: The Great Profile. 1941: The Invisible Woman. World Premiere. 1942: Playmates. *Screen Snapshots No 107.

BARRYMORE, Lionel (L. Blythe) 1878–1954
Irascible, versatile and popular character star brother of Ethel and John. Won an Academy Award in 1931 for A Free Soul and continued his career despite being crippled by a fall in 1937. Gained renewed popularity as crusty old Dr Gillespie in the M-G-M series of the thirties and forties. Also directed. Nominated for an Academy Award on A Free Soul. Received an Oscar nomination in the best director category for Madame X.
1911: *Fighting Blood. *The Battle. 1912: *An

Adventure in the Autumn Woods. *Brutality. *The Chief's Dilemma. *Friends. *The Chief's Blanket. *A Cry for Help. *Fate. The God Within. *Gold and Glitter. *Home Folks. *The Informer. *Love in an Apartment Hotel. *The Massacre. *The Musketeers of Pig Alley. *My Baby. *The New York Hat. *Oil and Water. *The One She Loved. *So Near and Yet So Far.*My Hero. *The Telephone Girl and the Lady). *Three Friends. 1913: *The Battle of Elderbrush Gulch. *Death's Marathon. *The House of Darkness. *Brute Force. *Just Gold. *The Lady and the Mouse. *A Misunderstood Boy. *Near to Earth. *The Perfidy of Mary. *The Rancher's Revenge. *The Sheriff's Baby. *The Switch Tower. *A Timely Interception. *The Wanderer. *The Yaqui Cur. *Her Father's Silent Partner. *Pa Says. *A Welcome Intruder. *Woman Against Woman. *The Fatal Wedding. *Father's Lesson. *His Inspiration. *Mister Jefferson Green. *So Runs the Way. *The Suffragette Minstrels. *The Vengeance of Galora. *Classmates. *The House of Discord. *The Power of the Press. *The Stolen Treaty. 1914: Men and Women. The Span of Life. Judith of Bethulia. Strongheart. The Woman in Black. The Seals of the Mighty. Under the Gaslight. 1915: Wildfire. The Romance of Elaine (serial). The Exploits of Elaine (serial). A Modern Magdalen. The Curious Life of Judge Legarde. The Flaming Sword. Dora Thorne. A Yellow Streak. 1916: Dorian's Divorce. The Quitter. The Upheaval. The Brand of Cowardice. 1917: The End of the Tour. His Father's Son. The Millionaire's Double. Life's Whirlpool. 1919: The Valley of Night. 1920: The Copperhead. The Master Mind. The Devil's Garden. 1921: The Great Adventure. Jim the Penman. 1922: Boomerang Bill. The Face in the Fog. 1923: The Enemies of Women. Unseeing Eyes. 1924: The Eternal City. Decameron Nights. America. Meddling Women. 1925: I am the Man. Die Frau mit dem schlechten Ruf. The Iron Man. Children of the Whirlwind. The Girl Who Wouldn't Work. The Wrongdoer. Fifty-Fifty. The Splendid Road. 1926: The Barrier. *Wife Tamers. Brooding Eyes. The Lucky Lady. Paris at Midnight. The Bells. The Temptress. 1927: The Show. Women Love Diamonds. Body and Soul. The Thirteenth Hour. 1928: Love (GB: Anna Karenina). Sadie Thompson. Drums of Love. West of Zanzibar. The Lion and the Mouse. Road House. The River Woman. 1929: Alias Jimmy Valentine. Hollywood Revue of 1929. Mysterious Island. 1930: Free and Easy. 1931: A Free Soul. The Yellow Ticket (GB: The Yellow Passport). Mata Hari. Guilty Hands. 1932: Broken Lullaby (GB: The Man I Killed). Arsene Lupin. Washington Masquerade (GB: Mad Masquerade). Grand Hotel. Rasputin and the Empress (GB: Rasputin the Mad Monk). 1933: Sweepings. Looking Forward (GB: Service). Dinner at Eight. Stranger's Return. Night Flight. One Man's Journey. Scarlet River. The Late Christopher Bean. Should Ladies Behave? 1934: This Side of Heaven. Carolina (GB: The House of Connelly). Cardboard City. Treasure Island. The Girl from Missouri (GB: 100 Per Cent Pure). 1935: Mark of the Vampire. The Little Colonel.

Public Hero Number One. The Return of Peter Grimm. 1936: Ah, Wilderness! The Voice of Bugle Ann. The Road to Glory. The Devil Doll. The Gorgeous Hussy. Camille. 1937: A Family Affair. Captains Courageous. Navy Blue and Gold. A Yank at Oxford. 1938: Test Pilot. You Can't Take It With You. Young Dr Kildare. 1939: Let Freedom Ring. Calling Dr Kildare. On Borrowed Time. Secret of Dr Kildare. 1940: Dr Kildare's Strange Case. Dr Kildare Goes Home. Dr Kildare's Crisis. 1941: The Bad Man (GB: Two-Gun Cupid). The Penalty. *Cavalcade of the Academy Awards. The People versus Dr Kildare (GB: My Life is Yours). Lady Be Good. Dr Kildare's Wedding Day (GB: Mary Names the Day). 1942: Dr Kildare's Victory (GB: The Doctor and the Debutante). Calling Dr Gillespie. Dr Gillespie's New Assistant. 1943: Tennessee Johnson (GB: The Man on America's Conscience). Thousands Cheer. Dr Gillespie's Criminal Case (GB: Crazy to Kill). A Guy Named Joe. *The Last Will and Testament of Tom Smith. 1944: Three Men in White. Dragon Seed (narrator). Since You Went Away. 1945: The Valley of Decision. Between two Women. 1946: Three Wise Fools. The Secret Heart. It's a Wonderful Life. Duel in the Sun. 1947: Dark Delusion (GB: Cynthia's Secret). 1948: Key Largo. 1949: Down to the Sea in Ships. Malaya (GB: East of the Rising Sun). 1950: Right Cross. *The Screen Actor. 1951: Bannerline. 1952: Lone Star. 1953: Main Street to Broadway.

As director: 1917: Life's Whirlpool. 1929: *Confession. Madame X. His Glorious Night. The Unholy Night. 1930: The Rogue Song. 1931: Ten Cents a Dance.

BARTHELMESS, Richard 1895–1963
Thoughtful, ultra-serious, dark-haired American leading man who came to films straight from college and was used memorably by D.W. Griffith in Broken Blossoms and Way Down East. Immensely popular in sensitive roles through the 1920s, but his appeal was never quite as strong after the coming of the talkies, when he rarely seemed able to give his lines a completely natural inflexion. Died from cancer. Oscar nominations for The Noose and The Patent Leather Kid.
1916: War Brides. Snow White. Gloria's Romance (serial). Just a Song at Twilight. 1917: The Seven Swans. The Valentine Girl.

Bab's Diary. Camille. The Soul of Magdalen. The Streets of Illusion. Bab's Burglar. Nearly Married. The Moral Code. For Valor. The Eternal Sin. Sunshine Man. 1918: Hit the Trail Holiday. Rich Man, Poor Man. The Hope Chest. Boots. A Wild Primrose. 1919: The Girl Who Stayed Home. Three Men and a Girl. Peppy Polly. Broken Blossoms. I'll Get Him Yet. Scarlet Days. 1920: The Idol Dancer. The Love Flower. Way Down East. 1921: Experience. Tol'able David. 1922: The Seventh Day. Sonny. Fury. The Bond Boy. 1923: The Bright Shawl. The Fighting Blade. 1924: Twenty One. The Enchanted Cottage. Classmates. 1925: New Toys. Soul Fire. Share Leave. The Beautiful City. 1926: Just Suppose. Ransom's Folly. The Amateur Gentleman. The White Black Sheep. 1927: The Patent Leather Kid. The Drop Kick (GB: Glitter). 1928: The Little Shepherd of Kingdom Come. The Noose. Kentucky Courage. Wheels of Chance. Out of the Ruins. Scarlet Seas. 1929: Weary River. Drag (GB: Parasites). Show of Shows. Young Nowheres. 1930: Son of the Gods. The Dawn Patrol. 1931: The Lash (GB: Adios). The Finger Points. The Last Flight. 1932: *The Stolen Jools (GB: The Slippery Pearls). Alias the Doctor. Cabin in the Cotton. 1933: Central Airport. Heroes for Sale. Massacre. 1934: A Modern Hero. Midnight Alibi. 1935: A Spy of Napoleon. Four Hours to Kill. 1939: Only Angels Have Wings. 1940: The Man Who Talked Too Much. 1942: The Mayor of 44th Street. The Spoilers.

BARTHOLOMEW, Freddie (Frederick Llewellyn) 1924–
Dark-haired, British-born Hollywood child star, mainly in gentle or 'sissified' roles. The subject of many legal tangles between various relations, it was once estimated he had been in court twice a month between 1934 and 1939. In the fifties, he moved to a career in advertising.
1930: Toyland. 1931: Fascination. Let's Go Naked. 1932: Lily Christine. 1935: David Copperfield. Anna Karenina. Professional Soldier. 1936: Little Lord Fauntleroy. The Devil is a Sissy (GB: The Devil Takes the Count). Lloyds of London. 1937: Captains Courageous. 1938: Kidnapped. Lord Jeff (GB: The Boy from Barnardo's). Listen, Darling. 1939: Spirit of Culver (GB: Man's Heritage). Two Bright Boys. 1940: Swiss Family Robin-

son. *Tom Brown's Schooldays. 1941: Naval Academy. 1942: Cadets on Parade. A Yank at Eton. Junior Army. 1944: The Town Went Wild. 1947: Sepia Cinderella. 1949: Outward Bound (TV). 1951: St Benny the Dip (GB: Escape If You Can).*

BARTOK, Eva (E. Szöke) 1926–
Striking, minxish, brunette Hungarian actress on the international scene who made more headlines than films, especially in a much-publicized marriage to Curt Jurgens (1955–1956) and an affair with Frank Sinatra. Made her debut in Hungary and claims to have had two lines in a second Hungarian film, although no trace of this 'appearance' seems to have survived. Left show business in the sixties for a life of 'peace and tranquillity' in Indonesia.
1947: Mezet Próféta (US: Prophet of the Fields). 1950: Madeleine. 1951: A Tale of Five Cities. 1952: Venetian Bird (US: The Assassin). The Crimson Pirate. 1953: Der letzte Walzer. Spaceways. Park Plaza 605 (US: Norman Conquest). Front Page Story. 1954: Meines Vaters Pferde. Carnival Story (German version). Rummelplatz der Liebe. Orient Express. Viktoria und ihr Husar. 1955: Dunja. Der Postmeister (GB: Her Crime Was Love). Von Himmel gefallen/Special Delivery. Break in the Circle. The Gamma People. 1956: Ohne Dich wird es Nacht. Durch die Wälder, durch die Auen. 1957: Ten Thousand Bedroooms. 1958: Operation Amsterdam. Der Arzt von Stalingrad. Madeleine – Tel 136211. 1959: Operation Caviare. SOS Pacific. Douze heures d'horloge. 1960: Ein Student ging vorbei. Beyond the Curtain. 12 Stunden Angst. 1961: Unter Ausschluss der Öffentlichkeit. Diesmal muss es Kaviar sein. The Woman with Red Hair. Es muss nicht immer Kaviar sein. 1962: Eheinstitut Aurora (US: Aurora Marriage Bureau). Winter im Ischia. 1963: Ferien wie noch nie. I'll See You in Hell. 1964: Sei donne per l'assassino (GB: Blood and Black Lace). 1965: Savina. 1974: Pele, King of Football.

BASEHART, Richard 1914–1984
Subdued, introverted, sandy-haired American actor, much at home with mental anguish, less at ease in action roles. After winning the New York Critics' Best Newcomer Award (1945), he was tipped for top stardom. When it didn't quite arrive, he went abroad, and played good roles in some excellent films until

his luck ran out in the late fifties. He later appeared in a string of unlikely roles. Long married to Valentina Cortese, but divorced in 1971. Died after a series of strokes.
1946: Cry Wolf. 1947: Repeat Performance. 1948: He Walked by Night. 1949: The Black Book (GB: Reign of Terror). Roseanna McCoy. Tension. 1950: Outside the Wall. 1951: Fourteen Hours. The House on Telegraph Hill. Fixed Bayonets. Decision Before Dawn. 1952: Titanic. 1953: The Stranger's Hand. 1954: La strada/The Road. Avanzi di galeria (US: Jailbirds). The Good Die Young. Cartouche. 1955: Canyon Crossroads. La veno d'oro (US: The Golden Touch). Il bidone (GB: The Spivs. US: The Swindlers). 1956: The Extra Day. The Intimate Stranger (US: Finger of Guilt). Moby Dick. 1957: So Soon to Die (TV). Time Limit. Dimas/Arriverderci, Dimas. 1958: The Brothers Karamozov. 1959: The Man Stalin Killed. A Dream of Treason (TV). Five Branded Women. The Restless and the Damned (GB: The Climbers. US: The Ambitious Ones). Jons und Erdman. 1960: Portrait in Black. The Hiding Place (TV). For the Love of Mike (GB: None But the Brave). 1961: Passport to China (GB: Visa to Canton). 1962: Hitler. The Savage Guns. 1963: Kings of the Sun. 1964: Four Days in November (narrator only). The Satan Bug. 1969: Un homme qui me plait (GB: A Man I Like. Love is a Funny Thing). The Sole Survivor (TV). 1971: City beneath the Sea (TV. GB cinemas: One Hour to Doomsday). The Death of Me Yet (TV). The Birdmen (TV. GB cinemas: Escape of the Birdmen). Chato's Land. 1972: Assignment Munich (TV). The Bounty Man (TV). Rage. The Sagittarius Mine. 1973: Dive to Danger (narrator only). And Millions Must Die. Maneater (TV). 1974: Valley Forge (TV). 1975: Mansion of the Doomed (GB: The Terror of Dr Chaney). 1976: 21 Hours at Munich (TV. GB: cinemas). Flood! (TV. GB: cinemas). Time Travelers (TV). 1977: The Island of Dr Moreau. The Great Georgia Bank Hoax. Stonestreet (TV). 1978: The Court Martial of Lt William Calley. WEB (TV). 1979: Being There. 1980: Marilyn: the Untold Story (TV. GB: cinemas). 1981: Knight Rider (TV).

BATES, Alan 1934–
Dark-haired, solid English stage actor who came to the screen with the wave of angry

young men in the early 1960s. Adept at playing rough diamonds insensitive to other people's feelings, Bates proved very popular in the middle and late 1960s, after which he got involved in several highly uncommercial enterprises, and concentrated on the theatre until the late 1970s. Further cinema roles continued by and large to be unworthy of his talents. Oscar nomination for *The Fixer*.
*1960: The Entertainer. 1961: Whistle Down the Wind. 1962: A Kind of Loving. 1963: The Running Man. The Caretaker (US: The Guest). Nothing But the Best. 1964: Zorba the Greek. 1965: Insh' Allah (narrator only). 1966: Georgy Girl. King of Hearts. 1967: Far from the Madding Crowd. 1968: The Fixer. 1969: Women in Love. 1970: Three Sisters. 1971: The Go-Between. A Day in the Death of Joe Egg. 1972: *Second Best. 1973: Impossible Object/The Story of a Love Story. 1974: Mikis Theodorakis: A Profile of Greatness. Butley. The Story of Jacob and Joseph (TV). 1975: In Celebration. Royal Flash. 1977: An Unmarried Woman. 1978: The Shout. 1979: The Rose. 1980: Very Like a Whale (TV). Nijinsky. 1981: Quartet. The Trespasser (TV). Rece do gory/Hands Up! 1982: The Return of the Soldier. Britannia Hospital. 1983: An Englishman Abroad (TV). The Wicked Lady. 1986: The Gift of the Heart.*

BATES, Barbara 1925–1969
Pretty, well-groomed brunette Fox ingenue who gave up modelling and ballet careers to concentrate on acting. Despite a leading role opposite Danny Kaye, and a memorable 'bit' at the end of *All About Eve*, ill-health dogged her later career (forcing her to withdraw from

the British *Campbell's Kingdom* in 1957) and she was dead at 43, a 'suicide by asphyxiation'.
1945: Salome, Where She Danced. This Love of Ours. Lady on a Train. Strange Holiday (GB: The Day after Tomorrow). 1946: A Night in Paradise. 1947: The Fabulous Joe. 1948: Johnny Belinda. Adventures of Don Juan. Romance on the High Seas (GB: It's Magic). June Bride. 1949: The House Across the Street. One Last Fling. The Inspector General. 1950: All About Eve. Quicksand. Cheaper by the Dozen. 1951: The Secret of Convict Lake. I'd Climb the Highest Mountain. Let's Make It Legal. 1952: Belles on Their Toes. The Outcasts of Poker Flat. 1953: All Ashore. The Caddy. 1954: Rhapsody. 1956: House of Secrets (US: Triple Deception). Town on Trial! 1958: Apache Territory.

BAXTER. Anne 1923–1985
Brown-haired American leading actress, particularly good at playing deceptively sweet young things, an outstanding example being her Eve in *All About Eve*, for which she received an Oscar nomination. An attempt to revise her image from dramatic actress to pin-up girl in the fifties proved unsuccessful. Academy Award in 1946 for *The Razor's Edge*. Married to John Hodiak (first of two) 1946–1953. Died following a stroke.
*1940: Twenty Mule Team. The Great Profile. 1941: Charley's Aunt. Swamp Water (GB: The Man Who Came Back). 1942: The Magnificent Ambersons. The Pied Piper. 1943: Crash Dive. Five Graves to Cairo. The North Star. 1944: The Sullivans. The Eve of St Mark. Guest in the House. Sunday Dinner for a Soldier. 1945: A Royal Scandal (GB: Czarina). Smoky. 1946: Angel on My Shoulder. The Razor's Edge. 1947: Mother Wore Tights (narrator only). Blaze of Noon. 1948: Homecoming. The Luck of the Irish. The Walls of Jericho. 1949: Yellow Sky. You're My Everything. 1950: A Ticket to Tomahawk. All About Eve. 1951: Follow the Sun. 1952: *Screen Snapshots No. 206. The Outcasts of Poker Flat. My Wife's Best Friend. O. Henry's Full House (GB: Full House). 1953: I Confess. The Blue Gardenia. 1954: Carnival Story. Rummelplatz der Liebe. 1955: One Desire. The Spoilers. 1956: The Come-On. The Ten Commandments. Three Violent People. 1958: The Right Hand Man (TV). Chase a Crooked Shadow. 1960:*

Cimarron. Summer of the 17th Doll (US: Season of Passion). 1961: Mix Me a Person. 1962: A Walk on the Wild Side. 1965: The Family Jewels. 1966: The Tall Women. 1967: Stranger on the Run (TV). The Busy Body. 1968: The Challengers (TV. GB: cinemas). Companions in Nightmare (TV). 1970: Ritual of Evil (TV). 1971: If Tomorrow Comes (TV). Fools' Parade (GB: Dynamite Man from Glory Jail). The Catcher (TV). 1972: The Late Liz. Lisa Bright and Dark (TV). Lapin 360. 1977: Nero Wolfe (TV). 1978: Little Mo (TV). 1980: Jane Austen in Manhattan (TV). 1983: The Architecture of Frank Lloyd Wright (narrator only). 1984: The Masks of Death (TV).

BAXTER, Jane (Feodora Forde) 1909–
Unpretty but personable, German-born Jane Baxter had a lovely smile and proved one of Britain's most popular leading ladies in gently upper-crust roles of the mid-1930s. She was Charles Laughton's leading lady in *Down River* and Richard Tauber's in *Blossom Time*. Her limited cinematic appeal soon waned when she reached her thirties, but she continued to appear to good effect on stage. Her first husband, a racing driver, was killed in a crash.
1930: Bedrock. Bed and Breakfast. 1931: Down River. 1932: Two White Arms (US: Wives Beware). Flat Number Nine. 1933: The Constant Nymph. 1934: The Night of the Party. The Double Event. Girls Please! Blossom Time (US: April Romance). We Live Again. 1935: Royal Cavalcade (US: Regal Cavalcade). Drake of England (US: Drake the Pirate). The Enchanted April. The Clairvoyant. Line Engaged. 1936: The Man behind the Mask. Dusty Ermine (US: Hideout in the Alps). 1937: Second Best Bed. 1938: The Ware Case. 1939: Confidential Lady. Murder Will Out. The Chinese Bungalow (US: Chinese Den). 1940: The Briggs Family. 1941: Ships with Wings. 1943: The Flemish Farm. 1951: Death of an Angel. 1953: All Hallowe'en.

BAXTER, Warner 1889–1951
Solid, dependable, moustachioed American leading man, whose very seriousness contrasted strangely with his most popular characterization, the Cisco Kid, in which guise he won an Academy Award in 1929. Hollywood's top money-earner in 1936, after which his

career gradually declined to lesser films. Died of bronchial pneumonia.
*1914: Her Own Money. 1918: All Woman. 1919: Lombardi Ltd. 1921: Cheated Hearts. First Love. 1922: Her Own Money. The Love Charm. Sheltered Daughters. If I Were Queen. The Girl in His Room. A Girl's Desire. 1923: Blow Your Own Horn. The Ninety and Nine. St Elmo. 1924: Alimony. In Search of a Thrill. Christine of the Hungry Heart. The Female. His Forgotten Wife. Those Who Dance. The Garden of Weeds. 1925: The Golden Bed. The Awful Truth. Welcome Home. Air Mail. A Son of His Father. Mannequin. The Best People. Rugged Water. 1926: Miss Brewster's Millions. The Runaway. Mismates. Aloma of the South Seas. The Great Gatsby. 1927: Drums of the Desert. Singed. The Coward. Telephone Girl. 1928: The Tragedy of Youth. Three Sinners. Ramona. A Woman's Way. Craig's Wife. Danger Street. 1929: Linda. Far Call. West of Zanzibar. In Old Arizona. Thru Different Eyes. Behind That Curtain. Romance of the Rio Grande. 1930: Happy Days. Such Men Are Dangerous. Arizona Kid. Renegades. Doctors' Wives. 1931: The Squaw Man (GB: The White Man). Daddy Long Legs. Their Mad Moment. The Cisco Kid. Surrender. 1932: Amateur Daddy. *The Stolen Jools (GB: The Slippery Pearls). Man about Town. Six Hours to Live. Dangerously Yours. 1933: Forty-Second Street. I Loved You Wednesday. Paddy the Next Best Thing. Penthouse (GB: Crooks in Clover). 1934: As Husbands Go. Stand Up and Cheer. Such Women Are Dangerous. Grand. Canary. Broadway Bill (GB: Strictly Confidential). Hell in the Heavens. 1935: One More Spring. Under the Pampas Moon. King of Burlesque. 1936: Robin Hood of El Dorado. The Prisoner of Shark Island. The Road to Glory. To Mary – With Love. White Hunter. 1937: Slave Ship. Vogues of 1938. Wife, Doctor and Nurse. Kidnapped. I'll Give a Million. 1939: Wife, Husband and Friend. Return of the Cisco Kid. Barricade. 1940: Earthbound. 1941: Adam Had Four Sons. 1943: The Crime Doctor. The Crime Doctor's Strangest Case (GB: The Strangest Case). 1944: Lady in the Dark. Shadows in the Night. 1945: The Crime Doctor's Courage (GB: The Doctor's Courage). Just Before Dawn. The Crime Doctor's Warning (GB: The Doctor's Warning). 1946: The Crime Doctor's Man Hunt. 1947: The Millerson Case. The Crime Doctor's*

Gamble (GB: The Doctor's Gamble). 1948: A Gentleman from Nowhere. Prison Warden. 1949: The Devil's Henchman. The Crime Doctor's Diary. 1950: State Penitentiary.

BEACHAM, Stephanie 1949–
Spectacularly-structured, slightly petulant-looking blonde British leading lady who was chosen to star with Marlon Brando in The Nightcomers, but was afterwards confined largely to screaming heroines in horror films which emphasized her physical attributes. Drifting away from the cinema, she proved herself a more than capable actress, especially in such long-running television series as Tenko. Has usually showed up best in unsympathetic roles.
1968: The Games. 1971: Tam Lin (GB: The Devil's Widow). The Nightcomers. 1972: Dracula AD 1972. The Aries Computer. 1973: Blue Movie Blackmail. And Now the Screaming Starts. 1975: Schizo. Mafia Junction. 1980: Inseminoid. (US: Horror Planet).

BEAL, John (James Bliedung) 1909–
Dark, compact American leading man of the sincere, sensitive, brooding type, often cast as men wrestling with their own consciences. He enjoyed some good roles at RKO in the 1930s, but failed to prove a dominant enough personality to sustain a star career. In the 1950s, he made some reputation on TV in largely macabre roles. During World War II, he had directed war training films, but never directed a feature film, spending most of the latter part of his career with stage touring companies.
1933: Another Language. 1934: Hat, Coat and

Glove. The Little Minister. 1935: Les Miserables. Laddie. Break of Hearts. 1936: M'Liss. We Who Are About to Die. 1937: The Man Who Found Himself. Border Cafe. Danger Patrol. Double Wedding. Madame X. Beg, Borrow or Steal. 1938: Port of Seven Seas. I Am the Law. The Arkansas Traveler. 1939: The Great Commandment. The Cat and the Canary. 1941: Ellery Queen and the Perfect Crime (GB: The Perfect Crime). Doctors Don't Tell. 1942: Atlantic Convoy. One Thrilling Night. 1943: Edge of Darkness. Let's Have Fun. 1948: Key Witness. So Dear to My Heart. 1949: Alimony. Song of Surrender. Chicago Deadline. 1950: Messenger of Peace. Hit the Deck (TV). 1952: My Six Convicts. 1953: Remains to be Seen. 1954: The Country Parson. 1957: That Night! The Vampire. 1959: The Sound and the Fury. 1960: Ten Who Dared. 1966: The Easter Angel (TV). 1974: The House That Cried Murder. 1975: The Legend of Lizzie Borden (TV). 1977: Eleanor and Franklin: the White House Years (TV). 1979: Jennifer: A Woman's Story (TV). 1983: Amityville 3D.

BEATTY, Robert 1909–
Dark-haired Canadian actor, in Britain from the 1930s. He entered films as an extra and stand-in, but was groomed into a minor star by Ealing Studios from 1943 and remained quite popular in leading parts until the mid-1950s. Also well-liked in radio serials as the detective Philip O'Dell. His velvet tones have been used so frequently in narration, mainly in documentary films, that this part of his work is listed separately here.
1938: Black Limelight. Murder in Soho (US: Murder in the Night). 1940: Mein Kampf – My Crimes. Dangerous Moonlight (US: Suicide Squadron). 1941: 49th Parallel (US: The Invaders). 1942: One of Our Aircraft is Missing. The First of the Few. Flying Fortress. Suspected Person. 1943: San Demetrio London. 1944: It Happened One Sunday. 1946: Appointment with Crime. Odd Man Out. 1947: Green Fingers. 1948: Against the Wind. Counterblast. Another Shore. Portrait from Life (US: The Girl in the Painting). 1949: The Twenty Questions Murder Mystery. 1950: Her Favourite Husband (US: The Taming of Dorothy). 1951: Captain Horatio Hornblower RN. Calling Bulldog Drummond. The Magic Box. 1952: Wings of Danger (US: Dead on Course). The Gentle Gunman. The Net (US:

Project M7). The Oracle (US: The Horse's Mouth). 1953: Man on a Tightrope. The Square Ring. The Broken Horseshoe. Albert RN (US: Break to Freedom). 1954: L'amante di Paride (GB: The Face That Launched a Thousand Ships). Out of the Clouds. 1955: Portrait of Alison (US: Postmark for Danger). 1957: Time Lock. Tarzan and the Lost Safari. Something of Value. 1959: The Shakedown. 1961: Tremor. 1962: The Amorous Prawn. 1964: Bikini Paradise. 1965: Die Todesstrahlen des Dr Mabuse. 1968: 2001: a Space Odyssey. Where Eagles Dare. 1972: Sitting Target. 1973: Man at the Top. 1974: The Spikes Gang. 1976: The Pink Panther Strikes Again. 1977: Golden Rendezvous. 1979: The Martian Chronicles (TV). The Spaceman and King Arthur (US: Unidentified Flying Oddball). 1981: The Amateur. 1983: Superman III. 1985: Minder on the Orient Express (TV).

As narrator:
1952: *Spotlight on Reuters. *World of Life (and ensuing series). *The Figurehead. 1953: *Modern Ireland. The Master of Ballantrae. 1954: *Spotlight on Food (and ensuing 'Spotlight' series). 1955: Paris in London. *Four Legs to Master. 1956: 48 Hours. *Have a Care. *Fur, Feathers and Finery. *Signs of Life. *June in January. 1957: *Operation Universe. The Savage Mountain. *And So Forth. *The Oyster and the Pearl. *Battleground. *Mountain Holiday. 1958: *Pooches on Parade. *Secret World. *Riviera Express. 1959: *Cuckoo Land. *The Isle and the Pussycat. *Wrecker's Coast. 1960: The Mad Twenties. 1962: *Six of the Best. A Short Memory. 1966: One Million Years BC.

BEATTY, Warren (W. Beaty) 1937–
Boyishly handsome, dark-haired American leading man with a powerful personality and careful preparation of role which tends to show on screen. The brother of Shirley MacLaine (qv), his career has varied between immense hits and disastrous flops. In the early 1970s, his prodigious love life won him more headlines than his acting, but when he turned to direction his talent behind the camera was immediately apparent, and he won the 1982 directing Oscar for Reds. Two films in the past 10 years, though, has meant meagre rations for his fans. Acting Oscar nominations for Bonnie and Clyde, Heaven Can Wait and Reds.

1961: *Splendor in the Grass. The Roman Spring of Mrs Stone.* 1962: *All Fall Down.* 1964: *Lilith.* 1965: *Mickey One.* 1966: *Promise Her Anything. Kaleidoscope.* 1967: *Bonnie and Clyde.* 1969: *The Only Game in Town.* 1970: *Arthur Penn, 1922: themes and variants.* 1971: *McCabe and Mrs Miller. $ (GB: The Heist).* 1973: *Year of the Woman.* 1974: *The Parallax View. The Fortune.* 1975: *Shampoo.* 1978: †*Heaven Can Wait.* 1981: ‡*Reds.* 1986: *Ishtar.*

† And co-directed
‡ And directed

BEERY, Wallace 1886–1949
Hollywood's big lummox: a bull in a china shop, whose early serio-comic roles, casting him as the rampaging tough guy, with or without heart of gold, later gave way to figures of outright farce, especially in comedies with Marie Dressler and Marjorie Main. He won an Oscar in 1931 as the washed-up boxer in *The Champ,* (after a nomination for *The Big House*) and was one of M-G-M's most popular stars in the early 1930s. Married to Gloria Swanson (qv) from 1916 to 1918, the first of two wives. Died from a heart attack at exactly the same age as his acting brother Noah Beery Sr. (1883–1946).
1914: **Sweedie and the Lord. *Sweedie and the Double Exposure. *Sweedie's Skate. *Sweedie Springs a Surprise. *The Fickleness of Sweedie. *Sweedie Learns to Swim. *She Landed a Big One. *Sweedie and the Trouble Maker. *Sweedie at the Fair. *Madame Double X. *The Plum Tree. *Sweedie the Swatter. *The Fable of the Bush League Lover Who Failed to Qualify. *The Broken Pledge. *Chick Evans Links with Sweedie.* 1915: **Sweedie's Suicide. *Sweedie and the Dog. *Two Hearts That Beat as Ten. *Sweedie's Hopeless Love. *Sweedie Goes to College. *Love and Trouble. *Sweedie Learns to Ride. *Sweedie's Hero. *The Slim Princess. *Sweedie in Vaudeville. *Sweedie's Finish.* 1916: **Sweedie the Janitor. *Teddy at the Throttle. *A Dash of Courage.* 1917: **Cactus Nell. *The Clever Dummy. *Maggie's First False Step. Patria (serial). The Little American.* 1918: *Johanna Enlists.* 1919: *The Love Burglar. The Unpardonable Sin. Life Line. Soldier of Fortune. Behind the Door. Victory. The Virgin of Stamboul.* 1920: *The Molly-coddle. The Roundup. The Last of the Mohicans. The Rookies Return.* 1921: *The Four*

Horsemen of the Apocalypse. 813. Patsy. A Tale of Two Worlds. The Golden Snare. The Last Trail. 1922: *Wild Honey. The Man from Hell's River. The Rosary. The Sagebrush Trail. Ridin' Wild. I Am the Law. Robin Hood. Trouble Associated. Hurricane's Gal. Only a Shop Girl.* 1923: *Stormswept. The Flame of Life. Bavu. Ashes of Vengeance. Drifting. The Eternal Struggle. The Spanish Dancer. Three Ages. Richard, the Lion Hearted. Drums of Jeopardy. White Tiger.* 1924: *The Sea Hawk. Unseen Hands. Madonna of the Streets. Dynamite Smith. Another Man's Wife. The Red Lily. The Signal Tower. So Big.* 1925: *Let Woman Alone. The Great Divide. Coming Through. The Devil's Cargo. Adventure. The Lost World. The Night Club. Rugged Water. In the Name of Love. Pony Express.* 1926: *Behind the Front. Volcano. Old Ironsides (GB: Sons of the Sea). We're in the Navy Now. The Wanderer.* 1927: *Casey at the Bat. Fireman, Save My Child. Now We're in the Air.* 1928: *Wife Savers. Partners in Crime. The Big Killing. Beggars of Life.* 1929: *Chinatown Nights. Stairs of Sand. River of Romance.* 1930: *Way for a Sailor. Billy the Kid. A Lady's Morals (GB: Jenny Lind). The Big House. Min and Bill.* 1931: *The Secret Six. Hell Divers. The Champ.* 1932: *Grand Hotel. Flesh. *The Stolen Jools (GB: The Slippery Pearls).* 1933: *Dinner at Eight. Tugboat Annie. The Bowery.* 1934: *The Mighty Barnum. Viva, Villa! Treasure Island.* 1935: *West Point of the Air. China Seas. O'Shaughnessy's Boy. Ah, Wilderness!* 1936: *A Message to Garcia. Old Hutch.* 1937: *Good Old Soak. Slave Ship.* 1938: *Bad Man of Brimstone. Port of Seven Seas. Stablemates.* 1939: *Stand Up and Fight. *Screen Snapshots No. 77. Sergeant Madden. Thunder Afloat.* 1940: *The Man from Dakota (GB: Arouse and Beware). Twenty Mule Team. Wyoming (GB: Bad Man of Wyoming).* 1941: *The Bad Man (GB: Two Gun Cupid). Barnacle Bill. The Bugle Sounds.* 1942: *Jackass Mail.* 1943: *Salute to the Marines.* 1944: *Rationing. Barbary Coast Gent.* 1945: *This Man's Navy.* 1946: *Bad Bascomb. The Mighty McGurk.* 1948: *Alias a Gentleman. A Date with Judy.* 1949: *Big Jack.*

BELAFONTE, Harry 1927–
Strikingly handsome black American singer-actor with mellifluous light voice who, stran-

gely, didn't do his own singing in his biggest film hit, *Carmen Jones.* He has remained principally a record star, having several hits with calypso-style ballads, developing later into a portrayer of scruffy types in the occasional film, in contrast to his continuously smooth image as a singer. In 1984, he turned producer with the successful *Beat Street.*
1953: *Bright Road.* 1954: *Carmen Jones.* 1957: *Island in the Sun.* 1959: *The World, the Flesh and the Devil. Odds Against Tomorrow.* 1970: *The Angel Levine. King: a Filmed Record … Montgomery to Memphis.* 1972: *Buck and the Preacher.* 1974: *Uptown Saturday Night.* 1983: *The Smoky.*

BEL GEDDES, Barbara 1922–
Round-faced, light-haired American actress of much warmth and appeal, who plays plain, sincere, lovable ladies. She made her stage debut at 17, but her wholesome image never really caught on in the cinema. Her career was also somewhat impaired by ill-health and the McCarthy witch-hunt; thus Hollywood let her best years escape the screen. Nominated for an Oscar in *I Remember Mama,* she has undoubtedly made too few films, but did become a familiar figure to television audiences of the 1980s as Miss Ellie in *Dallas.*
1947: *The Long Night. The Gangster.* 1948: *I Remember Mama. Blood on the Moon.* 1949: *Caught.* 1950: *Panic in the Streets.* 1951: *Fourteen Hours.* 1958: *Rumors of Evening (TV). Vertigo.* 1959: *The Five Pennies. Five Branded Women.* 1961: *By Love Possessed.* 1971: *Summertree. The Todd Killings.*

BELL, Tom 1933–
Dark, lean and angry-looking British actor who came to stardom on the wave of 'kitchen sink' dramas of the early 1960s, and quickly gained a reputation for upsetting the 'establishment' which, it was said, cost him much film and television work. As his features became more taut with the years, it was hard to imagine him in comedy – but he built up a formidable range of TV and theatre work without entirely losing his 'stormy petrel' image, having twice refused to appear in sequels to highly successful television series.
1960: *The Criminal (US: The Concrete Jungle). Echo of Barbara.* 1961: *Payroll. The Kitchen.* 1962: *HMS Defiant (US: Damn the Defiant!). A Prize of Arms. The L-Shaped Room.* 1964: *Ballad in Blue (US: Blues for*

*Lovers). 1965: He Who Rides a Tiger. 1967: In Enemy Country. 1968: The Long Day's Dying. 1969: Lock Up Your Daughters! The Violent Enemy. All the Right Noises. 1971: Quest for Love. *The Spy's Wife. 1972: Straight on Till Morning. 1975: Royal Flash. 1978: The Sailor's Return. 1985: The Innocent. Summer Lightning (TV). Hard Travelling (TV).*

BELLAMY, Ralph 1904–
Tall, fair-haired American actor of resolute features. Beginning on stage, he had his own theatre company at 23, but in films he was generally cast in too many parts which merely required him to be dull and dependable, often as pipe-smoking sleuth, family friend, or guy who fails to get the girl. In later years, he became a redoubtable craggy, often crusty character actor, and served four years as president of Actors' Equity. He was nominated for an Academy Award in *The Awful Truth*.
1931: The Secret Six. The Magnificent Lie. Surrender. West of Broadway. Disorderly Conduct. 1932: Young America (GB: We Humans). Forbidden. Rebecca of Sunnybrook Farm. The Woman in Room 13. Wild Girl (GB: Salomy Jane). Air Mail. Almost Married. 1933: Second Hand Wife. Parole Girl. Destination Unknown. Picture Snatcher. The Narrow Corner. Below the Sea. Headline Shooter (GB: Evidence in Camera). Blind Adventure. Ace of Aces. Flying Devils (GB: The Flying Circus). 1934: Ever in My Heart. Spitfire. This Man is Mine. Once to Every Woman. One is Guilty. Before Midnight. The Crime of Helen Stanley. Girl in Danger. 1935: Woman in the Dark. Helldorado. The Wedding

Night. Rendezvous at Midnight. Air Hawks. Eight Bells. The Healer. Gigolette (GB: Night Club). Navy Wife. 1936: Hands Across the Table. Dangerous Intrigue. The Final Hour. Roaming Lady. Straight from the Shoulder. Wild Brian Kent. 1937: Counterfeit Lady. The Man Who Lived Twice. The Awful Truth. Let's Get Married. 1938: The Crime of Dr Hallet. Fools for Scandal. Boy Meets Girl. Carefree. Girls' School. Trade Winds. 1939: Let Us Live. Blind Alley. Smashing the Spy Ring. Flight Angels. Coast Guard. His Girl Friday. 1940: Brother Orchid. Queen of the Mob. Dance, Girl, Dance. Public Deb No 1. Ellery Queen, Master Detective. Meet the Wildcat. 1941: Ellery Queen's Penthouse Mystery. Footsteps in the Dark. Affectionately Yours. Ellery Queen and the Perfect Crime (GB: The Perfect Crime). Dive Bomber. Ellery Queen and the Murder Ring (GB: The Murder Ring). The Wolf Man. 1942: The Ghost of Frankenstein. Lady in a Jam. Men of Texas (GB: Men of Destiny). The Great Impersonation. 1943: Stage Door Canteen. 1944: Guest in the House. 1945: Delightfully Dangerous. Lady on a Train. 1955: The Court Martial of Billy Mitchell (GB: One Man Mutiny). 1956: Heritage of Anger (TV). 1960: Sunrise at Campobello. 1966: The Professionals. 1967: Wings of Fire (TV). 1968: Rosemary's Baby. 1969: The Immortal (TV). 1971: Doctors' Wives. 1972: Something Evil (TV). Cancel My Reservation. 1973: Owen Marshall, Counsellor at Law (TV). 1974: Log of the Black Pearl (TV). 1975: Murder on Flight 502 (TV). Adventures of the Queen (TV). Search for the Gods (TV). 1976: McNaughton's Daughter (TV). Nightmare in Badham County (TV). Return to Earth (TV). The Boy in the Plastic Bubble (TV). 1977: Charlie Cobb: Nice Night for a Hanging (TV). Oh, God! 1978: The Clone Master (TV). The Millionaire. 1979: The Billion Dollar Threat (TV. GB: cinemas). Power (TV). 1980: The Memory of Eva Ryker (TV). 1983: Trading Places.

BELMONDO, Jean-Paul 1933–
The supremely Gallic leading man of the sixties; Belmondo's lazy charm won him an instant international following after his first big success, in Godard's *Breathless*. Thereafter, he tended to trade in on the image. He could be memorable in the right film, but flounder rather badly without a decent script.

Like the American Burt Reynolds, Belmondo likes to do his own stunt-work.
*1955: *Molière. 1956: Dimanche nous volerons. 1957: A pied, à cheval et en voiture. 1958: Sois belle et tais-toi (GB: Blonde for Danger). Drôle de Dimanche. Les tricheurs (GB: Youthful Sinners). *Charlotte et son Jules. Les copains de Dimanche. 1959: Mademoiselle Ange. A bout de souffle (GB and US: Breathless). A double tour (GB: Web of Passion. US: Leda). 1960: Moderato cantabile (GB: Seven Days … Seven Nights). Lettere di una novizia. La française et l'amour (GB: Love and the Frenchwoman). Les distractions (GB: Trapped by Fear). Classe tous risques (GB: The Big Risk). 1961: La viaccia. La ciociara (GB and US: Two Women). Léon Morin, Priest. Une femme est une femme. Amours célèbres. Un nommé La Rocca. 1962: Un singe en hiver (GB: It's Hot in Hell). Cartouche (GB: Swords of Blood). Le doulos. I Don Giovanni della Costa Azzurra. L'aîné des Ferchaux. 1963: Mare matto. I giorno piu corto … (GB and US: The Shortest Day). Dragées au poivre (GB: Sweet and Sour). Peau de banane (US: Banana Peel). 1964: L'homme de Rio (GB: That Man from Rio). Cent mille dollars au soleil. Echappement libre. La chasse à l'homme (GB: The Gentle Art of Seduction). Week-end à Zuydcoote (GB: Weekend at Dunkirk). 1965: Par un beau matin d'été (US: Crime on a Summer Morning). Pierrot le fou. 1966: Les tribulations d'un Chinois en Chine (GB: Up to His Ears. US: Chinese Adventure in China). Is Paris Burning? Tendre voyou. 1967: *La bande à Bébel. Casino Royale. Le voleur (GB and US: The Thief). 1968: Ho! 1969: Dieu a choisi Paris. Le cerveau (GB and US: The Brain). La sirène du Mississippi (GB and US: Mississippi Mermaid). Un homme qui me plaît (GB and US: A Man I Like). 1970: Borsalino. 1971: Les mariés de l'an deux (GB: The Scoundrel). Le casse (GB and US: The Burglars). 1972: Docteur Popaul (GB: Scoundrel in White. US: Tender Scoundrel). La scoumoune. 1973: L'héritier (GB: The Inheritor). 1974: Le magnifique (GB: How to Destroy the Reputation of the Greatest Secret Agent …). Stavisky. 1975: Peur sur la ville (GB: Night Caller. US: Fear over the City). 1977: L'animal. Le corps de mon ennemi. 1979: Flic ou voyou. 1980: Le guignolo. I piccioni di Piazza San Marco. 1981: Le professionnel. 1982: L'as des as/Ace of Aces 1983: Les morfalous (US: The Vultures). 1984: Joyeuses pâques/Happy Easter.*

BELUSHI, John 1949–1982
Dark, tubby, abrasive American TV comedian and comic actor who made his name, along with such as Chevy Chase and Dan Aykroyd (both qv), on the innovative, rule-breaking late-night TV show *Saturday Night Live*. A hard-cursing Lou Costello for modern times (Belushi used the kind of language *on* camera that Costello was reputed to use off), he took his partnership with Aykroyd into films, and after putting audience's backs up or (mostly) having them in stitches. He was mellowing his hard-hitting style towards mainline cinema when hard living caught up with him and his death, from an overdose of cocaine and other

drugs, robbed him of intended participation in several major box-office successes, notably *Ghost Busters*.

1975: La honte de la jungle (GB: Jungle Burger. US: Shame of the Jungle. Voice only). 1978: National Lampoon's Animal House. Goin' South. Old Boyfriends. 1979: 1941. 1980: The Blues Brothers. 1981: Neighbors. Continental Divide.

BENDIX, William 1906–1964
Likeable American character star, with fair, wavy hair and soft, Brooklynese voice, built like a barrel, and often cast as amiable, dim-witted thugs. Appeared in a memorable series of Paramount thrillers in the forties, but his later success in comedy meant his virtual loss to TV from 1953 on. Died from lobar pneumonia. Oscar nominee for *Wake Island*.

*1942: The McGuerins from Brooklyn. Woman of the Year. Brooklyn Orchid. Wake Island. The Glass Key. Star Spangled Rhythm. Who Done It? 1943: China. Hostages. The Crystal Ball. Taxi, Mister. Guadalcanal Diary. Lifeboat. 1944: The Hairy Ape. *Skirmish on the Home Front. Abroad with Two Yanks. Greenwich Village. It's in the Bag! (GB: The Fifth Chair). 1945: Duffy's Tavern. Don Juan Quilligan. A Bell for Adano. 1946: Two Years Before the Mast. The Blue Dahlia. The Dark Corner. Sentimental Journey. White Tie and Tails. I'll Be Yours. 1947: Blaze of Noon. Calcutta. Where There's Life. Variety Girl. The Web. 1948: The Time of Your Life. Race Street. The Babe Ruth Story. 1949: The Life of Riley. A Connecticut Yankee in King Arthur's*

Court. The Big Steal. †Two Knights in Brooklyn/Two Mugs from Brooklyn. Streets of Laredo. Cover Up. Johnny Holiday. 1950: Kill the Umpire! Gambling House. 1951: Submarine Command. Detective Story. 1952: Blackbeard the Pirate. A Girl in Every Port. Macao. 1954: Dangerous Mission. 1955: Crashout. *Hollywood Shower of Stars. 1956: Battle Stations. Going His Way (narrator only). 1957: The Deep Six. 1959: A Quiet Game of Cards (TV). Idle on Parade (US: Idol on Parade). The Rough and the Smooth (US: Portrait of a Sinner). 1961: Johnny Nobody. The Phoney American (GB: It's a Great Life). 1962: Boys' Night Out. *Cash on the Barrel Head. 1963: The Young and the Brave. For Love or Money. Law of the Lawless. 1964: Young Fury.*

† *Combined GB version of the McGuerins from Brooklyn/Taxi, Mister!*

BENJAMIN, Richard 1938–
Tall, slim, handsome (if too often grouchy-looking) American light actor with black, curly hair, at his most adept with black humour. His career limped along in the 1970s after a dynamic start in films, but his output increased dramatically at the end of the decade. In the 1980s, he became a director, with some quite promising results. Married to Paula Prentiss (qv) since 1961.

1969: Goodbye Columbus. 1970: Catch 22. Diary of a Mad Housewife. 1971: The Marriage of a Young Stockbroker. The Steagle. 1972: Portnoy's Complaint. 1973: The Last of Sheila. Westworld. 1975: The Sunshine Boys. 1978: House Calls. No Room to Run. Witches' Brew (released 1985). 1979: Love at First Bite. How to Beat the High Cost of Living. Scavenger Hunt. 1980: The Last Married Couple in America. First Family. 1981: Saturday the 14th. 1983: Packin' It In (TV).

As director:

1982: My Favorite Year. 1984: Racing with the Moon. City Heat. 1986: The Money Pit.

BENNETT, Bruce (Herman Brix) 1909–
Tall, taciturn, husky, fair-haired American actor with slow smile. US shot-putt champion from 1928 to 1932, he was introduced to films by Douglas Fairbanks Senior, but badly injured a shoulder while making his first movie, and missed out on the chance to become Tarzan. Resuming an acting career, the soft-voiced star was a serial king before

changing his name to Bruce Bennett and becoming a minor-league Gary Cooper. Being resident at Warners, he was always in Cooper's shadow, and never got the parts he seemed to deserve.

*1931: †Touchdown (GB: Playing the Game). 1933: †College Humor. 1934: †Student Tour. †Riptide. †Death on the Diamond. 1935: †The New Adventures of Tarzan (serial). †The New Adventures of Tarzan (feature version). 1936: †Silks and Saddles (GB: College Racehorse). †Shadow of Chinatown (serial). 1937: †Million Dollar Racket. †Two Minutes to Play. †Flying Fists. †Danger Patrol. 1938: †Tarzan and the Green Goddess (additional feature from 1935 serial). †The Lone Ranger (serial). †A Million to One. †Land of Fighting Men. †Hawk of the Wilderness (serial). †Fighting Devil-Dogs (serial). 1939: †Hi-Yo Silver (feature version of The Lone Ranger). †Daredevils of the Red Circle (serial). Café Hostess. My Son is Guilty (GB: Crime's End). Blondie Brings Up Baby. Invisible Stripes. 1940: Blazing Six-Shooters (GB: Stolen Wealth). West of Abilene (GB: The Showdown). The Lone Wolf Meets a Lady. Girls of the Road. The Secret Seven. Before I Hang. *The Heckler. *His Bridal Fright. *The Taming of the Snood. The Phantom Submarine. The Lone Wolf Keeps a Date. The Man with Nine Lives. *Boobs in the Woods. *A Bundle of Bliss. *How High is Up? *No Census, No Feelings. *The Spook Speaks. 1941: The Officer and the Lady. Honolulu Lu. *So Long, Mr Chumps. *Dutiful But Dumb. Three Girls About Town. Submarine Zone. Two Latins from Manhattan. 1942: Underground Agent. Tramp, Tramp, Tramp. Submarine Raider. Atlantic Convoy. Sabotage Squad. 1943: Frontier Fury. The More the Merrier. Murder in Times Square. Sahara. There's Something About a Soldier. 1944: I'm from Arkansas. U-Boat Prisoner (GB: Dangerous Mists). 1945: Danger Signal. Mildred Pierce. *Beer Barrel Polecats. 1946: The Man I Love. Stolen Life. 1947: Nora Prentiss. Dark Passage. Cheyenne. 1948: The Yellow Phantom (feature version of Shadow of Chinatown). Silver River. Smart Girls Don't Talk. Treasure of the Sierra Madre. The Younger Brothers. To the Victor. 1949: The House Across the Street. Without Honor. The Doctor and the Girl. Task Force. Undertow. 1950: Mystery Street. Shakedown. The Second Face. 1951: Angels in the Outfield (GB: Angels and the*

Pirates). The Great Missouri Raid. The Last Outpost. 1952: Sudden Fear. 1953: Dream Wife. Dragonfly Squadron. 1954: Stories of the Century No 1: Quantrill and His Raiders. 1955: Strategic Air Command. Robber's Roost. The Big Tip-Off. 1956: The Bottom of the Bottle (GB: Beyond the River). Love Me Tender. Hidden Guns. Three Outlaws. Daniel Boone – Trail Blazer. Three Violent People. 1957: Ain't No Time for Glory (TV). 1958: The Cosmic Man. Flaming Frontier. 1959: The Alligator People. 1961: The Outsider. Fiend of Dope Island. 1966: Lost Island of Kioga (feature version of Hawk of the Wilderness). 1972: Deadhead Miles. 1973: The Clones (GB: Clones). 1980: Hero's Return.

† As Herman Brix

BENNETT, Constance 1904–1965
Hell-raising, high-powered blonde American leading lady, the older sister of Joan Bennett and very much her antithesis. Her star career, chiefly distinguished by her performance in What Price Hollywood? – the forerunner of A Star is Born – soon burned itself out, but she continued in show business and, not surprisingly, ended up as Auntie Mame on stage. Died from a cerebral haemorrhage.
1915: The Valley of Decision. 1921: Reckless Youth. 1922: Evidence. What's Wrong With the Woman? 1924: Cytherea. Into the Net (serial). 1925: The Goose Hangs High. Married? Code of the West. Wandering Fires. My Son. My Wife and I. The Goose Woman. Sally, Irene and Mary. The Pinch Hitter. 1929: This Thing Called Love. Rich People. Clothes. 1930: Son of the Gods. Common Clay. Three Faces East. Lazy Lady. Sin Takes a Holiday. 1931: In Deep. The Easiest Way. Born to Love. Adam and Eve. The Common Law. Bought. 1932: Lady With a Past. What Price Hollywood? Two Against the World. Rockabye. 1933: Our Betters. Bed of Roses. After Tonight (GB: Sealed Lips). 1934: Moulin Rouge. The Affairs of Cellini. Outcast Lady (GB: A Woman of the World). 1935: After Office Hours. 1936: Everything is Thunder. Ladies in Love. 1937: Topper. 1938: Merrily We Live. Service De Luxe. 1939: Topper Takes a Trip. Tail Spin. 1941: Submarine Zone. Law of the Tropics. Two-Faced Woman. Wild Bill Hickok Rides. 1942: Sin Town. Madame Spy. 1945: Paris-Underground (GB: Madame Pimpernel). 1946: Centennial Summer. 1947: The Unsuspected. 1948: Smart Woman. Angel on the

Amazon (GB: Drums Along the Amazon). 1951: As Young As You Feel. 1953: It Should Happen to You. 1966: Madame X.

BENNETT, Hywel 1944–
Wide-eyed, fair-haired Welsh actor seen either as hapless innocent or characters whose baby faces concealed darker designs. Made several films with Hayley Mills, but left films in 1972 because he was (justifiably) unsatisfied with the calibre of his roles. Initial comebacks didn't seem to stick, but he did well on TV, both in comedy and drama, in the late seventies.
1966: The Family Way. 1967: Il marito e mio e l'àmmazzo quando mi pare. 1968: Twisted Nerve. 1969: The Virgin Soldiers. 1970: Loot. The Buttercup Chain. Percy. 1971: Endless Night. 1972: Alice's Adventures in Wonderland. The Love Ban. 1980: *Towards the Morning. 1985: Murder Elite. 1986: Frankie and Johnnie (TV).

BENNETT, Joan 1910–
Exquisitely beautiful, dark-haired (initially blonde) American socialite actress, sister of Constance Bennett. She gave her best performances in several Fritz Lang films of the forties, but her later film appearances were restricted after a shooting scandal.
1915: The Valley of Decision. 1923: The Eternal City. 1928: Power. 1929: Bulldog Drummond. Three Live Ghosts. Disraeli. Mississippi Gambler. 1930: Puttin' on the Ritz. Crazy That Way. Moby Dick. Maybe It's Love. Scotland Yard (GB: 'Detective Clive' – Bart). 1931: Many a Slip. Doctors' Wives. Hush Money. She Wanted a Millionaire. 1932: Care-

less Lady. The Trial of Vivienne Ware. Weekends Only. Me and My Gal. Wild Girl (GB: Salomy Jane). Arizona to Broadway. 1933: Little Women. 1934: The Pursuit of Happiness. 1935: The Man Who Reclaimed His Head. Mississippi. Private Worlds. Two for Tonight. The Man Who Broke the Bank at Monte Carlo. She Couldn't Take It (GB: Woman Tamer). 1936: Thirteen Hours by Air. Big Brown Eyes. Two in a Crowd. Wedding Present. 1937: Vogues of 1938. 1938: I Met My Love Again. The Texans. Artists and Models Abroad (GB: Stranded in Paris). 1939: Trade Winds. The Man in the Iron Mask. The Housekeeper's Daughter. 1940: Green Hell. The House Across the Bay. The Man I Married. Son of Monte Cristo. 1941: She Knew All the Answers. Wild Geese Calling. Manhunt. 1942: Confirm or Deny. Twin Beds. The Wife Takes a Flyer (GB: A Yank in Dutch). Girl Trouble. 1943: Margin for Error. 1944: The Woman in the Window. 1945: Nob Hill. Scarlet Street. 1946: Colonel Effingham's Raid (GB: Man of the Hour). The Macomber Affair. 1948: The Secret Beyond the Door. The Woman on the Beach. Hollow Triumph (GB: The Scar). 1949: The Reckless Moment. 1950: Father of the Bride. For Heaven's Sake. 1951: Father's Little Dividend. The Guy Who Came Back. 1954: Highway Dragnet. 1955: We're No Angels. 1956: There's Always Tomorrow. Navy Wife (GB: Mother – Sir). 1957: The Thundering Wave (TV). 1960: Desire in the Dust. 1970: House of Dark Shadows. Gidget Gets Married (TV). 1972: The Eyes of Charles Sand (TV). 1976: Suspiria. 1978: Suddenly It's Love (TV). 1981: This House Possessed (TV). 1982: Divorce Wars (TV).

BENNY, Jack (Benjamin Kubelsky) 1894–1974
Uniquely droll, dry-voiced, fiddle-playing American comedian with an air of faint bemusement, a fine sense of timing and a stream of jokes about his own age and parsimoniousness. The cinema never really captured his intimate appeal, mainly because Benny needed an audience off whom to react; but it never quite gave up trying. Married to his radio partner Mary Livingstone (Sadye Marks) from 1927.
1928: *Bright Moments. 1929: Hollywood Revue of 1929. *The Songwriters' Revue. 1930: Strictly Modern. *The Rounder. Chasing Rain-

bows. *Medicine Man. 1931: *A Broadway Romeo. *Cab Waiting. *Taxi Tangle. 1933: Mr Broadway. 1934: Transatlantic Merry-Go-Round. 1935: Broadway Melody of 1936. It's in the Air. 1936: The Big Broadcast of 1937. College Holiday. 1937: Artists and Models. Manhattan Merry-Go-Round (GB: Manhattan Music Box). 1938: Artists and Models Abroad (GB: Stranded in Paris). 1939: Man About Town. 1940: Buck Benny Rides Again. Love Thy Neighbor. 1941: Charley's Aunt. 1942: To Be or Not To Be. George Washington Slept Here. 1943: *Show Business at War. *Screen Snapshots No 109. The Meanest Man in the World. 1944: Hollywood Canteen. It's in the Bag! (GB: The Fifth Chair). 1945: The Horn Blows at Midnight. 1946: Without Reservations. 1948: *Screen Snapshots No 166. *Radio Broadcasting Today. 1949: The Lucky Stiff. The Great Lover. *A Rainy Day in Hollywood. 1952: Somebody Loves Me. *Memorial to Al Jolson (narrator only). 1953: *Hollywood's Pair of Jacks. 1954: Susan Slept Here. 1955: The Seven Little Foys. 1957: Beau James. 1958: *Fabulous Hollywood. *The Mouse That Jack Built. 1959: Who Was That Lady? 1962: Gypsy. 1963: It's a Mad, Mad, Mad, Mad World. 1967: A Guide for the Married Man. 1972: The Man.

BENSON, Robby (R. Segal) 1956–
Precocious, dark-haired, pale-eyed, soft-voiced Hollywood teenage acting prodigy, who has also contributed to the scripts of his own films. His most successful roles have been in tear-jerkers, often based on real-life stories: and he has yet to make a proper dramatic impact outside the genre, or to escape juvenile roles.
1972: Jory. 1973: Jeremy. 1974: All the Kind Strangers. The Virginia Hill Story (TV). 1975: Lucky Lady. 1976: Death Be Not Proud (TV). Ode to Billy Joe. 1977: The Death of Richie (TV). One on One. 1978: The End. Ice Castles. 1979: Walk Proud. 1980: Die Laughing. Tribute. The Chosen. 1981: National Lampoon Goes to the Movies (released 1983). 1982: Running Brave (released 1984). Two of a Kind (TV). 1984: Harry and Son. 1985: City Limits.

BENTLEY, John 1917–
Debonair, dark-haired British leading man who didn't film until he had turned 30, but

quickly became the second-feature detective par excellence. His raincoated figure was to be seen rescuing heroines and tracking crooks to their lairs throughout the fifties, and he played several sleuths of detective fiction, including Paul Temple and the Toff. A Hollywood contract in the fifties came too late to further his career.
1947: The Hills of Donegal. 1948: Calling Paul Temple. 1949: Torment (US: Paper Gallows). Bait. 1950: The Happiest Days of Your Life. She Shall Have Murder. Paul Temple's Triumph. 1951: Salute the Toff. The Woman's Angle. 1952: Hammer the Toff. The Lost Hours (US: The Big Frame). Tread Softly (US: Tread Softly, Stranger). Paul Temple Returns. 1953: Black Orchid. Men against the Sun. River Beat. 1954: Double Exposure. Profile. Final Appointment. Golden Ivory (US: White Huntress). The Scarlet Spear. 1955: Confession (US: The Deadliest Sin). Stolen Assignment. The Flaw. Dial 999 (US: The Way Out). Flight from Vienna. Count of Twelve. 1956: Escape in the Sun. 1957: Istanbul. 1958: Submarine Seahawk. 1960: The Singer Not the Song. An heiligen Wassern. 1961: Mary Had a Little ... The Sinister Man. 1962: The Fur Collar. 1963: Quest of the Damned. Shadow of Treason.

BERENGER, Tom 1949–
American actor with tight dark curly hair; his open-faced good looks seemed tinged with humour at the corners of the mouth, and his slight resemblance to Paul Newman (qv) got him cast as the young Butch Cassidy in Butch and Sundance The Early Days. Berenger studied journalism but took up acting in his early

twenties. In leading film roles after his psycho-killer in Looking for Mr Goodbar, he has held that status without yet moving into the superstar league.
1976: The Sentinel. 1977: Johnny, We Hardly Knew Ye (TV). Looking for Mr Goodbar. 1978: In Praise of Older Women. 1979: Butch and Sundance The Early Days. 1980: The Dogs of War. 1982: Oltre la porta (GB: Beyond the Door). Eddie and the Cruisers (released 1984). 1983: Fear City. The Big Chill. 1985: Rustlers' Rhapsody. 1986: If Tomorrow Comes. La Sposa americana. The Platoon.

BERGEN, Candice 1946–
Tall, icy, fair-haired, square-jawed actress, the daughter of ventriloquist Edgar Bergen (see below). The fervour lacking in her acting did express itself in her ardent feminism and in her later career as a photo-journalist. Married French director Louis Malle in 1980. Oscar-nominated for Starting Over.
1966: The Group. The Sand Pebbles. 1967: The Day the Fish Came Out. Vivre pour vivre. 1968: The Magus. 1970: Getting Straight. Soldier Blue. The Adventurers. 1971: Carnal Knowledge. The Hunting Party. 1972: T.R. Baskin (GB: A Date with a Lonely Girl). 1974: 11 Harrowhouse. 1975: Bite the Bullet. The Wind and the Lion. 1976: The Domino Killings. 1977: The End of the World, in Our Usual Bed, in a Night Full of Rain. 1978: Oliver's Story. 1979: Starting Over. 1981: Rich and Famous. 1982: Gandhi. 1983: Arthur the King (TV. Released 1985). 1984: Stick. 1986: Murder: By Reason of Insanity (TV).

BERGEN, Edgar 1903–1978
Dark, dapper, slit-mouthed (probably from concentrating on keeping it closed) American

ventriloquist who made a start in vaudeville before finding his greatest success (strange for a ventriloquist, but just like Britain's Peter Brough a decade later) on radio. That led to a few starring films between 1938 and 1944 (one with his radio vis-à-vis W.C. Fields) before nightclub work took over Bergen's career. Father of actress Candice Bergen. His most famous dummy, the smart-Alec Charlie McCarthy, still exists, bequeathed to the Smithsonian Institution. Bergen died from a heart attack in his sleep. Received a special Oscar in 1937.

1930: *The Operation. *The Office Scandal. 1933: *Africa Speaks ... English. *Free and Easy. 1934: *At the Races. *Pure Feud. 1935: *All American Drawback. *Two Boobs in a Balloon. 1936: *2 Minutes to Play. 1938: The Goldwyn Follies. Letter of Introduction. 1939: Charlie McCarthy, Detective. You Can't Cheat an Honest Man. 1941: Look Who's Laughing. 1942: Here We Go Again. 1943: Stage Door Canteen. 1944: Song of the Open Road. 1947: Fun and Fancy Free. 1948: I Remember Mama. 1949: Captain China. 1950: *Charlie McCarthy and Mortimer Snerd in Sweden. 1964: The Hanged Man (TV. GB: cinemas). 1965: One-Way Wahine. 1967: Don't Make Waves. Rogue's Gallery. 1969: The Phynx. 1971: The Homecoming (TV). 1975: Won Ton Ton, The Dog Who Saved Hollywood. 1979: The Muppet Movie.

BERGEN, Polly (Nellie Burgin) 1929–
Pretty, peppy American brunette who became popular as a radio singer in the post-war years and subsequently made a number of films. Although she projected a warm personality, she seemed somewhat difficult to cast, and was most successful on television, where she won an Emmy for her performance in Helen Morgan. Married/divorced actor Jerome Courtland (qv), first of two husbands.

1949:† Across the Rio Grande. 1950: At War With the Army. 1951: That's My Boy. Warpath. 1952: The Stooge. 1953: Arena. Half a Hero. Cry of the Hunted. Fast Company. Escape from Fort Bravo. 1957: Helen Morgan (TV). 1961: Belle Sommers. 1962: Cape Fear. 1963: The Caretakers. Move Over Darling. 1964: Kisses for My President. 1967: A Guide for the Married Man. 1973: Anatomy of Terror (TV). 1974: Death Cruise (TV). 1975: Murder on Flight 502 (TV). Telethon (TV). 1981:

The Million Dollar Face (TV). 1982: Born Beautiful (TV). 1986: Making Mr Right.

† As Polly Burgin

BERGER, Senta 1941–
One of those 'mittel-European' beauties whom the international cinema snapped up for its epic adventures of the early sixties. With a full-blown prettiness and even fuller-blown bust, Austrian-born Senta could hardly fail. But she seemed to lose some of her ambition after the mid-sixties, and some unworthy Hollywood roles were followed by a return to European features. Only Sam Peckinpah really did her simmering appeal justice, in Major Dundee.

1957: Die unentschuldige Stunde. Die Lindenwirtin vom Donanstrand. 1958: Der veruntreute Himmel. The Journey. 1959: Katia. Ich heirate herrn Direktor. 1960: The Good Soldier Schweik. O sole mio. 1961: The Secret Ways. Das Wunder des Malachias. Immer Arger mit dem Bett. Eine Hübscher als die Andere. Junge Leute brauchen Liebe. Adieu, Liebewohl, Goodbye. Ramona. Es muss nicht immer Kaviar sein. Diesmal muss es Kaviar Sein (US: The Reluctant Spy). 1962: Das Geheimnis der schwartzen Koffer (GB: Secret of the Black Trunk). Sherlock Holmes and the Deadly Necklace. The Testament of Dr Mabuse. Frauenarzt Dr Sibelius. 1963: The Victors. Jack and Jenny. The Waltz King. Kali-Yug, Goddess of Vengeance. Kali-Yug, Part II (GB: The Mystery of the Indian Temple). 1964: Full Hearts and Empty Pockets. See How They Run (TV). The Spy with My Face (TV). 1965: Major Dundee. The Glory Guys. 1966: The Spy With My Face. Du suif dans l'orient. Our Man in Marrakesh. The Poppy is Also a Flower (GB: Danger Grows Wild). Cast a Giant Shadow. The Quiller Memorandum. Lange Finger. 1967: Peau d'espion (GB and US: To Commit a Murder). Operazione San Gennaro (GB: The Treasure of San Gennaro. The Ambushers. The Miracle of Father Malachios. Paarungen. The Magnificent Thief (TV). Diabolically Yours. 1968: If It's Tuesday, This Must Be Belgium. Istanbul Express (TV. GB: cinemas). 1969: Les étrangers. De Sade. Cuore solitari. 1970: Quando le donne avevano la coda (US: When Women Had Tails). Der Graben. Canasova. Percy. 1971: L'amante dell' Orsa maggiore. Roma bene. Wer in Glashaus liebt ... Sancorsiap. Mamma dolce, mamma cara. Un anguilla

da trecento milione. Cobra. When Women Lost Their Tails. Causa di divorzio. 1972: The Scarlet Letter. Amore i gimnastica. Die Moral der Ruth Halbfass. 1973: Reigen (GB: Dance of Love. US: Merry-Go-Round). Bisturi, la mafia bianca (US: White Mafia). Di mamma ce n'e una sola. L'uomo senza memoria. 1974: La bellissima estate. 1975: The Swiss Conspiracy. Il ventro caldo della signora. Mitgift. Lonely Hearts. La guardia del corpo. Progliaccio d'amore. 1976: Signore e Signori buonanotte. 1977: Cross of Iron. Ritratto di Borghesia in Nero. 1978: Nest of Vipers. Sentimenti/Sentiments and Passions. La giacca verde. Das chinesische Wunder. 1979: I Miss You, Hugs and Kisses. Amanti, dell'orsa maggiore. 1985: The Flying Devils. Killing Cars.

BERGMAN, Ingrid 1915–1982
Square-built blonde Swedish actress who seemed born to play tragic, haunted heroines, never more memorably than in Casablanca, three years after she had gone to Hollywood. Married to director Roberto Rossellini (second of three husbands) from 1950 to 1958, a relationship which, in its pre-marital state, caused her ostracism from Hollywood in 1948. Three Oscars (for Gaslight, Anastasia and Murder on the Orient Express), plus several nominations. Additional Oscar nominations for For Whom the Bell Tolls, The Bells of St Mary's, Joan of Arc and Autumn Sonata. She died from cancer.

1934: Munkbrogreven. 1935: Bränningar. Swedenhielms. Valborgsmässoafton (US: Walpurgis Night). 1936: På Solsidan. Intermezzo. 1937: Juninatten. 1938: En Kvinnas Ansikte (GB and US: A Woman's face). Die vier Gesellen. Dollar. En Ende Natt. 1939: Intermezzo (GB: Escape to Happiness). 1941: Rage in Heaven. Adam Had Four Sons. Dr Jekyll and Mr Hyde. 1942: Casablanca. 1943: *Swedes in America (GB: Ingrid Bergman Answers). For Whom the Bell Tolls. 1944: Gaslight (GB: The Murder in Thornton Square). 1945: The Bells of St Mary's. Spellbound. Saratoga Trunk. 1946: Notorious. *The American Creed. Arch of Triumph. Joan of Arc. 1949: Under Capricorn. 1950: Stromboli. 1951: Europa/The Greatest Love. 1952: Siamo donne (GB: We the Women). 1954: Voyage to Italy (GB: The Lonely Woman. US: The Strangers). Joan at the Stake. Fear. 1956: Elena et les hommes (GB: Elena and

Men. US: Paris Does Strange Things). Anastasia. 1958: Indiscreet. The Inn of the Sixth Happiness. 1960: *The Camp (narrator only). 1961: Aimez-vous Brahms? (GB: Goodbye Again). 1964: The Yellow Rolls Royce. The Visit. 1966: Stimulantia. 1967: Fugitive in Vienna. 1969: Cactus Flower. A Walk in the Spring Rain. 1970: Henri Langlois. 1973: From the Mixed-Up Files of Mrs Basil E. Frankweiler (GB: The Hideaways). 1974: Murder on the Orient Express. 1976: A Matter of Time. 1978: Autumn Sonata. 1982: Golda (TV).

BERGNER, Elisabeth (E. Ettel) 1898–1986
Polish-born actress with wispy blonde hair, whose brief popularity in England in the thirties failed to survive long under the triple strain of her own advancing years, her quickly outdated persona (elfin, fey, almost little-girlish) and the imminence of forties' realism (Margaret Sullavan had much the same trouble). She did her best acting work in later years in the theatre. Academy Award for Escape Me Never.
1924: Der Evangelimann. 1925: Nju. 1926: Der Geiger von Florenz. Liebe. 1928: Queen Louise. Dona Juana. 1929: Fräulein Else (US: Miss Else). 1931: The Loves of Ariane. 1932: Der träumende Mund. 1934: Catherine the Great. 1935: Escape Me Never. 1936: As You Like It. 1937: Dreaming Lips. 1938: Stolen Life. 1941: Paris Calling. 49th Parallel (US: The Invaders). 1962: Die glücklichen Jahre der Thorwalds. 1970: Cry of the Banshee. 1971: Courier to the Tsar. 1973: Der Füssgänger. 1979: Der Pfingstausflug. 1981: Society Limited.

BERLE, Milton (Mendel Berlinger) 1908–
Breezy, Broadway-based comedian who never quite made a home for himself in films, although he made more movies than one might think. Enormously successful in TV in the forties and fifties, when he became known as 'Mr Television' in America. Started in films as a child and alleges that he made over 50. The first three were Tillie's Punctured Romance, Bunny's Little Brother and The Perils of Pauline, all in 1914.
Sound films: 1932: *Poppin' the Cork. 1937: New Faces of 1937. 1938: Radio City Revels. 1941: Tall, Dark and Handsome. Sun Valley Serenade. Rise and Shine. 1942: Whispering Ghosts. A Gentleman at Heart. 1943: Over My

Dead Body. Margin for Error. 1945: The Dolly Sisters. 1949: Always Leave Them Laughing. 1960: Let's Make Love. The Bellboy. 1963: It's a Mad, Mad, Mad, Mad World. 1965: The Loved One. 1966: The Oscar. Don't Worry, We'll Think of a Title. 1967: The Happening. The Silent Treatment. Who's Minding the Mint? 1968: Where Angels Go, Trouble Follows. For Singles Only. 1969: Can Hieronymous Merkin Ever Forget Mercy Humppe and Find True Happiness? Seven in Darkness (TV). The April Fools. 1970: Love, American Style (TV). Journey Back to Oz (voice only). 1972: Evil Roy Slade (TV). 1974: Lepke. 1975: The Legend of Valentino (TV). Won Ton Ton, the Dog Who Saved Hollywood. 1978: The Muppet Movie. 1979: 'Hey Abbott' (TV). 1983: Smorgasbord.

BEST, Edna 1900–1974
Charming, fair-haired, quietly-spoken, very British actress who rose to fame in the stage production of The Constant Nymph and continued in unspectacular stage and film roles until going to America in 1939, where she played a few mothers and wives. Married to Herbert Marshall 1928–1940, the second of her three husbands.
1921: Tilly of Bloomsbury. 1923: A Couple of Down and Outs. 1930: Sleeping Partners. Loose Ends. Escape. Beyond the Cities. 1931: Michael and Mary. The Calendar (US: Bachelor's Folly). 1932: The Faithful Heart (US: Faithful Hearts). 1934: The Key. The Man Who Knew Too Much. 1937: South Riding. 1938: Prison Without Bars. 1939: Return to Yesterday. Intermezzo (GB: Escape to Happiness). 1940: The Swiss Family Robinson. A Dispatch

from Reuter's (GB: This Man Reuter). 1947: The Late George Apley. The Ghost and Mrs Muir. 1948: The Iron Curtain.

BETTGER, Lyle 1915–
Fair-haired actor whose slightly sinister charm won him some good post-war roles on Broadway. On moving into films in 1950, his crooked smile, shifty eyes and husky voice qualified him for a whole range of treacherous villains. In the fifties he went into TV, and sixties' film roles proved to be only pale echoes of his meatier parts at Paramount and Universal.
1950: No Man of Her Own. Union Station. 1951: The First Legion. Dear Brat. 1952: The Greatest Show on Earth. Hurricane Smith. Denver and Rio Grande. 1953: All I Desire. The Vanquished. Forbidden. The Great Sioux Uprising. 1954: Carnival Story. Drums Across the River. Destry. 1955: The Sea Chase. 1956: The Lone Ranger. Explosion (TV. GB: cinemas). Showdown at Abilene. Gunfight at the OK Corral. 1959: Guns of the Timberland. Showdown at Sandoval (TV. GB: cinemas, as Gunfight at Sandoval). 1965: Town Tamer. 1966: Johnny Reno. Nevada Smith. Return of the Gunfighter. The Fastest Guitar Alive. 1968: The Golden Bullet. 1969: Impasse. 1970: The Hawaiians (GB: Master of the Islands). 1971: The Seven Minutes.

BEY, Turhan (T. Schultavey) 1920–
Austrian-born leading man (of Turkish-Czech parentage) with slick black hair and faintly oriental aspect. His sleekly handsome features flourished in Arabian Nights and other escapist adventures in the war years, but his career foundered after army service (1948–

1950) and he became a commercial photographer.

1941: Footsteps in the Dark. Raiders of the Desert. Burma Convoy. Shadows on the Stairs. The Gay Falcon. 1942: Junior G-Men of the Air (serial). The Falcon Takes Over. A Yank on the Burma Road (GB: China Caravan). Bombay Clipper. Drums of the Congo. Arabian Nights. Destination Unknown. The Unseen Enemy. The Mummy's Tomb. 1943: Danger in the Pacific. Adventures of Smilin' Jack (serial). White Savage (GB: White Captive). The Mad Ghoul. Background to Danger. 1944: Follow the Boys. The Climax. Dragon Seed. Bowery to Broadway. Ali Baba and the 40 Thieves. 1945: Frisco Sal. Sudan. 1946: A Night in Paradise. 1947: Out of the Blue. 1948: The Amazing Mr X (GB: The Spiritualist). Adventures of Casanova. 1949: Parole Inc. Song of India. 1953: Prisoners of the Casbah.

BEYMER, Richard (George Beymer Jr) 1939–

Boyish, dark-haired American leading man who was in films at 14 and gave some spritely accounts of himself as a teenager. His wooden performance in *West Side Story* effectively torpedoed his Hollywood star career, although he drifted on through a few more films before becoming a producer. Later he worked on documentary films, taught transcendental meditation and returned to the occasional acting assignment in character roles.

1953: So Big. Stazione termini/Indiscretion of an American Wife (GB: Indiscretion). 1957: Johnny Tremain. 1958: The Diary of Anne Frank. 1959: Dark December (TV). 1960: High Time. 1961: West Side Story. 1962: Five Finger Exercise. Hemingway's Adventures of a Young Man (GB: Adventures of a Young Man). Bachelor Flat. The Longest Day. 1963: The Stripper (GB: Woman of Summer). 1971: Scream Free! (completed 1969). 1974: †Innerview. 1983: Cross Country. 1985: Generation (TV).

† And directed

BICKFORD, Charles 1889–1967
Rugged, outspoken, curly-haired American star and later leading character player, of Irish ancestry. He never won an Oscar (perhaps because he was one of the banes of the Hollywood establishment), despite gruff, consistently good, characteristically intense performances over 38 years; he was nominated

three times – for *The Song of Bernadette, The Farmer's Daughter* and *Johnny Belinda.* Died from emphysema.

1929: Dynamite. South Sea Rose. Hell's Heroes. 1930: Passion Flower. Anna Christie. The Sea Bat. River's End. 1931: East of Borneo. The Squaw Man (GB: The White Man). Pagan Lady. The Men in Her Life. 1932: Thunder Below. Panama Flo. Scandal for Sale. The Last Man. Vanity Street. 1933: No Other Woman. This Day and Age. White Woman. The Red Waggon. Song of the Eagle. 1934: Little Miss Marker (GB: Girl in Pawn). A Wicked Woman. 1935: A Notorious Gentleman. Under Pressure. The Farmer Takes a Wife. East of Java (GB: Java Seas). 1936: Pride of the Marines. Rose of the Rancho. The Plainsman. 1937: Night Club Scandal. Daughter of Shanghai (GB: Daughter of the Orient). Thunder Trail. 1938: High, Wide and Handsome. Valley of the Giants. Gangs of New York. The Storm. Stand Up and Fight. 1939: Street of Missing Men. Romance of the Redwoods. Our Leading Citizen. One Hour to Live. Mutiny in the Big House. Of Mice and Men. 1940: Thou Shall Not Kill. Girl from God's Country. Queen of the Yukon. South to Karanga. 1941: Burma Convoy. Riders of Death Valley (serial). 1942: Reap the Wild Wind. Tarzan's New York Adventure. 1943: Mr Lucky. 1944: Song of Bernadette. A Wing and a Prayer. 1945: Captain Eddie. 1946: Fallen Angel. Duel in the Sun. 1947: The Farmer's Daughter. The Woman on the Beach. Brute Force. 1948: Four Faces West (GB: They Passed This Way). The Babe Ruth Story. Johnny Belinda. Command Decision. 1949: Whirlpool. Roseanna McCoy. Guilty of Treason (GB: Treason). 1950: Branded. Riding High. 1951: Jim Thorpe – All American (GB: Man of Bronze). The Raging Tide. Elopement. 1953: The Last Posse. 1954: A Star is Born. 1955: Prince of Players. Not As a Stranger. The Court-Martial of Billy Mitchell (GB: One Man Mutiny). 1956: You Can't Run Away from It. Forbidden Area (TV). Sincerely, Willis Wayde (TV). 1957: Mister Cory. Clipper Ship (TV). Dark Wave (and narrator). 1958: The Big Country. Days of Wine and Roses (TV). Free Week-End (TV). 1959: Out of Dust (TV). Della (TV). The Unforgiven. 1960: Tomorrow (TV). 1962: Days of Wine and Roses. 1966: A Big Hand for the Little Lady (GB: Big Deal at Dodge City).

BISHOP, Julie (Jacqueline Wells Brown) 1914–

Chestnut-haired American actress, the forthright heroine in many a thriller and western, or the girl back home in war films. Made a few films as a child, then acted as Jacqueline Wells from 1931, until she signed for Warner Brothers, who decided to change it to Julie Bishop. Since retiring from acting has become a painter of some repute.

*1923: ‡Maytime. ‡Bluebeard's Eighth Wife. ‡Children of Jazz. 1924: ‡Captain Blood. ‡Dorothy Vernon of Haddon Hall. 1925: ‡The Golden Bed. ‡The Home Maker. ‡Classified. 1931: †Pardon Us (GB: Jailbirds). *†Skip the Maloo! †Scareheads. 1932: **Heroes of the West (serial). *†The Knockout. *†Any Old Port. *†In Walked Charley. *†You're Telling Me. 1933: †Clancy of the Mounted (serial). †Tillie and Gus. †Tarzan the Fearless. †Alice in Wonderland. 1934: †The Black Cat (GB: The House of Doom). †Kiss and Make Up. †Happy Landing. †The Square Shooter. †The Loud Speaker (GB: The Radio Star). 1935: †Coronado. †Night Cargo. 1936: †The Bohemian Girl. 1937: †Frame-Up. †Little Miss Roughneck. †Counsel for Crime. †Paid to Dance. †Girls Can Play. 1938: †She Married an Artist. †When G-Men Step In. †Highway Patrol. †Flight into Nowhere. †My Son is a Criminal. †The Main Event. †The Little Adventuress. †Spring Madness. †Flight to Fame. 1939: †Behind Prison Gates. †Torture Ship. †Kansas Terrors. †My Son is Guilty (GB: Crime's End). 1940: †Young Bill Hickok. †The Girl in 313. †Her First Romance. †The Ranger and the Lady. 1941: †Back in the Saddle. The Nurse's Secret. International Squadron. Steel Against the Sky. Wild Bill Hickok Rides. 1942: I Was Framed. The Hidden Land. Lady Gangster. Busses Roar. Escape from Crime. The Hard Way. 1943: Northern Pursuit. Action in the North Atlantic. Princess O'Rourke. 1944: Hollywood Canteen. 1945: You Came Along. Rhapsody in Blue. 1946: Cinderella Jones. Murder in the Music Hall. Idea Girl. Strange Conquest. 1947: Last of the Redmen (GB: Last of the Redskins). High Tide. 1949: Deputy Marshal. The Threat. Sands of Iwo Jima. 1951: Westward the Women. 1953: Sabre Jet. 1954: Why Men Leave Home. The High and the Mighty. 1955: Headline Hunters. 1956: Survival (TV). 1957: The Big Land (GB: Stampeded!).*

‡ *As Jacqueline Brown* † *As Jacqueline Wells*
** *As Diane Duval*

BISHOP, William 1917–1959
Tall, dark, husky, handsome and virile American leading man who died from cancer at 42. Originally studied to be a lawyer but, after some acting experience, decided on a film career in the post-war years. His Hollywood days were spent mainly as cruel, laughing villains in Technicolor Columbia action films of the 1940s and 1950s.
1943: *A Guy Named Joe*. 1946: *Pillow to Post*. 1947: *Song of the Thin Man*. *The Romance of Rosy Ridge*. *Devil Ship*. 1948: *Thunderhoof (GB: Fury)*. *The Untamed Breed*. *Adventure in Silverado*. *Port Said*. *Coroner Creek*. *The Black Eagle*. 1949: *Anna Lucasta*. *The Walking Hills*. 1950: *The Tougher They Come*. *Harriet Craig*. *The Killer That Stalked New York (GB: Frightened City)*. 1951: *Lorna Doone*. *The Texas Rangers*. *The Frogmen*. *The Basketball Fix (GB: The Big Decision)*. 1952: *Breakdown*. *Cripple Creek*. *The Raiders/Riders of Vengeance*. 1953: *The Redhead from Wyoming*. *Gun Belt*. 1954: *Overland Pacific*. 1955: *Top Gun*. *Wyoming Renegades*. 1956: *The Boss*. *The White Squaw*. 1957: *The Phantom Stagecoach*. *Short Cut to Hell*. *The Star-Wagon (TV)*. 1959: *The Oregon Trail*.

BISSET, Jacqueline
(Winifred J. Bisset) 1944–
Striking British-born brunette glamour girl and presentable actress in international films who made an unlikely first impact as a spotty schoolgirl in *Two for the Road*. Her performances tend to be on the grave side but,
like Elizabeth Taylor at the same age, she has wisely stayed within her own range. Never quite able to carry a film by herself, although her acting did grow stronger within the years and she is always a pleasure to watch.
1965: †*The Knack . . . and how to get it*. 1966: †*Drop Dead Darling (US: Arrivederci Baby)*. †*Cul-de-Sac*. 1967: †*Two for the Road*. †*Casino Royale*. *The Sweet Ride*. *The Cape Town Affair*. 1968: *The Detective*. *Bullitt*. *La promesse (GB: Secret World)*. *The First Time (GB: You Don't Need Pyjamas at Rosie's)*. 1969: *L'echelle blanche*. *Airport*. 1970: *The Grasshopper*. *The Mephisto Waltz*. 1971: *Believe in Me*. 1972: *Secrets*. *Stand Up and Be Counted*. 1973: *The Life and Times of Judge Roy Bean*. *The Thief Who Came to Dinner*. *La nuit américaine (GB and US: Day for Night)*. *How to Destroy the Reputation of the Greatest Secret Agent/Le magnifique*. 1974: *Murder on the Orient Express*. 1975: *The Spiral Staircase*. *Der Richter und sein Henker/The Judge and His Hangman (GB: Deception. US: End of the Game)*. 1976: *St Ives*. *The Sunday Woman*. 1977: *The Deep*. 1978: *The Greek Tycoon*. *Who is Killing the Great Chefs of Europe? (GB: Too Many Chefs)*. 1979: *Amo non amo/I Love You, I Love You Not*. 1980: *Inchon! When Time Ran Out. . .* 1981: *Rich and Famous*. *Together?* 1982: *Forbidden*. 1983: *Class*. 1984: *Under the Volcano*. *Notes from Under the Volcano*. *Observations Under the Volcano*. 1985: *Anna Karenina (TV)*. 1986: *Choice (TV)*. *High Season*.

† *As Jackie Bisset*

BLACK, Karen (K. Ziegler) 1942–
Distinctive, talented and bewitchingly cross-eyed American actress often cast as mischievous or spiteful blondes from the wrong side of the tracks, but capable of a wide range of roles and interpretations, all of which (even flying a crippled plane over a mountain in *Airport 1975*), she seems to enjoy. Often turning up, especially in the late 1970s and 1980s, in fairly out-of-the-way projects, she remains an abrasive screen original, as (though not like) Katharine Hepburn (*qv*). Twice Oscar-nominated, for *Easy Rider* and *Five Easy Pieces*.
1959: *The Prime Time*. 1966: *You're a Big Boy Now*. 1968: *Hard Contract*. 1969: *Easy Rider*. 1970: *Five Easy Pieces*. *A Gunfight*. *Freedom*. 1971: *Drive, He Said*. *Cisco Pike*.
Born to Win. 1972: *Portnoy's Complaint*. 1973: *Rhinoceros*. *The Pyx*. *The Outfit*. 1974: *Owen. Law and Disorder*. *Little Laura and Big John*. *The Great Gatsby*. *Airport 1975*. 1975: *The Day of the Locust*. *Nashville*. *Crime and Passion/An Ace Up My Sleeve*. 1976: *Trilogy of Terror (TV)*. *Family Plot*. *Burnt Offerings*. 1977: *Capricorn One*. *The Strange Possession of Mrs Oliver (TV)*. *In Praise of Older Women*. 1978: *Because He's My Friend*. *The Big Rip-Off/The Rip-Off (US: The Squeeze)*. *Killer Fish*. 1979: *Mr Horn (TV)*. *The Last Word*. *Confessions of a Lady Cop/The Other Side of Fear (TV)*. 1980: *Miss Right*. *Mr Patman*. *Valentine*. *Where the Ladies Go (TV)*. 1981: *The Grass is Singing*. *Separate Ways*. *Chanel solitaire*. 1982: *Come Back to the 5 and Dime, Jimmy Dean, Jimmy Dean*. 1983: *Can She Bake a Cherry Pie? Growing Pains*. †*Breathless*. 1984: *Martin's Day*. *A Stroke of Genius*. 1985: *Cut and Run*. *Invaders from Mars*. *Savage Dawn*. 1986: *The Blue Man*. *Hostage*.

† *Scenes deleted from final release print*

BLACKMAN, Honor 1925–
Blonde British actress whose wartime career as a Home Office dispatch rider seemed to peg her as the adventurous sort. But the Rank Charm School took one look at her china-doll features and cast her as a succession of English roses, whence she slid into heroine roles in numerous second features. TV's *The Avengers* rescued the tiger in her by casting her as a leather-clad, judo-throwing adventuress.
1947: *Daughter of Darkness*. *Fame is the Spur*. 1948: *Quartet*. 1949: *A Boy, a Girl and a Bike*. *Conspirator*. *Diamond City*. 1950: *So Long at the Fair*. *Green Grow the Rushes*. 1951: *Come Die My Love*. 1954: *The Rainbow Jacket*. *The Yellow Robe*. *The Delavine Affair*. *Diplomatic Passport*. 1955: *The Glass Cage (GB: The Glass Tomb)*. 1956: *Breakaway*. 1957: *Suspended Alibi*. *You Pay Your Money*. *Account Rendered*. *Danger List*. 1958: *A Night to Remember*. *The Square Peg*. 1961: *A Matter of WHO*. 1962: *Serena*. *A Sense of Belonging*. 1963: *Jason and the Argonauts*. 1964: *Goldfinger*. 1965: *Life at the Top*. *The Secret of My Success*. 1966: *Moment to Moment*. 1967: *A Twist of Sand*. 1968: *Shalako*. *The Struggle for Rome*. 1969: *Twinky*. *The Struggle for Rome II*. 1970: *The Virgin and the Gypsy*. 1971: *The Last Grenade*. *Fright*. *Something*

Big. 1976: To the Devil a Daughter. 1977: Summer Rain. Age of Innocence. 1978: The Cat and the Canary. 1985: Minder on the Orient Express (TV).

BLAINE, Vivian (V. Stapleton) 1921–
Blonde American band singer whose acerbic personality was somewhat wasted in Fox musicals of the forties. But prolonged Broadway success compensated for a film career whose highlight was a repeat of a stage role – Adelaide in *Guys and Dolls*.
1942: Girl Trouble. It Happened in Flatbush. Through Different Eyes. 1943: He Hired the Boss. Jitterbugs. 1944: Greenwich Village. Something for the Boys. 1945: Nob Hill. State Fair. 1946: Doll Face (GB: Come Back to Me). If I'm Lucky. Three Little Girls in Blue. 1952: Skirts Ahoy. 1953: Main Street to Broadway. 1955: Guys and Dolls. 1957: Public Pigeon Number One. 1972: Richard. 1978: The Dark. Katie: Portrait of a Centerfold. 1979: Sooner or Later (TV). Fast Friends (TV). The Cracker Factory (TV). 1982: Parasite. 1983: I'm Going To Be Famous.

BLAIR, Betsy (Elizabeth Boger) 1923–
Quiet, intense American actress with silky brown hair whose facial structure and mannerisms made her just as natural for a demented inmate of *The Snake Pit* as for the shy wallflower of *Marty*, for which she won a British Oscar and an Academy Award nomination. Afterwards she moved to Europe, but was seen only occasionally in films. Married (first and second of three) to actor-dancer Gene Kelly (*qv*) and director Karel Reisz.

1947: The Guilt of Janet Ames. 1948: A Double Life. Another Part of the Forest. The Snake Pit. 1950: Mystery Street. 1951: Kind Lady. 1955: Marty. Othello. 1956: Calle Mayor. 1957: Il grido (GB: The Cry). The Halliday Brand. 1958: Die Hauptstrasse. 1960: Die Thronfolger. 1961: All Night Long. Senilita. 1968: Mazel Tov ou le mariage (GB and US: Marry Me, Marry Me!). 1973: A Delicate Balance. 1985: The Flight of the Spruce Goose.

BLAIR, Janet (Martha Lafferty) 1921–
Vivacious, petite, pretty American 'strawberry-blonde', singer-actress whose personality could be alternately sweet and demure, or sharp and peppy. Like Ann Miller later on, she often outshone the above-title stars without ever really becoming a star in her own right. Still does the occasional stint on stage or in TV.
*1941: Three Girls about Town. 1942: Two Yanks in Trinidad. Blondie Goes to College. Broadway. *Screen Snapshots No. 103. My Sister Eileen. 1943: Something to Shout About. 1944: Once Upon a Time. Tonight and Every Night. 1946: Tars and Spars. 1947: Gallant Journey. The Fabulous Dorseys. 1948: I Love Trouble. The Fuller Brush Man. (GB: That Mad Mr Jones). The Black Arrow (GB: The Black Arrow Strikes). 1957: Public Pigeon Number One. 1962: Night of the Eagle (US: Burn, Witch, Burn). Boys' Night Out. 1968: The One and Only Genuine Original Family Band. 1975: Won Ton Ton, the Dog Who Saved Hollywood.*

BLAIR, Linda 1959–
Chubby-faced, light-haired American actress who made an eye-opening start to her major

film career as the possessed girl in *The Exorcist* (it won her an Oscar nomination), then ran the predictable route to Hollywood maturity through the sex-and-drugs-in-the-headline syndrome, while growing into a pneumatic but sparky leading lady. As the 1980s progressed, she gave unexpectedly spirited performances in a number of contemporary exploitation films.
1970: The Way We Live Now. 1971: The Sporting Club. 1973: The Exorcist. 1974: Born Innocent (TV). Airport 1975. 1975: Sara T: Portrait of a Teenage Alcoholic (TV). Sweet Hostage (TV). Roman Grey (TV. GB: The Art of Crime). 1976: Victory at Entebbe (TV. GB: cinemas). 1977: Exorcist II: The Heretic. 1978: Summer of Fear/Stranger in Our House (TV). 1979: Roller Boogie. Hard Ride to Rantan. Wild Horse Hank. 1980: Ruckus. 1981: Hell Night. 1982: Chained Heat. 1983: Night Fighters (released 1986). Savage Island. 1984: Red Heat. Savage Streets. Night Patrol.

BLAKE, Robert (Michael Gubitosi) 1933–
Short, chunky, wisecracking, dark-haired Brooklyn-born Hollywood actor who started his screen career at six as a member of Our Gang in their comedy shorts, then moved on to a series of westerns with Wild Bill Elliott (*qv*). Following the teenage drug-taking trauma that seems to afflict so many child stars, Blake re-emerged as an adult actor in the late 1950s, had a highly successful TV series called *Baretta*, and almost (but not quite) became a box-office cinema star.
*1939: *†Joy Scouts. *†Auto Antics. *†Captain Spanky's Show Boat. †Bridal Suite. *†Time Out for Lessons. *†Alfalfa's Double. *†Bubbling Troubles. 1940: *†The Big Premiere. *†All About Hash. *†The New Pupil. *†Goin' Fishin'. *†Good Bad Boys. *†Waldo's Last Stand. *†Kiddie Cure. †I Love You Again. *†Fightin' Fools. 1941: *†Baby Blues. *†Ye Olde Minstrels. *†Come Back, Miss Pipps. *†1-2-3, Go! *†Robot Wrecks. *†Helping Hands. *†Wedding Worries. *†Melodies Old and New. 1942: *†Going to Press. *†I Don't Lie. *†Surprised Parties. *†Doin' Their Bit. *‡Rover's Big Chance. ‡Mokey. ‡Andy Hardy's Double Life. *‡Mighty Lak a Goat. *‡Unexpected Riches. ‡China Girl. 1943: *‡Benjamin Franklin Jnr. *‡Family Troubles. *‡Election Daze. ‡Lost Angel. *‡Calling All Kids. *‡Farm Hands.*

*‡*Little Miss Pinkerton.* *‡*Three Smart Guys.*
‡*Salute to the Marines.* ‡*Slightly Dangerous.*
1944: *‡*Radio Bugs.* *‡*Dancing Romeo.*
*‡*Tale of a Dog.* ‡*The Cherokee Flash.* ‡*Tucson Raiders.* ‡*Marshal of Reno.* ‡*The Big Noise.*
‡*The San Antonio Kid.* ‡*The Woman in the Window.* ‡*Meet the People.* ‡*The Seventh Cross.* ‡*Vigilantes of Dodge City.* ‡*Cheyenne Wildcat.* †*Sheriff of Las Vegas.* *1945:* ‡*The Great Stagecoach Robbery.* ‡*The Horn Blows at Midnight.* ‡*Bells of Rosarita.* ‡*Colorado Pioneers.* ‡*Wagon Wheels Westward.* ‡*Lone Texas Ranger.* ‡*Phantom of the Plains.* ‡*Dakota.* ‡*Marshal of Laredo.* ‡*Pillow to Post.* *1946:* ‡*California Gold Rush.* ‡*Sante Fé Uprising.* †*Sheriff of Redwood Valley.* ‡*Stagecoach to Denver.* ‡*Humoresque.* ‡*Home on the Range.* ‡*Sun Valley Cyclone.* ‡*Out California Way.* ‡*In Old Sacramento.* ‡*A Guy Could Change.* *1947:* ‡*The Last Round-Up.* ‡*Oregon Trail Scouts.* ‡*Homesteaders of Paradise Valley.* ‡*Marshal of Cripple Creek.* ‡*The Return of Rin Tin Tin.* ‡*Rustlers of Devil's Canyon.* ‡*Vigilantes of Boomtown.* *1948:* ‡*The Treasure of the Sierra Madre.* *1950:* ‡*The Black Rose.* ‡*Black Hand.* *1952:* ‡*Apache War Smoke.* *1953:* ‡*Treasure of the Golden Condor.* ‡*The Veils of Bagdad.* *1956:* ‡*Screaming Eagles.* ‡*Three Violent People.* ‡*The Rack.* *Rumble on the Docks.* *1957:* *The Beast of Budapest.* *The Tijuana Story.* *1958:* *Revolt in the Big House.* *1959:* *Battle Flame.* *The Purple Gang.* *Pork Chop Hill.* *1961:* *Town without Pity.* *1962:* *PT 109.* *The Connection.* *1965:* *The Greatest Story Ever Told.* *1966:* *This Property is Condemned.* *1967:* *In Cold Blood.* *1969:* *Tell Them Willie Boy is Here.* *1971:* *Corky/Ripped Off.* *1972:* *Tough Guy.* *1973:* *Electra Glide in Blue.* *1974:* *Busting.* *1978:* *The Hamster of Happiness* (later *Second Hand Hearts*). *1980:* *Coast to Coast.* *The Big Trade* (TV). *The Big Black Pill* (TV). *The Monkey Mission* (TV). *1981:* *Of Mice and Men* (TV). *1983:* *Blood Feud* (TV). *1985:* *Hell Town* (TV). *The Heart of a Champion: The Ray Mancini Story* (TV).

† *As Mickey Gubitosi.* ‡ *As Bobby Blake.*

BLANCHARD, Mari (Mary Blanchard)
1927–1970
Elegant, blonde Californian model whose exotic looks led to her type-casting in a series of 'easterns' and adventure stories, nearly all Technicolor co-features of the mid-fifties.

Away from her contract studio, Universal, she was busy at first, but her roles quickly declined when she reached 30. Increasingly ill in later years, she died from cancer.
1950: Mr Music. *1951: On the Riviera. Something to Live For. No Questions Asked. The Unknown Man. Bannerline. Overland Telegraph. Ten Tall Men.* *1952: The Brigand. Assignment – Paris! Back at the Front* (GB: *Willie and Joe in Tokyo*). *1953: Abbott and Costello Go to Mars. Veils of Bagdad.* *1954: Rails into Laramie. Black Horse Canyon. Destry.* *1955: Son of Sinbad. The Return of Jack Slade* (GB: *Texas Rose*). *The Crooked Web.* *1956: Stagecoach to Fury. The Cruel Tower.* *1957: Jungle Heat. She Devil. Machete.* *1958: No Place to Land* (GB: *Man Mad*). *Escort West.* *1962: Don't Knock the Twist.* *1963: Twice Told Tales. McLintock!*

BLONDELL, Joan 1909–1979
Cheerful, wisecracking Hollywood blonde, at her best in the 1930s, especially in films that paired her with James Cagney (qv). She held the glamour image until she was past 40, returning in the 1950s to bring a plump, warm brassiness to character roles. Married to Dick Powell (qv) from 1936 to 1945 and producer Mike Todd from 1947 to 1950, second and third of three husbands. Died from leukaemia. Oscar-nominated for *The Blue Veil.*
1930: *Devil's Parade.* *Broadway's Like That. The Office Wife. Sinners' Holiday. Other Men's Women.* *1931: Illicit. Millie. My Past. Public Enemy* (GB: *Enemies of the Public*). *God's Gift to Women* (GB: *Too Many Women*). *Big Business Girl. Night Nurse. The Reckless Hour. Blonde Crazy* (GB: *Larceny Lane*). *1932: Big City Blues. Union Depot* (GB: *Gentleman for a Day*). *The Greeks Had a Word for Them. The Crowd Roars. The Famous Ferguson Case. Make Me a Star. Miss Pinkerton. Three on a Match. Central Park. Lawyer Man.* *1933: Broadway Bad* (GB: *Her Reputation*). *Blondie Johnson. Gold Diggers of 1933. Goodbye Again. Footlight Parade. Havana Widows. Convention City. I've Got Your Number.* *1934: Smarty* (GB: *Hit Me Again*). *He was Her Man. Dames. Kansas City Princess.* *1935: Traveling Saleslady. Broadway Gondolier. We're in the Money. Miss Pacific Fleet.* *1936: Colleen. Sons o' Guns. Bullets or Ballots. Stage Struck. Three Men on a Horse. Gold Diggers of 1937. Talent Scout* (GB: *Studio*

Romance). *1937: The King and the Chorus Girl* (GB: *Romance is Sacred*). *A Day at Santa Anita. Back in Circulation. The Perfect Specimen.* *1938: Stand-In. There's Always a Woman.* *1939: Off the Record. East Side of Heaven. The Kid from Kokomo* (GB: *The Orphan of the Ring*). *Good Girls Go to Paris. The Amazing Mr Williams.* *1940: Two Girls on Broadway* (GB: *Choose Your Partner*). *I Want a Divorce.* *1941: Topper Returns. Model Wife. Three Girls About Town. Lady for a Night.* *1943: Cry Havoc.* *1944: A Tree Grows in Brooklyn.* *1945: Don Juan Quilligan. Adventure.* *1946: Christmas Eve.* *1947: The Corpse Came COD. Nightmare Alley.* *1950: For Heaven's Sake.* *1951: The Blue Veil.* *1956: The Opposite Sex.* *1957: Lizzie. This Could be the Night. Child of Trouble* (TV). *The Desk Set* (GB: *His Other Woman*). *Will Success Spoil Rock Hunter* (GB: *Oh! for a Man*). *1959: A Marriage of Strangers* (TV). *1960: Angel Baby.* *1964: Advance to the Rear* (GB: *Company of Cowards*). *1966: The Cincinnati Kid. Paradise Road. Ride Beyond Vengeance. The Spy in the Green Hat* (TV. GB: cinemas). *1967: Waterhole Number 3* (GB: *Waterhole 3*). *Winchester 73* (TV). *1968: Stay Away, Joe. Kona Coast.* *1969: The Delta Factor. The Phynx.* *1970: Battle at Gannon's Bridge* (TV). *1971: Support Your Local Gunfighter.* *1974: The Dead Don't Die* (TV). *1975: Winner Take All* (TV). *Big Daddy. Won Ton Ton, the Dog Who Saved Hollywood.* *1976: Death at Love House* (TV). *1977: Opening Night.* *1978: Grease. Battered* (TV). *1979: The Champ. Family Secrets* (TV). *The Glove* (released 1981). *1980: The Woman Inside.*

BLOOM, Claire (C. Blume) 1931–
Austerely beautiful dark-haired English actress given her first big film role by Chaplin in *Limelight.* She always seemed too dignified to play comedy, fantasy or sex-drama, although she had a go at all three, sometimes with notable success. But drama is her forte; although it never made her a box-office attraction, she was, and is, capable of both moving and biting performances. Married to Rod Steiger from 1959 to 1971.
1948: The Blind Goddess. *1952: Limelight.* *1953: Innocents in Paris. The Man Between.* *1955: Richard III.* *Ballet Girl* (narrator only). *1956: Alexander the Great.* *1958: The Brothers Karamazov. The Buccaneer.* *1959:*

Look Back in Anger. Misalliance (TV). Adventures of Mr Wonderbird (voice only). 1960: Schachnovelle (GB: Three Moves to Freedom. US: The Royal Game). 1961: The Chapman Report. 1962: The Wonderful World of the Brothers Grimm. 1963: The Haunting. 80,000 Suspects. Il maestro di Vigevano. 1964: The Outrage. Alta infideltà (GB: High Infidelity). 1965: The Spy Who Came in from the Cold. 1968: Charly. The Illustrated Man. 1969: Three into Two Won't Go. 1970: A Severed Head. 1971: Red Sky at Morning. 1973: A Doll's House (directed by Patrick Garland). 1976: Islands in the Stream. 1981: Clash of the Titans. 1985: Always (later Deja Vu). Florence Nightingale (TV). 1986: Promises to Keep (TV).

BLYTH, Ann 1928–

Diminutive singer-actress who, despite a minxish face, was cast mainly in demure roles. A notable exception was the vindictive daughter in *Mildred Pierce*, a role that won her an Oscar nomination. After a few big (but not good) M-G-M musicals, she suddenly left films at 29. Recovered well after breaking her back in 1945.

1944: Chip Off the Old Block. The Merry Monahans. Babes on Swing Street. 1945: Bowery to Broadway. Mildred Pierce. 1946: Swell Guy. 1947: Killer McCoy. A Woman's Vengeance. 1948: Another Part of the Forest. Mr Peabody and the Mermaid. 1949: Red Canyon. Once More, My Darling. Top o' the Morning. Free for All. You Can Change the World. 1950: Our Very Own. 1951: The Great Caruso. Katie Did It. The Golden Horde. Thunder on the Hill (GB: Bonaventure). I'll Never Forget You. 1952: The World in His Arms. Sally and Saint Anne. One Minute to Zero. 1953: All the Brothers Were Valiant. 1954: Rose Marie. The Student Prince. 1955: Kismet. The King's Thief. 1957: Slander. The Buster Keaton Story. The Helen Morgan Story (GB: Both Ends of the Candle).

BOGARDE, Dirk (Derek Van Den Bogaerde) 1921–

Handsome, dark-haired, youthful British leading man, a big box-office attraction in light-hearted star roles, but always at his most interesting as villains, or men of flawed or devious character. These latter parts dominated his career from the early sixties

onwards, when he was to be seen in increasingly gloomy roles.

*1939: Come on George (as extra). 1947: Dancing with Crime. 1948: Esther Waters. Quartet. Once a Jolly Swagman (US: Maniacs on Wheels). 1949: Dear Mr Prohack. Boys in Brown. The Blue Lamp. 1950: So Long at the Fair. The Woman in Question (US: Five Angles on Murder). Blackmailed. 1951: Hunted (US: The Stranger in Between). 1952: Penny Princess. The Gentle Gunman. 1953: Appointment in London. Desperate Moment. 1954: They Who Dare. Doctor in the House. The Sleeping Tiger. For Better, for Worse (US: Cocktails in the Kitchen). The Sea Shall Not Have Them. Simba. 1955: Doctor at Sea. Cast a Dark Shadow. 1956: The Spanish Gardener. Ill Met by Moonlight (US: Night Ambush). 1957: Doctor at Large. Campbell's Kingdom. 1958: A Tale of Two Cities. The Wind Cannot Read. 1959: The Doctor's Dilemma. Libel! 1960: Song without End. The Angel Wore Red. The Singer Not the Song. 1961: Victim. 1962: HMS Defiant (US: Damn the Defiant!). The Password is Courage. We Joined the Navy. The Mind Benders. 1963: I Could Go On Singing. Doctor in Distress. Hot Enough for June (US: Agent 8¾). The Servant. 1964: King and Country. The High Bright Sun (US: McGuire, Go Home!). 1965: Darling. 1966: Modesty Blaise. 1967: Accident. Our Mother's House. Sebastian. 1968: The Fixer. *Return to Lochaver. 1969: Oh! What a Lovely War. Justine. La caduta degli dei (GB and US: The Damned). 1970: *Upon This Rock. 1971: Death in Venice. 1973: The Serpent. 1974: The Night Porter. 1975: Permission to Kill. 1977: Providence. A Bridge Too Far. 1978: Despair. 1981: The Patricia Neal Story (TV).*

BOGART, Humphrey 1899–1957

Probably Hollywood's most charismatic and enduring star. Although not an actor of great range, he imposed the sharply-defined lines of his own abrasive but warm personality on every role he played. Oscar for *The African Queen*. Now hero-worshipped to an impossible degree, but imperishably associated with a certain kind of trench-coated, trilby-hatted, cigarette-smoking lone-wolf hero it is no longer possible to portray on today's screens. Died from throat cancer. Married to Lauren Bacall (his fourth wife) from 1945 until his

death. Further Oscar-nominated for *Casablanca* and *The Caine Mutiny*.

*1930: *Broadway's Like That. Up the River. A Devil With Women. 1931: Body and Soul. Bad Sister. Women of All Nations. A Holy Terror. Big City Blues. 1932: Love Affair. Three on a Match. 1934: Midnight. 1936: The Petrified Forest. Bullets or Ballots. Two Against the World (GB: The Case of Mrs Pembrook). China Clipper. Isle of Fury. Black Legion. The Great O'Malley. 1937: Marked Woman. Kid Galahad. San Quentin. Dead End. Stand-In. Swing Your Lady. 1938: Men Are Such Fools. Crime School. Racket Busters. The Amazing Dr Clitterhouse. Angels with Dirty Faces. 1939: King of the Underworld. The Oklahoma Kid. Dark Victory. You Can't Get Away with Murder. The Roaring Twenties. The Return of Dr X. Invisible Stripes. 1940: Virginia City. It All Came True. Brother Orchid. They Drive By Night (GB: The Road to Frisco). 1941: High Sierra. The Wagons Roll at Night. The Maltese Falcon. 1942: Across the Pacific. In This Our Life. All Through the Night. The Big Sleep. Casablanca. 1943: Action in the North Atlantic. *Show Business at War. Thank Your Lucky Stars. Sahara. 1944: Passage to Marseille. To Have and Have Not. 1945: Conflict. *Hollywood Victory Caravan. Two Guys from Milwaukee (GB: Royal Flush). 1946: The Big Sleep. Dead Reckoning. 1947: The Two Mrs Carrolls. Dark Passage. 1948: Always Together. The Treasure of the Sierra Madre. Key Largo. 1949: Knock on Any Door. Tokyo Joe. 1950: Chain Lightning. In a Lonely Place. The Enforcer (GB: Murder Inc). 1951: Sirocco. The African Queen. 1952: Deadline USA (GB: Deadline). Battle Circus. 1953: Beat the Devil. The Love Lottery. 1954: The Caine Mutiny. Sabrina (GB: Sabrina Fair). The Barefoot Contessa. We're No Angels. 1955: The Left Hand of God. The Desperate Hours. 1956: The Harder They Fall.*

BOLES, John 1895–1969

Handsome, affable, if rather stolid leading man and singer, who was at his best and most popular in such musicals as *The Desert Song*. But he also provided competent back-up for a number of powerful actresses in successful tear-jerkers of the thirties. Died from a heart attack.

1924: So This Is Marriage? 1925: Excuse Me. 1927: The Love of Sunya. 1928: The Shepherd

Forever and a Day. Stage Door Canteen. 1944: Four Jacks and a Jill. 1945: The Harvey Girls. 1949: Make Mine Laughs. Look for the Silver Lining. 1952: Where's Charley? 1953: April in Paris. 1961: Babes in Toyland. 1966: The Daydreamer. 1976: The Entertainer (TV). 1979: Just You and Me Kid. Heaven Only Knows (TV). Three on a Date (TV). The Runner Stumbles. 1984: That's Dancing!

† *Scenes deleted from final release print*

*of the Hills. We Americans (GB: The Heart of a Nation). The Bride of the Colorado. Fazil. The Water Hole. Virgin Lips. Man Made Woman. Romance of the Underworld. 1929: The Last Warning. Scandal. The Desert Song. Rio Rita. 1930: Song of the West. *Voice of Hollywood No. 1. Captain of the Guard. King of Jazz. One Heavenly Night. 1931: Seed. Resurrection. Good Sport. Frankenstein. 1932: Careless Lady. Back Street. Six Hours to Live. 1933: Child of Manhattan. My Lips Betray. Only Yesterday. Music in the Air. 1934: Beloved. Bottoms Up. I Believed in You. The Life of Vergie Winters. Wild Gold. The Age of Innocence. 1935: The White Parade. Orchids to You. Curly Top. Redheads on Parade. The Littlest Rebel. 1936: A Message to Garcia. Rose of the Rancho. Craig's Wife. 1937: As Good as Married. Stella Dallas. Fight for Your Lady. 1938: She Married An Artist. Romance in the Dark. Sinners in Paradise. 1942: The Road to Happiness. Between Us Girls. 1943: Thousands Cheer. 1952: Babes in Bagdad.*

BOLGER, Ray 1904–
Although immortalized as the Scarecrow in *The Wizard of Oz*, Bolger was never as big a box-office star in the cinema as he had become on the American stage. But, with horsey face, beaming smile and seemingly indiarubber legs, he could be funny, likeable or romantic. He was also capable of some amazing dance routines, and most of his few screen appearances were notable personal successes.
1936: The Great Ziegfeld. 1937: Rosalie. 1938: Sweethearts. †The Girl of the Golden West. 1939: The Wizard of Oz. 1941: Sunny. 1943:

BOND, Derek 1919–
Jovial, Scottish-born actor, mainly in lordly roles. Was effective as officers and gentlemen (although rather less so as Nicholas Nickleby), but his strictly upper-class image could not sustain his stardom beyond the early fifties. From 1959 onwards Bond directed innumerable segments of the Rank Organization's *Look at Life* series.
*1946: The Captive Heart. 1947: Nicholas Nickleby. The Lovers of Joanna Godden. Uncle Silas (US: The Inheritance). Broken Journey. 1948: The Weaker Sex. Scott of the Antarctic. 1949: Marry Me. Christopher Columbus. Poet's Pub. 1950: Tony Draws a Horse. 1951: The Quiet Woman. 1952: Distant Trumpet. Love's a Luxury (US: The Caretaker's Daughter). The Hour of 13. 1953: Trouble in Store. 1954: Svengali. Stranger from Venus (US: Immediate Decision). A Tale of Three Women. 1953: Three Cornered Fate. 1956: The High Terrace. *Behind the Screen (narrator only). 1957: Rogue's Yarn. 1958: Gideon's Day (US: Gideon of Scotland Yard). Stormy Crossing (US: Black Tide). 1960: The Hand. 1963: Saturday Night Out. 1964: Wonderful Life. 1966: Secrets of a Windmill Girl. Press for Time. 1971: When Eight Bells Toll. 1975: Hijack! Intimate Reflections. 1980: Dangerous Davies – the Last Detective (TV).*

BOONE, Pat (Charles Boone) 1934–
Bland, excessively clean-cut American singer of the fifties who made some popular musicals at Fox before trying hard to escape his own image in the early sixties. But the public wouldn't buy it, and Boone drifted out of films.
1957: Bernardine. April Love. 1958: Mardi Gras. 1959: Journey to the Center of the Earth. 1961: All Hands on Deck. 1962: State Fair. 1963: The Yellow Canary. The Main Attrac-

tion. The Horror of It All. 1964: Never Put It in Writing. Goodbye Charlie. 1965: The Greatest Story Ever Told. 1967: The Perils of Pauline. 1969: The Pigeon (TV). 1970: The Cross and the Switchblade.

BOONE, Richard 1917–1981
Sullen-featured American actor – a descendant of Daniel Boone – much in demand for villain roles before huge success in a TV western series, *Have Gun, Will Travel*, brought him better billing. He continued to appear mainly as tough men of action, until his death from cancer of the throat.
1950: Halls of Montezuma. 1951: Call Me Mister. The Desert Fox (GB: Rommel – Desert Fox). 1952: Kangaroo. Red Skies of Montana. Return of the Texan. 1953: Way of a Gaucho. Beneath the 12-Mile Reef. City of Bad Men. Man on a Tightrope. The Robe. Vicki. 1954: Dragnet. The Raid. The Siege at Red River. 1955: Man Without a Star. Robbers' Roost. Ten Wanted Men. The Big Knife (narrator only). 1956: Battle Stations. Away All Boats. Star in the Dust. 1957: Garment Center (GB: The Garment Jungle). Lizzie. The Tall T. 1958: I Bury the Living. 1959: The Tunnel (TV). 1960: The Alamo. Tomorrow (TV). 1961: A Thunder of Drums. 1964: Rio Conchos. 1965: The War Lord. 1966: Hombre. 1968: Kona Coast (TV. GB: cinemas). The Night of the Following Day. The Arrangement. The Kremlin Letter. 1970: Madron. 1971: Big Jake. The Century Turns (TV. GB: Hec Ramsey). In Broad Daylight (TV). 1972: Goodnight My Love (TV). Deadly Harvest (TV). 1974: The Great Niagara (TV). 1976:

Against a Crooked Sky. The Shootist. 1977: Winter Kills (released 1979). God's Gun. 1978: The Big Sleep. The Last Dinosaur. The Bushido Blade (released 1982). The Hobbit (TV. Voice only).

BOOTH, Adrian (Virginia Pound) 1918–
On the face of it Ginger Pound, who sang with Roger Pryor's band in the late 1930s, Lorna Gray, the 1940s' serial queen, Adrian Booth, the classy actress from so many of Republic's post-war outdoor adventures, and Mrs Virginia Davis of Southern California would seem to have had separate careers. But they are all the same person, a gritty auburn-haired lady who frequently lost the hero to the horse, but seems to have had no lack of variety in her life. Married to David Brian (*qv*) since 1949.
1938: †*Red River Range.* †*Smashing the Spy Ring.* †*Adventure in Sahara.* 1939: †*Three Sappy People.* †*Mr Smith Goes to Washington.* †*Flying G-Men (serial).* †*The Man They Could Not Hang.* †*The Lone Wolf Spy Hunt (GB: The Lone Wolf's Daughter).* †*Pest from the West.* †*The Stranger from Texas (GB: The Stranger).* 1940: †*Rockin' Through the Rockies.* †*Drums of the Desert.* †*Convicted Woman.* †*Up in the Air.* †*Deadwood Dick (serial).* †*Bullets for Rustlers (GB: On Special Duty).* 1941: †*Father Steps Out.* †*Tuxedo Junction (GB: The Gang Made Good).* †*City Limits.* 1942: †*Perils of Nyoka (serial).* †*Riding Down the Canyon.* 1943: †*O, My Darling Clementine.* †*So Proudly We Hail!* 1944: †*The Girl Who Dared.* †*Captain America (serial).* †*Tell It to a Star.* 1945: †*Adventures of Kitty O'Day.* †*Fashion Model.* †*Dakota.* †*Federal Operator 99 (serial).* 1946: *Daughter of Don Q (serial). Valley of the Zombies. Home on the Range. The Man from Rainbow Valley. Out California Way.* 1947: *Exposed. The Last Frontier (GB: The Last Frontier Uprising). Along the Oregon Trail. Spoilers of the North. Under Colorado Skies.* 1948: *California Firebrand. The Plunderers. The Gallant Legion. Lightnin' in the Forest.* 1949: *The Hideout. Brimstone. The Last Bandit.* 1950: *Rock Island Trail (GB: Transcontinent Express). The Savage Horde.* 1951: *Oh! Susanna. Yellowfin (GB: Yellow Fin). The Sea Hornet.*

† *As Lorna Gray*

BOOTH, James (David Geeves-Booth) 1930–
Slightly lugubrious-looking British actor who had a good run in the sixties with various sharpies, petty gang leaders and men on the make. The public was not attracted to him in leading roles, and he returned to playing rascals. Now lives in America, working mainly as a writer of film and TV scripts.
1959: *Jazzboat.* 1960: *Let's Get Married. The Trials of Oscar Wilde (US: The Man with the Green Carnation). In the Nick.* 1961: *The Hellions. In the Doghouse.* 1962: *Sparrows Can't Sing.* 1963: *Zulu.* 1964: *90 Degrees in the Shade. French Dressing.* 1965: *The Secret of My Success.* 1967: *Robbery.* 1968: *The Bliss of Mrs Blossom. Fraulein Doktor.* 1969: *Adam's Woman.* 1970: *The Man Who Had Power Over Women. Darker Than Amber.* 1971: *Revenge. Macho Callahan.* 1972: *Rentadick.* 1973: *That'll Be the Day. Penny Gold.* 1974: *Percy's Progress. Brannigan.* 1975: *I'm Not Feeling Myself Tonight.* 1977: *Airport 77.* 1978: *Murder in Peyton Place (TV).* 1979: *Jennifer – A Woman's Story (TV). Cabo Blanco.* 1980: *The Jazz Singer.* 1981: *Zorro the Gay Blade.* 1985: *Pray for Death.*

BOOTH, Shirley (Thelma Ford) 1907–
Leading American stage actress who, after being widowed in 1951, became a film star in her middle years, mostly as anguished women trying to hold on to their men. In her first (and best) film she won an Oscar, but hers was not a popular image and she returned to stage work.
1952: *Come Back, Little Sheba.* 1953: *Main

Street to Broadway. 1954: *About Mrs Leslie.* 1957: *The Hostess with the Mostess (TV).* 1958: *Hot Spell. The Matchmaker.* 1968: *The Smugglers (TV).*

BOOTHE, Powers 1939–
Powerfully built, large-headed, Texas-born actor with wispy brown hair and heavily charismatic presence. He looked to be a major star in the making when featured in *Southern Comfort*, but his career in films has perhaps not quite progressed in the right direction and one fears he may be in weighty character roles before long. He has, however, distinguished himself in the theatre and made the best Philip Marlowe for some time in two popular television series based on the detective novels of Raymond Chandler.
1977: *The Goodbye Girl.* 1979: *Guyana Tragedy: The Story of Jim Jones (TV).* 1980: *Cruising. A Cry for Love (TV). The Plutonium Incident (TV). The Cold Eye/My Darling Be Careful.* 1981: *Skag/The Wildcatters (TV). Southern Comfort.* 1984: *Red Dawn. A Breed Apart.* 1985: *The Emerald Forest.* 1986: *Extreme Prejudice.*

BORGNINE, Ernest (Ermes Borgnino) 1915–
Heavy-set American actor whose swarthy scowl was much in evidence as villains in thrillers and westerns after a late debut at 36. Roles for the kindlier image he projected in *Marty* (which won him an Oscar) proved difficult to find, and he gradually regressed to aggressive bigots, albeit leavened with humour. Five wives have included Katy

Jurado (1959–1964) and Ethel Merman (a few months in 1964).

1951: China Corsair. The Whistle at Eaton Falls (GB: Richer Than the Earth). The Mob (GB: Remember That Face). 1953: From Here to Eternity. The Stranger Wore a Gun. 1954: Demetrius and the Gladiators. The Bounty Hunter. Johnny Guitar. Vera Cruz. Bad Day at Black Rock. Run for Cover. 1955: Marty. Violent Saturday. The Last Command. The Square Jungle. 1956: Jubal. The Catered Affair (GB: Wedding Breakfast). The Best Things in Life Are Free. 1957: Three Brave Men. 1958: The Rabbit Trap. Torpedo Run. The Vikings. 1960: The Badlanders. Pay or Die! Man on a String (GB: Confessions of a Counterspy). Summer of the Seventeenth Doll (US: Season of Passion). 1961: Seduction of the South. Los guerrilleros. Go Naked in the World. Il giudizio universale. Barabbas. 1962: Il re di Poggioreale. 1964: McHale's Navy. 1965: The Flight of the Phoenix. 1966: The Oscar. 1967: The Dirty Dozen. Chuka. 1968: Ice Station Zebra. The Split. The Legend of Lylah Clare. 1969: The Wild Bunch. Vengeance is Mine. Rain for a Dusty Summer. 1970: Suppose They Gave a War and Nobody Came. The Adventurers. A Bullet for Sandoval. 1971: The Trackers (TV). Bunny O'Hare. Hannie Caulder. Willard. Sam Hill – Who Killed the Mysterious Mr Foster? (TV). 1972: The Revengers. Guns of the Revolution. Tough Guy. The Poseidon Adventure. 1973: Emperor of the North Pole (GB: Emperor of the North). The Neptune Factor. 1974: Law and Disorder. Sunday in the Country. Twice in a Lifetime (TV). 1975: The Devil's Rain. 1976: Future Cop (TV). Shoot. Cleaver and Haven (TV). Hustle. Natale in case di appuntamento. 1977: Fire! (TV. GB: cinemas). The Prince and the Pauper (US: Crossed Swords). The Greatest. 1978: Convoy. The Double McGuffin. Ravagers. The Cops and Robin (TV). The Ghost of Flight 401 (TV). 1979: The Black Hole. 1980: Super Snooper (US: Super Fuzz). 1981: Deadly Blessing. 1982: The Graduates of Malibu High. Hollywood Hookers. 1983: Young Warriors. Masquerade (TV). Carpool (TV). Airwolf (TV). 1984: The Last Days of Pompeii (TV). White Stallion. Man Hunt Warning. Codename Wildgeese. Love Leads the Way. 1985: The Dirty Dozen: Next Mission (TV). Blood Hunt.

BOTTOMS, Timothy 1949–
Sympathetic-looking, light-haired, slightly-built American actor. The best-known and most forthright of a trio of acting brothers, Bottoms started his Hollywood career with a bang in *The Last Picture Show*, but had slipped into co-starring roles in some productions by the late 1970s.

1971: The Last Picture Show. Johnny Got His Gun. 1972: Look Homeward, Angel (TV). Love and Pain and the whole damn thing. 1973: The Paper Chase. 1974: The White Dawn. The Crazy World of Julius Vrooder/Vrooder's Hooch. 1975: Operation Daybreak. 1976: A Small Town in Texas. 1977: Rollercoaster. A Shining Season (TV). 1978: The Gift of Love (TV). The Other Side of the Mountain – Pt 2.

1979: Hurricane. The First Hello. 1980: The High Country. Escape (TV). 1981: East of Eden (TV). 1983: Hambone and Hillie (GB: The Adventures of Hambone). 1984: Secrets of the Phantom Caverns. Love Leads the Way. The Census Taker. 1985: The Sea Serpent. Invaders from Mars. 1986: In the Shadow of Kilimanjaro. The Fantasist.

BOW, Clara 1905–1965
Known variously as the 'It' girl, the Jazz Baby and the Brooklyn Bonfire, Clara was a vivacious, petite redhead, who typified America in the mid-1920s. Her abrasive love life hardly matched her screen image, which soon palled with the public with the coming of sound. A weight problem (she was always dumpy by modern standards) hastened her early retirement. Married (from 1931) to cowboy star Rex Bell (1905–1962), she died from a heart attack.

1922: Beyond the Rainbow. Down to the Sea in Ships. 1923: Enemies of Women. Maytime. The Daring Years. 1924: Black Oxen. Poisoned Paradise. Daughters of Pleasure. Wine. Empty Hearts. Grit. Black Lightning. This Woman. 1925: Helen's Babies. Capital Punishment. The Adventurous Sex. My Lady's Lips. Parisian Love. Eve's Lover. Kiss Me Again. The Scarlet West. The Primrose Path. The Plastic Age. Keeper of the Bees. Lawful Cheaters. Free to Love. The Best Bad Man. 1926: Two Can Play. The Runaway. Mantrap. Kid Boots. The Ancient Mariner. My Lady of Whim. Dancing Mothers. The Shadow of the Law. 1927: Children of Divorce. It. Rough House Rosie. Wings. Hula. Get Your Man. 1928: Red Hair. Ladies

of the Mob. The Fleet's In. Three Weekends. 1929: The Wild Party. The Saturday Night Kid. Dangerous Curves. 1930: Paramount on Parade. True to the Navy. Love among the Millionaires. Her Wedding Night. 1931: No Limit. Kick In. 1932: Call Her Savage. 1933: Hoopla.

BOWIE, David (D. Jones) 1947–
Rangy, fair-haired British rock singer and actor of strained, faintly upper-class good looks, and deliberately enigmatic personality and sexuality. Enormously successful on record, he couldn't really get a film career going until Nicolas Roeg asked him to play the title character in *The Man Who Fell to Earth*, a role entirely suited to his at once magnetic and distant aura. After that he continued to play often unsettling characters with more regularity.

*1967: *The Image. 1968: Love You Till Tuesday (unfinished). 1969: The Virgin Soldiers. 1976: The Man Who Fell to Earth. 1978: Just a Gigolo/Arme Gigolo. 1981: Christiane F. 1982: Ziggy Stardust and the Spiders from Mars. Merry Christmas Mr Lawrence. *The Snowman. 1983: The Hunger. Yellowbeard. 1984: Jazzing for Blue Jean (video). 1985: Into the Night. Labyrinth. 1986: Absolute Beginners.*

BOWMAN, Lee 1910–1979
Sleek, gentlemanly, urbane, dark-haired American leading man with razor-thin moustache. From beginnings as a radio singer, he developed into a capable second-rank studio star (often in M-G-M films), even if he was

usually to be found playing second-fiddle to someone else. After the 1940s Bowman concentrated on TV, where he made a suave Ellery Queen, and rounded out his career in later years by coaching prominent men in the art of public speaking. With his velvet tones, few were better qualified. He died from a heart attack on Christmas Day, just three days away from his 69th birthday.

1936: Three Men in White. 1937: I Met Him in Paris. Internes Can't Take Money (GB: You Can't Take Money). Last Train from Madrid. This Way, Please. Sophie Lang Goes West. 1938: Having Wonderful Time. A Man to Remember. Tarnished Angel. Next Time I Marry. The First Hundred Years. 1939: Society Lawyer. Stronger Than Desire. Fast and Furious. Dancing Co-Ed (GB: Every Other Inch a Lady). The Lady and the Mob. Miracles for Sale. Love Affair. The Great Victor Herbert. 1940: Wyoming (GB: Bad Man of Wyoming). Florian. Gold Rush Maisie. Third Finger, Left Hand. 1941: Buck Privates (GB: Rookies). Model Wife. Washington Melodrama. Married Bachelor. Design for Scandal. 1942: Kid Glove Killer. We Were Dancing. Pacific Rendezvous. Tish. 1943: Bataan. Three Hearts for Julia. 1944: Cover Girl. The Impatient Years. Tonight and Every Night. 1945: She Wouldn't Say Yes. 1946: The Walls Came Tumbling Down. 1947: Smash-Up, the Story of a Woman (GB: A Woman Destroyed). 1949: My Dream is Yours. There's a Girl in My Heart. The House by the River. 1955: Double-Barreled Miracle. 1964: Youngblood Hawke. 1966: Fame is the Name of the Game (TV). 1968: Judd for the Defense: Fall of a Skylark (TV).

BOYD, Stephen (William Millar) 1928–1977

Handsome, Belfast-born actor with Kirk Douglas chin. Quickly caught on as an international star after a few roles in British films, but his career fell away in the late sixties after a succession of poor roles in which his performances became progressively less magnetic. Although he was a fitness fanatic, a heart attack killed him while he was playing golf.

1955: Born for Trouble. An Alligator Named Daisy. 1956: The Man who Never Was. A Hill in Korea (US: Hell in Korea). 1957: Seven Waves Away (US: Abandon Ship!). Island in

the Sun. Seven Thunders (US: The Beast of Marseilles). Les bijoutiers du clair de lune (GB: Heaven Fell That Night. US: The Night Heaven Fell). 1958: The Bravados. 1959: Ben-Hur. A Woman Obsessed. The Best of Everything. 1960: The Big Gamble. To the Sounds of Trumpets (TV). 1962: The Inspector (US: Lisa). Billy Rose's Jumbo. 1963: Imperial Venus. The Fall of the Roman Empire. 1964: The Third Secret. 1965: Genghis Khan. 1966: The Bible ... in the Beginning. The Poppy is Also a Flower (GB: Danger Grows Wild). The Oscar. Fantastic Voyage. 1967: Assignment K. The Caper of the Golden Bulls (GB: Carnival of Thieves). 1968: Shalako. 1969: Slaves. 1970: Marta. 1971: Hannie Caulder. 1972: Carter's Army (TV). Kill (US: Kill! Kill! Kill!). Bloody Mary. The Hands of Cormac Joyce (TV). Key West (TV). The Big Game. The Devil Has Seven Faces. 1973: The Man Called Noon. 1974: One Man Against the Organization. The Left Hand of the Law. 1975: Of Men and Women II (TV). Those Dirty Dogs. The Lives of Jenny Dolan (TV). 1976: Impossible Love. Potato Fritz. Montana Trap. Lady Dracula. Evil in the Deep. Frauenstation (US: Women in Hospital). 1977: The Squeeze.*

BOYD, William 1895–1972
Ohio-born Hollywood star who earned himself security, popularity and a niche in screen history when he started playing the western hero Hopalong Cassidy in 1935. A pillar of respectability and two-fisted justice, Cassidy was perhaps the only cowboy to match white hair with a black outfit. Boyd took the character with him into TV in 1948. Married four times, his last wife (from 1937) being actress Grace Bradley. Died from Parkinson's Disease.

1918: Old Wives for New. 1919: Why Change Your Wife? 1920: A City Sparrow. 1921: Brewster's Millions. Moonlight and Honeysuckle. The Affairs of Anatol (GB: A Prodigal Knight). Exit the Vamp. A Wise Fool. 1922: Bobbed Hair. Nice People. The Young Rajah. Manslaughter. On the High Seas. 1923: Enemies of Children. The Temple of Venus. Michael O'Halloran. Hollywood. 1924: Tarnish. Changing Husbands. Triumph. 1925: Forty Winks. The Road to Yesterday. The Golden Bed. The Midshipman. 1926: The Last Frontier. Eve's Leaves. Her Man O' War. The Volga Boatman. Steel Preferred. 1927: Two Arabian Knights. King of Kings. Dress Parade.

Wolves of the Air. Jim the Conqueror. Yankee Clipper. 1928: The Night Flyer. Power Skyscraper. The Cop. 1929: High Voltage. Lady of the Pavements (GB: Lady of the Night). The Flying Fool. The Leatherneck. Wolf Song. Locked Door. 1930: Those Who Dance. Officer O'Brien. His First Command. The Storm. 1931: The Gang Buster. The Painted Desert. Beyond Victory. The Big Gamble. Suicide Fleet. 1932: Carnival Boat. Men of America (GB: Great Decision). The Wiser Sex. Madison Square Garden. 1933: Lucky Devils. Emergency Call. 1934: Port of Lost Dreams. Cheaters. Flaming Gold. 1935: The Lost City. Transatlantic Merry-Go-Round. Night Life of the Gods. Racing Luck. Hop-A-Long Cassidy. Bar 20 Rides Again. Eagle's Brood. Call of the Prairie. Go Get 'Em Haines. 1936: Three on the Trail. Federal Agent. Burning Gold. Heart of the West. Hopalong Cassidy Returns. Trail Dust. Borderland. 1937: Hills of Old Wyoming. North of the Rio Grande. Rustlers' Valley. Hopalong Rides Again. Texas Trail. Partners of the Plains. Cassidy of Bar 20. 1938: Bar 20 Justice. Heart of Arizona. In Old Mexico. The Frontiersman. Pride of the West. Sunset Trail. 1939: Silver on the Sage. Law of the Pampas. Range War. Renegade Trail. 1940: Santa Fé Marshal. Showdown. Hidden Gold. Stagecoach War. Three Men from Texas. 1941: In Old Colorado. Doomed Caravan. Pirates on Horseback. Border Vigilantes. Wide Open Town. Secrets of the Wasteland. Stick to Your Guns. Twilight on the Trail. Outlaws of the Desert. Riders of the Timberline. 1942: Undercover Man. Lost Canyon. 1943: Leather Burners. Hoppy Serves a Writ. Border Patrol. False Colors. Colt Comrades. Bar 20. Riders of the Deadline. 1944: Texas Masquerade. Lumberjack. Forty Thieves. Mystery Man. 1946: The Devil's Playground. Fools' Gold. Unexpected Guest. Dangerous Venture. 1947: Hoppy's Holiday. The Marauders. 1948: Silent Conflict. The Dead Don't Dream. Strange Gamble. Sinister Journey. False Paradise. Borrowed Trouble. 1951: *Hopalong in Hoppyland. 1952: The Greatest Show on Earth.*

BOYER, Charles 1899–1978
The 'great lover' of the screen, every filmgoing lady's ideal of the romantic Frenchman. It was a reputation rendered imperishable by his portrayal of Pepe le Moko in *Algiers*, in which he did *not* ask Hedy Lamarr to 'Come wiz me

to de Casbah'. The charm turned deadly to great effect in *Gaslight*: in later years he played equally charming roués. Special Oscar in 1942 for 'cultural achievement'. Committed suicide a few days after the death of his wife, English actress Pat Paterson. Received acting Oscar nominations for his performances in *Conquest*, *Algiers*, *Gaslight* and *Fanny*.

1920: *L'homme du large. Le grillon du foyer.* 1921: *Chantelouve.* 1922: *L'esclave.* 1927: *La ronde infernale.* 1928: *Le capitaine Fracasse.* 1929: *Le procès de Mary Dugan.* 1930: *Barcarolle d'amour. Révolte dans la prison.* 1931: *Tumultes. I.F.1 ne reponde pas. The Magnificent Lie.* 1932: *The Man from Yesterday. Red Headed Woman.* 1933: *L'épervier. The Only Girl (US: Heart Song. French version: Moi et l'impératrice). Liliom.* 1934: *The Battle (US: Thunder in the East. French version: La bataille). Caravan (and French version). Le bonheur.* 1935: *Private Worlds. Break of Hearts. Shanghai. Mayerling.* 1936: *The Garden of Allah.* 1937: *Tovarich. Conquest (GB: Marie Walewska). History is Made at Night. Orage.* 1938: *Algiers.* 1939: *Love Affair. When Tomorrow Comes. Le corsaire (unfinished).* 1940: *All This and Heaven Too. The Heart of a Nation (narrator only).* 1941: *Back Street. Hold Back the Dawn. Appointment for Love.* 1942: *Tales of Manhattan.* 1943: *The Constant Nymph. Flesh and Fantasy.* **Little Isles of Freedom (narrator only).* 1944: *Gaslight (GB: The Murder in Thornton Square). Together Again.* 1945: *Bataille de Russie (narrator only). Le combattant (narrator only). Confidential Agent.* 1946: *Cluny Brown.* 1947: *A Woman's Vengeance.* 1948: *Arch of Triumph.* 1949: **On Stage.* 1950: **Hollywood-sur-Seine (narrator only).* 1951: *The First Legion. Thunder in the East. The Thirteenth Letter.* 1952: *The Happy Time.* 1953: *Madame de . . . (US: The Diamond Earrings).* 1954: *Nana.* 1955: *The Cobweb.* 1956: *La fortuna di essera donna (GB and US: Lucky to be a Woman). Paris-Palace Hôtel. Around the World in 80 Days.* 1957: *Une Parisienne. C'est arrivé à 36 chandelles.* 1958: *The Buccaneer. Le grande rencontre (narrator only). Maxime.* 1960: *Fanny.* 1961: *The Four Horsemen of the Apocalypse. Les démons de minuit (GB: Demons at Midnight). Adorable Julia.* **Son et lumière (narrator only).* 1963: *Love is a Ball (GB: All This and Money Too).* 1965: *A Very Special Favor. Is Paris Burning?* 1966: *How to Steal a Million.* 1967: *Casino Royale. Barefoot in the Park.* 1969: *The April Fools. The Madwoman of Chaillot. The Day the Hot Line Got Hot.* 1973: *Lost Horizon.* 1974: *Stavisky.* 1976: *A Matter of Time.*

BOYLE, Peter 1933–

Bald, aggressive, thick-set American actor, whose first starring role, as the foul-mouthed central character of *Joe*, was far from his own previous life as a monk in the Christian Brothers order. Quickly proving himself capable of a wide range of characterizations, Boyle sustained his rating as a star character actor well into the 1980s. He has reverted to playing largely unpleasant types in recent years.

1968: *The Virgin President. Medium Cool.* 1969: *Joe.* 1970: *Diary of a Mad Housewife.* 1971: *T R Baskin (GB: A Date with a Lonely Girl).* 1972: *Steelyard Blues. The Candidate.* 1973: *Slither. The Friends of Eddie Coyle. Kid Blue/Dime Box. The Man Who Could Talk to Kids (TV).* 1974: *Crazy Joe. Ghost in the Noonday Sun. Young Frankenstein.* 1976: *Swashbuckler (GB: The Scarlet Buccaneer). Taxi Driver. Tail Gunner Joe (TV).* 1978: *Hardcore (GB: The Hardcore Life). F.I.S.T.* 1979: *Beyond the Poseidon Adventure. The Brink's Job. In God We Trust.* 1980: *Where the Buffalo Roam. Hammett (released 1982).* 1981: *Outland.* 1983: *Yellowbeard.* 1984: *Johnny Dangerously.* 1985: *Turk 182!* 1986: *Citizen Joe.*

BRACKEN, Eddie 1920–

This stocky comic actor was usually cast as dynamic but dopey sub-Mickey Rooney types whose fast-talking backchat covered their own insecurity. But he did please wartime audiences and was funny in a couple of Preston Sturges' best films. His limited appeal soon faded in post-war years. When business ventures failed, he became a writer and occasional cameo performer.

1938: *Brother Rat.* 1940: *Too Many Girls.* 1941: *Life With Henry. Caught in the Draft. Reaching for the Sun.* 1942: *The Fleet's In. Sweater Girl. Star Spangled Rhythm.* 1943: *Young and Willing. Happy Go Lucky.* 1944: *The Miracle of Morgan's Creek. Hail the Conquering Hero. Rainbow Island.* 1945: *Bring on the Girls. Duffy's Tavern. Hold That Blonde. Out of This World.* 1946: *Ladies' Man.*

1947: *Fun on a Weekend.* 1949: *The Girl from Jones Beach.* 1950: *Summer Stock (GB: If You Feel Like Singing).* 1951: *Two Tickets to Broadway.* **Hollywood on a Sunday Afternoon.* 1952: *We're Not Married. About Face.* 1953: *A Slight Case of Larceny.* 1961: *Wild, Wild World.* 1962: *A Summer Sunday.* 1971: *Shinbone Alley (voice only).* 1983: *National Lampoon's Vacation.*

BRADY, Alice 1892–1939

Enchantingly appealing brunette American leading lady of silents, some of which were adaptations of hits she had already had on stage. Left films in 1923, and timed her comeback to Hollywood to perfection, this time in comedy character roles. She had just won an Oscar for a rare dramatic role in *In Old Chicago* (1938), when she learned she had terminal cancer. She died the following year, at 46. Also Oscar-nominated for *My Man Godfrey*.

1914: *As Ye Sow.* 1915: *The Boss. The Lure of Woman. The Cup of Chance.* 1916: *The Rack. The Ballet Girl. La Bohème. The Woman in 47. Then I'll Come Back to You. Tangled Fates. Miss Petticoats. The Gilded Cage. Bought and Paid For.* 1917: *A Hungry Heart. The Dancer's Peril. Darkest Russia. Maternity. The Divorce Game. A Self-Made Widow. Betsy Ross. A Maid of Belgium. A Woman Alone.* 1918: *The Trap. At the Mercy of Men. The Spurs of Sybil. The Knife. Woman and Wife. Her Silent Sacrifice. The Whirlpool. The Ordeal of Rosetta. The Death Dance. The Better Half. Her Great Chance. In the Hollow of Her Hand.* 1919: *The Indestructible Wife. The World to Live In. Marie Ltd. The Redhead. Her Bridal Night. A Dark Lantern. The Fear Market.* 1920: *Sinners. The New York Idea.* 1921: *Out of the Chorus. The Land of Hope. Dawn of the East. Little Italy. Hush Money.* 1922: *Anna Ascends. Missing Millions.* 1923: *The Snow Bride. The Leopardess.* 1933: *When Ladies Meet. Broadway to Hollywood. Beauty for Sale. Stage Mother. Should Ladies Behave?* 1934: *Miss Fane's Baby is Stolen. The Gay Divorcee (GB: The Gay Divorce).* 1935: *Let 'Em Have It (GB: False Faces). Gold Diggers of 1935. Lady Tubbs (GB: The Gay Lady). Metropolitan.* 1936: *The Harvester. My Man Godfrey. Go West, Young Man. Mind Your Own Business.* 1937: *Three Smart Girls. Call It a Day. One Hundred Men and a Girl. Mama*

Steps Out. Mr Dodd Takes the Air. Merry-Go-Round of 1938. 1938: Joy of Living. In Old Chicago. Goodbye Broadway. 1939: Zenobia (GB: Elephants Never Forget). Young Mr Lincoln.

BRADY, Scott (Gerald Tierney) 1924–1985
Rugged, handsome Hollywood leading man with light-brown hair, brother of Lawrence Tierney (qv). His forceful early acting promise was dissipated in a series of routine action roles for Universal-International, but he kept busy, in latter days as a pudgy and balding character star. Lost to TV from 1959–1962 as *Shotgun Slade* and from 1974 to 1978 as the barman in *Police Story*. Died from respiratory failure.
1947: Born to Kill (GB: Lady of Deceit). 1948: In This Corner. Canon City. Montana Belle (released 1952). He Walked by Night. 1949: The Gal Who Took the West. Port of New York. Undertow. I Was a Shoplifter. 1950: Kansas Raiders. Undercover Girl. 1951: The Model and the Marriage Broker. Untamed Frontier. 1952: Yankee Buccaneer. Bronco Buster. Bloodhounds of Broadway. 1953: A Perilous Journey. El Alamein (GB: Desert Patrol). Three Steps to the Gallows (released 1955. US: White Fire). 1954: The Law versus Billy the Kid. Johnny Guitar. 1955: They Were So Young. Gentlemen Marry Brunettes. The Vanishing American. 1956: Terror at Midnight. The Maverick Queen. Mohawk. 1957: The Storm Rider. Lone Woman (TV). The Restless Breed. 1958: Ambush at Cimarron Pass. Blood Arrow. 1959: Battle Flame. 1963: Operation Bikini. 1964: Stage to Thunder Rock. John Goldfarb, Please Come Home. 1965: Black Spurs. They Ran for Their Lives. 1966: Destination Inner Space. Castle of Evil. 1967: Red Tomahawk. Fort Utah. Journey to the Center of Time. 1968: Arizona Bushwhackers. 1969: Nightmare in Wax. Cain's Way. The Road Hustlers. Smashing the Crime Syndicate (released 1973). Marooned. The DA: Murder One (TV). 1970: Five Bloody Graves. Satan's Sadists. 1971: Doctors' Wives. The Mighty Gorga. $ (GB: The Heist). Hell's Bloody Devils. 1972: The Loners. The Night Strangler (TV). The Leo Chronicles. Bonnie's Kids. 1975: Wicked, Wicked. Roll, Freddy, Roll (TV). Kansas City Massacre (TV). 1976: Law and Order (TV). 1978: The China Syndrome. Suddenly Love (TV). Streets of Fear

(TV). Pressure Point (TV). When Every Day Was the Fourth of July (TV). 1979: The Last Ride of the Dalton Gang (TV). 1981: Dead Kids. Shadowland. 1983: This Girl for Hire (TV). 1984: Gremlins.

BRAND, Neville 1921–
A regular army man (the fourth most decorated American soldier of World War II), Brand became interested in acting when he took part in army training films ('I was always the sergeant, and Charlton Heston the captain'). After leaving the army in 1946, his thick-set, scowling, glowering features quickly became a regular feature of the villainy in Hollywood crime films, although some of his best performances (for example, the warder in *Birdman of Alcatraz*) have been in quieter, gently humorous roles.
1949: D.O.A. 1950: Kiss Tomorrow Goodbye. Where the Sidewalk Ends. Halls of Montezuma. 1951: Only the Valiant. The Mob (GB: Remember That Face). Red Mountain. Flame of Araby. *Benjy. 1952: Kansas City Confidential (GB: The Secret Four). The Turning Point. The Man from the Alamo. 1953: Stalag 17. Man Crazy. The Charge at Feather River. Gun Fury. 1954: Prince Valiant. The Lone Gun. Riot in Cell Block 11. Return from the Sea. 1955: The Prodigal. Raw Edge. The Return of Jack Slade (GB: Texas Rose). Bobby Ware is Missing. 1956: Fury at Gunsight Pass. Mohawk. Gun Brothers. Love Me Tender. Three Outlaws. 1957: The Tin Star. The Way to the Gold. The Lonely Man. 1958: Cry Terror! Galvanised Yankee (TV). Badman's Country. 1959: Five Gates to Hell. The Scarface Mob. 1960: The Adventures of Huckleberry Finn. Alcatraz Express (GB: TV). 1961: The Last Sunset. The George Raft Story (GB: Spin of a Coin). 1962: Birdman of Alcatraz. Hero's Island. 1965: That Darn Cat! 1967: Three Guns for Texas (TV). 1968: Backtrack (TV). 1969: The Desperados. 1970: Marriage: Year One (TV). Tora! Tora! Tora! Lock, Stock and Barrel (TV). 1971: Hitched (GB: Westward the Wagon) (TV). Two for the Money (TV). 1972: No Place to Run (TV). The Adventures of Nick Carter (TV). 1973: Cahill, United States Marshal (GB: Cahill). The Deadly Trackers. This is a Hi-Jack. 1974: Killdozer (TV). Death Stalk (TV). Scalawag. The Police Connection. 1975: Psychic Killer. The Mad Bomber. Barbary

Coast (TV. GB: In Old San Francisco). 1976: Eaten Alive (GB: Death Trap). 1977: Fire! (TV. GB: cinemas). The Mouse and His Child (voice only). Hi-Riders. Captains Courageous (TV). 1978: Seven from Heaven. Five Days from Home. 1979: Angels' Brigade. The Ninth Configuration/Twinkle, Twinkle, Killer Kane. 1980: Without Warning. 1983: Evils of the Night.

BRANDO, Marlon 1924–
Magnetic, husky American star who created painfully realistic characters that often gripped an audience with their primeval force. His blurred diction was much imitated, he gained a reputation for being 'difficult' and a Brando film was rarely less than controversial. His appeal to women faded in the 1960s, but he returned in triumph a decade later to win his second Oscar for *The Godfather*. His first was for *On the Waterfront*, and there have been five other nominations, for *A Streetcar Named Desire*, *Viva Zapata!*, *Julius Caesar*, *Sayonara* and *Last Tango in Paris*. Married to actresses Anna Kashfi (1957–1959) and Movita (1960–1968), first and second of three.
1950: The Men. 1951: A Streetcar Named Desire. 1952: Viva Zapata! 1953: Julius Caesar. The Wild One. 1954: On the Waterfront. Désirée. 1955: Guys and Dolls. 1956: The Teahouse of the August Moon. 1957: Sayonara. 1958: The Young Lions. 1959: The Fugitive Kind. 1960: One-Eyed Jacks. 1962: Mutiny on the Bounty. 1963: The Ugly American. 1964: Bedtime Story. *Tiger by the Tail. 1965: Morituri (GB: The Saboteur, Code Name Morituri). 1966: The Chase. *Meet Marlon Brando. The Appaloosa (GB: Southwest to Sonora). A Countess from Hong Kong. 1967: Reflections in a Golden Eye. 1968: The Night of the Following Day. Candy. 1969: Burn! (GB: Queimada!). 1971: The Nightcomers. 1972: The Godfather. 1973: Last Tango in Paris. 1976: The Missouri Breaks. 1978: Superman. 1979: Apocalypse Now. Raoni (narrator only). 1980: The Formula.

As director: 1960: One-Eyed Jacks.

BRAZZI, Rossano 1916–
A former lawyer who, after 15 years in the Italian cinema, became one of Hollywood's Latin lovers. The light-haired, courteous, romantic Italian he projected with such

relaxed ease was perhaps an extension of his own long and happy marriage. Unable or unwilling, however, to change the image, his international appeal decreased after a few years, and he became involved in a succession of increasingly unlikely ventures. Once claimed to have made 200 films.

1939: Processo e morte di Socrate. Il ponte di vetro. 1940: Kean. Ritorno. La forza bruta. Tosca. 1941: E' caduta una donna. Il re si diverte (US: The King's Jester). Il bravo di Venezia. 1942: Una signora dell'Ovest. I due Foscari. La Gorgona. Rendenzione. Noi vivi. Addio Kira! Maria Malibran. Il treno crociato. L'accusata. 1943: Baruffe chiozotte. Silenzio si gira! La case senza tempo. Damals. 1945: Le resa di titi (US: The Merry Chase). Malia. I dieci commandamenti/The Ten Commandments. 1946: L'aquila nera (GB: The Black Eagle). La grande aurora. Furia. 1947: Il passatore (US: Bullet for Stefano). I diavolo bianco. Il contrabbandieri del mare. La monaca di Monza. Il corriere del re. Eleanora Duse. 1948: Oliva. The Mistress of Treves. 1949: Little Women. Volcano. 1950: Gli inesorabili. Toselli. Romanzo d'amore. La corona negra. 1951: Incantesimo tragico. Plus fort que la haine. La vendetta di aquila nera. La leggenda di Genoveffa. 1952: La prigoniera della torre di fuoco. L'ingiusta condanna (US: Guilt is Not Mine). La spigolatride di Sapri. La donna che inventò l'amore. Eran trecento. La barriera della legga. Quelli che non muoiono. Il boia di Lilla. Il figlio di Legardère. 1953: C'era una volta Angelo Musco. Carne de horca. Il terrore dell'Andalusia (GB and US: Flesh and Desire). 1954: La contessa di Castiglione. Three Coins in the Fountain. Angela. The Barefoot Contessa. 1955: Il conte aquila. Summer Madness (US: Summertime). Gli ultimi cinque minuti. Faccia da mascalzone. 1956: Loser Takes All. 1957: Interlude. The Story of Esther Costello (US: Golden Virgin). Legend of the Lost. 1958: South Pacific. A Certain Smile. 1959: Count Your Blessings. L'assedio di Siracusa (GB and US: The Siege of Syracuse). Austerlitz (GB: The Battle of Austerlitz). 1962: The Light in the Piazza. Milady and the Musketeers. Mondo Cane. Die Rote. Les quatres verités (GB and US: Three Fables of Love). Rome Adventure. 1963: Dark Purpose/L'ingorgo. 1964: La ragazza in prestito (US: A Girl for Hire). Il marito latino. 1965: Un amore. The Battle of

the Villa Fiorita. Engagement Italiano. 1966: Per amore ... per magià ... The Christmas That Almost Wasn't. La ragazza del bersagliere. 1967: The Bobo. Woman Times Seven. One Step to Hell. 1968: Sette uomini e un cervello. Andante. Diario segreto di una minorenne. Krakatoa – East of Java. Salvare la faccia (US: Psychout for Murder). Il rubamento. 1969: The Italian Job. Assignment Istanbul. Honeymoon with a Stranger (TV). 1970: Intimà proibita di una giovane sposa. The Adventurers. 1971: Political Asylum. Il sesso del diavolo. Il giorno del giudizio. 1972: The Great Waltz. Clown. Morir per amar. Detras de esa puerta. 1973: Racconti proibiti di nulla vertiti (GB: Master of Love). Mr Kingstreet's War (TV). Frankenstein's Castle of Freaks. 1974: Drums of Vengeance/Drummer of Vengeance. 1976: Day of the Assassin. I telefoni bianchi. 1978: Caribia. 1979: Fatti nostri. 1980: The Final Conflict (later Omen III The Final Conflict). 1981: Io e Catherina. 1982: Il paramedico. La vocazione di Suor Teresa. La voce. 1983: Fear City. 1984: The Maltese Connection/Final Justice. 1985: Formula for a Murder.

As director: *1966: The Christmas That Almost Wasn't. 1968: Salvare la faccia (US: Psychout for Murder). Il rubamento.*

BRENT, Evelyn (Mary Riggs) 1899–1975
Dark-haired, oval-faced, sharp-featured American actress who started as a 15-year-old extra and remained popular throughout the silent period on both sides of the Atlantic (especially after making several films in Britain from 1920 to 1922) reaching a peak of achievement in von Sternberg's *Underworld* (1927). Never as popular after sound, she pursued her career doggedly, playing featured roles (albeit in small 'B' pictures) well into her forties. Died from a heart attack.

1914: A Gentleman from Mississippi. The Heart of a Painted Woman. The Pit. 1915: The Shooting of Dan McGrew. 1916: The Soul Market. The Spell of the Yukon. The Lure of Heart's Desire. The Iron Woman. Playing with Fire. The Weakness of Strength. 1917: Raffles, the Amateur Cracksman. To the Death. Who's Your Neighbor? The Millionaire's Double. 1918: Daybreak. 1919: The Other Man's Wife. Fool's Gold. Help, Help, Police. The Glorious Lady. Border River. Into the River. 1920: The

Shuttle of Life. The Law Divine. 1921: Sybil. Demos (US: Why Men Forget). Laughter and Tears. Sonia (US: The Woman Who Came Back). The Door That Has No Key. Circus Jim. 1922: Married to a Mormon. The Experiment. Pages of Life. Spanish Jade. Trapped by the Mormons. 1923: Held to Answer. Loving Lies. 1924: Arizona Express. The Cyclone Rider. The Desert Outlaw. The Lone Chance. My Husband's Wives. Silk Stocking Sal. The Plunderer. Shadow of the East (GB: Shadow of the Desert). 1925: Smooth As Satin. Alias Mary Flynn. The Dangerous Flirt. Broadway Lady. Forbidden Cargo (GB: The Dangerous Cargo). Lady Robin Hood. Midnight Molly. Three Wise Crooks (GB: Three of a Kind). 1926: The Flame of the Argentine. The Imposter. Love 'em and Leave 'em. Queen of Diamonds. The Jade Cup. Secret Orders. 1927: Blind Alley. Love's Greatest Mistake. Woman's Wares. Underworld (GB: Paying the Penalty). 1928: Beau Sabreur. A Night of Mystery. The Dragnet. The Last Command. The Mating Call. The Showdown. Interference. His Tiger Lady. 1929: Broadway. Darkened Rooms. Fast Company. Woman Trap. Why Bring That Up? 1930: Framed. Madonna of the Streets. Paramount on Parade. Slightly Scarlet. The Silver Horde. 1931: The Mad Parade (GB: Forgotten Women). Traveling Husbands. The Pagan Lady. 1932: High Pressure. Attorney for the Defense. The Crusader. 1933: The World Gone Mad (GB: The Public Be Hanged). 1935: Home on the Range. The Nitwits. Symphony of Living. 1936: It Couldn't Have Happened. The President's Mystery. Hopalong Cassidy Returns. Jungle Jim (serial). Penthouse Party (GB: Without Children). Song of the Trail. 1937: Night Club Scandal. King of the Gamblers. Daughter of Shanghai (GB: Daughter of the Orient). The Last Train from Madrid. 1938: Mr Wong, Detective. The Law West of Tombstone. Sudden Bill Dorn. Speed Limited. 1939: Daughter of the Tong. Panama Lady. The Mad Empress (GB: Carlotta, the Mad Empress). 1941: Forced Landing. Wide Open Town. Dangerous Lady. Emergency Landing. Holt of the Secret Service (serial). Ellery Queen and the Murder Ring (GB: The Murder Ring). 1942: The Wrecking Crew. The Pay-Off. Westward Ho! 1943: The Seventh Victim. Spy Train. Bowery Champs. Silent Witness (GB: The Attorney for the Defence). 1946: Raiders of the South. 1947: Robin Hood of Monterey. 1958: The Mystery of the Golden Eye (GB: The Golden Eye). Stage Struck. 1950: Again, Pioneers.

BRENT, George (G. B. Nolan) 1904–1979
Irish-born George Brent (he fled to America in the 1922 'troubles' with a price on his head) was a leading man, but never quite a star. He always seemed to be billed beneath the leading lady, most particularly Bette Davis, whom he supported on seven occasions. In the 1930s he moved from rugged action heroes to tender, courteous swains in much the same way as did Rock Hudson in the 1950s. He appeared out of the blue in 1978, playing a judge, but died from emphysema the following year. Married to Ruth Chatterton (1932–1934) and

Ann Sheridan (1942–1943), second and fourth of six wives.

1928: The K-Guy. 1930: Those We Love. Love, Honor and Betray. The Big Trail. Under Suspicion. 1931: Lightning Warrior (serial). Once a Sinner. Fair Warning. Homicide Squad. Charlie Chan Carries On. Ex-Bad Boy. 1932: So Big. Life Begins (GB: The Dawn of Life). The Rich Are Always with Us. Week-End Marriage (GB: Working Wives). Miss Pinkerton. The Purchase Price. The Crash. They Call It Sin (GB: The Way of Life). 1933: 42nd Street. The Keyhole. Luxury Liner. Lilly Turner. Private Detective 62. From Headquarters. Baby Face. Female. 1934: Housewife. Stamboul Quest. Desirable. The Painted Veil. 1935: Living on Velvet. Front Page Woman. Stranded. The Goose and the Gander. Special Agent. In Person. The Right to Live (GB: The Sacred Flame). Snowed Under. The Golden Arrow. The Case Against Mrs Ames. Give Me Your Heart (GB: Sweet Aloes). More Than a Secretary. God's Country and the Woman. 1937: The Go-Getter. Mountain Justice. Submarine D-1. 1938: Jezebel. Racket Busters. Gold Is Where You Find It. 1939: Secrets of an Actress. Dark Victory. The Old Maid. The Rains Came. Wings of the Navy. 1940: The Man Who Talked Too Much. 'Til We Meet Again. The Fighting 69th. Adventure in Diamonds. South of Suez. 1941: Honeymoon for Three. International Lady. They Dare Not Love. The Great Lie. 1942: The Gay Sisters. In This Our Life. Twin Beds. You Can't Escape for Ever. Silver Queen. My Reputation (released 1946). 1945: The Affairs of Susan. Experiment Perilous. The Spiral Staircase. 1946: Tomorrow is Forever. Lover Come Back. Temptation. 1947: Slave Girl. Out of the Blue. The Corpse Came COD. Christmas Eve. 1948: Luxury Liner (and 1933 film). Angel on the Amazon (GB: Drums Along the Amazon). Montana Belle (released 1952). 1949: Red Canyon. Illegal Entry. The Kid from Cleveland. Bride for Sale. 1951: FBI Girl. 1952: The Last Page (US: Manbait). 1953: Tangier Incident. 1955: †The Rains of Ranchipur. 1956: †Death of a Scoundrel. 1978: Born Again.

† Scenes deleted from final release print

BRIAN, David (Brian Davis) 1914–
Tall, fair-haired American actor who spent

many years on stage (he began as a theatre doorman) before Warners signed him to a contract in 1949. There, his sardonic smile and distinctive voice quickly had him typed as villains in crime movies, especially the melodramas of Joan Crawford. He left Warners after four years, and never seemed as effective outside their environment. Married to former Republic star Adrian Booth (*qv*) since 1949.

1949: G-Men (new prologue shot for reissue version of 1935 film). Flamingo Road. Beyond the Forest. Intruder in the Dust. 1950: The Damned Don't Cry. Breakthrough. The Great Jewel Robber. 1951: Inside Straight. Fort Worth. Inside the Walls of Folsom Prison. 1952: This Woman is Dangerous. Million Dollar Mermaid (GB: The One Piece Bathing Suit). Springfield Rifle. 1953: Ambush at Tomahawk Gap. A Perilous Journey. 1954: The High and the Mighty. Dawn at Socorro. 1955: Timberjack. 1956: Fury at Gunsight Pass. The First Traveling Saleslady. The White Squaw. No Place to Hide. Accused of Murder. 1958: Ghost of the China Sea. 1959: The Rabbit Trap. 1961: A Pocketful of Miracles. 1962: How the West Was Won. 1966: The Rare Breed. Castle of Evil. The Destructors. 1968: The Girl Who Knew Too Much. The Manhunter (TV). 1969: Childish Things. 1970: Tora! Tora! Tora! 1971: The Seven Minutes. 1972: Confessions of Tom Harris (TV).

BRIAN, Mary (Louise Dantzler) 1908–
Petite, brown-haired, personable Hollywood leading lady with wide blue eyes. She started her career as Wendy in *Peter Pan*, and was perhaps unfortunately tagged 'the sweetest

girl in motion pictures' by fan magazines. Possibly because of this, and despite some good films in Britain, her career petered out earlier than it should have done.

*1924: Peter Pan. 1925: The Little French Girl. The Air Mail. The Street of Forgotten Men. A Regular Fellow. 1926: Beau Geste. The Enchanted Hill. More Pay – Less Work. The Prince of Tempters. Brown of Harvard. Paris at Midnight. Behind the Front. Stepping Alone. 1927: Running Wild. Two Flaming Youths. Man Power. Knockout Reilly. Her Father Said No. Shanghai Bound. High Hat. 1928: Harold Teen. The Big Killing. Varsity. Under The Tonto Rim. Forgotten Faces. Someone to Love. Partners in Crime. 1929: River of Romance. The Man I Love. The Virginian. The Marriage Playground. Black Waters. 1930: The Light of Western Stars. The Royal Family of Broadway. Only Saps Work. The Social Lion. Paramount on Parade. Only the Brave. Burning Up. The Kibitzer (GB: Busybody). 1931: The Front Page. Gun Smoke. Captain Applejack. The Runaround. Homicide Squad (GB: The Lost Men). 1932: The Unwritten Law. It's Tough to Be Famous. Blessed Event. Manhattan Tower. 1933: Girl Missing. The World Gone Mad (GB: The Public Be Hanged). Hard to Handle. Song of the Eagle. One Year Later. Moonlight and Pretzels (GB: Moonlight and Melody). 1934: Shadows of Sing Sing. Fog. College Rhythm. Monte Carlo Nights. Ever Since Eve. Private Scandal. The Man on the Flying Trapeze (GB: The Memory Expert). 1935: Charlie Chan in Paris. *Star Night at the Cocoanut Grove. 1936: Killer at Large. Spendthrift. Three Married Men. Two's Company. The Amazing Quest of Ernest Bliss (US: Romance and Riches). 1937: Week-end Millionaire. Navy Blues. The Affairs of Cappy Ricks. 1943: I Escaped from the Gestapo (GB: No Escape). Danger! Women at Work. Calaboose. 1947: The Dragnet.*

BRIDGES, Beau 1941–
The elder son of Lloyd Bridges (*qv*), Beau gained some experience as a child actor in the 1940s; but he was older than most people imagined when he made his biggest impact as an innocent abroad, in *Gaily, Gaily* and *The Landlord*. Thereafter, though, his indeterminate features were the subject of much miscasting, and he was always more interesting as devious or low-key characters than

as upright heroes. One experiment in direction has not so far been followed up.

1948: No Minor Vices. Force of Evil. 1949: The Red Pony. Zamba (GB: Zamba the Gorilla). 1951: The Company She Keeps. 1961: The Explosive Generation. 1965: Valley of the Giants. 1967: The Incident. Attack on the Iron Coast. 1968: For Love of Ivy. 1969: Gaily, Gaily (GB: Chicago, Chicago). Adam's Woman. 1970: The Landlord. 1971: The Christian Licorice Store. 1972: Hammersmith is Out. Child's Play. 1973: Lovin' Molly. Your Three Minutes Are Up. The Man without a Country (TV). 1974: The Stranger Who Looks Like Me (TV). 1975: Medical Story (TV). The Other Side of the Mountain/A Window to the Sky. 1976: One Summer Love (TV). Swashbuckler (GB: The Scarlet Buccaneer). 1977: Greased Lightning. Behind the Iron Mask (GB: The Fifth Musketeer). 1978: The Four Feathers (US: TV). Two-Minute Warning. Something Light (US: Shimmering Light). The President's Mistress (TV). Norma Rae. 1979: The Runner Stumbles. The Child Stealer (TV). Silver Dream Racer. 1981: Honky Tonk Freeway. †The Kid from Nowhere (TV). 1982: Night Crossing. Love Child. Witness for the Prosecution (TV). 1983: Heart Like a Wheel. 1984: The Hotel New Hampshire. The Red-Light Sting (TV). 1986: Outrage! (TV). A Fighting Choice (TV).

† And directed

BRIDGES, Jeff 1949–
More rugged than his brother Beau, Jeff Bridges has also been acting from an early age. Despite a run of critically acclaimed pictures unparalleled in recent times by a young leading man, he doesn't seem quite to have acquired the charisma to become a bankable star. Despite his versatility, Bridges hit a bad patch with film roles in the late 1970s, but box-office success returned in the early 1980s, and he remains one of the most interesting of American stars in their thirties. Nominated for Academy Awards in *The Last Picture Show*, *Thunderbolt and Lightfoot* and *Starman*.
1951: The Company She Keeps. 1969: Silent Night, Lonely Night (TV). Halls of Anger. 1970: In Search of America. †The Yin and the Yang of Dr Go. 1971: The Last Picture Show. Fat City. 1972: Bad Company. 1973: The Last American Hero. Lolly Madonna XXX (GB: The Lolly Madonna War). The Iceman

Cometh. 1974: Thunderbolt and Lightfoot. Rancho de Luxe. 1975: Hearts of the West (GB: Hollywood Cowboy). Tilt. 1976: King Kong. Stay Hungry. 1977: Winter Kills (released 1979). 1978: Somebody Killed Her Husband. 1980: Heaven's Gate. Cutter and Bone (later Cutter's Way). The American Success Company (later $uccess). 1981: The Last Unicorn (voice only). 1982: Kiss Me Goodbye. Tron. 1984: Against All Odds. Starman. 1985: 8 Million Ways to Die. Jagged Edge. 1986: The Morning After.

† Unreleased

BRIDGES, Lloyd 1913–
Tallow-haired Hollywood actor in films after being spotted in off-Broadway plays. Bridges's screen characters were usually unreliable: braggarts who would back down; charmers who would let you down. He had a nice line in cynical sneers, and it was a pity he didn't rise above about fifth place on cast lists until the early fifties. TV gave him his greatest success in an underwater series called *Sea Hunt*, and he still works prodigiously in the medium.
*1941: Honolulu Lu. The Lone Wolf Takes a Chance. Cadets on Parade. Son of Davy Crockett. I Was a Prisoner on Devil's Island. Here Comes Mr Jordan. The Medico of Painted Springs (GB: Doctor's Alibi). Our Wife. Two Latins from Manhattan. Harmon of Michigan. Three Girls about Town. The Royal Mounted Patrol. Harvard, Here I Come (GB: Here I Come). You Belong to Me (GB: Good Morning, Doctor). 1942: The Wife Takes a Flyer (GB: A Yank in Dutch). Underground Agent. North of the Rockies (GB: False Clues). West of Tombstone. Blondie Goes to College (GB: The Boss Said No). Sing for Your Supper. Shut My Big Mouth. Canal Zone. Stand By All Networks. Tramp, Tramp, Tramp. Alias Boston Blackie. Hello, Annapolis (GB: Personal Honour). Sweetheart of the Fleet. Meet the Stewarts. Flight Lieutenant. Riders of the Northland. Atlantic Convoy. The Talk of the Town. Spirit of Stanford. A Man's World. Pardon My Gun. 1943: Commandos Strike at Dawn. Sahara. The Heat's On (GB: Tropicana). Hail to the Rangers (GB: Illegal Rights). *The Great Glover. Passport to Suez. The Crime Doctor's Strangest Case (GB: The Strangest Case). Destroyer. 1944: Two-man Submarine. Louisiana Hayride. Once Upon a*

Time. She's a Soldier Too. The Master Race. Saddle Leather Law (GB: The Poisoner). 1945: A Walk in the Sun. Strange Confession. Secret Agent X-9 (serial). 1946: Miss Susie Slagle's. Abilene Town. Canyon Passage. 1947: Ramrod. The Trouble With Women. Unconquered. 1948: Secret Service Investigator. Sixteen Fathoms Deep. Moonrise. *Mr Whitney Had a Notion. 1949: Red Canyon. Hide-Out. Home of the Brave. Calamity Jane and Sam Bass. Trapped. 1950: Colt '45. Rocketship XM. The White Tower. The Sound of Fury (GB: Try and Get Me). 1951: Little Big Horn (GB: The Fighting 7th). Three Steps North. The Whistle at Eaton Falls (GB: Richer Than the Earth). 1952: High Noon. Plymouth Adventure. Last of the Comanches (GB: The Sabre and the Arrow). The Tall Texan. 1953: City of Bad Men. The Kid from Left Field. The Limping Man. 1954: Pride of the Blue Grass (GB: Prince of the Blue Grass). 1955: Wichita: Apache Woman. Third Party Risk (US: The Deadly Game). 1956: Wetbacks: Heritage of Anger (TV). The Rainmaker. 1957: Ride Out for Revenge. 1958: The Goddess. 1962: Who Killed Julie Greer (TV). 1966: Around the World Under the Sea. 1967: The Daring Game. Attack on the Iron Coast. 1969: The Happy Ending. Lost Flight (TV). The Love War (TV). The Silent Gun (TV). Silent Night, Lonely Night (TV). 1970: Do You Take This Stranger? (TV). 1971: A Tattered Web (TV). To Find a Man. The Deadly Dream (TV). 1972: Crime Club (TV). Scuba (narrator only). Haunts of the Very Rich (TV). Trouble Comes to Town (TV). 1973: Running Wild. Death Race (TV). 1974: Stowaway to the Moon (TV). Deliver Us from Evil. 1975: The Return of Joe Forrester (TV). 1977: Behind the Iron Mask (GB: The Fifth Musketeer). The Force of Evil (TV). 1978: Something Light (US: Shimmering Light). The Great Wallendas (TV). Telethon (TV). 1979: Disaster on the Coastliner (TV. Later: Express to Terror). Bear Island. Mission Galactica (TV. GB: cinemas). The Critical List (TV). 1980: Airplane! 1982: Airplane II The Sequel. Life of the Party: The Story of Beatrice (TV). 1983: Grace Kelly (TV). 1985: Hollywood Air Force.

BRITTON, Barbara (B. Brantingham)
1919–1980
Radiant Hollywood redhead whose blue-eyed

charms proved a natural for outdoor action dramas of the forties. Films neglected her natural talent for light comedy and she enjoyed her greatest success on television, with a series, *Mr and Mrs North*, followed by a 12-year commercial stint on which she became known as 'the Revlon lady'. Remained active on stage and television, until her early death from gastric cancer.

1941: Secrets of the Wasteland. Louisiana Purchase. 1942: The Fleet's In. Beyond the Blue Horizon. Wake Island. Reap the Wild Wind. Mrs Wiggs of the Cabbage Patch. 1943: Young and Willing. *The Last Will and Testament of Tom Smith. So Proudly We Hail! 1944: The Story of Dr Wassell. Till We Meet Again. 1945: The Great John L (GB: A Man Called Sullivan). Captain Kidd. 1946: The Virginian. The Fabulous Suzanne. They Made Me a Killer. The Return of Monte Cristo (GB: Monte Cristo's Revenge). 1947: Gunfighters. 1948: Albuquerque (GB: Silver City). The Untamed Breed. Mr Reckless. 1949: I Shot Jesse James. Cover-Up. Loaded Pistols. 1950: Champagne for Caesar. Bandit Queen. 1952: The Raiders. 1953: Ride the Man Down. Bwana Devil. 1954: Dragonfly Squadron. 1955: Ain't Misbehavin'. The Spoilers. Night Freight.

BRITTON, Tony 1924–
Diffident English actor with wavy hair and shy smile, who turned to acting in his twenties after working for an estate agent and an aircraft company. His quiet authority and light touch in comedy made him a popular star of British films for some eight years. Later in character roles, with most notable success in television light comedy.

1951: Salute the Toff. 1956: Loser Takes All. 1957: The Birthday Present. 1958: Behind the Mask. Operation Amsterdam. 1959: The Heart of a Man. The Rough and the Smooth (US: Portrait of a Sinner). 1960: Suspect (US: The Risk). 1961: The Horsemasters. Stork Talk. 1962: The Break. The Last Winter. 1963: Dr Syn – Alias the Scarecrow. 1970: There's a Girl in My Soup. 1971: Sunday, Bloody Sunday. Mr Forbush and the Penguins. 1973: The Day of the Jackal. Night Watch. 1977: The People That Time Forgot. 1978: Agatha.

BRODIE, Steve (John Stevens) 1919–
Burly, surly, puff-cheeked, dark-haired American actor – he took his name from a

famous turn-of-the-century gambler – who mostly played bad guys with one hand in their pockets, but also bulldozed his way through a few leading roles in second-feature crime yarns of the 1940s. He played more benevolent characters in later years.

1944: Follow the Boys. Ladies Courageous. Thirty Seconds over Tokyo. *Easy Life. A Walk in the Sun. It's in the Bag! (GB: The Fifth Chair). 1945: *Fall Guy. The Crimson Canary. This Man's Navy. Anchors Aweigh. 1946: Badman's Territory. Criminal Court. Young Widow. The Falcon's Adventure. Sunset Pass. 1947: Desperate. Trail Street. Out of the Past (GB: Build My Gallows High). Crossfire. Thunder Mountain. Code of the West. 1948: Arizona Ranger. Bodyguard. Station West. Return of the Badmen. Guns of Hate. 1949: I Cheated the Law. Rose of the Yukon. Home of the Brave. Massacre River. Treasure of Monte Cristo. The Big Wheel. Tough Assignment. Brothers in the Saddle. The Rustlers. 1950: Winchester '73. It's a Small World. Kiss Tomorrow Goodbye. The Admiral Was a Lady. The Armored Car Robbery. The Great Plane Robbery. Counterspy Meets Scotland Yard. 1951: The Steel Helmet. Fighting Coast Guard. M. Sword of Monte Cristo. Two-Dollar Bettor (GB: Beginner's Luck). Only the Valiant. Joe Palooka in Triple Cross (GB: The Triple Cross). 1952: Army Bound. Bal Tabarin. Three for Bedroom C. Lady in the Iron Mask. The Will Rogers Story (GB: The Story of Will Rogers). 1953: White Lightning. Donovan's Brain. Sea of Lost Ships. The Charge at Feather River. The Beast from 20,000 Fathoms. 1954: The Far Country. The Caine Mutiny. 1956: The Cruel Tower. 1957: Gun Duel in Durango. The Crooked Circle. Under Fire. 1958: Sierra Baron. Spy in the Sky. 1959: Arson for Hire. 1960: Three Came to Kill. 1961: Blue Hawaii. 1962: A Girl Named Tamiko. 1963: Of Love and Desire. A Bullet for Billy the Kid. 1964: Roustabout. 1969: Cycle Savages. 1975: The Giant Spider Invasion. 1984: Mugsy's Girls. 1986: The Wizard of Speed and Time.

BROLIN, James (J. Bruderlin) 1940–
Tall, dark-haired, hunk-ish American leading man reminiscent of Clint Walker (*qv*). He had trouble getting decent roles in Hollywood until television success as the junior partner in *Marcus Welby MD*. His cinema portrait of

Clark Gable was not a popular success and, after a couple of box-office hits in the late 1970s, he was relegated to tough heroes of minor action films.

1963: Take Her, She's Mine. 1964: Goodbye Charlie. John Goldfarb, Please Come Home. 1965: Von Ryan's Express. Morituri (GB: The Saboteur Code Name Morituri). Our Man Flint. 1966: Way … Way Out. Fantastic Voyage. 1967: Capetown Affair. 1968: The Boston Strangler. 1972: Skyjacked. Westworld. A Short Walk to Daylight (TV). 1973: Trapped (TV. GB: cinemas as Doberman Patrol). Class of '63 (TV). 1975: Gable and Lombard. 1976: The Car. 1977: Capricorn One. 1978: Steel Cowboy (TV). Night of the Juggler. 1979: The Amityville Horror. 1981: High Risk/Big Bucks. Ambush Murders (TV). 1982: Mae West (TV). 1983: White Water Rebels (TV). Cowboy (TV). 1985: Beverly Hills Cowboy Blues (TV).

BRONSON, Charles (C. Buchinski) 1921–
Rugged, hatchet-faced, latterly moustachioed American star, a former juvenile delinquent, miner and boxer who turned to acting after World War II. For many years cast as villains and men of violence, he broke through to stardom only in 1968, after which he played *heroes* and men of violence at just as prolific a rate as before. One of the world's top box-office stars through most of the 1970s, he has been married (second) to British-born actress Jill Ireland (*qv*) since 1968.

1950: †USS Teakettle (later You're in the Navy Now). 1951: †The People Against O'Hara. †The Mob (GB: Remember That Face). 1952: †Red Skies of Montana. †My

Six Convicts. †The Marrying Kind. †Pat and Mike. †Diplomatic Courier. †Bloodhounds of Broadway. 1953: ‡House of Wax. ‡The Clown. ‡Miss Sadie Thompson. 1954: ‡Crime Wave (GB: The City is Dark). ‡Tennessee Champ. ‡Riding Shotgun. ‡Apache. ‡Vera Cruz. Drum Beat. 1955: Big House USA. Target Zero. 1956: Explosion (TV. GB: cinemas). Jubal. 1957: Run of the Arrow. 1958: Machine Gun Kelly. Gang War. Showdown at Boot Hill. When Hell Broke Loose. Ten North Frederick. 1959: Never So Few. 1960: The Magnificent Seven. 1961: Master of the World. A Thunder of Drums. X-15. 1962: Kid Galahad. This Rugged Land (TV. GB: cinemas). 1963: The Great Escape. Four for Texas. 1964: Guns of Diablo (TV. GB: cinemas). 1965: The Sandpiper. Battle of the Bulge. 1966: This Property is Condemned. 1967: The Dirty Dozen. Guns for San Sebastian. 1968: Adieu leami (GB: Farewell Friend). Villa Rides! Once Upon a Time … in the West. 1969: Twinky (US: Lola). Rider on the Rain. 1970: You Can't Win 'Em All. Violent City (US: The Family). De la part des copains (US: Cold Sweat). Red Sun. 1971. Quelqu'un derrière la porte (GB: Two Minds for Murder. US: Someone behind the Door). Chato's Land. 1972: The Mechanic (later Killer of Killers). The Valachi Papers. 1973: The Stone Killer. Valdez the Halfbreed (GB: The Valdez Horses. US: Chino). 1974: Mr Majestyk. Death Wish. 1975: Breakout. Hard Times (GB: The Streetfighter). From Noon Till Three. 1976: Breakheart Pass. St Ives. Raid on Entebbe (TV. GB: cinemas). 1977: Telefon. The White Buffalo. 1978: Love and Bullets. 1979: Cabo Blanco. 1980: Death Hunt. Borderline (GB: TV). 1981: Death Wish II. 1982: 10 to Midnight. 1983: The Evil That Men Do. 1985: Death Wish 3. Act of Vengeance (TV). 1986: Murphy's Law. Assassin. Death Wish IV.

† As Charles Buchinski   ‡ As Charles Buchinsky

BROOK, Clive (Clifford Brook) 1887–1974
British-born star of handsome if stern features. The son of an opera singer, Brook became a musician, but turned to acting after being invalided out of World War I in 1918. Equally adept at stiff upper-lip drama and sophisticated comedy, he had no difficulty holding his own in Hollywood (until his age

began to tell) after success in home-grown films. After World War II he devoted his time to the stage. Father of actors Faith and Lyndon Brook.
1920: Trent's Last Case. Kissing Cup's Race. 1921: Her Penalty. The Loudwater Mystery. Daniel Deronda. A Sportsman's Wife. Sonia. Christie Johnstone. 1922: *Vanity Fair: extract. *A Talr of Two Cities: extract. *Whispering. *The Sheik. Shirley. Married to a Mormon. Stable Companions. *Rigoletto: extract. *La Traviata: extract. The Experiment. *Sir Rupert's Wife. A Debt of Honour. Love and a Whirlwind. *The Parson's Fight. Through Fire and Water. 1923: This Freedom. Out to Win. *The Reverse of the Medal. The Royal Oak. Woman to Woman. The Money Habit. 1924: The White Shadow (US: White Shadows). *The City of Stars. The Wine of Life. The Passionate Adventure. Human Desires. Recoil. Christine of the Hungry Heart. The Mirage. 1925: When Love Grows Cold. Enticement. Seven Sinners. Declassée (GB: The Social Exile). *Peeps into Hollywood No. 9. Playing with Souls. If Marriage Fails. The Woman Hater. Compromise. The Home Maker. The Pleasure Buyers. 1926: Why Girls Go Back Home. For Alimony Only. You Never Know Women. The Popular Sin. Three Faces East. 1927: Afraid to Love. Barbed Wire. Underworld. Hula. The Devil Dancer. French Dressing (GB: Lessons for Wives). 1928: Midnight Madness. The Yellow Lily. The Perfect Crime. Forgotten Faces. The Four Feathers. 1929: Interference. A Dangerous Woman. Charming Sinners. The Return of Sherlock Holmes. The Laughing Lady. 1930: Slightly Scarlet. Paramount on Parade. Sweethearts and Wives. Anybody's Woman. 1931: East Lynne. Tarnished Lady. Scandal Sheet. The Lawyer's Secret. Silence. 24 Hours (GB: The Hours Between). Husband's Holiday. 1932: The Man from Yesterday. Sherlock Holmes. The Night of June 13. Shanghai Express. Make Me a Star. 1933: Gallant Lady. Cavalcade. Midnight Club. 1934: Where Sinners Meet (GB: The Dover Road). If I Were Free (GB: Behold We Live). Let's Try Again. 1935: Dressed to Thrill. The Dictator (US: The Loves of a Dictator). 1936: Love in Exile. The Lonely Road (US: Scotland Yard Commands). 1937: Action for Slander. 1938: The Ware Case. 1939: Return to Yesterday. 1940: Convoy. 1941: Freedom Radio (US: A Voice in the Night). Breach of Promise (US: Adventure in Blackmail). 1943: The Flemish Farm. The Shipbuilders. 1944: †On Approval. 1963: The List of Adrian Messenger.

† Also directed

BROOK, Lesley (L. Learoyd) 1916–
Quietly pretty, highly animated, sympathetic, dark-haired British actress handed a Warner Brothers contract at 19 (she made several films for their British arm, but none for Hollywood who would probably have misused her in Geraldine Fitzgerald fashion) and a star in her first film. Much seen in both comedies and thrillers of the late 1930s, she drifted away from the cinema soon after World War II.

1937: The Vulture. Side Street Angel. Patricia Gets Her Man. The Man Who Made Diamonds. The Dark Stairway. 1938: Quiet Please! Glamour Girl. The Viper. It's in the Blood. Dead Men Tell No Tales. The Return of Carol Deane. 1939: The Nursemaid Who Disappeared. 1940: The Briggs Family. 1942: Rose of Tralee. Variety Jubilee. 1943: When We Are Married. The Bells Go Down. I'll Walk Beside You. 1944: Twilight Hour. 1945: For You Alone. The Trojan Brothers. 1948: House of Darkness. 1949: The Fool and the Pincess.

BROOKE, Hillary (Beatrice Peterson) 1914–

Tall, determined-looking Hollywood blonde who often played predatory women and belongs up there with Lynn Bari, Merry Anders (both qv) and all those other actresses who kept their careers going for 20 years or more despite never becoming major stars. Miss Brooke was a first-rate bad girl and occasionally a strong-willed heroine. And, in common with others of her ilk, she had to play a lot of parts that weren't worthy of her talent.
1937: New Faces of 1937. 1939: Eternally Yours. The Adventures of Sherlock Holmes (GB: Sherlock Holmes). 1940: New Moon. The Philadelphia Story. Two Girls on Broadway (GB: Choose Your Partner). Florian. 1941: Dr Jekyll and Mr Hyde. Maisie Was a Lady. Mr and Mrs North. Married Bachelor. Unfinished Business. The Lone Rider Rides On. The Lone Rider in Frontier Fury (GB: Frontier Fury). 1942: Born to Sing. Ship Ahoy. Sleepy-time Gal. Wake Island. To the Shores of Tripoli. Counter Espionage. Calling Dr Gilles-

pie. *Sherlock Holmes and the Voice of Terror (GB: The Voice of Terror)*. 1943: *Sherlock Holmes Faces Death. The Crystal Ball. Happy Go Lucky. Ministry of Fear. Jane Eyre.* 1944: *Lady in the Dark. Practically Yours. And the Angels Sing. Standing Room Only.* 1945: *The Enchanted Cottage. The Crime Doctor's Courage (GB: The Doctor's Courage). The Woman in Green. Road to Utopia. Up Goes Maisie (GB: Up She Goes).* 1946: *Strange Impersonation. Monsieur Beaucaire. Earl Carroll's Sketchbook (GB: Hats Off to Rhythm). The Strange Woman. The Gentleman Misbehaves. Strange Journey.* 1947: *Big Town. I Cover Big Town (GB: I Cover the Underworld). Big Town After Dark.* 1948: *The Fuller Brush Man (GB: That Mad Mr Jones). Big Town Scandal. Let's Live Again.* 1949: *Alimony. Africa Screams.* 1950: *Unmasked. The Admiral Was a Lady. Bodyhold. Beauty on Parade. Vendetta.* 1951: *Lucky Losers. Insurance Investigator. Skipalong Rosenbloom. The Lost Continent.* 1952: *Confidence Girl. Abbott and Costello Meet Captain Kidd. Never Wave at a WAC (GB: The Private Wore Skirts).* 1953: *The Lady Wants Mink. Mexican Manhunt. Invaders from Mars. The Maze.* 1954: *The House Across the Lake (US: Heat Wave). Dragon's Gold.* 1955: *Bengazi.* 1956: *The Man Who Knew Too Much.* 1957: *Spoilers of the Forest.*

BROOKS, Geraldine (G. Stroock) 1925–1977

Dark-haired, small, pretty American actress of strong personality and performances. Although critics liked most of the few films she did make as a leading lady, she never fulfilled her potential. Later filmed on the continent, became a natural history photographer (a book of her bird studies, *Swan Watch*, was published) and poet, and appeared in the 1970s on television as Dan Dailey's secretary in the feature-length *Faraday and Co* series. Died from cancer. The actress Gloria Stroock is her sister.
1946: *Cry Wolf.* 1947: *Possessed.* 1948: *Embraceable You. An Act of Murder.* 1949: *The Younger Brothers. Challenge to Lassie. The Reckless Moment. Volcano.* 1950: *This Side of the Law.* 1951: *J'étais une pécheresse. Ho sognato il paradiso (US: Street of Sorrow). The Green Glove.* 1954: *La strada (GB: The Road. Dubbed voice only English-language version).*

1957: *Street of Sinners.* 1966: *Johnny Tiger.* 1973: *The Aspern Affair.* 1975: *Mr Ricco.*

BROOKS, Louise 1906–1985

Black-haired, dark-eyed American leading lady, a former Ziegfeld Follies girl, hailed by some critics as the greatest actress of her generation, derided by others as an overrated star who could not properly survive sound. Her mask-like face and luminous personality certainly lend a haunting quality to the two fine films she made in Germany. But she was snubbed on her return to Hollywood, and ended playing western heroines before ignominious retirement. Died from a heart attack.
1925: *The Street of Forgotten Men.* 1926: *The American Venus. A Social Celebrity. The Show-Off. Love 'Em and Leave 'Em. Just Another Blonde. It's the Old Army Game.* 1927: *Evening Clothes. Now We're in the Air. The City Gone Wild. Rolled Stockings.* 1928: *A Girl in Every Port. Beggars of Life.* 1929: *Die Büchse der Pandora (GB and US: Pandora's Box). The Canary Murder Case. Das Tagebuch einer Verlorenen (GB and US: Diary of a Lost Girl).* 1930: *Prix de beauté (GB: Miss Europe).* 1931: *It Pays to Advertise. God's Gift to Women (GB: Too Many Women). The Public Enemy (GB: Enemies of the Public). Other Men's Women/Steel Highway.* *Windy Riley Goes to Hollywood (GB: The Gas-Bag).* 1936: *Empty Saddles.* 1937: *When You're in Love (GB: For You Alone).* †*King of Gamblers.* 1938: *Overland Stage Raiders.*

† *Scenes deleted from final release print*

BROOKS, Mel (Melvin Kaminsky) 1926–

Extrovert, enormously self-confident Jewish–American director-comedian who started as a stand-up comic, then switched to comedy writing (first hit as writer: *New Faces*, 1954). In the 1970s the immense commercial success of some of his films enabled him to combine both talents in a hit-and-miss series of zany comedies that take satirical sideswipes at everything and range from crude to wittily hilarious. In the 1980s he became increasingly involved with his own film production company. Married to Anne Bancroft (*qv*) since 1964.
1963: *The Critic (narrator only).* 1967: *Putney Swope.* 1970: *The Twelve Chairs.* 1974: *Blazing Saddles.* 1976: *Silent Movie.* 1977:

High Anxiety. 1978: *The Muppet Movie.* 1981: *History of the World Part One.* 1983: *To Be or Not To Be.*

As director: 1967: *The Producers.* 1970: *The Twelve Chairs.* 1974: *Blazing Saddles. Young Frankenstein.* 1976: *Silent Movie.* 1977: *High Anxiety.* 1981: *History of the World Part One.*

BROOKS, Ray 1939–

Curly-haired, stocky, slightly sullen-looking British leading man, often in belligerent, swaggering or cocksure roles. He once described himself as 'the best actor under 30 in Britain', but most of his cinema roles did not live up to that tag by a long way, and his best work has been achieved in theatre and for television, where he has appeared in a number of successful plays and series.
1962: *Some People. HMS Defiant (US: Damn the Defiant!). Play It Cool.* 1965: *The Knack ... and how to get it.* 1966: *Daleks – Invasion Earth 2150 AD.* 1969: *The Last Grenade.* 1971: *Baffled! (TV. GB: cinemas).* 1972: *The Flesh and Blood Show. Alice's Adventures in Wonderland. Carry on Abroad.* 1973: *Tiffany Jones. Assassin.* 1974: *House of Whipcord.*

BROWN, Bryan 1947–

Dark-haired, eagle-featured, gimlet-eyed Australian actor, often in aggressive roles. Something like Jason Robards Jr (*qv*) in the way that he can be riveting in some roles and ineffective in others, Brown began his acting career with Britain's National Theatre in 1974. Performances in *Newsfront* and '*Breaker' Morant* brought him to international attention, and he also advanced his standing in the

TV series *A Town Like Alice*. British ventures were less successful and he is now based in California, where he married the British-born actress Rachel Ward (*qv*) in 1983.

*1975: *The Christmas Tree. 1977: The Love Letters from Teralba Road. 1978: The Irishman. Newsfront. Money Movers. Weekend of Shadows. The Chant of Jimmie Blacksmith. 1979: Cathy's Child. The Odd Angry Shot. Third Person Plural. 'Breaker' Morant. 1980: Palm Beach. *Con Man Harry and the Others. Stir. 1981: The Winter of Our Dreams. 1982: Far East. 1984: Give My Regards to Broad Street. Kim (TV). Bones (later Parker). 1985: Rebel. The Shiralee. F/X. The Empty Beach. 1986: The Umbrella Woman. Tai Pan. The Good Wife.*

BROWN, Jim 1935–

American former football hero who turned to acting in his thirties, and became popular for a short while as the unlikely black hero of a dozen tough and violent action melodramas.

1964: Rio Conchos. 1967: The Dirty Dozen. 1968: Dark of the Sun (GB: The Mercenaries). The Split. Ice Station Zebra. Riot. 1969: 100 Rifles. ... tick ... tick ... tick. 1970: The Grasshopper. Kenner. El Condor. 1972: Black Gunn. Slaughter. 1973: I Escaped from Devil's Island. Slaughter's Big Rip Off. The Slams. 1974: Three the Hard Way. 1975: Take a Hard Ride. 1977: Fingers. Kid Vengeance. 1982: One Down Two to Go. 1985: Lady Blue (TV).

BROWN, Joe E. 1892–1973

Ever-smiling, slick-haired American comedian said to have the widest mouth in show business. He had long experience in vaudeville dating back to the age of nine, when he began as a boy acrobat. In films, he usually played the innocent abroad and remained very popular from the beginning of sound to the early forties. In his case more than most, his face was his fortune. The 'E' stood for Evans.

*1928: Crooks Can't Wait. Me, Gangster. Road House. Dressed to Kill. The Circus Kid. Hit of the Show. Burlesque. *Don't Be Jealous. Take Me Home. 1929: On With the Show. Painted Faces. *The Dancing Instructor. In Old Arizona. Sunny Side Up. Molly and Me. My Lady's Past. Sally. The Cock-eyed World. The Ghost Talks. Protection. 1930: Song of the West. Hold Everything. Top Speed. Lottery Bride. Maybe It's Love. *Screen Snapshots No. 5. Up the River. Born Reckless. City Girl. 1931: Going Wild. Sit Tight. *Screen Snapshots No. 8. Broad Minded. Local Boy Makes Good. 1932: Fireman Save My Child. You Said a Mouthful. The Tenderfoot. *The Putter. *The Stolen Jools (GB: The Slippery Pearls). 1933: Elmer the Great. Son of a Sailor. *Hollywood on Parade No. 8. 1934: The Circus Clown. Six-Day Bike Rider. 1935: Alibi Ike. Bright Lights (GB: Funny Face). A Midsummer Night's Dream. 1936: Sons o' Guns. Earthworm Tractors (GB: A Natural Born Salesman). Polo Joe. 1937: When's Your Birthday? Riding on Air (GB: All is Confusion). Fit for a King. 1938: Wide Open Faces. The Gladiator. Flirting with Fate. 1939: A Thousand Dollars a Touchdown. 1940: *Rodeo Dough. Beware Spooks! So You Won't Talk. 1942: Shut My Big Mouth. Joan of Ozark (GB: Queen of Spies). The Daring Young Man. 1943: Chatterbox. 1944: Pin-Up Girl. Hollywood Canteen. Casanova in Burlesque. 1947: The Tender Years. 1951: Show Boat. 1952: *Memories of Famous Hollywood Comedians (narrator only). 1954: *Hollywood Fathers. 1956: Around the World in 80 Days. 1959: Some Like It Hot. 1963: It's a Mad, Mad, Mad, Mad World. Comedy of Terrors.*

BROWN, Johnny Mack 1904–1975

Husky, square-jawed, dark-haired former All-American football player who came to the screen in the late 1920s and co-starred twice with Greta Garbo (*qv*). He was also a notable Billy the Kid in 1930. From 1936 to 1952, he starred in almost nothing but 'B' feature westerns, retaining his popularity in the genre throughout that period. Later ran a restaurant. Died from a cardiac condition.

*1927: The Bugle Call. Slide, Kelly, Slide. Mockery After Midnight. The Fair Co-Ed (GB: The Varsity Girl). 1928: Our Dancing Daughters. Soft Living. Square Crooks. Play Girl. Annapolis (GB: Branded a Coward). Lady of Chance. The Divine Woman. A Woman of Affairs. 1929: Coquette. The Single Standard. The Valiant. Hurricane. Jazz Heaven. 1930: Montana Moon. Undertow. Billy the Kid. 1931: The Secret Six. The Great Meadow. Lasca of the Rio Grande. The Last Flight. Laughing Sinners. 1932: Flames. The Vanishing Frontier. 70,000 Witnesses. Malay Nights. 1933: Fighting with Kit Carson (serial). Saturday's Millions. Female. Son of a Sailor. Hollywood on Parade. 1934: Belle of the Nineties. Cross Streets. Marrying Widows. Three on a Honeymoon. 1935: St Louis Woman. Between Men. *Star Night at the Cocoanut Grove. The Courageous Avenger. The Rustlers of Red Dog (serial). The Right to Live. 1936: The Desert Phantom. Rogue of the Range. Riding the Apache Trail. Every Man's Law. Valley of the Lawless. Crooked Trail. Undercover Man. Lawless Land. 1937: Gambling Terror. Trail of Vengeance. Bar Z Bad Men. Guns in the Dark. Boot Hill Brigade. A Lawman is Born. Wells Fargo. Wild West Days (serial). 1938: Flaming Frontiers (serial). Born to the West. Land of Liberty. 1939: The Oregon Trail (serial). Desperate Trails. Oklahoma Frontier. Chip of the Flying U. 1940: West of Carson City. Riders of Pasco Basin. Bad Man from Red Butte. Son of Roaring Dan. Ragtime Cowboy Joe. Boss of Bullion City. Law and Order (GB: Lucky Ralston). 1941: The Masked Rider. Bury Me Not on the Lone Prairie. Rawhide Rangers. The Man from Montana (GB: Montana Justice). Law of the Range. Arizona Cyclone. 1942: Ride 'Em Cowboy. Fighting Bill Fargo. The Boss of Hangtown Mesa. Stagecoach Buckaroo. Little Joe the Wrangler. The Silver Bullet. 1943: The Old Chisholm Trail. The Ghost Rider. Raiders of San Joaquin. Six-Gun Gospel. The Texas Kid. Outlaws of Stampede Pass. Tenting Tonight on the Old Camp Ground. Cheyenne Round-Up. The Stranger from Pecos. Lone Star Trail. 1944: Land of the Outlaws. Range Law. West of the Rio Grande. Ghost Guns. Partners of the Trail. They Shall Have Faith (GB: The Right to Live). 1945: Navajo Trail. Gunsmoke. Stranger from Santa*

Fé. Frontier Feud. Law of the Valley. Raiders of the Border. Law Men. Lost Trail. Flame of the West. 1946: Drifting Along. Under Arizona Skies. The Haunted Mine. Shadows on the Range. Raiders of the South. Gentleman from Texas. Trigger Fingers. Silver Range. Border Bandits. 1947: Land of the Lawless. Valley of Fear. Trailing Danger. Flashing Guns. Prairie Express. Code of the Saddle. The Law Comes to Gunsight. Gun Talk. 1948: Triggerman. Frontier Agent. Overland Trail. Crossed Trails. The Fighting Ranger. The Sheriff of Medicine Bow. Backtrail. Hidden Danger. Gunning for Justice. 1949: Stampede. Law of the West. West of El Dorado. Trail's End. Range Justice. Western Renegades. 1950: Short Grass. Six Gun Mesa. Law of the Panhandle. Outlaw Gold. Over the Border. West of Wyoming. 1951: Oklahoma Outlaws. Man from Sonora. Colorado Ambush. Montana Desperado. Oklahoma Justice. Texas Lawmen. Blazing Bullets. 1952: Whistling Hills. Dead Man's Trail. Texas City. Canyon Ambush. Man from the Black Hills. 1953: The Marshal's Daughter. 1954: *Hollywood Fathers. 1965: Requiem for a Gunfighter. The Bounty Killer. 1966: Apache Uprising.

BRUCE, Brenda 1918–
Blonde British actress with distinctive, Scandinavian-type features, often seen with urchin haircut. Originally a dancer, she had her first big success in intimate revue before trying straight acting, demonstrating an unusual gamine appeal. Critics liked her looks and acting ability, but she was perhaps too cool for the public taste and did not become a major star. Still plays character roles on stage, in films and on TV.
1943: Millions Like Us. 1944: They Came to a City. 1945: I Live in Grosvenor Square (US: A Yank in London). Night Boat to Dublin. 1946: I See a Dark Stranger (US: The Adventuress). Piccadilly Incident. Carnival. While the Sun Shines. 1947: When the Bough Breaks. 1948: My Brother's Keeper. 1949: Marry Me. Don't Ever Leave Me. 1951: Two on the Tiles. 1953: The Final Test. 1958: Law and Disorder. Behind the Mask. 1959: Peeping Tom. 1963: Nightmare. 1964: The Uncle. 1973: That'll Be the Day. 1974: Swallows and Amazons. All Creatures Great and Small. 1976: The Man in the Iron Mask (TV). 1981: Käthe Kollwitz. 1985: Steaming. Time After Time (TV).

BRUCE, Virginia (Helen V. Briggs) 1910–1982
Ultra-blonde American actress, in quiet roles through the 1930s and early 1940s. The private life of this former Ziegfeld girl was less quiet; she married John Gilbert (1932–1934) in the years of his decline. Gilbert died two years after they parted, and her second husband, director J. Walter Ruben, died in 1942. Her third husband, Turkish director Ali Ipar, fell foul of his country's regime and was jailed for 18 months in 1960. They were later divorced.
1929: Fugitives. Blue Skies. Woman Trap. Illusion. The Love Parade. Why Bring That Up? 1930: Safety in Numbers. Only the Brave. Slightly Scarlet. Paramount on Parade. Follow Thru. Whoopee! Raffles. Young Eagles. Lilies of the Field. Social Lion. 1931: Hell Divers. Are You Listening? The Wet Parade. 1932: The Miracle Man. Sky Bride. Downstairs. Kongo. Winner Take All. A Scarlet Week-End. 1934: Jane Eyre. The Mighty Barnum. Dangerous Corner. 1935: Times Square Lady. Society Doctor. Shadow of Doubt. Let 'Em Have It (GB: False Faces). Here Comes the Band. Escapade. Metropolitan. The Murder Man. 1936: The Garden Murder Case. The Great Ziegfeld. *Pirate Party on Catalina Isle. Born to Dance. 1937: Women of Glamour. When Love is Young. Between Two Women. Wife, Doctor and Nurse. 1938: The First Hundred Years. Arsène Lupin Returns. Bad Man of Brimstone. Yellow Jack. Woman Against Woman. There Goes My Heart. There's That Woman Again. (GB: What a Woman). 1939: Let Freedom Ring! Society Lawyer. Stronger Than Desire. 1940: Flight Angels. The Man Who Talked Too Much. Hired Wife. 1941: The Invisible Woman. Adventure in Washington (GB: Female Correspondent). 1942: Pardon My Sarong. Butch Minds the Baby. Careful, Soft Shoulders. 1944: Brazil. Action in Arabia. 1945: Love, Honor and Goodbye. 1948: The Night Has a Thousand Eyes. 1949: State Dept – File 649 (GB: Assignment in China). 1953: Istanbul. 1955: The Reluctant Bride (US: Two Grooms for a Bride). 1960: Strangers When We Meet.

BRYNNER, Yul (Youl Bryner) 1915–1985
Bald-headed actor of Swiss–Mongolian parentage (born on an island off the coast of Siberia), whose career has been inextricably

tied up with his portrayals of the King of Siam in The King and I, and the mysterious gunfighter in black in The Magnificent Seven. His faint accent and clipped tones remained unique, but a further stage stint with The King and I in the late seventies signalled his departure from the screen. Married to Virginia Gilmore 1944–1960. Oscar for The King and I. Died from lung cancer.
1949: Port of New York. 1956: The King and I. The 10 Commandments. Anastasia. 1958: The Brothers Karamazov. The Buccaneer. The Journey. 1959: Le testament d'Orphée. Solomon and Sheba. The Sound and the Fury. 1960: Once More with Feeling. *Profile of a Miracle (narrator only). Surprise Package. The Magnificent Seven. 1961: Aimez-vous Brahms? (GB: Goodbye Again). Escape from Zahrain. 1962: Taras Bulba. 1963: Kings of the Sun. 1964: Flight from Ashiya. Invitation to a Gunfighter. 1965: Morituri (GB: The Saboteur Code Name Morituri). Is Paris Burning? 1966: Cast a Giant Shadow. Return of the Seven. The Poppy is Also a Flower (GB: Danger Grows Wild). Triple Cross. 1967: The Long Duel. The Double Man. 1968: Villa Rides! 1969: The Picasso Summer. The Battle of Neretva. The File of the Golden Goose. The Magic Christian. The Madwoman of Chaillot. 1970: Indio Black (GB: The Bounty Hunters. US: Adios Sabata). 1971: Romance of a Horsethief. Catlow. The Light at the Edge of the World. 1972: Fuzz. 1973: The Serpent. Westworld. 1975: The Ultimate Warrior. 1976: Con la rabbia agli occhi (GB: Anger in His Eyes. US: Death Rage). Futureworld.

As narrator: 1959: *Mission to No Man's Land. 1961: *My Friend Nicholas. 1962: Man is to Man.

BUCHANAN, Jack 1891–1957
Smooth, sophisticated musical entertainer, with dry Martini voice, a British Fred Astaire but with the accent on comedy, indelibly a product of the London stage in the twenties. The Scottish-born Buchanan was continually and painfully ill with spinal arthritis in his last years, but made a few very welcome reappearances in the fifties.
1917: Auld Lang Syne. 1919: Her Heritage. 1923: The Audacious Mr Squire. 1924: The Happy Ending. 1925: Settled Out of Court. *A Typical Budget. Bulldog Drummond's Third

Round. *Stage Stars Off Stage. 1927: Confetti. 1928: Toni. 1929: Paris. Show of Shows. 1930: Monte Carlo. *The Glee Quartette. 1931: Man of Mayfair. 1932: Goodnight Vienna (GB: Magic Night). ‡Yes Mr Brown. †That's a Good Girl. 1934: Brewster's Millions. Come Out of the Pantry. Limelight (US: Backstage). 1936: When Knights Were Bold. This'll Make You Whistle. 1937: Smash and Grab. The Sky's the Limit. 1938: Break the News. *Cavalcade of the Stars. 1939: The Gang's All Here (US: The Amazing Mr Forrest). The Middle Watch. 1940: Bulldog Sees It Through. 1944: *Some Like It Rough (narrator only). 1951: *A Boy and a Bike. 1952: *Giselle (narrator only). 1953: The Band Wagon. 1955: As Long As They're Happy. Josephine and Men. 1956: The Diary of Major Thompson (US: The French They Are a Funny Race).

† Also directed ‡ Also co-directed

BUCHHOLZ, Horst 1932–
Black-haired, boyishly handsome German leading man who became an international star in the early sixties, but failed to mature well and rang the bell at box-offices for only a few years. Gave all his most charismatic performances in his twenties.
1954: Marianne. Emil and the Detectives. 1955: Himmel ohne Sterne (US: Sky without Stars). 1956: Regine. Die Halbstarken (GB: Wolfpack. US: Teenage Wolfpack). Herrscher ohne Krone (GB: The King in Shadow). 1957: Die Bekenntnisse des Hochstaplers Felix Krull (GB: The Confessions of Felix Krull). Robinson soll nicht sterben. Monpti. Endstation Liebe. 1958: Nasser Asphalt. Resurrection. Das

Totenschiff. 1959: Tiger Bay. 1960: The Magnificent Seven. 1961: One, Two, Three. Fanny. 1962: Nine Hours to Rama. The Girl and the Legend (US: The Legend of Robinson Crusoe). 1963: La noia (GB and US: The Empty Canvas). Andorra. 1964: The Fabulous Adventures of Marco Polo (GB: Marco the Magnificent). That Man in Istanbul. 1966: Cervantes, the Young Rebel. Johnny Banco. 1968: L'astragale. Come, quando, perché (GB: How, When and with Whom). 1970: Le sauveur. La columba non deve volare. 1972: The Great Waltz. 1973: Aber Jonny! 1974: Lohngelder für Pitteville. 1975: The Catamount Killing. 1976: Raid on Entebbe (TV. GB: cinemas). The Savage Bees. Frauenstation (US: Women in Hospital). 1977: Dead of Night (TV). 1978: The Amazing Captain Nemo. 1979: Avalanche Express. Da Dunkerque alla vittoria (US: From Hell to Victory). 1981: Aphrodite 1983: Sahara. Berlin Tunnel 21 (TV). 1984: Wenn Ich Mich fürchte (US: Fear of Falling). 1985: Code Name: Emerald.

BUJOLD, Geneviève 1942–
Dark-haired, baby-faced Canadian actress with attractive, very slight French–Canadian accent. After a start in French films, she came on to the international scene when chosen to star as Anne Boleyn in Anne of the Thousand Days, a film that won her an Oscar nomination. Since then she has chosen roles that make stern demands of her in all kinds of ways – acting and physical. At her best at the centre of things; least effective when paired with male superstars. Married to director Paul Almond since 1967.
1954: French Can-Can. 1963: Amantia Pestilens. 1964: La terre à boire. La fleur de l'âge ou: les adolescentes. 1965: *Rouli – Roulant (voice only). 1966: La guerre est finie. Le roi de coeur (GB and US: King of Hearts). Le voleur. 1967: Isabel. Entre la mer et l'eau douce. 1969: Anne of the Thousand Days. 1970: Act of the Heart. *Marie-Christine. 1971: The Trojan Women. 1972: Epoh/Journey. 1973: Kamouraska. 1974: Earthquake. 1975: Obsession. L'incorrigible. 1976: Swashbuckler (GB: The Scarlet Buccaneer). Alex and the Gypsy. 1977: Un autre homme, une autre chance (GB: Another Man, Another Woman. US: Another Man, Another Chance). Coma. 1978: Sherlock Holmes: Murder by Decree (GB: Murder by Decree). 1979: The Last Flight of Noah's Ark.

1980: Final Assignment. 1981: Mistress of Paradise (TV). 1982: Monsignor. 1984: Tightrope. Choose Me. 1985: Trouble in Mind.

BURNS, Bob 'Bazooka' 1893–1956
Countrified, dark-haired, round-faced American comedian and entertainer, who followed vaudeville and radio success with some cheerful western comedy-musicals of the 1930s and 1940s. Much in the Will Rogers (qv) mould, he was known as The Arkansas Philosopher, and often played guileless rurals whose sheer goodness kept them afloat. Gained his nickname from a musical instrument he played and claimed to have invented.
1931: Quick Millions. 1935: The Phantom Empire (GB: Radio Ranch). The Singing Vagabond. *Restless Knights. 1936: The Courageous Avenger. Rhythm on the Range. Guns and Guitars. The Big Broadcast of 1937. 1937: Waikiki Wedding. Wells Fargo. Git Along, Little Dogies (GB: Serenade of the West). Public Cowboy No. 1. Yodelin' Kid from Pine Ridge (GB: The Hero of Pine Ridge). Hit the Saddle. 1938: Mountain Music. Tropic Holiday. Radio City Revels. The Arkansas Traveler. 1939: Our Leading Citizen. I'm from Missouri. Rovin' Tumbleweed. 1940: Alias the Deacon. Prairie Schooners (GB: Through the Storm). Comin' Round the Mountain. 1942: The Hillbilly Deacon. Call of the Canyon. 1944: Belle of the Yukon. Mystery Man. 1947: Saddle Pals. Twilight on the Rio Grande.

BURNS, George (Nathan Birnbaum) 1896–
Cigar-puffing American comedian of caustic wit, usually the victim of wife Gracie Allen's

(they married in 1926 and she died in 1964) harebrained ideas, most successful in radio and films in the thirties and television in the fifties. Started a whole new career when he returned to films in 1975 as a veteran vaudevillian in *The Sunshine Boys* and won an Academy Award.

1929: *Lamb Chops. 1930: *Fit To Be Tied. *Pulling a Bone. 1931: *The Antique Shop. *Once Over, Light. *One Hundred Percent Service. 1932: The Big Broadcast. *Oh My Operation.* The Babbling Book. 1933: International House. College Humor. *Hollywood on Parade. *Let's Dance. *Walking the Baby. 1934: We're Not Dressing. Six of a Kind. Many Happy Returns. 1935: Love in Bloom. Here Comes Cookie. The Big Broadcast of 1936. 1936: College Holiday. The Big Broadcast of 1937. A Damsel in Distress. 1938: College Swing (GB: Swing, Teacher, Swing). 1939: Honolulu. 1944: Two Girls and a Sailor. 1954: *Screen Snapshots No. 224. 1956: The Solid Gold Cadillac (narrator only). 1975: The Sunshine Boys. 1977: Oh, God! 1978: Sergeant Pepper's Lonely Hearts Club Band. The Comedy Company (TV). Movie Movie. 1979: Just You and Me, Kid. Going in Style. 1980: Oh, God! Book II. 1983: Two of a Kind (TV). 1984: Oh, God! You Devil.

BURR, Raymond 1917–
Tall, dark, heavy and menacing Canadian-born actor who played Hollywood villains for a decade (including a memorable white-haired maniac in *Rear Window*) before deserting films for such long-running TV series as *Perry Mason* and *A Man Called Ironside*. Has not been lucky in love: twice widowed, once divorced.

1946: San Quentin. Without Reservations. 1947: Code of the West. Desperate. 1948: Pitfall. Ruthless. Raw Deal. Fighting Father Dunne. Sleep My Love. I Love Trouble. Walk a Crooked Mile. Station West. 1949: Adventures of Don Juan (GB: The New Adventures of Don Juan). Abandoned. Black Magic. Criss Cross. Bride of Vengeance. Red Light. Love Happy (later Kleptomaniacs). 1950: Unmasked. Borderline. Key to the City. 1951: FBI Girl. M. The Magic Carpet. New Mexico. Bride of the Gorilla. His Kind of Woman. A Place in the Sun. The Whip Hand. Meet Danny Wilson. 1952: Mara Maru. Horizons West. 1953: Tarzan and the She-Devil. Serpent of

the Nile. The Blue Gardenia. Fort Algiers. Bandits of Corsica (GB: Return of the Corsican Brothers). Casanova's Big Night. 1954: Khyber Patrol. Gorilla at Large. Rear Window. Passion. Thunder Pass. 1955: Double Danger (TV. GB: cinemas). They Were So Young. A Man Alone. Count Three and Pray. You're Never Too Young. Godzilla (US: Godzilla, King of the Monsters). 1956: Great Day in the Morning. A Cry in the Night. The Brass Legend. Secret of Treasure Mountain. Ride the High Iron. Please Murder Me. The Greer Case (TV). 1957: Crime of Passion. Affair in Havana. The Lone Woman (TV). 1960: Desire in the Dust. 1968: P.J. (GB: New Face in Hell). 1971: The Priest Killer (TV). 1975: Mallory (TV). 1976: The Newspaper Game (TV). The Amazing World of Psychic Phenomena (narrator only). 1977: Kingston (TV). Tomorrow Never Comes. 1978: The Jordan Chance (TV). 1979: Centennial (TV). Love's Savage Fury (TV). 1980: Cebe/Out of the Blue. The Night the City Screamed (TV). 1981: The Return. 1982: Airplane II The Sequel. 1985: Godzilla 1985. 1986: The Return of Perry Mason (TV).*

BURSTYN, Ellen (Edna Gillooley) 1932–
Pretty, butter-haired American actress of much warmth and *joie-de-vivre* who went through several changes of name before making a reputation on stage and coming to Hollywood in the 1970s. A deserved Oscar for *Alice Doesn't Live Here Anymore* did not succeed in making her a bankable star, and she turned her attention to out-of-the-way projects. Also nominated for Academy Awards on *The Last Picture Show, The Exorcist, Same Time, Next Year* and *Resurrection.*

1964: †Goodbye Charlie. †For Those Who Think Young. 1969: †Pit Stop. Tropic of Cancer. 1970: Alex in Wonderland. 1971: The Last Picture Show. 1972: The King of Marvin Gardens. 1973: The Exorcist. 1974: Harry and Tonto. Thursday's Game (TV). Alice Doesn't Live Here Anymore. 1977: Providence. A Dream of Passion. 1978: Same Time, Next Year. 1980: Resurrection. The Silence of the North. 1981: Lee Strasberg and the Actors' Studio. 1982: The People vs Jean Harris (TV). 1984: The Ambassador. 1985: Twice in a Lifetime. Surviving (TV). Act of Vengeance (TV). Into Thin Air (TV). 1986: Brian Walker, Please Call Home (TV).

† As Ellen McRae

BURTON, Richard (R. Jenkins) 1925–1984
Welsh-born leading actor with rich, resonant speaking voice who went to Hollywood and projected youthful integrity for a few years, then middle-aged disillusionment. His choice of films in latter times did not always seem wise, but perhaps he was entitled to some degree of disillusion; he was nominated seven times for an Academy Award without winning once. From the 1960s on, his reputation for high living equalled that gained by his better acting performances. Married (second of three wives) to Elizabeth Taylor (*qv*) from 1964 to 1974; briefly remarried her two years later. Died from a cerebral haemorrhage.

1948: The Last Days of Dolwyn (US: Woman of Dolwyn). 1949: Now Barabbas was a robber... 1950: Waterfront (US: Waterfront Women). The Woman with No Name (US: Her Paneled Door). 1951: Green Grow the Rushes. 1952: My Cousin Rachel. 1953: The Desert Rats. The Robe. 1954: Prince of Players. 1955: The Rains of Ranchipur. *Thursday's Children (narrator only). 1956: Alexander the Great. 1957: Sea Wife. Bitter Victory. 1958: *March to Aldermaston (narrator only). A Midsummer Night's Dream (dubbed voice). 1959: Look Back in Anger. 1960: The Bramble Bush. Ice Palace. 1961: *Dylan Thomas. 1962: The Longest Day. 1963: Cleopatra. The VIPs. Zulu (narrator only). Becket. *Inheritance (narrator only). 1964: The Night of the Iguana. Hamlet. 1965: The Spy Who Came in from the Cold. The Sandpiper. What's New Pussycat? *Eulogy to 5.02 (narrator only). *The Days of Wilfred Owen (narrator only). 1966: The Taming of the Shrew. Who's Afraid of Virginia Woolf? 1967: Doctor Faustus. The Comedians. *The Comedians in Africa. 1968: Boom! Candy. A Wall in Jerusalem (narrator only). Where Eagles Dare. The Rime of the Ancient Mariner (narrator only). 1969: Anne of the Thousand Days. Staircase. 1971: Villain. Raid on Rommel. Under Milk Wood (narrator only). 1972: The Assassination of Trotsky. Hammersmith is Out. Bluebeard. 1973: Massacre in Rome. Sujetska (GB: The Fifth Offensive). 1974: Il viaggio (GB and US: The Voyage). The Klansman. 1975: Brief Encounter (TV). Volcano (voice only). Resistance. 1977: Exorcist II: The Heretic. Equus. 1978: The Medusa Touch. The Wild Geese. California Suite. Absolution (released 1981). 1979: Breakthrough/Sergeant Steiner, zweite Teil.

CAAN, James (J. Cahn) 1938–
Fuzzy-haired American leading man with slow but engaging smile, whose performances on the way to the top were rather better than those he gave when he got there. Capable of excellent work with strong direction, but in lighter roles often appeared to be having more fun than the audience. Oscar-nominated for *The Godfather*.
1963: *Irma La Douce*. 1964: *Lady in a Cage*. 1965: *The Glory Guys. Red Line 7000*. 1967: *El Dorado. Countdown. Journey to Shiloh. Submarine X-1. Games*. 1969: *The Rain People. Man Without Mercy (later Gone With the West)*. 1970: *Rabbit Run*. 1971: *T.R. Baskin (GB: A date with a Lonely Girl). Brian's Song (TV). The Godfather*. 1973: *Slither. Cinderella Liberty*. 1974: *Freebie and the Bean. The Conversation. The Gambler. The Godfather Part II*. 1975: *Funny Lady. Rollerball. The Killer Elite*. 1976: *Harry and Walter Go to New York. Silent Movie*. 1977: *A Bridge Too Far. Un autre homme, une autre chance (GB: Another Man, Another Woman, US: Another Man, Another Chance)*. 1978: *Comes a Horseman*. 1979: *Chapter Two*. 1980: †*Hide in Plain Sight*. 1981: *Thief (later and GB: Violent Streets). Les uns et les autres (US: The Ins and the Outs)*. 1982: *Kiss Me Goodbye*.

† *Also directed*

CABOT, Bruce (Etienne de Bujac) 1904–1972
Tall, taciturn, slick-haired American leading man of French extraction (and education) and a hell-raising private life, in the course of which he found time to marry and divorce

three times. His pictures (which included *King Kong*) were almost all action-adventures, with Cabot alternating between hero and villain. Hollywood kept him busy throughout the 1930s, but his career never regained what impetus it had after he returned from active service in World War II. Died from lung cancer. His second wife, actress Adrienne Ames (A. McClure, 1907–1947) also died from cancer.
1931: *Confessions of a Co-ed (GB: Her Dilemma)*. 1932: *What Price Hollywood? Lady with a Past (GB: Her Reputation). Roadhouse Murder*. 1933: *Scarlet River. Lucky Devils. Midshipman Jack. The Great Jasper. Ann Vickers. King Kong. Disgraced! Flying Devils*. 1934: *Shadows of Sing Sing. Murder on the Blackboard. Finishing School. Their Big Moment (GB: Afterwards). His Greatest Gamble. Redhead. Night Alarm. Penthouse Party (GB: Without Children)*. 1935: *Man of the Night. Let 'Em Have It (GB: False Faces). Show Them No Mercy (GB: Tainted Money). Without Children*. 1936: *Legion of Terror. Three Wise Guys. Fury. Sinner Take All. Don't Gamble with Love. The Last of the Mohicans. Don't Turn 'Em Loose. The Big Game. Robin Hood of Eldorado*. 1937: *Bad Guy. Love Takes Flight*. 1938: *Sinners in Paradise. Bad Men of Brimstone. Smashing the Rackets. Tenth Avenue Kid*. 1939: *Homicide Bureau. Dodge City. Traitor Spy (US: The Torso Murder Mystery). Mickey the Kid. You and Me. The Mystery of the White Room. My Son is Guilty (GB: Crime's End)*. 1940: *Susan and God (GB: The Gay Mrs Trexel). Girls under 21. Captain Caution*. 1941: *The Flame of New Orleans. Sundown. Wild Bill Hickok Rides*. 1942: *Silver Queen. Pierre of the Plains. The Desert Song*. 1945: *Divorce. Fallen Angel. Salty O'Rourke*. 1946: *Smoky. Avalanche*. 1947: *The Angel and the Badman. Gunfighters (GB: The Assassin)*. 1948: *The Gallant Legion*. 1949: *Sorrowful Jones*. 1950: *Fancy Pants. Rock Island Trail (GB: Transcontinent Express)*. 1951: *Best of the Badmen*. 1952: *Lost in Alaska. Kid Monk Baroni (GB: Young Paul Baroni)*. 1953: *William Tell (unfinished)*. 1956: *The Red Cloak. Rommel's Treasure. Toti lascia a raddoppia? 1957: La ragazza del Palio (GB: Girl of the Palio. US: The Love Specialist)*. 1958: *The Sheriff of Fractured Jaw. The Quiet American*. 1959: *Il terrore dei barbari (GB and US: Goliath and the Barbarians). John Paul Jones*.

1961: *The Comancheros*. 1962: *Hatari!* 1963: *McLintock! Law of the Lawless. Black Spurs*. 1965: *In Harm's Way. Town Tamer. Cat Ballou*. 1966: *The Chase*. 1967: *The War Wagon*. 1968: *Hellfighters. The Green Berets*. 1969: *The Undefeated*. 1970: *W.U.S.A. Chisum*. 1971: *Big Jake. Diamonds Are Forever*.

CABOT, Susan (Harriet Shapiro) 1927–
Raven-haired, dark-eyed American actress and singer whose ambitions to be another Kathryn Grayson were stillborn at the hands of studios who used her merely as decoration in colourful adventure stories. As a combination of Grayson and Ann Blyth, she was born five years too late and, following a break for marriage and children, appeared in a succession of progressively more unlikely roles that ended her cinema career.
1950: *On the Isle of Samoa. Tomahawk (GB: Battle of Powder River). The Enforcer (GB: Murder Inc.)*. 1951: *Flame of Araby*. 1952: *Son of Ali Baba. Battle at Apache Pass. Duel at Silver Creek*. 1953: *Gunsmoke!* 1954: *Ride Clear of Diablo*. 1957: *Viking Women. One and Only. Sorority Girl (GB: The Bad One)*. 1958: *Fort Massacre. War of the Satellites. Machine Gun Kelly*. 1959: *Surrender Hell! Wasp Woman*.

CAESAR, Sid 1922–
Flat-faced, dark-haired, fast-talking American comedian, a sour-looking equivalent of Britain's Bob Monkhouse, and enormously successful in vaudeville, radio and especially television. Attempts to establish him in films were not ambitious enough, and he has been

largely confined to guest spots and all-star movies.

1945: Tars and Spars. 1947: The Guilt of Janet Ames. 1963: It's a Mad, Mad, Mad, Mad World. 1966: The Spirit is Willing. The Busy Body. 1967: A Guide for the Married Man. 1973: Ten from Your Show of Shows. 1974: Airport 1975. 1976: Flight to Holocaust (TV). Silent Movie. 1977: Fire Sale. Barnaby and Me. Curse of the Black Widow (TV). 1978: Grease. The Cheap Detective. 1980: The Fiendish Plot of Dr Fu Manchu. 1981: History of the World Part I. The Munsters' Revenge (TV). 1982: Grease 2. 1983: Over the Brooklyn Bridge. Cannonball Run II. 1985: Stoogemania. Love is Never Silent (TV).

CAGE, Nicolas (N. Coppola) 1964–
Rangy, wild-haired, thick-lipped, sleepy-eyed American actor with fierce eyebrows and leering good looks, the nephew of director Francis (Ford) Coppola. Fear of reflected nepotism could have given him an inferiority complex, but he soon proved more personable and talented than many of the young American actors springing to prominence in the early 1980s, playing vicious, dumb or sensitive characters with equal conviction and offering deeply felt performances in his more emotional roles.
1981: The Best of Times (TV). 1982: Fast Times at Ridgemont High (GB: Fast Times). Valley Girl. 1983: Racing with the Moon. Rumble Fish. 1984: The Cotton Club. Birdy. 1985: The Boy in Blue. 1986: Peggy Sue Got Married. Miracle Mile. Raising Arizona.

CAGNEY, James 1899–1986
Short, jaunty, aggressive, gingery-haired Hollywood star, with much-imitated clockwork tippy-toe strut (probably inherited from his Broadway dancing days), rasping speech and truculence of manner. He usually played cocksure, punch-happy characters who rarely bit off more than they could chew, and remains one of the most sharply-defined stars from the American cinema's vintage years. Oscar for Yankee Doodle Dandy. Additionally Oscar-nominated for Angels with Dirty Faces and Love Me or Leave Me. Died from diabetes and circulatory failure.
1930: Sinner's Holiday. Doorway to Hell (GB: A Handful of Clouds). Other Men's Women/Steel Highway. 1931: The Millionaire. The Public Enemy (GB: Enemies of the Public).

Smart Money. Blonde Crazy (GB: Larceny Lane). Taxi!. *Practice Shots. 1932: *James Cagney. The Crowd Roars. Winner Take All. Hard to Handle. 1933: Lady Killer. *Hollywood on Parade No. 8. Picture Snatcher. The Mayor of Hell. Footlight Parade. 1934: Jimmy the Gent. He Was Her Man. *Screen Snapshots No. 11. Here Comes the Navy. *The Hollywood Gad-About. The St Louis Kid (GB: A Perfect Weekend). 1935: *A Trip Thru a Hollywood Studio. Devil Dogs of the Air. 'G' Men. The Irish in Us. The Frisco Kid. A Midsummer Night's Dream. Ceiling Zero. 1936: Great Guy (GB: Pluck of the Irish). 1937: Something to Sing About. 1938: *For Auld Lang Syne. Boy Meets Girl. Angels with Dirty Faces. 1939: The Oklahoma Kid. Each Dawn I Die. The Roaring Twenties. 1940: The Fighting 69th. Torrid Zone. City for Conquest. 1941: Strawberry Blonde. The Bride Came C.O.D. 1942: Captains of the Clouds. Yankee Doodle Dandy. 1943: *You, John Jones. *Show Business at War. Johnny Come Lately (GB: Johnny Vagabond). 1944: *Battle Stations (narrator only). 1945: Blood on the Sun. 1946: 13 Rue Madeleine. 1948: The Time of Your Life. 1949: White Heat. 1950: Kiss Tomorrow Goodbye. The West Point Story (GB: Fine and Dandy). 1951: Come Fill the Cup. Starlift. 1952: What Price Glory? 1953: A Lion is in the Streets. 1954: Run for Cover. 1955: The Seven Little Foys. Love Me or Leave Me. Mister Roberts. Tribute to a Bad Man. 1956: These Wilder Years. 1957: Man of a Thousand Faces. 1958: †Short Cut to Hell (introduction only). 1959: Shake Hands With the Devil. Never Steal Anything Small. 1960: The Gallant Hours. 1961: One, Two, Three. 1962: The Road to the Wall (narrator only). 1968: Arizona Bushwhackers (narrator only). 1981: Ragtime. 1984: Terrible Joe Moran (TV).

† Also directed

CAINE, Michael (Maurice Micklewhite) 1933–
Whatever qualities Caine has that made him a star, none of them are conventional. Often bespectacled, not especially handsome, with a pronounced London accent and un-fluid acting style, the fair-haired British actor nonetheless took films by storm in 1965 and has kept his place as a top box-office star, latterly in cynical roles, with only a slight dip in the latter half of the 1970s, when he went into

all-star films. Nominated for Oscars in Alfie, Sleuth and Educating Rita.
1956: A Hill in Korea (US: Hell in Korea). 1957: How to Murder a Rich Uncle. 1958: The Key. Carve Her Name with Pride. The Two-Headed Spy. Blind Spot. 1959: Danger Within (US: Breakout). Passport to Shame (US: Room 43). 1960: Foxhole in Cairo. The Bulldog Breed. 1961: The Day the Earth Caught Fire. 1962: Solo for Sparrow. The Wrong Arm of the Law. 1963: Zulu. 1965: The Ipcress File. 1966: Gambit. Alfie. The Wrong Box. Funeral in Berlin. Hurry Sundown. 1967: Billion Dollar Brain. Woman Times Seven. Tonite Let's All Make Love in London. Deadfall. 1968: Play Dirty. The Magus. 1969: The Italian Job. Battle of Britain. Too Late the Hero. 1970: The Last Valley. *Simon, Simon. Get Carter. 1971: Zee and Co (US: X, Y and Zee). Kidnapped. 1972: Pulp. Sleuth. 1974: The Marseille Contract (US: The Destructors). The Black Windmill. The Wilby Conspiracy. 1975: The Man Who Would Be King. The Romantic Englishwoman. Peeper. 1976: Harry and Walter Go to New York. The Eagle Has Landed. 1977: A Bridge Too Far. Silver Bears. 1978: The Swarm. California Suite. 1979: Ashanti. Beyond the Poseidon Adventure. 1980. The Island. Dressed to Kill. 1981: The Hand. Escape to Victory (US: Victory). 1982: Deathtrap. 1983: The Jigsaw Man. Educating Rita. Beyond the Limit (GB: The Honorary Consul). Blame It on Rio. 1985: Water. The Holcroft Covenant. Sweet Liberty. 1986: Half Moon Street. The Whistle Blower. Mona Lisa. Travelling Man. Hannah and Her Sisters. Surrender. The Fourth Protocol.

CALHOUN, Rory (Francis Durgin) 1922–
Almost too handsome, black-haired ex-juvenile delinquent, lumberjack, cowboy, miner and firefighter who struggled on his first visit to Hollywood after being discovered by Alan Ladd, then succeeded second time around as the hero of vigorous outdoor action films, and became one of the film world's busiest men about town. Married to actress-singer Lita Baron from 1949 to 1970.
1944: †Something for the Boys. †Sunday Dinner for a Soldier. 1945: †The Bullfighters. †Nob Hill. †The Great John L (GB: A Man Called Sullivan). 1947: The Red House. Adventure Island. That Hagen Girl. 1948: Miraculous Journey. 1949: Sand. Massacre River. 1950:

A Ticket to Tomahawk. County Fair. I'd Climb the Highest Mountain. Rogue River. Return of the Frontiersman. 1951: Meet Me After the Show. 1952: With a Song in My Heart. Way of a Gaucho. 1953: The Silver Whip. Powder River. How to Marry a Millionaire. 1954: River of No Return. The Yellow Tomahawk. A Bullet is Waiting. Dawn at Socorro. Four Guns to the Border. 1955: The Looters. Ain't Misbehavin'. The Treasure of Pancho Villa. The Spoilers. 1956: Red Sundown. Raw Edge. Flight to Hong Kong. 1957: The Hired Gun. The Domino Kid. Utah Blaine. Ride Out for Revenge. The Big Caper. 1958: Apache Territory. The Saga of Hemp Brown. 1960: The Colossus of Rhodes. Thunder in Carolina. 1961: Marco Polo. The Treasure of Monte Cristo (US: The Secret of Monte Cristo). 1963: A Face in the Rain. The Gun Hawk. The Young and the Brave. 1964: Young Fury. Operation Delilah. Black Spurs. 1965: Apache Uprising. Finger on the Trigger. 1966: Il gioco delle spie (US: Our Men in Bagdad). 1967: La Muchacha del Nilo (GB: The Emerald of Artatama). 1968: Dayton's Devils. 1969: Operation Cross Eagles. 1972: Night of the Lepus. 1973: Blood Black and White. 1975: Mulefeathers/The West is Still Wild. Won Ton Ton – the Dog Who Saved Hollywood. 1976: Flight to Holocaust (TV). 1977: Kino, the Padre on Horseback. Love and the Midnight Auto Supply. 1978: Bitter Heritage. Flatbed Annie and Sweetiepie: Lady Truckers (TV. GB: Girls of the Road). The Father Kino Story. 1979: Just Not the Same without You. Okinagan's Day. The Main Event. 1980: Running Hot. Motel Hell. 1982: The Circle of Crime. 1983: Angel. 1984: Avenging Angel. 1985: Half Nelson (TV).

† As Frank McCown

CALLARD, Kay 1933–

Bright, chirpy, Canadian-born blonde with provocative personality and attractive croaky voice, seen to advantage in leading roles in a number of British second-features of the 1950s which were considerably enlivened by her presence.
1953: They Who Dare. 1954: The Stranger Came Home (US: The Unholy Four). 1955: Stolen Assignment. The Reluctant Bride (US: Two Grooms for a Bride). Dial 999 (US: The Way Out). Secret File (TV. GB: cinemas). Joe Macbeth. Assignment Abroad (TV. GB: cinemas). 1956: Find the Lady. 1957: West of

Suez (US: Fighting Wildcats). The Hypnotist (US: Scotland Yard Dragnet). Man in the Shadow. Cat Girl. The Flying Scot (US: Mailbag Robbery). Undercover Girl. 1958: Escapement (US: Zex/The Electronic Monster). Intent to Kill. A Woman Possessed. Links of Justice. The Great Van Robbery. 1959: Top Floor Girl. 1961: Freedom to Die.

CALVERT, Phyllis
(Phyllis Bickle) 1915–

Dark-haired British leading lady, a former child dancer and actress who only came to star roles in films in her mid-twenties. Her ladylike carriage and upper-class personality proved no bar to popularity and her tremulous lower lip and liquid brown eyes made her a big hit in weepies and regency romance. A trip to Hollywood in the late forties was not successful.
1927: The Land of Heart's Desire/The Arcadians. 1935: School for Stars. 1938: Inspector Hornleigh. Two Days to Live. 1940: They Came by Night. Let George Do It. Charley's (Big-Hearted) Aunt. Neutral Port. Inspector Hornleigh Goes to It (US: Mail Train). 1941: Kipps (US: The Remarkable Mr Kipps). 1942: The Young Mr Pitt. Uncensored. 1943: The Man in Grey. 1944: Fanny by Gaslight (US: Man of Evil). 2,000 Women. Madonna of the Seven Moons. 1945: They Were Sisters. 1946: Men of Two Worlds. The Magic Bow. 1947: The Root of All Evil. Time Out of Mind. Broken Journey. 1948: My Own True Love. 1949: The Golden Madonna. Appointment with Danger. 1950: The Woman with No Name (US: Her Panelled Door). 1951: Mr

Denning Drives North. 1952: Mandy (US: Crash of Silence). The Net (US: Project M-7). 1956: It's Never Too Late. Child in the House. 1958: The Young and the Guilty. Indiscreet. A Lady Mislaid. 1960: Oscar Wilde. 1965: The Battle of the Villa Fiorita. 1968: Twisted Nerve. 1969: Oh! What a Lovely War. 1970: The Walking Stick.

CALVET, Corinne (C. Dibos) 1925–

Tawny-haired, sultry-looking Parisienne brought to Hollywood by producer Hal Wallis (after making only four French films) as a kind of combination Lauren Bacall and Rita Hayworth. Calvet didn't quite have that kind of smouldering personality but decorated a number of colourful double-feature films. Married four times, once to actor John Bromfield.
1946: La part de l'ombre. Nous ne sommes pas mariés. 1947: Pétrus. Le château de la dernière chance. 1949: Rope of Sand. When Willie Comes Marching Home. 1950: My Friend Irma Goes West. 1951: Quebec. *Hollywood on a Sunday Afternoon. On the Riviera. Peking Express. Sailor Beware. 1952: Thunder in the East. What Price Glory? 1953: Powder River. Flight to Tangier. 1954: The Far Country. So This is Paris. The Adventures of Casanova. The Girls of San Frediano. Four Women in the Night. Bonnes à tuer. 1955: Napoléon. 1958: The Plunderers of Painted Flats. 1960: Bluebeard's Ten Honeymoons. 1962: Hemingway's Adventures of a Young Man (GB: Adventures of a Young Man). 1965: Apache Uprising. 1970: Pound. 1974: The Phantom of Hollywood (TV). 1976: Too Hot to Handle (GB: She's Too Hot to Handle). 1979: She's Dressed to Kill (TV). 1980: Dr Heckyl and Mr Hype. 1982: The Sword and the Sorceror.

CAMERON, Rod (Nathan R. Cox) 1910–1983

Rugged was really the only word for this tall, dark-haired square-jawed Canadian star, built like a redwood tree, who, after ten years in construction work and a slow start to his belated film career, played a slew of good-humoured men of action at Universal and Republic in the 1940s and 1950s.
1939: †The Old Maid. Heritage of the Desert. 1940: If I Had My Way. Rangers of Fortune. Northwest Mounted Police. The Quarterback. Christmas in July. Stagecoach War. Those

Small Town Girl. The Big Leaguer. Code Two. Escape from Fort Bravo. 1954: The High and the Mighty. The Fast and the Furious. 1955: Battle Cry. Running Wild. Cell 2455 – Death Row. Man without a Star. Man in the Vault. 1956: Backlash. Love Me Tender. Walk the Proud Land. 1957: Eighteen and Anxious. 1958: The Naked and the Dead. Money, Women and Guns. The Sheriff of Fractured Jaw. 1960: Natchez Train. 1963: The Young Racers. The Secret Invasion. Dementia 13 (GB: The Haunted and the Hunted). Hush ... Hush, Sweet Charlotte. 1966: Blood Bath. Track of the Vampire. 1971: Pretty Maids All in a Row. 1972: Black Gunn. 1974: Dirty Mary, Crazy Larry.

Were the Days. 1941: Henry Aldrich for President. The Monster and the Girl. Nothing But the Truth. I Wanted Wings (voice only). Buy Me That Town. Pacific Blackout (GB: Midnight Angel). Among the Living. The Parson of Panamint. The Night of January 16th. 1942: The Fleet's In. The Remarkable Andrew. Star Spangled Rhythm. Priorities on Parade. Wake Island. True to the Army. The Forest Rangers. 1943: No Time for Love. Gung Ho! The Commandos Strike at Dawn. G-Man versus the Black Dragon (serial). The Good Fellows. Honeymoon Lodge. The Kansan (GB: Wagon Wheels). Secret Service in Darkest Africa (serial. GB: Desert Agent). Riding High (GB: Melody Inn). 1944: Beyond the Pecos (GB: Beyond the Seven Seas). Boss of Boomtown. Mrs Parkington. Trigger Trail. The Old Texas Trail (GB: Stagecoach Line). Renegades of the Rio Grande. (GB: Bank Robbery). Riders of the Santa Fé (GB: Mile a Minute). 1945: Frontier Gal (GB: The Bride Wasn't Willing). Salome, Where She Danced. Swing Out, Sister. 1946: The Runaround. 1947: Pirates of Monterey. 1948: River Lady. Panhandle. Strike It Rich. Belle Starr's Daughter. The Plunderers. 1949: Brimstone. Stampede. 1950: Stage to Tucson (GB: Lost Stage Valley). Dakota Lil. Short Grass. 1951: Oh! Susanna. Cavalry Scout. The Sea Hornet. 1952: Ride the Man Down. Woman of the North Country. Wagons West. Fort Osage. 1953: The Jungle. The Steel Lady (GB: Treasure of Kalifa). San Antone. 1954: Southwest Passage (GB: Camels West). Hell's Outpost. 1955: Sante Fé Passage. The Fighting Chance. Headline Hunters. Double Jeopardy (GB: The Crooked Ring). 1956: Passport to Treason. Yaqui Drums. 1957: Spoilers of the Forest. 1958: The Man Who Died Twice. Escapement (later Zex. US: the Electronic Monster). 1963: The Gun Hawk. Bullet and the Flesh. 1964: Las pistoles no discuten/Bullets Don't Argue/ Die letzten zwei von Rio Bravo (released 1967). I sentieri dell'odio. 1965: The Bounty Killer. Requiem for a Gunfighter. 1966: Winnetou and His Friend Old Firebrand (GB: Thunder at the Border). 1967: Ride the Wind (TV. GB: cinemas). 1971: The Last Movie. Evel Knievel. 1972: Redneck. 1975: The Kirlian Force. Psychic Killer. 1976: Jessie's Girls (GB: Wanted Women). 1977: Love and the Midnight Auto Supply.

† *Scenes deleted from final release print*

CAMPBELL, Beatrice 1923–1980
Blue-eyed Irish brunette with sympathetic, Phyllis Calvert-style looks who broke into British films at the end of World War II via an ENSA tour of Northern Ireland. Became adept at waiting women and providing leading men with shoulders to cry on, but was disappointing as Errol Flynn's leading lady, and was little seen subsequently in the cinema. Married to Nigel Patrick (*qv*) from 1951 until her death.
1946: Wanted for Murder. Odd Man Out. The Laughing Lady. Meet Me at Dawn. 1947: The Hangman Waits. My Brother Jonathan. 1948: Things Happen at Night. 1949: Now Barabbas was a robber ... Silent Dust. No Place for Jennifer. 1950: Last Holiday. The Mudlark. 1951: Laughter in Paradise. The House in the Square (US: I'll Never Forget You). 1953: Grand National Night (US: Wicked Woman). The Master of Ballantrae. 1955: Cockleshell Heroes.

CAMPBELL, William 1926–
Black-haired American actor whose youthful looks and smiling sneer qualified him for a good run of sharpies, conceited Romeos and psychopaths in the fifties, ever willing to swap sides at the drop of a dollar. His Death Row study of Caryl Chessman was much admired, but, growing older and heavier without being able to shed the punk image, he regressed to minor roles.
1950: The Breaking Point. Breakthrough. 1951: Inside the Walls of Folsom Prison. Operation Pacific. The People Against O'Hara. 1952: Holiday for Sinners. 1953: Battle Circus.

CANNON, Dyan
(Samille Friesen, later legally changed) 1937–
Feline American actress whose career as tawny temptresses was swiftly interrupted by meeting Cary Grant, living with him from 1961–1964, being married to him from 1965–1968, then getting a much-publicized divorce. She quickly became a star on resumption of her career, but soon tired of playing busty blonde bitches and opted out of films for four years. Her early performances are pure plastic, but she blossomed in comedy in the late seventies. Nominated for Academy Awards in *Bob & Carol & Ted & Alice* and *Heaven Can Wait*.
1959: This Rebel Breed. The Rise and Fall of Legs Diamond. 1969: Bob & Carol & Ted & Alice. 1970: Doctors' Wives. 1971: The Anderson Tapes. The Love Machine. Le casse (GB and US: The Burglars). 1972: Such Good Friends. Shamus. 1973: The Last of Sheila. 1974: Child Under a Leaf. The Virginia Hill Story (TV). 1978: Lady of the House (TV). The Revenge of the Pink Panther. Heaven Can Wait. 1979: For the First Time. 1980: Coast to Coast. Honeysuckle Rose. 1982: Deathtrap. Author! Author! Having It All. 1983: Arthur the King (TV. Released 1985). 1984: Master of the Game (TV).
As director: *1975: Number One. 1979: For the First Time.*

CANOVA, Judy (Juliet Canova) 1916–1983
Dark-haired American singer-comedienne with wide grin whose unique brand of scatterbrained hillbilly humour and ear-splitting

yodel were enough to keep her going in second-feature comedy films through three decades. The actress Diana Canova, of TV's *Soap* fame, is her daughter.

*1935: In Caliente. Going Highbrow. Broadway Gondolier. 1937: Artists and Models. Thrill of a Lifetime. 1940: Scatterbrain. 1941: Sis Hopkins. Puddin' Head (GB: Judy Goes to Town). *Meet Roy Rogers. 1942: Joan of Ozark (GB: The Queen of Spies). True to the Army. Sleepytime Gal. 1943: Chatterbox. Sleepy Lagoon. 1944: Louisiana Hayride. 1945: Hit the Hay. 1946: Singin' in the Corn. 1951: Honeychile. 1952: Oklahoma Annie. 1953: The WAC from Walla Walla (GB: Army Capers). 1954: Untamed Heiress. 1955: Carolina Cannonball. 1956: Lay That Rifle Down. 1960: The Adventures of Huckleberry Finn. 1976: Cannonball (GB: Carquake).*

CANTOR, Eddie
(Edward Iskowitz) 1892–1964
Pop-eyed American singer and comedian who was the centrepiece to some wild and spectacular musical comedies of the early thirties. Received a special Academy Award in 1956. Died from a heart attack.

*1926: Kid Boots. 1927: *The Speed Hound. Follies. Special Delivery. 1929: Glorifying the American Girl. *That Party in Person. 1930: Whoopee! *Insurance. 1931: Palmy Days. 1932: The Kid from Spain. 1933: Roman Scandals. 1934: Kid Millions. *Hollywood Cavalcade. *Screen Snapshots No. 11. 1936: Strike Me Pink. 1937: Ali Baba Goes to Town. 1940: Forty Little Mothers. 1943: Thank Your Lucky Stars. 1944: Hollywood Canteen. Show Busi-*

ness. 1945: Rhapsody in Blue. 1948: If You Knew Susie. 1952: The Story of Will Rogers. 1953: The Eddie Cantor Story. 1956: Seidman and Son (TV).

CARDINALE, Claudia 1939–
Despite a bust best described as generous, an urchin face, an attractively raucous voice and a curriculum vitae that parallels that of Sophia Loren (*qv*), in that she married the producer who discovered her, Cardinale didn't make it to the same extent as an international star, lacking in some ways Loren's depth and some of her elegance and style; also, her English, though as fluent, was less seductive. Still, after a lull in the early 1970s, she keeps busy into her forties, having produced or co-produced some of her recent films.

*1956: *Chaînes d'or. 1957: Goha. 1958: I soliti ignoti (GB: Persons Unknown. US: Big Deal on Madonna Street). Totò e Marcellino. Tre straniere a Roma. La prima notte. 1959: Il magistrato. Un maledetto imbroglio (US: The Facts of Murder). Upstairs and Downstairs. Audace colpo dei soliti ignoti. Vento del sud. Austerlitz (GB: The Battle of Austerlitz). 1960: La ragazza con la valigia. Il bell'Antonio. I delfini. Rocco and His Brothers. 1961: Les lions sont lâchés. Senilità. La viaccia (US: The Love Makers). 1962: Cartouche (GB: Swords of Blood). The Leopard. 1963: Eight and a Half. Time of Indifference. Bebo's Girl. Circus World (GB: The Magnificent Showman). The Pink Panther. 1964: Il magnifico cornuto (US: The Magnificent Cuckold). 1965: Vaghe stelle dell'orsa (GB: Of a Thousand Delights. US: Sandra). 1966: Una rosa per tutti (US: A Rose for Everyone). Le fate (GB: Sex Quartet. US: The Queens). Lost Command. The Professionals. 1967: Don't Make Waves. *Piero Gheradi. Il giorno della civetta (US: Mafia). 1968: The Hell with Heroes. Once Upon a Time ... in the West. A Fine Pair. 1969: The Red Tent. Nell'anno del signore. The Adventures of Gérard. Certo, certissimo, anzi ... probabile. 1970: Popsy Pop (GB: The 21 Carat Snatch. US: The Butterfly Affair). 1971: Les pétroleuses (GB and US: The Legend of Frenchie King). L'udienza. Bello, onesto, emigrato Australia sposerebbe compaesana illibata. 1972: La scoumoune 1973: Libera, amore rio. I guappi. Un uomo (GB: Fury). 1974: Il giorno del furore. Conversation Piece. 1975: Il profeta di ferro. A mezzanotte va la ronda del piacere.*

Beato lore. Il comune senso del pudore. Qui comincia l'avventura (GB: Midnight Pleasures. US: Lucky Girls). 1977: Un jour peut-être à San Pedro ou ailleurs. La part du feu. 1978: Escape to Athena. Good Bye and Amen. L'arma. La petite fille en velours bleu (US: The Girl in Blue Velvet). Cocktails for Three. 1979: L'ingorgo (US: Traffic Jam). Corleone. The Immortal Bachelor. Si salve chi vuole. 1980: Le cadeau/The Gift. I briganti. 1981: The Salamander. La pelle. 1982: Fitzcarraldo. Burden of Dreams. 1983: The Ruffian. Princess Daisy (TV). Stelle emigranti. Enrico IV. 1984: Claretta. 1985: L'été prochain. La storia (History). The Woman of Wonders.

CAREY, Harry 1878–1947
Grim, unsmiling, light-haired hero of masses of silent westerns, many of them directed by the young John Ford, in which Carey was often the bad guy reformed by the love of the heroine. Left films in 1928 to train his voice for the coming of sound and, on his return in 1931, continued as tough men of action, with sympathetic character roles as the years wore on. Died from a coronary thrombosis. His son Harry Carey Jr (1921–) is the Hollywood character actor. Oscar-nominated for *Mr Smith Goes to Washington*.

*1911: *Bill Sharkley's Last Game. *Riding de Trail. *The Informer. *My Hero. 1912: *An Unseen Enemy. *A Cry for Help. *The Musketeers of Pig Alley. *In the Aisles of the Wild. *Friends. *Heredity. *Two Men of the Desert. *The Unwelcome Quest. *An Adventure in the Autumn Woods. 1913: *Love in an Apartment Hotel. *Broken Ways. *Pirate Gold. *Brothers. *The Sheriff's Baby. *Three Friends. *The Ranchero's Revenge. *The Left-Handed Man. *The Hero of Little Italy. *Olaf – an Atom. 1914: *Travelin' On. Judith of Bethulia. McVeagh of the South Seas (GB: Brute Island). 1915: Graft (serial). Judge Not, Or The Woman of Mona Diggins. 1916: The Three Godfathers. Behind the Lines. A Knight of the Range. 1917: The Almost Good Man. Red Saunders Plays Cupid. Beloved Jim. Two Guns. The Fighting Gringo. Straight Shooting. The Secret Man. A Marked Man. Bucking Broadway. The Soul Herder. Cheyenne's Pal. 1918: Wild Women. Three Mounted Men. Thieves' Gold. Hell Bent. A Regular Fellow. Fighting Through. God's Outlaw. The Mayor of Filbert. The Scarlet Drop (GB: Hillybilly). The Phan-*

*tom Riders. A Woman's Fool. 1919: Roped. Blind Husbands. Bare Fists. Riders of Vengeance. The Outcasts of Poker Flat. A Fight for Love. Ace of the Saddle. A Gun Fightin' Gentleman. Rider of the Law. Marked Men. Sure Shot Morgan. The Fighting Brothers. By Indian Post. The Rustlers. Gun Law. The Gun Packer. The Last Outlaw. 1920: Overland Red. West is West. Sundown Slim. Hitchin' Posts. Human Stuff. Bullet Proof. Blue Streak McCoy. 1921: 'If Only' Jim. The Freeze Out. The Wallop. Hearts Up. Desperate Trails. The Fox. 1922: Man to Man. Canyon of the Fools. The Kickback. Good Men and True. 1923: Crashin' Thru. Desert Driven. The Night Hawk. The Miracle Baby. 1924: The Man from Texas. Roaring Rails. Tiger Thompson. The Lightning Rider. Flaming Frontiers. 1925: Beyond the Border. Soft Shoes. The Texas Trail. The Man from Red Gulch. The Prairie Pirate. The Bad Lands. Wanderer. Silent Sanderson. 1926: Driftin' Thru. Satan Town. The Frontier Trail. The Seventh Bandit. 1927: Slide, Kelly, Slide. A Little Journey. 1928: The Trail of '98. Border Patrol. Burning Bridges. 1931: Trader Horn. Bad Company. The Vanishing Legion (serial). Across the Line. Double Sixes. Horse Hoofs. The Hurricane Rider. 1932: Cavalier of the West. Border Devils. Without Honor. Law and Order. Last of the Mohicans (serial). The Devil Horse. Night Rider. 1933: Man of the Forest. Sunset Pass. 1934: The Thundering Herd. 1935: Rustlers' Paradise. Powdersmoke Range. Barbary Coast. Wagon Trail. Wild Mustang. Last of the Clintons. 1936: Sutter's Gold. Last of the Outlaws. The Accusing Finger. Valiant is the Word for Carrie. The Prisoner of Shark Island. Little Miss Nobody. The Three Mesquiteers. The Man Behind the Mask. 1937: Ghost Town. Racing Lady. Born Reckless. Kid Galahad. Souls at Sea. Border Café. Annapolis Salute (GB: Salute to Romance). *Lest We Forget. Danger Patrol. Aces Wild. 1938: The Port of Missing Girls. You and Me. The Law West of Tombstone. Gateway. Sky Giant. King of Alcatraz (GB: King of the Alcatraz). 1939: Burn 'Em Up O'Connor. Mr Smith Goes to Washington. Street of Missing Men. Inside Information. Code of the Streets. My Son is Guilty (GB: Crime's End). 1940: Outside the 3-Mile Limit (GB: Mutiny of the Seas). Beyond Tomorrow. They Knew What They Wanted. 1941: Among the Living. Shepherd of the Hills. Sundown. Parachute Battalion. 1942: The Spoilers. 1943: Happy Land. Air Force. 1944: The Great Moment. 1945: China's Little Devils. 1946: Duel in the Sun. 1947: The Angel and the Badman. Sea of Grass. 1948: So Dear to My Heart. Red River.*

CAREY, Macdonald

(Edward M. Carey) 1913–

Bland-looking American leading man, all eyes, eyebrows and lazy smile. His film career, already a late starter, was seriously disrupted by four-year service in the US Marines and, in its latter stages, contained far too many vapid comedies and lukewarm adventure yarns. He was an excellent smiling villain, an ability that remained much under-used.

*1942: Dr Broadway. Take a Letter, Darling (GB: The Green-Eyed Woman). Wake Island. Star Spangled Rhythm. 1943: Shadow of a Doubt. Salute for Three. 1947: Suddenly It's Spring. Variety Girl. 1948: Hazard. Dream Girl. 1949: Streets of Laredo. Bride of Vengeance. The Great Gatsby. Song of Surrender. South Sea Sinner (GB: East of Java). 1950: Comanche Territory. The Lawless (GB: The Dividing Line). Copper Canyon. Mystery Submarine. The Great Missouri Raid. 1951: Excuse My Dust. Meet Me After the Show. Cave of Outlaws. Let's Make It Legal. 1952: My Wife's Best Friend. 1953: Count the Hours (GB: Every Minute Counts). Hannah Lee (later Outlaw Territory). 1954: Malaga (US: Fire over Africa). 1956: Strangers at My Door. In Times Like These (TV. GB: cinemas). Odongo. *Edge of the Law. Miracle on 34th Street (TV. GB: cinemas). 1958: Man or Gun. Natchez (TV). 1959: Blue Denim (GB: Blue Jeans). John Paul Jones. 1961: The Damned (US: These Are the Damned). 1962: Stranglehold. The Devil's Agent. 1963: Tammy and the Doctor. 1965: The Redeemer (voice only). Broken Sabre (TV. GB: cinemas). 1971: Gidget Gets Married (TV). 1973: Ordeal (TV). 1975: Who is the Black Dahlia? 1977: End of the World. Foes. 1978: Stranger in Our House/Summer of Fear (TV). Pressure Point (TV). 1980: American Gigolo.*

CAREY, Phil 1925–

Tall, rugged American actor whose film career unaccountably went astray after he had proved himself adept at heroes and villains alike. He made an excellent Philip Marlowe in a TV

series, but has been too little seen in recent times. Billed as Philip in some early films. *1949: Daughter of the West. 1950: Operation Pacific. 1951: I Was a Communist for the FBI. Inside the Walls of Folsom Prison. This Woman is Dangerous. The Tanks are Coming. 1952: Springfield Rifle. Cattle Town. The Man Behind the Gun. 1953: Calamity Jane. The Nebraskan. Gun Fury. 1954: Pushover. Massacre Canyon. Outlaw Stallion. They Rode West. The Long Gray Line. 1955: Wyoming Renegades. Three Stripes in the Sun (GB: The Gentle Sergeant). Count Three and Pray. Mister Roberts. 1956: Port Afrique. Wicked As They Come. 1957: The Shadow on the Window. 1958: Screaming Mimi. Return to Warbow. 1959: Tonka. 1960: The Trunk. 1963: Black Gold. 1964: Dead Ringer (GB: Dead Image). FBI Code 98. The Time Travelers. 1965: The Great Sioux Massacre. 1967: Three Guns for Texas. 1969: Once You Kiss a Stranger. 1970: Sudden Death. 1971: The Seven Minutes. 1974: Shadow of Fear (TV). Scream of the Wolf (TV). Hard Day at Blue Nose. 1976: Fighting Mad.*

CARLSON, Richard 1912–1977

Quiet, soft-spoken American leading man who came to Hollywood as a writer, but found himself the juvenile lead in a fistful of films before war service. He failed to regain the same footing from 1947, but looked brainy enough to play the scientist hero of several interesting science-fiction films, having a hand in the writing and direction of some of these, and others. Died from a cerebral haemorrhage.

1938: The Young in Heart. Duke of West Point. Little Accident. Dancing Co-Ed (GB: Every Other Inch a Lady). These Glamour Girls. Winter Carnival. 1940: Beyond Tomorrow. Too Many Girls. The Ghost Breakers. No, No, Nanette. The Howards of Virginia (GB: The Tree of Liberty). 1941: West Point Widow. The Little Foxes. Back Street. Hold That Ghost! Secrets of G-32. 1942: My Heart Belongs to Daddy. The Silver Spoon. Fly by Night. White Cargo. Highways by Night. The Affairs of Martha (GB: Once Upon a Thursday). The Magnificent Ambersons. 1943: Presenting Lily Mars. Young Ideas. A Stranger in Town. The Man from Down Under. 1947: So Well Remembered. 1948: Behind Locked Doors. 1950: Try and Get Me (GB: The Sound of Fury). King

Solomon's Mines. 1951: The Blue Veil. Valentino. A Millionaire for Christy. 1952: Whispering Smith Hits London (US: Whispering Smith versus Scotland Yard). Retreat Hell! 1953: The Magnetic Monster. The Maze. Flat Top (GB: Eagles of the Fleet). All I Desire. Seminole. Riders to the Stars. It Came from Outer Space. 1954: The Creature from the Black Lagoon. 1955: The Last Command. Bengazi. An Annapolis Story (GB: The Blue and the Gold. Narrator only). 1956: Three for Jamie Dawn. 1957: The Helen Morgan Story (GB: Both Ends of the Candle). 1959: Della (TV). 1960: Tormented. 1965: Kid Rodelo. 1966: The Doomsday Flight. 1967: The Power. 1969: The Valley of Gwangi. Change of Habit.

As director: 1953: Riders to the Stars. 1954: Four Guns to the Border. 1958: Appointment with a Shadow (GB: The Big Story). The Saga of Hemp Brown. 1965: Kid Rodelo.

CARLSON, Veronica 1944–
Statuesque British blonde actress whose fortunes rose and fell with those of Hammer horror films, for whom she proved a spirited as well as decorative leading lady after one or two very small roles. She showed considerable signs of an interesting acting talent in *The Ghoul*, but then seemed to opt out of show business for painting and family life.
1967: Smashing Time. The Magnificent Two. 1968: Hammerhead. Dracula Has Risen from the Grave. 1969: Crossplot. Frankenstein Must Be Destroyed. 1970: The Horror of Frankenstein. Pussycat, Pussycat, I Love You. 1974: Vampira (US: Old Dracula). The Ghoul.

CARMICHAEL, Ian 1920–
Fair-haired British light comedy actor of the 'I say, old chap' school who was an enormous success in the fifties as the quintessential dithering blunderer, a character once described as 'the muddle-headed pawn in life's game of chess'. Found new fame in the seventies on television as the gentleman sleuth Lord Peter Wimsey, and as P.G. Wodehouse's Bertie Wooster.
1948: Bond Street. 1949: Trottie True (US: Gay Lady). Dear Mr Prohack. 1952: Time Gentlemen Please! Ghost Ship. 1953: Meet Mr Lucifer. 1954: The Colditz Story. Betrayed. 1955: Storm over the Nile. Simon and Laura. 1956: Private's Progress. The Big Money. Bro-

thers in Law. 1957: Lucky Jim. Happy is the Bride! 1959: Left, Right and Centre. I'm All Right, Jack. 1960: School for Scoundrels. Light Up the Sky. 1961: Double Bunk. 1962: The Amorous Prawn. 1963: Heavens Above! Hide and Seek. 1964: The Case of the 44s. 1967: Smashing Time. 1971: The Magnificent Seven Deadly Sins. 1973: From Beyond the Grave. 1979: The Lady Vanishes.

CARNEY, Art 1918–
Square-built, phlegmatic American actor and comedian who built himself a big reputation on television, and then, after beating an alcohol problem, went on to become one of the world's leading character stars in the seventies, following an Oscar for his performance in *Harry and Tonto*.
1941: Pot o' Gold (GB: The Golden Hour). 1957: Charley's Aunt (TV). 1958: The Fabulous Irishman (TV). 1959: The Velvet Alley (TV). 1964: The Yellow Rolls Royce. 1967: A Guide for the Married Man. 1972: The Female Instinct (TV. GB: The Snoop Sisters). 1974: Harry and Tonto. 1975: W.W. and the Dixie Dancekings. Won Ton Ton the Dog Who Saved Hollywood. Death Scream (TV). Katherine (TV). 1976: Lanigan's Rabbi (TV). 1977: The Late Show. Scott Joplin – King of Ragtime. 1978: Ravagers. Movie Movie. House Calls. 1979: Defiance. Sunburn. You Can't Take It with You (TV). Going in Style. Letters from Frank. Steel. 1980: Roadie. Alcatraz: The Whole Shocking Story (TV). 1981: St Helens. Take This Job and Shove It. 1982: Ménage à Trois/Summer Lovers. Bitter Harvest (TV). 1984: Firestarter. The Naked

Face. A Doctor's Story (TV). The Muppets Take Manhattan. The Night They Saved Christmas (TV). Terrible Joe Moran (TV). 1985: The Undergrads/The Undergraduates. Izzy and Mo (TV). 1986: Time Flyer (TV). Miracle of the Heart: a Boys' Town Story (TV).

CAROL, Martine
(Marie-Louise de Mourer) 1921–1967
Blonde, voluptuous, full-lipped French actress with a mature, Dresden shepherdess-type face. She became the first French postwar sex symbol, and millions flocked to see her as a series of courtesans in films that included *Nana* and the *Caroline Chérie* series. She made one or two international films, but her best roles were behind her when she died from a heart attack at 45.
1942: Les inconnus dans la maison. 1943: La ferme aux loups. 1945: Bifur III. L'extravagante mission. Trente et quarante. 1946: Voyage surprise. En êtes-vous bien sûr? 1947: La fleur de l'age. Miroir. L'île aux enfants perdus. 1948: Les amants de Vérone. Je n'aime que toi. Les souvenirs ne sont pas à vendre. 1949: Une nuit de noces. Méfiez-vous des blondes. 1950: Caroline Chérie. Nous irons à Paris. 1951: El Deseo y el Amor. 1952: Adorable créatures. Une nuit avec Caroline. Les belles de nuit. Lucrezia Borgia. 1953: Un caprice de Caroline Chérie. Destinées (GB: Love, Soldiers and Women. US: Daughters of Destiny). La spiaggia (GB and US: The Beach). 1954: Secrets d'alcove/The Bed. Il letto della Pompadour. Madame DuBarry. 1955: Nana. Lola Montès. 1956: Scandale à Milan. The Diary of Major Thompson (US: The French They Are a Funny Race). Around the World in 80 Days. Defendo il mio amour. 1957: Action of the Tiger. Au bord du volcan. 1958: Les noces Venetiennes. Le passager clandestin (GB: The Stowaway). Nathalie, agent secret (GB and US: The Foxiest Girl in Paris). Ten Seconds to Hell. La prima notte. 1959: Austerlitz (GB: The Battle of Austerlitz). 1960: Love and the Frenchwoman. Operation Gold Ingot. 1961: Le cave se rebiffe (GB: Counterfeiters of Paris. US: The Sucker Strikes Back). Vanina vanini. Un soir sur la plage. En plein cirage. Rape of the Sabines (US: Romulus and the Sabines). 1962: I Don Giovanni della Costa Azzurra (US: Beach Casanova). 1963: Hell is Empty (released 1967).

CARON, Leslie 1931–
Immensely appealing brunette French gamine, mainly in Hollywood, who could carry a musical with her elegant dancing, or touch the heartstrings in the fifties when, mostly at M-G-M, she produced several performances of tremendous charm. Received Oscar nominations for *Lili* and *The L-Shaped Room*.
1951: *An American in Paris. The Man with a Cloak.* 1952: *Glory Alley. Lili.* 1953: *The Story of Three Loves.* 1954: *The Glass Slipper.* 1955: *Daddy Long Legs.* 1956: *Gaby.* 1958: *Gigi.* 1959: *The Doctor's Dilemma. The Man Who Understood Women. Austerlitz (GB: The Battle of Austerlitz).* 1960: *The Subterraneans.* 1961: *Fanny.* 1962: *Guns of Darkness. The L-Shaped Room. Les quatres vérités (GB: Three Fables of Love).* 1964: *Father Goose.* 1965: *A Very Special Favor. Promise Her Anything. Is Paris Burning?* 1967: *Il padre di famiglia (US: Head of the Family).* 1970: *Madron.* 1971: *Chandler.* 1972: *Purple Night.* 1974: *QB VII (TV).* 1975: *James Dean – the First American Teenager.* 1976: *Sérail.* 1977: *Valentino. L'homme qui aiment les femmes.* 1979: *Goldengirl. Tous vedettes.* 1980: *Kontrakt.* 1981: *Chanel solitaire.* 1982: *The Imperative. Die Unerreichbare (TV).* 1985: *La diagonale du fou (US: Dangerous Moves). Reel Horror.*

CARPENTER, Paul
(Patrick P. Carpenter) 1921–1964
A former professional ice-hockey player, then popular band singer, Canadian-born Carpenter's acting career in British films hit fewer headlines than his riotous style of living until he suddenly broke from the ranks of supporting players to become the leading man of a rash of second-features in the fifties. But regressed to small roles after 1960. Married (2nd) to actress Kim Parker from 1955 to 1958. Collapsed and died in his dressing-room while appearing in a play.
1946: *This Man is Mine. School for Secrets.* 1948: *Uneasy Terms.* 1949: *Landfall.* 1953: *Albert RN (US: Break to Freedom). The Weak and the Wicked.* 1954: *Face the Music (US: The Black Glove). Johnny on the Spot. Duel in the Jungle. The House Across the Lake (US: Heatwave). The Young Lovers (US: Chance Meeting). The Last Moment. Five Days. Diplomatic Passport. The Stranger Came Home. Night People. The Sea Shall Not Have Them. Shadow of a Man. The Red Dress.* 1955: *Double Jeopardy. Miss Tulip Stays the Night. One Jump Ahead. The Hornet's Nest. Dust and Gold. Doctor at Sea. The Diamond Expert. Stock Car.* 1956: *The Narrowing Circle. Women Without Men (US: Blonde Bait). Fire Maidens from Outer Space. Behind the Headlines. The Iron Petticoat. No Road Back. Reach for the Sky.* 1957: *Murder Reported. The Hypnotist (US: Scotland Yard Dragnet). Black Ice. Les espions. Undercover Girl.* 1958: *Action Stations. Intent to Kill.* 1959: *Jet Storm.* 1960: *The Big Arena (narrator only). Incident at Midnight. I Aim at the Stars.* 1962: *Dr Crippen.* 1963: *Panic. Call Me Bwana. Maigret voit rouge.* 1964: *The Beauty Jungle (US: Contest Girl). First Men in the Moon.*

CARRADINE, David 1936–
Tall, heavy-lidded, fair-haired, sulky-looking American actor, son of character star John Carradine (Richmond Carradine 1906–). In the 1960s he became best known for his 'hippie' lifestyle, and a flagging career was twice saved by TV series – *Shane* in the mid-1960s, after which he played western villains and, more recently, *Kung Fu*. He has since done well as the rakehell hero of way-out action films, but attempts to widen his appeal were not too successful and latterly his performances have been rather better than this films.
1965: *Taggart. Too Many Thieves (TV. GB: cinemas). Bus Riley's Back in Town.* 1967: *The Violent Ones. Dr Terror's Gallery of Horrors.* 1968: *Heaven with a Gun.* 1969: *The Good Guys and the Bad Guys. Young Billy Young. The McMasters ... Tougher Than the West Itself!* 1970: *Macho Callahan. A Gunfight. Maybe I'll Come Home in the Spring (TV).* 1971: *McCabe and Mrs Miller.* 1972: *Boxcar Bertha.* 1973: *House of Dracula's Daughter. Mean Streets. The Long Goodbye.* 1974: ‡*Around.* †*You and Me.* 1975: *Death Race 2000. Long Way Home (TV).* 1976: *Cannonball (GB: Carquake). Bound for Glory.* 1977: *The Serpent's Egg. Gray Lady Down. Thunder and Lightning.* 1978: *The Silent Flute. Fast Charlie – the Moonbeam Rider. Deathsport 2000. Roger Corman – Hollywood's Wild Angel.* 1979: *The Perfect Merry-Go-Round.* ‡*Kansas (A Country Mile). Cloud Dancer. Mr Horn (TV). Gauguin – the Savage.* 1980: *The Long Riders. Carradines in Concert. High Noon: Part II (TV).* 1981: *Rally (later Safari 3000).* †*Americana.* 1982: *'Q' The Winged Serpent/'Q'/The Winged Serpent. The Bad Seed (TV). Trick or Treats.* 1983: *Lone Wolf McQuade. Jealousy (TV).* 1984: *Distant Scream. The Warrior and the Empress (Kain of Dark Planet). On the Line.* 1985: *Behind Enemy Lines/POW The Escape.* 1986: *Kung Fu The Movie (TV). The Jade Jungle.*

† *And directed*
‡ *Unreleased*

CARRADINE, Keith 1950–
Light-haired, gaunt-looking American leading man with cynical smile, the son of John Carradine and younger half-brother of David Carradine (qv). Became early in his career associated with director Robert Altman, and consequently found himself in films that were critically better received than those of his father and half-brother, if further away from the Hollywood mainline. Also a guitarist, composer and singer.
1970: *A Gunfight.* 1971: *McCabe and Mrs Miller. Man on a String (TV).* 1973: *Hex. The Emperor of the North Pole (GB: Emperor of the North). Antoine et Sebastian.* 1974: *You and Me. Thieves Like Us. Idaho Transfer. Run Run Joe. The Godchild (TV).* 1975: *Nashville. Russian Roulette.* 1976: *Lumière. Welcome to LA.* 1977: *Pretty Baby. The Duellists.* 1978: *Old Boyfriends. Sergeant Pepper's Lonely Hearts Club Band.* 1979: *An Almost Perfect Affair (released 1983).* 1980: *The Long Riders. Carradines in Concert.* 1981: *Southern*

Comfort. 1984: Maria's Lovers. Choose Me. Scorned and Swindled (TV). 1985: Trouble in Mind. The Tigress. Blackout. 1986: A Winner Never Quits (TV). The Inquiry.

CARRERA, Barbara 1951–
Tall, olive-complexioned, black-haired, dark-eyed, full-lipped Nicaraguan beauty with feline grace and predatory air, a highly successful model who gradually broke into films in decorative roles. She always seemed to be a must for a James Bond film, and indeed eventually played the luscious Fatima Blush in Sean Connery's 'comeback' to the role in *Never Say Never Again*.
1970: Puzzle of a Downfall Child. 1975: The Master Gunfighter. Embryo. 1977: The Island of Dr Moreau. 1978: Centennial (TV). 1980: Masada (TV. GB: cinemas – abridged – as The Antagonists). When Time Ran Out ... 1981: Condorman. I, the Jury. 1983: Never Say Never Again. Lone Wolf McQuade. 1984: Sins of the Past. 1985: Wild Geese II.

CARROLL, John
(Julian La Faye) 1905–1979
Brawny, handsome, moustachioed singer from New Orleans who led a colourful early life and stayed in Hollywood from the mid-thirties after an abortive first fling there. Carroll didn't make it as a musical star, despite a pleasant voice and personality, but enjoyed a goodish run as a rugged action hero. Married to actress Steffi Duna (1913–) from 1936 to 1940, his off-screen amours had the fan magazines buzzing and in 1956 *Confidential*

finally, inevitably, 'told all'. Died from leukaemia.
1929: Devil-May-Care. Hearts in Exile. Marianne. 1930: Rogue Song. Doughboys. New Moon. Monte Carlo. Reaching for the Moon. 1935: Go into Your Dance. Hi, Gaucho. 1936: Muss 'Em Up (GB: House of Fate). The Accusing Finger. Murder on the Bridal Path. 1937: Zorro Rides Again (serial). Death in the Air. We Who Are About to Die. 1938: Rose of the Rio Grande. I Am a Criminal. 1939: Only Angels Have Wings. Wolf Call. 1940: Congo Maisie. Phantom Raiders. Susan and God (GB: The Gay Mrs Trexel). Hired Wife. Go West. 1941: This Woman is Mine. Sunny. Lady Be Good. 1942: Rio Rita. Pierre of the Plains. Flying Tigers. 1943: The Youngest Profession. Hit Parade of 1943. 1945: Bedside Manner. A Letter for Evie. 1947: Fiesta. Wyoming. The Fabulous Texan. The Flame. 1948: I, Jane Doe (GB: Diary of a Bride). Old Los Angeles. Angel in Exile. 1950: The Avengers. Surrender. Hit Parade of 1951. 1951: Belle Le Grand. 1953: The Farmer Takes a Wife. Geraldine. 1955: The Reluctant Bride (US: Two Grooms for a Bride). 1957: Decision at Sundown. 1958: The Plunderers of Painted Flats.

CARROLL, Madeleine
(Marie-Madeleine O'Carroll) 1906–
Exquisite English blonde actress with glazed-china face. Her enormous popularity in British films inevitably led to an exit for Hollywood, but her films there included too few worthy of her beauty and talents. Best remembered as the handcuffed lady in *The 39 Steps* (Hitchcock version), her four marriages include one to actor Sterling Hayden, from 1942 to 1946.
*1927: The Guns of Loos. 1928: What Money Can Buy. The First Born. Instinct. *Gaumont Mirror No. 82. 1929: The Crooked Billet. The American Prisoner. Atlantic. 1930: The 'W' Plan. Young Woodley. French Leave. Escape. The School for Scandal. Kissing Cup's Race. 1931: Madame Guillotine. Fascination. The Written Law. 1933: Sleeping Car. I Was a Spy. *Peace or War? 1934: The World Moves On. 1935: The Dictator (US: Loves of a Dictator). The 39 Steps. 1936: Secret Agent. *The Story of Papworth. The Case Against Mrs Ames. The General Died at Dawn. Lloyd's of London. 1937: On the Avenue. It's All Yours. The Prisoner of Zenda. 1938: Blockade. 1939:*

Café Society. Honeymoon in Bali (GB: Husbands or Lovers). My Son, My Son. 1940: Safari. North West Mounted Police. 1941: Virginia. One Night in Lisbon. Bahama Passage. 1942: My Favorite Blonde. 1946: *La petite république. 1947: White Cradle Inn (US: High Fury). 1948: An Innocent Affair (later Don't Trust Your Husband). 1949: The Fan (GB: Lady Windermere's Fan).*

CARROLL, Nancy
(Ann La Hiff) 1904–1965
Petite, pert, blue-eyed redhead who looked a little like Clara Bow, sang in a tinkly, happy voice and became one of the sound era's first big stars. In recent years, she has built up a cult following. Was discovered dead kneeling in front of her television set. An autopsy yielded no explanation and a verdict of 'natural causes' was returned. Received Oscar nomination for *The Devil's Holiday*.
1927: Ladies Must Dress. 1928: Abie's Irish Rose. Easy Come, Easy Go. Chicken à la King. The Water Hole. Manhattan Cocktail. 1929: The Shopworn Angel. The Wolf of Wall Street. Sin Sister. Close Harmony. The Dance of Life. Illusion. Sweetie. 1930: Dangerous Paradise. Paramount on Parade. Follow Thru. The Devil's Holiday. Honey. Laughter. Two Against Death. 1931: Stolen Heaven. The Night Angel. Revolt. Personal Maid. 1932: Broken Lullaby (GB: The Man I Killed). Wayward. Scarlet Dawn. Hot Saturday. Undercover Man. 1933: Child of Manhattan. The Woman Accused. The Kiss Before the Mirror. I Love That Man. 1934: Springtime for Henry. Transatlantic Merry-Go-Round. Jealousy. Broken Melody. 1935: I'll Love You Always. After the Dance. Atlantic Adventure. 1938: There Goes My Heart. That Certain Age.

CARSON, Jack 1910–1963
Beefy, bulldozing, Canadian-born Hollywood character star, in residence at Warners from 1941 to 1950, often as comedy relief in musicals, or the guy who doesn't get the girl. Elmer was Carson's middle name, and it suited his speciality: happy-go-lucky Joes without too much brain. He made a couple of very funny comedies as star towards the end of the forties, and surprised many by revealing subtler dramatic talents in the fifties. Married four times, once to Lola Albright (1952–1958). Died from stomach cancer.
*1935: *Knife No. 5. Circle of Death. 1937: *A*

Rented Riot. Stage Door. You Only Live Once. Stand-In. It Could Happen to You. Reported Missing. Too Many Wives. On Again, Off Again. †A Damsel in Distress. High Flyers. Music for Madame. The Toast of New York. 1938: The Saint in New York. Vivacious Lady. Carefree. This Marriage Business. The Girl Downstairs. Condemned Women. Go Chase Yourself. Crashing Hollywood. Law of the Underworld. Everybody's Doing It. Night Spot. Having Wonderful Time. Maid's Night Out. Quick Money. She's Got Everything. Bringing Up Baby. Mr Doodle Kicks Off. 1929: Destry Rides Again. Fifth Avenue Girl. The Kid from Texas. The Escape. The Honeymoon's Over. Mr Smith Goes to Washington. Legion of Lost Flyers. 1940: I Take This Woman. The Girl in 313. Shooting High. Sandy Gets Her Man. Alias the Deacon. Enemy Agent (GB: Secret Enemy). Queen of the Mob. Typhoon. Love Thy Neighbor. Parole Fixer. Lucky Partners. Young As You Feel. I Take This Woman. 1941: Mr and Mrs Smith. Love Crazy. The Strawberry Blonde. The Bride Came COD. Blues in the Night. Navy Blues. 1942: Larceny Inc. Wings for the Eagle. Gentleman Jim. The Hard Way. The Male Animal. 1943: Thank Your Lucky Stars. Princess O'Rourke. Arsenic and Old Lace. 1944: Shine On Harvest Moon. The Doughgirls. Hollywood Canteen. *The Shining Future. Make Your Own Bed. *Road to Glory. 1945: Roughly Speaking. Mildred Pierce. 1946: The Time, the Place and the Girl. One More Tomorrow. Two Guys from Milwaukee (GB: Royal Flush). 1947: Love and Learn. 1948: Always Together. Two Guys from Texas (GB: Two Texas Nights). Romance on the High Seas (GB: It's Magic). April Showers. 1949: John Loves Mary. My Dream is Yours. It's a Great Feeling. *Rough But Hopeful. 1950: Bright Leaf. The Good Humor Man. 1951: The Groom Wore Spurs. Mr Universe. 1953: Dangerous When Wet. 1954: A Star is Born. Red Garters. Phffft! *Hollywood Cowboy Stars. 1955: Ain't Misbehavin'. 1956: Magnificent Roughnecks. Bottom of the Bottle (GB: Beyond the River). 1957: The Tattered Dress. Three Men on a Horse (TV). The Tarnished Angels. 1958: Rally 'Round the Flag, Boys! Cat on a Hot Tin Roof. The Long March (TV). 1960: The Bramble Bush. 1961: King of the Roaring Twenties (GB: The Big Bankroll). 1962:

Sammy the Way-Out Seal (TV. GB: cinemas).

† Scenes deleted from final release print

CARSON, Jeannie (Jean Shufflebottom) 1928–
Vivacious red-headed British star, of Scottish parentage, from musicals and revues on stage, where she made a tremendous hit at only 21 in a show called Love from Judy. British films could never find the right vehicle for her, and she now lives in America with her husband, actor Biff McGuire.
1948: †A Date with a Dream. 1953: †Love in Pawn. 1955: †As Long As They're Happy. †An Alligator Named Daisy. 1958: Rockets Galore (US: Mad Little Island). 1962: Seven Keys.

† As Jean Carson

CARSON, John (J. Carson-Parker) 1927–
Velvet-voiced (aurally a dead ringer for James Mason), suave, dark-haired, Ceylon-born actor who played silky-smooth villains in the 1960s, but has for many years been lost to voice-overs for television commercials. Raised in Ceylon (now Sri Lanka), Oxford University and New Zealand, where he acted until 1955. Married to actress Luanshya Greer, he has six children.
1955: The Adventures of Quentin Durward (US: Quentin Durward). 1956: Ramsbottom Rides Again. 1958: Intent to Kill. The Lady is a Square. 1959: Beyond This Place (US: Web of Evidence). 1960: Identity Unknown. 1962: Guns of Darkness. Seven Keys. Locker 69. The

Set-Up. 1963: Master Spy. Accidental Death. 1964: Act of Murder. Smokescreen. 1965: The Plague of the Zombies. The Night Caller (US: Blood Beast from Outer Space). 1967: Thunderbird 6 (voice only). 1968: The Last Shot You Hear. 1970: The Man Who Haunted Himself. Taste the Blood of Dracula. 1972: Captain Kronos – Vampire Hunter.

CARTER, Janis (J. Dremann) 1917–
Personable, fair-haired American leading lady with bright, cheery smile and attractive personality. She enlivened a number of Hollywood second-features in the 1940s, playing good girls and bad girls with equal facility. But she seemed to lack the driving force to move on to bigger things, and retired early after a successful second marriage.
1941: Cadet Girl. 1942: Secret Agent of Japan. Who is Hope Schuyler? Just Off Broadway. I Married an Angel. Girl Trouble. Thunder Birds. That Other Woman. 1943: Swing Out the Blues. Lady of Burlesque. The Ghost That Walks Alone. 1944: Girl in the Case (GB: The Silver Key). The Missing Juror. One Mysterious Night. Mark of the Whistler (GB: The Marked Man). 1945: The Fighting Guardsman. One Way to Love. Power of the Whistler. 1946: Night Editor (GB: The Trespasser). The Notorious Lone Wolf. 1947: I Love Trouble. Framed (GB: Paula). 1949: Miss Grant Takes Richmond (GB: Innocence is Bliss). Slightly French. And Baby Makes Three. I Married a Communist (GB: The Woman on Pier 13). 1950: A Woman of Distinction. Her Wonderful Lie. 1951: My Forbidden Past. Flying Leathernecks. Sante Fé. 1952: The Half Breed. 1954: Second Face (GB: Double Profile).

CASSAVETES, John 1929–
Slight, dark, lean-and-hungry-looking American actor who largely escaped the gangster roles for which his Italianate features seemed to destine him. In 1959 he turned director and has had several immense critical successes, although the public have stayed away from the same films in droves. His biggest popular success was a TV series called Johnny Staccato. Long married to actress Gena Rowlands (qv), who appears in his films. Oscar-nominated for The Dirty Dozen.
1951: †Fourteen Hours. 1953: Taxi. 1955: The Night Holds Terror. 1956: Crime in the Streets. 1957: Winter Dreams (TV). Edge of the City

(GB: *A Man is 10 Feet Tall*). *Affair in Havana. 1958: Saddle the Wind. Virgin Island/ Our Virgin Island. 1959: Shadows. 1962: The Webster Boy. 1964: The Killers. 1967: The Dirty Dozen. The Devil's Angels. 1968: Rosemary's Baby. Gli intoccabili (GB and US: Machine Gun McCain). Roma coma Chicago (GB: The Violent Four. US: Bandits in Rome). 1969: If It's Tuesday, This Must Be Belgium. 1970: Husbands. 1971: Minnie and Moskowitz. 1975: Capone. 1976: Two-Minute Warning. Mikey and Nicky. 1977: Opening Night. 1978: The Fury. Brass Target. 1979: Flesh and Blood (TV). 1981: Incubus. Whose Life Is It, Anyway? 1982: Tempest. 1983: Marvin and Tige. Love Streams. 1984: Like Father and Son. I'm Almost Not Crazy … 1986: The Third Day Comes.*

As director: *1959: Shadows. 1961: Too Late Blues. 1962: A Child is Waiting. 1968: Faces. 1970: Husbands. 1971: Minnie and Moskowitz. 1974: A Woman Under the Influence. 1976: The Killing of a Chinese Bookie. 1977: Opening Night. 1980: Gloria. 1983: Love Streams.*

1956: The Happy Road. 1957: A pied, à cheval et en voiture. La peau de l'ours. *Les surmenés. 1958: Le desordre et la nuit. En cas de malheur. Et ta soeur? 1959: Sacrée jeunesse. La marraine de Charley. Les jeux de l'amour (US: The Love Game). 1960: Le farceur (US: The Joker). Candide. 1961: L'amant de cinq jours (US: The Five-Day Lover). Les sept péchés capitaux (GB: The Seven Deadly Sins. US: Seven Capital Sins). La gamberge. Napoléon II: l'aiglon. 1962: Le caporal epinglé (US: The Vanishing Corporal. US: The Elusive Corporal). Arsène Lupin contre Arsène Lupin. Cyrano et d'Artagnan. 1963: Nunca pasa nada. Les plus belles escroqueries du monde. *Cabrioles (narrator only). 1964: Alta infideltà (GB and US: High Infidelity). Un monsieur de compagnie (US: Male Companion). La ronde. 1965: Those Magnificent Men in Their Flying Machines. Les fêtes galantes. Is Paris Burning? 1966: Jeu de massacre (US: The Killing Game). La dolci signore. 1968: L'ours et la poupée. 1969: Oh! What a Lovely War. L'armée des ombres. 1970: La rupture. 1971: Le bateau sur l'herbe. Malpertuis. 1972: Baxter! (US: The Boy). Le charme discret de la bourgeoisie (GB and US: The Discreet Charm of the Bourgeoisie). 1973: Il magnate. The Three Musketeers: The Queen's Diamonds. 1974: Le mouton enragé (GB and US: The French Way). Murder on the Orient Express. The Four Musketeers: The Revenge of Milady. 1975: Docteur Françoise Gailand (US: No Time for Breakfast). That Lucky Touch. 1976: Folies bourgeoises/The Twist. 1978: Les rendez-vous d'Anna. Who is Killing the Great Chefs of Europe? (GB: Too Many Chefs). 1979: Da Dunkerque alla vittoria (US: From Hell to Victory). Superman II. 1980: Alice. Le soleil en face. 1981: La vie continue. 1985: Tranches de la vie.

CASSEL, Jean-Pierre (J.-P. Crochon) 1932–
Tall, sandy-haired wry-faced French leading man who began as a dancer, and started his film career in a Hollywood film partly shot in his native Paris. His Gallic good looks faded rather early, but he remained in demand for character roles in both continental and international films until the early 1980s. In style and looks, something of a throwback to the melancholy heroes in the French cinema of the 1930s.

CASTLE, Don
(Marion Goodman Jr.) 1919–1966
Slim, dark, often moustachioed American actor, a cross between Guy Madison and Don Ameche. His promising career – he was considered a major star in the making – was interrupted by war service and his roles thereafter were confined to leading men in small second-features. Later became a producer, but was badly injured in a car smash. Died from a drug overdose.
1938: Love Finds Andy Hardy. Rich Man, Poor Girl. Out West with the Hardys. 1939:

These Glamour Girls. 1940: I Take This Woman. Susan and God (GB: The Gay Mrs Trexel). You're the One. 1941: Power Dive. World Premiere. 1942: Tombstone, the Town Too Tough to Die. Wake Island. 1946: Lighthouse. The Searching Wind. Born to Speed. 1947: The Invisible Wall. Seven Were Saved. Roses are Red. High Tide. The Guilty. In Self Defense. 1948: Perilous Waters. I Wouldn't Be in Your Shoes. Strike It Rich. Who Killed 'Doc' Robbin? (GB: Sinister House). 1949: Stampede. 1950: Motor Patrol. 1956: Gunfight at the OK Corral. 1957: The Big Land (GB: Stampeded!).

CASTLE, Peggie 1926–1973
Tall, sultry, green-eyed blonde actually spotted by a talent scout while she was lunching in a Beverly Hills restaurant. She was usually somebody's 'woman' rather than a girl-friend and her career was confined to colourful co-features. After four years in a TV western series, she left show business in 1962. Later developed an alcohol problem, and died of cirrhosis of the liver.
1949: Mr Belvedere Goes to College. 1950: Shakedown. I Was a Shoplifter. Bright Victory (GB: Lights Out). Woman in Hiding. Buccaneer's Girl. The Prince Who Was a Thief. 1951: The Golden Horde. Air Cadet (GB: Jet Men of the Air). Payment on Demand. 1952: Harem Girl. Invasion USA. Wagons West. Cow Country. 1953: 99 River Street. Son of Belle Star. I the Jury. 1954: The Long Wait. Jesse James' Women. The Yellow Tomahawk. The White Orchid. Southwest Passage (GB: Camels West). Overland Pacific. 1955: Tall Man Riding. Target Zero. Finger Man. 1956: Miracle in the Rain. Two Gun Lady. Oklahoma Woman. Quincannon - Frontier Scout (GB: Frontier Scout). The Counterfeit Plan. 1957: Back from the Dead. Hell's Crossroads. The Beginning of the End. 1958: The Seven Hills of Rome. The Money.

CAULFIELD, Joan
(Beatrice J. Caulfield) 1922–
Demurely pretty blonde American star, who came to films via modelling. At her best being winsomely sexy in light comedies, and, seemingly not able to provide much depth to more dramatic characterizations, she had only a few years at the top.
1944: Miss Susie Slagle's (released 1946). 1945: Duffy's Tavern. 1946: Blue Skies. Monsieur Beaucaire. 1947: Welcome Stranger. Dear

Ruth. Variety Girl. The Unsuspected. 1948: The Sainted Sisters. Larceny. 1949: Dear Wife. 1950: The Petty Girl (GB: Girl of the Year). 1951: The Lady Says No. 1955: The Rains of Ranchipur. 1963: Cattle King (GB: Guns of Wyoming). 1967: Red Tomahawk. 1968: Buckskin. 1973: The Magician (TV). 1975: The Hatfields and the McCoys (TV). 1976: Pony Express Rider. 1977: The Daring Dobermans (TV). 1978: The Space-Watch Murders (TV).

CHAMBERLAIN, Richard 1935–
Fair-haired, boyishly handsome American actor who achieved immense success as television's Dr Kildare in the sixties. His early cinema roles proved too bland for public taste but, after stage experience, he established himself as a serious screen actor, if not quite as a top star.
1960: The Secret of the Purple Reef. 1961: A Thunder of Drums. 1963: Twilight of Honor (GB: The Charge is Murder). 1965: Joy in the Morning. 1968: Petulia. 1969: The Madwoman of Chaillot. 1970: Julius Caesar. The Music Lovers. 1972: Lady Caroline Lamb. 1973: The Three Musketeers. The Woman I Love (TV). 1974: The Last of the Belles (TV). The Count of Monte-Cristo (TV. GB: cinemas). The Towering Inferno. The Four Musketeers. 1976: The Slipper and the Rose. The Man in the Iron Mask (TV). 1977: The Last Wave. 1978: The Swarm. 1980: Shogun (TV. GB: cinemas in abbreviated version). 1981: Bells (later Murder by Phone). 1983: Cook and Peary: The Race to the Pole (TV). 1984: Wallenberg, the Lost Hero. 1985: King Solomon's Mines. Quartermain. 1986: Allan Quartermain and the City of Gold.

CHAKIRIS, George 1933–
Smooth, dark-haired, sharp-featured boyish American musical star, first a boy singer, then dancer in the chorus of fifties' musicals. An Oscar for *West Side Story* skyrocketed his career, but his acting proved not quite strong enough in subsequent dramatic outings.
1947: Song of Love. 1951: The Great Caruso. 1953: The 5,000 Fingers of Dr T. Give a Girl a Break. Gentlemen Prefer Blondes. 1954: White Christmas. There's No Business Like Show Business. Brigadoon. 1955: The Girl Rush. 1956: †Meet Me in Las Vegas (GB: Viva las Vegas!). 1957: Under Fire. 1961: West Side Story. 1962: Two and Two Make Six. Diamond Head. 1963: Kings of the Sun. Bebo's Girl. 1964: The High Bright Sun (US: McGuire, Go Home!). 633 Squadron. Flight from Ashiya. 1965: Is Paris Burning? Le voleur de la Joconde. 1967: The Young Girls of Rochefort. 1968: The Day the Hot Line Got Hot. 1969: The Big Cube. 1979: Why Not Stay for Breakfast?

† As George Kerris

CHAMPION, Marge
(Marjorie Belcher) 1921–
Personable dancer with lovely legs and a winning smile who briefly hit the big time in M-G-M musicals with then-husband Gower, pictured above with Marge, (married 1947– 1971). Gower (1921–1980) turned to directing on the Broadway stage and, after the divorce, Marge devoted her attentions to choreography, winning an Emmy for her work on a 1974 TV movie, *Queen of the Stardust Ballroom*. A

† indicates a film with Gower, who died from a rare blood cancer. She later married director Boris Sagal, but he was killed in an accident in 1981.
1939: ‡The Story of Vernon and Irene Castle. ‡Sorority House (GB: The Girl from College). ‡Honor of the West. ‡Pinocchio (voice only). 1950: †Mr Music. 1951: †Show Boat. 1952: †Lovely to Look At. †Everything I Have is Yours. 1953: † Give a Girl a Break. 1955: †Jupiter's Darling. †Three for the Show. 1967: The Swimmer. 1968: The Party. 1969: The Cockeyed Cowboys of Calico Country (GB TV: A Woman for Charlie).
‡ As Marjorie Bell

CHANCE, Naomi 1930–
Aristocratic, elegant, honey-voiced blonde British actress who co-starred with a number of visiting American stars in home-grown thrillers of the early 1950s. She seemed to lose interest in a star career after marrying director Guy Hamilton in 1954 (they were later divorced), and was thereafter seen only in minor roles. Always looked more at home in furs than jeans.
1952: Wings of Danger (US: Dead on Course). It Started in Paradise. The Gambler and the Lady. 1953: Blood Orange. Strange Stories. The Saint's Return (US: The Saint's Girl Friday). 1954: Dangerous Voyage (US: Terror Ship). The End of the Road. 1956: A Touch of the Sun. 1957: Suspended Alibi. 1958: The Man Inside. 1959: Operation Bullshine. 1960: The Trials of Oscar Wilde (US: The Man with the Green Carnation). 1963: The Comedy Man. 1965: He Who Rides a Tiger.

CHANDLER, Jeff
(Ira Grossel) 1918–1961
Square-jawed hero of Hollywood action yarns of the fifties, with prematurely grey hair, fierce, scowling features and harsh, aggressive voice. In early films was often cast as Red Indians – he made his name as Cochise in three movies – or other dark-skinned nationals. His death caused something of a scandal as it followed a routine minor operation. The official cause was blood poisoning. He was nominated for an Oscar in *Broken Arrow*.
1947: Johnny O'Clock. The Invisible Wall. Roses Are Red. 1949: Mr Belvedere Goes To College. Abandoned. Sword in the Desert. 1950: Deported. Double Crossbones (narrator only).

Two Flags West. Broken Arrow. 1951: Bird of Paradise. Iron Man. Flame of Araby. Smuggler's Island. Meet Danny Wilson. 1952: The Battle at Apache Pass. The Red Ball Express. Yankee Buccaneer. Because of You. 1953: East of Sumatra. War Arrow. The Great Sioux Uprising. 1954: Taza, Son of Cochise. *Queens of Beauty. Yankee Pasha. Sign of the Pagan. 1955: Foxfire. Female on the Beach. The Spoilers. 1956: Away All Boats. Pillars of the Sky (GB: The Tomahawk and the Cross). *The Nat King Cole Musical Story (and narrator). Toy Tiger. 1957: Drango. The Tattered Dress. Jeanne Eagels. Man in the Shadow (GB: Pay the Devil). 1958: The Lady Takes a Flyer. Raw Wind in Eden. Ten Seconds to Hell. 1959: Thunder in the Sun. Stranger in My Arms. The Jayhawkers. 1960: A Story of David. The Plunderers. 1961: Return to Peyton Place. Merrill's Marauders.

CHANEY, Lon
(Alonso Chaney) 1883–1930

American character star, known as 'the man with a thousand faces' because of the ingenious and sometimes painful make-up devices with which he changed his appearance from film to film. The child of deaf-and-dumb parents, he became a master pantomimist, bringing great pathos to such creations as Fagin, Quasimodo and the Phantom of the Opera. Died from throat cancer.
1913: *The Sea Urchin. *Poor Jake's Demise. *The Trap. *Almost an Actress. *Back to Life. *Red Margaret – Moonshiner. *Bloodhounds of the North. *The Lie. 1914: *Remember Mary Magdalen. *The Honor of the Mounted. Discord

and Harmony. *The Menace to Carlotta. *The Embezzler. The Lamb, the Woman and the Wolf. *The End of the Feud. *The Tragedy of Whispering Creek. *The Unlawful Trade. *The Old Cobbler. The Small Town Girl. The Forbidden Room. *A Ranch Romance. *Her Grave Mistake. *By the Sun's Ray. *A Miner's Romance. The Adventures of Francois Villon (serial). *Her Bounty. *The Pipes of Pan. Richelieu. *Virtue Its Own Reward. *Her Life's Story. *Lights and Shadows. *The Lion, the Lamb, the Man. *A Night of Thrills. *Her Escape. *The Sin of Olga Brandt. *The Star of the Sea. 1915: *The Measure of a Man. *The Threads of Fate. When the Gods Played a Badger Game. *Such is Life. *Where the Forest Ends. *All for Peggy. *Outside the Gates. *The Desert Breed. *Maid of the Mist. *The Girl of the Night. *The Stool Pigeon. The Grind. *For Cash. *Her Chance. *An Idyll of the Hills. *The Stronger Mind. *The Oyster Dredger. *The Violin Maker. *Steady Company. *The Trust. Bound on the Wheel. *Mountain Justice. *Quits. *The Chimney's Secret. *The Pine's Revenge. The Fascination of Fleur de Lis. *Alas and Alack. *A Mother's Atonement. *Lon of Lone Mountain. The Millionaire Paupers. Father and the Boys. *Under a Shadow. *Stronger Than Death. 1916: *Dolly's Scoop. The Grip of Jealousy. Tangled Hearts. The Gilded Spider. Bobbie of the Ballet. Grasp of Greed. The Mark of Cain. If My Country Should Call. Place Beyond the Winds. *Felix on the Job. Accusing Evidence. The Price of Silence. The Piper's Price (GB: Storm and Sunshine). 1917: Hell Morgan's Girl. *The Mask of Love. The Girl in the Checkered Coat. The Flashlight. A Doll's House. Vengeance of the West. The Rescue. Fires of Rebellion. Pay Me. Triumph. The Empty Gun. Bondage. Anything Once. The Scarlet Car. 1918: Broadway Love. The Kaiser, the Beast of Berlin. The Grand Passion. Fast Company. A Broadway Scandal. Riddle Gawne. That Devil, Bateese. The Talk of the Town. Danger – Go Slow. 1919: The Wicked Darling. False Faces. Paid in Advance. A Man's Country. The Miracle Man. When Bearcat Went Dry. Victory. 1920: Daredevil Jack (serial). Treasure Island. The Gift Supreme. Nomads of the North. The Penalty. 1921: Outside the law. For Those We Love. Bits of Life. Ace of Hearts. 1922: The Trap (GB: Heart of a Wolf). Voices of the City. Flesh and Blood. The Light in the Dark. Oliver Twist. Shadows. Quincy Adams Sawyer. A Blind Bargain. 1923: All the Brothers Were Valiant. While Paris Sleeps. The Shock. The Hunchback of Notre Dame. 1924: The Next Corner. He Who Gets Slapped. 1925: The Monster. The Unholy Three. The Phantom of the Opera. The Tower of Lies. 1926: The Blackbird. The Road to Mandalay. Tell It to the Marines. 1927: Mr Wu. The Unknown. Mockery. London after Midnight (GB: The Hypnotist). 1928: The Big City. Laugh, Clown, Laugh. While the City Sleeps. West of Zanzibar. 1929: Where East is East. Thunder. 1930: The Unholy Three (remake).

As director: 1915: *The Stool Pigeon. *For

Cash. *The Oyster Dredger. *The Violin Maker. *The Trust. *The Chimney's Secret.

CHANEY, Lon Junior
(Creighton Chaney) 1905–1973

Big, ugly, dark-haired, hulking American actor, the son of Lon Chaney. A star in horror films, but a supporting player elsewhere, he was always best as simple-minded brutes unable to cope when dramatic events overtook them – whether they took the shape of men turning into werewolves or worse, or, in the best performance of his career, the pitiable Lenny in Of Mice and Men. Died from cancer.
1932: †The Sign of the Cross. †Girl Crazy. †Bird of Paradise. †The Last Frontier (serial). 1933: †Lucky Devils. †Scarlet River. †Son of the Border. †The Three Musketeers (serial). 1934: †Girl o' My Dreams. †The Life of Vergie Winters. †Sixteen Fathoms Deep. 1935: Captain Hurricane. Accent on Love. Hold 'Em Yale (GB: Uniform Lovers). Shadow of Silk Lennox. The Marriage Bargain (GB: Woman of Destiny). Scream in the Night. 1936: Undersea Kingdom (serial). The Singing Cowboy. Killer at Large. The Old Corral (GB: Texas Serenade). Ace Drummond (serial). Rhythm on the Range. 1937: Secret Agent X-9 (serial). Midnight Taxi. Angel's Holiday. Wild and Woolly. Wife, Doctor and Nurse. Love and Hisses. The Lady Escapes. One Mile from Heaven. This is My Affair (GB: His Affair). City Girl. Second Honeymoon. That I May Live. Born Reckless. Thin Ice (GB: Lovely to Look At). Charlie Chan on Broadway. Slave Ship. Life Begins in College (GB: The Joy Parade). 1938: Mr Moto's Gamble. Straight, Place and Show (GB: They're Off). Walking Down Broadway. Alexander's Ragtime Band. Passport Husband. Road Demon. Submarine Patrol. Speed to Burn. Happy Landing. Josette. 1939: Jesse James. Union Pacific. Frontier Marshal. Charlie Chan in City of Darkness (GB: City of Darkness). Of Mice and Men. 1940: One Million BC (GB: Man and His Mate). Northwest Mounted Police. Riders of Death Valley (serial). 1941: Billy the Kid. San Antonio Rose. Too Many Blondes. Badlands of Dakota. The Wolf Man. Man Made Monster (GB: The Electric Man). 1942: The Ghost of Frankenstein. Overland Mail (serial). North to the Klondike. The Mummy's Tomb. *Keeping Fit. 1943: Frankenstein Meets the Wolf Man. Eyes of the Underworld. Son of Dracula. Fron-

tier Badman. Crazy House. Calling Doctor Death. 1944: Follow the Boys. Ghost Catchers. Weird Woman. Cobra Woman. The Mummy's Ghost. Dead Man's Eyes. The Mummy's Curse. House of Frankenstein. 1945: Here Come the Coeds. The Frozen Ghost. House of Dracula. Pillow of Death. Strange Confession. The Daltons Ride Again. 1947: My Favorite Brunette. 1948: Sixteen Fathoms Deep. Albuquerque (GB: Silver City). Abbott and Costello Meet Frankenstein (GB: Abbott and Costello Meet the Ghosts). The Counterfeiters. 1949: There's a Girl in My Heart. Captain China. 1950: Once a Thief. 1951: Inside Straight. Only the Valiant. Flame of Araby. Behave Yourself! 1952: Bride of the Gorilla. Thief of Damascus. The Battles of Chief Pontiac. Springfield Rifle. High Noon. The Black Castle. The Bushwhackers (GB: The Rebel). 1953: A Lion is in the Streets. Raiders of the Seven Seas. Casanova's Big Night. 1954: Jivaro (GB: Lost Treasure of the Amazon). The Boy from Oklahoma. Passion. The Big Chase. The Black Pirates. 1955: Big House USA. I Died a Thousand Times. The Indian Fighter. The Silver Star. 1956: Pardners. Manfish (GB: Calypso). The Indestructible Man. Daniel Boone – Trail Blazer. The Black Sleep. 1957: Cyclops. 1958: Money, Women and Guns. The Defiant Ones. 1959: La casa del terror (US: Face of the Screaming Werewolf). The Alligator People. The Devil's Messenger. 1961: The Phantom. Rebellion in Cuba. 1963: The Haunted Palace. Law of the Lawless. 1964: Witchcraft. Stage to Thunder Rock. Young Fury. 1965: Black Spurs. House of the Black Death. Town Tamer. Apache Uprising. 1966: Johnny Reno. The Vulture. Night of the Beast. Welcome to Hard Times (GB: Killer on a Horse). 1967: Hillbillys in a Haunted House. Dr Terror's Gallery of Horrors. 1968: Buckskin. Cannibal Orgy (US: Spider Baby). 1969: Jungle Terror (US: Fireball Jungle). 1970: Blood of Frankenstein (US: Dracula versus Frankenstein). Satan's Sadists.

† *As Creighton Chaney*

CHAPLIN, Sir Charles 1889–1977
British-born pantomimist with dark, curly hair who became the most popular comedian of Hollywood's silent era. His legendary character The Tramp, complete with bowler hat, cane, toothbrush moustache and splay-

footed walk, triumphed with great ingenuity and sublime comic timing over life's pitfalls and a mountain of hulking villains. He became less popular after World War II, when his private life did not suit America's tastes, and his films were overtaken by pathos and autocracy. Given special Oscars in 1928 (specifically in connection with *The Circus*) and 1972, he won an Academy Award for his *Limelight* music in 1952. Married four times including (third) Paulette Goddard (*qv*) from 1936 to 1942. Knighted in 1975. Received an acting Oscar nomination for *The Great Dictator*.

1914: Making a Living. Kid Auto Races at Venice. Mabel's Strange Predicament. Between Showers. A Film Johnnie. Tango Tangles. His Favorite Pastime. Cruel, Cruel Love. The Star Boarder. Mabel at the Wheel. Twenty Minutes of Love. The Knockout. †Tillie's Punctured Romance. Caught in a Cabaret. Caught in the Rain. A Busy Day. The Fatal Mallet. Her Friend the Bandit. Mabel's Busy Day. Mabel's Married Life. Laughing Gas. The Property Man. The Face on the Bar-Room Floor. Recreation. The Masquerader. His New Profession. The Rounders. The New Janitor. Those Love Pangs. Dough and Dynamite. Gentlemen of Nerve. His Musical Career. His Trysting Place. Getting Acquainted. His Prehistoric Past. 1915: His New Job. A Night Out. The Champion. In the Park. A Jitney Elopement. The Tramp. By the Sea. His Regeneration. Work. A Woman. The Bank. Shanghaied. A Night in the Show. †Carmen/Charlie Chaplin's Burlesque on Carmen. 1916: Police. The Floorwalker. The Fireman. The Vagabond. One A.M. The Count. The Pawn Shop. Behind the Screen. The Rink. 1917: Easy Street. The Cure. The Immigrant. The Adventurer. 1918: How to Make Movies. The Bond. A Dog's Life. Triple Trouble. †Shoulder Arms. Charles Chaplin in a Liberty Loan Appeal. 1919: Sunnyside. A Day's Pleasure. 1920: †The Kid. †The Mollycoddle. 1921: †The Nut. The Idle Class. 1922: Pay Day. Nice and Friendly. 1923: †The Pilgrim. †Souls for Sale. †A Woman of Paris. 1925: †The Gold Rush. 1926: †A Woman of the Sea. 1927: †The Circus. 1928: †Show People. †The Woman Disputed. 1931: †City Lights. 1936: †Modern Times. 1940: †The Great Dictator. 1947: †Monsieur Verdoux. 1952: †Limelight. 1957: †A King in New York. 1966: †A Countess from Hong Kong.

As narrator of compilation film: *1959: The Chaplin Revue.*

Chaplin directed (or co-directed) all the above except the first 13, plus *His Regeneration, The Nut, Souls for Sale* and *Show People.*

All shorts, except features (†)

CHAPLIN, Geraldine 1944–
Wan-faced, toothy, brunette American actress, oldest daughter of Charles Chaplin's fourth marriage. Most of her early performances are as pale as her complexion, and she has never been a power at the box-office. But the seventies showed a stronger actress emerging, perhaps through her long personal and working association with the Spanish director Carlos Saura.

*1952: Limelight. 1964: *Dernier soir. Par un beau matin d'été. 1965: Doctor Zhivago. Andremo in città. 1966: A Countess from Hong Kong. 1967: I Killed Rasputin. Stranger in the House (US: Cop-Out). Peppermint frappé. 1968: Stres es tres, tres. 1969: La Madriguera (US: The Honeycomb). 1970: El Jardín de las Delicias. The Hawaiians (GB: Master of the Islands). Sur un arbre perché. 1971: ZPG (GB: Zero Population Growth). 1972: Innocent Bystanders. La Casa sin fronteras. 1973: Aña and the Wolves. The Three Musketeers. Verflucht, dies Amerika. Y El Projimo? 1974: Le marriage à la mode. The Four Musketeers. Summer of Silence. 1975: Nashville. The Gentleman Tramp. Cria cuervos (GB: Raise Ravens. US: Cria!). 1976: Elisa, vida mia. Noroît. Buffalo Bill and the Indians. Scrim. Welcome to LA. 1977: Une page d'amour. Roseland. In Memoriam. 1978: The Masked Bride. Remember My Name. L'adoption. Savage Weekend. A Wedding. Los ojos vendados. Mais où et donc ornicar? 1979: Tout est à nous. Mama cumple cien años. La viuda de Montiel. Le voyage en douce. 1980: The Mirror Crack'd. 1981: Les uns et les autres (US: The Ins and the Outs). Bolero. 1983: La vie est un roman (GB and US: Life is a Bed of Roses). 1984: L'amour par terre (GB: Love on the Ground). 1985: The Corsican Brothers (TV). Hidden Talent.*

CHAPMAN, Marguerite 1920–
Marguerite was a treat in Technicolor. The blue-eyed brunette with the fabulous complexion remained queen of Columbia's double-feature output from 1942 until 1948. But subsequent roles wasted her warmth and

latent sensuality and she spent most of the fifties in TV. Now lives in Hawaii, and was occasionally glimpsed in episodes of the television series *Hawaii Five-O*.
1940: *On Their Own. Charlie Chan at the Wax Museum*. 1941: *Navy Blues. A Girl, a Guy and a Gob (GB: The Navy Steps Out). You're in the Army Now. The Body Disappears*. 1942: *Submarine Raider. Parachute Nurse. A Man's World. Spy Smasher (serial). The Spirit of Stanford. The Daring Young Man*. 1943: *Murder in Times Square. Appointment in Berlin. My Kingdom for a Cook. Destroyer. One Dangerous Night*. 1944: *Strange Affair*. 1945: *Counter Attack. Pardon My Past. One Way to Love. A Thousand and One Nights*. 1946: *The Walls Came Tumbling Down*. 1947: *Mr District Attorney*. 1948: *Relentless. Coroner Creek. The Gallant Blade*. 1949: *The Green Promise (GB: Raging Waters)*. 1950: *Kansas Raiders*. 1951: *Flight to Mars*. 1952: *The Last Page (US: Man Bait). Sea Tiger. Bloodhounds of Broadway*. 1955: *The Seven Year Itch*. 1960: *The Amazing Transparent Man*.

CHARISSE, Cyd (Tula Finklea) 1921–
Tall, stately, serious-looking American dancing star with lovely legs and a smoulder that only really caught fire in dancing scenes. An elegant, eye-catching partner for both Fred Astaire and Gene Kelly. Since 1948 has been married to second husband Tony Martin, with whom, glamorous as ever, she still makes night-club and television appearances.
1941: *Rhumba Serenade. *Poème. *I Knew It Would Be This Way. *Did Anyone Call?* 1942: †*Something to Shout About. *This Love of Mine. Mission to Moscow*. 1943: *Thousands Cheer*. 1944: *Ziegfeld Follies (released 1946)*. 1945: *The Harvey Girls*. 1946: *Three Wise Fools. Till the Clouds Roll By*. 1947: *Fiesta. The Unfinished Dance*. 1948: *On an Island with You. Words and Music. The Kissing Bandit*. 1949: *Tension. East Side, West Side*. 1951: *Mark of the Renegade*. 1952: *The Wild North. Singin' in the Rain*. 1953: *Sombrero. The Band Wagon. Easy to Love*. 1954: *Deep in My Heart. Brigadoon*. 1955: *It's Always Fair Weather*. 1956: *Meet Me in Las Vegas (GB: Viva Las Vegas)*. 1957: *Invitation to the Dance. Silk Stockings*. 1958: *Twilight for the Gods. Party Girl*. 1960: *Black Tights*. 1961: *Five Golden Hours*. 1962: *Something's Gotta Give (unfinished). Two Weeks in Another Town*. 1963: *Il

segreto del vestito rosso (GB: Assassin … Made in Italy. US: Assassination in Rome). 1966: *The Silencers. Maroc 7*. 1972: *Call Her Mom (TV)*. 1975: *Won Ton Ton – the Dog Who Saved Hollywood*. 1978: *Warlords of Atlantis*. 1980: *Portrait of an Escort (TV)*.

† *As Lily Norwood*

CHASE, Chevy
(Cornelius Chase) 1949–
Moon-faced American satirist and comic actor with high forehead, dark hair and laconic smile (he looks like a benevolent Henry Silva). Broke into public limelight with his abrasively aggressive style on a late-night TV satire show, *Saturday Night Live*, along with John Belushi, Dan Aykroyd (both *qv*) and others. Film stardom was longer in coming, but *Fletch* was a personal *tour-de-force* which seems to have established him at the top.
1974: *The Groove Tube*. 1976: *Tunnelvision*. 1978: *Foul Play*. 1980: *Caddyshack. Oh Heavenly Dog. Seems Like Old Times*. 1981: *Modern Problems. Under the Rainbow*. 1983: *Deal of the Century. National Lampoon's Vacation*. 1984: *Fletch*. 1985: *National Lampoon's European Vacation. Sesame Street Presents: Follow That Bird. Spies Like Us*. 1986: *The Three Amigos*.

CHATTERTON, Ruth 1893-1961
Pretty, dark-haired American stage star (an immense hit in gamine roles of the 1920s) for whom film talkies came almost too late. She was a major star in them, but for only a few years. Returned to the stage in the late 1930s, having been nominated for Academy Awards in *Madame X* and *Sarah and Son*. In her

later years she became a modestly successful novelist. Married three times, the first two being film stars Ralph Forbes (1924–1932) and George Brent (1932–1934).
1928: *Sins of the Fathers*. 1929: *The Doctor's Secret. The Dummy. Madame X. Charming Sinners. The Laughing Lady*. 1930: *Sarah and Son. Paramount on Parade. The Lady of Scandal (GB: The High Road). Anybody's Woman. The Right to Love*. 1931: *Unfaithful. The Magnificent Lie. Once a Lady*. 1932: *Tomorrow and Tomorrow. The Rich Are Always with Us. The Crash*. 1933: *Frisco Jenny. Lilly Turner. Female*. 1934: *Journal of a Crime*. 1936: *Lady of Secrets. Girls' Dormitory. Dodsworth*. 1937: *The Rat*. 1938: *A Royal Divorce*.

CHERRY, Helen 1915–
Attractive auburn-haired British actress of sympathetic personality, long married to Trevor Howard. Her upper-class voice, slightly old-fashioned looks and theatrical style probably kept her from star roles in films, although she has been very much successful on stage, with many successes at Stratford-upon-Avon.
1947: *The Courtneys of Curzon Street (US: The Courtney Affair). The Mark of Cain*. 1949: *For Them That Trespass. Adam and Evelyne (US: Adam and Evalyn)*. 1950: *Morning Departure (US: Operation Disaster). They Were Not Divided. Last Holiday. The Woman with No Name (US: Her Panelled Door)*. 1951: *Young Wives' Tale. His Excellency*. 1952: *Castle in the Air*. 1955: *Three Cases of Murder*. 1956: *Run for the Sun*. 1957: *High Flight*. 1961: *The Naked Edge*. 1962: *Tomorrow at Ten. The Devil's Agent*. 1964: *Flipper's New Adventure (GB: Flipper and the Pirates)*. 1968: *The Charge of the Light Brigade*. 1969: *Hard Contract*. 1974: *11 Harrowhouse*. 1975: *Conduct Unbecoming*. 1978: *No Longer Alone*. 1985: *Time After Time (TV)*.

CHEVALIER, Maurice 1888–1972
French actor and crooner of long stage background and international reputation. With twinkling eyes, Gallic charm and leering lower lip, Chevalier became a big star of early Hollywood musical comedies, especially opposite Jeanette MacDonald. Everyone imitated him singing 'Louise' – even the Marx Brothers. Returned in the fifties, still lecherous but more avuncular. Given a special

Academy Award in 1958. Died from a heart attack. He was nominated for best actor Oscars on *The Love Parade* and *The Big Pond*. 1908: *Trop crédule. 1911: *Un marie qui se fait attendre. *Par habitude. 1912: *La valse renversante. 1917: *Une soirée mondaine. 1921: Le mauvais garçon. 1922: *Le match Criqui-Ledoux. Gonzague. 1923: L'affaire de la Rue de Lourcine. Jim Bougne, boxeur. 1924: Par habitude (remake). 1928: Bonjour New York! 1929: †Innocents of Paris. †The Love Parade. 1930: †Paramount on Parade. †The Big Pond. †Playboy of Paris. 1931: †The Smiling Leutenant. *El Cliente Seductor. 1932: †One Hour with You. Make Me a Star. *Hollywood on Parade No.5. Love Me Tonight. *The Stolen Jools (GB: The Slippery Pearls). *Stopping the Show (voice only). *Battling Georges. 1933: A Bedtime Story. †The Way to Love. 1934: †The Merry Widow. 1935: Folies Bergère (GB: The Man from Folies Bergère). 1936: †The Beloved Vagabond. L'homme du jour. Avec le sourire. 1938: Break the News. 1939: Pièges (US: Personal Column). 1946: Paris 1900. Le silence est d'or (US: Man About Town). 1949: Le roi (US: A Royal Affair). 1950: Ma pomme. 1952: *Jouons le jeu ... l'Avarice. 1953: *Chevalier de Ménilmontant. Schlager-Parade. 1954: A Hundred Years of Love. I Had Seven Daughters. *Caf'Conc. 1954: *Sur toute la gamme (narrator only). 1957: Love in the Afternoon. Rendez-vous avec Maurice Chevalier (series). The Heart of Show Business. 1958: Gigi. 1959: Count Your Blessings. 1960: Can-Can. Black Tights. A Breath of Scandal. Pepe. 1961: Jessica. Fanny. 1962: In Search of the Castaways. 1963: Panic Button. A New Kind of Love. 1964: I'd Rather Be Rich. La Chance et l'amour. 1967: Monkeys, Go Home! 1970: The Aristocats (voice only).

† Also starred in French-language version

CHRISTIAN, Paul
See Hubschmid, Paul

CHRISTIANS, Mady (Margarethe Christians) 1900–1951
Fluffy Viennese blonde, the Mary Pickford of Austro-German films, in which she commanded a huge and faithful following. Left Germany in 1934, and quickly established herself as a Hollywood character actress,

although in later years she seemed to prefer the stage, where she had scored her first US triumph in 1938 as Gertrude in a production of *Hamlet*. Shortly before her death from a cerebral haemorrhage, she was blacklisted in Hollywood during the investigations of the House Un-American Activities Committee.
1916: Audrey. 1917: Das verlorene Paradies. Die Krone von Kerkyra. Frau Marias Erlebnis. 1918: Am andern Ufer. Am Scheidewege. Die Dreizehn. Die Verteidigerin. Nachtsschatten. 1919: Die Nacht des Grauens. Der goldene

Klub. Die Peruanerin. Die Sühne der Martha Marx. Eine junge Dame von Welt. Fidelio. Not und Verbrechen. 1920: Die Gesunkenen. Wer unter Euch ohne Sünde ist... Der Mann ohne Namen. 1921: Der Schicksalstag. Das Weib des Pharao (US: The Loves of Pharaoh). 1922: Es leuchtet meine Liebe. Kinder der Seit. Ein Glas Wasser. Malmaison. 1923: Die Buddenbrooks. Der verlorene Schuh. Der Wetterwart. Die Finanzen des Grossherzogs (US: The Grand Duke's Finances). 1924: Mensch gegen Mensch. Soll und Haben. 1925: Der Abenteurer. Die vom Niederrhein. Der Farmer aus Texas. Ein Walzertraum (GB and US: The Waltz Dream). Die Verrufenen (US: Slums of Berlin). 1926: Die geschiedene Frau. Nanette macht alles. La duchesse de 'Les Folies'/Die Königin vom Moulin Rouge. Die Welt will belogen sein. Wien, wie es weint und lacht. Zopf und Schwert. 1927: Königin Luise (US: Queen Luise). Grand Hotel ...! Heimveh. Der Sohn der Hagar (US: Out of the Mist). Königin Luise II. 1928: Fräulein Chauffeur. Eine Frau von format. Priscillas Fahrt ins Gluck. Duel. 1929: Das brennende Herz (GB and US: The Burning Heart). Meine Schwester und ich. Dich hab'ich geliebt (US: Because I Loved You). Leutnant warst du einst bei den Husaren. The Runaway Princess. 1931: Das Schicksal der Renate Langen. Die Frau, von der Man spricht. 1932: Der schwartze Husar. Friederike. 1933: Ich und die Kaiserin. The Only Girl (US: Heart Song). Manolescu. Salon Dora Green. 1934: Mon amour. Wicked Woman. 1935: Escapade. Ship Café. 1936: Come and Get It. 1937: Seventh Heaven. Heidi. The Woman I Love. 1943: Tender Comrade. 1944: Address Unknown. 1948: All My Sons. Letter from an Unknown Woman. 1950: The Morning After (TV).

CHRISTIE, Julie 1940–
India-born British actress with corn-coloured hair who suddenly seemed to be the spirit of the swinging sixties. This 'spirit' was rewarded with an Oscar for *Darling* (she was nominated again later for *McCabe and Mrs Miller*), but most of the critics deserted her when she attempted to widen her range, and her later performances were felt to lack the passion and colour of the earlier ones. But she returned to something like her best form in *Heaven Can Wait* and stepped up her work-rate in the 1980s, regaining some of her lost standing, if not box-office power, in some prestigious projects.
1962: Crooks Anonymous. 1963: The Fast Lady. Billy Liar. 1964: Young Cassidy. 1965: Darling. Doctor Zhivago. 1966: Fahrenheit 451. 1967: Far from the Madding Crowd. Tonite Let's All Make Love in London. 1968: Petulia. In Search of Gregory. 1970: The Go-Between. 1971: McCabe and Mrs Miller. 1973: Don't Look Now. 1975: Shampoo. Nashville. 1977: Demon Seed. 1978: Heaven Can Wait. 1981: Memoirs of a Survivor. Les quarantièmes rugissants (The Roaring Forties). The Animals Film (narrator only). 1982: The Return of the Soldier. 1983: Heat and Dust. The Gold Diggers. 1985: Power. 1986: Miss Maggie. The Easter Egg Chase.

CHURCHILL, Diana 1913–
Cool, blonde, elegant, pleasing British leading lady, a resilient wisecracking heroine of some late 1930s' comedy-thrillers, but mostly on stage after World War II. Widow of Barry K. Barnes (qv), her one-time co-star, whom she nursed through many years of ill-health until

his death in 1975. In 1976 she married actor Mervyn Johns (*also qv*).
1931: *Service for Ladies* (US: *Reserved for Ladies*). 1932: *Sally Bishop*. 1935: *Foreign Affaires*. 1936: *Pot Luck. Dishonour Bright. Sensation! The Dominant Sex*. 1937: *School for Husbands*. 1938: *Housemaster. Jane Steps Out. Yes, Madam?* 1939: *The Spider. Midnight Mail*. 1940: *Law and Disorder. The Flying Squad. The House of the Arrow* (US: *Castle of Crimes*). 1948: *Scott of the Antarctic*. 1949: *The History of Mr Polly*. 1966: *The Winter's Tale*.

CHURCHILL, Marguerite 1909–
Gravely beautiful brown-haired American actress of the 1930s, often seen in spunky roles. Chiefly remembered as John Wayne's leading lady in *The Big Trail*, but her performances almost always had that little extra sparkle. Married to western star George O'Brien (*qv*) from 1933 to 1949 (neither has remarried), she interrupted her career after the birth of her first child and retired after the second. Now lives in Portugal.
1929: *The Valiant. Pleasure Crazed. They Had to See Paris. Seven Faces*. 1930: *Good Intentions. Born Reckless. Harmony at Home. The Big Trail*. 1931: *Girls Demand Excitement. Charlie Chan Carries On. Quick Millions. Riders of the Purple Sage. Ambassador Bill*. 1932: *Forgotten Commandments*. 1933: *Girl without a Room*. 1934: *Penthouse Party* (US: *Without Children*). 1935: *Man Hunt*. 1936: *Alibi for Murder. The Walking Dead. Dracula's Daughter. Murder by an Aristocrat. The Final Hour. Legion of Terror*. 1950: *Bunco Squad*.

CHURCHILL, Sarah 1914–
Red-haired, green-eyed British actress, elder daughter of statesman Sir Winston Churchill. Plain but personable, she flirted with films in the 1930s and 1940s, before overcoming an alcohol problem to become a poetess, painter and authoress. She was married to Vic Oliver (first of four husbands) from 1936 to 1945.
1937: *Who's Your Lady Friend?* 1940: *Spring Meeting*. 1941: *He Found a Star*. 1947: *Daniele Cortis. Sinfonia fatale* (GB: *When in Rome*). 1948: *All Over the Town*. 1949: **Back to Sorrento* (narrator only). 1950: *Royal Wedding* (GB: *Wedding Bells*). 1956: *Sincerely, Willis Wayde* (TV). 1959: *Serious Charge*

(US: *A Touch of Hell*). 1973: **Churchill the Man*.

CILENTO, Diane 1933–
Talented blonde actress (born in New Guinea), principally in British films, with feline smile and stunning figure. Adept at playing tarts with hearts, but born into the wrong era: 20 years earlier in Hollywood she would undoubtedly have become a much bigger star. As it is, she has given some strong performances, but got herself into far too many unworthy films. Married to Sean Connery (*qv*) 1962–1972. Oscar-nominated for *Tom Jones*.

1952: *Wings of Danger* (US: *Dead on Course*). *Moulin Rouge*. 1953: *Meet Mr Lucifer. All Hallowe'en*. 1954: *The Angel Who Pawned Her Harp. The Passing Stranger*. 1955: *Passage Home. The Woman for Joe*. 1957: *The Admirable Crichton* (US: *Paradise Lagoon*). 1958: *The Truth about Women*. 1959: *Jet Storm*. 1961: *The Full Treatment* (US: *Stop Me Before I Kill!*). *The Naked Edge*. 1962: *I Thank a Fool*. 1963: *Tom Jones*. 1964: *The Third Secret. Rattle of a Simple Man*. 1965: *The Agony and the Ecstasy*. 1966: *Hombre*. 1968: *Negatives*. 1972: *ZPG* (GB: *Zero Population Growth*). 1973: *Hitler: the Last Ten Days. The Wicker Man*. 1975: *The Tiger Lily*. 1981: *Duet for Four*. 1982: *For the Term of His Natural Life* (TV). 1985: *The Boy Who Had Everything*.

CLARE, Diane 1937–
Demure, small faced British blonde of the 1960s, who perhaps looked a little too much

like all the British blondes of the 1960s rolled into one to build up a strong individual career. But she made an impression as the nurse killed off early on in *Ice Cold in Alex* and later got a few leading roles in some offbeat horror films.
1958: *Indiscreet. The Reluctant Debutante. Ice Cold in Alex* (US: *Desert Attack*). 1960: *Let's Get Married*. 1961: *The Green Helmet. Whistle down the Wind. The Clock Struck Three. The Naked Edge. Go to Blazes*. 1962: *Mrs Gibbons' Boys. The L-Shaped Room. Lunch Hour*. 1963: *Tamahine. The Double*. 1964: *Witchcraft*. 1965: *The Plague of the Zombies*. 1966: *The Wrong Box. The Hand of Night. The Vulture*. 1967: *The Trygon Factor*.

CLARK, Dane (Bernard Zanville) 1913–
Grim-faced, wiry American tough-guy actor with light-brown wavy hair, at his peak in the 1940s (a law graduate in the 1930s, he turned to acting), generally in grouchy roles as guys with chips on their shoulders. Continued in the same morose vein on television, a medium in which he worked solidly from the 1950s to the 1980s.
1942: *†The Glass Key. †Sunday Punch. †Pride of the Yankees. †Tennessee Johnson* (GB: *The Man on America's Conscience*). *†Wake Island*. 1943: *†Heaven Can Wait. †Action in the North Atlantic. Destination Tokyo*. 1944: *The Very Thought of You. Hollywood Canteen*. 1945: *God is My Co-Pilot. Pride of the Marines* (GB: *Forever in Love*). 1946: *Her Kind of Man. A Stolen Life*. 1947: *That Way with Women. Deep Valley*. 1948: *Embraceable You. Moonrise. Whiplash*. 1949: *Without Honor*. 1950:

Backfire. Barricade. Le traqué (GB: Gunman in the Streets). Highly Dangerous. 1951: Never Trust a Gambler. Fort Defiance. 1952: The Gambler and the Lady. 1954: Go Man Go. Five Days (US: Paid to Kill). Thunder Pass. Port of Hell. 1955: Murder by Proxy (US: Blackout. Completed 1953). Toughest Man Alive. Time Running Out. One Life (TV. GB: cinemas). 1956: The Man is Armed. Massacre. 1957: Outlaw's Son. Reunion (TV). 1966: Flojten. 1969: The McMasters . . . tougher than the west itself! 1971: The Face of Fear (TV). 1972: The Family Rico (TV). Say Goodbye, Maggie Cole (TV). 1974: The Hunters (TV). 1975: Days in My Father's House. The Return of Joe Forrester (TV). Murder on Flight 502 (TV). 1976: James Dean (TV). 1978: A Chance to Live (TV). Narc (TV). 1980: The Woman Inside.

† As Bernard Zanville

CLARK, Petula 1932–
Brunette (now blonde) English actress who became a radio star in the war years, having started as a band singer at the age of eight. Played a string of sweet young things as a straight actress, then reverted to singing, most successfully after settling in France.
*1944: Medal for the General. Strawberry Roan. 1945: Murder in Reverse. I Know Where I'm Going. *Trouble at Townsend. 1946: London Town (US: My Heart Goes Crazy). 1947: Vice Versa. Easy Money. 1948: Here Come the Huggetts. 1949: Vote for Huggett. Don't Ever Leave Me. The Huggetts Abroad. The Romantic Age (US: Naughty Arlette). 1950: Dance Hall. 1951: White Corridors. Madame Louise. 1952: The Card (US: The Promoter). Made in Heaven. 1954: The Runaway Bus. The Gay Dog. The Happiness of Three Women. Track the Man Down. 1957: That Woman Opposite (US: City After Midnight). 1958: Six-Five Special. 1963: A couteaux tirés (GB: Daggers Drawn). 1965: Questi pazzi, pazzi Italiani. 1968: Finian's Rainbow. 1969: Goodbye, Mr Chips. 1980: Second Star to the Right and on till Morning. Never Never Land.*

CLARK, Susan 1940–
Tall, willowy, brunette, Canadian-born leading lady in Hollywood, talented in both comedy and drama, but in a forthright sort of role she was never given until the mid-1970s. In

the film capital from 1966, always as a leading lady, but never, despite a warm personality, quite as a marquee name, even after winning an Emmy for the TV film *Babe* in 1975.
1967: Banning. 1968: The Challengers (TV. GB: cinemas). Something for a Lonely Man. Madigan. Coogan's Bluff. 1969: The Forbin Project. Tell Them Willie Boy is Here. Skullduggery. 1970: Valdez is Coming. 1971: Skin Game. The Astronaut (TV). 1973: Trapped (TV. GB: cinemas as Doberman Patrol). Showdown. 1974: The Midnight Man. The Apple Dumpling Gang. Airport 1975. 1975: Night Games. Babe (TV). 1976: Amelia Earhart (TV). McNaughton's Daughter (TV). 1978: City on Fire. North Avenue Irregulars (GB: Hill's Angels). Sherlock Holmes: Murder by Decree (GB: Murder by Decree). 1979: Promises in the Dark. Double Negative. 1980: The Choice (TV). 1981: Porky's. Nobody's Perfekt. Jimmy B & André (TV). 1982: Maid in America (TV).

CLARKE, Mae (Violet Klotz) 1907–
American honey-blonde actress who leapt to brief stardom after dancing in the chorus (with Barbara Stanwyck) and became adept at good-time dames with hearts of gold. She always looked older than her years and after 1931, her peak year (*Frankenstein*, *The Front Page* and getting a grapefruit in the face from Cagney in *The Public Enemy*), her career ran all the way downhill to bit parts, though she kept working into her sixties.
1929: Big Time. Nix on Dames (GB: Don't Trust Dames). 1930: The Fall Guy (GB: Trust Your Wife). The Dancers. Men on Call. 1931:

Reckless Living. The Front Page. The Good Bad Girl. Waterloo Bridge. The Public Enemy (GB: Enemies of the Public). Frankenstein. 1932: Final Edition (GB: Determination). Night World. Breach of Promise. The Penguin Pool Murder (GB: The Penguin Pool Mystery). Impatient Maiden. Three Wise Girls. As the Devil Commands. 1933: Parole Girl. Turn Back the Clock. Penthouse (GB: Crooks in Clover). Fast Workers. 1934: Lady Killer. Flaming Gold. Let's Talk It Over. This Side of Heaven. Nana. The Man with Two Faces. 1935: The Daring Young Man. The Silk Hat Kid. 1936: Hitch Hike Lady (GB: Eventful Journey). Wild Brian Kent. Hats Off. Hearts in Bondage. The House of 1,000 Candles. 1937: Great Guy (GB: Pluck of the Irish). Trouble in Morocco. Outlaws of the Orient. 1940: Women in War. 1941: Sailors on Leave. 1942: Flying Tigers. The Lady from Chungking. 1944: Here Come the Waves. And Now Tomorrow. 1945: Kitty. 1948: Daredevils of the Clouds. 1949: Streets of San Francisco. Gun Runner. King of the Rocket Men (serial). 1950: Annie Get Your Gun. Duchess of Idaho. Mrs O'Malley and Mr Malone. Royal Wedding (GB: Wedding Bells). The Yellow Cab Man. 1951: The Unknown Man. The People Against O'Hara. The Great Caruso. Three Guys Named Mike. Love Is Better than Ever (GB: The Light Fantastic). Mr Imperium (GB: You Belong to My Heart). Callaway Went Thataway (GB: The Star Said No). 1952: Thunderbirds. Pat and Mike. Shirts Ahoy! Fearless Fagan. Singin' in the Rain. Horizons West. Because of You. 1953: Confidentially Connie. 1954: Magnificent Obsession. 1955: Wichita. Not As a Stranger. Women's Prison. I Died a Thousand Times. 1956: Come Next Spring. Mohawk. The Catered Affair (GB: Wedding Breakfast). The Desperadoes Are in Town. Ride the High Iron. 1958: The Voice in the Mirror. 1959: Ask Any Girl. 1966: A Big Hand for the Little Lady (GB: Big Deal at Dodge City). 1967: Thoroughly Modern Millie. 1970: Watermelon Man.

CLARKE, Robert 1920–
Moustachioed, solidly-built American actor with dark, curly hair. After getting a break on radio, he began his Hollywood career in small supporting roles. Later, he played leads in several very minor films between 1950 and 1962, showing a liking for frightening slices

of science-fiction, occasionally having a hand in writing, producing and directing them. Married one of the King Sisters and later joined The King Family Singing Tour.
1944: The Falcon in Hollywood. 1945: First Yank into Tokyo (GB: Mask of Fury). The Enchanted Cottage. The Body Snatcher. Man Alive. Radio Stars on Parade. Wanderer of the Wasteland. A Game of Death. Those Endearing Young Charms. 1946: Sunset Pass. Bedlam. San Quentin. Criminal Court. Genius at Work. Lady Luck. The Bamboo Blonde. 1947: Desperate. Dick Tracy Meets Gruesome (GB: Dick Tracy's Amazing Adventure). Code of the West. The Farmer's Daughter. Under the Tonto Rim. Thunder Mountain. 1948: Return of the Bad Men. If You Knew Susie. Fighting Father Dunne. 1949: Ladies of the Chorus. Riders of the Range. 1950: Outrage. A Modern Marriage. 1951: Hard, Fast and Beautiful. The Man from Planet X. Casa Manana. Pistol Harvest. Street Bandits. 1952: Sword of Venus (GB: Island of Monte Cristo). Tales of Robin Hood. The Fabulous Senorita. Captive Women (GB: 3000 AD). The Sword of D'Artagnan. 1953: Captain John Smith and Pocahontas (GB: Burning Arrows). 1954: The Black Pirates. Her Twelve Men. 1955: †The Hideous Sun Demon (GB: Blood on His Lips. Released 1959). King of the Carnival (serial). 1956: Secret File (TV. GB: cinemas). My Man Godfrey. 1957: Outlaw Queen. Miss Body Beautiful. The Deep Six. Band of Angels. The Astounding She Monster (GB: The Mysterious Invader). 1958: Timbuktu. 1959: The Incredible Petrified World. 1960: Beyond the Time Barrier. 1962: Terror of the Bloodhunters. 1965: Zebra in the Kitchen. 1970: The Brotherhood of the Bell (TV).

† And directed

CLAYBURGH, Jill 1941–
Tawny-haired American actress with honeyed tones who made no sort of impact on film until she reached 30, remaining very much her own woman in the sorts of parts she would play. Later recognized as a comedienne of Carole Lombard warmth, and a dramatic actress of considerable emotional range, highlighted by her performance in *An Unmarried Woman*, which won her an Oscar nomination.
1966: The Wedding Party. 1971: The Telephone Book. 1972: Portnoy's Complaint. The Female Instinct (TV. GB: The Snoop Sisters). 1973: Tiger on a Chain (TV). The Thief Who Came to Dinner. Shock-a-Bye Baby (TV). 1974: The Terminal Man. 1975: Roman Grey (TV. GB: The Art of Crime). Hustling (TV). 1976: Silver Streak. Gable and Lombard. 1977: Semi-Tough. Griffin and Phoenix (GB: Today is Forever. Originally for TV). An Unmarried Woman. 1979: La luna. Starting Over. 1980: It's My Turn. 1981: First Monday in October. 1982: I'm Dancing As Fast As I Can. 1983: Hanna. 1985: Where Are the Children? 1986: Shy People.

CLEMENTS, Sir John 1910–
Smooth, cheerful British leading man in sterling, upper-class roles, a look-alike for Michael Denison, with whom he shared a preference for the stage. Had some good roles for Alexander Korda in the thirties, but his image quickly palled with the cinemagoing public in post-war years. Long married to Kay Hammond (*qv*), with whom he became very popular in radio panel games. Knighted in 1968.
*1934: Once in a New Moon. 1935: *No Quarter. The Divine Spark. Ticket of Leave. 1936: Things to Come. Rembrandt. 1937: Knight Without Armour. South Riding. 1938: Star of the Circus (US: Hidden Menace). 1939: The Four Feathers. 1940: Convoy. 1941: This England. Ships with Wings. 1942: Tomorrow We Live (US: At Dawn We Die). 1943: Undercover (US: Underground Guerrillas). 1944: They Came to a City. 1948: †Call of the Blood. 1949: Train of Events. 1958: The Silent Enemy. 1962: The Mind Benders. 1969: Oh! What a Lovely War. 1982: Gandhi. 1984: The Jigsaw Man.*

† And directed

CLIFT, Montgomery
(Edward M. Clift) 1920–1966
Dark, boyish-looking, intense American actor, in soul-searching or romantic roles. On stage as a teenager, but most popular in the early 1950s, until a bad car smash changed his facial structure (and, some said, his personality) giving him a more wasted look. Also sustained brain concussion, from which he may never have fully recovered, although the official cause of death was a heart attack. He was nominated for an Academy Award for *The Search*, his first film, as well as for *A Place in the Sun*, *From Here to Eternity* and *Judgment at Nuremberg*.

MONTGOMERY CLIFT

1948: The Search. Red River. 1949: The Heiress. 1950: The Big Lift. 1951: A Place in the Sun. 1952: I Confess. 1953: From Here to Eternity. 1954: Stazione termini (GB: Indiscretion. US: Indiscretion of an American Wife). 1957: Raintree County. 1958: The Young Lions. 1959: Lonelyhearts. Suddenly Last Summer. 1960: Wild River. 1961: The Misfits. Judgment at Nuremberg. 1962: Freud (GB: Freud – the Secret Passion). 1966: L'espion/The Defector.

CLIVE, Colin (C. C. Greig) 1898–1937
Dark, handsome, but rather worried-looking English actor, often in tortured roles. He went to Hollywood to repeat his stage success in *Journey's End* and stayed to become immortalized for horror fans as Henry Frankenstein in two classic fantasy films. French-born Clive died somewhat mysteriously at 39 from a 'pulmonary and intestinal ailment'. Married to character actress Jeanne de Casalis (1896–1966).
1930: Journey's End. 1931: The Stronger Sex. Frankenstein. 1932: Lily Christine. 1933: Christopher Strong. Looking Forward (GB: Service). 1934: Jane Eyre. The Key. One More River (GB: Over the River). 1935: The Right to Live (GB: The Sacred Flame). Clive of India. Mad Love (GB: The Hands of Orlac). The Girl from Tenth Avenue (GB: Men on Her Mind). The Man Who Broke the Bank at Monte Carlo. Bride of Frankenstein. 1936: The Widow from Monte Carlo. 1937: History is Made at Night. The Woman I Love.

CLOONEY, Rosemary 1928–
Chirpy, brown-haired American singing star who became hugely popular on record – chiefly for a song called *Come On a My House* – and shot to stardom in films, revealing a husky speaking voice and bright personality. But the initial sparkle soon faded, and she returned to nightclub work. Her middle years were unhappy ones, and she recounted her prolonged experiences under mental care in her autobiography, published in 1977. Married/divorced José Ferrer (*qv*).
1953: The Stars Are Singing. Here Come the Girls. 1954: Red Garters. White Christmas. Deep in My Heart.

CLYDE, June (J. Tetrazini) 1909–
Gracious, likeable, sparkling-eyed, peppy blonde American actress, singer and dancer, in vaudeville from seven (as Baby Tetrazini) and films at 19. She married director Thornton Freeland at 20 (they're still married) and came to Britain with him in 1934, starring there in several popular light musicals and comedies, and returning to America only with the outbreak of war. The Freelands returned to Britain in 1946, and she played the odd cameo role here and there before retirement.
1920: The Sea Wolf. 1929: Tanned Legs. Why Bring That Up? 1930: Hit the Deck. The Cuckoos. Midnight Mystery. 1931: The Mad Parade (GB: Forgotten Women). Morals for Women (GB: Farewell Party). Arizona (GB: The Virtuous Wife). Men Are Like That. The Secret Witness. 1932: The All-American (GB: Sport of a Nation). The Cohens and Kellys

in Hollywood. Racing Youth. Radio Patrol. Steady Company. The Thrill of Youth. Strange Adventure. Back Street. File 113. Branded Men. 1933: Only Yesterday. Tess of the Storm Country. Her Resale Value. A Study in Scarlet. Hold Me Tight. Forgotten. 1934: I Hate Women. Hollywood Hoodlum (GB: What Price Fame?). Hollywood Party. 1935: Dance Band. She Shall Have Music. Charing Cross Road. No Monkey Business. 1936: Land Without Music (US: Forbidden Music). Aren't Men Beasts! King of the Castle. 1937: Intimate Relations. School for Husbands. Let's Make a Night of It. Make Up. Sam Small Leaves Town. 1938: Weddings Are Wonderful. His Lordship Goes to Press. 1939: Poison Pen. 1941: Sealed Lips. Unfinished Business. Country Fair. 1942: Hi' Ya Chum (GB: Everything Happens to Us). 1944: Seven Doors to Death. 1945: Hollywood and Vine (GB: Daisy (the Dog) Goes Hollywood). 1946: Behind the Mask. 1951: Night Without Stars. 1952: 24 Hours of a Woman's Life (GB: Affair in Monte Carlo). Treasure Hunt. 1953: The Love Lottery. 1957: The Story of Esther Costello (US: Golden Virgin). After the Ball.

COBB, Lee J.
(Leo Jacoby) 1911–1976
Thick-set, mean-looking American actor in tough, growly roles, mostly as bosses, gangsters and men who rode roughshod over the law. Always looked older than his years and so enjoyed a fine run of middle-aged aggressors, topped by his union racketeer in *On the Waterfront*. His thick, crinkly hair hid the reality of a bald head. Died of a heart attack. Oscar-nominated for *On the Waterfront* and *The Brothers Karamazov*.
1934: Vanishing Shadow (serial). 1937: North of the Rio Grande. Rustler's Valley. Ali Baba Goes to Town. 1938: Danger on the Air. 1939: The Phantom Creeps (serial). Golden Boy. 1941: This Thing Called Love. Men of Boys' Town. Paris Calling. 1942: How to Operate Behind Enemy Lines. The Moon is Down. 1943: Buckskin Frontier (GB: The Iron Road). Tonight We Raid Calais. The Song of Bernadette. 1944: Winged Victory. 1946: Anna and the King of Siam. 1947: Boomerang. Captain from Castile. Johnny O'Clock. Carnival in Costa Rica. 1948: Miracle of the Bells. Call Northside 777. The Luck of the Irish. 1949: The Dark Past. Thieves' Highway. 1950: The

Man Who Cheated Himself. 1951: Sirocco. The Family Secret. 1952: The Fighter. 1953: The Tall Texan. 1954: On the Waterfront. Yankee Pasha. Gorilla at Large. The Day of Triumph. 1955: The Racers (GB: Such Men Are Dangerous). The Road to Denver. The Left Hand of God. 1956: The Man in the Gray Flannel Suit. Miami Exposé. 1957: Twelve Angry Men. The Three Faces of Eve. The Garment Jungle. Panic Button (TV). 1958: The Brothers Karamazov. Man of the West. The Trap (GB: The Baited Trap). 1959: Green Mansions. Project Immortality (TV). But Not for Me. 1960: Exodus. 1962: The Brazen Bell (TV. GB: cinemas). The Four Horsemen of the Apocalypse. How the West Was Won. 1963: Come Blow Your Horn. 1965: Our Man Flint. 1967: In Like Flint. Il giorno della civetta (US: Mafia). 1968: Mackenna's Gold. Las Vegas 500 milliones (GB and US: They Came to Rob Las Vegas). Coogan's Bluff. 1970: The Liberation of L. B. Jones. Macho Callahan. 1971: Heat of Anger (TV). Lawman. 1973: Double Indemnity (TV). The Man Who Loved Cat Dancing. The Exorcist. La polizia sta a guardare. 1974: Dr Max (TV). The Great Ice Rip-Off (TV). Trapped Beneath the Sea (TV). 1975: Ultimatum alla citta (US: Ultimatum). That Lucky Touch. Venditore di Pallancini (GB: Last Moments. US: The Last Circus Show). La legge violenta della squadra anticrimine (US: Cross Shot). Mark il poliziotto (US: Blood, Sweat and Fear). 1976: Nick the Sting. 1979: Arthur Miller — on Home Ground.

COBURN, Charles 1877–1961
American actor whose paunch, monocle, cigar and thick lips lent superb character to a series of lovable but perceptive upper-class gentlemen with rasping voices and hearts of pure gold. Like Sydney Greenstreet (*qv*), he did not become a film regular until past 60, but was an instant success with the public and stayed for 20 years, often in near-leading roles. Academy Award in 1943 for *The More the Merrier*. Died of a heart ailment. Also Oscar-nominated for *The Devil and Miss Jones* and *The Green Years*.
1933: Boss Tweed. 1935: The People's Enemy. 1938: Of Human Hearts. Yellow Jack. Lord Jeff (GB: The Boy from Barnardo's). Vivacious Lady. 1939: Idiot's Delight. Made for Each Other. The Story of Alexander Graham

Bell (GB: The Modern Miracle). Bachelor Mother. In Name Only. The Captain is a Lady. 1940: The Road to Singapore. 1941: Three Faces West. Our Wife. Kings' Row. H. M. Pulham Esq. The Devil and Miss Jones. Unexpected Uncle. The Lady Eve. 1942: In This Our Life. George Washington Slept Here. 1943: The Constant Nymph. Forever and a Day. The More the Merrier. Heaven Can Wait. Princess O'Rourke. 1944: Knickerbocker Holiday. Wilson. The Impatient Years. Together Again. 1945: A Royal Scandal (GB: Czarina). Shady Lady. Over 21. Rhapsody in Blue. 1946: Colonel Effingham's Raid (GB: Man of the Hour). The Green Years. 1947: Lured (GB: Personal Column). The Paradine Case. 1948: B. F.'s Daughter (GB: Polly Fulton). Green Grass of Wyoming. 1949: Everybody Does It. The Doctor and the Girl. Yes Sir, That's My Baby. Impact. The Gal Who Took the West. Peggy. 1950: Louisa. Mr Music. 1951: The Highwayman. *Oh Money, Money. 1952: Monkey Business. Has Anybody Seen My Gal? 1953: Trouble Along the Way. Gentlemen Prefer Blondes. 1954: The Rocket Man. The Long Wait. 1955: How to be Very, Very Popular. 1956: Around the World in 80 Days. The Power and the Prize. Town on Trial! 1957: The Story of Mankind. How to Murder a Rich Uncle. 1959: Stranger in My Arms. The Remarkable Mr Pennypacker. John Paul Jones. 1960: Pepe.

COBURN, James 1928–
Lean, gangling American actor with tooth-filled smile whose villainy proved so personable that he made the almost inevitable progression to stardom. His cheetah-like mobility made him a good bet for 'supermen' spies, but he seemed to prefer more gutsy and offbeat roles.
1959: Ride Lonesome. Face of a Fugitive. 1960: The Magnificent Seven. 1962: Hell is for Heroes! The Murder Men (TV. GB: cinemas). 1963: The Great Escape. Charade. The Man from Galveston (TV. GB: cinemas). 1964: The Americanisation of Emily. 1965: Major Dundee. A High Wind in Jamaica. The Loved One. Our Man Flint. 1966: What Did You Do in the War, Daddy? Dead Heat on a Merry-Go-Round. 1967: In Like Flint. Waterhole No. 3 (GB: Waterhole 3). The President's Analyst. 1968: Duffy. Candy. Hard Contract. 1969: Last of the Mobile Hot-Shots (later Blood

Kin). 1971: Giù la testa (GB: A Fistful of Dynamite. US: Duck, You Sucker!). 1972: The Honkers. The Carey Treatment. A Reason to Live, a Reason to Die (US: Massacre at Fort Holman). 1973: Pat Garrett and Billy the Kid. The Last of Sheila. Harry Never Holds (GB: Harry in Your Pocket). 1974: The Internecine Project. 1975: Hard Times (GB: The Streetfighter). Bite the Bullet. 1976: Sky Riders. The Last Hard Men. White Rock. A Fast Drive in the Country (and narrator). Midway (GB: Battle of Midway). 1977: Cross of Iron. 1978: The Dain Curse (TV). California Suite. 1979: The Muppet Movie. The Baltimore Bullet. Goldengirl. Firepower. 1980: Big Bucks/High Risk. Mr Patman. Loving Couples. The Fall Guy (TV). 1981: Looker. 1983: Crossover. Malibu (TV). Digital Dreams. 1984: Martin's Day. Draw! (TV. Originally for cinemas). 1985: Sins of the Father (TV). Leonski – The Brown Out Murders. 1986: Death of a Soldier.

COCHRAN, Steve
(Robert Cochran) 1917–1965
Dark, handsome, young-looking American actor whose beetle brows made him slightly menacing, and got him cast as good-looking snakes-in-the-grass, hoodlums with slicked-back hair who were also ladies' men. Never quite made the top, but his off-screen love life, which rivalled that of Errol Flynn, kept him in the public eye. Died of acutely swollen lung tissue sustained aboard his boat when caught in a hurricane with his three-girl crew.
1943: Stage Door Canteen. 1945: Wonder Man. Boston Blackie Booked on Suspicion (GB: Booked on Suspicion). The Gay Senorita. Boston Blackie's Rendezvous (GB: Blackie's Rendezvous). 1946: The Kid from Brooklyn. The Best Years of Our Lives. The Chase. 1947: Copacabana. 1948: A Song is Born. 1949: White Heat. 1950: The Damned Don't Cry. Highway 301. Storm Warning. The West Point Story (GB: Fine and Dandy). Dallas. 1951: Raton Pass (GB: Canyon Pass). The Tanks Are Coming. Inside the Walls of Folsom Prison. Jim Thorpe – All American (GB: Man of Bronze). Tomorrow is Another Day. 1952: The Lion and the Horse. Operation Secret. 1953: She's Back on Broadway. The Desert Song. Back to God's Country. Shark River. 1954: Carnival Story. Private Hell 36. 1956: Come Next Spring. Slander. The Weapon. 1957: Il grido (GB: The Cry. US:

Outcry). 1958: I, Mobster. Quantrill's Raiders. 1959: The Beat Generation (GB: This Rebel Age). The Big Operator. 1961: The Deadly Companions. 1963: Of Love and Desire. 1964: Tell Me in the Sunlight (and directed). 1965: Mozambique.

COLBERT, Claudette
(Lily Chauchoin) 1903–
Pert, petite and sparkling French-born Hollywood star who excelled in sophisticated comedy, also played Poppaea and Cleopatra and sustained her stardom for over 20 years. All her characters in the thirties were impish and spirited in one way or another, none more so than Ellie Andrews in It Happened One Night, which won her an Academy Award. Married (first of two) to actor/director Norman Foster, from 1928 to 1935. Also Oscar-nominated for Since You Went Away.
1927: For the Love of Mike. 1929: The Hole in the Wall. The Lady Lies. 1930: †The Big Pond. Young Man of Manhattan. Manslaughter. L'enigmatique Monsieur Parkes. 1931: †The Smiling Lieutenant. Honor Among Lovers. Secrets of a Secretary. His Woman. 1932: The Wiser Sex. The Misleading Lady. The Man from Yesterday. Make Me a Star. The Phantom President. The Sign of the Cross. 1933: Tonight is Ours. I Cover the Waterfront. Three Cornered Moon. Torch Singer (GB: Broadway Singer). 1934: Four Frightened People. It Happened One Night. Cleopatra. Imitation of Life. 1935: The Gilded Lily. Private Worlds. She Married Her Boss. The Bride Comes Home. 1936: Under Two Flags. 1937: Maid of Salem. Tovarich. I Met Him in Paris. 1938: Bluebeard's Eighth Wife. Zaza. 1939: Midnight. Drums Along the Mohawk. It's a Wonderful World. 1940: Boom Town. Arise, My Love. 1941: Skylark. Remember the Day. 1942: The Palm Beach Story. 1943: So Proudly We Hail. No Time for Love. 1944: Since You Went Away. 1945: Practically Yours. Guest Wife. Tomorrow is Forever. 1946: Without Reservations. The Secret Heart. 1947: The Egg and I. 1948: Sleep My Love. Family Honeymoon. 1949: Bride for Sale. 1950: Three Came Home. The Secret Fury. 1951: Thunder on the Hill (GB: Bonaventure). Let's Make It Legal. 1952: The Planter's Wife (US: Outpost in Malaya). 1953: Destinées (GB: Love and the Frenchwoman. US: Daughters of Destiny). Si Versailles m'était conté (GB: Versailles. US:

Royal Affairs in Versailles). 1955: Texas Lady. 1957: One Coat of White (TV). 1961: Parrish.

† *And French Version*

COLE, George 1925–
British actor of dark, wavy hair and worried mien who can adapt his cultured tones to cockney or other regional English accents at the drop of a lip. Started in straight roles as a teenager, but soon specialized in shy young bachelors who were all thumbs with girls and life in general, following great personal success in radio's *A Life of Bliss*, and became very popular in 1950s' comedies. Later still he moved to prominence on television, at first with more serious portrayals of middle-aged men, but then back in comedy vein, especially in the hit series *Minder*, which ran for several seasons. Married actresses Eileen Moore (1954–1966) and Penny Morrell (1968 on).
*1941: Cottage to Let (US: Bombsite Stolen). 1942: Those Kids from Town. 1943: *Fiddling Fuel. The Demi-Paradise (US: Adventure for Two). 1944: Henry V. 1945: Journey Together. 1948: My Brother's Keeper. Quartet. 1949: The Spider and the Fly. 1950: Morning Departure (US: Operation Disaster). Gone to Earth (US: The Wild Heart). 1951: Flesh and Blood. Laughter in Paradise. Scrooge. Lady Godiva Rides Again. 1952: The Happy Family (US: Mr Lord Says No). Who Goes There! (US: The Passionate Sentry). Top Secret (US: Mr Potts Goes to Moscow). Folly to be Wise. 1953: Will Any Gentleman? The Intruder. Our Girl Friday (US: The Adventures of Sadie). The Clue of the Missing Ape. 1954: An Inspector Calls. Happy Ever After (US: Tonight's the Night). The Belles of St Trinian's. 1955: A Prize of Gold. Where There's a Will. The Constant Husband. The Adventures of Quentin Durward. 1956: It's a Wonderful World. The Green Man. The Weapon. 1957: Blue Murder at St Trinian's. 1959: Too Many Crooks. Don't Panic Chaps! The Bridal Path. 1960: The Pure Hell of St Trinian's. 1963: Dr Syn alias the Scarecrow. Cleopatra. 1964: One Way Pendulum. 1965: The Legend of Young Dick Turpin. 1966: The Great St Trinian's Train Robbery. 1968: *The Green Shoes. 1970: The Vampire Lovers. 1971: Fright. 1972: Madigan: The London Beat (TV). 1973: Take Me High. 1976: The Blue Bird. 1983: *Perishing Solicitors. 1985: Minder on the Orient Express (TV).*

COLEMAN, Nancy 1917–
Auburn-haired, pretty, roundfaced, sad-looking American actress in quiet roles, most notably Anne Brontë in *Devotion*. Under contract to Warners for a few years, but married the studio publicity head, had twins and disappointingly worked mostly thereafter (sporadically) for stage and television.
1941: Dangerously They Live. Kings Row. 1942: The Gay Sisters. Desperate Journey. 1943: Devotion (released 1946). Edge of Darkness. 1944: In Our Time. 1946: Her Sister's Secret. 1947: Violence. Mourning Becomes Electra. 1953: That Man from Tangier. 1969: Slaves.

COLLEANO, Bonar
(B. Sullivan II) 1924–1958
Dark-haired, angular-faced American-born actor in British films, familiar as wisecracking GI or sharpster on the make. From a circus family of acrobats (he was performing with them at five) he had a few semi-leads, but was in supporting roles when killed in a car crash at 34. Married to Susan Shaw. Initially billed as Bonar Colleano Junior.
*1943: Starlight Serenade. 1944: *We the People. 1945: The Way to the Stars (US: Johnny in the Clouds). 1946: Wanted for Murder. A Matter of Life and Death (US: Stairway to Heaven). While the Sun Shines. 1947: Broken Journey. 1948: Merry-Go-Round. One Night with You. Good Time Girl. Sleeping Car to Trieste. Once a Jolly Swagman (US: Maniacs on Wheels). 1949: Give Us This Day (US: Salt to the Devil). 1950: Dance Hall. Pool of London. 1951: A Tale of Five Cities*

(US: A Tale of Five Women). 1952: Eight Iron Men. 1953: Is Your Honeymoon Really Necessary? Escape by Night. 1954: The Flame and the Flesh. Time is My Enemy. The Sea Shall Not Have Them. 1955: Joe Macbeth. 1956: Stars in Your Eyes. Zarak. 1957: Interpol (US: Pickup Alley). Fire Down Below. Death over My Shoulder. 1958: Them Nice Americans. No Time to Die! (US: Tank Force).

COLLINS, Joan 1933–
A classic example of how to make a provocative face, a stunning figure and a great deal of determination go a very long way. A sultry, dark-haired British actress, soon in international films; her temptresses' social standings have improved with the longevity of her career, even if one feels the appeal is still very much on the surface. In the 1980s she became a queen of American soap opera in the series *Dynasty*. Her three marriages, to actors Maxwell Reed and Anthony Newley and producer Ron Kass, all ended in divorce.
1951: Lady Godiva Rides Again. The Woman's Angle. Judgment Deferred. 1952: I Believe in You. Decameron Nights. Cosh Boy (US: The Slasher). 1953: Turn the Key Softly. The Square Ring. Our Girl Friday (US: The Adventures of Sadie). 1954: The Good Die Young. 1955: Land of the Pharaohs. The Virgin Queen. The Girl in the Red Velvet Swing. 1956: The Opposite Sex. 1957: Sea Wife. Island in the Sun. The Wayward Bus. Stopover Tokyo. 1958: The Bravados. Rally 'round the Flag, Boys! 1959: Seven Thieves. 1960: Esther and the King. 1962: The Road to Hong Kong. 1964: La congiuntura. 1967: Warning Shot. 1968: Subterfuge. Can Hieronymus Merkin Ever Forget Mercy Humppe and Find True Happiness? 1969: Drive Hard, Drive Fast (TV). If It's Tuesday, This Must Be Belgium. Breve amore. 1970: Up in the Cellar (GB: Three in the Cellar). The Executioner. 1971: Quest for Love. Revenge (US: Inn of the Frightened People). 1972: The Aquarian. Fear in the Night. Tales from the Crypt. 1973: Tales that Witness Madness. Dark Places. 1974: Call of the Wolf. The Referee (later Football Crazy). 1975: Alfie Darling. The Bawdy Adventures of Tom Jones. I Don't Want to Be Born. 1976: The Great Adventure. 1977: Empire of the Ants. 1978: The Stud. The Big Sleep. The Day of the Fox. Zero to Sixty. 1979: The Bitch. Sunburn.

Game for Vultures. 1980: Growing Pains. Homework. 1982: Nutcracker. The Wild Women of Chastity Gulch (TV). 1983: The Making of a Male Model (TV). 1984: The Cartier Affair (TV). Her Life as a Man (TV).

COLMAN, Ronald 1891–1958
Elegant, strong, moustachioed British-born star who moved easily from Latin lovers of the twenties to men of honour in the thirties. Colman made a few films in England before heading for Hollywood, where he became number one box-office attraction for three consecutive years in the late twenties, and stayed on to star in some of the sound cinema's most beguiling entertainments. Long-deserved Oscar finally won for *A Double Life* (1948). Married to Benita Hume (second wife) from 1938. Died from pneumonia. Previously nominated for Academy Awards in *Bulldog Drummond, Condemned* and *Random Harvest*.
1917: *The Live Wire. 1919: The Toilers. A Daughter of Eve. Sheba. Snow in the Desert. 1920: A Son of David. Anna the Adventuress. The Black Spider. 1921: Handcuffs or Kisses. 1923: The Eternal City. The White Sister. Twenty Dollars a Week. 1924: Tarnish. Her Night of Romance. Romola. A Thief in Paradise. 1925: His Supreme Moment. The Sporting Venus. Her Sister from Paris. The Dark Angel. Stella Dallas. Lady Windermere's Fan. 1926: Kiki. Beau Geste. The Winning of Barbara Worth. 1927: The Night of Love. The Magic Flame. 1928: Two Lovers. 1929: The Rescue. Bulldog Drummond. Condemned (GB: Condemned to Devil's Island). 1930: Raffles. The Devil to Pay. 1931: The Unholy Garden. Arrowsmith. 1932: Cynara. 1933: The Masquerader. 1934: Bulldog Drummond Strikes Back. 1935: Clive of India. The Man Who Broke the Bank at Monte Carlo. A Tale of Two Cities. 1936: Under Two Flags. 1937: Lost Horizon. The Prisoner of Zenda. 1938: If I Were King. 1940: Lucky Partners. The Light That Failed. 1941: My Life with Caroline. 1942: The Talk of the Town. Random Harvest. 1944: Kismet. 1946: The Late George Apley. 1948: A Double Life. 1950: Champagne for Caesar. 1953: *The Globe Playhouse (narrator only). 1956: Around the World in 80 Days. 1957: The Story of Mankind.*

COMINGORE, Dorothy 1913–1971
Ethereal-looking, chubby-faced Hollywood blonde whose own rise and fall (she was stuck

in bit parts and comedy shorts for years before stardom) so paralleled that of Susan Alexander Kane, whom she played in *Citizen Kane*, that it was uncanny. Still, she was good when it mattered, unlike poor Mrs K. McCarthy blacklisting finally finished her career in 1951.
1938: †*Campus Cinderella.* †*Comet over Broadway.* †*Prison Train. 1939:* †*Blondie Meets the Boss.* †*Trade Winds.* †**The Awful Goof.* †*North of the Yukon.* †*Mr Smith Goes to Washington.* †*Scandal Sheet.* †*Café Hostess. 1940:* †**The Hecklers.* †**Rockin' through the Rockies. Pioneers of the Frontier. Street of Missing Women. 1941: Citizen Kane. 1944: The Hairy Ape. 1949: Any Number Can Play. 1951: The Big Night.*

† *As Linda Winters*

COMPSON, Betty 1896–1974
Petite, blue-eyed, bow-lipped redhead (although her hair colour varies from film to film) popular in early silent comedies, but increasingly accepted as a dramatic actress from 1919 on. Survived the coming of sound to become an equally delightful character actress. Married/divorced director James Cruze (first of three). Academy Award nominee for *The Barker*.
1914: *Wanted – a Leading Lady. Some Chaperone. Jed's Trip to the Fair. Where the Heater Blooms. Their Quiet Honeymoon. 1915: Hist at Six O'Clock. Love and a Savage. Mingling Spirits. Her Steady Car Fare. When the Losers Won. A Quiet Supper for Four. Her Friend the Doctor. When Lizzie Disappeared. Cupid Trims His Lordship. The Deacon's Waterloo.*

Love and Vaccination. He Almost Eloped. The Janitor's Busy Day. A Leap Year Tangle. Eddie's Night Out. The Newlywed's Mix Up. Lem's College Career. Potts Bungles Again. He's a Devil. The Wooing of Aunt Jemima. 1916: Her Celluloid Hero. All Over a Stocking. Almost a Widow. Wanted – a Husband. His Baby. The Making Over of Mother. A Brass Buttoned Romance. Some Kid. Cupid's Uppercut. Out for the Coin. Her Crooked Career. Her Friend the Chauffeur. Small Change. Hubby's Night Out. 1917: A Bold Bad Night. As Luck Would Have It. Suspended Sentence. His Last Pill. Those Wedding Bells. Almost a Scandal. Down by the Sea. Won in a Cabaret. Crazy by Proxy. Betty's Big Idea. Love and the Locksmiths. Almost a Bigamist. Almost Divorced. 1918: Betty Makes Up. Nearly a Papa. Betty's Adventure. Their Seaside Tangle. Many a Slip. Whose Wife? Cupid's Camouflage. Somebody's Baby. All Dressed Up. A Seminary Scandal. The Sheriff. Border Raiders. 1919: The Terror of the Range (serial). The Prodigal Liar. The Miracle Man. The Devil's Trail. The Little Diplomat. Light of Victory. 1921: Prisoners of Love. For Those We Love. Ladies Must Live. At the End of the World. The Little Minister. The Law and the Woman. 1922: The Green Temptation. Over the Border. Always the Woman. The Bonded Woman. To Have and to Hold. 1923: The White Flower. Kick In. The Rustle of Silk. The Woman with Four Faces. Hollywood. Woman to Woman. The Royal Oak. The Prude's Fall. 1924: The White Shadow (US: White Shadows). The Stranger. Miami. The Enemy Sex. Ramshackle House. The Female. The Garden of Weeds. The Fast Set. 1925: New Lives for Old. Pony Express. Paths to Paradise. Beggar on Horseback. Eve's Secret. Locked Doors. 1926: The Counsel for Defense. The Wise Guy. The Belle of Broadway. The Palace of Pleasure. 1927: Twelve Miles Out. The Ladybird. Temptations of a Shop Girl. Say It with Diamonds. Cheating Cheaters. 1928: Big City. The Desert Bride. Love's Mockery. The Masked Angel. Love Me and the World is Mine. Scarlet Seas. The Docks of New York. Court Martial. The Barker. 1929: Woman to Woman (remake). Weary River. The Time, the Place and the Girl. The Show of Shows. Street Girl. The Great Gabbo. Skin Deep. On with the Show. 1930: The Midnight Mystery. Blaze o' Glory. The Case of Sergeant Grischa. Czar of Broadway. Inside the Lines. Isle of Escape. Boudoir Diplomat. Those Who Dance. The Spoilers. She Got What She Wanted. 1931: The Lady Refuses. Three Who Loved. Virtuous Husband. The Gay Diplomat. 1932: The Silver Lining. Guilty or Not Guilty. 1933: Destination Unknown. West of Singapore. Notorious but Nice. 1935: False Pretences. The Millionaire Kid. August Weekend. 1936: Laughing Irish Eyes. Bulldog Edition (GB: Lady Reporter). Hollywood Boulevard. Killer at Large. 1937: Circus Girl. Federal Bullets. Two Minutes to Play. 1938: Torchy Blane in Panama (GB: Trouble in Panama). A Slight Case of Murder. Port of Missing Girls. Blondes at Work. Two Gun Justice. Under the Big Top (GB: The Circus Comes to Town). 1939: The Mystic Circle Murder. News is Made at Night. Cow-

boys from Texas. 1940: Mad Youth. Laughing at Danger. 1941: Mr and Mrs Smith. The Road of the Press. The Invisible Ghost. 1943: Danger! Women at Work. Her Adventurous Night. 1946: Claudia and David. 1947: Hard Boiled Mahoney. Second Chance. 1948: Here Comes Trouble.

COMPTON, Fay
(Virginia C. Mackenzie) 1894–1978
Dominant, auburn-haired English actress, sister of novelist Sir Compton Mackenzie. A much-revered figure on the London stage between the two World Wars, she forsook leading roles for some demanding character parts thereafter. Third and fourth marriages were to actors Leon Quartermaine and Ralph Michael.
1914: She Stoops to Conquer. 1917: One Summer's Day. The Labour Leader. 1920: Judge Not. 1921: A Woman of No Importance. The Old Wives' Tale. 1922: The House of Peril. Diana of the Crossways. A Bill for Divorcement. 1923: This Freedom. The Loves of Mary Queen of Scots. 1924: Claude Duval. The Happy Ending. The Eleventh Commandment. 1925: *Stage Stars Off Stage. 1926: London Love. 1927: Robinson Crusoe. Somehow Good. 1928: Zero. 1929: Fashions in Love. 1930: Cape Forlorn (US: The Love Storm). 1931: Uneasy Virtue. Tell England (US: The Battle of Gallipoli). 1934: Waltzes from Vienna (US: Strauss's Great Waltz). Autumn Crocus. The Phantom Light. Song at Eventide. 1936: Wedding Group (US: Wrath of Jealousy). The Mill on the Floss. 1938: *Cavalcade of the Stars. 1939: So This is London. 1941: The Prime Minister. 1946: Odd Man Out. 1947: Nicholas Nickleby. 1948: London Belongs to Me (US: Dulcimer Street). Esther Waters. 1949: Britannia Mews (US: Forbidden Street). 1950: Blackmailed. 1951: Othello. Laughter in Paradise. 1952: I vinti. 1954: Aunt Clara. 1956: Doublecross. Town on Trial! 1957: The Story of Esther Costello (US: Golden Virgin). 1962: In the Cool of the Day. 1963: Uncle Vanya. The Haunting. 1969: I Start Counting. 1970: The Virgin and the Gypsy.

CONNERY, Sean 1930–
Tall, dark, Scottish-born star whose rather bland youthful looks became much more interesting in middle age. Not everyone's ideal James Bond, he created the part on screen in 1962 and quickly made it his own. Has since

defied receding hair to continue in a variety of rugged leading roles. Married to Diane Cilento (first of two) 1962–72.
1954: Lilacs in the Spring (US: Let's Make Up). 1956: No Road Back. 1957: Time Lock. Hell Drivers. Action of the Tiger. 1958: Darby O'Gill and the Little People. Another Time, Another Place. A Night to Remember. 1959: Tarzan's Greatest Adventure. 1961: The Frightened City. On the Fiddle (US: Operation Snafu). 1962: The Longest Day. Dr No. 1963: From Russia with Love. 1964: Woman of Straw. Goldfinger. Marnie. 1965: The Hill. Thunderball. 1966: A Fine Madness. 1967: You Only Live Twice. *The Castles of Scotland (narrator only). 1968: Shalako. 1969: The Molly Maguires. The Red Tent. †The Bowler and the Bonnet. 1971: The Anderson Tapes. Diamonds Are Forever. 1972: Something like the Truth (later The Offence). 1973: Zardoz. 1974: Murder on the Orient Express. Ransom (US: The Terrorists). *The Vocation (narrator only). 1975: The Wind and the Lion. The Man Who Would Be King. 1976: Robin and Marian. The Next Man. 1977: A Bridge Too Far. 1978: The First Great Train Robbery. 1979: Meteor. Cuba. 1981: Time Bandits. Outland. 1982: The Man with the Deadly Lens. Five Days One Summer. *Burning (narrator only). 1983: Never Say Never Again. Sword of the Valiant. 1985: Highlander. 1986: The Name of the Rose. Travelling Man.

† Also directed

CONNORS, Chuck
(Kevin Connors) 1921–
Big, tall, fair-haired, hatchet-faced American leading man, a former basketball and baseball

professional who took up acting when he quit sport. Swiftly in demand for ethnic bad guys, he later became a big star in TV series, but never in films: the title role in Geronimo was the nearest he came. Still on screen for the occasional monolithic villain. Married (second) to Kamala Devi 1963–1972.
1952: Pat and Mike. 1953: Trouble along the Way. Code Two. South Sea Woman. 1954: Naked Alibi. Dragonfly Squadron. The Human Jungle. 1955: Target Zero. Good Morning, Miss Dove. Three Stripes in the Sun (GB: The Gentle Sergeant). 1956: Hold Back the Night. Hot Rod Girl. Walk the Dark Street. 1957: Tomahawk Trail. Designing Woman. Death in Small Doses. Old Yeller. The Hired Gun. The Lady Takes a Flyer. 1958: The Big Country. 1962: Geronimo. 1963: Flipper. Move Over, Darling. 1965: Synanon (GB: Get Off My Back). Broken Sabre (TV. GB: cinemas). 1966: Ride Beyond Vengeance. 1968: Captain Nemo and the Underwater City. Kill Them All and Come Back Alone. 1969: The Profane Comedy/Set This Town on Fire (TV). 1970: The Deserter. 1971: Pancho Villa. Support Your Local Gunfighter. The Birdmen (TV. GB cinemas: Escape of the Birdmen). 1972: Night of Terror (TV). Horror at 37,000 Feet (TV). Embassy. The Proud and the Damned (GB: TV). The Mad Bomber. 1973: Soylent Green. Police Story (TV. GB: cinemas). 1974: 99 and 44/100ths % Dead (GB: Call Harry Crown). Wolf Larsen (US: Sea Wolf). The Police Connection. 1975: Pancho Villa. 1976: Banjo Hackett (TV). Nightmare in Badham County (TV). 1978: Tourist Trap. The Night They Took Miss Beautiful (TV). Standing Tall (TV). 1980: Virus. 1981: Day of the Assassin. Red Alert West. Las mujeres de Jeramias (US: Garden of Venus). The Capture of Grizzly Adams (TV). 1982: Target Eagle. Airplane II The Sequel. 1983: The Vals (released 1985). 1985: Rattlers. Spenser: For Hire (TV). Sakura Killers. Balboa.

CONNORS, Michael (Kreker Ohanian) 1925–
Dark-haired, heftily built, plastically handsome American star who had a not-too-successful career as a second-league leading man under the name Touch Connors. Then, under his new name, he hit the big time on television, especially in the detective series Mannix, which ran from 1967 to 1974. Hollywood welcomed him back but continued to give him

one-dimensional roles, and he returned to the small screen.

1952: †Sudden Fear. 1953: †Island in the Sky. †The 49th Man. †Sky Commando. 1954: †The Day of Triumph. †Naked Alibi. 1955: †Five Guns West. †Swamp Women. †The Twinkle in God's Eye. 1956: †Jaguar. †Shake, Rattle and Rock. †The Ten Commandments. †Flesh and the Spur. 1958: Suicide Battalion. Live Fast, Die Young. 1963: Panic Button. 1964: Good Neighbor Sam. Where Love Has Gone. 1965: Situation Hopeless But Not Serious. Harlow. 1966: Stagecoach. 1967: Kiss the Girls and Make Them Die. 1973: Beg, Borrow or Steal (TV). 1975: The Killer Who Wouldn't Die (TV). 1976: Revenge for a Rape (TV). 1977: Stigma (TV). 1978: Long Journey Back (TV). Cruise Missile. 1979: Avalanche Express. High Midnight (TV). Casino (TV. GB: SS Casino). 1980: The Death of Ocean View Park (TV). 1981: NightKill (made for cinemas but shown only on TV). 1984: Too Scared to Scream.

† As Touch Connors

CONNORS, Touch
See Connors, Michael

CONRAD, Jess (Gerald James) 1936–
Dark, well-built, clean-cut, good-looking British pop singer – a teenage idol for a couple

of years – who succeeded in sustaining an acting career in dribs and drabs in some odd countries and even odder roles (one co-starring with Jayne Mansfield). Infrequently seen in films since the mid-1960s.

1959: The Ugly Duckling. Serious Charge (US: A Touch of Hell). Friends and Neighbours. Follow a Star. Too Young to Love. 1960: The Queen's Guards. 1961: Konga. Rag Doll. 1962: Alibi. The Boys. KIL 1. 1963: Hell is Empty (released 1967). 1964: When Strangers Meet (US: Dog Eat Dog). The Golden Head. 1965: The Amorous Adventures of Moll Flanders. 1968: The Assassination Bureau. 1970: Cool It Carol! (US: The Dirtiest Girl I Ever Met). 1972: The Flesh and Blood Show. 1979: The Great Rock 'n' Roll Swindle.

CONRAD, William 1920–
Bulky American actor with heavy black moustache and forceful style who changed from writing for radio to playing villains in films. Kept his eye in with an occasional stab at

writing and direction before winning worldwide acclaim as television's fat and balding sleuth, *Cannon*. His beady eyes and inimitable rasping voice (he was also the unseen narrator on the long-running TV series *The Fugitive*) stole many scenes.

1946: The Killers. 1947: Body and Soul. 1948: Arch of Triumph. Four Faces West (GB: They Passed This Way). To the Victor. Sorry, Wrong Number. Joan of Arc. 1949: Any Number Can Play. Tension. East Side, West Side. 1950: The Milkman. Dial 1119 (GB: The Violent Hour). One Way Street. 1951: Cry Danger. The Sword of Monte Cristo. The Racket. 1952: Lone Star. 1953: Cry of the Hunted. The Desert Song. 1954: The Naked Jungle. 1955: The Cowboy (narrator only). Five Against the House. The Naked Sea (narrator only). 1956: The Conqueror. Johnny Concho. 1957: The Ride Back. 1959: –30– (GB: Deadline Midnight). 1970: The Brotherhood of the Bell (TV). The DA: Conspiracy to Kill (TV). 1976: Moonshine County Express. 1977: Night Cries. The City (TV. Narrator only). 1978: Keefer (TV). 1980: The Murder That Wouldn't Die (TV). The Return of Frank Cannon (TV). 1982: The Mikado (TV). Shock – Trauma (TV). 1985: In Like Flynn (TV). 1986: Killing Cars.

As director: *1963: The Man from Galveston (TV. GB: cinemas). 1965: My Blood Runs Cold. Brainstorm. Two on a Guillotine. 1981: Side Show (TV).*

CONSTANTINE, Eddie 1917–
Squat, dark, tough-looking American actor who broke into French films after radio work, and was an almost instant success in Bogart-

style private eye roles, especially as detectives Nick Carter and Lemmy Caution. Many others (notably George Nader) followed his example but none was as successful. Later widened his range and, although failing to make a decisive dent in the international market, he remained popular in continental potboilers.

1953: Egypt by Three. La môme vert-de-gris (US: Poison Ivy). Cet homme est dangereux. Les femmes s'en balancent. 1954: Votre devoué Blake. Avanzi di galeria. Ça va Barder (US: There Goes Barder). Repris de justice. 1955: Vous pigez. Je suis un sentimental (GB: Headlines of Destruction). 1956: Les truands. Folies-Bergère. L'homme et l'enfant. 1957: Le grand bluff. Ces dames préfèrent le mambo. Incognito. 1958: Hoppla jetzt kommt Eddie. 1959: Passport to Shame (US: Room 43). The Treasure of San Teresa (US: Long Distance). Du rififi chez les femmes. SOS Pacific. Ravissante. 1960: Bomben auf Monte Carlo. Comment qu'elle est? Ne faire ça à moi. Ça va être ta fête. 1961: Chien de pique. Hands Up! The Seven Deadly Sins. Bonne chance, Charlie. Lemmy pour les dames. Une grosse tête. Cause toujours mon lapin. En plein bagarre. 1962: Cleo de 5 à 7. Les femmes d'abord (GB: Riff Raff Girls). L'empire de la nuit. Nous irons à Deauville. Comme s'il en pleuvat. 1963: Comment trouvez-vous ma soeur? Des frissons partout. A toi de faire, Mignonne. 1964: Lucky Joe. Nick Carter va tout casser. Laissez tirer les tirurs. Ces dames s'en mêlent. Alphaville. 1965: Feu à volonté. Je vous salue Maffia (US: Hail Mafia). Cartes sur table (US: Attack of the Robots). Nick Carter et le trèfle rouge. 1967: Residencia para Espias. 1968: A tout casser (GB: The Great Chase). Les gros malins. 1969: Lions' Love. 1970: Malatesta. 1971: Warnung vor einer heiligen Nutte (US: Beware of a Holy Whore). Eddie geht weiter. 1974: Une baleine qui avait mal aux dents. 1975: Der zweite Frühling. Souvenir of Gibraltar. 1976: Le couple temoin. Raid on Entebbe (TV. GB: cinemas). 1977: Mort au sang donneur/Blood-Relations. 1978: It Lives Again! 1979: Die dritte Generation. The Long Good Friday. 1980: Box Office. Exit . . . nur keine Panik! Tango durch Deutschland. Rote Liebe. 1981: Freak Orlando. 1983: Flight to Berlin. 1985: Paul Chevrolet en de ultieme hallucinatie. 1986: Frankenstein's Aunt.

CONTE, Richard
(Nicholas Conte) 1914–1975
Dark-haired Italianate American actor, mostly in crime dramas as life's underdogs from the wrong side of the tracks. He had some fine leading roles in realist thrillers at Twentieth Century-Fox in the late forties and, although top stardom had slipped away by the late fifties, he continued working steadily until his early death from a heart attack.

1939: †Heaven with a Barbed-Wire Fence. 1943: Guadalcanal Diary. 1944: The Purple Heart. 1945: A Bell for Adano. Captain Eddie. The Spider. A Walk in the Sun. 1946: Somewhere in the Night. 13 Rue Madeleine. 1947: The Other Love. Call Northside 777. 1948: Cry of the City. 1949: House of Strangers. Thieves' Highway. Whirlpool. Big Jack. 1950:

The Sleeping City. Under the Gun. 1951: Hollywood Story. The Raging Tide. 1952: The Fighter. The Raiders. 1953: The Blue Gardenia. Desert Legion. Slaves of Babylon. Highway Dragnet. 1954: Mask of Dust (US: Race for Life). Little Red Monkey (US: The Case of the Little Red Monkey). 1955: New York Confidential. Target Zero. The Big Combo. The Big Tip-Off. Bengazi. I'll Cry Tomorrow. 1956: Full of Life. Overnight Haul (TV. GB: cinemas). 1957: The Brothers Rico. This Angry Age (GB: The Sea Wall). 1959: They Came to Cordura. 1960: Ocean's Eleven. Pepe. 1963: Who's Been Sleeping in My Bed? The Eyes of Annie Jones. 1964: Circus World (GB: The Magnificent Showman). 1965: Synanon (GB: Get Off My Back). The Greatest Story Ever Told. 1966: Assault on a Queen. Hotel. 1967: Tony Rome. Death Sentence. 1968: Lady in Cement. The Challengers (TV. GB: cinemas). 1969: Explosion. Operation Cross Eagles. 1971: The Godfather. 1972: L'onorata famiglia (Uccidere è Cosa Nostra. US: The Big Family). 1973: Tony Arzenta/Big Guns. La polizia vuole giustizia (US: The Violent Professionals). Piazza Pulita (GB and US: Pete, Pearl and the Pole). Il boss (GB: Murder Inferno. US: The New Mafia). My Brother Anastasia. The Inspector is Killed. 1974: Il poliziotto è marcio (US: Shoot First, Die Later). Anna quel particolare piacere (GB: Secrets of a Call Girl. US: Anna: the Pleasure, the Torment). 1975: No Way Out. Roma violenta (GB: Street Killers). The Spectres. The Evil Eye. Un urlo dalle tenebre (GB: Naked Exorcism. US: Who Are You Satan?). The Citizen Needs Self Protection. The Police Accuse.

As director: 1969: Operation Cross Eagles.

† As Nicholas Conte

CONTI, Tom 1942–

Black-haired Scottish actor of wry-faced handsomeness who won praise on television (especially for the series The Glittering Prizes) and in the theatre, but had problems finding his slot in films until he played the dissolute lothario poet in Reuben, Reuben, which won him an Oscar nomination. He still looks uncomfortable, though, playing straightforward leading men, and is best suited to a script on which he can impose his dominant offbeat personality.

1974: Flame. Galileo. 1976: Eclipse. Full

Circle. 1977: The Duellists. 1980: Blade on the Feather (TV). 1981: The Wall (TV). 1982: Reuben, Reuben. Merry Christmas, Mr Lawrence. 1985: American Dreamer. Saving Grace. 1986: Miracles. Io e D'Annunzio. The Beate Klarsfeld Story (TV). Heavenly Pursuits.

CONWAY, Tom
(Thomas Sanders) 1904–1967

Russian-born international actor of British parents, brother of George Sanders, whom he followed to Hollywood in 1939. Well remembered as the suave, moustachioed hero of many a minor thriller, most notably as The Falcon, in a series he inherited from his brother. Sustained stardom in black-and-white thrillers until well into his fifties, when high living and heavy drinking took its toll. Died from cirrhosis of the liver.

1940: Sky Murder. 1941: The Trial of Mary Duggan. Free and Easy. The People versus Dr Kildare (GB: My Life Is Yours). Wild Man of Borneo. Mr and Mrs North. Lady Be Good. Tarzan's Secret Treasure. The Bad Man (GB: Two Gun Cupid). 1942: Rio Rita. Grand Central Murder. Mrs Miniver. The Falcon's Brother. Cat People. 1943: The Seventh Victim. I Walked with a Zombie. The Falcon Strikes Back. The Falcon in Danger. The Falcon and the Co-Eds. One Exciting Night. 1944: The Falcon Out West. The Falcon in Hollywood. The Falcon in Mexico. A Night of Adventure. 1945: Two O'Clock Courage. The Falcon in San Francisco. 1946: The Falcon's Alibi. Whistle Stop. Criminal Court. The Falcon's Adventure. Runaway Daughters. 1947: Repeat Performance. Fun on a Week-End. Lost Honey-

moon. 1948: The Checkered Coat. The Challenge. Thirteen Lead Soldiers. Bungalow 13. One Touch of Venus. 1949: I Cheated the Law. 1950: The Great Plane Robbery. 1951: Painting the Clouds with Sunshine. 1952: Bride of the Gorilla. Confidence Girl. 1953: Paris Model. Tarzan and the She-Devil. Peter Pan (voice only). Blood Orange. Park Plaza 605 (US: Norman Conquest). 1954: Prince Valiant. Three Stops to Murder. 1955: Barbados Quest (US: Murder on Approval). 1956: Breakaway. The Last Man to Hang? Operation Murder. Death of a Scoundrel. The She-Creature. 1957: Voodoo Woman. 1959: Atomic Submarine. 1960: Twelve to the Moon. 1961: One Hundred and One Dalmatians (voice only). 1964: What a Way to Go!

COOGAN, Jackie 1914–1984

American child star whose floppy fair hair and lovelorn expression endeared him to millions. In the 1930s he was involved in court battles with his parents over earnings (he was left with $125,000 out of an original $4 million) and his unique box-office appeal vanished (so, too, did the hair) with adulthood. After unsuccessful attempts to stay in leading roles, he reappeared in the 1950s as a plump character actor. Married (first of four) to Betty Grable (qv) from 1937 to 1939. Died from a heart ailment.

1916: Skinner's Baby. 1919: A Day's Pleasure. 1920: The Kid. 1921: Peck's Bad Boy. 1922: My Boy. Oliver Twist. Trouble. 1923: Daddy. Circus Days. 1924: Long Live the King. A Boy of Flanders. Little Robinson Crusoe. The Rag Man. 1925: Johnny Get Your Gun. Old Clothes. 1926: Johnny Get Your Hair Cut. 1927: The Bugle Call. Buttons. 1930: *Voice of Hollywood No.2. Tom Sawyer. 1931: Huckleberry Finn. 1935: Home on the Range. 1936: *Love in September. 1938: College Swing (GB: Swing, Teacher, Swing). 1939: Million Dollar Legs. Sky Patrol. 1947: Kilroy Was Here. 1948: French Leave (GB: Kilroy on Deck). 1951: Skipalong Rosenbloom. Varieties on Parade. 1952: Outlaw Women. 1953: The Actress. 1954: Mesa of Lost Women/Lost Women. 1956: Forbidden Area (TV). The Proud Ones. 1957: The Buster Keaton Story. The Joker is Wild. The Star-Wagon (TV). Eighteen and Anxious. The Troublemakers. 1958: High School Confidential. Lonelyhearts. No Place to Land (GB: Man Mad). The Space Children. Night of the Quarter Moon. 1959:

Yonder (GB: Thunder Across the Pacific).
Rich, Young and Pretty. 1952: Carbine Williams. My Man and I. The Wild North. 1953:
Laughing Anne. Jamaica Run. 1954: Hell's
Half Acre. Rear Window. Fireman Save My
Child. 1955: The Big Knife. 1956: The Killer
is Loose. The Bold and the Brave. The Rack.
The Rainmaker. 1957: Loving You. 1958: The
Light in the Forest. 1959: Alias Jesse James.
1964: Blood on the Arrow. 1965: Broken Sabre
(TV. GB: cinemas). Agent for H.A.R.M. 1966:
Waco. Women of the Prehistoric Planet. Picture
Mommy Dead. 1967: Red Tomahawk. Cyborg
2087. 1968: Buckskin. The Starmaker. The
Astro Zombies.

CORRI, Adrienne (A. Riccoboni) 1930–
Tempestuous red-headed Scottish-born
actress with a reputation for living life to the
full. Has, on the whole, not been seen in many
films that showcased her particular talent to
advantage. Married/divorced actor Daniel
Massey (qv).
1949: The Romantic Age (US: Naughty
Arlette). 1951: The River. Quo Vadis? 1953:
The Kidnappers (US: The Little Kidnappers).
The Sinners. 1954: Devil Girl from Mars. Meet
Mr Callaghan. Lease of Life. Make Me an
Offer. 1955: *The Man Who Stayed Alive.
Triple Blackmail. 1956: The Feminine Touch
(US: The Gentle Touch). Behind the Head-
lines. The Shield of Faith. Three Men in a Boat.
1957: Second Fiddle. The Big Chance. The
Surgeon's Knife. 1958: Corridors of Blood.
1959: The Rough and the Smooth (US: Por-
trait of a Sinner). 1960: The Tell-Tale Heart.
Sword of Freedom. 1961: The Hellfire Club.
1962: Dynamite Jack. 1963: Lancelot and
Guinevere (US: Sword of Lancelot). 1965:
Bunny Lake is Missing. A Study in Terror.
Doctor Zhivago. 1967: The Viking Queen.
Woman Times Seven. Africa – Texas Style!
1968: The File of the Golden Goose. Cry Wolf.
1969: Moon Zero Two. 1971: A Clockwork
Orange. Vampire Circus. 1974: Madhouse.
Rosebud. 1978: Revenge of the Pink Panther.
1979: The Human Factor.

CORTESE, Valentina 1924–
Italian-born (on New Year's Day) actress
whose auburn hair, green eyes and appealing
emotional style brought her to the notice of
film producers even before she had left
Rome's Academy of Dramatic Art. Her inter-

national career was fairly brief (1949–1956)
but she later proved her talent in more mature
roles. Long married to Richard Basehart, but
divorced in 1971. Surname spelt Cortesa in
American films.
1940: Orizzonte dipinto. 1941: Il bravo di
Venezia. La cena delle beffe. Regina di
Navarra. Primo amore. 1942: Soltanto un
bacio. Una signora dell'Ovest. Orrizonte di
sangue. Quarta pagina. Giorni felici. L'angelo
bianco. 1943: Quattro regazze sognano. Chi
l'ha visto? Nessuno torna indietro. 1945: Un
americano in vacanza (US: A Yank in Rome).
1946: Roma, città libera. 1947: Il passatore. Gli
uomini sono nemici. Les misérables. Il corriere
del re. L'ebreo errante. 1948: Le carrefour des
passions (GB: Crossroads of Passion). 1949:
Donne senza nome (GB: Unwanted Women).
The Glass Mountain. Thieves' Highway. Black
Magic. Malaya (GB: East of the Rising Sun).
1950: Shadow of the Eagle. 1951: The House
on Telegraph Hill. 1952: Secret People. Lulu.
1953: La passeggiata. Donne proibite/Forbidden
Women (US: Angels of Darkness). 1954: The
Barefoot Contessa. Avanzi di galera. Il matrimonio. Répris de justice. Addio mia bella signora.
1955: Il conte Aquila. Le amiche. Adriana
Lecouvreur. Faccia da mascalzone. 1956:
Magic Fire. Calabuch. 1959: Amore e guai.
*Béatrice. 1961: Square of Violence. Barabbas.
1962: Axel Munthe. 1963: The Evil Eye. 1964:
The Visit. 1965: The Possessed. Juliet of the
Spirits. 1966: Le soleil noir. 1968: The Legend
of Lylah Clare. Scusi, faciamo l'amore. 1969:
Tòh, è morta la nonna! Les caprices de Marie.
1970: First Love. Madly. 1971: Le bateau sur
l'herbe. 1972: L'iguana dalla lingua di fuoco.
Brother Sun, Sister Moon. Imputazione di
omicidio per uno studente. The Assassination of
Trotsky. 1973: Il bacio. La nuit américaine
(GB and US: Day for Night). 1974: Appa-
sionata. Tendre Dracula. Amore mio non farme
male. 1975: La chair de l'orchidée. La città
sconvolta – caccia spietata ai rapitori. Dracula
in Brianza. 1976: Friends of Nick Hazard. Le
grand escogriffe. Kidnap Syndicate. 1977: Nido
de viudas/Widow's Nest. 1978: Sentimenti e
passione. Tanto va la gatta al lardo. 1980:
When Time Ran Out . . . 1982: La Ferdinanda.

CORTEZ, Ricardo
(Jacob Krantz) 1899–1977
Black-haired American actor groomed for
stardom in the Valentino mould in the twen-

ties. His square, stern and rather immobile
features proved more suitable for villainy with
the coming of sound and he drifted on in
routine roles until giving up the screen for
business interests.
1923: Sixty Cents an Hour. Children of Jazz.
Call of the Canyon. 1924: The Next Corner. A
Society Scandal. The Bedroom Window. Feet
of Clay. The City That Never Sleeps. Argentine
Love. 1925: The Spaniard (GB: Spanish
Love). The Swan. Not So Long Ago. In the
Name of Love. The Pony Express. 1926: Iban-
ez's Torrent (GB: The Torrent). The Cat's
Pajamas. The Sorrows of Satan. The Eagle of
the Sea. New York. 1927: Mockery. The Pri-
vate Life of Helen of Troy. 1928: Ladies of
the Night Club. Excess Baggage. 1929: The
Younger Generation. The Phantom in the
House. 1930: The Lost Zeppelin. Montana
Moon. Her Man. Illicit. 1931: Big Business
Girl. Ten Cents a Dance. Behind Office Doors.
The Maltese Falcon. White Shoulders. Trans-
gression. Bad Company. Reckless Living. 1932:
Men of Chance. No One Man. Phantom of
Crestwood. Flesh. Thirteen Woman. Is My Face
Red? Symphony of Six Million (GB: Melody
of Life). 1933: Broadway Bad (GB: Her
Reputation). Midnight Mary. Big Executive.
Torch Singer (GB: Broadway Singer). The
House on 56th Street. 1934: The Big Shake-
down. Mandalay. Wonder Bar. The Man with
Two Faces. Hat, Coat and Glove. The Firebird.
Lost Lady. 1935: Special Agent. The Frisco
Kid. Shadow of Doubt. I Am a Thief. White
Cockatoo. Manhattan Moon (GB: Sing Me a
Love Song). 1936: Man Hunt. The Walking
Dead. The Murder of Dr Harrigan. Postal
Inspector. The Case of the Black Cat. Talk of
the Devil. 1937: The Californian (GB: Beyond
the Law). West of Shanghai. Her Husband
Lies. 1938: City Girl. 1939: Mr Moto's Last
Warning. Charlie Chan in Reno. 1940: Murder
Over New York. 1941: Romance of the Rio
Grande. A Shot in the Dark. World Premiere.
I Killed That Man. 1942: Rubber Racketeers.
Who is Hope Schuyler? Tomorrow We Live.
1944: Make Your Own Bed. 1946: The Inner
Circle. The Locket. 1947: Blackmail. 1948:
Mystery in Mexico. 1950: Bunco Squad. 1958:
The Last Hurrah.
As director: 1938: City Girl. 1939: The Inside
Story. Chasing Danger. Heaven with a Barbed
Wire Fence. The Escape. City of Chance. 1940:
Free, Blonde and 21. The Girl in 313.

COSTELLO, Dolores 1905–1979

Pale, square-faced, initially dark-haired (later blonde) American actress of fragile appearance, who was married to John Barrymore (qv) from 1928 to 1935. Returned to the screen after the break-up of her marriage but soon found that her silent screen image had dated and left films for good in the 1940s. Daughter of early silent actor Maurice Costello, sister of actress Helene Costello and mother of actor John Drew Barrymore (John Barrymore Jr). Died from emphysema.

1911: *The Meeting of the Ways. His Sister's Children. The Child Crusoes. The Geranium.* 1912: *A Juvenile Love Affair. Wanted, a Grandmother. Ida's Christmas. The Money King. The Troublesome Stepdaughters.* 1913: *The Hindoo Charm.* 1923: *The Glimpses of the Moon. Lawful Larceny.* 1925: *Greater Than a Crown. Bobbed Hair.* 1926: *Mannequin. The Little Irish Girl. The Sea Beast. Bride of the Storm. The Third Degree.* 1927: *When a Man Loves (GB: His Lady). Old San Francisco. A Million Bid. The Heart of Maryland. The College Widow.* 1928: *Glorious Betsy. Tenderloin.* 1929: *Glad Rag Doll. The Redeeming Sin. Madonna of Avenue A. Hearts in Exile. The Show of Shows. Noah's Ark.* 1930: *Second Choice.* 1931: *Expensive Women.* 1936: *Yours for the Asking. Little Lord Fauntleroy.* 1938: *The Beloved Brat (GB: A Dangerous Age). Breaking the Ice.* 1939: *Whispering Enemies. Outside These Walls. King of the Turf.* 1942: *The Magnificent Ambersons.* 1943: *This is the Army.*

COSTELLO, Lou

See ABBOTT and COSTELLO

COTTEN, Joseph 1905–

Quiet, taciturn, crinkly-haired American actor with distinctive rasping voice, much associated with Orson Welles. Came late to films after drama criticism and stage experience, but has worked steadily since, most notably in films for Welles and Hitchcock, and in progressively less worthy ones in recent years. Had been married to first wife for 30 years when she died: since 1960 has been married to Patricia Medina (qv).
1938: †*Too Much Johnson.* 1941: *Citizen Kane. Lydia.* 1942: *The Magnificent Ambersons. Journey into Fear.* 1943: *Hers to Hold. Shadow of a Doubt.* 1944: *Gaslight (GB:*

Murder in Thornton Square). Since You Went Away. I'll Be Seeing You. 1945: *Love Letters.* 1946: *Duel in the Sun.* 1947: *The Farmer's Daughter.* 1948: *Portrait of Jennie (GB: Jennie).* 1949: *The Third Man. Under Capricorn. Beyond the Forest. Walk Softly, Stranger.* 1950: *Gone to Earth (US: The Wild Heart) (narrator only). Two Flags West. September Affair.* 1951: *Half Angel. Peking Express. The Man with a Cloak.* 1952: *Untamed Frontier. The Steel Trap.* 1953: *Niagara. A Blueprint for Murder. Egypt by Three (narrator only).* 1955: *Special Delivery. The Killer is Loose.* 1956: *The Bottom of the Bottle (GB: Beyond the River).* **Nobody Runs Away.* 1957: *The Halliday Brand. Edge of Innocence (TV).* 1958: *Touch of Evil. From the Earth to the Moon.* 1960: *The Angel Wore Red.* 1961: *The Last Sunset.* 1964: *Hush ... Hush, Sweet Charlotte.* 1965: *The Money Trap. The Great Sioux Massacre. Krakatoa (narrator only).* 1966: *The Oscar. Some May Live (TV. GB: cinemas). Gli uomini dal passo pesante (GB and US: The Tramplers). I crudeli (GB and US: The Hellbenders). Brighty of Grand Canyon.* 1967: *Jack of Diamonds.* 1968: *Rio Hondo (GB: White Comanche). Petulia. Gangster '70 (US: Days of Fire).* 1969: *The Lonely Profession (TV). Cutter's Trail (TV). Latitude Zero. Keene.* 1970: *The Grasshopper. Tora! Tora! Tora! E venne l'ora della vendetta. Do You Take This Stranger? (TV). Assault on the Wayne (TV).* 1971: *Lady Frankenstein. The Screaming Woman (TV). The Abominable Dr Phibes. City Beneath the Sea (TV. GB cinemas: One Hour to Doomsday).* 1972: *Lo scopone scientifico (US: The Scientific Cardplayer). The Devil's Daughter (TV). Doomsday Voyage. Gli orrori del castello di Norimberga (GB: Baron Blood).* 1973: *Soylent Green. F for Fake. Timber Tramp.* 1974: *A Delicate Balance.* 1975: *Il giustiziere sfida la citta (US: Syndicate Sadists).* 1976: *The Lindbergh Kidnapping Case (TV). A Whisper in the Dark.* 1977: *Airport 77. Twilight's Last Gleaming.* 1978: *L'ordre et la sécurité du monde. Caravans. The Fish Men.* 1979: *Guyana: The Crime of the Century. The House Where Death Lives (re-released 1982 as The House Where Evil Dwells). Island of Mutations. Casino (TV. GB: SS Casino). Trauma. The Concorde Affair.* 1980: *The Hearse. Heaven's Gate.* 1981: *The Survivor.* 1982: *Screamers (The Fish Men with added footage).*

† *Unreleased*

COURT, Hazel 1926–

A small, shapely, green-eyed, red-haired British actress with impishly aristocratic looks, Hazel was a Technicolor technician's dream. Hollywood would have starred her in easterns or earthy period roles, but British films wasted her, as shy sisters and heroines of (black and white!) second-feature crime dramas. A few horror films in the sixties belatedly revealed her as a good Technicolor bad girl. Married to actors Dermot Walsh (1949–1963) and Don Taylor.

1944: *Champagne Charlie. Dreaming.* 1946: *Gaiety George (US: Showtime). Carnival.* 1947: *Meet Me at Dawn. The Root of All Evil. Dear Murderer. Holiday Camp.* 1948: *My Sister and I. Bond Street. Forbidden.* 1952: *Ghost Ship.* 1953: *Counterspy (US: Undercover Agent).* 1954: *Devil Girl from Mars. The Scarlet Web. A Tale of Three Women.* 1956: *The Narrowing Circle. Behind the Headlines. The Curse of Frankenstein.* 1957: *Hour of Decision.* 1958: *A Woman of Mystery.* 1959: *Model for Murder. Breakout. The Man Who Could Cheat Death. The Shakedown.* 1960: *The Man Who Was Nobody.* 1961: *Dr Blood's Coffin. Mary Had a Little.* 1962: *The Premature Burial.* 1963: *The Raven.* 1964: *The Masque of the Red Death.*

COURTENAY, Tom 1937–

Unhappy-looking British actor briefly in star roles as undernourished working-class misfits, but whose working life has been principally

committed to the theatre. Oscar-nominated for *Doctor Zhivago* and *The Dresser*.
1962: The Loneliness of the Long Distance Runner. Private Potter. 1963: Billy Liar! 1964: King and Country. 1965: Operation Crossbow (US: The Great Spy Mission). King Rat. Doctor Zhivago. 1966: The Night of the Generals. 1967: The Day the Fish Came Out. 1968: A Dandy in Aspic. Otley. 1971: Catch Me a Spy. One Day in the Life of Ivan Denisovitch. 1972: *Today Mexico – Tomorrow the World. 1973: I Heard the Owl Call My Name (TV). 1983: The Dresser. 1985: Happy New Year.

COURTLAND, Jerome (C. Jourolmon) 1926–
Very tall, dark, bland-looking, spindly American actor who came to the screen at 17 and played a succession of fresh young innocents in Columbia westerns and musicals. Later gave up a flagging acting career to become a production executive with Walt Disney Productions, for whom he also produced a couple of pictures. Married/divorced Polly Bergen (*qv*), first of two.
1944: Together Again. 1945: Kiss and Tell. 1948: The Man from Colorado. 1949: The Walking Hills. Tokyo Joe. Make Believe Ballroom. Battleground. 1950: A Woman of Distinction. The Palomino (GB: Hills of the Brave). When You're Smiling. 1951: Santa Fé. The Texas Rangers. Sunny Side of the Street. The Barefoot Mailman. 1952: Cripple Creek. 1953: Take the High Ground. 1955: The Bamboo Prison. 1958: Tonka. 1960: O sole mio. 1961: The Adventures of Mary Read (GB: Hell Below Deck). Tharus, Son of Attila. 1962: Café Oriental. 1965: Black Spurs. The Restless Ones.

COURTNEIDGE, Dame Cicely 1893–1980
Ever-cheerful, much-loved, brown-haired, Australian-born entertainer, a personable comedienne of limitless energy who could sing and dance as well. Her angular features enjoyed their greatest successes on stage but with her husband Jack Hulbert (*qv*) she became very popular for a while in early sound musical comedies, some of which she virtually turned into one-woman shows. Created Dame in 1972.
1928: *British Screen Tatler No 10. 1930: Elstree Calling. 1931: The Ghost Train. 1932:

Jack's the Boy (US: Night and Day). Happy Ever After. 1933: Soldiers of the King (US: The Woman in Command). Falling for You. Aunt Sally (US: Along Came Sally). 1934: Things Are Looking Up. 1935: Me and Marlborough. The Perfect Gentleman (GB: The Imperfect Lady). 1936: Everybody Dance. 1937: Take My Tip. 1940: Under Your Hat. 1955: Miss Tulip Stays the Night. 1960: The Spider's Web. 1962: The L-Shaped Room. 1965: Those Magnificent Men in Their Flying Machines. 1966: The Wrong Box. 1972: Not Now Darling.

COWARD, Sir Noël 1899–1973
Multi-talented British playwright and entertainer, noted for his charm and sophisticated wit, and the toast of London's theatreland in the twenties and thirties. His film appearances were as rare as they were often eccentric, but most of his plays were filmed, and enormous successes, encapsulating as they did the mood of Britain at the given time. Knighted in 1970. Died from a heart attack. Special Academy Award 1942.
1918: Hearts of the World. 1935: The Scoundrel. 1942: †In Which We Serve. 1950: The Astonished Heart. 1956: Around the World in 80 Days. 1959: Our Man in Havana. 1960: Surprise Package. 1963: Paris When It Sizzles. 1965: Bunny Lake is Missing. 1968: Boom! 1969: The Italian Job.

† *Also co-directed*

COYOTE, Peter 1945–
Tall, fair-haired, laconic-looking, strong-faced American actor seen in dominating leading and semi-leading roles of the 1980s. A

late arrival to cinema screens, Coyote was for many years a leading light in the San Francisco theatre world before bringing his sardonic tones to a wider audience, proving equally at home in gentle or cruel roles, but an attention-grabber in anything.
1980: Die Laughing. Tell Me a Riddle. In the Child's Best Interest (TV). 1981: Isabel's Choice (TV). The People vs Jean Harris (TV). Southern Comfort. Pursuit/The Pursuit of D B Cooper. 1982: E.T. the Extra Terrestrial. Timerider – The Adventure of Lyle Swann. Out. Endangered Species. 1983: Strangers Kiss. Cross Creek. 1984: Scorned and Swindled (TV). Best Kept Secrets (TV). Slayground. 1985: The Legend of Billie Jean. Jagged Edge. Heartbreakers. 1986: Time Flyer (TV). Outrageous Fortune.

CRABBE, Larry 'Buster' (Clarence Crabbe) 1907–1983
Olympic swimming champion who won a bronze medal for America in 1928 and a gold in 1932, before becoming as famous playing intergalactic heroes Flash Gordon and Buck Rogers as another swimming champ, Johnny Weissmuller (*qv*) did playing Tarzan. Crabbe became a 'B' western star of the 1940s before moving into business and becoming an executive in water sports. In 1971 he broke the world 400-metre freestyle record for oversixties! Died from a heart attack.
1930: Good News. 1931: Maker of Men. 1932: Island of Lost Souls. The Most Dangerous Game (GB: The Hounds of Zaroff). That's My Boy. 1933: Tarzan the Fearless (serial). King of the Jungle. To The Last Man. Man of

the Forest. *Hollywood on Parade (B7). The Sweetheart of Sigma Chi (GB: Girl of My Dreams). The Thundering Herd. 1934: Search for Beauty. You're Telling Me. Badge of Honor. She Had to Choose. We're Rich Again. The Oil Raider. 1935: Hold 'em Yale (GB: Uniform Lovers). Wanderer of the Wasteland. Nevada. 1936: Drift Fence. Desert Gold. Rose Bowl (GB: O'Reilly's Luck). Flash Gordon (serial). Arizona Raiders. Lady, Be Careful. Arizona Mahoney. 1937: Murder Goes to College. Sophie Lang Goes West. Daughter of Shanghai (GB: Daughter of the Orient). King of Gamblers. Forlorn River. Thrill of a Lifetime. 1938: Red Barry (serial). Tip-Off Girls. Hunted Men. Flash Gordon's Trip to Mars (serial). Illegal Traffic. 1939: Unmarried (GB: Night Club Hostess). Million Dollar Legs. Buck Rogers (serial). Colorado Sunset. Call a Messenger. 1940: Sailor's Lady. Flash Gordon Conquers the Universe (serial). 1941: Billy the Kid Wanted. Billy the Kid's Roundup. Jungle Man. 1942: Billy the Kid Trapped. Law and Order (GB: Double Alibi). Jungle Siren. Wildcat. Mysterious Rider. Sheriff of Sage Valley. Billy the Kid's Smoking Guns (GB: Smoking Guns). Queen of Broadway. 1943: The Kid Rides Again. Fugitive of the Plains. Western Cyclone. Devil Riders. The Drifter. The Renegade. Cattle Stampede. Blazing Frontier. 1944: Thundering Gunslingers. Nabonga (GB: The Jungle Woman). Frontier Outlaws. Oath of Vengeance. Fuzzy Settles Down. The Contender. Valley of Vengeance. Rustlers' Hideout. Wild Horse Phantom. 1945: Shadows of Death. Border Badmen. Stagecoach Outlaws. Fighting Bill Carson. Lightning Raiders. Prairie Rustlers. Gangsters' Den. His Brother's Ghost. 1946: Overland Raiders. Outlaws of the Plains. Prairie Badmen. Gentlemen with Guns. Ghost of Hidden Valley. Terrors on Horseback. Swamp Fire. 1947: Last of the Redmen (GB: Last of the Redskins). The Sea Hound (serial). 1948: Caged Fury. 1950: Pirates of the High Seas (serial). Captive Girl. 1952: King of the Congo (serial). 1954: Desert Outpost (TV. GB: cinemas). 1956: Gun Brothers. 1957: The Lawless Eighties. 1958: Badman's Country. 1960: Gunfighters of Abilene. 1965: The Bounty Killers. Arizona Raiders (and 1936 version). 1971: The Comeback Trail (released 1982). 1979: Swim Team. 1981: The Alien Dead (released 1985).

CRAIG, James (John Meador) 1912–1985
Rugged, black-haired, latterly moustachioed, chubby-faced American leading man, a minor-league Clark Gable in tough action roles, with the occasional romantic lead thrown in. A second-line star from 1942 to 1959, following a solid performance in *All That Money Can Buy*, which gave him his first important role, his stormy marriages included one (1959–1962) to actress Jil Jarmyn. Died from lung cancer.
1937: Sophie Lang Goes West. Born to the West. Thunder Trail. 1938: The Big Broadcast of 1938. The Buccaneer. Pride of the West. 1939: Blondie Meets the Boss. The Lone Wolf Spy Hunt (GB: The Lone Wolf's Daughter). North of Shanghai. Romance of the Redwoods.

A Woman is the Judge. Café Hostess. *Skinny the Moocher. Good Girls Go to Paris. Missing Daughters. Taming of the West. Flying G-Men (serial). Overland with Kit Carson (serial). Behind Prison Gates. The Man They Could Not Hang. Konga, the Wild Stallion (GB: Konga). 1940: Winners of the West. The House Across the Bay. Zanzibar. Enemy Agent (GB: Secret Enemy). Seven Sinners. Two-Fisted Rangers. Law and Order (GB: Lucky Ralston). South to Karanga. I'm Nobody's Sweetheart Now. Scandal Sheet. Kitty Foyle. 1941: All That Money Can Buy/The Devil and Daniel Webster/Daniel and the Devil. Unexpected Uncle. 1942: Friendly Enemies. The Omaha Trail. Northwest Rangers. Valley of the Sun. Seven Miles from Alcatraz. 1943: Swing Shift Maisie (GB: The Girl in Overalls). The Human Comedy. Lost Angel. The Heavenly Body. 1944: Kismet. Marriage is a Private Affair. Gentle Annie. 1945: Dangerous Partners. Our Vines Have Tender Grapes. She Went to the Races. 1946: Boys' Ranch. Little Mr Jim. 1947: Dark Delusion (GB: Cynthia's Secret). 1948: The Man from Texas. Northwest Stampede. 1949: Side Street. 1950: A Lady without Passport. 1951: The Strip. Drums in the Deep South. 1952: Hurricane Smith. 1953: Code Two. Fort Vengeance. 1955: Last of the Desperadoes. 1956: Women of Pitcairn Island. Massacre. While the City Sleeps. 1957: Shootout at Medicine Bend. Cyclops. Ghost Diver. Naked in the Sun. The Persuader. 1958: Man or Gun. 1959: Four Fast Guns. 1967: Fort Utah. Hostile Guns. The Doomsday Machine. 1968: The Devil's Brigade. Arizona Bushwhackers. If He Hollers, Let Him Go! 1969: Bigfoot.

CRAIG, Michael (M. Gregson) 1928–
Tall, clean-cut, light-haired, British, slightly stuffy actor (born in India) who, through the Rank Organisation, enjoyed a good run of virile leading roles from 1956 to 1963, later giving some interesting performances in character parts. In the middle and late seventies, was seen in leading roles in Australian films. He has also written screenplays.
1949: †Passport to Pimlico. 1953: Malta Story. 1954: The Love Lottery. Forbidden Cargo. The Embezzler. Svengali. 1955: Passage Home. Handcuffs London. 1956: The Black Tent. Yield to the Night (US: Blonde Sinner). Eyewitness. House of Secrets (US: Triple Decep-

tion). 1957: High Tide at Noon. Campbell's Kingdom. 1958: The Silent Enemy. Nor the Moon by Night (US: Elephant Gun). Sea of Sand (US: Desert Patrol). 1959: Life in Emergency Ward 10. Sapphire. Upstairs and Downstairs. 1960: The Angry Silence. Cone of Silence (US: Trouble in the Sky). Doctor in Love. 1961: Payroll. No, My Darling Daughter! A Pair of Briefs. 1962: Mysterious Island. La citta prigioniera (GB: The Captive City. US: The Conquered City). Life for Ruth (US: Walk in the Shadow). The Iron Maiden (US: The Swingin' Maiden). 1963: Stolen Hours. 1965: Vaghe stelle dell'orsa (GB: Of a Thousand Delights). Life at the Top. 1966: Modesty Blaise. Sandra. 1968: Star! 1969: Twinky. The Royal Hunt of the Sun. Country Dance (US: Brotherly Love). 1971: A Town Called Bastard. The Fourth Mrs Anderson. The Night of the Assassin. 1973: Vault of Horror. 1974: Last Rites (TV). Inn of the Damned. 1975: Port Essington. Ride a Wild Pony. 1976: The Emigrants. 1977: The Timeless Land (TV). The Irishman. Roses Bloom Twice (TV). 1981: Turkey Shoot. 1983: Stanley.

† As crowd player: and probably more in this capacity

CRAIN, Jeanne 1925–
Green-eyed, auburn-haired, sweet-faced American actress, a beauty contest winner at 16 and cast almost exclusively for 11 years by Fox as nice young things with deep, inner feelings. In these forties' films she was often touching and sometimes funny, but her career took a questionable turn in the fifties when

she forsook this image for pin-up glamour – even if she did look pretty good for a lady with seven children. An Oscar nominee for her performance in *Pinky*.
1943: *The Gang's All Here (GB: The Girls He Left Behind)*. 1944: *Home in Indiana. In the Meantime, Darling. Winged Victory.* 1945: *State Fair. Leave Her to Heaven. *All-Star Bond Rally.* 1946: *Margie. Centennial Summer.* 1948: *Apartment for Peggy. You Were Meant for Me.* 1949: *A Letter to Three Wives. The Fan (GB: Lady Windermere's Fan). Pinky.* 1950: *Cheaper by the Dozen. I'll Get By.* 1951: *Take Care of My Little Girl. People Will Talk. The Model and the Marriage Broker.* 1952: *Belles on Their Toes. O. Henry's Full House (GB: Full House).* 1953: *Dangerous Crossing. City of Bad Men. Vicki.* 1954: *Duel in the Jungle.* 1955: *Man Without a Star. Gentlemen Marry Brunettes. The Second Greatest Sex.* 1956: *The Fastest Gun Alive.* 1957: *The Tattered Dress. The Joker is Wild.* 1958: *The Great Gatsby (TV).* 1959: *Meet Me in St Louis (TV). Guns of the Timberland.* 1961: *With Fire and Sword. Pontius Pilate. Nerfertiti, regina del Nilo (GB and US: Queen of the Nile). Twenty Plus Two (GB: It Started in Tokyo).* 1962: *Madison Avenue.* 1964: *52 Miles to Terror (re-released 1967 as Hot Rods to Hell).* 1971: *The Night God Screamed (GB: Scream).* 1972: *Skyjacked.*

CRAWFORD, Anne
(Imelda Crawford) 1920–1956
Sharply oval-faced, Palestinian-born, cool blonde actress in British films, equally at home as heroines, funny ladies or shrews. Perhaps because of her versatility, she didn't quite find her niche in the cinema, although stealing the notices was possibly reward enough. Died of leukemia at 35.
1938: *Prison without Bars.* 1940: *Ferry Pilot.* 1942: *They Flew Alone (US: Wings and the Woman). The Peterville Diamond. The Night Invader.* 1943: *The Dark Tower. Millions Like Us. Headline. The Hundred Pound Window.* 1944: *2,000 Women.* 1945: *They Were Sisters.* 1946: *Caravan. Bedelia.* 1947: *Master of Bankdam. Daughter of Darkness.* 1948: *Night Beat. The Blind Goddess. It's Hard to be Good.* 1950: *Tony Draws a Horse. Trio.* 1951: *Thunder on the Hill (GB: Bonaventure).* 1953: *Street Corner (US: Both Sides of the Law).*

1954: *Knights of the Round Table. Mad About Men.*

CRAWFORD, Broderick
(William B. Crawford) 1910–1986
Big, beefy, powerful American actor, the son of Helen Broderick. Began as Damon Runyon-style gangsters and serio-comic western villains, progressing to corrupt politicians and businessman. His career suffered several gradual declines, but he always managed to come back into the limelight. Academy Award for *All the King's Men* (1949). Very popular in TV series *Highway Patrol*. Died following a series of strokes.
1937: *Woman Chases Man. Submarine D-1. The Woman's Touch.* 1938: *Start Cheering. Sudden Money.* 1939: *Ambush. Undercover Doctor. Island of Lost Men. The Real Glory. Eternally Yours. Beau Geste.* 1940: *Slightly Honorable. When the Daltons Rode. Trail of the Vigilantes. I Can't Give You Anything But Love, Baby. Seven Sinners. Texas Rangers Ride Again.* 1941: *The Black Cat. Tight Shoes. South of Tahiti (GB: White Savage). Badlands of Dakota.* 1942: *Butch Minds the baby. Broadway. *Keeping Fit. North to the Klondike. Larceny Inc. Men of Texas (GB: Men of Destiny). Sin Town.* 1946: *The Runaround. The Black Angel.* 1947: *Slave Girl. The Flame.* 1948: *The Time of Your Life. Sealed Verdict. Bad Men of Tombstone.* 1949: *A Kiss in the Dark. Night unto Night. Anna Lucasta. All the King's Men.* 1950: *Born Yesterday. Cargo to Capetown. Convicted.* 1951: *The Mob (GB: Remember That Face).* 1952: *Lone Star. Scandal Sheet (GB: The Dark Page). Last of the Comanches (GB: The Sabre and the Arrow). Stop, You're Killing Me.* 1953: *The Last Posse.* 1954: *Night People. Human Desire. Down Three Dark Streets.* 1955: *New York Confidential. Big House USA. Il bidone (GB and US: The Swindlers). Not As a Stranger.* 1956: *The Fastest Gun Alive. Between Heaven and Hell.* 1958: *The Decks Ran Red.* 1960: *La vendetta di Ercole (GB: Goliath and the Dragon. US: The Revenge of Hercules).* 1961: *Nasilje na Trgu (GB: Square of Violence).* 1962: *The Castilian. Convicts Four (GB: Reprieve!).* 1964: *A House is Not a Home.* 1965: *Up from the Beach. Kid Rodelo.* 1966: *The Oscar. El Escuadrón de la Muerte (US: Mutiny at Fort Sharp). The Texican. The Vulture.* 1967: *Red Tomahawk.* 1968: *The Fakers. Gregorio and the Angel.*

1969: *Smashing the Crime Syndicate (released 1973).* 1970: *How Did a Nice Girl Like You Get into This Business? Maharlika. The Challenge (TV).* 1971: *Ransom Money. A Tattered Web (TV). Forbidden Knowledge (TV).* 1972: *The Candidate (voice only). House of Dracula's Daughter. Embassy.* 1973: *The Adventures of Nick Carter (TV). Terror in the Wax Museum.* 1974: *The Phantom of Hollywood (TV).* 1975: *Won Ton Ton, the Dog Who Saved Hollywood.* 1976: *Mayday at 40,000 Feet! (TV. GB: cinemas).* 1977: *Look What's Happened to Rosemary's Baby (TV). Proof of the Man. The Private Files of J. Edgar Hoover.* 1979: *Supertrain (TV. Later: Express to Terror). Just Not the Same Without You. A Little Romance. Harlequin. There Goes the Bride.* 1981: *The Upper Crust. Liar's Moon.*

CRAWFORD, Joan
(Lucille LeSueur) 1904–1977
Dark-haired (earlier blonde), thick-browed, dominating American actress. After an apprenticeship playing bitchy, hard-headed flappers, the Crawford of the forties and fifties, great haunted eyes and jagged mouth to the fore, excelled as women born to suffer. Still in leading roles when past 50, she remains one of the few actresses to create their own genre, with its ingredients of melodrama, mayhem, murder and mink. Academy Award for *Mildred Pierce*. Married to actors Douglas Fairbanks Jr. (1929–1933), Franchot Tone (1935–1939) and Philip Terry (1942–1946). Her last husband, a businessman, left her a widow in 1959. Died from a heart attack. Also Oscar-nominated for *Possessed* and *Sudden Fear*.
1925: *Miss MGM. Lady of the Night. Proud Flesh. Pretty Ladies. The Merry Widow. The Circle. The Only Thing (GB: Four Flaming Days). Old Clothes. Sally, Irene and Mary.* 1926: *The Boob (GB: The Yokel). Paris (GB: Shadows of Paris). Tramp, Tramp, Tramp.* 1927: *Winners of the Wilderness. The Taxi Dancer. West Point (GB: Eternal Youth). The Understanding Heart. The Unknown. Twelve Miles Out. Spring Fever.* 1928: *The Law of the Range. Rose Marie. Across to Singapore. Dream of Love. Four Walls. Our Dancing Daughters.* 1929: *The Duke Steps Out. Our Modern Maidens. Untamed. Hollywood Revue of 1929.* 1930: *Montana Moon. Our Blushing Brides. Paid (GB: Within the Law).* 1931:

Dance, Fools, Dance. Laughing Sinners. This Modern Age. Possessed. 1932: Grand Hotel. *The Stolen Jools (GB: The Slippery Pearls). Letty Lynton. Rain. 1933: Today We Live. Dancing Lady. 1934: Sadie McKee. Forsaking All Others. Chained. 1935: No More Ladies. I Live My Life. 1936: The Gorgeous Hussy. Love on the Run. 1937: The Last of Mrs Cheyney. The Bride Wore Red. Mannequin. 1938: The Shining Hour. 1939: Ice Follies of 1939. The Women. 1940: Strange Cargo. Susan and God (GB: The Gay Mrs Trexel). 1941: When Ladies Meet. A Woman's Face. 1942: They All Kissed the Bride. Reunion/Reunion in France (GB: Mademoiselle France). 1943: Above Suspicion. 1944: Hollywood Canteen. 1945: Mildred Pierce. 1946: Humoresque. 1947: Possessed. Daisy Kenyon. 1949: Flamingo Road. It's a Great Feeling. 1950: The Damned Don't Cry. Harriet Craig. 1951: Goodbye, My Fancy. This Woman is Dangerous. 1952: Sudden Fear. 1953: Torch Song. 1954: Johnny Guitar. 1955: *Hollywood Mothers. Female on the Beach. Queen Bee. 1956: Autumn Leaves. 1957: The Story of Esther Costello (US: Golden Virgin). 1959: The Best of Everything. Della (TV). 1962: What Ever Happened to Baby Jane? 1963: The Caretakers (GB: Borderlines). 1964: Strait-Jacket. 1965: I Saw What You Did. 1967: Berserk! The Karate Killers (TV. GB: cinemas). 1969: Night Gallery (TV). 1970: Trog. 1975: We're Going to Scare You to Death (TV).

CRAWFORD, Michael
(M. Dumble-Smith) 1942–
Light-haired, ingenuous-looking British comedy actor whose early career was spent playing hapless young heroes with two left feet. Broadened his horizons in the seventies and, from 1972 to 1980 concentrated entirely on stage and television. Later scored a big personal hit in the leading role of the stage musical *Barnum*, which occupied much of his time in the early 1980s.
1957: Soapbox Derby. 1958: Blow Your Own Trumpet. 1960: A French Mistress. 1961: Two Living One Dead. 1962: The War Lover. Two Left Feet. 1965: The Knack ... and how to get it. 1966: A Funny Thing Happened on the Way to the Forum. The Jokers. 1967: How I Won the War. 1968: The Games. 1969: Hello Dolly! 1970: Hello – Goodbye. 1971: Prelude to

Taurus. 1972: Alice's Adventures in Wonderland. 1981: Condorman.

CRAZY GANG, The
See Flanagan, Bud

CREGAR, Laird
(Samuel L. Cregar) 1916–1944
Massively overweight American actor who built up a tremendous reputation in just a

few years, after making his name in a stage production of the life of Oscar Wilde. Particularly good at cynics and tormented men of evil, culminating in his portrayals of Jack the Ripper and George Harvey Bone. Died from a heart attack following a crash diet.
1940: Oh, Johnny, How You Can Love! Granny Get Your Gun. Hudson's Bay. 1941: Blood and Sand. Charley's Aunt (GB: Charley's American Aunt). I Wake Up Screaming (GB: Hot Spot). 1942: Joan of Paris. Rings on Her Fingers. This Gun for Hire. The Black Swan. Ten Gentlemen from West Point. 1943: Hello, Frisco, Hello. Holy Matrimony. Heaven Can Wait. 1944: The Lodger. 1945: Hangover Square.

CRENNA, Richard 1926–
Few actors have spent a greater part of their career in television than this quiet, self-effacing American star. Despite several attempts to launch him as a big name in films, his taciturn personality had little box-office drawing power and he always returned to the happy hunting grounds of the small screen.
1951: Red Skies of Montana. 1952: Pride of St Louis. It Grows on Trees. 1955: Our Miss

Brooks. 1956: Over-Exposed. 1964: John Goldfarb, Please Come Home. 1965: Made in Paris. 1966: The Sand Pebbles. 1967: Wait Until Dark. 1968: Star! 1969: Midas Run (GB: A Run on Gold). Marooned. 1970: Red Sky at Morning. Doctors' Wives. La spina dorsale del Diavolo/The Deserter. 1971: Catlow. Thief (TV). 1972: Un Flic (GB: Dirty Money). The Man Called Noon. Footsteps (TV). 1973: Double Indemnity (TV). Nightmare (TV). Jonathan Livingston Seagull (voice only). Shootout in a One-Dog Town (TV). 1974: Honky Tonk (TV). A Girl Named Sooner (TV). 1975: Breakheart Pass. 1977: The War Between the Tates (TV). Cry Demon. 1978: Devil Dog, the Hound of Hell (TV). A Fire in the Sky (TV). First, You Cry (TV). The Evil. 1979: The Sin Sniper. Death Ship. Mayflower: The Pilgrims' Adventure (TV). 1980: Stone Cold Dead. 1981: Body Heat. The Ordeal of Bill Carney (TV). 1982: Table for Five. First Blood. The Day the Bubble Burst (TV). 1984: Squaring the Circle (narrator only). The Flamingo Kid. Passions (TV). 1985: Summer Rental. Rambo: First Blood Part II. The Rape of Richard Beck (TV). 1986: A Case of Deadly Force (TV).

As director. 1979: Better Late Than Never (TV). 1980: Fugitive Family (TV).

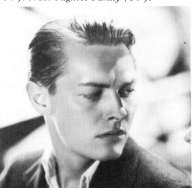

CROMWELL, Richard (Roy Radabaugh)
1910–1960
Blond-haired, lazy-lidded, sensitive-looking, very fresh-faced American actor with the smooth good looks of a 1930s' Richard Chamberlain (qv). The son of an inventor, he began his career in Hollywood creating 'masks' of the stars, but his ambitions switched from art to acting, especially when his enthusiasm and boyish appeal won him the leading role in Tol'able David (only his second film). He continued to play youthful and occasionally headstrong roles (most notably as Henry Fonda's brother in Jezebel) through the 1930s, but never really picked up the threads of his acting career after World War II service with the US Coast Guard, and worked mainly in ceramics before his early death from cancer. Briefly married (1945–46) to Angela Lansbury (qv).
1930: The King of Jazz. Tol'able David. 1931: Fifty Fathoms Deep. Shanghaied Love. Maker of Men. 1932: Age of Consent (GB: Are These Our Children?). The Strange Love of Molly

Louvain. That's My Boy. Emma. Tom Brown of Culver. 1933: This Day and Age. Hoopla. Above the Clouds. 1934: Carolina (GB: The House of Connelly). Among the Missing. Name the Woman. When Strangers Meet. Most Precious Thing in Life. 1935: The Lives of a Bengal Lancer. Life Begins at Forty. McFadden's Flats. Men of the Hour. The Unknown Woman. Annapolis Farewell (GB: Gentlemen of the Navy). 1936: Poppy. 1937: Our Fighting Navy (US: Torpedoed!). The Road Back/Return of the Hero. The Wrong Road. 1938: Jezebel. Come On, Leathernecks! Storm Over Bengal. 1939: Young Mr Lincoln. 1940: Enemy Agent (GB: Secret Enemy). The Villain Still Pursued Her. Village Barn Dance (GB: Dance Your Cares Away). 1941: Parachute Battalion. Riot Squad. 1942: Baby Face Morgan. 1943: Crime Doctor. 1948: Bungalow 13.

CROSBY, Bing (Harry Crosby) 1901–1977
Fair-haired, sleepy-looking singer with rich, soothing voice whose warm and friendly image, despite an unexceptional talent, made him into one of Hollywood's biggest stars, especially in the forties, when he was No. 1 box-office attraction in the country. Won an Oscar for *Going My Way* (1944), although his best work was in the 'Road' films with Bob Hope and as a dramatic actor in *The Country Girl* (1954). Married to actresses Dixie Lee (1930–1952) who died of cancer, and Kathryn Grant (1957 on). So much of Crosby's screen work consisted of gag guest spots in other people's (mostly Hope's) films that such appearances have been marked (G). Died from a heart attack after a round of golf. Also Oscar-nominated for *The Bells of St Mary's* and *The Country Girl*.
1930: *Ripstitch the Tailor. *Two Plus Fours. King of Jazz. Check and Double Check. 1931: *I Surrender Dear. *One More Chance. *At Your Command. Reaching for the Moon. Confessions of a Co-Ed (GB: Her Dilemma). 1932: *The Billboard Girl. *Hollywood on Parade No. 2. *Dream House. *Hollywood on Parade No. 4. The Big Broadcast. 1933: *Blue of the Night. *Please. *Sing, Bing, Sing. College Humor. Too Much Harmony. Going Hollywood. 1934: *Just an Echo. We're Not Dressing. Here is My Heart. She Loves Me Not. 1935: *Star Night at the Cocoanut Grove. Mississippi. Two for Tonight. The Big Broadcast of 1936.

1936: Anything Goes. Rhythm on the Range. Pennies from Heaven. 1937: Waikiki Wedding. Double or Nothing. 1938: Sing You Sinners. *Don't Hook Now. Dr Rhythm. 1939: Paris Honeymoon. The Star Maker. East Side of Heaven. 1940: *Swing with Bing. Rhythm on the River. Road to Singapore. If I Had My Way. 1941: Birth of the Blues. Road to Zanzibar. 1942: My Favorite Blonde (G). Holiday Inn. *Angels of Mercy. Road to Morocco. Star Spangled Rhythm. 1943: Dixie. 1944: *The Road to Victory. The Princess and the Pirate (G). The Shining Future. Going My Way. Here Comes the Waves. 1945: Road to Utopia. *All Star Bond Rally. *Hollywood Victory Caravan. Duffy's Tavern (G). Out of This World (voice only). The Bells of St Mary's. 1946: Monsieur Beaucaire (G). Blue Skies. 1947: Welcome Stranger. My Favorite Brunette (G). Road to Rio. Variety Girl (G). 1948: The Emperor Waltz. *Rough But Hopeful. 1949: *The Road to Peace. *It's in the Groove. *Honor Caddie. You Can Change the World (G). A Connecticut Yankee in King Arthur's Court (GB: A Yankee in King Arthur's Court). The Adventures of Ichabod and Mr Toad (narrator only). Top o' the Morning. 1950: Riding High. Mr Music. 1951: Here Comes the Groom. Angels in the Outfield (GB: Angels and the Pirates) (G). A Millionaire for Christy (voice only). 1952: The Greatest Show on Earth (G). Son of Paleface (G). Just for You. Road to Bali. 1953: Little Boy Lost. Off Limits (GB: Military Policemen) (G). Scared Stiff (G). *Faith, Hope and Hogan (G). 1954: White Christmas. The Country Girl. 1955: *Bing Presents Oreste. *Hollywood Fathers. 1956: Anything Goes. High Society. 1957: The Heart of Show Business (narrator only). Man on Fire. 1958: *Showdown at Ulcer Gulch. 1959: Alias Jesse James (G). *This Game of Golf. *Your Caddie, Sir (G). Say One for Me. 1960: Let's Make Love (G). High Time. Pepe (G). 1961: *Kitty Caddy (voice only). 1962: The Road to Hong Kong. 1964: Robin and the Seven Hoods. 1965: Bing Crosby's Cinerama Adventures / Cinerama's Russian Adventure (narrator only). 1966: Stagecoach. 1968: *Bing Crosby's Washington State. 1970: *Golf's Golden Years (narrator only). Goldilocks (TV). Dr Cook's Garden (TV). 1972: Cancel My Reservation (G). 1974: That's Entertainment!

CROSS, Ben 1948–
Dark-haired, usually unsmiling, hook-nosed, earnest-looking British actor, good looking in a bony-featured sort of way, who had a hard climb to the top after leaving school at 15 and starting life as a window-cleaner. A personable man with a forthright singing voice, Cross sprang to the attention of major casting directors with his performance in the London cast of the stage musical *Chicago*, then successfully projected his own brand of sincerity in the popular TV series *The Citadel* and *The Far Pavilions*. Films few so far, but he is becoming a man in demand.
1975: Great Expectations (TV. GB: cinemas). 1977: A Bridge Too Far. 1981: Chariots of

Fire. 1984: Coming Out of the Ice. The Assisi Underground. 1985: L'attenzione/The Lie.

CULP, Robert 1930–
Tall, dark, long-faced American actor, good at cynicism and world-weariness. Has had several good leading roles as well as a top-rating television series (*I Spy*), but his screen personality was not sympathetic or likeable enough to enable him to become a box-office star in the cinema. Much TV work from 1956 to 1961. Married actress France Nuyen – later divorced.

1962: PT 109. Sammy the Way Out Seal (TV. GB: cinemas). 1963: Sunday in New York. 1964: Rhino! The Raiders (TV. GB: cinemas). The Hanged Man (TV. GB: cinemas). 1967: The Movie Maker (TV). 1969: †Operation Breadbasket (narrator only). Bob & Carol & Ted & Alice. 1970: *This Land is Mine (narrator only). ‡The Grove. 1971: See the Man Run (TV). Hannie Caulder. 1972: A Cold Night's Death (TV). †Hickey and Boggs. 1973: Outrage (TV). A Name for Evil/The Dead Are Alive. The Lie (TV). 1974: The Castaway Cowboy. Houston, We've Got a Problem (TV). Strange Homecoming (TV). 1975: A Cry for Help (TV). Inside Out. Give Me Liberty. 1976: Sky Riders. Flood! (TV. GB: cinemas). Breaking Point. The Great Scout and Cathouse Thursday. 1977: Spectre (TV). 1978: A Cry for Justice (TV). Last of the Good Guys (TV). Thou Shalt Not Kill (TV). 1979: Goldengirl. Hot Rod (TV). 1980: The Night the City Screamed (TV). Word Games (TV). 1981: Killjoy (TV). 1982: National Lampoon's Movie Madness. 1984: Her Life As a Man (TV). Turk 182! 1985: Brothers-in-Law (TV). Calendar Girl Murders (TV). 1986: The Gladiator (TV).

† Also directed ‡ Unreleased

CUMMINGS, Constance
(C. C. Halverstadt) 1910–

Sparkling, sophisticated, brown-haired (often blonde) American leading lady of attractively angular features who, after being sacked from her first film, came back to become not only a thirties' star on both sides of the Atlantic, but a much-respected actress of the London stage (and occasionally screen) through several decades. Married (from 1933 to his death in 1973) to the playwright Benn Levy.

1931: The Criminal Code. The Love Parade. Lover Come Back. Guilty Generation. Traveling Husbands. 1932: The Big Timer. Behind the Mask. Movie Crazy. Night after Night. An American Madness. The Last Man. Washington Merry-Go-Round (GB: Invisible Power). Attorney for the Defense. 1933: Heads We Go (US: The Charming Deceiver). Channel Crossing. Billion Dollar Scandal. Broadway Thru a Keyhole. The Mind Reader. 1934: Glamour. Looking for Trouble. This Man is Mine. 1935: Remember Last Night? 1936: Seven Sinners (GB: Doomed Cargo). Strangers on a Honeymoon. 1940: Busman's Honeymoon (US: Haunted Honeymoon). 1941: This England. 1942: The Foreman Went to France (US: Somewhere in France). 1945: Blithe Spirit. 1950: Into the Blue (US: The Man in the Dinghy). 1953: Three's Company. 1954: The Scream. 1955: John and Julie. 1956: The Intimate Stranger (US: Finger of Guilt). 1959: The Battle of the Sexes. 1962: Sammy Going South (US: A Boy Ten Feet Tall). 1963: In the Cool of the Day. 1970: Jane Eyre (TV. GB: cinemas). 1986: Dead Man's Folly.

CUMMINGS, Robert
(Charles R. Cummings) 1908–

Perennially young, ever-smiling, black-haired American leading man, most at home in light comedy-romance where his skill at throwaway humour was best displayed. But he could be effectively used in drama, as proved by Sam Wood in King's Row and Hitchcock in Saboteur. One of the earliest Hollywood entrants into TV, where he had his own show from 1955 to 1961. Made film debut as crowd player under the name Blade Stanhope

Conway. Recently billed (since 1962) as Bob Cummings.

1933: Sons of the Desert (GB: Fraternally Yours). 1935: So Red the Rose. Millions in the Air. The Virginia Judge. 1936: Arizona Mahoney. Forgotten Faces. Desert Gold. Border Flight. Three Cheers for Love. Hollywood Boulevard. The Accusing Finger. 1937: Wells Fargo. Hideaway Girl. Last Train from Madrid. Souls at Sea. 1938: College Swing (GB: Swing, Teacher, Swing). Touchdown Army (GB: Generals of Tomorrow). You and Me. The Texans. I Stand Accused. 1939: The Underpup. Rio. Everything Happens at Night. Charlie McCarthy, Detective. Three Smart Girls Grow Up. 1940: Spring Parade. Private Affairs. One Night in the Tropics. And One Was Beautiful. 1941: The Devil and Miss Jones. Free and Easy. Moon over Miami. It Started with Eve. Kings Row. 1942: Saboteur. Between Us Girls. 1943: Forever and a Day. Princess O'Rourke. Flesh and Fantasy. 1945: You Came Along. 1946: The Bride Wore Boots. The Chase. 1947: Heaven Only Knows. The Lost Moment. 1948: Sleep My Love. The Accused. Let's Live a Little. 1949: Free for All. The Black Book (GB: Reign of Terror). Tell It to the Judge. 1950: Paid in Full. The Petty Girl (GB: Girl of the Year). For Heaven's Sake. 1951: The Barefoot Mailman. 1952: The First Time. 1953: Marry Me Again. 1954: Dial M for Murder. Lucky Me. 1955: How to Be Very, Very Popular. 1958: Bomber's Moon (TV). 1962: My Geisha. 1963: Beach Party. 1964: What a Way to Go! The Carpetbaggers. 1966: Promise Her Anything. Stagecoach. 1967: Five Golden Dragons. 1969: Gidget Grows Up (TV). 1972: The Great American Beauty Contest (TV). 1973: Partners in Crime (TV).

CUMMINS, Peggy 1925–

Petite Welsh-born Peggy was so pretty of face – plus blonde hair, green bedroom eyes and a fabulous figure – that no-one minded that she wasn't much of an actress. If she had been, her forties visit to Hollywood might have resulted in her becoming a very big international star. As it was, she graced British and American screens for over 20 years without ever seeming to get any older.

1939: Dr O'Dowd. 1942: Salute John Citizen. Old Mother Riley – Detective. 1944: Welcome Mr Washington. English Without Tears (US: Her Man Gilbey). 1946: The Late George

Apley. 1947: Moss Rose. 1948: Green Grass of Wyoming. Escape. 1949: Gun Crazy. That Dangerous Age (US: If This Be Sin). 1950: My Daughter Joy (US: Operation X). 1952: Who Goes There! (US: The Passionate Sentry). 1953: Street Corner (US: Both Sides of the Law). Always a Bride. Meet Mr Lucifer. 1954: To Dorothy a Son (US: Cash on Delivery). The Love Lottery. 1956: The March Hare. 1957: Carry on Admiral (US: The Ship was Loaded). Hell Drivers. Night of the Demon (US: Curse of the Demon). 1958: The Captain's Table. 1959: Your Money or Your Wife. 1960: Dentist in the Chair. 1961: In the Doghouse.

CURTIS, Jamie Lee 1958–

Lithe, long-legged, light-haired, sumptuously-built American actress, the daughter of Janet Leigh and Tony Curtis (both qv). By no means as pretty as that union would indicate, her unconventional looks, low voice and brooding presence soon boosted her into leading roles, although she found it difficult to escape type-casting: first as a 'screamie' queen in gory horror films, then in roles that traded on her physical assets – although these also revealed more of the actress beneath the low-lidded gaze.

1977: Operation Petticoat (TV). 1978: Halloween. 1979: The Fog. Terror Train. 1980: Prom Night. 1981: Halloween II. Roadgames/ Road Games. She's in the Army Now (TV). Death of a Centerfold (TV). 1982: Coming Soon (TV). Money on My Side/ Money on the Side (TV). 1983: Trading Places. Love Letters/My Love Letters. 1984: Grandview USA. 1985: Perfect. Annie Oakley (TV). 1986: As Summers Die (TV).

CURTIS, Tony
(Bernard Schwartz) 1925–
Bronx-born American actor with a mop of unruly black hair (which thinned as the years wore on) and East Side voice. After World War II service with the US Navy, he became the teenage rage of the early 1950s, baring his chest in a series of lavish sword-and-sandal adventures. Later he proved himself a good actor as well as a pin-up (being nominated for an Oscar in *The Defiant Ones*), but the 1960s heralded a return to the bland comedies in which he had dabbled before, and the downswing of his career. Married (first two of three) to actresses Janet Leigh (1951–1962) and Christine Kaufmann (1963–1967). Billed as Anthony Curtis in his first 10 films.
1948: Criss Cross. 1949: City Across the River. Take One False Step. The Lady Gambles. Francis. Johnny Stool Pigeon. 1950: Sierra. I Was a Shoplifter. Winchester 73. Kansas Raiders. The Prince Who Was a Thief. 1951: Meet Danny Wilson. Flesh and Fury. 1952: No Room for the Groom. Son of Ali Baba. 1953: All-American (GB: The Winning Way). Forbidden. 1954: Beachhead. Johnny Dark. The Black Shield of Falworth. So This is Paris. 1955: Six Bridges to Cross. The Purple Mask. The Square Jungle. 1956: The Rawhide Years. Trapeze. 1957: Mister Cory. The Midnight Story (GB: Appointment with a Shadow). Sweet Smell of Success. 1958: The Vikings. The Defiant Ones. Kings Go Forth. The Perfect Furlough (GB: Strictly for Pleasure). 1959: Some Like It Hot. Operation Petticoat. Who Was That Lady? 1960: Spartacus. Pepe. The Young Juggler (TV). The Rat Race. 1961: The Great Impostor. The Outsider. 1962: 40 Pounds of Trouble. Taras Bulba. 1963: Captain Newman MD. The List of Adrian Messenger. Paris When It Sizzles. 1964: Wild and Wonderful. Goodbye Charlie. Sex and the Single Girl. 1965: The Great Race. Boeing Boeing. 1966: Chamber of Horrors. Not with My Wife, You Don't. Drop Dead Darling (US: Arrivederci, Baby). 1967: La cintura di castità (GB: The Chastity Belt. US: A Funny Thing Happened on the Way to the Crusades). Don't Make Waves. 1968: The Boston Strangler. Rosemary's Baby (voice only). 1969: Monte Carlo or Bust! (US: Those Daring Young Men in Their Jaunty Jalopies). 1970: You Can't Win 'Em All. Suppose They Gave a War and Nobody Came. 1973: The Third Girl from the Left (TV). 1974: Lepke. The

Count of Monte Cristo (TV. GB: cinemas). 1975: The Big Rip-Off (TV). 1976: The Last Tycoon. 1977: Casanova and Co (GB: The Rise and Rise of Casanova). Sextette. The Manitou. 1978: Vega (TV). The Bad News Bears Go to Japan. The Users (TV). 1979: It Rained All Night the Day I Left. Little Miss Marker. The Million Dollar Face (TV). 1980: Title Shot. The Mirror Crack'd. 1981: Inmates: A Love Story (TV). 1982: Brainwaves. Othello the Black Commando. 1984: Where is Parsifal? King of the City. 1985: Insignificance. Half Nelson (TV). Balboa. 1986: Mafia Princess (TV). The Last of Philip Banter.

CUSHING, Peter 1913–
Dark-haired, gaunt-faced British actor with distinctive receding temples and a cold, cultured personality. His career was going nowhere in particular until sudden success in television (British TV Actor of the Year 1955), especially in a production of *1984*, launched him into a long run in horror films, chiefly as scientists meddling in things Best Left Alone. Started his film career in Hollywood.
*1939: The Man in the Iron Mask. A Chump at Oxford. 1940: Vigil in the Night. *Dreams. *The Hidden Master. The Howards of Virginia (GB: The Tree of Liberty). Women in War. Laddie. 1941: They Dare Not Love. *We All Help. *The New Teacher. *Safety First. 1947: *It Might Be You. 1948: Hamlet. 1952: Moulin Rouge. 1954: The Black Knight. The End of the Affair. 1956: Magic Fire. Alexander the Great. Time without Pity. The Curse of Frankenstein. 1957: The Abominable Snowman (US: The Abominable Snowman of the Himalayas). Violent Playground. 1958: Dracula (US: The Horror of Dracula). The Revenge of Frankenstein. 1959: John Paul Jones. The Hound of the Baskervilles. The Mummy. The Flesh and the Fiends (US: Mania). 1960: Suspect (US: The Risk). Cone of Silence (US: Trouble in the Sky). The Brides of Dracula. Sword of Sherwood Forest. 1961: Fury at Smugglers' Bay. The Hellfire Club. The Naked Edge. 1962: Cash on Demand. The Devil's Agent. Captain Clegg (US: Night Creatures). The Man Who Finally Died. 1964: The Evil of Frankenstein. The Gorgon. Dr Terror's House of Horrors. 1965: She. Dr Who and the Daleks. The Skull. 1966: Island of Terror. Some May Live (TV. GB: cinemas). Daleks – Invasion Earth 2150 AD. 1967: Frankenstein Created Woman. Night of the Big Heat (US: Island of the Burning Damned). Torture Garden. Caves of Steel. The Blood Beast Terror*

*(US: The Vampire Beast Craves Blood). The Mummy's Shroud (narrator only). 1968: Corruption. 1969: One More Time. Frankenstein Must Be Destroyed. Scream and Scream Again. 1970: The Vampire Lovers. I, Monster. The House that Dripped Blood. Incense for the Damned (US: Bloodsuckers). Death Corps (later Shock Waves. GB: Almost Human). 1971: Twins of Evil. 1972: Fear in the Night. Asylum. Dr Phibes Rises Again. Dracula AD 1972. Nothing But the Night. Tales from the Crypt. The Creeping Flesh. Panico en el Transiberio (GB and US: Horror Express). 1973: The Satanic Rites of Dracula (US: Dracula and His Vampire Bride). Frankenstein and the Monster from Hell. And Now the Screaming Starts. From Beyond the Grave. 1974: The Beast Must Die. The Legend of the Seven Golden Vampires (US: The Seven Brothers Meet Dracula). Madhouse. Tendre Dracula/La grande trouille. The Ghoul. Shatter. Legend of the Werewolf. 1976: The Devil's Men (US: Land of the Minotaur). At the Earth's Core. Trial by Combat (US: Dirty Knight's Work). 1977: The Uncanny. Star Wars. Die Standarte (US: Battle Flag). The Great Houdinis (TV). 1978: Touch of the Sun. *The Detour (narrator only). Hitler's Son. 1979: Arabian Adventure. 1980: Monster Island. 1981: A Tale of Two Cities (TV. Released 1985). Black Jack. 1982: House of the Long Shadows. 1983: Sword of the Valiant/Sword of the Valiant – The Legend of Gawain and the Green Knight. Helen and Teacher. 1984: Top Secret! The Masks of Death (TV). 1986: Biggles.*

CUTTS, Patricia 1926–1974
Fair-haired, pretty British actress with lovely smile but cold voice, the daughter of director Graham Cutts. In show business from childhood, her attempts at establishing an adult film career as a leading lady (one under a different name) were not successful. Committed suicide by taking an overdose of pills.
*1932: Self-Made Lady. 1946: *Flying with Prudence. 1947: Just William's Luck. 1948: Bond Street. 1949: Madness of the Heart. The Adventures of PC 49: The Case of the Guardian Angel. 1950: †Your Witness (US: Eye Witness). 1951: †The Long Dark Hall. 1952: Those People Next Door. 1954: The Happiness of Three Women. The Man Who Loved Redheads. 1958: Merry Andrew. 1959: The Tingler. Battle of the Coral Sea. 1971: Private Road.*

† As Patricia Wayne

as a glamourpuss, following a Rank contract, but did well later on as beleaguered, delicate but resourceful heroines. Seemed to lack the career drive to make herself a big star.

1943: The Bells Go Down. 1947: Dancing with Crime. Uncle Silas (US: The Inheritance). 1948: Love in Waiting/Ladies in Waiting. 1949: Don't Ever Leave Me. 1950: The Dancing Years. 1952: Hammer the Toff. Castle in the Air. Paul Temple Returns. Tread Softly (US: Tread Softly Stranger). 1953: Operation Diplomat. 1956: No Road Back. 1957: The Passionate Stranger (US: A Novel Affair). At the Stroke of Nine. 1959: Witness in the Dark. 1960: The House in Marsh Road. Ticket to Paradise. 1961: The Third Alibi.

DALE, Jim (James Smith) 1935–
Lanky, cheery, rubber-faced British actor/comedian who has stage-managed his film career cleverly without quite reaching the big time. First a stand-up comic, then pop star, he joined the Carry On team, but devoted most of his time from the mid-sixties to (often classical) stage work. A return to films in the seventies included several appearances, with varying success, in Walt Disney productions.

1958: Six-Five Special. 1961: Raising the Wind. 1962: Nurse on Wheels. The Iron Maiden. 1963: Carry On Cabby. Carry On Jack. 1964: Carry On Spying. Carry On Cleo. 1965: The Big Job. Carry On Cowboy. 1966: Carry On Screaming. Don't Lose Your Head. The Winter's Tale. 1967: The Plank. Follow That Camel. Carry On Doctor. 1969: Lock Up Your Daughters! Carry On Again, Doctor. 1972: Adolf Hitler – My Part in His Downfall. 1973: Digby – the Biggest Dog in the World. The National Health. 1976: Joseph Andrews. 1977: Pete's Dragon. 1978: Hot Lead and Cold Feet. 1979: The Spaceman and King Arthur (US: Unidentified Flying Oddball). 1983: Scandalous.

DAHL, Arlene 1924–
Willowy blue-eyed American redhead who progressed from saucy girl-friends to minxish schemers, before leaving films to become a beauty columnist. Five times married, the first being actors Lex Barker (1951–1952) and Fernando Lamas (1954–1960).

1947: Life with Father. My Wild Irish Rose. 1948: The Bride Goes Wild. A Southern Yankee (GB: My Hero). 1949: The Black Book (GB: Reign of Terror). Scene of the Crime. Ambush. 1950: The Outriders. Three Little Words. Watch the Birdie. 1951: Inside Straight. No Questions Asked. 1952: Caribbean (GB: Caribbean Gold). 1953: Desert Legion. Jamaica Run. Sangaree. The Diamond Queen. Here Come the Girls. 1954: Bengal Brigade (GB: Bengal Rifles). Woman's World. 1956: Slightly Scarlet. Wicked As They Come. 1957: Fortune is a Woman (US: She Played with Fire). 1959: Journey to the Centre of the Earth. 1964: Kisses for My President. 1968: Les Poneyettes. 1969: Land Raiders. The Road to Katmandu. 1970: Du blé en liasses.

DAILEY, Dan 1914–1978
Fair-haired, blue-eyed, cheerful song-and-dance man, at first billed as Dan Dailey Jr. From a family of vaudevillians, he worked in a minstrel show as a boy. He was never the greatest of musical stars, but the public took a shine to him and kept him at the top for ten good post-war years. His pleasing, often understated, acting style was a help. Came to look increasingly cadaverous in later years, and died of anaemia. Three times married and

divorced. Nominated for an Academy Award in *When My Baby Smiles at Me.*

1939: The Captain is a Lady. 1940: Hullabaloo. Susan and God (GB: The Gay Mrs Trexel). The Mortal Storm. Dulcy. 1941: Ziegfeld Girl. Moon over Her Shoulder. Lady Be Good. The Wild Man of Borneo. Washington Melodrama. The Get-Away. Down in San Diego. 1942: Mokey. Panama Hattie. Sunday Punch. Timber. Give Out, Sister. 1947: Mother Wore Tights. 1948: You Were Meant for Me. Give My Regards to Broadway. Chicken Every Sunday. When My Baby Smiles at Me. 1949: You're My Everything. 1950: When Willie Comes Marching Home. A Ticket to Tomahawk. I'll Get By. My Blue Heaven. 1951: I Can Get It for You Wholesale (GB: This is My Affair). Call Me Mister. 1952: What Price Glory? Meet Me at the Fair. The Pride of St Louis. 1953: The Girl Next Door. Taxi. The Kid from Left Field. 1954: There's No Business Like Show Business. 1955: It's Always Fair Weather. 1956: Meet Me in Las Vegas (GB: Viva Las Vegas!). The Best Things in Life Are Free. 1957: The Wings of Eagles. Oh, Men! Oh, Women! The Wayward Bus. 1958: Underwater Warrior. 1960: Pepe. 1962: Hemingway's Adventures of a Young Man (GB: Adventures of a Young Man). 1971: Mr and Mrs Bo Jo Jones (TV). 1972: Michael O'Hara the Fourth (TV). 1974: The Daughters of Joshua Cabe Return (TV). 1977: The Private Files of Edgar J. Hoover.

DAINTON, Patricia 1930–
Blue-eyed Dresden China blonde, born in Scotland, and on stage as a teenager. Started

DALL, John (J. Thompson) 1918–1971
Tall, rangy, toothily-handsome American actor with light-brown hair and fascinating, slightly awkward presence. Although his film and television careers played a decided second fiddle to the theatre in his life, he was involved memorably in at least three films – as the coalminer/student taught by Bette Davis in *The Corn is Green* (a role which won him an Oscar nomination), as one of the two young psy-

chotic murderers in Hitchcock's *Rope*, and as the war veteran-turned-bank robber in *Gun Crazy*. A heart attack killed him at 52.
1939: *For Love of Mary*. 1945: *The Corn is Green*. 1947: *Something in the Wind*. 1948: *Rope. Another Part of the Forest*. 1949: *Gun Crazy/Deadly is the Female*. 1950: *The Man Who Cheated Himself*. 1960: *Spartacus*. 1961: *L'Atlantide (GB: Atlantis, the Lost Continent. US: Journey Beneath the Desert)*.

DALTON, Audrey 1934–
Irish-born actress with dark hair and pretty, heart-shaped face: one of three girls who won a world-wide talent contest to appear in *The Girls of Pleasure Island*. Stayed longer than the other two (Joan Elan, Dorothy Bromily) to decorate a number of Hollywood adventures and horror films, but was never a very strong actress, and spent most of her career after the mid-1950s on television.
1952: *The Girls of Pleasure Island. My Cousin Rachel. Dreamboat*. 1953: *Titanic. Casanova's Big Night*. 1954: *Drum Beat*. 1955: *The Prodigal. Confession (US: The Deadliest Sin)*. 1956: *The Empty Room (TV. GB: cinemas). Hold Back the Night*. 1957: *The Monster That Challenged the World*. 1958: *The Lone Texan. Thundering Jets. Separate Tables*. 1959: *This Other Eden*. 1961: *Mr Sardonicus (GB: Sardonicus)*. 1962: *Six Gun Law (TV. GB: cinemas)*. 1964: *Kitten with a Whip*. 1965: *The Bounty Killer*.

DAMON, Mark 1933–
Boyishly handsome, dark-haired American

leading man, a chubbier-cheeked version of Robert Wagner. In 1963 he became one of the first Hollywood actors to make a career in the new breed of Italian action film. Without doing a Clint Eastwood he was quite successful. In the seventies he returned to America, where he now heads a producer sales organization.
1955: *Inside Detroit*. 1956: *Screaming Eagles. Between Heaven and Hell. The Hefferan Family (TV. GB: cinemas). In Times Like These (TV. GB: cinemas)*. 1957: *Young and Dangerous*. 1958: *Life Begins at 17. The Party Crashers*. 1960: *This Rebel Breed. The Fall of the House of Usher*. 1962: *The Longest Day. Beauty and the Beast. The Reluctant Saint*. 1963: *The Young Racers. Black Sabbath. Sfida al re di Castiglia (GB: Kingdom of Violence. US: The Tyrant of Castile). Mas cornadas da el hombre (US: Wounds of Hunger)*. 1964: *The 100 Horsemen. Son of Cleopatra. Island Affair. Agente 777 – Operazione mistero*. 1965: *Son of El Cid*. 1966: *Johnny Oro (GB: Ringo and His Golden Pistol). Il camaleonte d'oro. Johnny Yuma*. 1967: *Requiescat. A Train for Durango. Anzio (GB: The Battle for Anzio). Sette vergine per il diavolo (GB: and US: The Young, the Evil and the Savage)*. 1968: *Tutto per tutto. Dio cometi amo*. 1969: *Rassenschande*. 1970: *Arm of Fire*. 1971: *The Norman Sword*. 1972: *Lo chinamavano 'Verita'/They Called Him Truth. Crypt of the Living Dead (GB: Vampire Woman). Don't Cry for Me, Little Mother. Byleth. The Age of Pisces*. 1973: *Il plenilunio delle vergini (US: The Devil's Wedding Night). Posate le pistole, reverendo*. 1976: *There is No 13*. 1982: *Stuck on You!*

DANDRIDGE, Dorothy 1923–1965
Coffee-coloured American singer and dancer of immense drive who, after a few bit parts, became a successful night-club entertainer in the 1940s. Success in the musical *Carmen Jones* the following decade (it won her an Oscar nomination) launched her into a different sort of stardom in which suitable film roles proved difficult to find. Seemingly not able to cope with these new stresses, and declared bankrupt in 1962, she was found dead from an overdose of pills mixed with alcohol.
1937: *A Day at the Races*. 1938: *Going Places*. 1940: *Irene*. 1941: *The Lady from Louisiana. Sundown. Sun Valley Serenade. Bahama Pass-*

age. 1942: *Lucky Jordan. Drums of the Congo*. 1943: *Hit Parade of 1943*. 1944: *Since You Went Away. Atlantic City*. 1945: *Pillow to Post*. 1947: *Ebony Parade*. 1951: *Tarzan's Peril (GB: Tarzan and the Jungle Queen). The Harlem Globetrotters*. 1953: *Bright Road. Remains to be Seen*. 1954: *Carmen Jones*. 1956: *The Happy Road*. 1957: *Island in the Sun*. 1958: *The Decks Ran Red*. 1959: *Porgy and Bess. Tamango*. 1960: *Moment of Danger (US: Malaga)*. 1962: *The Murder Men (TV. GB: cinemas)*.

DANE, Karl (K. Daen) 1886–1934
Tall, hefty, angular Danish actor (on stage in his native country as a juvenile) who became very popular with silent-screen American audiences after his success as Slim in *The Big Parade*. Later successfully teamed with tiny Briton George K. Arthur (G. K. A. Brest, 1899–) in an amusing series of broad comedies for M-G-M. But his career collapsed with the coming of sound (his thick accent did not match his characters) and, after spells as a carpenter and a fast-food operator, Dane shot himself at 47.
1918: *My Four Years in Germany. To Hell with the Kaiser*. 1925: *Lights of Old Broadway. The Big Parade. La Boheme. His Secretary. The Everlasting Whisper*. 1926: *Bardelys the Magnificent. Son of the Sheik. The Scarlet Letter. War Paint. Monte Carlo*. 1927: *The Red Mill. Slide, Kelly, Slide. Rookies. The Enemy*. 1928: *Show People. The Trail of 98. Detectives. Baby Mine. Brotherly Love. Circus Rookies. Alias Jimmy Valentine. Wyoming*. 1929: *Speedway. All at Sea. Hollywood Revue of 1929. China Bound. The Duke Steps Out. The Voice of the Storm. The Gob*. 1930: *Mon-*

tana Moon. The Big House. Navy Blues. Free and Easy. Numbered Men. Billy the Kid. On to Singapore. 1932: Speak Easily. 1933: The Whispering Shadow (serial).

D'ANGELO, Beverly 1954–

Diminutive but exuberant blonde American actress who began her working life at 17 as a cartoonist who wanted to be an animator in films. Sang with a rock band, drifted into acting and now excels in fast-moving, scatterbrained comedy roles with the occasional excursion into heavy drama. Surprised many with her vibrant singing voice as the doomed Patsy Cline in Coal Miner's Daughter.
1976: The Sentinel. Hey Marilyn. 1977: Annie Hall. First Love. 1978: Every Which Way But Loose. 1979: Hair. Flashpoint. 1980: Coal Miner's Daughter. 1981: Honky Tonk Freeway. Paternity. 1983: National Lampoon's Vacation. 1984: A Streetcar Named Desire (TV). Finders Keepers. 1985: National Lampoon's European Vacation.

DANIELS, Bebe
(Virginia Daniels) 1901–1971

Dark-haired, effervescent American actress, on stage at three and a leading lady in Harold Lloyd's slapstick silents at 15. Later married actor Ben Lyon, and moved to Britain, where they became one of entertainment's most popular couples, especially for their radio series Hi Gang! in which Bebe blossomed as a singer and comedienne. Another successful series, Life with the Lyons, led to a couple of films. Died of a cerebral haemorrhage after a long period of ill-health.

1908: *A Common Enemy. 1914: The Savage. Anne of the Golden West. 1916: *Luke Laughs Out. *Luke Laughs Last. *Luke Foils the Villain. *Luke and the Rural Roughnecks. *Luke's Double. *Luke Pipes the Pippins. *Luke and the Bomb Throwers. *Luke's Late Lunches. *Luke's Fatal Flivver. *Luke's Washful Waiting. *Luke Rides Roughshod. *Luke Crystal Gazer. *Luke's Lost Lamb. *Luke Does the Midway. *Luke and the Mermaids. *Luke Joins the Navy. *Luke's Society Mix-Up. *Luke and the Bang-Tails. *Luke's Speedy Club Life. *Luke, the Chauffeur. *Luke's Newsie Knockout. *Luke, Gladiator. *Luke's Preparedness Preparation. *Luke, Patent Provider. *Luke Locates the Loot. *Luke's Fireworks Fizzle. *Luke's Movie Muddle. *Luke's Shattered Sleep. 1917: *Luke's Busy Days. *Luke's Trolley Trouble. *Lonesome Luke, Lawyer. *Luke's Last Liberty. *Luke Wins Ye Ladye Faire. *Lonesome Luke's Lively Rifle. *Lonesome Luke on Tin Can Alley. *Lonesome Luke's Lively Life. *Lonesome Luke's Honeymoon. *Lonesome Luke, Plumber. *Stop! Luke! Listen! *Lonesome Luke, Messenger. *Lonesome Luke, Mechanic. *Lonesome Luke's Wild Women. *Lonesome Luke Loses Patients. *From London to Laramie. *Over the Fence. *Pinched. *By the Sad Sea Waves. *Birds of a Feather. *Bliss. *Rainbow Island. *Love, Laughs and Lather. *The Flirt. *Clubs Are Trumps. *All Aboard. *We Never Sleep. *Move On. *Bashful. *The Tip. 1918: *The Big Idea. *The Lamb. *Hit Him Again. *Beat It. *A Gasoline Wedding. *Let's Go. *Look Pleasant, Please. *On the Jump. *Here Come the Girls. *Follow the Crowd. *Pipe the Whiskers. *It's a Wild Life. *Hey There! *Kicked Out. *The Non-Stop Kid. *Two-Gun Gussie. *Fireman, Save My Child. *That's Him. *The City Slicker. *Sic 'Em Towser. *Somewhere in Turkey. *Bride and Gloom. *Are Crooks Dishonest? *An Ozark Romance. *Kicking the Germ Out of Germany. *Two Scrambled. *Bees in His Bonnet. *Swing Your Partners. *Why Pick On Me? *Nothing But Trouble. *Hear 'Em Rave. *Take a Chance. *She Loves Me Not. 1919: *Wanted: $5,000. *Going! Going! Gone! *Ask Father. *On the Fire. *I'm on My Way. *Look Out Below. *The Dutiful Dub. *Next Aisle Over. *A Sammy in Siberia. *Young Mr Jazz. *Just Dropped In. *Crack Your Heels. *Si, Senor. *Before Breakfast. *The Marathon. *Swat the Cook. *Off the Trolley. *Spring Fever. Billy Blazes Esquire. *At the Old Stage Door. *A Jazzed Honeymoon. *Chop Suey and Co. *Count Your Change. *Heap Big Chief. *Don't Shove. *Be My Wife. *The Rajah. *He Leads, Others Follow. *Soft Money. *Count the Votes. *Pay Your Dues. *His Only Father. *Never Touched Me. *Just Neighbors. *Bumping into Broadway. Male and Female (GB: The Admirable Crichton). Everywoman. Captain Kidd's Kids. 1920: Sick Abed. Feet of Clay. Why Change Your Wife? The Dancin' Fool. 1921: The Affairs of Anatol (GB: A Prodigal Knight). Oh Lady, Lady. She Couldn't Help It. One Wild Week. The Speed Girl. Ducks and Drakes. You Never Can Tell. The March Hare. Two Weeks with Pay. 1922: Nancy from Nowhere. The Game Chicken. Nice

People. North of the Rio Grande. Singed Wings. Pink Gods. *A Trip to Paramounttown. 1923: The Exciters. The World's Applause. Glimpses of the Moon. His Children's Children. 1924: Sinners in Heaven. Daring Youth. Dangerous Money. Monsieur Beaucaire. Argentine Love. Heritage of the Desert. Unguarded Women. 1925: The Manicure Girl. The Crowded Hour. Wild, Wild Susan. Lovers in Quarantine. Miss Bluebeard. 1926: The Splendid Crime. Stranded in Paris. Mrs Brewster's Millions. The Palm Beach Girl. Volcano. The Campus Flirt. 1927: She's a Sheik. A Kiss in a Taxi. Senorita. Swim, Girl, Swim. 1928: Feel My Pulse. The Fifty-Fifty Girl. Take Me Home. What a Night! Hot News. 1929: Rio Rita. 1930: Alias French Gertie (GB: Love Finds a Way). Dixiana. Love Comes Along. Lawful Larceny. 1931: Reaching for the Moon. *Screen Snapshots No. 7. My Past. The Maltese Falcon. Honor of the Family. 1932: Silver Dollar. *Radio Girl. *The Stolen Jools (GB: The Slippery Pearls). 1933: *Hollywood on Parade No. 3. 42nd Street. *Hollywood on Parade No. 7. Cocktail Hour. The Song You Gave Me. A Southern Maid. 1934: Counsellor at Law. Registered Nurse. 1935: Music is Magic. 1936: Not Wanted on Voyage (US: Trickery on the High Seas). 1938: The Return of Carol Deane. 1941: Hi Gang! 1947: The Fabulous Joe. 1953: Life with the Lyons (US: Family Affair). 1954: Adventures with the Lyons (serial). The Lyons in Paris.

DANIELY, Lisa
(Elizabeth Bodington) 1930–

Raven-haired British actress who made a big impact with the star role in her first film, but whose career gradually slid into lesser things. Now acts on television under her real name, with her days as a curvaceous pin-up girl forgotten.

1950: Lilli Marlene. 1952: Hindle Wakes (US: Holiday Week). 1953: The Wedding of Lilli Marlene. Operation Diplomat. 1955: Tiger by the Tail (US: Crossup). 1956: The Man in the Road. 1957: The Tommy Steele Story (US: Rock Around the World). The Vicious Circle (US: The Circle). 1959: High Jump. 1960: *The Last Train. Danger Tomorrow. An Honourable Murder. The Man Who Was Nobody. 1961: The Middle Course. Two Wives at One Wedding. 1962: The Lamp in Assassin Mews. 1964: Curse of Simba (US: Curse of *the Voodoo*). *1967: Stranger in the House (US: Cop-Out).*

DANNING, Sybil 1950–
Voluptuous, satin-skinned Viennese-born blonde glamour star who seems happy to be regarded as a sex symbol rather than a serious actress and as such a throwback to the bombshells of old; one is surprised she hasn't yet been seen walking through Beverly Hills with a leopard on a leash. In California for seven years as a child (the explanation of the fluent English), she was a dental assistant in Salzburg when persuaded to appear in soft-porn West German films; rather precariously she made the jump into the international market in the mid-1970s and has since fared best as fascinatingly wicked women, often in costume spectaculars.
1971: Urlaubsreport (GB: Swedish Love Games). Siegfried und das sagenhafte Liebesleben der Nibelungen (GB: The Erotic Adventures of Siegfried). US: The Long Swift Sword of Siegfried). Ehemänner Report (GB: Freedom for Love). Das Mädchen mit der heissen Masche (GB: The Loves of a French Pussycat). L'occhio nel labirinto (GB: Blood). Liebesmarkt in Dänemark (GB: Only in Denmark). 1972: Die liebestollen Apothekerstöchter (GB and US: Passion Pill Swingers). Lorelei. Bluebeard. 1973: The Three Musketeers (The Queen's Diamonds). 1974: Joe e Margherito (GB and US: Run Run Joe). The Four Musketeers (The Revenge of Milady). Sam's Song (released 1980 as The Swap). 1975: Der flüsternde Tod (GB: Death in the Sun). 1977: The Prince and the Pauper (US: Crossed Swords). Entebbe: Operation Thunderbolt. 1979: Kill Castro! The Concorde – Airport '79 (GB: Airport 80 . . . The Concorde). Meteor. 1980: Battle Beyond the Stars. How to Beat the High Cost of Living. The Man with Bogart's Face. 1981: The Day of the Cobra. Julie Darling. NightKill (GB: TV). The Salamander. 1983: The Seven Magnificent Gladiators (released 1985). Hercules. Black Diamond. Cat in the Cage/Chained Heat. 1984: Jungle Warriors. They're Playing with Fire. The Wild Life. 1985: The Tomb. Howling II . . . Your Sister is a Werewolf. Malibu Express. Clair/Private Passions. 1986: Pompeii. Young Lady Chatterley II. Reform School Girls.

DANTINE, Helmut
(H. Guttman) 1917–1982
Tall, dark, smooth-looking Austrian actor with cleanly delineated features. Dantine made no films in his native country, fleeing to Hollywood in 1938, and breaking into movies there three years later. Attracted attention for a while in the absence of many top stars on war service, but found the going tough when hostilities ended, and later moved into production and direction. Later took small roles in films with whose production he had been involved. Died 'after a massive coronary'.
1941: International Squadron. 1942: Desperate Journey. To Be Or Not To Be. Mrs Miniver. The Pied Piper. The Navy Comes Through. Casablanca. 1943: Edge of Darkness. Mission to Moscow. Northern Pursuit. 1944: Passage to Marseille (GB: Passage to Marseilles). Hollywood Canteen. 1945: Hotel Berlin. Escape in the Desert. 1946: Shadow of a Woman. 1947: Whispering City. 1952: Guerilla Girl. 1953: Call Me Madam. 1954: Stranger from Venus (US: Immediate Decision). 1956: War and Peace. Alexander the Great. 1957: Clipper Ship (TV). The Story of Mankind. Hell on Devil's Island. 1958: Fraulein. Tempest. 1960: The Hiding Place (TV). 1965: Operation Crossbow (US: The Great Spy Mission). 1974: The Wilby Conspiracy. Bring Me the Head of Alfredo Garcia. 1975: The Killer Elite. 1977: Behind the Iron Mask (GB: The Fifth Musketeer).

As director: *1958: Thundering Jets.*

DANTON, Ray 1931–
Narrow-faced, black-haired, snake-eyed (but handsome) American actor who was a great

success in his first film as a smiling villain, and repeated the trick four years later with his portrait of gangster Legs Diamond. Otherwise he has perhaps failed to make the most of the chances proffered, although he made a series of colourful adventure yarns on the continent, and later emerged, albeit briefly, as a determined independent director of shockers. Married to Julie Adams (*qv*).
1955: The Looters. Chief Crazy Horse (GB: Valley of Fury). The Spoilers. I'll Cry Tomorrow. 1956: Outside the Law. 1957: The Night Runner. 1958: Too Much, Too Soon. Onionhead. Tarawa Beachhead. 1959: The Big Operator. Yellowstone Kelly. The Beat Generation. The Rise and Fall of Legs Diamond. 1960: Ice Palace. 1960. A Fever in the Blood. 1961: The George Raft Story (GB: Spin of a Coin). Portrait of a Mobster. A Majority of One. The Chapman Report. 1962: The Longest Day. 1963: Sandokan alla riscossa (GB and US: Sandokan Fights Back). 1964: FBI Code 98. Sandokan Against the Leopard of Sarawak (GB: The Return of Sandokan). 1965: Höllenjagd auf heisse Ware (GB: The Spy Who Went Into Hell). 1966: New York chiama Superdrago. Ballata da milliardo. 1968: The Candy Man. L'ultima mercenario. 1971: Triangle. Banyon (TV). 1972: The Ballad of Billie Blue. A Very Missing Person (TV). The Sagittarius Mine. 1973: Runaway (TV. GB: cinemas: The Runaway Train). 1974: †Mystic Mountain Massacre. Centerfold Girls. 1976: Our Man Flint Dead on Target (TV). Pursuit (TV). Six-Pack Annie.

As director: *1972: Crypt of the Living Dead (GB: Vampire Woman). 1973: Deathmaster (GB: The Deathmaster). 1975: Psychic Killer. 1986: The Return of Mike Hammer (TV). † unreleased.*

DARBY, Kim (Deborah Zenby) 1947–
Fresh-faced, appealing, girlish (actually married and divorced young) actress who failed to sustain the impression she created as the gutsy young westerner in *True Grit*, yet still seems capable of great emotional depths. If her time is past, then she's been unlucky.
1963: Bye Bye Birdie (as extra). 1965: The Restless Ones. Bus Riley's Back in Town. 1967: The Karate Killers (TV. GB: cinemas). Flesh and Blood (TV). 1969: Generation (GB: A Time for Giving). True Grit. 1970: Norwood. The Strawberry Statement. 1971: The Grissom

Gang. *The People (TV). Red Sky at Morning. 1973: Don't Be Afraid of the Dark (TV). 1974: This is the West That Was (TV). Pretty Boy Floyd (GB: The Story of Pretty Boy Floyd) (TV). 1977: The One and Only. 1978: Flatbed Annie and Sweetiepie: Lady Truckers (TV. GB: Girls of the Road). 1979: The Last Convertible (TV). 1980: The Flight of the Enola Gay (TV). 1981: The Capture of Grizzly Adams (TV). 1983: Summer Girl (TV). 1985: First Steps (TV). Better off Dead.*

DARIN, Bobby
(Walden Cassotto) 1934–1973
Pop star turned actor whose popularity waned along with the collapse of his marriage (1960–1967) to Sandra Dee. His intensive, explosive acting style was dissipated in vapid comedies, although not before he had been nominated for an Oscar. Darin remarried and was making a new start to an acting career when he died at 39 following heart surgery. Oscar-nominated for *Captain Newman MD.*
1960: Pepe. Heller in Pink Tights. 1961: Come September. State Fair. Too Late Blues. 1962: Pressure Point. Hell is for Heroes. If a Man Answers. 1963: Captain Newman MD. 1965: That Funny Feeling. 1967: Gunfight in Abilene. Stranger in the House (US: Cop-Out). 1969: The Happy Ending. 1973: Run Stranger Run.

DARNELL, Linda
(Manetta Darnell) 1921–1965
Dark-haired American actress, seldom well cast by her studio, Twentieth Century-Fox, who used her as lovely decoration or (after *Forever Amber*) a lightweight sex symbol.

Only occasional films, such as *My Darling Clementine* and *This is My Love,* used properly the qualities of wilfulness, hard-heartedness and deep-seated sexual smoulder that could have made her a tragedienne of the first order. Died in a fire at her home. Three times married and divorced.
*1939: Elsa Maxwell's Hotel for Women (GB: Hotel for Women). Daytime Wife. 1940: Brigham Young – Frontiersman (GB: Brigham Young). Star Dust. Chad Hanna. The Mark of Zorro. 1941: Blood and Sand. Rise and Shine. 1942: The Loves of Edgar Allan Poe. 1943: City Without Men. The Song of Bernadette. *Show Business at War. 1944: Buffalo Bill. It Happened Tomorrow. Summer Storm. Sweet and Low Down. 1945: *All-Star Bond Rally. The Great John L (GB: A Man Called Sullivan). Hangover Square. Fallen Angel. 1946: Anna and the King of Siam. Centennial Summer. My Darling Clementine. 1947: Forever Amber. 1948: The Walls of Jericho. Unfaithfully Yours. 1949: A Letter to Three Wives. Everybody Does It. Slattery's Hurricane. 1950: No Way Out. Two Flags West. 1951: The Thirteenth Letter. The Lady Pays Off. The Guy Who Came Back. 1952: Saturday Island (US: Island of Desire). Blackbeard the Pirate. Night Without Sleep. 1953: Donne proibite (GB: Forbidden Women. US: Angels of Darkness). Second Chance. 1954: This is My Love. 1955: Gli ultimi cinque minuti. 1956: Dakota Incident. 1957: Zero Hour. Homeward Borne (TV). 1963: El Valle de las Espados. 1964: Black Spurs.*

DARRIEUX, Danielle 1917–
For five decades this green-eyed blonde French actress has been staring straight out of the screen, playing pretty well every kind of woman (with perhaps a slight preference for the experienced woman with something to teach the younger man). Made a star by the first version of *Mayerling,* she has made fewer international appearances than her contemporaries, but that was France's gain, and she is still as beautiful as ever.
1931: Le bal. 1932: Coquecigrole. Le coffret de laque. Panurge. 1933: Château de rêve. L'or dans la rue. 1934: Mauvaise graine. Dedée. La crise est finie (GB: The Slump is Over). Mon coeur t'appelle. Volga en flammes. 1935: Quelle drôle de gosse! J'aime toutes les femmes. Le contrôleur des wagon-lits. Le domino vert. Made-

moiselle Mozart (US: Meet Miss Mozart). 1936: Mayerling. Tarass Boulba. Port-Arthur. Club de femmes. Un mauvais garçon. 1937: Abus de confiance. Mademoiselle ma mère. 1938: Katia. Retour à l'aube. The Rage of Paris. 1939: Battement de coeur. 1941: Premier rendezvous (US: Her First Affair). Caprices. 1942: La fausse maîtresse. 1945: Adieu Chérie. 1946: Au petit bonheur. 1947: Bethsabée. Ruy Blas. 1948: Jean de la Lune. 1949: Occupe-toi d'Amélie. 1950: La ronde. Toselli. 1951: Rich, Young and Pretty. Le plaisir. La maison Bonnadieu. La vérité sur Bébé Donge. 1952: Five Fingers. Adorables créatures. 1953: Madame de ... (US: The Diamond Earrings). Le bon Dieu sans confession. Châteaux en Espagne. 1954: Napoléon. Escalier de service. Bonnes à tuer. Le rouge et le noir. 1955: Lady Chatterley's Lover. Si Paris nous était conté. L'affaire des poisons. 1956: Alexander the Great. Typhon sur Nagasaki. Le salaire du péché. 1957: Pot-Bouille. Le septième ciel. 1958: Le désordre et la nuit. La vie à deux. Un drôle de dimanche. 1959: Marie-Octobre. Les yeux de l'amour. 1960: Meurtre en 45 tours (GB: Murder at 45 RPM). 1961: The Greengage Summer (US: Loss of Innocence). Les lions sont lâchés. Les bras de la nuit. 1962: Vive Henri IV, vive l'amour. The Devil and the 10 Commandments. Landru. Le crime ne paie pas. Pourquoi Paris? 1963: Du grabuge chez les veuves. Méfiez-vous, mesdames! 1964: Patate. 1965: Le coup de grâce. L'or du Duc. Le dimanche de la vie. 1966: L'homme à la Buick. 1967: The Young Girls of Rochefort. Birds in Peru. 1968: 24 Hours in a Woman's Life. 1969: La maison de campagne. 1972: Roses rouges et piments verts. 1975: Divine. 1976: L'année sainte. 1979: Le cavaleur. 1982: Une chambre en ville. 1983: En haut des marches.

DARVI, Bella (Bayla Wegier) 1927–1971
Dark-haired, Polish-born actress who was modelling in France when 'discovered' by Darryl F. Zanuck and taken to Hollywood with a Twentieth Century-Fox contract. Things did not go well for Zanuck's protégée and after three films she returned to France, although it was in Monte Carlo at the age of 43 that she committed suicide by gassing herself.
1954: Hell and High Water. The Egyptian. 1955: The Racers (GB: Such Men Are Dangerous). Je suis un sentimental (GB: Head-

lines of Destruction). 1956: Je reviendra à Kandara. 1957: Le gorille vous salue bien (US: Mask of the Gorilla). Raffles sur la ville (GB: Trap for a Killer). 1958: Pia de' Tolomei (US: Pia of Ptolemy). 1959: Enigme aux Folies-Bergère. Il rossetto (GB: Red Lips. US: Lipstick). Sinners of Paris. 1960: Le pain de Jules. 1971: Les petites filles modèles (GB: Good Little Girls).

DAUPHIN, Claude
(C. Franc-Nohan) 1903–1978
Dapper, stocky little French actor, adept at inspectors, doctors and psychiatrists – a more straightforward version of Claude Rains. Dauphin brought an air of relaxed sophistication to all he did and gradually became more in demand internationally after World War II.

1930: Langrevin père et fils. 1931: La fortune. Mondanités. Aux urnes citoyens. Figuration. 1932: Un homme heureux. Faubourg Montmartre. Une jeune fille et un million. Clair de lune. Paris soleil. Tout s'arrange. 1933: L'Abbé Constantin. La fille du régiment. Pas besoin d'argent. Les surprises du Sleeping. Je suis un homme perdu. Maître chez soi. Le billet de mille. Le rayon des amours. 1934: Dédée. Voyage imprevu. Nous ne sommes plus des enfants. D'amour et d'eau fraîche. 1935: Retour au Paradis. Les pantoufles (US: The Slipper Episode). 1936: La route heureuse. Faisons un rêve. 1937: La fessée. Les perles de la couronne. Entrée des artistes (US: The Curtain Rises). Conflit. L'affair Lafont. 1939: Paris – New York. Menaces. Cavalcade d'amour. Le monde tremblera. Battements de coeur. 1940: Les surprises de la radio. 1941: Les petits riens. L'étrange Suzy. Les deux timides. Les hommes sans peur. Une femme dans la nuit. Une femme disparaît. 1942: Promesse à l'inconnue. Félicie Nanteuil. La belle aventure. 1943: The Gentle Sex. 1944: Salut à la France. English without Tears (US: Her man Gilbey). 1945: Dorothée cherche l'amour. La femme coupée en morceaux. Cyrano de Bergerac. Nous ne sommes pas mariés. 1946: Tombe du ciel. Rendez-vous à Paris. L'eventail (US: Twilight). Parade du rire. 1947: Croisère pour l'inconnu. Route sans issue. La Passion d'Evelyne Cléry. Paris 1900. 1948: L'impeccable Henri. L'inconnue d'un soir. Ainsi finit la nuit. Le bal des pompiers. Jean de la Lune. 1949: La petite chocolatière. La renaissance du rail. 1950: Deported. 1951:

Le plaisir. Casque d'or. 1952: April in Paris. Mademoiselle Modiste (US: Naughty Martine). 1953: Little Boy Lost. Innocents in Paris. 1954: Phantom of the Rue Morgue. 1955: Les mauvaises rencontres. 1956: Le temps de l'amour. 1957: Mon coquin de père. 1958: The Quiet American. Pourquoi viens-tu si tard? 1959: Passeport pour le monde (narrator only). 1961: The Full Treatment (US: Stop Me Before I Kill). 1962: The Devil and the 10 Commandments. Tiara Tahiti. 1963: Symphonie pour un massacre. La bonne soupe. 1964: The Visit. 1965: The Sleeping Car Murders. Lady L. Is Paris Burning? 1966: Da Berlino l'Apocalisse (GB: The Spy Pit). Grand Prix. 1967: Two for the Road. L'une et l'autre (US: The Other One). Lamiel. Barbarella. 1968: ou l'age tendre. Hard Contract. 1969: The Madwoman of Chaillot. 1970: Berlin Affair (TV). 1971: Eglantine. 1972: La piu bella serata della mia vita. Au rendez-vous de la mort joyeuse. 1973: Vogliamo i colonelli. 1974: L'important c'est d'aimer. (US: That Most Important Thing: Love). Rosebud. 1975: La course a l'echalotte. 1976: The Tenant. Mado. 1977: La vie devant soi (GB and US: Madame Rosa). Le point de mire. 1978: Le pion. Les misérables (TV)

DAVENPORT, Nigel 1928–
Dark, strong, moustachioed, thick-eyebrowed British actor of rasping delivery and scowling visage, which can break into tough, he-man smile. Can play heroes, villains, drunkards and weaklings with equal conviction. Arrived too late on the film scene to claim top stardom, but almost made just that rating in the late 1960s and early 1970s before slipping back to top character roles.

1959: Look Back in Anger. Desert Mice. Peeping Tom. 1960: The Entertainer. 1962: Lunch Hour. In the Cool of the Day. Operation Snatch. 1963: Return to Sender. Ladies Who Do. 1964: The Verdict. The Third Secret. 1965: A High Wind in Jamaica. Where the Spies Are. Sands of the Kalahari. Life at the Top. 1966: A Man for All Seasons. 1967: Sebastian. Red and Blue. 1968: The Strange Affair. Play Dirty. 1969: Sinful Davey. The Virgin Soldiers. The Mind of Mr Soames. The Royal Hunt of the Sun. 1970: No Blade of Grass. 1971: The Last Valley. Villain. Mary, Queen of Scots. L'attentat (GB: Plot). 1972: Living Free. Charley One-Eye. 1973: Dracula.

Phase IV. The Picture of Dorian Gray (TV). 1975: La regenta. 1977: Stand Up Virgin Soldiers. The Island of Dr Moreau. 1978: Cry of the Innocent (TV). 1979: Zulu Dawn. The London Connection (US: The Omega Connection). 1980: The Ordeal of Dr Mudd (TV). 1981: Chariots of Fire. Nighthawks. The Upper Crust. 1984: A Christmas Carol (TV). Greystoke the Legend of Tarzan Lord of the Apes. 1986: Caravaggio.

DAVIES, Marion
(Marion Douras) 1897–1961
Bright, chirpy, round-faced Hollywood blonde whose talent for comedy went largely unappreciated in its day because she was the mistress of newspaper magnate William Randolph Hearst whose money kept her in leading roles for 20 years. Nowadays critical opinion, looking objectively at Marion's career, seems to be that the fun-loving girl with the delightful stutter would probably have done very nicely without her protector. She died from cancer.

1917: Runaway Romany. 1918: Cecilia of the Pink Roses. The Burden of Proof. 1919: The Cinema Murder. The Dark Star. The Belle of New York. Getting Mary Married. 1920: April Folly. Restless Sex. 1921: Buried Treasure. Enchantment. 1922: The Bride's Play. Beauty's Worth. The Young Diana. When Knighthood Was in Flower. 1923: Adam and Eva. Little Old New York. 1924: Yolanda. Janice Meredith (GB: The Beautiful Rebel). 1925: Zander the Great. Lights of Old Broadway (GB: Merry Wives of Gotham). 1926: Beverly of Graustark. 1927: Quality Street. The Fair Co-Ed (GB: The Varsity Girl). The Red Mill. Tillie the Toiler. 1928: The Patsy (GB: The Politic Flapper). The Cardboard Lover. Show People. 1929: Hollywood Revue of 1929. Marianne. †The Five O'Clock Girl. 1930: Not So Dumb (GB: Dulcy). The Florodora Girl (GB: The Gay Nineties). 1931: Bachelor Father. It's a Wise Child. Five and Ten (GB: Daughter of Luxury). 1932: Polly of the Circus. Blondie of the Follies. *Jackie Cooper's Christmas (GB: The Christmas Party). Peg o' My Heart. 1933: Going Hollywood. 1934: Operator 13 (GB: Spy 13). 1935: Page Miss Glory. 1936: Hearts Divided. Cain and Mabel. *Pirate Party on Catalina Isle. 1937: Ever Since Eve.

†unreleased

DAVIS, Bette
(Ruth Elizabeth Davis) 1908–

Dark-haired (blonde until 1938), showy, intense American actress with inimitably clipped speech who became one of Hollywood's biggest stars after a long apprenticeship in the early 1930s. Her habit of spitting out her dialogue, or biting off the ends of her lines, made her the target for a thousand imitators, but few players were as adept as her at expressing a grand passion. Academy Awards in 1935 for *Dangerous* and in 1938 for *Jezebel*. Eight further nominations between 1939 and 1962. Married (fourth of four) to actor Gary Merrill from 1950 to 1960.

1931: *The Bad Sister. Seed. Waterloo Bridge. Way Back Home (GB: Old Greatheart). 1932: Hell's House. So Big. The Dark Horse. The Menace. The Man Who Played God (GB: The Silent Voice). The Rich are Always with Us. Cabin in the Cotton. Three on a Match. 20,000 Years in Sing Sing. 1933: Parachute Jumper. Ex-Lady. The Working Man. Bureau of Missing Persons. Fashions (GB: Fashion Follies of 1934). 1934: The Big Shakedown. Jimmy the Gent. Fog over Frisco. Housewife. Of Human Bondage. Bordertown. 1935: Front Page Woman. Special Agent. Dangerous. The Girl from 10th Avenue (GB: Men on her Mind). 1936: The Golden Arrow. The Petrified Forest. Satan Met a Lady. *A Day at Santa Anita. 1937: Kid Galahad. Marked Woman. That Certain Woman. It's Love I'm After. 1938: Jezebel. The Sisters. 1939: The Private Lives of Elizabeth and Essex. Dark Victory. Juarez. The Old Maid. 1940: All This and Heaven Too. The Letter. 1941: The Little Foxes. The Great Lie. Shining Victory. The Bride Came COD. The Man Who Came to Dinner. 1942: In This Our Life. Now, Voyager. 1943: Watch on the Rhine. Thank Your Lucky Stars. *Show Business at War. *A Present with a Future. *Stars on Horseback. Old Acquaintance. 1944: Mr Skeffington. Hollywood Canteen. 1945: The Corn is Green. 1946: Deception. A Stolen Life. 1948: Winter Meeting. June Bride. 1949: Beyond the Forest. 1950: All About Eve. 1951: Another Man's Poison. Payment on Demand. 1952: Phone Call from a Stranger. The Star. 1955: The Virgin Queen. 1956: The Catered Affair (GB: Wedding Breakfast). Storm Center. 1959: The Scapegoat. John Paul Jones. 1961: Pocketful of Miracles. 1962: What Ever Happened to Baby Jane? 1963: La noia (GB*

and US: The Empty Canvas). 1964: Dead Ringer (GB: Dead Image). Hush ... Hush, Sweet Charlotte. Where Love Has Gone. 1965: The Nanny. 1967: The Anniversary. 1969: Connecting Rooms. 1971: Bunny O'Hare. Madame Sin (TV. GB: cinemas). 1972: The Judge and Jake Wyler (TV). The Scientific Card-Player. 1973: Scream Pretty Peggy (TV). 1976: Burnt Offerings. The Disappearance of Aimee (TV). 1977: Return to Witch Mountain. 1978: Death on the Nile. The Children of Sanchez. 1979: Strangers (TV). 1980: White Mama (TV). 1981: The Watcher in the Woods. Skyward (TV). Family Reunion (TV). A Piano for Mrs Cimino (TV). 1982: Little Gloria – Happy at Last (TV). 1983: Right of Way (TV). 1985: Murder with Mirrors (TV). As Summers Dip (TV).

DAVIS, Jim (Marlin Davis) 1915–1981

Husky, slow-speaking, black-haired, diffident-looking six-footer who was unsuccessful in a star role opposite Bette Davis early in his career, and was thereafter confined to leading parts in 'B' westerns and supporting roles in bigger features. Middle age seemed to suit him, and he gave some good performances in the 1970s. Later still, he became familiar to TV viewers as Jock Ewing of the soap opera *Dallas*, before dying following surgery for a perforated ulcer. Billed in some 1940s' films as James Davis.

1940: *Safari. 1941: Revenge of the Zombies. 1942: White Cargo. *Keep 'Em Sailing. Riding Through Nevada. 1943: Frontier Fury. Salute to the Marines. Swing Shift Maisie (GB: The Girl in Overalls). 1944: Cyclone Prairie Rangers. Thirty Seconds over Tokyo. 1945: What Next, Corporal Hargrove? Up Goes Maisie (GB: Up She Goes). 1946: Gallant Bess. 1947: The Fabulous Texan. Merton of the Movies. The Beginning or the End? The Romance of Rosy Ridge. 1948: Winter Meeting. 1949: Brimstone. Hellfire. Mississippi Rhythm. Yes Sir, That's My Baby. Red Stallion in the Rockies. 1950: California Passage. The Showdown. The Cariboo Trail. Hi-Jacked. Square Dance Katy. The Savage Horde. 1951: Silver Canyon. Oh! Susana. Cavalry Scout. Little Big Horn (GB: The Fighting Seventh). The Sea Hornet. Three Desperate Men. 1952: Woman of the North Country. Rose of Cimarron. The Big Sky. The Blazing Forest. 1953: Ride the Man Down. The Woman They Almost*

Lynched. 1954: The Last Command. The Outcast (GB: The Fortune Hunter). Jubilee Trail. Hell's Outpost. The Big Chase. The Outlaw's Daughter. 1955: Timberjack. Last of the Desperadoes. The Vanishing American. 1956: Blonde Bait. Bottom of the Bottle (GB: Beyond the River). The Maverick Queen. The Wild Dakotas. The Quiet Gun. Frontier Gambler. Duel at Apache Wells. 1957: The Restless Breed. Raiders of Old California. Apache Warrior. Last Stagecoach West. The Monster from Green Hell. Guns Don't Argue. 1958: Toughest Gun in Tombstone. Flaming Frontier. The Badge of Marshal Brennan. Wolf Dog (GB: Lust to Kill). 1959: Noose for a Gunman. Alias Jesse James. 1961: Frontier Uprising. The Gambler Wore a Gun. 1965: Zebra in the Kitchen. Iron Angel. They Ran for Their Lives (released 1968). 1966: Fort Utah. Jesse James Meets Frankenstein's Daughter. Hondo and the Apaches (TV. GB: cinemas). 1967: Border Lust. El Dorado. 1969: The Road Hustlers. 1970: Blood of Frankenstein (US: Dracula versus Frankenstein). The Gun Riders. Five Bloody Graves. Rio Lobo. Vanished (TV). Monte Walsh. 1971: Big Jake. The Trackers (TV). 1972: The Honkers. Bad Company. 1973: Fire-Eaters. Deliver Us from Evil (TV). One Little Indian. 1974: The Parallax View. 1975: Satan's Triangle (TV). The Runaway Barge (TV). Inferno in Paradise (TV). 1976: The Deputies (TV). 1977: The Choirboys. Just a Little Inconvenience (TV). 1978: Comes a Horseman. Trail of Danger (TV). Stone/Killing Stone (TV). 1979: The Day Time Ended. 1981: Don't Look Back (TV).

DAVIS, Joan
(Madonna Davis) 1907–1961

Wide-mouthed, copper-haired, rubber-faced American clown, a rival to Judy Canova (*qv*) in the female B-movie comedy stakes of the forties and early fifties. Crowned her career with phenomenal success in the television comedy series *I Married Joan*. Died from a heart attack.

1935: *Way Up Thar. Millions in the Air. 1936: Bunker Bean (GB: His Majesty Bunker Bean). 1937: The Holy Terror. On the Avenue. Nancy Steele is Missing. The Great Hospital Mystery. Time Out for Romance. Thin Ice (GB: Lovely to Look At). Life Begins in College (GB: The Joy Parade). Love and Hisses. Angel's Holiday. You Can't Have Everything. Wake Up and Live. Sing and Be Happy. 1938:*

Hold That Co-Ed (GB: Hold That Girl). Tail Spin. Sally, Irene and Mary. Josette. My Lucky Star. Just Around the Corner. 1939: Day-Time Wife. Too Busy to Work. 1940: Free, Blonde and 21. Sailor's Lady. Manhattan Heartbeat. 1941: Sun Valley Serenade. Hold That Ghost. Two Latins from Manhattan. For Beauty's Sake. 1942: Yokel Boy (GB: Hitting the Headlines). Sweetheart of the Fleet. 1943: He's My Guy. Two Senoritas from Chicago. Around the World. 1944: Beautiful but Broke. Show Business. Kansas City Kitty. 1945: George White's Scandals. She Gets Her Man. 1946: She Wrote the Book. 1948: If You Knew Susie. 1949: Make Mine Laughs. The Traveling Saleswoman. 1950: Love That Brute. 1951: The Groom Wore Spurs. 1952: Harem Girl.

DAVIS, Sammy Jr 1925–
Dynamic, pint-sized black American singer and actor who describes himself as 'the first one-eyed Jewish negro' and often gives performances twice as large as the part demands. On stage as a child, he lost an eye in a car crash in 1954, just before coming to Hollywood. Films could never really restrain him, and he has remained at his best as a nightclub performer. Married (second of three) to Swedish actress May Britt (Maj-britt Wilkens 1933–   ).
1933: Rufus Jones for President. 1956: The Benny Goodman Story. 1958: Anna Lucasta. 1959: Porgy and Bess. 1960: Ocean's Eleven. Pepe. 1962: The Threepenny Opera/Der Dreigroschenoper. Convicts Four (GB: Reprieve!). Sergeants Three. 1963: Johnny Cool. 1964: Robin and the Seven Hoods. Nightmare in the Sun. 1966: A Man Called Adam. 1968: Salt and Pepper. Sweet Charity. 1969: Man without Mercy (later Gone with the West). The Pigeon (TV). 1970: One More Time. 1971: The Trackers (TV). Poor Devil (TV). 1973: Save the Children. 1975: James Dean – the First American Teenager. 1978: Sammy Stops the World. 1981: The Cannonball Run II. 1984: Cry of the City. That's Dancing!

DAY, Doris (D. von Kappelhoff) 1924–
Chirpy blonde American singer with white, white teeth and an engaging smile. The girl-next-door of Warners' family musicals of the late forties and early fifties, she later became accepted as a competent dramatic actress, and then not only sustained her career but became

America's number one box-office star, with a series of fluffy sex comedies from 1958 on. At her best she was endearingly vulnerable. But her finest performances remain in musicals where her characters mixed vivacity with gusto: *The Pajama Game* and *Calamity Jane.* Nominated for an Academy Award in *Pillow Talk.*
*1948: Romance on the High Seas (GB: It's Magic). 1949: My Dream is Yours. It's a Great Feeling. Young Man with a Horn (GB: Young Man of Music). 1950: The West Point Story (GB: Fine and Dandy). Tea for Two. Storm Warning. 1951: Lullaby of Broadway. Starlift. On Moonlight Bay. I'll See You in My Dreams. 1952: The Winning Team. *Screen Snapshots No. 206. April in Paris. 1953: By the Light of the Silvery Moon. Calamity Jane. *So You Want a Television Set. 1954: Lucky Me. Young at Heart. 1955: Love Me or Leave Me. 1956: The Man Who Knew Too Much. Julie. 1957: The Pajama Game. 1958: Teacher's Pet. The Tunnel of Love. 1959: It Happened to Jane. Pillow Talk. 1960: Midnight Lace. Please Don't Eat the Daisies. 1961: Lover Come Back. 1962: That Touch of Mink. Billy Rose's Jumbo. 1963: The Thrill of It All. Move Over, Darling. 1964: Send Me No Flowers. 1965: Do Not Disturb. 1966: The Glass Bottom Boat. 1967: Caprice. The Ballad of Josie. 1968: Where Were You When the Lights Went Out? With Six You Get Egg Roll.*

DAY, Frances (F. Schenk) 1908–1984
Blonde American-born musical-comedy star of strong personality, who made her name on the English stage in the late twenties and

early thirties, but was not popular with some sections of press and public. Her glamorous image remained most effective on stage and she, too, seemed most at home there.
*1928: The Price of Divorce. 1930: *OK Chief. Big Business. 1932: The First Mrs Frazer. 1933: The Girl from Maxim's. 1934: Two Hearts in Waltztime. Temptation. Oh Daddy. 1936: Public Nuisance No. 1. You Must Get Married. Dreams Come True. 1937: Who's Your Lady Friend? The Girl in the Taxi. 1938: Kicking the Moon Around (US: The Playboy). 1940: Room for Two. 1944: Fiddlers Three. 1949: Scrapbook for 1933. 1952: Tread Softly (US: Tread Softly, Stranger). 1957: There's Always a Thursday. 1960: Climb Up the Wall.*

DAY, Laraine (LaRaine Johnson) 1917–
Quiet, sensitive American actress with demure features and fairish brown hair. A middle-range star from 1939 to 1949, she remains fixed in most minds as Nurse Mary Lamont in the Dr Kildare series, a role she played seven times. She has devoted most of her latter days to the Mormon church into which she was born.
*1937: ‡The Law Commands. ‡Doomed at Sundown. †Stella Dallas. 1938: †Border G-Man. †Scandal Sheet. †The Painted Desert. 1939: †The Arizona Legion. †Sergeant Madden. †*Think First. Tarzan Finds a Son! Calling Dr Kildare. Secret of Dr Kildare. 1940: My Son, My Son. And One Was Beautiful. Dr Kildare's Strange Case. I Take This Woman. Foreign Correspondent. Dr Kildare Goes Home. Dr. Kildare's Crisis. 1941: The Bad Man (GB: Two Gun Cupid). The People versus Dr Kildare (GB: My Life is Yours). The Trial of Mary Dugan. Unholy Partners. Kathleen. Dr Kildare's Wedding Day (GB: Mary Names the Day). 1942: Journey for Margaret. Fingers at the Window. A Yank on the Burma Road (GB: China Caravan). 1943: Mr Lucky. 1944: The Story of Dr Wassell. Bride by Mistake. 1945: Keep Your Powder Dry. Those Endearing Young Charms. 1946: The Locket. 1947: Tycoon. 1948: My Dear Secretary. 1949: I Married a Communist (GB: The Woman on Pier 13). Without Honor. 1954: The High and the Mighty. 1956: Toy Tiger. Three for Jamie Dawn. 1959: The Third Voice. Dark As the Night (TV). 1972: House of Dracula's Daughter. 1975: Murder on Flight 502 (TV).*

‡*As Lorraine Hayes*
†*As Laraine Johnson*

DAY, Vera 1936–
Fluffy, petite British blonde actress, a pint-sized Diana Dors and a forerunner of Barbara Windsor (*both qv*). In fact, if she could have got into the Carry On film comedies, her career might have been considerably longer, but her talents were, surprisingly, more effective in quiet drama. Too many glamour poses may well have proved her eventual downfall. Made debut at only 17 – appropriately in *The Crowded Day*.
*1954: The Crowded Day. Dance Little Lady. 1955: A Kid for Two Farthings. Fun at St Fanny's. It's a Great Day. 1956: Stars in Your Eyes. 1957: Quatermass II (US: Enemy from Space). The Prince and the Showgirl. Hell Drivers. The Flesh is Weak. 1958: *A Clean Sweep. Up the Creek. Womaneater. I Was Monty's Double (US: Monty's Double). Grip of the Strangler (US: The Haunted Strangler). Them Nice Americans. 1959: Too Many Crooks. Trouble with Eve (US: In Trouble with Eve). 1960: And the Same to You. The Trunk. 1961: Watch It Sailor! 1963: A Stitch in Time. Saturday Night Out.*

DEAN, James 1931–1955
Fair-haired American star whose Adonis-like good looks, appeal to the youth market and anguished, intense style of playing shot him to gigantic international stardom in his first leading role, in *East of Eden*. Two films later he was killed in a car crash, and the public sorrow was unequalled since the death of

Valentino. Nominated for Academy Awards in *East of Eden* and *Giant*.
1951: Fixed Bayonets! Hill Number One. Sailor Beware. 1952: Has Anybody Seen My Gal? 1953: Trouble Along the Way. 1954: East of Eden. 1955: Rebel without a Cause. 1956: Giant.

DE BANZIE, Brenda 1915–1981
Fair-haired, matronly British actress, mostly seen on stage. After her performance in the 1954 version of *Hobson's Choice*, she became Britain's most unexpected star of the fifties – albeit for only a few years – before moving on to character roles. Died after surgery for a non-malignant tumour.
1951: The Long Dark Hall. 1952: I Believe in You. Private Information. Never Look Back. 1953: A Day to Remember. Don't Blame the Stork! 1954: Hobson's Choice. What Every Woman Wants. The Purple Plain. The Happiness of Three Women (US: Wishing Well). 1955: As Long as They're Happy. A Kid for Two Farthings. Doctor at Sea. 1956: The Man Who Knew Too Much. House of Secrets (US: Triple Deception). 1959: Too Many Crooks. Passport to Shame (US: Room 43). The 39 Steps. 1960: The Entertainer. 1961: The Mark. Flame in the Streets. Come September. 1962: A Pair of Briefs. I Thank a Fool. 1963: The Pink Panther. 1967: Pretty Polly (US: A Matter of Innocence).

DE CARLO, Yvonne
(Peggy Y. Middleton) 1922–
Pretty Yvonne Middleton from Vancouver, Canada, laboured hard for three years as decoration on the fringe of Hollywood exotica and college comedies. But when they dressed

her up in a yashmak and bangles, and called her Yvonne de Carlo, she became a star. Although no great actress, she put plenty of fire into a colourful series of easterns and westerns from 1945 to 1960 and even revealed a more delicate shade of beauty in the occasional quieter role.
*1941: *I Look at You. Harvard, Here I Come (GB: Here I Come). 1942: *Kink of the Campus. This Gun for Hire. *The Lamp of Memory. Youth on Parade. Road to Morocco. Lucky Jordan. 1943: The Crystal Ball. Rhythm Parade. Salute for Three. For Whom the Bell Tolls. So Proudly We Hail! Let's Face It. True to Life. The Deerslayer. 1944: Practically Yours. Standing Room Only. The Story of Dr Wassell. Kismet. Rainbow Island. *Fun Time. Here Come the Waves. 1945: Bring on the Girls. Salome Where She Danced. Frontier Gal (US: The Bride Wasn't Willing). 1947: Song of Scheherezade. Slave Girl. Brute Force. 1948: Casbah. River Lady. Black Bart (GB: Black Bart – Highwayman). 1949: The Gal Who Took the West. Calamity Jane and Sam Bass. Criss Cross. 1950: Buccaneer's Girl. The Desert Hawk. Tomahawk (GB: Battle of Powder River). 1951: Hotel Sahara. Silver City (GB: High Vermilion). 1952: The San Francisco Story. Hurricane Smith. Scarlet Angel. 1953: Sea Devils. Sombrero. The Captain's Paradise. Fort Algiers. La contessa di Castiglione. 1954: Border River. Happy Ever After (US: Tonight's the Night/O'Leary Night). Passion. 1955: Flame of the Islands. Shotgun. 1956: Magic Fire. Raw Edge. The Ten Commandments. Death of a Scoundrel. 1957: Band of Angels. 1958: La spada e la croce. Verdict of Three (TV). 1959: Timbuktu. 1963: McLintock! A Global Affair. Law of the Lawless. 1966: Munster Go Home! 1967: The Power. Hostile Guns/Huntsville. 1968: Arizona Bushwhackers. 1970: The Delta Factor. 1971: The Seven Minutes. 1974: The Girl on the Late, Late Show (TV). The Mark of Zorro (TV). 1975: Arizona Slim. Won Ton Ton, the Dog Who Saved Hollywood. 1976: It Seemed Like a Good Idea at the Time. La casa de las sombras. Blazing Stewardesses. 1977: Satan's Cheerleaders. 1978: Nocturna. 1979: Guyana: The Crime of the Century. The Man with Bogart's Face. 1981: The Munsters' Revenge (TV). Liar's Moon. 1982: Play Dead. 1983: Vultures in Paradise/Flesh and Bullets. 1986: A Masterpiece of Murder (TV).*

DEE, Frances (Jean F. Dee) 1907–
Gravely beautiful blue-eyed brunette American actress, noted for her calmness and serenity, who gave many touching and appealing performances without quite making the foremost rank. Married to Joel McCrea since 1933. Plucked from the legions of extras by Maurice Chevalier for her first leading role (in *Playboy of Paris*).
1929: Words and Music. 1930: A Man from Wyoming. Follow Through. Monte Carlo. Manslaughter. Playboy of Paris. Along Came Youth. True to the Navy. 1931: An American Tragedy. Caught. Rich Man's Folly. June Moon. Working Girls. 1932: If I Had a Million.

Middle of the Night. The Wonderful Country. 1965: Gammera the Invincible. 1967: Come Spy with Me. 1969: The Wild Bunch.

DELON, Alain 1935–
Dark-haired, open-faced, boyishly handsome French romantic lead, the successor in that country to Gérard Philipe, but much more successful internationally. His career has had its share of clangers (mainly the films made in Britain and America) but his good looks have enabled him to ride them and, since the mid-sixties, he has become increasingly involved in the production of his own films, the most successful of which have had a gangster theme. Married to Nathalie Delon from 1964 to 1969.
1957: Quand la femme s'en mêle (GB: Send a Woman When the Devil Fails). 1958: Sois belle et tais-toi (GB: Blonde for Danger). Christine. Faible femmes (GB: Women Are Weak. US: Three Murderesses). 1959: Le chemin des écoliers. Plein soleil (GB: Purple Noon). 1960: Rocco and His Brothers. 1961: Che gioia viviere. Les amours célèbres. The Eclipse. 1962: The Devil and the 10 Commandments. Mélodie en sous-sol (GB: The Big Snatch). The Leopard. Marco Polo (unfinished). Carambolages. 1963: The Black Tulip. 1964: Les félins (GB: The Love Cage. US: Joy House). L'insoumis. The Yellow Rolls-Royce. 1965: Once a Thief. Is Paris Burning? 1966: Lost Command. Texas Across the River. Les aventuriers (GB: The Last Adventure). 1967: Le samourai. Histoires extraordinaires (GB: Tales of Mystery. US: Spirits of the Dead). Diabolically Yours. 1968: Girl on a Motorcycle. Adieu l'ami (GB: Farewell Friend. US: So Long, Pal). La piscine (GB: The Sinners). 1969: Jeff. The Sicilian Clan. 1970: Borsalino. Le cercle rouge. Madly. Crepa, padrone, crepa tranquillo (unfinished). 1971: Doucement les basses! Red Sun. Fantasia chez les ploucs. La veuve Couderc. 1972: The Assassination of Trotsky. Un flic (GB: Dirty Money). Le prima notte di quiete. Traitement du choc (GB: The Doctor in the Nude. US: Shock Treatment). Il était une fois un flic. 1973: Tony Arzenta/Big Guns. Deux hommes dans la ville. Les granges brûlées (GB: TV, as The Investigator). 1974: La race des 'Seigneurs'. Les seins de glace. Borsalino & Co (GB: Blood on the Streets). Le gifle (US: The Slap). 1975: Zorro. Le gitan. Flic story. Creezy. 1976: Mr Klein. Comme un boomerang. 1977: Amer-

ica at the Movies (narrator only). L'homme pressé (GB: TV, as The Hurried Man). Armageddon. Mort d'un pourri. Attention, les enfants regardent. 1978: Le toubib. 1979: Harmonie. The Concorde – Airport '79 (GB: Airport '80 ... The Concorde). Teheran Incident/Teheran 1943. 1980: Trois hommes à abattre. 1981: †Pour la peau d'un flic (US: For a Cop's Hide). 1982: Le choc. 1983: †Le battant (US: The Cache). Swann in Love/Un amour de Swann. 1984: Notre histoire (GB: Our Story). Separate Rooms. 1985: The Untouchable. Paróle de flic (US: Cop's Honor). Les mocassins Italiens.

†Also directed

DEL RIO, Dolores
(Lolita de Martinez) 1905–1983
Beautiful, dark-haired, aristocratic-looking Mexican actress, at her loveliest in exotic roles of the late 1920s and early 1930s. She stayed in the acting profession after her Hollywood days were over and became a much-admired performer in Mexican and international films. Her beauty became graver with the years, but she remained as striking as ever.
1925: Joanna. 1926: High Steppers. The Whole Town's Talking. Pals First. What Price Glory? 1927: Resurrection. The Loves of Carmen. 1928: The Gateway of the Moon. The Trail of '98. No Other Woman. The Red Dance (GB: The Red Dancer of Moscow). Ramona. Revenge. 1929: Evangeline. 1930: The Bad One. 1932: The Bird of Paradise. The Girl of the Rio (GB: The Dove). 1933: Flying Down to Rio. 1934: Wonder Bar. Madame Dubarry. *Hollywood on Parade No 13. 1935: In Caliente. I Live for Love (GB: I Live for You). *A Trip thru a Hollywood Studio. The Widow from Monte Carlo. 1936: Accused. 1937: The Devil's Playground. Lancer Spy. Ali Baba Goes to Town. 1938: International Settlement. 1940: The Man from Dakota (GB: Arouse and Beware). 1942: Journey into Fear. 1943: Flor silvestre. Maria Candelaria (GB and US: Portrait of Maria). 1944: Bugambilia. Las abandonas. 1945: La selva de fuego. 1946: La otra. 1947: The Fugitive. 1948: Historia de una mala mujer. 1949: Le malquerida. La casa chica. 1950: Dona perfecta. 1951: Deseada. 1953: Reportaje. El nino y la niebla. 1954: Senora Ama. 1965: Torero. 1958: La cucaracha (GB: The Bandit). A donde van nuestros hijos. 1960:

Flaming Star. Pecado de una madre. 1964: Cheyenne Autumn. 1966: La dama del Alba. Casa de mujeres. 1967: C'era una volta/Once Upon a Time (GB: Cinderella Italian Style. US: More Than a Miracle). Rio Blanco. 1978: The Children of Sanchez.

DE MARNEY, Derrick 1906–1978
Unforceful British leading man with dark, wavy hair and lantern-shaped face: good-looking but slightly sinister. Kept pretty busy in unmemorable leading roles before World War II. Independent production ventures afterwards were not too successful, and he spent his last few films in small roles. Brother of actor Terence de Marney (1909–1971).
1928: The Little Drummer Boys. Adventurous Youth. The Forger. Valley of the Ghosts. 1931: Shadows. Stranglehold. 1932: Laughter of Fools. 1933: The Private Life of Henry VIII. 1934: Once in a New Moon. Music Hall. The Scarlet Pimpernel. 1935: The Immortal Gentleman. Windfall. 1936: Things to Come. Café Mascot. Born That Way. Land without Music (US: Forbidden Music). 1937: Victoria the Great. Young and Innocent (US: The Girl Was Young). 1938: Sixty Glorious Years (US: Queen of Destiny). Blonde Cheat. 1939: Flying Fifty Five. The Spider. The Lion Has Wings. 1940: The Second Mr Bush. Three Silent Men. 1941: Dangerous Moonlight (US: Suicide Squadron). 1942: The First of the Few (US: Spitfire). *The Call of the Sea. 1945: Latin Quarter. 1947: Uncle Silas (US: The Inheritance). 1948: Sleeping Car to Trieste. 1950: She Shall Have Murder. 1954: Meet Mr Callaghan. 1956: Private's Progress. The March Hare. 1962: Doomsday at Eleven. 1966: The Projected Man.

DEMONGEOT, Mylène
(Marie-Hélène Demongeot) 1936–
Very slim and shapely French blonde actress with charming smile. More likeable than Bardot and Cardinale and, maybe because of that, not quite so successful as an international star. From 1960 on her peaches-and-cream complexion has been seen in less and less interesting roles.
1944: ‡Les enfants de l'amour. 1955: ‡Futures vedettes (GB: Sweet Sixteen). ‡Frou Frou. 1956: ‡Quand vient l'amour. †It's a Wonderful World. 1957: The Witches of Salem. Une manche et la belle (GB: The Evil That is Eve). 1958: Bonjour Tristesse. Sois belle et tais-toi

(GB: Blonde for Danger). Cette nuit-là (GB: Night Heat). Faibles femmes (GB: Women Are Weak. US: Three Murderesses). 1959: Le vent se lève (GB: Operation Time Bomb). Upstairs and Downstairs. The Battle of Marathon (GB: The Giant of Marathon). Entrée de service. 1960: Under Ten Flags. The Three Musketeers. Un amore a Roma. Les garçons. The Singer Not the Song. 1961: Rape of the Sabines (US: Romulus and the Sabines). Le chevalier noir. 1962: Copacabana Palace. Gold for the Caesars. L'inassouvie. I Don Giovanni della Costa Azzurra (US: Beach Casanova). A cause d'une femme. 1963: Cherchez l'idole (GB: The Chase). Doctor in Distress. L'appartement des filles. Vengeance of the Three Musketeers. 1964: Fantômas. Gangster, Gold und flötte Mädchen. 1965: Furia a bakla pour OSS 117 (GB: Mission for a Killer). Fantômas revient (GB and US: The Vengeance of Fantomas). Uncle Tom's Cabin. Fantômas se dechaîne (GB and US: Fantomas Strikes Back). 1966: Tendre voyou. Fantômas contre Scotland Yard. 1968: The Private Navy of Sergeant O'Farrell. Une cigarette pour un ingénu. 1969: Twelve Plus One (US: The Twelve Chairs). 1970: Le champignon. 1971: L'explosion. 1972: Les pavillons de verre. 1974: Les noces de porcelaine. 1976: Par le sang des autres. A Few Acres of Snow. 1977: L'echappatoire. 1983: Surprise Party. Le bâtard. 1984: Americonga. 1985: Paulette. 1986: Tenue de soirée.

†as Mylene Nicole
‡as Mylène-Nicole Demongeot

DENCH, Judi 1934–
Chubbily pretty, light-haired British actress, most at home on stage, where an amazing variety of work ranges from tragedy to musicals. She has been hardly seen in the cinema, where her sporadic appearances have varied from the distinctive to the disastrous, but a hit comedy series on TV, *A Fine Romance*, opposite actor-husband Michael Williams, brought her face more to the fore. Won a British Academy Award for *Four in the Morning*.
1964: The Third Secret. 1965: Four in the Morning. A Study in Terror (US: Fog). He Who Rides a Tiger. 1968: A Midsummer Night's Dream. 1973: Luther. 1974: Dead Cert. 1983: Saigon – year of the Cat (TV). 1985: Wetherby. The Angelic Conversation (voice only). A Room with a View. 1986: 84 Charing Cross Road.

DENEUVE, Catherine
(Catherine Dorléac) 1943–
Blonde French actress with open, questioning face, the sister of actress Françoise Dorléac (1942–1967). Has worked for most of the major continental directors, plus a few largely fruitful international sorties. With such outward iciness it's surprising she never made a film for Hitchcock, especially as she often exhibits such steel beneath the surface.
1956: Les collégiennes. 1959: Les petits chats. 1960: L'homme à femmes. Les portes claquent. 1961: Les Parisiennes. 1962: Vice and Virtue..... Et Satan conduit le bal. Vacances portugaises. 1963: Les plus belles escroqueries du monde. 1964: Les parapluies de Cherbourg. La chasse à l'homme. Un monsieur de compagnie. Le costanza della ragione. Repulsion. 1965: Le chant du monde. La vie de château. Das Liebeskarussell (GB: Who Wants to Sleep?). 1966: Les créatures. 1967: Belle de jour. The Young Girls of Rochefort. 1968: Benjamin. Manon 70. Mayerling. La chamade. 1969: The April Fools. Mississippi Mermaid. Don't Be Blue. 1970: Tristana. Peau d'âne (GB: Once Upon a Time. US: The Magic Donkey). Henri Langlois. 1971: Liza. Ça n'arrive qu'aux autres. 1972: Un flic (GB: Dirty Money). Melampo. 1973: L'évènement le plus important depuis que l'homme a marché sur la lune (GB: The Slightly Pregnant Man). Touche pas à la femme blanche. 1974: Fatti di gente perbene/La grande bourgeoise (US: The Murri Affair). Zig-Zig (US: Zig-Zag). La femme aux bottes rouges. 1975: Hustle. Le sauvage (US: Lovers Like Us). L'agression (US: Act of Aggression). 1976: Il cassotto (US: The Beach Hut). Si c'était à refaire (GB: Second Chance). 1977: Coup de foudre. March or Die! 1978: Ecoute voir. L'argent des autres. Si je suis comme ça, c'est la faute de papa (US: When I Was a Kid, I Didn't Dare). Anima persa. 1979: A nous deux (US: An Adventure for Two). Ils sont grands, ces petits. 1980: Courage fuyons. Le dernier métro. Je vous aime. 1981: Le choix des armes. Reporters. Hotel des Amériques. 1982: Le choc. L'Africain. 1983: The Hunger. Daisy Chain. 1984: Fort Saganne. Parôles et musiques. 1985: Let's Hope It's a Girl. Babette's Dinner. 1986: La mauvaise herbe. Le lieu du crime.

DE NIRO, Robert 1943–
Lean, dark and sallow American actor of great drive and intensity, often seen in Italianate or working-class New Yorker roles. After a slow start, and despite offering a somewhat unvarying performance, he rose quickly to the top following the winning of an Oscar in *The Godfather Part II*. In 1981 he took a second Oscar for *Raging Bull*. Also an Oscar nominee for *Taxi Driver* and *The Deer Hunter*.
1965: Trois chambres à Manhattan. 1966: The Wedding Party. 1968: Greetings. 1969: Bloody Mama. 1970: Hi, Mom! 1971: Jennifer on My Mind. The Gang That Couldn't Shoot Straight. Born to Win. 1973: Bang the Drum Slowly. Mean Streets. 1974: Sam's Song (later The Swap). The Godfather Part II. 1976: Taxi Driver. 1900. The Last Tycoon. 1977: New York, New York. 1978: The Deer Hunter. 1980: Raging Bull. 1981: True Confessions. 1982: The King of Comedy. Elia Kazan, Outsider. 1983: Once Upon a Time in America. 1984: Brazil. Falling in Love. 1986: The Mission. Angel Heart.

DENISON, Michael 1915–
Gently polite but firm upper-class English actor with rich voice, very similar to John Clements, and so popular in British post-war films that it comes as a surprise to find that he made so few. But both he and his wife Dulcie Gray (married 1939) have remained very active in the English theatre.
1939: Inspector Hornleigh on Holiday (US: Inspector Hornleigh on Leave). 1940: Tilly of Bloomsbury. 1946: Hungry Hill. 1948: My Brother Jonathan. The Blind Goddess. 1949: The Glass Mountain. Landfall. 1951: The Franchise Affair. The Magic Box. 1952: Angels One Five. The Importance of Being Earnest.

Tall Headlines. There Was a Young Lady. 1955: Contraband Spain. 1958: The Truth about Women. 1960: Faces in the Dark. 1961: *The Friendly Inn (narrator only). 1982: *The Rocking Horse Winner.

DENNING, Richard
(Ludwig, later Louis Denninger) 1914–

Tall, fair-haired, breezy, athletic American actor with natural smile who served a crowded apprenticeship before war service, but whose leading man career afterwards was confined almost entirely to second-features. He found some popularity in TV series in the 1950s and has for many years now lived in Hawaii. His wife was actress Evelyn Ankers (*qv*) whom he married in 1942. Most recently, he was seen regularly as the Governor in the long-running TV series *Hawaii Five-O*. His later credits sometimes get mixed up with those of a British actor (mainly on stage) of the same name.

1937: On Such a Night. Daughter of Shanghai. Hold 'Em Navy (GB: That Navy Spirit). Our Neighbors the Carters. 1938: Give Me a Sailor. King of Alcatraz (GB: King of the Alcatraz). The Texans. Her Jungle Love. The Buccaneer. Touchdown Army (GB: Generals of Tomorrow). College Swing (GB: Swing, Teacher, Swing). Campus Confessions (GB: Fast Play). Illegal Traffic. The Big Broadcast of 1938. The Arkansas Traveler. Say It in French. Ambush. 1939: Grand Jury Secrets. Some Like It Hot. King of Chinatown. Star Maker. Million Dollar Legs. I'm from Missouri. Persons in Hiding. Night of Nights. Television Spy. Geronimo. Zaza. Hotel Imperial. The Gracie Allen Murder Case. Union Pacific. Sudden Money. Disputed Passage. Undercover Doctor. 1940: The

Farmer's Daughter. Parole Fixer. Emergency Squad. Golden Gloves. Seventeen. Queen of the Mob. Love Thy Neighbor. Those Were The Days (GB: Good Old Schooldays). Northwest Mounted Police. 1941: Adam Had Four Sons. West Point Widow. Ice Capades. 1942: Calgary Stampede. Star Spangled Rhythm. Quiet Please, Murder. The Glass Key. Ice Capades Revue (GB: Rhythm Hits the Ice). 1946: Black Beauty. The Fabulous Suzanne. 1947: Seven Were Saved. 1948: Unknown Island. Caged Fury. Disaster. Lady at Midnight. When My Baby Smiles at Me. 1950: Double Deal. Harbor of Missing Men. No Man of Her Own. 1951: Flame of Stamboul. Insurance Investigator. Weekend with Father. 1952: Okinawa. Scarlet Angel. Hangman's Knot. 1953: The 49th Man. The Glass Web. Target Hong Kong. Jivaro (GB: Lost Treasure of the Amazon). 1954: The Creature from the Black Lagoon. Why Men Leave Home. Battle of Rogue River. Target Earth. 1955: The Magnificent Matador (GB: The Brave and the Beautiful). Air Strike. The Creature with the Atom Brain. The Crooked Web. The Gun That Won the West. The Day the World Ended. 1956: Naked Paradise. Assignment Redhead (US: Million Dollar Manhunt/Requirement for a Redhead). Girls in Prison. Oklahoma Woman. 1957: An Affair to Remember. Buckskin Lady. The Black Scorpion. The Lady Takes a Flyer. 1958: Desert Hell. 1963: Twice Told Tales.

DENNIS, Sandy 1937–

Toothy, tawny-haired, blue-eyed American actress, mostly in roles which involve much torment of the character's inner self. Her habit of chewing over lines makes her a distinctive star, and she has great drive, if at times her all-consuming style can overpower a film. After five years at the top, it seemed that the public tired of her; but in the studio days she would probably have been built into a major female star along Bette Davis lines. Oscar for *Who's Afraid of Virginia Woolf?*

1961: Splendor in the Grass. 1966: The Three Sisters. Who's Afraid of Virginia Woolf? 1967: Up the Down Staircase. The Fox. 1968: Sweet November. *Teach Me! 1969: That Cold Day in the Park. A Touch of Love (US: Thank You All Very Much). 1970: The Out-of-Towners. The Only Way Out is Dead. 1972: Something Evil (TV). 1975: Mr Sycamore. 1976: Nasty Habits. Demon. The Three Sisters

(remake). 1977: Perfect Gentlemen (TV). 1978: Day of Terror, Night of Fear (TV). 1981: The Four Seasons. The Animals Film. 1982: Come Back to the 5 and Dime, Jimmy Dean, Jimmy Dean. 1985: The Execution (TV).

DENNY, Reginald
(R. Daymore) 1891–1967

Tall, dark, square-jawed, oft-moustachioed British actor of the 'Bad luck, old girl!' school. A dashing hero of comedy-action films in Hollywood's silent era, he became a genial and slightly stuffy 'other man' with the coming of sound. Never lost his essential Britishness and made an impeccable Algy in the Bulldog Drummond series of the 1930s. Also a talented designer of light aircraft. Died after a stroke.

1912: The Melting Pot. 1919: The Oakdale Affair. Bringing up Betty. 1920: 39 East. Experience. A Dark Lantern. 1921: Footlights. Disraeli. Paying the Piper. The Iron Trail. Tropical Love. The Price of Possession. 1922: *Let's Go. The Kentucky Derby. *Round Two. *Payment Through the Nose. Sherlock Holmes (GB: Moriarty). *A Fool and His Money. *The Taming of the Shrew. *Whipsawed. *He Raised Kane. *Young King Cole. *When Kane Met Abel. *Chickasha Bone Crusher. 1923: *Strike Father, Strike Son. *The Wandering Two. The Thrill. *Don Coyote. The Abysmal Brute. *The Widower's Mite. *Something for Nothing. *Barnaby's Grudge. *Columbia the Gem and the Ocean. *He Loops to Conquer. *That Kid from Madrid. 1924: Sporting Youth. *Swing Bad the Sailor. The Reckless Age. *Girls Will Be Girls. The Fast Worker. *The City of Stars. *A Tough Tenderfoot. *Big Boy Blue. Captain Fearless. 1925: I'll Show You the Town. Oh, Doctor! California Straight Ahead. Skinner's Dress Suit. Where Was I? 1926: What Happened to Jones? Take It from Me. Rolling Home. 1927: Jaws of Steel. Out All Night. Fast and Furious. The Cheerful Fraud. On Your Toes. 1928: The Night Bird. Good Morning, Judge. That's My Daddy. 1929: Red Hot Speed. Clear the Decks. His Lucky Day. One Hysterical Night. 1930: Embarrassing Moments. Madame Satan. What a Man! Those Three French Girls. A Lady's Morals (GB: Jenny Lind). Oh, for a Man. 1931: Private Lives. Kiki. Stepping Out. Parlor, Bedroom and Bath (GB: Romeo in Pyjamas). 1932: Strange Justice. The Iron

Master. 1933: The Barbarian (GB: A Night in Cairo). Only Yesterday. The Big Bluff (GB: Worthy Deceiver). 1934: The Lost Patrol. One More River (GB: Over the River). The Richest Girl in the World. Of Human Bondage. Dancing Man. Fog. The Little Minister. We're Rich Again. The World Moves On. Penthouse Party (GB: Without Children). 1935: Anna Karenina. Lottery Lover. Vagabond Lady. No More Ladies. Here's to Romance. Midnight Phantom. Remember Last Night? The Lady in Scarlet. 1936: It Couldn't Have Happened. Two in a Crowd. More Than a Secretary. Romeo and Juliet. The Rest Cure (GB: We're in the Legion Now). The Preview Murder Mystery. 1937: Bulldog Drummond Comes Back. The Great Gambini. Join the Marines. Beg, Borrow or Steal. Bulldog Drummond Escapes. Women of Glamour. Let's Get Married. Jungle Menace (serial). Bulldog Drummond's Revenge. 1938: Four Men and a Prayer. Bulldog Drummond's Peril. Blockade. Bulldog Drummond in Africa. Everybody's Baby. 1939: Bulldog Drummond's Bride. Arrest Bulldog Drummond! Bulldog Drummond's Secret Police. 1940: Spring Parade. Rebecca. Seven Sinners. 1941: Appointment for Love. International Squadron. One Night in Lisbon. 1942: Thunder Birds. Sherlock Holmes and the Voice of Terror. Over My Dead Body. Captains of the Clouds. Eyes in the Night. 1943: Ghost Ship. Crime Doctor's Strangest Case (GB: The Strangest Case). 1944: Song of the Open Road. 1945: Love Letters. 1946: Tangier. The Locket. 1947: My Favorite Brunette. The Macomber Affair. The Secret Life of Walter Mitty. Escape Me Never. Christmas Eve. 1948: Mr Blandings Builds His Dream House. 1950: The Iroquois Trail (GB: The Tomahawk Trail). 1953: The Hindu (later Sabaka). Fort Vengeance. Abbott and Costello Meet Dr Jekyll and Mr Hyde. 1954: World for Ransom. Bengal Brigade (GB: Bengal Rifles). The Snow Creature. 1955: Escape to Burma. 1956: Around the World in 80 Days. 1957: Street of Sinners. The Story of Mankind. 1964: Advance to the Rear (GB: Company of Cowards). 1965: Cat Ballou. 1966: Assault on a Queen. Batman.

DEPARDIEU, Gérard 1948–
I must admit that the merits of France's own Incredible Hulk have up to now escaped me. The energies of this huge, Punch-chinned actor, who looks uncomfortable in tweed suits

and ties, are, however, undeniable. He has lumbered his giant country-man's build from film to film – almost 50 of them in 15 years, a phenomenal workrate by today's standards. Attempting to his credit a wide range of roles, he has looked most relaxed as figures of history, such as Wajda's Danton. Still comparatively little known outside Europe, he is in France (if he will pardon the expression) massive.

1965: *Le beatnik et le minet. A Christmas Carol (unfinished). 1967: Rendez-vous à Badenberg (TV). 1970: Le cri du cormoran, le soir au-dessus des jonques. 1971: Le viager. Le tueur. Un peu de soleil dans l'eau froide. 1972: Nathalie Granger. La scoumoune (GB: Scoundrel. US: The Jinx). Au rendez-vous de la mort joyeuse. L'affaire Dominici. 1973: Un monsieur bien rangé (TV). Deux hommes dans la ville. Rude journée pour la reine. Les Gaspards (US: The Holes). Les valseuses (GB: Making It. US: Going Places). L'inconnu (TV). 1974: Stavisky... La femme du Gange. Vincent, François, Paul... et les autres. Pas si méchant que ça (GB: TV as This Wonderful Crook. US: The Wonderful Crook). 1975: 7 morts sur ordonnance. Je t'aime, moi non plus (GB: I Love You, I Don't). Bertolucci secundo il cinéma. 1976: Maîtresse. 1900. L'ultima donna (GB: The Last Woman). Barocco. René la canne. Baxter – Vera Baxter. 1977: Le camion. Die linkshändige Frau (GB: The Left-Handed Woman). Dites-lui que j'aime (GB: This Sweet Sickness). Préparez vos mouchoirs (GB and US: Get Out Your Handkerchiefs). Violenta. La nuit tous les chats sont gris. 1978: Rêve de singe/Bye Bye Monkey. Le sucre. Les chiens. Le grand embouteillage. 1979: Loulou. Rosy la bourrasque. Buffet froid. Mon oncle d'Amérique. 1980: Je vous aime. The Last Métro. Inspecteur la bavure. 1981: La femme d'à côté (GB and US: The Woman Next Door). La chèvre. Le grand frère. Le choix des armes (US: Choice of Arms). Trois hommes à abattre. 1982: L'Africain. Danton. Le retour de Martin Guerre (GB and US: The Return of Martin Guerre). 1983: La lune dans le caniveau (GB and US: The Moon in the Gutter). 1984: Fort Saganne. †Le tartuffe. Les compères (GB: Fathers' Day). 1985: Une femme ou deux. Paris Moliers. Jean de Florette. Police. Rive droite, rive gauche. Manon des sources. 1986: Rue de depart. Tenue de Soirée. Les fugitifs. 1987: The Possessed.

†And directed

DEREK, Bo (Mary Collins) 1956–
Fair-haired, firm-bodied American actress with pale blue eyes, facially not unlike Raquel Welch. Married to John Derek (qv), who masterminds her career, she seemed set at one time to become the cinema's sex symbol for the 1980s. But films produced by her and directed by her husband endured stormy passages before emerging to critical scorn and public apathy. Pretentiousness was at the root of their failure, but the lady does have a way with comic double-entendres and may well live to fight another day.

1975: And Once Upon a Time (US: Fantas-

ies). 1977: Orca – Killer Whale. 1978: Love You. 1979: '10'. 1980: A Change of Seasons. 1981: Tarzan the Ape-Man. 1984: Bolero.

DEREK, John (Derek Harris) 1926–
Handsome American leading man with black, wavy hair, who moved from juvenile delinquents, headstrong pilots and gunslingers to dashing men of action somewhere between Cornel Wilde and Tony Curtis (both qv). It is hard to say why Derek did not become a bigger star, unless it was his subservience to the career of his one-time wife Ursula Andress (qv), or his partiality for directing, a facet which has latterly extended to soft-core films featuring his current wife Bo Derek (qv). In between, he was also married to actress Linda Evans.

1944: †I'll Be Seeing You. 1948: A Double Life. 1949: Knock on Any Door. All the King's Men. 1950: Rogues of Sherwood Forest. 1951: Saturday's Hero (GB: Idols in the Dust). Mask of the Avenger. Scandal Sheet (GB: The Dark Page). The Family Secret. 1952: Thunderbirds. 1953: Mission over Korea (GB: Eyes of the Skies). The Last Posse. Prince of Pirates. Ambush at Tomahawk Gap. 1954: Sea of Lost Ships. The Outcast (GB: The Fortune Hunter). The Adventures of Hajji Baba. Run for Cover. Prince of Players. 1955: Annapolis Story (GB: The Blue and the Gold). 1956: *Mr Rhythm's Holiday. The Leather Saint. The Ten Commandments. Massacre at Sand Creek (TV). 1957: Omar Khayyam. Fury at Showdown. The Flesh is Weak. Il corsaro della mezzaluna. 1958: High Hell. Prisoners of the Volga (GB: The Boatmen. US: The Volga Boatman). 1960: Exodus. 1963: Nightmare in the Sun. 1966: *Once Before I Die.* 1969: *Childish Things.* 1975: *And Once Upon a Time.* 1978: *Love You.*

As director: 1966: *Once Before I Die.* 1969: *Childish Things.* 1972: †*Confessions of Tom Harris.* 1975: *And Once Upon a Time (US: Fantasies).* 1978: *Love You.* 1981: *Tarzan the Ape-Man.* 1984: *Bolero.*
† Co-directed.

DERN, Bruce 1936–
Tall, gangling American actor with toothy grin who specialized for many years in hairy psychotics, but was such a distinctive performer that leading roles were bound to come eventually. Since stardom caught up with him in the early seventies, he has been seen in a variety of parts, but the more straightforward the role, the less effective he has been, and there is still a hint of madness behind his more compelling characters. Nominated for an Academy Award in *Coming Home.*
1960: *Wild River.* 1961: *The Crimebusters.* 1963: *Bedtime Story.* 1964: *Marnie. Hush ... Hush, Sweet Charlotte.* 1967: *The Saint Valentine's Day Massacre. The War Wagon. The Wild Angels. Waterhole No. 3 (GB: Waterhole 3). Will Penny. The Trip. Rebel Rousers* (released 1969). *Hang 'Em High.* 1968: *Psych-Out. Support Your Local Sheriff. Castle Keep.* 1969: *Number One. They Shoot Horses, Don't They? Bloody Mama.* 1970: *Drive, He Said. The Incredible Two-Headed Transplant. Cycle Savages.* 1971: *The Cowboys. Sam Hill: Who Killed the Mysterious Mr Foster? (TV). Silent Running.* 1972: *Thumb Tripping. The King of Marvin Gardens. The Laughing Policeman (GB: An Investigation of Murder).* 1974: *The Great Gatsby. Smile.* 1975: *Posse. Won Ton Ton – the Dog Who Saved Hollywood.* 1976: *Folies bourgeoises/The Twist. Family Plot. Black Sunday.* 1978: *Coming Home. The Driver (GB: Driver).* 1979: *Middle Age Crazy.* 1980: *Tattoo.* 1981: *Harry Tracy – Desperado.* 1982: *That Championship Season.* 1984: *On the Edge.* 1985: *Toughlove (TV).*

DE SICA, Vittorio 1894–1974
Distinguished Italian actor and director, a vanguard neo-realist director of the post-war

years, a time when he won Oscars for *Shoeshine* and *Bicycle Thieves.* In the thirties he was a charming romantic actor but later, when his dark hair had turned to silver, he was cast in increasingly lightweight and unworthy roles, and all his best post-war work was done from the director's chair. He won two more Academy Awards – for *Yesterday, Today and Tomorrow* and *The Garden of the Finzi-Continis.* Also Oscar-nominated for his performance in *A Farewell to Arms.*
1918: *L'affaire Clemenceau.* 1926: *La bellezza del mondo.* 1928: *La compagnia dei matti.* 1932: *La vecchia signora. Gli uomini, che mascalzoni! Due cuori felici.* 1933: †*La canzone del sole. La segretaria per tutti. Il signore desidera? Un cattivo soggetto. Lisetta. Passa l'amore.* 1934: *Tempo massimo.* 1935: *Amo te sola. Darò un milione. Lohengrin. Non ti conosco più.* 1936: *Ma non è una cosa seria. L'uomo che sorride. Questi ragazzi.* 1937: *Il signor Max. Hanno rapito un uomo. Napoli di altri tempi. Le dame e i cavalieri.* 1938: *L'orologio a cucù. Le due madri. La mazurka di papà. Partire.* †*Castelli in aria. Giochi di società.* 1939: *Napoli che non muore. Grandi magazzini. Finesce sempre cosi. Ai vostri ordini, signora!* 1940: *Manon Lescaut. Pazza di gioia. La peccatrice. Rose scarlatte/Due dozzine di rose scarlatte.* 1941: *Teresa Venerdi. Maddalena zero in condotta. L'avventuriera del piano di sopra.* 1942: *Un garibaldino in convento. Se io fossi onesto. La guardia del corpo.* 1943: *I nostri sogni. L'ippocampo. Nessuno torna indietro. Dieci minuti di vita* (unfinished). 1944: *Non sono superstizioso ... ma!* 1945: *Lo sbaglio di essere vivo. Il mondo vuole cosi.* 1946: *Roma città libera. Abbasso la ricchezza!* 1947: *Natale al campo 119. Sperduti nel buio.* 1948: *Lo sconosciuto di San Marino. Cuore.* 1950: *Domani è troppo tardi (US: Tomorrow is Too Late).* 1951: *Cameriera bella presenza offresi. Altri tempi (US: Times Gone By). Gli uomini non guardano il cielo.* 1952: *Buongiorno, elefante! (GB and US: Hello Elephant!). Tempi nostri.* 1953: *Pane, amore e fantasia (GB and US: Bread, Love and Dreams). Villa Borghese. Il matrimonio. Madame de ... (US: The Diamond Earrings). Secrets d'alcôve. A Hundred Years of Love.* 1954: *Pane, amore e gelosia (GB: Bread, Love and Jealousy. US: Frisky). La vergine moderna. L'oro di Napoli. L'allegro squadrone. Peccato che sia una canaglia (GB and US: Too Bad She's Bad).* 1955: *Il segno di Venere. Gli*

ultimi cinque minuti. *La bella mugnaia. Pane, amore e ... (GB and US: Scandal in Sorrento). Racconti romani. Il bigamo (US: A Plea for Passion).* 1956: *Nero's Weekend (US: Nero's Mistress). The Monte Carlo Story. Tempo di villeggiatura. It Happened in Rome. Noi siamo le colonne. Padri e figli.* 1957: *Amore e chiacchiere. Il conte Max. A Farewell to Arms. Totò Vittorio e la dottoresa (US: The Lady Doctor). La donna che venne dal mare. Il medico e lo stregone. Vacanze ad Ischia (US: Holiday Island).* 1958: *Casino de Paris. Anna of Brooklyn (US: Fast and Sexy). Pane, amore e Andalusia. Ballerina e buon Dio (GB and US: Angel in a Taxi). L'ambitieuse. Les noces Venitiennes. Domenica è sempre domenica. Kanonenserenade. La ragazza di piazza San Pietro. Gli zitelloni. La prima notte.* 1959: *Nel blu dipinto di blu/Volare. Uomini e nobiluomini. Il nemico di mia moglie (US: My Wife's Enemy). Policarpo, uficiale di scrittura. Vacanza d'inverno. The Moralist. Il Generale Della Rovere. Gastone. Ferdinand I, King of Naples. Il mondo dei miracoli. Austerlitz. Three Etcs and the Colonel.* 1960: *The Angel Wore Red. Fontana di Trevi. Il vigile. It Started in Naples. The Millionairess. The Pillars of Hercules. Un amore a Roma. Gli incensurati.* 1961: *Il giudizio universale. The Wonders of Aladdin. L'onorata società. Gli attendenti. Lafayette.* 1962: *The Two Colonels. Boccaccio 70. Vive Henri IV, vive l'amour.* 1965: *The Amorous Adventures of Moll Flanders. Io, io, io ... e gli altri.* 1966: *After the Fox. The Biggest Bundle of Them All.* 1967: *Caroline Chérie. Un italiano in America. Gli altri, gli altri, noi.* 1968: *The Shoes of the Fisherman.* 1969: *If It's Tuesday, This Must Be Belgium. Twelve Plus One (US: The Twelve Chairs).* 1970: *Cose di 'Cosa Nostra'.* 1971: *Trastevere. L'odeur des fauves. Io non vedo, tu none parli, lui non sente.* 1972: *Snow Job (GB: Ski Raiders). Ettore lo fusto. Pinocchio (TV). Siamo tutti in libertà provvisoria.* 1973: *Il delitto Matteoli. Small Miracle (TV). Storia de fratelli e di cortelli.* 1974: *Viaggia, ragazza, viaggia. Andy Warhol's Dracula (GB: Blood for Dracula). C'eravamo tanto amati (US: We All Loved Each Other So Much). Vittorio de Sica: il regista, l'attore l'uomo (TV).*

As director: 1940: *Rose scarlatte/Due dozzine di rose scarlatte. Maddalena zero in condotta.* 1941: *Teresa Venerdi.* 1942: *Un garibaldino al convento.* 1943: *The Children Are Watching Us.* 1944: *La porta del cielo* (released 1946). *Shoeshine.* 1948: *Bicycle Thieves.* 1950: *Miracle in Milan.* 1952: *Umberto D.* 1953: *Stazione Termini (GB: Indiscretion. US: Indiscretion of an American Wife).* 1954: *L'oro di Napoli.* 1956: *Il tetto.* 1961: *Il giudizio universale. Two Women.* 1962: *Boccaccio 70 (episode). The Condemned of Altona.* 1963: *Il boom.* 1964: *Yesterday, Today and Tomorrow. Marriage Italian Style.* 1965: *Un mondo nuovo.* 1966: *After the Fox. The Witches (episode).* 1967: *Woman Times Seven.* 1968: *Amanti/A Place for Lovers.* 1969: *Sunflower.* 1970: *Le coppie (episode).* 1971: *The Garden of the Finzi-Continis.* 1972: *Lo chiamaremo Andrea.* 1973: *Una breve vacanza.* 1974: *The Journey.*
†and German version.

DEVANE, William 1939–
Dark, square-faced, black-browed American
actor, a little like a smaller Dale Robertson,
but with distinctive rasping tones and strong
acting style. He was a New York stage actor
until the seventies when his screen career
picked up, at first in TV movies, then when
Hitchcock cast him as the villain of *Family
Plot*. Adept at smiling villains and men you
can't quite trust. Less prominent in the 1980s.
*1970: The Pursuit of Happiness. 1971: The
Three Hundred Year Weekend. Lady Liberty.
McCabe and Mrs Miller. Glory Boy (GB:
My Old Man's Place). 1973: The Bait (TV).
Crime Club (TV). 1974: The Missiles of
October (TV). Operation Undercover (US:
Report to the Commissioner). 1975: Fear on
Trial (TV). Irish Whiskey Rebellion. 1976:
Family Plot. Marathon Man. 1977: Rolling
Thunder. Red Alert (TV). The Bad News
Bears in Breaking Training. 1978: The Dark.
Yanks. 1981: The Red Flag. Honky Tonk Free-
way. The Fifth Victim (TV) 1982: Hadley's
Rebellion. 1983: Jane Doe (TV). Testament.
1984: Intent to Kill (TV).*

DE WILDE, Brandon
(Andre B. de Wilde) 1942–1972
Fair-haired American juvenile actor, on television at nine and hauntingly memorable as
the boy who worships the mysterious gunman
in *Shane*, a role which won him an Academy
Award nomination. Never made the same
impact in adult roles, and was killed in a car
crash at 29.
*1952: The Member of the Wedding. 1953:
Shane. 1956: Goodbye My Lady. All Mine to*

Give *(US: The Day They Gave Babies Away).
1957: Night Passage. 1958: The Missouri
Traveler. 1959: Blue Denim (GB: Blue Jeans).
1962: All Fall Down. 1963: Hud. 1964: Those
Calloways. The Tenderfoot (TV. GB:
cinemas). 1965: In Harm's Way. 1967: The
Trip. 1969: God Bless You, Uncle Sam. 1970:
The Deserter. 1972: Wild in the Sky.*

DEXTER, Anthony
(Walter Fleischmann) 1919–
Black-haired, aristocratic-looking American
actor who, with no previous film experience,
was chosen to play Rudolph Valentino in a
1951 biopic. The picture was not terribly successful and – apart from the next one, *The
Brigand* – the rest of Dexter's films did little
to establish him at the top.
*1951: Valentino. 1952: The Brigand. 1953:
Captain John Smith and Pocahontas (GB:
Burning Arrows). 1954: Captain Kidd and
the Slave Girl. The Black Pirates. 1956: Fire
Maidens from Outer Space. He Laughed Last.
1957: The Parson and the Outlaw. The Story
of Mankind. 1960: Three Blondes in his Life.
Twelve to the Moon. 1962: The Phantom
Planet. 1965: Saturday Night Bath in Apple
Valley. 1967: Thoroughly Modern Millie.*

DICKINSON, Angie
(Angeline Brown) 1931–
Long-legged, blonde American actress who
entered films via beauty contests. Most film
writers patently think Miss Dickinson hard
done-by in the cinema but to me she has
always been rather plastic, a mould that clearly
hardened to polystyrene in her TV series

Policewoman. It took French director Roger
Vadim (in *Pretty Maids All in a Row*) to make
her seem really sexy, and she began working
regularly in France in the seventies. Married
to composer Burt Bacharach 1965–1980.
*1954: Lucky Me. 1955: The Man with the Gun
(GB: The Trouble Shooter). The Return of
Jack Slade (GB: Texas Rose). Tennessee's
Partner. Hidden Guns. 1956: Gun the Man
Down. The Black Whip. Tension at Table Rock.
The Unfinished Task. Down Liberty Road.
1957: Calypso Joe. I Married a Woman. Shoot-
Out at Medicine Bend. Run of the Arrow (voice
only). China Gate. 1958: Cry Terror! Frontier
Rangers (TV. GB: cinemas). 1959: Rio Bravo.
The Bramble Bush. 1960: A Fever in the Blood.
Ocean's Eleven. 1961: The Sins of Rachel Cade.
I'll Give My Life. Jessica. 1962: Rome Adven-
ture (GB: Lovers Must Learn). 1963: Captain
Newman MD. 1964: The Killers. 1965: The
Art of Love. 1966: The Chase. Cast a Giant
Shadow. The Poppy is Also a Flower (GB:
Danger Grows Wild). 1967: Point Blank. The
Last Challenge (GB: The Pistolero of Red
River). 1968: A Case of Libel (TV). 1969:
Sam Whiskey. The Love War (TV). Young
Billy Young. 1970: Some Kind of Nut. 1971:
The Resurrection of Zachary Wheeler (GB:
TV). Thief (TV). See the Man Run (TV).
Pretty Maids All in a Row. 1972: Un homme
est mort (GB: The Outside Man). The Scorpio
Scarab). 1973: The Norliss Tapes (TV). 1974:
Pray for the Wildcats (TV). Big Bad Mama.
1977: A Sensitive, Passionate Man (TV).
1978: Le labyrinthe (US: Labyrinths). Over-
board (TV). 1979: L'homme en colère. Klon-
dike Fever. The Suicide's Wife. 1980:
Dressed to Kill. 1981: Death Hunt. Charlie
Chan and the Curse of the Dragon Queen. Dial
M for Murder (TV). 1982: One Shoe Makes
it Murder. 1983: Jealousy (TV). 1984: A
Touch of Scandal (TV).*

DIETRICH, Marlene
(Maria Magdalene Dietrich) 1901–
Alphabetical order ungraciously places two of
the best pairs of twentieth-century legs next
to each other. Dietrich, a blonde German
actress who slaved through a fistful of bit parts
before being spotted for *The Blue Angel* in
1930, is, next to Garbo, the most magical
face and voice from the early sound era. Her
ageless charms enabled her to make several
comebacks after lulls in her career. And her

husky singing voice made her a successful night-club entertainer from the fifties on. Received an Oscar nomination for *Morocco*.
1922: *So sind die Männer/Der Kleine Napoleon.* 1923: *Tragödie der Liebe. Der Sprung ins Leben. Der Mensch am Wege.* 1925: *Die freudlose Gasse* (GB and US: *Joyless Street*). *Manon Lescaut.* 1926: *Eine DuBarry von Heute* (GB: *A Modern Dubarry*). *Madame wünscht keine Kinder* (US: *Madame Wants No Children*). *Kopf hoch, Charly! Der Juxbaron.* 1927: *Sein grosser Bluff. Café Electric.* 1928: *Prinzessin Olala.* **Die glückliche Mutter.* 1929: *Die Frau, nach der Man sich sehnt. Ich küsse ihre Hand, Madame. Liebesnächte. Das Schiff der verlorene Menschen.* 1930: *The Blue Angel. Morocco.* 1931: *Dishonored.* 1932: *Shanghai Express. Blonde Venus.* 1933: *Song of Songs.* 1934: *The Scarlet Empress.* 1935: *The Devil is a Woman.* 1936: *Desire. The Garden of Allah. I Loved a Soldier* (unfinished). 1937: *Knight without Armour. Angel.* 1939: *Destry Rides Again.* 1940: *Seven Sinners.* 1941: *Manpower. The Flame of New Orleans.* 1942: *The Lady is Willing. The Spoilers. Pittsburgh.* 1943: **Screen Snapshots No. 103.* **Show Business at War.* 1944: *Follow the Boys. Kismet.* 1946. *Martin Roumagnac* (US: *The Room Upstairs*). 1947: *Golden Earrings.* 1948: *A Foreign Affair.* 1949: *Jigsaw. Stage Fright.* 1951: *No Highway* (US: *No Highway in the Sky*). 1952: *Rancho Notorious.* 1956: *Around the World in 80 Days. The Monte Carlo Story.* 1957: *Witness for the Prosecution.* 1958: *Touch of Evil.* 1961: *Judgment at Nuremberg.* 1962: *The Black Fox* (narrator only). 1963: *Paris When It Sizzles.* 1978: *Just a Gigolo.* 1984: *Marlene.*

DIFFRING, Anton 1918–
Fair-haired, cold-eyed, cruel-looking German actor, who came to Britain after spending four years as an internee in Canada. After playing numerous nasties and Nazis, Diffring almost became a star of the British cinema in the late 1950s, but his lack of warmth did not help him stay in the top rank, and he eventually returned to Germany. Some sources insist that Diffring appeared in two 1940 films, *Convoy* and *Sailors Three* (US: *Three Cockeyed Sailors*), but fail to explain how he could have managed this.
1950: *State Secret* (US: *The Great Manhunt*). *Highly Dangerous.* 1951: *Hotel*

Sahara. Appointment with Venus (US: *Island Rescue*). *The Woman's Angle.* 1952: *Song of Paris* (US: *Bachelor in Paris*). *Top Secret* (US: *Mr Potts Goes to Moscow*). 1953: *Never Let Me Go. The Red Beret* (US: *Paratrooper*). *Albert RN* (US: *Break to Freedom*). *Park Plaza 605* (US: *Norman Conquest*). *Operation Diplomat.* 1954: *Betrayed. The Sea Shall Not Have Them. The Colditz Story.* 1955: *I Am a Camera.* 1956: *Doublecross. The Black Tent. House of Secrets* (US: *Triple Deception*). *Reach for the Sky.* 1957: *The Traitors* (US: *The Accused*). *The Crooked Sky. Lady of Vengeance. Seven Thunders* (US: *The Beasts of Marseilles*). 1958: *A Question of Adultery. Mark of the Phoenix.* 1959: *The Man Who Could Cheat Death.* 1960: *Circus of Horrors.* 1961: *Enter Inspector Duval.* 1962: *Incident at Midnight.* 1964: *Vorsicht, Mister Dodd. Liane, Queen of the Amazons.* 1965: *The Heroes of Telemark.* 1966: *The Blue Max. Fahrenheit 451.* 1967: *The Double Man. Counterpoint.* 1968: *Where Eagles Dare.* 1969: *Michael Kohlhaas.* 1971: *Zeppelin. L'iguana della lingua di fuoco. The Day the Clown Cried* (unfinished). 1972: *Don't Cry for Me, Little Mother. Hexen: geschandet und zu Tode geqvalt.* 1973: *Sujetska* (GB: *The Fifth Offensive*). *Sieben Tote in der Augen der Katze. Tony Arzenta/ Big Guns. Dead Pigeon in Beethoven Street.* 1974: *The Beast Must Die. Borsalino & Co* (GB: *Blood on the Streets*). *Shatter.* 1975: *Mark of the Devil Pt II. Operation Daybreak. The Swiss Conspiracy.* 1976: *Potato Fritz. Vanessa. Io sono mia.* 1977: *Valentino. Anna Ferroli. Le mutant. Les Indiens sont encore loin. Waldrausch.* 1978: *L'imprecateur. Das Einhorn. Hitler's Son.* 1979: *Tusk.* 1981: *Escape to Victory* (US: *Victory*). 1982: *SAS Malko.* 1984: *The Masks of Death* (TV). 1985: *Marie Ward.* 1986: *Der Sommer des Samurai.*

DILLER, Phyllis (P. Driver) 1917–
Madcap, crow-voiced, explosive American comedienne with accentuated witch-like looks who followed success on television with a few appearances in films that found it hard to contain her firework style in the framework of a plot. She returned to television and to the nightclub work which had first brought her success. Began her career at 40 after bringing up a family of five.
1960: *Splendor in the Grass.* 1966: *The Fat Spy. Boy, Did I Get a Wrong Number.* 1967:

Eight on the Lam (GB: *Eight on the Run*). *Mad Monster Party* (voice only). 1968: *The Private Navy of Sergeant O'Farrell. Did You Hear the One about the Traveling Saleslady?* 1969: *The Adding Machine.* 1970: *Love American Style* (TV). 1982: *Pink Motel* (GB: *Motel*).

DILLMAN, Bradford 1930–
Lean, dark, curly-haired, brooding American actor, mostly in sombre roles, whose career got off to a cracking start in *Compulsion*. But he suffered a few disasters, and was thereafter unable to command the kind of parts he wanted, being seen mainly as bad guys with half a screw loose. Said the once-choosy star in the mid-seventies: 'I'm motivated by financial necessity. I'll accept just about everything I'm offered.' His TV career bears witness to that. Married to ex-actress Suzy Parker (Cecelia Parker 1932–   ).
1958: *A Certain Smile. In Love and War.* 1959: *Compulsion.* 1960: *Crack in the Mirror. Circle of Deception.* 1961: *Sanctuary. Francis of Assisi.* 1963: *The Case against Paul Ryker* (TV. Released to GB and US cinemas 1968 as *Sergeant Ryker*). *Jane.* 1965: *A Rage to Live.* 1966: *The Plainsman.* 1967: *The Helicopter Spies* (TV. GB: cinemas). 1968: *Jigsaw.* 1969: *Black Water Gold* (TV). *The Bridge at Remagen. Fear No Evil* (TV). 1970: *The Mephisto Waltz. Suppose They Gave a War and Nobody Came. Brother John.* 1971: *Escape from the Planet of the Apes. The Resurrection of Zachary Wheeler* (GB: TV). *Five Desperate Women* (TV). *Revenge!* (TV). 1972. *Moon of the Wolf* (TV). *The Delphi Bureau* (TV). *The Eyes of Charles Sand* (TV). 1973: *Deliver Us from Evil* (TV). *The Iceman Cometh. The Way We Were.* 1974: *The Disappearance of Flight 412* (TV). *Gold. Deborah/A Black Ribbon for Deborah. Murder or Mercy?* (TV). *The Last Bride of Salem* (TV). *99 and 44/100% Dead* (GB: *Call Harry Crown*). 1975: *Widow* (TV). *Michèle. Bug. Demon, Demon* (TV). *Force Five* (TV). *Please Call It Murder* (TV). *Adventures of the Queen* (TV). 1976: *The Enforcer. The Newspaper Game* (TV). *Mastermind. Kingston* (TV). *Street Killing* (TV). 1977: *The Amsterdam Kill. The Lincoln Conspiracy.* 1978: *Final Judgment* (TV). *The Swarm. The Hostage Heart* (TV). *Love and Bullets. Piranha.* 1979: *Guyana: the Crime of the Century. Before and After* (TV). *The*

Legend of Walks Far Woman (TV). Jennifer (TV). 1980: The Memory of Eva Ryker (TV). Tourist (TV). 1983: Sudden Impact. 1984: The Treasure of the Amazon/Treasure of Doom. 1986: The Tuscaloosan.

DILLON, Matt 1964–

Long-jawed, slim, dark American young actor of Bowery-style handsomeness, mainly in teenage rebel roles. The great-nephew of cartoonist Alex Raymond, who created the comic strips *Flash Gordon* and *Jungle Jim*, Dillon was in leading roles at 15 and, although part of ensemble performances in his first few successes, branched out on his own with *The Flamingo Kid* and subsequent roles and now looks like being a top movie pin-up.

1979: Over the Edge. 1980: Little Darlings. My Bodyguard. 1981: Fallen Angel (TV). Liar's Moon. 1982: The Great American Fourth of July and Other Disasters (TV). Tex. 1983: The Outsiders. Rumble Fish. 1984: The Flamingo Kid. 1985: Target. Rebel. 1986: Native Son.

DILLON, Melinda 1939–

Square-faced, rather plaintive-looking American actress with distinctive lips and a mass of light curly hair, a dab hand at emotional performances. A prominent Broadway player from the early 1960s, she seemed to have come too late to films for big success, but a lower-grade stardom did find her after her appealing performance as the mother in *Close Encounters of the Third Kind* and she was nominated for Academy Awards both for that and for her hapless victim in *Absence of Malice*.

1969: The April Fools. 1976: Bound for Glory. 1977: Slap Shot. Close Encounters of the Third Kind. 1978: The Critical List (TV). F.I.S.T. 1979: Transplant (TV). 1980: Marriage is Alive and Well (TV). Hellinger's Law (TV). The Special Edition of Close Encounters of the Third Kind. Reunion (TV). 1981: Absence of Malice. 1983: Right of Way (TV). A Christmas Story. 1985: Songwriter. Shattered Spirits (TV).

DIX, Richard

(Ernest Brimmer) 1894–1949

Dark-haired, square-faced, usually unsmiling American leading man, enormously popular in silents, whose career gradually declined after the early thirties, when he had been nominated for an Oscar in *Cimarron*. Died from heart trouble.

*1919: One of the Finest. 1921: The Sin Flood. Not Guilty. All's Fair in Love. The Old Nest. The Poverty of Riches. Dangerous Curve Ahead. 1922: The Glorious Fool. Yellow Men and Gold. The Bonded Women. The Wallflower. Fools First. 1923: The Christian. Racing Hearts. The Woman with Four Faces. The Ten Commandments. Souls for Sale. The Call of the Canyon. To the Last Man. Quicksands. 1924: Sinners in Heaven. Icebound. The Iron Horse. Manhattan. The Stranger. Unguarded Women. 1925: The Vanishing American. The Shock Punch. The Lucky Devil. Too Many Kisses. A Man Must Live. The Lady Who Lied. Men and Women. 1926: Woman-Handled. The Quarterback. Say It Again. Fascinating Youth. Let's Get Married. 1927: Quicksands (remake). Knock-out Reilly. Manpower. Shanghai Bound. Paradise for Two. 1928: Easy Come, Easy Go. Moran of the Marines. Sporting Goods. The Gay Defender. Warming Up. 1929: Nothing But the Truth. Redskin. The Wheel of Life. The Love Doctor. Seven Keys to Baldpate. 1930: Lovin' the Ladies. Shooting Straight. 1931: Cimarron. Young Donovan's Kid (GB: Donovan's Kid). Secret Service. Public Defender. 1932: The Lost Squadron. Hell's Highway. *The Stolen Jools (GB: The Slippery Pearls). Roar of the Dragon. The Conquerors. Liberty Road. 1933: No Marriage Ties. The Ace of Aces. The Great Jasper. Day of Reckoning. 1934: Stingaree. West of the Pecos. His Greatest Gamble. 1935: The Tunnel (US: Transatlantic Tunnel). The Arizonian. 1936: The Devil's Squadron. Special Investigator. Yellow Dust. 1937: The Devil is Driv-*

ing. It Happened in Hollywood. Once a Hero. The Devil's Playground. 1938: Blind Alibi. Sky Giant. 1939: Man of Conquest. Reno. Here I Am a Stranger. 1940: The Marines Fly High. Cherokee Strip (GB: Fighting Marshal). Men Against the Sky. 1941: The Roundup. Badlands of Dakota. 1942: American Empire (GB: My Son Alone). Tombstone, The Town Too Tough to Die. 1943: Buckskin Frontier (GB: The Iron Road). The Kansan (GB: Wagon Wheels). Eyes of the Underworld. Top Man. The Ghost Ship. 1944: The Whistler. The Mark of the Whistler (GB: The Marked Man). 1945: The Power of the Whistler. 1946: The Voice of the Whistler. The Mysterious Intruder. The Secret of the Whistler. 1947: The Thirteenth Hour.

DOLENZ, George 1908–1963

Italian-born leading man with dark, wavy hair whose handsome but crafty features were equally well equipped to portray swashbuckling heroes or cunning villains. Started his career as an opera singer, but enjoyed a fair run of success in wartime Hollywood in the absence of more powerful stars. Best remembered in Britain for his TV series *The Count of Monte-Cristo*. Father of actor-musician Micky Dolenz, once of The Monkees. Died from a heart attack.

1927: The Ring. 1941: Unexpected Uncle. Faculty Row. 1942: Take a Letter, Darling (GB: The Green-Eyed Woman). She's for Me. Calling Dr Death. 1943: Young Ideas. Fired Wife. The Strange Death of Adolf Hitler. Moonlight in Vermont. 1944: In Society. The Climax. Enter Arsene Lupin. Bowery to Broadway. 1945: The Royal Mounted Rides Again (serial). Song of the Sarong. Easy to Look At. Girl on the Spot. 1946: Idea Girl. A Night in Paradise. 1947: Song of Scheherezade. 1950: Vendetta. 1952: My Cousin Rachel. 1953: Wings of the Hawk. Thunder Bay. Scared Stiff. 1954: Sign of the Pagan. The Last Time I Saw Paris. 1955: Such Men Are Dangerous (GB: The Racers). The Purple Mask. A Bullet for Joey. 1957: The Sad Sack. 1959: Timbuktu. 1961: Look in Any Window. 1962: The Four Horsemen of the Apocalypse.

DOMERGUE, Faith 1925–

Dark-haired, brown-eyed American leading lady, on the sultry side. She was a protegée of Howard Hughes, who, after starring her in one film, kept her under wraps for several

years, then relaunched her in a blaze of Jane Russell-style publicity. Public and critics did not take to her, and her star bubble burst almost at once, although she subsequently performed competently in a number of routine thrillers and action films.

1946: Young Widow. 1950: Where Danger Lives. Vendetta. 1952: The Duel at Silver Creek. 1953: The Great Sioux Uprising. 1954: This is My Love. 1955: Cult of the Cobra. This Island Earth. It Came from Beneath the Sea. Santa Fé Passage. Timeslip (US: The Atomic Man). 1956: Soho Incident (US: Spin a Dark Web). 1957: Man in the Shadow. Il cielo brucia. 1958: Live in Fear. 1959: Escort West. 1963: California. 1966: Prehistoric Planet Women. 1967: Track of Thunder. 1969: One on Top of the Other. The Gamblers. Le sorelle/So Evil My Sister. 1970: L'amore breve. 1971: Legacy of Blood. L'uomo dagli occhi di ghiaccio (US: The Man with the Icy Eyes). 1973: The House of the Seven Corpses.

DONAHUE, Troy
(Merle Johnson) 1936–
Big, beefy, baby-faced American actor with butter-coloured hair, the pin-up of a million teenage girls in the late 1950s and early 1960s. An attempt to widen his range beyond the teenage dream was not entirely successful and after he had left the aegis of his studio, Warners, he found the going very tough indeed. He now plays lesser roles but, with a little Hollywood tongue-in-cheek, was cast as 'Merle Johnson' in The Godfather Part II. Married to actresses Suzanne Pleshette (qv) in 1964 and Valerie Allen (from 1966).
1957: Man Afraid. The Tarnished Angels.

1958: The Voice in the Mirror. Live Fast. Die Young. This Happy Feeling. Summer Love. Wild Heritage. Monster on the Campus. The Perfect Furlough (GB: Strictly for Pleasure). 1959: Imitation of Life. A Summer Place. 1960: The Crowded Sky. 1961: Parrish. Susan Slade. 1962: Rome Adventure (GB: Lovers Must Learn). 1963: Palm Springs Weekend. 1964: A Distant Trumpet. 1965: My Blood Runs Cold. 1967: Rocket to the Moon (US: Those Fantastic Flying Fools). Come Spy with Me. 1969: The Lonely Profession (TV). 1971: Sweet Saviour. 1973: Seizure. 1974: Born to Kill (GB: Cockfighter). The Godfather Part II. 1977: The Legend of Frank Woods. 1982: Tin Man. 1983: Malibu (TV). 1984: Grandview USA. 1985: Savage Sunday. 1986: Low-Blow.

DONALD, James 1917–
Scottish actor who threw up a university career to join Edinburgh Repertory Company, and thence went into British films where he played serious, thoughtful roles, in keeping with his dark, unsmiling looks. A star from 1948 to 1952, but began to look gaunt in early middle age and was soon in character roles, mostly of dry, literate, office-bound types.
1942: The Missing Million. Went the Day Well? In Which We Serve. 1943: San Demetrio London. 1944: The Way Ahead. 1947: Broken Journey. 1948: The Small Voice (US: Hideout). 1949: Edward My Son. Trottie True (US: Gay Lady). 1950: Cage of Gold. 1951: White Corridors. Brandy for the Parson. *Persian Story (narrator only). 1952: Gift Horse (US: Glory at Sea). The Pickwick Papers. The Net (US: Project M 7). 1954: Beau Brummell. 1956: Lust for Life. 1957: The Bridge on the River Kwai. 1958: The Vikings. 1959: Third Man on the Mountain. 1963: The Great Escape. 1965: King Rat. Cast a Giant Shadow. 1966: The Jokers. 1967: Quatermass and the Pit (US: Five Million Miles to Earth). 1968: Hannibal Brooks. 1969: The Royal Hunt of the Sun. David Copperfield (TV. GB: cinemas). Destiny of a Spy (TV). 1975: Conduct Unbecoming. 1978: The Big Sleep.

DONAT, Robert 1905–1958
Cheerful, chunky, good-looking British leading man who could do very little wrong in films in the thirties. His forthright, pleasing, open acting style endeared him to audiences,

produced a memorable series of characterizations and culminated in his Academy Award for Goodbye Mr Chips! Later, blighted by persistent asthma, he was less successful by his own high standards, although his mellifluous voice patterns made him ever-popular on radio. Married (second) to actress Renee Asherson, although they were separated at the time of his death from a cerebral thrombosis brought on by chronic bronchial asthma. An Oscar-nominee for The Citadel.
1932: Men of Tomorrow. That Night in London (US: Overnight). 1933: Cash (US: For Love or Money). The Private Life of Henry VIII. 1934: The Count of Monte-Cristo. 1935: The 39 Steps. The Ghost Goes West. 1937: Knight without Armour. 1938: The Citadel. 1939: Goodbye Mr Chips! 1941: *Cavalcade of the Academy Awards. The Young Mr Pitt. 1943: The Adventures of Tartu (US: Tartu). 1945: Perfect Strangers (US: Vacation from Marriage). 1947: Captain Boycott. *The British – Are They Artistic? 1948: The Winslow Boy. 1949: †The Cure for Love. 1951: The Magic Box. 1953: *Royal Heritage (narrator only). 1954: Lease of Life. 1956: *The Stained Glass at Fairford. 1958: The Inn of the Sixth Happiness.

†Also directed

DONLAN, Yolande 1920–
American actress (daughter of character actor James Donlan: 1889–1938) and dancer who slaved away for years on the sidelines in Hollywood before taking them by storm on the London stage as the heroine of Born Yesterday. Although her appeal was primarily that of the dizzy blonde, she played some enchanting

variations on it in the British cinema of the late forties and early fifties. Married (second) to British director Val Guest.

1936: *Pennies from Heaven. After the Thin Man.* 1937: *The Champagne Waltz. Rosalie.* 1938: *Love Finds Andy Hardy. Sweethearts.* 1939: *The Oklahoma Kid. The Great Man Votes. Idiot's Delight. Man About Town.* 1940: *I Take this Woman.* †*Turnabout.* †*Cross Country Romance.* †*Dark Streets of Cairo.* †*Devil Bat.* 1941: †*Road Show.* †*Under Age.* †*Unfinished Business.* 1942: †*DuBarry Was a Lady.* 1943: †*Girl Crazy.* 1949: *Traveller's Joy. Miss Pilgrim's Progress.* 1950: *The Body Said No! Mr Drake's Duck.* 1952: *Penny Princess.* 1955: *They Can't Hang Me.* 1957: *Tarzan and the Lost Safari.* 1959: *Expresso Bongo.* 1962: *Jigsaw.* 1963: *80,000 Suspects.* 1970: *The Adventurers.* 1976: *Seven Nights in Japan.*

† *as Yvonne Mollot*

DONLEVY, Brian
(Grosson B. Donlevy) 1899–1972
Heavy-set, gloweringly handsome, strong, moustachioed, Irish-born Hollywood actor. After an adventurous early life (including World War I service in Lafayette Escadrille) he drifted into acting, although it was 1935 before he settled permanently in Hollywood. A tough villain of the 1930s, he became a popular semi-star of rugged thrillers and action films in the succeeding decade after his success in the title role of *The Great McGinty*. Although Donlevy suffered from drinking problems, his forthright performances remained good value to the end. Died from cancer of the throat. Oscar-nominated for his sadistic sergeant in *Beau Geste*.

1923: *Jamestown.* 1924: *Monsieur Beaucaire. Damaged Hearts.* 1925: *School for Wives.* 1926: *A Man of Quality.* 1928: *Mother's Boy.* 1929: *Gentlemen of the Press.* 1932: *A Modern Cinderella.* 1935: *Another Face (GB: It Happened in Hollywood). Barbary Coast. Mary Burns. Fugitive.* 1936: *Strike Me Pink. High Tension. Crack-Up. Human Cargo. Half Angel. Thirteen Hours by Air. 36 Hours to Kill.* 1937: *Born Reckless. Midnight Taxi. This is My Affair (GB: His Affair).* 1938: *We're Going to be Rich. In Old Chicago. Battle of Broadway. Sharpshooters.* 1939: *Jesse James. Union Pacific. Behind Prison Gates. Beau Geste. Destry Rides Again. Allegheny Uprising*

(GB: The First Rebel). 1940: *The Great McGinty (GB: Down Went McGinty). Brigham Young – Frontiersman (GB: Brigham Young). When the Daltons Rode.* 1941: *I Wanted Wings. Birth of the Blues. Hold Back the Dawn. Billy the Kid. South of Tahiti (GB: White Savage).* 1942: *The Great Man's Lady. The Remarkable Andrew. A Gentleman After Dark. Wake Island. The Glass Key. Nightmare. Stand by for Action (GB: Cargo of Innocents). Two Yanks in Trinidad.* 1943: *Hangmen Also Die. The City That Stopped Hitler – Heroic Stalingrad (narrator only).* 1944. *An American Romance. The Miracle of Morgan's Creek.* 1945: *Duffy's Tavern. The Trouble with Women (released 1947).* 1946: *Our Hearts Were Growing Up. The Virginian. Canyon Passage. Two Years Before the Mast.* 1947: *The Beginning or the End. Song of Scheherezade. Heaven Only Knows. Kiss of Death. Killer McCoy.* 1948: *A Southern Yankee (GB: My Hero). Impact. Command Decision.* 1949: *The Lucky Stiff.* 1950: *Shakedown. Kansas Raiders.* 1951: *Fighting Coast Guard. Hoodlum Empire. Slaughter Trail.* 1952: *Ride the Man Down.* 1953: *The Woman They Almost Lynched.* 1955: *The Big Combo. The Quatermass Xperiment (US: The Creeping Unknown).* 1956: *A Cry in the Night.* 1957: *Quatermass 2 (US: Enemy from Space).* 1958: *Escape from Red Rock. Cowboy.* 1959: *Juke Box Rhythm. Never So Few.* 1960: *The Girl in Room 13.* 1961: *The Errand Boy.* 1962: *The Pigeon That Took Rome.* 1964: *The Curse of the Fly.* 1965: *Gammera the Invincible. How to Stuff a Wild Bikini.* 1966: *The Fat Spy. Waco.* 1967: *Hostile Guns.* 1968: *Arizona Bushwhackers. Rogue's Gallery.* 1969: *Pit Stop.*

DORLEAC, Françoise 1942–1967
More extrovert sister of Catherine Deneuve, this dark-haired, rangy French actress with attractive personality was on the verge of becoming as big an international star as her sister when we was killed in a car crash at 25.

1957: *Mensonges.* 1959: *Les loups dans la bergerie (GB: The Damned and the Daring).* 1960: *Les portes claquent (US: The Door Slams).* 1961: *La gamberge. Le jeu de la verité. All the Gold in the World. Ce soir ou jamais. La fille aux yeux d'or (US: The Girl with the Golden Eyes).* 1962: *Arsène Lupin contre*

Arsène Lupin. 1964: *That Man from Rio. La peau douce (GB: Silken Skin). La Ronde (US: Circle of Love). La chasse a l'homme.* 1965: *Where the Spies Are. Genghis Khan.* 1966: *Cul-de-sac.* 1967: *The Young Girls of Rochefort. Billion Dollar Brain.*

DORN, Philip
(Hein Van Der Niet) 1901–1975
Dutch stage actor who fled the Germans in 1939 and ended up in Hollywood where, despite his comparative lack of film experience, he was eagerly snapped up for a series of sincere if stolid continentals of varying nationality. He was usually distinctive, however, and occasionally (as in *I Remember Mama*) quite memorable. A stroke in 1946 disrupted his film career and he was forced to retire in 1955 following an accident in a stage play. Died from a heart attack.

1936: †*De Kribbebyter (GB: The Cross-Patch).* 1937: †*Der Tiger von Eschnapur.* †*Das Indische Grabmal.* 1938: †*Reise nach Tilsit.* 1939: *Confessions of a Nazi Spy.* 1940: *Ski Patrol. Diamond Frontier. Escape. Enemy Agent (GB: Secret Enemy).* 1941: *Ziegfeld Girl. Tarzan's Secret Treasure. Underground.* 1942: *Reunion/Reunion in France (GB: Mademoiselle France). Calling Dr Gillespie. Random Harvest.* 1943: *Paris After Dark (GB: The Night is Ending). Chetniks.* 1944: *Passage to Marseille (GB: Passage to Marseilles). Blonde Fever.* 1945: *Escape in the Desert. Paris Underground (GB: Madame Pimpernel).* 1946: *Concerto (later and GB: I've Always Loved You).* 1948: *I Remember Mama.* 1949: *The Fighting Kentuckian.* 1950: *Spy Hunt (GB: Panther's Moon).* 1951: *Sealed Cargo. Der träumende Mund.* 1954: *Salto mortale.*

† *As Fritz Van Dongen*

DORNE, Sandra (Joanna Smith) 1925–
Alphabetical order produces more discomfort by squeezing next to one another Britain's two busty blondes from the forties and fifties. For me, Sandra certainly had more sex appeal, if perhaps less acting ability, but was locked away in second-features for three-quarters of her career. And her private life was less sensational than that of La Dors, which meant she hit fewer international headlines. Married to Patrick Holt since 1954. Still occasionally on TV.

1947: *Eyes That Kill.* 1948: *A Piece of Cake. Once a Jolly Swagman* (US: *Maniacs on Wheels*). *All Over the Town. Saraband for Dead Lovers* (US: *Saraband*). 1949: *Marry Me. Don't Ever Leave Me. Golden Arrow* (US: *The Gay Adventure*). *Traveller's Joy.* 1950: *Don't Say Die. The Clouded Yellow. Helter Skelter.* 1951: *Happy Go Lovely.* 1952: *13 East Street. Hindle Wakes* (US: *Holiday Week*). *The Yellow Balloon. Alf's Baby.* 1953: *Wheel of Fate. The Beggar's Opera. Marilyn/Roadhouse Girl. The Case of Express Delivery. The Weak and the Wicked. The Good Die Young.* 1955: *Police Dog. The Final Column. Diplomatic Error.* 1956: *The Gelignite Gang. Alias John Preston. The Iron Petticoat. Operation Murder.* 1957: *Three Sundays to Live.* 1958: *Orders to Kill.* **Portrait of a Matador. The Bank Raiders.* 1960: *Not a Hope in Hell. The House in Marsh Road* (US: *The Invisible Creature*). *The Malpas Mystery.* 1962: *The Amorous Prawn* (US: *The Playgirl and the War Minister*). 1963: *Devil Doll.* 1964: *The Secret Door.* 1971: *All Coppers Are...* 1976: *Joseph Andrews.* 1978: *The Playbirds.*

1946: *The Shop at Sly Corner. Dancing with Crime.* 1947: *Holiday Camp.* 1948: *Good Time Girl. Penny and the Pownall Case. The Calendar. My Sister and I. Oliver Twist. Here Come the Huggetts.* 1949: *It's Not Cricket. Vote for Huggett. Diamond City. A Boy, a Girl and a Bike.* 1950: *Dance Hall.* 1951: *Lady Godiva Rides Again. Worm's Eye View.* 1952: *The Last Page* (US: *Manbait*). *My Wife's Lodger. The Great Game.* 1953: *Is Your Honeymoon Really Necessary? It's a Grand Life. The Weak and the Wicked* (US: *Young and Willing*). 1955: *As Long As They're Happy. A Kid for Two Farthings. Miss Tulip Stays the Night. Value for Money. An Alligator Named Daisy.* 1956: *Yield to the Night* (US: *Blonde Sinner*). *I Married a Woman.* 1957: *The Unholy Wife. La ragazza del Palio* (GB: *The Love Specialist* US: *Girl of the Palio*). *The Long Haul.* 1958: *Tread Softly Stranger.* 1959: *Passport to Shame* (US: *Room 43*). 1960: *Scent of Mystery* (GB: *Holiday in Spain*). 1961: *On the Double. King of the Roaring Twenties* (GB: *The Big Bankroll*). 1962: *Mrs Gibbons' Boys. Encontra a Mallorca.* 1963: *West 11.* 1964: *Allez France* (US: *The Counterfeit Constable*). 1966: *The Sandwich Man.* 1967: *Berserk! Danger Route.* 1968: *Hammerhead. Baby Love.* 1970: *There's a Girl in My Soup. Deep End.* 1971: *Hannie Caulder. The Pied Piper.* 1972: *The Amazing Mr. Blunden. Nothing But the Night.* 1973: *Theatre of Blood. From Beyond the Grave. Steptoe and Son Ride Again. Craze.* 1974: *The Amorous Milkman. Swedish Wildcats* (GB: *What the Swedish Butler Saw.* US: *The Groove Room*). *Bedtime with Rosie. Three for All.* 1975: *Adventures of a Taxi Driver.* 1976: *Keep It Up Downstairs.* 1977: *Adventures of a Private Eye.* 1979: *Confessions from the David Galaxy Affair.* 1981: *Dick Turpin* (TV). 1984: *Steaming.*

Academy Awards in *Champion, The Bad and the Beautiful* and *Lust for Life.*
1946: *The Strange Love of Martha Ivers.* 1947: *I Walk Alone. Out of the Past* (GB: *Build My Gallows High*). *Mourning Becomes Electra.* 1948: *My Dear Secretary. The Walls of Jericho.* 1949: *A Letter to Three Wives. Champion. Young Man with a Horn* (GB: *Young Man of Music*). 1950: *The Glass Menagerie.* 1951: *Along the Great Divide. The Big Carnival* (GB: *Ace in the Hole*). *Detective Story.* 1952: *The Big Sky. The Big Trees. The Bad and the Beautiful.* 1953: *The Story of Three Loves. The Juggler. Act of Love. Ulysses.* 1954: *20,000 Leagues under the Sea. The Racers* (GB: *Such Men Are Dangerous*). *The Indian Fighter.* 1956: *Lust for Life. Gunfight at the OK Corral.* 1957: *Paths of Glory. Top Secret Affair* (GB: *Their Secret Affair*). 1958: *The Vikings.* 1959: *Last Train from Gun Hill. The Devil's Disciple.* 1960: *Spartacus. Strangers When We Meet.* 1961: *The Last Sunset. Town without Pity.* 1962: *Lonely Are the Brave. Two Weeks in Another Town.* 1963: *The List of Adrian Messenger. For Love or Money. The Hook.* 1964: *Seven Days in May.* 1965: *In Harm's Way. The Heroes of Telemark. Is Paris Burning?* 1966: *Cast a Giant Shadow.* 1967: *The Way West. The War Wagon.* 1968: *A Lovely Way to Die* (GB: *A Lovely Way to Go*). **French Lunch. The Brotherhood.* 1969: *The Arrangement.* 1970: *There Was a Crooked Man. A Gunfight.* 1971: *The Light at the Edge of the World. Catch Me a Spy.* 1972: *A Man to Respect* (US: *The Master Touch*). 1973: *Mousey* (TV. GB: cinemas: *Cat and Mouse*). †*Scalawag.* 1974: *Once is Not Enough.* 1975: †*Posse.* 1976: *Victory at Entebbe* (TV. GB: cinemas). 1977: *Holocaust 2000* (US: *The Chosen*). 1978: *The Fury.* 1979: *The Villain* (GB: *Cactus Jack*). 1980: *Home Movies. Saturn 3. The Final Countdown. Remembrance of Love* (TV). 1981: *The Man from Snowy River.* 1983: *Eddie Macon's Run.* 1984: *Draw!* (TV). 1985: *Amos* (TV). 1986: *Tough Guys.*

†*Also directed*

DORS, Diana (D. Fluck) 1931–1984
Platinum blonde British actress with sexy smile whose career had as many curves and swerves as her once hourglass figure. One of her first films, *Good Time Girl,* summed up her early career, but she proved herself a real actress in *Yield to the Night,* only to throw the reputation away on an abortive and wildly over-publicized visit to Hollywood. Extremely good in some early 1970s' character roles, she was latterly given less worthy material. Died from cancer.

DOUGLAS, Kirk
(Issur Danielovitch, later Demsky) 1916–
Forceful, fair-haired, powerfully-built American star with dimpled chin and fierce grin, apt to get hold of a role and tear it apart, but a magnetic attraction at the box office from *Champion,* in 1949 – a typical audience-crunching role as a boxer – right up to the early sixties. Father of Michael Douglas (qv). Belatedly turned director, making one disaster and one fairly good western. Nominated for

DOUGLAS, Melvyn
(M. Hesselberg) 1901–1981
Elegant American leading man with pencil moustache and a precise sense of romantic comedy (the zanier the comedy, the more at

home he was). His splendidly modulated voice often wittily betrayed the tongue in his cheek. Forsaking Hollywood when his days as a star were over, Douglas spent a rewarding ten years on stage before returning to films as a fine character actor of grouchy but sterling old men. Academy Award for *Hud*, and again in 1980 for *Being There*. Also nominated for *I Never Sang for My Father*.

*1931: Tonight or Never. 1932: Prestige. The Wiser Sex. Broken Wing. The Old Dark House. As You Desire Me. 1933: Nagana. The Vampire Bat. 1934: Counsellor at Law. Dangerous Corner. Woman in the Dark. 1935: Mary Burns – Fugitive. She Married Her Boss. Annie Oakley. People's Enemy. 1936: The Lone Wolf Returns. The Gorgeous Hussy. And So They Were Married. Theodora Goes Wild. 1937: Angel. Captains Courageous. Women of Glamour. I Met Him in Paris. 1938: Arsene Lupin Returns. The Toy Wife (GB: Frou Frou). Fast Company. The Shining Hour. There's Always a Woman. There's That Woman Again. That Certain Age. 1939: Good Girls Go to Paris. Tell No Tales. Ninotchka. The Amazing Mr Williams. 1940: Too Many Husbands (GB: My Two Husbands). Third Finger, Left Hand. He Stayed for Breakfast. 1941: Our Wife. Two-Faced Woman. That Uncertain Feeling. This Thing Called Love (GB: Married But Single). A Woman's Face. 1942: They All Kissed the Bride. We Were Dancing. 1943: Three Hearts for Julia. 1947: The Guilt of Janet Ames. Sea of Grass. *Make Way for Youth (narrator only). 1948: Mr Blandings Builds His Dream House. My Own True Love. 1949: A Woman's Secret. The Great Sinner. 1950: My Forbidden Past. 1951: On the Loose. 1954: You Can Win Elections (narrator only). 1957: The Greer Case (TV). 1958: The Plot to Kill Stalin (TV). The Return of Ansel Gibbs (TV). 1961: *The Highest Commandment (narrator only). 1962: Billy Budd. 1963: Hud. 1964: Advance to the Rear (GB: Company of Cowards). The Americanization of Emily. 1965: Rapture. *The Fast I Have Chosen (narrator only). 1966: Hotel. 1967: Companions in Nightmare (TV). 1969: I Never Sang for My Father. 1970: Hunters Are for Killing (TV). 1971: Death Takes a Holiday (TV). The Going Up of David Lev (TV). 1972: The Candidate. One is a Lonely Number. 1973: Death Squad (TV) 1974: Murder or Mercy (TV). 1975: Benjamin Franklin: the Statesman (TV). 1976: The Tenant. 1977: Twilight's Last Gleaming. Intimate Strangers (TV). 1978: Battered! (TV). 1979: The Changeling. The Seduction of Joe Tynan. Being There. 1980: Tell Me a Riddle. Ghost Story. Hot Touch.*

DOUGLAS, Michael 1944–

Intense, hard-driving, brown-haired (usually centre-parted), green-eyed American actor whose face and distinctive voice both reflect his father, Kirk Douglas (*qv*). He evaded his father's image by playing hippie roles in his early films, then went 'legitimate' as a popular TV cop in *The Streets of San Francisco*. Tried to devote himself to producing in the mid-1970s, but acting wouldn't let him go and the

unexpected smash success of *Romancing the Stone* in 1984 pushed him close to superstardom. A long personal relationship with Brenda Vaccaro (*qv*) fell through in 1977, and he subsequently married a non-professional.

*1968: The Experiment (TV). 1969: Hail, Hero! 1970: Adam at 6am. 1971: Summertree. Napoleon and Samantha. When Michael Calls (TV). 1977: *Minestrone. Coma. 1978: The China Syndrome. 1979: Running (TV). 1980: It's My Turn. Three Mile Island. Tell Me a Riddle. 1983: The Star Chamber. 1984: Romancing the Stone. 1985: A Chorus Line. The Jewel of the Nile.*

DOUGLAS, Paul 1907–1959

Big, beaming American sports commentator (above, being kissed by Ginger Rogers) who found, via stooging for comedians, a talent for acting and excelled as a series of affable, big-hearted, sometimes slow-witted gorillas, both comic and tragic. Also involved with the short series *Paul Douglas' Sports Review* in the forties, although this may not have included any on-screen appearances. Married (fifth of five) to Jan Sterling from 1950 until his death in 1959 from a heart attack. His fourth wife was actress Virginia Field.

*1949: A Letter to Three Wives. It Happens Every Spring. Everybody Does It. 1950: The Big Lift. Panic in the Streets. Love That Brute. 1951: Fourteen Hours. The Guy Who Came Back. Rhubarb. Angels in the Outfield (GB: Angels and the Pirates). 1952: When in Rome. Clash by Night. We're Not Married. Never Wave at a WAC (GB: The Private Wore Skirts). 1953: Forever Female. *The Javanese*

*Dagger. *The Sable Scarf. 1954: Executive Suite. The Maggie (US: High and Dry). Green Fire. 1955: Joe Macbeth. 1956: The Leather Saint. The Hefferan Family (TV. GB: cinemas). The Solid Gold Cadillac. The Gamma People. 1957: This Could Be the Night. Beau James. Fortunella. 1958: The Dungeon (TV). 1959: The Raider (TV). The Mating Game. Judgment at Nuremburg (TV).*

DOUGLAS, Robert
(Robert D. Finlayson) 1909–

Floridly handsome, light-haired, moustachioed British actor who went to Hollywood in 1948, and used his world-class prowess as a swordsman to give himself eight years of swashbuckling villains. Later became a director and worked prolifically in television.

1930: P.C. Josser. 1931: Many Waters. 1933: The Blarney Stone (US: The Blarney Kiss). 1935: Death Drives Through. 1937: Our Fighting Navy (US: Torpedoed!). London Melody (US: Girls in the Street). Over the Moon. 1938: The Challenge. 1939: The Lion Has Wings. Chinese Bungalow (US: Chinese Den). 1947: The End of the River. 1948: Adventures of Don Juan (GB: The New Adventures of Don Juan). The Decision of Christopher Blake. 1949: The Fountainhead. Homicide. The Lady Takes a Sailor. 1950: Barricade. Buccaneer's Girl. This Side of the Law. The Flame and the Arrow. Spy Hunt (GB: Panther's Moon). Kim. Mystery Submarine. 1951: Thunder on the Hill (GB: Bonaventure). Target Unknown. At Sword's Point (GB: Sons of the Musketeers). 1952: Ivanhoe. The Prisoner of Zenda. 1953: The Desert Rats. Fair Wind to Java. Flight to Tangier. 1954: Saskatchewan (GB: O'Rourke of the Royal Mounted). King Richard and the Crusaders. 1955: The Virgin Queen. Helen of Troy. The Scarlet Coat. Good Morning Miss Dove. 1959: The Young Philadelphians (GB: The City Jungle). Tarzan the Ape-Man. 1960: The Lawbreakers (TV. GB: cinemas). 1974: The Questor Tapes (TV).

As director: 1964: Night Train to Paris. 1976: Future Cop (TV).

DOUGLAS, Warren 1917–

Most of my colleagues in the film world seem not to have heard of Warren Douglas. But 1940s' audiences certainly knew this laughing-eyed, dark-haired American actor as the chun-

kily-built hero of a fistful of low-budget dramas and thrillers. As his acting career dimmed in the 1950s, Douglas was already turning to writing, producing dozens of screenplays between *Torpedo Alley* (1952) and *The Night of the Grizzly* (1966), before going into television.

1938: Freshman Year. 1939: First Offenders. 1943: Northern Pursuit. Adventure in Iraq. Murder on the Waterfront. Destination Tokyo. Mission to Moscow. 1944: The Doughgirls. 1945: *Law of the Badlands. God is My Co-Pilot. Pride of the Marines (GB: Forever in Love). 1946: Below the Deadline. The Man I Love. The Inner Circle. The Pilgrim Lady. 1947: High Conquest. The Magnificent Rogue. The Trespasser. The Chinese Ring. The Red Hornet. 1948: Homicide for Three (GB: An Interrupted Honeymoon). Incident. Lightnin' in the Forest. The Babe Ruth Story. 1949: Task Force. Post Office Investigator. Homicide. Forgotten Women. 1950: County Fair. Square Dance Katy. The Great Jewel Robber. 1951: Cuban Fireball. Northwest Territory. Yellowfin (GB: Yellow Fin). 1952: Secrets of Monte Carlo. 1953: Fangs of the Arctic. 1954: Cry Vengeance. 1955: Double Danger. 1957: The Helen Morgan Story (GB: Both Ends of the Candle). The Deep Six. Dragoon Wells Massacre. 1973: The Red Pony (TV. GB: cinemas, in abridged version).

DOW, Peggy (Margaret Varnadow) 1928–
Spectacularly beautiful green-eyed blonde who swopped medical studies for acting when discovered by Universal. No sooner had she demonstrated a wide range of talents than she

retired to become Mrs Walter Helmerich III.
1949: Undertow. Woman in Hiding. 1950: Shakedown. The Sleeping City. Bright Victory (GB: Lights Out). Harvey. 1951: Reunion in Reno. You Never Can Tell (GB: You Never Know). I Want You.

DOWLING, Joan 1928–1954
Blonde, blue-eyed British actress whose career progressed from cheerful cockney teenagers to put-upon waifs to sluttish other women. Had difficulty finding a good range of adult roles and, at 26, was found dead in a gas-filled room. Married to Harry Fowler (from 1951).
1947: Hue and Cry. 1948: Bond Street. No Room at the Inn. *Pathe Pictorial No 132. 1949: For Them That Trespass. A Man's Affair. Landfall. Train of Events. 1950: Murder Without Crime. 1951: The Magic Box. Pool of London. 1952: 24 Hours in a Woman's Life (US: Affair in Monte Carlo). Women of Twilight (US: Twilight Women). 1953: The Case of Gracie Budd.

DOWN, Lesley-Anne 1954–
Eye-catching, headline-snatching, dark-haired British actress, in films at 15, at first as schoolgirls, but later as hard-edged decoration in big-budget movies. With her determination to succeed, surface brightness and lack of inhibition about what she tackles, she shows every sign of becoming the Joan Collins of the 1990s and beyond.
1969: †The Smashing Bird I Used to Know. All the Right Noises. 1970: Sin un Adios. Countess Dracula. Assault. 1972: Pope Joan. 1973:

From Beyond the Grave. Scalawag. 1975: Brannigan. 1976: A Little Night Music. The Pink Panther Strikes Again. 1978: The Betsy. The One and Only Phyllis Dixey (TV). The First Great Train Robbery. 1979: Hanover Street. 1980: Roughcut. Sphinx. 1981: Offbeat. Murder is Easy (TV). 1982: The Hunchback of Notre Dame (TV). 1983: The Devil Impostor. 1984: Arch of Triumph (TV). 1985: Nomads.

† As Lesley Down

DOWNS, Cathy 1924–1976
A natural, fresh beauty, this brown-haired, blue-eyed American model-turned-actress was starred by John Ford in the title role of *My Darling Clementine.* But hers was a quiet and unassertive talent, and the rest of her career was a steady downhill slide. Married to actor Joe Kirkwood (1949 on).
1945: The Dolly Sisters. Billy Rose's Diamond Horseshoe (GB: Diamond Horseshoe). State Fair. 1946: The Dark Corner. Do You Love Me? My Darling Clementine. 1947: For You I Die. 1948: The Noose Hangs High. Panhandle. 1949: Massacre River. The Sundowners (GB: Thunder in the Dust). 1950: Short Grass. 1951: Joe Palooka in Triple Cross (GB: The Triple Cross). 1952: Gobs and Gals (GB: Cruising Casanovas). 1953: The Flaming Urge. Bandits of the West. 1955: The Phantom from 10,000 Leagues. Narcotics Squad. The Big Tip-Off. 1956: Kentucky Rifle. The She-Creature. Oklahoma Woman. 1957: The Amazing Colossal Man. 1959: Missile to the Moon.

DRAKE, Charlie
(Charles Springall) 1925–
Cherubic, pint-sized British comedian with unruly fair hair and squeaky voice, who, after

roles with Universal via radio success as detective Sam Spade. Often cast as double-shaded characters who died at the end, but his career nosedived with the end of the studio contract system. Married to Ida Lupino 1951–1968.
1947: Brute Force. 1948: The Naked City. All My Sons. 1949: Illegal Entry. Woman in Hiding. Red Canyon. Calamity Jane and Sam Bass. Johnny Stoolpigeon. 1950: Spy Hunt (GB: Panther's Moon). Shakedown. 1951: The Lady From Texas. Steel Town. 1952: The Roar of the Crowd. Models Inc./Call Girl (later and GB: That Kind of Girl). 1953: Spaceways. Tanganyika. Jennifer. 1954: The Yellow Mountain. Private Hell 36. 1955: Women's Prison. Flame of the Islands. 1956: While the City Sleeps. Blackjack Ketchum, Desperado. The Broken Star. 1957: Sierra Stranger. 1962: Boys' Night Out. Le sette folgori di Assur (GB: The Thunderbolt. US: War Gods of Babylon). 1963: Sardanapalus the Great. La congiura dei Borgia. 1967: Panic in the City. 1969: The DA: Murder One (TV). 1970: In Search of America (TV). 1971: A Little Game (TV). 1972: Snatched (TV). 1973: The Heist (TV. GB: Suspected Person). 1974: Tight As a Drum (TV). 1977: The Late Show. 1978: A Wedding. Battered! (TV). In the Glitter Palace (TV). Ski Lift to Death (TV). 1979: Kramer vs. Kramer. Double Negative. Family Secrets (TV). The Young Maverick (TV). 1980: Valentine Magic on Love Island (TV). Oh, God! Book II. 1982: The Wild Women of Chastity Gulch (TV). 1983: This Girl for Hire (TV). 1985: Love on the Run (TV). 1986: Monster in the Closet. Deceit.

DUKE, Patty (Anna Duke) 1946–
Puffy-cheeked, light-haired American actress who won an Academy Award for recreating her stage role as Helen Keller in *The Miracle Worker*, and had her own television show at 17. After the commercial failure of *Me Natalie* in 1969, she no longer seemed a potential superstar and has been seen infrequently in films since. Married actor John Astin and from 1973 to 1982 was billed as Patty Duke Astin. Later divorced and remarried.
1955: I'll Cry Tomorrow. 1956: Somebody Up There Likes Me. 1958: The Goddess. Country Music Holiday. 1959: Happy Anniversary. The

4-D Man. 1961: The Power and the Glory (TV. GB: cinemas). 1962: The Miracle Worker. 1965: Billie. 1966: The Daydreamer (voice only). 1967: Valley of the Dolls. 1969: Me Natalie. My Sweet Charlie (TV). 1971: Two on a Bench (TV). If Tomorrow Comes (TV). She Waits (TV). Deadly Harvest (TV). You'll Like My Mother. 1973: Nightmare (TV). 1974: Miss Kline, We Love You (TV). Hard Day at Blue Nose. 1977: Fire! (TV. GB: cinemas). Rosetti and Ryan: Men Who Love Women (TV). Look What's Happened to Rosemary's Baby (TV). The Storyteller (TV). Curse of the Black Widow (TV). 1978: The Swarm. Having Babies III (TV). Killer on Board (TV). 1979: The Miracle Worker (TV). A Family Upside Down (TV). Hanging by a Thread (TV). Before and After (TV). 1980: The Women's Room (TV). The First Nine Months are the Hardest (TV). Mom, the Wolfman and Me (TV). The Babysitter (TV). 1981: By Design. 1982: The Violation of Sarah McDavid (TV). Something So Right (TV). September Gun (TV). 1984: Best Kept Secrets. 1985: A Time to Triumph (TV). 1986: Willy/Milly.

DULLEA, Keir 1936–
Lean, good-looking, pale-eyed American leading man, reminiscent of Tab Hunter, but generally in more cerebral roles. After a very bright start, his roles have too often seemed ordinary and routine, and his performances have lacked the intensity of earlier years.
1959: Mrs Miniver (TV). 1961: The Hoodlum Priest. 1962: David and Lisa. 1963: Mail Order Bride (GB: West of Montana). 1964: The Thin Red Line. The Naked Hours. 1965: Bunny Lake is Missing. Madame X. 1967: The Fox. 1968: 2001: a Space Odyssey. 1969: De Sade. Black Water Gold (TV). 1972: Paperback Hero. 1973: Il diavolo nel cervello. Last of the Big Guns. 1974: Paul and Michelle. Black Christmas. 1976: Full Circle. Law and Order (TV). 1977: Welcome to Blood City. Leopard in the Snow. 1978: Because He's My Friend. 1979: The Legend of the Golden Gun (TV). 1980: The Hostage Tower. Brave New World (TV). 1981: No Place to Hide (TV). 1982: The Next One. Brainwaves. 1983: Blind Date. 1984: 2010.

DUNAWAY, Faye 1941–
Blonde American actress with childlike face, horsey smile and purposeful air, not unlike Jane Fonda in acting approach and sub-surface smoulder. It's noticeable that both have been successful as gutsy women of pioneer days. Both are also Oscar-winners, Ms (impossible to think of Faye as Miss) Dunaway for her foul-mouthed TV executive in *Network*. Also Oscar-nominated for *Bonnie and Clyde* and *Chinatown*.
1966: The Happening. Hurry Sundown. 1967: Bonnie and Clyde. 1968: The Extraordinary Seaman. The Thomas Crown Affair. Amanti (GB and US: A Place for Lovers). 1969: The Arrangement. 1970: Little Big Man. Puzzle of a Downfall Child. 1971: Doc. The Deadly Trap. 1972: The Woman I Love (TV). 1973: Oklahoma Crude. The Three Musketeers. 1974: The Towering Inferno. The Four Musketeers. Chinatown. 1975: Three Days of the Condor. 1976: The Disappearance of Aimée (TV). Voyage of the Damned. Network. 1978: Eyes of Laura Mars. The Champ. 1979: Arthur Miller – on Home Ground. 1980: The First Deadly Sin. 1981: Mommie Dearest. Evita Peron (TV). 1983: The Wicked Lady. Supergirl. 1984: Ordeal by Innocence. 1985: Thirteen at Dinner (TV). 1986: Beverly Hills Madam (TV).

DUNN, James 1901–1967
Genial, smooth-faced Hollywood actor of Irish extraction, a lightweight Pat O'Brien who always looked older than his years. Made a sensational debut, played beautifully opposite Shirley Temple and won an Acad-

emy Award for *A Tree Grows in Brooklyn*. But there was an awful lot of dross, even after the Oscar. Died after a stomach operation. Married (second of three) to Frances Gifford (*qv*) from 1938 to 1941.

1931: Bad Girl. Sob Sister (GB: The Blonde Reporter). Over the Hill. 1932: Society Girl. Dance Team. Handle with Care. 1933: Hello, Sister! The Girl in 419. Hold Me Tight. Sailor's Luck. Jimmy and Sally. Take a Chance. Arizona to Broadway. 1934: Hold That Girl! Have a Heart. Change of Heart. Stand Up and Cheer. Baby Take a Bow. 365 Nights in Hollywood. Bright Eyes. She Learned about Sailors. 1935: George White's 1935 Scandals. The Pay-Off. Welcome Home. The Daring Young Man. Bad Boy. 1936: Hearts in Bondage. Don't Get Personal. Come Closer, Folks. Two-Fisted Gentleman. 1937: Mysterious Crossing. Living on Love. We Have Our Moments. Venus Makes Trouble. 1938: Shadows over Shanghai. 1939: Pride of the Navy. Mercy Plane (GB: Wonder Plane). 1940: Son of the Navy. Hold That Woman. A Fugitive from Justice. 1942: The Living Ghost. 1943: The Ghost and the Guest. Government Girl. 1944: Leave It to the Irish. A Tree Grows in Brooklyn. 1945: The Caribbean Mystery. 1946: That Brennan Girl. 1947: Killer McCoy. 1948: Texas, Brooklyn and Heaven (GB: The Girl from Texas). 1950: The Golden Gloves Story. 1951: A Wonderful Life. 1960: The Bramble Bush. Journey to the Day (TV). 1962: The Nine Lives of Elfego Baca (TV. GB: cinemas). Hemingway's Adventures of a Young Man (GB: Adventures of a Young Man). Six Gun Law (TV. GB: cinemas). 1966: The Oscar. 1967: The Movie Maker (TV). 1968: Shadow over Elveron (TV).

DUNNE, Irene (I. Dunn) 1898–
Ladylike but spunky leading actress, one of Hollywood's brightest stars in the thirties and early forties. Trained as a singer, she came to straight acting with sound, and proved capable of conveying a wide range of moods, from soapy melodrama to lunatic comedy. One of those careers that was unlucky not to have an Oscar in it along the way: she was nominated five times but never won.

1930: Leathernecking (GB: Present Arms). 1931: Consolation Marriage (GB: Married in Haste). Cimarron. Bachelor Apartment. The

*Great Lover. 1932: Symphony of Six Million (GB: Melody of Life). Thirteen Women. *The Stolen Jools (GB: The Slippery Pearls). Back Street. 1933: The Secret of Madame Blanche. No Other Woman. The Silver Cord. Ann Vickers. If I Were Free (GB: Behold We Live). 1934: This Man is Mine. Stingaree. The Age of Innocence. 1935: Magnificent Obsession. Sweet Adeline. Roberta. 1936: Show Boat. Theodora Goes Wild. 1937: High, Wide and Handsome. The Awful Truth. 1938: Joy of Living. 1939: Invitation to Happiness. Love Affair. When Tomorrow Comes. 1940: My Favorite Wife. 1941: Penny Serenade. Unfinished Business. 1942: Lady in a Jam. 1943: *Show Business at War. A Guy Named Joe. 1944: Together Again. The White Cliffs of Dover. 1945: Over 21. 1946: Anna and the King of Siam. 1947: Life with Father. 1948: I Remember Mama. 1950: Never a Dull Moment. The Mudlark. 1952: It Grows on Trees.*

DUPREZ, June 1918–1984
Lovely, dark-haired British leading lady who sprang to prominence as Ethne in the 1939 version of *The Four Feathers*. After *The Thief of Bagdad*, also for Alexander Korda, she stayed in Hollywood and made a few more films there before retiring to marry. Daughter of character actor Fred Duprez (1884–1938).

1935: The Amateur Gentleman. 1936: The Crimson Circle. The Cardinal. 1939: The Spy in Black (US: U-Boat 29). The Four Feathers. The Lion Has Wings. 1940: The Thief of Bagdad. 1941: Don Winslow of the Coast Guard (serial). 1942: Little Tokyo USA. They Raid by Night. 1943: Forever and A Day. Tiger Fangs. 1944: None but the Lonely Heart. 1945: The Brighton Strangler. And Then There Were None (GB: Ten Little Niggers). 1946: Calcutta. That Brennan Girl. 1961: The Kinsey Report.

DURANTE, Jimmy 'Schnozzle'
1893–1980
Big-nosed, gravel-voiced, piano-playing American comedian with a unique repertoire of inspired comic songs. Under contract to M-G-M for many years, but the studio never really projected his personality properly, and he remained at his best in solo spots, night clubs and records. Died from pneumonia.

1930: Roadhouse Nights. 1931: Cuban Love

*Song. The New Adventures of Get-Rich-Quick Wallingford. 1932: The Wet Parade. The Passionate Plumber. The Phantom President. Speak Easily. *Hollywood on Parade No. 3. Blondie of the Follies. 1933: Hell Below. What! No Beer? Meet the Baron. Broadway to Hollywood (GB: Ring Up the Curtain). 1934: George White's Scandals. She Learned about Sailors. Hollywood Party. Strictly Dynamite. Palooka (GB: The Great Schnozzle). Student Tour. Carnival. 1938: Start Cheering. Little Miss Broadway. Forbidden Music. Sally, Irene and Mary. 1940: Melody Ranch. 1941: You're in the Army Now. The Man Who Came to Dinner. 1944: Two Girls and a Sailor. Music for Millions. 1946: Two Sisters from Boston. 1947: It Happened in Brooklyn. This Time for Keeps. 1948: On an Island with You. 1950: The Milkman. The Great Rupert. 1957: Beau James. 1960: Pepe. 1961: Il giudizio universale (US: The Last Judgment). 1962: Billy Rose's Jumbo (GB: Jumbo). 1963: It's a Mad, Mad, Mad, Mad World.*

DURBIN, Deanna
(Edna Mae Durbin) 1921–
Auburn-haired, blue-eyed, oval-faced Canadian songstress with fresh, natural appeal who, almost single-handed, kept her studio (Universal) financially afloat with her appealing charms and lilting soprano until Abbott and Costello came along a few years later. Special Academy Award 1938. Married (third of three) French director Charles David in 1950 and retired to live in France.

*1936: *Every Sunday. Three Smart Girls.*

1937: One Hundred Men and a Girl. 1938: That Certain Age. Mad About Music. 1939: Three Smart Girls Grow Up. First Love. 1940: Spring Parade. It's a Date. 1941: Nice Girl? It Started with Eve. 1943: The Amazing Mrs Holliday. Hers to Hold. His Butler's Sister. 1944: Christmas Holiday. *The Shining Future. Can't Help Singing. 1945: Lady on a Train. Because of Him. 1946: I'll Be Yours. 1947: Something in the Wind. 1948: Up in Central Park. For the Love of Mary.

DURYEA Dan 1907–1968
Tall, fair-haired, lean, laconic, mean-looking American actor who came late to films but quickly made himself a fixture. He was one of the cinema's finest purveyors of nastiness: his villains were vindictive and even his heroes were unscrupulous. Briefly in star roles at the end of the forties, but later mostly as western bad guys with a whining, wheedling charm. Died from cancer.
1941: The Little Foxes. Ball of Fire. 1942: That Other Woman. The Pride of the Yankees. 1943: Sahara. Ministry of Fear. 1944: Mrs Parkington. None But the Lonely Heart. The Woman in the Window. Main Street After Dark. Man from Frisco. 1945: Scarlet Street. Lady on a Train. Along Came Jones. The Great Flamarion. Valley of Decision. 1946: Black Angel. White Tie and Tails. 1948: Black Bart (GB: Black Bart Highwayman). River Lady. Larceny. Another Part of the Forest. 1949: Criss Cross. Too Late for Tears. Manhandled. Johnny Stool Pigeon. 1950: One Way Street. Winchester 73. The Underworld Story. 1951: Chicago Calling. Al Jennings of Oklahoma. 1953: Sky Commando. Thunder Bay. Ride Clear of Diablo. 1954: World for Ransom. 36 Hours (US: Terror Street). Rails into Laramie. Silver Lode. This is My Love. 1955: Foxfire. The Marauders. Storm Fear. The Burglar. 1956: Battle Hymn. Smoke Jumpers (TV). 1957: Night Passage. Slaughter on 10th Avenue. 1958: Kathy O'. 1959: Showdown at Sandoval (TV. GB: cinemas as Gunfight at Sandoval). 1960: Platinum High School (GB: Rich, Young and Deadly). 1961: Six Black Horses. 1963: He Rides Tall. Walk a Tightrope. 1964: Taggart. Do You Know This Voice? 1965: The Bounty Killer. The Flight of the Phoenix. 1966: Incident at Phantom Hill. Un fiume di dollari (GB: The Hills Run Red). 1967: Five Golden Dragons. Stranger on the

Run (TV). Winchester '73 (TV). 1968: The Bamboo Saucer/Collision Course.

DUVALL, Robert 1931–
Slight, balding, generally unsmiling, but forceful and personable American actor with distinctive thin, outlined lips and pale blue eyes. A Korean War veteran, he turned to acting and could probably have made a lifetime career out of psychotic villains had not a desire for versatility been stronger. In leading roles – with odd little regressions to support or even unbilled guest appearances – since the early 1970s, he was nominated three times for an Academy Award (The Godfather, Apocalypse Now, The Great Santini) before winning the Best Actor Oscar for Tender Mercies.
1960: John Brown's Raid (TV). Destiny's Tot (TV). 1962: To Kill a Mockingbird. 1963: Captain Newman MD. Nightmare in the Sun. 1965: The Chase. 1966: Fame is the Name of the Game (TV). 1967: Cosa Nostra: An Arch Enemy of the FBI (TV. GB: cinemas). 1968: Countdown. Bullitt. The Detective. 1969: True Grit. The Rain People. M*A*S*H. 1970: Lawman. 1971: The Revolutionary. THX 1138. Tomorrow (released 1975). 1972: The Godfather. The Great Northfield Minnesota Raid. Joe Kidd. 1973: Badge 373. Lady Ice. The Outfit. 1974: The Conversation. The Godfather Part II. 1975: Breakout. The Killer Elite. 1976: Network. The Seven Per Cent Solution. The Eagle Has Landed. 1977: The Greatest. 1978: Invasion of the Body Snatchers. The Betsy. 1979: The Great Santini. Apocalypse Now. 1981: True Confessions. The Pursuit of D B Cooper. 1982: Tender Mercies. 1983: The Terry Fox Story (made for TV, but later shown in cinemas). 1984: The Natural. The Stone Boy. 1985: The Lightship. Belizaire the Cajun. 1986: Let's Get Harry. Hotel Colonial.

As director: 1974: We're Not the Jet Set. 1983: Angelo My Love.

DUVALL, Shelley 1949–
Very thin, dark-haired American actress with huge, brown, bird-like eyes, long thin nose and thick, if attractive, lips: as one might expect, she is good at nervousness and insecurity. Chiefly seen in films by Robert Altman, and especially good in his Three Women. Perfectly cast as Olive Oyl in Popeye,

but little heard of since that film was made in 1980.
1970: Brewster McCloud. 1971: McCabe and Mrs Miller. 1974: Thieves Like Us. Un homme qui dort (voice only). 1975: Nashville. 1976: Buffalo Bill and the Indians, or: Sitting Bull's History Lesson. Bernice Bobs Her Hair. 1977: Annie Hall. Three Women. 1980: The Shining. Popeye. 1981: Time Bandits. 1985: Annie Oakley (TV. Narrator only).

DVORAK, Ann
(Anna McKim) 1911–1979
Brunette (later blonde) American actress, daughter of silent actress Anna Lehr. Her prominent nose and slanty green eyes may have been the cause of her getting cast so often (after a brilliant early performance in Scarface) in sluttish or spiteful roles. But her career was not helped by her fight with Warners over better roles. Married (first of three) to British-born actor-director Leslie Fenton from 1932 to 1946.
1916: †Ramona. 1920: †The Five Dollar Plate. 1929: The Hollywood Revue of 1929. 1930: Free and Easy. Love in the Rough. Way Out West. Lord Byron of Broadway (GB: What Price Melody?). 1931: Son of India. Susan Lenox, Her Fall and Rise (GB: The Rise of Helga). The Guardsman. Just a Gigolo (GB: The Dancing Partner). Politics. This Modern Age. Dance, Fools, Dance. La Sevillana. 1932: Sky Devils. The Crowd Roars. The Strange Love of Molly Louvain. Love is a Racket. Scarface. Stranger in Town. Three on a Match. Crooner. 1933: The Way to Love. College Coach (GB: Football Coach). 1934: Heat Lightning. Massacre. Side Streets (GB:

Woman in her Thirties). Friends of Mr Sweeney. Midnight Alibi. Housewife. I Sell Anything. Gentlemen Are Born. Murder in the Clouds. 1935: Sweet Music. 'G' Men. * A Trip thru a Hollywood Studio. Bright Lights (GB: Funnyface). Folies Bergère de Paris (GB: The Man from Folies Bergère). Dr Socrates. Thanks a Million. 1936: We Who Are about to Die. 1937: Racing Lady. Midnight Court. Manhattan Merry-Go-Round (GB: Manhattan

Music Box). The Case of the Stuttering Bishop. She's No Lady. 1938: Merrily We Live. Gangs of New York. 1939: Blind Alley. Café Hostess (GB: Street of Missing Women). Stronger than Desire. 1940: Street of Missing Women. Girls of the Road. 1941: Don Winslow of the Navy (serial). This Was Paris. 1942: Squadron Leader X. 1943: Escape to Danger. There's a Future in It. 1945: Flame of the Barbary Coast. Masquerade in Mexico. Abilene Town. 1946:

The Bachelor's Daughters (GB: Bachelor Girls). 1947. The Long Night. The Private Affairs of Bel Ami. Out of the Blue. 1948: The Walls of Jericho. 1950: A Life of Her Own. Mrs O'Malley and Mr Malone. Our Very Own. The Return of Jesse James. 1951: The Secret of Convict Lake. I Was an American Spy.

† *as Baby Anna Lehr.*

Doyenne dames (*grande* variety). Bette Davis and Olivia de Havilland get to grips in *Hush ... Hush, Sweet Charlotte* in 1964.

Eastwood (Clint) and Everloving friend (Clyde) in 1978's *Every Which Way But Loose*. That's Clint on the left ...

F for family Fonda. Father Henry and daughter Jane together on location in 1981 for his Oscar-winning *On Golden Pond*.

EASTWOOD, Clint 1930–

Tall, dark American actor with soft, deliberate speech who came to fame in the TV western series *Rawhide* (1958–1965), then went to Italy and gained even bigger stardom as ultra-tough, silent western heroes who blew their opponents apart at the twitch of a nostril. Back in Hollywood, he mixed westerners with equally brutish police detectives, but his ventures into direction, although erratic, revealed a more interesting, and talented, side of his nature.

1955: *Revenge of the Creature. Francis in the Navy. Lady Godiva (GB: Lady Godiva of Coventry). Tarantula!* 1956: *Away All Boats. Never Say Goodbye. Star in the Dust. The First Traveling Saleslady.* 1957: *Escapade in Japan. Lafayette Escadrille (GB: Hell Bent for Glory).* 1958: *Ambush at Cimarron Pass.* 1964: *A Fistful of Dollars.* 1965: *For a Few Dollars More.* 1966: *The Good, the Bad and the Ugly. The Witches.* 1967: *Hang 'Em High.* 1968: *Coogan's Bluff. Where Eagles Dare.* 1969: *Paint Your Wagon. Two Mules for Sister Sara.* 1970: *Kelly's Heroes. The Beguiled.* 1971: *Dirty Harry. Play 'Misty' for Me.* 1972: *Joe Kidd. High Plains Drifter.* 1973: *Magnum Force. Breezy.* 1974: *Thunderbolt and Lightfoot.* 1975: *The Eiger Sanction.* 1976: *The Outlaw Josey Wales. The Enforcer.* 1977: *The Gauntlet.* 1978: *Every Which Way But Loose.* 1979: *Escape from Alcatraz.* 1980: *Bronco Billy. Any Which Way You Can.* 1982: *Firefox.* 1983: *Honkytonk Man. Sudden Impact.* 1984: *City Heat. Tightrope.* 1985: *Pale Rider.* 1986: *Heartbreak Ridge.*

As director:
1971: *Play 'Misty' for Me.* 1972: *High Plains Drifter.* 1973: *Breezy.* 1975: *The Eiger Sanction.* 1976: *The Outlaw Josey Wales.* 1977: *The Gauntlet.* 1980: *Bronco Billy.* 1982: *Firefox.* 1983: *Honkytonk Man. Sudden Impact.* 1985: *Pale Rider.*

EATON, Shirley 1936–

Bright, bouncy British blonde, a teenage sex-pot and her own best publicist. A sexy stooge on radio at 16, she seemed to be everywhere in the fifties, singing, dancing, panel-gaming, acting or just being interviewed. The potential to make her into a top star, though, was never quite there and her appearances had dwindled significantly a decade on.

1954: *You Know What Sailors Are. The Belles of St Trinian's. Doctor in the House.* 1955: *The Love Match.* 1956: *Charley Moon. Sailor Beware! (US: Panic in the Parlor). Three Men in a Boat.* 1957: *Doctor at Large. Date with Disaster. The Naked Truth (US: Your Past is Showing).* 1958: *Carry On Sergeant. Further Up the Creek. Life is a Circus.* 1959: *Carry On Nurse. In the Wake of a Stranger.* 1960: *Carry on Constable.* 1961: *A Weekend with Lulu. Nearly a Nasty Accident. Dentist on the Job (US: Get On with It!). What a Carve Up! (US: Home Sweet Homicide).* 1963: *The Girl Hunters.* 1964: *Goldfinger. The Naked Brigade.* 1965: *Around the World Under the Sea. Ten Little Indians.* 1966: *The Scorpio Letters (TV. GB: cinemas). Eight on the Lam (GB: Eight on the Run).* 1967: *Sumuru (US: The 1,000,000 Eyes of Sumuru).* 1968: *The Blood of Fu Manchu (US: Kiss and Kill/Fu Manchu and the Kiss of Death).* 1969: *The Seven Men of Sumuru.*

EBSEN, Buddy (Christian Ebsen) 1908–

Lanky, dark-haired, disgruntled-looking American actor-dancer who proved extremely tenacious career-wise after he came to Hollywood in 1935 with sister and stage partner Vilma. Specializing in 'countrified characters', Ebsen faltered after war service, then found one profitable slot after another, first playing second-fiddle to Fess Parker in the Davy Crockett series, then on TV as head of *The Beverly Hillbillies.* At 64, he found audience favour again on TV as Barnaby Jones, a sort of elderly Will Rogers-type sleuth. 'On TV,' he says, 'they had fat detectives, young detectives, girl detectives – everything but old, tall

detectives.' If they ever make a series about an old folks' home, the odds are that Ebsen'll be right in there.

1935: *Broadway Melody of 1936.* 1936: *Captain January. Banjo on My Knee. Born to Dance.* 1937: *Broadway Melody of 1938.* 1938: *Yellow Jack. My Lucky Star. The Girl of the Golden West.* 1939: *Four Girls in White. The Kid from Texas.* 1941: *Parachute Battalion. They Met in Argentina.* 1942: *Sing Your Worries Away.* 1950: *Under Mexicali Stars.* 1951: *Silver City Bonanza. Thunder in God's Country. Rodeo King and the Senorita. Utah Wagon Train.* 1954: *Red Garters. Night People. Davy Crockett – King of the Wild Frontier.* 1955: *Davy Crockett and the River Pirates.* 1956: *Between Heaven and Hell. Attack!* 1958: *Frontier Rangers.* 1959: *Mission of Danger. A Trip to Paradise (TV). Free Weekend (TV).* 1961: *Breakfast at Tiffany's.* 1962: *The Interns.* 1963: *Mail Order Bride (GB: West of Montana).* 1968: *The One and Only Genuine Original Family Band.* 1972: *The Daughters of Joshua Cabe (TV).* 1973: *Horror at 37,000 Feet (TV. GB: cinemas). Tom Sawyer. The President's Plane is Missing (TV).* 1976: *Smash-Up on Interstate Five (TV).* 1978: *Leave Yesterday Behind (TV). The Critical List (TV).* 1979: *Final Judgment (TV. Originally material from the 'Barnaby Jones' series). The Paradise Connection (TV).* 1980: *Nightmare in Hawaii (TV).* 1981: *Fire on the Mountain (TV). The Return of the Beverly Hillbillies (TV).*

EDDY, Nelson 1901–1967

Very blond, square-shouldered, serious-looking American baritone who, with Jeanette

MacDonald (*qv*), became the cinema's most successful singing team in a series of thirties' musicals which, despite phenomenal box-office success and public adulation, brought Eddy a critical panning for his stiff and awkward attempts at dramatic acting. Became a successful night-club entertainer in later years, and died from a stroke shortly after a performance.

1933: Broadway to Hollywood (GB: Ring Up the Curtain). Dancing Lady. 1934: Student Tour. 1935: Naughty Marietta. 1936: Rose Marie. 1937: Maytime. Rosalie. 1938: Girl of the Golden West. Sweethearts. 1939: Let Freedom Ring. Balalaika. 1940: New Moon. Bitter Sweet. 1941: The Chocolate Soldier. 1942: I Married an Angel. 1943: The Phantom of the Opera. 1944: Knickerbocker Holiday. 1946: Make Mine Music (voice only). 1947: Northwest Outpost (GB: End of the Rainbow).

EDEN, Barbara (B. Huffman) 1934–
Durable blonde American actress and singer with pert face and lithe, curvy figure. Had she been around a decade earlier, Universal would have welcomed her with open arms to their easterns; but in the early sixties at Fox she had difficulty establishing herself. Since then, with the help of a successful TV series – *I Dream of Jeannie* (1965–1969) – and a widening range, she has clung tenaciously to her career as a leading actress. Married to Michael Ansara (1922–   ) from 1958 to 1973.

1956: Back from Eternity. 1957: Will Success Spoil Rock Hunter (GB: Oh! for a Man). The Wayward Girl. 1959: A Private's Affair. 1960: The Schnook (GB: Double Trouble). Twelve Hours to Kill. From the Terrace. Flaming Star. 1961: All Hands on Deck. Voyage to the Bottom of the Sea. 1962: Five Weeks in a Balloon. The Interns. The Wonderful World of the Brothers Grimm. Swingin' Along (revised version of The Schnook). 1963: The Yellow Canary. 1964: The Brass Bottle. The New Interns. The Seven Faces of Dr Lao. Ride the Wild Surf. The Confession (GB: TV as Quick! Let's Get Married). 1970: The Feminist and the Fuzz (TV). 1971: A Howling in the Woods (TV). 1972: The Woman Hunter (TV). 1973: Guess Who's Sleeping in My Bed (TV). 1974: The Stranger Within (TV). 1975: Let's Switch (TV). 1976: How to Break Up a Happy Divorce (TV). 1977: The Amazing Dobermans. Stonestreet (TV). 1978: Harper Valley PTA. 1979: The

Girls in the Office (TV). 1981: Return of the Rebels (TV). 1983: Jaws 3-D. 1984: Chattanooga Choo Choo. 1986: I Dream of Jeannie: 15 Years Later (TV).

EDWARDS, Henry (Ethelbert Edwards) 1882–1952
Tall, dark, sober-faced, stalwart British leading man of silent days who also directed many of his films. He married his oft-time co-star Chrissie White (*qv*), and they became Britain's most popular film couple of the silent era. After World War II, Edwards began a new career as a character actor, mostly as men of authority, but it was destined to last only a few years.

*1914: A Bachelor's Love Story. *Clancarty. 1915: Alone in London. My Old Dutch. Lost and Won/Odds Against. Far from the Madding Crowd. The Man Who Stayed at Home. A Welsh Singer. 1916: Doorsteps. Grim Justice. East is East. 1917: Merely Mrs Stubbs. The Cobweb. The Failure. Broken Threads. Nearer My God to Thee. 1918: The Touch of a Child. The Hanging Judge. *A New Version. *The Message. *Against the Grain. *Anna. *Her Savings Saved. *The Street. *The Refugee. *Tares. Towards the Light. *The Poet's Windfall. *Old Mother Hubbard. *The Inevitable. *What's the Use of Grumbling? 1919: *Broken in the Wars. The Kinsman. Possession. The City of Beautiful Nonsense. His Dearest Possession. 1920: A Temporary Vagabond. Aylwin. The Amazing Quest of Mr Ernest Bliss. John Forrest Finds Himself. 1921: The Bargain. The Lunatic at Large. 1922: Simple Simon. Tit for Tat. 1923: Lily of the Alley. Boden's Boy. The Naked Man. 1924: The World of Wonderful Reality. 1926: *Screen Magazine No. 3. The Flag Lieutenant. 1927: The Fake. Further Adventures of the Flag Lieutenant. 1928: Ein Mödel und drei Clowns. Angst. Der Faschingskönig. Indizienbeweiss. 1929: The Three Kings. Ringing the Changes. 1930: The Call of the Sea. 1931: The Girl in the Night. 1932: The Flag Lieutenant (remake). 1933: General John Regan. 1934: D'Ye Ken John Peel? (US: Captain Moonlight). The Rocks of Valpré (US: High Treason). 1937: Captain's Orders. 1940: East of Piccadilly (US: The Strangler). Spring Meeting. 1946: The Magic Bow. Green for Danger. 1947: Take My Life. 1948: Woman Hater. Oliver Twist. London Belongs to Me (US: Dulcimer Street). Quartet. The Brass*

Monkey (later Lucky Mascot). All Over the Town. 1949: Dear Mr Prohack. Elizabeth of Ladymead. 1950: Golden Salamander. Double Confession. Madeleine. Trio. 1951: Othello. The Rossiter Case. White Corridors. The Magic Box. The Lady with a Lamp. 1952: Never Look Back. Trent's Last Case. Something Money Can't Buy. The Long Memory.

As director:

1915: A Welsh Singer. 1916: Doorsteps. East is East. 1917: Merely Mrs Stubbs. Dick Carson Wins Through. Broken Threads. 1918: The Hanging Judge. Towards the Light. 1919: His Dearest Possession. The Kinsman. Possession. The City of Beautiful Nonsense. 1920: A Temporary Vagabond. Aylwin. The Amazing Quest of Mr Ernest Bliss. John Forrest Finds Himself. 1921: The Lunatic at Large. The Bargain. 1922: Simple Simon. Tit for Tat. 1923: Lily of the Alley. The Naked Man. Boden's Boy. 1924: The World of Wonderful Reality. 1925: King of the Castle. A Girl of London. One Colombo Night. 1926: The Island of Despair. 1931: The Girl in the Night. Stranglehold. 1932: Brother Alfred. The Flag Lieutenant. The Barton Mystery. 1933: General John Regan. 1934: The Man Who Changed His Name. The Lash. Lord Edgware Dies. Are You a Mason? 1935: The Lad. Vintage Wine. Squibs. Scrooge. The Private Secretary. 1936: Eliza Comes to Stay. In the Soup. Juggernaut. 1937: Beauty and the Barge. The Vicar of Bray. Song of the Forge. 1940: Spring Meeting.

EDWARDS, Jimmy 1920–
Bluff, hearty British comedian with large, round face and handlebar moustache, immensely successful on post-war radio after leaving the RAF with the Distinguished Flying Cross. A bombastic stand-up funnyman, in the character of a hectoring schoolmaster ('Wake up at the back there'), he was heard at his best in radio's long-running *Take It from Here*, followed later by his portrait of the headmaster of Chiselbury School in *Whack-O!* Films could not cope with his explosive style, but there have been some barnstorming latter-day performances, full of ad-libs, for theatre audiences to relish.

*1948: Trouble in the Air. 1949: Murder at the Windmill (US: Murder at the Burlesque). Helter Skelter. 1952: Treasure Hunt. *Sport and Speed. 1953: Innocents in Paris. 1955: An*

Alligator Named Daisy. 1956: Three Men in a Boat. 1960: Bottoms Up! 1961: Nearly a Nasty Accident. 1967: The Plank. A Ghost of a Chance. 1968: Lionheart. 1969: The Bed Sitting Room. 1970: Rhubarb. 1971: The Magnificent Six and a Half (3rd series). 1972: Anoop and the Elephant.

EDWARDS, Penny (Millicent Edwards) 1928–

As pretty a prairie flower as ever rode the range, Penny Edwards languished in Roy Rogers westerns and made too few films. The blonde American actress was in the Ziegfeld Follies at 12 and films at 19. Fox made a brief attempt to build her into a bigger star, but nothing much seemed to happen. Her daughter is actress Deborah Winters, who inherited her mother's precocity by marrying at 15.

1947: That Hagen Girl. My Wild Irish Rose. 1948: Two Guys from Texas (GB: Two Texas Knights). Feudin', Fussin', and a-Fightin'. 1949: Tucson. 1950: Sunset in the West. North of the Great Divide. Trail of Robin Hood. 1951: Spoilers of the Plains. Heart of the Rockies. In Old Amarillo. Utah Wagon Train. Missing Women. The Wild Blue Yonder (GB: Thunder Across the Pacific). Million Dollar Pursuit. Street Bandits. 1952: Captive of Billy the Kid. Pony Soldier (GB: MacDonald of the Canadian Mounties). Woman in the Dark. 1953: Powder River. 1957: Ride a Violent Mile. The Dalton Girls. Johnny Bravo (TV. GB: cinemas).

EDWARDS, Vince (Vincento Edouardo Zoino) 1926–

Dark, squarely built, thick-haired, slightly soulful-looking American actor who was an Olympic swimming prospect before taking acting lessons in such distinguished company as Grace Kelly, John Cassavetes and Anne Bancroft. His immobile features often got him cast in faintly dangerous roles before success in the title role of television's Ben Casey gave him a softer image and a pin-up's mail-bag. Has made films only inconsistently (his main body of work has been for TV), but also has talents as a singer and a photographer.

1951: Mr Universe. Sailor Beware. 1952: Hiawatha. 1954: Rogue Cop. 1955: The Night Holds Terror. 1956: The Killing. Serenade. Cell 2455 Death Row. Hit and Run. 1957: The Hired Gun. 1958: Island Women. Ride Out

for Revenge. 1959: City of Fear. Murder by Contract. The Scavengers. 1961: The Outsider. 1963: The Victors. 1967: The Devil's Brigade. 1968: Hammerhead. The Marauders (TV). 1969: The Desperados. 1970: Sole Survivor (TV). Dial Hot Line (TV). 1971: Do Not Fold, Spindle or Mutilate (TV). 1972: The Mad Bomber. 1973: Firehouse (TV). 1974: The Police Connection. 1975: Death Stalk (TV). 1977: Cover Girls (TV). 1978: The Courage and the Passion (TV). A Chance to Live (TV). 1981: The Seduction. Knight Rider (TV). 1983: Space Raiders. 1984: Texas Sno-Line. 1985: The Fix (filmed in 1983 as The Agitators). 1986: Vasectomy, a Delicate Matter. The Return of Mike Hammer (TV).

As co-director:
1979: Mission Galactica – the Cylon Attack (TV. GB: cinemas).

EGAN, Richard 1921–

Big, beefy American leading man with square face and wide, white-toothed smile. At one time spoken of as a successor to Clark Gable but, although he was popular in rugged roles after a good performance in Split Second, there was nothing to suggest that Egan possessed Gable's gift for comedy or, indeed, his range, and he slid rapidly into television after the late fifties.

1950: Return of the Frontiersman. The Good Humor Man. The Damned Don't Cry. The Killer That Stalked New York (GB: The Frightened City). Wyoming Mail. Kansas Raiders. Undercover Girl. Bright Victory (GB: Lights Out). 1951: Hollywood Story. Up Front. The Golden Horde. Highway 301. Flame

of Araby. 1952: Battle at Apache Pass. The Devil Makes Three. One Minute to Zero. Cripple Creek. Blackbeard the Pirate. 1953: Split Second. The Glory Brigade. Wicked Woman. The Kid from Left Field. 1954: Gog. Demetrius and the Gladiators. Khyber Patrol. Underwater. 1955: Untamed. Violent Saturday. Seven Cities of Gold. The View from Pompey's Head (GB: Secret Interlude). 1956: The Revolt of Mamie Stover. Love Me Tender. Tension at Table Rock. 1957: Slaughter on 10th Avenue. 1958: These Thousand Hills. Voice in the Mirror. The Hunters. 1959: A Summer Place. 1960: Pollyanna. Esther and the King. 1962: The 300 Spartans. This Rugged Land (TV. GB: cinemas). 1966: The Destructors. 1967: Valley of Mystery. 1968: Chubasco. 1969: The Big Cube. 1970: The Day of the Wolves. Moonfire. The House That Wouldn't Die (TV). 1972: The Left Hand of Gemini. 1973: Shoot-Out in a One-Dog Town (TV). 1976: Throw Out the Anchor (TV). 1977: The Amsterdam Kill. Kino, the Padre on Horseback. 1978: Ravagers. The Sweet Creek County War.

EGE, Julie 1943–

Shapely, sultry Norwegian pin-up girl who decorated the pages of many British newspapers and magazines in various states of undress before bringing her charms to the cinema. A leading role in Creatures the World Forgot revealed her acting as too awkward to make her a second Raquel Welch, and she moved to decoration in comedies.

1969: On Her Majesty's Secret Service. 1970: Every Home Should Have One. Creatures the World Forgot. 1971: Up Pompeii. Rentadick. The Magnificent Seven Deadly Sins. 1972: The Alf Garnett Saga. Go for a Take. Not Now Darling. 1973: The Final Programme. Craze. 1974: Percy's Progress. The Amorous Milkman. The Legend of the Seven Golden Vampires. The Mutations. Kanari Fuglen. 1975: Bortreist pa Ubestemt Tid. Flexnes. 1976: Sherlock Jones. Sekretaerena som Forsuant.

EGGAR, Samantha (Victoria S. Eggar) 1938–

Pretty, chestnut-haired British leading lady of natural, 'outdoor' appeal. Reminiscent of America's Katharine Ross (qv), she was mainly seen as resourceful heroines, especially in her earlier days. It's difficult to analyse why

she did not progress further up the ladder to international stardom; some of her later performances perhaps reflect her disappointment at not having achieved this, as she mingled TV drama 'guest' spots with some often bizarre motion pictures. Oscar-nominated for *The Collector*.

1961: *The Wild and the Willing*. 1962: *Dr Crippen*. 1963: *Doctor in Distress. Psyche 59*. 1965: *Return from the Ashes. The Collector*. 1966: *Walk Don't Run*. 1967: *Doctor Dolittle*. 1968: *The Molly Maguires*. 1970: *The Walking Stick. The Lady in the Car with Glasses and a Gun*. 1971: *L'etrusco uccide ancora* (US: *The Dead Are Alive*). *The Light at the Edge of the World*. 1973: *Double Indemnity* (TV). *A Name for Evil* (TV). 1974: *All the Kind Strangers* (TV). *Help on My Terms* (TV). 1976: *The Seven-Per-Cent Solution. The Killer Who Wouldn't Die* (TV). *Why Shoot the Teacher?* 1977: *The Uncanny. Welcome to Blood City. Il grande attacca* (US: *The Biggest Battle*). 1978: *Ziegfeld: The Man and His Women* (TV). 1979: *Hagen* (TV). *The Brood*. 1980: *The Exterminator. Macabra* (US: *Demonoid*). *French Kiss*. 1981: *Hot Touch. Curtains* (released 1983).

EILERS, Sally (Dorothea Sallye Eilers) 1908–1978
Brunette (blonde from late 1931 on) American actress of Jewish-Irish ancestry who entered Hollywood with school-friend Carole Lombard, and led just as active a social life. On screen, she was alternately seen in romantic or vampish roles. Beset by illness in later years. Married (first and second of four) to

western star Hoot Gibson (1930–1933) and producer Harry Joe Brown (1933–1943).

1927: **The Campus Carmen. *The Campus Vamp. *Matchmaking Mammas. Sunrise. Paid to Love. The Red Mill. Slightly Used*. 1928: *The Crowd. Cradle Snatchers. Dry Martini. Broadway Daddies* (GB: *Girl of the Night*). *The Good-Bye Kiss*. 1929: *Broadway Babies. Trial Marriage. The Show of Shows. The Long, Long Trail. Sailor's Holiday*. 1930: *Let Us Be Gay. She Couldn't Say No. Doughboys* (GB: *Forward March*). *Trigger Tricks. Roaring Ranch*. 1931: *Reducing. Quick Millions. The Black Camel. Clearing the Range. Parlor, Bedroom and Bath* (GB: *Romeo in Pyjamas*). *Bad Girl. Over the Hill. Dance Team. Holy Terror*. 1932: *Disorderly Conduct. Hat Check Girl* (GB: *Embassy Girl*). *Second Hand Wife* (GB: *The Illegal Divorce*). 1933: *State Fair. Made on Broadway* (GB: *The Girl I Made*). *I Spy* (US: *The Morning After*). *Sailor's Luck. Central Airport. Hold Me Tight. Walls of Gold*. 1934: *She Made Her Bed. Three on a Honeymoon*. 1935: *Carnival. Pursuit. Alias Mary Dow. Remember Last Night?* 1936: *Strike Me Pink. Don't Get Personal. Without Orders. Florida Special*. 1937: *We Have Our Moments. Danger Patrol. Lady Behave. Talk of the Devil*. 1938: *Condemned Women. The Nurse from Brooklyn. Tarnished Angel. Everybody's Doing It*. 1939: *They Made Her a Spy. Full Confession*. 1941: *I Was a Prisoner on Devil's Island*. 1942: **First Aid*. 1944: *A Wave, a Wac and a Marine*. 1945: *Out of the Night* (GB: *Strange Illusion*). 1948: *Coroner Creek*. 1950: *Stage to Tucson* (GB: *Lost Stage Valley*).

EKBERG, Anita 1931–
Big, tall, sultry-looking Swedish blonde, Miss Sweden of 1951 and subsequently briefly under contract to Howard Hughes. Her buxom and well-publicized charms, during a period in which she was known as The Ice Maiden, proved top box-office from the mid 1950s to the early 1960s. Married to actors Anthony Steel (1956–1962) and Rik Van Nutter (1963–1975). Suffered from on-off weight problems in later years.

1951: *Terras förster No 5*. 1953: *Abbott and Costello Go to Mars. Take Me to Town. The Golden Blade. Mississippi Gambler*. 1955: *Blood Alley. Artists and Models. Man in the Vault*. 1956: *War and Peace. Hollywood or

Bust. Back from Eternity. Zarak*. 1957: *Interpol* (US: *Pick-Up Alley*). *Valerie*. 1958: *Paris Holiday. Screaming Mimi. The Man Inside. Nel segno di Roma* (GB: *Sign of the Gladiator*). 1959: *La dolce vita. Apocalisse sul fiume giallo* (GB: *Last Train to Shanghai*. US: *The Dam on the Yellow River*). *Le tre ecetera del colonnello*. 1960: *Les cocottes* (GB: *The Call Girl Business*. US: *Little Girls and High Finance*). *A porte chiuse* (GB: *Behind Closed Doors*. US: *Behind Locked Doors*). 1961: *Il giudizio universale* (US: *The Last Judgement*). *The Mongols*. 1962: *Boccaccio 70*. 1963: *Call Me Bwana. Four for Texas*. 1964: *L'incastro. Bianco, rosso, giallo, rosa*. 1965: *Das Liebeskarussel* (GB and US: *Who Wants to Sleep?*). *The Alphabet Murders*. 1966: *Way ... Way Out. Scusi, lei e'favorevole o contrario? Come imparai ad amare le donne* (GB: *How I Learned to Love Women*). 1967: *The Cobra. Woman Times Seven. La sfinge d'oro* (GB: *The Glass Sphinx*). *Das Gewisse etwas der Frauen*. 1968: *Malenka, the Vampire's Niece*. 1969: *If It's Tuesday, This Must Be Belgium. Blonde Köder für den Mörder. La morte bussa due volte*. 1970: *Il debito coniugale. Il divorzio. The Clowns*. 1972: *North-East of Seoul*. 1973: *Fangs of the Living Dead*. 1974: *Das Tal der Witwen* (US: *Valley of the Widows*). 1975: *Death Knocks Twice*. 1978: *Suor omicidio* (GB: *The Killer Nun*). 1979: *Gold of the Amazon Women*. 1981: *Daisy Chain*.

EKLAND, Britt (Britt-Marie Eklund) 1942–
Blonde, kittenish Swedish actress, on the international scene since 1964; better known as the consort of famous men than for her acting ability, although this is not as negligible as some alleged. Her pin-up looks gained her endless newspaper coverage, as well as some interesting roles. Married to Peter Sellers, 1963–1968.

1962: *Kort ar Sommaren*. 1963: *Det är Hos Mig Han Her Varit. Il comandante. Il diavolo*. 1964: *Carol for Another Christmas* (TV). 1965: *Too Many Thieves* (TV. GB: *cinemas*). 1966: *After the Fox*. 1967: *The Double Man. The Bobo*. 1968: *The Night They Raided Minsky's*. 1969: *Stiletto. Nell'anno del Signore. Machine Gun McCain*. 1970: *Percy. I cannibali/The Cannibals. Get Carter. Tinto Mara*. 1971: *Endless Night. Night Hair Child. A Time for Loving*. 1972: *Asylum. Baxter!* 1973: *The*

Wicker Man. 1974: The Man with the Golden Gun. The Ultimate Thrill (US: The Ultimate Chase). 1975: Royal Flash. 1976: High Velocity. 1977: Casanova and Co (GB: The Rise and Rise of Casanova). Slavers. 1978: King Solomon's Treasure. Ring of Passion (TV). The Great Wallendas (TV). 1980: The Monster Club. The Hostage Tower. 1981: Dark Eyes (later Satan's Mistress). 1983: Erotic Images. 1984: Hellhole. 1985: Fraternity Vacation. Marbella. Love Scenes.

ELLIOTT, Denholm 1922–
Gentlemanly British actor who played true-blue fresh young men, often under fire in war, in British films of the fifties. Returned in the sixties in altogether different persona – that of dog-eared ex-public school type eager to sell his own mother up the river for money or personal advancement. Married to Virginia McKenna 1954–1956.
1949: Dear Mr Prohack. 1952: The Sound Barrier (US: Breaking the Sound Barrier). The Ringer. The Holly and the Ivy. 1953: The Cruel Sea. The Heart of the Matter. 1954: They Who Dare. Lease of Life. The Man Who Loved Redheads. 1955: The Night My Number Came Up. 1956: Pacific Destiny. 1960: Scent of Mystery (GB: Holiday in Spain). 1962: Station Six Sahara. 1963: Nothing But the Best. 1964: The High Bright Sun (US: McGuire Go Home!). 1965: You Must Be Joking! King Rat. 1966: Alfie. The Spy with a Cold Nose. Maroc 7. 1967: Here We Go round the Mulberry Bush. 1968: The Night They Raided Minsky's. 1969: The Sea Gull. Too Late the Hero. 1970: The Rise and Fall of Michael Rimmer. The House That Dripped Blood. Percy. 1971: Quest for Love. Madame Sin (TV. GB: cinemas). 1973: A Doll's House (Garland). Vault of Horror. 1974: Percy's Progress. The Apprenticeship of Duddy Kravitz. 1975: Russian Roulette. The Last Chapter. 1976: To the Devil a Daughter. Partners. Robin and Marian. Voyage of the Damned. 1977: A Bridge Too Far. The Hound of the Baskervilles. 1978: Sweeney 2. The Little Girl in Blue Velvet. The Boys from Brazil. Watership Down (voice only). 1979: Game for Vultures. Saint Jack. Zulu Dawn. Cuba. 1980: Rising Damp. Les séducteurs/Sunday Lovers. Bad Timing (US: Bad Timing/A Sensual Obsession). 1981: Raiders of the Lost Ark. 1982: Brimstone and Treacle. The Missionary.

1983: The Wicked Lady. The Hound of the Baskervilles (and 1977 film). Trading Places. 1984: A Private Function. Camille (TV). The Razor's Edge. 1985: Underworld. Defence of the Realm. A Room with a View. Hotel du Lac (TV). 1986: The Whoopee Boys. Mrs Delafield Wants to Marry (TV).

ELLIOTT, Sam 1944–
Dark-haired, muscular American leading man with thick moustache, often seen as faintly roguish types who come out all right in the end. Now turned 40, Elliott still seems to be having a tough time establishing himself as a consistent box-office star, despite one outstanding performance, in Lifeguard, in which the vulnerability behind his chunky façade was fully exposed. Long professionally and privately associated with actress Katharine Ross (qv); the couple married in 1984.
1968: The Games. 1970: Assault on the Wayne (TV). The Challenge (TV). 1971: Molly and Lawless John. 1972: Frogs. 1973: The Blue Knight (TV. GB: cinemas). 1975 I Will Fight No More Forever (TV). Evel Knievel (TV). 1976: Lifeguard. 1978: The Legacy. 1979: Wild Times (TV). The Sacketts (TV). The Last Convertible (TV). 1981: Murder in Texas (TV). 1982: The Shadow Riders (TV). 1984: Mask.

ELLIOTT, William 'Wild Bill' (Gordon Nance) 1903–1965
Tall, taciturn western star in the William S. Hart (qv) tradition, with deep-brown voice and purposeful air. A top rodeo rider at 16, he went to Hollywood and won some good featured roles in silents. After a long career in

minor and even extra roles in the early sound years, Elliott became a popular star of countless 'B' westerns before being promoted in his mid-forties to leading man in a series of surprisingly high-quality 'A' westerns in the late 1940s. He never did achieve his ambition of starring in the life story of Hart, his idol, and died from cancer at 62.
1925: †The Plastic Age. 1926: †Napoleon Junior. 1927: †The Drop Kick (GB: Glitter). †The Private Life of Helen of Troy. †The Arizona Wildcat. 1928: †Beyond London's Lights. †Valley of Hunted Men. †The Passion Song. †Restless Youth. 1929: †Broadway Scandals. 1930: †The Great Divide. †The Midnight Mystery. †Sunny. †She Couldn't Say No. *†Fast Work. 1931: †City Streets. †Delicious. †Peach o' Reno. †Palmy Days. †Convicted. †The Magnificent Lie. †Reaching for the Moon. †Platinum Blonde. 1932: †Merrily We Go to Hell (GB: Merrily We Go to ———). †Night After Night. †Lady with a Past (GB: My Reputation). †One Hour with You. †The Rich Are Always with Us. †Vanity Fair. †Crooner. †Jewel Robbery. 1933: †Little Giant. †The Keyhole. †Private Detective 62. † Gold Diggers of 1933. †Dancing Lady. 1934: †Registered Nurse. †Wonder Bar. †The Case of the Howling Dog. †Twenty Million Sweethearts. †Here Comes the Navy. †Housewife. †Desirable. †A Modern Hero. †The Secret Bride (GB: Concealment). 1935: †Broadway Hostess. †Living on Velvet. †Page Miss Glory. †Broadway Gondolier. †Dangerous. †Alibi Ike. †Devil Dogs of the Air. †I Live for Love (GB: I Live for You). †The Story of Louis Pasteur. †Stars over Broadway. †Gold Diggers of 1935. †Doctor Socrates. †Moonlight on the Prairie. †Go Into Your Dance. †A Night at the Ritz. †Bright Lights (GB: Funny Face). †Ceiling Zero. †The Traveling Saleslady. †While the Patient Slept. †The Woman in Red. *†Romance of the West. †The Goose and the Gander. †The Girl from 10th Avenue (GB: Men on Her Mind). †'G' Men. †Man of Iron. 1936: †The Case of the Black Cat. †The Golden Arrow. †China Clipper. †The Case of the Velvet Claws. †Romance in the Air. †Trailin' West (GB: On Secret Service). †The Walking Dead. †The Singing Kid. †Bullets or Ballots. †Polo Joe. †Down the Stretch. †Two Against the World (GB: The Case of Mrs Pembrook). †Murder by an Aristocrat. †The Big Nose. †The Murder of Dr Harrigan. 1937: †Melody for Two. †Midnight Court. †Fugitive in the Sky. †Speed to Spare. †Guns of the Pecos. †Roll Along Cowboy. †Wife, Doctor and Nurse. †Love Takes Flight. †Swing It, Professor (GB: Swing It Buddy). †Boy of the Streets. †Boots and Saddles. † You Can't Have Everything. 1938: †Tarzan's Revenge. †Valley of Hunted Men. †The Devil's Party. †Letter of Introduction. †Lady in the Morgue (GB: The Case of the Missing Blonde). **The Great Adventures of Wild Bill Hickock. **Frontier of '49. **In Early Arizona. 1939: **Overland with Kit Carson (serial). **Lone Star Pioneers (GB: Unwelcome Visitors). **The Law Comes to Texas. **The Taming of the West. **The Return of Wild Bill (GB: False Evidence). 1940: **Prairie Schooners (GB: Through the

Storm). **Pioneers of the Frontier (GB: The Anchor). **The Man from Tumbleweeds. **Beyond the Sacramento (GB: Power of Justice). **Wildcat of Tucson (GB: Promise Fulfilled). 1941: **Across the Sierras (GB: Welcome Stranger). **North from the Lone Star. **Hands Across the Rockies. **King of Dodge City. **Meet Roy Rogers. **Roaring Frontiers. **Where Did You Get That Girl? **The Son of Davy Crockett (GB: Blue Clay). **The Return of Daniel Boone (GB: The Mayor's Nest). **Lone Star Vigilantes (GB: The Devil's Price). 1942: **The Valley of Vanishing Men (serial). **North of the Rockies (GB: False Clues). **Bullets or Bandits. **The Devil's Trail (GB: Rogues' Gallery). **Prairie Gunsmoke. **Vengeance of the West. 1943: @Calling Wild Bill Elliott. @The Man from Thunder River. @Wagon Tracks West. @Overland Mail Robbery. @Bordertown Gunfighters. @Death Valley Manhunt. 1944: @Mojave Firebrand. @Tucson Raiders. @The San Antonio Kid. @Vigilantes of Dodge City. @Cheyenne Wildcat. @Marshal of Reno. @Hidden Valley Outlaws. @Sheriff of Las Vegas. 1945: @The Great Stagecoach Robbery. @Lone Texas Ranger. @Phantom of the Plains. @Marshal of Laredo. @Colorado Pioneers. @Wagon Wheels Westward. @Bells of Rosarita. 1946: @Sheriff of Redwood Valley. @Sun Valley Cyclone. @Conquest of Cheyenne. ‡In Old Sacramento. ‡The Plainsman and the Lady. 1947: ‡Wyoming. ‡The Fabulous Texan. 1948: ‡Old Los Angeles. ‡The Gallant Legion. ‡Hellfire. 1949: ‡The Savage Horde. ‡The Last Bandit. 1950: ‡The Showdown. 1951: @The Longhorn. 1952: @Waco (GB: The Outlaw and the Lady). @Fargo. @Kansas Territory. 1953: @The Homesteaders. @Rebel City. @Topeka. 1954: @Bitter Creek. @Vigilante Terror. @The Forty-Niners. 1955: **Dial Red O. **Sudden Danger. 1956: **Calling Homicide. **Chain of Evidence. 1957: **Footsteps in the Night.
†As Gordon Elliott
**As Bill Elliott
@As Wild Bill Elliott
‡As William Elliott

ELLISON, James or Jimmy (James E. Smith) 1910–
Tall, dull, brown-haired American leading man, pleasant enough in routine leading roles, or as youngish western sidekicks, but never seeming to progress to very much more. It

seems surprising now that he lasted over 20 years in the Hollywood mill, but in 1952 he gave up acting, apart from sporadic favours for friends, and moved into real estate.
1932: Play Girl. 1934: Carolina (GB: The House of Connelly). Death on the Diamond. The Winning Ticket. *Buried Loot. 1935: Reckless. Hop-a-Long Cassidy. The Eagle's Brood. Bar 20 Rides Again. Call of the Prairie. 1936: The Leathernecks Have Landed (GB: The Marines Have Landed). Three on the Trail. The Plainsman. Hopalong Cassidy Returns. Heart of the West. Trail Dust. Hitch Hike Lady (GB: Eventful Journey). 1937: Borderland. Annapolis Salute (GB: Salute to Romance). 23½ Hours' Leave. The Barrier. 1938: Vivacious Lady. Mother Carey's Chickens. Next Time I Marry? 1939: Zenobia (GB: Elephants Never Forget). Elsa Maxwell's Hotel for Women (GB: Hotel for Women). Fifth Avenue Girl. Almost a Gentleman (GB: Magnificent Outcast). Sorority House (GB: That Girl from College). 1940: You Can't Fool Your Wife. Anne of Windy Poplars (GB: Anne of Windy Willows). Playgirl. 1941: Charley's Aunt (GB: Charley's American Aunt). Ice-Capades. They Met in Argentina. Lone Star Law Man. 1942: Army Surgeon. Mr District Attorney in the Carter Case (GB: The Carter Case). Careful, Soft Shoulders. The Undying Monster (GB: The Hammond Mystery). 1943: The Gang's All Here (GB: The Girls He Left Behind). Dixie Dugan. I Walked with a Zombie. That Other Woman. 1944: Lady Let's Dance. Johnny Doesn't Live Here Any More. Trocadero. 1945: Hollywood and Vine (GB: Daisy (the Dog) Goes Hollywood). 1946: GI War Brides. 1947: Calendar Girl. The Ghost Goes Wild. 1949: Last of the Wild Horses. Hostile Country. 1950: Crooked River. Marshal of Heldorado. Colorado Ranger. West of the Brazos. Fast on the Draw (later Sudden Death). I Killed Geronimo. The Texan meets Calamity Jane. 1951: Texas Lawmen. Oklahoma Justice. Kentucky Jubilee. Whistling Hills. 1952: Texas City. Dead Man's Trail. The Man from the Black Hills. 1956: Ghost Town. 1963: Girls Take Over.

EMERSON, Faye 1917–1983
Flamboyant, glamorous blonde American actress who came to movies ten years too late – her natural wit and vivacity would have made her a great wisecracking girl-friend of the

thirties. As it was, she was more successful in high society than on the screen, as her studio, Warners, put her into a string of unsuitable roles. But in the fifties she became a popular TV personality, being dubbed 'television's First Lady'. Died from cancer of the stomach.
1941: The Nurse's Secret. Man Power. Blues in the Night. Bad Men of Missouri. Affectionately Yours. Nine Lives Are Not Enough. Wild Bill Hickok Rides. 1942 Murder in the Big House. Juke Girl. The Hard Way. Secret Enemies. Lady Gangster. 1943: The Desert Song. Destination Tokyo. Air Force. Find the Blackmailer. 1944: Hollywood Canteen. The Mask of Dimitrios. Between Two Worlds. The Very Thought of You. In Our Time. Uncertain Glory. Crime by Night. 1945: Hotel Berlin. Danger Signal. 1946: Nobody Lives Forever. Her Kind of Man. 1950: Guilty Bystander. 1953: Main Street to Broadway. 1957: A Face in the Crowd.

ERICSON, John (Joseph Meibes) 1927–
Fair-haired German-born leading man, under contract to M-G-M in the fifties, but lacking in sufficient mobility or personality to promote him to the top rank. His best screen work was probably the title role of Pretty Boy Floyd, but he has remained very busy on television in routine action roles.
1950: Saturday's Children (TV). 1951: Teresa. 1954: The Student Prince. Green Fire. Rhapsody. Bad Day at Black Rock. 1955: The Return of Jack Slade (GB: Texas Rose). 1956: The Cruel Tower. Heritage of Anger (TV). 1957: Forty Guns. Oregon Passage. 1958: Day of the Bad Man. The Innocent Sleep (TV). 1960: Under Ten Flags. Pretty Boy Floyd. 1962: Slave Queen of Babylon/I, Semiramis. 1964: The Seven Faces of Dr Lao. 1965: Operation Atlantic. 1966: The Destructors. 1967: Odio per odio. Los Siete de Pancho Villa (GB and US: Treasure of Pancho Villa). 1968: The Money Jungle. The Bamboo Saucer/Collision Course. 1969: Testa o croce (US: Heads or Tails). 1971: Bedknobs and Broomsticks. 1972: The Bounty Man (TV). 1974: Murder Impossible. 1976: Hustler Squad (GB: The Dirty Half Dozen). Crash.

ERROL, Leon 1881–1951
Bald, explosive, Australian-born comedian, with india-rubber legs and twitching, lugubrious features, often seen as the henpecked

drunk, in dozens of short comedies throughout the thirties and forties. Died from a heart attack.

1924: Yolanda. 1925: Clothes Make the Pirate. Sally. 1927: Lunatic at Large. 1929: One Heavenly Night. 1930: *Let's Merge. Paramount on Parade. Queen of Scandal. Only Saps Work. 1931: Her Majesty, Love. Finn and Hattie. *Practice Shots. 1933: Alice in Wonderland. *Poor Fish. *Three Little Swigs. *Hold Your Temper. 1934: We're Not Dressing. The Captain Hates the Sea. *No More Bridge. *Autobuyography. *Service with a Smile. *Good Morning, Eve. *Perfectly Mismated. *Fixing a Stew. *One Too Many. 1935: Princess O'Hara. Coronado. *Hit and Rum. *Salesmanship Ahoy. *Home Work. *Honeymoon Bridge. *Counselitis. 1936: *Down the Ribber. *Pirate Party on Catalina Isle. *Wholesailing Along. *One Live Ghost. 1937: Make a Wish. *Wrong Romance. *Should Wives Work? *A Rented Riot. *Dummy Owner. 1938: *His Pest Friend. *The Jitters. *Stage Fright. *Major Difficulties. *Crime Rave. *Berth Quakes. 1939: The Girl from Mexico. Career. Dancing Co-Ed (GB: Every Other Inch a Lady). Mexican Spitfire. *Home Boner. *Moving Vanities. *Ring Madness. *Wrong Room. *Truth Aches. *Scrappily Married. 1940: *Bested by a Beard. *He Asked for It. *Tattle Television. *The Fired Man. Pop Always Pays. Mexican Spitfire Out West. The Golden Fleecing. 1941: Six Lessons from Madame La Zonga. Where Did You Get That Girl? Hurry, Charlie, Hurry. Mexican Spitfire's Baby. Melody Lane. Moonlight in Hawaii. Never Give a Sucker an Even Break (GB: What a Man!). *When Wifie's Away. *A Polo Phony. *A Panic in the Parlor. *Man I Cured. *Who's a Dummy? *Home Work. 1942: Mexican Spitfire at Sea. *Mexican Spitfire Sees a Ghost. Mexican Spitfire's Elephant. *Wedded Blitz. *Framing Father. *Mail Trouble. *Dear! Dear! *Pretty Dolly. 1943: *Double Up. *A Family Feud. *Gem Jams. *Radio Runaround. *Seeing Nellie Home. *Cutie on Duty. *Wedtime Stories. Cowboy in Manhattan. Strictly in the Groove. Mexican Spitfire's Blessed Event. Follow the Band. Higher and Higher. Gals Inc. 1944: Hat Check Honey. The Invisible Man's Revenge. Slightly Terrific. Twilight on the Prairie. Babes on Swing Street. *Say Uncle. *Poppa Knows Worst. *Prices Unlimited. *Girls, Girls, Girls. *Triple

Trouble. *He Forgot to Remember. 1945: She Gets Her Man. What a Blonde! Under Western Skies. Mama Loves Papa. *Birthday Blues. *Let's Go Stepping. *It Shouldn't Happen to a Dog. *Double Honeymoon. *Beware of Redheads. 1946: *Oh, Professor, Behave. *Maid Trouble. *Twin Husbands. *I'll Take Milk. *Follow That Blonde. Joe Palooka, Champ. Gentleman Joe Palooka. 1947: Joe Palooka in the Knockout. *Wife Tames Wolf. *In Room 303. *Hired Husband. *Blondes Away. *The Spook Speaks. 1948: Joe Palooka in Fighting Mad. The Noose Hangs High. Variety Time. *Bet Your Life. *Don't Fool Your Wife. *Secretary Trouble. *Bachelor Blues. *Uninvited Blonde. *Backstage Follies. 1949: Joe Palooka in the Big Fight. Joe Palooka in Counterpunch. Joe Palooka Meets Humphrey. *Dad Always Pays. *Cactus Cut-Up. *I Can't Remember. *Oil's Well That Ends Well. *Sweet Cheat. *Shocking Affair. 1950: *High and Dizzy. Joe Palooka in Humphrey Takes a Chance (GB: Humphrey Takes a Chance). *Texas Tough Guy. *Spooky Wooky. 1951: *Chinatown Chump. *Punchy Pancho. *One Wild Night. *Deal Me In. *Lord Epping Returns. *Too Many Wives. Footlight Varieties.

ERWIN, Stuart 1902–1967
Fair-haired American actor with open, puzzled face, the Eddie Bracken of his day in roles of hapless innocence, first as fresh college kids, then as honest Joes. He was very successful in television from 1949 onwards, initially in his own show with his wife, actress June Collyer (1907–1968). Nominated for an Academy Award in Pigskin Parade.
1928: Mother Knows Best. 1929: Speakeasy. Happy Days. The Exalted Flapper. New Year's Eve. Thru Different Eyes. Sweetie. The Cockeyed World. The Trespasser. This Thing Called Love. Dangerous Curves. The Sophomore. 1930: Men without Women. Paramount on Parade. Young Eagles. Dangerous Nan McGrew. Only Saps Work. Playboy of Paris. Love among the Millionaires. Maybe It's Love. Along Came Youth. 1931: No Limit. Up Pops the Devil. The Magnificent Lie. Dude Ranch. Working Girls. 1932: *Hollywood on Parade No. 2. Two Kinds of Women. Make Me a Star. The Big Broadcast. The Misleading Lady. Strangers in Love. 1933: Face in the Sky. The Crime of the

Century. International House. Hold Your Man. The Stranger's Return. Day of Reckoning. Before Dawn. Going Hollywood. He Learned about Women. Under the Tonto Rim. 1934: Viva Villa! Palooka (GB: The Great Schnozzle). Chained. Have a Heart. Bachelor Bait. The Band Plays On. The Party's Over. 1935: Ceiling Zero. After Office Hours. 1936: Exclusive Story. Absolute Quiet. Women Are Trouble. Pigskin Parade (GB: The Harmony Parade). All American Chump (GB: The Country Bumpkin). 1937: Dance, Charlie, Dance. Second Honeymoon. Slim. I'll Take Romance. Checkers. Small Town Boy. 1938: Three Blind Mice. Mr Boggs Steps Out. Passport Husband. 1939: It Could Happen to You. Back Door to Heaven. Hollywood Cavalcade. The Honeymoon's Over. 1940: When the Daltons Rode. Our Town. Sandy Gets Her Man. A Little Bit of Heaven. 1941: Cracked Nuts. The Bride Came COD. 1942: The Adventures of Martin Eden. Blondie for Victory (GB: Trouble through Billets). Drums of the Congo. 1943: He Hired the Boss. 1944: The Great Mike. 1945: Pillow to Post. 1947: Killer Dill. Heaven Only Knows. Heading for Heaven. 1948: Strike It Rich. 1950: Father is a Bachelor. 1953: Main Street to Broadway. 1956: †Snow Shoes (TV). 1958: †The Right Hand Man (TV). 1959: †A Diamond is a Boy's Best Friend (TV). 1960: †Wrong Way Mooche (TV). †For the Love of Mike (GB: None But the Brave). 1963: †Son of Flubber. 1964: †The Misadventures of Merlin Jones. 1968: Shadow over Elveron (TV).

†As Stu Erwin

ESTEVEZ, Emilio 1962–
Stocky, worried-looking, jaunty young American actor who looks and sounds a lot like his father, Martin Sheen (qv) and seems destined for much the same sort of career pattern. Into TV movies, then films, direct from high school, the talented Estevez has a second string to his bow with writing, contributing the screenplay to his 1985 feature That Was Then, This is Now. He has an acting brother, Charlie Sheen, and his plans to play Charley's Aunt on stage seem to reveal an inclination to break away from the family 'seriousness'.
1980: Seventeen Going Nowhere (TV). 1981: To Climb a Mountain (TV). 1982: Tex. In the Custody of Strangers (TV). 1983: The

ETAIX

138

Outsiders. Nightmares. 1984: Repo Man. The Breakfast Club. 1985: St Elmo's Fire. That Was Then, This is Now. 1986: Overdrive. †Wisdom.

†Also Directed

ETAIX, Pierre 1928–
Mournful-looking, dark-haired, poker-faced, slightly built French comedian of rigid, stick-like gait. After starting his film career on the production side, Etaix worked with Jacques Tati before branching out on his own. At first his character of the man who, riotously, can do no wrong, was an immense success, but his later films were slower and less popular, and he has not directed one since 1971, occupying his time with his own 'Ecole du Cirque', at which he teaches clowning and mimicry.
1958: Mon oncle. 1959: Pickpocket. 1960: *Le pèlerinage. 1961: Tire-au-flanc 62. *†Rupture. *†Happy Anniversary. 1962: †The Suitor/Le soupirant. 1963: Une grosse tête. *†Insomnia. *†Nous n'irons plus au bois. 1964: †Yoyo. 1965: †As Long As You're Healthy. 1966: Le voleur. 1968: †Le grand amour. 1969: *La mayonnaise. 1970: †Pays de cocagne. 1971: The Day the Clown Cried (unfinished). *†La Polonaise. 1973: ‡Bel ordure. 1974: Sérieux comme le plaisir. 1986: Max mon amour.

† And directed
‡Scenes deleted from final release print

never had the same momentum afterwards and he was seen mostly in 'B' films as police inspectors or treacherous men of affluence and influence.
1935: The River House Mystery. 1936: Ourselves Alone (US: River of Unrest). The Tenth Man. Calling The Tune. A Woman Alone. 1937: The Mutiny of the Elsinore. Mademoiselle Docteur. La mort du Sphinx. 1938: 13 Men and a Gun. Luck of the Navy. 1939: His Brother's Keeper. The Proud Valley. At the Villa Rose (US: House of Mystery). 1940: Fingers. The Flying Squad. The House of the Arrow (US: Castle of Crimes). 1941: Freedom Radio. The Saint Meets the Tiger. Love on the Dole. Penn of Pennsylvania (US: The Courageous Mr Penn). 1942: Suspected Person. The Foreman Went to France (US: Somewhere in France). 1943: The Flemish Farm. 1947: The Silver Darlings. While I Live. 1949: The Twenty Questions Murder Mystery. A Run for Your Money. 1952: Escape Route (US: I'll Get You). 1953: Valley of Song (US: Men Are Children Twice). The Straw Man. †The Case of the Marriage Bureau. The Case of Express Delivery. The Case of Gracie Budd. †The Case of the Last Dance. Point of No Return. The Case of Canary Jones. The Case of the Burnt Alibi. †The Case of the Black Falcon. 1954: Solution by Phone. The Case of Soho Red. The Accused. †The Case of the Second Shot. Companions in Crime. †The Case of Diamond Annie. †The Case of Uncle Henry. *Fool Notions. The Red Dress. The Case of the Bogus Count. The Yellow Robe. 1955: The Gilded Cage. The Diamond Expert. *Ring of Greed. The Case of the Pearl Payroll. 1956: Passport to Treason. 1957: At the Stroke of Nine. Face in the Night (US: Menace in the Night). The Heart Within. Violent Playground. 1958: *Man with a Dog. 1959: SOS Pacific. 1961: The Curse of the Werewolf. 1962: Kiss of the Vampire (US: Kiss of Evil). 1963: The Long Ships. 1967: A Twist of Sand. 1969: One Brief Summer.

† Three (35-minute) films shown as a single feature on the continent

life. Widowed at 17, she had lost three of her six children before they were 21. Fourteen grandchildren are hopefully some consolation.
1940: The East Side Kids. 1942: Orchestra Wives. Rhythm Hits the Ice. Girl Trouble. 1943: Here Comes Elmer. Hoosier Holiday (GB: Farmyard Follies). Swing Your Partner. The West Side Kid. In Old Oklahoma (GB: War of the Wildcats). 1944: Casanova in Burlesque. San Fernando Valley. Yellow Rose of Texas. Song of Nevada. 1945: Utah. Lights of Old Santa Fé. The Big Show-Off. The Man from Oklahoma. Don't Fence Me In. Hitchhike to Happiness. Bells of Rosarita. Sunset in Eldorado. Along the Navajo Trail. 1946: Song of Arizona. My Pal Trigger. Under Nevada Skies. Roll On Texas Moon. Home in Oklahoma. Rainbow over Texas. Out California Way. Heldorado. 1947: Apache Rose. Bells of San Angelo. The Trespasser. 1948: Slippy McGee. 1949: Down Dakota Way. Susanna Pass. The Golden Stallion. 1950: Twilight in the Sierras. Bells of Coronado. Trigger Jr. 1951: South of Caliente. Pals of the Golden West.

EVANS, Dame Edith 1888–1976
Forthright English actress whose films as a silent screen leading lady were lamentably few, but who touched her every character portrayal in later years with eccentric brilliance. Few could match the richness and resonance of her diction and her indignation as Lady Bracknell in The Importance of Being Earnest is one of the cinema's most treasurable occasions. Created Dame in 1946. Died after a short illness following a stroke and heart attack. Oscar-nominated for Tom Jones, The Chalk Garden and The Whisperers.
1915: A Honeymoon for Three. A Welsh Singer. 1916: East is East. 1948: The Queen of Spades. 1949: The Last Days of Dolwyn (US: Woman of Dolwyn). 1952: The Importance of Being Earnest. 1958: The Nun's Story. 1959: Look Back in Anger. 1963: Tom Jones. The Chalk Garden. 1964: Young Cassidy. 1966: The Whisperers. 1967: Fitzwilly (GB: Fitzwilly Strikes Back). 1968: Prudence and the Pill. Crooks and Coronets (US: Sophie's Place). 1969: The Madwoman of Chaillot. David Copperfield (TV GB: cinemas). 1970: Scrooge. Upon This Rock. 1973: A Doll's House (Garland). Craze. 1974: QB VII (TV). 1976: The Slipper and the Rose. Nasty Habits.

EVANS, Clifford 1912–1985
Black-haired Welsh actor mainly seen in thoughtful, serious roles who had just worked his way up to star billing in big films when World War II intervened. His film career

EVANS, Dale (Frances Smith) 1912–
Red-headed American vocalist who doubtless deserved the luck she had when she met and married Roy Rogers and prolonged her career, for she was a lady with a lot of tragedy in her

EVANS, Madge 1909–1981

Fluffy blonde American actress at her most popular as a child star of the early silent days, when she was known as Baby Madge. As an adult she took glamorous, sophisticated, rather empty roles, and was never more than a second-rank star. After 1938 she deserted the cinema completely for the theatre (she married playwright Sidney Kingsley in 1939), although she was seen occasionally on television in the 1950s.

*1914: †The Sign of the Cross. 1915: †Zaza. †Alias Jimmy Valentine. †The Garden of Lies. 1916: †Seven Sisters. †Sudden Riches. †Seventeen. †Broken Chairs. †The Hidden Scar. †Husband and Wife. 1917: †The Little Duchess. †The Volunteer. †The Burglar. †The Little Patriot. †Beloved Adventuress. †The Adventures of Carol. †Maternity. †Web of Desire. †The Corner Grocer. 1918: †Woman and Wife. †Gates of Gladness. †The Power and the Glory. †The Golden Wall. †Stolen Orders. †Neighbors. †Wanted – a Mother. 1919: †The Love Nest. †Home Wanted. †The Love Defender. †Seventeen (and 1916 film). 1921: Heidi. 1923: On the Banks of the Wabash. 1924: Classmates. 1930: *Envy. 1931: Sporting Blood. Son of India. Guilty Hands. Heartbreak. 1932: Are You Listening? West of Broadway. Lovers Courageous. The Greeks Had a Word for Them. Huddle (GB: Impossible Lover). 1933: Hallelujah, I'm a Bum (GB: Hallelujah, I'm a Tramp). Hell Below. The Nuisance (GB: Accidents Wanted). Dinner at Eight. Broadway to Hollywood (GB: Ring Up the Curtain). Day of Reckoning. Beauty for Sale (GB: Beauty). Mayor of Hell. Made on Broadway (GB: The Girl I Made). 1934: The Show Off. Fugitive Lovers. Death on the Diamond (GB: Death on the Sports Field). Grand Canary. What Every Woman Knows. Paris Interlude. 1935: Helldorado. David Copperfield. Age of Indiscretion. Men without Names. The Tunnel (US: Transatlantic Tunnel). Calm Yourself. 1936: Moonlight Murder. Piccadilly Jim. Exclusive Story. Pennies From*

Heaven. 1937: Espionage. The Thirteenth Chair. 1938: Army Girl. Sinners in Paradise.

† *As Baby Madge*

EVANS, Peggy 1924–

Blonde British actress with china doll looks and wide blue, even scared, eyes; on stage from childhood as a dancer, but mainly used in films as gangsters' girls, most notably in *The Blue Lamp*, and despite a spirited showing as a girl investigator in *Penny and the Pownall Case*. Dropped out of show business after a few post-war roles.

1938: The Mikado. 1940: Charley's (Big-Hearted) Aunt. 1946: School for Secrets (US: Secret Flight). A Matter of Life and Death (US: Stairway to Heaven). 1947: The Woman in the Hall. Penny and the Pownall Case. 1948: Love in Waiting. Look Before You Love. 1949: The Blue Lamp. 1951: Calling Bulldog Drummond. 1953: Murder at 3 am.

EWELL, Tom (S. Yewell Tompkins) 1909–

American actor who played gullible sorts or inept woman chasers, with the occasional wisecracking friend on the side. Not really discovered by Hollywood until into his forties, when his mournful features found their way into several classic comedies. But the qualities of the roles offered quickly fell away, and he returned to his first love, the stage

*1940: They Knew What They Wanted. 1941: Desert Bandit/The Kansas Kid. 1949: *Caribbean Capers. *Southward Ho! Ho! Adam's Rib. 1950: An American Guerilla in the Philippines (GB: I Shall Return). Mr Music. A Life of Her Own. 1951: Up Front. Finders Keepers. 1952: Lost in Alaska. Back at the Front (GB: Willie and Joe in Tokyo). 1955: The Seven Year Itch. The Lieutenant Wore Skirts. 1956: The Great American Pastime. 1957: The Girl Can't Help It. 1958: A Nice Little Bank That Should Be Robbed (GB: How to Rob a Bank). 1961: Tender is the Night. 1962: State Fair. 1965: *Wonders of Kentucky (narrator only). 1970: Suppose They Gave a War and Nobody Came. 1971: To Find a Man. 1972: They Only Kill Their Masters. 1974: †The Great Gatsby. The Spy Who Returned from the Dead. 1975: Promise Him Anything (TV). 1979: Return of the Mod Squad (TV).*

† *Scenes deleted from final version*

EYTHE, William 1918–1957

Diffident American leading man whose great promise on stage did not generally reflect itself in his screen performances. His self-opinionated attitudes made him unpopular in Hollywood and his career there petered out after 13 films. Developed an alcohol problem in the fifties and died from complications arising from acute hepatitis.

1942: The Ox-Bow Incident (GB: Strange Incident). 1943: The Song of Bernadette. 1944: The Eve of St Mark. A Wing and a Prayer. Wilson. 1945: The House on 92nd Street. A Royal Scandal (GB: Czarina). Colonel Effingham's Raid (GB: Man of the Hour). 1946: Centennial Summer. 1947: Meet Me at Dawn. 1948: Mr Reckless. 1949: Special Agent. 1950: Customs Agent.

FABIAN (F. Forte Bonaparte) 1942–
Beefy, handsome American pop singer with dark, wavy hair. Fox gave him a few semi-leading roles in the sixties on the strength of his popularity as a rockin' teenage idol, and he has continued to crop up from time to time in between night-club engagements.
1959: Rock 'n' Roll. Hound Dog Man. 1960: North to Alaska. High Time. Love in a Goldfish Bowl. 1962: Mr Hobbs Takes a Vacation. The Longest Day. Five Weeks in a Balloon. 1964: Ride the Wild Surf. 1965: Dear Brigitte . . . Ten Little Indians. 1966: Fireball 500. Dr Goldfoot and the Girl Bombs (GB: Dr G and the Love Bomb). 1967: Thunder Alley. 1968: The Devil's Eight. Maryjane. The Wild Racers. 1970: †A Bullet for Pretty Boy. 1972: †Lovin' Man. †Matthew. 1974: †Little Laura and Big John. 1976: †The Day the Lord Got Busted. 1977: Getting Married. 1978: Disco Fever. Katie: Portrait of a Centerfold (TV). 1979: †Crisis in Mid-Air. 1983: †Get Crazy.

† As Fabian Forte

FAIRBANKS, Douglas Jnr 1909–
In films from an early age, Fairbanks followed his father in swashbuckling mould in several films, although he was a more versatile, if less dominant performer. Gave up movies even earlier than his father and went into production, with just the occasional foray into films or theatre. Married (first of two) to Joan Crawford (qv) from 1929 to 1933. Wore a moustache from 1933.
1923: Stephen Steps Out. 1924: The Air Mail. 1925: The American Venus. Wild Horse Mesa. Stella Dallas. 1926: Padlocked. Man Bait.

Broken Hearts of Hollywood. 1927: Women Love Diamonds. Is Zat So? A Texas Steer. Dead Man's Curve. 1928: Modern Mothers. The Toilers. The Power of the Press. A Woman of Affairs. The Barker. 1929: The Jazz Age. Fast Life. Our Modern Maidens. The Careless Age. The Forward Pass. The Show of Shows. Party Girl. 1930: Loose Ankles. The Little Accident. The Dawn Patrol. The Way of All Men (GB: The Sin Flood). Outward Bound. One Night at Susie's. Little Caesar. 1931: Chances. I Like Your Nerve. Union Depot (GB: Gentlemen for a Day). L'aviateur. L'athlete malgré lui. 1932: It's Tough to be Famous. Love is a Racket. Le plombier amoureux. Scarlet Dawn. *Hollywood on Parade No. 3. *The Stolen Jools (GB: The Slippery Pearls). 1933: Parachute Jumper. The Life of Jimmy Dolan (GB: The Kid's Last Fight). The Narrow Corner. Captured! Morning Glory. Catherine the Great. 1934: Success At Any Price. 1935: Man of the Moment. The Amateur Gentleman. Mimi. 1936: Accused. 1937: Jump for Glory (US: When Thief Meets Thief). The Prisoner of Zenda. 1938: The Joy of Living. The Rage of Paris. Having Wonderful Time. The Young in Heart. 1939: Gunga Din. The Sun Never Sets. Rulers of the Sea. 1940: Green Hell. Safari. Angels over Broadway. 1941: The Corsican Brothers. 1947: Sinbad the Sailor. The Exile. 1948: That Lady in Ermine. The Fighting O'Flynn. 1950: State Secret (US: The Great Manhunt). Mr Drake's Duck. 1953: Three's Company. The Triangle. The Genie. Thought to Kill (narrator only). 1954: *International Settlement. *The Journey. Destination Milan. Forever My Heart. The Last Moment. 1955: *Hollywood Fathers. 1957: Chase a Crooked Shadow. 1962: The Shadowed Affair (TV). 1967: Red and Blue. The Funniest Man in the World (narrator only). 1972: The Crooked Hearts (TV). 1973: Churchill the Man (narrator only). 1980: The Hostage Tower. 1981: Ghost Story.

FAIRBANKS, Douglas Snr (D. Ulman) 1883–1939
Florid, moustachioed, ever-cheerful, athletic American actor, one of the biggest stars of the Hollywood silent era, and its swashbuckler par excellence, doing all his own spectacular stunts against equally spectacular sets. When sound came, his time was over. Married to Mary Pickford (second of three) from 1920 to

1936. Father of Douglas Fairbanks Jnr. (by first wife). Died from a heart attack.
1915: The Lamb. Double Trouble. 1916: The Habit of Happiness. His Picture in the Papers. The Good Bad Man. Reggie Mixes In (GB: Mysteries of New York). *The Mystery of the Leaping Fish. The Half-Breed. Flirting with Fate. Manhattan Madness. Intolerance. American Aristocracy. The Matrimaniac. The Americano. 1917: In Again – Out Again. Wild and Wooly. Down to Earth. The Man from Painted Post. Reaching for the Moon. A Modern Musketeer. *War Relief. 1918: Headin' South. Mr Fix-It. Say! Young Fellow. He Comes Up Smiling. *Sic 'em Sam! Arizona. *Fire the Kaiser. Bound in Morocco. 1919: The Knickerbocker Buckaroo. His Majesty, the American (GB: One of the Blood). When the Clouds Roll By. 1920: The Mollycoddle. The Mark of Zorro. 1921: The Nut. *Screen Snapshots No. 24. The Three Musketeers. 1922: Robin Hood. 1924: Thief of Bagdad. 1925: Don Q, Son of Zorro. 1926: The Black Pirate. 1927: The Gaucho. 1928: Show People. 1929: The Iron Mask. The Taming of the Shrew. 1930: *Voice of Hollywood No. 2. Reaching for the Moon. 1931: Around the World in 80 Minutes. 1932: Mr Robinson Crusoe. 1934: The Private Life of Don Juan. 1955: *Hollywood Fathers.

FAITH, Adam (Terence Nelhams) 1940–
Fair-haired, bony-faced, undernourished-looking singer, actor and entrepreneur who has occasionally cropped up in films in anything from comedy (as hapless innocents) to heavy drama (as cockney hard-men or wheeler-dealers). A great pop idol in his day,

he was also enormously successful as the central character in the TV series *Budgie*, about a small-time crook.

1959: 'Beat' Girl (US: Wild for Kicks). 1960: Never Let Go. 1961: What a Whopper! What a Carve-Up! (US: Home Sweet Homicide). 1962: Mix Me a Person. 1974: Stardust. 1979: Yesterday's Hero. Foxes. 1980: McVicar. 1985: Minder on the Orient Express (TV).

FALK, Peter 1927–
Short, dark, Brooklynese Hollywood star character actor who found it hard to fight clear of the gangster stereotype before his enormous success as television's rumpled, never-fail detective Columbo. Has remained most successful on television despite some promising looking film material in the seventies. A tumour caused the loss of his right eye when he was three. Nominated for Academy Awards in *Murder Incorporated* and *Pocketful of Miracles*.

1958: Wind Across the Everglades. 1959: The Bloody Brood. The Rebel Set. Pretty Boy Floyd. 1960: A Death of Princes (TV. GB: cinemas). The Secret of the Purple Reef. Murder Incorporated. 1961: Cry Vengeance (TV). The Million Dollar Incident (TV). Pocketful of Miracles. 1962: Pressure Point. The Balcony. 1963: It's A Mad, Mad, Mad, Mad World. 1964: Robin and the Seven Hoods. Italiano Brava Gente (US: Attack and Retreat). 1965: The Great Race. Too Many Thieves (TV. GB: cinemas). 1966: Penelope. 1967: Luv. 1968: Anzio (GB: The Battle for Anzio). Prescription: Murder (TV). 1969: Rosolino paternò soldato (US: Operation Snafu). Machine Gun McCain. Castle Keep. 1970: Husbands. A Step Out of Line (TV). 1971: Ransom for a Dead Man (TV. GB: cinemas). 1972: *The Politics Film (narrator only). 1974: A Woman under the Influence. 1976: Murder by Death. Mikey and Nicky. Griffin and Phoenix (GB: Today is Forever). 1977: Opening Night. 1978: The Cheap Detective. The Brink's Job. 1979: The In-Laws. 1981: The Great Muppet Caper. All the Marbles (GB: The California Dolls). 1984: Big Trouble. 1985: Happy New Year.

FALKENBURG, Jinx (Eugenia Falkenburg) 1919–
Tall, attractive, brunette, fresh-looking, Spanish-born actress in Hollywood films.

Raised in Chile, she rose to be that country's champion free-style swimmer before becoming America's number one model, her entrée to films. Her vivacious personality and bursting-with-health appearance made her popular in comedies and light musicals of the wartime years. A biography of her eventful life was published as early as 1951.

1936: †Big Brown Eyes. 1937: †Nothing Sacred. 1938: †Song of the Buckaroo. 1939: †The Lone Ranger Rides Again (serial). †Professional Model. 1941: Sing for Your Supper. 1942: Two Latins from Manhattan. Sweetheart of the Fleet. Lucky Legs. Laugh Your Blues Away. 1943: Two Senoritas from Chicago (GB: Two Senoritas). She Has What It Takes. The Cover Girl. 1944: Nine Girls. Tahiti Nights. 1946: The Gay Senorita. Meet Me on Broadway. Talk about a Lady. 1947: *Brains Can Be Beautiful. 1949: *Straw Hat Cinderella.

† *As Jinx Falken*

FARMER, Frances 1910–1970
Determined-looking American actress, a harsher version of Joan Fontaine. She became unpopular in the Hollywood of the thirties, where alcoholism and mental illness put a stop to her career. After seven years in an asylum (1943–1950), she eventually made a comeback in the mid-fifties, and became quite well known as a TV hostess. Died from cancer of the throat. Married to Leif Erickson (first of three) from 1936–1942. Her harrowing life story was filmed several times in the early 1980s.

1936: Too Many Parents. Border Flight. Come

and Get It. Rhythm on the Range. 1937: The Toast of New York. Ebb Tide. Exclusive. 1938: Ride a Crooked Mile (GB: Escape from Yesterday). 1940: South of Pago Pago. Flowing Gold. 1941: World Premiere. Badlands of Dakota. Among the Living. 1942: Son of Fury. 1957: Reunion (TV). 1958: The Party Crashers.

FARMER, Suzan 1943–
Shapely British blonde actress of brisk and efficient manner that, one would have thought, made her ideal casting for nurses. She was a child actress before coming to adult roles in the early 1960s, quickly graduating to leads in horror films. Marriage to Ian McShane (1965–1968) seemed to slow her progress, and she has latterly been seen mainly on television and with stage touring companies.

1959: The Dawn Killer (serial). 1962: The Wild and the Willing. 1963: The Scarlet Blade (US: The Crimson Blade). The Devil Ship Pirates. 80,000 Suspects. 1964: 633 Squadron. 1965: Monster of Terror (US: Die, Monster, Die). Dracula – Prince of Darkness. Rasputin the Mad Monk. 1966: Doctor in Clover. Where the Bullets Fly. 1967: *Talk of the Devil. 1974: Persecution. 1976: The Chiffy Kids (serial).

FARR, Derek 1912–1986
Quiet, dark, brooding English leading man with distinctive receding hairline, who forsook schoolteaching for acting after work as an extra in films of the late thirties. Usually cast as nice young chaps who were sometimes falsely accused of murder. Maintained leading man status from 1940 to 1951, co-star until

1961, but most latterly in small character roles with bigger parts on TV. Married (second of two) to Muriel Pavlow from 1947. Died from cancer.

1939: Inspector Hornleigh on Holiday (US: Inspector Hornleigh on Leave). The Outsider. Q Planes (US: Clouds over Europe). Black Eyes. 1940: Spellbound (US: The Spell of Amy Nugent). 1941: Freedom Radio (US: A Voice in the Night). Quiet Wedding. 1943: *Camouflage. 1946: Quiet Weekend. Wanted for Murder. The Shop at Sly Corner (US: The Code of Scotland Yard). 1947: Teheran (US: The Plot to Kill Roosevelt). 1948: Bond Street. Noose (US: The Silk Noose). The Story of Shirley Yorke. 1949: Silent Dust. Man on the Run. 1950: Double Confession. Murder without Crime. 1951: Young Wives' Tale. Reluctant Heroes. 1952: Little Big Shot. 1953: Front Page Story. Eight O'Clock Walk. 1954: Bang! You're Dead (US: Game of Danger). 1955: The Dam Busters. Value for Money. 1956: The Man in the Road. Town on Trial! 1957: Doctor at Large. The Vicious Circle (US: The Circle). 1958: The Truth about Women. 1961: Attempt to Kill. 1966: The Projected Man. 1967: 30 is a Dangerous Age, Cynthia. 1971: The Johnstown Monster. 1972: Pope Joan.

FARR, Felicia 1932–

Attractive, tawny-haired, brown-eyed American actress of substantial, warm personality, in star roles from the onset of her film career. She played a few strong-willed heroines in upper-class westerns, but has been only sporadically seen in films and on television since marrying Jack Lemmon (qv) in 1960.

1955: †Big House USA. Timetable. 1956: Jubal. The First Texan. Reprisal! 1957: 3:10 to Yuma. The Last Wagon. The Country Husband (TV. GB: cinemas). 1958: Onionhead. 1960: Hell Bent for Leather. 1964: Kiss Me Stupid. 1966: The Venetian Affair. 1967: Asylum for a Spy (TV). 1970: Lock, Stock and Barrel (TV). 1971: Kotch. 1973: Charley Varrick.

† As Randy Farr

FARRAR, David 1908–

Strong, silent, dark, saturnine, resolute-looking British leading man who came late to acting after a spell in journalism, but quickly established himself as stalwart types (including Sexton Blake three times), moving on in post-war years to subtler roles. His decision

to go to Hollywood in the early 1950s was an unqualified disaster. He was cast as nothing but villains in increasingly silly costume epics and his special qualities never re-emerged. Now retired and living in South Africa.

1937: Head Over Heels (US: Head Over Heels in Love). Return of A Stranger. Silver Top. 1938: Sexton Blake and the Hooded Terror. A Royal Divorce. 1941: Danny Boy. Sheepdog of the Hills. Penn of Pennsylvania (US: The Courageous Mr Penn). 1942: Suspected Person. Went the Day Well? (US: 48 Hours). The Night Invader. 1943: The Dark Tower. They Met in the Dark. Headline. The Hundred Pound Window. 1944: For Those in Peril. Meet Sexton Blake. The World Owes Me a Living. 1945: The Echo Murders. The Trojan Brothers. 1946: Lisbon Story. 1947: Black Narcissus. Frieda. 1948: Mr Perrin and Mr Traill. The Small Back Room. 1949: Diamond City. 1950: Cage of Gold. Gone to Earth (US revised version: The Wild Heart). 1951: The Late Edwina Black (US: Obsessed). Night without Stars. The Golden Horde (GB: The Golden Horde of Genghis Khan). 1954: Duel in the Jungle. The Black Shield of Falworth. Lilacs in the Spring (US: Let's Make Up). 1955: Escape to Burma. Pearl of the South Pacific. The Sea Chase. Lost (US: Tears for Simon). 1957: Triangle on Safari (US: Woman and the Hunter). I Accuse! 1958: Son of Robin Hood. 1959: John Paul Jones. Watusi. Solomon and Sheba. 'Beat' Girl (US: Wild for Kicks). 1962: The Webster Boy. The 300 Spartans.

FARRELL, Charles 1901–

Gentle, tousle-haired, romantic American leading man, now all but forgotten, but immensely popular in the late twenties and early thirties in a series of lyrical love stories opposite Janet Gaynor, one of which, *Seventh Heaven*, won an Academy Award. Left films in 1941 to go into the sports club business, but made a comeback on TV in the fifties. Married to Virginia Valli (V. McSweeney 1895–1968) from 1932 until her death.

1923: Rosita. The Cheat. The Hunchback of Notre Dame. The Ten Commandments. 1925: The Love Hour. The Freshman (GB: College Days). Wings of Youth. *The Gosh-darn Mortgage. Clash of the Wolves. 1926: Old Ironside (GB: Sons of the Sea). Sandy. A Trip to Chinatown. 1927: The Rough Riders (GB: The Trumpet Call). Seventh Heaven. 1928: Street Angel. The Red Dance (GB: The Red Dancer of Moscow). The River. Fazil. 1929: City Girl. Sunny Side Up. Lucky Star. Happy Days. 1930: Liliom. The Princess and the Plumber. The Man Who Came Back. High Society Blues. 1931: Body and Soul. Heartbreak. Merely Mary Ann. Delicious. 1932: After Tomorrow. The First Year. Tess of the Storm Country. Wild Girl (GB: Salomy Jane). 1933: Girl Without a Room. Aggie Appleby, Maker of Men (GB: Cupid in the Rough). The Big Shakedown. 1934: Change of Heart. Falling in Love (US: Trouble Ahead). 1935: Fighting Youth. Forbidden Heaven. 1936: The Flying Doctor. 1937: Moonlight Sonata. Midnight Menace (US: Bombs over London). 1938: Flight to Fame. Just Around the Corner. Tail Spin. 1941: The Deadly Game.

FARRELL, Glenda 1904–1971

Buoyant, witty, blonde American actress with lived-in charm and long, pencilled eyebrows. Many people's favourite wisecracking woman-of-the-world from Hollywood films of the 1930s, she is perhaps most fondly recalled as the intrepid girl reporter Torchy Blane. Was once said to have delivered a 400-word speech in 40 seconds. Won an Emmy in 1963. Died from lung cancer.

1929: Lucky Boy. 1930: Little Caesar. *The Lucky Break. 1931: Night Nurse. 1932: Three on a Match. *Position and Backswing. Life Begins (GB: The Dawn of Life). The Match King. Scandal for Sale. I Am a Fugitive from a Chain Gang. 1933: The Mystery of the Wax Museum. Central Airport. Girl Missing. Grand Slam. The Keyhole. Gambling Ship. Lady for a Day. Bureau of Missing Persons. Mary Stevens,

MD. Man's Castle. Havana Widows. The Mayor of Hell. 1934: I've Got Your Number. Dark Hazard. Kansas City Princess. Hi, Nellie! The Big Shakedown. The Personality Kid/ Information Please. The Merry Wives of Reno. Heat Lightning. The Secret Bride (GB: Concealment). 1935: In Caliente. Go Into Your Dance (GB: Casino de Paree). Traveling Saleslady. Gold Diggers of 1935. We're in the Money. Little Big Shot. Miss Pacific Fleet. 1936: Smart Blonde. The Law in Her Hands. Snowed Under. Nobody's Fool. Here Comes Carter! (GB: The Voice of Scandal). High Tension. Gold Diggers of 1937. 1937: Breakfast for Two. Blondes at Work. Hollywood Hotel. Fly-Away Baby. Dance, Charlie, Dance. You Live and Learn. The Adventurous Blonde/ Torchy Blane the Adventurous Blonde. 1938: The Road to Reno. Stolen Heaven. Torchy Gets Her Man. Prison Break. Exposed. 1939: Torchy Blane in Chinatown. Torchy Runs for Mayor. 1941: Johnny Eager. 1942: A Night for Crime. The Talk of the Town. Twin Beds. 1943: Klondike Kate. City without Men. 1944: Ever Since Venus. 1947: Heading for Heaven. I Love Trouble. Mary Lou. 1948: Lulu Belle. 1952: Apache War Smoke. 1953: Girls in the Night (GB: Life After Dark). 1954: Secret of the Incas. Susan Slept Here. 1955: The Girl in the Red Velvet Swing. 1959: Middle of the Night. 1964: The Disorderly Orderly. Kissin' Cousins. 1966: Dead Heat on a Merry-Go-Round. 1968: Tiger by the Tail.

FARROW, Mia (Maria Farrow) 1945–
Fair-haired, fragile-looking American actress of expressive brown eyes and fey charm, the daughter of Maureen O'Sullivan (qv) and director John Farrow. She enjoyed something of a reputation as a wild spirit in her younger days, but then gradually came to prominence in the cinema with a series of wistful, vulnerable heroines, sometimes not quite all there. Married to Frank Sinatra (1966–1968) and conductor André Previn (1970–1979), she has been associated both privately and professionally in recent times with the filmmaker/comedian Woody Allen (qv).
1959: John Paul Jones. 1963: *The Age of Curiosity. 1964: Guns at Batasi. 1967: Johnny Belinda (TV). 1968: A Dandy in Aspic. Rosemary's Baby. 1969: Secret Ceremony. John and Mary. 1971: Blind Terror (US: See No Evil). Goodbye Raggedy Ann (TV). Follow Me (US:

The Public Eye). 1972: Docteur Popaul (GB and US: Scoundrel in White). 1974: The Great Gatsby. 1975: Peter Pan (TV). 1976: Full Circle. 1978: Death on the Nile. A Wedding. Avalanche. 1979: Hurricane. 1981: The Last Unicorn (voice only). Sarah/The Seventh Match. 1982: A Midsummer Night's Sex Comedy. 1983: Zelig. 1984: Supergirl. Broadway Danny Rose. 1985: The Purple Rose of Cairo. 1986: Hannah and Her Sisters.

FAWCETT, Farrah 1946–
Lithe, fluffily blonde American actress who rose to the top on the success of a TV series (Charlie's Angels) and her flashing toothpaste smile. Her career seemed to be faltering in the late 1970s, when her private life – married/divorced Lee Majors (qv), then live-in companion of Ryan O'Neal (qv) – gained her more notices than her disappointing acting performances. But some courageous portrayals on stage and TV in the 1980s brought her the belated respect of her critics.
1969: Un homme qui me plaît (US: Love is a Funny Thing). 1970: Myra Breckinridge. The Feminist and the Fuzz (TV). 1972: The Great American Beauty Contest (TV). 1974: Of Men and Women II (TV). The Girl Who Came Gift Wrapped (TV). 1975: Murder on Flight 502 (TV). 1976: Logan's Run. 1978: †Somebody Killed Her Husband. 1979: An Almost Perfect Affair. Sunburn. 1980: Saturn 3. The Fall Guy (TV). 1981: The Cannonball Run. Murder in Texas (TV). 1984: The Red-Light Sting (TV). The Burning Bed (TV). 1985: Extremities. 1986: Unfinished Business (TV). Between Two Women (TV). The Beate Klarsfeld Story (TV).

† As Farrah Fawcett-Majors

FAYE, Alice (A. Leppert) 1912–
Blonde, round-faced American singer with a warm smile and voice to match. Starting as a singer with Rudy Vallee's band, she became much in demand for sympathetic roles in musicals of the thirties and early forties, before retiring (too) early to concentrate on consolidating her marriage to Phil Harris (1941 on, her second husband). Comeback roles in later years did not show her to advantage. First married to Tony Martin (1937–1940).
1934: George White's Scandals. She Learned about Sailors. Now I'll Tell. (GB: When New

York Sleeps). 365 Nights in Hollywood. 1935: George White's Scandals of 1935. Music is Magic. Every Night at Eight. 1936: Poor Little Rich Girl. Sing, Baby, Sing. King of Burlesque. Stowaway. 1937: On the Avenue. Wake Up and Live. You Can't Have Everything. You're a Sweetheart. 1938: In Old Chicago. Sally, Irene and Mary. Alexander's Ragtime Band. Tail Spin. 1939: Hollywood Cavalcade. Barricade. Rose of Washington Square. 1940: Lillian Russell. Little Old New York. Tin Pan Alley. 1941: That Night in Rio. The Great American Broadcast. Weekend in Havana. 1943: Hello, Frisco, Hello. The Gang's All Here (GB: The Girls He Left Behind). 1944: Four Jills in a Jeep. 1945: Fallen Angel. 1962: State Fair. 1975: Won Ton Ton – the Dog Who Saved Hollywood. 1978: The Magic of Lassie.

FELDMAN, Marty 1933–1982
Tiny, bug-eyed, hook-nosed British comedian who moved from writing to performing and became a huge success on television in the late 1960s. His film performances did not evoke the same laughter and remained over-indulgent. Died from a heart attack.
1969: The Bed Sitting Room. 1970: Every Home Should Have One. 1974: Young Frankenstein. 1975: The Adventure of Sherlock Holmes' Smarter Brother. 40 gradi all'ombra del lenzuolo (GB and US: Sex with a Smile). 1976: Silent Movie. 1977: †The Last Remake of Beau Geste. 1979: †In God We Trust. 1982: Slapstick/Slapstick of Another Kind. 1983: Yellowbeard.

† Also directed

FENECH, Edwige 1948–

Lovely dark-haired Algerian-born actress and pin-up, probably the most physically beautiful continental star since Hedy Lamarr. Alas, she has seemed content to remain lovingly photographed in the shallows of glossy Italian and West German sexploitation films (the English titles speak for themselves), belatedly dipping her toes into international waters with *Il grande attacca* in 1977. Her appearances in skinshow comedies have made her a big attraction in Europe, although barely (!) known elsewhere.

1967: Toutes folles de lui. 1968: Madame und ihre Nichte (GB: House of Pleasure). Komme, liebe Maid und mache . . . (GB: Sex is a Pleasure). Il figlio del Aquila Nera. Frau Wirtin hat auch einen Grafin (GB: Sexy Susan Sins Again. US: Sexy Susan at the King's Court). Samoa, Queen of the Jungle. Sensation!/Top Sensation (US: The Seducers). 1969: Der Mann mit dem goldenen Pinsel. Madame Bovary/Die ñackte Bovary (GB: Play the Game or Leave the Bed. US: The Sins of Madame Bovary). Testa o croce. L'année de la contestation. Alle Kätzen naschen gern (GB: The Blonde and the Black Pussycat). Frau Wirtin hat auch eine Nichte. Die tolldreisten Geschichten des Honoré de Balzac (GB: the Bawdy Women of Balzac). 1970: Swinging Young Seductresses. Le caldi notti de Don Giovanni (GB: Don Giovanni's Hot Nights. US: The Loves of Don Juan). Le Mans, scorciatoia per l'inferno. Cinque bambole per la luna d'agosto (GB and US: Five Dolls for an August Moon). Lo stranio vizio della Signora Ward. La tela del ragno. Satiricosissimo. 1971: Deserto di fuoco (US: Desert of Fire). Next Victim. 1972: La bella Antonia (GB: Naughty Nun). Perche quelle strane groce di angue sul corpo di Jennifer? (GB: Erotic Blue). Il tuo vizio e una stanza chiusa e solo io ne ho la chiave (GB: Excite Me. US: Eye of the Black Cat). Quando la donne si chiamavano 'Madonne'. Tutti i colori del buio. 1973: Dio, sei un Padretemo (US: Mean Frank and Crazy Tony). Fiori uno, sotto un altro, arriva 'il Passatore'. Quel gran pezzo dell' Ubalda (US: Ubalda, All Naked and Warm). Giovanna coscialunga disonorata con onore. 1974. Anna, quel particolare Piacere (GB: Secrets of a Call Girl). La signora gioca bene a scopa? (GB: Poker in Bed. Later, The Good, the Bad and the Sexy). La vedova inconsolabile ringrazia quanti la consolarono (US: The Win-

some Widow). Il suo nome faceva tremare . . . Interpol in allarme. Innocenza e turbamento. 1975: Il vizio di famiglia (GB and US: Vices in the Family). Grazie nonna (GB: Lover Boy). L'insegnante (GB: Sexy Schoolteacher). La moglie vergine (GB and US: The Virgin Wife). 40 gradi all'ombra del lenzuolo (GB and US: Sex with a Smile). Nude per l'assassino (GB: Strip Nude for Your Killer). La poliziotta fa carriera (US: Confessions of a Lady Cop). 1976: Cattavi pensieri (GB and US: Evil Thoughts). 1977: Gioia (GB: Erotic Exploits of a Sexy Seducer. US: Bull by the Horns). Il grande attacca/The Biggest Battle. 1979: The Lady Next Door. My Loves. Jekyll Junior. La patata bollente (US: Hot Potato). Il ladrone (US: The Good Thief. 1980: La moglie in Vacanza, l'amante in casa (US: While the Wife's Away . . .). Io sono fotogenico. Zucchero, miele e peperoncino. 1981: Tais-toi quand tu parles! Io e Caterina. Lo spiritoso. Asso. Swing! 1982: Il paramedico (US: The Orderly). Pizza, prosciutto e fichi. La poliziotta in New York. Roma X112X. L'avventura ideale. 1984: Vacanze in America.

FERNANDEL (Fernand Contandin) 1903–1971

This genial horse-faced French star comedian was around from the beginning of sound, but became internationally popular only after World War II. Whether as an unctuous flatterer of ladies, a hapless adventurer or the ubiquitous Don Camillo, he was a very funny man. Died from cancer.

1930: Le blanc et le noir. La fine combine. Coeur de lilas. On purge bébé. La meilleure bobonne. 1931: Attaque nocturne. Paris-Béguin. Restez dîner. J'ai quelque chose à vous dire. Pas un mot à man femme. Beau jour de noces. La veine d Anatole. Une brume piquante. Bric-a-brac et cie. 1932: Le judgement de minuit Lidoire. Les gaietés de l'escadron. Le parteuse de pain. Le rosier de Madame Husson. 1933: L'ordonnance. L'homme sans nom. Le coq du régiment. Adhémar aviateur. 1934: Le garrison amoureuse. Angèle. Ma ruche. Nuit de folies. D'amour et d'eau fraîche. Le chéri de sa concièrge. Les bleus de la marine. L'hôtel du libre exchange. 1935: Le train de huit heures. Le cavalier Lafleur. Ferdinand le noceur. Les gaietés de la finance. Jim la Houlette. 1936: Les rois du sport. Les dégourdis de la onzième. François premier. Josette. Un de la legion. 1937: Ignace. Regain.

Hercule. Un carnet de bal (US: Life Dances On). Ernest le Rebelle. 1938: Barnabé. Schpountz. Tricoche et Cacdet. Raphaël le Tatoué. Les cinq sous de Lavarède. 1939: Christine. Berlingot et cie. C'était moi. Fric-Frac. 1940: Monsieur Hector. L'héritier des Montdésir. La fille du puisatier. L'acrobate. Une chapsan de paille d'Italie. L'âge d'or. 1941: La nuit merveilleuse. Le club des soupirants. Les petits viens. Une vie de chien. 1942: La bonne étoile. Simplet. Ne le criez pas sur les toits. 1943: Adrien. La cavalcade des heures. Guignol, marionette de France. 1944: Les gueux du paradis. Naïs. Irma la voyante. 1945: L'aventure de Cabasson. La carrière du grand café. Le mystère Saint-Val. 1946: Pétrus Coeur de coq. Comédians ambulants. 1947: Edition spéciale. Emile l'Africain. 1948: Si ça peut vous faire plaisir. L'armoire volante. 1949: Je suis de la revue. On demande un assassin. Casimir. L'heroïque Monsieur Boniface. 1950: Topaze. Meurtres. Tu m'as sauvé la vie. Uniformes et grandes manoeuvres. Boniface somnambule (GB: The Sleepwalker). 1951: The Red Inn. Adhémar. La table aux crevés (GB: Village Feud). The Little World of Don Camillo. 1952: Coiffeur pour dames (GB: An Artist with Ladies). Forbidden Fruit. Le boulanger de Valargue. The Return of Don Camillo. 1953: Carnaval. Santarellina. Mam'zelle Nitouche. Public Enemy No. 1. 1954: The Sheep Has Five Legs. Ali-Baba. Le printemps, l'automne et l'amour. 1955: La grande bagarre de Don Camillo (GB: Don Camillo's Last Round). 1956: Le couturier de ces dames (GB: Fernandel the Dressmaker). Honoré de Marseille. Quatre pas dans les nuages. 1956: L'art d'être papa (TV). Around the World in 80 Days. 1957: L'homme à l'impermeable. Ex-fugue pour clarinette. Le chômeur de Clochemerle. Sénéchal the Magnificent. 1958: Paris Holiday. La vie à deux (GB: The Two of Us). La loi c'est la loi. Le grand chef. Le confident de ces dames. The Cow and I. Sous le ciel de Provence. 1959: Crésus. Les vignes du Seigneur. 1960: Le caïd. Cocagne. Dynamite Jack. 1961: Don Camillo Monseigneur. Cet imbecile de Rimoldi. L'assassin est dans l'annaire. Il giudizio universale. 1962: En avant la musique. The Devil and the 10 Commandments. Voyage to Biarritz. 1963: La cuisine au beurre (US: My Wife's Husband). Blague dans le coin. 1964: L'âge ingrat. Relaxe-toi, chérie. Le bon roi Dagobert. 1965: La bourse et la vie. Don Camillo in Moscow. 1966: Le voyage du père. 1967: L'homme à la Buick. 1970: Heureux qui comme Ulysse.

FERRER, José (J. Vicente F. Otero y Cintron) 1909–

Glowering, long-faced, thick-lipped Puerto Rican actor who made himself a reputation for versatility in his first few films (which included an Academy Award for *Cyrano de Bergerac*) after coming to the cinema at 40. Later indulged a penchant for direction with variable results. He received additional Academy Award nominations for *Joan of Arc* and *Moulin Rouge*. Marriages to actress Uta Hagen and singer Rosemary Clooney were among three that ended in divorce.

*1946: *Bolivia (narrator only). 1948: Joan of*

Arc. 1949: Whirlpool. *The Sydenham Plan (narrator only). 1950: The Secret Fury. Crisis. Cyrano de Bergerac. 1952: Anything Can Happen. Moulin Rouge. *Article 55 (narrator only). 1953: Miss Sadie Thompson. 1954: The Caine Mutiny. Deep in My Heart. 1955: The Shrike. Cockleshell Heroes. 1956: The Great Man. 1957: I Accuse! 1959: The High Cost of Loving. 1961: Forbid Them Not (narrator only). Leggi di guerra. 1962: Lawrence of Arabia. Cyrano and D'Artagnan. Nine Hours to Rama. *Progress for Freedom (narrator only). 1963: Verspätung in Marienborn (GB: Stop Train 349). 1965: The Greatest Story Ever Told. Ship of Fools. 1966: Enter Laughing. 1968: Le avventure e gli amori di Miguel Cervantes (GB: Cervantes. US: Cervantes, the Young Rebel). A Case of Libel (TV). 1969: *The Little Drummer Boy. 1970: The Aquarians (TV). 1971: Banyon (TV). The Cable Car Mystery (later Crosscurrent) (TV). 1973: The Marcus-Nelson Murders (TV). El Clan de los Immorales (GB: Order to Kill). 1974: The Missing Are Deadly (TV). 1975: e'Lollipop (US: Forever Young, Forever Free). Paco. Medical Story (TV). Roman Grey (GB: The Art of Crime) (TV). 1976: Crash. The Sentinel. The Big Bus. Voyage of the Damned. 1977: Exo-Man (TV). Who Has Seen the Wind? Behind the Iron Mask (GB: The Fifth Musketeer). Zoltan, Hound of Dracula (US: Dracula's Dog). J. Edgar Hoover, Godfather of the FBI Later and (GB: The Private Files of J. Edgar Hoover). 1978: The Swarm. The Amazing Captain Nemo (TV. GB: cinemas). Fedora. 1979: Natural Enemies. 1980: Bittercreek Brawl. The Red Tide (later Blood Tide). Easter Sunday. The Murder That Wouldn't Die (TV). Bloody Birthday. 1981: Berlin Tunnel 21 (TV). 1982: A Midsummer Night's Sex Comedy. 1983: To Be or Not to Be. The Being. This Girl for Hire (TV). Blood Feud (TV). 1984: Dune. The Evil That Men Do. Samson and Delilah (TV). 1985: Hitler's SS: Portrait in Evil (TV. GB: cinemas).

As director:
1955: The Shrike. Cockleshell Heroes. 1956: The Great Man. 1957: I Accuse! 1958: The High Cost of Loving. 1961: Return to Peyton Place. 1962: State Fair.

FERRER, Mel (Melchior Ferrer) 1917–
Gaunt, sensitive-looking leading man with receding hair, employed to best advantage in the early fifties, when he proved he could project sensitivity and meanness to equal effect. Went into production (he was a producer-director before acting in films) in the seventies after an increasingly lacklustre series of costume epics. Married to Audrey Hepburn (fourth of five) from 1954 to 1968.

1949: Lost Boundaries. 1950: Born to be Bad. 1951: The Brave Bulls. 1952: Rancho Notorious. Scaramouche. Lili. 1953: Saadia. 1954: Knights of the Round Table. 1955: Proibito (US: Forbidden). Oh, Rosalinda!! 1956: War and Peace. Elena et les hommes (GB and US: Paris Does Strange Things). 1957: The Vintage. The Sun Also Rises. 1958: Fraulein. Mayerling (TV). 1959: The World, the Flesh and the Devil. 1960: The Hands of Orlac. L'homme à femmes. Et mourir de plaisir. 1961: Charge of the Black Lancers. Blood and Roses. Leggi di guerra. 1962: The Longest Day. Kriegsgesetz. The Devil and the 10 Commandments. The Fall of the Roman Empire. 1964: Paris When It Sizzles. Sex and the Single Girl. El Greco. El Señor de la Salle. 1967: Every Day's a Holiday. 1969: Who Are My Own? 1971: Time for Loving. 1975: The Black Pirate. Brannigan. The Girl from the Red Cabaret. 1976: Eaten Alive (GB: Death Trap). Das Netz. The Antichrist (US: The Tempter). 1977: Hi-Riders. Pyjama Girl. 1978: The Fish Men. La ragazza in pigiama giallo. The Amazing Captain Nemo (TV. GB: cinemas). The Norsemen. Zwischengleis (US: Yesterday's Tomorrow). Sharon: Portrait of a Mistress (TV). 1979: The Visitor. Top of the Hill (TV). The Fifth Floor. 1980: Sfida all'ultimo paradiso. Avvoltoi sulla city/Vultures over the City. The Memory of Eva Ryker (TV) Nightmare City. Buitres sobre la ciudad. Fugitive Family (TV). Lili Marleen. Mangiati vivi dai cannibali (GB: Eaten Alive. US: Doomed to Die). 1981: Mille milliards de dollars. Die Jäger (US: Deadly Game). 1982: Screamers (The Fish Men with added footage). One Shoe Makes It Murder. 1986: Outrage! (TV).

As director:
1945: The Girl of the Limberlost. 1950: The Secret Fury. Vendetta (co-directed). 1958: Green Mansions. 1965: Cabriola (US: Every Day is a Holiday).

FEUILLÈRE, Edwige (Caroline E. Cunati-Koenig) 1907–
Beautiful, faintly spiteful-looking French actress, only occasionally seen in international roles. In post-war years, she became best known for her parts as sensual, mature women teaching young men about love, or being confounded by fate. Her chestnut-haired, brown-eyed loveliness has graced the London stage on a number of occasions, although she made just one British film.

1931: Cordon-bleu. Mam'zelle Nitouche. *La fine combine. 1932: La perle. Topaze. Monsieur Albert. Maquillage. Une petite femme dans le train. 1933: Toi que j'adore. Les aventures du Roi Pausole. Matricule 33. L'appel de la nuit. Ces messieurs de La Santé. 1934: Le miroir des alouettes. 1935: Lucrecia Borgia. Barcarolle. Stradivarius. Amore. Golgotha. La route heureuse. 1936: Mister Flow (US: Compliments of Mister Flow). 1937: Marthe Richard au service de la France (GB: Au Service de la France). Feu! La dame de Malacca. 1938: J'étais une aventurière. 1939: L'émigrante. Sans lendemain. 1940: De Mayerling à Sarajevo. 1941: Mam'zelle Bonaparte. La Duchesse de Langeais. L'honorable Catherine. 1943: Lucrèce. 1945: Tant que je vivrai. La parte de l'ombre (US: Blind Desire). 1946: L'idiot. Il suffit d'une fois. 1947: L'aigle a deux têtes. 1948: Woman Hater. 1949: Julie de Carneilhan. 1950: Olivia (US: Pit of Loneliness). Souvenirs perdus (GB: Lost Property). 1951: Le Cap de l'Esperance. 1952: Adorables créatures/Adorable Creatures. 1953: Le blé en herbe (GB: Ripening Seed. US: The Game of Love). 1954: Les fruits de l'été (US: Fruits of the Summer). 1957: Quand la femme s'en mêle. Le septième commandment (GB: The Seventh Commandment). 1958: En cas de malheur (GB and US: Love is My Profession). La vie à deux/The Two of Us. 1961: Amours célèbres. 1962: Le crime ne paie pas. 1964: Aimez-vous les femmes? (GB: Do You Like Women? US: A Taste for Women). 1967: *La route d'un homme (narrator only). 1968: Scusi, facciamo l'amore. 1970: Le clair de terre. 1974: La chair de l'orchidée.

FIELD, Betty 1918–1973
Neat, versatile American actress, seen in her younger days mostly as girls with some kind of defect, physical or mental, in their make-up. She had some interesting roles (the farm-slut in *Of Mice and Men*, Daisy in the 1949 version of *The Great Gatsby*), but showed preference for the stage and also aged quickly, returning to films from time to time as

troubled or repressed women. Died from a cerebral haemorrhage.
1939: What a Life. Of Mice and Men. 1940: Seventeen. Victory. 1941: Shepherd of the Hills. Blues in the Night. 1942: King's Row. Are Husbands Necessary? 1943: Flesh and Fantasy. 1944: The Great Moment. Tomorrow the World. 1945: The Southerner. 1949: The Great Gatsby. 1955: Picnic. 1956: Bus Stop. 1957: Peyton Place. 1959: Hound Dog Man. 1960: Butterfield 8. 1962: Bird Man of Alcatraz. 1965: Seven Women. 1968: How to Save a Marriage – and Ruin Your Life. Coogan's Bluff.

FIELD, Sally 1946–
Tiny, pug-faced American actress with sexy figure who played cute young things in TV series throughout the 1960s. Her career seemed to be over by the early 1970s, when she suddenly re-emerged as a big star with a series of tough, determined little ladies that only her one previous film appearance had hinted at. Subsequently, she took Academy Awards for *Norma Rae* and *Places in the Heart*. Stepdaughter of Jock Mahoney (*qv*).
1967: The Way West. 1970: Marriage Year One (TV). Maybe I'll Come Home in the Spring (TV). 1971: Hitched (TV. GB: Westward the Wagon). Mongo's Back in Town (TV). 1972: Home for the Holidays (TV). 1976: Bridger (TV). Stay Hungry. Sybil (TV. GB: cinemas). 1977: Smokey and the Bandit. Heroes. 1978: Hooper. The End. Norma Rae. 1979: Beyond the Poseidon Adventure. 1980: Smokey and the Bandit II (GB: Smokey and the Bandit Ride Again). 1981: Back Roads. Absence of Malice. No Small

Affair. 1982: Kiss Me Goodbye. 1984: Places in the Heart. 1985: Murphy's Romance.

FIELD, Shirley Ann(e) 1936–
Busty, brunette British actress with cheerful smile and jaunty manner. A multiplicity of pin-up pictures was followed by success as a panellist in the TV quiz game *Yakity Yak*. Her film roles, though increasing in size, remained strictly decorative until 1960, when she surprisingly blossomed as an actress (and added the 'e' to Ann). She was unwisely cast after that, and her career disappointingly petered out into TV commercials, although she came back in TV drama in 1980.
1955: Simon and Laura. All for Mary. Lost (US: Tears for Simon). 1956: The Weapon. It's Never Too Late. It's a Wonderful World. Dry Rot. Loser Takes All. The Silken Affair. Yield to the Night (US: Blonde Sinner). 1957: The Flesh is Weak. Seven Thunders (US: The Beasts of Marseilles). The Good Companions. 1959: Horrors of the Black Museum. Upstairs and Downstairs. Once More with Feeling. Beat Girl. 1960: And the Same to You. Peeping Tom. The Entertainer. Saturday Night and Sunday Morning. Man in the Moon. 1961: The Damned (US: These Are the Damned). 1962: The War Lover. Lunch Hour. 1963: Kings of the Sun. Hell is Empty (released 1967). 1965: Wedding March. 1966: Doctor in Clover. Alfie. 1969: With Love in Mind. 1970: A Touch of the Other. 1973: House of the Living Dead (GB: Dr Maniac). 1985: My Beautiful Laundrette.

FIELD, Sid 1904–1950
Crazy, fast-talking British comedian, an

immense success in the music-halls, particularly in the provinces, where his cross-talking routines with stooge Jerry Desmonde (especially the famous golfing sketch) frequently brought the house down. His three films tried to do too much with him as a situation-comedy actor and failed to capture his special appeal. Died from a heart attack.
1940: That's the Ticket. 1946: London Town (US: My Heart Goes Crazy). 1948: Cardboard Cavalier.

FIELDS, Dame Gracie (Grace Stansfield) 1898–1979
Bubbling, dark-haired British comedienne/singer, whose Lancashire-slanted mixture of comic songs and romantic ballads made her the most popular recording star of her day. Despite coming to films in her thirties, she quickly became Britain's (and, briefly, the world's) highest-paid film star, cruising her chirpy personality through a series of soft-centred, artfully-contrived tragi-comedies. Lost her popularity (and her British film career) when deciding to live abroad during World War II. Married (second of three) director/comedian Monty Banks (1897–1950). Created Dame in 1979. Died from a heart attack.
1931: Sally in Our Alley. 1932: Looking on the Bright Side. 1933: This Week of Grace. 1934: Love, Life and Laughter. Sing As We Go. 1935: Look Up and Laugh. 1936: Queen of Hearts. 1937: The Show Goes On. 1938: We're Going to be Rich. Keep Smiling (US: Smiling Along). 1939: Shipyard Sally. 1943: Stage Door Canteen. Holy Matrimony. 1944: Molly and Me. 1945: Paris Underground (GB: Madame Pimpernel).

FIELDS, W. C. (William Claude Dukenfield) 1879–1946
Burly, round-faced, red-nosed American juggler and comedian, with a long history in vaudeville before his serious film career began in the mid-twenties. With sound, his own peculiar, abrasive, embittered, alcohol-oriented delivery really came into its own and, as henpeck or charlatan in turn, he created a series of comedy classics. Wore a fake moustache in films until 1932. Died, from a com-

bination of dropsy, a liver ailment and heart failure, on the day he moaned about more than any other – Christmas Day.

1915: *Pool Sharks. *His Lordship's Dilemma. 1924: Janice Meredith (GB: The Beautiful Rebel). 1925: Sally of the Sawdust. That Royle Girl. 1926: So's Your Old Man. It's the Old Army Game. 1927: The Potters. Running Wild. Two Flaming Youths (GB: The Side Show). 1928: Tillie's Punctured Romance (GB: Marie's Millions). Fools for Luck. 1930: *The Golf Specialist. 1931: Her Majesty Love. 1932: *The Dentist. If I Had a Million. Million Dollar Legs. 1933: *The Fatal Glass of Beer. *The Pharmacist. *Hip Action. *Hollywood on Parade (B7). *The Barber Shop. International House. Tillie and Gus. Alice in Wonderland. 1934: Six of a Kind. You're Telling Me! The Old Fashioned Way. It's a Gift. Mrs Wiggs of the Cabbage Patch. 1935: David Copperfield. Mississippi. The Man on the Flying Trapeze (GB: The Memory Expert). 1936: Poppy. 1938: The Big Broadcast of 1938. 1939: You Can't Cheat an Honest Man. 1940: My Little Chickadee. The Bank Dick (GB: The Bank Detective). 1941: Never Give a Sucker an Even Break (GB: What A Man!). 1942: †Tales of Manhattan. 1944: Follow the Boys. Song of the Open Road. Sensations of 1945.

† Sequences deleted from final release print

FINCH, Jon 1941–
Dark-haired, handsome, brooding, young-looking British actor who shot to stardom in the early 1970s, especially in the title role of Roman Polanski's *Macbeth*. But good roles

in British films seemed elusive, and he was looking further afield from the mid-1970s. He did not, however, regain his place at the top in cinematic terms, despite some good supporting roles and one or two further leads.

1970: The Vampire Lovers. The Horror of Frankenstein. 1971: L'affaire Martine Desclos. Sunday, Bloody Sunday. Macbeth. 1972: Frenzy. Lady Caroline Lamb. 1973: The Final Programme (US: The Last Days of Man on Earth). 1974: Diagnosis: Murder. 1976: Une femme fidèle. The Man with the Green Cross. 1977: El segundo poder. Die Standarte (US: Battle Flag). 1978: El borracho. Death on the Nile. 1979: The Sabina. 1980: Breaking Glass. Gary Cooper, que estas en los cielos. 1981: The Threat. 1982: Giro City (TV. US: And Nothing But the Truth). 1984: Pop Pirates.

FINCH, Peter (William Mitchell) 1916–1977
Dark-haired, British-born portrayer of strong characters. He made his name in Australia before returning to England where he slowly became much admired as hero, villain and all-round good actor. In the sixties he became an international star, but his roles were less consistently good. A hell-raiser who lived life to the full, he died from a heart attack, and was posthumously given an Oscar for his last film, *Network*. Also Oscar-nominated for *Sunday, Bloody Sunday*.

1935: †Magic Shoes. 1938: Dad and Dave Come to Town. Mr Chedworth Steps Out. 1939: Ants in His Pants. 1940: The Power and the Glory. 1942: Another Threshold. While There's Still Time. 1943: South-West Pacific. Red Sky at Morning (released 1951 as Escape at Dawn). 1944: Rats of Tobruk. Jungle Patrol (narrator only). 1945: *Indonesia Calling (narrator only). 1946: A Son is Born. *Native Earth (narrator only). 1947: *The Nomads (narrator only). 1948: Eureka Stockade (US: Massacre Hill). The Hunt (narrator only). 1949: *The Corroboree (narrator only). Train of Events. 1950: The Wooden Horse. The Miniver Story. 1952: The Story of Robin Hood and His Merrie Men. 1953: The Story of Gilbert and Sullivan (US: The Great Gilbert and Sullivan). The Heart of the Matter. 1954: Father Brown (US: The Detective). Elephant Walk. Make Me an Offer. 1955: Passage Home. The Dark Avenger (US: The Warriors). Simon

and Laura. Josephine and Men. 1956: A Town Like Alice (US: The Rape of Malaya). The Queen in Australia (narrator only). *Melbourne – Olympic City (narrator only). The Battle of the River Plate (US: Pursuit of the Graf Spee). The Royal Tour of New South Wales (narrator only). 1957: The Shiralee. Robbery Under Arms. Windom's Way. 1958: A Far Cry (narrator only). Operation Amsterdam. 1959: The Nun's Story. 1960: The Trials of Oscar Wilde (US: The Man with the Green Carnation). Kidnapped. No Love for Johnnie. 1961: The Sins of Rachel Cade. 1962: I Thank a Fool. 1963: In the Cool of the Day. Girl with Green Eyes. 1964: First Men in the Moon. The Pumpkin Eater. 1965: Judith. The Flight of the Phoenix. 1966: 10.30 pm Summer. 1967: Far from the Madding Crowd. 1968: The Legend of Lylah Clare. 1969: The Red Tent. *The Greatest Mother of Them All. 1971: Sunday, Bloody Sunday. Something to Hide. 1972: England Made Me. Lost Horizon. 1973: Bequest to the Nation (US: The Nelson Affair). 1974: The Abdication. 1976: Raid on Entebbe (TV. GB: cinemas). Network.

As director:
1962: *The Day
† Unreleased

FINLAY, Frank 1926–
Stocky, hollow-cheeked, black-browed British character star, good at provincials, union officials and police inspectors. After several years in supporting roles, he looked like drifting into stardom in the early 1970s. The prospect seemed to repel him and he became a dedicated theatre man again, in leading roles and, especially in the British stage production of *Amadeus*, to fine critical reviews. He returned to films in the 1980s, although his choice of roles has sometimes seemed less sure. Nominated for an Oscar in *Othello*.

1962: The Loneliness of the Long Distance Runner. The Longest Day. Life for Ruth (US: Walk in the Shadow). Private Potter. 1963: Doctor in Distress. The Informers. The Comedy Man. Hot Enough for June (US: Agent 8¾). The Wild Affair. 1965: A Study in Terror (US: Fog). Othello. 1966: The Sandwich Man. The Jokers. 1967: The Deadly Bees. I'll Never Forget What's 'is Name. *The Spare Tyres. Robbery. 1968: The Molly Maguires. The Shoes of the Fisherman. Inspector Clouseau. Twisted Nerve. 1970: Cromwell. The

Body (narrator only). Assault (US: The Devil's Garden). 1971: Gumshoe. Danny Jones. 1972: Sitting Target. Neither the Sea Nor the Sand. 1973: Shaft in Africa. The Three Musketeers. 1974: The Four Musketeers. 1978: The Wild Geese. The Thief of Baghdad. Sherlock Holmes: Murder by Decree (GB: Murder by Decree). 1982: Enigma. The Return of the Soldier. 1983: The Ploughman's Lunch. 1984: Sakharov. A Christmas Carol (TV). 1919. The Key. Arch of Triumph (TV). 1985: Life Force (formerly Space Vampires). The Secret State.

FINNEY, Albert 1936–

Beefy, scowling, tow-haired British leading actor, one of the original angry young brigade of the early 1960s. His best roles (Tom Jones, Saturday Night and Sunday Morning, Gumshoe, The Dresser) have been so good as to make the rest of his film career seem desperately unsatisfactory by comparison. Married to actresses Jane Wenham (1957 to 1961) and Anouk Aimee (qv; 1970 to 1978). Nominated for Academy Awards in Tom Jones, Murder on the Orient Express and The Dresser. 1960: The Entertainer. Saturday Night and Sunday Morning. 1963: Tom Jones. The Victors. Night Must Fall. 1967: Two for the Road. †Charlie Bubbles. 1969: The Picasso Summer. 1970: Scrooge. 1971: Gumshoe. 1972: Alpha Beta (copyrighted and released 1975). 1974: Murder on the Orient Express. 1975: The Adventure of Sherlock Holmes' Smarter Brother. 1977: The Duellists. 1980: Loophole. 1981: Wolfen. Shoot the Moon. 1982: Annie. 1983: The Dresser. 1984: Under the Volcano. Pope John Paul II (TV). Notes from Under the Volcano. Observations Under the Volcano.

† And directed

FIRTH, Peter 1953–

Slight, fair-haired, boyish-looking British actor who had a few minor roles and juvenile leads in films before making his name on stage as the tormented youth in Equus, a role he repeated with some (but not as much) success on screen, although it won him an Oscar nomination. It seems he may not be distinctive enough to become a star in the international cinema, a field in which he continues to make sporadic appearances.
1972: Diamonds on Wheels. Brother Sun, Sister

Moon. 1973: Daniel and Maria. 1976: Aces High. Joseph Andrews. 1977: Equus. 1979: Tess. When You Comin' Back, Red Ryder? 1983: The Aerodrome (TV). 1984: White Elephant. 1985: The Flight of the Spruce Goose. Letter to Brezhnev. Life Force (formerly Space Vampires). 1986: A State of Emergency.

FISHER, Carrie 1956–

Diminutive but forceful, dark-haired American actress, daughter of Debbie Reynolds (qv) and singer Eddie Fisher, and on stage with her mother at 12. Despite landing the female lead in the Star Wars films, she hasn't quite as yet established a definite image for herself and her remaining roles don't linger in the mind. Some filmographies credit her with appearances in I Wanna Hold Your Hand (1978) and Wise Blood (1979), but she doesn't seem to be in either. Married singer Paul Simon (of Simon and Garfunkel) in 1984.
1975: Shampoo. 1977: Star Wars. 1978: Leave Yesterday Behind (TV). 1979: Mr Mike's Mondo Video. 1980: The Empire Strikes Back. The Blues Brothers. 1981: Under the Rainbow. 1983: Return of the Jedi. 1984: Garbo Talks! 1985: Mischief/The Man with the One Red Shoe. 1986: Hannah and Her Sisters. Hollywood Vice Squad.

FITZGERALD, Barry (William Shields) 1888–1961

Diminutive Irish actor (at the Abbey Theatre from 1915) with rumpled features and twinkling blue eyes, who won an Academy Award as the Catholic priest (in real life he was a Protestant) in Going My Way, and remained

Hollywood's favourite Irishman from 1936 to 1952. Died a few weeks after brain surgery.
1929: Juno and the Paycock (US: The Shame of Mary Boyle). 1934: Guests of the Nation. 1936: When Knights Were Bold. The Plough and the Stars. 1937: Ebb Tide. 1938: Pacific Liner. Bringing Up Baby. The Dawn Patrol. Four Men and a Prayer. Marie Antoinette. 1939: The Saint Strikes Back. Full Confession. 1940: The Long Voyage Home. San Francisco Docks. 1941: The Sea Wolf. Tarzan's Secret Treasure. How Green Was My Valley. 1943: Two Tickets to London. The Amazing Mrs Holliday. Corvette K-225 (GB: The Nelson Touch). 1944: Going My Way. None But the Lonely Heart. I Love a Soldier. 1945: And Then There Were None (GB: 10 Little Niggers). Duffy's Tavern. Incendiary Blonde. The Stork Club. 1946: Two Years Before the Mast. California. 1947: Welcome Stranger. Easy Come, Easy Go. Variety Girl. 1948: The Naked City. The Sainted Sisters. Miss Tatlock's Millions. 1949: Top o' the Morning. 1950: The Story of Seabiscuit (GB: Pride of Kentucky). Union Station. 1951: Silver City (GB: High Vermilion). 1952: The Quiet Man. Il filo d'erba. 1954: Happy Ever After (US: Tonight's the Night). 1956: The Catered Affair (GB: Wedding Breakfast). 1958: Rooney. 1959: The Cradle of Genius. Broth of a Boy.

FITZGERALD, Geraldine 1912–

Dark-haired Irish actress with classic 'colleen' complexion and strong personality. She went to Hollywood after a start in British films, but her ideals were too high for Warners, who suspended her a number of times for refusing roles, and her film career stuttered to a halt in the late forties. Has latterly become a barnstorming character actress and nightclub singer. Nominated for an Academy Award in *Wuthering Heights*.

1934: *Blind Justice. Open All Night.* 1935: *The Lad. The Ace of Spades. Three Witnesses. Lieutenant Daring RN. Turn of the Tide. Radio Parade of 1935. Bargain Basement/Department Store.* 1936: *Debt of Honour. Café Mascot. The Mill on the Floss.* 1939: *Wuthering Heights. Dark Victory.* 1940: *A Child is Born. 'Til We Meet Again.* 1941: *Shining Victory. Flight from Destiny.* 1942: *The Gay Sisters.* 1943: *Watch on the Rhine.* 1944: *Ladies Courageous. Wilson.* 1945: *The Strange Affair of Uncle Harry (GB: Uncle Harry).* 1946: *Three Strangers. OSS. Nobody Lives Forever.* 1948: *So Evil My Love.* 1951: *The Late Edwina Black (US: Obsessed).* 1958: *10 North Frederick.* 1959: *The Moon and Sixpence (TV).* 1961: *The Fiercest Heart.* 1965: *The Pawnbroker.* 1968: *Rachel, Rachel.* 1971: †*Believe in Me.* 1973: *The Last American Hero.* 1974: *Harry and Tonto.* 1975: *Cold Sweat. Echoes of a Summer.* 1977: *Ciao Male/Bye Bye Monkey!/The Monkey's Uncle. The Mango Tree. Yesterday's Child (TV). The Quinns (TV).* 1979: *Tristan and Isolt (unreleased).* 1980: *Arthur.* 1982: *The Link.* 1983: *Kennedy (TV). Easy Money.* 1985: *Do You Remember Love? (TV).* 1986: *Poltergeist II.*

FLANAGAN, Bud (Reuben Weintrop, later Robert Winthrop) 1896–1968
Genial Jewish East Londoner who, after music-hall experience as a magician, formed half of a smash-hit comedy team with lean, poker-faced Chesney Allen (1893–1982). Their sense of humour, at once bawdy and lunatic, was amalgamated in the late thirties with fellow comedy teams Nervo and Knox and Naughton and Gold to form The Crazy Gang. Flanagan, customarily in dented porkpie hat and enormous fur coat, led the Gang and also wrote and sang (with Allen) some enormously successful London-based songs. The team ultimately split because of Allen's ill-health but, ironically, it was Flanagan who died first, from a heart attack.

1932: **The Bailiffs.* 1933: **They're Off. *The Dreamers.* 1934: *Wild Boy.* 1935: *A Fire Has Been Arranged.* 1937: *Underneath the Arches. Okay for Sound.* 1938: *Alf's Button Afloat.*

1939: *The Frozen Limits.* 1940: *Gasbags.* 1941: **Listen to Britain. *The Crazy Gang Argue About Lending Money (Gaumont-British newsreel).* 1942: *We'll Smile Again.* 1943: *Theatre Royal.* 1944: *Dreaming.* 1945: *Here Comes the Sun.* 1951: †*Judgment Deferred.* 1958: *Dunkirk. Life is a Circus.* 1963: †*The Wild Affair.*

†*Without Chesney Allen*

FLEMING, Rhonda (Marilyn Louis) 1922–
So what was wrong with Marilyn Louis? At any rate, the change of name did this stunning, green-eyed American redhead little good until she was selected as Bing Crosby's leading lady in *A Connecticut Yankee*. Then she rapidly became known as Queen of Technicolor in a series of self-reliant, but slightly too self-aware performances in which she never quite seemed to let herself go. Married (fourth of four) producer-director Hall Bartlett from 1966 to 1971.

1943: *In Old Oklahoma (later War of the Wildcats).* 1944: *When Strangers Marry (later Betrayed). Since You Went Away.* 1945: *Spellbound. The Spiral Staircase. Abilene Town.* 1947: *Adventure Island. Out of the Past (GB: Build My Gallows High).* 1949: *A Connecticut Yankee in King Arthur's Court. The Great Lover.* 1950: *The Eagle and the Hawk. The Redhead and the Cowboy. Cry Danger.* 1951: *The Last Outpost. Little Egypt (GB: Chicago Masquerade). Hong Kong. Crosswinds.* 1952: *The Golden Hawk. Tropic Zone.* 1953: *Pony Express. Those Redheads from Seattle. Serpent of the Nile. Inferno.* 1954: *Jivaro (GB: Lost Treasure of the Amazon). Yankee Pasha. The Courtesan of Babylon (GB: The Slave Woman. US: Queen of Babylon).* 1955: *Tennessee's Partner.* 1956: *The Killer is Loose. Slightly Scarlet. *Hollywood Beauty. While the City Sleeps. Odongo. *Hollywood Première. Gunfight at the OK Corral.* 1957: *The Buster Keaton Story. Gun Glory.* 1958: *Bullwhip. Home Before Dark.* 1959: *Alias Jesse James. The Big Circus.* 1960: *The Revolt of the Slaves. The Crowded Sky.* 1964: *The Patsy. Una moglie americana (US: Run for Your Wife).* 1968: *Backtrack (TV).* 1975: *Last Hours Before Morning (TV). Won Ton Ton, the Dog Who Saved Hollywood.* 1979: *Love for Rent (TV).* 1980: *The Nude Bomb.*

FLEMYNG, Robert 1912–
Elegant, brown-haired British leading man who seems in retrospect to have been in scores of films since his debut as a smooth young foil for Jessie Matthews, but has in fact made comparatively few. Always authoritative and in command of the situation, whether as officer, lawyer, teacher, politician or, latterly, judge. His principal work, to which he has brought commanding presence and ringing tones, has remained for the theatre.

1937: *Head over Heels (GB: Head over Heels in Love).* 1948: *Bond Street. The Guinea Pig.* 1949: *Conspirator. The Blue Lamp.* 1950: *Blackmailed.* 1951: *The Magic Box.* 1952: *The Holly and the Ivy.* 1955: *Cast a Dark Shadow. The Man Who Never Was.* 1956: *Funny Face.* 1957: *Let's Be Happy. Windom's Way.* 1959: *Blind Date. A Touch of Larceny. Chance Meeting.* 1960: *Radius.* 1962: **The King's Breakfast. L'orribile segreto del Dottor Hichcock (GB: The Terror of Dr Hichcock. US: The Horrible Doctor Hichcock).* 1963: *Mystery Submarine (US: Decoy).* 1966: *The Quiller Memorandum. The Deadly Affair. The Spy with a Cold Nose.* 1967: *The Blood Beast Terror (US: Deathshead Avenger).* 1969: *The Body Stealers. Oh! What a Lovely War. Battle of Britain.* 1970: *The Firechasers.* 1971: *The Darwin Adventure. Young Winston.* 1972: *Travels with My Aunt.* 1977: *The Medusa Touch. Golden Rendezvous.* 1978: *The Four Feathers (TV. GB: cinemas). The Thirty-Nine Steps.* 1980: *Rebecca (TV).*

FLYNN, Errol 1909–1959
Tasmanian-born star whose colourful early years, spent mainly in various forms of ship-

ping, led him to film in Australia, England and finally Hollywood, where, soon moustachioed, he became the film capital's swashbuckler *par excellence* in a series of expensively-mounted action films. His vivid, womanizing, booze-hitting private life included marriages to actresses Lily Damita (1935–1942) and Patrice Wymore (1950; separated 1957), first and third of three. Died from a heart attack.

1932: *Dr H. Erben's New Guinea Expedition.* 1933: *In the Wake of the Bounty.* 1934: *Murder at Monte Carlo.* 1935: *The Case of the Curious Bride. Don't Bet on Blondes. Captain Blood.* 1936: *The Charge of the Light Brigade.* **Pirate Party on Catalina Isle.* 1937: *Green Light. The Prince and the Pauper. Another Dawn. The Perfect Specimen.* 1938: *The Adventures of Robin Hood. The Sisters. Four's a Crowd. The Dawn Patrol.* 1939: *Dodge City. The Private Lives of Elizabeth and Essex.* 1940: *Virginia City. Santa Fé Trail. The Sea Hawk.* 1941: *Footsteps in the Dark. Dive Bomber. They Died with Their Boots On* 1942: *Desperate Journey. Gentleman Jim.* 1943: *Edge of Darkness. Northern Pursuit. Thank Your Lucky Stars.* 1944: *Uncertain Glory.* 1945: *Objective Burma. San Antonio.* 1946: *Never Say Good-bye. Cry Wolf. Escape Me Never. Always To-gether.* 1948: *Silver River. Adventures of Don Juan (GB: The New Adventures of Don Juan).* 1949: *That Forsyte Woman (GB: The Forsyte Saga). It's a Great Feeling. Montana.* 1950: *Rocky Mountain. Hello God. Kim. The Adventures of Captain Fabian.* 1952: **Cruise of the Zaca. Maru Maru. Against All Flags.* **Deep Sea Fishing.* 1953: *The Master of Ballantrae. Crossed Swords.* †*William Tell.* 1954: *Lilacs in the Spring (US: Let's Make Up).* 1955: *The Dark Avenger (US: The Warriors). King's Rhapsody.* 1956: *Istanbul. The Sword of Villon (TV). The Big Boodle (GB: Night in Havana).* 1957: *The Sun Also Rises. Without Incident (TV).* 1958: *The Roots of Heaven. Too Much, Too Soon.* 1959: *Cuban Rebel Girls.*

†*Unfinished*

FOCH, Nina (N. Fock) 1924–
Aristocratic, cool, resourceful blonde Dutch-born Hollywood actress, the daughter of composer-conductor Dirk Fock and actress Consuelo Flowerton (1900–1965). She gave some excellent performances in the mid-forties that

might have set her up for a star career, but she lacked a definitive personality and, after a spell in television and theatre, was confined to top supporting roles. Oscar-nominated for *Executive Suite.*

1943: **Wagon Wheels West. Return of the Vampire.* 1944: *Curse of the Werewolf. Strange Affair. Nine Girls. She's a Soldier Too. Shadows in the Night. She's a Sweetheart.* 1945: *Prison Ship. Escape in the Fog. My Name is Julia Ross. I Love a Mystery. A Song to Remember. Boston Blackie's Rendezvous (GB: Blackie's Rendezvous).* 1947: *The Guilt of Janet Ames. Johnny O'Clock.* 1948: *The Dark Past.* 1949: *Johnny Allegro (GB: Hounded). The Undercover Man.* 1951: *St Benny the Dip (GB: Escape If You Can). An American in Paris. Young Man with Ideas.* 1952: *Scaramouche. Fast Company.* 1953: *Sombrero.* 1954: *Executive Suite. Four Guns to the Border.* 1955: *One Life (TV. GB: cinemas). You're Never Too Young. Yacht on the High Sea (TV. GB: cinemas). Illegal.* 1956: *The Ten Commandments. Heritage of Anger (TV).* 1957: *The Playroom (TV). Three Brave Men.* 1958: *Free Weekend (TV).* 1959: *Cash McCall.* 1960: *Spartacus.* 1967: *Prescription Murder (TV).* 1969: *Gidget Grows Up (TV).* 1971: *Such Good Friends.* 1972: *Female Artillery (TV).* 1973: *Salty.* 1974: *A Little Bit Like Murder (TV). Oh! Baby, Baby, Baby ... (TV).* 1975: *Mahogany.* 1977: *The Great Houdinis (TV).* 1978: *Jennifer. Ebony, Ivory and Jade (TV). Child of Glass (TV).* 1981: *Rich and Famous.* 1985: *Shadow Chasers (TV).*

FONDA, Henry 1905–1982
Dark, handsome, youthful-looking American leading man whose sincerity, sensitivity and memorable speaking voice enabled him to give any number of fine performances in the cinema, amazingly without winning an Academy Award until the year of his death, although nominated for *The Grapes of Wrath* in 1940. His prolific narration is listed separately below. Married (first of five) to Margaret Sullavan (*qv*) from 1931 to 1933. Father of Jane and Peter Fonda. In 1981 Fonda received an honorary Academy Award, then finally won a best actor Oscar for *On Golden Pond*, a few months before his death from heart trouble.

1935: *The Farmer Takes a Wife. Way Down*

East. *I Dream Too Much.* 1936: *The Trail of the Lonesome Pine. Spendthrift. The Moon's Our Home.* 1937: *Slim. Wings of the Morning. That Certain Woman. You Only Live Once.* 1938: *Blockade. I Met My Love Again. The Mad Miss Manton. Jezebel. Spawn of the North.* 1939: *Jesse James. The Story of Alexander Graham Bell (GB: The Modern Miracle). Let Us Live. Drums Along the Mohawk. Young Mr Lincoln.* 1940: *The Grapes of Wrath. The Return of Frank James. Lillian Russell. Chad Hanna.* 1941: *The Lady Eve. Wild Geese Calling. You Belong to Me (GB: Good Morning, Doctor).* 1942: *Rings on Her Fingers. The Male Animal. The Magnificent Dope. The Big Street. Tales of Manhattan. The Ox-Bow Incident (GB: Strange Incident).* 1943: *The Immortal Sergeant.* 1946: *My Darling Clementine.* 1947: *The Fugitive. Daisy Kenyon. The Long Night.* 1948: *Fort Apache. A Miracle Can Happen (later and GB: On Our Merry Way).* 1949: *Jigsaw.* 1953: †*Main Street to Broadway.* 1955: *Mister Roberts.* 1956: *12 Angry Men. The Wrong Man. War and Peace.* 1957: *The Tin Star.* 1958: *Stage Struck.* **Fabulous Hollywood.* 1959: *Warlock. The Man Who Understood Women.* 1962: *Advise and Consent. The Longest Day. How the West Was Won.* 1963: *Spencer's Mountain.* 1964: *The Best Man. Fail Safe. Sex and the Single Girl.* 1965: *The Rounders. In Harm's Way. Battle of the Bulge. La guerre secrète (GB and US: The Dirty Game).* 1966: *A Big Hand for the Little Lady (GB: Big Deal at Dodge City). Welcome to Hard Times (GB: Killer on a Horse).* 1967: *Firecreek. Stranger on the Run (TV). All About People.* 1968: *Yours, Mine and Ours. Madigan. The Boston Strangler. Once Upon a Time in the West.* 1969: *Too Late the Hero.* 1970: *There Was a Crooked Man. The Cheyenne Social Club.* 1971: *Sometimes a Great Notion (GB: Never Give an Inch). Directed by John Ford.* 1972: *The Serpent.* 1973: *Ash Wednesday. The Alpha Caper (TV. GB: cinemas, as Inside Job). The Red Pony (TV. GB: cinemas, in abbreviated version). My Name is Nobody.* 1974: *Mussolini: The Last Act/Mussolini: The Last Four Days.* 1976: *Midway (GB: Battle of Midway). Collision Course. Tentacles.* 1977: *Rollercoaster. The Last of the Cowboys (later The Great Smokey Roadblock). Il grande attacca/The Biggest Battle.* 1978: *The Swarm. Fedora. Wanda Nevada. City on Fire.* 1979: *Home to Stay (TV). Meteor.* 1980: *Gideon's Trumpet (TV). The Oldest Living Graduate (TV).* 1981: *On Golden Pond. Summer Solstice (TV).*

As narrator:
1942: **The Battle of Midway.* 1943: **It's Everybody's War.* 1950: **Home of the Homeless.* 1951: **Grant Wood.* **Benjy.* **The Growing Years.* 1952: *The Impressionable Years.* 1958: **Reach for Tomorrow.* 1963: **Rangers of Yellowstone.* 1967: *The Golden Flame.* 1968: *Born to Buck.* 1969: **An Impression of John Steinbeck – Writer.* 1974: *Valley Forge.* 1977: **Alcohol Abuse – The Early Warning Signs.* 1978: **Big Yellow Schooner to Byzantium.* 1979: *The Man Who Loved Bears.* 1981:

America's Sweetheart: The Mary Pickford Story.

† *Scenes deleted from final release print*

FONDA, Jane 1937–
Tawny-haired American actress, daughter of Henry Fonda. Started out as bright, knowing city girls, graduated to pin-up roles, then suddenly, at the end of the sixties, burst on the film scene as a fine actress, later picking up Oscars for *Klute* and *Coming Home*. She has inherited much of her father's movingly deep sincerity and, given the right role, is now one of the best two or three actresses in America. Married (first of two) to director Roger Vadim (1965–1973) and noted for her espousal of women's rights, anti-Vietnam and provocative minority causes. Also Oscar-nominated for *They Shoot Horses, Don't They?*, *Julia*, *The China Syndrome* and *On Golden Pond*.
1960: *Tall Story*. 1961: *The Chapman Report*. *A String of Beads (TV)*. 1962: *A Walk on the Wild Side*. *Period of Adjustment*. 1963: *In the Cool of the Day*. *Sunday in New York*. 1964: *Les félins (GB: The Love Cage. US: Joyhouse)*. *La ronde*. 1965: *Cat Ballou*. *The Chase*. 1966: *La curée (GB: The Game is Over)*. *Any Wednesday (GB: abridged as Bachelor Girl Apartment)*. *Hurry Sundown*. 1967: *Barefoot in the Park*. *Histoires extraordinaires (GB: Tales of Mystery. US: Spirits of the Dead)*. *Barbarella*. 1969: *They Shoot Horses, Don't They?* 1971: *Klute*. 1972: *Steelyard Blues*. *Tout va bien*. *FTA*. 1973: *A Doll's House*. *Jane Fonda on Vietnam*. 1974: *Vietnam Journey*. 1976: *The Blue Bird*. *Fun with Dick and Jane*. 1977: *Sois belle et tais-toi*. *Julia*. 1978: *Coming Home*. *Comes a Horseman*. *California Suite*. *The China Syndrome*. 1979: *The Electric Horseman*. 1980: *9 to 5*. *No Nukes*. 1981: *On Golden Pond*. *Lee Strasburg and The Actors' Studio*. *Roll-Over*. 1984: *The Dollmaker (TV)*. 1985: *Agnes of God*. 1986: *The Morning After*.

As director:
1974: *Vietnam Journey (co-directed)*

FONDA, Peter 1939–
Tall, rangy, sensitive-looking American actor, son of Henry Fonda. His fair hair and blue eyes at first qualified him for glossily innocuous roles, against which he soon rebelled. His success in *Easy Rider* type-cast him again, this time as a bike-riding tearaway, and he has not

commanded the same calibre of role maintained by his father and sister Jane.
1963: *Tammy and the Doctor*. *The Victors*. 1964: *Carol for Another Christmas (TV)*. *The Young Lovers*. 1965: *Lilith*. 1965: *The Rounders*. 1966: *The Wild Angels*. 1967: *The Trip*. *Histoires extraordinaires (GB: Tales of Mystery. US: Spirits of the Dead)*. 1969: *Easy Rider*. 1971: *The Hired Hand*. *The Last Movie*. 1973: *Not So Easy*. *Motorcycle Safety*. *Two People*. 1974: *Open Season*. *Dirty Mary, Crazy Larry*. 1975: *92 in the Shade*. *Race with the Devil*. *The Diamond Mercenaries (US: Killer Force)*. 1976: *Fighting Mad*. *Future World*. 1977: *Outlaw Blues*. *High-Ballin'*. 1978: *Roger Corman: Hollywood's Wild Angel*. *Wanda Nevada*. 1980: *The Hostage Tower*. 1981: *The Cannonball Run*. *Death Bite (later Spasms)*. 1982: *Split Image/Captured!* *Dance of the Dwarfs*. 1984: *Peppermint Frieden/Peppermint Freedom*. *A Reason to Live (TV)*. 1985: *Certain Fury*. *Come the Day*. 1986: *Hawker*.

As director:
1971: *The Hired Hand*. 1973: *Idaho Transfer*

FONTAINE, Joan (J. de Havilland) 1917–
Purposeful, fair-haired Hollywood actress, born in Japan of English parentage, and the sister of Olivia de Havilland. Not such an instant success as her sister, she worked hard in the thirties and early forties to become a star as vulnerable, innocent heroines for whom things ended happily, such as her roles in *Rebecca*, *Suspicion* (for which she won an Oscar) and *Jane Eyre*. As she passed 30 her features hardened, and the quality of her roles fell away fairly rapidly. Married (first of four)

to Brian Aherne from 1939 to 1945. Also nominated for Academy Awards in *Rebecca* and *The Constant Nymph*.
1935: *No More Ladies*. 1937: *Quality Street*. *Music for Madame*. *A Damsel in Distress*. *You Can't Beat Love*. 1938: *The Man Who Found Himself*. *Sky Giant*. *Blonde Cheat*. *Maid's Night Out*. 1939: *The Duke of West Point*. *Gunga Din*. *Man of Conquest*. *The Women*. 1940: *Rebecca*. 1941: *Suspicion*. 1942: *This Above All*. 1943: *The Constant Nymph*. 1944: *Jane Eyre*. *Frenchman's Creek*. 1945: *The Affairs of Susan*. 1946: *From This Day Forward*. 1947: *Ivy*. 1948: *Letter from an Unknown Woman*. *Kiss the Blood Off My Hands (GB: Blood on My Hands)*. *The Emperor Waltz*. 1949: *You Gotta Stay Happy*. 1950: *Born to Be Bad*. *September Affair*. 1951: *Darling, How Could You? (GB: Rendezvous)*. *Something to Live For*. 1952: *Ivanhoe*. *Decameron Nights*. *Othello*. 1953: *Flight to Tangier*. *The Bigamist*. *Casanova's Big Night*. 1956: *Serenade*. *Beyond a Reasonable Doubt*. 1957: *Island in the Sun*. *Until They Sail*. 1958: *A Certain Smile*. 1961: *Voyage to the Bottom of the Sea*. *Tender is the Night*. 1966: *The Witches (GB: The Devil's Own)*. 1978: *The Users (TV)*. 1982: *All By Myself*.

† *As Joan Burfield*

FORAN, Dick (John Foran) 1910–1979
Very tall, genial, fair-haired American actor with coat-hanger shoulders. Was once a railroad investigator before becoming a singer, forming his own orchestra and turning film star. From 1936 he was Warners' first (and only) singing cowboy. Later played light 'B' heroes or good guys who didn't get the girl. Died at 69, leaving a wife and four children: in real life, he seems to have been the good guy who did get the girl.
1934: *Change of Heart*. *Stand Up and Cheer*. *Gentlemen Are Born*. 1935: *Lottery Lover*. *One More Spring*. *It's a Small World*. *Ladies Love Danger*. *Moonlight on the Prairie*. *The Farmer Takes a Wife*. *Accent on Youth*. *Shipmates Forever*. *Dangerous*. 1936: *Song of the Saddle*. *Treachery Rides the Range*. *The Petrified Forest*. *Guns of the Pecos*. *Trailin' West (GB: On Secret Service)*. *The Case of the Velvet Claws*. *The Big Noise (GB: Modern Madness)*. *The Golden Arrow*. *Earthworm Tractors (GB: A Natural Born Salesman)*. *California Mail*. *Public Enemy's Wife (GB: G-Man's Wife)*

1937: Black Legion. Land Beyond the Law. Blazing Sixes. *Sunday Round-up. Devil's Saddle Legion. Empty Holsters. Prairie Thunder. Cherokee Strip (GB: Strange Laws). The Perfect Specimen. She Loved a Fireman. Over the Wall. 1938: Cowboy from Brooklyn (GB: Romance and Rhythm). Love, Honor and Behave. Four Daughters. Secrets of a Nurse. Heart of the North. Boy Meets Girl. The Sisters. 1939: Daughters Courageous. Hero for a Day. Inside Information. I Stole a Million. The Fighting 69th. Four Wives. Private Detective. 1940: My Little Chickadee. The House of the Seven Gables. Rangers of Fortune. The Mummy's Hand. Four Mothers. Winners of the West (serial). 1941: In the Navy. Horror Island. Mob Town. Ride 'Em Cowboy. Riders of Death Valley (serial). Unfinished Business. The Kid from Kansas. Keep 'Em Flying. Road Agent. 1942: The Mummy's Tomb. Butch Minds the Baby. Behind the Eight Ball (GB: Off the Beaten Track). Private Buckaroo. *Keeping Fit. 1943: Hi, Buddy. He's My Guy. 1945: Guest Wife. 1947: Easy Come, Easy Go. 1948: Fort Apache. 1949: Deputy Marshal. El Paso. 1951: Al Jennings of Oklahoma. 1954: Treasure of Ruby Hills. 1955: Miracle on 34th Street (TV. GB: cinemas). 1956: Please Murder Me! 1957: Sierra Stranger. Chicago Confidential. 1958: Thundering Jets. The Fearmakers. Violent Road. 1959: Atomic Submarine. The Sounds of Eden (TV). 1960: The Big Night. Studs Lonigan. 1962: Donovan's Reef. 1964: Taggart. 1967: Brighty of Grand Canyon (GB: Brighty).

FORBES, Bryan (John Clarke) 1926–
Stocky, black-haired, worried-looking English actor whose career as a player never rose above the occasional lead in B-features but who proved himself first as a writer in the mid-fifties, then as a sensitive director in the sixties. An ill-fated spell as head of production for Associated British (1969–1972) heralded a slight falling away from the directorial highpoints of ten years earlier. Married to actresses Constance Smith (1951–1954) and Nanette Newman (1954 on).
1943: *The Tired Man. 1948: The Small Back Room. All Over the Town. 1949: Dear Mr Prohack. 1950: The Wooden Horse. Saturday Night. Green Grow the Rushes. 1952: The World in His Arms. Flesh and Fury. 1953: Appointment in London. Sea Devils. Wheel of

Fate. The Million Pound Note (US: Man with a Million). 1954: An Inspector Calls. The Colditz Story. Up to His Neck. 1955: Passage Home. 1956: Now and Forever. The Baby and the Battleship. It's Great to be Young. The Extra Day. Satellite in the Sky. The Last Man to Hang? 1957: Quatermass 2 (US: Enemy from Space). 1958: The Key. I Was Monty's Double. 1959: Yesterday's Enemy. 1960: The Angry Silence. The League of Gentlemen. 1961: The Guns of Navarone. 1962: The L-Shaped Room. 1964: A Shot in the Dark. Of Human Bondage. 1970: The Raging Moon (US: Long Ago Tomorrow). (voice only). 1974: The Stepford Wives. 1976: The Slipper and the Rose. 1978: International Velvet. 1984: The Naked Face. 1985: Restless Natives.

As director:
1961: Whistle Down the Wind. 1962: The L-Shaped Room. 1963: Seance on a Wet Afternoon. 1965: King Rat. 1966: The Wrong Box. The Whisperers. 1968: Deadfall. 1969: The Madwoman of Chaillot. 1970: The Raging Moon (US: Long Ago Tomorrow). 1974: The Stepford Wives. 1976: The Slipper and the Rose. 1978: International Velvet. 1980: Sunday Lovers (co-directed). 1982: Ménage à trois/Better Late Than Never. 1984: The Naked Face.

FORD, Glenn (Gwyllyn Newton) 1916–
Dark-haired, serious-looking Canadian-born actor whose determined style coupled with a lack of warmth caused him to be cast as slightly unsympathetic heroes, notably in films opposite Rita Hayworth. A study of 'method' acting in the early fifties, and a change of hair-style, enabled Ford to really hit the jackpot and remain one of America's most popular actors, mainly in tortured roles, for almost ten years. Married (first and second of three) to actresses Eleanor Powell (1943–1959) and Kathryn Hays (1966–1968).
1937: *Night in Manhattan. 1939: Heaven with a Barbed Wire Fence. My Son is Guilty (GB: Crime's End). 1940: Convicted Woman. Babies for Sale. Men without Souls. Blondie Plays Cupid. The Lady in Question. 1941: Texas. So Ends Our Night. Go West, Young Lady. 1942: The Adventures of Martin Eden. Flight Lieutenant. 1943: Destroyer. Desperadoes. *Hollywood in Uniform. 1946: Gilda. A Stolen Life. 1947: Gallant Journey. Framed (GB: Paula). 1948: The Mating of Millie. The

Loves of Carmen. The Return of October (GB: Date with Destiny). The Man from Colorado. 1949: The Undercover Man. Lust for Gold. Mr Soft Touch (GB: House of Settlement). The Doctor and the Girl. *Hollywood Goes to Church. 1950: The White Tower. Convicted. The Flying Missile. The Redhead and the Cowboy. 1951: Follow the Sun. The Secret of Convict Lake. Young Man with Ideas. The Green Glove. 1952: Affair in Trinidad. 1953: The Man from the Alamo. Time Bomb (US: Terror on a Train). Plunder of the Sun. The Big Heat. Appointment in Honduras. 1954: Human Desire. The Americano. City Story (narrator only). 1955: The Violent Men (GB: Rough Company). Interrupted Melody. *Hollywood Fathers. Blackboard Jungle. Trial. Ransom! 1956: Jubal. *Hollywood Goes a-Fishing. The Fastest Gun Alive. The Teahouse of the August Moon. 1957: 3:10 to Yuma. Don't Go Near the Water. 1958: The Sheepman. Cowboy. Torpedo Run. Imitation General. 1959: It Started with a Kiss. The Gazebo. 1960: Cimarron. 1961: Cry for Happy. Pocketful of Miracles. The Four Horsemen of the Apocalypse. 1962: Experiment in Terror (GB: The Grip of Fear). 1963: The Courtship of Eddie's Father. Love is a Ball (GB: All This and Money Too). Advance to the Rear (GB: Company of Cowards). 1964: Fate is the Hunter. Dear Heart. 1965: The Money Trap. The Rounders. Seapower (narrator only). Is Paris Burning? 1966: Rage. 1967: A Time for Killing (GB: The Long Ride Home). The Last Challenge (GB: The Pistolero of Red River). 1968: Day of the Evil Gun. 1970: The Brotherhood of the Bell (TV). 1971: Slayride (TV). 1972: The Gold Diggers (TV). Santee. 1973: Jarrett (TV). 1974: Punch and Jody (TV). The Greatest Gift (TV). The Disappearance of Flight 412 (TV). 1975: Long Way Home (TV). 1976: Midway (GB: The Battle of Midway). 1977: The 3,000 Mile Chase (TV). 1978: Superman. No Margin for Error (TV). 1979: The Visitor. The Sacketts (TV). The Family Holvack (TV). 1980: Virus. 1981: Happy Birthday to Me. Day of the Assassin.

FORD, Harrison 1942–
Aggressive, youthful-looking into his forties, light-haired American actor who had several bites at the Hollywood cherry before hitting the big-time as Han Solo in Star Wars. He was billed as Harrison J. Ford until 1970 to

avoid any confusion with the silent screen actor of the same name (1892–1957). After settling in as a middle-range star in a variety of popular films, Ford hit the jackpot when he accepted the role rejected by Tom Selleck (*qv*) in *Raiders of the Lost Ark,* and has been in superstar category since then. Academy Award nomination for *Witness.*

1966: Dead Heat on a Merry-Go-Round. 1967: Luv. Journey to Shiloh. A Time for Killing (GB: The Long Ride Home). 1970: The Intruders (TV). †Zabriskie Point. Getting Straight. 1973: American Graffiti. 1974: The Conversation. 1976: Dynasty (TV). 1977: The Trial of Lt Calley (TV). Star Wars. Heroes. 1978: The Possessed (TV). Force Ten from Navarone. 1979: Hanover Street. Apocalypse Now. The Frisco Kid. 1980: The Empire Strikes Back. 1981: Raiders of the Lost Ark. The Making of Raiders of the Lost Ark. 1982: Blade Runner. 1983: Return of the Jedi. 1984: Indiana Jones and the Temple of Doom. 1985: Witness. 1986: The Mosquito Coast.

† *Scenes deleted*

FORMBY, George 1904–1961
Toothy, ever-grinning, gormless-looking Lancashire comedian who sang smutty songs in between whose verses he frantically strummed a small ukulele. Born blind, the son of another comedian, he recovered his sight in a coughing fit, and went on to become Britain's second biggest box-office star, after Gracie Fields, of the thirties and early forties. Died from a heart attack. The George Formby in *No Fool Like an Old Fool (1914)* is Formby Senior.

*1915: By the Shortest of Heads. 1934: Boots! Boots! 1935: Off the Dole. No Limit. 1936: Keep Your Seats Please. 1937: Keep Fit. Feather Your Nest. 1938: I See Ice. *Cavalcade of the Stars. It's in the Air (US: George Takes the Air). 1939: Come on George. Trouble Brewing. 1940: Let George Do It. Spare a Copper. 1941: Turned Out Nice Again. South American George. 1942: Much Too Shy. 1943: Bell Bottom George. Get Cracking. 1944: He Snoops to Conquer. 1945: I Didn't Do It. 1946: George in Civvy Street.*

FORREST, Frederic 1947–
Light-haired, slightly-built, intense American actor specializing in slightly off-centre characters. Started as a star in his first major film,

but was subsequently seen in a mixture of top featured roles, subservient leading roles, or TV movies. His career doesn't seem to have sustained its initial impetus and, although his personal notices have remained good, his has not become a familiar face at the top. Oscar nominee for *The Rose.*

1969: Futz. 1972: When the Legends Die. 1973: The Don is Dead. 1974: The Dion Brothers (TV. GB: cinemas, as The Gravy Train). The Conversation. Larry (TV). 1975: Permission to Kill. Promise Him Anything (TV). 1976: The Missouri Breaks. 1977: It Lives Again! 1979: The Survival of Dana (TV). The Rose. Ruby and Oswald (TV). Apocalypse Now. 1982: Hammett (completed 1980). One from the Heart. Valley Girl. 1983: Who Will Love My Children? (TV. GB: cinemas). Saigon – Year of the Cat (TV). Jealousy (TV). 1984: The Stone Boy. Best Kept Secrets (TV). Calamity Jane (TV). The Parade (TV). 1985: Right to Kill (TV). Return! Where Are the Children? 1986: Valentino Returns.

FORREST, Sally (Katharine Feeney) 1928–
Appealing American actress with curly blonde hair. She danced away happily in the chorus of M-G-M musicals of the 1940s before Ida Lupino (*qv*) saw her in a small acting role, 'discovered' her and changed her name. She was much in demand then for two or three years, but appeared to lose her career drive (something she seems in later years to have regretted) after marrying late in 1951.

1946: †Till the Clouds Roll By. 1947: †Fiesta. 1948: †The Pirate. †Easter Parade. †The Kissing Bandit. †Are You With It? †The Daring

Miss Jones. 1949: †Mr Belvedere Goes to College. Not Wanted. Never Fear. 1950: Mystery Street. Vengeance Valley. 1951: Excuse My Dust. Hard, Fast and Beautiful. The Strip. Bannerline. Valentino. The Strange Door. 1953: Code Two. 1955: Son of Sinbad. 1956: While the City Sleeps. Ride the High Iron.

† *As Katharine Feeney (when billed)*

FORREST, Steve (William F. Andrews) 1924–
Square-jawed American leading man with fair, curly hair, but less personality than his looks – handsome, mobile features with a hint of a smile – suggested. But he has maintained his leading man status, more or less, through the years, largely through working extensively in television from 1957. Brother of Dana Andrews (*qv*).

1942: †Crash Dive. 1943: †The Ghost Ship. 1951: †Geisha Girl. †Sealed Cargo. 1952: †Last of the Comanches (GB: The Sabre and the Arrow). The Bad and the Beautiful. Dream Wife. 1953: Battle Circus. The Clown. So Big. Take the High Ground. The Band Wagon. 1954: Rogue Cop. Prisoner of War. Phantom of the Rue Morgue. 1955: Bedevilled. 1957: Clipper Ship (TV). The Living Idol. 1959: It Happened to Jane. 1960: Heller in Pink Tights. Flaming Star. Five Branded Women. 1961: The Second Time Around. 1962: The Longest Day. 1963: The Yellow Canary. 1969: Rascal. 1971: The Wild Country. 1972: The Sagittarius Mine. The Late Liz. 1973: Chant of Silence (TV). 1974: The Hanged Man (TV). 1975: SWAT Squad (TV). The Hatfields and the McCoys (TV). The Deadly Tide (TV). 1976: The Running Man (TV). The Siege (TV). Wanted: the Sundance Woman (TV). 1978: Captain America (TV). Man-eaters Are Loose! The Deerslayer (TV). 1979: North Dallas Forty. 1980: Roughnecks (TV). 1981: Mommie Dearest. 1982: Hotline (TV). 1983: Malibu (TV). Sahara. 1985: Spies Like Us.

† *As William Andrews*

FORSTER, Robert (R. Foster) 1941–
Offbeat American actor in the rebel mould, with tousled dark hair and off-centre gaze. He brought his downtown New York tones to films after a stage career in which he had made a speciality of playing Stanley Kowalski in *A Streetcar Named Desire.* Subsequently in a

variety of 'loner' roles, often as vulnerable heroes. Less effective in top supporting roles, he turned director in the mid-1980s.
1967: Reflections in a Golden Eye. 1968: The Stalking Moon. 1969: Justine. Medium Cool. 1970: Pieces of Dreams. Cover Me Babe. 1971: Run Shadow Run. Banyon (TV). The City (TV). 1972: Journey Through Rosebud. 1973: Death Squad (TV). The Don Is Dead. 1974: Nakia (TV). 1977: Stunts. 1978: Avalanche. Standing Tall (TV). 1979: The Black Hole. The Darker Side of Terror (TV). Crunch. 1980: Royce (TV). Alligator. 1981: Kinky Coaches and the Pom Pom Pussycats. 1982: Vigilante. 1983: Walking the Edge. 1985: †Hollywood Harry. 1986: The Delta Force.

†And directed

FORSYTH, Rosemary 1944–
A sad but classic example of a promising career that went sour. She was feted for her performances in her first two films but, after that, the tall, delicate-looking, blue-eyed Canadian blonde seemed to alienate media and audiences alike. Roles appeared hard to come by and, truth to tell, she was not especially good in them. Her last cinema appearance to date, in *Gray Lady Down*, was reduced to a single short scene by the time the film was released.
1965: Shenandoah. The War Lord. 1966: Texas across the River. 1969: Where It's At. Whatever Happened to Aunt Alice? 1970: How Do I Love Thee? The Brotherhood of the Bell (TV). 1971: City beneath the Sea (TV. GB: cinemas, as One Hour to Doomsday). Triple Play (TV). The Death of Me Yet (TV).

1973: One Little Indian. Black Eye. 1975: My Father's House (TV). 1977: Gray Lady Down. 1986: The Gladiator (TV).

FORSYTHE, John (John Freund) 1918–
Solid, dependable American leading man, with dark, wavy hair, at his best as pressurized heroes in films for such directors as Hitchcock and Robert Wise. Most of his career has been spent on Broadway and in television. A burst of cinematic activity in the fifties seemed to come too late to make him a star. Became a major television personality in the 1980s with his success in the soap opera *Dynasty*.
1943: Destination Tokyo. 1952: The Captive City. 1953: It Happens Every Thursday. The Glass Web. Escape from Fort Bravo. 1955: The Trouble with Harry. 1956: The Ambassador's Daughter. Everything but the Truth. 1964: See How They Run (TV). 1965: Kitten with a Whip. 1966: Madame X. Death Pays in Dollars. 1967: In Cold Blood. 1968: Shadow on the Land (TV). 1969: Topaz. The Happy Ending. 1971: Murder Once Removed (TV). 1972: The Letters (TV). Lisa Bright and Dark (TV). 1974: Cry Panic (TV). The Healers (TV). Terror on the Fortieth Floor (TV). 1975: The Deadly Tower (TV). 1976: The Feather and Father Gang (TV). Amelia Earhart (TV). Tail Gunner Joe. 1977: Emily, Emily (TV). 1978: The Users (TV). With This Ring (TV). Good Bye and Amen. Cruise into Terror (TV). 1979: And Justice for All. 1981: Sizzle (TV).

FOSTER, Barry 1931–
Versatile British actor with fair, curly hair, who looks like a serious Jon Pertwee. His most successful work has been for television and he has made fewer films than one expected, although his contribution as the murderer in Hitchcock's *Frenzy* should not be underestimated.
1956: The Battle of the River Plate (US: Pursuit of the Graf Spee). The Baby and the Battleship. 1957: High Flight. Yangtse Incident (US: Battle Hell). 1958: Sea Fury. Sea of Sand. Dunkirk. 1959: Yesterday's Enemy. 1962: Playback. 1964: King and Country. 1966: The Family Way. 1967: Robbery. 1968: Inspector Clouseau. Twisted Nerve. The Guru. 1969: Battle of Britain. 1970: Ryan's Daughter. 1972: Frenzy. 1974: Quiet Day in Belfast. Der letzte Schrei. 1976: Sweeney!

1978: The Wild Geese. The Three Hostages (TV). 1980: Danger on Dartmoor. 1981: The Bomber. 1982: Heat and Dust. 1984: To Catch a King (TV. GB: cinemas). 1985: Hotel du Lac (TV). 1986: The Whistle Blower.

FOSTER, Dianne (D. Laruska) 1928–
Striking chestnut-haired Canadian actress who started her film career in Britain before she had some success in Hollywood from 1953 to 1958, mainly in westerns and gangland thrillers. Her warm, sympathetic performances in a variety of roles belied her pin-up looks, but she was not quite a strong enough personality to remain a star.
1951: The Quiet Woman. 1952: The Lost Hours (US: The Big Frame). 1953: The Steel Key. Isn't Life Wonderful! Three's Company. Bad for Each Other. 1954: Drive a Crooked Road. Three Hours to Kill. The Bamboo Prison. 1955: The Violent Men (GB: Rough Company). The Kentuckian. 1957: Monkey on My Back. Night Passage. The Brothers Rico. 1958: The Deep Six. The Last Hurrah. Gideon's Day (US: Gideon of Scotland Yard). 1961: King of the Roaring Twenties (GB: The Big Bankroll). 1963: Who's Been Sleeping in My Bed?

FOSTER, Jodie 1963–
Fair-haired, blue-eyed American actress whose rasping tones soon betrayed acerbic edges to the little-girl charm of her early Disney appearances. Before she was 14 she had played a gangster's moll, a murderess and a prostitute. One hopes such precocious talents

aren't so wasted as those of the slightly similar Tuesday Weld but recent appearances have certainly been less memorable. Oscar-nominee for *Taxi Driver*.

1971: Napoleon and Samantha. 1972: Kansas City Bomber. Menace on the Mountain (TV. GB: cinemas). 1973: Rookie of the Year (TV). Tom Sawyer. One Little Indian. 1974: Smile Jenny, You're Dead (TV). Alice Doesn't Live Here Anymore. 1975: Echoes of a Summer. 1976: Freaky Friday. The Little Girl Who Lives Down the Lane. Bugsy Malone. Taxi Driver. Il cassotto (GB: The Beach Hut). 1977: Candleshoe. Moi, fleur bleue (US: Stop Calling Me Baby!) 1978: Movies Are My Life. 1979: Foxes. Carny. 1981: O'Hara's Wife. 1983: Svengali (TV). Le sang des autres. 1984: The Hotel New Hampshire. 1985: Mesmerized.

FOSTER, Julia 1941–
Fluffily blonde British actress who overcame early roles that required her to look wistful and take her clothes off, to specialize in slightly scatterbrained secretaries and girl-friends. After *Half a Sixpence*, which might have made her an international star but didn't, she seemed to turn her back on the cinema, and concentrate on theatre and TV.

*1962: Term of Trial. The Loneliness of the Long-Distance Runner. Two Left Feet. 1963: The Small World of Sammy Lee. 1964: The System (GB: The Girl Getters). The Bargee. One-Way Pendulum. 1966: Alfie. 1967: Half a Sixpence. *The Ride of the Valkyrie. 1970: *Simon, Simon. Percy. 1971: All Coppers Are . . . 1974: The Great McGonagall. 1976: F. Scott Fitzgerald in Hollywood (TV).*

FOSTER, Preston 1900–1970
As a boy, I was hopelessly confused between Robert Preston and Preston Foster. Both were dark, well built, often moustachioed and with strong white smiles that qualified them equally for heroes and villains. Foster was the older of the two, a former opera singer who was at his best in films of the early thirties, but continued in middling roles until going into television in 1954.

*1928: Pusher-in-the-Face. 1929: Nothing But the Truth. 1930: Follow the Leader. Heads Up. 1931: His Woman. 1932: Life Begins (GB: The Dawn of Life). The All American (GB: Sport of a Nation). You Said a Mouthful. Two Seconds. Doctor X. The Last Mile. I Am a Fugitive from a Chain Gang. 1933: Elmer the Great. Ladies They Talk About. Corruption. Danger Crossroads. The Man Who Dared. Hoopla. The Devil's Mate (GB: He Knew Too Much). Sensation Hunters. 1934: Heat Lightning. Sleepers East. Wharf Angel. The Band Plays On. 1935: The People's Enemy. Strangers All. *A Night at the Biltmore Bowl. The Informer. Annie Oakley. The Arizonian. The Last Days of Pompeii. 1936: We're Only Human. Love Before Breakfast. The Plough and the Stars. Muss 'Em Up (GB: House of Fate). We Who Are About to Die. 1937: The Outcasts of Poker Flat. Sea Devils. You Can't Beat Love. First Lady. The Westland Case. 1938: Everybody's Doing It. Submarine Patrol. Double Danger. The Lady in the Morgue (GB: The Case of the Missing Blonde). Up the River. The Last Warning. White Banners. Army Girl (GB: The Last of the Cavalry). The Storm. 1939: Twenty Thousand Men a Year. Chasing Danger. Missing Evidence. News is Made at Night. Society Smugglers. 1940: Café Hostess. Geronimo. Moon Over Burma. North West Mounted Police. 1941: The Roundup. Unfinished Business. 1942: Secret Agent of Japan. Little Tokyo U.S.A. A Gentleman After Dark. A Night in New Orleans. American Empire (GB: My Son Alone). Thunder Birds. 1943: My Friend Flicka. Guadalcanal Diary. 1944: Roger Touhy, Gangster (GB: The Last Gangster). Bermuda Mystery. Thunderhead, Son of Flicka. 1945: The Valley of Decision. Abbott and Costello in Hollywood. Twice Blessed. Blonde from Brooklyn. The Harvey Girls. 1946: Inside Job. Tangier. Strange Alibi. 1947: King of the Wild Horses (GB: King of the Wild). Ramrod. 1948: The Hunted. Thun-*

derhoof (GB: Fury). 1949: The Big Cat. I Shot Jesse James. 1950: Tomahawk (GB: Battle of Powder River). The Tougher They Come. 1951: The Big Night. Three Desperate Men. The Big Gusher. 1952: Montana Territory. Face to Face. Kansas City Confidential (GB: The Secret Four). 1953: I, the Jury. Law and Order. The Marshal's Daughter. 1957: Destination 60,000. 1963: Advance to the Rear (GB: Company of Cowards). 1964: The Time Travelers. The Man from Galveston (TV. GB: cinemas). 1967: You've Got to be Smart. 1968: Chubasco.

FOSTER, Susanna (Susanne Larson) 1924–
Strawberry blonde American singer and actress who starred in operatic chillers and other Universal fol-de-rols of the early forties. Following an acrimonious divorce from fellow-singer Wilbur Evans (her first and only marriage: 1948–1956) she left show business altogether.

1939: The Great Victor Herbert. 1941: The Hard-Boiled Canary (later There's Magic in Music). Glamour Boy. 1942: Star Spangled Rhythm. 1943: Phantom of the Opera. Top Man. 1944: Follow the Boys. The Climax. This is the Life. Bowery to Broadway. 1945: Frisco Sal. That Night with You.

FOX, Edward 1937–
Gravely aristocratic English actor, for years under the shadow of his younger brother James. After James temporarily forsook the arts for religion, the fair-haired, blue-eyed Edward scored some notable and deserved critical successes, yet has failed to develop into

a big box-office star. Married/divorced actress Tracy Reed.

1962: *The Mind Benders*. 1965: *Morgan – a Suitable Case for Treatment (US: Morgan)*. 1966: *The Frozen Dead. The Jokers*. 1967: *I'll Never Forget What's 'is Name. The Long Duel. The Naked Runner*. 1968: *The Breaking of Bumbo*. 1969: *Battle of Britain. Oh! What a Lovely War. Skullduggery*. 1970: *The Go-Between*. 1973: *The Day of the Jackal*. 1974: *Galileo. A Doll's House (Losey)*. 1977: *The Squeeze. A Bridge Too Far. The Duellists*. 1978: *The Big Sleep. Survival Run. Force 10 from Navarone. The Cat and the Canary. Soldier of Orange*. 1980: *The Mirror Crack'd*. 1982: *Gandhi*. 1983: *The Dresser. Never Say Never Again*. 1984: *The Bounty. The Shooting Party*. 1985: *Wild Geese II*.

FOX, James (William Fox) 1939–
British child actor with fair hair and blue eyes, who grew up to play facile, upper-class types. Reached a peak of popularity in the mid-1960s, then turned to evangelism, making only one religion-slanted film in the next 13 years until making a low-key return to mainstream cinema in 1983.

1950: †*The Miniver Story*. †*The Magnet*. 1951: †*One Wild Oat*. †*The Lavender Hill Mob*. 1958: †*Timbuktu*. 1960: †*The Queen's Guards*. 1961: †*The Secret Partner*. 1962: †*She Always Gets Their Man*. †*What Every Woman Wants*. †*The Loneliness of the Long Distance Runner*. 1963: *Tamahine. The Servant*. 1965: *Those Magnificent Men in Their Flying Machines. The Chase. King Rat*. 1967: *Arabella. Thoroughly Modern Millie*. 1968: *Duffy*. 1969: *Isadora*. 1970: *Performance*. 1978: *No Longer Alone*. 1983: *Runners. Greystoke: The Legend of Tarzan, Lord of the Apes*. 1984: *A Passage to India. Pavlova*. 1986: *Absolute Beginners. The Whistle Blower. High Season*.

† *As William Fox*

FOX, Sidney (S. Liefer) 1910–1942
One of those 'So what happened?' careers. There certainly weren't many prettier young leading ladies in the Hollywood of the early 1930s than this tiny (4′11′), dark-haired ingénue with an attractively coquettish acting style. She had studied law before turning to acting; she and Bette Davis (*qv*) played sisters in her first film but, whereas Davis's career

solidified, Fox's gradually slid away – despite getting good reviews in a wide variety of genres. She married script editor Charles Beahan in 1932; they were divorced in 1934 and remarried in 1935. There was a little theatre, and film projects after 1935 that 'failed to materialize' and then she was found dead at 31, from 'a possible overdose of sleeping pills'.

1931: *Bad Sister. Strictly Dishonorable. Six Cylinder Love*. 1932: *Nice Women. Murders in the Rue Morgue. The Mouthpiece. The Cohens and Kellys in Hollywood. Once in a Lifetime. Le roi pausole (GB and US: The Merry Monarch). Afraid to Talk*. 1933: *Don Quixote*. 1934: *Midnight. Down to Their Last Yacht (GB: Hawaiian Nights)*. 1935: *School for Girls*.

FRANCIOSA, Anthony (A. Papaleo) 1928–
Italianate American actor, lean and ever-smiling with piercing blue eyes. Made a big reputation on stage before coming to Hollywood where he got some good roles, but showed a certain lack of warmth. Since 1963 he has been heavily involved with television in less demanding roles, but still profitably stretched his talent in the occasional interesting film, such as *A Man Called Gannon*. Married to Shelley Winters (first of two) from 1957 to 1960. Oscar-nominated for *A Hatful of Rain*.

1957: *A Face in the Crowd. This Could Be the Night. A Hatful of Rain. Wild is the Wind*. 1958: *The Long Hot Summer. The Naked Maja*. 1959: *The Story on Page One. Career*.

1960: *Go Naked in the World. Let No Man Write My Epitaph*. 1961: *Senilità*. 1962: *Period of Adjustment*. 1964. *Rio Conchos*. 1965: *The Pleasure Seekers*. 1966: *Assault on a Queen. A Man Could Get Killed. The Swinger. Fame is the Name of the Game (TV)*. 1967: *Fathom. The Sweet Ride*. 1968: *In Enemy Country. A Man Called Gannon*. 1971: *The Catcher (TV). Nella stretta morsa del magno. The Deadly Hunt (TV). Earth II (TV). In the Grip of the Spider*. 1972: *Across 110th Street. Dracula im Schloss des Schreckens*. 1974: *Ghost in the Noonday Sun. This is the West That Was (TV)*. 1975: *Matt Helm (TV). The Drowning Pool*. 1977: *Curse of the Black Widow (TV)*. 1979: *Firepower. The World is Full of Married Men. The Concorde Affair*. 1980: *La cicala. Texas Legend*. 1981: *Aiutami a sognare. Side Show (TV). Julie Darling*. 1982: *Death Wish II. Kiss My Grits. Tenebrae*. 1986: *Stagecoach (TV)*.

FRANCIS, Anne 1930–
Tall, sulky-looking American blonde whose cool talents were ill-used by two studios, Twentieth Century-Fox, who gave her the 'big chance' in the mediocre *Lydia Bailey*, an unsuitable role, and M-G-M, who promoted her as a blonde sexpot to succeed Lana Turner. Low-key drama and sophisticated comedy would have been closer to her abilities, but she rarely got either.

1946: *Summer Holiday (released 1948)*. 1947: *This Time for Keeps*. 1948: *Portrait of Jennie (GB: Jennie)*. 1950: *So Young, So Bad*. 1951: *Elopement. The Whistle at Eaton Falls (GB: Richer than the Earth)*. 1952: *Lydia Bailey. Dreamboat*. 1953: *A Lion is in the Streets*. 1954: *The Rocket Man. Rogue Cop. Bad Day at Black Rock. Battle Cry. Susan Slept Here*. 1955: *Blackboard Jungle. The Scarlet Coat*. 1956: *Forbidden Planet. The Rack. The Great American Pastime*. 1957: *The Hired Gun. Don't Go Near the Water*. 1960: *The Crowded Sky. Girl of the Night*. 1964: *The Satan Bug*. 1965: *Brainstorm*. 1967: *The Intruders (TV)*. 1968: *Impasse. Funny Girl. More Dead Than Alive*. 1969: *Lost Flight (TV). Hook, Line and Sinker. The Love God?* 1970: *Wild Women (TV). The Intruders (TV). Bourbon in Suburbia. Gun Quest (TV)*. 1971: *The Forgotten Man (TV). Mongo's Back in Town (TV)*. 1972: *Fireball Forward (TV). Pancho Villa. Haunts of the Very Rich (TV)*. 1973: *Night*

Life (TV). Chant of Silence (TV). 1974: Cry Panic (TV). The FBI versus Alvin Karpis (TV). 1975: The Last Survivors (TV). A Girl Named Sooner (TV). 1976: Banjo Hackett: Roamin' Free (TV). Survival. 1978: Little Mo (TV). Born Again. 1980: Detour to Terror (TV). 1982: Mazes and Monsters/Rona Jaffe's Mazes and Monsters (TV).

FRANCIS, Kay (Katharine Gibbs) 1903–1968

Grave, gentle, ladylike, brunette American actress. Essentially a star of the thirties, she starred in some classic light comedies and weepie melodramas, and seemed quite lost in the forties. Married to actor Kenneth Mackenna (third of three) from 1931 to 1933. Died from cancer. Some sources give date of birth as 1899, but 1903 seems the most likely. Acted as Katharine Francis until 1929.

1929: Gentlemen of the Press. The Cocoanuts. Dangerous Curves. Illusion. The Marriage Playground. Honest Finder. 1930: Behind the Makeup. Paramount on Parade. Raffles. The Children. A Notorious Affair. The Virtuous Sin (GB: Cast Iron). For the Defense. Let's Go Native. Passion Flower. Street of Chance. 1931: Scandal Sheet. The Vice Squad. Ladies' Man. Guilty Hands. Transgression. The False Madonna (GB: The False Idol). Girls About Town. 24 Hours (GB: The Hours Between). 1932: Strangers in Love. Man Wanted. House of Scandal. Jewel Robbery. Street of Women. One-Way Passage. Trouble in Paradise. Cynara. 1933: The Keyhole. The House on 56th Street. Mary Stevens MD. I Loved a Woman. Storm at Daybreak. 1934: Mandalay. Dr Monica. Wonder Bar. British Agent. 1935: Living on Velvet. Stranded. The Goose and the Gander. I Found Stella Parrish. 1936: The White Angel. Give Me Your Heart (GB: Sweet Aloes). Stolen Holiday. 1937: Another Dawn. First Lady. Confession. 1938: My Bill. Women Are Like That. Comet Over Broadway. Secrets of an Actress. 1939: In Name Only. King of the Underworld. Women in the Wind. 1940: It's a Date. When the Daltons Rode. Little Men. 1941: Play Girl. Charley's Aunt (GB: Charley's American Aunt). The Feminine Touch. The Man Who Lost Himself. 1942: Always in My Heart. Between Us Girls. 1943: *Show Business at War. 1944: Four Jills in a Jeep. 1945: Divorce. Allotment Wives (GB:

Woman in the Case). 1946: Wife Wanted (GB: Shadow of Blackmail).

FRANCISCUS, James 1934–

Handsome, fair-haired American actor with equine, Heston-ish features. He looked to be destined for good things until the disaster of Youngblood Hawke, after which he went through a barren patch until settling for routine fodder. But he could still give hints of what might have been when occasionally given the opportunity.

1956: Four Boys and a Gun. 1958: The Mugger. 1959: I Passed for White. 1961: The Outsider. 1962: The Miracle of the White Stallions (GB: Flight of the White Stallions). 1964: Youngblood Hawke. 1968: Operation Deep Yellow (GB: Snow Treasure). Shadow over Elveron (TV). Trial Run (TV). Hellboats. 1969: The Valley of Gwangi. Marooned Beneath the Planet of the Apes. 1970: Cat o' Nine Tails. Night Slaves (TV). 1973: The 500 Pound Jerk (GB: The Strong Man) (TV). 1974: Aloha Means Goodbye (TV). 1975: The Dream Makers (TV). The Trial of Chaplain Jensen (TV). One of My Wives is Missing (TV). 1976: The Amazing Dobermans. The Man Inside. 1977: Surf. 1978: Secrets of Three Hungry Wives (TV). The Greek Tycoon. Good Guys Wear Black. City on Fire. Puzzle. Killer Fish. The Pirate (TV). 1979: The Concorde Affair. 1980: When Time Ran Out ... 1981: Butterfly. Nightkill. L'ultimo squalo (GB: Shark. US: Great White). 1982: Jacqueline Bouvier Kennedy (TV). The Courageous. 1985: Secret Weapons (TV). Sexpionage (video).

FRANKLIN, Pamela 1949–

British actress with dark hair and round, open face, just as well used for spitefulness or innocence. Began as a child star and, like others of that ilk, seemed anxious to prove herself in 'adult' roles. Although she gave some interesting performances, her films have been few and she did not become any sort of power at the box office. Born in Japan.

1961: The Innocents. 1962: The Lion. The Horse without a Head. 1964: The Third Secret. See How They Run (TV). Flipper's New Adventure (GB: Flipper and the Pirates). 1965: The Nanny. 1967: Our Mother's House. 1968: The Prime of Miss Jean Brodie. 1969: Sinful Davey. David Copperfield (TV. GB:

cinemas). 1970: And Soon the Darkness. 1972: The Letters (TV). Necromancy. 1973: The Legend of Hell House. Satan's School for Girls (TV). Ace Eli and Rodger of the Skies. 1975: Crossfire (TV). 1976: The Food of the Gods.

FRANKLYN, William 1926–

British actor with dark (now grey) curly hair, a suave, smooth hero of 'B' features in the late 1950s and early 1960s. The son of Whitehall farceur Leo Franklyn, he was brought up in Australia before making his acting career in Britain. Films lost him when he became the voice-over spokesman for Schweppes commercials for nine years. Later, he mixed acting with being front-man, master of ceremonies and comedy star in various TV shows. Also directs in the theatre.

1954: Time is My Enemy. The Love Match. 1955: Out of the Clouds. Above Us the Waves. 1957: Quatermass II (US: Enemy from Space). That Woman Opposite (US: City After Midnight). The Flesh is Weak. 1958: The Snorkel. 1959: Danger Within (US: Breakout). 1960: The Big Day. 1961: Fury at Smuggler's Bay. Pit of Darkness. 1964: The Intelligence Men. 1965: The Legend of Young Dick Turpin. 1966: Cul-de-Sac. 1972: Ooh ... You Are Awful (US: Get Charlie Tully). 1973: The Satanic Rites of Dracula. (US: Dracula and His Vampire Bride). 1982: Nutcracker.

FRANZ, Arthur 1920–

Curly-haired American leading man whose pleasant features, naturally inclined towards a smile, were mostly seen wearing a thin-lipped, embittered look in roles of tension or neurosis.

Had the leading role in his first film, and stayed a minor star, notably in low-budget successes from Stanley Kramer, until 1959, after which he turned to television and the theatre, returning occasionally to films in small character roles.

1948: *Jungle Patrol.* 1949: *The Doctor and the Girl. Sands of Iwo Jima. Red Stallion in the Rockies. The Red Light. Roseanna McCoy.* 1950: *Three Secrets. Tarnished.* 1951: *Abbott and Costello Meet the Invisible Man. Submarine Command. Strictly Dishonourable. Flight to Mars.* 1952: *Rainbow 'round My Shoulder. Member of the Wedding. The Sniper. Eight Iron Men.* 1953: *Bad for Each Other. The Eddie Cantor Story. Invaders from Mars.* 1954: *The Caine Mutiny. Flight Nurse. Battle Taxi. Steel Cage.* 1955: *New Orleans Uncensored (GB: Riot on Pier 6). Bobby Ware is Missing.* 1956: *Beyond a Reasonable Doubt. The Wild Party. Running Target.* 1957: *The Devil's Hairpin. The Unholy Wife. Hellcats of the Navy. Back from the Dead.* 1958: *The Young Lions. The Flame Barrier. Monster on the Campus.* 1959: *Atomic Submarine.* 1963: *The Carpetbaggers.* 1966: *Alvarez Kelly.* 1967: *Anzio (GB: The Battle for Anzio). The Sweet Ride.* 1974: *Murder or Mercy? (TV).* 1975: *The 'Human' Factor.* 1976: *Sisters of Death.* 1979: *Jennifer: A Woman's Story (TV).* 1982: *That Championship Season.*

FRASER, John 1931–
Fresh-faced, young-looking Scottish actor, a pin-up of the fifties who did not mellow into more mature roles, although he tackled a wider variety of characters than one might

think. Divided his time between the cinema and theatre from 1953 to 1965, but afterwards was seen almost entirely in plays, with the occasional foray into films and televison.

1953: *Valley of Song (US: Men Are Children Twice). The Good Beginning.* 1954: *The Face That Launched a Thousand Ships.* 1955: *The Dam Busters. Touch and Go (US: The Light Touch).* 1957: *The Good Companions.* 1958: *The Wind Cannot Read.* 1960: *The Trials of Oscar Wilde (US: The Man with the Green Carnation). Tunes of Glory.* 1961. *Fury at Smuggler's Bay. The Horsemasters. El Cid.* 1962: *Waltz of the Toreadors.* 1963: *Tamahine.* 1964: *Repulsion.* 1965: *Operation Crossbow (US: The Great Spy Mission).* 1965: *A Study in Terror (US: Fog). Doctor in Clover.* 1969: *Isadora.* 1972. *The Man and the Snake.* 1976: *Schizo.*

FRAZEE, Jane (Mary J. Frahse) 1918–1985
Sunny, likeable, well-liked strawberry blonde American star with pinchedly pretty face. Contralto, dancer, comedienne and actress, and pretty useful at all four, the sparkling Miss Frazee brightened several minor musicals and comedies of the 1940s, after starting in two-reelers as one of the Frazee Sisters. Her appearances in the Joe McDoakes short comedies of the mid-1950s were a bonus for her fans. Married to comedian Glenn Tryon from 1942 to 1947, she later became a successful businesswoman. Died from pneumonia following a series of strokes that had enforced her retirement two years earlier.

1936: *Study and Understudy.* 1939: *Swing Styles. Arcade Varieties. Rollin' in Rhythm.* 1940: *Buck Privates (GB: Rookies). Melody and Moonlight.* 1941: *Moonlight in Hawaii. What's Cookin' (GB: Wake Up and Dream). Hellzapoppin. Sing Another Chorus. Don't Get Personal. Angels with Broken Wings. San Antonio Rose. Music in the Morgan Manner.* 1942: *Moonlight Masquerade. Almost Married. Sweetheart of the Fleet. Hi'Ya Chum (GB: Everything Happens to Us). Get Hep to Love (GB: She's My Lovely). Moonlight in Havana.* 1943: *Keep 'em Slugging. Two Senoritas from Chicago. Rhythm of the Islands. Beautiful But Broke. When Johnny Comes Marching Home.* 1944: *Cowboy Canteen (GB: Close Harmony). She's a Sweetheart. The Big Bonanza. Kansas City Kitty. Swing in the*

Saddle (GB: *Swing and Sway*). *Rosie the Riveter (GB: In Rosie's Room).* 1945: *Practically Yours. A Guy Could Change. Ten Cents a Dance (GB: Dancing Ladies). Swingin' on a Rainbow.* 1946: *Calendar Girl.* 1947: *Springtime in the Sierras. On the Old Spanish Trail. The Gay Ranchero.* 1948: *Under California Stars. Homicide for Three. Grand Canyon Trail. Incident. Last of the Wild Horses.* 1951: *Rhythm Inn.* 1954: *So You Want to Be Your Own Boss. So You Want to Go to a Nightclub. So You're Taking in a Roomer.* 1955: *So You Don't Trust Your Wife. So You Want to Be a Gladiator. So You Want to Build a Model Railroad.* 1956: *So You Think the Grass is Greener.*

FREDERICK, Pauline (Beatrice P. Libbey) 1883–1938
Dark-haired, bird-like American actress who started as a chorus girl and developed into one of the *grandes dames* of the Broadway stage. Her best film work came in a series of roles for Samuel Goldwyn, playing strong-willed and sometimes tragic figures, beginning with the definitive version of *Madame X*, which she also played for 10 months on the London stage. Her cinema career was in decline when an acute asthma attack killed her at 55.

1915: *The Eternal City. Bella Donna. Lydia Gilmore. Sold. Zaza.* 1916: *Her Honor, the Governor. The Moment Before. The Woman in the Case. Audrey. The Spider. Ashes of Embers.* 1917: *Sleeping Fires. Slave Island. The Love That Lives. Hungry Heart.* 1918: *Fedora. Tosca. Resurrection. Mrs Dane's Defense. Her Final Reckoning. Madame Jealousy.* 1919: *One Week of Love. The Peace of the Roaring River. Paid in Full. Bonds of Love. Out of the Shadow.* 1920: *The Paliser Case. Madame X. A Slave of Vanity.* 1921: *Mistress of Shenstone. Salvage. Roads of Destiny. The Sting of the Lash. The Lure of Jade.* 1922: *The Woman Breed. The Glory of Clementina/The Glorious Clementina. Two Kinds of Women.* 1924: *The Fast Set. Smouldering Fires. Married Flirts. Let No Man Put Asunder.* 1925: *The Lady. Three Women.* 1926: *Devil's Island. Her Honor, the Governor (remake). Josselyn's Wife.* 1927: *The Nest. Mumsie.* 1928: *Woman from Moscow. On Trial.* 1929: *The Sacred Flame. Evidence.* 1931: *This Modern Age.* 1932: *Wayward. The Phantom of Crestwood.* 1933: *Self Defense.* 1934: *Social Register.* 1935: *My Marriage.*

1936: Ramona. 1937: Thank You, Mr Moto. 1938: The Buccaneer.

FREEMAN, Mona (Monica Freeman) 1926–

Pretty, chubby-cheeked, blue-eyed blonde American actress, very popular as brattish kid sisters and teenage spitfires in the forties. She found herself repeating the role well into her twenties and discovered it difficult to settle into routine heroine roles in the fifties.
1944: Double Indemnity. Here Come the Waves. Till We Meet Again. National Velvet. Our Hearts Were Young and Gay. Together Again. 1945: Junior Miss. Roughly Speaking. Danger Signal. 1946: Black Beauty. Our Hearts Were Growing Up. That Brennan Girl. 1947: Mother Wore Tights. Variety Girl. Dear Ruth. 1948: Isn't It Romantic? 1949: Streets of Laredo. The Heiress. Dear Wife. 1950: Branded. I Was a Shoplifter. Copper Canyon. 1951: Dear Brat. Darling, How Could You? (GB: Rendezvous). The Lady from Texas. 1952: Flesh and Fury. Jumping Jacks. Angel Face. The Greatest Show on Earth. Thunderbirds. 1954: Battle Cry. 1955: Before I Wake (US: Shadow of Fear). Dial 999 (US: The Way Out). The Road to Denver. 1956: Men Against Speed (TV. GB: cinemas). Hold Back the Dawn. Seidman and Son (TV). Huk. 1957: Dragoon Wells Massacre. Three Men on a Horse (TV). 1958: The World Was His Jury. The Long March (TV). 1971: Welcome Home, Johnny Bristol (TV).

FRIEND, Philip 1915–

Fresh-faced, youthful-looking British leading man who went to Hollywood in 1946 (on the recommendation of Alfred Hitchcock) and enjoyed middling success there as dashing adventurers, although he always looked a little too much like Richard Greene for his own good. Returned to Britain in 1952, but could not regain his place there as a major star.
1939: The Midas Touch. Inquest. 1940: Old Bill and Son. 1941: Pimpernel Smith (US: Mister V). Dangerous Moonlight (US: Suicide Squadron). Sheepdog of the Hills. 1942: In Which We Serve. Back Room Boy. The Next of Kin. The Day Will Dawn (US: The Avengers). 1943: We Dive at Dawn. The Bells Go Down. Warn That Man. The Flemish Farm. 1944: 2,000 Women. I Want to be an Actress. 1945: Great Day. 1948: My Own True Love.

*Enchantment. 1949: Sword in the Desert. Buccaneer's Girl. 1950: Spy Hunt (GB: Panther's Moon). 1951: Smuggler's Island. The Highwayman. Thunder on the Hill (GB: Bonaventure). 1953: Desperate Moment. Background (US: Edge of Divorce). 1954: The Diamond (US: Diamond Wizard). Triple Blackmail. 1955: Cloak Without Dagger (US: Operation Conspiracy). 1956: *Dick Turpin – Highwayman. 1957: *Danger List. 1958: The Betrayal. Son of Robin Hood. 1959: Web of Suspicion. 1962: Stranglehold. The Fur Collar. 1964: Manutara. 1966: The Vulture.*

FULLER, Leslie 1889–1948

Big, aggressive, loud-voiced, concert-party comedian whose bull-at-a-gate style rang the British box-office bell in regional comedies throughout the thirties. His appeal faded rapidly during the war years and when he died of a heart attack at 59, he was all but forgotten.
1930: Not So Quiet on the Western Front. Kiss Me Sergeant. Why Sailors Leave Home. 1931: Old Soldiers Never Die. Poor Old Bill. Bill's Legacy. What a Night! Tonight's the Night. 1932: Old Spanish Customers. The Last Coupon. 1933: Hawleys of High Street. The Pride of the Force. A Political Party. 1934: The Outcast. Lost in the Legion. Doctor's Orders. 1935: Strictly Illegal/Here Comes a Policeman. The Stoker. Captain Bill. 1936: One Good Turn. 1937: Boys Will be Girls. 1939: The Middle Watch. 1940: Two Smart Men. 1941: My Wife's Family. 1942: Front Line Kids. 1945: What Do We Do Now?

FUNICELLO, Annette 1942–

Pretty, ever-smiling, pert and cheerful Disney singer and actress of the 1950s and early 1960s, with tinkling voice, dark hair and dark eyes. Like Kathryn Grayson before her, she played down a formidable bustline to trade in sweetness and light, and had a second career as star of the American-International beach comedy-musicals of the mid-1960s. Began as a child on Disney's *Mickey Mouse Club* TV show. A comeback was announced in *Grease 2* (1982) but, to the disappointment of her fans, it didn't materialize.
1957: Johnny Tremain. 1959: †The Shaggy Dog. 1961: †The Horsemasters. †Babes in Toyland. 1962: †Escapade in Florence (TV. GB: cinemas). †Six Gun Law (TV. GB: cinemas). †The Golden Horseshoe Revue. 1963: †The Misadventures of Merlin Jones. Beach Party. 1964: Bikini Beach. Pajama Party. Muscle Beach Party. 1965: Dr Goldfoot and the Bikini Machine (GB: Dr G and the Bikini Machine). †The Monkey's Uncle. 1965: Beach Blanket Bingo (GB: Malibu Beach). How to Stuff a Wild Bikini. 1966: Fireball 500. Pajama Party in a Haunted House. 1967: Thunder Alley. 1968: Head. 1970: Divorce American Style (TV).

†As Annette

FURNEAUX, Yvonne (Y. Scatcherd) 1928–

French-born leading lady who spent most of her early life in Britain. Her dark-haired, green-eyed dusky looks qualified her immediately for slave queens of Babylon. British studios knew not what to do with her, and she spent most of her career roaming Europe in search of decent parts.

1952: 24 Hours in a Women's Life (US: Affair in Monte Carlo). Meet Me Tonight. 1953: The Beggar's Opera. The Master of Ballantrae. The House of the Arrow. 1954: The Genie. 1955: Il principe della maschera rossa. The Dark Avenger (US: The Warriors). Cross Channel. L'aigle rouge. 1956: Lisbon. Le amiche. 1959. The Mummy. La dolce vita. 1960: A noi piace freddo ...! Run with the Devil. The Tank of September 8. 1961: Dox, caccia all' uomo. The Count of Monte-Cristo. Charge of the Black Lancers. Lui, lei e il nonno. Via Margutta/La rue des amours faciles. 1962: Io, Semiramide (GB: I, Semiramis. US: Slave Queen of Babylon). 1963: Enough Rope/Le meurtrier. Il criminale. I quatro tassisti. 1964: The Lion of Thebes. Repulsion. 1965: Die Todesstrahlen des Dr Mabuse. Night Train to Milan. 1966: Le scandale (GB: The Champagne Murders).

1972: In nome del popolo italiano. 1973: Versuchung in Sommerwind. 1983: Frankenstein's Great Aunt Tillie (released 1985).

FYFFE, Will 1884–1947

Big, thickly-built Scottish actor, singer and comedian, who was performing at the age of 11 and a music hall star in his twenties, playing the archetypal drunken Scot and singing *I Belong to Glasgow*. He transferred his gruff old Scotsmen to films in the thirties and became a popular character star. Fell to his death from a hotel window in St Andrew's.

1930: Elstree Calling. 1934: Happy. 1935: Rolling Home. 1936: Debt of Honour. King of Hearts. Love in Exile. Men of Yesterday. Annie Laurie. Well Done Henry. 1937: Spring Handicap. Cotton Queen. Said O'Reilly to McNab (US: Sez O'Reilly to McNab). Owd Bob (US: To the Victor). 1939: Rulers of the Sea. The Mind of Mr Reeder (US: The Mysterious Mr Reeder). The Missing People. 1940: They Came By Night. For Freedom. Neutral Port. 1941: The Prime Minister. *Camp Concert. 1943: *Scottish Savings No. 2. 1944: Heaven is Round the Corner. Give Me the Stars. 1947: The Brothers.

GABIN, Jean

(J. Alexis G. Moncourge) 1904–1976

Solidly-built French actor with thick, tousled sandy hair and grimly humorous features who became perhaps more identified with the French cinema of the thirties, forties and fifties than any other one actor. He began his career with small roles at the Folies Bergère, then appeared in music halls, cafés and the Moulin Rouge before entering films in 1930. His characters always had a certain charm beneath their world-weariness, and he remained immensely popular in tough roles until his death from a heart attack.

*1930: Chacun sa chance. Coeur de lilas. Méphisto. 1931: Paris-Béguin. Tout ça ne vaut pas l'amour. 1932: Les gaiétés de l'escadron. La belle marinière. Gloria. La foule hurle. 1933: L'étoile de Valencia. Adieu les beaux jours. Le tunnel. Du haut en bas. 1934: Zouzou. Maria Chapdelaine. Golgotha. La bandera. Variétés. 1936: La belle équipe. Les bas-fonds. Pépé le Moko. 1937: Le messager. La grande illusion. Gueule d'amour. 1938: Quai des brumes. La bête humaine (GB: Judas Was a Woman). 1939: Le jour se lève. La récif de corail. Remorques. 1942: Moontide. 1943: The Imposter. 1946: Martin Roumagnac (GB and US: The Man Upstairs). 1947: Le miroir/The Mirror. 1948: Au delà des grilles. 1949: La Marie du port. 1950: E più facile che un camelo. 1951: Victor. La nuit est mon royaume. Le plaisir. La verité sur bébé Donge (GB: The Truth about Our Marriage). 1952: The Moment of Truth. Bufere. *Echos de plateau. 1953: Leur dernière nuit. La vierge du Rhin. Touchez pas au grisbi*

(GB: Honour Among Thieves). 1954: L'air de Paris. Napoléon. Le port du désir. French Can-Can. Razzia sur la chnouf (GB: Chnouf). 1955: Chiens perdus sans collier. Gas-Oil. Des gens sans importance. Voici le temps des assassins (GB: Twelve Hours to Live). Le sang à la tête. La traversée de Paris. 1956: Crime and Punishment. The Case of Dr Laurent. 1957: Le rouge est mis. Maigret tend un piège (GB: Maigret Sets a Trap). Les misérables. Le désordre et la nuit. 1958: En cas de malheur (GB: and US: Love is My Profession). Les grandes familles. Archimède le clochard. 1959: Maigret et l'affair Saint-Fiacre. Rue des Prairies. 1960: Le baron de l'écluse. Les Vieux de la vieille (GB: The Old Guard). 1961: Le président. Le cave se rebiffe. 1962: Un singe en hiver (GB: It's Hot in Hell). Le gentleman d'Epsom. Mélodie en sous-sol (GB: The Big Snatch). 1963: Maigret voit rouge. 1964: Monsieur. L'âge ingrat. 1965: Le tonnerre de Dieu. Du Rififi à Paname. 1966: Le jardinier d'argenteuil. 1967: Le soleil des voyous (GB and US: Action Man). Le pacha. 1968: Sous le signe du taureau. Le tatoué. 1969: The Sicilian Clan. Fin de journée. 1970: La Horse. 1971: Le chât. Le drapeau noir flotte sur la marmite. 1972: Le tueur. 1973: L'affaire Dominici. Deux hommes dans la ville. 1974: Verdict. 1976: L'année sainte.

GABLE, Clark 1901–1960

Jug-eared, moustachioed, smilingly handsome American leading man with dark hair and a great deal of rough, rugged masculine charm. Equally at home in comedy or drama, he became the 'King of Hollywood' in the 1930s, a period in which he won an Oscar for *It Happened One Night*, and which culminated in his triumph (another Oscar nomination) in *Gone With the Wind*. His rough on-screen treatment of his leading ladies endeared him to his legions of female fans and, although he was never quite the same after the war years, he managed one last great performance in *The Misfits*. Married (third of five) to Carole Lombard from 1939 to her death in 1942. Died from a heart attack.

1924: Forbidden Paradise. White Man. 1925: The Merry Widow. Déclassée. The Pacemakers. 1926: Fighting Blood (series). The Johnstown Flood (GB: The Flood). North Star. The Plastic Age. 1930: The Painted Desert. 1931: The Easiest Way. Dance, Fools, Dance. The Finger

*Points. Laughing Sinners. The Secret Six. Night Nurse. A Free Soul. Sporting Blood. Susan Lenox, Her Fall and Rise (GB: The Rise of Helga). Possessed. 1932: Hell Divers. Polly of the Circus. Strange Interlude (GB: Strange Interval). Red Dust. No Man of Her Own. *Jackie Cooper's Christmas (GB: The Christmas Party). 1933: Hold Your Man. The White Sister. Night Flight. Dancing Lady. 1934: Men in White. It Happened One Night. Manhattan Melodrama. Chained. *Hollywood on Parade No. 13. Forsaking All Others. 1935: After Office Hours. Call of the Wild. China Seas. Mutiny on the Bounty. 1936: Wife Versus Secretary. San Francisco. Cain and Mabel. Love on the Run. 1937: Parnell. Saratoga. 1938: Too Hot to Handle. Test Pilot. 1939: Idiot's Delight. Gone With the Wind. 1940: Strange Cargo. Boom Town. Comrade X. 1941: They Met in Bombay. Honky Tonk. 1942: Somewhere I'll Find You. *Wings Up (narrator only). Aerial Gunner. *Hollywood in Uniform. 1944: Combat America. *Be Careful! (narrator only). 1945: Adventure. 1947: The Hucksters. 1948: Command Decision. Homecoming. 1949: Any Number Can Play. 1950: Key to the City. To Please a Lady. *The Screen Actor. 1951: Across the Wide Missouri. Callaway Went Thataway (GB: The Star Said No!). 1952: Lone Star. 1953: Never Let Me Go. *Memories in Uniform. 1954: Mogambo. Betrayed. 1955: Soldier of Fortune. The Tall Men. 1956: The King and Four Queens. 1957: Band of Angels. 1958: Teacher's Pet. Run Silent, Run Deep. 1959: But Not for Me. 1960: It Started in Naples. 1961: The Misfits.*

GABOR, Zsa Zsa (Sari Gabor) 1919–

A former Miss Hungary, Zsa Zsa was (and is!) a slinky-looking blonde who went to Hollywood, called everybody 'darlink' and got into more society columns than films. Someone once described her as a professional guest star and that's about right. Married to George Sanders (third of four) from 1949 to 1957.

1952: We're Not Married. Lovely to Look At. Moulin Rouge. Lili. 1953: The Story of Three Loves. Public Enemy Number 1. 1954: Three Ring Circus. Sang et lumières. Ball der Nationen. 1955: Man of Taste(TV). 1956: Death of a Scoundrel. The Greer Case (TV). 1957: The Girl in the Kremlin. Circle of the Day (TV). The Man Who Wouldn't Talk. 1958: Touch of Evil. Queen of Outer Space.

Country Music Holiday. 1959: For the First Time. La contessa azzurra. 1960: Pepe. 1962: Boys' Night Out. 1966: Picture Mommy Dead. Drop Dead Darling (US: Arrivederci, Baby!). 1967: Jack of Diamonds. 1972: Up the Front. 1975: Won Ton Ton, the Dog Who Saved Hollywood. 1983: Frankenstein's Great Aunt Tillie (released 1985). 1986: Smart Alec.

GAM, Rita 1928–
Dark-haired, full-lipped American leading lady on the slinky side. After theatrical and television experience, she began in films as the tenement temptress in the wordless The Thief and, finding it hard to break the mould, seemed to lose interest in the medium. Has made very occasional returns from Broadway for character roles. In the early eighties, turned documentary director.
1952: The Thief. 1953: Saadia. 1954: Night People. Sing of the Pagan. 1956: Magic Fire. Mohawk. 1958: Sierra Baron. 1959: Côte d'Azure (US: Wildcats on the Beach). Hannibal. 1961: King of Kings. 1962: No Exit. 1971: Klute. Shoot Out. 1972: Such Good Friends. 1974: Law and Disorder. 1975: The Gardener (later Seeds of Evil).

GARBO, Greta (G. Gustafsson) 1905–
Magnetic, fair-haired Swedish actress whose haunting qualities were especially well employed in tragic situations where she was required, for one reason or another, to forsake her true love. She went to America in 1925 and swiftly became the Hollywood love goddess of the twenties and thirties. Later her vehicles became more elaborate and she drifted away

from her public and, finally, films themselves, apparently losing confidence in herself, and only remembered by most for her catchphrase 'I want to be alone'. Alone she has been, now, for over 40 years. Given a Special Academy Award in 1954. Nominated for best actress Oscars on Anna Christie, Romance, Camille and Ninotchka.
1921: *How Not to Dress. Fortune Hunter. 1922: *Our Daily Bread. Peter the Tramp. 1924: Gösta Berlings Saga (GB: The Atonement of Gosta Berling. US: The Story of Gosta Berling). 1925: Die freudlose Gasse (GB: Joyless Street. US: Street of Sorrow). 1926: The Torrent. The Temptress. 1927: Flesh and the Devil. 1928: Love (GB: Anna Karenina). The Mysterious Lady. The Divine Woman. A Woman of Affairs. 1929: Wild Orchids. The Single Standard. The Kiss. A Man's Man. 1930: †Anna Christie. Romance. 1931: Susan Lenox – Her Fall and Rise (GB: The Rise of Helga). Inspiration. 1932: Mata Hari. Grand Hotel. As You Desire Me. 1933: Queen Christina. 1934: The Painted Veil. 1935: Anna Karenina. 1936: Camille. 1937: Conquest ((GB: Marie Walewska). 1939: Ninotchka. 1941: Two-Faced Woman.

† and German and Swedish versions

GARDNER, Ava (Lucy Johnson) 1922–
Strikingly beautiful green-eyed brunette American actress, built by M-G-M into their last great sex symbol. She remained best as characters whose passionate natures ruled their destinies, but was also good at expressing cynicism and world weariness. The glamorous image persisted into her three marriages, all to entertainers: Mickey Rooney (1942–1943), bandleader Artie Shaw (1945–1947) and Frank Sinatra (1951–1957).
1941: *Fancy Answers. H. M. Pulham Esq. 1942: *Joe Smith – American (GB: Highway to Freedom). We Were Dancing. Sunday Punch. *Mighty Lak a Goat. This Time for Keeps. Kid Glove Killer. Calling Dr Gillespie. Reunion/Reunion in France (GB: Mademoiselle France). 1943: Pilot No. 5. Hitler's Madman. Ghosts on the Loose (GB: Ghosts in the Night). Young Ideas. Lost Angel. Du Barry Was a Lady. 1944: Swing Fever. Music for Millions. Three Men in White. Blonde Fever. Two Girls and a Sailor. Maisie Goes to Reno (GB: You Can't Do That to Me). 1945: She Went to the

Races. 1946: Whistle Stop. The Killers. 1947: Singapore. The Hucksters. 1948: One Touch of Venus. 1949: The Bribe. The Great Sinner. East Side, West Side. 1950: Pandora and the Flying Dutchman. 1951: My Forbidden Past. Show Boat. 1952: Lone Star. The Snows of Kilimanjaro. 1953: Ride, Vaquero! Mogambo. The Band Wagon. 1954: Knights of the Round Table. The Barefoot Contessa. 1956: Bhowani Junction. 1957: The Little Hut. The Sun Also Rises. 1959: On the Beach. 1960: The Angel Wore Red. 1962: 55 Days at Peking. 1964: Seven Days in May. The Night of the Iguana. 1966: The Bible ... in the beginning. 1968: Mayerling. 1971: Tam Lin (GB: The Devil's Widow). 1972: The Life and Times of Judge Roy Bean. 1974: Earthquake. 1975: Permission to Kill. 1976: The Sentinel. The Cassandra Crossing. The Blue Bird. 1978: City on Fire. 1980: Priest of Love. The Kidnapping of the President. 1982: Roma Regina.

GARFIELD, John
(Julius Garfinkle) 1912-1952
Dark-haired American actor who played loners, losers and rebels. His 'chip on the shoulder' image was unusual in the late thirties and early forties, and won him great popularity, especially with the younger set. But the Communist witch-hunt of the late forties hit an already wavering career, and he had been virtually out of work for 18 months when he died from a heart attack. Oscar-nominated in Four Daughters and Body and Soul.
1938: †Secrets of an Actress. Four Daughters. Blackwell's Island. 1939: Juarez. They Made Me a Criminal. Daughters Courageous. Dust Be My Destiny. 1940: Saturday's Children. Flowing Gold. East of the River. Castle on the Hudson (GB: Years Without Days). 1941: The Sea Wolf. Out of the Fog. 1942: Tortilla Flat. Dangerously They Live. 1943: Air Force. Destination Tokyo. Thank Your Lucky Stars. The Fallen Sparrow. 1944: Between Two Worlds. Hollywood Canteen. 1945: Pride of the Marines (GB: Forever in Love). 1946: The Postman Always Rings Twice. Nobody Lives Forever. Humoresque. 1947: Daisy Kenyon. Body and Soul. 1948: Gentleman's Agreement. Force of Evil. 1949: We Were Strangers. Jigsaw. 1950: Under My Skin. The Breaking Point. Difficult Years (narrator only). 1951: He Ran All the Way.

† Scenes deleted from final release print

GARGAN, William 1905–1979
American actor of Irish extraction, similar in looks to James Dunn, and largely seen in the same sort of roles, persisting as the hero of 'B' features, notably the last few 'Ellery Queens', until the late forties. His voice was reduced to a whisper after an operation for cancer of the larynx in 1960, although he had long become entrenched in television. Died of cancer, but did much good work for the American Cancer Society. Oscar-nominated for *They Knew What They Wanted*.
1917: *Mother's Darling*. 1929: *My Mother's Eyes (later Lucky Boy)*. 1930: *Follow the Leader*. 1931: *His Woman*. 1932: *Rain. The Sport Parade. Misleading Lady. The Animal Kingdom (GB: The Woman in His House)*. 1933: *Sweepings. The Story of Temple Drake. Emergency Call. Aggie Appleby – Maker of Men (GB: Cupid in the Rough). Night Flight. Lucky Devils. Headline Shooter (GB: Evidence in Camera)*. 1934: *British Agent. Things Are Looking Up. Four Frightened People. The Line-Up (GB: Identity Parade). Strictly Dynamite*. 1935: *Black Fury. A Night at the Ritz. Traveling Saleslady. Bright Lights (GB: Funny Face). Don't Bet on Blondes. Broadway Gondolier*. 1936: *Manhunt. The Sky Parade. Alibi for Murder. Blackmailer. Lucky Corrigan. The Milky Way. Navy Born. Flying Hostess*. 1937: *Breezing Home. Fury and the Woman. You Only Live Once. Wings over Honolulu. Some Blondes Are Dangerous. Behind the Mike. Reported Missing. She Asked for It. You're a Sweetheart*. 1938: *The Crowd Roars. The Devil's Party. Personal Secretary. The Crime of Dr Hallet. Women in the Wind*. 1939: *Within the Law. Broadway Serenade. The Housekeeper's Daughter. Three Sons. House of Fear. Joe and Ethel Turp Call on the President*. 1940: *Isle of Destiny. They Knew What They Wanted. Turnabout. Star Dust. Sporting Blood. Double Alibi*. 1941: *Flying Cadets. Sealed Lips. Cheers for Miss Bishop. I Wake Up Screaming (GB: Hot Spot). Keep 'em Flying*. 1942: *Bombay Clipper. Miss Annie Rooney. A Close Call for Ellery Queen (GB: A Close Call). Who Done It? Enemy Agents Meet Ellery Queen (GB: The Lido Mystery). Destination Unknown. The Mayor of 44th Street. A Desperate Chance for Ellery Queen (GB: A Desperate Chance)*. 1943: *No Place for a Lady. Swing Fever. Harrigan's Kid. The*

Canterville Ghost. 1945: *She Gets Her Man. One Exciting Night. Midnight Manhunt. Song of the Sarong. The Bells of St Mary's. Follow That Woman. Behind Green Lights*. 1946: *Strange Impersonation. Night Editor (GB: The Trespasser). Murder in the Music Hall. Hot Cargo. Rendezvous 24. Till the End of Time. Swell Guy*. 1948: *The Argyle Secrets. Waterfront at Midnight*. 1949: *Dynamite*. 1955: *Man on the Ledge (TV. GB: cinemas)*. 1956: *Miracle in the Rain. The Rawhide Years*.

GARLAND, Beverly (B. Fessenden) 1926–
Brown-eyed blonde American actress of the sultry kind, a sort of cross between Audrey Totter and Gloria Grahame (both *qv*). Allegedly blacklisted in Hollywood for remarks she made about her first film and quarrels with the press, she was more or less out of work for nearly five years, then spent most of her screen time being menaced by mobsters and monsters. Television has at least kept this wasted talent fully occupied since 1954.
1949: †*DOA*. 1950: *A Life of Her Own*. 1951: *Strictly Dishonorable*. 1952: *Fearless Fagan*. 1953: *The Glass Web. Problem Girls*. 1954: *Bitter Creek. The Go-Getter. The Desperado. Two Guns and a Badge. The Rocket Man. The Miami Story. Killer Leopard*. 1955: *New Orleans Uncensored (GB: Riot on Pier 6). The Desperate Hours. Sudden Danger*. 1956: *It Conquered the World. Gunslinger. Swamp Women. Curucu, Beast of the Amazon. The Steel Jungle*. 1957: *Not of This Earth. The Joker is Wild. Naked Paradise. Badlands of Montana. Chicago Confidential. Bombers B-52 (GB: No Sleep Till Dawn)*. 1958: *The Saga of Hemp Brown*. 1959: *The Alligator People. Gunfight at Sandoval (TV. GB: cinemas)*. 1963: *Twice Told Tales. Stark Fear*. 1965: *The Dog That Bit You*. 1967: *The Man in the Middle. Trial by Error (TV)*. 1968: *Pretty Poison*. 1969: *Cutter's Trail (TV)*. *The Day God Died. The Mad Room*. 1972: *Say Goodbye, Maggie Cole (TV). The Voyage of the Yes (TV). The Weekend Nun (TV)*. 1974: *Where the Red Fern Grows. Deadly Volley (TV). The Day the Earth Moved (TV). The Healers (TV). Unwed Father (TV). Airport 1975*. 1977: *Sixth and Main*. 1979: *Roller Boogie*. 1980: *It's My Turn*. 1983: *This Girl for Hire (TV)*.

† *As Beverly Campbell*

GARLAND, Judy
(Frances Gumm) 1922–1969
Small, chubby, dark, peppy and intense American singer and actress with strong, warm, vibrant, throbbing voice. After fantastic success as a teenager (including a special Oscar in 1939, the year she sang 'Over the Rainbow' in *The Wizard of Oz*), her private life buckled under the pressures of her public one, into a mess of pills, psychiatry and attempted suicide. Married to director Vincente Minnelli 1945–1950 (third of five): Liza Minnelli (*qv*) is their daughter. Died from 'an accidental overdose of sleeping pills'. Academy Award nominations for *A Star Is Born* and *Judgment at Nuremberg*.
1929: *†The Meglin Kiddie Revue*. 1930: *†Holiday in Storyland. *†The Wedding of Jack and Jill*. 1931: *†The Old Lady in the Shoe*. 1935: †*La Fiesta de Santa Barbara*. 1936: *Every Sunday. Pigskin Parade (GB: The Harmony Parade)*. 1937: *Broadway Melody of 1938. Thoroughbreds Don't Cry*. 1938: *Everybody Sing. Love Finds Andy Hardy. Listen, Darling*. 1939: *The Wizard of Oz. Babes in Arms*. 1940: *Andy Hardy Meets Debutante. Strike Up the Band. Little Nellie Kelly*. 1941: *Life Begins for Andy Hardy. Ziegfeld Girl. Babes on Broadway. *Meet the Stars No. 4. *Cavalcade of the Academy Awards*. 1942: *For Me and My Gal (GB: For Me and My Girl). *We Must Have Music*. 1943: *Presenting Lily Mars. Girl Crazy. Thousands Cheer*. 1944: *Ziegfeld Follies (released 1946). Meet Me in St Louis*. 1945: *The Clock (GB: Under the Clock). The Harvey Girls*. 1946: *Till the Clouds Roll By*. 1948: *The Pirate. Words and Music. Easter Parade*. 1949: *In the Good Old Summertime*. 1950: *Summer Stock (GB: If You Feel Like Singing)*. 1954: *A Star is Born*. 1960: *Pepe (voice only)*. 1961: *Judgment at Nuremberg*. 1962: *Gay Purr-ee (voice only)*. 1963: *A Child is Waiting. I Could Go on Singing*.

† *As one of The Gumm Sisters*

GARNER, James (J. Baumgarner) 1928–
Tall, beefy, happy-looking American actor with black curly hair and lopsided grin. Specialized in offbeat heroes who got the better of the villain by means other than muscular. He did not quite make the big time in a cinema

unable to pigeonhole him, and returned to television (scene of his greatest success, the western series *Maverick*) to gain renewed popularity in the mid-seventies. Academy Award nomination for *Murphy's Romance*.
*1956: Toward the Unknown (GB: Brink of Hell). The Girl He Left Behind. Explosion (TV. GB: cinemas). 1957: Sayonara. Shoot-Out at Medicine Bend. 1958: Darby's Rangers (GB: The Young Invaders). Girl on the Subway (TV. GB: cinemas). 1959: Up Periscope. Alias Jesse James. Cash McCall. 1961: The Children's Hour (GB: The Loudest Whisper). 1962: Boys' Night Out. 1963: The Thrill of It All. Move Over, Darling. The Great Escape. The Wheeler Dealers (GB: Separate Beds). 1964: The Americanization of Emily. 36 Hours. 1965: The Art of Love. Mister Buddwing (GB: Woman without a Face). 1966: A Man Could Get Killed. Duel at Diablo. Grand Prix. 1967: Hour of the Gun. 1968: The Pink Jungle. How Sweet It Is! Support Your Local Sheriff. 1969: Marlowe. 1970: A Man Called Sledge (GB: Sledge). 1971: Skin Game. Support Your Local Gunfighter. 1972: They Only Kill Their Masters. *Just to Prove It (narrator only). 1973: One Little Indian. 1974: The Castaway Cowboy. 1978: The New Maverick (TV). 1979: Health. 1981: The Fan. The Long Summer of George Adams (TV). 1982: Victor/Victoria. 1983: Tank. 1984: The Glitter Dome (TV. GB: cinemas). Heartsounds (TV). 1985: Murphy's Romance.*

GARNER, Peggy Ann 1931–1984
Fair-haired, brown-eyed American actress, outstanding as a child (special Academy Award 1945). She was not given roles that

demanded enough of her after that, and her career fell away before she was 21. In later years she made her living selling at first houses, then cars. Married to Albert Salmi (1956 to 1963), second of three. Died from cancer.
1938: Little Miss Thoroughbred. 1939: In Name Only. Blondie Brings Up Baby. 1940: Abe Lincoln in Illinois (GB: Spirit of the People). 1942: The Pied Piper. Eagle Squadron. 1943: Jane Eyre. 1944: The Keys of the Kingdom. 1945: A Tree Grows in Brooklyn. Nob Hill. Junior Miss. 1946: Home Sweet Homicide. 1947: Thunder in the Valley (GB: Bob, Son of Battle). Daisy Kenyon. 1948: The Sign of the Ram. 1949: The Lovable Cheat. The Big Cat. Bomba the Jungle Boy. 1951: Teresa. 1954: Eight Witnesses. Black Widow. 1955: The Black Forest. 1966: Cat! 1978: A Wedding Betrayal (TV).

GARR, Teri 1952–
This Hollywood actress of the 1970s and 1980s is facially a throwback to the slinky, sulky film noir blondes of 20 years before – but with a kooky sense of humour which has caused her to be successfully cast in high comedy. The daughter of actor Edward Garr (1900–1956), who made a few films, she combined careers in acting and dancing until 1974, when a big break in *Young Frankenstein* made her concentrate on the former. She has, alas, subsequently been, as one writer put it, 'cruelly marginalized' in many of her films. *Mr Mom* wasn't the success its performances warranted; now she needs another break.
1968: Head. 1969: Changes/Chances. 1970: The Moonshine War. 1974: Young Frankenstein. The Conversation. 1975: Won Ton Ton, the Dog Who Saved Hollywood. 1976: Law and Order (TV). 1977: Oh, God! Close Encounters of the Third Kind. 1978: Once Upon a Brothers Grimm (TV). Witches' Brew (released 1985). 1979: The Black Stallion. Mr Mike's Mondo Video. 1980: The Special Edition of Close Encounters of the Third Kind. 1981: Prime Suspect (TV). Honky Tonk Freeway. 1982: The Escape Artist. One from the Heart. Tootsie. 1983: The Sting II. The Black Stallion Returns. Mr Mom (GB: Mr Mum). 1984: To Catch a King (TV). 1985: After Hours. First Born. Intimate Strangers (TV). 1986: Heavenly Pursuits. Miracles.

GARRETT, Betty 1919–
Energetic American singer-dancer-comedienne with dark, curly hair, perky personality and happy, broadly-smiling face, whose musical career was taking great strides to stardom when it was stopped cold by the Communist witch-hunt and never regained impetus. Married to Larry Parks from 1944 until his death in 1975. Probably best remembered now as Frank Sinatra's taxi-driving love interest in *On the Town*.
1948: The Big City. Words and Music. 1949: Take Me Out to the Ball Game (GB: Everybody's Cheering). Neptune's Daughter. On the Town. 1955: My Sister Eileen. 1957: Shadow on the Window.

GARSON, Greer 1908–
Red-haired, Irish-born, ladylike star (known as the Duchess of Garson in her London theatre days). M-G-M took her to Hollywood at the late age of 31, but she quickly became a very big star, winning one Oscar (for *Mrs Miniver*), being nominated for five more, and forming a very successful acting partnership with Walter Pidgeon which lasted through eight popular films. Married to Richard Ney (1917– , second of three) from 1943 to 1947.
*1939: Goodbye Mr Chips! Remember? 1940: Pride and Prejudice. 1941: Blossoms in the Dust. When Ladies Meet. 1942: Mrs Miniver. Random Harvest. 1943: The Youngest Profession. Madame Curie. *A Report from Miss Greer Garson. 1944: Mrs Parkington. *The Miracle of Hickory. 1945: The Valley of Decision. Adventure. 1947: Desire Me. 1948: Julia Misbehaves. 1949: That Forsyte Woman*

(GB: The Forsyte Saga). 1950: The Miniver Story. 1951: The Law and the Lady. 1952: Scandal at Scourie. 1953: Julius Caesar. 1954: Her Twelve Men. 1955: Strange Lady in Town. 1960: Sunrise at Campobello. Pepe. 1966: The Singing Nun. 1967: The Happiest Millionaire. 1978: Little Women (TV). The Little Drummer Boy (TV. Voice only).

GASSMAN, Vittorio 1922–

Dark, sharply-handsome Italian leading man, always more popular – and acclaimed – in his own country, where he has received a greater, and more demanding, variety of work. Briefly, but unhappily, under contract to M-G-M in the early fifties.

1946: Preludio d'amore. 1947: Daniele Cortis. Le avventure di Pinocchio. L'ebreo errante. La figlia del capitano. 1948: Il cavaliere misterioso. 1949: Riso amaro (GB and US: Bitter Rice). Lo sparviero del Niro. Il lupo della Sila. 1950: Una voce nel tuo cuore. No sognato il paradiso. I fuorillegge. 1951: Il leone di Amalfi. Tradimento. J'étais une pêcheresse. Anna. 1952: Il sogno di Zorro. La corona negra. Umanita'. La tratta delle bianchi. 1953: The Glass Wall. Cry of the Hunted. Sombrero. 1954: Rhapsody. 1955: Mambo. La donna più bella del mondo (GB and US: Beautiful But Dangerous). 1956: War and Peace. Difendo il mio amore. 1957: Giovanni dalle bande nere (US: The Violent Patriot). †Kean, Genius or Scoundrel. La ragazza del Palio (GB: The Love Specialist). 1958: I soliti ignoti. 1959: The Miracle. La grande guerra. Il mattatore. Audace colpo dei soliti ignoti. Le sorprese dell' amore. 1960: La cambiale. Crimen (GB: Killing in Monte Carlo). 1961: Il giudizio universale. I briganti Italiani (GB and US: Seduction of the South). Barabbas. Una vita difficile. 1962: Fantasmi a Roma (GB: Phantom Lovers). Anima nera. Il sorpasso. La smania addosso. La marcia su Roma. Erotica. 1963: The Shortest Day. L'amore difficile. Il successo. I mostri. 1964: Se permettete parliamo di donne. Frenesia d'estate. The Gaucho. La congiuntura. 1965: Una vergine per il principe (GB: A Virgin for the Prince). La guerre secrète (GB: The Dirty Game). Slalom. The Devil in Love. Spione unter sich. 1966: L'armata Brancaleone. 1967: Lo scatenato (GB and US: Catch As Catch Can). Woman Times Seven. Il tigre (GB and US: The Tiger and the Pussycat). Le piacevoli notti. 1968: Il pro-

feta (GB and US: Mr Kinky). Ghosts Italian Style. La pecora nera. The Alibi. 1969: Dova vai tutta nuda? (GB and US: Where Are You Going All Naked?). L'arcangelo. Twelve Plus One. La contestazione generale. 1970: Il divorzio. Scipione, detto anche l'Africano. 1971: Brancaleone alle crociate. L'udienza. I fakiri. 1972: In nome del popolo Italiano. Senza famiglia. 1973: Che c'entriamo noi con la revoluzione. Tosca. 1974: That Female Scent. C'eravamo tanto amati (US: We All Loved Each Other So Much). 1975: A mezzanotte va la ronda del piacere. 1976: Virginity. Signore e signorini, buona notte. Midnight Pleasures. Telefoni bianchi. 1977: Le desert des Tartares. Anima persa. I nuovi mostri. 1978: A Wedding. Quintet. Due pezzi di pane (US: Happy Hobos). Caro padre. 1979: Bugsy. The Immortal Bachelor. The Return of Maxwell Smart. 1980: Io sono fotogenico. La terrazza. 1981: Sharky's Machine. Il turno/Night Shift. 1982: La fuite à Varennes. Tempest. From Father to Son. Il conte Tacchia. 1983: La vie est un roman (GB and US: Life is a Bed of Roses). Benvenuta. 1985: Power of Evil/Le pouvoir du mal. I soliti ignoti 20 anni doppo (US: Big Deal on Madonna Street – Update).

† *Also co-directed*

GASTONI, Lisa 1935–

Italian-born actress with sexy smoulder, who became a pin-up blonde of British comedies and light dramas of the 1950s. Returned to Italy in 1961, turned brunette and gained a reputation as a strong actress (after some costume fol-de-rols) in torrid melodramas.

1953: You Know What Sailors Are. 1954: Doctor in the House. The Runaway Bus. They Who Dare. Dance Little Lady. Beautiful Stranger (US: Twist of Fate). 1955: Man of the Moment. Josephine and Men. Dust and Gold. 1956: The Baby and the Battleship. Three Men in a Boat. 1957: Face in the Night (US: Menace in the Night). Second Fiddle. Suspended Alibi. Man from Tangier (US: Thunder over Tangier). Blue Murder at St Trinian's. The Truth about Women. 1958: Family Doctor (US: RX Murder). The Strange Awakening (US: Female Fiends). Intent to Kill. Chain of Events. Hello London. 1959: The Treasure of San Teresa (US: Long Distance). Wrong Number. 1960: Visa to Canton (US: Passport to China). 1961: The

GATES, Nancy 1926–

Pretty brown-haired American actress, a radio singer at 13 and under contract to RKO at 15. She broke off her career in 1946 to study for 18 months at university and subsequently found film roles hard to get. It was the mid-fifties before she established herself as a leading lady and after the birth of twin sons in 1959 she left the cinema to devote more time to her family.

1942: The Tuttles of Tahitti. The Magnificent Ambersons. Come on, Danger. The Great Gildersleeve. 1943: Hitler's Children. Gildersleeve's Bad Day. This Land is Mine. 1944: Bride by Mistake. The Master Race. Nevada. A Night of Adventure. 1945: The Spanish Main. 1947: Cheyenne Takes Over. Check Your Guns. 1949: Roll Thunder Roll. 1951: At Sword's Point (GB: Sons of the Musketeers). 1952: The Atomic City. The Greatest Show on Earth. Target Hong Kong. The Member of the Wedding. 1953: Torch Song. 1954: Hell's Half Acre. Suddenly. Masterson of Kansas. 1955: Top of the World. Stranger on Horseback. No Man's Woman. 1956: Bottom of the Bottle (GB: Beyond the River). Magnificent Roughnecks. The Brass Legend. World without End. Wetbacks. Death of a Scoundrel. The Search for Bridey Murphy. 1957: The Rawhide Breed. 1958: Some Came Running. 1959: Gunfight at

Dodge City. 1960: Comanche Station. 1972: The Age of Pisces.

GAYNOR, Janet (Laura Gainor) 1906–1984

Sweet-faced, tousle-haired, petite American actress and occasional singer – a big star in simple, sentimental, romantic stories of the late 1920s and early 1930s, when she presented a portrait of the ragged-skirted optimist in the midst of the Depression that endeared her to millions. Her image inevitably dated quickly, but it remains a potent one. Married to (Gilbert) Adrian, the M-G-M costume designer, from 1939 to his death in 1959 (second of three). Oscar as best actress 1927 (the first) for *Seventh Heaven/Sunrise/Street Angel.* Never fully recovered from a bad car crash in 1982. Died from pneumonia. Also Oscar-nominated for *A Star is Born.*

1925: *The Spooney Age. *The Haunted Honeymoon. *The Cloud Rider. 1926: The Johnstown Flood (GB: The Flood). The Shamrock Handicap. The Midnight Kiss. The Blue Eagle. The Return of Peter Grimm. 1927: Two Girls Wanted. Seventh Heaven. Sunrise. Street Angel. Four Devils. *Fox Talent Movietone. 1929: Christina. Lucky Star. Sunny Side Up. 1930: Happy Days. High Society Blues. The Man Who Came Back. 1931: Daddy Long Legs. Merely Mary Ann. Delicious. 1932: Tess of the Storm Country. State Fair. Cardboard City. 1933: The First Year. Paddy. The Next Best Thing. Adorable. 1934: Carolina (GB: The House of Connelly). Change of Heart. Servants' Entrance. 1935: One More Spring. The Farmer Takes a Wife. 1936: Small Town Girl. Ladies in Love. 1937: A Star is Born. 1938: Three Loves Has Nancy. The Young in Heart. 1957: Bernardine.

GAYNOR, Mitzi

(Francesca M. von Gerber) 1930–

Long-legged singing and dancing star with peppy personality and lots of snap and crackle. A teenage stage star, she was signed by Fox at 20, but didn't *quite* make the top musical rank, despite some fizzy performances. *South Pacific* seemed to give her a second chance, but she was more fizzle than fizz as Nellie Forbush, and thereafter performed mainly for night-clubs and TV.

1950: My Blue Heaven. 1951: Take Care of My Little Girl. Golden Girl. 1952: We're Not

Married. Bloodhounds of Broadway. 1953: The 'I Don't Care' Girl. Down Among the Sheltering Palms. 1954: Three Young Texans. There's No Business Like Show Business. 1956: The Birds and the Bees. Anything Goes. 1957: The Joker is Wild. Les Girls. 1958: South Pacific. 1959: Happy Anniversary. 1960: Surprise Package. 1963: For Love or Money. 1969: For the First Time.

GAYSON, Eunice (E. Sargaison) 1931–

Striking raven-haired British actress, a frequent cover girl whose bright style of prettiness was very popular in the fifties when, after frequent TV appearances, she was briefly in leading film roles. Despite an unhappy private life, she has kept her career going, being seen mainly in the theatre in the seventies.

1948: My Brother Jonathan. 1949: Melody in the Dark. 1950: Dance Hall. 1951: To Have and to Hold. 1952: Miss Robin Hood. Down Among the Z Men. 1953: The Case of the Last Dance. Street Corner (US: Both Sides of the Law). The Case of the Bogus Count. 1954: Dance Little Lady. 1955: Out of the Clouds. One Just Man. 1956: Count of Twelve. The Second Crime. The Last Man to Hang? Zarak. House of Secrets (US: Triple Deception). 1957: Carry on Admiral (US: The Ship was Loaded). Light Fingers. 1958: The Revenge of Frankenstein. Hello London. 1962: Dr No. 1963: From Russia with Love.

GAZZARA, Ben

(Biago Gazzara) 1930–

Dark, floridly good-looking, Italianate leading actor whose career has been one of much

promise but little fulfilment. A critical rave in his first film (unfortunately it was also uncommercial), his best notices since have been won in films with his friends Peter Falk and John Cassavetes. In more commercial projects, his performances have too often smacked of disinterest. Later, he developed a marvellous grating voice. Married (second) to Janice Rule (qv) from 1961 to 1979.

1954: The Alibi Kid (TV). 1957: The Troublemakers (TV). The Strange One (GB: End As a Man). 1958: The Violent Heart (TV). 1959: Anatomy of a Murder. 1960: Risate di gioia (GB: The Passionate Thief). 1961: The Young Doctors. Cry Vengeance (TV). 1962: Convicts Four (GB: Reprieve!). La citta prigoniera (GB: The Captive City. US: The Conquered City). 1964: Carol for Another Christmas (TV). 1965: A Rage to Live. 1966: *Celebration (narrator only). 1968: The Bridge at Remagen. If It's Tuesday, This Must Be Belgium. 1970: Husbands. King: a filmed record. Montgomery to Memphis. 1971: When Michael Calls (TV). 1972: Afyon – Opium (US: The Sicilian Connection). Fireball Forward (TV). The Family Rico (TV). Pursuit (TV). 1973: The Neptune Factor. Maneater (TV). 1974: QB VII (TV). 1975: Capone. 1976: The Death of Ritchie (TV). High Velocity. Voyage of the Damned. The Killing of a Chinese Bookie. 1977: Opening Night. The Trial of Lee Harvey Oswald (TV). 1979: Bloodline/Sidney Sheldon's Bloodline. Saint Jack. 1981: Inchon! They All Laughed. Tales of Ordinary Madness. A Question of Honor (TV). 1982: La ragazza di Trieste. 1983: Boogie Woogie. Uno scandalo perbene/Only for Love. 1984: Richie (TV). The Professor/Il camorrista. The Woman of Wonders. 1986: An Early Frost (TV). A Letter to Three Wives (TV).

GEESON, Judy 1948–

Fair-haired British actress whose career faltered after she followed the predictable route from stage school through child roles to teenage blonde sex nymphet. Much in demand in the late sixties, when she rarely seemed to be seen with her clothes on, she has had poor roles in horror films and sex farces since then, obtaining much more interesting work on television. Tends to look older than her years. Married actor Kristoffer Tabori in 1985.

1963: Wings of Mystery. 1966: To Sir, with

Love. 1967: *Berserk! Here We Go Round the Mulberry Bush.* 1968: *Two Gentlemen Sharing. Prudence and the Pill. Hammerhead.* 1969: *Three into Two Won't Go.* 1970: *Goodbye Gemini. The Executioner. 10 Rillington Place. One of Those Things. Nightmare Hotel.* 1971: *Sam Hill – Who Killed the Mysterious Mr Foster? (TV).* 1972: *Doomwatch. Fear in the Night.* 1973: *A Candle for the Devil.* 1974: *Percy's Progress. Diagnosis: Murder.* 1975: *Brannigan. Adventures of a Taxi Driver.* 1976: *Carry on England. The Eagle Has Landed.* 1978: *Dominique.* 1980: *Inseminoid (US: Horror Planet). *Towards the Morning.* 1982: *The Plague Dogs (voice only).*

GENN, Leo 1905–1978
Smooth, urbane, dark-haired British actor who forsook the legal profession in the early thirties. As the forties progressed, he found himself in increasing demand to play confidants, people of calm authority and unflappable officer types. He had some success in Hollywood in the fifties but, after *Moby Dick* in 1956, his roles grew less interesting and he turned up in an odd bunch of films in his later years. His velvet voice was often heard as narrator in documentaries. Oscar-nominated for *Quo Vadis?*
1935: *The Immortal Gentleman.* 1936: *The Dream Doctor.* 1937: *The Cavalier of the Streets. Jump for Glory (US: When Thief Meets Thief). The Squeaker (US: Murder on Diamond Row). The Rat.* 1938: *Consider Your Verdict. The Drum (US: Drums). Kate Plus Ten. Ripe Earth (narrator only). Governor Bradford. Dangerous Medicine. Pygmalion.* 1939: *Ten Days in Paris (US: Missing Ten*

Days). 1940: *Law and Disorder. Contraband (US: Blackout).* 1941: *The Young Mr Pitt.* 1943: *Desert Victory (narrator only). Tunisian Victory (narrator only).* 1944: *The Way Ahead. Return of the Viking. Henry V.* 1945: **Julius Caesar. Caesar and Cleopatra.* 1946: *Green for Danger.* 1947: *The Velvet Touch. Mourning Becomes Electra.* 1948: *The Snake Pit.* 1949: *No Place for Jennifer.* 1950: *The Undefeated (voice only). The Wooden Horse. The Miniver Story.* 1951: *The Magic Box. Quo Vadis?* 1952: **The Changing Face of Europe (narrator only). *The Good Life (narrator only). Plymouth Adventure. 24 Hours in a Woman's Life (US: Affair in Monte Carlo).* 1953: *The Girls of Pleasure Island. Elizabeth is Queen (narrator only). The Red Beret (US: Paratrooper). Personal Affair.* 1954: *The Green Scarf.* 1955: *The Lowest Crime. Lady Chatterley's Lover.* 1956: *Beyond Mombasa. Moby Dick.* 1957: *The Steel Bayonet. Land of Laughter (narrator only). I Accuse!* 1958: *No Time to Die! (US: Tank Force). *The Immortal Land (narrator only).* 1959: **Greek Sculpture (narrator only). Invitation to Monte Carlo (narrator only). Mrs Miniver (TV).* 1960: *Era notte a Roma (GB: Wait for the Dawn). Too Hot to Handle (US: Playgirl After Dark).* 1961: **The State Opening of Parliament (narrator only). The Life of Hitler (narrator only).* 1962: *The Longest Day. 55 Days at Peking.* 1963: *Give My Love a Gun.* 1965: *Ten Little Indians. Circus of Fear (US: Psycho-Circus). Die Todesstrahlen des Dr Mabuse.* 1968: *Dr Jekyll and Mr Hyde (TV).* 1969: *Connecting Rooms.* 1970: *Der Hexentöter von Blackmoor (US: The Bloody Judge). Die Screaming, Marianne.* 1971: *Endless Night. A Lizard in a Woman's Skin.* 1973: *The Mackintosh Man. The Silent One.* 1974: *The Martyr. Sie sind frei, Dr Korczak!* 1975: *Escape to Nowhere.*

GEORGE, Gladys (G. Clare) 1900–1954
From 1936 to 1942 wry-faced Gladys George was the queen of Hollywood's brassy blondes with hearts of gold. They had seen better days and they never got the hero – but they usually stole the picture. Nominated for an Academy Award (and unlucky not to win it) for *Valiant is the Word for Carrie*, she was married and divorced four times, and suffered from cancer in later years. Died from a brain haemorrhage.

1919: *The Oath.* 1920: *Woman in the Suitcase. Home Spun Folks. Red Hot Dollars.* 1921: *The Easy Road. Chickens. The House That Jazz Built.* 1934: *Straight is the Way.* 1936: *Valiant is the Word for Carrie.* 1937: *Stand In. Madame X. They Gave Him a Gun.* 1938: *Love is a Headache. Marie Antoinette.* 1939: *I'm from Missouri. Here I Am a Stranger. The Roaring Twenties.* 1940: *A Child is Born. The House Across the Bay. The Way of All Flesh.* 1941: *The Maltese Falcon. The Lady from Cheyenne. Hit the Road.* 1942: *The Hard Way.* 1943: *The Crystal Ball. Nobody's Darling.* 1944: *Christmas Holiday. Minstrel Man.* 1945: *Steppin' in Society.* 1946: *The Best Years of Our Lives.* 1947: *Millie's Daughter.* 1948: *Alias a Gentleman.* 1949: *Flamingo Road.* 1950: *Undercover Girl. Bright Leaf.* 1951: *Detective Story. Lullaby of Broadway. He Ran All the Way. Silver City (GB: High Vermilion).* 1953: *It Happens Every Thursday.*

GEORGE, Susan 1950–
Another of Britain's stage-school-to-child actress-to blonde sex kitten stars. Her private life pouted and smouldered its way through hundreds of newspapers (one of which made up a 'top eleven' football team of her lovers), but she didn't actually make too many films until a little burst in the early 1980s. Those she has made have usually revealed her as better than her often exploitative material. Screen debut at five in a film whose title she cannot remember.
1962: *Come Fly With Me.* 1965: *Cup Fever. Davey Jones' Locker.* 1966: **Liz and Sally.* 1967: *The Sorcerers. Up the Junction. Billion Dollar Brain.* 1968: *The Strange Affair. All Neat in Black Stockings.* 1969: *The Looking Glass War. Twinky (US: Lola). Spring and Port Wine.* 1970: *Eyewitness (US: Sudden Terror). Die Screaming, Marianne.* 1971: *Fright. Straw Dogs.* 1973: *Dr Jekyll and Mr Hyde (TV). J and S, a Criminal Story of the Far West (US: Sonny and Jed).* 1974: *Dirty Mary, Crazy Larry. Mandingo.* 1975: *Out of Season.* 1976: *A Small Town in Texas.* 1977: *Tintorera. The Final Eye (TV). Tomorrow Never Comes.* 1978: *Blue Orchids.* 1981: *Venom. Texas Legend. Enter the Ninja.* 1982: *The House Where Evil Dwells. Kiss My Grits.* 1983: *The Jigsaw Man.* 1986: *The White Stallion.*

GERE, Richard 1949–

Fresh-faced, dark-haired, youthfully good-looking (if a shade mournful) American actor whose impassioned and charismatic performances in the late 1970s pushed him towards superstar status. He made his first impression in the original stage version of *Grease* in 1973 and has since remained prominent in rebel-type roles. Tried to extend his range in the mid-1980s with varying results.
1974: Operation Undercover (US: Report to the Commissioner). 1975: Strike Force (TV). 1976: Baby Blue Marine. 1977: Looking for Mr Goodbar. 1978: Bloodbrothers. Days of Heaven. Yanks. 1979: American Gigolo. 1981: An Officer and a Gentleman. Reporters. 1983: Breathless. Beyond the Limit (GB: The Honorary Consul). 1984: The Cotton Club. 1985: King David. Power. 1986: No Mercy.

GERRARD, Gene

(Eugene O'Sullivan) 1892–1971

Effervescent, ever-smiling, crinkle-haired leading man in British musical comedies of the thirties. A former tailor's cutter, he turned to the stage at 18 and made his film debut in an unknown Hepworth film of 1912. Often co-directed and co-wrote his own films and after 1938 went over to direction entirely.
1931: Let's Love and Laugh (US: Bridegroom for Two). My Wife's Family. Out of the Blue. 1932: Brother Alfred. Lucky Girl. Let Me Explain, Dear. 1933: Leave It to Me. The Love Nest. 1934: There Goes Susie (US: Scandals of Paris). 1935: It's a Bet. Joy Ride. Royal Cavalcade (US: Regal Cavalcade). The Guv'nor (US: Mr. Hobo). No Monkey Busi-

ness. *1936: Faithful. Where's Sally? Such is Life. Wake Up Famous. 1938: Glamour Girl. 1945: Dumb Dora Discovers Tobacco.*

As co-director: *1931: Out of the Blue. 1932: Lucky Girl. Let Me Explain, Dear.* As director: *1936: Wake Up Famous. 1938: It's in the Blood.*

GIANNINI, Giancarlo 1942–

Fierce, dark-haired (greying early), chunkily-built Italian actor with piercing blue eyes, usually seen as poor-born figures enjoying love-hate relationships with women. Very successful in films by Lina Wertmüller, but his international assignments, seeing him as a sort of sad-eyed Omar Sharif, have not made a good job of showcasing his particular talents. In the mid-1980s he also began showing an interest in direction. Oscar-nominated for *Seven Beauties*.
1965: Fango sulla metropoli. Libido. 1966: Rita la Zanzara. 1967: The Battle for Anzio (GB: Anzio). Arabella. Non stuzzicate la zanzara. Stasere mi butto. 1968: Fräulein Doktor. Stasere mi butto – i due bagnani. 1969: Le sorelle/The Sisters. The Secret of Santa Vittoria. Una macchia rosa. 1970: Drama della gelosia (US: The Pizza Triangle). 1971: Mio padre Monsignore. La tarantola del ventre nero (GB and US: The Black Belly of the Tarantula). Mazzabubu ... quante come stranno quaggiù? Un aller simple. Ettore Lo Fusto. Una prostituta al servizio del pubblico ... 1972: La prima notte di quiete. Mimi Metallurgico ferito nell'onore (US: The Seduction of Mimi). 1973: Film d'amore e d'anarchia (US: Love and Anarchy). Sono stato io. Paulo il caldo (GB: The Sensual Man. US: The Sensuous Sicilian). Sesso matto. 1974: Il bestione (GB: The 8-Wheeled Beast). Fatti di gente per bene. Travolti da un in solito destino nell'azzurro mare d'agosto (GB and US: Swept Away). Tutto a posto e niente in ordine (US: All Screwed Up). 1975: A mezzanotte va la ronda del piacere. Pasqualino settebellezze (GB and US: Seven Beauties). 1976: L'innocente (GB and US: The Innocent). How Funny Can Sex Be? 1977: In una notte piena di poggia. The End of the World in Our Usual Bed in a Night Full of Pain. I nuovi mostri. 1978: Vengeance/Revenge. Shimmy, lugano, tarantelle e vino. 1979: Sidney Sheldon's Bloodline/Bloodline. Travels with Anita. The Immortal Bachelor. Suffer or Die.

1980: Lili Marleen. 1981: Lovers and Liars. 1982: Bello mio, bellezza mia. La vite e bella. 1983: Escape. 1984: †I capitoni (US: Small Fry and Big Fish). American Dreamer. 1985: Saving Grace. Fever Pitch. 1986: †I numeri del lotto.

† And directed

GIBSON, Hoot

(Edward Gibson) 1892–1962

Fair-haired American western star, a real-life westerner who had worked in circuses, as a law enforcement officer and rodeo performer before coming to Hollywood, initially in 1910 and then again in 1914. Got his nickname from a passion for hunting owls when a boy. Married to Sally Eilers from 1930 to 1933 (third of four). Died from cancer.
1910: Two Brothers. 1911: Shotgun Jones. 1912: His Only Son. 1914: The Hazards of Helen (serial). 1915: The Ring of Destiny. 1916: A Daughter of Daring (serial). Night Riders. A Knight of the Range. The Cactus Kid. The Wedding Guest. Passing of Hell's Crown. 1917: Straight Shooting. A 44 Calibre Mystery. Voice of the Wire. Shameless Salvation. The Golden Bullet. The Secret Man. A Marked Man. 1918: The Midnight Flyer. The Trail of the Holdup Man. Play Straight or Fight. The Double Holdup. Headin' South. The Branded Man. The Crow. Ace High. 1919: Black Jack – Horse Bandit. Kingdom Come. The Face in the Watch. The Tell Tale Watch. Love Letters. The Jaybird. The Lone Hand. West is Best. Jack o' Hearts. The Sheriff's Oath. 1920: Saddle King. Double Dancer. Roaring Dan. One Law for All. The Big Catch. A Gamblin' Fool. The Shootin' Kid. Harmony Ranch. Cinders. The Champion Liar. The Smilin' Kid. Some Shooter. The Fightin' Terror. The Rustlers. The Stranger. The Marryin' Kid. The Texas Kid. Running Straight. A Nose in a Book. 1921: Superstition. Teacher's Pet. The Rustler's Kiss. A Pair of Twins. The Marrying Margin. The Bronco Kid. Wolf Tracks. Thieves' Clothes. Action. Red Courage. 1922: Surefire. The Bearcat. The Fire Eater. Headin' West. Step on It! Trimmed. The Loaded Doors. The Gallopin' Kid. The Denver Dude. Ridin' Wild. 1923: Dead Game. Double Dealing. The Ramblin' Kid. The Gentleman from Arizona. Kindled Courage. Shootin' for Love. Single Handed. Out of Luck. Blinky. The Thrill Chaser. 1924: Ride for Your Life. The Ridin'

Kid from Powder River. *The City of Stars. The Sawdust Trail. Hook and Ladder. Hit and Run. Broadway or Bust. Forty-Horse Hawkins. 1925: Spook Ranch. Taming the West. Let 'Er Buck. The Hurricane Kid. The Calgary Stampede. The Saddle Hawk. The Arizona Sweepstakes. 1926: Chip of the Flying U. The Phantom Bullet. The Man in the Saddle. Flaming Frontier. The Buckaroo Kid. The Texas Streak. 1927: Galloping Fury. The Rawhide Kid. The Denver Dude (remake). *The Hawaiian Serenaders. Hero on Horseback. Hey! Hey! Cowboy. Straight Shootin' (different from 1917 film). The Silent Rider. Painted Ponies. The Prairie King. 1928: The Flyin' Cowboy. Danger Rider. Clearing the Trail. Riding for Fame. A Trick of Hearts. The Wild West Show. 1929: The Lariat Kid. Smilin' Guns. Burning the Wind. King of the Rodeo. The Long, Long Trail. The Winged Horseman. Points West. Courtin' Wildcats. 1930: Roaring Ranch. Trailin' Trouble. Trigger Tricks. Spurs. The Concentratin' Kid. The Mounted Stranger. 1931: Hard Hombre. The Gay Buckaroo. *Screen Snapshots No.8. Clearing the Range. Wild Horse. 1932: Local Bad Man. Boiling Point. Spirit on the West. A Man's Land. Cowboy Counsellor. 1933: The Dude Bandit. The Fighting Parson. 1935: Powdersmoke Range. Sunset Range. Rainbow's End. 1936: Frontier Justice. Swifty. The Riding Avenger. Lucky Terror. Cavalcade of the West. Feud of the West. The Last Outlaw. 1937: The Painted Stallion (serial). 1943: Blazing Guns. Wild Horse Stampede. Death Valley Rangers. The Law Rides Again. Westward Bound. 1944: Arizona Whirlwind. The Outlaw Trail. Trigger Law. The Utah Kid. Sonora Stagecoach. Marked Trails. 1946: Flight to Nowhere. 1953: The Marshal's Daughter. 1959: The Horse Soldiers. 1960: Ocean's Eleven.

GIBSON, Mel 1956–
Dark-haired, well-built, boyishly-handsome, unsmiling Australian-raised actor whose quiet, brooding, blue-eyed charisma had female temperatures rising in the cinema of the early 1980s. Born in New York, one of 11 children, he went to Australia at 12 and made his film debut there, shooting to top stardom as the futuristic desert wanderer in the Mad Max films. Hollywood swooped but made the mistake of pairing him with female stars who provided rather more acting competition that

he could yet handle. Back in Australia, he revived his superstar status in a third Mad Max saga.
1977: Summer City. 1978: Tim. 1979: Mad Max. 1980: Attack Force Z. 1981: Gallipoli. Mad Max 2 (US: The Road Warrior). 1982: The Year of Living Dangerously. 1984: The Bounty. The River. Mrs Soffel. 1985: Mad Max III (GB and US: Mad Max Beyond Thunderdome).

GIBSON, Wynne (Winnifred Gibson) 1899–
Fair-haired, square-faced American actress (a chorus girl at 15) who started her film career late in life (although studio biographies advanced her date of birth by varying numbers of years), but enjoyed a good run of golddigging blondes while with Paramount in the early 1930s. Left acting in the 1950s to become an actors' agent for the remainder of her working life.
1929: Nothing But the Truth. 1930: Children of Pleasure. The Fall Guy (GB: Trust Your Wife). 1931: June Moon. City Streets. Kick-In. Ladies of the Big House. Man of the World. The Gang Buster. Road to Reno. 1932: If I Had a Million. Night After Night. Lady and Gent. The Strange Case of Clara Deane. The Devil is Driving. Two Kinds of Women. *The Stolen Jools (GB: The Slippery Pearls). 1933: Aggie Appleby, Maker of Men (GB: Cupid in the Rough). Emergency Call. Her Bodyguard. Crime of the Century. 1934: Gambling. The Crosby Case (GB: The Crosby Murder Case). Sleepers East. The Captain Hates the Sea. 1935: Admirals All. The Crouching Beast. 1936: Come Closer, Folks! 1937: Michael O'Halloran. Trapped by G-Men. Racketeers in Exile. 1938: Flirting with Fate. Gangs of New York. 1939: My Son is Guilty (GB: Crime's End). 1940: Forgotten Girls. Café Hostess. A Miracle on Main Street. 1941: Double Cross. 1942: A Man's World. 1943: The Falcon Strikes Back. Mystery Broadcast.

GIELGUD, Sir John (Arthur J. Gielgud) 1904–
Tall, slim, stern-looking British actor who achieved greatest distinction in Shakespearian roles on stage. He appeared briefly as an aesthetic leading man in a few pre-war films, but most post-war parts were cameos that were unworthy both of the actor and his reedily

mellifluous voice. Knighted in 1953. Won an Academy Award for Arthur. Also nominated for Becket.
1924: Who is the Man? 1929: The Clue of the New Pin. 1932: Insult. 1933: The Good Companions. 1936: The Secret Agent. 1937: *Full Fathom Five (voice only). 1939: Hamlet. 1941: The Prime Minister. *An Airman's Letter to His Mother (voice only). 1944: *Unfinished Journey (narrator only). *Shakespeare's Country (voice only). 1945: A Diary for Timothy. 1953: Julius Caesar. 1954: Romeo and Juliet. 1955: Richard III. 1956: Around the World in 80 Days. 1957: The Barretts of Wimpole Street. Saint Joan. 1958: The Immortal Land (narrator only). 1962: To Die in Madrid (narrator only). 1963: Hamlet. 1964: Becket. 1965: The Loved One. 1966: Chimes at Midnight (US: Falstaff). 1967: Sebastian. October Revolution (narrator only). Assignment to Kill. 1968: The Shoes of the Fisherman. The Charge of the Light Brigade. 1969: Oh! What a Lovely War. 1970: Julius Caesar. Eagle in a Cage. 1972: Lost Horizon. Probe (TV). 1973: Frankenstein: the True Story (TV. GB: cinemas). Luther. 1974: QB VII (TV). 11 Harrowhouse. Gold. Murder on the Orient Express. Galileo. 1976: Aces High. Joseph Andrews. 1977: A Portrait of the Artist as a Young Man. Providence. 1978: Les Miserables (TV). Caligula. Sherlock Holmes: Murder by Decree (GB: Murder by Decree). 1979: Omar Mukhtar: Lion of the Desert. The Human Factor. 1980: Dyrygent/The Conductor. Sphinx. Priest of Love. Arthur. 1981: Chariots of Fire. The Elephant Man. 1982: The Hunchback of Notre Dame (TV). Wagner (TV). Gandhi. 1983: The Wicked Lady. The Scarlet and the Black (TV). Invitation to the Wedding. Scandalous! 1984: The Shooting Party. Camille (TV). 1985: Plenty. Romance on the Orient Express (TV). Leave All Fair. 1986: The Whistle Blower. Time After Time (TV).

GIFFORD, Frances (Mary F. Gifford) 1920–
Stunning blue-eyed brunette American actress whose career seemed to be coming to a peak at M-G-M when she suffered serious head injuries in a 1948 car accident from which, despite a couple of minor roles later on, she has never really recovered, spending long periods in hospital. Best remembered by nostalgia fans as the screen's first Nyoka in

the serial *Jungle Girl*. Married to James Dunn 1938–41.

1937: *Woman Chases Man. New Faces of 1937. Stage Door. Living on Love.* 1938: *Having Wonderful Time.* 1939: *Mr Smith Goes to Washington.* 1940: *Mercy Plane. Hold That Woman.* 1941: *The Reluctant Dragon. Jungle Girl (serial). Border Vigilantes. West Point Widow. Louisiana Purchase.* 1942: *My Heart Belongs to Daddy. American Empire (GB: My Son Alone). The Glass Key. Beyond the Blue Horizon. The Remarkable Andrew. Tombstone, the Town Too Tough to Die. Star Spangled Rhythm.* 1943: *Cry Havoc. Tarzan Triumphs.* 1944: *Marriage is a Private Affair.* 1945: *Thrill of a Romance. Our Vines Have Tender Grapes. She Went to the Races.* 1946: *Little Mr Jim.* 1947: *The Arnelo Affair.* 1948: *Luxury Liner.* 1950: *Riding High.* 1953: *Sky Commando.*

GILBERT, John (J. Pringle) 1895–1936
Dashing, moustachioed, sharp-faced American actor with very dark hair, an enormous success as a great lover on the silent screen, especially in roles opposite Greta Garbo. His inability to modulate his exaggerated acting style to sound films, coupled with an unappealing voice, led to the rapid decline of his career. He became an alcoholic and died from a heart attack at 40. Besides his well-publicized off-screen affair with Garbo, he was married to actresses Leatrice Joy (1922–1924), Ina Claire (1929–1931) and Virginia Bruce (1932–1934): 2nd, 3rd and 4th of four.
1915: *The Mother Instinct.* 1916: *Hell's Hinges. The Phantom. The Eye of the Night. The Apostle of Vengeance. Bullets and Brown*

Eyes. Shell 43. 1917: *Princess of the Dark. Happiness. The Millionaire Vagrant. Hater of Men. The Devil Dodger. Doing Her Bit. Golden Rule Kate.* 1918: *Sons of Men. Nancy Comes Home. Three X Gordon. More Trouble. Shackled. Wedlock. The Mask. The Dawn of Understanding.* 1919: *The Busher. Widow by Proxy. Should a Woman Tell? The White Heather. The Red Viper. Heart o' the Hills.* 1920: *The White Circle. Deep Waters. The Great Redeemer. The Servant in the House.* 1921: *Ladies Must Live. Shame. The Bait. †Love's Penalty.* 1922: *Gleam o' Dawn. The Yellow Stain. Arabian Love. The Count of Monte Cristo. Honor First. The Love Gambler. Calvert's Valley (GB: Calvert's Folly).* 1923: *Cameo Kirby. The Exiles. A California Romance. Saint Elmo. Truxton King (GB: Truxtonia). The Glory of Love. The Madness of Youth. While Paris Sleeps.* 1924: *The Wolf Man. Just Off Broadway. A Man's Mate. Romance Ranch. The Lone Chance. His Hour. The Snob. Wife of the Centaur. He Who Gets Slapped. Married Flirts.* 1925: *The Merry Widow. The Big Parade.* 1926: *La Bohème. Bardelys The Magnificent.* 1927: *The Show. Flesh and the Devil. Twelve Miles Out. Man, Woman and Sin.* 1928: *Love (GB: Anna Karenina). Four Walls. *Voices across the Sea. The Cossacks. Masks of the Devil.* 1929: *Desert Nights. A Man's Man. Hollywood Revue of 1929. His Glorious Night. A Woman of Affairs.* 1930: *Redemption. Way for a Sailor.* 1931: *Gentleman's Fate. The Phantom of Paris.* 1932: *West of Broadway. Downstairs.* 1933: *Fast Workers. Queen Christina.* 1934: *The Captain Hates the Sea.*

† *Also directed*

GILMORE, Virginia
(Sherman V. Poole) 1919–1986
Exquisitely pretty brown-eyed blonde American actress (of British parentage) who gave some glowingly warm performances in romantic roles, but lacked a screen personality and was mainly a theatre actress after 1943. Married to Yul Brynner from 1944 to 1960; after their divorce she became a drama coach. Died of complications from emphysema.
1939: *Winter Carnival.* 1939–40: *†Raffles.* 1940: *Laddie. Jennie. Manhattan Heartbeat.* 1941: *Western Union. Swamp Water (GB: The Man Who Came Back). Mr District*

Attorney in The Carter Case (GB: The Carter Case). 1942: *Tall, Dark and Handsome. The Loves of Edgar Allan Poe. Orchestra Wives. Berlin Correspondent. Pride of the Yankees. Sundown Jim. That Other Woman.* 1943: *Chetniks.* 1945: *Wonder Man.* 1948: *Close-Up.* 1952: *Walk East on Beacon (GB: Crime of the Century).*

† *Scenes deleted from final release print*

GIRARDOT, Annie 1931–
Dark-haired, personable French actress with impishly angular features, much in demand for romantic roles calling for warmth and depth. Tackled a wide variety of characters following a belated arrival (at 24) on the film scene after five years of dramatic training and some stage work. Her dearth of ventures into the international scene hardly qualifies her for a place in this book, so the fact that she is the author's favourite continental star will have to suffice. Won a César (French Oscar) in 1976 for *Docteur Françoise Gailland*.
1955: *Treize à table.* 1956: *L'homme aux clés d'or. Réproduction interdite. Le rouge est mis (US: Speaking of Murder).* 1957: *L'amour est un jeu. Maigret tend un piège (GB: Maigret Sets a Trap. US: Inspector Maigret).* 1958: *Le desert de Pigalle.* 1959: *Le corde raide (US: Lovers on a Tightrope).* 1960: *La Française et l'amour (GB and US: Love and the Frenchwoman). Rocco e i suoi fratelli (GB and US: Rocco and His Brothers). Recours en grâce.* 1961: *La proie pour l'ombre. Le rendez-vous. Les amours célèbres.* 1962: *Smog. Le bateau d'Emile. Le crime ne paie pas (GB and US: Crime Does Not Pay).* 1963: *Vice and Virtue. La bonne soupe (US: Careless Love). Il giorno più corto commedia umaristica (US: The Shortest Day). I compagni (US: The Organizer).* 1964: *Le mari de la femme à barbe (US: The Ape Woman). L'autre femme. Un monsieur de compagnie (US: Male Companion).* 1965: *I fourlegge del matrimonio. La ragazza in prestito. Une voglia di morire. La belle famiglie. Declic et des claques. Guerre secrète (GB and US: The Dirty Game).* 1966: *Trois chambres à Manhattan. Le streghe (US: The Witches).* 1967: *Vivre pour vivre (GB and US: Live for Life).* 1968: *Le bande à Bonnot. La vie, l'amour, la mort. Les gauloises bleus. Dillinger is Dead. Erotissimo.* 1969: *Metti une sera, a cena. Le voleur des crimes. Il seme dell'uomo (US: The Seed of Man). Le clair de terre. Un*

homme qui me plaît (US: A Man I Like. US: Love is a Funny Thing). Il pleut dans mon village. The Story of a Woman. 1970: Elle boit pas, elle fume pas, elle drague pas … mais elle cause. Les novices. 1971: Mourir d'aimer. La vieille fille. La mandarine. Les feux de la chandeleur. 1972: Elle cause plus … elle flingue. Traitement de choc (GB: The Doctor in the Nude/Shock Treatment. US: Shock!). Il n'y a pas de fumée sans feu (US: Where There's Smoke). 1973: Juliette et Juliette. Mission dans l'Italie fasciste. Ursule et Grélu. 1974: Le gifle (US: The Slap). Il sospetto. 1975: It is Raining on Santiago. Il faut vivre dangereusement. Le Gitan. Un cri. D'amour et d'eau fraîche. 1976: Docteur Françoise Gailland (US: No Time for Breakfast). Cours après moi que je t'attrape (US: Run After Me – Until I Catch You!). A chacun son enfer. Autopsie d'un monstre. 1977: Le dernier baiser. Jambon d'Ardenne. La zizanie. Tendre poulet (GB: Dear Detective. US: Dear Inspector). Le point de mire. Le commissaire a de jolies menottes. L'affaire. 1978: La clé sur la porte. Justices. Vas-y maman. Fais-moi rêver. L'ingorgo. 1979: Le cavaleur (US: The Skirt Chaser). L'amour en question. L'embouteillage. Allo, je craque. Bobo Jacco. 1980: Autres femmes (US: The Mother Beast). Cause toujours … tu m'interesse. On a volé la cuisse de Jupiter. Le coeur à l'envers. 1981: All Night Long. La vie continue. 1982: Une robe noire pour un tueur. 1984: Io e il duce (US: Mussolini and I). Liste noire/Blacklist. Souvenirs, souvenirs. 1985: Partir revenir. Olga's Family.

GISH, Dorothy (right above)
(D. de Guiche) 1898–1968
Long-faced, solemn, tawny-haired American actress, almost as popular as her prettier sister Lillian at her peak. Played much the same kind of 'sweet girl' roles, but without Lillian's dramatic intensity. Deserted films for the theatre in 1928, but never retired. Died from bronchial pneumonia.
1912: Oil and Water. The New York Hat. The Musketeers of Pig Alley. An Unseen Enemy. Gold and Glitter. My Hero. A Cry for Help. 1913: The Perfidy of Mary. Just Gold. The Lady and the Mouse. Her Mother's Oath. Almost a Wild Man. Pa Says. The Widow's Kids. The House of Discord. The Lady in Black. The Vengeance of Galora. Those Little Flowers. The Adopted Brother. 1914: †Judith of Bethu-

lia. Her Father's Silent Partner. The Old Man. The Newer Woman. Her Old Teacher. The Mysterious Shot. †The Floor Above. Liberty Belles. †The Mountain Rat. Silent Sandy. The Better Way. Arms and the Gringo. The Suffragettes Battle in Nuttyville. †Home Sweet Home. The Painted Lady. The Tavern of Tragedy. The City Beautiful. Their First Acquaintance. Her Mother's Necklace. A Lesson in Mechanics. Granny. His Lesson. †A Fair Rebel. †The Wife. Sands of Fate. Down the Road to Creditville. The Warning. Back to the Kitchen. The Availing Prayer. The Sisters. The Saving Grace. †Man's Enemy. 1915: Minerva's Mission. How Hazel Got Even. The Lost Lord Lowell. An Old-Fashioned Girl. Her Grandparents. †Her Mother's Daughter. †Old Heidelberg. †Bred in the Bone. †Jordan is a Hard Road. The Little Catamount. The Mountain Girl. Victorine. 1916: †Betty of Greystone. †Little Meena's Romance. †Atta Boy's Last Race. Gretchen the Greenhorn. †Children of the Feud. †Susan Rocks the Boat (GB: Sweet Seventeen). †The Little Schoolma'am. 1917: †The Little Yank. †Her Official Fathers. †Stage Struck. 1918: †Hearts of the World. †The Hun Within. †Battling Jane. 1919: †Boots. †Peppy Polly. †Nugget Nell. †I'll Get Him Yet. †Turning the Tables. †Out of Luck. †The Hope Chest. 1920: †Mary Ellen Comes to Town. †Little Miss Rebellion. †Remodeling Her Husband. †Flying Pat. 1921: †The Ghost in the Garret. †Oh, Jo! 1922: †Orphans of the Storm. †The Country Flapper. 1923: †Fury. †The Bright Shawl. 1924: †Romola. 1925: †Night Life of New York. †Clothes Make the Pirate. †The Beautiful City. †Nell Gwyn. 1926: †London. 1927: †Madame Pompadour. †Tip Toes. 1930: †Wolves (US: Wanted Men). 1944: †Our Hearts Were Young and Gay. 1946: †Centennial Summer. 1951: †The Whistle at Eaton Falls (GB: Richer Than the Earth). 1963: †The Cardinal.

All shorts except †Features

GISH, Lillian (L. de Guiche) 1896–
Small, delicately pretty, tawny-haired American actress with heart-shaped face. Became famous with her sister Dorothy in films of D. W. Griffith and developed into one of Hollywood's finest actresses, not only in silent films but in character roles in talkies following a sojourn in the theatre. Some sources give

birthdate as 1893, but this seems unlikely. Special Oscar 1970. Nominated for an Oscar in *Duel in the Sun*. Has never married.
1912: *Oil and Water. *The New York Hat. *The Musketeers of Pig Alley. *An Unseen Enemy. *Gold and Glitter. *My Baby. *A Cry for Help. *Two Daughters of Eve. *In the Aisles of the Wild. *The Burglar's Dilemma. *The Unwelcome Guest. 1913: *Just Gold. *The Lady and the Mouse. *A Misunderstood Boy. *House of Darkness. *The Left-Handed Man. *During the Round-Up. *The Mothering Heart. *An Indian's Loyalty. *The Madonna of the Storm. *A Woman in the Ultimate. *A Timely Interception. *A Modest Hero. *The Battle of Elderbush Gulch. 1914: Judith of Bethulia. Home Sweet Home. *The Green-Eyed Devil. The Escape. *Silent Sandy. The Tear That Burned. The Quicksands. *The Sisters. The Battle of the Sexes. Lord Chumley. *The Hunchback. Man's Enemy. His Lesson. The Rebellion of Kitty Belle. *The Folly of Anne. The Wife/A Wife. *The Angel of Contention. 1915: Enoch Arden (GB: As Fate Ordained). The Birth of a Nation. Captain Macklin. The Lost House. The Lily and the Rose. 1916: Intolerance. Sold for Marriage. Flirting with Fate. Daphne and the Pirate. An Innocent Magdalene. Diane of the Follies. Pathways of Life. The Children Pay. 1917: Souls Triumphant. The House Built Upon Sand. 1918: Hearts of the World. *Buy Liberty Bonds. The Great Love. The Greatest Thing in Life. 1919: Broken Blossoms. True Heart Susie. The Greatest Question. A Romance of Happy Valley. 1920: Way Down East. 1922: Orphans of the Storm. 1923: The White Sister. 1924: Romola. 1926: La Bohème. The Scarlet Letter. 1927: Annie Laurie. 1928: The Enemy. The Wind. 1930: One Romantic Night. 1933: His Double Life. 1942: Commandos Strike at Dawn. 1943: Top Man. 1944: Miss Susie Slagle's (released 1946). 1946: Duel in the Sun. 1948: Portrait of Jennie (GB: Jennie). 1955: The Cobweb. 1955: *Salute to the Theatres. Night of the Hunter. 1958: Orders to Kill. 1959: The Unforgiven. 1966: Follow Me, Boys! Warning Shot. 1967: The Comedians. Arsenic and Old Lace (TV). 1970: Henri Langlois. 1976: Twin Detectives (TV). 1978: A Wedding. 1980: Thin Ice (TV). 1983: Hobson's Choice (TV). Hambone and Hillie (GB: The Adventures of Hambone). 1985: Sweet Liberty.

As director: *1920: Remodeling Her Husband.*

GLEASON, Jackie
(Herbert John Gleason) 1916–
Portly American comedian with a nice line in easy-going humour. He played a few small roles as comic relief at the beginning of the 1940s, then made a sensational impact with his first big dramatic role in *The Hustler*, which won him an Academy Award nomination. Disappointingly, he returned to comedy roles and his film career again stuttered. But he has been very successful on television.
1941: Navy Blues. 1942: †Larceny Inc. All Through the Night. Lady Gangster. Escape from Crime. Orchestra Wives. Springtime in the

Rockies. 1950: The Desert Hawk. 1961: The Hustler. 1962: Requiem for a Heavyweight (GB: Blood Money). Gigot. 1963: Papa's Delicate Condition. Soldier in the Rain. 1968: Skidoo. 1969: Don't Drink the Water. How to Commit Marriage. 1970: How Do I Love Thee? 1977: Mr Billion. Smokey and the Bandit. 1980: Smokey and the Bandit II (GB: Smokey and the Bandit Ride Again). 1982: The Toy. 1983: The Sting II. Smokey and the Bandit – Part 3. 1984: Fools Die. 1985: Izzy and Mo (TV). 1986: Nothing in Common.

† *As Jack C. Gleason*

GLENN, Scott 1942–

Lean, laconic, leathery, whippy actor in the James Coburn mould who does all his own stunts and has the reputation of being one of the fittest American actors in films. An ex-Marine and one-time reporter, Glenn came up the hard way, not getting his first film role until he was 29 and then having to wait another 10 years for stardom. A real-life hero who saved three children from drowning in 1979, Glenn looks capable of something superior to the action heroes he usually plays. *1971: The Baby Maker. Angels Hard As They Come. 1972: Gargoyles (TV). 1973: Hex. 1975: Nashville. 1976: Fighting Mad. 1977: She Came to the Valley (released 1979). 1979: Apocalypse Now. Cattle Annie and Little Britches. More American Graffiti/The Party's Over/Purple Haze. 1980: Urban Cowboy. 1982: The Challenge (The Equals). Personal Best. 1983: The Right Stuff. The Keep. 1984: The River. Countdown to Looking Glass (TV). 1985: Wild Geese II. Silverado. 1986: As Summers Die (TV).*

GODDARD, Paulette

(Pauline G. Levee) 1911–
Petite, svelte American brunette who rose from the chorus. One of the few leading ladies 'introduced' by Charlie Chaplin to prove that she could stand on her own feet afterwards. With her verve and vivacity (plus a cute figure), she was equally at home in costume or comedy, as nice girls or minxes. Married to Chaplin (1936–1942), Burgess Meredith (1944–1949) and author Erich Maria Remarque (1958 on): second, third and fourth of four. Remarque died in 1970. Oscar-nominated for *So Proudly We Hail!*

*1929: The Locked Door. *Berth Marks. 1931: The Girl Habit. City Streets. 1932: The Kid from Spain. Pack Up Your Troubles. *Young Ironsides. *Girl Grief. The Mouthpiece. *Show Business. 1933: Roman Scandals. 1934: Kid Millions. 1936: The Bohemian Girl. Modern Times. 1938: The Young in Heart. Dramatic School. 1939: The Women. The Cat and the Canary. 1940: The Great Dictator. The Ghost Breakers. Northwest Mounted Police. 1941: Second Chorus. Nothing but the Truth. Hold Back the Dawn. Pot o' Gold (GB: The Golden Hour). 1942: The Lady Has Plans. The Forest Rangers. Reap the Wild Wind. Star Spangled Rhythm. 1943: So Proudly We Hail. The Crystal Ball. 1944: Standing Room Only. I Love a Soldier. 1945: Duffy's Tavern. Kitty. 1946: The Diary of a Chambermaid. 1947: Suddenly It's Spring. Variety Girl. Unconquered. 1948: A Miracle Can Happen (later On Our Merry Way). An Ideal Husband. Hazard. 1949: Bride of Vengeance. Anna Lucasta. 1950: The Torch (GB: Bandit General). 1952: Babes in Bagdad. 1953: Vice Squad (GB: The Girl in Room 17). Paris Model. Sins of Jezebel. 1954: Charge of the Lancers. The Stranger Came Home (US: The Unholy Four). 1963: Gli indifferenti (GB and US: Time of Indifference). 1972: The Female Instinct (TV. GB: The Snoop Sisters).*

GORCEY, Leo 1915–1969

Pint-sized, fast-talking (out of the side of his mouth), dark-haired American actor of Swiss parentage, whose round, wise-guy face, Brooklyn voice and success as one of the tough teenagers in the stage and film versions of *Dead End*, typed him in the same mould for the rest of his career. A member of the Dead End Kids from 1937–1940, then the East Side

Kids from 1940–1945, then leader of the Bowery Boys in a long series of simple comedies which convulsed Americans and proved largely painful to audiences elsewhere. The series quickly died when Gorcey decided to leave in 1956.

1937: Portia on Trial (GB: The Trial of Portia Merriman). Dead End. 1938: Crime School. Mannequin. Angels with Dirty Faces. 1939: Hell's Kitchen. Private Detective. Angels Wash Their Faces. The Battle of City Hall. They Made Me a Criminal. The Dead End Kids on Dress Parade. 1940: That Gang of Mine. Gallant Sons. Boys of the City (GB: East Side Kids). Angels with Broken Wings. Junior G-Men (serial). Invisible Stripes. Pride of the Bowery (GB: Here We Go Again). 1941: Sea Raiders (serial). Bowery Blitzkrieg (GB: Stand and Deliver). Out of the Fog. Spooks Run Wild. Road to Zanzibar. Down in San Diego. 1942: Mr Wise Guy. Sunday Punch. Smart Alecks. 'Neath Brooklyn Bridge. Let's Get Tough. Born to Sing. Junior G-Men of the Air (serial). Maisie Gets Her Man (GB: She Got Her Man). 1943: Clancy Street Boys. Mr Muggs Steps Out. Destroyer. 1944: Block Busters. Bowery Champs. Follow the Leader. The Million Dollar Kid. 1945: One Exciting Night. Midnight Manhunt. Mr Muggs Rides Again. Docks of New York. Live Wires. Come Out Fighting. 1946: Mr Hex (GB: Pride of the Bowery). In Fast Company. Spook Busters. Bowery Bombshell. 1947: Hard-Boiled Mahoney. News Hounds. Pride of Broadway. Bowery Buckaroos. 1948: Jinx Money. So This is New York. Angels' Alley. Trouble Makers. Smugglers' Cove. 1949: Angels in Disguise. Fighting Fools. Master Minds. Hold That Baby. 1950: Blues Busters. Triple Trouble. Blonde Dynamite. Lucky Losers. 1951: Ghost Chasers. Bowery Battalion. Crazy over Horses. Let's Go Navy. 1952: Here Come the Marines. Hold That Line. No Holds Barred. Feudin' Fools. 1953: Jalopy. Loose in London. Clipped Wings. Private Eyes. 1954: Paris Playboys. The Bowery Boys Meet the Monsters. Jungle Gents. 1955: Bowery to Bagdad. High Society. Jail Busters. Spy Chasers. 1956: Dig That Uranium. Crashing Las Vegas. 1963: It's a Mad Mad Mad Mad World. 1965: Second Fiddle to a String Guitar. 1969: The Phynx.

GORING, Marius 1912–

Fair-haired, blue-eyed British actor whose suavely sinister looks often got him cast as

foreign villains – with the occasional romantic lead thrown in. Attractive but slightly unbalanced characters were also a Goring speciality. He made an excellent Scarlet Pimpernel in a British television series of the 1950s and was also successful later on TV as *The Expert*, a forerunner of Hollywood's *Quincy*. Long married to Lucie Mannheim (*qv*). Widowed in 1976.

1935: *The Amateur Gentleman.* 1936: *Rembrandt.* 1938: *Dead Men Tell No Tales. Consider Your Verdict.* 1939: *The Last Straw. The Spy in Black (US: U-Boat 29). Flying Fifty-Five.* 1940: *Pastor Hall. The Case of the Frightened Lady (US: The Frightened Lady).* 1941: *The Big Blockade.* 1942: *The Night Invader.* 1943: *When We Are Married.* 1944: **The True Story of Lilli Marlene.* 1945: *Night Boat to Dublin.* 1946: *A Matter of Life and Death (US: Stairway to Heaven).* 1947: *Take My Life.* 1948: *The Red Shoes. Mr Perrin and Mr Traill.* 1950: *Odette. Highly Dangerous. Pandora and the Flying Dutchman.* 1951: *Circle of Danger. The Magic Box.* 1952: *So Little Time. Nachts auf den Strassen. The Man Who Watched Trains Go By (GB: Paris Express). Rough Shoot (US: Shoot First).* 1953: **The Mirror and Markheim (narrator only).* 1955: *Break in the Circle. The Adventures of Quentin Durward (US: Quentin Durward). The Barefoot Contessa.* 1957: *Ill Met by Moonlight (US: Night Ambush). *The Magic Carpet (narrator only). The Truth About Women. The Moonraker.* 1958: *Family Doctor (US: RX Murder). Son of Robin Hood. I Was Monty's Double (US: Monty's Double).* 1959: *Whirlpool. The Angry Hills. The Treasure of San Teresa (US: Long Distance). Desert Mice.* 1960: *Beyond the Curtain. The Unstoppable Man. Exodus.* 1961: *The Life of Hitler (narrator only).* 1962: *The Inspector (US: Lisa). The Devil's Daffodil (US: The Daffodil Killer). The Devil's Agent.* 1963: *This Garden England (narrator only).* 1964: *The Crooked Road.* 1965: *Up from the Beach.* 1967: *The 25th Hour.* 1968: *Girl on a Motorcycle. Subterfuge.* 1970: *First Love.* 1978: *The Little Girl in Blue Velvet.*

GOUGH, Michael 1917–

Malaya-born actor in British films. He moved from dark, sensitive intense young men in the 1940s to more outright villains and then along the Peter Cushing (*qv*) trail to leading roles in horror films, mostly as scientists whose creations got the better of them. In smaller roles since the end of the 1960s.

1947: *Blanche Fury. Anna Karenina.* 1948: *Saraband for Dead Lovers (US: Saraband). The Small Back Room.* 1950: *Blackmailed. Ha'penny Breeze.* 1951: *No Resting Place. The Man in the White Suit. Night Was Our Friend.* 1953: *Twice Upon a Time. Rob Roy the Highland Rogue. The Sword and the Rose.* 1955: *Richard III.* 1956: *Reach for the Sky.* 1957: *Ill Met by Moonlight (GB: Night Ambush). The House in the Woods.* 1958: *Dracula (US: The Horror of Dracula). The Horse's Mouth.* 1959: *Model for Murder. Horrors of the Black Museum.* 1961: *Konga. Mr Topaze (US: I Like Money). What a Carve Up! (US: Home Sweet Homicide).* 1962: *Candidate for Murder. The Phantom of the Opera.* 1963: *Black Zoo. Tamahine.* 1964: *Dr Terror's House of Horrors.* 1965: *Game for Three Losers. The Skull.* 1967: *They Came from Outer Space. Berserk!* 1968: *Un soir, un train. Curse of the Crimson Altar (US: Crimson Cult).* 1969: *Women in Love. A Walk with Love and Death.* 1970: *Julius Caesar. Trog. The Corpse.* 1971: *The Go-Between.* 1972: *Henry VIII and His Six Wives. Savage Messiah.* 1973: *Horror Hospital. The Legend of Hell House.* 1974: *Galileo. QB VII (TV). Monet in London (narrator only).* 1976: *Satan's Slave.* 1978: *The Boys from Brazil.* 1979: *L'amour en question.* 1981: *Venom.* 1982: *Witness for the Prosecution (TV).* 1983: *Memed My Hawk. The Dresser. Arthur the King (TV. Released 1985).* 1984: *A Christmas Carol (TV. GB: cinemas). Top Secret! Oxford Blues.* 1985: *Out of Africa. Hard Travelling (TV). Shattered Spirits (TV).* 1986: *Caravaggio.*

GOULD, Elliott (E. Goldstein) 1938–

Thick-lipped, heavy-featured, mournful-looking American star who can express both cynicism and sincerity. Very popular from 1969 to 1971, but fell victim to his own temperament and was off screen for two years. Lately he has returned in more commercial, if less penetrating, roles. Married to Barbra Streisand (first of two) 1963–1969. Received an Academy Award nomination for *Bob and Carol and Ted and Alice*.

1964: *The Confession (GB. TV: Quick, Let's Get Married!).* 1968: *The Night They Raided Minsky's.* 1969: *Bob and Carol and Ted and Alice.* 1970: *M*A*S*H. Getting Straight. I Love My Wife. Move. The Touch.* 1971: *Little Murders.* 1973: *The Long Goodbye. Busting.* 1974: *SPYS. California Split. Who?* 1975: *Nashville. Whiffs (GB: C*A*S*H). I Will, I Will . . . for Now. Mean Johnny Barrows.* 1976: *Harry and Walter Go to New York.* 1977: *A Bridge Too Far. Capricorn One.* 1978: *The Silent Partner. Matilda. The Muppet Movie. Escape to Athena.* 1979: *The Lady Vanishes. The Last Flight of Noah's Ark. Falling in Love Again.* 1980: *Dirty Tricks. The Devil and Max Devlin. A New Life.* 1981: *The Rules of Marriage (TV).* 1983: *Over the Brooklyn Bridge.* 1984: *The Naked Face. The Muppets Take Manhattan.* 1985: *Inside Out.* 1986: *The Myth. Boogie Woogie.*

GRABLE, Betty
(Elizabeth Grasle) 1916–1973

Was Betty really a chorus girl at 12 (she was born in December)? Every reference gives the same date of birth, so it must be true: in which case, no wonder she had had enough of powder-puff musicals by the time she was 40. The peaches-and-cream blonde with the healthy, swim-star figure laboured for ten years on the Hollywood scene before a lucky break (Alice Faye's illness) launched her to top stardom in *Down Argentine Way*. Her 'million-dollar legs' subsequently made her the queen of World War II pin-ups. Married to Jackie Coogan (1937–1940) and Harry James (1943–1965). Died from cancer.

1929: *Happy Days. Let's Go Places (GB: Mirth and Melody).* 1930: *Fox Movietone Follies of 1930 (GB: New Movietone Follies of 1930). Whoopee!* 1931: *Kiki. Palmy Days. *Ex-Sweeties. †*Crashing Hollywood.* 1932: *†*Hollywood Luck. †*Hollywood Lights.*

*Lady, Please. *Over the Counter. *The Flirty Sleepwalker. The Greeks Had a Word for Them. Child of Manhattan. Probation (GB: Second Chances). Hold 'Em Jail. The Kid from Spain. 1933: *Air Tonic. Cavalcade. The Sweetheart of Sigma Chi (GB: Girl of My Dreams). Melody Cruise. What Price Innocence? (GB: Shall the Children Pay?). 1934: *Susie's Affairs. The Gay Divorcee (GB: The Gay Divorce). Student Tour. Hips, Hips, Hooray! By Your Leave. *Love Detectives. *Business is a Pleasure. 1935: The Nitwits. Old Man Rhythm. *A Quiet Fourth. *A Night at the Biltmore Bowl. *Drawing Rumors. *The Spirit of 1976. 1936: Pigskin Parade (GB: The Harmony Parade). Follow the Fleet. Don't Turn 'Em Loose. Collegiate (GB: The Charm School). 1937: This Way Please. Thrill of a Lifetime. 1938: College Swing (GB: Swing, Teacher, Swing). Campus Confessions (GB: Fast Play). Give Me a Sailor. 1939: Man About Town. Million Dollar Legs. The Day the Bookies Wept. 1940: Down Argentine Way. Tin Pan Alley. 1941: A Yank in the RAF. I Wake Up Screaming (GB: Hot Spot). Moon over Miami. 1942: Footlight Serenade. Song of the Islands. Springtime in the Rockies. 1943: Coney Island. Sweet Rosie O'Grady. 1944: Four Jills in a Jeep. Pin-Up Girl. 1945: Billy Rose's Diamond Horseshoe (GB: Diamond Horseshoe). The Dolly Sisters. *All Star Bond Rally. 1946: Do You Love Me? The Shocking Miss Pilgrim. *Hollywood Park. 1947: Mother Wore Tights. 1948: That Lady in Ermine. When My Baby Smiles at Me. 1949: The Beautiful Blonde from Bashful Bend. 1950: Wabash Avenue. My Blue Heaven. 1951: Call Me Mister. Meet Me After the Show. 1953: The Farmer Takes a Wife. How to Marry a Millionaire. 1955: Three for the Show. How to Be Very, Very Popular.

† As Frances Dean

GRAHAME, Gloria
(G. G. Hallward) 1924–1981
Green-eyed blonde of sulky appearance and unique slightly lisping delivery (reminiscent of Humphrey Bogart, with whom she once co-starred). She painted a superb gallery of bad girls – Oscar-nominated as early as 1947, finally winning best supporting actress for *The Bad and the Beautiful* in 1952 – but could be surprisingly inept when called on to project a sympathetic character. Four times married,

including (first) Stanley Clements (1945–1948) and (second) director Nicholas Ray (1948–1952). Died from cancer.
1943: Cry Havoc. 1944: Blonde Fever. 1945: Without Love. 1946: It's a Wonderful Life. 1947: It Happened in Brooklyn. Merton of the Movies. Song of the Thin Man. Crossfire. 1948: A Woman's Secret. 1949: Roughshod. 1950: In a Lonely Place. Macao (released 1952). 1952: Sudden Fear. The Greatest Show on Earth. The Bad and the Beautiful. 1953: Man on a Tightrope. The Glass Wall. The Big Heat. Prisoners of the Casbah. 1954: The Good Die Young. Human Desire. Naked Alibi. 1955: Oklahoma! The Cobweb. Not As a Stranger. 1956: The Man Who Never Was. 1957: Ride Out for Revenge. 1959: Odds Against Tomorrow. 1966: Ride Beyond Vengeance. 1971: Blood and Lace. Chandler. The Todd Killings. Black Noon. Escape (TV). 1972: The Loners. Julio and Stein. 1973: Tarot. 1974: Mama's Dirty Girls. The Girl on the Late, Late Show (TV). 1975: Mansion of the Doomed (GB: The Terror of Dr Chaney). 1979: Chilly Scenes of Winter/Head Over Heels. The Nesting. 1980: Melvin and Howard. The Biggest Bank Robbery (TV).

GRAHAME, Margot 1911–1982
Britain's first ('aluminium') blonde bombshell. A bright, fluffy-haired blonde (in later years a redhead), she was so successful in British films of the early 1930s that she went to Hollywood, where she started strongly but gradually declined, returning to Britain before the war and latterly appearing more often on the stage than in the cinema. Died from chronic bronchitis.
1922: Lady of the Camelias. 1930: Rookery Nook (US: One Embarrassing Night). Compromising Daphne (US: Compromised!). To Live Happy. The Love Habit. 1931: Uneasy Virtue. The Rosary. Glamour. Creeping Shadows (US: The Limping Man). Stamboul. 1932: Postal Orders. A Letter of Warning. Illegal. Innocents of Chicago (US: Why Saps Leave Home). Yes Mr Brown. 1933: Forging Ahead. Timbuctoo. Prince of Arcadia. House of Dreams. Sorrell and Son. I Adore You. 1934: Without You. Easy Money. The Broken Melody. Falling in Love. 1935: The Informer. The Arizonian. The Three Musketeers. Two in the Dark. 1936: Trouble Ahead. Falling in Love. Crime over London. Make Way for a Lady. Night Waitress. Counterfeit. 1937: The

Soldier and the Lady (GB: Michael Strogoff). Criminal Lawyer. Fight for Your Lady. 1938: The Buccaneer. 1943: The Shipbuilders. 1947: Forever Amber. The Fabulous Joe. Broken Journey. 1949: The Romantic Age (US: Naughty Arlette). Black Magic. 1951: Lucky Nick Cain (GB: I'll Get You for This). 1952: Venetian Bird (US: The Assassin). The Crimson Pirate. 1953: The Beggar's Opera. 1954: Orders Are Orders. 1957: Saint Joan.

GRANGER, Farley 1925–
Dark, brooding American leading man with boyish good looks and liquid brown eyes. Signed by Samuel Goldwyn at 18, Granger alternated romantic leads with disturbed youths, but was seen to best advantage as flawed heroes, especially in Hitchcock's *Strangers on a Train*. After a career hiatus, he re-emerged for a few years in the 1970s in Italian exploitation films, mostly as handsome ne'er-do-wells.
1943: North Star. 1944: The Purple Heart. 1947: They Live By Night (released 1949). 1948: Rope. Enchantment. 1949: Roseanna McCoy. 1950: Edge of Doom (GB: Stronger Than Fear). Side Street. Our Very Own. 1951: Strangers on a Train. I Want You. Behave Yourself! 1952: O Henry's Full House (GB: Full House). Hans Christian Andersen . . . and the dancer. 1953: Small Town Girl. The Story of Three Loves. 1954: Senso. 1955: The Naked Street. 1956: The Girl in the Red Velvet Swing. Men Against Speed (TV. GB: cinemas). Seidman and Son (TV). 1957: The Clouded Image (TV). 1967: Laura (TV). Rogue's Gallery. 1968: The Challengers (TV. GB: cinemas). Those Days in the Sun. 1970: Planet Venus. They Call Me Trinity. Qual cosa striscia nel buio (GB: Something Creeping in the Dark. US: Shadows in the Dark). Maharlika. La tela del ragno. 1971: Il posso dell' assassino. Alla ricera del piacere (GB and US: Hot Bed of Sex). 1972: Replica di un delitto (US: Violence). The Serpent. La rossa dalla pelle che Scotta. Confessions of a Sex Maniac. 1973: White Fang. The Man Called Noon. Arnold. 1974: The Slasher. The Haunting of Penthouse D (TV). 1975: La polizie chiede aiuto. Death Shall Have Your Eyes. Widow (TV). So Sweet, So Dead/Bad Girls. The Lives of Jenny Dolan (TV). 1981: Rosemary's Killer. The Prowler. 1984: Deathmask. 1986: The Imagemaker. The Whoopee Boys. Very Close Quarters.

GRANGER, Stewart

(James Stewart) 1913–

Tall, dark, debonair British actor who, after a hard apprenticeship, was invalided out of war service and promptly shot to stardom portraying a series of dashing romantic adventurers. He went to Hollywood at the late age of 37, but still enjoyed half-a-dozen good years in bigger-budget M-G-M facsimiles of his British successes. He ended his star career in continental action films. Married to Elspeth March 1939–1949 and Jean Simmons (1950–1960): first and second of three.

1933: I Spy (US: The Morning After. As stand-in only). A Southern Maid. 1934: Give Her a Ring. Over the Garden Wall. 1937: Mademoiselle Docteur (US: Street of Shadows). 1939: So This is London. 1940: Convoy. 1942: Secret Mission. 1943: Thursday's Child. The Lamp Still Burns. The Man in Grey. 1944: Love Story (US: A Lady Surrenders). Fanny by Gaslight (US: Man of Evil). Madonna of the Seven Moons. Waterloo Road. 1945: Caesar and Cleopatra. 1946: Caravan. The Magic Bow. 1947: Captain Boycott. Blanche Fury. 1948: Saraband for Dead Lovers (US: Saraband). Woman Hater. 1949: Adam and Evelyne. 1950: King Solomon's Mines. 1951: Soldiers Three. The Light Touch. 1952: Scaramouche. The Wild North. The Prisoner of Zenda. 1953: Young Bess. All the Brothers Were Valiant. Salome. 1954: Beau Brummell. Green Fire. 1955: Moonfleet. Footsteps in the Fog. 1956: The Last Hunt. Bhowani Junction. 1957: The Little Hut. Gun Glory. 1958: The Whole Truth. Harry Black (US: Harry Black and the Tiger). 1960: North to Alaska. 1961: The Secret Partner. Swordsman of Siena. 1962: La congiura dei Dieci. The Last Days of Sodom and Gomorrah. 1963: Il giorno piu corto commedia umaristica (US: The Shortest Day). March or Die (GB: The Legion's Last Patrol. US: Commando). 1964: The Secret Invasion. The Crooked Road. Among Vultures (US: Frontier Hellcat). 1965: Der Ölprinz (GB and US: Rampage at Apache Wells). Old Surehand, erste Teil (GB and US: Flaming Frontier). 1966: Das Geheimnis der drei Dschunken (US: Red Dragon). Das Geheimnis der gelben Mönche (US: Target for Killing). Der Chef schickt seinen besten Mann (US: Requiem for a Secret Agent). Gern hab' ich die Frauen gekillt. 1967: The Last Safari. The Trygon Factor. 1969:

Any Second Now (TV). 1972: The Hound of the Baskervilles (TV). 1978: The Wild Geese. 1984: The Royal Romance of Charles and Diana (TV). 1986: Hell Hunters.

GRANT, Cary (Archibald Leach) 1904–

Dark-haired, British-born Hollywood star who originally went to America as an acrobat, but stayed to become a top star for over 30 years. His smooth elegance, dry delivery of a line, unique voice, hints of depths (of villainy and heroism) and delicious sense of the absurd built an immensely likeable screen personality apparently at odds with an explosive private life. Married to actresses Virginia Cherrill (1933–1935), Betsy Drake (1949–1960) and Dyan Cannon (1965–1968): first, third and fourth of four. Amazingly never won an Oscar (even his two nominations were not for his best roles); he was finally given an honorary one in 1969 for 'his unique mastery of the art of screen acting'.

*1931: This is the Night. *Singapore Sue. 1932: Merrily We Go to Hell (GB: Merrily We Go To ——) Sinners in the Sun. Hot Saturday. The Devil and the Deep. Blonde Venus. Madame Butterfly. 1933: Woman Accused. I'm No Angel. She Done Him Wrong. The Eagle and the Hawk. Gambling Ship. Alice in Wonderland. 1934: Thirty-Day Princess. Born to be Bad. Ladies Should Listen. Kiss and Make Up. Enter Madame. 1935: Wings in the Dark. The Last Outpost. Sylvia Scarlett. 1936: The Amazing Quest of Ernest Bliss (US: Romance and Riches). *Pirate Party on Catalina Isle. Wedding Present. Big Brown Eyes. Suzy. 1937: When You're in Love (GB: For You Alone). The Toast of New York. Topper. The Awful Truth. 1938: Holiday (GB: Free to Live/Unconventional Linda). Bringing Up Baby. 1939: Only Angels Have Wings. Gunga Din. In Name Only. His Girl Friday. 1940: My Favorite Wife. The Howards of Virginia (GB: The Tree of Liberty). The Philadelphia Story. 1941: Penny Serenade. Suspicion. 1942: The Talk of the Town. Once Upon a Honeymoon. 1943: Mr Lucky. Destination Tokyo. Arsenic and Old Lace. 1944: Once Upon a Time. *Road to Victory. *The Shining Future. None But the Lonely Heart. 1946: Night and Day. Without Reservations. Notorious. 1947: The Bachelor and the Bobby Soxer (GB: Bachelor Knight). 1948: The Bishop's Wife. Mr Blandings Builds His Dream House. Every Girl Should Be Married. 1949: I Was a Male War Bride (GB:*

*You Can't Sleep Here). 1950: Crisis. 1951: People Will Talk. 1952: Room for One More. Monkey Business. 1953: Dream Wife. 1955: To Catch a Thief. 1956: The Pride and the Passion. 1957: An Affair to Remember. Kiss Them for Me. 1958: Indiscreet. Houseboat. 1959: North by Northwest. Operation Petticoat. 1960: The Grass is Greener. 1961: *Captive Islands. 1962: That Touch of Mink. 1963: Charade. 1964: Father Goose. 1966: Walk, Don't Run. 1970: Elvis – That's the Way It Is.*

GRANT, Kirby (K. G. Hoon) 1911–1985

There can't be many bandleaders who became western stars, but this genial, fair-haired actor-musician from the wilds of Montana was certainly one. A child prodigy on the violin, he formed his own dance orchestra in his twenties and made occasional acting appearances before the war years, when spots with his band in low-budget Universal romps brought him back into demand for films. His acting career seemed to be petering out in the late 1940s, when Poverty Row studio Monogram came along with the offer of a series of films starring Grant as a Canadian Mountie, with a talented white husky as co-star. Several of these rugged little numbers were not at all bad, but with the demise of the second feature market Grant returned to night-club work. Killed in a car crash.

1938: Lawless Valley. Red River Range. 1939: †Three Sons. 1940: †Bullet Code. The Marines Fly High. 1941: Blondie Goes Latin. 1942: Hello, Frisco, Hello. My Favorite Blonde. The Stranger from Pecos. 1943: Bombardier. 1944: Hi Good Lookin'. Babes on Swing Street. Ghost Catchers. Destination Tokyo. In Society. 1945: Trail to Vengeance. I'll Remember April. Penthouse Rhythm. Bad Men of the Border. 1946: Code of the Lawless. Easy to Look At. 1946: Spider Woman Strikes Back. She Wrote the Book. Gun Town. Gunman's Code. The Lawless Breed. Rustlers' Roundup. 1948: Song of Idaho. 1949: Black Midnight. Feudin' Rhythm. Trail of the Yukon. Wolf Hunters. 1950: Snow Dog. Indian Territory. Call of the Klondike. 1951: Comin' Round the Mountain. The Celebrated Jumping Frog (of Calaveras County)(TV). Rhythm Inn. Yukon Manhunt. Northwest Territory. 1952: Yukon Gold. 1953: Cavalcade of America (TV). Northern Patrol. 1954: Yukon Vengeance. 1955: The Court Martial of Billy Mitchell (GB: One Man Mutiny).

† As Robert Stanton

GRANT, Lee (Lyova Rosenthal) 1929–
Dark-haired, forceful American actress. Nominated for an Academy Award in her first role, she submerged her handsome looks beneath a series of writhing neurotics. Hollywood could find no niche for her and she spent most of her time on stage and TV, only re-emerging, albeit mainly in character roles (but more commercial ones), into films and TV movies in the late sixties. Finally won an Oscar for *Shampoo*. Also Oscar-nominated for *The Landlord* and *Voyage of the Damned*.

1951: *Detective Story*. 1955: *Storm Fear*. 1959: *Middle of the Night*. 1962: *The Balcony*. 1963: *Pie in the Sky*. 1965: *An Affair of the Skin*. 1966: *Terror in the City*. 1967: *In the Heat of the Night*. *Divorce American Style*. *Valley of the Dolls*. 1968: *Buona Sera Mrs Campbell*. *The Big Bounce*. 1969: *Perilous Voyage* (*TV*). *Marooned*. 1970: *There Was a Crooked Man*. *Night Slaves* (*TV*). *The Landlord*. 1971: *Plaza Suite*. *Ransom for a Dead Man* (*TV*. *GB: cinemas*). *The Neon Ceiling* (*TV*). *Portnoy's Complaint*. 1972: *Lt. Schuster's Wife* (*TV*). 1973: *Partners in Crime* (*TV*). *What Are Best Friends For?* (*TV*). 1974: *The Internecine Project*. 1975: *Shampoo*. *Man Trouble* (*TV*). 1976: *Voyage of the Damned*. *Perilous Voyage* (*TV*). 1977: *Airport 77*. *The Spell* (*TV*). 1978: *Damien – Omen II*. *The Swarm*. *Thou Shalt Not Kill* (*TV*). *The Mafu Cage*. 1979: *When You Comin' Back, Red Ryder?* *You Can't Go Home Again* (*TV*). *The Million Dollar Face* (*TV*). 1980: *Little Miss Marker*. 1981: *Charlie Chan and the Curse of the Dragon Queen*. *The Fright*. 1982: *Visiting Hours*. 1983: *A Matter of Sex* (*TV*). 1984: *Trial Run*. *Teachers*. *Will There Really Be a Morning?* (*TV*). *A Billion for Boris*.

As director: 1980: *Tell Me a Riddle*. 1981: *The Willmar 8*. *For Ladies Only* (*TV*). 1985: *What Sex Am I?* 1986: *Nobody's Child* (*TV*).

GRANVILLE, Bonita 1923–
Long-nosed, lantern-jawed (but attractive) American actress with light brown hair. Played brats and smart-Alec teenagers through the thirties, most notably the abhorrent Mary in *These Three* (1936), which won her an Oscar nomination. Her career went slowly downhill in the forties, and she seemed to lose interest in acting after her marriage in

1947, becoming associated with the 'Lassie' TV series for nearly 20 years on the production side. Said to have made small appearances in shorts from 1930 to 1932.
1932: *Westward Passage*. *Silver Dollar*. 1933: *Cavalcade*. *The Cradle Song*. 1934: *The Life of Vergie Winters*. *Anne of Green Gables*. *A Wicked Woman*. 1935: *Ah, Wilderness!* 1936: *These Three*. *Song of the Saddle*. *The Plough and the Stars*. *The Garden of Allah*. 1937: *Maid of Salem*. *Call It a Day*. *Quality Street*. *It's Love I'm After*. *The Life of Emile Zola*. 1938: *Merrily We Live*. *White Banners*. *My Bill*. **For Auld Lang Syne*. *The Beloved Brat* (*GB: A Dangerous Age*). *Hard to Get*. *Nancy Drew, Detective*. 1939: *Nancy Drew, Reporter*. *Nancy Drew, Trouble Shooter*. *Nancy Drew and the Hidden Staircase*. *Angels Wash Their Faces*. 1940: *Those Were the Days*. *The Mortal Storm*. *Forty Little Mothers*. *Third Finger, Left Hand*. *Escape*. *Gallant Sons*. 1941: *The Wild Man of Borneo*. *The People vs. Dr Kildare* (*GB: My Life is Yours*). *H. M. Pulham Esq.* *Down in San Diego*. 1942: *Syncopation*. *The Glass Key*. *Now, Voyager*. 1943: *Seven Miles from Alcatraz*. *Hitler's Children*. *What a Woman!* 1944: *Andy Hardy's Blonde Trouble*. *Youth Runs Wild*. *Song of the Open Road*. 1945: *Senorita from the West*. *The Beautiful Cheat* (*GB: What a Woman!*). 1946: *Love Laughs at Andy Hardy*. *Breakfast in Hollywood* (*GB: The Mad Hatter*). *Suspense*. *The Truth About Murder* (*GB: The Lie Detector*). 1947: *The Guilty*. 1948: *Strike It Rich*. 1950: *Guilty of Treason* (*GB: Treason*). 1956: *The Lone Ranger*. 1958: *The Velvet Alley* (*TV*). 1981: *The Legend of the Lone Ranger*.

GRAVES, Peter (P. Aurness) 1925–
Tall, well-built American actor, brother of James Arness. His fair hair, blue eyes and faintly oriental looks seemed to qualify him for a profitable run of handsome villains, especially after his treacherous Price in *Stalag 17*. But from 1955 he became involved as increasingly artificial men-of-action in successive television series. His film leads since then have been largely in 'Z' movies.
1950: *Rogue River*. 1951: *Fort Defiance*. 1952: *Red Planet Mars*. *Stalag 17*. 1953: *East of Sumatra*. *War Paint*. *Beneath the 12-Mile Reef*. *Killers from Space*. 1954: *The Raid*. *The Yellow Tomahawk*. *The Long Gray Line*. *Black Tuesday*. 1955: *The Naked Street*. *Robbers'*

Roost. *Wichita*. *Night of the Hunter*. *The Court-Martial of Billy Mitchell* (*GB: One Man Mutiny*). *Fort Yuma*. 1956: *Hold Back the Night*. *Canyon River*. *It Conquered the World*. 1957: *Death in Small Doses*. *Bayou*. *The Beginning of the End*. 1958: *Wolf Larsen*. 1959: *Stranger in My Arms*. 1963: *The Case Against Paul Ryker* (*TV*. *GB and US cinemas 1968 as Sergeant Ryker*). 1965: *A Rage to Live*. 1966: *Texas Across the River*. 1967: *The Ballad of Josie*. *Valley of Mystery*. 1969: *The Five Man Army*. *Mission Impossible vs. the Mob* (*TV*. *GB: cinemas*). 1971: *The President's Plane is Missing* (*TV*). 1972: *Call to Danger* (*TV*). 1974: *Sidecar Racers*. *Where Have All the People Gone?* (*TV*). *The Underground Man* (*TV*). *Scream of the Wolf* (*TV*). 1975: *Dead Man on the Run* (*TV*). *Bigfoot: the Mysterious Monster* (*narrator only*). 1976: *Spree*. 1977: *SST Death Flight* (*TV*). 1978: *Missile X*. *High Seas Hijack*. 1979: *The Clonus Horror*. *Death Car on the Freeway* (*TV*). *Teheran Incident/Teheran 1943*. *The Rebels* (*TV*). 1980: *Trieste File*. *Airplane!* *Survival Run*. *The Memory of Eva Ryker* (*TV*). 1981: *300 Miles for Stephanie* (*TV*). *The Guns and the Fury*. 1982: *Savannah Smiles*. *Airplane II The Sequel*. 1986: *Number One with a Bullet*.

GRAY, Coleen (Doris Jensen) 1922–
Petite, full-lipped, showy-looking fair-haired American actress, always in leading roles, but almost entirely in co-features. Of Danish parentage, she was a relative latecomer to films at 23, but stayed around in a variety of colourful pot-boilers until her late thirties. Most

interesting as semi-bad girls, a role in which she wasn't often cast.

1945: State Fair. 1946: Three Little Girls in Blue. 1947: Kiss of Death. Nightmare Alley. 1948: Red River. Fury at Furnace Creek. 1949: Will James' Sand (GB: Sand). 1950: Riding High. Father is a Bachelor. The Sleeping City. 1951: Apache Drums. Lucky Nick Cain (GB: I'll Get You for This). 1952: Models Inc (GB: That Kind of Girl). Kansas City Confidential (GB: The Secret Four). 1953: The Fake. Sabre Jet. The Vanquished. 1954: Arrow in the Dust. 1955: Las Vegas Shakedown. The Twinkle in God Eye's. Tennessee's Partner. 1956: Star in the Dust. The Wild Dakotas. The Killing. Frontier Gambler. Death of a Scoundrel. The Black Whip. 1957: Destination 60,000. The Vampire. Copper Sky. God is My Partner. 1958: Hell's Five Hours. Johnny Rocco. 1959: The Leech Woman. 1962: Phantom Planet. 1965: Town Tamer. 1968: P.J. (GB: New Face in Hell). 1971: Ellery Queen: Don't Look Behind You (TV). 1972: The Late Liz. 1979: The Best Place to Be (TV). 1986: Cry from the Mountain.

of Paris. *1952: Saturday Island (US: Island of Desire). 1954: The Diamond (US: Diamond Wizard). Burnt Evidence. 1955: Timeslip (US: The Atomic Man). 1956: Satellite in the Sky. The Secret Tent. Supersonic Saucer.*

his initial British film *Murder at Monte Carlo.*
1927: *A Daughter of the Night. The Silver Lining. Poppies of Flanders. One of the Best. 1928: Moulin Rouge. Smashing Through. Lockendes Gift (GB: Sweet Pepper). Villa Falconieri. Die Abenteuer GmbH (GB: The Secret Adversary). 1930: The Loves of Robert Burns. Why Sailors Leave Home. Night Birds. 1931: Midnight. The Wickham Mystery. 1933: The Flaw. The Bermondsey Kid. Smithy. 1934: The Crimson Candle. Guest of Honour. Murder at Monte Carlo. Womanhood. Big Business. What's in a Name? 1935: Death on the Set (GB: Murder on the Set). *Just for Tonight. Three Witnesses. Bargain Basement (later Department Store). Scrooge. The Last Journey. 1936: Twice Branded. Such is Life. They Didn't Know. Jury's Evidence. The Happy Family. 1937: Pearls Bring Tears. When the Devil Was Well. The Vicar of Bray. The Strange Adventures of Mr Smith. Fifty Shilling Boxer. Who Killed Fen Markham?/The Angelus. Silver Blaze (US: Murder at the Baskervilles). 1938: The Awakening. His Lordship Regrets. 1951: One Good Turn.

GRAY, Lorna
See Booth, Adrian

GRAY, Dolores 1924–
Blonde, catlike American singer of spectacularly striking face and figure. Combined with a fine singing voice that sounded like liquid honey, these attributes, plus a sensual smoulder, soon made her a top star of stage musicals. She never set the screen on fire in quite the same way, in spite of a few good tries.

1944: Mr Skeffington. 1954: It's Always Fair Weather. 1955: Kismet. 1956: The Opposite Sex. 1957: Designing Woman.

GRAY, Donald
(Eldred Tidbury) 1914–1979
South African-born leading man with brown, wavy hair and pleasantly square-shaped, if intent-looking, face. His promising career in British films looked to be over when he lost an arm in World War II, but he courageously carried on acting, and found a niche as a detective called Mark Saber in a long-running British television series, which in turn led to a few more film parts.

1936: Strange Experiment. 1937: Well Done, Henry. 1938: Murder in the Family. 13 Men and a Gun. 1939: The Four Feathers. Sword of Honour. 1942: We'll Meet Again. 1948: Idol

GRAY, Dulcie (D. Bailey) 1919–
Pretty, appealing, ultra-English brunette actress (actually born in Malaya), never given much chance to realize her capabilities in films, and mostly confined to milk-and-water waiting women. Not surprisingly, she quit films in 1952, and concentrated on dual careers as stage actress and novelist. A great hit as Miss Marple on stage in the seventies. Married to Michael Denison (qv) since 1939.

1944: *Victory Wedding. 2,000 Women. Madonna of the Seven Moons. 1945: A Place of One's Own. They Were Sisters. 1946: Wanted for Murder. The Years Between. 1947: A Man About the House. Mine Own Executioner. 1948: My Brother Jonathan. 1949: The Glass Mountain. 1951: The Franchise Affair. 1952: Angels One Five. There Was a Young Lady. 1966: A Man Could Get Killed.

GRAY, Eve 1904–
Blue-eyed blonde known in early sound days as the most beautiful girl in British films. Brought up in Australia (although English-born), she was a big hit on the London stage in the mid-1920s. She turned down Hollywood offers, but did make some films for UFA in Germany. Remaining popular throughout the 1930s, when she concentrated heavily on films, often playing bad girls, she is now best remembered as Errol Flynn's leading lady in

GRAY, Nadia (N. Kujnir-Herescu) 1923–
Glamorous, chestnut-haired international leading lady, born in Berlin of Russian parents, and raised in Rumania. After lending her distinctive, spiky personality to films in several European countries over a period of 20 years, she emigrated to America. In the

late seventies she launched herself as a night-club singer.

1948: L'inconnu d'un soir. 1949: Monseigneur. The Spider and the Fly. 1951: Night without Stars. Valley of the Eagles. 1952: Top Secret (US: Mr Potts Goes to Moscow). 1953: Gran varietà. Puccini. La vierge du Rhin. Les femmes s'en balancent. Inganno. Moglie per una notte (GB: Wife for a Night). 1954: Carosello Napoletano (GB: Neapolitan Fantasy). Crossed Swords. Casta diva. Casa Ricordi. Casanova (GB: The Adventures of Casanova. US: Sins of Casanova. Ivan, il figlio del diavolo bianco. 1955: Il falco d'oro. Musik im Blut. 1956: Folies Bergère. Senechal the Magnificent. 1957: Il diavolo nero. Une Parisienne. One Week with Love. 1958: The Captain's Table. 1959: La dolce vita. Vacanze ad Ischia. 1960: Candide. 1961: Les crouants se porte bien. Le jeu de la vérité. Le pavé de Paris (GB: The Pavements of Paris). Jeunesse de nuit. Mr Topaze (US: I Like Money). 1962: Rocambole. Maniac. Adventurer from Tortuga. 1963: Zwei Whisky und ein Sofa. 1964: Begegnung in Salzburg. The Crooked Road. 1965: Up from the Beach. 1966: Winnetou und sein Freund Old Firehand (GB: Thunder at the Border). 1967: The Oldest Profession. The Naked Runner. Two for the Road. 1976: Rue Haute.

GRAY, Sally (Constance Stevens) 1916–
Beautiful British blonde actress with wolf-whistle figure, dancing in a minstrel show at 14 and popular in British films at 19. Suffered a breakdown attributed to overwork in 1941, and retired. Came back in 1946 looking more stunning than ever and made a few more male hearts flutter in the cinema before marrying into the aristocracy in 1953.

1930: School for Scandal. 1935: Radio Pirates. The Dictator (US: The Loves of a Dictator). Limelight (US: Backstage). Cross Currents. Lucky Days. Checkmate. Marry the Girl. 1936: Olympic Honeymoon. Café Colette (US: Danger in Paris). Cheer Up! Calling the Tune. 1937: Over She Goes. Saturday Night Revue. 1938: Mr Reeder in Room 13 (US: Mystery of Room 13). Hold My Hand. Lightning Conductor. 1939: The Lambeth Walk. The Saint in London. Sword of Honour. A Window in London (US: Lady in Distress). 1940: Honeymoon Merry-Go-Round. 1941: The Saint's Vacation. Dangerous Moonlight (US: Suicide Squadron). 1946: Carnival. Green for Danger.

1947: They Made Me a Fugitive (US: I Became a Criminal). The Mark of Cain. 1948: Obsession (US: The Hidden Room). 1949: Silent Dust. 1952: Escape Route (US: I'll Get You).

GRAYSON, Kathryn
(Zelma K. Hedrick) 1922–
Dark-haired, brown-eyed, almost absurdly pretty American singing star who trilled her coloratura soprano voice across M-G-M sound stages for 13 years and played in some of their best musicals. She played down her sexy hour-glass figure until later in her career, although it was then that she gave two of her most attractive performances – as Magnolia in Show Boat and Katharine in Kiss Me Kate. Her latter-day appearances showed that the once-svelte star had gained weight dramatically.

1941: Andy Hardy's Private Secretary. The Vanishing Virginian. 1942: Rio Rita. Seven Sweethearts. 1943: Thousands Cheer. 1944: Ziegfeld Follies (released 1946). 1945: Anchors Aweigh. 1946: Two Sisters from Boston. Till the Clouds Roll By. 1947: It Happened in Brooklyn. 1948: The Kissing Bandit. 1949: That Midnight Kiss. 1950: The Toast of New Orleans. Grounds for Marriage. 1951: Show Boat. 1952: Lovely to Look At. 1953: The Desert Song. So This Is Love (GB: The Grace Moore Story). Kiss Me Kate. 1956: The Vagabond King. 1957: Lone Woman (TV). 1978: Beverly Hills High (TV).

GRECO, Juliette 1927–
Dark-haired, dark-eyed French night-club chanteuse who had a sporadic career in French

films. Her acerbic songs had made her the darling of Paris Left-Bank existentialist cellars, when she was 'discovered' by Darryl F. Zanuck who put her under contract to Twentieth Century-Fox for five years. She seemed to lose interest in the cinema in the sixties and has long been married (second) to Michel Piccoli (1925–   ).

1949: Au royaume des cieux. 1950: *Désordre. Sans laisser d'adresse. 1951: The Green Glove. 1952: La route de bonheur. 1953: Boum sur Paris! Quand tu liras cette lettre. 1956: La châtelaine du Liban. Elena et les hommes (GB: Paris Does Strange Things). L'homme et l'enfant (GB and US: Man and Child). 1957: C'est arrivé a 36 chandelles. The Sun Also Rises. 1958: The Naked Earth. Roots of Heaven. Bonjour Tristesse. 1959: Whirlpool. 1960: Crack in the Mirror. 1961: The Big Gamble. Malefices. 1962: Canzoni nel mondo (US: 38–24–36). 1965: Uncle Tom's Cabin. 1966: The Night of the Generals.

GREEN, Mitzi (M. Keno) 1920–1969
Happy-looking, raven-haired child star of the early sound days (having made her vaudeville debut at three), a talented mimic who could also sing and dance – usually cast in movies as junior wiseacres. She stayed in show business when her childhood days were over, mainly as a middle-range Broadway performer. Married to director Joseph Pevney from 1942 until her death from cancer.

1929: The Marriage Playground. Honey. 1930: Paramount on Parade. Love among the Millionaires. Santa Fé Trail. Tom Sawyer. 1931: Finn and Hattie. Huckleberry Finn. Dude Ranch. Skippy. Newly Rich. 1932: Little Orphan Annie. *The Stolen Jools (GB: The Slippery Pearls). Girl Crazy. 1934: Transatlantic Merry-Go-Round. 1940: Walk with Music. 1952: Lost in Alaska (GB: Abbott and Costello Lost in Alaska). Bloodhounds of Broadway.

GREENE, Richard 1918–1985
Tall, dark, strongly-built, boyishly handsome British leading man whose acting was somewhat restricted, but who might have become an even bigger Hollywood star had the war not interrupted his career. When he returned to America, he was confined to increasingly minor swashbucklers, but a British television series, Robin Hood, was an immense success, made him a household name, and enabled him

to retire in middle age. Married to Patricia Medina (first of two) 1941–1951. Never fully recovered from a brain tumour operation in 1982.

1934: †*Sing As We Go*. 1938: *Four Men and a Prayer. My Lucky Star. Kentucky. Submarine Patrol*. 1939: *The Hound of the Baskervilles. Stanley and Livingstone. The Little Princess. Here I Am a Stranger*. 1940: *I Was an Adventuress. Little Old New York*. 1942: *Unpublished Story. Flying Fortress*. 1943: *Yellow Canary*. 1944: *Don't Take It to Heart*. 1946: *Gaiety George (US: Showtime)*. 1947: *Forever Amber*. 1948: *The Fighting O'Flynn*. 1949: *The Fan (US: Lady Windermere's Fan). That Dangerous Age (US: If This Be Sin). Now Barabbas was a robber . . .* 1950: *My Daughter Joy (US: Operation X). Shadow of the Eagle. The Desert Hawk*. 1951: *Peter Ibbetson (TV). Lorna Doone*. 1952: *The Black Castle*. 1953: *Rogue's March. Captain Scarlett. The Bandits of Corsica (GB: Return of the Corsican Brothers)*. 1955: *Contraband Spain*. 1960: *Beyond the Curtain*. 1961: *Sword of Sherwood Forest*. 1967: *Island of the Lost*. 1968: *The Blood of Fu Manchu (US: Kiss and Kill/Fu Manchu and the Kiss of Death). The Castle of Fu Manchu*. 1972: *Tales from the Crypt*. 1984: *Special Effects*.

† *Scenes deleted from final release print*

GREENSTREET, Sydney 1879–1954
Huge English actor with impeccable diction and tiny, hostile features above a bulky body that at one time reached 325 pounds. A massive hit in more ways than one as the fat man in *The Maltese Falcon* – his first film at 60 – and a regular in Warner Brothers films after that throughout the forties. Ill-health forced him to retire earlier than the studio would have wished. Most popular of all in films that teamed him with Peter Lorre (*qv*) – a kind of Laurel and Hardy in Hell. Died from Bright's Disease complicated by diabetes. Oscar-nominated for *The Maltese Falcon*.

1941: *The Maltese Falcon. They Died with Their Boots On*. 1942: *Across the Pacific. In This Our Life. Casablanca*. 1943: *Devotion (released 1946). Background to Danger*. 1944: *Passage to Marseille. Hollywood Canteen. Between Two Worlds. The Mask of Dimitrios. The Conspirators*. 1945: *Pillow to Post. Christmas in Connecticut. Conflict*. 1946: *Three Strangers. The Verdict*. 1947: *That Way with Women. The Hucksters. The Woman in White*. 1948: *Ruthless. The Velvet Touch*. 1949: *Flamingo Road. It's a Great Feeling. Malaya (GB: East of the Rising Sun)*.

GREENWOOD, Joan 1921–
Pixieish, plummy-voiced, green-eyed blonde, a sort of demure Fenella Fielding. Ideally cast as Lady Caroline Lamb in the otherwise poor *The Bad Lord Byron*, she was mostly seen as *femmes fatales*, although she tried to vary her range and, like most screen bad girls, found it difficult to prolong her film career into her thirties. Married to André Morell from 1960 until his death in 1978.

1940: *John Smith Wakes Up*. 1941: *My Wife's Family. He Found a Star*. 1943: *The Gentle Sex*. 1945: *They Knew Mr Knight. Latin Quarter*. 1946: *A Girl in a Million*. 1947: *The Man Within (US: The Smugglers). The October Man. The White Unicorn (US: Bad Sister)*. 1948: *Saraband for Dead Lovers (US: Saraband). The Bad Lord Byron*. 1949: *Whisky Galore (US: Tight Little Island). Kind Hearts and Coronets*. 1951: *Flesh and Blood. Young Wives' Tale. The Man in the White Suit. Monsieur Ripos (US: Mr Peek-a-Boo)*. 1952: *The Importance of Being Earnest*. 1954: *Knave of Hearts (US: Lovers, Happy Lovers). Father Brown (US: The Detective)*. 1955: *Moonfleet*. 1958: *Stage Struck*. 1962: *Mysterious Island. The Amorous Prawn*. 1963: *Tom Jones. The Moon-Spinners*. 1971: *Girl Stroke Boy*. 1977: *The Uncanny. The Hound of the Baskervilles*. 1978: *The Water Babies*. 1979: *The Flame is Love (TV)*. 1986: *Little Dorrit I. Little Dorrit II*.

GREER, Jane (Bettejane Greer) 1924–
Strikingly pretty brunette American actress with chiselled features who recovered from Bell's palsy as a child to become a useful actress who didn't get the breaks to make her a top star. Could be warm and sympathetic or cold and calculating: it was in the latter vein that she did her best film work, at her first studio, RKO, where she had become one of Howard Hughes' protégées in 1943. Married to Rudy Vallee (first of two) 1943–1944.

1945: †*Two O'Clock Courage*. †*Pan-Americana*. †*George White's Scandals. Dick Tracy (GB: Split Face)*. 1946: *The Falcon's Alibi. The Bamboo Blonde. Sunset Pass*. 1947: *Sinbad the Sailor. They Won't Believe Me. Out of the Past (GB: Build My Gallows High)*. 1948: *Station West*. 1949: *The Big Steal*. 1950: *USS Teakettle (later You're in the Navy Now)*. 1951: *The Company She Keeps*. 1952: *You for Me. The Prisoner of Zenda. Desperate Search*. 1953: *The Clown. Down Among the Sheltering Palms*. 1955: *One Man Missing (TV)*. 1956: *Run for the Sun*. 1957: *Man of a Thousand Faces*. 1958: *No Time At All (TV)*. 1964: *Where Love Has Gone*. 1965: *Billie*. 1973: *The Outfit*. 1982: *The Shadow Riders (TV)*. 1983: *Against All Odds*. 1985: *Something in Common*.

† *As Bettejane Greer*

GREGSON, John 1919–1975
Diffident, well-liked British star of Irish background, with dark curly hair. Eventually succeeded, after some initial tough times, as shy young heroes with steely inner cores. His film career faded after ten good years, but he found

new popularity as a top cop in the successful TV series *Gideon's Way*. Married for nearly 30 years until his death (from a heart attack) to actress Thea Gregory.

1948: *Saraband for Dead Lovers* (US: *Saraband*). *London Belongs to Me* (US: *Dulcimer Street*). *Scott of the Antarctic*. 1949: *The Hasty Heart*. *Whisky Galore* (US: *Tight Little Island*). *Train of Events*. 1950: *Treasure Island*. *Cairo Road*. 1951: *The Lavender Hill Mob*. 1952: *Angels One Five*. *The Brave Don't Cry*. *The Holly and the Ivy*. *Venetian Bird* (US: *The Assassin*). 1953: *The Titfield Thunderbolt*. *Genevieve*. *The Weak and the Wicked* (US: *Young and Willing*). 1954: *The Crowded Day*. *Conflict of Wings*. *To Dorothy a Son* (US: *Cash on Delivery*). 1955: *Above Us the Waves*. *Three Cases of Murder*. *Value for Money*. 1956: *Jacqueline*. *The Battle of the River Plate* (US: *Pursuit of the Graf Spee*). *True As a Turtle*. 1957: *Miracle in Soho*. 1958: *Rooney*. *Sea of Sand* (US: *Desert Patrol*). *The Captain's Table*. 1959: *SOS Pacific*. 1960: *Faces in the Dark*. *Flight from Treason*. *Hand in Hand*. 1961: *The Treasure of Monte Cristo* (US: *The Secrets of Monte Cristo*). *The Frightened City*. 1962: *Live Now – Pay Later*. *Tomorrow at Ten*. *The Longest Day*. 1963: *Anatomy of a Disaster* (narrator only). 1964: *The Yellow Golliwog*. 1966: *The Night of the Generals*. 1970: *70 Years On* (narrator only). 1971: *Fright*. 1975: *The Tiger Lily*.

GREY, Anne (Aileen Ewing) 1907–
Tall, dark-haired British actress – a former journalist – with upper-class, Penelope Keith-type looks. Tremendously popular in the early days of sound, she was often cast in aristocratic roles, sometimes as girls of independent spirit, sometimes as 'other women'. Married Lester Matthews (1900–1975) in 1931, and went with him to Hollywood in 1935, making a few films there. Returned to England when the marriage broke up, but could not regain her place in the front rank, and surprisingly did not have a second career as a character player.
1927: *The Constant Nymph*. 1928: *What Money Can Buy*. *The Warning*. *Master and Man*. 1929: *Taxi for Two*. *The Nipper/The Brat*. 1930: *The Squeaker*. *Crossroads*. *The School for Scandal*. *Guilt*. 1931: *The Man at Six* (US: *The Gables Mystery*). *Other People's Sins*. *The Calendar* (US: *Bachelor's Folly*). *The Happy Ending*. *The Old Man*. 1932: *Mur-*

der at Covent Garden. *Lily Christine*. *The Faithful Heart* (US: *Faithful Hearts*). *Number Seventeen*. *Arms and the Man*. *Leap Year*. 1933: *She Was Only a Village Maiden*. *One Precious Year*. *The Lost Chord*. *The Golden Cage*. *The Blarney Stone* (US: *The Blarney Kiss*). *The Lure*. *The Fire Raisers*. *Just Smith* (US: *Leave It to Smith*). *The Wandering Jew*. *Colonel Blood*. *The House of Trent*. 1934: *Borrowed Clothes*. *The Scoop*. *Lady in Danger*. *Road House*. *The Poisoned Diamond*. 1935: *Bonnie Scotland*. *Break of Hearts*. 1936: *Just My Luck*. *Too Many Parents*. 1937: *Dr Sin Fang*. 1938: *Chinatown Nights*.

GREY, Virginia 1917–
Pretty in a pinched, anguished-looking way, this gentle-mannered, soft-haired American blonde was one of Hollywood's most durable actresses, with a career extending over 40 years, during which time she was a perennial juvenile lead supporting the stars, with one or two better leading roles, although in minor films, in the late forties and early fifties. Long romantically involved with Clark Gable, she lost him to Carole Lombard, and has never married.
1927: *Uncle Tom's Cabin*. 1928: *Heart to Heart*. *Jazz Mad*. *The Michigan Kid*. 1931: *Misbehaving Ladies*. 1933: *Secrets*. 1934: *Dames*. *The Firebird*. *St Louis Kid* (GB: *A Perfect Weekend*). 1935: *She Gets Her Man*. *Gold Diggers of 1935*. 1936: *Old Hutch*. *The Great Ziegfeld*. *Secret Valley* (GB: *The Gangster's Bride*). **Violets in Spring*. 1937: *Bad Guy*. *Rosalie*. 1938: *Test Pilot*. *Dramatic School*. **The Canary Comes Across*. *Shopworn Angel*. *Youth Takes a Fling*. *Ladies in Distress*. *Rich Man, Poor Girl*. 1939: *Thunder Afloat*. *Broadway Serenade*. *The Hardys Ride High*. *Idiot's Delight*. *The Women*. *Another Thin Man*. 1940: *Three Cheers for the Irish*. *The Captain is a Lady*. *Hullabaloo*. *The Golden Fleecing*. 1941: *Blonde Inspiration*. *Keeping Company*. *Washington Melodrama*. *The Big Store*. *Mr and Mrs North*. *Whistling in the Dark*. 1942: *Tish*. *Grand Central Murder*. *Bells of Capistrano*. *Tarzan's New York Adventure*. 1943: *Idaho*. *Sweet Rosie O'Grady*. *Secrets of the Underground*. *Stage Door Canteen*. 1944: *Strangers in the Night*. 1945: *Blonde Ransom*. *Flame of the Barbary Coast*. *Grissly's Millions*. *The Men in her Diary*. 1946: *Smooth As Silk*. *Swamp Fire*. *House of Horrors*.

(GB: *Joan Medford is Missing*). 1947: *Unconquered*. *Wyoming*. 1948: *Glamour Girl*. *So This is New York*. *Miraculous Journey*. *Mexican Hayride*. *When My Baby Smiles at Me*. *Unknown Island*. *Who Killed 'Doc' Robbin?* (GB: *Sinister House*). *Leather Gloves* (GB: *Loser Take All*). 1949: *Jungle Jim*. *The Threat*. 1950: *Highway 301*. 1951: *The Bullfighter and the Lady*. *Three Desperate Men*. *Slaughter Trail*. 1952: *Desert Pursuit*. *The Fighting Lawman*. 1953: *Captain Scarface*. *A Perilous Journey*. *Hurricane at Pilgrim Hill*. 1954: *The Forty-Niners*. *Target Earth*. 1955: *The Eternal Sea*. *The Last Command*. *All That Heaven Allows*. 1956: *The Rose Tattoo*. *Accused of Murder*. 1957: *Crime of Passion*. *Jeanne Eagels*. 1958: *The Great Gatsby* (TV). *The Restless Years*. 1959: *No Name on the Bullet*. 1960: *Portrait in Black*. 1961: *Tammy Tell Me True*. *Flower Drum Song*. *Bachelor in Paradise*. *Back Street*. 1963: *Black Zoo*. 1964: *The Naked Kiss*. *Love Has Many Faces*. 1966: *Madame X*. 1968: *Rosie!* 1969: *Airport*. 1975: *The Lives of Jenny Dolan* (TV).

GRIFFITH, Andy 1926–
Slow-drawling, light-haired, large-faced, solidly-built American actor and entertainer who made a major impression in his first film role but was thereafter most successful on television, where his 'country-boy' wit and sly charm made him a favourite with his own show from 1960 to 1971, one of the longest runs on record. Later he appeared in a few TV movies as redneck, but warm-hearted, sheriffs, preserving his star status well into his fifties.
1957: *A Face in the Crowd*. 1958: *No Time for Sergeants*. *The Male Animal* (TV). *Onionhead*. 1961: *The Second Time Around*. 1969: *Angel in My Pocket*. 1972: *The Strangers in 7A* (TV). 1973: *Winter Kill* (TV). 1975: *Hearts of the West* (GB: *Hollywood Cowboy*). *Adams of Eagle Lake* (TV). 1976: *The Girl in the Empty Grave* (TV). 1977: *The Deadly Game* (TV). 1978: *Salvage-1* (TV). 1981: *Murder in Texas* (TV). 1983: *The Demon Murder Case* (TV). *Murder in Coweta County* (TV). 1985: *Rustler's Rhapsody*. *Crime of Innocence* (TV). 1986: *Diary of a Perfect Murder* (TV).

GRIFFITHS, Jane 1929–1975
Attractive green-eyed brunette British actress who created quite a stir in 1953 when cast

opposite Gregory Peck in *The Million Pound Note*. The demure Jane's film career did not live up to that beginning, partly because she lacked a strong enough personality, partly because she seemed more interested in the stage. Her later years were dogged by ill-health.

1950: Double Confession. 1952: The Gambler and the Lady. 1953: The Million Pound Note (US: Man with a Million). 1954: The Green Scarf. Shadow of a Man. 1957: The Traitor (US: The Accused). Three Sundays to Live. 1958: Tread Softly Stranger. 1961: The Impersonator. The Third Alibi. 1962: The Durant Affair. Dead Man's Evidence. 1963: The Double.

GRODIN, Charles 1935–
Diffident, chubby, dark-haired American actor, good in light comedy and comedy-thrillers and seemingly on the verge of stardom in the mid-1970s. But it didn't quite happen and he later seemed happy just to back up the stars of the film. Also writes screenplays and has directed on stage.

1968: Rosemary's Baby. 1970: Sex and the College Girl. Catch 22. 1973: The Heartbreak Kid. 1974: 11 Harrowhouse. 1976: King Kong. Thieves. 1978: The Grass is Always Greener over the Septic Tank (TV). Just Me and You (TV). Heaven Can Wait. Sunburn. 1979: Real People/Real Life. 1980: The Incredible Shrinking Woman. It's My Turn. Seems Like Old Times. 1981: The Great Muppet Caper. 1983: The Lonely Guy. 1984: The Woman in Red. 1985: Movers and Shakers. 1986: Last Resort. Ishtar.

GUARDINO, Harry 1925–
Worried-looking, dark-haired American actor whose early career gave him a lot of struggle but few parts. Much busier from 1958 onwards, he hasn't quite made the most of the best opportunities that have come his way, remaining a face to which one may have a little difficulty in putting the name. Heavily employed as TV guest star.

1951: Purple Heart Diary (GB: No Time for Tears). 1952: Flesh and Fury. 1955: Hold Back Tomorrow. 1958: Houseboat. 1959: The Five Pennies. The Killers of Mussolini (TV). Pork Chop Hill. Made in Japan (TV). Five Branded Women. 1961: King of Kings. The Pigeon That Took Rome. 1962: Hell is for Heroes! 1964: Rhino! 1965: The Adventures of Bullwhip Griffin. 1966: Moving Target (TV). Operazione San Gennaro (US: The Treasure of San Gennaro). 1967: Valley of Mystery. 1968: Jigsaw. Madigan. The Hell with Heroes. 1969: Lovers and Other Strangers. The Lonely Profession (TV). 1971: Red Sky at Morning. Octaman. Dirty Harry. Slingshot. The Last Child (TV). 1972: They Only Kill Their Masters. 1973: Partners in Crime (TV). Police Story (TV. GB: cinemas). 1974: Get Christie Love! (TV). Indict and Convict (TV). 1975: Capone. Whiffs (GB: C.A.S.H.). 1976: St Ives. Having Babies (TV). The Enforcer. 1977: Contract on Cherry Street (TV). Street Killing (TV). Rollercoaster. 1978: Pleasure Cove (TV). Blue Orchids. Matilda. No Margin for Error (TV). 1979: Goldengirl. 1980: Any Which Way You Can. 1983: The Lonely Guy.

GUINNESS, Sir Alec
(A. Guinness de Cuffe) 1914–
Fair-haired, shy-looking, fresh-faced British actor who made his name as a man of many faces (most notably as eight brothers and sisters in *Kind Hearts and Coronets*), playing mainly loveable scoundrels in a brilliant run of Ealing comedies from the late forties to the late fifties. Later, he continued to tackle offbeat roles as a character star, winning an Oscar (and British Oscar) for *The Bridge on the River Kwai*. Knighted in 1959. Special Academy Award 1980. Received further Oscar nominations for *The Lavender Hill Mob* and *Star Wars*.

1934: Evensong (as extra). 1946: Great Expectations. 1948: Oliver Twist. 1949: Kind Hearts

and Coronets. A Run for Your Money. 1950: Last Holiday. 1951: The Mudlark. The Lavender Hill Mob. The Man in the White Suit. The Card (US: The Promoter). 1953: The Captain's Paradise. Malta Story. 1954: Father Brown (US: The Detective). The Stratford Adventure. To Paris with Love. 1955: The Prisoner. *Rowlandson's England (narrator only). The Ladykillers. 1956: The Swan. 1957: The Bridge on the River Kwai. Barnacle Bill (US: All at Sea). 1958: The Horse's Mouth. 1959: The Scapegoat. Our Man in Havana. 1960: Tunes of Glory. 1961: A Majority of One. 1962: HMS Defiant (US: Damn the Defiant!). Lawrence of Arabia. 1963: The Fall of the Roman Empire. 1965: Situation Hopeless . . . but not serious. Doctor Zhivago. 1966: Hotel Paradiso. The Quiller Memorandum. 1967: The Comedians. 1970: Cromwell. Scrooge. 1972: Brother Sun, Sister Moon. 1973: Hitler: the Last Ten Days. 1976: Murder by Death. 1977: Star Wars. 1980: The Empire Strikes Back. Raise the Titanic! 1981: Little Lord Fauntleroy. 1983: Lovesick. Return of the Jedi. 1984: A Passage to India. 1986: Little Dorrit I. Little Dorrit II.*

GUTTENBERG, Steve 1958–
Well-built, ever-smiling, young-looking American actor with dark, curly hair. Worked his way up from messenger at an actors' agency, through bit parts in the late 1970s, to leading roles in the 1980s, most notably the parking-lot attendant who becomes a police cadet in the *Police Academy* films. The fact that he's interesting even in supporting roles probably indicates he's here to stay.

1977: *The Last Chance. Rollercoaster. The Chicken Chronicles. Something for Joey (TV). 1978: The Boys from Brazil. 1979: Players. 1980: Can't Stop the Music. To Race the Wind (TV). 1981: Miracle on Ice (TV). 1982: Diner. 1983: The Day After (TV). The Man Who Wasn't There. 1984: Police Academy. 1985: Police Academy 2: Their First Assignment. Cocoon. Bad Medicine. 1986: Short Circuit. Police Academy 3.*

GWENN, Edmund 1875–1959
Gnome-like Welsh-born character star, often in unsympathetic roles in his British films of the thirties. After some American films, he went permanently to Hollywood in 1940 with retirement vaguely in mind, but they wouldn't hear of it, keeping him exuding testy benevolence as shepherds, scientists and scoundrels, winning a best supporting Oscar for his Kris Kringle in *Miracle on 34th Street* (1947), for another 15 years. Further Oscar-nominated for *Mister 880*.
*1916: *The Real Thing at Last. 1920: The Skin Game. Unmarried. 1930: How He Lied to Her Husband. 1931: Hindle Wakes. Money for Nothing. The Skin Game (remake). Frail Women. Condemned to Death. 1932: Love on Wheels. Tell Me Tonight (US: Be Mine Tonight). 1933: The Good Companions. Cash (US: For Love or Money). Early to Bed. I Was a Spy. Channel Crossing. Smithy. Friday the Thirteenth. Marooned. 1934: The Admiral's Secret. Passing Shadows. Waltzes from Vienna (US: Strauss's Great Waltz). Warn London. Java Head. Father and Son. Spring in the Air. 1935: The Bishop Misbehaves (GB: The Bishop's Misadventures). Sylvia Scarlett. 1936: Laburnum Grove. Anthony Adverse. The Walking Dead. All-American Chump (GB: Country Bumpkin). Mad Holiday. 1937: Parnell. South Riding. A Yank at Oxford. 1938: Penny Paradise. 1939: Cheer Boys Cheer. *Happy Families. An Englishman's Home (US: Madmen of Europe). 1940: The Doctor Takes a Wife. The Earl of Chicago. Pride and Prejudice. Foreign Correspondent. 1941: Scotland Yard. Cheers for Miss Bishop. The Devil and Miss Jones. One Night in Lisbon. 1942: A Yank at Eton. *The Greatest Gift. 1943: The Meanest Man in the World. Forever and a Day. Lassie Come Home. 1944: Between Two Worlds. Keys of the Kingdom. 1945: Bewitched. Dangerous Partners. She Went to the Races.*

1946: Of Human Bondage. Undercurrent. 1947: Miracle on 34th Street (GB: The Big Heart). Thunder in the Valley (GB: Bob, Son of Battle). Green Dolphin Street. Life with Father. 1948: Apartment for Peggy. Hills of Home (GB: Master of Lassie). 1949: Challenge to Lassie. 1950: A Woman of Distinction. Mister 880. Pretty Baby. Louisa. For Heaven's Sake. 1951: Peking Express. 1952: Sally and Saint Anne. Bonzo Goes to College. Les Misérables. Something for the Birds. 1953: Mr Scoutmaster. The Bigamist. 1954: Them. The Student Prince. 1955: It's a Dog's Life. The Trouble with Harry. 1956: Calabuch (US: Rocket from Calabuch). 1957: The Greer Case (TV). Winter Dreams (TV).*

GWYNNE, Anne
(Marguerite G. Trice) 1918–
The slightly startled look on the face of this willowy ex-model with strawberry-blonde hair and hazel eyes might be attributed to the medley of monsters Universal forced her to meet in the 1940s. She was mainly used as decoration in horror and outdoor films and a return to acting in the late 1960s after an absence of many years did not lead to any meatier roles.
*1939: *Swimming Underwater. Charlie McCarthy, Detective. Flash Gordon Conquers the Universe (serial). Oklahoma Frontier. Unexpected Father (GB: Sandy Takes a Bow). Little Accident. 1940: The Green Hornet (serial). Framed. Bad Man from Red Butte. Black Friday. Sandy is a Lady. Spring Parade. Man from Montreal. Give Us Wings. 1941: Honeymoon Deferred. Jailhouse Blues. The Black Cat. Nice Girl? Washington Melodrama. Give Us Wings. Tight Shoes. Ride 'Em Cowboy. Mob Town. Man Made Monster (GB: The Electric Man). 1942: The Strange Case of Dr RX. Melody Lane. Broadway. Men of Texas (GB: Men of Destiny). Don't Get Personal. Road Agent. *Keeping Fit. You're Telling Me. Sin Town. 1943: We've Never Been Licked (GB: Texas to Tokyo). Top Man. Frontier Bad Men. 1944: Weird Woman. Ladies Courageous. Moon over Las Vegas. South of Dixie. House of Frankenstein. 1945: I Ring Doorbells. Murder in the Blue Room. Babes on Swing Street. 1946: Fear. The Glass Alibi. 1947: The Ghost Goes Wild. Dick Tracy Meets Gruesome (GB: Dick Tracy's Amazing Adventure). Killer Dill. 1948: Panhandle. Arson Inc. 1949: The Enchanted Valley. 1950: The Blazing Sun.*

Call of the Klondike. 1951: **Dead Man's Voice. **The Man Who Wasn't There. **The Yellow Ticket. **The Innocent Lion. **The Bandaged Hand. 1952: Breakdown. 1953: King of the Bullwhip. 1955: Phantom of the Jungle. 1957: Teenage Monster (GB: Meteor Monster). 1969: Adam at 6 am.*

*** US TV shorts shown in GB cinemas*

GYNT, Greta
(Margrethe Woxholt) 1916–
Glamorous Norwegian blonde actress, on stage as teenager, and in British films from 1937, remaining a box-office attraction for 15 years (although her Hollywood chance came too late: she had lost her spark), even if prudes raised eyebrows at her high-flying high-society private life. Although her career lost some momentum in the fifties, she worked regularly until 1960.
*1934: ‡Sången Till Henne. 1935: ‡It Happened in Paris. †Boys Will Be Girls. 1937: The Road Back/Return of the Hero. The Last Curtain. Second Best Bed. 1938: Sexton Blake and the Hooded Terror. The Last Barricade. 1939: Too Dangerous to Live. Dark Eyes of London (US: The Human Monster). The Arsenal Stadium Mystery. The Middle Watch. She Couldn't Say No. 1940: Two for Danger. Bulldog Sees It Through. Room for Two. Crook's Tour. 1941: The Common Touch. 1942: Tomorrow We Live (US: At Dawn We Die). It's That Man Again. 1944: Mr Emmanuel. 1946: London Town (US: My Heart Goes Crazy). 1947: Take My Life. Dear Murderer. Easy Money. 1948: The Calendar. Mr Perrin and Mr Traill. 1950: Shadow of the Eagle. 1951: Lucky Nick Cain (GB: I'll Get You for This). Soldiers Three. Whispering Smith Hits London (US: Whispering Smith versus Scotland Yard). 1952: I'm a Stranger. The Ringer. 1953: Three Steps in the Dark. 1954: Forbidden Cargo. Destination Milan. The Last Moment. Devil's Point (US: Devil's Harbor). 1955: *Dead on Time. See How They Run. Born for Trouble. The Blue Peter (US: Navy Heroes). 1956: Keep It Clean. My Wife's Family. 1957: Fortune is a Woman (US: She Played with Fire). Morning Call (US: The Strange Case of Dr Manning). 1959: The Crowning Touch. The Witness. 1960: Bluebeard's 10 Honeymoons. 1964: The Runaway.*

‡ As Margrethe Woxholt † As Greta Woxholt

G for Great Lovers ... Greta Garbo and John Gilbert, partners in many an epic screen romance, in this case *Flesh and the Devil* (1927)

She had played Eliza Doolittle. He'd later be Henry Higgins (and Dr Dolittle). Here Wendy Hiller and Rex Harrison are in *Major Barbara* (1941).

I, J and K . . . Glenda Jackson and Ben Kingsley look all set to race Ivan the Turtle back to the sea in *Turtle Diary* (1985).

Okay! George Kennedy and Sally Kellerman find unexpected romance behind the mountains of *Lost Horizon* (1972).

HAAS, Hugo 1901–1968

One of the foremost figures of the Czech cinema in the thirties, Haas never quite recovered from having to leave his homeland when war threatened. Slow to settle in Hollywood, he became a stocky character actor with guttural accent, before writing and directing a series of tawdry moralizing dramas, most (although not all) of which deserved their critical hammering. Was preparing to return to his native land in 1968 when the Russians moved in. Died of heart failure or, as friends put it, 'of a broken heart'.

1925: *Jedenacte Přikazami. Z Českych Mlynu.* 1930: *Kariera Pavla Camrdy. Když Struny Lkaji.* 1931: *The Good Soldier Schweik. Obrácení Ferdyše Pištory. Muži v Offsidu. Načaderec, Král Kibiců.* 1932: *Sestra Angelika. Zapadlí Vlastenci.* 1933: *Život je Pes. Dům na Předměstí. Její Lékař. Madla z Cihelny. Okénko.* 1934: *Poslední muž. Mazlíček.* 1935: *Ať žije Nebožtík. Jedenácté Přikazání.* 1936: *Velbloud uchem jehly. Ulička v Raji. Švadlenka. Mravnost nade vše. Tři Muži ve Snehu.* 1937: *Kvocna. Tři Vejce do Skla. Děvčata, nedějte se! Bílá.* 1938: *Andula Vyhrala. Svět Kde se Žebrá. Co se Šeptá.* 1939: *The Sea in Flames. Our Combat (narrator).* 1940: *Skeleton on Horseback. Documents secrets.* 1943: *Days of Glory.* 1944: *The Princess and the Pirate. Summer Storm. Mrs Parkington. Strange Affair.* 1945: *A Bell for Adano. Dakota. Jealousy. What Next, Corporal Hargrove?* 1946: *Holiday in Mexico. Two Smart People.* 1947: *Northwest Outpost (GB: End of the Rainbow). The Foxes of Harrow. Fiesta. The Private Affairs of Bel Ami. Merton*

of the Movies. 1948: *Casbah. My Girl Tisa. For the Love of Mary.* 1949: *The Fighting Kentuckian.* 1950: *King Solomon's Mines. Vendetta.* 1951: *Pickup. Girl on the Bridge.* 1952: *Strange Fascination.* 1953: *Thy Neighbor's Wife. One Girl's Confession.* 1954: *Bait. The Other Woman.* 1955: *Hold Back Tomorrow. The Tender Trap.* 1956: *Edge of Hell.* 1957: *Hit and Run. Paradise Alley (released 1962). Lizzie.* 1959: *Night of the Quarter Moon. Born to be Loved.*

As director: 1937: *Děvčata, nedějte se! (co-directed). Bíla Nemoc.* 1938: *Co se Šepta.* 1939: *Our Combat.* 1951: *Pickup. Girl on the Bridge.* 1952: *Strange Fascination.* 1953: *Thy Neighbor's Wife. One Girl's Confession.* 1954: *Bait. The Other Woman.* 1955: *Hold Back Tomorrow.* 1956: *Edge of Hell.* 1957: *Hit and Run. Lizzie. Paradise Alley (released 1962).* 1959: *Night of the Quarter Moon. Born to be Loved.* 1967: *The Crazy Ones.*

HACKETT, Joan 1934–1983

Brunette American actress who, after years of success on Broadway, made her film debut as one of the girls in *The Group*. In subsequent movies she was normally seen as forthright, independent, strong-willed, unglamorous women; on the whole her screen roles, her character in *Will Penny* apart, were none too rewarding, and she remained primarily a Broadway star. Nominated for an Oscar in *Only When I Laugh.* Died from cancer.

1965: †*The Satan Bug.* 1966: *The Group.* 1967: *Will Penny.* 1968: *Assignment to Kill.* 1969: *Support Your Local Sheriff.* 1970: *How Awful about Allan (TV). The Other Man (TV). The Young Country (TV).* 1971: *Five Desperate Women (TV).* 1972: *The Rivals.* 1973: *The Last of Sheila. Class of '63 (TV).* 1974: *Reflections of Murder (TV). The Terminal Man.* 1975: *Mackintosh and T J.* 1976: *Treasure of Matecumbe.* 1977: *Stonestreet (TV).* 1978: *The Possessed (TV).* 1979: *Pleasure Cove (TV). Mr Mike's Mondo Video.* 1979: *The North Avenue Irregulars (GB: Hill's Angels).* 1980: *One Trick Pony. The Long Days of Summer (TV).* 1981: *Only When I Laugh (GB: It Hurts Only When I Laugh). The Long Summer of George Adams (TV).* 1982: *The Escape Artist.* 1983: *Flicks.*

† *Scenes deleted from final release print*

HACKMAN, Gene 1930–

Stocky, curly-haired American actor of unsettling personality who began to get featured roles in Hollywood after an Oscar nomination for *Bonnie and Clyde. The French Connection* (1971) – for which he is said to have been sixth choice – jetted him to stardom and a variety of plum roles for the next four years. His career wavered after a series of poor films in the late seventies, and in 1979 he announced his retirement, but was soon back. Further Oscar nomination for *I Never Sang for My Father.*

1961: *Mad Dog Coll.* 1964: *Lilith.* 1966: *Hawaii. Les espions. A Covenant with Death.* 1967: *Banning. First to Fight. Bonnie and Clyde.* 1968: *The Split. Riot. Shadow on the Land (TV).* 1969: *Downhill Racer. The Gypsy Moths. Marooned.* 1970: *I Never Sang for My Father.* 1971: *Doctors' Wives. The Hunting Party. The French Connection.* 1972: *Cisco Pike. Prime Cut. The Poseidon Adventure.* 1973: *Scarecrow.* 1974: *The Conversation. Young Frankenstein. Zandy's Bride. Bite the Bullet.* 1975: *French Connection II (GB: French Connection No. 2). Lucky Lady. Night Moves.* 1976: *The Domino Killings (released 1978).* 1977: *A Bridge Too Far. March or Die. A Look at Liv.* 1978: *Superman. Speed Fever.* 1980: *Superman II.* 1981: *All Night Long. Reds.* 1982: *Eureka.* 1983: *Misunderstood. Under Fire. Uncommon Valor.* 1985: *Twice in a Lifetime. Target. Power.* 1986: *Hoosiers. Deceit. Superman IV.*

HAGEN, Jean
(Jean Ver Hagen) 1924–1977

Bright, chirpy American blonde actress,

equally at home in comedy and drama, although perhaps less happy with sympathetic roles. Memorable both as the moll in *The Asphalt Jungle* and the squeaky-voiced silent-film star in *Singin' in the Rain*, by which time she had become a sort of minor league Judy Holliday. Died from throat cancer. Oscar nomination for *Singin' in the Rain*.
1949: *Side Street. Adam's Rib.* 1950: *The Asphalt Jungle. Ambush. A Life of Her Own.* 1951: *Night into Morning. Shadow in the Sky. No Questions Asked.* 1952: *Singin' in the Rain. Carbine Williams.* 1953: *Arena. Half a Hero. Latin Lovers.* 1955: *The Big Knife.* 1957: *Spring Reunion.* 1959: *The Shaggy Dog.* 1960: *Sunrise at Campobello.* 1962: *Panic in Year Zero.* 1964: *Dead Ringer* (GB: *Dead Image*). 1977: *Alexander – The Other Side of Dawn* (*TV*).

HAGMAN, Larry (L. Hageman) 1939–
Wry, dark-haired American actor with large face and small eyes, the son of Mary Martin (*qv*) by her first marriage. In TV programmes as a teenager, he looked at first the natural successor to such actors as Tony Randall (*qv*). He had a good running role in the TV comedy series *I Dream of Jeannie* from 1965 to 1969, but never really made his mark in show business until asked to play the abominable JR in TV's *Dallas*, a persona with which he has been synonymous since 1978.
1958: *The Member of the Wedding* (*TV*). 1960: *Once Around The Block* (*TV*). 1964: *Ensign Pulver. Fail Safe.* 1965: *In Harm's Way.* 1966: *The Group. The Cavern.* 1969: *Three's a Crowd* (*TV*). 1970: *Up in the Cellar* (GB: *Three in the Cellar*). 1971: †*Beware! The Blob* (GB: *Son of Blob*). *Vanished* (*TV*). *Triple Play* (*TV*). *A Howling in the Woods* (*TV*). 1972: *Getting Away From It All* (*TV*). *No Place to Run* (*TV*). 1973: *The Alpha Caper* (*TV. GB: cinemas, as Inside Job*). *Blood Sport* (*TV*). *What Are Best Friends For?* (*TV*). *Antonio.* 1974: *Sidekicks* (*TV*). *Hurricane* (*TV*). *Stardust. Harry and Tonto. Mother, Jugs and Speed* (released 1976). 1975: *Sara T: Portrait of a Teenage Alcoholic* (*TV*). *The Big Ripoff* (*TV*). *The Big Bus. The Eagle Has Landed. Crash. The Return of the World's Greatest Detective* (*TV*). 1977: *Intimate Strangers* (*TV*). 1978: *The President's Mistress* (*TV*). *Superman. Last of the Good Guys*

(*TV*). 1981: *SOB.* 1982: *Deadly Encounter* (*TV*).

†*Also directed*

HAIGH, Kenneth 1929–
Chunky, businesslike, usually tight-lipped, dark-haired British actor who was the original Jimmy Porter in the stage version of *Look Back in Anger*, and has remained in rebellious mould ever since. Gained great TV success in *Man at the Top* (another aggressive, working-class role), but hasn't quite made it in films.
1953: *The Case of the Last Dance.* 1954: *Companions in Crime. The Case of the Bogus Count.* 1956: *My Teenage Daughter* (US: *Teenage Bad Girl*). 1957: *Saint Joan. High Flight.* 1963: *Cleopatra.* 1964: *Week-End à Zuydcoote* (GB and US: *Weekend at Dunkirk*). *A Hard Day's Night.* 1966: *The Deadly Affair.* 1968: *A Lovely Way to Die* (GB: *A Lovely Way to Go*). 1970: *Eagle in a Cage.* 1973: *Man at the Top.* 1976: *Robin and Marian.* 1978: *En vandring i solen* (GB TV: *Walking in the Sun*). 1979: *The Bitch.* 1985: *Wild Geese II. A State of Emergency.*

HALE, Barbara 1921–
Glamorous brunette American star of cheerful and friendly manner who gave some solid performances in juicy roles towards the end of the forties after a small-parts start via the model and beauty queen route. Her looks became motherly rather early (like Rosemary De Camp), but she found a successful second career as Della Street in the long-running *Perry Mason* series on TV from 1957 to 1965. Married to Bill Williams from 1946. Mother of William Katt (1951–).

1943: *Gildersleeve's Bad Day. Higher and Higher. The Seventh Victim. Mexican Spitfire's Blessed Event. The Iron Major. Gildersleeve on Broadway. Government Girl. Around the World.* 1944: *Goin' to Town.* *Prunes and Politics. Heavenly Days. The Falcon Out West. The Falcon in Hollywood. Belle of the Yukon.* 1945: *West of the Pecos. First Yank into Toyko* (GB: *Mask of Fury*). 1946: *Lady Luck.* 1947: *A Likely Story.* 1948: *The Boy with Green Hair.* 1949: *The Clay Pigeon. The Window.* 1950: *Jolson Sings Again. And Baby Makes Three. The Jackpot. Emergency Wedding* (GB: *Jealousy*). 1951: *Lorna Doone. The First Time.* 1952: *Last of the Comanches* (GB: *The Sabre and the Arrow*). 1953: *Seminole. Lone Hand. A Lion is in the Streets.* 1955: *Unchained. The Far Horizons. The Country Husband* (TV. GB: cinemas). 1956: *Seventh Cavalry. The Houston Story.* 1957: *The Oklahoman. Slim Carter.* 1958: *Desert Hell.* 1966: *Buckskin.* 1969: *Airport.* 1971: *Soul Soldier* (GB: *Men of the Tenth*). 1975: *The Giant Spider Invasion.* 1978: *Big Wednesday.* 1986: *The Return of Perry Mason* (*TV*).

HALE, Sonnie
(John Robert Hale Monro) 1902–1959
It seems hard to understand now that Britain's small, bespectacled, owlish-looking Sonnie Hale not only had legions of followers as a romantic leading man but wooed and won two of musical comedy's brightest and most beautiful stars. But he had and he did. He also possessed a ready wit, a gift for mimicry, could act and sing with equal facility and write as well. Married to Evelyn Laye from 1926 to 1930 and Jessie Matthews from 1931 to 1944. Died of myelofibrosis, a blood disease.
1927: *On with the Dance.* *The Parting of the Ways.* 1932: *Happy Ever After. Tell Me Tonight* (US: *Be Mine Tonight*). 1933: *Friday the Thirteenth. Early to Bed.* 1934: *Evergreen. Wild Boy. Are You a Mason? My Song for You. My Heart is Calling.* 1935: *Marry the Girl. First a Girl.* 1936: *It's Love Again.* 1938: *The Gaunt Stranger* (US: *The Phantom Strikes*). 1939: *Let's Be Famous.* 1944: *Fiddlers Three.* 1946: *London Town* (US: *My Heart Goes Crazy*).

As director: 1937: *Head over Heels* (US: *Head over Heels in Love*). *Gangway.* 1938: *Sailing Along.*

HALEY, Jack 1899–1979
Chunky, cheery, dark-haired American musical comedy star of hearty manner, mainly on vaudeville and stage, but quite popular in films from 1935–1945, especially after his performance as the Tin Man in *The Wizard of Oz*. Died from a heart attack.
1927: *Broadway Madness*. 1930: **Harlequins*. *Follow Thru*. 1932: *Redheads on Parade*. 1933: *Sitting Pretty*. *Mr Broadway*. 1934: *Here Comes the Groom*. 1935: *The Girl Friend*. *Coronado*. *Spring Tonic*. 1936: *Pigskin Parade* (GB: *The Harmony Parade*). *Poor Little Rich Girl*. *F-Man*. *Mister Cinderella*. 1937: *Wake Up and Live*. *Pick a Star*. *She Had to Eat*. *Danger Love at Work*. 1938: *Rebecca of Sunnybrook Farm*. *Alexander's Ragtime Band*. *Hold That Co-Ed* (GB: *Hold That Girl*). *Thanks for Everything*. 1939: *The Wizard of Oz*. 1941: *Moon over Miami*. *Navy Blues*. 1942: *Beyond the Blue Horizon*. 1943: *Higher and Higher*. 1944: *One Body Too Many*. 1945: *George White's Scandals*. *People Are Funny*. *Scared Stiff*. *Sing Your Way Home*. 1946: *Vacation in Reno*. 1949: *Make Mine Laughs*. 1970: *Norwood*. 1972: *Rolling Man (TV)*.

HALL, Huntz
(Henry Hall) 1920–
Long-faced, pop-eyed, thin-lipped, fair-haired American actor who sprang to prominence as one of the street kids in the stage and film versions of *Dead End*. Later became the gormless Satch of The Bowery Boys: he was the one who got the laughs while partner Leo Gorcey (*qv*) expressed exasperation. Hall stayed with the series until the bitter end, and continued working fairly regularly in character roles until the late 1970s.
1937: *Dead End*. 1938: *Crime School*. *Little Tough Guy*. *Angels with Dirty Faces*. 1939: *Hell's Kitchen*. *Call a Messenger*. *Angels Wash Their Faces*. *The Battle of City Hall*. *The Return of Doctor X*. *They Made Me a Criminal*. *The Dead End Kids on Dress Parade*. 1940: *That Gang of Mine*. *Give Us Wings*. *You're Not So Tough*. *Gallant Sons*. *Boys of the City* (GB: *East Side Kids*). *Angels with Broken Wings*. *Junior G-Men (serial)*. *Invisible Stripes*. *Pride of the Bowery* (GB: *Here We Go Again*). 1941: *Sea Raiders (serial)*. *Hit the Road*. *Bowery Blitzkrieg* (GB: *Stand and Deliver*). *Zis Boom Bah*. *Spooks Run Wild*. *Mob Town*. 1942: *Junior Army*. *Private Buckaroo*. *Mr Wise Guy*. *Sunday Punch*. *Tough As They Come*. *Smart Alecks*. '*Neath Brooklyn Bridge*. *Let's Get Tough*. *Junior G-Men of the Air (serial)*. 1943: *Clancy Street Boys*. *Mug Town*. *Kid Dynamite*. *Mr Muggs Steps Out*. *Keep 'em Slugging*. *Ghosts on the Loose*. 1944: *Block Busters*. *Bowery Champs*. *Follow the Leader*. *The Million Dollar Kid*. 1945: *Wonder Man*. *A Walk in the Sun*. *Bring on the Girls*. *Mr Muggs Rides Again*. *Live Wires*. *Docks of New York*. *Come Out Fighting*. 1946: *Mr Hex* (GB: *Pride of the Bowery*). *In Fast Company*. *Spook Busters*. *Bowery Bombshell*. 1947: *Hard-Boiled Mahoney*. *News Hounds*. *Pride of Broadway*. *Bowery Buckaroos*. 1948: *Jinx Money*. *Angels' Alley*. *Trouble Makers*. *Smugglers' Cove*. 1949: *Angels in Disguise*. *Fighting Fools*. *Master Minds*. *Hold That Baby*. 1950: *Blues Busters*. *Triple Trouble*. *Blonde Dynamite*. *Lucky Losers*. 1951: *Ghost Chasers*. *Bowery Battalion*. *Crazy over Horses*. *Let's Go Navy*. 1952: *Here Come the Marines*. *Hold That Line*. *No Holds Barred*. *Feudin' Fools*. 1953: *Jalopy*. *Loose in London*. *Clipped Wings*. *Private Eyes*. 1954: *Paris Playboys*. *The Bowery Boys Meet the Monsters*. *Jungle Gents*. 1955: *Bowery to Bagdad*. *High Society*. *Jail Busters*. *Spy Chasers*. 1956: *Dig That Uranium*. *Crashing Las Vegas*. *Hold That Hypnotist*. 1957: *Spook Chasers*. *Looking for Danger*. *Up in Smoke*. 1958: *In the Money*. 1965: *Second Fiddle to a Steel Guitar*. 1967: *Gentle Giant*. 1969: *The Phynx*. 1971: *Escape (TV)*. 1974: *Herbie Rides Again*. *The Manchu Eagle Murder Caper Mystery*. 1975: *Won Ton Ton, the Dog Who Saved Hollywood*. 1977: *Valentino*. 1979: *Gas Pump Girls*. 1982: *The Escape Artist*.

HALL, Jon
(Charles H. Locher) 1913–1979
The king of the Technicolor, if slightly tatty, eastern (and western) of the 1940s, husky, dark-haired Hall probably blacked up to play South Sea islander or Arabian adventurer more times than any other Hollywood hero. When his waist thickened, like that of Johnny Weissmuller (*qv*), Hall, who was the son of Swiss-born character actor Felix Locher (1882–1969), forsook films to devote more time to photography. Married to Frances Langford (1938 to 1955) and Raquel Torres (1959 on) – second and third of three. After being bedridden for nine months following

surgery for bladder cancer, Hall shot himself.
1935: †*Here's to Romance*. †*Women Must Dress*. †*Charlie Chan in Shanghai*. 1936: †*The Lion Man*. †*Winds of the Wasteland*. †*The Clutching Hand (serial)*. †*The Mysterious Avenger*. ††*Mind Your Own Business*. 1937: ††*Girl from Scotland Yard*. *The Hurricane*. 1940: *South of Pago Pago*. *Sailor's Lady*. *Kit Carson*. 1941: *Aloma of the South Seas*. 1942: *The Tuttles of Tahiti*. *Eagle Squadron*. *Invisible Agent*. *Arabian Nights*. 1943: *White Savage* (GB: *White Captive*). *Ali Baba and the Forty Thieves*. 1944: *Lady in the Dark*. *Cobra Woman*. *Gypsy Wildcat*. *The Invisible Man's Revenge*. *San Diego, I Love You*. 1945: *Men in Her Diary*. *Sudan*. 1947: *Last of the Redmen* (GB: *Last of the Redskins*). *The Michigan Kid*. *The Vigilantes Return* (GB: *The Return of the Vigilantes*). 1948: *The Prince of Thieves*. 1949: *Zamba* (GB: *Zamba the Gorilla*). *The Mutineers*. *Deputy Marshal*. 1950: *On the Isle of Samoa*. 1951: *When the Redskins Rode*. *China Corsair*. *Hurricane Island*. 1952: *Brave Warrior*. *Last Train from Bombay*. 1953: *White Goddess* (GB: *Ramar of the Jungle*). *Eyes of the Jungle* (GB: *Destination Danger*). 1955: *Phantom of the Jungle*. *Thunder over Sangoland*. 1957: *Hell Ship Mutiny*. 1958: *Forbidden Island*. 1965: ***The Beachgirls and the Monster/Monster from the Surf*.

† *As Charles Locher*
†† *As Lloyd Crane* ** *Also directed*

HAMILL, Mark 1951–
Fair-haired, blue-eyed, baby-faced, pocket-sized, energetic American actor who shot to stardom in his first cinema role, as the hero of *Star Wars*, but found a good range of roles

hard to come by. Before that, he had been
acting since 1969, his light voice gaining him
much employment in voice-overs for TV car-
toon series. In the 1980s he turned to the stage
with considerable personal success.
*1975: Delancy Street (TV). Mallory (TV).
Eric (TV). Sara T: Portrait of a Teenage
Alcoholic (TV). 1977: Wizards (voice only).
The City (TV). Star Wars. 1978: Corvette
Summer (GB: The Hot One). 1979: Samuel
Fuller and The Big Red One. 1980: The Big
Red One. The Empire Strikes Back. 1981: The
Night the Lights Went Out in Georgia. 1982:
Britannia Hospital. 1983: Return of the Jedi.*

HAMILTON, George 1939–
Dark, brooding, thick-lipped but extremely
handsome American leading man who made
a powerful start in his first two films, but was
not well served for the remainder of his
M-G-M days and had difficulty re-estab-
lishing himself as a top star until he hit the
jackpot with *Love at First Bite* in 1979.
*1959: Crime and Punishment U.S.A. 1960:
Home from the Hill. All the Fine Young Can-
nibals. Angel Baby. 1961: Where the Boys Are.
By Love Possessed. A Thunder of Drums. 1962:
The Light in the Piazza. Two Weeks in Another
Town. 1963: The Victors. Act One. 1964: The
Turncoat (TV). Looking for Love. Your
Cheatin' Heart. 1965: Viva Maria! 1966:
That Man George. 1967: Doctor, You've Got
to Be Kidding! The Power. A Time for Killing
(GB: The Long Ride Home). Jack of
Diamonds. 1970: Togetherness. Double Image.
1972: The Scorpio Scarab. Evel Knievel. 1973:
The Man Who Loved Cat Dancing. 1974:
Medusa. The Dead Don't Die (TV). Once is
Not Enough. 1977: Sextette. The Happy
Hooker Goes to Washington. The Strange Pos-
session of Mrs Oliver (TV). 1978: Killer on
Board (TV). The Users (TV). The Mag-
nificent Hustle (TV). Institute for Revenge
(TV). The Deadly Price of Paradise (TV).
(GB: Nightmare at Pendragon's Castle). 1979:
Supertrain (TV). Da Dunkerque alla vittoria
(US: From Hell to Victory). Love at First
Bite. The Seekers (TV). Death Car on the
Freeway (TV). 1980: The Great Cash Get-
away (TV). 1981: Zorro the Gay Blade.*

HAMILTON, Neil
(James N. Hamilton) 1899–1984
Stocky, light-haired, boyishly handsome
American leading man, especially popular

during the latter days of the silent era. Sincerity was his strong point, and his appeal
was somewhat akin to a less intense Richard
Barthelmess. He seemed to have made the
transition to sound stardom, but lacked a
definite image and from 1935 he was slipping.
Retired in 1969. Died from asthmatic complications.
*1918: The Beloved Impostor. 1919: The Great
Romance. 1923: The White Rose. America.
1924: The Side Show of Life. Isn't Life Wonderful? 1925: Men and Women. The Little
French Girl. Street of Forgotten Men. New
Brooms. The Golden Princess. The Splendid
Crime. 1926: Desert Gold. Beau Geste. Dip-
lomacy. The Great Gatsby. The Music Mak-
er/The Music Master. 1927: 10 Modern Com-
mandments. The Joy Girl. The Spotlight. Shield
of Honor. Mother Machree. 1928: The Show-
down. Something Always Happens. Don't
Marry. The Grip of the Yukon. Hot News. The
Patriot. Take Me Home. Three Week-Ends.
What a Night! 1929: Why Be Good? A
Dangerous Woman. The Studio Murder
Mystery. The Insidious Dr Fu Manchu (later
the Mysterious Dr Fu Manchu). The Love
Trap. Darkened Rooms. 1930: The Kibitzer
(GB: Busybody). Anybody's Woman. The Cat
Creeps. The Dawn Patrol. The New Adventures
of Dr Fu Manchu (later The Return of Dr Fu
Manchu). Ladies Must Play. The Widow from
Chicago. Ex-Flame (GB: Mixed Doubles).
1931: Command Performance. Strangers May
Kiss. The Sin of Madelon Claudet (GB: The
Lullaby). The Great Lover. Laughing Sinners.
The Spy. This Modern Age. 1932: Tarzan the
Ape Man. The Animal Kingdom (GB: The
Woman in His House). Are You Listening? The
Wet Parade. Payment Deferred. The Woman
in Room 13. What Price Hollywood? Two
Against the World. 1933: Terror Aboard. The
World Gone Mad (GB: The Public Be
Hanged). Ladies Must Love. The Silk Express.
One Sunday Afternoon. As the Devil
Commands. 1934: Once to Every Bachelor. One
Exciting Adventure. Fugitive Lady. Tarzan
and His Mate. Here Comes the Groom. Blind
Date. By Your Leave. 1935: Keeper of the
Bees. The Daring Young Man. 1936: Honey-
moon Limited. Mutiny Ahead. Southern Roses.
Everything in Life. You Must Get Married.
Parisienne Life/La vie Parisienne. 1937: Mr
Stringfellow Says No. Secret Lives (US: I
Married a Spy). The Gang's All Here (US:
The Amazing Mr Forrest). Portia on Trial*

*(GB: The Trial of Portia Merriman). Lady
Behave! 1938: Army Girl (GB: The Last of
the Cavalry). The Hollywood Stadium Mys-
tery/The Stadium Murders. 1939: The Saint
Strikes Back. 1940: Queen of the Mob. 1941:
King of the Texas Rangers (serial). Father
Takes a Wife. Federal Fugitives. Dangerous
Lady. Look Who's Laughing. They Meet Again.
1942: Too Many Women. X Marks the Spot.
The Lady is Willing. 1943: Secrets of the
Underground. All by Myself. Bombardier. The
Sky's the Limit. 1944: When Strangers Marry.
1945: Brewster's Millions. 1961: The Little
Shepherd of Kingdom Come. 1962: The Devil's
Hand. 1964: The Patsy. Good Neighbor Sam.
Strategy of Terror. 1965: The Family Jewels.
1966: Madame X. Batman. 1970: Which Way
to the Front? (GB: Ja, Ja, Mein General! But
Which Way to the Front?). Vanished (TV).*

HAMMOND, Kay
(Dorothy Standing) 1909–1980
Glamorous, high-spirited English leading
lady with a mass of blonde curls and an attractive, honeyed voice. Particularly effective in
comedy, she was popular in British and American films of the early thirties, but won greater
fame as a stage and (latterly) radio star. Her
later career was dogged by ill-health, and she
was forced to retire after a stroke that left her
confined to a wheelchair. Daughter of Sir Guy
Standing; mother of John Standing (1934–).
Married to Sir John Clements (second of two)
from 1946.
*1929: The Trespasser. Her Private Affair.
1930: Abraham Lincoln. Children of Chance.
1931: Fascination. A Night in Montmartre.
Almost a Divorce. Out of the Blue. Carnival
(US: Venetian Nights). The Third String.
1932: A Night Like This. Nine Till Six. Sally
Bishop. Money Means Nothing. 1933: Yes,
Madam. Sleeping Car. Britannia of Billings-
gate. The Umbrella. Bitter Sweet. Racetrack.
Double Harness. 1934: Eight Girls in a Boat.
By-Pass to Happiness. 1936: Two on a
Doorstep. 1941: Jeannie (US: Girl in
Distress). 1945: Blithe Spirit. 1948: Call of
the Blood. 1961: Five Golden Hours.*

HAMMOND, Peter 1923–
Tousle-haired, pleasant young leading man of
British films of the 1940s, with perennial boy-
next-door looks, usually seen as boyfriend,
weakling or harassed hero. Left acting in the
late 1950s, after a period in smaller film roles,

to concentrate on writing and direction, mainly in television, where he has made dozens of episodes in drama series.
1944: Waterloo Road. 1945: They Knew Mr Knight. 1947: Holiday Camp. 1948: Fly Away Peter. Here Come the Huggetts. Vote for Huggett. 1949: Fools Rush In. The Huggetts Abroad. Helter Skelter. 1950: Morning Departure (US: Operation Disaster). The Reluctant Widow. The Adventurers (US: The Great Adventure). 1952: Father's Doing Fine. Come Back Peter. Alf's Baby. 1954: The Crowded Day. 1955: Confession (US: The Deadliest Sin). 1956: The Secret Tent. Soho Incident (US: Spin a Dark Web). It's Never Too Late. X the Unknown. 1959: Model for Murder.

As director: *1969: Spring and Port Wine.*

HAMPSHIRE, Susan 1938–
Blonde, sweet-faced English leading lady with tip-tilted nose and engaging smile. Throughout her career has fought enthusiastically against typecasting in milk-and-water roles, winning her biggest audiences in television 'sagas' and becoming a highly-rated stage star in the seventies.
1947: The Woman in the Hall. 1959: Expresso Bongo. Upstairs and Downstairs. Idle on Parade (US: Idol on Parade). 1961: During One Night. The Long Shadow. 1963: Night Must Fall. The Three Lives of Thomasina. 1964: Wonderful Life (US: Swingers' Paradise). 1965: Paris in August. 1966: The Fighting Prince of Donegal. 1967: The Trygon Factor. 1969: The Violent Enemy. Monte Carlo or Bust! (US: Those Daring Young Men in Their Jaunty Jalopies). David Copperfield (TV. GB: cinemas). 1971: Time for Loving. Baffled! Mal-

pertuis (GB: The Legend of Doom House). 1972: Living Free. Roses rouges et piments verts (US: The Lonely Woman). Neither the Sea Nor the Sand. 1973: Dr Jekyll and Mr Hyde (TV). 1976: Bang! 1980: Dick Turpin (GB: TV).

HANCOCK, Tony 1924–1968
Lugubrious dark-haired British comedian with hangdog look, usually seen as aggressive, gullible, self-opinionated loafers. Riotously funny on radio and TV, he led a stormy, alcoholic private life. His intolerance of advice led him to fall fairly flat in films, and his career went downhill rapidly. Committed suicide by taking an overdose of pills.
1954: Orders Are Orders. 1961: The Rebel (US: Call Me Genius). 1962: The Punch and Judy Man. 1965: Those Magnificent Men in Their Flying Machines. 1966: The Wrong Box.

HANDLEY, Tommy 1894–1949
Round-faced British comedian with chorus-boy looks and dark, boot-polish hair, who became the country's most popular entertainer in the war years with his radio show *ITMA*. His few films were nowhere near as successful, not capturing the zaniness of his humour. Died after a stroke.
*1928: *Pathe Pictorial No. 548. *Gaumont Mirror No. 94. 1930: Elstree Calling. 1933: *Making a Christmas Pudding. *A Tail of Tails (voice only). This is Paris! That Was!! (narrator only). 1934: *Hot Airman. 1936: *Leslie Jeffries and His Orchestra. 1937: *BBC Musicals No. 2. 1938: Two Men in a Box. 1942: It's That Man Again. 1943: Pictorial Revue of 1943. Time Flies. 1945: *Worker and Warfront Magazine. 1945: *Tommy Handley's Victory*

*Song. 1946: *Tom Tom Topia. 1949: Scrapbook for 1933.*

HANLEY, Jimmy 1918–1970
Cherubic, fair-haired British actor who began as a likeable teenage star, then blinked his way myopically through what seemed like dozens of boy-friends, cub reporters and other ranks for the next 20-odd years, before throwing it all up to don his spectacles as the genial, much-liked host of a TV advertising magazine and, later, radio shows. Died from cancer. Married (first of two) to Dinah Sheridan (*qv*) from 1942 to 1953.
*1933: Red Wagon. 1934: Those Were the Days. Little Friend. 1935: Royal Cavalcade (US: Regal Cavalcade). Brown on Resolution/For Ever England (US: Born for Glory). Boys Will be Boys. The Tunnel (US: Transatlantic Tunnel). 1936: Landslide. 1937: Cotton Queen. Night Ride. 1938: Housemaster. Coming of Age. 1939: *Beyond Our Horizon. There Ain't No Justice! 1940: Gaslight (US: Angel Street). 1942: Salute John Citizen. 1943: The Gentle Sex. 1944: The Way Ahead. Kiss the Bride Goodbye. Henry V. 1945: For You Alone. 29 Acacia Avenue (US: The Facts of Love). Murder in Reverse. 1946: The Captive Heart. 1947: Holiday Camp. Master of Bankdam. It Always Rains on Sunday. 1948: Here Come the Huggetts. It's Hard to Be Good. 1949: The Huggetts Abroad. Don't Ever Leave Me. Boys in Brown. The Blue Lamp. 1950: Room to Let. 1951: The Galloping Major. 1954: Radio Cab Murder. The Black Rider. 1955: The Deep Blue Sea. 1956: Satellite in the Sky. *Look This Way. 1968: The Lost Continent.*

HARDIN, Ty
(Orson Hungerford, later legally changed) 1930–
Fair-haired, blue-eyed, clean-cut, beefy American actor who changed his name from Hungerford to Hardin (the 'Ty' is a boyhood nickname) and became the star of the television western series *Bronco* in the late 1950s and early 1960s. He never managed to impose a personality on his cinema roles and, after being briefly jailed for drug-trafficking in Spain in 1974, became a self-styled minister in 1979, touring America with Bible readings until he ceased active ministry in 1984. Married six times.
1958: †As Young As We Are. †The Space

Children. †*I Married a Monster from Outer Space.* †*The Buccaneer.* 1959: *Last Train from Gun Hill.* 1961: *The Chapman Report.* 1962: *PT 109. Merrill's Marauders.* 1963: *Palm Springs Weekend. Wall of Noise.* 1964: ‡*Boudine. L'uomo della valle muledetta.* 1965: *Battle of the Bulge.* 1966: *Savage Pampas. Custer of the West.* 1967: *Berserk! One Step to Hell (US: King of Africa). Bersaglio mobile (GB and US: Death on the Run).* 1970: *Sacramento. The Last Rampage/Last Train to Berlin.* 1971: *Acquasanta Joe. The Last Rebel.* 1974: *Drums of Vengeance/Drummer of Vengeance.* 1977: *Fire! (TV. GB: cinemas).*

† *As Ty Hungerford*
‡ *Also directed*

HARDING, Ann
(Dorothy Gatley) 1901–1981
Stunning blue-eyed blonde, of genteel manner, good at suffering in thirties' soap operas. Her career suffered from type-casting, also from the fact that she moved over to 'mother' and character roles rather too early. Her throatily attractive voice, however, continued to be heard in the cinema until 1956, and on television until 1965, when she retired. Academy Award nomination for *Holiday*.
1929: *Paris Bound. Her Private Affair. Condemned (GB: Condemned to Devil's Island).* 1930: *Girl of the Golden West. Holiday.* 1931: *East Lynne. Devotion.* 1932: *Prestige. Westward Passage. The Conquerors. The Animal Kingdom (GB: The Woman in His House).* 1933: *When Ladies Meet. Double Harness. Right to Romance. Gallant Lady.* 1934: *The Life of Vergie Winters. The Fountain.* 1935:

Enchanted April. The Flame Within. Peter Ibbetson. Biography of a Bachelor Girl. 1936: *The Lady Consents. The Witness Chair.* 1937: *Love from a Stranger.* 1942: *Eyes in the Night.* 1943: *Mission to Moscow. North Star.* 1944: *Nine Girls. Janie.* 1945: *Those Endearing Young Charms.* 1946: *Janie Gets Married.* 1947: *Christmas Eve/Sinners' Holiday. It Happened on Fifth Avenue.* 1950: *The Magnificent Yankee (GB: The Man with 30 Sons). Two Weeks with Love.* 1951: *The Unknown Man.* 1955: *The Late George Apley (TV. GB: cinemas).* 1956: *I've Lived Before. The Man in the Gray Flannel Suit. Strange Intruder.* 1957: *Young Man from Kentucky (TV. GB: cinemas).*

HARDWICKE, Sir Cedric 1893–1964
Scholarly-looking, high-domed English actor with imposing, fruitily booming voice, a former medical student and army officer who took to the London stage in the early thirties and played some choice theatre and film roles. He went to America in 1938, at first with some success as a character star, but then in progressively inferior parts. His last film role, however, was one of his best. Knighted in 1934.
1913: *Riches and Rogues.* 1926: *Nelson.* 1931: *Dreyfus (US: The Dreyfus Case).* 1932: *Rome Express.* 1933: *Orders is Orders. The Ghoul. The Lady is Willing.* 1934: *Bella Donna. Nell Gwyn. Jew Süss (US: Power). The King of Paris.* 1935: *Peg of Old Drury. Les Misérables. Becky Sharp.* 1936: *Things to Come. Laburnum Grove. Tudor Rose (US: Nine Days a Queen). Calling the Tune.* 1937: *King Solomon's Mines. The Green Light.* 1939: *On Borrowed Time. The Hunchback of Notre Dame. Stanley and Livingstone.* 1940: *Tom Brown's Schooldays. The Invisible Man Returns. The Howards of Virginia (GB: The Tree of Liberty). Victory.* 1941: *Suspicion. Sundown.* 1942: *The Ghost of Frankenstein. Valley of the Sun. Invisible Agent. The Commandos Strike at Dawn.* 1943: *The Moon is Down. The Cross of Lorraine.* †*Forever and a Day.* 1944: *The Lodger. Wilson. A Wing and a Prayer. The Keys of the Kingdom.* 1945: *The Picture of Dorian Gray (narrator only).* 1946: *Beware of Pity. Sentimental Journey. The Imperfect Lady (GB: Mrs Loring's Secret).* 1947: *Lured (GB: Personal Column). A Woman's Vengeance. Ivy. Nicholas Nickleby. Tycoon.* 1948: *Song of My*

Heart. The Winslow Boy. Rope. I Remember Mama. A Connecticut Yankee in King Arthur's Court (GB: A Yankee in King Arthur's Court). 1949: *Now Barabbas was a robber . . .* 1950: *The White Tower. Mr Imperium (GB: You Belong to My Heart).* 1951: *The Desert Fox (GB: Rommel – Desert Fox). The Green Glove.* 1952: *Caribbean (GB: Caribbean Gold). The War of the Worlds (narrator only).* *Hollywood Night at 21 Club.* 1953: *Salome. Botany Bay.* 1954: *Bait. Helen of Troy.* 1955: *Richard III. Diane.* 1956: *Gaby. Mr and Mrs McAdam (TV). The Vagabond King. The Power and the Prize. The Ten Commandments. Around the World in 80 Days.* 1957: *Baby Face Nelson. The Story of Mankind.* 1961: *The Magic Fountain.* 1962: *Five Weeks in a Balloon.* 1964: *The Pumpkin Eater.*

† *Also co-directed*

HARDY, Oliver (Norvell Hardy, later legally changed) 1892–1957
Tie-twiddling, camera-appealing, button-moustached, ultra-courtly fat half of the Laurel and Hardy team, in show business from the age of eight (he ran away to sing in a minstrel show). Now rated by many critics as highly as his partner – they teamed in 1927. Died after a stroke.
1913: *Outwitting Dad.* 1914: *Back to the Farm. Pins Are Lucky. The Soubrette and the Simp. The Smuggler's Daughter. The Female Cop. What He Forgot. Cupid's Target. Spaghetti and Lottery. Gus and the Anarchists. Shoddy the Tailor.* 1915: *The Paper Hanger's Helper. Spaghetti a la Mode. Charley's Aunt. Artists and Models. The Tramps. Prize Baby. An Expensive Visit. Cleaning Time. Mixed Flats. Safety Worst. Twin Sisters. Baby. Who Stole the Dogies? A Lucky Strike. The New Butler. Matilda's Legacy. Her Choice. The Cannibal King. What a Cinch! The Dead Letter. Avenging Bill. The Haunted Hat. The Simp and the Sophomores. Babe's Schooldays. Ethel's Romeos. A Bungalow Bungle. Three Rings and a Goat. A Rheumatic Joint. Something in Her Eye. A Janitor's Joyful Job. Fatty's Fatal Fun. Ups and Downs. This Way Out. Chickens. A Frenzied Finance. Busted Hearts.* 1916: *A Sticky Affair. Bungles' Rainy Day. The Try-Out. One Two Many. Bungles Enforces the Law. The Serenade. Bungles' Elopement. Nerve and Gasoline. Bungles Lands a Job. Their*

(US: *Murder for Sale*). 1931: *Princesse à vos ordres. Nie wieder Liebe. Calais – Douvres.* †*Congress Dances. Ihre Holeit befiehlt.* 1932: *Zwei Herzen und ein Schlag. La fille et le garçon.* †*Quick.* †*Happy Ever After.* †*The Only Girl.* 1933: *My Lips Betray. My Weakness. König der Clows.* 1934: *I Am Suzanne. Let's Live Tonight.* 1935: *Mein ist die Rache. Did I Betray? (later Black Roses). Invitation to the Waltz.* 1936: †*Glückskinder.* 1937: *Sieben Ohrfeigen/Seven Slaps. Fanny Elssler.* 1938: *Capriccio.* 1939: *Castellia in Aria. Frau am Steuer.* 1940: *Serenade. Miquette et sa mère.* 1950: *Herrliche Zeiten.* 1958: *Das gags nur einmal.* 1960: *Das kommt nich wieder.*

† *Plus French/English/German versions as appropriate*

HASSO, Signe (Signe Larsson) 1910–
Forceful, grave-looking blonde Swedish actress who won the first Swedish 'Oscar' in 1938 for *Karriär*. Belatedly went to Hollywood in 1942, and biographies for many years gave her date of birth as 1915 to help prolong her career there. She never quite settled in American films, nor did they use her cool, low-key appeal to best advantage. Returned to Sweden in 1950: now divides her acting time between the two countries.
1933: †*Tystnadens Hus (US: House of Silence).* 1937: *Häxnatten.* 1938: *Karriär. Geld fällt vom Himmel.* 1939: *Pengar från Skyn. Vi Trå. Emilie Höggvist.* 1940: *Vildmarkens Sång. Stöl. Far och Son. Än en gång Gösta Ekman. Stora Fammen.* 1941: *Bartard. Den ljusnande Framtid.* 1942: *Journey for Margaret.* 1943: *Assignment in Brittany. Heaven Can Wait.* 1944: *The Story of Dr Wassel. The Seventh Cross.* 1945: *Dangerous Partners. Johnny Angel. The House on 92nd Street.* 1946: *Strange Triangle. A Scandal in Paris (GB: Thieves' Holiday).* 1947: *Where There's Life. Aitanga.* 1948: *To the Ends of the Earth. A Double Life.* 1950: *Outside the Wall. Crisis. Sånt Händer inte Här (GB: High Tension).* 1953: *Maria Johanna.* 1954: *Die Sonne von St Moritz. Den unter Brara Lognen. Taxi 13.* 1955: *The True and the False.* 1966: *Picture Mommy Dead.* 1967: *Code Name: Heraclitus (TV).* 1971: *A Reflection of Fear.* 1973: *The Magician (TV).* 1974: *QB VII (TV).* 1975: *Shell Game (TV).* 1976: *The Black Bird. Sherlock Holmes in New York (TV).* 1977: *I*

Never Promised You a Rose Garden. 1985: Mirrors (TV).

† *as Signe Larsson*

HATFIELD, Hurd 1918–
Cold, handsome, aloof-looking, ascetic American actor whose career ran sadly downhill in just five years from the leading role in *The Picture of Dorian Gray* to support in *Tarzan and the Slave Girl*. Has since acted mainly on stage, and still looks absurdly young. 'I guess I must have a portrait in the attic,' he says.
1944: *Dragon Seed.* 1945: *The Picture of Dorian Gray.* 1946: *The Diary of a Chambermaid.* 1947: *The Beginning or the End? The Unsuspected.* 1948: *The Checkered Coat. Chinatown at Midnight. Joan of Arc.* 1950: *Tarzan and the Slave Girl. Destination Murder.* 1957: *The Last Man (TV).* 1958: *The Left Handed Gun.* 1961: *King of Kings. El Cid.* 1965: *Mickey One. Harlow.* 1968: *The Boston Strangler.* 1970: *Von Richthofen and Brown (GB: The Red Baron).* 1971: *Thief (TV).* 1973: *The Norliss Tapes (TV).* 1979: *You Can't Go Home (TV).* 1985: *King David. Lime Street (TV).* 1986: *Crimes of the Heart.*

HAUER, Rutger 1944–
Very fair-haired, blue-eyed, unsmiling, ambitious Dutch actor who, after becoming known as the 'Paul Newman of Holland', aimed to become an international star, but left it late. He seemed most fitted for villainous roles and indeed Hollywood saw him that way at first. Later he widened his range, but has not yet achieved the stature to which he aspires. Began his career in a pantomime company.

1973: *Repelstweltje. Turks fruit (GB and US: Turkish Delight).* 1974: *The Wilby Conspiracy. Pusteblume (GB: Hard to Remember).* 1975: *Le vent de la violence. Keetje tippel. La donneuse (GB: Naked and Lustful).* 1976: *Max Havelaar.* 1977: *Soldier of Orange.* 1978: *Femme entre chien et loup. Jewel in the Deep.* 1981: *Nighthawks. Chanel solitaire.* 1982: *Blade Runner. Eureka. Grijpstra and De Gier (US: Outsider in Amsterdam).* 1983: *The Osterman Weekend. Spetters.* 1984: *A Breed Apart.* 1985: *LadyHawke. Flesh and Blood.* 1986: *The Hitcher.*

HAVER, June
(J. Stovenour) 1925–
Bright, bouncy blonde American singer and actress with pleasing smile and warm personality. A dance band vocalist at 14, her career ran roughly parallel to that of Betty Grable at the same studio (Fox): they actually appeared together in *The Dolly Sisters*. Considered becoming a nun in the early fifties. Now married to Fred MacMurray (second) since 1954.
1942: **Swing's the Thing.* **Trumpet Serenade.* 1943: *Casanova in Burlesque. The Gang's All Here (GB: The Girls He Left Behind).* 1944: *Home in Indiana. Irish Eyes are Smiling.* 1945: *Where Do We Go from Here? The Dolly Sisters.* 1946: *Three Little Girls in Blue. Wake Up and Dream.* 1947: *I Wonder Who's Kissing Her Now.* 1948: *Scudda-Hoo! Scudda-Hay! (GB: Summer Lightning).* 1949: *Oh, You Beautiful Doll! Look for the Silver Lining.* 1950: *The Daughter of Rosie O'Grady. I'll Get By.* 1951: *Love Nest.* 1953: *The Girl Next Door.*

HAVOC, June
(Ellen Hovick) 1916–
Bright blue-eyed blonde American dancer, singer and later dramatic actress of cool personality, sister of Gypsy Rose Lee. On stage as soon as she could walk. Around 1918, made two or three two-reelers with Harold Lloyd, as Baby June. I have not been able to trace individual titles. Married three times, the first two at 13 and 19. But since 1949, has been married to director William Spier.
1941: *Four Jacks and a Jill.* 1942: *Powder Town. My Sister Eileen. Sing Your Worries Away.* 1943: *Hello, Frisco, Hello! No Time for Love. Hi Diddle Diddle. Casanova in Burlesque.* 1944: *Sweet and Low Down. Timber Queen.*

1945: Brewster's Millions. 1947: Intrigue. Gentleman's Agreement. 1948: When My Baby Smiles at Me. The Iron Curtain. 1949: The Story of Molly X. Red Hot and Blue. Chicago Deadline. 1950: Mother Didn't Tell Me. Once a Thief. 1951: Follow the Sun. 1952: Lady Possessed. 1956: Three for Jamie Dawn. 1970: The Boy Who Stole the Elephants (TV). 1977: J. Edgar Hoover, Godfather of the FBI (Later and GB: The Private Files of J. Edgar Hoover). 1980: Can't Stop the Music.

HAWKINS, Jack 1910–1973
Tall, powerful, well-built British actor with square jaw and cheerful grin who emerged in the early fifties from years of solid supporting roles to feature throughout the decade in stiff-upper-lip roles as one of Britain's biggest stars. His finest asset was his rich and fruity voice: sadly this disappeared in 1966 after an operation for throat cancer removed his vocal chords. His death seven years later resulted from haemorrhaging following an operation to implant a 'voice box'. Married (first of two) to Jessica Tandy from 1932 to 1944.
1930: Birds of Prey (US: The Perfect Alibi). 1932: The Lodger (US: The Phantom Fiend). 1933: The Lost Chord. The Good Companions. I Lived with You. The Jewel. A Shot in the Dark. 1934: Lorna Doone. Autumn Crocus. Death at Broadcasting House. 1935: Peg of Old Drury. 1937: Beauty and the Barge. The Frog. 1938: Who Goes Next? A Royal Divorce. 1939: Murder Will Out. 1940: The Flying Squad. 1942: The Next of Kin. 1948: The Fallen Idol. Bonnie Prince Charlie. The Small Back Room. 1950: The Black Rose. The Elusive Pimpernel (US: The Fighting Pimpernel). State Secret (US: The Great Manhunt). The Adventurers (US: The Great Adventure). 1951: No Highway (US: No Highway in the Sky). Home at Seven (US: Murder on Monday). 1952: Mandy (US: Crash of Silence). The Planter's Wife (US: Outpost in Malaya). Angels One Five. 1953: The Cruel Sea. *Pathway into Light (narrator only). Twice Upon a Time. Malta Story. The Intruder. *Prince Philip (narrator only). Front Page Story. 1954: The Seekers (US: Land of Fury). 1955: Land of the Pharaohs. The Prisoner. Touch and Go (US: The Light Touch). 1956: The Long Arm (US: The Third Key). The Man in the Sky (US: Decision Against Time). 1957: *The Battle for Britain (narrator only). Fortune is a Woman (US: She Played with Fire). The Bridge on the River Kwai. 1958: Gideon's Day (US: Gideon of Scotland Yard). The Two-Headed Spy. 1959: Ben-Hur. 1960: The League of Gentlemen. 1961: La Fayette. Two Loves (US: Spinster). 1962: Lawrence of Arabia. Five Finger Exercise. Rampage. 1963: Zulu. 1964: The Third Secret. Guns at Batasi. Masquerade. Lord Jim. 1965: Judith. 1966: The Poppy is Also a Flower (GB: Danger Grows Wild). 1967: †Great Catherine. 1968: †Shalako. 1969: †Oh! What a Lovely War. †Monte Carlo or Bust (US: Those Daring Young Men in Their Jaunty Jalopies). †Twinky (US: Lola). †The Adventures of Gerard. 1970: †The Beloved (GB: TV, as Sin). †Jane Eyre (TV. GB: cinemas). †Waterloo. 1971: †When Eight Bells Toll. †Kidnapped. †Nicholas and Alexandra. †Young Winston. 1972: †Escape to the Sun. 1973: †Theatre of Blood. †Tales That Witness Madness. †The Last Lion. 1974: †QB VII (TV).

† Voice dubbed by other actors (Charles Gray, Robert Rietty)

HAWN, Goldie 1945–
Large-eyed, doll-faced, petite, volatile American actress who shot to fame as the daffy, squeaky pin-up of the long-running TV comedy show Laugh-In, and plays free-living, loveable scatterbrains. Won an Academy Award (best supporting actress) in her second film, Cactus Flower. Also nominated for Private Benjamin. Married (third) actor Kurt Russell (qv) in 1986.
1968: The One and Only Genuine Original Family Band. 1969: Cactus Flower. 1970: There's a Girl in My Soup. 1971: $ (GB: The Heist). 1972: Butterflies Are Free. 1973: The Sugarland Express. 1974: The Girl from Petrovka. 1975: Shampoo. 1976: The Duchess and the Dirtwater Fox. 1978: Foul Play. 1979: Travels with Anita (US: A Trip with Anita). 1980: Private Benjamin. Seems Like Old Times. 1981: Lovers and Liars. 1982: Best Friends. 1983: Swing Shift. 1984: Protocol. 1985: Wildcats.

HAY, Will 1888–1949
Solidly-built, light-haired British music-hall comedian. His chief character, the disreputable (and frequently incompetent) figure of tatty authority, was built up of coughs, grunts and snuffles, plus a pair of pince-nez and a shifty look, and perfected on stage before he launched it on film to provide a series of unparalleled comedy classics, often in partnership with cherubic Graham Moffatt and doddery Moore Marriott. Died after a series of strokes.
1933: *Know Your Apples. 1934: Those Were the Days. Radio Parade of 1935 (US: Radio Follies). 1935: Dandy Dick. Boys Will Be Boys. 1936: Where There's a Will. Windbag the Sailor. 1937: Good Morning, Boys. Oh, Mr Porter. 1938: Convict 99. Hey! Hey! USA. Old Bones of the River. 1939: Ask a Policeman. Where's That Fire? 1941: The Ghost of St Michael's. †The Black Sheep of Whitehall. The Big Blockade. 1942: *Go to Blazes! †The Goose Steps Out. 1943: †My Learned Friend.

† And co-directed

HAYAKAWA, Sessue
(Kintaro Hayakawa) 1889–1973
Good-looking, solidly built Japanese actor who tried his luck in early Hollywood silents, and had a great run of success as sensuous orientals from 1914 until the mid-twenties. After that he made his career mainly on stage, with occasional film forays through the years, mostly as Japanese wartime commanders. Died from cerebral thrombosis complicated by pneumonia. Received an Oscar nomination for The Bridge on the River Kwai.
1914: The Typhoon. The Wrath of the Gods. The Last of the Line. The Vigil. The Ambassador's Envoy. 1915: The Cheat. The Clue. The Secret Sin. After Five. 1916: Honorable Friend. Alien Souls. The Soul of Kura-San. Temptation. 1917: Forbidden Paths. The Jagu-

ar's Claw. The Debt. Honor Redeemed (GB: The Victoria Cross). Hashimure Togo. The Bottle Imp. The Call of the East. The Secret Game. Each to His Kind. 1918: Hidden Pearls. The City of Dim Faces. His Birthright. The Temple of Dusk. White Man's Law. The Honor of His House. The Bravest Way. 1919: The Tong Man. The Dragon Painter. Courageous Coward. Heart in Pawn. Gray Horizon. The Man Beneath. Bonds of Honor. His Debt. 1920: The Devil's Claim. Li-ting Lang. An Arabian Knight. The Brand of Lopez. The Beggar Prince. 1921: Black Roses. The First Born. Where Lights Are Low. The Swamp. 1922: The Vermilion Pencil. Five Days to Live. 1923: La bataille (GB: The Battle. US: The Danger Line). J'ai tué (GB: The First Born). 1924: The Great Prince Shan. Sen Yan's Devotion. 1925: Loyalty. The Darling of the Gods. 1929: *The Man Who Laughed Last. 1930: *Voice of Hollywood No. 2. 1931: Daughter of the Dragon. 1933: Tohjin Okichi. 1937: Yoshiwara. Die Tochter des Samurai. 1938: Forfaiture. Tempête sur l'Asie. 1939: Macao. l'enfer du jeu (GB: Gambling Hell). 1940: Patrouille blanche. 1946: Le cabaret du grand large. Quartier chinois. 1949: Tokyo Joe. 1950: Three Came Home. Les misérables. 1953: Higego no Shogun Yamashita Yasubumi. 1955: House of Bamboo. 1957: The Bridge on the River Kwai. 1958: The Geisha Boy. 1959: Green Mansions. 1960: The Swiss Family Robinson. Hell to Eternity. 1962: The Big Wave. 1966: The Daydreamer.

HAYDEN, Linda (L. Higginson) 1951–
Languorous British blonde actress pegged as a teenage sexpot after her first big role (in

Baby Love). It was a slot she found impossible to escape and, despite some interesting dramatic roles, she soon slid into Confessions-style comedies, later discovering better acting opportunities on television.
1968: The Lion in Winter. Baby Love. 1970: Taste the Blood of Dracula. Satan's Skin (later Blood on Satan's Claw). 1971: Something to Hide. 1972: Barcelona Kill. 1973: Night Watch. 1974: Vampira (US: Old Dracula). Madhouse. Confessions of a Window Cleaner. 1975: Exposé. 1977: Confessions from a Holiday Camp. Let's Get Laid! 1978: The Boys from Brazil. 1985: Minder on the Orient Express (TV).

HAYDEN, Sterling
(Christian Walter, later legally changed). 1916–1986
Tall, strong blond American leading man of Dutch parentage, idyllically good-looking in his early years when he became famous as a sea-going adventurer before taking up the cinema. After a distinguished war career in the Marines, he returned as the strong, silent, sometimes semi-corrupt hero with the occasional plum amid a waste of routine action films. Quit Hollywood in 1958 and now acts according to financial necessity. Married (first of three) to Madeleine Carroll, 1942–1946. Died from cancer.
1941: †Virginia. †Bahama Passage. 1947: Variety Girl. Blaze of Noon. 1949: El Paso. Manhandled. 1950: The Asphalt Jungle. 1951: Journey into Light. Flaming Feather. 1952: Denver and Rio Grande. The Golden Hawk. Hellgate. Flat Top (GB: Eagles of the Fleet). 1953: Take Me to Town. Kansas Pacific. Fighter Attack. So Big. The Star. Crime Wave (GB: The City is Dark). 1954: Arrow in the Dust. Johnny Guitar. Naked Alibi. Suddenly! Prince Valiant. Battle Taxi. 1955: Timberjack. The Eternal Sea. Shotgun. The Last Command. Top Gun. 1956: The Come-On. The Killing. 1957: Five Steps to Danger. Crime of Passion. The Iron Sheriff. A Sound of Different Drummers (TV). Valerie. Zero Hour. Gun Battle at Monterey. The Last Man (TV). 1958: Terror in a Texas Town. The Long March (TV). Ten Days to Tulara. Old Man (TV). 1963: Dr Strangelove, or: How I Learned to Stop Worrying and Love the Bomb. 1964: Carol for Another Christmas (TV). 1969: Sweet Hunters. Hard Contract. 1970: Loving. 1971: Cobra/Le saut

de l'ange. 1972: The Godfather. Le grand départ. 1973: The Long Goodbye. The Final Programme (US: The Last Days of Man on Earth). 1974: Deadly Strangers. 1975: Cry Onion. 1976: 1900. 1977: Winter Kills (released 1979). 1978: King of the Gypsies (released 1980). 1980: Gas. 9 to 5. 1981: Possession. Charlie Chan and the Curse of the Dragon Queen. Venom. 1983: Leuchtturm des Chaos.

† As Stirling Hayden

HAYES, Allison
(Mary Jane Hayes) 1930–1977
Strong, statuesque, chestnut-haired actress who started her professional career as a pianist with symphony orchestras, but was persuaded to try acting after winning a number of beauty contests. Nowadays has something of a cult following for her performance in Attack of the 50-Foot Woman, one of several chilly, low-budget horror films in which she appeared. Died from blood poisoning.
1954: Francis Joins the WACs. Sign of the Pagan. So This is Paris. The Purple Mask. 1955: Chicago Syndicate. Double Jeopardy (GB: Crooked Ring). Count Three and Pray. 1956: Gunslinger. Mohawk. The Steel Jungle. 1957: The Unearthly. The Disembodied. The Undead. Zombies of Mora Tau (GB: The Dead That Walk). Voodoo Woman. 1958: Attack of the 50-Foot Woman. Wolf Dog (GB: Lust to Kill). Hong Kong Confidential. 1959: Counterplot. Pier 5 – Havana. 1960: The Hypnotic Eye. The High Powered Rifle. 1963: Who's Been Sleeping in My Bed? The Crawling Hand. 1965: Tickle Me.

HAYES, Helen
(Helen H. Brown) 1900–
Fair-haired American child actress who became one of the great Broadway stars of the twenties. Her theatrical style was unsuited to films, nor was she a great film-star beauty, and, despite an Academy Award for The Sin of Madelon Claudet, she soon returned to the stage. Her return to films in later years was more successful, and she won another Academy Award in Airport. Married to writer Charles MacArthur (died 1956); actor James MacArthur (qv) is their adopted son.
1910: *Jean and the Calico Doll. 1917: The Weavers of Life. 1920: Babs. 1931: The Sin of Madelon Claudet (GB: The Lullaby). Arrow-

smith. 1932: A Farewell to Arms. The Son-Daughter. 1933: The White Sister. Another Language. Night Flight. 1934: What Every Woman Knows. Crime Without Passion. 1935: Vanessa, Her Love Story. 1943: Stage Door Canteen. 1952: My Son John. 1953: Main Street to Broadway. 1956: Anastasia. 1957: Four Women in Black (TV). 1959: Third Man on the Mountain. 1969: Airport. 1972: The Female Instinct (GB: The Snoop Sisters) (TV). 1973: Do Not Fold, Spindle or Mutilate (TV). Herbie Rides Again. 1975: One of Our Dinosaurs is Missing. 1976: Victory at Entebbe (TV. GB: cinemas). 1977: Candleshoe. 1979: A Family Upside Down (TV). 1981: Hopper's Silence (voice only). Murder is Easy (TV). 1983: A Caribbean Mystery (TV. GB: Murder in the Caribbean). 1985: Murder with Mirrors (TV).

HAYMES, Dick 1916–1980
Toothy, light-haired, Argentine-born American singer, whose fine baritone voice got him into a succession of film roles in the forties. In looks, he was rather reminiscent of Johnnie Ray. The song was fine, but wine, women and hard living got the better of him and he declared bankruptcy twice, in 1960 and 1971, before making a night-club comeback in the seventies. Married to Joanne Dru 1941–1949 and Rita Hayworth 1953–1954, second and fourth of six. Ended his days as an Irish citizen. Died from lung cancer.
1938: Dramatic School. 1943: Du Barry Was a Lady. 1944: Four Jills in a Jeep. Irish Eyes Are Smiling. 1945: State Fair. Billy Rose's Diamond Horseshoe (GB: Diamond Horse-

shoe). 1946: Do You Love Me? 1947: Carnival in Costa Rica. The Shocking Miss Pilgrim. 1948: Up in Central Park. One Touch of Venus. 1951: St Benny the Dip (GB: Escape If You Can). 1953: All Ashore. Cruisin' down the River. 1974: The Betrayal (TV). 1975: Won Ton Ton, the Dog Who Saved Hollywood.

HAYWARD, Louis
(Seafield Grant) 1909–1985
Dark-haired, laughing-eyed South African-born leading man with mocking smile. He began his career in British films, then went to Hollywood in 1935, where he played debonair heroes and was ideally cast as The Saint. Later, he rather surprisingly became typed in double-feature swashbucklers, and drifted out of films in his forties. Married to Ida Lupino 1939–1945, first of three.
1932: Self Made Lady. 1933: The Thirteenth Candle. The Man Outside. I'll Stick to You. Chelsea Life. Sorrell and Son. 1934: The Love Test. 1935: The Flame Within. A Feather in Her Hat. 1936: Absolute Quiet. Trouble for Two (GB: The Suicide Club). Anthony Adverse. The Luckiest Girl in the World. 1937: The Woman I Love. 1938: Midnight Intruder. The Rage of Paris. The Saint in New York. Condemned Women. The Duke of West Point. 1939: The Man in the Iron Mask. 1940: My Son, My Son. Dance, Girl, Dance. Son of Monte Cristo. 1941: Ladies in Retirement. 1942: The Magnificent Ambersons. 1945: And Then There Were None (GB: Ten Little Niggers). 1946: Young Widow. The Strange Woman. The Return of Monte Cristo (GB: Monte Cristo's Revenge). 1947: Repeat Performance. 1948: Ruthless. The Black Arrow Strikes (GB: The Black Arrow). Walk a Crooked Mile. 1949: The Pirates of Capri (GB: The Masked Pirate). The House by the River. 1950: The Fortunes of Captain Blood. 1951: The Lady and the Bandit (GB: Dick Turpin's Ride). Son of Dr Jekyll. 1952: Lady in the Iron Mask. Captain Pirate (GB: Captain Blood – Fugitive). 1953: The Saint's Return (US: The Saint's Girl Friday). Storm over Africa (US: Royal African Rifles). 1954: Duffy of San Quentin (GB: Men Behind Bars). 1955: The Voyage of Captain Tom Jones, Pirate (TV). 1956: The Search for Bridey Murphy. 1967: Chuka. The Christmas Kid.

Electric Man. 1969: The Phynx. 1973: Terror in the Wax Museum.

HAYWARD, Susan
(Edythe Marrenner) 1917–1975
There was an inner driving force behind the career of this American star that belied the pretty face in the chestnut curls and showed itself in the set of the lips and the look behind the eyes. It led her swiftly from 'sweet' heroines to tough ladies in the Stanwyck mould – but with more problems. First nominated for an Oscar for her alcoholic in Smash-Up (a role that set the pace for the remainder of her career), she was up for the Academy Award several times after that, finally winning for I Want to Live! ten years later. Died from a brain tumour.
1937: Hollywood Hotel. 1938: I Am the Law. *Campus Cinderella. The Sisters. Girls on Probation. The Amazing Dr Clitterhouse. Comet over Broadway. 1939: Our Leading Citizen. $1,000 a Touchdown. Beau Geste. 1941: Adam Had Four Sons. Sis Hopkins. Among the Living. 1942: Reap the Wild Wind. I Married a Witch. Star Spangled Rhythm. *A Letter from Bataan. Forest Rangers. 1943: Hit Parade of 1943. Young and Willing. Jack London. 1944: The Fighting Seabees. The Hairy Ape. *Skirmish on the Home Front. And Now Tomorrow. 1946: Deadline at Dawn. Canyon Passage. 1947: Smash-Up, the Story of a Woman (GB: A Woman Destroyed). The Lost Moment. They Won't Believe Me. 1948: Tap Roots. The Saxon Charm. 1949: Tulsa. House of Strangers. My Foolish Heart. 1950: Rawhide. 1951: I Can Get It For You Wholesale (GB: This is My Affair). I'd Climb the Highest Mountain. David and Bathsheba. 1952: With a Song in My Heart. The Snows of Kilimanjaro. The Lusty Men. 1953: The President's Lady. White Witch Doctor. 1954: Demetrius and the Gladiators. Garden of Evil. 1955: Untamed. Soldier of Fortune. I'll Cry Tomorrow. 1956: The Conqueror. 1957: Top Secret Affair (GB: Their Secret Affair). 1958: I Want to Live! 1959: Woman Obsessed. Thunder in the Sun. 1960: The Marriage-Go-Round. 1961: Ada. Back Street. 1962: I Thank a Fool. 1963: Stolen Hours. 1964: Where Love Has Gone. 1966: The Honey Pot. 1967: Valley of the Dolls. 1971: Heat of Anger (TV). 1972: The Revengers. Say Goodbye, Maggie Cole (TV).

HAYWORTH, Rita
(Margarita Cansino) 1918–

Dark-haired American dancer and actress, born to show-business parents (and cousin of Ginger Rogers) and dancing professionally at 14. After a series of minor roles, her wide smile and flashing eyes, allied to a sumptuous figure, propelled her forward as one of the foremost and dreamiest-looking love goddesses of the forties. Her beauty faded with the decade and she lapsed into middle-aged roles as soon as she turned 40. Even so, her appearance in *Gilda* and some of her early musicals, can still take the breath away. Married to Orson Welles 1943–1947 and Dick Haymes 1953–1954, second and fourth of five. Recently in poor health, a sufferer from Alzheimer's disease, a wasting of the brain.

1926: †*La Fiesta. 1934: †Cruz Diablo. 1935: †*Rose de Francia. †Under the Pampas Moon. †Dante's Inferno. †Charlie Chan in Egypt. †In Caliente. †Silk Legs. †Paddy O'Day. 1936: †Human Cargo. †A Message to Garcia. †Rebellion. †Meet Nero Wolfe. 1937: †Hit the Saddle. †Trouble in Texas. †Old Louisiana (GB: Treason). Criminals of the Air. The Game That Kills. Paid to Dance. Girls Can Play. The Shadow (GB: The Circus Shadow). 1938: There's Always a Woman. Who Killed Gail Preston? Juvenile Court. Convicted. Homicide Bureau. 1939: The Lone Wolf Spy Hunt (GB: The Lone Wolf's Daughter). Renegade Ranger. Only Angels Have Wings. Special Inspector (GB: Across the Border). 1940: Music in My Heart. Susan and God (GB: The Gay Mrs Trexel). Blondie on a Budget. The Lady in Question. Angels over Broadway. 1941: The Strawberry Blonde. Affectionately Yours. Blood and Sand. You'll Never Get Rich. 1942: My Gal Sal. Tales of Manhattan. You Were Never Lovelier. 1943: *Show Business at War. 1944: Cover Girl. Tonight and Every Night. 1946: Gilda. 1947: Down to Earth. 1948: The Loves of Carmen. The Lady from Shanghai. 1952: Affair in Trinidad. 1953: Salome. Miss Sadie Thompson. 1954: Champagne Safari. *Screen Snapshots No. 225. 1957: Fire Down Below. Pal Joey. 1958: Separate Tables. 1959: They Came to Cordura. The Story on Page One. 1962: The Happy Thieves. 1964: Circus World (GB: The Magnificent Showman). 1965: The Money Trap. 1966: The Poppy is Also a Flower (GB: Danger Grows Wild). L'avventuriero/The Rover. 1968: I bastardi/

Sons of Satan. 1970: The Road to Salina. 1971: The Naked Zoo. 1972: The Wrath of God. 1976: Circle.

† *As Rita Cansino (when billed)*

HAZELL, Hy
(Hyacinth Hazel O'Higgins) 1920–1970

Long-legged British musical-comedy star with bubbly blonde hair. Her singing and dancing talents were seldom displayed to advantage in British films, where she was deployed as more of a sex symbol. On stage at seven. Made a great principal boy in pantomime. Choked to death on a piece of steak.

1943: †The Dummy Talks. †My Learned Friend. 1947: Meet Me at Dawn. Just William's Luck. 1949: Paper Orchid. Celia. 1950: The Body Said No! Dance Hall. The Lady Craved Excitement. 1951: The Franchise Affair. 1952: The Night Won't Talk. The Yellow Balloon. 1953: Forces' Sweetheart. 1955: Stolen Assignment. 1956: Up in the World. Anastasia. 1957: Light Fingers. The Key Man. *The Mail Van Murder. 1958: The Whole Truth. 1960: Trouble with Eve. 1961: Five Golden Hours. 1962: What Every Woman Wants. 1970: Every Home Should Have One.

† *As Derna Hazell*

HEALEY, Myron 1922–

Big, fair-haired, blue-eyed, mean-looking American actor who mostly played villains in 'B' westerns, but was good in some minor leading roles of the 1950s. Our photograph catches a rare, in films at least, Healey smile.

A child violinist and pianist; also wrote some screenplays.

1942: *For the Common Defense. *Keep 'Em Sailing. 1943: Salute to the Marines. I Dood It (GB: By Hook or By Crook). Thousands Cheer. The Iron Major. 1944: See Here, Private Hargrove. Meet the People. 1946: The Time of Their Lives. Crime Doctor's Man Hunt. 1947: The Corpse Came COD. It Had to Be You. Buck Privates Come Home (GB: Rookies Come Home). Down to Earth. 1948: Blondie's Reward. The Man from Colorado. Hidden Danger. Across the Rio Grande. Wake of the Red Witch. I, Jane Doe (GB: Diary of a Bride). You Gotta Stay Happy. Ladies of the Chorus. Range Justice. 1949: Trail's End. *The Girl from Gunsight. Knock on Any Door. South of Rio. Lawless Code. Haunted Trails. Western Renegades. Gun Law Justice. Riders of the Dusk. Slightly French. Rusty's Birthday. Brand of Fear. Laramie. 1950: Salt Lake Raiders. Trail of the Rustlers. Pioneer Marshal. Emergency Wedding. Over the Border. A Woman of Distinction. My Blue Heaven. The Fuller Brush Girl (GB: The Affairs of Sally). I Killed Geronimo. Outlaw Gold. Between Midnight and Dawn. West of Wyoming. Fence Riders. Law of the Panhandle. Hot Rod. In a Lonely Place. Short Grass. 1951: Colorado Ambush. Montana Desperado. Bonanza Town. The Big Night. The Texas Rangers. Roar of the Iron Horse (serial). The Longhorn. Lorna Doone. Bomba and the Elephant Stampede. *Baby Sitters' Jitters. Silver City (GB: High Vermilion). The Wild Blue Yonder (GB: Thunder Across the Pacific. Voice only). Slaughter Trail. Night Riders of Montana. 1952: The Kid from Broken Gun. Rodeo. Desperadoes' Outpost. West of Wyoming. The Maverick. Fort Osage. Storm over Tibet. Montana Territory. Apache War Smoke. Monsoon. Fargo. 1953: White Lightning. Vigilante Terror. Texas Bad Man. Kansas Pacific. Private Eyes. Saginaw Trail. Son of Belle Starr. Combat Squad. The Fighting Lawman. Hot News. 1954: Cattle Queen of Montana. Silver Lode. Rails into Laramie. 1955: Man without a Star. Panther Girl of the Kongo (serial). Rage at Dawn. Gang Busters. Ma and Pa Kettle at Waikiki. Yacht on the High Sea (TV. GB: cinemas). Tennessee's Partner. Jungle Moon Men. African Manhunt. The Man from Bitter Ridge. Count Three and Pray. 1956: Magnificent Roughnecks. The Claw Monsters (feature version of Panther Girl of the Kongo). Border Showdown (TV. GB: cinemas). Dig That Uranium. Thunder over Sangoland. Slightly Scarlet. The First Texan. The Young Guns. The White Squaw. Calling Homicide. Running Target. 1957: The Restless Breed. Guns Don't Argue. Shoot-Out at Medicine Bend. Hell's Crossroads. Crime Beneath the Sea (GB: Undersea Girl). The Hard Man. The Unearthly. 1958: Quantrill's Raiders. Escape from Red Rock. Cole Younger, Gunfighter. Apache Territory. 1959: Gunfight at Dodge City. Rio Bravo. 1961: The George Raft Story (GB: Spin of a Coin). 1962: Convicts Four (GB: Reprieve!). The Final Hour (TV. GB: cinemas). Varan the Unbelievable. 1964: He Rides Tall. 1965: Harlow (Carroll Baker ver-

sion). *Mirage.* 1966: *Shadow on the Land (TV).* 1967: *Journey to Shiloh.* 1969: *True Grit.* 1970: *The Cheyenne Social Club. Which Way to the Front? (GB: Ja! Ja! Mein General, But Which Way to the Front?).* 1975: *Smoke in the Wind.* 1977: *The Incredible Melting Man.* 1978: *The Other Side of the Mountain: Part 2.* 1979: *Spider-Man The Dragon's Challenge (TV. GB: cinemas).*

HEARD, John 1946–
American leading man of warmth and versatility, with light brown hair, lantern jaw and laconic good looks slightly along the lines of George Segal (*qv*). After theatrical training in Chicago and New York, he stayed a stage actor until his early thirties; he has not quite fulfilled his first promise in films but there may still be time. Very briefly (six days!) married to Margot Kidder (*qv*).
1977: *First Love. Between the Lines.* 1978: *On the Yard.* 1979: *Heart Beat. Head Over Heels.* 1980: *Misdeal (released 1982).* 1981: *Cutter and Bone (GB: Cutter's Way).* 1982: *Cat People.* 1983: *Legs (TV). Best Revenge. Will There Really Be a Morning? (TV).* 1984: *C.H.U.D. Too Scared to Scream.* 1985: *Heaven Help Us/Catholic Boys. After Hours. The Trip to Bountiful.*

HEARNE, Richard 1908–1979
British circus comedian, acrobatic tumbler and stage actor, of amiable mien, benign expression and fair, wavy hair. In supporting cameos for many years before his character of the doddering, accident-prone Mr Pastry made him a national celebrity on stage and TV. The character even made an appearance in a few, largely quite presentable, low-budget comedy films. Died from a heart attack.
1934: *Give Her a Ring.* 1935: *Dance Band. No Monkey Business.* 1936: *Millions.* 1937: *Splinters in the Air.* 1943: *Miss London Ltd. The Butler's Dilemma.* 1948: *One Night with You. Woman Hater.* 1949: *Helter Skelter.* 1950: *Something in the City.* **Mr Pastry Does the Laundry.* 1951: *Captain Horatio Hornblower RN. Madame Louise.* 1952: **What a Husband. Miss Robin Hood.* 1955: *The Time of His Life.* 1956: *Tons of Trouble.* 1962: **The King's Breakfast.*

HEDLEY, Jack (J. Hawkins) 1930–
Rather solemn-looking British actor with blue eyes and fair, wavy hair: gained a few star roles on the strength of his success as the hero of TV mystery serials by Francis Durbridge. His dour, somewhat colourless acting was not well suited to the cinema, and he has made only a few appearances on the big screen.
1957: *The Pack.* 1958: *Behind the Mask. Room at the Top.* 1959: *Left, Right and Centre.* 1960: *Make Mine Mink. Cone of Silence (US: Trouble in the Sky).* 1962: *Never Back Losers. In the French Style. The Longest Day. Lawrence of Arabia. Nine Hours to Rama.* 1963: *The Very Edge. The Scarlet Blade.* 1964: *Witchcraft. Of Human Bondage. The Secret of Blood Island.* 1967: *How I Won the War. The Anniversary.* 1969: *Goodbye, Mr Chips.* 1975: *Brief Encounter (TV).* 1977: *The Devil's Advocate. Sophia Loren – Her Own Story (TV).* 1981: *For Your Eyes Only.*

HEDREN, Tippi
(Nathalie Hedren) 1935–
Ultra-slender blonde American model, faci-ally a cross between Grace Kelly and Martha Hyer, and discovered by Alfred Hitchcock for films. Despite extremely interesting performances in *The Birds* and *Marnie*, her film roles since then have been very lacklustre. Perhaps it needed Hitchcock to bring out her special disturbing qualities. She became interested in animal welfare – particularly of big cats – in later years.
1950: *The Petty Girl (GB: Girl of the Year).* 1963: *The Birds.* 1964: *Marnie.* 1965: *Satan's Harvest.* 1966: *A Countess from Hong Kong.* 1968: *Tiger by the Tail.* 1969: *The Man with the Albatross.* 1973: *Mister Kingstreet's War (GB: TV). The Harrad Experiment.* 1975: *Adonde Mucre el Viento.* 1980: *Roar.* 1985: *Alfred Hitchcock Presents (TV).* 1986: *Foxfire Light.*

HEFLIN, Van
(Emmet Evan Heflin) 1910–1971
Sandy-haired, square-faced, thin-lipped, friendly-looking American actor and one of Hollywood's most interesting and underrated stars. Not able to bring much to poor leading roles, he often gave quite exceptional performances in meaty, well-written parts. Academy Award 1942 (best supporting actor) in *Johnny Eager.* Died following a massive stroke sustained while swimming.
1936: *A Woman Rebels.* 1937: *The Outcasts of Poker Flat. Flight from Glory. Annapolis Salute (GB: Salute to Romance). Saturday's Heroes.* 1939: *Back Door to Heaven.* 1940: *Santa Fé Trail.* 1941: *The Feminine Touch. H. M. Pulham Esq. Johnny Eager.* 1942: *Seven Sweethearts. Kid Glove Killer. Grand Central Murder. Tennessee Johnson (GB: The Man on America's Conscience).* 1943: *Presenting Lily Mars. *Hollywood in Uniform.* 1946: *Till the Clouds Roll By. The Strange Love of Martha Ivers.* 1947: *Possessed. Green Dolphin Street.* 1948: *Act of Violence. Tap Roots. B. F.'s Daughter (GB: Polly Fulton). The Three Musketeers. The Secret Land (narrator only).* 1949: *Madame Bovary. East Side, West Side.* 1950: *Tomahawk (GB: Battle of Powder River).* 1951: *The Prowler. Week-End with Father.* 1952: *My Son John. South of Algiers (US: The Golden Mask).* 1953: *Wings of the Hawk. Shane.* 1954: *Tanganyika. The Raid. Black Widow. Woman's World.* 1955: *Count Three and Pray. Battle Cry.* 1956: *Patterns (GB: Patterns of Power).* 1957: *3:10 to Yuma. The Dark Side of Earth (TV).* 1958: *Gunman's Walk. Tempest.* 1959: *They Came to*

Cordura. Five Branded Women. Rank and File (TV). 1960: Under 10 Flags. The Wastrel. The Cruel Day (TV). 1963: Cry of Battle/To Be a Man. 1965: The Greatest Story Ever Told. Once a Thief. 1966: Stagecoach. 1967: The Man Outside. 1968: Ognuno per se/Das Geld von Sam Cooper (GB: Every Man for Himself. US: The Ruthless Four). A Case of Libel (TV). 1969: Airport. The Big Bounce. 1971: The Last Child (TV).

HEMINGWAY, Mariel 1961–
Tall (5′ 11″), dark-haired (later sometimes blonde) American actress, the granddaughter of Ernest Hemingway and very pretty in a faintly anguished-looking sort of way. The sister of sometime actresses Margaux and Muffet Hemingway, she made her film debut at 14 and was nominated for an Oscar three years later for her affecting performance in *Manhattan*. Her height has somewhat limited the number of further appearances, and she has yet to establish a definite personality on screen.
1976: Lipstick. I Want to Keep My Baby (TV). 1979: Manhattan. 1982: Personal Best. 1983: Star 80. 1985: The Mean Season. Creator.

HEMMINGS, David 1941–
Chubby-faced, slightly scruffy and rather sad-looking fair-haired British leading man who progressed from cheeky schoolboys to slightly wayward teenagers. His leading-man period, which began with *Blow-Up*, lasted only a few years, even though he was, for a short while, a much-publicized cult figure. He was playing

(and looking the part) middle-aged character roles in his thirties, but has shown some interesting ideas as a director. Married to Gayle Hunnicutt (*qv*) from 1968 to 1974.
1950: Night and the City. 1954: The Rainbow Jacket. 1957: Five Clues to Fortune. Saint Joan. The Heart Within. 1959: In the Wake of a Stranger. No Trees in the Street. Men of Tomorrow. 1961: The Wind of Change. The Painted Smile (US: Murder Can Be Deadly). 1962: Some People. Play It Cool. Two Left Feet. 1963: West 11. Live It Up (US: Sing and Swing). 1964: The System (US: The Girl Getters). Be My Guest. 1965: Dateline Diamonds. 1966: Eye of the Devil. Blow-Up. 1967: Camelot. Barbarella. 1968: The Charge of the Light Brigade. Only When I Larf. The Long Day's Dying. The Best House in London. 1969: Alfred the Great. 1970: The Walking Stick. Fragment of Fear. *Simon, Simon. 1971: Unman, Wittering and Zigo. The Love Machine. 1972: *Today Mexico, Tomorrow the World. Autobiography. 1973: Voices. 1974: Juggernaut. Mister Quilp. No es nada, Mama, solo un juego. 1975: Profundo rosso/Deep Red. 1976: Islands in the Stream. 1977: Squadra antitruffa. Blood Relatives. The Squeeze. The Prince and the Pauper (US: Crossed Swords). The Heroin Busters. 1978: Power Play. Sherlock Holmes: Murder by Decree (GB: Murder by Decree). The Disappearance. Just a Gigolo. 1979: Thirst. Charlie Muffin (TV). Harlequin. 1980: Beyond Reasonable Doubt. Dr Jekyll and Mr Hyde (TV). 1982: Man, Woman and Child. 1983: Airwolf (TV). 1984: Calamity Jane (TV).

As director: *1972: Running Scared. 1973: The 14. 1978: Just a Gigolo. 1981: The Survivor. Race for the Yankee Zephyr. 1985: Come the Day.*

HENDRIX, Wanda
(Dixie W. Hendrix) 1928–1981
This dark-haired, green-eyed American actress was another case of a talented teenager failing to maintain the same level of stardom as an adult, even though she developed into a petite, Madonna-like beauty. Briefly, and very stormily, married to Audie Murphy (first of three) 1949–1950. Died from double pneumonia.
1945: Confidential Agent. *Magical Movieland. 1947: Welcome Stranger. Variety Girl.

Nora Prentiss. Ride the Pink Horse. 1948: Miss Tatlock's Millions. My Own True Love. 1949: Prince of Foxes. Song of Surrender. Captain Carey USA (GB: After Midnight). 1950: Saddle Tramp. Sierra. The Admiral Was a Lady. 1951: My Outlaw Brother. The Highwayman. 1952: Montana Territory. South of Algiers (US: The Golden Mask). 1953: The Last Posse. Sea of Lost Ships. 1954: Highway Dragnet. The Black Dakotas. 1961: The Boy Who Caught a Crook. 1963: Johnny Cool. 1964: Stage to Thunder Rock. 1974: †Mystic Mountain Massacre. The Oval Portrait.

† unreleased

HENDRY, Ian 1931–1984
Forceful, fluent, brown-haired British actor, good in a variety of roles, but at his best as persuasive con-men, a type which brought him quickly to stardom in the early 1960s. Declining to wear a toupé to cover his receding hair, he regressed to less worthy roles by the end of the decade, but remained to bring the occasional acerbic touch to unlikely assignments, until his early death from a heart attack. Married (first of two) to Janet Munro from 1963 to 1971. He remembered a couple of walk-on roles in the mid-fifties, but not the names of the films.
1958: Room at the Top. 1959: In the Nick. 1960: Sink the Bismarck! 1962: Live Now – Pay Later. 1963: Girl in the Headlines (US: The Model Murder Case). Children of the Damned. This is My Street. 1964: The Beauty Jungle (US: Contest Girl). Repulsion. 1965: The Hill. 1966: The Sandwich Man. 1967: Casino Royale. 1968: Cry Wolf. 1969: Doppelganger (US: Journey to the Far Side of the Sun). The Southern Star. 1970: The MacKenzie Break. Get Carter. 1971: The Jerusalem File. All Coppers Are ... 1972: Tales from the Crypt. Captain Kronos – Vampire Hunter. 1973: Theatre of Blood. Assassin. 1974: The Internecine Project. 1975: Professione: Reporter (GB and US: The Passenger). 1976: Intimate Games. 1978: Damien – Omen II. 1979: The Bitch. 1980: McVicar.

HENIE, Sonja 1910–1969
Blonde, Norwegian-born Olympic champion with winning smile who went to America and did for ice in the thirties what Esther Williams did for water in the forties. Died from leu-

kemia, on board an aeroplane bound for her native city, Oslo.

*1927: Syv Dager for Elisabeth. 1936: One in a Million. 1937: Thin Ice (GB: Lovely to Look At). 1938: Happy Landing. My Lucky Star. *Snow Fun. 1939: Second Fiddle. Everything Happens at Night. 1941: Sun Valley Serenade. 1942: Iceland (GB: Katina). 1943: Wintertime. 1945: It's a Pleasure. 1948: The Countess of Monte Cristo. 1952: *Hollywood Night at 21 Club. 1954: *Laughing Water. 1958: Hello London.*

Worlds. *1945: The Spanish Main. 1946: Of Human Bondage. Deception. 1947: Song of Love. 1948: Hollow Triumph (GB: The Scar). 1949: Rope of Sand. Dans la vie, tout s'arrange. 1950: So Young, So Bad. Last of the Buccaneers. Pardon My French (GB: The Lady from Boston). 1951: For Men Only/The Tall Lie. 1952: Stolen Face. Thief of Damascus. 1953: Mantrap (US: Woman in Hiding). Siren of Bagdad. 1954: Kabarett. Deep in My Heart. 1955: Pirates of Tripoli. 1956: Meet Me in Las Vegas (GB: Viva Las Vegas!). A Woman's Devotion (GB: War Shock). 1957: One Coat of White (TV). Ten Thousand Bedrooms. 1959: Holiday for Lovers. Never So Few. 1962: The Four Horsemen of the Apocalypse. 1965: Operation Crossbow. 1967: Peking Remembered (narrator only). 1969: The Madwoman of Chaillot. 1970: Double Image. 1971: The Failing of Raymond (TV). 1975: Mrs R/Death Among Friends (TV). 1977: Exorcist II: The Heretic. 1982: On the Road to Hollywood.*

As director: *1951: For Men Only/The Tall Lie. 1956: A Woman's Devotion (GB: War Shock). 1958: Girls on the Loose. Live Fast, Die Young. 1964: Dead Ringer (GB: Dead Image). Ballad in Blue (US: Blues for Lovers). 1971: †Forbidden Knowledge (TV).*
† Co-directed

HENREID, Paul
(P. von Hernried) 1908–
Austrian-born actor with light, wavy hair and thoughtful expression. After a beginning in Austrian films, he fled to England, where he became a useful supporting player, then to Hollywood. Here, he seemed forever to be the refugee or stateless person, soon as star or semi-star opposite a number of dominant actresses in 'women's pictures'. He escaped typing in these, only to become equally bogged down in garishly lightweight swashbucklers. Has also directed. Billed until his Hollywood years as Paul von Hernried.
1933: Morgenrot. 1934: Hohe Schule. 1935: Nur ein Komödiant. Eva. Lachen am Freibad (US: Laugh at the Lido). 1937: Victoria the Great. 1939: Goodbye Mr Chips! An Englishman's Home (US: Madmen of Europe). 1940: Under Your Hat. Night Train to Munich (US: Night Train). 1941: Joan of Paris. 1942: Now, Voyager. Casablanca. 1943: In Our Time. Devotion (released 1946). 1944: Hollywood Canteen. The Conspirators. Between Two

HENRY, William (Bill) 1918–
Sandy-haired American actor with small, pleasant, yet slightly strained features. In show business from the age of eight, he was a teenage Hollywood player before leading roles reached out for him as one of C. Aubrey Smith's four sons in *Four Men and a Prayer*. The others – George Sanders, Richard Greene and David Niven – all moved on to top stardom. But Henry, perhaps held back by lack of stature and of a forthright personality, never rose above minor action leads and, towards the late 1940s, gradually slipped back to third or fourth billing in minor westerns, then into character roles.
1926: Lord Jim. 1933: Best of Enemies. Adorable. 1934: The Thin Man. A Wicked Woman. 1935: Only Eight Hours. Society Doctor. China Seas. 1936: Tarzan Escapes! Exclusive Story. 1937: Double or Nothing. Madame X. Mama Runs Wild. 1938: Campus Confessions (GB: Fast Play). A Man to Remember. Jezebel. Four Men and a Prayer. Yellow Jack. The Arizona

Wildcat. *1939: Ambush. I'm from Missouri. Persons in Hiding. Television Spy. Geronimo. 1940: Emergency Squad. The Way of All Flesh. Parole Fixer. Queen of the Mob. Cherokee Strip (GB: Frontier Marshal). 1941: Blossoms in the Dust. Dance Hall. Scattergood Meets Broadway. Harmon of Michigan. 1942: A Gentleman After Dark. There's One Born Every Minute. Klondike Fury. Pardon My Stripes. Stardust on the Sage. Rubber Racketeers. Sweater Girl. 1943: I Escaped from the Gestapo (GB: No Escape). Sarong Girl. Alaska Highway. False Faces (GB: The Attorney's Dilemma). Calaboose. Johnny Come Lately (GB: Johnny Vagabond). Tornado. Women in Bondage. Nearly Eighteen. 1944: The Navy Way. The Lady and the Monster (GB: The Lady and the Doctor). Call of the South Seas. The Adventures of Mark Twain. The Silent Partner. 1946: The Invisible Informer. GI War Brides. The Mysterious Mr Valentine. The Fabulous Suzanne. 1947: Gun Talk. 1948: Women of the Night. Trail to San Antone. The Denver Kid. 1949: Death Valley Gunfighter. Streets of San Francisco. King of the Gamblers. 1950: The Old Frontier. Motor Patrol. Federal Man. 1951: Fury of the Congo. Valentino. 1952: What Price Glory? Torpedo Alley. Canadian Mounties vs. the Atomic Invaders (serial). Marshal of Cedar City. Savage Frontier. 1954: Secret of the Incas. Masterson of Kansas. 1955: New Orleans Uncensored (GB: Riot on Pier 6). A Bullet for Joey. Jungle Moon Men. A Life at Stake. Mister Roberts. Paris Follies of 1956. 1957: The Wings of Eagles. Spook Chasers. 1958: The Last Hurrah. The Lone Ranger and the Lost City of Gold. Gunsmoke in Tucson. 1959: The Horse Soldiers. 1960: Sergeant Rutledge. The Alamo. 1961: Two Rode Together. 1962: How the West Was Won. The Man Who Shot Liberty Valance. 1963: Donovan's Reef. 1964: Cheyenne Autumn. Taggart. 1967: El Dorado.*

HENSON, Leslie 1891–1957
British concert-party and revue comedian of lizard eyes, stocky build and florid complexion, popular in a few frantic farces from the British cinema of the 1930s, but almost entirely on stage, where he had started at 18. Married (second of three) to character actress Gladys Henson from 1926 to 1943. Father of actor Nicky Henson (qv).
*1916: *Wanted a Widow. *The Real Thing*

at Last. The Lifeguardsman. 1920: *Broken Bottles. Alf's Button. 1924: Tons of Money. 1927: *On with the Dance (series). 1930: A Warm Corner. 1931: The Sport of Kings. 1933: It's a Boy! The Girl from Maxim's. 1935: Oh Daddy! 1943: The Demi-Paradise (US: Adventure for Two). 1956: Home and Away.

HENSON, Nicky 1945–

Light-haired, youthful-looking British actor, mostly in light comedy roles calling for dash and aggressive masculinity. Like his father, stage comedian Leslie Henson (qv), he has had leading roles in films, but they have not made him a permanent star of the cinema. In the mid-1970s Henson seemed to be flavour-of-the-month in British films, but it soon melted away. Married to Una Stubbs (1938–) from 1969 to 1975. Later romantically involved with Susan Hampshire (qv) for several years, but this too broke up.

1963: Father Came Too. 1966: Doctor in Clover. 1967: Here We Go Round the Mulberry Bush. 1968: Witchfinder-General (US: The Conqueror Worm). Mosquito Squadron. Crooks and Coronets (US: Sophie's Place). 1970: There's a Girl in My Soup. 1971: All Coppers Are … 1972: The Love Ban. Psychomania (US: The Death Wheelers). 1973: Penny Gold. 1974: Vampira (US: Old Dracula). Bedtime with Rosie. 1975: The Bawdy Adventures of Tom Jones. 1977: No 1 of the Secret Service.

HEPBURN, Audrey
(Edda Hepburn-Ruston) 1929–
Wide-mouthed, dark-eyed, pencil-slim, Belgian-born actress of mixed parentage. She

made a few British and continental films before going to Hollywood and taking the movie capital by storm with her Oscar-winning performance in *Roman Holiday*. Her captivating charm and inimitable delivery kept her at the top in a number of glossily successful dramas, comedies and thrillers for the next 15 years. Comebacks since 1967 revealed her aspect as much changed, and were not terribly successful. Married to Mel Ferrer (first of two) from 1954 to 1968. Also Oscar-nominated for *Sabrina*, *The Nun's Story*, *Breakfast at Tiffany's* and *Wait Until Dark*.

1948: Nederland in 7 Lessen. 1951: Nous irons à Monte Carlo (GB: Monte Carlo Baby). Laughter in Paradise. One Wild Oat. Young Wives' Tale. The Lavender Hill Mob. 1952: Secret People. 1953: Roman Holiday. 1954: Sabrina (GB: Sabrina Fair). 1956: War and Peace. Funny Face. 1957: Love in the Afternoon. 1958: Mayerling (TV). The Nun's Story. Green Mansions. 1959: The Unforgiven. 1961: Breakfast at Tiffany's. 1962: The Children's Hour (GB: The Loudest Whisper). 1963: Charade. Paris When It Sizzles. 1964: My Fair Lady. 1966: How to Steal a Million. 1967: Two for the Road. Wait Until Dark. 1976: Robin and Marian. 1979: Bloodline/ Sidney Sheldon's Bloodline. 1981: They All Laughed.

HEPBURN, Katharine 1907–

Distinctively individual, copper-haired American actress with attractively grating New England diction and finely-structured features that exude determination and individuality. Usually seen as indomitable feminist aggressors or figures of history but also a whizz at sophisticated screwball comedy. Very choosy about scripts, she has had her ups and downs at the box-office, but gathered four Best Actress Oscars (*Morning Glory*, *Guess Who's Coming to Dinner*, *The Lion in Winter* and *On Golden Pond*) and seven further nominations along the way. For 25 years she was associated publicly and privately with Spencer Tracy, with whom she made eight films. Continued acting into her seventies despite suffering from Parkinson's Disease.

1933: Christopher Strong. Morning Glory. Little Women. 1934: Spitfire. Break of Hearts. The Little Minister. 1935: Alice Adams. Sylvia Scarlett. 1936: Mary of Scotland. A Woman Rebels. 1937: Quality Street. Stage Door.

1938: Bringing Up Baby. Holiday/ Unconventional Linda (GB: Free to Live). 1940: The Philadelphia Story. 1941: Woman of the Year. 1942: Keeper of the Flame. 1943: Stage Door Canteen. Women in Defense (narrator only). 1944: Dragon Seed. 1945: Without Love. 1946: Undercurrent. 1947: Song of Love. Sea of Grass. 1948: State of the Union (GB: The World and His Wife). 1949: Adam's Rib. 1951: The African Queen. 1952: Pat and Mike. 1955: Summer Madness (US: Summertime). 1956: The Rainmaker. The Iron Petticoat. 1957: Desk Set (GB: His Other Woman). 1959: Suddenly Last Summer. 1962: Long Day's Journey into Night. 1967: Guess Who's Coming to Dinner. 1968: The Lion in Winter. 1969: The Madwoman of Chaillot. 1971: The Trojan Women. 1973: The Glass Menagerie (TV). 1974: A Delicate Balance. 1975: Love Among the Ruins (TV. GB: cinemas). Rooster Cogburn. 1978: The Corn is Green (TV). Olly, Olly, Oxen Free. 1981: On Golden Pond. 1984: The Ultimate Solution of Grace Quigley (GB: Grace Quigley) 1986: Mrs Delafield Wants to Marry (TV).

HERLIE, Eileen (E. Herlihy) 1919–

Scottish-born actress with dark hair, twinkling brown eyes, high cheekbones and glowing complexion. She began her career with the Scottish National theatre company and has remained largely a stage star. The British cinema offered her some good roles (to which she brought her own inbuilt warmth), but not a career.

1946: Hungry Bill. 1948: Hamlet. 1950: The Angel with the Trumpet. 1953: The Story of Gilbert and Sullivan (US: The Great Gilbert and Sullivan). Isn't Life Wonderful! 1954: For Better, For Worse (US: Cocktails in the Kitchen). 1958: She Didn't Say No! 1962: Freud (GB: Freud – the Secret Passion). 1964: Hamlet. 1966: Heartbreak House (TV). 1969: The Sea Gull.

HERSHEY, Barbara (B. Herztine) 1947–

Pretty, smooth-skinned, dark-haired American actress with olive complexion and statuesque figure, at first in Disneyesque roles (e.g. TV's *The Monroes*), but soon in high drama that called for maximum exposure of her physical assets. Became one of Hollywood's great free spirits, living with David Carradine from 1969 to 1975 but, since their break-up,

cinema and TV have hardly maximized her undoubted talent. Acted as Barbara Seagull from 1973 to 1975.

1968: With Six You Get Egg Roll. Heaven with a Gun. 1969: Last Summer. The Liberation of L B Jones. 1970: The Pursuit of Happiness. 1971: The Baby Maker. 1972: Boxcar Bertha. Dealing: Or the Berkeley-to-Boston-Forty Bricks-Lost-Bag Blues. 1973: †Time to Run. 1974: †Vrooder's Hooch/The Crazy World of Julius Vrooder. †You and Me. 1975: †Diamonds. Love Comes Quietly. 1976: Trial by Combat (US: Dirty Knights' Work). The Last Hard Men. Flood! (TV). 1977: In the Glitter Palace (TV). Sunshine Christmas (TV). The Stuntman (released 1980). 1978: Just a Little Inconvenience (TV). 1979: A Man Called Intrepid (TV). 1980: Angel on My Shoulder (TV). 1981: Take This Job and Shove It. Americana. The Entity. 1983: The Right Stuff. 1984: The Natural. 1985: My Wicked, Wicked Ways – The Legend of Errol Flynn (TV). Hannah and Her Sisters. 1986: Passion Flower (TV). Hoosiers.

† As Barbara Seagull

HERSHOLT, Jean 1886–1956

Square-faced Danish actor, sometimes moustachioed, with a bush of dark hair. A handsome leading man (and sometimes villain) of silent films. After he reached the top in the early twenties, his accent and age led him into character roles with sound, and he soon became the screen's best-known doctor. His most famous character, Dr Christian, a kindly country physician, was created on radio, and

carried through into films and, later, television. Two special Oscars, one for Motion Picture Relief Fund work, the other for services to the industry. Also has an Oscar – the Jean Hersholt Humanitarian Award – named after him. Died from cancer.

*1913: *Short film in Denmark. 1915: The Disciple. Don Quixote. 1916: Hell's Hinges. The Aryan. The Deserter. Kinkaid – Gambler. Bullets and Brown Eyes. 1917: Love Aflame. The Terror. Southern Justice. The Saintly Sinner. Stormy Knights. 49–17. The Greater Law. Fighting for Love. The Show-Down. The Soul Herder. 1918: Princess Virtue. Madame Spy. 1919: In the Land of the Setting Sun. 1920: Merely Mary Ann. The Red Lane. The Servant in the House. The Deceiver. 1921: The Golden Trail. A Certain Rich Man. The Four Horsemen of the Apocalypse. Man of the Forest. 1922: Tess of the Storm Country. The Gray Dawn. Golden Dreams. When Romance Rides. The Stranger's Banquet. Heart's Haven. 1923: Quicksand. Red Lights. Greed (released 1925). Jazzmania. Torment. 1924: Sinners in Silk. Cheap Kisses. So Big. *The City of Stars. The Woman on the Jury. Her Night of Romance. 1925: A Woman's Faith. If Marriage Fails. Dangerous Innocence. Fifth Avenue Models. Stella Dallas. Don Q, Son of Zorro. 1926: My Old Dutch. Flames. The Greater Glory. It Must Be Love. The Old Soak. 1927: The Wrong Mr Wright. 1928: Alias the Deacon. The Student Prince in Old Heidelberg (GB: The Student Prince). The Secret Hour. Jazz Mad. Give and Take. The Battle of the Sexes. 13 Washington Square. 1929: Abie's Irish Rose. The Younger Generation. The Girl on the Barge. Modern Love. You Can't Buy Love. 1930: The Cat Creeps. Hell Harbor. Mamba. The Climax. The Case of Sergeant Grischa. East is West. Third Alarm. Viennese Nights. A Soldier's Plaything (GB: A Soldier's Pay). 1931: Susan Lenox, Her Fall and Rise (GB: The Rise of Helga). The Sin of Madelon Claudet (GB: The Lullaby). Phantom of Paris. Transatlantic. Private Lives. Daybreak. 1932: Beast of the City. Grand Hotel. Are You Listening? Night Court (GB: Justice for Sale). Emma. Skyscraper Souls. New Morals for Old. Hearts of Humanity. Unashamed. Flesh. The Mask of Fu Manchu. 1933: The Crime of the Century. Son of the Eagle. Dinner at Eight. The Late Christopher Bean (GB: Christopher Bean). 1934: Men in White. The Cat and the Fiddle. The Fountain. The Painted Veil. 1935: Break of Hearts. Mark of the Vampire. Murder in the Fleet. 1936: Sins of Man. The Tough Guy. The Country Doctor. Reunion (US: Hearts in Reunion). One in a Million. His Brother's Wife. 1937: Heidi. Seventh Heaven. 1938: I'll Give a Million. Happy Landing. Alexander's Ragtime Band. Five of a Kind. 1939: Mr Moto in Danger Island (GB: Mr Moto on Danger Island). Meet Dr Christian. 1940: Courageous Dr Christian. Dr Christian Meets the Women. Remedy for Riches. 1941: Melody for Three. They Meet Again. 1943: Stage Door Canteen. 1948: *Jean Hersholt Party. 1949: Dancing in the Dark. 1952: *Hollywood Night at 21 Club. 1954: Run for Cover. 1955: *Hollywood Shower of Stars.*

HESTON, Charlton

(John C. Carter) 1923–

Granite-faced, deep-voiced, light-haired American star, a big man with barrel chest, aquiline nose and noble bearing. He started in outdoor action films, but could express anguish, sincerity and zeal with equal conviction, assets which prompted Cecil B. DeMille to set him up for a lifetime of epic service by casting him as Moses in *The 10 Commandments*. *Ben-Hur* won him an Academy Award; small-scale successes like *Will Penny* revealed more of the man beneath the muscle. Married actress Lydia Clarke in 1944.

*1941: Peer Gynt. 1949: Julius Caesar. 1950: Dark City. 1952: The Greatest Show on Earth. The Savage. Ruby Gentry. 1953: Pony Express. The President's Lady. Arrowhead. Bad for Each Other. *Three Lives. 1954: Secret of the Incas. The Naked Jungle. The Far Horizons. 1955: The Private War of Major Benson. Lucy Gallant. 1956: Three Violent People. Forbidden Area (TV). The 10 Commandments. 1958: Touch of Evil. Point of No Return (TV). The Buccaneer. The Big Country. 1959: The Wreck of the Mary Deare. Ben-Hur. 1961: El Cid. 1962: *Five Cities of June (narrator only). The Pigeon That Took Rome. 55 Days at Peking. Diamond Head. 1964: Major Dundee. 1965: The Greatest Story Ever Told. The Agony and the Ecstasy. The War Lord. *The Egyptologists (narrator only). 1966: Khartoum. *While I Run This Race (narrator only). 1967: Counterpoint. All About People. Planet of the Apes. Will Penny. 1969: Rowan and Martin at the Movies. Number One. The Heart of Variety. Beneath the Planet of the Apes. The Festival Game. 1970: Julius Caesar. King: a Filmed Record . . . Montgomery to Memphis (and narrator). The Hawaiians (GB: Master of the Islands). 1971: The Omega Man. †Antony and Cleopatra. 1972: Skyjacked. Call of the Wild. *Our Active Earth (narrator only). 1973: Soylent Green. The Three Musketeers (The Queen's Diamonds). *Lincoln's Gettysburg Address (narrator only). 1974: Earthquake. The Four Musketeers (The Revenge of Milady). Airport 1975. 1975: *The Fun of Your Life (narrator only). 1976: The Last Hard Men. Two Minute Warning. Midway (GB: Battle of Midway). America at the Movies (narrator only). 1977: The Prince and the Pauper (US: Crossed Swords). Gray Lady Down. 1979: The Mountain Men. 1980: The*

Awakening. 1982: †Mother Lode. 1984: Nairobi Affair (TV).

† And directed

HEYWOOD, Anne
(Violet Pretty) 1930–
Dark-haired, widely-smiling British actress with distinctive high cheekbones: a beauty contest winner who worked hard to become recognized as a serious actress. Although successful, especially in one film, *The Fox*, she has not often been fortunate in her choice of parts, and has accepted some pretty weird assignments. Still, there can be few better-looking women of her age in the world. Married for more than 20 years to producer Raymond Stross.
1951: †Lady Godiva Rides Again. 1956: Find the Lady. Checkpoint. 1957: Doctor at Large. The Depraved. Dangerous Exile. Violent Playground. 1958: Floods of Fear. 1959: The Heart of a Man. Upstairs and Downstairs. Carthage in Flames. 1960: A Terrible Beauty (US: The Night Fighters). 1961: Petticoat Pirates. Stork Talk. 1962: Vengeance (US: The Brain). 1963: The Very Edge. 1964: 90 Degrees in the Shade. 1967: The Fox. 1968: The Awful Story of the Nun of Monza. 1969: The Chairman (GB: The Most Dangerous Man in the World). Midas Run (GB: A Run on Gold). 1971: I Want What I Want. 1972: Assassino ... e al telefono (GB: The Killer is on the Phone). 1973: The Nun and the Devil. Trader Horn. 1975: Dance in the Open Air Under the Elms. 1978: Good Luck, Miss Wyckoff. 1979: Ring of Darkness. 1984: Secrets of the Phantom Caverns.

† As Violet Pretty

HICKS, Sir Seymour
(Arthur S. Hicks) 1871–1949
British star of stage comedies, and actor-manager who married his oft-time stage partner, Ellaline Terriss (1871–1971). After a few early silents, he became the first British actor to take a company to the World War II battlefront. With the coming of sound Hicks, now a character star, transferred several of his stage hits to the screen. Knighted in 1934.
*1907: Seymour Hicks edits the Tatler. 1913: *Seymour Hicks and Ellaline Terriss. David Garrick. Scrooge. 1914: Always Tell Your Wife. 1915: A Prehistoric Love Story. 1923:*

*Always Tell Your Wife (remake). 1927: Blighty. 1930: *Tell Tales. †Sleeping Partners. The Love Habit. 1931: ‡Glamour. Money for Nothing. 1934: The Secret of the Loch. 1935: Royal Cavalcade (US: Regal Cavalcade). Mr What's-His-Name. Vintage Wine. Scrooge (remake). 1936: Eliza Comes to Stay. It's You I Want. 1937: Change for a Sovereign. 1939: The Lambeth Walk. Young Man's Fancy. 1940: Pastor Hall. Busman's Honeymoon (US: Haunted Honeymoon). 1947: Fame is the Spur. 1948: Silent Dust.*

† Also directed ‡ Also co-directed

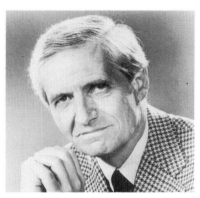

HILL, Arthur 1922–
Soft-spoken, sandy-haired (now grey), concerned-looking Canadian actor who began in British films, but spent most of his time on stage and television before taking a wide variety of second leads in the cinema from the early 1960s, proving most effective in sympathetic roles although clearly enjoying the occasional corrupt man-at-the-top.
1949: I Was a Male War Bride (GB: You Can't Sleep Here). Miss Pilgrim's Progress. 1950: The Undefeated. 1951: Scarlet Thread. Salute the Toff. 1952: Paul Temple Returns. 1953: A Day to Remember. 1954: Life with the Lyons (US: Family Affair). The Crowded Day. 1955: The Deep Blue Sea. Raising a Riot. 1961: The Young Doctors. 1962: The Ugly American. Focus (TV). 1963: In the Cool of the Day. 1965: Moment to Moment. 1966: Harper (GB: The Moving Target). 1967: Desperate Hours (TV). 1968: Petulia. The Fatal Mistake (TV). Don't Let the Angels Fall. 1969: The Chairman (GB: The Most Danger-

ous Man in the World). 1970: Rabbit, Run. The Andromeda Strain. The Pursuit of Happiness. The Other Man (TV). Vanished (TV). 1971: Owen Marshall – Counselor at Law (TV). 1973: Ordeal (TV). 1975: The Killer Elite. The Rivalry (TV). 1976: Futureworld. Judge Horton and the Scottsboro Boys (TV). Death Be Not Proud (TV). 1977: Tell Me My Name (TV). A Bridge Too Far. 1978: The Champ. 1979: Butch and Sundance The Early Days. A Little Romance. Hagen (TV). 1980: Dirty Tricks. The Ordeal of Dr Mudd (TV). The Return of Frank Cannon (TV). Revenge of the Stepford Wives (TV). 1981: Angel Dusted (TV). The Amateur. 1982: Making Love. 1983: Miss Lonelyhearts. 1984: The Guardian (TV). Love Leads the Way. 1985: A Fine Mess. One Magic Christmas.

HILL, Benny
(Alfred Hill) 1925–
Chubby, youthful-looking, brown-haired British comedian of leering innocence, once known as 'Britain's brightest boy'. His cheerful comedy made him immensely popular in the 1950s but despite a promising star debut in his first film no big career in the cinema followed. His periodic TV shows are rough-edged celebrations of picture-postcard vulgarity, with Hill himself doing broad impressions and singing leery madrigals.
*1956: Who Done It? 1960: Light Up the Sky. 1965: Those Magnificent Men in Their Flying Machines. 1968: Chitty Chitty Bang Bang. 1969: The Italian Job. *The Waiters. 1974: The Best of Benny Hill (TV material reshown in cinemas). 1984: Benny and Friends (video).*

HILL, Terence (Mario Girotti) 1939–
German-born star with piercing blue eyes, in Italian films as a teenager. For 15 years he played leads in home produce and supports in international ventures, before a change of hair colour (from dark to fair) and name nudged him to world-wide stardom in spaghetti westerns, often in tandem with Bud Spencer (Carlo Pedersoli, 1931–). Recent English-language films have oddly done less well, and Hill has returned to knockabout action in Italy with Spencer.
1951: †Vacanze col gangster. †La voca del silencio. 1953: †Villa Borghese. 1954: †Divisione folgore. 1955: †Gli sbandati. †La vena d'oro. 1956: †Mamma sconosciuta. †Guaglione.

†*Bambino. 1957: †La grande strada azzurra.*
†*Lazzarella. 1958: †La spada e la croce. 1959:*
†*Hannibal. †Carthage in Flames. †Il padrone*
delle ferriere. †Cerasella. 1960: †Un militaro e
mezzo. †Giuseppe venduto dei fratelli (GB:
Sold into Egypt. US: Joseph and his Brethren).
1961: †The Wonders of Aladdin. †Magdalena.
†*Seven Seas to Calais. 1962: †The Leopard.*
1964: †Die Lady (GB: Frustration. US:
Games of Desire). †Unter Geiern (GB: Among
Vultures. US: Arizona Wildcat). †La rivincita
di Ivanhoe. 1965: †Der Ölprinz (GB and US:
Rampage at Apache Wells). †Old Surehand:
erste Teil (GB and US: Flaming Frontier).
†*Duell vor Sonnenuntergang. †Winnetou II*
(GB and US: Last of the Renegades). †Du suif
dans l'Orient. †Ruf der Wälder. 1966: †La
grosse pagaille. †El Misterioso Senor Van Eyck.
†*Die Nibelungen I – Siegfried. †Die Nibelungen*
II – Whom the Gods Destroy (GB: Whom the
Gods Wish to Destroy). 1967: †Io non protesto,
io amo. Dio perdona, io no (GB: Blood River).
Rita of the West. 1968: Preparati la bara. I
quattro dell' Ave Maria (GB: Revenge in El
Paso). 1969: Barbaglia. La collina degli stivali
(US: Boot Hill). 1970: They Call Me Trinity.
The True and the False. La collera del vento.
1971: Trinity is Still My Name. 1972: Baron
Blood. E poi lo chiamarono il Magnifico (GB:
Man of the East). Piu forte ragazzi (GB: All
the Way Boys!). 1973: My Name is Nobody.
1974: Altrimenti ci Arrambiamo (GB: Watch
Out, We're Mad!). 1975: Porgi d'altra
guancia. Un genio, due compari, un pollo (US:
Nobody's the Greatest). 1976: Crime Busters.
1977: Mr Billion. March or Die. 1978: Super
Cops. Odds and Evens. 1979: I'm for the Hip-
popotamus. 1980: Super Snooper (US: Super
Fuzz). 1981: The Super Fire Busters. A Friend
is a Treasure. 1982: ‡Don Camillo. Hands Off
the Island. 1983: Go For It! 1984: The Crew.
1985: Don Camillo II.

† *As Mario Girotti*   ‡ *And directed*

HILLER, Dame Wendy 1912–

Pretty, chestnut-haired British actress with
rosy cheeks and fierce eyebrows. Filmed only
from time to time, but made her name with
an unmistakable voice and a series of deter-
minedly independent heroines. Drifted too
soon into a more mature kind of role in which
her individual approach was less effective,
although she took a best supporting actress
Oscar in *Separate Tables*. Created Dame in

1975. Further Oscar-nominated for *A Man
for All Seasons*.
*1937: Lancashire Luck. 1938: Pygmalion.
1941: Major Barbara. 1945: I Know Where
I'm Going. 1951: *To Be a Woman (narrator
only). Outcast of the Islands. 1953: Single-
Handed (US: Sailor of the King). 1957: How
to Murder a Rich Uncle. Something of Value.
*Bernard Shaw. 1958: Separate Tables. 1960:
Sons and Lovers. 1963: Toys in the Attic. 1966:
A Man for All Seasons. 1969: David Cop-
perfield (TV. GB: cinemas). 1974: Murder
on the Orient Express. 1976: Voyage of the
Damned. 1978: The Cat and the Canary. 1980:
The Elephant Man. 1982: Making Love. Wit-
ness for the Prosecution (TV). 1983: Attracta
(TV). 1985: The Importance of Being Earnest
(TV).*

HOBSON, Valerie 1917–

Tall, elegant, full-lipped, long-faced, Irish-
born leading lady in British films. Began at
16, spending two years in Hollywood in her
teens before returning to Britain, where she
remained quite popular, despite limited
output, for the next 15 years in upper-bracket
roles. In fact, it was a surprise when she
retired at 37. Now spends most of her time
working for Lepra, a leprosy relief charity
organization.
*1933: Eyes of Fate. 1934: The Path of Glory.
Two Hearts in Waltztime. Badger's Green.*
†*Great Expectations. Life Returns (released
1938). 1935: Oh, What a Night! Strange
Wives. Rendezvous at Midnight. Bride of
Frankenstein. The Werewolf of London. The
Mystery of Edwin Drood. 1936: Chinatown*

*Squad. The Great Impersonation. Tugboat
Princess. The Secret of Stamboul. No Escape.
1937: Jump for Glory (US: When Thief Meets
Thief). 1938: The Drum (US: Drums). This
Man is News. 1939: Q Planes (US: Clouds
Over Europe). The Spy in Black (US: U-
Boat 29). The Silent Battle (US: Continental
Express). This Man in Paris. 1940: Con-
traband (US: Blackout). 1941: Atlantic Ferry
(US: Sons of the Sea). 1942: Unpublished
Story. 1943: Adventures of Tartu (US:
Tartu). 1946: The Years Between. Great
Expectations. 1947: Blanche Fury. 1948: The
Small Voice (US: Hideout). 1949: Kind
Hearts and Coronets. Train of Events. The
Interrupted Journey. The Rocking Horse
Winner. 1952: The Card (US: The Promoter).
Who Goes There? (US: The Passionate
Sentry). Meet Me Tonight. The Voice of Mer-
rill (US: Murder Will Out). 1953: Back-
ground. 1954: Knave of Hearts (US: Lovers,
Happy Lovers).*

† *Scenes deleted from final release print*

HODIAK, John 1914–1955

Forthright, sincere, often-moustachioed
American leading actor with a harsh voice but
smoothly ingratiating manner. He tended to
be a bit stiff at times, but spent nine quite
profitable years at M-G-M, where he made
almost all of his films. Married to Anne Baxter
1946–1953. Died from a coronary thrombosis.
*1943: A Stranger in Town. I Dood It (GB:
By Hook or By Crook). Swing Shift Maisie
(GB: The Girl in Overalls). Song of Russia.
1944: Ziegfeld Follies (released 1946). Maisie
Goes to Reno (GB: You Can't Do That to
Me). Lifeboat. Sunday Dinner for a Soldier.
Marriage is a Private Affair. 1945: A Bell for
Adano. 1946: The Harvey Girls. Two Smart
People. Somewhere in the Night. 1947: Love
from a Stranger (GB: A Stranger Walked
In). The Arnelo Affair. Desert Fury. 1948:
Homecoming. Command Decision. The Bribe.
1949: Malaya (GB: East of the Rising Sun).
Battleground. Ambush. 1950: The Miniver
Story. A Lady without Passport. 1951: The
People against O'Hara. Night unto Morning.
Across the Wide Missouri. 1952: The Sellout.
*Screen Snapshots No. 206. Battle Zone. 1953:
Mission over Korea (GB: Eyes of the Skies).
Ambush at Tomahawk Gap. Conquest of Coch-
ise. 1954: Dragonfly Squadron. 1955: Trial.
1956: On the Threshold of Space.*

Lucasta. 1950: The White Tower. 1951: Der schweigende Mund. 1952: Top Secret (US: Mr Potts Goes to Moscow). 1953: The House of the Arrow. 1954: Prisoner of War. 1955: The Seven Year Itch. 1956: War and Peace. 1957: A Farewell to Arms. 1958: The Plot to Kill Stalin (TV). Tempest. The Key. Heart of Darkness (TV). 1960: In the Presence of Mine Enemies (TV). Assassination Plot at Teheran (TV). Victory (TV). 1961: Mr Sardonicus (GB: Sardonicus). 1962: Boys' Night Out. The Wonderful World of the Brothers Grimm. The Mooncussers (TV. GB: cinemas). 1963: The Long Ships. 1964: Joy in the Morning. 1966: Funeral in Berlin. 1967: Billion Dollar Brain. Assignment to Kill. The Happening. Jack of Diamonds. 1968: Dr Jekyll and Mr Hyde (TV). The Madwoman of Chaillot. 1970: The Executioner. Song of Norway. 1974: The Tamarind Seed. 1975: One of Our Own (TV). The Curse of the Hope Diamond (TV).

HOPE, Bob (Leslie Hope) 1903–
Dark-haired, ski-slope-nosed, English-born Hollywood star comedian, in America from childhood. After a slow start, his film career really blossomed with The Cat and the Canary and he remained at his funniest throughout the forties, a period which saw the beginning of his friendly rivalry with Bing Crosby – in and out of the 'Road' films – and made him one of the world's most popular stars, in roles which highlighted his ability to get into situations which exposed the yellow streak running down his back. From the mid-fifties the standard of his material fell away. Special Oscars 1940, 1944, 1952, 1965.
1934: *Paree, Paree. *Going Spanish. *Soup for Nuts. 1935: *Watch the Birdie. *The Old Grey Mayor. *Double Exposure. 1936: *Calling all Tars. *Shop Talk. 1938: The Big Broadcast of 1938. College Swing (GB: Swing, Teacher, Swing). Give Me a Sailor. Thanks for the Memory. *Don't Hook Now. 1939: Never Say Die. Some Like It Hot. The Cat and the Canary. 1940: Road to Singapore. The Ghost Breakers. 1941: Caught in the Draft. *Cavalcade of the Academy Awards. Road to Zanzibar. Louisiana Purchase. Nothing But the Truth. 1942: Road to Morocco. My Favorite Blonde. Star Spangled Rhythm. They Got Me Covered. 1943: *Welcome to Britain. Let's Face It. *Show Business at War. 1944: The Princess and the Pirate. 1945: *All-Star Bond Rally.

Duffy's Tavern. Road to Utopia. *Hollywood Victory Caravan. 1946: Monsieur Beaucaire. 1947: My Favorite Brunette. Variety Girl. Where There's Life. Road to Rio. 1948: *Radio Broadcasting Today. The Paleface. *Screen Snapshots No. 166. *Rough But Hopeful. 1949: *Honor Caddie. Sorrowful Jones. The Great Lover. 1950: Fancy Pants. *On Stage Everybody! 1951: My Favorite Spy. The Lemon Drop Kid. 1952: The Greatest Show on Earth. Son of Paleface. Road to Bali. Off Limits (GB: Military Policemen). *A Sporting Oasis. 1953: Scared Stiff. Here Come the Girls. Casanova's Big Night. 1954: *Screen Snapshots No. 224. 1955: The Seven Little Foys. 1956: That Certain Feeling. The Iron Petticoat. 1957: Beau James. *The Heart of Show Business. 1958: Paris Holiday. *Showdown at Ulcer Gulch. 1959: The Five Pennies. Alias Jesse James. 1960: The Facts of Life. 1961: Bachelor in Paradise. *Kitty Caddy (voice only). 1962: The Road to Hong Kong. 1963: Critic's Choice. A Global Affair. Call Me Bwana. 1965: I'll Take Sweden. 1966: The Oscar. Boy, Did I Get a Wrong Number. *Hollywood Star-Spangled Revue. Not With My Wife You Don't. 1967: Eight on the Lam (GB: Eight on the Run). The Movie Maker (TV). 1968: The Private Navy of Sergeant O'Farrell. 1969: How to Commit Marriage. 1972: Cancel My Reservation. 1978: The Muppet Movie. 1979: Ken Murray's Shooting Stars. 1985: Spies Like Us. 1986: A Masterpiece of Murder (TV).

HOPKINS, Anthony 1937–
Stocky, dark-haired Welsh actor capable of playing a wide range of ages. From the beginning, he expressed disinterest in becoming a conventional leading man and showed a preference for the stage. Still, leading roles have pursued the reluctant star, who has most recently been seen as characters under various kinds of unusual stresses.
1967: The White Bus. 1968: The Lion in Winter. 1969: Hamlet. The Looking Glass War. 1971: When Eight Bells Toll. Young Winston. 1973: A Doll's House (Garland). 1974: QB VII (TV). Juggernaut. The Girl from Petrovka. All Creatures Great and Small. 1975: Dark Victory (TV). 1976: The Lindbergh Kidnapping Case (TV). Victory at Entebbe (TV. GB: cinemas). 1977: Audrey Rose. A Bridge Too Far. 1978: International Velvet. Magic. 1979: Mayflower: the Pilgrims'

Adventure (TV). 1980: A Change of Seasons. The Elephant Man. 1981: The Bunker (TV). Peter and Paul (TV). 1982: The Hunchback of Notre Dame (TV). 1984: Io e il duce (US: Mussolini and I). Arch of Triumph (TV). The Bounty. 1985: Guilty Conscience (TV). 1986: The Good Father (TV). 84 Charing Cross Road.

HOPKINS, Miriam
(Ellen M. Hopkins) 1902–1972
A blue-eyed American blonde who looked just like a thirties version of Cybill Shepherd, Miriam Hopkins was exactly right for her time, her theatrically chic and faintly bitchy sophistication dovetailing beautifully with Lubitsch comedies and other high-gloss offerings to give her star charisma. The passing of the thirties reduced her to ordinariness and she faded from the cinema scene. Married to director Anatole Litvak (1937–1939), third of four. Died from a heart attack.
1928: *The Home Girl. 1930: Fast and Loose. 1931: The Smiling Lieutenant (and French-language version). Twenty Four Hours (GB: The Hours Between). Dr Jekyll and Mr Hyde. 1932: The World and the Flesh. Two Kinds of Women. Trouble in Paradise. Dancers in the Dark. 1933: The Story of Temple Drake. Design for Living. The Stranger's Return. 1934: All of Me. She Loves Me Not. The Richest Girl in the World. 1935: Barbary Coast. Becky Sharp. Splendor. 1936: These Three. Men Are Not Gods. 1937: Woman Chases Man. The Woman I Love (GB: The Woman Between). 1938: Wise Girl. 1939: The Old Maid. 1940: Virginia City. The Lady with Red Hair. 1942: A Gentleman After Dark. 1943: Old Acquaintance. 1944: *Skirmish on the Home Front. 1949: The Heiress. 1951: The Mating Season. 1952: Carrie. The Outcasts of Poker Flat. 1962: The Children's Hour (GB: The Loudest Whisper). 1965: Fanny Hill. 1966: The Chase. 1970: Comeback (later copyrighted 1973 as Savage Intruder).

HOPPER, Dennis 1935–
Fair-haired, sharp-featured American actor, distantly related to Hedda and William Hopper. Began as bad brothers and whining, wild-eyed psychopaths, then graduated to hippy heroes. Took the world by storm with Easy Rider and, although his pet project The Last Movie was much less successful, he was something of a cult figure by the late 1970s.

1954: *Johnny Guitar.* 1955: *I Died a Thousand Times. Rebel Without a Cause.* 1956: *The Steel Jungle. Giant. Gunfight at the OK Corral.* 1957: *The Story of Mankind.* 1958: *From Hell to Texas* (GB: *Manhunt*). 1959: *The Young Land.* 1960: *Key Witness.* 1961: *Night Tide.* 1963: *Tarzan and Jane Regained . . . Sort Of.* 1965: *The Sons of Katie Elder.* 1966: *Planet of Blood.* 1967: *The Glory Stompers. Cool Hand Luke. Panic in the City. Hang 'Em High. The Trip.* 1968: *Head.* 1969: *True Grit.* †*Easy Rider.* 1970: *The American Dreamer.* 1971: †*The Last Movie. Crush Proof.* 1973: *Kid Blue/Dime Box. Hex.* 1975: *James Dean – The First American Teenager. The Sky is Falling.* 1976: *Tracks. Mad Mog Morgan* (GB: *Mad Dog*). 1977: *The American Friend. Les apprentis sorciers.* 1978: *L'ordre et la sécurité du monde. Couleur chair. The Human Highway* (released 1983). 1979: *Apocalypse Now. Wild Times* (TV). 1980: †*Cebe/Out of the Blue. King of the Mountain.* 1981: *Reborn.* 1982: *Bikers' Heaven.* 1983: *White Star* (released 1985). *Jungle Warriors. The Osterman Weekend. Rumble Fish.* 1984: *The Utterly Monstrous Mind-Roasting Summer of O C and Stiggs. The Inside Man.* 1985: *My Science Project. Running Out of Luck. Stark* (TV). 1986: *The American Way. Blue Velvet. The Texas Chainsaw Massacre 2. River's Edge. Hoosiers. Black Widow.*

† *And directed*

HOPPER, Hedda (Elda Furry) 1890–1966
Svelte, glamorous, dark-haired American actress of above-average height. After more than 100 films in semi-leads ranging from heroine's friend to society matron, she opted for a new (and fabulously successful) career in middle-age, as a gossip columnist on the movie scene, becoming one of the two or three most powerful such ladies in Hollywood. Mother of character player/second lead William Hopper (1915–1970). Like her son, she died from pneumonia.

1916: *Battle of Hearts.* 1917: *Her Excellency, the Governor. Nearly Married. Seven Keys to Baldpate. The Food Gamblers.* 1919: *By Right of Purchase. Virtuous Wives. The Third Degree. Isle of Conquest.* 1920: *The Man Who Lost Himself. The New York Idea.* 1921: *Heedless Moths. Conceit.* 1922: *Women Men Marry. Sherlock Holmes. What's Wrong with Women?* 1923: *Reno. Has the World Gone Mad?* 1924: *Free Love. Another Scandal. Happiness. Miami. Gambling Wives. Sinners in Silk. Why Men Leave Home. The Snob.* 1925: *Déclassée. Zander the Great. Raffles the Amateur Cracksman. Borrowed Finery. Dangerous Innocence. The Teaser. Her Market Value.* 1926: *Lew Tyler's Wives. Don Juan.* *Mona Lisa. Fools of Fashion. Dance Madness. Skinner's Dress Suit. The Silver Treasure. The Caveman. Pleasures of the Rich. Obey the Law.* 1927: *The Drop Kick. Orchids and Ermine. Venus of Venice. Children of Divorce. Wings. Adam and Evil. The Cruel Truth. One Woman to Another. Matinee Ladies. A Reno Divorce. Black Tears.* 1928: *Giving In. Diamond Handcuffs. Green Grass Widows. Runaway Girls. The Whip Woman. Port of Missing Girls. Love and Learn. The Chorus Kid. Undressed. The Companionate Marriage* (GB: *The Jazz Bride*). 1929: *Girls Gone Wild. Song of Kentucky. The Last of Mrs Cheyney. His Glorious Night. Hurricane. The Racketeer* (GB: *Love's Conquest*). *Half Marriage.* 1930: *Our Blushing Brides. War Nurse. Murder Will Out. High Society Blues. Such Men Are Dangerous. Divorcee. Let Us Be Gay. Holiday.* 1931: *Shipmates. Up for Murder. Flying High* (GB: *Happy Landing*). *The Prodigal. The Easiest Way. Men Call It Love. Strangers May Kiss. Rebound. Mystery Train. Good Sport. Common Law. A Tailor Made Man.* 1932: *West of Broadway. Night World. Speak Easily. Skyscraper Souls. Downstairs. As You Desire Me. The Unwritten Law.* *The Stolen Jools* (GB: *The Slippery Pearls*). *The Man Who Played God.* 1933: *Pilgrimage. Man Must Fight. Beauty for Sale* (GB: *Beauty*). *The Barbarian* (GB: *A Night in Cairo*). 1934: *Little Man, What Now? Harold Teen* (GB: *The Dancing Fool*). *Bombay Mail. Let's Be Ritzy* (GB: *Millionaire for a Day*). *No Ransom* (GB: *Bonds of Honour*). 1935: *One Frightened Night. Lady Tubbs* (GB: *The Gay Lady*). *Alice Adams. I Live My Life. Society Fever. Three Kids and a Queen* (GB: *The Baxter Millions*). 1936: *Bunker Bean* (GB: *His Majesty Bunker Bean*). *Dracula's Daughter. Dark Hour. Doughnuts and Society* (GB: *Stepping into Society*). 1937: *You Can't Buy Luck. Topper. Nothing Sacred. Dangerous Holiday. Artists and Models. Vogues of 1938.* 1938: *Thanks for the Memory. Maid's Night Out. Tarzan's Revenge. Dangerous to Know.* 1939: *The Women. That's Right – You're Wrong. Midnight. Laugh It Off. What a Life!*

1940: *Cross Country Romance. Queen of the Mob.* 1941: *Life with Henry. I Wanted Wings.* 1942: *Reap the Wild Wind.* 1946: *Breakfast in Hollywood* (GB: *The Mad Hatter*). 1950: *Sunset Boulevard.* 1960: *Pepe.* 1964: *The Patsy.* 1966: *The Oscar.*

HORNE, Lena 1917–
Lithe, dynamic, barnstorming songstress who put more emotion into songs – hot or sweet – than some did into acting. Her splendid voice and pleasant personality made her the first black performer to sign a long-term contract with a major studio (M-G-M), but they frittered her away in all-black films and guest appearances.

1938: *The Duke is Tops.* 1940: *Harlem Hotshots.* 1942: *Boogie Woogie Dream. Harlem on Parade. Panama Hattie.* 1943: *I Dood It* (GB: *By Hook Or By Crook*). *Swing Fever. Thousands Cheer. Cabin in the Sky. Stormy Weather.* 1944: *Ziegfeld Follies* (released 1946). *Broadway Rhythm. Two Girls and a Sailor.* 1946: *Till the Clouds Roll By.* *Studio Visit.* *Mantan Messes Up.* 1948: *Words and Music.* 1950: *Duchess of Idaho.* 1956: *Meet Me in Las Vegas* (GB: *Viva Las Vegas!*). 1969: *Death of a Gunfighter.* 1978: *The Wiz.*

HORTON, Robert
(Mead Howard Horton) 1924–
Husky is the only word for this Hollywood six-footer with sandy hair, broad smile and big baritone voice. Signed a contract with M-G-M, but didn't get the musical roles that came the way of his first wife Barbara Ruick (1932–1974). The studio put him into muscular action films. He failed to make the front rank, but subsequently enjoyed tremendous

popular acclaim as the scout in TV's *Wagon Train* (1957–1961). After minor leading roles, he left films to sing in nightclubs with his second wife.

1951: The Tanks Are Coming. Return of the Texan. 1952: Pony Soldier (GB: MacDonald of the Canadian Mounties). Apache War Smoke. 1953: Code Two. Bright Road. Arena. The Story of Three Loves. 1954: Men of the Fighting Lady. Prisoner of War. 1956: This Man is Armed. Lady in Fear (TV. GB: cinemas). 1966: The Dangerous Days of Kiowa Jones (TV. GB: cinemas). 1969: The Green Slime. The Spy Killer (TV). 1970: Foreign Exchange (TV).

HOUSTON, Donald 1923–
Handsome golden-haired Welshman who shot to prominence when given the star role in his first film. But his immobile style was of little help in some gloomy melodramas, and he gradually lost his star status as the fifties wore on. Later mixed comedy with men of violence. Brother of actor Glyn Houston (1926–). Married actress Brenda Hogan (1928–).

*1949: The Blue Lagoon. A Run for Your Money. 1950: Dance Hall. 1952: My Death is a Mockery. Crow Hollow. 1953: The Red Beret (US: Paratrooper). Small Town Story. The Large Rope. *Point of No Return. The Case of Express Delivery. 1954: Doctor in the House. Devil's Point (US: Devil's Harbor). The Happiness of Three Women (US: Wishing Well). 1955: The Flaw. Doublecross. Return to the Desert. 1956: Find the Lady. The Girl in the Picture. 1957: Yangtse Incident (US: Battle Hell). The Surgeon's Knife. *Every Valley (narrator only). 1958: A Question of Adultery. The Man Upstairs. Room at the Top. 1959: *Jessy. Danger Within (US: Breakout). 1961: The Mark. *A Letter for Wales (and narrator). 1962: The 300 Spartans. Twice Round the Daffodils. The Longest Day. The Prince and the Pauper. Maniac. 1963: Doctor in Distress. Carry On Jack (US: Carry On Venus). 1964: 633 Squadron. 1965: A Study in Terror (US: Fog). 1967: The Viking Queen. 1968: Where Eagles Dare. The Bushbaby. 1969: A Prince for Wales (narrator only). 1970: My Lover, My Son. 1972: Sunstruck. 1973: Tales that Witness Madness. 1976: Voyage of the Damned. 1980: The Sea Wolves. 1981: Clash of the Titans.*

HOWARD, John (J. Cox) 1913–
Sturdy, businesslike, oft-moustachioed, brown-haired American actor. He made a forthright Bulldog Drummond in a series of films at Paramount, but his career, not helped by being cast as stuffy 'other men', seemed to be torpedoed by his (distinguished) wartime service. He found it impossible to regain his prewar footing, but did gain a measure of success in two popular television series of the fifties.

1935: †Four Hours to Kill. †Car 99. Annapolis Farewell (GB: Gentlemen of the Navy). Millions in the Air. 1936: Soak the Rich. 13 Hours by Air. Border Flight. Easy to Take. Valiant is the Word for Carrie. 1937: Let Them Live! (GB: Let Them Love). Mountain Music. Hold 'Em Navy (GB: That Navy Spirit). Hitting a New High. Penitentiary. Bulldog Drummond Comes Back. Lost Horizon. 1938: Touchdown Army (GB: Generals of Tomorrow). Bulldog Drummond's Revenge. Bulldog Drummond's Peril. Prison Farm. Arrest Bulldog Drummond. Bulldog Drummond in Africa. 1939: Disputed Passage. Bulldog Drummond's Secret Police. Bulldog Drummond's Bride. Grand Jury Secrets. What a Life. 1940: Green Hell. Man from Dakota (GB: Arouse and Beware). Texas Rangers Ride Again. The Mad Doctor (GB: A Date with Destiny). The Philadelphia Story. 1941: Father Takes a Wife. Tight Shoes. The Invisible Woman. Three Girls About Town. A Tragedy at Midnight. The Man Who Returned to Life. 1942: Submarine Raider. Isle of Missing Men. The Undying Monster (GB: The Hammond Mystery). 1945: The Way to the Stars (US: Johnny in the Clouds). 1946: Le bataillon du ciel. 1947: Love from a Stranger (GB: A Stranger Walked In). 1948: I Jane Doe (GB: Diary of a Bride). 1949: The Fighting Kentuckian. 1950: Experiment Alcatraz. Radar Secret Service. 1951: ‡Dead Man's Voice. ‡The Man Who Wasn't There. ‡The Yellow Ticket. ‡The Innocent Lion. ‡The Bandaged Hand. ‡Where Time Stood Still. 1952: Models Inc (later Call Girl. GB: That Kind of Girl). 1954: Make Haste to Live. The High and the Mighty. 1957: Unknown Terror. 1966: Destination Inner Space. The Destructors. 1970: The Sky Bike. 1971: Buck and the Preacher. 1975: Capone.

† *As John Cox* ‡ *US TV shorts shown in GB cinemas*

HOWARD, Leslie
(L. H. Stainer, originally possibly Laszlo Horvarth) 1893–1943
Tall, sensitive and intelligent-looking British actor (from a Hungarian family) with unruly fair wavy hair. His faintly distant romantic appeal made him enormously popular in Britain in the 1930s, and he repeated his success in Hollywood, where his youthful looks kept him in important star roles well into his forties. But he was never more happily cast than in Britain as *The Scarlet Pimpernel*. He went missing on a wartime flight between Portugal and England: his plane was believed shot down. Nominated for Academy Awards in *Berkeley Square* and *Pygmalion*.

*1914: *The Heroine of Mons. 1917: The Happy Warrior. 1918: The Lackey and the Lady. 1920: *Five Pounds Reward. *Bookworms. 1930: Outward Bound. 1931: Never the Twain Shall Meet. A Free Soul. Devotion. Service for Ladies (US: Reserved for Ladies). Five and Ten (GB: Daughter of Luxury). 1932: Smilin' Through. The Animal Kingdom (GB: The Woman in His House). 1933: The Lady is Willing. Secrets. Berkeley Square. Captured. 1934: British Agent. Of Human Bondage. *Hollywood on Parade No. 13. The Scarlet Pimpernel. 1936: Romeo and Juliet. The Petrified Forest. 1937: It's Love I'm After. Stand-In. 1938: *Pygmalion. 1939: Gone with the Wind. Intermezzo: a Love Story (GB: Escape to Happiness). 1940: *Common Heritage (narrator only). 1941: †Pimpernel Smith (US: Mister V). *From the Four Corners. 49th Parallel (US: The Invaders). *The White Eagle (narrator only). 1942: †The First of the Few (US: Spitfire). 1943: ‡The Gentle Sex.*

† *Also directed* ‡ *Also co-directed*

HOWARD, Ron 1953–
Fresh-faced, fair-haired American actor (and latterly director), in show business from early childhood. He moved from *enfants terribles* to teenage innocents, then had an enormous hit on TV with *Happy Days*. 'I'm kind of dull' he has said about himself, which is true of Howard the actor and one good reason why he has concentrated more and more on his skills as director, becoming one of Hollywood's hottest behind-the-camera bets in the mid-1980s following his box-office hits with *Splash* and *Cocoon*.

1956: †*Frontier Woman.* 1958: †*The Journey.* 1959: †*Black December* (*TV*). 1961: †*The Music Man.* 1963: †*The Courtship of Eddie's Father.* 1965: †*The Village of the Giants.* 1966: †*Door-to-Door Maniac.* 1967: †*A Boy Called Nuthin'* (*TV*). 1970: *Smoke* (originally for *TV*). 1971: *The Wild Country.* 1973: *American Graffiti. Happy Mother's Day. Love George/Run, Stranger, Run.* 1974: *The Spikes Gang. The Migrants* (*TV*). *Huckleberry Finn* (*TV*). *Locusts* (*TV*). 1975: *The First Nudie Musical.* 1976: *Eat My Dust! The Shootist.* 1977: *Grand Theft Auto.* 1978: *Roger Corman: Hollywood's Wild Angel.* 1979: *More American Graffiti/The Party's Over/Purple Haze.* 1980: *Act of Love* (*TV*). 1981: *Fire on the Mountain* (*TV*). 1982: *Bitter Harvest* (*TV*).

† *As Ronny Howard*

As director: 1969: **Deed of Derring-Do.* 1977: *Grand Theft Auto.* 1979: *Cotton Candy* (*TV*). 1980: *Through the Magic Pyramid* (*TV*). 1981: *Skyward* (*TV*). 1982: *Night Shift.* 1983: *Rainbow Warrior.* 1984: *Splash.* 1985: *Cocoon.* 1986: *Gung Ho.*

HOWARD, Ronald (R. H. Stainer) 1916–
Suave, scholarly-looking British actor with fair, wavy hair, son of Leslie Howard. He forsook a journalistic career to devote himself full time to acting in the late forties, but was far too stolid to have his father's unique appeal and was usually to be found in British 'B' features. Despite presentable performances in a few international incursions (notably *Drango*), he did not become a big name. Mostly seen in later days as ex-Army types.

1941: *Pimpernel Smith* (*US: Mister V*). 1946: *While the Sun Shines.* 1947: *My Brother Jonathan. Night Beat.* 1948: *Bond Street. The Queen of Spades.* 1949: *Now Barabbas was a robber ...* 1950: *Portrait of Clare. Double Confession.* 1951: *Flesh and Blood. The Browning Version. Assassin for Hire. Night Was Our Friend.* 1952: *Wide Boy.* 1953: **La même route. Black Orchid. Street Corner* (*US: Both Sides of the Law*). *Noose for a Lady. Glad Tidings. Flannelfoot. The World's a Stage* (series: narrator only). 1954: *The Thirteenth Green.* 1956: *Drango. The Hideout.* 1957: *Light Fingers. The House in the Woods. I Accuse!* 1958: *Moment of Indiscretion. Gideon's Day* (*US: Gideon of Scotland Yard*). 1959: *No Trees in the Street. Man Accused. Babette Goes to War. Compelled. The Malpas Mystery.* 1961: *The Naked Edge. Murder She Said. Come September. The Monster of Highgate Ponds. Bomb in the High Street. The Spanish Sword.* 1962: *KIL 1. Fate Takes a Hand. Live Now – Pay Later. Nurse on Wheels.* 1963: *The Bay of Saint Michel* (*US: Pattern for Plunder*). *Siege of the Saxons.* 1964: *The Curse of the Mummy's Tomb. Week-End à Zuydcoote* (*GB and US: Weekend at Dunkirk*). 1965: *You Must Be Joking!* 1967: *Africa – Texas Style.* 1969: *Run a Crooked Mile* (*TV*). 1971: *The Hunting Party.* 1974: *Persecution.* 1975: *Take a Hard Ride.* 1980: *Act of Love* (*TV*).

HOWARD, Sydney 1884–1946
Portly British comedian whose clenched teeth and twisted expression could as easily express disdain or despair. Popular in concert parties, he came to films with the beginnings of sound and soon became the star of a number of medium-budget comedies which capitalized on his flapping gestures and dignified panics. He tried top character roles with some success in the war years; a press campaign to have him restored to major comedies in the postwar period was foiled by his early death from a heart attack at 61.

1929: *Splinters.* 1930: *French Leave.* 1931: *Tilly of Bloomsbury. Almost a Divorce. Splinters in the Navy. Up for the Cup.* 1932: *The Mayor's Nest. It's a King!* 1933: *Up for the Derby. Night of the Garter. Trouble.* 1934: *It's a Cop!* 1935: *Where's George?/The Hope of His Side.* 1936: *Fame. Chick.* 1937: *Splinters in the Air. What a Man!* 1939: *Shipyard Sally.*

1940: *Tilly of Bloomsbury* (remake). 1941: *Once a Crook.* **Mr Proudfoot Shows a Light.* 1943: *When We Are Married.* 1945: *Flight from Folly.*

HOWARD, Trevor 1916–
Brown-haired, sandpaper-voiced, intensely-staring British actor who moved from stage to films in his late twenties, rose rapidly to the top via *Brief Encounter* and proved equally at home as hero or villain in a star run of 20 years. Although there were too many red-faced unworthy cameos in later years, the right part showed that Howard still had the stuff of great acting in him. Married to Helen Cherry (qv) since 1944. Oscar nominee for *Sons and Lovers.*

1944: *Volga-Volga* (dubbed voice). *The Way Ahead.* 1945: *The Way to the Stars* (*US: Johnny in the Clouds*). *Brief Encounter.* 1946: *I See a Dark Stranger* (*US: The Adventuress*). *Green for Danger.* 1947: *So Well Remembered. They Made Me a Fugitive* (*US: I Became a Criminal*). 1948: *The Passionate Friends* (*US: One Woman's Story*). 1949: *The Third Man.* 1950: *Golden Salamander. Odette. The Clouded Yellow.* 1951: *Lady Godiva Rides Again. Outcast of the Islands.* 1952: *Gift Horse* (*US: Glory at Sea*). 1953: *The Heart of the Matter.* 1954: *The Stranger's Hand. Les Amants du tage* (*GB: The Lovers of Lisbon*). **April in Portugal* (voice only). 1955: *Cockleshell Heroes.* 1956: *Deception* (*TV. GB: cinemas*). *Around the World in 80 Days. Run for the Sun.* 1957: *Interpol* (*US: Pickup Alley*). *Manuela* (*US: Stowaway Girl*). 1958: *The Roots of Heaven. The Key.* 1960: *Moment of Danger* (*US: Malaga*). *The Hiding Place* (*TV*). *Sons and Lovers.* 1962: *Mutiny on the Bounty. The Lion.* 1963: *Man in the Middle.* 1964: *Father Goose.* 1965: *Operation Crossbow* (*US: The Great Spy Mission*). *The Liquidator. Morituri* (*GB: The Saboteur – Code Name Morituri*). *Von Ryan's Express.* 1966: *The Poppy is Also a Flower* (*GB: Danger Grows Wild*). *Triple Cross.* 1967: *The Long Duel. Pretty Polly* (*US: A Matter of Innocence*). 1968: *The Charge of the Light Brigade.* 1969: *Battle of Britain. Twinky* (*US: Lola*). 1970: *Ryan's Daughter.* 1971: *The Night Visitor. Mary, Queen of Scots. Catch Me a Spy. Kidnapped.* 1972: *Ludwig. Pope Joan. The Offence.* 1973: *A Doll's House* (Losey). *Catholics* (*TV*). *Craze.* 1974: *11 Harrowhouse. Per-*

secution. *The Count of Monte Cristo* (*TV. GB: cinemas*). *Who?* 1975: *Hennessy. Death in the Sun. The Bawdy Adventures of Tom Jones. Conduct Unbecoming.* 1976: *Aces High.* 1977: *The Last Remake of Beau Geste. Eliza Frazer* (*GB: TV as The Rollicking Adventures of Eliza Fraser*). *Slavers.* 1978: *Die Rebellen/One Take Two* (*GB: TV, as Flashpoint Africa*). *Superman. Stevie.* *How to Score ... a Movie.* 1979: *Meteor.* *Night Flight. Hurricane. The Shillingbury Blowers* (*TV*). 1980: *Sir Henry at Rawlinson End. The Sea Wolves. Windwalker.* 1981: *Les années lumières* (*GB and US: Light Years Away*). 1982: *Gandhi. Inside the Third Reich* (*TV*). *The Deadly Game* (*TV*). *The Missionary.* 1983: *Sword of the Valiant. The Devil Impostor.* 1985: *Dust. Time After Time* (*TV*). 1986: *Foreign Body. Rumplestiltskin.*

HOWERD, Frankie
(Francis Howard) 1921–

Lugubrious, crabbed-looking, purse-lipped, curly-haired British comedian whose unique, audience-belabouring style shot him to radio stardom immediately after World War II. Film roles have proved less riotous, but he has made invaluable contributions to seemingly unsaveable comedies.

*1954: The Runaway Bus. 1955: An Alligator Named Daisy. The Ladykillers. 1956: Jumping for Joy. A Touch of the Sun. 1958: Further Up the Creek. 1959: *Three Seasons. 1961: Watch It Sailor! 1962: The Fast Lady. The Cool Mikado. 1963: The Mouse on the Moon. 1966: The Great St Trinian's Train Robbery. 1967: Carry on Doctor. 1969: Carry on Up the Jungle. 1971: Up Pompeii. Up the Chastity Belt. Up the Front. 1973: The House in Nightmare Park. 1978: Sergeant Pepper's Lonely Hearts Club Band.*

HOWES, Sally Ann 1930–

Lovely fair-haired British actress, mostly in light comedies, the daughter of thirties' stage musical star Bobby Howes (1895–1972). As a teenager, she gave attractive performances in several films, but a run of poor movies stopped her adult career. Later, she enjoyed stage success as a musical star but, like her father, she has made only a handful of films.

1943: Thursday's Child. 1944: Halfway House. 1945: Dead of Night. Pink String and Sealing Wax. 1947: Nicholas Nickleby. 1948: Anna Karenina. My Sister and I. 1949: The

History of Mr Polly. Fools Rush In. Stop Press Girl. 1951: *Honeymoon Deferred.* 1957: *The Admirable Crichton* (*US: Paradise Lagoon*). 1968: *Chitty Chitty Bang Bang.* 1972: *Female Artillery* (*TV*). *The Hound of the Baskervilles* (*TV*). 1979: *Death Ship.*

HUBSCHMID, Paul 1917–

Dark-haired, virile, handsome, cheerful-looking Swiss-born leading man whose reputation survived working in German films during World War II sufficiently for him to be offered work in Hollywood in 1949, under a new name – Paul Christian. Although he returned to Germany a few years later, he was for many years still billed as Paul Christian in the English-speaking world, on those of his films (mostly swashbuckling adventures) that reached the international market.

1938: Füsilier Wipf. 1939: Der letzte Appel (*unfinished*). *Maria Ilona. 1940: My Dream. Mir lönd nüd lugg. Die Missbrauchten/Die missbrauchten Briefe. 1942: Der Fall Rainer. Meine Freundin Josephine. Altes Herz wird wieder jung. 1943: Liebesbriefe. Der gebieterische Ruf. Wilder Urlaub. 1944: Das Gesetz der Liebe. 1945: Das seltsame Fräulein Sylvia. 1948: Der himmlische Walzer. 1949: Geheimnisvolle Tiefe. Gottes Engel sind überall. Arlberg Express. Bagdad. 1950: The Thief of Venice* (*released 1953*). *1952: No Time for Flowers. 1953: The Beast from 20,000 Fathoms. Venus of Tivoli. Maske in blau. Le mystère du Palace-hotel. Musik bei nacht. Mit siebzehn beginnt das Leben. Les cloches n'ont pas sonné* (*US: Hungarian Rhapsody*). *1954: Glückliche Reise. Schule für Eheglück. 1955: Ingrid. Die Frau des Botshafters. Rommel's Treasure. 1956: Heute heiratet mein*

Mann. Du bist Musik. Liebe die den Kopf verliert. Die goldene Brücke. 1957: *Salzburger Geschichten. Glücksritter. Die Zürcher Verlobung.* 1958: *Ihr 106. Geburtstag. La morte viene dallo spazio* (*GB: Death Comes from Outer Space. US: The Day the Sky Exploded*). *Scampolo. Italienreise – Liebe inbegriffen. Meine schöne Mama. Der Tiger von Eschnapur. Das indische Grabmal.* 1959: *Zwei Gitarren. Liebe Luft und lauter Lügen. Heldinnen. Alle Tage ist kein Sonntag. Marili. Auskunft im Cockpit.* 1960: ‡*Journey to the Lost City. The Red Hand. Die junge Sünderin.* 1961: *Schwartze Rose, Rosemarie* (*US: Festival*). 1962: *Ich bin auch nur eine Frau.* 1963: *Elf Jahre und ein Tag. And So to Bed.* 1964: *Die Lady* (*GB: Frustration: US: Games of Desire*). *Le grain de sable. Die Diamantenhölle am Mekong. Heirate mich, Chéri!* 1965: *The Devil's Agent. Playgirl* (*US: That Woman*). *Rüf der Wälder. Die Herren. Ich suche einen Mann. Der Mann mit den 1,000 Masken. Die schwedische Jungfrau. Die Unmoralischen. Mozambique.* 1966: *Funeral in Berlin. Caroline und die Männer über vierzig. A belles dents. Upperseven. Ein gewisses Verlangen.* 1967: *In Enemy Country. Karriere.* 1968: *Negresco. Manon '70.* 1969: *Taste of Excitement. Skullduggery.* 1973: *Versuchung im Sommerwind.*

‡ *Abridged US version* (*in one film*) *of Der Tiger von Eschnapur and Das indische Grabmal*

HUDSON, Rochelle 1914–1972

Very pretty, dark-haired, square-faced American actress in films at 16, but mainly as repressed daughters and submissive wives. Stayed an actress all her working life, until illness curtailed her career in her fifties.

1930: Laugh and Get Rich. 1931: Fanny Foley Herself (*GB: Top of the Bill*). *Are These Our Children?* 1932: *Hell's Highway. Beyond the Rockies. The Penguin Pool Murder* (*GB: The Penguin Pool Mystery*). *Liberty Road. Mysteries of the French Police.* 1933: *Wild Boys of the Road* (*GB: Dangerous Days*). *Love is Like That. She Done Him Wrong. Lucky Devils. Scarlet River. The Savage Girl. Love is Dangerous* (*GB: Women Are Dangerous*). *Notorious But Nice. Doctor Bull. Mr Skitch. Walls of Gold.* 1934: *Harold Teen* (*GB: The Dancing Fool*). *Bachelor Bait. Judge Priest. The Mighty Barnum. Such Women Are Dangerous. Imitation of Life.* 1935: *I've Been*

Around. Life Begins at Forty. Les Miserables. Curly Top. Way Down East. Show Them No Mercy (GB: Tainted Money). 1936: The Music Goes Round. The Country Beyond. Poppy. Everybody's Old Man. Reunion (GB: Hearts in Reunion). 1937: Born Reckless. Woman Wise. That I May Live. She Had to Eat. 1938: Mr Moto Takes a Chance. Rascals. Storm over Bengal. 1939: Pride of the Navy. A Woman is the Judge. Smuggled Cargo. Pirates of the Skies. Missing Daughters. Konga, the Wild Stallion (GB: Konga). 1940: Convicted Woman. Babies for Sale. Island of Doomed Men. Men without Souls. Girls under 21. 1941: Meet Boston Blackie. The Stork Pays Off. The Officer and the Lady. 1942: Queen of Broadway. Rubber Racketeers. 1947: Bush Pilot. 1948: The Devil's Cargo. 1949: Sky Liner. 1955: Rebel without a Cause. 1964: Strait-Jacket. 1965: The Night Walker. Broken Sabre (TV. GB: cinemas). 1967: Dr Terror's Gallery of Horrors.

foot. Magnificent Obsession. 1955: All That Heaven Allows. One Desire. 1956: Never Say Goodbye. Written on the Wind. Battle Hymn. Four Girls in Town. Giant. 1957: The Tarnished Angels. A Farewell to Arms. Something of Value. 1958: Twilight for the Gods. 1959: This Earth is Mine. Pillow Talk. 1961: The Last Sunset. Lover Come Back. Come September. 1962: The Spiral Road. 1963: A Gathering of Eagles. Marilyn (narrator only). 1964: Send Me No Flowers. Man's Favorite Sport? 1965: Strange Bedfellows. A Very Special Favor. *The Nurse (narrator only). 1966: Blindfold. Seconds. Tobruk. 1968: Ice Station Zebra. 1969: Darling Lili. A Fine Pair. The Undefeated. 1970: Hornets' Nest. 1971: Pretty Maids All in a Row. 1973: Showdown. 1975: Embryo. 1978: Avalanche. 1979: The Martian Chronicles (TV). 1980: The Mirror Crack'd. 1984: The Ambassador. The Vegas Strip War (TV).

Riders in the Sky. The Devil's Henchman. Square Dance Jubilee. Young Man with a Horn (GB: Young Man of Music). 1950: Holiday Rhythm. 1951: Passage West (GB: High Venture). Close to My Heart. 1954: Highway Dragnet. Loophole. 1955: Las Vegas Shakedown. 1956: Dig That Uranium. 1957: Gun Battle at Monterey. 1958: No Time at All (TV). 1974: The Working Girls. 1977: How's Your Love Life?

HULBERT, Claude 1900–1964

Moon-faced, light-haired British star comedian with jutting upper lip, usually to be found as blustering, babbling, upper-class 'silly asses' who shared the limelight with, and stole scenes from, the star. A hit on stage in the twenties and thirties: later a useful foil for Will Hay. Married actress Enid Trevor in 1924. Brother of Jack Hulbert.

1928: Champagne. 1929: Naughty Husbands. 1932: A Night Like This. Thark. The Mayor's Nest. Let Me Explain Dear. The Face at the Window. 1933: Heads We Go (US: The Charming Deceiver). Radio Parade. Their Night Out. The Song You Gave Me. 1934: Love at Second Sight (US: The Girl Thief). The Girl in Possession. A Cup of Kindness. Big Business. Lilies of the Field. 1935: Hello Sweetheart. Man of the Moment. Bulldog Jack (US: Alias Bulldog Drummond). 1936: Where's Sally? Wolf's Clothing. The Interrupted Honeymoon. Hail and Farewell. Olympic Honeymoon (later Honeymoon Merry-Go-Round). Take a Chance. The Vulture. 1937: Ship's Concert. It's Not Cricket. You Live and Learn. 1938: Simply Terrific. It's in the Blood. The Viper. His Lordship Regrets. Many Tanks Mr Atkins. 1940: Sailors Three (US: Three Cockeyed Sailors). 1941: The Ghost of St Michael's. 1943: The Dummy Talks. My Learned Friend. 1946: London Town (US: My Heart Goes Crazy). 1947: The Ghost of Berkeley Square. 1948: Under the Frozen Falls. 1949: Cardboard Cavalier. 1955: Fun at St Fanny's. 1960: Not a Hope in Hell.

HUDSON, Rock (Roy Scherer) 1925–1985

A gentle giant: a big, beefy American actor with dark, curly hair. His intrinsically quiet and intellectual nature contrasted with the rugged man-of-action roles he was called upon to play in his early Universal-International days, a studio at which he became a star inside three years. Although nominated for an Oscar in Giant, he proved to be at his best in a series of smooth, battle-of-the-sexes comedies in the late 1950s and early 1960s in which Doris Day and Paula Prentiss had him looking like a baffled panda. After that good material eluded him and several of his subsequent films were scarcely seen outside America. His losing battle with AIDS made many unsavoury headlines in 1985.

1948: Fighter Squadron. 1949: Undertow. 1950: I Was a Shoplifter. Winchester 73. One Way Street. Peggy. The Desert Hawk. Shakedown. Double Crossbones. Tomahawk (GB: Battle of Powder River). Bright Victory (GB: Lights Out). 1951: Iron Man. The Fat Man. Air Cadet (GB: Jet Men of the Air). 1952: Has Anybody Seen My Gal? Bend of the River (GB: Where the River Bends). Scarlet Angel. Here Come the Nelsons. Horizons West. The Lawless Breed. 1953: Gun Fury. Seminole. The Golden Blade. Back to God's Country. Sea Devils. 1954: Taza, Son of Cochise. Bengal Brigade (GB: Bengal Rifles). Captain Light-

HUGHES, Mary Beth 1919–

Full-lipped, baby-faced blonde, in films direct from college plays and brief stage experience, in leading roles by the mid-forties, mostly in minor films, and almost equally as good girls and bad girls. Carried on in supporting roles in fifties' films before retiring around 1963. Unexpectedly reappeared in two low-budget seventies' movies.

1939: Broadway Serenade. Bridal Suite. The Covered Trailer. Dancing Co-Ed (GB: Every Other Inch a Lady). The Women. These Glamour Girls. Fast and Furious. 1940: Free, Blonde and 21. Lucky Cisco Kid. Star Dust. Sleepers West. Four Sons. The Great Profile. 1941: Ride on, Vaquero. Charlie Chan in Rio. The Cowboy and the Blonde. Dressed to Kill. The Great American Broadcast. Design for Scandal. Blue, White and Perfect. 1942: Over My Dead Body. The Night Before the Divorce. Orchestra Wives. The Ox-Bow Incident (GB: Strange Incident). 1943: Good Morning, Judge. Never a Dull Moment. Melody Parade. Follow the Band. 1944: Men on Her Mind. I Accuse My Parents. Take it Big. Timber Queen. 1945: The Great Flamarion. The Lady Confesses. Rockin' in the Rockies (GB: Partners in Fortune). 1948: Return of Wildfire (GB: The Black Stallion). Joe Palooka in Winner Take All (GB: Winner Take All). Caged Fury. Waterfront at Midnight. Inner Sanctum. Last of the Wild Horses. 1949: Rimfire. El Paso. Grand Canyon.

HULBERT, Jack 1892–1978

Jaunty Jack had a chin like a trowel, a prominent nose, a lick of hair and a gap in his teeth. But such was the impact of his happy-go-lucky personality, dry voice and great personal charm that he remained a favourite of London theatregoers, and, later, cinemagoers, as com-

edian, dancer, singer and light actor for nigh on 30 years. Married his stage partner, Cicely Courtneidge (qv), in 1916.
1928: *British Screen Tatler No. 10. 1930: Elstree Calling. 1931: The Ghost Train. Sunshine Susie (US: The Office Girl). 1932: Jack's the Boy (US: Night and Day). Love on Wheels. Happy Ever After. 1933: Falling for You. 1934: Jack Ahoy! The Camels Are Coming. 1935: Bulldog Jack (US: Alias Bulldog Drummond). 1936: Jack of All Trades (US: The Two of Us). 1937: Take My Tip. Paradise for Two (US: The Gaiety Girls). 1938: Kate Plus Ten. 1940: Under Your Hat. 1948: *Highwaymen. 1950: Into the Blue (US: The Man in the Dinghy). 1951: The Magic Box. 1955: Miss Tulip Stays the Night. 1960: The Spider's Web. 1972: Not Now Darling. The Cherry Picker.

HUME, Benita 1906–1967

Dark, sweetly pretty, serious-looking British leading lady. In films as a teenager, she became a big star of British films before leaving for Hollywood in 1935, after a visit two years earlier. Her career here was short and sweet: she met and married Ronald Colman and retired. They were married from 1938 until his death in 1958. In the same year she married George Sanders.
1924: The Happy Ending. 1925: *They Wouldn't Believe Me. *Her Golden Hair Was Hanging Down Her Back. 1926: Second to None. 1927: Easy Virtue. The Constant Nymph. 1928: A South Sea Bubble. A Light Woman. The Wrecker. The Lady of the Lake. Balaclava (US: Jaws of Hell). 1929: The Clue of the New Pin. High Treason. 1930: The House

of the Arrow. Symphony in Two Flats. 1931: The Flying Fool. *Healthy, Wealthy and Why. A Honeymoon Adventure (US: Footsteps in the Night). The Happy Ending. Service for Ladies (US: Reserved for Ladies). 1932: Women Who Play. Diamond Cut Diamond (US: Blame the Woman). Sally Bishop. Help Yourself. Men of Steel. Lord Camber's Ladies. Discord. 1933: The Little Damozel. Worst Woman in Paris? Clear All Wires. Gambling Ship. Only Yesterday. Looking Forward (GB: Service). 1934: The Private Life of Don Juan. Jew Süss (US: Power). 1935: The Divine Spark. 18 Minutes. The Gay Deception. 1936: The Garden Murder Case. Suzy. Moonlight Murder. Rainbow on the River. Tarzan Escapes. 1937: The Last of Mrs Cheyney. 1938: Peck's Bad Boy with the Circus.

HUNNICUTT, Gayle 1942–

Chestnut-haired American actress who, after a late start, played strong-nerved heroines in Hollywood, British and French films of the 1970s. Her film career seemed (surprisingly) to go adrift in the later years of the decade. Married to David Hemmings (qv) from 1968 to 1974, she now lives in Britain and works mainly in the theatre. Early 1980s' interviews revealed that she had completely lost her American accent.
1967: The Wild Angels. P.J. (GB: New Face in Hell). 1968: The Smugglers (TV). 1969: Marlowe. Eye of the Cat. 1970: Freelance. Fragment of Fear. 1971: The Love Machine. 1972: *Today Mexico – Tomorrow the World. Scorpio. Running Scared. 1973: The Legend of Hell House. Nuits rouges/L'homme sans visage (GB: Shadowman). Voices. 1975: The Sellout. The Spiral Staircase. 1976: Blazing Magnum (US: Strange Shadows in an Empty Room). Tony Saitta/Tough Tony. 1978: Die Rebellen/One Take Two (GB: TV, as Flashpoint Africa). Once in Paris. 1979: The Martian Chronicles (TV). A Man Called Intrepid (TV). The Million Dollar Face (TV). 1980: Kiss of Gold (TV). 1983: Return of the Man from UNCLE (TV). 1985: Target. Dream Lover. 1986: Turnaround.

HUNT, Marsha

(Marcia Hunt) 1917–
Pretty, petite brunette American actress who usually played demure but plucky heroines in 'B' movies and gentle or tragic supporting

roles in bigger films. She began to get an interesting variety of roles in the late forties, but her career was virtually ended when she was blacklisted in the Communist witch-hunts. Played a few mother roles later on, and remains actively involved in civil rights, the United Nations and charity work. Married director Jerry Hopper (1938–1943) and screenwriter Robert Presnell (1946 on).
1935: The Virginia Judge. 1936: Desert Gold. Gentle Julia. The Accusing Finger. Arizona Raiders. Easy to Take. Hollywood Boulevard. College Holiday. 1937: Annapolis Salute (GB: Salute to Romance). Murder Goes to College. Easy Living. Thunder Trail. Born to the West. 1938: The Long Shot. Come on Leathernecks. 1939: The Hardys Ride High. The Star Reporter. These Glamour Girls. Joe and Ethel Turp Call on the President. Winter Carnival. 1940: *Women in Hiding. Flight Command. Pride and Prejudice. Irene. Ellery Queen, Master Detective. 1941: Blossoms in the Dust. The Trial of Mary Dugan. I'll Wait for You. Cheers for Miss Bishop. The Penalty. Unholy Partners. 1942: Kid Glove Killer. The Affairs of Martha. Seven Sweethearts. Panama Hattie. Joe Smith, American (GB: Highway to Freedom). 1943: Bride by Mistake. Thousands Cheer. The Human Comedy. Pilot No. 5. Lost Angel. Cry Havoc. 1944: None Shall Escape. Music for Millions. 1945: A Letter for Evie. The Valley of Decision. 1947: Smash-Up, the Story of a Woman (GB: A Woman Destroyed). Carnegie Hall. 1948: The Inside Story. Raw Deal. 1949: Jigsaw. Take One False Step. Mary Ryan, Detective. 1952: Actors and Sin. The Happy Time. 1954: Diplomatic Passport. 1956: No Place to Hide. 1957: Man of the Law (TV. GB: cinemas). Bombers B-52 (GB: No Sleep Till Dawn). Back from the Dead. 1959: Blue Denim (GB: Blue Jeans). 1960: The Plunderers. 1969: Fear No Evil (TV). 1971: Johnny Got His Gun. 1972: Jigsaw (TV). 1976: The Siege (TV). 1981: Rich and Famous.

HUNTER, Ian 1900–1975

Tall, solid, pleasant, light-haired South African-born leading man who had long careers in Britain and Hollywood, mostly as quiet, dependable types. Although perhaps not dynamic enough to become a top star, his range was wider than his constant casting as 'other men' or members of the aristocracy

Yug Goddess of Vengeance. Kali-Yug – the Mystery of the Indian Tomb.

would suggest and he gave a fascinating performance as the Christ-figure in _Strange Cargo_ (1940).

1924: Not for Sale. 1925: Mr Oddy (later Confessions). A Girl of London. 1927: Downhill (US: When Boys Leave Home). Easy Virtue. His House in Order. The Ring. 1928: The Physician. The Thoroughbred. Valley of the Ghosts. 1929: Syncopation. 1930: Cape Forlorn (US: The Love Storm). Escape. 1931: Sally in Our Alley. 1932: The Water Gipsies. The Sign of Four. The Man from Toronto. Marry Me. 1933: Orders is Orders. *Skipper of the Osprey. The Silver Spoon. 1934: The Night of the Party. Something Always Happens. The Church Mouse. No Escape. Death at Broadcasting House. Lazybones. The Phantom Light. 1935: The Morals of Marcus. Jalna. The Girl from 10th Avenue (GB: Men on Her Mind). A Midsummer Night's Dream. I Found Stella Parish. 1936: The White Angel. To Mary, with Love. Stolen Holiday. The Devil is a Sissy (GB: The Devil Takes the Count). 1937: Another Dawn. Confession. Call It a Day. 52nd Street. That Certain Woman. 1938: The Adventures of Robin Hood. Always Goodbye. Secrets of an Actress. The Sisters. Comet over Broadway. 1939: Broadway Serenade. Tarzan Finds a Son. Yes, My Darling Daughter. The Little Princess. Maisie. Tower of London. Bad Little Angel. 1940: Broadway Melody of 1940. Strange Cargo. Bitter Sweet. Dulcy. Gallant Sons. The Long Voyage Home. 1941: Ziegfeld Girl. Billy the Kid. Dr Jekyll and Mr Hyde. Smilin' Through. Come Live with Me. Andy Hardy's Private Secretary. 1942: A Yank at Eton. It Comes Up Love (US: A Date with an Angel). 1943: Forever and a Day. 1946: Bedelia. 1947: White Cradle Inn (US: High Fury). The White Unicorn (US: Bad Sister). 1949: Edward My Son. 1951: Hunted (US: The Stranger in Between). 1952: It Started in Paradise. 1953: Appointment in London. Don't Blame the Stork! Eight O'Clock Walk. 1954: Fire One. 1956: The Battle of the River Plate (US: Pursuit of the Graf Spee). *The Door in the Wall. 1957: Fortune is a Woman (US: She Played with Fire). 1958: Rockets Galore (US: Mad Little Island). 1959: North West Frontier (US: Flame over India). 1960: The Bulldog Breed. 1961: Dr Blood's Coffin. The Treasure of Monte Cristo (US: The Secret of Monte Cristo). The Queen's Guards. 1962: Guns of Darkness (US: Act of Mercy). 1963: Kali-

HUNTER, Jeffrey

(Henry McKinnies) 1925–1969

Tall, dark, virile, young-looking American leading man, a favourite target for fan mail throughout the fifties at Twentieth Century-Fox, where his career ran parallel to that of Robert Wagner, with whom he often appeared in films. Away from Fox, Hunter got himself into a variety of out-of-the-way projects, some worthy, some not, that were not given wide distribution, and his name dropped from the popularity polls. Married to Barbara Rush (first of three) from 1950 to 1955. Died after surgery following injuries sustained in a fall.

1948: A Date with Judy. 1949: Julius Caesar. 1951: Call Me Mister. Fourteen Hours. Take Care of My Little Girl. The Frogmen. Red Skies of Montana. 1952: Belles on Their Toes. Dreamboat. Lure of the Wilderness. 1953: Single-Handed (US: Sailor of the King). 1954: Three Young Texans. Princess of the Nile. 1955: White Feather. Seven Angry Men. Seven Cities of Gold. 1956: A Kiss Before Dying. The Empty Room (TV. GB: cinemas). The Proud Ones. The Searchers. Gun for a Coward. The Great Locomotive Chase. Four Girls in Town. 1957: The True Story of Jesse James (GB: The James Brothers). No Down Payment. Count Five and Die. The Way to the Gold. 1958: Mardi Gras. In Love and War. The Last Hurrah. 1960: Key Witness. Hell to Eternity. Sergeant Rutledge. 1961: Man-Trap. King of Kings. The Secret Mission (TV). 1962: No Man is an Island. The Longest Day. Gold for the Caesars. 1963: The Man from Galveston (TV. GB: cinemas). 1964: The Woman Who Wouldn't Die. 1965: Murieta (GB: Vendetta). Brainstorm. 1966: Dimension 5. Witch without a Broom. 1967: The Christmas Kid. A Guide for the Married Man. Custer of the West. Frozen Alive. 1968: The Private Navy of Sergeant O'Farrell. Frau Wirtin hat auch eine Nichte (GB: Sexy Susan Sins Again. US: Sexy Susan at the King's Court). Joe ... Look for a Place to Die (GB and US: Joe – Find a Place to Die). 1969: The Hostess Also Has a Country. Viva America. Mafia Mob.

HUNTER, Kim

(Janet Cole) 1922–

Sweet-faced, intelligent American actress with dark, coppery hair who sprang to pro-

minence with good performances in low-budget films, was selected by British director Michael Powell to play 'a typical American girl' in 1945, and won a 'Best Supporting Actress' Oscar in 1951 for _A Streetcar Named Desire_. Despite all that, she has never become more than a vaguely familiar name at the box-office and was briefly blacklisted in the McCarthy era. Some filmographies credit her with an appearance in _A Canterbury Tale_ (1944), but she doesn't appear to be in it.

1943: The Seventh Victim. Tender Comrade. 1944: When Strangers Marry. 1945: You Came Along. A Matter of Life and Death (US: Stairway to Heaven). 1951: A Streetcar Named Desire. 1952: Deadline USA (GB: Deadline). Anything Can Happen. 1954: Fire One. 1956: Storm Center. The Comedian (TV). Bermuda Affair. 1957: The Young Stranger. The Dark Side of the Earth (TV). 1958: Before I Die (TV). Money, Women and Guns. Free Week-End (TV). 1959: The Sounds of Eden (TV). 1960: Alas, Babylon (TV). 1964: Lilith. 1967: Planet of the Apes. 1968: The Swimmer. The Young Loner (TV). 1969: Beneath the Planet of the Apes. 1970: Dial Hot Line (TV). In Search of America (TV). 1971: Escape from the Planet of the Apes. 1973: The Magician (TV). 1974: Bad Ronald (TV). Born Innocent (TV). Unwed Father (TV). 1975: Ellery Queen (TV). The Impersonation Murder Case (TV). 1976: The Hancocks (TV). The Dark Side of Innocence (TV). 1979: Dark August. The Golden Gate Murders (TV). 1981: Skokie (GB: TV, as Once They Marched Through a Thousand Towns). FDR: The Last Year (TV). 1985: Three Sovereigns for Sarah (TV).

HUNTER, Tab

(Arthur Gelien) 1931–

Tall, rangy actor with close-cropped fair hair, prime teenage bait at Warner Brothers, for whom he became a hot property in the fifties. Outside their environment, he has swam in some strange waters, vainly searching for his former popularity, latterly in continental action films.

1950: †The Lawless (GB: The Dividing Line). 1952: Saturday Island (US: Island of Desire). 1953: The Steel Lady (GB: Treasure of Kalifa). Gun Belt. 1954: Return to Treasure Island. Track of the Cat. 1955: The Sea Chase. Battle Cry. 1956: The Burning Hills. The Girl

face and unhappy mouth seemed to doom her to roles of anguish and suffering at both ends of the social bracket. A graduate of Sydney Box's 'company of youth' and the post-war Rank charm school, she had some meaty roles in the forties, but slipped into second-features in the following decade. Long married to actor Peter Dyneley (1921–1977). First husband was producer Euan Lloyd. Died from a heart attack.

1946: †The Years Between. Daybreak. Girl in a Million. 1947: Dear Murderer. The Upturned Glass. Holiday Camp. When the Bough Breaks. It Always Rains on Sunday. Jassy. 1948: My Sister and I. Good Time Girl. My Brother's Keeper. Here Come the Huggetts. 1949: Passport to Pimlico. 1950: Dance Hall. 1951: The Quiet Woman. Out of True. 1952: Tall Headlines. It Started in Paradise. 1953: The Weak and the Wicked (US: Young and Willing).

1954: Burnt Evidence. 1955: Secret Venture. Laughing in the Sunshine. 1957: You Pay Your Money. 1959: Violent Moment. Deadly Record. Devil's Bait. Night Train to Inverness. The Split (US: The Monster). 1960: Circus of Horrors. 1961: House of Mystery. 1963: Bitter Harvest. 1978: The Wild Geese.

† As Gwen Clark.

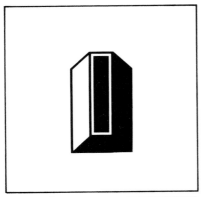

IRELAND, Jill 1936–

Perky British blonde actress, with distinctive urchin cut in her early days. A favourite magazine pin-up, although saucy rather than sexy, she appeared in supporting parts in British films before going to Hollywood, initially with her first husband, David McCallum. Later leading roles with second husband Charles Bronson revealed her acting as shaky, although she was good in one role – in *The Streetfighter/Hard Times*. Recovered from breast cancer in the mid-1980s.

1955: *Oh Rosalinda!! The Woman for Joe. Simon and Laura*. 1956: *The Big Money. Three Men in a Boat*. 1957: *There's Always a Thursday. Robbery under Arms. Hell Drivers*. 1959: *The Desperate Man*. *The Ghost Train Murder. Carry on Nurse*. 1960: *Girls of Latin Quarter*. 1961: *So Evil, So Young. Raising the Wind. Jungle Street*. 1962: *Twice round the Daffodils. The Battleaxe*. 1967: *The Karate Killers (TV. GB: cinemas)*. 1968: *Villa Rides!* 1969: *Rider on the Rain*. 1970: *Violent City (US: The Family)*. 1971: *Quelqu'un derrière la porte (GB: Two Minds for Murder). Cold Sweat*. 1972: *The Mechanic (reissued as Killer of Killers). The Valachi Papers*. 1973: *Valdez the Halfbreed (GB: The Valdez Horses. US: Chino)*. 1975: *Hard Times (GB: The Streetfighter). Breakheart Pass. From Noon Till Three*. 1978: *Love and Bullets*. 1981: *Death Wish II*. 1983: *The Girl, the Gold Watch and Everything (TV)*.

IRELAND, John 1914–

Tough-looking, heavy-browed, slim, narrow-faced, broad-shouldered, very dark-haired Canadian actor who rose nicely from supporting roles, mostly as villains, to star parts, but failed to maintain his expected position at the head of cast lists. A decline into featured parts, or leads in American and British 'B' movies in the 1950s took him into quite small roles in succeeding years. Married (second of three) to Joanne Dru from 1949 to 1958. Half-brother of actor/comedian Tommy Noonan (*qv*). Nominated for an Oscar in *All the King's Men*.

1945: *A Walk in the Sun*. 1946: *Behind Green Lights. It Shouldn't Happen to a Dog. My Darling Clementine. Wake Up and Dream. Somewhere in the Night (voice only)*. 1947: *The Gangster. Railroaded! Red River. I Love Trouble. Repeat Performance (narrator only)*. 1948: *Open Secret. Raw Deal. Joan of Arc. A Southern Yankee (GB: My Hero)*. 1949: *Roughshod. I Shot Jesse James. The Walking Hills. The Doolins of Oklahoma (GB: The Great Manhunt). Mr Soft Touch (GB: House of Settlement). Anna Lucasta. Undercover Man (narrator only). All the King's Men*. 1950: *Cargo to Capetown. The Return of Jesse James*. 1951: *Vengeance Valley. The Scarf. Little Big Horn (GB: The Fighting 7th). The Basketball Fix (GB: The Big Decision). The Bushwhackers (GB: The Rebel). Red Mountain. This is Korea (narrator only)*. 1952: *Hurricane Smith*. 1953: *The 49th Man. Combat Squad*. †*Hannah Lee (later Outlaw Territory)*. 1954: *The Good Die Young. Security Risk*. †*The Fast and the Furious. South West Passage (GB: Camels West). The Steel Cage*. 1955: *The Glass Cage (US: The Glass Tomb). Queen Bee. Hell's Horizon*. 1956: *Gunslinger. Gunfight at the OK Corral*. 1957: *Without Incident (TV). A Sound of Different Drummers (TV)*. 1958: *Stormy Crossing (US: Black Tide). No Place to Land (GB: Man Mad). Party Girl*. 1960: *Faces in the Dark. Spartacus. No Time to Kill (released 1963)*. 1961: *Wild in the Country. Return of a Stranger. Brushfire!* 1962: *55 Days at Peking*. 1963: *The Ceremony. The Fall of the Roman Empire*. 1965: *I Saw What You Did. Day of the Nightmare*. 1966: *Fort Utah*. 1967: *Flight of the Hawk. War Devils/The Devil's Man. Caxambu! Odio per odio. Dalle Ardenne all'inferno (GB: The Dirty Heroes). Arizona Bushwhackers*. 1968: *Villa Rides! Corri uomo corri (US: Run, Man, Run). El Chè Guevara (GB: Rebel with a Cause). Sparare è meglio, fidarsi*

è bene. *Tutto per tutto. Una pistola per cento bare. T'ammazzo! – raccomandanti a Dio*. 1969: *Una sull'altra (GB and US: One on Top of the Other). Rider on the Rain. La sfida dei Mackenna (US: The Challenge of the Mackennas). Zenabel. Femmine insaziabili (US: Carnal Circuit). Quanto costa morire. Quel caldo maledetto giorno di fuoco*. 1970: *The Adventurers*. 1972: *The Mechanic (reissued as Killer of Killers). Escape to the Sun. North-East to Seoul. Der Würger kommt auf leisen Socken (US: The Mad Butcher)*. 1973: *Welcome to Arrow Beach (US: Tender Flesh). The House of the Seven Corpses*. 1974: *Go for Broke. The Phantom of Hollywood (TV). The Girl on the Late, Late Show (TV). Ten Whites Killed by One Little Indian!* 1975: *Farewell, My Lovely. The Swiss Conspiracy. La furie du désir. We're No Angels. Il letto in piazza (GB: Sex Diary)*. 1976: *Captain Midnight/On the Air Live with Captain Midnight. Delta Fox*. 1977: *Salon Kitty (US: Madame Kitty). Assault on Paradise (US: Maniac. GB: TV, as Ransom). The Moon and a Murmur (unfinished). Satan's Cheerleaders. The Perfect Killer. Tomorrow Never Comes. Love and the Midnight Auto Supply. Kino, the Padre on Horseback*. 1978: *Kavik the Wolf Dog (GB: TV, as The Courage of Kavik the Wolf Dog). The Millionaire (TV). Verano sangrieto*. 1979: *Crossbar (TV). The Shape of Things to Come. Guyana: The Crime of the Century*. 1980: *Tourist (TV). Marilyn: the Untold Story (TV)*. 1981: *Incubus. Las majeres de Jeremias/Garden of Venus*. 1984: *Martin's Day. The Treasure of the Amazon/Treasure of Doom*. 1985: *The Hitchhiker. Thunder Run*. 1986: *Miami Galom*.

† *And co-directed*

IRONS, Jeremy 1948–

Tall, slim, erect and handsome in a taut and faintly forlorn-looking kind of way, this romantic British actor (born in the Isle of Wight) played guitar and sang in his early twenties, starting his show business career busking in London's West End. A far cry from the co-starring role with Meryl Streep in *The French Lieutenant's Woman* and his enormous popular success in the TV series *Brideshead Revisited*, although Irons's roles since then have been sufficiently off the beaten track for him to have not quite consolidated his position as a leading star of 1980s British cinema. Married actress Sinead Cusack. Once described as 'the thinking girl's pin-up'.

1980: Nijinsky. 1981: The French Lieutenant's Woman. 1982: Moonlighting. The Masterbuilders (narrator only). The Captain's Doll (TV). Betrayal. 1983: The Wild Duck. Un amour de Swann/Swann in Love. 1984: The Lie. 1986: The Mission.

IVES, Burl 1909–

Genial, jovial folk-singer who made a few appearances in outdoor adventure tales in the forties before unexpectedly becoming a dramatic heavyweight, in both senses, in the fifties. Singing has remained his first love, but he has continued to pop up occasionally, mostly as elderly characters as cantankerous as his forties' portraits were good-humoured. Academy Award (best supporting actor) in *The Big Country*.

1946: Smoky. 1948: Green Grass of Wycoming. Station West. So Dear to My Heart. 1950: Sierra. 1954: East of Eden. 1956. The Power and the Prize. 1957: The Miracle Worker (TV). 1958: Desire under the Elms. The Big Country. Cat on a Hot Tin Roof. Wind Across the Everglades. 1959: Our Man in Havana. Day of the Outlaw. 1960: Let No Man Write My Epitaph. 1962: The Flying Clipper (narrator only). The Spiral Road. Summer Magic. 1964: The Brass Bottle. Ensign Pulver. 1966: The Daydreamer (voice only). 1967: Rocket to the Moon (US: Those Fantastic Flying Fools). 1968: The Sound of Anger (TV). 1969: The Whole World is Watching (TV). The Only Way Out is Dead (US: TV as The Man Who Wanted to Live Forever). The McMasters ... tougher than the West itself! 1976: Baker's Hawk. Hugo the Hippo (voice only). 1978: The Bermuda Depths (TV). The New Adventures of Heidi (TV). Just You and Me, Kid. 1981: Earthbound. 1982: White Dog. 1984: The Ewok Adventure (TV. GB: cinemas, as Caravan of Courage. Narrator only). 1985: Uphill All the Way.

JACKSON, Anne 1925–

Gawky, red-haired, toothy American actress with an easy talent for wisecracks, seen occasionally as ordinary working women. Born ten years too late; a decade earlier, she would have been in hot demand for loveable loyal secretaries and witty best-friends. An attempt to make her into a star of the sixties was successful only with the critics. Married to Eli Wallach (*qv*) since 1948.

1950: *So Young, So Bad.* 1958: *The Journey.* 1960: *Tall Story.* 1967: *How to Save a Marriage . . . and Ruin Your Life. The Tiger Makes Out.* 1968: *The Secret Life of an American Wife.* 1969: *Zigzag (GB: False Witness).* 1970: *The Angel Levine. Lovers and Other Strangers. Dirty Dingus Magee.* 1976: *Nasty Habits. Twenty Shades of Pink (TV).* 1979: *The Bell Jar. The Shining.* 1980: *Family Man (TV). A Private Battle (TV). Blinded by the Light (TV).* 1981: *Leave 'Em Laughing (TV).* 1984: *Sam's Son.*

JACKSON, Glenda 1936–

Distinctive dark-haired English actress with precise, tart tones who looks as though she would stand no more nonsense than the original Mary Poppins. Remained a stage actress throughout her early career, then suddenly burst on the film scene as tempestuous, destiny-changing females, won two Oscars in four years (for *Women in Love* and *A Touch of Class*), continued building her stage reputation and endeared herself to British TV millions with her straight-faced sense of comedy on *The Morecambe and Wise Show.* Although now nearing her fifties, she is still in demand for leading roles. Also nominated for Oscars on *Sunday, Bloody Sunday* and *Hedda.*

1963: *This Sporting Life.* 1966: *The Persecution and Assassination of Jean Paul Marat . . . (The Marat/Sade). Benefit of the Doubt.* 1967: *Tell Me Lies.* 1968: *Negatives.* 1969: *Women in Love.* 1970: *The Music Lovers.* 1971: *Sunday, Bloody Sunday. The Boy Friend. Mary, Queen of Scots.* 1972: *The Triple Echo. A Touch of Class.* 1973: *Bequest to the Nation (US: The Nelson Affair). Il sorriso del grande tentatore (GB: The Tempter. US: The Devil is a Woman).* 1974: *The Maids.* 1975: *The Romantic Englishwoman. Hedda.* 1976: *Nasty Habits. The Incredible Sarah.* 1978: *House Calls. The Class of Miss MacMichael. Stevie.* 1979: *Lost and Found. Health. *Build Me a World (narrator only).* 1980: *Hopscotch.* 1981: **Stop Polio. The Patricia Neal Story (TV).* 1982: *The Return of the Soldier. Giro City (TV. US: And Nothing But the Truth).* 1984: *Sakharov.* 1985: *Turtle Diary.*

JACKSON, Gordon 1923–

Fair-haired, shy-seeming Scottish actor, briefly in engineering before deciding finally on an acting career after service in World War II. Initially as young soldiers and juvenile leads, later in minor leading roles and a good variety of supporting parts in bigger films. Won his greatest popularity in the seventies in the long-running TV series *Upstairs Downstairs.* Married to Rona Anderson since 1951.

1942: *The Foreman Went to France (US: Somewhere in France). Nine Men.* 1943: *San Demetrio London. Millions Like Us.* 1945: *Pink String and Sealing Wax.* 1946: *The Captive Heart.* 1948: *Against the Wind. Eureka Stockade.* 1949: *Floodtide. Stop Press Girl. Whisky Galore! (US: Tight Little Island).* 1950: *Bitter Springs.* 1951: *The Lady with a Lamp. Happy-Go-Lovely.* 1952: *Castle in the Air.* 1953: *Malta Story. Death Goes to School. Meet Mr Lucifer. The Love Lottery.* 1954: *The Delavine Affair.* 1955: *Passage Home. Windfall. The Quatermass Xperiment (US: The Creeping Unknown).* 1956: *Pacific Destiny. Women without Men (US: Blonde Bait). The Baby and the Battleship. Sailor Beware! (US: Panic in the Parlor).* 1957: *Seven Waves Away (US: Abandon Ship!). Black Ice. Let's Be Happy. Hell Drivers. Man in the Shadow.* 1958: **Scotland Dances (narrator only). Blind Spot. Rockets Galore (US: Mad Little Island). Three Crooked Men.* 1959: *Yesterday's Enemy. Blind Date. The Bridal Path. Devil's Bait. The Navy Lark.* 1960: *Cone of Silence (US: Trouble in the Sky). The Price of Silence. Tunes of Glory. Snowball.* 1961: *Greyfriars Bobby. Two Wives at One Wedding.* 1962: *Mutiny on the Bounty.* 1963: *The Long Ships. The Great Escape.* 1964: *Daylight Robbery.* 1965: *Cast a Giant Shadow. The Ipcress File. Those Magnificent Men in their Flying Machines. Operation Crossbow.* 1966: *The Fighting Prince of Donegal. The Night of the Generals. Triple Cross.* 1967: *Danger Route.* 1968: *The Prime of Miss Jean Brodie.* 1969: *On the Run. Run Wild, Run Free. Hamlet.* 1970: *Scrooge. The Music Lovers.* 1971: *Kidnapped. Madame Sin (TV. GB: cinemas).* 1975: *Russian Roulette.* 1977: *Golden Rendezvous. The Medusa Touch. Spectre (TV).* 1979: *Raising Daisy Rothschild (GB: TV as The Last Giraffe).* 1984: *The Shooting Party. The Masks of Death (TV).* 1986: *The Whistle Blower.*

JACOBSSON, Ulla 1929–1982

Plump-cheeked, light-haired, anxious-looking Swedish actress who gained international reputation of a sort (rather as Hedy Lamarr had done in the 1930s) with her sensational nude scenes in *One Summer of Happiness.* It was 1962, however, before she ventured outside European films, but she made no sort of impact at all, and returned to Sweden, her film career tailing away. Died from bone cancer.

1951: *Bärande Har (US: The Rolling Sea). Hon Dansade en Sommar (GB and US: One*

Summer of Happiness). 1953: All Jordens Frojd (US: All the Joy of the Earth). 1954: ...und ewig bleibt die Liebe (US: Eternal Love). Karin Månsdotter. Sir Arne's Treasure. 1955: Die heilige Lüge (US: The Sacred Lie). Der Pfarrer von Kirchfeld. Sommernattens Leende (GB: and US: Smiles of a Summer Night). 1956: Crime and Punishment. Sangen om den Eldröda Blomman (US: Song of the Scarlet Flower). 1957: Die letzten Werden die ersten sein. 1958: Körkarlen (US: The Phantom Carriage). Unruhige Nacht (US: The Restless Night). 1959: Llegaron dos hombres...und das am Montagmorgen. 1960: Im Name einer Mutter. 1961: Una domenica d'estate. Riviera Story. 1962: The Final Hour. 1963: Love is a Ball (GB: All This and Money Too). Zulu. 1965: Nattmara/Nightmare. The Heroes of Telemark. 1967: Alle Jahre Wieder. The Double Man. 1968: Bamse (US: Teddy Bear). Adolphe – ou l'âge tendre. 1969: The Servant. 1970: Atem der Lust. 1975: Faustrecht der Freiheit (GB: Fox. US: Fox and His Friends).

JAGGER, Dean (D. Jeffries) 1903–

Noble-looking, light-haired American actor of intelligent, deep-set features whose career came in waves. After one false start, he came to Hollywood in the thirties and played supporting roles, returning in 1940 in near-star parts after his portrayal of Brigham Young. In 1949 he revealed himself as a balding character star and promptly won an Academy Award for 12 O'Clock High.

1928: Handcuffed. 1929: The Woman from Hell. 1930: Whoopee! 1934: College Rhythm. You Belong to Me. Behold My Wife. 1935: Home on the Range. Wanderer of the Wasteland. Car 99. Wings in the Dark. Men without Names. People Will Talk. 1936: Woman Trap. Thirteen Hours by Air. Revolt of the Zombies. Star for a Night. Pepper. 1937: Woman in Distress. Song of the City. Under Cover of Night. Dangerous Number. Escape by Night. Exiled to Shanghai. 1938: Having Wonderful Time. 1940: Brigham Young – Frontiersman (GB: Brigham Young). 1941: The Men in Her Life. Western Union. 1942: Valley of the Sun. The Omaha Trail. 1943: North Star (later Armored Attack). I Escaped from the Gestapo (GB: No Escape). 1944: Alaska. When Strangers Marry. 1945: I Live in Grosvenor Square (US: A Yank in London). 1946: Sister Kenny. Pursued. 1947: Driftwood. 1949: 12 O'Clock

High. C-Man. 1950: Sierra. Dark City. 1951: Rawhide. Warpath. 1952: My Son John. Denver and Rio Grande. It Grows on Trees. 1953: The Robe. 1954: Executive Suite. Private Hell 36. White Christmas. Bad Day at Black Rock. 1955: The Eternal Sea. It's a Dog's Life. 1956: Red Sundown. On the Threshold of Space. Smoke Jumpers (TV). X the Unknown. The Great Man. 1957: The Dark Side of the Earth (TV). Three Brave Men. 40 Guns. Bernardine. 1958: The Proud Rebel. King Creole. The Nun's Story. 1959: Cash McCall. 1960: Elmer Gantry. 1961: Parrish. The Honeymoon Machine. 1962: Jumbo/Billy Rose's Jumbo. 1967: First to Fight. Firecreek. 1968: Tiger by the Tail. Day of the Evil Gun. 1969: Smith! The Lonely Profession (TV). The Kremlin Letter. 1970: Remember (TV). Incident in San Francisco (TV). 1971: The Brotherhood of the Bell (TV). Vanishing Point. 1972: The Delphi Bureau (TV). The Stranger (TV). The Glass House (TV. GB: cinemas). 1974: The Great Lester Boggs. So Sad About Gloria. The Hanged Man (TV). 1976: God Bless Dr Shagetz. The Lindbergh Kidnapping Case (TV). 1977: End of the World. 1978: Game of Death (US: Bruce Lee's Game of Death). 1980 Alligator. Gideon's Trumpet. Haywire (TV).

JAMES, Sidney 1913-1976

Dark, crinkly-haired South African-born character actor (in England from 1946) with battered features (a conspiracy between boxing and nature) and distinctive raucous laugh. Whether as cockney crook or loud-mouthed American, he became one of those faces to which one couldn't quite add the name, until TV's Hancock's Half Hour (1956–1960) revealed his facility for comedy. After Hancock broke up the partnership, James became the mainstay of the 'Carry On' films: his Henry VIII is especially treasurable. Died from a heart attack while performing on stage.

1947: Black Memory. The October Man. 1948: No Orchids for Miss Blandish. Night Beat. Once a Jolly Swagman (US: Maniacs on Wheels). The Small Back Room. 1949: Paper Orchid. The Man in Black. Give Us This Day (US: Salt to the Devil). 1950: Last Holiday. The Lady Craved Excitement. 1951: Talk of a Million (US: You Can't Beat the Irish). Lady Godiva Rides Again. The Lavender Hill Mob. The Magic Box. The Galloping Major. 1952:

I Believe in You. Emergency Call (US: Hundred Hour Hunt). Gift Horse (US: Glory at Sea). Cosh Boy (US: The Slasher). Miss Robin Hood. Time Gentlemen Please! Father's Doing Fine. Venetian Bird (US: The Assassin). Tall Headlines. The Yellow Balloon. 1953: The Wedding of Lilli Marlene. Escape by Night. The Titfield Thunderbolt. The Square Ring. Will Any Gentleman? The Weak and the Wicked (US: Young and Willing). Park Plaza 605 (US: Norman Conquest). The Flanagan Boy (US: Bad Blonde). Is Your Honeymoon Really Necessary? 1954: The Rainbow Jacket. The House Across the Lake (US: Heatwave). Father Brown (US: The Detective). Seagulls over Sorrento (US: Crest of the Wave). The Crowded Day. Orders Are Orders. Aunt Clara. For Better, for Worse (US: Cocktails in the Kitchen). The Belles of St Trinian's. 1955: Out of the Clouds. Joe Macbeth. The Deep Blue Sea. A Kid for Two Farthings. The Glass Cage (US: The Glass Tomb). A Yank in Ermine. It's a Great Day. John and Julie. 1956: Ramsbottom Rides Again. The Extra Day. Wicked As They Come. The Iron Petticoat. Dry Rot. Trapeze. 1957: Quatermass II (US: Enemy from Space). Interpol (US: Pickup Alley). The Smallest Show on Earth. The Shiralee. Hell Drivers. Campbell's Kingdom. A King in New York. The Story of Esther Costello (US: Golden Virgin). 1958: The Silent Enemy. Another Time, Another Place. Next to No Time! The Man Inside. I Was Monty's Double. The Sheriff of Fractured Jaw. 1959: Too Many Crooks. Make Mine a Million. The 39 Steps. Upstairs and Downstairs. Tommy the Toreador. Desert Mice. Idle on Parade (US: Idol on Parade). 1960: Carry on Constable. Watch Your Stern. And the Same to You. The Pure Hell of St Trinian's. 1961: Double Bunk. A Weekend with Lulu. The Green Helmet. What a Carve Up! (US: No Place like Homicide). Raising the Wind (US: Roommates). What a Whopper! Carry on Regardless. 1962: Carry on Cruising. We Joined the Navy. 1963: Carry on Cabby. 1964: The Beauty Jungle (US: Contest Girl). Carry on Cleo. Three Hats for Lisa. 1965: The Big Job. Carry on Cowboy. 1966: Where the Bullets Fly. Don't Lose Your Head. 1967: Carry on Doctor. 1968: Carry on Up the Khyber. 1969: Carry on Camping. Carry on Again, Doctor. Carry on Up the Jungle. 1970: Carry on Loving. Carry on Henry. 1971: Carry on at Your Convenience. Tokoloshe, the Evil Spirit. 1972: Carry on Matron. Bless This House. Carry on Abroad. 1973: Carry on Girls. 1974: Carry on Dick.

JANNINGS, Emil (Theodor E. Janenz) 1882–1950

Big, beefy, glowering, dominant Swiss-born actor whose speciality was great men destined for tragic decline. He became a leading figure in the German cinema in silent days and, when some of his films did well in America, went to Hollywood in 1926. Here, he enjoyed only a few years of popularity, for sound revealed his guttural accent and sent him back to Germany, where his efforts for the Third Reich in wartime led him to spend his final

years in virtual exile. Oscar in 1928, jointly, for *The Way of All Flesh* and *The Last Command*. Died from cancer.

1914: Arme Eva. Im Banne der Leidenschaft. Im Schützengraben. 1915: Passionels Tagebuch. Frau Eva. 1916: Nächte des Grauens. Stein unter Steinen. Unheilbar. Die Ehe der Luise Rohrbach. Im Angesicht des Toten. Aus Mangel an Beweisen. Der zehnte Pavillon der Zitadelle. Die Bettlerin von St Marien. 1917: Das Leben ein Traum. Der Ring der Giuditta Foscari. Ein fideles Gefängnis. Lulu. Wenn vier dasselbe tun. Das Geschäft. 1918: Nach zwanzig jahren. Die Augen der Mumie Mâ (GB: The Eyes of the Mummy). Keimendes Leben Part I. Keimendes Leben Part II. 1919: Der Mann der Tat. Die Tochter des Mehemed. Madame Dubarry (US: Passion). Rose Bernd. Kohlhiesels Töchter. 1920: Vendetta. Algol. Anna Boleyn (US: Deception). Colombine. Das grosse Licht. Der Schädel der Pharaonentochter. Der Stier von Oliviera. The Brothers Karamazov. 1921: Danton (US: All for a Woman). Das Weib des Pharao (GB and US: The Loves of Pharaoh). Der Schwur des Peter Hergatz. Die Ratten. 1922: Othello. Peter the Great. Die Gräfin von Paris. 1923: Alles für Geld (US: Fortune's Fool). Tragödie der Liebe. Quo Vadis? 1924: Der letzte Mann (GB and US: The Last Laugh). Nju (US: Husbands or Lovers). Das Wachsfigurenkabinett (GB and US: Waxworks). 1925: Liebe macht blind. Tartüff. Variety (US: Vaudeville). 1926: Faust. 1927: The Way of All Flesh. 1928: The Last Command. The Patriot. Sins of the Fathers. The Street of Sin (GB: King of Soho). 1929: Fighting the White Slave Traffic. Betrayal. 1930: Der blaue Engel/The Blue Angel. Liebling der Götter. 1931: Stürme der Leidenschaft. 1932: König Pausole (GB: The Merry Monarch). 1934: Der schwarze Walfisch. 1935: Der alte und der junge König. 1936: Traumulus. 1937: Der Herrscher. Der zerbrochene Krug (US: The Broken Jug). 1939: Robert Koch, der Bekämpfer des Todes. 1941: Ohm Krüger. 1942: Die Entlassung. 1943: Altes Herz wird wieder jung. 1945: †Wo ist Herr Belling?

†*Unfinished*

JANSSEN, David (D. Meyer) 1930–1980
Dark-haired (with distinctive high temples), gravel-voiced, seldom-smiling American

actor, in show business as a child. After an apprenticeship at Universal, he became perhaps television's most successful actor ever, especially in the series *Richard Diamond* (1957–1959), *The Fugitive* (1963–1966) and *Harry O* (1973–1975).He exuded cynicism, world-weariness and integrity, and was sometimes quite hypnotic to watch, although not so in films. Died from a heart attack. Has said that he played dozens of walk-on roles as a child in World War II films, but no records of these seem to exist.

1945: It's a Pleasure. 1946: Swamp Fire. 1952: Yankee Buccaneer. Francis Goes to West Point. No Room for the Groom. Bonzo Goes to College. 1955: Chief Crazy Horse (GB: Valley of Fury). The Private War of Major Benson. Cult of the Cobra. To Hell and Back. Francis in the Navy. The Square Jungle. All That Heaven Allows. 1956: Never Say Goodbye. Away All Boats. Toy Tiger. Francis in the Haunted House. Showdown at Abilene. The Girl He Left Behind. 1957: Lafayette Escadrille (GB: Hell Bent for Glory). Darby's Rangers (GB: The Young Invaders). 1958: The Money. 1960: Hell to Eternity. 1961: Dondi. Twenty Plus Two (GB: It Started in Tokyo). Man-Trap. Ring of Fire. King of the Roaring Twenties (GB: The Big Bankroll). 1962: Belle Sommers. 1963: My Six Loves. 1967: Warning Shot. 1968: The Green Berets. The Shoes of the Fisherman. 1969: Where it's At. Generation (GB: A Time for Giving). Marooned. 1970: Night Chase (TV). Macho Callahan. 1971: Operation Cobra (TV). 1972: The Longest Night (TV). Moon of the Wolf (TV). 1973: Pioneer Woman (TV). Birds of Prey (TV. GB: cinemas). Harry O (TV). Hijack (TV). 1974: Prisoner in the Middle (GB: TV. US: Warhead). Once is Not Enough/ Jacqueline Susann's Once is Not Enough. Smile Jenny, You're Dead (TV). 1975: The Swiss Conspiracy. Fer-de-Lance (TV. GB: cinemas as Death Dive). 1976: Farrell (TV). Two-Minute Warning. Mayday at 40,000 Feet (TV. GB: cinemas). 1977: Golden Rendezvous. A Sensitive, Passionate Man (TV). 1978: Sono stato un agente CIA (US: Covert Action). Stalk the Wild Child (TV). Nowhere to Run (TV). Pressure Point (TV). 1979: Superdome (TV). SOS Titanic (TV. GB: cinemas). Panic on Page One (TV. Later: City in Fear). High Ice. Specter on the Bridge/The Golden Gate Murders (TV). 1980: Inchon!

JAYNE, Jennifer (J. J. Jones) 1932–
Copper-haired British actress whose film career was undistinguished for ten years. Then she got her first leading role in the same year (1958) as a smash-hit television series, *William Tell,* which she followed with another, *Whiplash*. If her acting was moderate, she was so easy on the eye, it was hard to see why success hadn't come earlier. Wrote the screenplay for *Tales That Witness Madness* (1973) under the pseudonym Jay Fairbank.

1948: Once a Jolly Swagman (US: Maniacs on Wheels). 1949: The Blue Lamp. A Boy, a Girl and a Bike. 1950: Trio. 1951: There is Another Sun (later Wall of Death). Black Widow. 1953: It's a Grand Life. 1955: A Yank in Ermine. 1957: The End of the Line. 1958: A Woman of Mystery. Carve Her Name with Pride. Mark of the Phoenix. The Man Who Wouldn't Talk. The Trollenberg Terror (US: The Crawling Eye). 1961: Raising the Wind. 1962: Band of Thieves. On the Beat. 1963: Clash by Night (US: Escape by Night). 1963: Hysteria. Dr Terror's House of Horrors. 1965: The Liquidator. 1967: They Came from Beyond Space. 1978: The Medusa Touch.

JEAN, Gloria (G. J. Schoonover) 1928–
Dark-haired American child star and teenage singer and dancer. Gloria Jean was a kind of teenybopper's Diana Lynn. Kept at Universal as a minor-league rival to Deanna Durbin, Gloria was as pretty as paint and as cute as a button. Her youthful freshness enlivened many a penny-pinching swing session, and she deserved better than her relatively brief career.

1939: The Under-Pup. 1940: If I Had My Way. A Little Bit of Heaven. 1941: *Winter Serenade. Never Give a Sucker an Even Break. 1942: What's Cookin'? (GB: Wake Up and Dream). Get Hep to Love (GB: She's My Lovely). It Comes Up Love (GB: A Date with an Angel). When Johnny Comes Marching Home. 1943: Mister Big. Moonlight in Vermont. 1944: Follow the Boys. Ghost Catchers. Destiny. Pardon My Rhythm. The Reckless Age. 1945: Easy to Look At. I'll Remember April. River Gang (GB: Fairy Tale Murder). 1947: Copacabana. 1948: I Surrender, Dear. An Old-Fashioned Girl. 1949: Manhattan Angel. There's a Girl in My Heart. 1955: Air Strike. 1961: The Ladies' Man. 1963: The Madcaps.

JENKINS, Megs 1917–
Prettily plump, dark-haired British actress who moved swiftly from sisters to mothers, via a couple of interesting leading roles, in the British cinema of the immediate post-war years. Memorable as a nurse in *Green for Danger* and as the 'plump woman' in *The History of Mr Polly*. Since in a variety of kindly or worried parts and still active in television and on the stage.

1939: Inspector Hornleigh on Holiday (US: Inspector Hornleigh on Leave). The Silent Battle (US: Continental Express). Poison Pen. 1943: Millions Like Us. The Lamp Still Burns. It's in the Bag. 1945: 29 Acacia Avenue (US: The Facts of Love). Painted Boats (US: The Girl on the Canal). 1946: Green for Danger. 1947: The Brothers. 1948: Saraband for Dead Lovers (US: Saraband). The Monkey's Paw. 1949: The History of Mr Polly. A Boy, a Girl and a Bike. No Place for Jennifer. 1951: White Corridors. 1952: Ivanhoe. Secret People. 1953: Rough Shoot (US: Shoot First). The Cruel Sea. Trouble in Store. Personal Affair. 1954: The Gay Dog. 1955: Out of the Clouds. *Ring of Greed. John and Julie. 1956: The Man in the Sky (US: Decision Against Time). 1957: The Passionate Stranger. The Story of Esther Costello (US: Golden Virgin). 1958: Indiscreet. 1959: Tiger Bay. Jet Storm. Friends and Neighbours. 1960: Conspiracy of Hearts. 1961: The Green Helmet. Macbeth. The Innocents. The Barber of Stamford Hill. 1962: Life for Ruth (US: Walk in the Shadow). The Wild and the Willing. 1964: Murder Most Foul. 1965: Bunny Lake is Missing. 1967: Stranger

in the House (US: Cop-Out). 1968: Oliver! 1969: The Smashing Bird I Used to Know. David Copperfield (TV. GB: cinemas). 1972: Asylum. 1974: The Amorous Milkman.

JOBERT, Marlène 1943–
Red-haired, freckle-faced, green-eyed Algerian-born leading lady in French films, with bonily attractive facial features. She very quickly went into international films, but without noticeable response from the public. In the 1970s she quietly built up a solid reputation with her performances in mainline French pictures.

1965: Masculin féminin. 1966: Martin Soldat (GB: Kiss Me, General). Le voleur (US: The Thief of Paris). 1967: Alexandre le bienheureux (GB: Alexander). 1968: Faut pas prendre les enfants du bon Dieu pour des canards sauvages. Léontine. L'astragale. 1969: Rider on the Rain. Dernier domicile connu (US: Last Known Address). 1970: Les mariés de l'ân II. 1971: Catch Me a Spy. La poudre d'escampette. Le décade prodigieux (and English-language version: Ten Days' Wonder). 1972: Nous ne vieillirons pas ensemble. Repressailles. Docteur Popaul (GB: Scoundrel in White). 1973: Juliette et Juliette. 1974: Le secret. Pas si méchant que ça (GB: This Wonderful Crook. US: The Wonderful Crook). 1975: Folle à tuer. Trop ce trop/Touch and Go. Le bon et les méchants (US: The Good and the Bad). 1976: Julie pot de colle/The Chains off Pity. 1977: L'imprecateur. 1978: Va voir maman, papa travaille. 1979: Il giocatto. Grandison. La guerre des polices. 1980: Une sale affaire. 1981: L'amour nu. 1982: Effraction. 1983: Les cavaliers de l'orage.

JOHN, Rosamund (Nora R. Jones) 1913–
Grey-eyed British actress with red-blonde hair and gentle, well-bred air. She came to star roles a little late in life, but did give several compelling performances in the forties before declining into lesser films.

1934: The Secret of the Loch. 1942: The First of the Few (GB: Spitfire). 1943: The Gentle Sex. The Lamp Still Burns. 1944: Tawny Pipit. Soldier, Sailor. 1945: The Way to the Stars (US: Johnny in the Clouds). 1946: Green for Danger. 1947: The Upturned Glass. When the Bough Breaks. Fame is the Spur. 1949: No Place for Jennifer. 1950: She Shall Have

Murder. 1952: *Sports Page No. 6 – Football. Never Look Back. Here's to the Memory! 1953: Street Corner (US: Both Sides of the Law). 1956: Operation Murder.

JOHNS, Glynis 1923–
Blue-eyed blonde daughter of Mervyn Johns, born in South Africa. Her direct stare and attractively reedy voice made her a distinctive star of the British cinema: her sex-appeal was apparent even in ordinary roles and she was perfectly cast as Miranda the amorous mermaid. Later career interrupted by illness. Received an Academy Award nomination for *The Sundowners*.

1937: South Riding. 1938: Murder in the Family. Prison without Bars. 1939: On the Night of the Fire (US: The Fugitive). 1940: The Briggs Family. Under Your Hat. 1941: The Prime Minister. 49th Parallel (US: The Invaders). 1943: Adventures of Tartu (US: Tartu). 1944: Halfway House. 1945: Perfect Strangers (US: Vacation from Marriage). 1946: This Man is Mine. 1947: Frieda. An Ideal Husband. 1948: Miranda. Third Time Lucky. 1949: Dear Mr Prohack. Helter Skelter. The Blue Lamp. 1950: State Secret (US: The Great Manhunt). 1951: Flesh and Blood. Appointment with Venus (US: Island Rescue). Encore. The Magic Box. No Highway (US: No Highway in the Sky). 1952: The Card (US: The Promoter). 1953: The Sword and the Rose. Personal Affair. Rob Roy the Highland Rogue. The Weak and the Wicked (US: Young and Willing). 1954: The Seekers (US: Land of Fury). The Beachcomber. Mad About Men. 1955: Josephine and Men. The

Court Jester. 1956: Loser Takes All. All Mine to Give (US: The Day They Gave Babies Away). Around the World in 80 Days. 1958: Another Time Another Place. 1959: Shake Hands with the Devil. Last of the Few. 1960: The Spider's Web. The Sundowners. 1961: The Chapman Report. 1962: The Cabinet of Caligari. 1963: Papa's Delicate Condition. 1964: Mary Poppins. 1965: Dear Brigitte ... 1967: Don't Just Stand There! 1969: Lock Up Your Daughters! 1971: Under Milk Wood. 1973: Vault of Horror. 1982: Little Gloria – Happy at Last (TV).

JOHNS, Mervyn 1899–
Chunky, earnest-looking Welsh actor with dark, wavy hair who, in the absence of more high-powered leading men, unexpectedly became a star of the British cinema in the wartime years, doing well in a succession of unusual and rewarding parts. Later dropped back into character roles. His first wife died in 1971 after many years of marriage and, in 1976, he married Diana Churchill (1913–). Father of Glynis Johns.
1934: Lady in Danger. 1935: The Tunnel (US: Transatlantic Tunnel). The Guv'nor (US: Mister Hobo). Foreign Affaire. 1936: Everything is Thunder. In the Soup. Pot Luck. Dishonour Bright. 1937: Storm in a Teacup. Song of the Forge. 1938: Almost a Gentleman. 1939: Jamaica Inn. The Midas Touch. 1940: Convoy. Saloon Bar. The Girl in the News. 1942: The Foreman Went to France (US: Somewhere in France). The Next of Kin. Went the Day Well? (US: 48 Hours). 1943: The Bells Go Down. My Learned Friend. San Demetrio London. 1944: Halfway House. Twilight Hour. 1945: They Knew Mr Knight. Dead of Night. Pink String and Sealing Wax. 1946: The Captive Heart. 1947: Captain Boycott. Easy Money. 1948: Quartet. Counterblast. 1949: Edward My Son. Helter Skelter. Diamond City. 1950: Tony Draws a Horse. 1951: The Magic Box. Scrooge. 1952: Tall Headlines. The Oracle (US: The Horse's Mouth). 1953: Valley of Song (US: Men Are Children Twice). The Master of Ballantrae. 1954: Romeo and Juliet. 1955: The Blue Peter (US: Navy Heroes). 1984. 1956: The Intimate Stranger (US: Finger of Guilt). The Shield of Faith. Find the Lady. Moby Dick. The Counterfeit Plan. 1957: Doctor at Large. *Danger List. The Vicious Circle (US: The Circle). The Gypsy and the

Gentleman. The Surgeon's Knife. 1959: The Devil's Disciple. Once More with Feeling. 1960: Never Let Go. No Love for Johnnie. Echo of Barbara. The Sundowners. 1961: The Rebel. Francis of Assisi. 1962: The Day of the Triffids. 55 Days at Peking. The Old Dark House. 1963: 80,000 Suspects. The Victors. A Jolly Bad Fellow. 1965: The Heroes of Telemark. 1966: Who Killed the Cat? 1973: The National Health. 1974: QB VII (TV). 1975: House of Mortal Sin. 1979: Game for Vultures. 1980: Kill and Kill Again.

JOHNSON, Ben 1919–
Fresh-faced, personable, dark-haired American western star with rich, slow-drawling voice, a former cowboy, rodeo champion and stunt rider. His career built up in John Ford westerns, but he didn't quite make it as a top star, reappearing in the 1960s as a leathery and weatherbeaten character star. The Academy Award that he won for his role in The Last Picture Show gained him a whole new series of varied and interesting roles.
1945: The Naughty Nineties. 1946: Badman's Territory. 1948: Fort Apache. Three Godfathers. 1949: She Wore a Yellow Ribbon. Mighty Joe Young. 1950: Wagonmaster. Rio Grande. 1951: Fort Defiance. 1952: Wild Stallion. 1953: Shane. 1956: Rebel in Town. 1957: War Drums. Fort Bowie. Slim Carter. 1960: Ten Who Dared. 1961: Tomboy and the Champ. One-Eyed Jacks. 1964: Cheyenne Autumn. Major Dundee. 1966: The Rare Breed. 1967: Will Penny. Hang 'Em High. 1969: The Wild Bunch. The Undefeated. Ride a Northbound Horse (TV. GB: cinemas). 1970: Chisum. 1971: The Last Picture Show. Something Big. Corky. 1972: Junior Bonner. The Getaway. 1973: Dillinger. Kid Blue. Bloodsport (TV). Runaway (TV. GB: cinemas, as The Runaway Train). The Train Robbers. The Red Pony (TV. GB: cinemas, in abridged version). 1974: Locusts (TV). The Sugarland Express. 1975: Bite the Bullet. Hustle. 1976: The Savage Bees (TV. GB: cinemas). Breakheart Pass. 1977: The Town That Dreaded Sundown. The Greatest. Grayeagle. 1978: The Swarm. True Grit: A Further Adventure (TV). 1979: The Sacketts (TV). Wild Times (TV). 1980: Ruckus. The Hunter. Soggy Bottom USA. Terror Train. 1981: High Country Pursuit. 1982: Tex. The Shadow Riders (TV).

1983: Champions. 1984: Red Dawn. 1985: Wild Horses (TV). 1986: Cherry 2000. Let's Get Harry.

JOHNSON, Dame Celia 1908–1982
Dark-haired (with distinctive wave), pretty but plaintive-looking British actress, almost entirely a stage personality until well into her thirties. Despite her clipped, upper-class tones, she projected real warmth and feeling in several forties' classics, notably Brief Encounter, that confirmed her as one of Britain's leading actress. With a face that seems born for suffering, it was much to her credit that she got as many lively roles as she did. Died following a stroke. She received an Academy Award nomination for her performance in Brief Encounter.
1934: Dirty Work. 1941: *We Serve. *A Letter from Home. 1942: In Which We Serve. 1943: Dear Octopus (US: The Randolph Family). 1944: This Happy Breed. 1945: Brief Encounter. 1950: The Astonished Heart. 1952: I Believe in You. The Holly and the Ivy. 1953: The Captain's Paradise. 1955: A Kid for Two Farthings. 1957: The Good Companions. 1968: The Prime of Miss Jean Brodie. 1978: Les Miserables (TV). 1980: The Hostage Tower.

JOHNSON, Chic
See OLSEN AND JOHNSON

JOHNSON, Kay (Catherine Townsend) 1904–1975
Fair-haired American actress, notably unpretty, but effective in fragile or genteel roles to which she often brought unexpected hon-

esty and spirit. Her career got off to a tremendous start in a film on which she had some notable fights with Cecil B. DeMille, but she gradually regressed into supporting parts in a career not well-handled either by herself or her studios. Married to director John Cromwell from 1928 to 1948.

1929: Dynamite. 1930: This Mad World. Passion Flower. Billy the Kid. The Ship from Shanghai. The Spoilers. Madam Satan. 1931: The Single Sin. The Spy. 1932: American Madness. Thirteen Women. 1934: Eight Girls in a Boat. Of Human Bondage. This Man is Mine. Their Big Moment. 1935: Jalna. Village Tale. 1938: White Banners. 1939: The Real Glory. 1942: Son of Fury. 1943: Mr Lucky. 1944: The Adventures of Mark Twain.

JOHNSON, Richard 1927–

Dark, saturnine, smoothly good-looking British actor. He remained a little-known stage player until suddenly bursting into star film roles in the early sixties. Subsequently, his cinema career floundered after he got himself cast in a very high percentage of silly or below-par big-budget films. Married and divorced from actresses Sheila Sweet and Kim Novak.

1951: Captain Horatio Hornblower RN. Calling Bulldog Drummond. 1952: Lady in the Fog (US: Scotland Yard Inspector). 1953: Saadia. 1959: Never So Few. 1963: Cairo. The Haunting. 80,000 Suspects. 1964: L'autre femme. The Pumpkin Eater. 1965: The Amorous Adventures of Moll Flanders. Operation Crossbow (US: The Great Spy Mission). 1966: Khartoum. Deadlier than the Male. La strega in amore/The Witch in Love. L'avventuriero/The Rover. 1967: Danger Route. A Twist of Sand. Oedipus the King. 1968: Lady Hamilton (GB: Emma Hamilton). Some Girls Do. 1969: Gott mit uns. 1970: The Beloved (GB: TV, as Sin). Julius Caesar. 1971: The Tyrant. 1972: The Fifth Day of Peace. 1974: Chi Sei? (GB: Devil within Her. US: Behind the Door). 1975: Hennessy. Night Child. The Cursed Medallion. 1976: Aces High. The Message (narrator only). The Last Day of Spring. Stella. 1977: Take All of Me. The Comeback. 1978: The Fish Men. The Four Feathers. 1979: The Delessi Affair. Zombi 2 (GB: Zombie Flesh-Eaters. US: Zombie). Island of Mutations. The Biggest Bank Robbery (TV). The Flame is Love (TV). 1980: The Monster Club. 1981: Portrait of a Rebel (TV). 1982:

Screamers (The Fish Men with added footage). 1983: The Aerodrome (TV). 1984: Secrets of the Phantom Caverns. 1985: Lady Jane. Turtle Diary.*

JOHNSON, Rita (R. McSean) 1912–1965

Lovely blonde American actress who despite consistently good critical notices and one outstanding lead performance – as Spencer Tracy's wife in *Edison, the Man* – was not promoted by her studio, M-G-M, as a star. By the middle forties she was typed in 'other woman' roles, and her career was virtually ended after a serious brain operation in 1948 following an accident at home with a hair dryer. Died from a brain haemorrhage.

1931: The Spy. 1937: London by Night. My Dear Miss Aldrich. 1938: Man Proof. Rich Man, Poor Girl. Letter of Introduction. Smashing the Rackets. 1939: Honolulu. Six Thousand Enemies. They All Come Out. Stronger Than Desire. Within the Law. Broadway Serenade. The Girl Downstairs. Nick Carter, Master Detective. 1940: Congo Maisie. The Golden Fleecing. Forty Little Mothers. Edison, the Man. 1941: Appointment for Love. Here Comes Mr Jordan. 1942: The Major and the Minor. 1943: My Friend Flicka. 1944: Thunderhead – Son of Flicka. 1945: The Naughty Nineties. The Affairs of Susan. 1946: The Perfect Marriage. Pardon My Past. 1947: They Won't Believe Me. The Michigan Kid. 1948: Sleep My Love. The Big Clock. Family Honeymoon. 1950: The Second Face. 1954: Susan Slept Here. 1955: †Unchained. 1956: Emergency Hospital. All Mine to Give (GB: The Day They Gave Babies Away).

† Scenes deleted from final release print

JOHNSON, Van (Charles V. Johnson) 1916–

American leading actor whose Swedish ancestry showed in his blue eyes, red-gold hair and boyish, rather hurt-looking expression. He took advantage of the absence of top talent away in wartime (he was himself unfit for service following a car smash which left him with a metal plate in his head) to storm to stardom at M-G-M, where he remained for 15 years. His boyish charm wore thin in the fifties and he has been less seen in recent times.

*1940: Too Many Girls. 1941: Murder in the Big House. 1942: *For The Common Defense. The War Against Mrs Hadley. Somewhere I'll Find You. Dr Gillespie's New Assistant. 1943: The Human Comedy. Ziegfeld Follies (released 1946). Madame Curie. Dr Gillespie's Criminal Case (GB: Crazy to Kill). Pilot No. 5. A Guy Named Joe. 1944: Three Men in White. Between Two Women. White Cliffs of Dover. Two Girls and a Sailor. Thirty Seconds over Tokyo. 1945: Weekend at the Waldorf. Thrill of a Romance. 1946: Till the Clouds Roll By. Easy to Wed. No Leave, No Love. 1947: High Barbaree. The Romance of Rosy Ridge. 1948: State of the Union (GB: The World and His Wife). Command Decision. The Bride Goes Wild. 1949: Mother is a Freshman (GB: Mother Knows Best). Battleground. In the Good Old Summertime. Scene of the Crime. 1950: Grounds for Marriage. The Big Hangover. Duchess of Idaho. 1951: Too Young to Kiss. Go for Broke. It's a Big Country. Three Guys Named Mike. Invitation. 1952: Washington Story (US: Target for Scandal). When in Rome. Plymouth Adventure. 1953: Confidentially Connie. Remains to be Seen. Easy to Love. 1954: The Caine Mutiny. Men of the Fighting Lady. The Siege at Red River. The Last Time I Saw Paris. Brigadoon. 1955: The End of the Affair. 1956: 23 Paces to Baker Street. The Bottom of the Bottle (GB: Beyond the River). Slander. Miracle in the Rain. 1957: Kelly and Me. Action of the Tiger. The Pied Piper of Hamelin (TV. GB: cinemas). 1958: The Last Blitzkrieg. Subway in the Sky. 1959: Beyond This Place (GB: Web of Evidence). 1960: The Enemy General. 1963: Wives and Lovers. 1967: Divorce American Style. The Doomsday Flight (TV. GB: cinemas). 1968: Yours, Mine and Ours. Where Angels Go ... Trouble Follows. 1969: Il prezzo del potere (GB: The Price of Power). El Largo dia Del (GB: The Professional). La battaglia d'Inghilterra (GB: Battle Squadron). 1970: Company of Killers (TV. GB: cinemas). San Francisco International Airport (TV). Wheeler and Murdoch (TV). 1971: Eye of the Spider. 1972: Call Her Mom (TV). Man in the Middle (TV). 1974: The Girl on the Late, Late Show (TV). Eagle over London. 1977: Getting Married (TV). 1979: From Corleone to Brooklyn. Superdome (TV). 1980: The Kidnapping of the President. 1981: Absurd! 1985: The Purple Rose of Cairo.*

JOLSON, Al (Asa Yoelson) 1885–1950

Square-faced, exuberant, larger-than-life Russian-born Hollywood entertainer who made history by starring in the first part-talkie, *The Jazz Singer*. His popularity faded in the thirties, but he came to the fore again with his efforts for Allied troops during World War II, and the smash-hit release of *The Jolson Story* in 1946, for which he supplied the vocals and long-shot dances. Married (second of three) to Ruby Keeler, 1928–1939. Died from a heart attack.

*1926: *April Showers. 1927: The Jazz Singer. 1928: The Singing Fool. 1929: Sonny Boy. New York Nights. Say It with Songs. 1930: Mammy. Big Boy. Showgirl in Hollywood. 1933: Hallelujah, I'm a Bum (GB: Hallelujah I'm a Tramp). 1934: Wonder Bar. 1935: Go into Your Dance (GB: Casino de Paree). *Kings of the Turf. 1936: The Singing Kid. 1939: Rose of Washington Square. Hollywood Cavalcade. Swanee River. 1941: *Cavalcade of the Academy Awards. 1945: Rhapsody in Blue. 1946: The Jolson Story. 1948: *Screen Snapshots No. 166. 1949: Jolson Sings Again (voice only).*

JONES, Allan 1907–

Light-haired American singer, of Welsh parentage and cheerful disposition, a singing straight man for the Marx Brothers and a rival to Nelson Eddy for the screen affections of Jeanette MacDonald. His best role – and performance – came in the 1936 *Show Boat*, but his career nosedived after he fell out with Louis B. Mayer at M-G-M and was forced to work for other studios. Married to Irene

Hervey (1910–) from 1936 to 1957, second of four wives.

*1935: Reckless. A Night at the Opera. 1936: The Great Ziegfeld (voice only). Rose Marie. Ramona. Show Boat. 1937: *Lest We Forget. A Day at the Races. The Firefly. 1938: Everybody Sing. 1939: Honeymoon in Bali (GB: Husbands or Lovers). The Great Victor Herbert. 1940: The Boys from Syracuse. One Night in the Tropics. 1941: There's Magic in Music. 1942: Moonlight in Havana. True to the Army. When Johnny Comes Marching Home. 1943: You're a Lucky Fellow, Mr Smith. Rhythm of the Islands. Larceny with Music. Crazy House. 1944: The Singing Sheriff. Sing a Jingle (GB: Lucky Days). 1945: Honeymoon Ahead. The Senorita from the West. 1964: Stage to Thunder Rock. 1965: A Swingin' Summer.*

JONES, Buck (Charles Gebhardt, later legally changed) 1889–1942

Sharply good-looking, dark-haired American actor, popular for over 20 years in second-feature westerns, often featuring himself providing both the action and 'hick from the sticks' style comedy relief. Came from a long background of rodeo shows. Died from burns sustained in a fire while trying to rescue people still trapped.

1913: †Unidentified '101' western. 1917: †Blood Will Tell. 1919: The Speed Maniac. Pitfalls of a Big City. True Blue. Western Blood. The Wilderness Trail. The Rainbow Trail. Riders of the Purple Sage. 1920: Desert Rat. Brother Bill. The Uphill Climb. The Two Doyles. The Last Straw. The Cyclone. Forbidden Trails. Square Shooter. Straight from the Shoulder. 1921: Just Pals. Two Moons. Firebrand Trevision. The Big Punch. Sunset Sprague. Riding with Death. To a Finish. 1922: Trooper O'Neil. Bells of San Juan. West of Chicago. Bar Nothin'. The Boss of Camp Four. Pardon My Nerve. Western Speed. Fast Mail. 1923: Footlight Ranger. Snowdrift. Big Dan. Hell's Hole. The Eleventh Hour. Second Hand Love. Skid Proof. Cupid's Fireman. 1924: The Desert Outlaw. The Circus Cowboy. Against All Odds. Western Luck. The Vagabond Trail. Not a Drum Was Heard. Winner Take All. 1925: The Trail Rider. The Man Who Played Square. The Timber Wolf. Arizona Romeo. Gold and the Girl. Hearts and Spurs. Lazybones. Durand of the Bad Lands. Good As Gold. The Desert's Price. 1926: The Cowboy

*and the Countess. The Fighting Buckaroo. A Man Four Square. The Gentle Cyclone. 30 Below Zero. 1927: The Flying Horseman. Chain Lightning. Hills of Peril. *Life in Hollywood No. 4. Whispering Sage. War Horse. 1928: Blood Will Tell (remake). The Big Hop. The Branded Sombrero. 1930: Stranger from Arizona. The Lone Rider. Shadow Ranch. Men without Law. 1931: Fugitive Sheriff. South of the Rio Grande. The Texas Ranger. Border Law. Branded. Range Feud. Ridin' for Justice. Desert Vengeance. The Avenger. Sundown Trail. 1932: Born to Trouble/Hello Trouble. White Eagle. McKenna of the Mounted. Deadline. High Speed. One Man Law. Reckless Romance. Riders of Death Valley. 1933: Gordon of Ghost City (serial). Unknown Valley. California Trail. Forbidden Trail. Treason. Child of Manhattan. Thrill Hunter. The Fighting Sheriff. The Sundown Rider. 1934: The Red Rider (serial). The Fighting Rangers. The Dawn Trail. Rocky Rhodes. The Man Trailer. The Fighting Code. When a Man Sees Red. Texas Ranger. 1935: The Roaring West (serial). Outlawed Guns. Border Brigands. Stone of Silver Creek. The Crimson Trail. The Square Shooter. The Throwback. The Ivory Handled Gun. 1936: The Phantom Rider (serial). Silver Spurs. The Boss of Gun Creek. The Cowboy and the Kid. Sunset of Power. For the Service. Empty Saddles. Ride 'Em Cowboy! 1937: Headin' East. Pony Express. Law for Tombstone. Sandflow. Smoke Tree Range. The Left-Handed Law. Hollywood Round-Up. Black Aces. Boss of Lonely Valley. 1938: Sudden Bill Dorn. Law of the Texan. Overland Express. California Frontier. Stranger from Arizona. 1939: Unmarried (GB: Night Club Hostess). 1940: Wagons Westward. 1941: Riders of Death Valley (serial). The Gunman from Bodie. Arizona Bound. Forbidden Trails. White Eagle (serial). 1942: West of the Law. Ghost Town Law. Down Texas Way. Below the Border. Down on the Great Divide. Riders of the West.*

† As Charles Gebhardt

JONES, Carolyn 1929–1983

Raven-haired American actress with narrow face and unusual, villainess-type features. Attracted a good deal of critical attention in the mid-fifties but her career gradually slid away into television, a medium in which she remained active. Occasionally blonde. Died from cancer. Nominated for an Academy Award in *The Bachelor Party*.

1952: *The Turning Point. Road to Bali. Off Limits (GB: Military Policemen).* 1953: *House of Wax. War of the Worlds. The Big Heat. Geraldine.* 1954: *Make Haste to Live. The Saracen Blade. Three Hours to Kill. Shield for Murder. Desiree. East of Eden.* 1955: *Cavalcade (TV. GB: cinemas). The Seven-Year Itch. The Tender Trap.* 1956: *The Hefferan Family (TV. GB: cinemas). The Man Who Knew Too Much. Invasion of the Body Snatchers. The Opposite Sex.* 1957: *The Bachelor Party. Johnny Trouble. Baby Face Nelson. The Last Man (TV).* 1958: *Marjorie Morningstar. King Creole.* 1959: *A Hole in the Head. Last Train from Gun Hill. Career. The Man in the Net.* 1960: *Ice Palace.* 1961: *Sail a Crooked Ship.* 1962: *How the West Was Won.* 1963: *A Ticklish Affair.* 1968: *Heaven with a Gun.* 1969: *Color Me Dead.* 1976: *Eaten Alive (GB: Death Trap).* 1977: *Halloween with the Addams Family (TV). Little Ladies of the Night (TV).* 1978: *Good Luck Miss Wyckoff.* 1981: *Midnight Lace (TV).*

JONES, Dean 1933–
Young-looking, light-haired American comedy actor with wry smile who played bright young chaps on whom fortune never smiled until the happy ending. He had a spotty early career, but from 1965 worked for the Disney studio and made a major contribution – his look of hurt bewilderment was second only to that of James Stewart – to most of their biggest comedy hits. Began his show business career as a blues singer. In 1978 he became a born-again Christian and left showbusiness to work for the charismatic worship movement.

1956: *Gaby. These Wilder Years. The Opposite Sex. The Great American Pastime. The Rack. Somebody Up There Likes Me. Tea and Sympathy.* 1957: *Ten Thousand Bedrooms. Designing Woman. Until They Sail. Jailhouse Rock.* 1958: *Handle with Care. Imitation General. Torpedo Run.* 1959: *Night of the Quarter Moon. Never So Few.* 1963: *Under the Yum Yum Tree. The New Interns.* 1964: *Two on a Guillotine.* 1965: *That Darn Cat!* 1966: *Any Wednesday (GB: abridged, as Bachelor Girl Apartment). The Ugly Dachshund.* 1967: *Monkeys, Go Home. Blackbeard's Ghost.* 1968: *The Horse in the Gray Flannel Suit. The Mickey Mouse Anniversary Show (narrator*

only). 1969: *The Love Bug.* 1970: *Mr Superinvisible.* 1971: *Million Dollar Duck. The Great Man's Whiskers (TV).* 1973: *Snowball Express. Guess Who's Sleeping in My Bed (TV).* 1976: *The Shaggy D.A.* 1977: *Herbie Goes to Monte Carlo. Once Upon a Brothers Grimm (TV).* 1978: *When Every Day Was the Fourth of July (TV). Born Again.*

JONES, Emrys
(E. Whittaker-Jones) 1915–1972
Light-haired, quietly-spoken British actor with large, open face, not tall but powerfully built. He built up his career well in the forties, but lacked the strength of personality to become a big star and was soon in some rather glum second-features, whence he did well to return to, and concentrate on, his stage career. Died from a heart attack.

1942: *One of Our Aircraft is Missing.* 1943: **Tired Man. The Shipbuilders.* 1944: *Give Me The Stars.* 1945: *The Wicked Lady. The Rake's Progress (US: Notorious Gentleman).* 1946: *Beware of Pity.* 1947: *Nicholas Nickleby. Holiday Camp.* 1948: *This Was a Woman. The Small Back Room.* 1949: *Blue Scar. Dark Secret. Miss Pilgrim's Progress.* 1953: *Deadly Nightshade.* 1955: *Three Cases of Murder.* 1956: *The Shield of Faith.* 1960: *The Trials of Oscar Wilde (US: The Man with the Green Carnation). Ticket to Paradise.* 1962: *Serena.* 1963: *On the Run.*

JONES, Griffith 1910–
Light-haired, long-faced very romantic-looking British actor, at his most appealing in the thirties. His post-war roles were far less

interesting and his cinema career tapered off in the fifties with supporting roles and leads in some dreary second-features, when he appeared unsuited to harsher, more modern times. Father of actors Gemma Jones and Nicholas Jones.

1932: *The Faithful Heart. Money Talks.* 1933: *Catherine the Great.* 1934: *Leave It to Blanche.* 1935: *Escape Me Never. First a Girl.* 1936: *The Mill on the Floss. Line Engaged.* 1937: *Wife of General Ling. Return of a Stranger (US: The Face Behind the Scar). A Yank at Oxford.* 1939: *The Four Just Men (US: The Secret Four). Young Man's Fancy.* 1941: *Atlantic Ferry (US: Sons of the Sea). This Was Paris.* 1942: *The Day Will Dawn (US: The Avengers). Uncensored.* 1944: *Henry V.* 1945: *The Wicked Lady. The Rake's Progress (US: Notorious Gentleman).* 1947: *They Made Me a Fugitive (US: I Became a Criminal).* 1948: *Miranda. Good Time Girl. Look Before You Love.* 1949: *Once Upon a Dream.* 1951: *Honeymoon Deferred.* 1954: *Star of My Night. The Sea Shall Not Have Them. Scarlet Web.* 1957: *Face in the Night (US: Menace in the Night). Not Wanted on Voyage. Account Rendered. Kill Her Gently.* 1958: *The Truth About Women. Hidden Homicide.* 1959: *The Crowning Touch.* 1965: *Strangler's Web.* 1968: *Decline and Fall ... of a Birdwatcher.*

JONES, Jennifer (Phylis Isley) 1919–
It seemed that this dark-haired American actress with her alabaster beauty, was forever after roles as tempestuous women of destiny (perhaps to escape her saintly Oscar for *The Song of Bernadette*) when what she was best at, in terms of getting an audience to respond to the character, were the Jennies, the Miss Doves and the Cluny Browns of this world. Married to Robert Walker (1939–1945) and David O. Selznick (1949 until his death in 1965). She also received Oscar nominations for *Since You Went Away, Love Letters, Duel in the Sun* (making four consecutive years) and *Love is a Many-Splendored Thing*.

1939: *†Dick Tracy's G-Men (serial). †The New Frontier.* 1940: *†The Ranger Rides Again (serial).* 1943: *The Song of Bernadette.* 1944: *Since You Went Away.* 1945: *Love Letters.* 1946: *Cluny Brown. *The American Creed. Duel in the Sun.* 1948: *Portrait of Jennie (GB: Jennie).* 1949: *We Were Strangers. Madame*

Bovary. 1950: Gone to Earth (US: The Wild Heart). 1952: Carrie. Ruby Gentry. 1953: Stazione termini (GB: Indiscretion. US: Indiscretion of an American Wife). Beat the Devil. 1955: Love is a Many-Splendored Thing. Good Morning, Miss Dove. 1956: The Man in the Gray Flannel Suit. 1957: The Barretts of Wimpole Street. A Farewell to Arms. 1961: Tender is the Night. 1966: The Idol. 1969: Angel, Angel, Down You Go/Cult of the Damned. 1974: The Towering Inferno. 1980: Patricia.

† *As Phylis Isley*

JONES, Shirley 1933–

Sweet-faced, sweet-voiced, corn-haired American singer who soared to fame in two big Fox musicals of the mid-fifties. Despite her Academy Award as the prostitute in *Elmer Gantry*, she has remained underrated and underused as a dramatic actress with warmth to spare – although she has kept busy.

1955: Oklahoma! 1956: Carousel. The Big Slide (TV). 1957: April Love. 1959: Never Steal Anything Small. Bobbikins. 1960: Elmer Gantry. Pepe. 1961: Two Rode Together. 1962: The Music Man. 1963: The Courtship of Eddie's Father. A Ticklish Affair. Dark Purpose. 1964: Bedtime Story. 1965: Fluffy. The Secret of My Success. 1969: Silent Night, Lonely Night (TV). The Happy Ending. 1970: The Cheyenne Social Club. But I Don't Want to Get Married (TV). 1973: The Girls of Huntingdon House (TV). 1975: The Lives of Jenny Dolan (TV). The Family Nobody Wanted (TV). Winner Take All (TV). 1977: Yesterday's Child (TV). 1978: A Last Cry for Help (TV). 1979: Beyond the Poseidon Adventure. Who'll Save Our Children? (TV). 1980: The Children of An Lac (TV). 1981: Inmates: a Love Story (TV). 1983: Tank. 1985: There Were Times Dear.

JONES, Tommy Lee 1946–

Dark, handsome, gauntly-boned and slightly dangerous-looking American actor who, despite a late start, has tackled some extremely demanding leading roles, as well as proving a useful sounding-board for some powerhouse leading ladies of the 1970s and 1980s. His unsettling presence makes him something of a lightweight, better-looking Jack Palance (*qv*) but, in the cinema at least, he has not quite found a slot at the top.

1970: Love Story. 1976: Smash-Up on Interstate Five (TV). Charlie's Angels (TV). Jackson County Jail. 1977: Rolling Thunder. The Amazing Howard Hughes (TV). Eliza's Horoscope. 1978: The Betsy. Eyes of Laura Mars. 1980: Coal Miner's Daughter. 1981: Back Roads. 1982: The Executioner's Song (TV. GB: cinemas). 1983: Savage Islands. Nate and Hayes. 1984: The River Rat. 1985: Black Moon Rising. The Park is Mine (TV). 1986: Double Image (TV).

JORDAN, Richard 1938–

Films almost passed up on this chunkily-built, blink-eyed, good-looking American actor with tightly curly fair hair and a vague resemblance to the British actor Derren Nesbitt (*qv*). A stage actor until he was 32, Jordan was brought to films to play a couple of young western tearaways. A TV series called *Captains and the Kings* brought him more popularity and meatier roles for a short while. After a few years away on stage in the early 1980s, he returned to films to play some plainly dangerous characters. Married to actress Kathleen Widdoes.

1970: Valdez is Coming. Lawman. 1971: Chato's Land. 1972: The Trial of the Catonsville Nine. 1973: Incident at Vichy (TV). The Friends of Eddie Coyle. 1974: The Yakuza. 1975: Rooster Cogburn. Kamouraska. 1976: Logan's Run. 1978: Interiors. Old Boyfriends. The Defection of Simas Kudirka (TV). Les Misérables (TV). 1980: The Biggest Bank Robbery (TV). Raise the Titanic! The French Atlantic Affair (TV). 1981: Washington Mistress (TV). The Bunker (TV). 1984: Dune.

A Flash of Green. 1985: The Mean Season. 1986: The Men's Club.

JORY, Victor 1902–1982

Tall, dark, Alaska-born Hollywood actor. If you needed a villain from 1932 to 1957, all you had to do was get out the black jacket and floral waistcoat and call for Victor Jory. Grim-faced Jory's bad guys looked as if they would brook very little mercy and he menaced most of the screen's cowboy heroes. Also a very sinister Oberon in *A Midsummer Night's Dream*. Died from a heart attack.

1930: Renegades. 1932: The Pride of the Legion. Second Hand Wife (GB: The Illegal Divorce). 1933: Handle with Care. Infernal Machine. State Fair. Broadway Bad (GB: Her Reputation). Sailor's Luck. Trick for Trick. I Loved You Wednesday. Devil's in Love. My Woman. Smoky. 1934: He Was Her Man. I Believed in You. Pursued. Madame Du Barry. Murder in Trinidad. White Lies. 1935: Mills of the Gods. Too Tough to Kill. Escape from Devil's Island. Streamline Express. Party Wire. A Midsummer Night's Dream. 1936: Hell Ship Morgan. The King Steps Out. Meet Nero Wolfe. Rangle River. 1937: Glamorous Night. Bulldog Drummond at Bay. First Lady. 1938: The Adventures of Tom Sawyer. 1939: Dodge City. Man of Conquest. Women in the Wind. Wings of the Navy. Each Dawn I Die. Susannah of the Mounties. Men with Whips. I Stole a Million. Gone with the Wind. Call a Messenger. Blackwell's Island. 1940: Cherokee Strip (GB: Fighting Marshal). Knights of the Range. The Green Archer (serial). The Light of Western Stars. The Lone Wolf Meets a Lady. River's End. The Girl from Havana. Lady with Red Hair. Give Us Wings. The Shadow (serial). 1941: Charlie Chan in Rio. Border Vigilantes. Wide Open Town. Bad Men of Missouri. Riders of the Timberline. Secrets of the Lone Wolf (GB: Secrets). The Stork Pays Off. 1942: Tombstone, the Town Too Tough to Die. Shut My Big Mouth. 1943: The Kansan (GB: Wagon Wheels). Hoppy Serves a Writ. Buckskin Frontier (GB: The Iron Road). Bar 20. The Unknown Guest. Colt Comrades. The Leather Burners. Power of the Press. 1947: A Voice is Born: the Story of Niklos Grafni (voice only). 1948: The Loves of Carmen. The Gallant Blade. 1949: A Woman's Secret. South of St Louis. Canadian Pacific. Fighting Man of the Plains. 1950: The Capture. The Cariboo Trail.

1951: *Cave of Outlaws. Flaming Feather. The Highwayman.* 1952: *Toughest Man in Arizona. Son of Ali Baba.* 1953: *The Hindu (GB: Sabaka). Cat Women of the Moon. The Man from the Alamo.* 1954: *Valley of the Kings.* 1956: *Introduction to Erica. Lady in Fear (TV. GB: cinemas). Manfish (GB: Calypso). Death of a Scoundrel. Mr and Mrs McAdam (TV). Blackjack Ketchum, Desperado.* 1957: *Diary of a Nurse (TV). The Man Who Turned to Stone. Last Stagecoach West.* 1960: *The Fugitive Kind.* 1962: *The Miracle Worker.* 1964: *Cheyenne Autumn.* 1965: *Who Has Seen the Wind (TV).* 1967: *Ride the Wind (TV. GB: cinemas).* 1968: *Jigsaw (TV).* 1969: *Mackenna's Gold (narrator only). A Time for Dying. Perilous Voyage (TV).* 1970: *Flap (GB: The Last Warrior).* 1974: *Papillon. Frasier the Sensuous Lion.* 1976: *Perilous Voyage (TV).* 1977: *Kino, the Padre on Horseback.* 1978: *Devil Dog – the Hound of Hell (TV).* 1980: *The Mountain Men.*

JOURDAN, Louis (L. Gendre) 1919–
Debonair, dark-haired French charmer with smilingly handsome face. He was in Hollywood films soon after the end of World War II, but has made fewer than one might think in a 40-year career.
1939: *Le corsaire. Félicie Nanteuil.* 1940: *Untel père et fils. Le comédie du bonheur.* 1941: *Premier rendez-vous (GB: First Appointment). Nous les jeunes. Parade en sept nuits.* 1942: *L'arlésienne. La belle aventure. La vie de bohème.* 1943: *Les petites du quai aux fleurs.* 1947: *The Paradine Case.* 1948: *Letter from an Unknown Woman. No Minor Vices.* 1949: *Madame Bovary.* 1951: *Bird of Paradise. Anne of the Indies.* 1952: *The Happy Time. Decameron Nights.* 1953: *Rue de l'étrapade (GB: Françoise Steps Out).* 1954: *Three Coins in the Fountain.* 1955: *The Swan.* 1956: *Julie. Eloise (TV). La mariée est trop belle (GB and US: The Bride is Too Beautiful).* 1957: *Escapade. Dangerous Exile.* 1958: *Gigi.* 1959: *The Best of Everything.* 1960: *Les vierges de Rome/The Virgins of Rome.* 1961: *Dark Journey. Léviathan. Le compte de Monte-Cristo/The Story of the Count of Monte-Cristo.* 1962: *Le désordre/Disorder. Mathias Sandorf.* 1963: *The V.I.P.s* 1965: *Made in Paris. Les sultans.* 1966: *Cervantes.* 1967: *Peau d'espion (GB: To Commit a Murder).* 1968: *To Die in Paris (TV). A Flea in Her Ear.* 1969: *Fear No Evil (TV). Run a Crooked Mile (TV). Ritual of Evil (TV).* 1972: *The Great American Beauty Contest (TV).* 1974: *The Count of Monte-Cristo (TV. GB: cinemas).* 1976: *The Man in the Iron Mask (TV).* 1977: *Silver Bears.* 1981: *Double Deal.* 1982: *Swamp Thing.* 1983: *Octopussy.* 1986: *Beverly Hills Madam (TV).*

JOYCE, Brenda (Betty Leabo) 1918–
Fresh, bright, athletic, healthy-looking Hollywood blonde of the 1940s. A former model, she showed up well in a number of second leads in 'A' pictures before becoming the screen's second-best-known Jane (in Tarzan films) after Maureen O'Sullivan. She left films when deciding to quit the jungle adventure series in 1949.
1939: *Here I Am a Stranger. The Rains Came.* 1940: *Little Old New York. Maryland. Public Deb No 1.* 1941: *Private Nurse. Marry the Boss's Daughter. Right to the Heart/Knockout.* 1942: *Whispering Ghosts. The Postman Didn't Ring. Little Tokyo USA.* 1943: *Thumbs Up.* 1945: *Tarzan and the Amazons. The Enchanted Forest. Pillow of Death. Strange Confession. I'll Tell the World.* 1946: *Little Giant (GB: On the Carpet). Spider Woman Strikes Back. Tarzan and the Leopard Woman. Danger Woman.* 1947: *Tarzan and the Huntress. Stepchild.* 1948: *Tarzan and the Mermaids.* 1949: *Tarzan's Magic Fountain.*

JUDD, Edward 1932–
Tall, well-built, gentle-looking, Shanghai-born leading man who had several tiny roles in British films before being suddenly elevated to stardom in 1961. He surprisingly lasted only six years in star roles, but returned later, balding and seemingly with a tougher streak, in character parts. Married to actresses Gene Anderson (1931–1965) and Norma Ronald.
1948: *The Guinea Pig. Once a Jolly Swagman (US: Maniacs on Wheels). The Small Voice (US: Hideout).* 1949: *Boys in Brown.* 1953: *The Large Rope.* 1954: *Adventure in the Hopfields. The Good Die Young.* 1956: *X the Unknown. Battle of the River Plate (US: Pursuit of the Graf Spee).* 1958: *I Was Monty's Double. Subway in the Sky. The Man Upstairs. Carry on Sergeant.* 1959: *The Shakedown. No Safety Ahead.* 1960: *The Challenge. The Criminal (US: The Concrete Jungle).* 1961: *The Day the Earth Caught Fire.* 1962: *Mystery Submarine.* 1963: *The World Ten Times Over (US: Pussycat Alley). Stolen Hours. The Long Ships.* 1964: *First Men in the Moon.* 1965: *Strange Bedfellows. Invasion.* 1966: *Island of Terror.* 1968: *The Vengeance of She.* 1971: *Universal Soldier.* 1972: *Living Free. The Rape.* 1973: *O Lucky Man! Vault of Horror. Assassin.* 1975: *Feelings (US: Whose Child Am I?)* 1976: *The Incredible Sarah.* 1979: *The House on Garibaldi Street.* 1983: *The Boys in Blue. The Hound of the Baskervilles.*

JURADO, Katy (Maria J. Garcia) 1927–
Fiery, dark-haired Mexican actress with pouting lips and flashing eyes: with those looks Katy really couldn't have come from anywhere else. Her firecracker acting style brought her to Hollywood, but they were reluctant to let her do much more than toss her curls, wear off-the-shoulder peasant blouses and smoulder. Married to Ernest Borgnine 1959–1963. Nominated for an Academy Award in *Broken Lance.*
1943: *No Maturas.* 1944: *La Vida Inutil de Pito Perez.* 1945: *La Sombra de Chuco el Roto. El Museo del Crimen. Bartolo Toco la Flauta. Soltera y con Gemelos.* 1946: *La Viuda Celosa. Rosa del Caribe.* 1948: *Nosotros los Pobres. Prision de Sueños.* 1949: *Hay Lugar para Dos. El Seminarista. Mujer de Medica Noche.* 1950: *Cabellera Blanca.* 1951: *Cárcel de Mujeres. The Bullfighter and the Lady.* 1952: *El Bruto. High Noon.* 1953: *San Antone. Arrowhead.* 1954: *Broken Lance. Tehuantepec. El Corazón y la Espada (US: The Sword of Granada).* 1955: *The Racers (GB: Such Men Are Dangerous). Trial.* 1956: *The Man from Del*

Chan at the Opera. 1937: Night Key. West of Shanghai. *Cinema Circus. 1938: The Invisible Menace. Mr Wong, Detective. 1939: Son of Frankenstein. The Mystery of Mr Wong. The Man They Could Not Hang. Mr Wong in Chinatown. Tower of London. Devil's Island. 1940: The Fatal Hour (GB: Mr Wong at Headquarters). British Intelligence (GB: Enemy Agent). Black Friday. The Man with Nine Lives (GB: Behind the Door). Doomed to Die (GB: The Mystery of the Wentworth Castle). Before I Hang. The Ape. You'll Find Out. 1941: *Information Please No 8. The Devil Commands. *Information Please No 12. 1942: The Boogie Man Will Get You. 1944: The Climax. House of Frankenstein. 1945: The Body Snatcher. Isle of the Dead. 1946: Bedlam. 1947: The Secret Life of Walter Mitty. Lured (GB: Personal Column). Dick Tracy Meets Gruesome (GB: Dick Tracy's Amazing Adventure). Unconquered. 1948: Tap Roots. 1949: Abbott and Costello Meet the Killer Boris Karloff. 1951: The Strange Door. The Emperor's Nightingale (narrator only). 1952: The Black Castle. 1953: The Hindu (GB: Sabaka). Colonel March Investigates. Abbott and Costello Meet Dr Jekyll and Mr Hyde. Il monstro dell'isola/Monster of the Island. 1956: Rendezvous in Black (TV). 1957: Voodoo Island. *The Juggler of Our Lady (narrator only). 1958: Grip of the Strangler (US: The Haunted Strangler). Frankenstein 1970. Heart of Darkness (TV). Corridors of Blood. 1960: To the Sound of Trumpets (TV). 1963: The Raven. The Terror. Comedy of Terrors. Black Sabbath. *Today's Teens (narrator only). 1964: Bikini Beach. 1965: Monster of Terror (US: Die, Monster, Die). Mondo balordo/Strange World (narrator only). 1966: The Ghost in the Invisible Bikini. The Daydreamer (voice only). The Venetian Affair. The Sorcerers. 1967: Mad Monster Party (voice only). El coleccionista de cadaveres (GB: Cauldron of Blood. US: Blind Man's Buff). 1968: Targets. Curse of the Crimson Altar (US: The Crimson Cult). 1969: Isle of the Snake People/Snake People. The Incredible Invasion. †The Fear Chamber. †House of Evil.

† *Unreleased*

KAYE, Danny (David D. Kaminsky) 1913–
Red-haired, long-legged American zany comedian and singer of tongue-twisting comic songs, almost always on the run from villains

and the victim of his own wild imagination. After a big star build-up at the Goldwyn Studio, he made some fun, funny, firecracker, freewheeling entertainments – especially *The Secret Life of Walter Mitty, Wonder Man, Knock on Wood* and *The Court Jester* – before too many of his films somehow began to reflect the dreamy sentimentalism of his much-publicized work for children's charities. Special Oscars 1954 and 1982.
1937: *Dime a Dance. *Cupid Takes a Holiday. 1938: *Money or Your Life. *Getting an Eyeful. 1942: *Night Shift. 1944: Up in Arms. 1945: Wonder Man. 1946: The Kid from Brooklyn. 1947: The Secret Life of Walter Mitty. 1948: A Song is Born. 1949: The Inspector General. It's a Great Feeling. 1951: On the Riviera. 1952: Hans Christian Andersen ... and the dancer. 1954: *Assignment Children. Knock on Wood. White Christmas. *Hula from Hollywood. 1955: The Court Jester. 1958: Merry Andrew. Me and the Colonel. 1959: The Five Pennies. 1961: On the Double. 1963: The Man from the Diners' Club. 1969: The Madwoman of Chaillot. 1975: Peter Pan (TV) 1977: Pinocchio (TV). 1981: Skokie (TV. GB: Once They Marched Through a Thousand Towns).

KEACH, Stacy (Walter S. Keach Jr) 1941–
Light-haired (thinning from his twenties) broad-shouldered American actor with slight but distinctive cleft upper lip (latterly covered with moustache); usually seen as slightly off-centre and sometimes downright eccentric characters. He had some powerful leading roles in the early 1970s but by the end of the decade his career seemed, to some observers, to have lost its way. He was jailed in Britain for several months in 1984/1985 on narcotics charges, but soon picked up his career.
1968: †The Heart is a Lonely Hunter. 1969: End of the Road. 1970: The Traveling Executioner. Brewster McCloud. 1971: Doc. Fat City. 1972: The New Centurions (GB: Precinct 45: Los Angeles Police). Luther. The Life and Times of Judge Roy Bean. Orville and Wilbur (TV). 1973: Particular Men (TV). 1974: The Dion Brothers (TV. GB: cinemas, as The Gravy Train). Watched. One by One (narrator only). All the Kind Strangers (TV). 1975: James Dean – The First American Teenager (and narrator). Conduct Unbecoming. *Hamburger Hamlet. The Killer Inside Me.

1976: Dynasty (TV). Gli esecutori (GB: The Sicilian Cross. US: Street People). Jesus of Nazareth (TV). 1977: The Squeeze. Gray Lady Down. The Duellist (narrator only). Il grande attacca/The Biggest Battle. 1978: The Mountain in the Jungle (GB: Prisoner of the Cannibal God. US: Primitive Desires). Deux Solitudes. Up in Smoke. 1979: The Search for Solutions (narrator only). The Ninth Configuration/Twinkle, Twinkle, Killer Kane. Diary of a Young Comic (TV). 1980: The Long Riders. A Rumor of War (TV). 1981: Road Games. Butterfly. Cheech and Chong's Nice Dreams. 1982: That Championship Season. 1983: Murder Me, Murder You (TV). More Than Murder (TV). 1984: Mistral's Daughter (video). 1985: Intimate Strangers (TV). 1986: The Return of Mike Hammer (TV).

As director: *1971: *The Repeater.*

† *as Stacy Keach Junior*

KEATON, Buster (Joseph Keaton) 1895–1966
Expressionless, dark-haired, soulful-eyed American silent-screen comedian. Dubbed 'The Great Stone Face', he brought the mechanics of visual comedy down to a fine art, but struggled (both with his work and an alcohol problem) with the coming of sound. Much revered in post-war times, especially in Europe, he found fresh inspiration in his last few years. Special Academy Award 1959. Died from lung cancer.
1917: *A Reckless Romeo. *The Butcher Boy. *The Rough House. *His Wedding Night. *A Country Hero (released 1920). *Coney Island. *Oh Doctor! 1918: *Out West. *The Bell Boy. *Moonshine. *Good Night Nurse. *The Cook. 1919: *Love. *A Desert Hero. *Back Stage. *The Hayseed. *The Garage. 1920: *The Round Up. †*One Week. †*The High Sign. The Saphead. *†The Scarecrow. †*Neighbors. †*Convict 13. 1921: †*Hard Luck. †*The Goat. †*The Boat. †*The Paleface. †*The Playhouse. 1922: †*The Electric House. †*The Frozen North. †*My Wife's Relations. †*The Blacksmith. †*Daydreams. †*Cops. 1923: †*The Balloonatic. *The Love Nest. †The Three Ages. †Our Hospitality. 1924: ‡Sherlock Junior. ‡The Navigator. 1925: ‡Seven Chances. ‡Go West. 1926: †The General. Battling Butler. 1927: College. 1928: Steamboat Bill Junior. The Cameraman. 1929: Hollywood

*Revue of 1929 (and German version). Spite Marriage (and French version). 1930; Free and Easy (and Spanish version). Doughboys (GB: Forward March). 1931: Parlor, Bedroom and Bath (GB: Romeo in Pyjamas. And German and French versions). Sidewalks of New York. 1932: Speak Easily. The Passionate Plumber (and French version). 1933: What! No Beer? 1934: Le roi des Champs-Elysées. 1935: L'horloger amoureux. The Invaders (US: An Old Spanish Custom). *La Fiesta de Santa Barbara. *Allez-Oop. *The Serenade. *The Gold Ghost. *Palooka from Paducah. Hayseed Romance. *Stars and Stripes. *The E Flat Man. *One Run Elmer. 1936: *The Timid Young Man. *Three on a Limb. *Grand Slam Opera. *Blue Blazes. *The Chemist. Three Men on a Horse. *Mixed Magic. 1937: *Jail Bait. *Ditto. *Love Nest on Wheels. 1939: *Pest from the West. *Mooching through Georgia. The Jones Family in Hollywood. Hollywood Cavalcade. *Nothing But Pleasure. The Jones Family in Quick Millions. 1940: Li'l Abner (GB: Trouble Chaser). *The Villain Still Pursued Her. *Pardon My Berth Marks. *The Spook Speaks. *The Taming of the Snood. 1941: *His Ex Marks the Spot. *General Nuisance. *She's Oil Mine. *So You Won't Squawk. 1943: Forever and a Day. 1944: San Diego, I Love You. Two Girls and a Sailor. 1945: That Night with You. That's the Spirit. 1946: God's Country. El moderno Barba Azul. 1948: Un duel à mort. 1949: In the Good Old Summertime. The Loveable Cheat. You're My Everything. 1950: Sunset Boulevard. 1952: Limelight. Paradise for Buster. 1953: L'incantevole nemica. 1956: Around the World in 80 Days. 1960: The Adventures of Huckleberry Finn. 1962: Ten Girls Ago. 1963: It's a Mad, Mad, Mad, Mad World. *The Triumph of Lester Snapwell. 1964: Pajama Party. 1965: The Railrodder. Sergeant Deadhead. Buster Keaton Rides Again. Beach Blanket Bingo (GB: Malibu Beach). Film. How to Stuff a Wild Bikini. Due Marines e uno generale. 1966: A Funny Thing Happened on the Way to the Forum. *The Scribe.*

Also as director: *1938: Hollywood Handicap. Life in Sometown USA. Streamlined Swing.*

‡ *Also directed* † *Also co-directed*

KEATON, Diane (D. Hall) 1946–
Fascinating, bird-like, light-haired American

actress and singer, with naturalistic style. She rose to fame in Woody Allen vehicles (and won an Oscar in his *Annie Hall*), but soon proved she could stand on her own feet with a magnetic performance for Richard Brooks in *Looking for Mr Goodbar.*
1970: Lovers and Other Strangers. 1972: The Godfather. 1973: Play It Again Sam. 1974: Sleeper. The Godfather Part II. 1975: Love and Death. I Will . . . I Will . . . for Now. 1976: Harry and Walter Go to New York. 1977: Annie Hall. Looking for Mr Goodbar. 1978: Interiors. 1979: Manhattan. 1981: Shoot the Moon. Reds. 1984: Mrs Soffel. The Little Drummer Girl.

KEEL, Howard (Harold Leek) 1917–
Round-faced American actor with big baritone singing voice and swaggering style. Not too well used by his studio, M-G-M, who cast him in straight roles in second-features as well as some pretty lumpish musicals. He did enjoy a good run in the early fifties with *Kiss Me Kate, Calamity Jane* and *Seven Brides for Seven Brothers*, but then slipped into routine action films.
1948: †The Small Voice (US: Hideout). 1950: Annie Get Your Gun. Pagan Love Song. 1951: Three Guys Named Mike. Texas Carnival. Show Boat. Across the Wide Missouri (narrator only). Callaway Went Thataway (GB: The Star Said No!). 1952: Lovely to Look At. Desperate Search. 1953: Fast Company. I Love Melvin. Ride, Vaquero! Calamity Jane. Kiss Me Kate. 1954: Rose Marie. Seven Brides for Seven Brothers. Deep in My Heart. 1955: Jupiter's Darling. Kismet. 1958: Floods of Fear. 1959: The Big Fisherman. 1961: Armored Command. 1962: The Day of the Triffids. 1964: The Man from Button Willow (voice only). 1966: Waco. 1967: Red Tomahawk. The War Wagon. 1968: Arizona Bushwhackers.

† *As Harold Keel*

KEELER, Ruby (Ethel Keeler) 1909–
Dark-haired Canadian-born star of Hollywood musicals of the thirties, often in tandem with Dick Powell. The famous initial description of Astaire on his arrival in Hollywood – 'Can't act, can't sing, can dance a little' – would have fitted Ruby, though even her clackety-clack dancing was hopeful and energetic rather than hep. Still, she was pretty,

and whenever the leading lady broke a leg, Ruby went out there and became a star. Married (first of two) to Al Jolson from 1928 to 1939.
*1928: *Ruby Keeler. 1933: 42nd Street. Gold Diggers of 1933. Footlight Parade. 1934: Dames. Flirtation Walk. 1935: Go into Your Dance (GB: Casino de Paree). Shipmates Forever. 1936: Colleen. 1937: Ready, Willing and Able. 1938: Mother Carey's Chickens. 1941: Sweetheart of the Campus (GB: Broadway Ahead). 1969: The Phynx.*

KEITEL, Harvey 1947–
Dark-haired, pugnacious American actor who began in intense, often violent working-class roles. A sort of skid-row Fredric March (an actor he also resembles facially), Keitel has not achieved quite the prominence one would have thought probable a few years ago. His unsettling qualities may keep him in more rewarding if not giant-sized roles. Still tends to play loners with problems.
1968: Who's That Knocking at My Door? 1970: Street Scene. 1973: Mean Streets. 1974: Alice Doesn't Live Here Anymore. Mother, Jugs and Speed (released 1976). The Virginia Hill Story (TV). 1975: That's the Way of the World (later Shining Star). 1976: Taxi Driver. Welcome to LA. Buffalo Bill and the Indians, or: Sitting Bull's History Lesson. 1977: The Duellists. Fingers. 1978: Eagle's Wing. Blue Collar. 1979: La mort en direct/Deathwatch. 1980: Bad Timing (US: Bad Timing: a Sensual Obsession). Saturn 3. 1981: The Border. La nuit de Varennes. 1982: The New World. 1983: Order of Death/Cop Killer.

Une pierre dans la bouche. Exposed. 1984: Falling in Love. 1985: Camorra. Wiseguys. Un complicato intrig di donne, vicoli e delitti (US: Back Alley of Naples). El caballero del dragon. La sposa americana. 1986: The Men's Club. Off Beat. Corsa in discesa/Downhill Race. The Inquiry.

KEITH, Brian (Robert B. Keith) 1921–
Tough-looking, heavy-set American actor with thick mop of light brown hair. The son of Robert Keith (although nothing like his father), he was cast as rugged frontier scouts, grouchy fathers and craggy types with hearts of gold. Became more gruff and granite-like as the years progressed.
1924: †Pied Piper Malone. 1947: Boomerang! Kiss of Death. The Naked City. 1948: Portrait of Jennie (GB: Jennie). 1951: Fourteen Hours. 1953: Arrowhead. Jivaro (GB: Lost Treasure of the Amazon). 1954: Alaska Seas. The Violent Men (GB: Rough Company). The Bamboo Prison. 1955: Tight Spot. Five Against the House. 1956: Storm Center. Nightfall. 1957: Run of the Arrow. Chicago Confidential. Hell Canyon Outlaws (GB: The Tall Trouble). Dino (GB: Killer Dino). 1958: Sierra Baron. Villa! Violent Road. Fort Dobbs. Appointment with a Shadow (GB: The Big Story). Desert Hell. 1959: The Young Philadelphians (GB: The City Jungle). 1960: Ten Who Dared. 1961: The Parent Trap. The Deadly Companions. 1962: Moon Pilot. 1963: Savage Sam. A Tiger Walks. 1964: The Tenderfoot (TV, GB: cinemas). The Raiders. Those Calloways. 1965: The Pleasure Seekers. The Hallelujah Trail. 1966: The Russians Are Coming, the Russians Are Coming. The Rare Breed. Way ... Way Out. Nevada Smith. 1967: Reflections in a Golden Eye. 1968: With Six You Get Eggroll. Krakatoa, East of Java. 1969: Gaily, Gaily (GB: Chicago, Chicago). 1970: Suppose They Gave a War and Nobody Came. The Mackenzie Break. 1971: Scandalous John. Second Chance (TV). Something Big. 1974: The Yakuza. 1975: The Wind and the Lion. 1976: Joe Panther (GB: TV). Nickelodeon. 1977: In the Matter of Karen Ann Quinlan (TV). The Loneliest Runner (TV). 1978: Hooper. The Court Martial of George Armstrong Custer (TV). 1979: Meteor. The Mountain Men. 1980: ‡Hammett (released 1982). Charlie Chan and the Curse of the Dragon Queen. 1981: Sharky's Machine. 1982: Cry

for the Strangers (TV). 1984: Dream One (Nemo). 1986: Death Before Dishonour.

† As Robert Keith Junior
‡ Scenes deleted from final release print

KEITH, David 1954–
Pugnacious American actor with light, tufty hair. Often in cocksure roles, he can also play sensitive characters when the occasion demands. Similar in style to Dennis Quaid (qv) and The Monkees' Micky Dolenz, Tennessee-born Keith began to play forceful leading roles from 1982, often as men trapped in some way or another.
1979: Co-Ed Fever (TV). Friendly Fire (TV). The Rose. The Great Santini. 1980: Brubaker. 1981: Back Roads. Take This Job and Shove It. An Officer and a Gentleman. 1982: Independence Day (later Restless). The Lords of Discipline. 1983: The Golden Moment (TV). 1984: Firestarter. Gulag (cable TV. GB: cinemas). 1986: If Tomorrow Comes.

KELLER, Marthe (Marte Keller) 1945–
Dark-haired, well-scrubbed, Swiss-born actress whose budding dancing career was cut short by a skiing accident. Turning to acting, she built up a solid reputation on stage before becoming a sporadic visitor to the screen. Hollywood took her up belatedly in 1976, publicists knocking years off her age in trying to build her up as a young romantic star. But after six years of American films she returned to the continent.
1966: Funeral in Berlin. 1968: Le diable par le queue. 1969: Les caprices de Marie (US: Give Her the Moon). 1971: La vieille fille. Un

cave/The Loser. 1972: Elle court, elle court la banlieue (GB: TV, as Love in the Suburbs). 1973: Toute une vie (GB and US: And Now My Love). 1974: Die Antwort kennt nur der Wind. 1975: Par le antiche scale (GB and US: Down the Ancient Stairs). Le guépier. 1976: Marathon Man. Black Sunday. 1977: Bobby Deerfield. 1978: Fedora. 1980: The Formula. Les uns et les autres. 1981: The Amateur. 1982: Wagner (TV). 1983: Femmes de personne. 1985: Joan Lui. Rouge baiser.

KELLERMAN, Sally 1938–
Lanky, braless Hollywood blonde, with gawky gait, distinctive wide mouth and appealingly offbeat personality. Her successful period was limited both by its lateness after disheartening years of struggle, and by the slim number of films she chose to accept after her hit as Lt 'Hot Lips' in M*A*S*H, a role which won her an Oscar nomination. Now in character roles, but still an intriguing performer. Also a singer.
1957: Reform School Girl. 1960: Hands of a Stranger (released 1962). 1965: The Third Day. The Lollipop Cover (voice only). The Movie Maker (TV). 1968: The Boston Strangler. 1969: The April Fools. M*A*S*H. 1970: Brewster McCloud. 1971: A Reflection of Fear. 1972: Last of the Red Hot Lovers. Lost Horizon. 1973: Slither. 1974: Rafferty and the Gold Dust Twins. 1976: The Big Bus. Welcome to LA. 1977: The Mouse and His Child (voice only). 1978: She'll Be Sweet/Magee and the Lady. 1978: It Rained All Night the Day I Left. Verna: USO Girl (TV). 1979: A Little Romance. Foxes. 1980: Head On. Serial. Big Blonde (TV). Loving Couples. Melvin and Howard. 1981: Sweet Sixteen and Pregnant (TV. Narrator only). 1982: For Lovers Only (TV). 1983: Dempsey (TV). September Gun (TV). 1985: Meatballs III. Secret Weapons (TV). Moving Violations. Sesame Street Presents: Follow That Bird (voice only). Sexpionage (video). 1986: The Right Hand Man. Back to School.

KELLY, Gene (Eugene Kelly) 1912–
Dark-haired American dancer of Irish extraction, who could also sing in a light but distinctive way. Never able to convince purely as an actor, he was one of M-G-M's – and Hollywood's – top stars in musicals from 1945 to 1955 and responsible, with director Stanley

Donen, for several memorably innovative entertainments, in most of which he seems, on recollection, to have been a sailor on leave. Astaire's only real rival as a dancing star – though their styles were very different, Kelly's image being much less elegant – he was given a special Oscar in 1951. Married (first of two) to Betsy Blair from 1941 to 1957. Oscar nomination for *Anchors Aweigh*.

1942: For Me and My Gal (GB: For Me and My Girl). 1943: Dubarry Was a Lady. Pilot No. 5. Thousands Cheer. The Cross of Lorraine. 1944: Cover Girl. Christmas Holiday. Ziegfeld Follies (released 1946). 1945: Anchors Aweigh. 1947: Living in a Big Way. 1948: Words and Music. The Pirate. The Three Musketeers. 1949: On the Town. Take Me Out to the Ball Game (GB: Everybody's Cheering). 1950: Summer Stock (GB: If You Feel Like Singing). The Black Hand. 1951: An American in Paris. It's a Big Country. 1952: Singin' in the Rain. The Devil Makes Three. Love is Better than Ever. 1954: Seagulls over Sorrento (US: Crest of the Wave). Brigadoon. Deep in My Heart. 1955: It's Always Fair Weather. Invitation to the Dance. 1956: The Happy Road. 1957: Les Girls. 1958: Marjorie Morningstar. 1960: Inherit the Wind. Let's Make Love. 1964: What a Way to Go! 1967: The Young Girls of Rochefort. 1973: 40 Carats. 1974: That's Entertainment! 1976: That's Entertainment Part Two. 1977: Viva Knievel! 1980: Xanadu. 1981: Reporters. America's Sweetheart; the Mary Pickford Story (narrator only). 1985: That's Dancing!

As director: *1949: On the Town (co-directed). 1952: Singin' in the Rain (co-directed). 1955: Invitation to the Dance. 1956: The Happy Road. 1958: The Tunnel of Love. 1962: Gigot. 1967: A Guide for the Married Man. 1969: Hello, Dolly! 1970: The Cheyenne Social Club. 1975: Woman of the Year (TV). 1976: That's Entertainment Part Two (new sequences). 1985: That's Dancing!*

KELLY, Grace 1928–1982
Straight-faced blonde American actress, mostly in strait-laced leading roles although Alfred Hitchcock did his best to bring out her latent sexuality in her three films for him. Very striking in *High Noon* and strikingly drab in *The Country Girl*, for which she won an Oscar. Her career remained frustratingly

unfulfilled, however, when the 'fair Miss Frigidaire' (as Sinatra called her character in *High Society*) married Prince Rainier of Monaco in 1956 and retired. Died from a brain haemorrhage after a car crash. Also received an Oscar nomination for *Mogambo*.

1951: Fourteen Hours. 1952: High Noon. 1953: Mogambo. 1954: Rear Window. Dial M for Murder. The Country Girl. Green Fire. The Bridges at Toko-Ri. 1955: To Catch a Thief. 1956: High Society. The Swan. 1959: Invitation to Monte Carlo. 1978: The Children of Theatre Street (narrator only).

KELLY, Judy 1913–
Australian-born blonde star of British films in the thirties. Never settled down as a top star, seeming to alternate between leads and supporting roles. Her sophisticated personality often got her cast as 'other women', and with the realism of wartime, her popularity wavered.

1928: Adam's Apple (US: Honeymoon Ahead). 1931: Sleepless Nights. 1932: Money Talks. Lord Camber's Ladies. 1933: Hawleys of High Street. Their Night Out. The Love Nest. The Private Life of Henry VIII. Crime on the Hill. Mannequin. The Black Abbot. Four Masked Men. 1934: Anything Might Happen. Things Are Looking Up. 1935: It's a Bet. Royal Cavalcade (US: Regal Cavalcade). Marry the Girl. Charing Cross Road. Captain Bill. 1936: Under Proof. First Offence. A Star Fell from Heaven. The Limping Man. Aren't Men Beasts! 1937: Ship's Concert. Make Up. Boys Will Be Girls. The Price of Folly. Over She Goes. The Last Chance. 1938: Jane Steps Out.

Luck of the Navy (US: North Sea Patrol). Première (US: One Night in Paris). Queer Cargo (US: Pirates of the Seven Seas). 1939: Dead Man's Shoes. The Midas Touch. At the Villa Rose (US: House of Mystery). 1940: George and Margaret. Saloon Bar. 1942: Tomorrow We Live (US: At Dawn We Die). 1943: The Butler's Dilemma. 1944: It Happened One Sunday. 1945: Dead of Night. 1947: Dancing with Crime. 1948: Warning to Wantons.

KELLY, Nancy 1921–
Dark-haired, ladylike, decorous American actress. A child model-and-occasional actress, she was only really in films from 1938 to 1946, before taking up the stage career on which she had set her heart. Her brother, Jack Kelly (1927–), has also had a sporadic film career. Married to Edmond O'Brien 1941–1942. Received an Oscar nomination for *The Bad Seed*.

1926: Mismates. Untamed Lady. 1929: The Girl on the Barge. 1934: Convention Girl (GB: Atlantic City Romance). 1938: Submarine Patrol. Tailspin. 1939: Jesse James. Frontier Marshal. Stanley and Livingstone. 1940: He Married His Wife. Private Affairs. Sailor's Lady. One Night in the Tropics. 1941: Scotland Yard. A Very Young Lady. Parachute Battalion. 1942: Fly By Night (GB: Secret of G. 32). To the Shores of Tripoli. Friendly Enemies. 1943: Tornado. Women in Bondage. Tarzan's Desert Mystery. 1944: Show Business. Gambler's Choice. 1945: Song of the Sarong. Betrayal from the East. Double Exposure. The Woman Who Came Back. Follow That Woman. 1946: Murder in the Music Hall. 1956: The Bad Seed. Crowded Paradise. 1977: Murder at the World Series (TV). 1975: The Imposter (TV).

KELLY, Paul 1899–1956
Tall, upright, grim-looking American actor (of Irish parentage), in films as a child. Went grey early – hardly surprising as he was jailed in 1927 for the manslaughter of his mistress's husband (he married her in 1931 and she was killed in a car crash in 1940) after a fight. On his release from prison he became a staunch star of 'B' features and occasional villain of bigger films, but did all his finest work on stage. Died from a heart attack.

*1908: *A Good Little Devil. 1911: *Captain Barnacle, Diplomat. *How Milly Became an Actress. 1912: *A Juvenile Love Affair. *Cap-*

tain Barnacle's Waif. *An Expensive Shine. 1913: *The Mouse and the Lion. *Counsellor Bobby. 1914: *Buddy's First Call. *Buddy's Downfall. *Heartease. Lillian's Dilemma. 1915: *The Jarr Family Discovers Harlem (and subsequent 48-film series). *The Shabbies. *A Family Picnic. 1916: *Myrtle the Manicurist. *Claudia. 1917: Knights of the Square Table. 1918: Fit to Fight. 1919: Anne of Green Gables. 1920: Uncle Sam of Freedom Ridge. 1921: The Old Oaken Bucket. The Great Adventure. 1926: The New Klondike. 1927: Special Delivery. Slide, Kelly, Slide. 1932: The Girl from Calgary. 1933: Broadway thru a Keyhole. 1934: Side Streets (US: Woman in Her Thirties). Blind Date. Death on the Diamond. The Love Captive. School for Girls. 1935: When a Man's a Man. The President Vanishes (GB: Strange Conspiracy). Silk Hat Kid. Speed Devils. Public Hero Number One. Star of Midnight. My Marriage. 1936: Here Comes Trouble. It's a Great Life. The Song and Dance Man. Women Are Trouble. The Accusing Finger. The Country Beyond. Murder with Pictures. 1937: The Frame-Up. Join the Marines. Parole Racket. Fit for a King. Navy Blue and Gold. It Happened Out West. 1938: The Nurse from Brooklyn. Torchy Blane in Panama (GB: Trouble in Panama). Juvenile Court. Adventure in Sahara. Island in the Sky. The Missing Guest. The Devil's Party. 1939: Forged Passport. The Flying Irishman. Within the Law. 6,000 Enemies. The Roaring Twenties. Invisible Stripes. 1940: The Howards of Virginia (GB: The Tree of Liberty). Girls Under 21. Wyoming (GB: Bad Man of Wyoming). Queen of the Mob. Flight Command. 1941: Ziegfeld Girl. Parachute Battalion. Mystery Ship. I'll Wait for You. Mr and Mrs North. 1942: Call Out the Marines. Tarzan's New York Adventure. Tough As They Come. The Secret Code (serial). Flying Tigers. Gang Busters (serial). Not a Ladies' Man. 1943: The Man from Music Mountain. 1944: The Story of Dr Wassell. Dead Man's Eyes. Faces in the Fog. 1945: China's Little Devils. Grissly's Millions. Allotment Wives (GB: Woman in the Case). San Antonio. 1946: The Cat Creeps. Deadline for Murder. Strange Journey. The Glass Alibi. 1947: Fear in the Night. Spoilers of the North. Adventure Island. Crossfire. 1949: Thelma Jordon (GB: The File on Thelma Jordon). Side Street. There's a Girl in My Heart. 1950: Frenchie. The Secret Fury. Guilty of Treason

(GB: Treason). 1951: The Painted Hills. 1952. Springfield Rifle. 1953: Gunsmoke! Split Second. 1954: Duffy of San Quentin (US: Men Behind Bars). Johnny Dark. The High and the Mighty. The Steel Cage. 1955: The Square Jungle. Narcotics Squad. 1956: Storm Center. 1957: Bail Out at 43,000 (GB: Bale Out at 43,000).

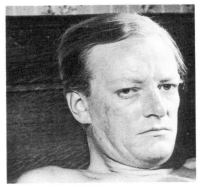

KEMP, Jeremy (Edmund Walker) 1934–
Scottish actor of red-gold hair and florid features who achieved his first big success in the TV series Z Cars, then went into films, taking a number of character lead roles by the scruff of the neck and visibly shaking them around. He has kept featured billing but despite one or two eye-catching performances has not so far become a box-office star.

1963: Cleopatra. 1964: Dr Terror's House of Horrors. Face of a Stranger. 1965: Operation Crossbow (US: The Great Spy Mission). Cast a Giant Shadow. 1966: The Blue Max. 1967: A Twist of Sand. Assignment K. 1968: The Strange Affair. The Games. 1969: Darling Lili. 1970: Eyewitness. 1972: Pope Joan. 1973: The Belstone Fox. The Blockhouse. 1976: The Seven-Per-Cent Solution. East of Elephant Rock. 1977: The Thoroughbreds (later Treasure Seekers). A Bridge Too Far. Leopard in the Snow. 1978: Keefer (TV). 1979: The Prisoner of Zenda. Caravans. 1982: The Return of the Soldier. 1983: Uncommon Valor. 1984: Top Secret!

KENDALL, Henry 1897–1962
Dark-haired, thickly-built British stage star with distinctive personality and wide range.

He became a big star of the British cinema in the thirties, making an enormous number of light comedies and dramas, often as bespectacled hero who came through half by luck and half by judgment. Returned to the stage in 1938: thereafter only filmed occasionally. Died from a heart attack.

1921: Mr Pim Passes By. Tilly of Bloomsbury. 1930: French Leave. 1931: The House Opposite. The Flying Fool. Rich and Strange (US: East of Shanghai). 1932: Mr Bill the Conqueror (US: The Man Who Won). Watch Beverly. The Innocents of Chicago (US: Why Saps Leave Home). The Iron Stair. 1933: The Shadow. Counsel's Opinion. The Ghost Camera. This Week of Grace. The Flaw. King of the Ritz. Timbuctoo. The Man Outside. Great Stuff. The Stickpin. 1934: Without You. The Girl in Possession. The Man I Want. Death at Broadcasting House. Crazy People. Sometimes Good. Leave It to Blanche. Guest of Honour. 1935: Death on the Set (US: Murder on the Set). Lend Me Your Wife. Three Witnesses. A Wife or Two. 1936: Twelve Good Men. The Amazing Quest of Ernest Bliss (US: Romance and Riches). The Mysterious Mr Davis. Take a Chance. 1937: Side Street Angel. It's Not Cricket. The Compulsory Wife. Ship's Concert. School for Husbands. 1943: The Butler's Dilemma. 1945: 29 Acacia Avenue (US: The Facts of Love). 1949: Helter Skelter. 1952: The Voice of Merrill (US: Murder Will Out). 1955: An Alligator Named Daisy. 1961: The Shadow of the Cat. Nothing Barred.

KENDALL, Kay (Justine Kendall McCarthy) 1926–1959
Effervescent redhead with a sparkling sense of sophisticated comedy that it took British films a long time (she was a chorus girl at 12, in films at 17) to discover. She was just becoming a big international star when struck down by leukaemia. Married to Rex Harrison from 1957 to her death.

1944: Fiddlers Three. Champagne Charlie. Dreaming. 1945: Waltz Time. Caesar and Cleopatra. 1946: Spring Song (US: Spring Time). London Town (US: My Heart Goes Crazy). 1950: Night and the City. Dance Hall. Happy Go Lovely. 1951: Lady Godiva Rides Again. 1952: Wings of Danger (US: Dead on Course). Curtain Up. It Started in Paradise. 1953: Mantrap (US: Man in Hiding). Street of Shadows (US: Shadow Man). Genevieve. The Square Ring. Meet Mr Lucifer. 1954: Fast and Loose. Doctor in the House. Abdullah's Harem (GB: Abdullah the Great). 1955: The Constant Husband. Simon and Laura. The Adventures of Quentin Durward (US: Quentin Durward). 1957: Les Girls. 1958: The Reluctant Debutante. 1959: Once More, with Feeling!

KENDALL, Suzy (Frieda Harrison) 1944–
Light-haired, sharp-featured, bird-like British leading lady, not unlike Julie Christie to look at. A former fashion model, she matured into a competent enough actress to make one wonder why she disappeared from the film scene. Married/divorced actor-comedian-musician Dudley Moore (qv).
1965: The Liquidator. Up Jumped a Swagman. Circus of Fear (US: Psycho-Circus). 1966: The Sandwich Man. To Sir, With Love. 1967: The Penthouse. 30 is a Dangerous Age, Cynthia. Up the Junction. 1968: Fraulein Doktor. 1969: The Gamblers. Color Me Dead. The Bird with the Crystal Plumage (GB: The Gallery Murders). 1970: Assault (US: In the Devil's Garden). Darker than Amber. 1972: Fear is the Key. 1973: Tales That Witness Madness. Craze. I corpi presentano tracce di violenza carnale/Torso. Storia di una monaca di clasura. 1975: Spasmo. To the Bitter End. 1977: Adventures of a Private Eye.

KENNEDY, Arthur (John A. Kennedy) 1914–
It's a long way down from City for Conquest and High Sierra to Emmanuelle on Taboo Island, but poor Arthur Kennedy has travelled every step of the way. This fair-haired American actor with a slightly fretful look and crooked smile spent six years on stage before deciding on a film career. He became a star without quite heading the cast, was five times Oscar-nominated, and ran up a good row of often likeable western villains. His roles deteriorated in quality from 1958, and in the seventies became increasingly frenzied. Some sources refer to a 1934 film debut, which I have not been able to trace.
1940: City for Conquest. Santa Fé Trail. 1941: High Sierra. Knockout. Highway West, Strange Alibi. They Died with their Boots On. Bad Men of Missouri. 1942: Desperate Journey. 1943: Air Force. Devotion (released 1946). 1947: Boomerang. Cheyenne. 1949: The Window. Champion. Too Late for Tears. The Walking Hills. Chicago Deadline. 1950: The Glass Menagerie. Bright Victory (GB: Lights Out). 1951: Red Mountain. 1952: Rancho Notorious. The Girl in White (GB: So Bright the Flame). Bend of the River (GB: Where the River Bends). The Lusty Men. 1954: Impulse. 1955: Crashout. The Man from Laramie. The Naked Dawn. Trial. The Desperate Hours. 1956: The Rawhide Years. 1957: Peyton Place. 1958: Twilight for the Gods. Some Came Running. 1959: A Summer Place. Home is the Hero. 1960: Elmer Gantry. In the Presence of Mine Enemies (TV). 1961: Claudelle Inglish (GB: Young and Eager). Murder She Said. 1962: Barabbas. Hemingway's Adventures of a Young Man (GB: Adventures of a Young Man). Lawrence of Arabia. 1964: Cheyenne Autumn. Italiano brave gente (GB: Attack and Retreat). 1965: Murieta (GB: Vendetta). Joy in the Morning. 1966: Nevada Smith. Fantastic Voyage. The Brave Rifles (narrator only). 1967: Anzio (GB: The Battle for Anzio). Shark! (released 1970). Il Chica del Lunes (US: Monday's Child). 1968: A Minute to Pray, a Second to Die (GB: Dead or Alive). Day of the Evil Gun. The Prodigal Gun. 1969: Hail Hero. 1970: The Movie Murderer (TV). 1971: Glory Boy (GB: My Old Man's Place). A Death of Innocence (TV). The President's Plane is Missing (TV). 1972: Crawlspace (TV). 1973: Ricco/The Dirty Mob. Baciamo le mane (GB: Family Killer. US: Mafia War). 1974: Nakia (TV). The Living Dead at the Manchester Morgue. The Antichrist (US: The Tempter). 1975: Killer Cop/The Police Can't Move. 1976: The Sentinel. Roma a mano armata (US: Brutal Justice). Nove ospiti per un delitto. 1977: Porco Mondo. Cyclone. The Last Angels. Emmanuelle on Taboo Island. 1978: La cueva de los triburones (GB: The Sharks' Cave. US: Cave of Sharks). Ab Morgen sind wir reich und ehrlich/Rich and Respectable. Covert Action. 1979. The Humanoid. 1980: Due nelle stelle.

KENNEDY, George 1925–
Scowling, glowering, powerfully-built American actor with thinning fair hair. He turned to an acting career after 16 years in the army and surprised many people by becoming a star – mainly on the strength of his Academy Award for Cool Hand Luke in 1967. The tran-

sition from villains to good-hearted Joes was almost immediate, but he has been a valuable asset to some poor films.
1961: The Little Shepherd of Kingdom Come. 1962: Lonely Are the Brave. 1963: The Man from the Diners' Club. Charade. 1964: Strait-Jacket. Island of the Blue Dolphins. McHale's Navy. Silent Witness. Hush … Hush, Sweet Charlotte. 1965: In Harm's Way. Shenandoah. Mirage. The Sons of Katie Elder. The Flight of the Phoenix. See How They Run (TV). 1967: Hurry Sundown. The Dirty Dozen. Cool Hand Luke. The Ballad of Josie. 1968: Bandolero! The Pink Jungle. The Boston Strangler. The Legend of Lylah Clare. 1969: Guns of the Magnificent Seven. The Good Guys and the Bad Guys. Gaily Gaily (GB: Chicago Chicago). …tick…tick…tick. Airport. 1970: Zigzag (GB: False Witness). Dirty Dingus Magee. 1971: Fool's Parade (GB: Dynamite Man from Glory Jail). The Badge or the Cross (TV). The Priest Killer (TV). 1972: A Great American Tragedy (TV. GB: Man at the Crossroads). Lost Horizon. 1973: A Cry in the Wilderness (TV). Deliver Us from Evil (TV). Cahill: United States Marshal (GB: Cahill). 1974: Thunderbolt and Lightfoot. Earthquake. Airport 1975. 1975: The Blue Knight 2 (TV). The 'Human' Factor. The Eiger Sanction. 1977: Airport 77. 1978: Brass Target. Death on the Nile. Mean Dog Blues. Search and Destroy (released 1981). 1979: The Double McGuffin. Steel. The Concorde – Airport '79 (GB: Airport '80 … the Concorde). Proof of the Man. Never Say Never (TV). 1980: Death Ship. Hotwire. Virus. Just Before Dawn. 1981: Modern Romance. Carnauba/A Rare Breed. 1982: Wacko. The Jupiter Menace. 1984: Bliss (TV). Bolero. Chattanooga Choo Choo. Radioactive Dreams. Rigged/Hit and Run. 1985: Half Nelson (TV). Savage Dawn. International Airport (TV). 1986: The Delta Force.

As director: 1965: *Three Songs.

KENNEY, James 1930–
Fair-haired British boy actor with clean-cut looks, the son of radio and music-hall comic Horace Kenney. After Cosh Boy, one of the first British films to get an X certificate, he became typed in callow roles. In the sixties he spent four years in Australia and two in America, but lately has been little seen.
1942: The Young Mr Pitt. 1946: London Town

(US: My Heart Goes Crazy). 1947: Circus Boy. Vice Versa. 1948: The Guinea Pig. 1949: Trapped by the Terror. 1951: Captain Horatio Hornblower RN. The Magic Box. Outcast of the Islands. 1952: Gift Horse (US: Glory at Sea). Cosh Boy (US: The Slasher). The Gentle Gunman. 1953: Thought to Kill. 1954: The Good Die Young. The Sea Shall Not Have Them. The Red Dress. 1955: The Love Match. Above Us the Waves. Doctor at Sea. 1956: The Gelignite Gang. 1957: Yangtse Incident (US: Battle Hell). Seven Thunders (US: The Beasts of Marseilles). Son of a Stranger. 1958: Hidden Homicide. 1959: No Safety Ahead. 1962: Ambush in Leopard Street. 1966: A Big Hand for the Little Lady (GB: Big Deal at Dodge City).

KENT, Jean (Joan Summerfield) 1921–
Strawberry-blonde British actress with knowing smile and faintly haughty mien, in show business at 12. Could play spiteful hussies and *femmes fatales* with the best of them and in the late forties got typed in the role. Later expressed regret at not having renewed her studio contract in 1952: as a freelance she was never the same force. Still active in the theatre.
1934: †*The Rocks of Valpré* (US: High Treason). 1935: †*How's Your Father?* 1939: ‡*Frozen Limits.* 1940: ‡*Hullo Fame!* 1942: It's That Man Again. 1943: Miss London Ltd. Warn That Man. 1944: Bees in Paradise. Fanny by Gaslight (US: Man of Evil). Waterloo Road. Champagne Charlie. Soldier, Sailor. 2,000 Women. Madonna of the Seven Moons. 1945: The Wicked Lady. The Rake's Progress (US: Notorious Gentleman). 1946: Carnival.

Caravan. The Magic Bow. 1947: The Man Within (US: The Smugglers). The Loves of Joanna Godden. 1948: Good Time Girl. Bond Street. Sleeping Car to Trieste. 1949: Trottie True (US: Gay Lady). 1950: The Woman in Question (US: Five Angles on Murder). Her Favourite Husband (US: The Taming of Dorothy). The Reluctant Widow. 1951: The Browning Version. 1952: The Lost Hours (US: The Big Frame). 1955: Before I Wake (US: Shadow of Fear). 1957: The Prince and the Showgirl. 1958: Bonjour Tristesse. Grip of the Strangler (US: The Haunted Strangler). 1959: Beyond This Place (US: Web of Evidence). Please Turn Over. 1960: Bluebeard's Ten Honeymoons. 1976: Shout at the Devil.

† As Joan Summerfield
‡ As Jean Carr

KERR, Deborah (D. Kerr-Trimmer) 1921–
Lovely red-haired Scottish-born leading lady whose angular beauty got her cast in gentle, ladylike roles. A star of the British cinema in only her third film, she went to Hollywood in 1947, where her struggle to break the well-bred image was unsuccessful, despite her torrid love scenes in *From Here to Eternity*; the vivacious, fun-loving lady of real life remained a suppressed image for the screen, although she did make some extremely good films within that image between 1956 and 1961. Nominated six times for the best actress Oscar but never won; perhaps her unluckiest losing performance was in *The Sundowners*.
1940: †*Contraband* (US: Blackout). 1941: Major Barbara. Love on the Dole. Hatter's Castle. Penn of Pennsylvania (US: The Courageous Mr Penn). 1942: The Day Will Dawn (US: The Avengers). 1943: The Life and Death of Colonel Blimp (US: Colonel Blimp). 1945: Perfect Strangers (US: Vacation from Marriage). 1946: I See a Dark Stranger (US: The Adventuress). 1947: Black Narcissus. The Hucksters. 1948: If Winter Comes. 1949: Edward My Son. Please Believe Me. 1950: King Solomon's Mines. 1951: Quo Vadis? Thunder in the East. 1952: The Prisoner of Zenda. 1953: Julius Caesar. Young Bess. Dream Wife. From Here to Eternity. 1955: The End of the Affair. 1956: The King and I. The Proud and Profane. Tea and Sympathy. 1957: Heaven Knows, Mr Allison. An Affair to Remember. 1958: Separate Tables. Bonjour

Tristesse. The Journey. 1959: Count Your Blessings. Beloved Infidel. 1960: The Sundowners. The Grass is Greener. 1961: The Naked Edge. The Innocents. 1963: The Chalk Garden. 1964: The Night of the Iguana. 1965: Marriage on the Rocks. 1966: Eye of the Devil. 1967: Casino Royale. 1968: Prudence and the Pill. 1969: The Arrangement. The Gypsy Moths. 1982: Witness for the Prosecution (TV). 1985: The Assam Garden. Reunion at Fairborough (TV). 1986: Hold the Dream.

†*Scenes deleted from final release print*

KEYES, Evelyn 1919–
Cat-like American blonde with lithe figure and knowing smile. Mostly played decorative minxes, but was occasionally very good in dramatic roles. A swinger in private life, as evidenced by the publication of her somewhat scarlet memoirs in the seventies. Her first husband shot himself a month after they separated; her second and third, Charles Vidor (1943–1945) and John Huston (1946–1950) were directors. Her fourth husband, in 1957, was seven times-wed bandleader Artie Shaw. They're still married.
1937: Artists and Models. 1938: The Buccaneer. Men with Wings. Artists and Models Abroad (GB: Stranded in Paris). Sons of the Legion. Dangerous to Know. 1939: Paris Honeymoon. Union Pacific. Sudden Money. Slightly Honorable. Gone with the Wind. 1940: Before I Hang. Beyond the Sacramento (GB: Power of Justice). The Lady in Question. 1941: The Face behind the Mask. Here Comes Mr Jordan. Ladies in Retirement. 1942: The Adventures of Martin Eden. Flight Lieutenant. 1943: There's Something About a Soldier. Dangerous Blondes. The Desperadoes. 1944: Nine Girls. Strange Affair. 1945: A Thousand and One Nights. 1946: The Jolson Story. Renegades. The Thrill of Brazil. 1947: Johnny O'Clock. 1948: Enchantment. The Mating of Millie. 1949: Mrs Mike. Mr Soft Touch (GB: House of Settlement). 1950: The Killer That Stalked New York (GB: The Frightened City). 1951: Smuggler's Island. Iron Man. The Prowler. 1952: One Big Affair. Rough Shoot (US: Shoot First). 1953: 99 River Street. 1954: Hell's Half Acre. It Happened in Paris. 1955: Top of the World. The Seven Year Itch. 1956: Around the World in 80 Days. 1972: Across 110th Street. 1985: Artie Shaw: Time is All You've Got.

Betrayal. 1984: Camille (TV). 1985: Turtle Diary. 1986: Harem.

KIDDER, Margot (Margaret Kidder) 1948–
Attractively sharp-faced actress with centre-fold figure, wild dark hair and strong personality. The girl from the wilds of Northwest Canada (born in Yellow Knife to a mining engineer) broke into acting when her family moved to Toronto. She had a low-key career as a leading lady before marriage to writer Thomas McGuane brought retirement to a ranch in Montana. After the divorce, she returned to films as Lois Lane in *Superman* (although she hardly seemed ideal casting). She has on the whole not found roles that extended her undoubted talent. Further married to actor John Heard (*qv*), for six days, and to director Philippe de Broca since 1983.
1968: The Best Damn Fiddler from Calabogie to Kaladar. 1969: Gaily Gaily (GB: Chicago, Chicago). 1970: Quackser Fortune Has a Cousin in the Bronx. 1971: Suddenly Single (TV). 1972: The Bounty Man (TV). Sisters (GB: Blood Sisters). 1973: A Quiet Day in Belfast/Quiet Days at Belfast. Such Dust As Dreams Are Made On (TV). The Suicide Club (TV). 1974: Honky Tonk (TV). The Dion Brothers (TV. GB: cinemas, as The Gravy Train). The Reincarnation of Peter Proud. Black Christmas. 1975: 92 in the Shade. The Great Waldo Pepper. 1978: Superman. 1979: The Amityville Horror. Mr Mike's Mondo Video. 1980: Miss Right. Willie & Phil. Superman II. 1981: Some Kind of Hero. Shoot the Sun Down (completed 1976). 1982: Heartaches. Trenchcoat. 1983: Louisiana. Superman III. 1984: The Glitter Dome (originally for TV, and shown there in 1983). 1985: Little Treasure. 1986: Picking Up the Pieces (TV). GoBots: Battle of the Rock Lords (voice only).

As director: *1975: And Again.*

KINGSLEY, Ben (Krishna Banji) 1944–
Small, balding, part-Indian British star actor with distinctive features who, after being chosen from almost nowhere to star as *Gandhi* in 1981 (released 1982) and deservedly winning an Academy Award for his performance, quickly became Britain's most perceptive and intelligent character star since Alec Guinness (*qv*), offering fully-rounded and amazingly-detailed portraits of everyday men in *Betrayal* and *Turtle Diary*.
1972: Fear is the Key. 1982: Gandhi. 1983:

KINSKI, Nastassja (N. Nakszynski) 1959–
No wonder they cast this dark-haired German actress (daughter of Klaus Kinski) in *Cat People*. She looks cat-like and dangerous. Full-lipped, with tautly attractive features, she was in uninhibited roles from an early age, playing haunted heroines whose sexual magnetism is often the axis on which the plot turns. Credited as 'Nastassia' in some films.

1975: †Falsche Bewegung (GB: Wrong Movement. US: The Wrong Move). 1976: To the Devil a Daughter. 1978: Leidenschaftliche Blumchen (GB: TV, as Passion Flower Hotel. US: Virgin Campus). Cosi come sei (GB and US: Stay As You Are). 1979: Tess. 1982: One from the Heart. Cat People. Reifezeugnis (GB and US: For Your Love Only. Copyrighted 1982, but originally made in 1976 for West German TV). 1983: Frühlingssinfonie. Exposed. La lune dans le caniveau (GB and US: The Moon in the Gutter). Unfaithfully Yours. 1984: The Hotel New Hampshire. Paris, Texas. Maria's Lovers. 1985: Revolution. 1986: Harem.

† *As Nastassja Naksynski*

KIRK, Phyllis (P. Kirkegaard) 1926–
Pencil-slim brunette with chirpy personality who switched from modelling to acting in her early twenties. M-G-M signed her and dropped her; Warners used her as decoration in a variety of colour films; but she was really at her best as the spunky heroine of several low-budget black-and-white thrillers. Played Nora Charles in a TV series of *The Thin Man* from 1957 to 1959.

1950: Our Very Own. Two Weeks with Love. A Life of Her Own. Mrs O'Malley and Mr Malone. 1951: Three Guys Named Mike. 1952: About Face. The Iron Mistress. 1953: House of Wax. Crime Wave (GB: The City is Dark). Thunder over the Plains. 1954: River Beat. 1955: Canyon Crossroads. 1956: Johnny Concho. Back from Eternity. Made in Heaven (TV). 1957: That Woman Opposite (US: City after Midnight). The Sad Sack. Men in Her Life (TV).

KIRKWOOD, Pat 1921–
Raven-haired, strong-voiced, forceful British musical star with seemingly unlimited energy, too much it seemed for films and film audiences, who never really took to her. At first in ingenue roles (including one in Hollywood); later became well known for impersonations of old-time music-hall stars whose traditions she had inherited. Three times married and divorced, latterly to actor Hubert Gregg (1914–).
1938: Save a Little Sunshine. 1939: Me and My Pal. Come on George. Band Waggon. 1944: Flight from Folly. 1946: No Leave, No Love. 1950: Once a Sinner. 1956: Stars in Your Eyes. 1957: After the Ball.

KITT, Eartha 1928–
Black, feline American nightclub singer (a former Katherine Dunham dancer) who became known as 'That Bad Eartha' from the sexy way she wove her reedy voice through such songs as 'Just an Old-Fashioned Girl', 'I Want to be Evil' and 'Santa Baby'. Most films tried to make her into something other

than a sinuous siren, and were notably unsuccessful.

1948: Casbah. 1954: New Faces. 1957: St Louis Blues. 1958: Anna Lucasta. Mark of the Hawk/The Accused. Heart of Darkness (TV). 1961: Saint of Devil's Island. 1965: Uncle Tom's Cabin. Synanon (GB: Get Off My Back). 1971: Up the Chastity Belt. 1972: Lt Schuster's Wife (TV). 1975: Friday Foster. 1978: Streets of Fear (TV). To Kill a Cop (TV). 1979: The Last Resort. 1982: All by Myself. 1985: The Serpent Warriors.

KNEF, Hildegarde 1925–
Cool, sultry-looking, tallish blonde German actress, cartoonist and writer. Came to international films (where she was billed as Hildegarde Neff) as husky-voiced European ladies with bedroom eyes, often involved in espionage. Returned to German films (and stronger roles) in the late fifties, and has sporadically pursued an acting career there since then. Survived numerous operations to remove cancerous growths in the early 1970s.
1945: Fahrt ins Glück. Unter den Brücken. 1946: Die Mörder sind unter uns. Träumerei. 1947: Zwischen Gestern und Morgen. 1948: Film ohne Titel. 1950: Die Sünderin (GB and US: The Sinner). 1951: Es geschehen noch Wunder. Nachts auf den Strassen. Decision before Dawn. 1952: The Snows of Kilimanjaro. Night without Sleep. Diplomatic Courier. La fête à Henriette. Alraune. Illusion in Moll. 1953: The Man Between. Eine Liebegeschichte. 1954: Gestandnis unter vier Augen. Svengali. La fille de Hambour/The Girl from Hamburg.

Madeleine und der Legionär (US: Escape from Sahara). 1956: Subway in the Sky. 1957: Der Mann, der sich verkanfte. 1959: La strada dei giganti. 1960: Valley of the Doomed. 1962: Landru. Ballade pour un voyou. The Threepenny Opera. Lulu. Catherine of Russia. 1963: Gibraltar (GB: The Spy). And So to Bed/Das Liebeskarussell. 1964: Wartezimmer zum Jeinseits. 1965: Verdammt zur Sünde. Mozambique. 1968: The Lost Continent. 1975: Jeder stirbt für sich allein (GB TV: Death Always Comes Alone). 1978: Fedora. 1979: Warum die UFOs unseren Salat klauen. 1980: Checkpoint Charlie. 1984: L'avenir d'Emilie.

KNIGHT, David (D. Mintz) 1927–
Sensitive-looking, dark-haired, Canadian-born leading man with high forehead, in Britain since 1952. A former teacher, he became a star in his first film, but his personality was too diffident for him to remain at the top, and he was not easy to cast. Gradually regressed to minor films, then dropped from cinematic sight in the 1960s.
1954: The Young Lovers (US: Chance Meeting). 1955: Out of the Clouds. Lost (US: Tears for Simon). On Such a Night. 1956: Eyewitness. 1957: Across the Bridge. 1958: Battle of the V1 (US: V1/Unseen Heroes). 1960: Clue of the Twisted Candle. A Story of David. 1962: The Devil's Agent. 1963: Nightmare.

KNIGHT, Esmond 1906–
Serious, scholarly-looking dark-haired British actor who progressed to star roles by the mid-thirties, but was blinded on active service

during World War II. Partially regained the use of one eye later, and continued his career in stalwart character roles. Long married to his second wife, Nora Swinburne (qv).
1928: The Blue Peter. 1931: 77 Park Lane. Romany Love. Deadlock. The Ringer. 1933: The Bermondsey Kid. 1934: Waltzes from Vienna (US: Strauss's Great Waltz). Lest We Forget. The Blue Squadron. Womanhood. The King of Wales. Girls Will Be Boys. Father and Son. My Old Dutch. 1935: Dandy Dick. Black Rose. Some Day. Crime Unlimited. 1936: Pagliacci (US: A Clown Must Laugh). Did I Betray? 1937: The Vicar of Bray. 1938: *What Men Live By. Weddings Are Wonderful. The Drum (US: Drums). 1939: The Arsenal Stadium Mystery. 1940: Contraband (US: Blackout). Fingers. 1941: This England. 1943: The Silver Fleet. 1944: Halfway House. A Canterbury Tale. Henry V. 1947: Black Narcissus. Holiday Camp. Uncle Silas (US: The Inheritance). The End of the River. 1948: Hamlet. The Red Shoes. 1950: Gone to Earth (US: The Wild Heart). 1951: The River. 1952: Girdle of Gold. 1953: The Steel Key. 1954: Helen of Troy. 1955: Richard III. 1956: The Battle of the River Plate (US: Pursuit of the Graf Spee). 1957: The Prince and the Showgirl. 1958: Battle of the V1 (US: V1/Unseen Heroes). 1959: Sink the Bismarck! 1960: Peeping Tom. 1963: Decision at Midnight. 1965: The Spy Who Came in from the Cold. 1966: The Winter's Tale. 1969: Where's Jack? 1970: Anne of the Thousand Days. 1972: The Boy Who Turned Yellow. 1973: Yellow Dog. 1976: Robin and Marian. The Man in the Iron Mask (TV). 1984: Forbrydelsens Element/The Element of Crime.

KNIGHT, Shirley 1937–
Ethereal, slender American blonde actress who has sought the intelligent roles for which she seemed suited, but has not to date had a satisfactory screen career. Married to British dramatist John Hopkins, she was occasionally billed in the 1970s as Shirley Knight Hopkins. Twice nominated for an Oscar – in The Dark at the Top of the Stairs and Sweet Bird of Youth.
1959: Five Gates to Hell. 1960: Ice Palace. The Dark at the Top of the Stairs. The Shape of the River (TV). 1962: The Couch. Sweet Bird of Youth. House of Women. 1963: Flight

from Ashiya. 1966: The Group. 1967: The Counterfeit Killer (TV. GB: cinemas). Dutchman. The Outsider (TV). 1968: Shadow over Elveron (TV). Petulia. 1969: The Rain People. 1971: Secrets. 1974: Juggernaut. 1975: Friendly Persuasion (TV). Medical Story (TV). 1976: Return to Earth (TV). 21 Hours at Munich (TV. GB: cinemas). 1977: Champions, a Love Story (TV). 1978: The Defection of Simas Kudirka (TV). 1979: Beyond the Poseidon Adventure. 1980: Playing for Time (TV). 1981: Endless Love. 1982: The Sender. 1984: With Intent to Kill (TV).

KNOTTS, Don 1924–

Scrawny, bulbous-eyed, squawk-voiced American cabaret comedian, who moved his 'nervous' character into TV and films in 1958, and starred in a big-budget series of comedies in the sixties that were more popular in America than abroad. Later as comic relief in Disney films, although retaining star billing.

1958: No Time for Sergeants. 1960: Wake Me When It's Over. 1961: The Last Time I Saw Archie. 1963: Move Over, Darling. The Incredible Mr Limpet. It's a Mad, Mad, Mad, Mad World. 1966: The Ghost and Mr Chicken. 1967: The Reluctant Astronaut. I Love a Mystery (TV). 1968: The Shakiest Gun in the West. 1969: The Love God? 1971: How to Frame a Figg. 1974: The Apple Dumpling Gang. 1976: No Deposit, No Return. Gus. 1977: Herbie Goes to Monte Carlo. 1979: The Apple Dumpling Gang Rides Again. The Prize Fighter. 1980: The Private Eyes. 1983: Cannonball Run II.

KNOWLES, Patric (Reginald Knowles) 1911–

Solidly-built British actor with light, crinkly hair (and moustache to match) who, after five years in British films, decided to take his chances in Hollywood in 1936, and remained a semi-star there in suave roles until the early fifties. Perhaps a little lightweight for the Flynn-type roles for which his looks seemed suited, but a useful foil for some high-powered Hollywood ladies.

1932: Men of Tomorrow. 1934: The Girl in the Crowd. Irish Hearts (US: Norah O'Neale). The Poisoned Diamond. 1935: Abdul the Damned. Royal Cavalcade (US: Regal Cavalcade). The Student's Romance. Honours Easy. The Guv'nor (US: Mr Hobo). 1936:

The Brown Wallet. Crown v Stevens. Wedding Group (US: Wrath of Jealousy). Two's Company. Fair Exchange. Irish for Luck. Give Me Your Heart (GB: Sweet Aloes). The Charge of the Light Brigade. 1937: It's Love I'm After. Expensive Husbands. 1938: The Patient in Room 18. The Adventures of Robin Hood. Four's a Crowd. Storm over Bengal. The Sisters. Heart of the North. 1939: Torchy Blane in Chinatown. Beauty for the Asking. Five Came Back. Another Thin Man. The Spellbinder. Two's Company. The Honeymoon's Over. 1940: Married and in Love. A Bill of Divorcement. Women in War. Anne of Windy Poplars (GB: Anne of Windy Willows). 1941: How Green Was My Valley. The Wolf Man. 1942: The Mystery of Marie Roget. The Strange Case of Dr RX. Lady in a Jam. Who Done It? Sin Town. Eyes of the Underworld. 1943: Frankenstein Meets the Wolf Man. Forever and a Day. All By Myself. Hit the Ice. Always a Bridesmaid. Crazy House. 1944: Chip Off the Old Block. This is the Life. Pardon My Rhythm. 1945: Kitty. Masquerade in Mexico. 1946: O.S.S. The Bride Wore Boots. Monsieur Beaucaire. Of Human Bondage. 1947: Variety Girl. Ivy. 1948 Dream Girl. Isn't It Romantic? 1949: The Big Steal. 1950: Three Came Home. 1951: Quebec. 1952: Tarzan's Savage Fury. Mutiny. 1953: Jamaica Run. Flame of Calcutta. 1954: World for Ransom. Khyber Patrol. 1955: No Man's Woman. 1956: The Empty Room (TV. GB: cinemas). 1957: Band of Angels. 1958: From the Earth to the Moon. 1959: Auntie Mame. 1962: Six Gun Law (TV. GB: cinemas). 1967: In Enemy Country. The Way West. 1968: The Devil's Brigade. 1969: The DA: Murder One (TV). 1970: Chisum. 1972: The Man. 1973: Terror in the Wax Museum. 1974: Arnold.

KNOX, Alexander 1907–

Quietly-spoken, earnest-looking, dark-haired Canadian actor who usually played characters older than his own age. Acted almost exclusively on the British stage throughout the thirties, then went to Hollywood and immediately won leading roles, most notably the title role in *Wilson*, which earned him an Oscar nomination. When his parts grew less interesting, he returned to England, but has since been seen only in supporting roles. Also writes novels.

1931: The Ringer. 1938: The Gaunt Stranger

(US: The Phantom Strikes). 1939: Cheer Boys Cheer. The Four Feathers. 1940: The Sea Wolf. 1942: Commandos Strike at Dawn. This Above All. 1944: None Shall Escape. Wilson. 1945: Over 21. 1946: Sister Kenny. 1948: The Sign of the Ram. The Judge Steps Out (GB: Indian Summer). 1949: Tokyo Joe. 1951: I'd Climb the Highest Mountain. Two of a Kind. Man in the Saddle (GB: The Outcast). Saturday's Hero (GB: Idols in the Dust). Son of Dr Jekyll. 1952: Paula (GB: The Silent Voice). Europa 51. 1954: The Sleeping Tiger. The Divided Heart. 1955: The Night My Number Came Up. 1956: Reach for the Sky. Alias John Preston. 1957: High Tide at Noon. Davy. Hidden Fear. 1958: Chase a Crooked Shadow. The Vikings. Passionate Summer. The Two-Headed Spy. Operation Amsterdam. Intent to Kill. 1959: Crack in the Mirror. The Wreck of the Mary Deare. 1960: Oscar Wilde. 1961: The Damned (US: These Are the Damned). 1962: The Share Out. The Longest Day. In the Cool of the Day. 1963: Man in the Middle. Woman of Straw. 1964: Mister Moses. Bikini Paradise. 1965: Crack in the World. The Psychopath. 1966: Modesty Blaise. Khartoum. 1967: Accident. How I Won the War. The 25th Hour. You Only Live Twice. 1968: Villa Rides! Shalako. Fraulein Doktor. 1969: Run a Crooked Mile (TV). Skullduggery. 1970 Puppet on a Chain. 1971: Nicholas and Alexandra. 1977: Holocaust 2000. 1978: Cry of the Innocent (TV). 1983: Gorky Park. Helen and Teacher. 1985: Joshua Then and Now.

KOCH, Marianne 1930–

Brown-haired, round-faced German actress (a former medical student) of pleasing personality, very popular in her own country until, amid much publicity, Universal signed her up for Hollywood roles. The 'stardom' lasted two films, and she returned to Germany, appearing in parts that made decreasing demands on her ability, and seeming to lose interest in the cinema after the mid-1960s. Usually billed in Britain and America as Marianne Cook, she retired in 1970.

1950: *Der Mann, der zweimal Leben wollte. Dr Holl/The Affairs of Dr Holl.* 1951: *Das Geheimnis einer Ehe. Czardas der Herzen. Mein Freund, der Dieb.* 1952: *Der keusche Lebemann. Wetterluchten am Dachstein. Skandal im Mädchenpensionat.* 1953: *Die grosse Schuld. Schloss Hubertus. Der Klösterjäger. Liebe und Trompetenblasen.* 1954: *Night People. Angelika. Der Schmied von St Bartholomä. Geh mach dein Fensterl auf.* 1955: *Ludwig II. Zwei blauen Augen. Des Teufels General/The Devil's General. Und der Himmel lacht dazu. Solange du lebst. Königswalzer. Christine.* 1956: *Die Ehe des Dr med.Danwitz. Wenn wir alle Engel wären. Salzburger Geschichten. Four Girls in Town.* 1957: *Interlude. Der Stern von Afrika. Vater sein dagegen sehr. Der Fuchs von Paris/Mission diabolique. Gli italiani sono matti. Die Landärztin. ... und nichts als die Wahrheit.* 1959: *Frau im besten Mannes alter.* 1960: *Heldinnen. Mit Himbeergeist geht alles besser. Der Frau am dunkeln Fenster.* 1961: *Pleins feux sur l'assassin. Unter Ausschluss der Öffentlichkeit. Napoléon II, l'aiglon.* 1962: *Heisser Hafen Hongkong (GB: Secrets of Buddha). Der schwartze Panther von Ratana. The Devil's Agent. Die Fledermaus. Liebling, ich muss dich erschiessen.* 1964: *Last Ride to Santa Cruz. The Monster of London City. Coast of Skeletons. A Fistful of Dollars. Frozen Alive. Sunscorched.* 1965: *A Place Called Glory.* 1966: *Trunk to Cairo. $5,000 für der Kopf von Jonny R.* 1968: *Schreie in der Nacht. Clint, il solitario.* 1969: *España, otra vez. Sandy the Seal.*

KORTNER, Fritz (F. Kohn) 1892–1970
Suave, stocky, plump-cheeked, brown-haired (going grey early) master character star from Austria, often in insidious roles. An unconventional star of the German theatre in the years following World War I, he fled the country in 1933 and played leading character roles in British and Hollywood films, often as smooth and dispassionate criminals. He

returned to Germany in 1948 and soon re-established his reputation on stage, a medium in which he spent most of his later years.

1915: *Manya, die Türkin. Das Geheimnis von D 14. Police Nummer 1111. Im Banne der Vergangenheit. Die grosse Gefahr. Sonnwendfeuer.* 1916: *Das zweite Leben.* 1917: *Der Brief einer Toten.* 1918: *Der Stärkere. Der Märtyrer seines Herzens. Das andere Ich. Gregor Marold. Frauenehre.* 1919: *Elese von Erlenhof. Prinz Kuckuck. Das Auge des Buddha. Ohne Zeugen. Satanas.* 1920: *Va banque. Gerechtigkeit. Katharina die Grosse/Catherine the Great. Die Brüder Karamasoff/The Brothers Karamazov. Weltbrand. Der Schädel der Pharaonentochter. Die Nacht der Königin Isabeau.* 1921: *Danton (US: All for a Woman). Die Hintertreppe (US: Backstairs). Die Lieblingsfrau des Maharadscha, dritte Teil. Das Haus zum Mond. Das Haus der Qualen. Die Verschwörung zu Genua. Landstrasse und Grosstadt. Am roten Kliff. Die Jagd nach Wahrheit. Aus dem Schwartzbuch eines Polizeikommissars. Der Eisenbahnkönig I. Der Eisenbahnkönig II.* 1922: *Luise Millerin. Die Mausefalle. Peter der Grosse/Peter the Great. Der Ruf des Schicksals. Der Graf von Esse. Am Rande der Grosstadt. Die Finsternis und ihr Eigentum. Sterbende Völker I. Sterbende Völker II.* 1923: *Nora. Der stärkste Trieb. Ein Weib, ein Tier, ein Diamant. Arme Sünderin. Schatten (US: Warning Shadows).* 1924: *Moderne Ehen. Armes kleines Mädchen. Dr Wislizenus.* 1925: *Orlacs Hände/The Hands of Orlac.* 1926: *Dürfen wir schweigen.* 1927: *Beethoven. Mata Hari/The Red Dancer. Primanerliebe. Alpentragödie. Maria Stuart I. Die Ausgestossenen. Die Geliebte des Gouveneurs. Mein Leben für das Deine. Maria Stuart II.* 1928: *Frau Sorge. Marquis d'Eon, der Spion der Pompadour. Der Büchse der Pandora/Pandora's Box. Revolutionhochzeit (US: The Last Night). Die Frau auf der Folter (US: A Scandal in Paris).* 1929: *Die Frau, nach der man sich sehnt (US: Three Loves). Somnambul. Atlantik. Die Frau im Talar. Die Nacht des Schreckens. Giftgas.* 1930: *Der Andere. Dreyfus (US: The Dreyfus Case). Die grosse Sehnsucht. Menschen im Käfig.* 1931: *Danton (remake). Der Mörder Dimitri Karamasoff (GB: The Brothers Karamazov. US: The Murderer Dimitri Karamazov. And French-language version).* 1934: *Chu-Chin-Chow. Evensong.* 1935: *Abdul the Damned. The Crouching Beast.* 1937: *Midnight Menace (US: Bombs over London).* 1943: *The Strange Death of Adolf Hitler. The Purple V.* 1944: *The Hitler Gang.* 1946: *The Wife of Monte Cristo. Somewhere in the Night. The Razor's Edge.* 1947: *The Brasher Doubloon (GB: The High Window).* 1948: *Berlin Express.* 1949: *The Last Illusion.* 1950: *Epilog.* 1951: *Bluebeard/Blaubart.* 1966: *Fritz Kortner spricht Monologe für eine Schallplatte.*

As director: 1918: *Gregor Marold.* 1919: *Elese von Erlenhof.* 1931: *Der brave Sünder (US: The Upright Sinner).* 1932: *So eine Mädel vergisst man nicht.* 1954: *Die Stadt ist voller Geheimnisse.* 1955: *Sarajewo/Sarajevo.* 1960: *Die Sendung der Lysistrata (TV).*

KOSCINA, Sylva 1933–
Brunette (often blonde in films), sexy-looking Yugoslavian actress with pouting lower lip, dazzling smile, very upright carriage and breathtaking figure. She began her 30-year career in Italian films, but was soon in great demand for movies the world over, jetting bewilderingly from one country to another, mainly as lovely decoration, with an equal assortment of heroines and villainesses. Most popular in the mid-1960s. At 25, played the mother of a 16-year-old!

1956: *Il ferroviere (GB: Man of Iron. US: The Railroad Man). Michael Strogoff. Guendalina.* 1957: *La nonna Sabella (GB: Oh! Sabella). Le fatiche di Ercole (GB and US: Hercules). La Gerusalemme liberata (GB: The Mighty Crusaders. US: The Mighty Invaders). I fidanzati della morte. L'impossibile Isabelle. Femmine tre volte. Ladro lui, ladro lei. Giovani mariti. La naif aux quarante enfants.* 1958: *Ercole e la regina di Lidia (GB: Hercules Unchained. US: Hercules and the Queen of Sheba). La nipote Sabella. Racconti d'estate (GB: Girls for the Summer. US: Love on the Riviera). Le confidant de ces dames. Mogli pericolose. Totò a Parigi. Parisien malgré lui. Totò nella luna.* 1959: *Erode il grande. Totò innamorato. La cambiale. Poveri millionari. Le sorprese dell'amore. Tempi duri per i vampiri (GB: Uncle Was a Vampire. US: Hard Times for Vampires). L'assedio di Siracusa (GB and US: Siege of Syracuse). I genitori in blue-jeans.* 1960: *Les distractions (GB: Trapped by Fear). Crimen (GB: Killing in Monte Carlo). Ravissante. Le pillole di Ercole (GB: The Pillars of Hercules). Il sicario. I piaceri dello scapolo. Il vigile. Femmine di lusso (GB: Traveling in Luxury). Mariti in pericolo.* 1961: *Swordsman of Siena/Le mercenaire. Jessica.* 1962: *Copacabana Palace (US: Girl Game). Cyrano and D'Artagnan. Les quatres vérités (GB and US: Three Fables of Love). Le massaggiatrici.* 1963: *Il giorno più corto commedia umoristica (US: The Shortest Day). Hot Enough for June (US: Agent 8¾). Il fornaretto di Venezia. Le monachine (US: The Little Nuns). Judex. Amore in quattro dimensioni (GB: Love in Four Dimensions). L'appartement des filles.* 1964: *The Dictator's Guns (GB: Guns for the Dictator). Se permettete - parliamo di donne (GB: Let's Talk About Women). Cadavere per signora. Juliet of the Spirits. That Man in Istanbul. L'idea fissa. Gangster, Gold und flotte*

Mädchen. 1965: Monnaie de singe (GB: Monkey Money). Thrilling. Il morbidone (US: The Dreamer). Made in Italy. Io, io, io ... a gli altri. I soldi. Baraka sur X 13. 1966: Una storia di notte. Jonny Banco. Three Bites of the Apple. Deadlier than the Male. Layton ... karatè e bambole. Racconti a due piazze. 1967: The Secret War of Harry Frigg. Das gemüsse etwas der Frauen. 1968: Kampf um Rom. The Battle of Neretva/Battle for Neretva. I protagonisti. Baraka X-77. A Lovely Way to Die (GB: A Lovely Way to Go). 1969: Kampf um Rom II. L'assoluto naturale/He and She. Justine ovvero le disavventure della virtù. Vendo nudo. 1970: Hornets' Nest. Le modification. Vertige pour un tueur. Mazzabubù ... quante corna stanno quaggiù? Les jambes en l'air. 1971: Perchè non ci lasciate in pace?/Why Don't You Leave Us in Peace? La colomba non deve volare. Nini Tirabusciò, Trittico. Boccaccio. Il sesso del diavolo. 1972: Sette scialli di seta gialla (GB: Crimes of the Black Cat). Uccidere in silenzio. Beati i ricchi. La 'mala' ordina (GB: Manhunt in Milan). Rivelazione di un maniaco al capo della squadra mobile (US: Confessions of a Sex Maniac). Homo Eroticus (US: Man of the Year). African Story. No desearas la mujer de vicino. 1973: La strana legge del Dr Menga. Qualcuno l'ho vista uccidere. Il tuo piacere e il mio. 1974: The Slasher. The Student Connection. So Naked, So Dead (US: Bad Girls/So Sweet, So Dead). Delitto d'autore. 1975: House of Exorcism (US: Lisa and the Devil). Dracula in Brianza. Un par de Zapatos del '39. Las Corrieras del Visconde Arnau. Clara and Nora. 1977: Casanova & Co (GB: The Rise and Rise of Casanova). 1980: Sunday Lovers/ Les séducteurs. 1981: L'asso. 1983: Stelle emigranti. 1984: Cinderella '80. 1986: Deadly Sanctuary.

KOVACS, Ernie 1919–1962
Black-haired, black-moustached, cigar-chewing, thickly-built American comedian with extravagant lifestyle who played loud-mouthed extroverts, and was very funny indeed in his few Columbia features of the late fifties and early sixties. Married to Edie Adams (1927–   ). Killed in a car crash.
1957: Operation Mad Ball. Topaze (TV). 1958: Bell, Book and Candle. *Showdown at Ulcer Gulch. 1959. It Happened to Jane. Our Man in Havana. 1960: Wake Me When It's Over. Strangers When We Meet. North to

Alaska. Pepé. 1961: Five Golden Hours. Sail a Crooked Ship.

KRISTEL, Sylvia 1952–
Dark-haired, sulky-looking Dutch actress, a beauty contest winner who made a few sexploitation films before appearing in the sensational Emmanuelle. Not surprisingly, she became typed as sexual adventuresses. More staid international ventures lit no fires, but she did better at the box-office as experienced women teaching callow youths the facts of life, even if most of these ventures were critical disasters.
1973: Frank and Eva. Naked over the Fence. Because of the Cats (GB: The Rape). 1974: Es war nicht die Nachtigall (GB: Julia. US: Julia: Innocence Once Removed). Emmanuelle. Un linceul n'a pas de poches. 1975: Emmanuelle 2. Le jeu avec le feu. 1976: René la canne. La marge (GB: The Streetwalker). Alice ou la dernière fugue. Une femme fidèle (GB: When a Woman in Love ...). 1977: Die eiserne Maske/ Behind the Iron Mask (GB: The 5th Musketeer). 1978: Goodbye Emmanuelle. The Madonna of the Sleeping Cars. Mysteries. Pastorale 1943. 1979: Letti selvaggi (released 1985 as Tigers in Lipstick). The Concorde – Airport '79 (GB: Airport '80 ... The Concorde). The Million Dollar Face (TV). 1980: Amore in prima classe. Private Lessons. The Nude Bomb. 1981: Lady Chatterley's Lover. 1983: Mata Hari (released 1985). Private School. Emmanuelle IV. 1984: Red Heat. Hot Cruise. 1986: The Big Bet.

KRISTOFFERSON, Kris 1936–
Well-built American country-and-western singer who drifted into films in his mid-thirties. Within a couple of years his handsome features, bearded then but later clean-shaven, had made him a world star. In 1978 he declared that he was quitting films to return to full-time music. Although he returned to the cinema some 18 months later, his standing since has not seemed quite the same, even though his looks bely a man just past 50. Married fellow singer Rita Coolidge, but later divorced.
1971: The Last Movie. 1972: Cisco Pike. 1973: The Gospel Road. Blume in Love. Pat Garrett and Billy the Kid. 1974: Bring Me the Head of Alfredo Garcia. Alice Doesn't Live Here Anymore. 1975: Vigilante Force. 1976: The Sailor Who Fell from Grace with the Sea. A Star is Born. 1977: Semi-Tough. 1978: Convoy. 1979: Freedom Road (longer version serialized on TV). 1980: Heaven's Gate. 1981: Roll-Over. The Million Dollar Face (TV). 1984: The Lost Honor of Kathryn Beck (TV. GB: Acts of Passion). Flashpoint. 1985: Songwriter. Trouble in Mind. 1986: Stagecoach (TV). The Last Days of Frank and Jessie James (TV).

KRÜGER, Hardy (Eberhardt Krüger)
1928–
Very blond, square-faced, young-looking German leading man who marched with Hitler's youth, and began his career in wartime; but he found all doors open to him after his engaging performance as the continually escaping German prisoner-of-war in The One That Got Away. Since then he has been seen in largely sympathetic roles in films from many countries.
1944: †Junge Adler. 1949: Das Fräulein und der Vagabond. Diese Nacht vergess ich nie. Kätchen für Alles. 1950: Das Mädchen aus der Südsee. Insel ohne Moral. Schön muss man sein. 1951: Mein Freund, der Dieb. Ich heisse Niki. 1952: Alle Kann ich nicht heiraten. Illusion in Moll. 1953: Die Jungfrau auf dem Dach. Solange du da bist. Ich und Du. The Moon is Blue (German version, released 1958). Muss man such gleich scheiden lassen? 1954: Der letzte Sommer. 1955: Der Himmel ist nie ausverkauft. Alibi. An der schönen blauen Donau. 1956: Die Christel von der Post. Liane – Jungle Goddess. Das Mädchen aus dem Urwald. 1957: Monpti. Bankstresor 713. The One That Got Away. 1958: Bachelor of Hearts. Gestehen sie, Dr

Corda! (GB: Confess Dr Corda). Mit dem kopf durch die Wand. Mission diabolique/Der Fuchs von Paris. 1959: Der Rest ist Schweigen (GB and US: The Rest is Silence). Bumerang (GB: Cry Double Cross). Blind Date. Die Gans von Sedan. Die Näckte und der Satan. 1960: Taxi pour Tobruk. 1961: Zwei unter Millionen. Traum von Lieschen Müller. 1962: Les dimanches de ville d'Avray/Sundays and Cybèle. Les quatres vérites (GB: Three Fables of Love). Hatari! 1963: Le gros coup. 1964: Le chant du monde. 1965: The Flight of the Phoenix. Les pianos mécaniques (US: The Uninhibited). 1966: La grande sauterelle. The Defector. 1967: Le Franciscain de Bourges. 1968: Battle for Neretva. The Awful Story of the Nun of Monza. 1969: The Red Tent. The Secret of Santa Vittoria. 1970: El Castillo de la Pureza. 1971: Night Hair Child. Le moine. 1972: Tod eines Fremden (GB: The Execution. US: Death of a Stranger). 1974: Paper Tiger. Un solitaire. 1975: Barry Lyndon. 1976: Autopsie d'un monstre. A chacun son enfer. Potato Fritz/Montana Trap. 1977: A Bridge Too Far. Down.

Horizons. 1978: The Wild Geese. Blue Fin. 1981: Society Limited. 1982: Wrong is Right/ The Man with the Deadly Lens. 1984: The Inside Man.

† As Eberhardt Krüger

KWAN, Nancy 1938–
Lovely Eurasian leading lady who shot to prominence when Hollywood gave her two plum roles in a row in her first two movies. Despite some appealing performances since then, she has gradually faded from prominence. Born in Hong Kong.
1960: The World of Suzie Wong. 1961: Flower Drum Song. 1962: The Main Attraction. 1963: Tamahine. 1964: Fate is the Hunter. The Wild Affair. Honeymoon Hotel. 1966: Drop Dead Darling (US: Arrivederci, Baby). Lt. Robin Crusoe USN. The Peking Medallion (US: The Corrupt Ones). 1967: Nobody's Perfect. 1968: The Wrecking Crew. The Girl Who Knew Too Much. 1969: The McMasters ... Tougher than

the West Itself! The Girl from Peking. 1973: Wonder Women. 1975: Supercock. The Pacific Connection. 1976: Project: Kill. 1978: Devil Cat (US: Night Creature). The Falcon's Ultimatum. 1979: Streets of Hong Kong. 1981: Angkor. Kampuchea Express. 1983: Walking the Edge. 1985: Blade in Hong Kong (TV).

LADD, Alan 1913–1964

Although born in Hot Springs, Arkansas, Ladd was cool and taciturn – and too short at 5ft 6in for the thirties when he got more work in radio than films. Came the forties (and a second marriage, to an astute agent, Sue Carol) and Ladd suddenly appeared as a kind of fair-haired avenging angel, teaming up with equally pint-sized Veronica Lake, shooting to world stardom in *This Gun for Hire* and making a string of similar tough-guy films. When the genre passed, so did his top stardom and he took to drink in later years, dying in bed from a mixture of medication and alcohol.

*1932: Once in a Lifetime. Island of Lost Souls. Tom Brown of Culver. 1933: Saturday's Millions. No Man of Her Own. 1936: Anything Goes. Pigskin Parade (GB: The Harmony Parade). 1937: Last Train from Madrid. Hold 'Em Navy (GB: That Navy Spirit). All Over Town. Rustlers' Valley. Souls at Sea. 1938: The Goldwyn Follies. Come on Leathernecks. †Born to the West. Freshman Year. The Texans. 1939: Rulers of the Sea. *Rita Rio and Her Orchestra. The Green Hornet (serial). Goose Step (GB: Hitler – Beast of Berlin). 1940: Gangs of Chicago. Brother Rat and a Baby (GB: Baby Be Good). Light of Western Stars. The Howards of Virginia (GB: The Tree of Liberty). Her First Romance. In Old Missouri. Meet the Missus. Captain Caution. Wildcat Bus. Those Were the Days (GB: Good Old School Days). Cross Country Romance. 1941: Great Guns. The Parson of Panamint. *I Look at You. Paper Bullets. Petticoat Politics. The Reluctant Dragon. They Met in Bombay. The Black Cat. Cadet Girl. Citizen*

*Kane. 1942: Joan of Paris. This Gun for Hire. The Glass Key. Star Spangled Rhythm. Lucky Jordan. 1943: China. *Hollywood in Uniform. *Letter from a Friend. 1944: *Skirmish on the Home Front. And Now Tomorrow. 1945: Duffy's Tavern. Salty O'Rourke. *Hollywood Victory Caravan. 1946: Two Years Before the Mast. The Blue Dahlia. OSS. 1947: Variety Girl. My Favorite Brunette. Calcutta. Wild Harvest. 1948: Saigon. Beyond Glory. Whispering Smith. 1949: *Eyes of Hollywood. *Variety Club Hospital. Chicago Deadline. The Great Gatsby. Captain Carey USA (GB: After Midnight). 1950: Branded. *The Road to Hope. 1951: Appointment with Danger (completed 1949). Thunder in the East (released 1953). Red Mountain. 1952: The Iron Mistress. *The Sporting Oasis. 1953: Shane. Botany Bay. The Red Beret (US: Paratrooper). Desert Legion. Hell Below Zero. 1954: The Black Knight. Saskatchewan (GB: O'Rourke of the Royal Mounted). Drum Beat. 1955: The McConnell Story (GB: Tiger in the Sky). Hell on Frisco Bay. 1956: Santiago (GB: The Gun Runner). A Cry in the Night (narrator only). 1957: The Big Land (GB: Stampeded!). Boy on a Dolphin. 1958: The Deep Six. The Proud Rebel. The Badlanders. 1959: The Man in the Net. Guns of the Timberland. 1960: All the Young Men. One Foot in Hell. 1961: Orazi e curiazi/Duel of Champions. 1962: 13 West Street. 1963: The Carpetbaggers.*

† *Scene deleted from final release print*

LAINE, Frankie (F. LoVecchio) 1913–

Dark, square-faced, beefy American singer with wide smile whose record sales were third only to Crosby and Sinatra in the 1940s and 1950s. Made several (over-) bright musicals for the Richard Quine–Blake Edwards team at Columbia in the 1950s, but is probably best remembered by filmgoers as the breathy, powerful voice singing theme songs behind the credits to a whole posse of westerns, notably *Gunfight at the OK Corral*, *3:10 to Yuma* and *Blazing Saddles*. In his youth, a record-breaking marathon dancer! Married to Nan Grey (Eschal Miller, 1918–) since 1950.

*1949: Make-Believe Ballroom. 1950: When You're Smiling. 1951: Sunny Side of the Street. 1952: Rainbow 'Round My Shoulder. 1955: Bring Your Smile Along. 1956: *Mr Rhythm's*

*Holiday. Meet Me in Las Vegas (GB: Viva Las Vegas!). He Laughed Last. 1957: *Rock 'Em Cowboy.*

LAKE, Veronica (Constance Ockleman) 1919–1973

Petite, slinky blonde with sleepy eyes, and unique peek-a-boo hairstyle which, draped over her right eye, swept the country until spoilsports cavilled that factory girls could get such hair caught in machinery. She was highly effective as the icy, husky-voiced femme fatale in night-life thrillers with Alan Ladd, but soon lost her distinctive looks, and Hollywood quickly cast her aside when her peak days were over. Her drink problems were well publicized and she was four times married and divorced. Died from acute hepatitis.

*1939: †All Women Have Secrets. †Sorority House (GB: That Girl from College). †Dancing Co-Ed (GB: Every Other Inch a Lady). ‡*Wrong Room. 1940: †Forty Little Mothers. †Young As You Feel. 1941: I Wanted Wings. Hold Back the Dawn. Sullivan's Travels. 1942: This Gun for Hire. The Glass Key. Star Spangled Rhythm. I Married a Witch. 1943: So Proudly We Hail! 1944: The Hour Before the Dawn. Miss Susie Slagle's (released 1946). 1945: Bring on the Girls. Out of This World. Duffy's Tavern. Hold That Blonde. 1946: The Blue Dahlia. 1947: Variety Girl. Ramrod. 1948: Saigon. The Sainted Sisters. Isn't It Romantic? 1949: Slattery's Hurricane. 1951: Stronghold. 1966: Footsteps in the Snow. 1970: Flesh Feast.*

† *as Constance Keane* ‡ *as Connie Keane*

LAMARR, Hedy (Hedwig Kiesler) 1913–

Perhaps the most beautiful actress ever to appear on screen. A kittenishly pretty face surrounded by raven-black hair; and a sublime figure. Hedy was physical perfection and quite enough to take one's breath away – which she did when sensationally appearing nude in the Czech film *Extase*. She married a millionaire and was out of show business for five years before Louis B. Mayer signed her up for M-G-M – but never really allowed her to let loose the sensuality that played about the lips and could have made her a screen immortal. Ultimately married and divorced six times, including (third) John Loder from 1943 to 1947. Born in Austria.

1930: †Geld auf der Strasse. 1931: †Sturm im

Wasserglas. †Wir brauchen kein Geld. †Die
Koffer des Herrn O.F. †Die Blumenfrau von
Lindenau. 1932: †Extase/Ecstasy. 1938:
Algiers. 1939: Lady of the Tropics. I Take
This Woman. *Screen Snapshots No. 10. 1940:
Comrade X. Boom Town. 1941: Come Live
with Me. H.M. Pulham Esq. Ziegfeld Girl.
1942: Tortilla Flat. Crossroads. White Cargo.
1943: *Show Business at War. The Heavenly
Body. The Conspirators. 1944: Experiment
Perilous. 1945: Her Highness and the Bellboy.
1946: The Strange Woman. 1947: Dishonored
Lady. 1948: Let's Live a Little. 1949: Samson
and Delilah. 1950: A Lady without Passport.
Copper Canyon. 1951: My Favourite Spy.
1953: The Loves of Three Queens/The Love of
Three Women. 1954: L'amante di Pari-
de/Eterna femmina (GB and US: The Face
That Launched a Thousand Ships). 1957: The
Story of Mankind. The Female Animal.
‡Slaughter on 10th Avenue.

† as Hedy Kiesler ‡scenes deleted from final
release print

LAMAS, Fernando 1915–1982
Slightly cruel-looking in his extremely handsome way, Argentine's Lamas made no Hollywood films until he was 35 and already greying. But his few years with M-G-M gained
him a world-wide reputation as a Latin lover
and also showed people he could sing. He
went into stage musicals from 1956 and later
divided his time between performing in night-
clubs and directing for television. Married
(third) Arlene Dahl, 1954–1960, and Esther
Williams (fourth) from 1967 until his death
from cancer.

1942: Frontera Sur. En ul Ultime Piso. 1945:
Villa Rica del Espiritu Santo. 1947: Navidad
de los Pobres. Evasion. El Tango Vuelve a Paris.
1948: Historia de una Mala Mujer/Lady Windermere's Fan. La Rubia Mireya. La Otra y
Yo. 1949: Vidalita. De Padre Desconocido.
1950: La Historia del Tango. The Avengers.
1951: Rich, Young and Pretty. The Law and
the Lady. 1952: The Merry Widow. The Girl
Who Had Everything. 1953: Dangerous When
Wet. Jivaro (GB: Lost Treasure of the
Amazon). Sangaree. Diamond Queen. 1954:
Rose Marie. 1955: The Girl Rush. 1960: The
Lost World. 1961: †The Magic Fountain.
1962: Duello nella Sila. 1963: D'Artagnan
against the Three Musketeers (US: Revenge
of the Musketeers). 1967: †The Violent Ones.
Valley of Mystery. Kill a Dragon. 1968: Back-
track (TV). 1969: The Lonely Profession
(TV). 100 Rifles. 1970: Powderkeg (TV. GB:
cinemas). 1971: Taxi to Terror. 1975: Won
Ton Ton, the Dog Who Saved Hollywood.
Murder on Flight 502 (TV). 1978: The Cheap
Detective. 1980: Sunday Games (TV).

† Also directed

LAMBERT, Christopher (Christophe
Lambert) 1957–
Tall, rangy, light-haired actor, born in America but raised in Switzerland. He was set for
a career on the London Stock Exchange when
he decided to become an actor and, given
three years by his parents to make it, moved
to Paris to achieve his ambition. But it was
his casting as Tarzan in a British film that
gave him the breakthrough to stardom which
his faintly Belmondo-like looks are helping
him consolidate.
1981: Le bar du telephone. 1983: Legitime violence. 1984: Greystoke – The Legend of Tarzan
Lord of the Apes. Paroles et musique. 1985:
Subway. 1986: Highlander. I Love You.

LAMONT, Molly 1910–
Bright, well-groomed, Transvaal-born actress
with light-brown (sometimes blonde) hair and
impish personality. A beauty contest winner
in South Africa, she came to Britain and was
successfully groomed for stardom at Elstree
Studios. She went to Hollywood in 1935 but
never enjoyed quite the same success, her
best roles probably coming as Cary Grant's
luckless fiancée in The Awful Truth and in the

lead of a minor 1943 offering called A Gentle
Gangster.
1930: The Black Hand Gang. 1931: Uneasy
Virtue. Old Soldiers Never Die. What a Night!
Shadows. The House Opposite. My Wife's
Family. Dr Josser KC. 1932: Strictly Business.
The Strangler. Lord Camber's Ladies. Brother
Alfred. The Last Coupon. Lucky Girl. Josser
on the River. His Wife's Mother. 1933: Letting
in the Sunshine. Leave It to Me. Paris Plane.
1934: *Wedding Anniversary. White Ensign.
Irish Hearts (US: Norah O'Neale). The Third
Clue. Murder at Monte Carlo. 1935: Oh, What
a Night! Handle with Care. Rolling Home.
Alibi Inn. Another Face (GB: It Happened in
Hollywood). Jalna. 1936: Muss 'Em Up (GB:
House of Fate). Sylvia Scarlett. A Woman
Rebels. Mary of Scotland. The Jungle Princess.
1937: A Doctor's Diary. The Awful Truth.
1942: The Moon and Sixpence. 1943: A Gentle
Gangster. 1944: The White Cliffs of Dover.
Follow the Boys. Mr Skeffington. Minstrel
Man. 1946: So Goes My Love (GB: A Genius
in the Family). The Dark Corner. 1947: Ivy.
Christmas Eve. Scared to Death. 1949: South
Sea Sinner (GB: East of Java). 1951: The
First Legion.

LAMOUR, Dorothy (Mary D. Slaton)
1914–
How anyone so American as dark-haired, sloe-
eyed, pencil-eyebrowed Dorothy Lamour
could become Hollywood's queen of South
Sea Island pictures is a bit of a mystery. But
she'll always be remembered as the maiden
bursting into sarong and the good-humoured
decoration in the 'Road' pictures. Fortunately,

she could also sing (rather well, if a bit syrupy) and act (a bit) and so sustained her star career. The public always liked her, and it was a hideous misjudgment of their taste to offer her only a cameo role in the last 'Road' film in 1962.

1936: *The Stars Can't Be Wrong. College Holiday. The Jungle Princess. 1937: Swing High, Swing Low. High, Wide and Handsome. Last Train from Madrid. The Hurricane. Thrill of a Lifetime. 1938: Her Jungle Love. The Big Broadcast of 1938. Tropic Holiday. Spawn of the North. 1939: St Louis Blues. Man About Town. Disputed Passage. 1940: Typhoon. Johnny Apollo. Moon Over Burma. Road to Singapore. Chad Hanna. 1941: Aloma of the South Seas. Road to Zanzibar. Caught in the Draft. 1942: Beyond the Blue Horizon. Road to Morocco. The Fleet's In. Star Spangled Rhythm. They Got Me Covered. 1943: Dixie. Riding High (GB: Melody Inn). 1944: Rainbow Island. And the Angels Sing. 1945: Road to Utopia. Duffy's Tavern. A Medal for Benny. Masquerade in Mexico. 1947: My Favorite Brunette. Variety Girl. Road to Rio. Wild Harvest. 1948: A Miracle Can Happen (later On Our Merry Way). Lulu Belle. The Girl from Manhattan. 1949: Slightly French. Manhandled. The Lucky Stiff. 1951: Here Comes the Groom. 1952: The Greatest Show on Earth. Road to Bali. *Screen Snapshots No. 205. 1962: The Road to Hong Kong. 1963: Donovan's Reef. 1964: Pajama Party. 1969: The Phynx. 1975: Won Ton Ton, the Dog Who Saved Hollywood. 1976: Death at Love House (TV).

LANCASTER, Burt (Burton Lancaster) 1913–
Muscular, fair-haired American actor with flashing smile tinged with menace. A former circus acrobat – and remarkably nimble for such a big man – he developed a taste for acting in wartime troop shows. Although he started in black thrillers, he became best known in swashbucklers, swinging spectacularly around on ropes. Some regret the drift into excessive seriousness that followed, although he did win an Oscar in 1960 for his fire-eating preacher in Elmer Gantry, and was also nominated for From Here to Eternity, Birdman of Alcatraz and, many years later, Atlantic City USA.

1946: The Killers. 1947: Desert Fury. Brute Force. Variety Girl. I Walk Alone. 1948: Sorry

Wrong Number. Kiss the Blood Off My Hands (GB: Blood on My Hands). 1949: Criss Cross. Rope of Sand. 1950: The Flame and the Arrow. Mister 880. 1951: Vengeance Valley. Jim Thorpe – All American (GB: Man of Bronze). Ten Tall Men. 1952: The Crimson Pirate. Come Back, Little Sheba. 1953: South Sea Woman. From Here to Eternity. His Majesty O'Keefe. Three Sailors and a Girl. 1954: Apache. Vera Cruz. 1955: †The Kentuckian. The Rose Tattoo. 1956: Trapeze. The Rainmaker. Gunfight at the O K Corral. 1957: Sweet Smell of Success. *Playtime in Hollywood. 1958: Separate Tables. Run Silent, Run Deep. 1959: The Devil's Disciple. The Unforgiven. 1961: The Young Savages. Judgment at Nuremberg. 1962: A Child is Waiting. Birdman of Alcatraz. The Leopard. 1963: The List of Adrian Messenger. 1964: Seven Days in May. 1965: The Train. The Hallelujah Trail. 1966: The Professionals. 1967: The Swimmer. 1968: The Scalphunters. 1969: Castle Keep. Airport. The Gypsy Moths. 1970: King: a Filmed Record ... Montgomery to Memphis. 1971: Lawman. Valdez is Coming. 1972: Ulzana's Raid. 1973: Scorpio. 1974: ‡The Midnight Man. Conversation Piece. 1975: Moses. 1976: Buffalo Bill and the Indians. 1900. Victory at Entebbe (TV. GB: cinemas). The Cassandra Crossing. 1977: The Island of Dr Moreau. Twilight's Last Gleaming. Go Tell the Spartans. 1979: Zulu Dawn. 1980: Cattle Annie and Little Britches. Atlantic City USA (GB and US: Atlantic City). 1981: La pelle. 1983: Local Hero. The Osterman Weekend. 1985: Little Treasure. Scandal Sheet (TV). 1986: Tough Guys.

† Also directed ‡ Also co-directed

LANDI, Elissa (Elisabeth-Marie-Christine Kühnelt) 1904–1948
Bright, vital, fair-haired, Austrian-born actress and authoress, supposedly the granddaughter of Elisabeth of Austria. In the late twenties and early thirties she made films in several countries, but was most successful in Hollywood, and especially as the haunting heroine of Sign of the Cross. Died from cancer.
1926: London. 1928: Bolibar. Underground. Le leur sur la cime (GB and US: The Betrayal). 1929: Broch och Brett (GB and US: Sin). The Inseparables. 1930: The Parisian (English-language version of Mon gosse de père). Knowing Men. The Price of Things. Children of

Chance. 1931: Body and Soul. Always Goodbye. Wicked. The Yellow Ticket (GB: The Yellow Passport). 1932: The Devil's Lottery. Sign of the Cross. The Woman in Room 13. A Passport to Hell (GB: Burnt Offering). 1933: The Masquerader. The Warrior's Husband. I Loved You Wednesday. 1934: Sisters under the Skin. By Candlelight. Man of Two Worlds. The Count of Monte Cristo. Enter Madame. The Great Flirtation. 1935: Without Regret. Koenigsmark. The Amateur Gentleman. 1936: Mad Holiday. After the Thin Man. 1937: The Thirteenth Chair. 1943: Corregidor.

LANDIS, Carole (Frances Ridste) 1919–1948
An All-American blonde bombshell, Carole Landis was four times married and divorced, and committed suicide at 29 allegedly from frustration over her desire to marry Rex Harrison (qv). Round-faced, bubbly and as sexy as all-get-out, she was one of the original sweater girls and a favourite pin-up of World War II troops.
1937: A Day at the Races. A Star is Born. The Adventurous Blonde. Broadway Melody of 1938. The Emperor's Candlesticks. Hollywood Hotel. Varsity Show. Blondes at Work. 1938: Gold Diggers in Paris (GB: The Gay Impostors). Over the Wall. Boy Meets Girl. Four's a Crowd. Men Are Such Fools. When Were You Born? 1939: Daredevils of the Red Circle (serial). Three Texas Steers (GB: Danger Rides the Range). Cowboys from Texas. 1940: One Million BC (GB: Man and His Mate). Mystery Sea Raider. Turnabout. Road Show. 1941: Topper Returns. I Wake Up Screaming (GB: Hot Spot). Dance Hall. Moon over Miami. Cadet Girl. 1942: A Gentleman at Heart. It Happened in Flatbush. Manila Calling. Orchestra Wives. My Gal Sal. 1943: The Powers Girl (GB: Hello! Beautiful). Wintertime. *Screen Snapshots No. 2 (new series). 1944: Secret Command. Four Jills in a Jeep. Having Wonderful Crime. 1946: Behind Green Lights. It Shouldn't Happen to a Dog. Scandal in Paris. 1947: Out of the Blue. 1948: Noose (US: The Silk Noose). The Brass Monkey (US: Lucky Mascot).

LANE, Abbe 1932–
Vivacious, red-haired American singer of exotic looks, on radio and stage from the age of 14. Married her bandleader, Xavier Cugat

(they were later divorced), and decorated a number of American and Italian pictures in 'spitfire' roles, before guesting in TV series and, ultimately, concentrating on a nightclub singing career.

1953: Wings of the Hawk. Ride Clear of Diablo. 1954: The Americano. 1955: Chicago Syndicate. Donetella. I girovaghi/The Wanderers. Lo scopolo. 1956: Tempo di villeggiatura. Parola di ladro. Sunset in Naples. 1957: La dottoressa (US: Lady Doctor). 1958: Maracaibo. Sailors, Women – Trouble/Morinai, donne e guai. Susanna y Yo. Totò, Vittorio e la dottoressa. 1959: I baccanali di Tiberio (US: Tiberius). 1960: My Friend Jekyll. 1983: The Twilight Zone (GB: Twilight Zone – the Movie).

LANE, Allan 'Rocky' (Harold Albershart) 1901–1973
Allan Lane was tall, dark and handsome, a top American football player who turned to acting when his sporting days were through. He could act enough to make one regret the mediocrity of his roles in the thirties, playing upright juvenile leads in crime films. Suddenly, in the mid-forties, he became the two-fisted star of second-feature westerns, one of the best of his kind. Died from a bone marrow disorder. Some sources are adamant that Lane's year of birth was 1909.

1929: The Forward Pass. *Knights Out. *Detectives Wanted. Not Quite Decent. 1930: Madam Satan. Love in the Rough. 1931: Night Nurse. The Star Witness. *War Mamas. Local Boy Makes Good. Honor of the Family. 1932: The Famous Ferguson Case. Miss Pinkerton.

Winner Takes All. One Way Passage. Crooner. It's Tough to be Famous. The Tenderfoot. The Crash. 1933: *Heavens! My Husband. 1936: Stowaway. 1937: Charlie Chan at the Olympics. Laughing at Trouble. Big Business. Fifty Roads to Town. The Duke Comes Back (GB: Call of the Ring). Sing and Be Happy. 1938: Crime Ring. The Law West of Tombstone. Having Wonderful Time. Night Spot. Pacific Liner. Maid's Night Out. Fugitives for a Night. The Marriage Business. 1939: They Made Her a Spy. Panama Lady. Twelve Crowded Hours. Conspiracy. The Spellbinder. 1940: Grand Old Opry. King of the Royal Mounted (serial). 1941: All-American Co-Ed. 1942: King of the Mounties (serial. And feature version: Yukon Patrol). 1943: Daredevils of the West (serial). The Dancing Masters. 1944: The Tiger Woman (serial). Call of the South Seas. Stagecoach to Monterey. Sheriff of Sundown. The Silver City Kid. 1945: Topeka Terror. Bells of Rosarita. Corpus Christi Bandits. Trail of Kit Carson. 1946: Gay Blades. Night Train to Memphis. A Guy Could Change. Out California Way. Stagecoach to Denver. Sante Fé Uprising. 1947: Oregon Trail Scouts. Marshal of Cripple Creek. Bandits of Dark Canyon. Homesteaders of Paradise Valley. Vigilantes of Boomtown. Rustlers of Devil's Canyon. The Wild Frontier. 1948: Oklahoma Badlands. Carson City Raiders. Desperadoes of Dodge City. Sundown in Santa Fé. The Bold Frontiersman. Marshal of Amarillo. The Denver Kid. Renegades of Sonora. 1949: Sheriff of Wichita. Frontier Investigator. Bandit King of Texas. Powder River Rustlers. Death Valley Gunfighters. The Wyoming Bandit. Navajo Trail Raiders. 1950: Gunmen of Abilene. Salt Lake Raiders. Vigilante Hideout. Frisco Tornado. Code of the Silver Sage. Covered Wagon Raiders. Rustlers on Horseback. Trail of Robin Hood. 1951: Rough Riders of Durango. Wells Fargo Gunmaster. The Desert of Lost Men. Night Riders of Montana. Fort Dodge Stampede. 1952: Leadville Gunslinger. Thundering Caravans. Black Hills Ambush. Captive of Billy the Kid. Desperadoes' Outpost. 1953: Marshal of Cedar Rock. Bandits of the West. Savage Frontier. El Paso Stampede. 1958: The Saga of Hemp Brown. 1960: Hell Bent for Leather. 1961: Posse from Hell. 1962: Geronimo's Revenge (TV. GB: cinemas).

LANE, Jackie (later Jocelyn) 1936–
Poutily pretty, dark-haired, dark-eyed starlet, almost a British Bardot. The younger sister of Mara Lane (qv), Jackie pursued her career with diligence, appearing mostly in provocative roles, and even changing her name to Jocelyn when she went to Hollywood in 1964. Even so, her acting was never more than adequate – and slightly colourless for a firecracker type – and her films petered out.

1954: For Better, For Worse (US: Cocktails in the Kitchen). Men of Sherwood Forest. April in Portugal. 1955: Dust and Gold. The Gamma People. 1956: Zarak. 1957: These Dangerous Years (US: Dangerous Youth). The Truth about Women. 1958: Wonderful Things! 1959: The Angry Hills. Jet Storm. 1960: Robin Hood and the Pirates. 1961: Aimez-vous Brahms?/

Goodbye Again. 1962: I tromboni di Fra' Diavolo (US: The Bandits of 'Fra Diavolo'). Mars, God of War. Le sette folgori di Assur (GB: 7th Thunderbolt. US: War Gods of Babylon). Operation Snatch. Two and Two Make Six. 1963: La congiura dei Borgia. 1965: †Tickle Me. †Sword of Ali Baba. 1966: †Bel Ami 2000 (GB: How to Seduce a Playboy). †The Poppy is Also a Flower (GB: Danger Grows Wild). †Incident at Phantom Hill. 1969: †Hell's Belles. †Land Raiders. 1970: †A Bullet for Pretty Boy.

† As Jocelyn Lane

LANE, Mara 1930–
Dark-haired, full-lipped, sultry-looking, petite, Austrian-born ballet dancer who got sexy roles in British (and a couple of Hollywood) pictures, then did some continental fol-de-rols before retiring in the early 1960s. Much photographed in her time and a frequent cover girl for fan magazines. Sister of Jackie Lane (qv).

1951: Hell is Sold Out. 1952: Treasure Hunt. Something Money Can't Buy. It Started in Paradise. Decameron Nights. 24 Hours in a Woman's Life (US: Affair in Monte Carlo). 1953: Innocents in Paris. 1954: Susan Slept Here. Angela. Uomini ombra/Shadow Men. The Adventures of Casanova. 1956: Pulverschnee nach Übersee. Fremdenführer von Lissabon. Bonsoir Paris, bonjour l'amour. 1957: Monpti. 1958: Der Elefant im Porzellanladen. Peter Voss, der Millionendieb. 1959: Schlag auf Schlag. Paradies der Matrosen. Bobby Dodd greift ein. 1960: Mal drunter – mal drüber. 1961: 79 AD. 1962: The Old Testament.

LANE, Priscilla (P. Mullican) 1917–
Prettiest, blondest and most personable of five acting sisters, two of whom, Rosemary (1913–1974) and Lola (1909–1981) appeared in films with her. Equally at ease with romantic or madcap comedy roles, she did all of her best work at Warners, where she was under contract from 1937 to 1941.
*1937: Varsity Show. 1938: Love, Honor and Behave. Cowboy from Brooklyn (GB: Romance and Rhythm). Four Daughters. Men Are Such Fools. Brother Rat. 1939: Daughters Courageous. Yes, My Darling Daughter. Dust Be My Destiny. The Roaring Twenties. Four Wives. 1940: Brother Rat and a Baby (GB: Baby Be Good). Three Cheers for the Irish. Ladies Must Live. 1941: Four Mothers. Million Dollar Baby. Blues in the Night. 1942: Saboteur. Silver Queen. 1943: The Meanest Man in the World. *Stars on Horseback. Arsenic and Old Lace. 1947: Fun on a Weekend. 1948: Bodyguard.*

LANG, June (Winifred J. Vlasek) 1915–
Very pretty, delicate-looking American actress with wide blue eyes and auburn hair. Beginning her career as a dancer, she moved on to become a likeably decorative star of light comedies and adventure yarns, much in the Piper Laurie (*qv*) mould. She might have moved on to more dramatic things, but her studio tore up her contract in 1939 because of her association with convicted criminal John Roselli (they were briefly married from 1940). Miss Lang's career never recovered, although she was quoted as saying a few years ago that she would 'love to act again'. Also married

and divorced (third of three) British actor Joss Ambler.
1931: †Young Sinners. 1932: †Chandu, the Magician. 1933: †I Loved You Wednesday. †The Man Who Dared. 1934: Music in the Air. 1935: Bonnie Scotland. Every Saturday Night. 1936: Captain January. The Country Doctor. The Road to Glory. White Hunter. 1937: Nancy Steele is Missing. Wee Willie Winkie. Ali Baba Goes to Town. 1938: One Wild Night. International Settlement. Meet the Girls. 1939: Captain Fury. Zenobia (GB: Elephants Never Forget). For Love or Money (GB: Tomorrow at Midnight). Forged Passport. 1940: Inside Information. Convicted Woman. 1941: Redhead. The Deadly Game. 1942: Too Many Women. Footlight Serenade. City of Silent Men. 1943: Stage Door Canteen. Flesh and Fantasy. 1947: Lighthouse.

† *As June Vlasek*

LANG, Matheson 1879–1948
Formidable, craggy, heavy-headed, dark-haired star of the British stage who, despite a somewhat theatrical style, became a dominant personality of the British cinema for 20 years between stage runs, mostly in larger-than-life roles that exercised his mastery of disguise. He was born in Canada to a Scottish clergyman, but brought up in Scotland, where he began acting at 18. He spent his later years working on his autobiography (*Mr Wu Looks Back*, a reference to one of his several 'oriental' roles) and in retirement in the Bahamas, where he died.
*1916: The Merchant of Venice. 1917: *Everybody's Business. Masks and Faces. The Ware Case. The House Opposite. 1918: Victory and Peace. 1919: Mr Wu. 1921: Carnival. 1922: Dick Turpin's Ride to York. A Romance of Old Bagdad. 1923: The Wandering Jew. Guy Fawkes. 1924: White Slippers. Henry – King of Navarre. Slaves of Destiny/Miranda of the Balcony. 1925: The Qualified Adventurer. The Secret Kingdom (US: Beyond the Veil). 1926: Island of Despair. The Chinese Bungalow. 1927: The King's Highway. 1928: The Blue Peter. The Triumph of the Scarlet Pimpernel (US: The Scarlet Daredevil). 1930: The Chinese Bungalow (remake). 1931: Carnival (remake. US: Venetian Nights). 1933: Channel Crossing. 1934: Little Friend. The Great Defender. 1935: Drake of England (US: Drake*

the Pirate). Royal Cavalcade (US: Regal Cavalcade). 1936: The Cardinal.

LANGDON, Harry 1884–1944
Baby-faced, pale-complexioned American silent-screen comedian whose speciality was blank bewilderment at life's vicissitudes. Won great popularity briefly at the end of the twenties, but quarrelled with those around him, failed as his own director and was declared bankrupt in 1931. Although he worked on, he never regained his popularity. Died from a cerebral haemorrhage.
*1918: The Master Mystery (serial). 1923: *Picking Peaches. 1924: *Smile Please. *Feet of Mud. *Shanghaied Lovers. *Flickering Youth. *The Luck o' the Foolish. *All Night Long. *The Cat's Meow. *His New Mamma. *The First Hundred Years. *The Hansom Cabman. 1925: *Boobs in the Woods. *Plain Clothes. *Lucky Stars. *There He Goes. *The Sea Squawk. *His Marriage Wow. *Remember When? *Horace Greeley Junior. *The White Wing's Bride. 1926: *Saturday Afternoon. *The Soldier Man. *Fiddlesticks. His First Flame. Ella Cinders. Tramp Tramp Tramp. The Strong Man. 1927: Long Pants. †Three's a Crowd. 1928: †The Chaser. †Heart Trouble. 1929: *Hotter Than Hot. *Shy Boy. *Skirt Shy. 1930: See America Thirst. A Soldier's Plaything (GB: A Soldier's Pay). *The Head Guy. *The Fighting Parson. *The Big Kick. *The King. *The Shrimp. 1932: *The Big Flash. 1933: Hallelujah, I'm a Bum (GB: Hallelujah I'm a Tramp). My Weakness. *Amateur Night. *The Hitch Hiker. *Knight Duty. *Tied for Life. *Hooks and Jabs. *Tired Feet. *Marriage Humor. *The Stage Hand. *Leave It to Dad. 1934: No Sleep on the Deep. *On Ice. *A Roaming Romeo. *A Circus Hoodoo. *Petting Preferred. *Council on De Fence. *Trimmed in Furs. *Shivers. 1935: Atlantic Adventure. *The Leather Necker. *His Marriage Mix-Up. *His Bridal Sweet. *I Don't Remember. 1937: Mad About Money (US: He Loved an Actress). 1938: *A Doggone Mixup. *Sue My Lawyer. There Goes My Heart. He Loved an Actress. 1939: Zenobia (GB: Elephants Never Forget). 1940: Misbehaving Husbands. *Goodness, a Ghost. *Cold Turkey. 1941: Road Show. All-American Co-Ed. Double Trouble. 1942: House of Errors. *What Makes Lizzie Dizzy. *Carry Harry. *Piano Mooners. *A Blitz on the Fritz. *Tireman, Spare My Tires. 1943:*

Warrior. *1959: Frontier Rangers/Northwest Rangers* (TV. GB: cinemas). *1961: Fury River* (TV. GB: cinemas). *1965: Women of the Prehistoric Planet. 1967: Caxambu! 1968: Mission Batangas. The Omegans. 1975: Trap on Cougar Mountain.*

As director: *1968: Mission Batangas. 1975: Trap on Cougar Mountain.*

LAUGHTON, Charles 1899–1962
Seldom if ever can so fat and ugly a man have become so big a star. But this light-haired, rubber-faced, thick-lipped English actor ran up such a string of brilliant characterizations in Hollywood (after winning an Oscar for his British-made Henry VIII) that his precise and plummy tones became the most imitated of all. Captain Bligh, Mr Barrett, Rembrandt, Ruggles of Red Gap, Javert in *Les Miserables*, Nero and, perhaps best of all, Quasimodo: they were all memorably Laughton. From 1945 till 1954 his overripe performances were the despair of his supporters. But he came good again in his last few films (adding an Oscar nomination for *Witness for the Prosecution* to the one he had received for *Mutiny on the Bounty*) before his death from spinal cancer. Married to Elsa Lanchester from 1929.
*1928: *Bluebottles. *Daydreams. 1929: Piccadilly. Comets. 1930: Wolves (US: Wanted Men). 1931: Down River. 1932: The Old Dark House. Payment Deferred. The Devil and the Deep. Sign of the Cross. If I Had a Million. Island of Lost Souls. 1933: The Private Life of Henry VIII. White Woman. 1934: The Barretts of Wimpole Street. Mutiny on the Bounty. Les Miserables. 1935: Ruggles of Red Gap. *Frankie and Johnny. 1936: Rembrandt. 1937: I Claudius (unfinished). 1938: Vessel of Wrath (US: The Beachcomber). St Martin's Lane (US: Sidewalks of London). 1939: Jamaica Inn. The Hunchback of Notre Dame. 1940: They Knew What They Wanted. 1941: It Started with Eve. 1942: The Tuttles of Tahiti. Tales of Manhattan. Stand by for Action (GB: Cargo of Innocents). 1943: This Land is Mine. The Man from Down Under. Forever and a Day. 1944: The Canterville Ghost. 1945: The Suspect. Captain Kidd. 1946: Because of Him. 1947: *The Queen's Necklace. 1948: The Paradine Case. Arch of Triumph. The Girl from Manhattan. The Big Clock. 1949: The Bribe.*

*The Man on the Eiffel Tower. 1951: The Blue Veil. The Strange Door. 1952: O. Henry's Full House (GB: Full House). Abbott and Costello Meet Captain Kidd. 1953: Young Bess. Salome. 1954: Hobson's Choice. 1957: Witness for the Prosecution. 1958: *Fabulous Hollywood. 1960: Under Ten Flags. Spartacus. 1962: Advise and Consent.*

As director: *1955: Night of the Hunter.*

LAUREL, Stan (Arthur S. Jefferson) 1890–1965
Red-haired British comedian, from the music-halls, who went to Hollywood in his twenties and eventually became the thin half of the Laurel and Hardy team. The inspiration behind most of their comedy routines, his trade marks included the scratching of his unruly mop of hair, the blank look, the ear-wiggle and dissolving into tears. A man with a somewhat contentious private life (he was fired more than once by his long-time boss, Hal Roach), Laurel was given a special Academy Award in 1960. He died from a heart attack. Foreign-language versions also exist of several of the early 1930s' Laurel and Hardy shorts.
1917: Lucky Dog. Nuts in May. The Evolution of Fashion. 1918: Hoot Mon. Whose Zoo? Just Rambling Along. Phoney Photos. It's Great To Be Crazy. Hickory Hiram. Huns and Hyphens. No Place Like Jail. Bears and Bad Men. Frauds and Frenzies. Do You Love Your Wife? 1919: Mixed Nuts. Scars and Stripes. Hustling for Health. 1921: The Rent Collector. 1922: The Pest. The Week-End Party. The Egg. Mud and Sand. 1923: When Knights Were Cold. The Noon Whistle. Pick and Shovel. Gas and Air. The Handy Man. A Man About Town. Scorching Sands. Roughest Africa. Mother's Joy. Collars and Cuffs. White Wings. Kill or Cure. Short Orders. The Whole Truth. Save the Ship. Frozen Hearts. Under Two Jags. The Soilers. 1924: Wild Bill Hiccup/Wide Open Spaces. Detained. Zeb vs. Paprika. Smithy. Near Dublin. Short Kilts. Rupert of Hee-Haw/Rupert of Coleslaw. West of Hot Dog. Postage Due. Brothers Under the Chin. Monsieur Don't Care. 1925: Madam Mix-Up/Mandarin Mix-Up. Pie-Eyed. Navy Blue Days. The Sleuth. Half a Man. Somewhere in Wrong. The Snow Hawk. Twins. Dr Pyckle and Mr Pride. 1926: Atta Boy. On the Front Page (GB: The

Editor). Get 'Em Young. 45 Minutes from Hollywood. 1927: Duck Soup. Slipping Wives. Love 'Em and Weep. Eve's Love Letters. Should Tall Men Marry? Why Girls Love Sailors. With Love and Hisses. Sugar Daddies. Sailors, Beware!/Ship's Hero. Call of the Cuckoo. Flying Elephants. Hats Off. Do Detectives Think? (GB: The Bodyguard). Let George Do It. Putting Pants on Philip. The Second Hundred Years. The Battle of the Century. Now I'll Tell One. Seeing the World. 1928: Leave 'Em Laughing. The Finishing Touch. From Soup to Nuts. You're Darn Tootin' (GB: The Music Blasters). Their Purple Moment. Should Married Men Go Home? Early to Bed. Two Tars. Habeas Corpus. We Faw Down (GB: We Slip Up). 1929: Liberty. Wrong Again. That's My Wife. Big Business. Unaccustomed As We Are. Double Whoopee. Berth Marks. Men o' War/ Man o' War. Perfect Day. They Go Boom. Bacon Grabbers. The Hoose-Gow. †Hollywood Revue of 1929. Angora Love. 1930: The Night Owls. Blotto. Brats. †The Rogue Song. Hog Wild (GB: Aerial Antics). The Laurel and Hardy Murder Case. Another Fine Mess. Below Zero. 1931: Be Big. Chickens Come Home. The Stolen Jools (GB: The Slippery Pearls). Laughing Gravy. Our Wife. †Pardon Us (GB: Jail Birds). Come Clean. One Good Turn. †Beau Hunks (GB: Beau Chumps). On the Loose. Helpmates. 1932: Any Old Port. The Music Box. The Chimp. Scram! County Hospital. †Pack Up Your Troubles. Their First Mistake. Towed in a Hole. 1933: Twice Two. Me and My Pal. †The Devil's Brother (GB: Fra Diavolo). The Midnight Patrol. Busy Bodies. Wild Poses. Dirty Work. †Sons of the Desert (GB: Fraternally Yours). 1934: Oliver the Eighth (GB: The Private Life of Oliver the Eighth). †Hollywood Party. Going Bye-Bye! Them Thar Hills. †Babes in Toyland. The Live Ghost. 1935: Tit for Tat. The Fixer Uppers. Thicker Than Water. †Bonnie Scotland. 1936: On the Wrong Trek. †The Bohemian Girl. †Our Relations. 1937: †Way Out West. †Pick a Star. 1938: †Swiss Miss. Block-Heads. 1939: †The Flying Deuces. †A Chump at Oxford. 1940: †Saps at Sea. 1941: †Great Guns. 1942: †A-Haunting We Will Go. Tree in a Test Tube. 1943: †Air Raid Wardens. †Jitterbugs. †The Dancing Masters. 1944: †The Big Noise. †Nothing But Trouble. 1945: †The Bull Fighters. 1951: †Atoll K (GB: Robinson Crusoeland. US: Utopia).

All shorts except † features

LAURIE, Piper (Rosetta Jacobs) 1932–
Red-haired, a photographer's dream, Piper really was a pretty package, with full lips, appealing hazel eyes, a cute nose and a figure that set male mouths gaping as it wriggled its way through a maze of iron bars in the easterns with Tony Curtis that made them a hot romantic team. After six years as a Casbah spitfire, Piper went away and gradually proved herself as a serious actress, eventually chalking up two Oscar nominations for *The Hustler* and *Carrie*. Married to film critic Joseph Morgenstern since 1962.

Another Town. 1963: Il demonio. La frustra e il corpo (GB: Night is the Phantom. US: What!). And So to Bed. 1964: Old Shatterhand (GB: Apaches' Last Battle). Lord Jim. Celestina. D.M. – Killer. Ou suif dans l'orient. 1965: Ten Little Indians. 1966: The Silencers. The Spy with a Cold Nose. 1967: Casino Royale. Rocket to the Moon (US: Those Fantastic Flying Fools). 1968: Nobody Runs Forever. 1969: Some Girls Do. 1971: Catlow.

1950: Louisa. The Milkman. The Prince Who Was a Thief. 1951: Francis Goes to the Races. 1952: Has Anybody Seen My Gal? No Room for the Groom. Son of Ali Baba. 1953: Mississippi Gambler. The Golden Blade. 1954: Dangerous Mission. Johnny Dark. Dawn at Socorro. *Queens of Beauty. 1955: Smoke Signal. Ain't Misbehavin'. 1956: Mr and Mrs McAdam (TV). 1957: Kelly and Me. Until They Sail. 1958: The Days of Wine and Roses (TV). 1961: The Hustler. 1976: Carrie. 1977: Ruby. In the Matter of Karen Ann Quinlan (TV). 1978: The Boss's Son. Rainbow (TV). Tim. 1980: Skag/The Wildcatters (TV). 1981: The Bunker (TV). 1982: Mae West (TV). 1984: Tender is the Night (TV). 1985: That Was Then, This is Now. Return to Oz. Toughlove (TV). 1986: Children of a Lesser God. Love, Mary (TV).

LAW, John Phillip 1937–
Tall, blonde, blue-eyed, well-built American leading man without excessive personality, who has worked equally in America and Italy. Has been acting since his early teens.
1950: The Magnificent Yankee (GB: The Man with Thirty Sons). 1964: Alta infidelità (GB: High Infidelity). Tre notti d'amore. La' frustra e il corpo (GB: Night is the Phantom. (US: What!). 1966: The Russians Are Coming, the Russians Are Coming. 1967: Death Rides a Horse. Hurry Sundown. Barbarella. Diabolik (GB: Danger: Diabolik). 1968: Skidoo. The Sergeant. 1969: Certo, certissimo, anzi ... probabile. 1970: The Hawaiians (GB: Master of the Islands). 1971: Von Richthofen and Brown (GB: The Red Baron). The Love Machine. The Last Movie. Michael Strogoff. 1973: The Golden Voyage of Sinbad. 1974: Open Season. Diary of a Telephone Operator. Polvere di Stella. 1975: The Spiral Staircase. Dr Justice. 1976: The Cassandra Crossing. Tigers Don't Cry. Your God and My Hell. A Whisper in the Dark. 1978: The Crystal Man. Der Schimmelreiter. The Devil's Bed. Ring of Darkness. Colpo secco. 1980: Attack Force Z. 1981: Tarzan the Ape-Man. 1982: Tin Man. 1984: Stormrider. No Time to Die. 1985: Night Train to Terror. Rainy Day Friends. Die Jagd der goldenen Tiger. 1986: American Commandos/Hitman.

LAVI, Daliah (D. Levenbuch) 1940–
Raven-haired, olive-skinned, flashing-eyed Israeli actress, never as well used as in her first major international film, Lord Jim (supposedly her debut, although she had been in films quite a few years). Afterwards, she was seen mainly as shapely decoration in spy thrillers, and never seemed to appear in more serious roles. Pursued a singing career after 1970.
1955: Hemsöborna. 1960: Burning Sands. Candide. 1961: The Return of Dr Mabuse. Un soir sur la plage (GB: Violent Summer). La fête espagnole. Le jeu de la vérité. 1962: The Black, White and Red Four-Poster. Cyrano and D'Artagnan. Le massaggiatrici. Two Weeks in

LAWFORD, Peter 1923–1984
Bland, inoffensive, elegant brown-haired British leading man, a staple ingredient of M-G-M films from 1942 to 1952 as light romantic interest. The thick eyebrows which always made him look a little quizzical became beetling in middle-age, when he became a member of the notorious Sinatra clan and a character

as benign and lightweight as he had been a star. An actor since childhood, Lawford died from kidney and liver complications.
1930: Poor Old Bill (US: Old Bill). 1931: A Gentleman of Paris. 1938: Lord Jeff (GB: The Boy from Barnardo's). 1942: Eagle Squadron. Mrs Miniver. Thunder Birds. Junior Army. A Yank at Eton. The London Blackout Murders (GB: Secret Motive). Random Harvest. 1943: Girl Crazy. The Purple V. Pilot No. 5. The Immortal Sergeant. The Man from Down Under. Someone to Remember. Above Suspicion. Sherlock Holmes Faces Death. The Sky's the Limit. Flesh and Fantasy. Corvette K-225 (GB: The Nelson Touch). Assignment in Brittany. Paris After Dark. Sahara. West Side Kid. 1944: The Adventures of Mark Twain. The Canterville Ghost. The White Cliffs of Dover. Mrs Parkington. 1945: The Picture of Dorian Gray. Son of Lassie. 1946: Cluny Brown. My Brother Talks to Horses. Two Sisters from Boston. 1947: It Happened in Brooklyn. Good News. 1948: Easter Parade. Julia Misbehaves. On an Island with You. 1949: Little Women. The Red Danube. 1950: Please Believe Me. Royal Wedding (GB: Wedding Bells). 1952: Just This Once. You for Me. Rogues' March. Kangaroo. The Hour of 13. 1954: It Should Happen to You. 1956: Sincerely, Willis Wayde (TV). 1959: Never So Few. 1960: Ocean's Eleven. Exodus. Pepe. 1962: The Longest Day. Advise and Consent. Sergeants Three. 1964: Dead Ringer (GB: Dead Image). 1965. Sylvia. Harlow. 1966: The Oscar. A Man Called Adam. How I Spent My Summer Vacation (TV. GB cinemas as Deadly Roulette). 1967: Dead Run. Deux billets pour Mexique. 1968: Skidoo. Salt and Pepper. Buona Sera, Mrs Campbell. 1969: The April Fools. The Big Blast. Hook, Line and Sinker. 1970: One More Time. Togetherness. A Step Out of Line (TV). 1971: The Deadly Hunt (TV). Ellery Queen: Don't Look Behind You (TV). Clay Pigeon (GB: Trip to Kill). Journey Back to Oz (voice only). 1972: They Only Kill Their Masters. 1974: That's Entertainment. Rosebud. The Phantom of Hollywood (TV). 1975: Won Ton Ton, the Dog Who Saved Hollywood. 1977: Fantasy Island (TV). 1978: Seven from Heaven. 1979: Island of Sister Teresa (TV. Later: Mysterious Island of Beautiful Women). Angels' Brigade. 1981: Body and Soul. 1983: Where is Parsifal?

LAWRENCE, Delphi 1928–
Tawny blonde, too-cool British actress of Anglo-Hungarian parentage. She gave up an ambition to be a concert pianist to turn to acting, and was quite busy in British films after 1953. Played heroines in 'B' features, and catty, worldly-wise 'other women' in bigger productions. Went to America in 1966 and stayed.
1953: Blood Orange. 1954: Meet Mr Callaghan. Duel in the Jungle. 1955: Murder by Proxy (US: Blackout. Completed 1953). Barbados Quest (US: Murder on Approval). The Gold Express. 1956: The Feminine Touch (US: The Gentle Touch). Doublecross. It's Never Too Late. 1957: Strangers' Meeting. Just My Luck. 1958: Blind Spot. Son of Robin Hood. Too Many Crooks. 1959: The Man Who Could Cheat Death. 'Beat' Girl (US: Wild for Kicks). 1960: Cone of Silence (US: Trouble in the Sky). 1961: *The Square Mile Murder. The Fourth Square. 1962: Seven Keys. *Dawn Rendezvous. 1963: On the Run. Farewell Performance. 1964: Frozen Alive. 1965: Bunny Lake is Missing. 1967: The Last Challenge (GB: The Pistolero of Red River). 1973: Cops and Robbers.

LAWRENCE, Gertrude (G. Lawrence-Klasen) 1898–1952
Jaunty, spring-heeled, irrepressible star of post-World War I revue, the top British star of her type in the twenties, with much of her material written especially for her by Noël Coward. She never came to terms with the cinema any more than it came to terms with her, although Julie Andrews told her story in

Star! Suffered much from ill-health in later years. Died from cancer of the liver.
1925: *Stage Stars Off Stage. 1928: *Gertrude Lawrence Singing 'I Don't Know'. 1929: The Battle of Paris. *Early Mourning. 1932: Lord Camber's Ladies. Women Who Play. Aren't We All? 1933: No Funny Business. 1935: Mimi. 1936: Rembrandt. Men Are Not Gods. 1943: Stage Door Canteen. 1950: The Glass Menagerie.

LAWSON, Sarah 1928–
Warmly attractive, full-lipped redhead equally at home in glamorous or homespun parts. Born in London, she made her acting debut in Edinburgh, then won leading roles almost as soon as she came to films from the repertory company she had formed herself. But her movies were mostly second-features and her career (which might perhaps have blossomed more fully in Hollywood) has long taken second place to that of her husband Patrick Allen (1927–), the Canadian actor she married in 1956.
1951: The Browning Version. 1952: The Night Won't Talk. 1953: Street Corner (US: Both Sides of the Law). Three Steps in the Dark. Meet Mr Malcolm. You Know What Sailors Are. 1955: The Blue Peter (US: Navy Heroes). 1956: It's Never Too Late. 1958: *Man With a Dog. Links of Justice. Three Crooked Men. The Solitary Child. 1962: Night Without Pity. 1963: On the Run. The World Ten Times Over (US: Pussycat Alley). 1967: Night of the Big Heat (US: Island of the Burning Damned). 1968: The Devil Rides Out (US: The Devil's Bride). 1969: Battle of Britain. 1978: The Stud.

LAWSON, Wilfrid (W. Worsnop) 1900–1966
Raucous-voiced, abrasive, distinctive British character star. In spite of alcohol problems that made him difficult to employ, he became a star of the British cinema from 1938 to 1947 (before spending a long sojourn on stage) with fruitful excursions to Hollywood. Even in his last years, was still capable of stealing scenes from the leading players. Died from a heart attack.
1931: East Lynne on the Western Front. 1933: Strike It Rich. 1935: Turn of the Tide. 1936: Ladies in Love. White Hunter. 1937: The Man Who Made Diamonds. Bank Holiday (US: Three on a Weekend). 1938: The Terror. Yel-

low Sands. The Gaunt Stranger (US: The Phantom Strikes). Pygmalion. Stolen Life. 1939: Dead Man's Shoes. Allegheny Uprising (GB: The First Rebel). 1940: The Long Voyage Home. Pastor Hall. Gentleman of Venture (US: It Happened to One Man). The Farmer's Wife. The Man at the Gate (US: Men of the Sea). 1941: Danny Boy. Jeannie. The Tower of Terror. Hard Steel. 1942: The Night Has Eyes (US: Terror House). The Great Mr Handel. 1943: Thursday's Child. 1944: Fanny by Gaslight (US: Man of Evil). 1945: *Macbeth. 1947: The Turners of Prospect Road. 1954: Make Me an Offer. 1955: The Prisoner. An Alligator Named Daisy. 1956: Now and Forever. War and Peace. 1957: Hell Drivers. Miracle in Soho. The Naked Truth (US: Your Past is Showing). Doctor at Large. 1958: Tread Softly Stranger. Room at the Top. 1959: Expresso Bongo. The Naked Edge. Nothing Barred. Over the Odds. Go to Blazes. 1962: Postman's Knock. 1963: Becket. Tom Jones. 1966: The Wrong Box. 1967: The Viking Queen.

LAWTON, Frank (F. L. Mokeley Jnr.) 1904–1969
Gentle-looking, light-haired British leading man of some charm, mostly in sensitive roles. Went to Hollywood with *Cavalcade*, and played a few film roles there, then returned to Britain and resumed his stage career. Later a character actor, mostly as upper-class types of military bearing. Not unlike John Mills. Married to Evelyn Laye from 1934.
1930: Birds of Prey (US: The Perfect Alibi). Young Woodley. 1931: The Skin Game. The Outsider. Michael and Mary. 1932: After

the Glen. 1955: Cast a Dark Shadow. 1976: The Slipper and the Rose.

LODER, John (J. Lowe) 1898–
Square-built, light-haired, cheerfully handsome, globe-trotting British actor who began in German films after giving up a military career. Then made films in Britain (four spells), France, Hollywood (two spells), India and Argentina. Too stiff ever to become a big star, but a useful sounding-board for some dominant leading ladies. Married (third of five) to Hedy Lamarr, 1943–1947.

1926: Madame wünscht keine kinder (US: Madame Wants No Children). Alraune. Die letzte Waltz. The Sinister Man. 1927: Dancing Mad. Der grosse Unbekannte. Die Sünderin. Die weisse Spinne. 1928: Casanova's Erbe. Frejwild. Wenn die Mutter und die Tochter ... The First Born. 1929: Black Waters. Sunset Pass. The Ivory Hunters. The Unholy Night. The Doctor's Secret. The Racketeer (GB: Love's Conquest). Her Private Affair. Rich People. 1930: The Seas Beneath. Lilies of the Field. The Man Hunter. Love's Conquest. The Second Floor Mystery. Sweethearts and Wives. 1931: One Night at Susie's. Hot Dogs. Men of the Sky. 1932: *On the Loose. Wedding Rehearsal. Money Means Nothing. 1933: Money for Speed. The Private Life of Henry VIII. You Made Me Love You. Paris Plane. 1934: Love, Life and Laughter. The Battle (US: Thunder in the East). Rolling in Money. Warn London. Java Head. Sing As We Go. Lorna Doone. My Song Goes Round the World. 1935: The Silent Passenger. It Happened in Paris. 18 Minutes. 1936: Whom the Gods Love (US: Mozart). Queen of Hearts. Ourselves Alone (US: River of Unrest). Sabotage (US: A Woman Alone). The Man Who Changed His Mind (US: The Man Who Lived Again). Guilty Melody. 1937: King Solomon's Mines. Dr Syn. Non-Stop New York. Owd Bob (US: To the Victor). Mademoiselle Docteur. Paix sur le Rhin. Menaces. 1938: Katia. Anything to Declare. 1939: The Silent Battle (US: Continental Express). Confidential Lady. Meet Maxwell Archer (US: Maxwell Archer Detective). Murder Will Out. 1940: Diamond Frontier. Tin Pan Alley. Adventure in Diamonds. 1941: Scotland Yard. One Night in Lisbon. How Green Was My Valley. Confirm or Deny. 1942: *Stars on Horseback. Eagle Squadron. Now, Voyager. Gentleman Jim. The Gorilla

Man. 1943: The Mysterious Doctor. Murder on the Waterfront. Old Acquaintance. Adventure in Iraq. 1944: Passage to Marseille. The Hairy Ape. Abroad with Two Yanks. 1945: The Brighton Strangler. The Fighting Guardsman. A Game of Death. Jealousy. The Woman Who Came Back. 1946: The Wife of Monte Cristo. One More Tomorrow. 1947: Dishonored Lady. 1952: †The Army Story. 1955: *Dead on Time. The Curse of the Cobra. 1957: Woman and the Hunter (GB: Triangle on Safari). The Story Of Esther Costello (US: Golden Virgin). Small Hotel. 1958: Gideon's Day (US: Gideon of Scotland Yard). The Secret Man. Josette from New Orleans. 1965: Esquiú. 1970: The Firechasers.

†*Unreleased*

LOLLOBRIGIDA, Gina 1927–
Raven-haired Italian actress with beauty-queen figure, who became Italy's first postwar sex symbol. A number of home-grown films as slinky flirt got her known internationally as 'La Lollo' and appearances in Hollywood movies made her a world-wide pin-up. Kept going fairly strongly until the early seventies, although long before that overtaken in popularity by Sophia Loren.

1946: L'aquila nera. L'elisir d'amore. Lucia di Lammermoor. 1947: Follie per l'opera/Mad about Opera. Il delitto di Giovanni Episcopo. La danse de mort. Il segreto di Don Giovanni. A Man About the House. 1948: I Pagliacci. 1949: Campane a martello. La sposa non puo' attendere. Miss Italia. 1950: Vita da cane. Cuori senza frontiera. Alina. Moglie per una notte. La citta' si difende. 1951: Amor non ho, pero' ... pero'. L'ora della fantasia. Fanfan La Tulipe. Altri tempi (US: Times Gone By). A Tale of Five Cities (US: A Tale of Five Women). Enrico Caruso, leggenda di una voce (US: The Young Caruso). Achtung, banditti! 1952: Les belles de nuit (GB and US: Night Beauties). Le infideli. The Wayward Wife. 1953: La provinciale. Pane, amore e gelosia/Bread, Love and Jealousy, Pane, amore e fantasia/Bread, Love, and Dreams. Crossed Swords. Beat the Devil. 1954: Le bella di Roma/Woman of Rome. Le grand jeu (GB: The Card of Fate). 1955: La donna più bella del mondo. 1956: Trapeze. The Hunchback of Notre Dame. 1957: Anna of Brooklyn. 1958: La loi (GB: Where the Hot Wind Blows).

1959: Solomon and Sheba. Never So Few. 1961: Go Naked in the World. Come September. 1962: La bellezza d'Ippolito. Mare matto. 1963: Vénus impériale. Woman of Straw. 1964: Strange Bedfellows. 1965: Le bambole (GB: Four Kinds of Love). The Sultans. 1966: Io, io, io ... e gli altri. Hotel Paradiso. Cervantes, the Young Rebel. 1967: Le piacevoli notti. La morte ha fatta l'uovo (GB: A Curious Way to Love. US: Plucked). 1968: Buona Sera, Mrs Campbell. The Private Navy of Sgt O'Farrell. Un bellissimo Novembre. 1970: Stuntman. 1971: Bad Man's River. L'avventure di Pinocchio. 1972: Laddove volano le pallottole. Roses rouges et piments verts (US: The Lonely Woman). King, Queen, Knave. 1977: Widow's Nest. 1983: Stelle emigranti. 1985: Deceptions.

LOM, Herbert (H. Schluderpacheru) 1917–
Smooth, dark-haired Czech actor who could be romantic, sinister, or even funny. His career hardly got started before he was on the run from the Nazis, landing in British films where his faintly menacing charm had some dubbing him a British Boyer, even though his characters usually ended up dead. Looked further afield for acting opportunities from 1959, but had a successful British TV series, *The Human Jungle*, which cast him in more sympathetic light. Latterly the hapless inspector in the 'Pink Panther' films.

1937: Žena Pod Křížem. 1940: Mein Kampf My Crimes. 1942: The Young Mr Pitt. Secret Mission. Tomorrow We Live (US: At Dawn We Die). 1943: The Dark Tower. 1944: Hotel Reserve. 1945: The Seventh Veil. Night Boat to Dublin. 1946: Appointment with Crime. 1947: Dual Alibi. Snowbound. 1948: Good Time Girl. Portrait from Life (US: The Girl in the Painting). The Brass Monkey/Lucky Mascot. 1949: The Lost People. 1950: Golden Salamander. Night and the City. State Secret (US: The Great Manhunt). The Black Rose. Cage of Gold. 1951: Hell is Sold Out. Two on the Tiles. Mr Denning Drives North. Whispering Smith Hits London (US: Whispering Smith versus Scotland Yard). 1952: The Ringer. The Net (US: Project M7). The Man Who Watched Trains Go By (US: Paris Express). 1953: Rough Shoot (US: Shoot First). The Love Lottery. Star of India. 1954: Beautiful Stranger (US: Twist of Fate). 1955: The Ladykillers. 1956: War and Peace. 1957: Fire

Down Below. Hell Drivers. Action of the Tiger. I Accuse! 1958: Chase a Crooked Shadow. The Roots of Heaven. Intent to Kill. 1959: No Trees in the Street. The Big Fisherman. Passport to Shame (US: Room 43). Northwest Frontier (US: Flame over India). Third Man on the Mountain. 1960: I Aim at the Stars. Spartacus. 1961: Mr Topaze (US: I Like Money). El Cid. Mysterious Island. The Frightened City. 1962: The Phantom of the Opera. The Treasure of Silver Lake. Tiara Tahiti. 1963: The Horse without a Head (US: TV). 1964: A Shot in the Dark. 1965: Return From the Ashes. Uncle Tom's Cabin. 1966: Our Man in Marrakesh (US: Bang Bang You're Dead). Gambit. Die Nibelungen (GB: Whom the Gods Wish to Destroy). 1967: Die Nibelungen II. Assignment to Kill. The Karate Killers (TV. GB: cinemas). 1968: The Face of Eve (US: Eve). Villa Rides! 99 Women (US: Island of Despair). 1969: Doppelganger (US: Journey to the Far Side of the Sun). Mister Jericho (US: TV). 1970: Count Dracula. Dorian Gray. Hexen bis aufs blut geqvält. 1971: Murders in the Rue Morgue. 1972: Asylum. 1973: Dark Places. Mark of the Devil. Blue Blood. And Now the Screaming Starts. 1974: The Return of the Pink Panther. Death in Persepolis. And Then There Were None. 1976: The Pink Panther Strikes Again. 1977: Charleston. 1978: Revenge of the Pink Panther. 1979: The Lady Vanishes. The Man with Bogart's Face. 1980: Hopscotch. 1982: Trail of the Pink Panther. 1983: Memed My Hawk. The Dead Zone. Curse of the Pink Panther. 1985: King Solomon's Mines. 1986: Whoops Apocalypse!

LOMBARD, Carole (Jane Peters, later legally changed) 1908–1942
One of Hollywood's most popular blondes. A kind of freewheeling, sophisticated Jean Harlow and good at everything from sensitive drama to screwball comedy. A car crash in 1926 almost ruined her budding career. But she recovered to match wits and words with some of Hollywood's biggest stars. Married to William Powell from 1931–1933 and Clark Gable from 1939 on. Killed in a plane crash. Nominated for an Academy Award in My Man Godfrey.
1921: ‡A Perfect Crime. 1925: †Marriage in Transit. †Hearts and Spurs. †Durand of the Badlands. †Gold and the Girl. 1927: †*Smith's

Pony. †*The Girl from Everywhere. †*Hold That Pose. †*The Campus Vamp. †*The Campus Carmen. †*A Gold Digger of Weepah. †The Fighting Eagle. 1928: †*Run Girl Run. †The Divine Sinner. †*The Beach Club. †*The Best Man. †*Matchmaking Mammas. †*The Swim Princess. †*The Bicycle Flirt. †*The Girl from Nowhere. †*His Unlucky Night. †Power. †Show Folks. †Me, Gangster. †Ned McCobb's Daughter. 1929: †High Voltage (GB: Wanted). †Big News. †The Racketeer (GB: Love's Conquest). 1930: †The Arizona Kid. Safety in Numbers. Fast and Loose. 1931: It Pays to Advertise. Ladies' Man. Take This Woman. Up Pops the Devil. Man of the Wild. 1932: Sinners in the Sun. No One Man. No Man of Her Own. No More Orchids. Virtue. 1933: Supernatural. From Hell to Heaven. The Eagle and the Hawk. White Woman. Brief Moment. 1934: Twentieth Century. Bolero. We're Not Dressing. Now and Forever. The Gay Bride. Lady by Choice. 1935: Rumba. Hands Across the Table. 1936: My Man Godfrey. The Princess Comes Across. Love Before Breakfast. 1937: Swing High, Swing Low. True Confession. Nothing Sacred. 1938: Fools for Scandal. 1939: In Name Only. Made for Each Other. 1940: *Picture People No. 4. Vigil in the Night. They Knew What They Wanted. 1941: Mr and Mrs Smith. 1942: To Be or Not To Be.

‡As Jane Peters †As Carol Lombard

LONDON, Julie (J. Peck) 1926–
Acting careers didn't come much more sporadic than that of this tawny-haired American actress. But in the mid-fifties she suddenly became an enormously popular torch-style singer, especially with a million-selling record called Cry Me a River. Cropped up much later in a seventies' TV series, looking not a year older. Married to Jack Webb (qv) from 1945 to 1953, then to actor/drummer Bobby Troup.
1944: Nabonga (GB: The Jungle Woman). 1945: On Stage Everybody. Billy Rose's Diamond Horseshoe (GB: Diamond Horseshoe). 1946: A Night in Paradise. 1947: The Red House. 1948: Tap Roots. 1949: Task Force. 1950: Return of the Frontiersman. 1951: The Fat Man. 1955: The Fighting Chance. 1956: The Girl Can't Help It. The Great Man. Crime Against Joe. 1957: Without Incident (TV).

Drango. 1958: Saddle the Wind. Man of the West. A Question of Adultery. Voice in the Mirror. 1959: The Third Voice. Night of the Quarter Moon. The Wonderful Country. 1961: The George Raft Story (GB: Spin of a Coin). 1967: The Helicopter Spies (TV. GB: cinemas). 1971: Emergency (TV). 1978: Survival on Charter No. 220.

LONG, Audrey 1923–
Coolly-attractive, light-haired (sometimes brunette), hazel-eyed American actress, supposed to have played dozens of walk-ons at Universal and Warners (few records of which seem to exist) before embarking on the major part of her career with RKO. A former model, she was always poised, but her roles were almost entirely confined to chic heroines in second-feature thrillers, and her film career was played out at 29.
1942: The Male Animal. Eagle Squadron. The Great Impersonation. Pardon My Sarong. 1944: Tall in the Saddle. A Night of Adventure. 1945: Pan-Americana. Wanderer of the Wasteland. A Game of Death. 1946: Perilous Holiday. 1947: Born to Kill (GB: Lady of Deceit). Desperate. In Self Defence. 1948: Song of My Heart. The Adventures of Gallant Bess. Stage Struck. Perilous Waters. Homicide for Three. Grand Canyon Trail. Miraculous Journey. 1949: The Duke of Chicago. Alias the Champ. Air Hostess. The Red Danube. Post Office Investigator. 1950: Trial without Jury. David Harding, Counterspy. Blue Blood. The Petty Girl (GB: Girl of the Year). 1951: Cavalry Scout. Insurance Investigator. Sunny Side of the Street. 1952: Indian Uprising.

LONGDEN, John 1900–1971
Tall, sharp-faced, grave-looking, brown-haired leading man of British films. Born in the West Indies, the son of a Wesleyan minister, he was a miner for a time before turning to acting, and making a big impact on the British cinema, especially in Quinneys and several early Hitchcock films. His career was hit by an alcohol problem and by a visit to Australia that produced only three films in four years. On his return he played a few police inspectors, then dropped to small supporting roles.
1926: The House of Marney. The Ball of Fortune. 1927: The Arcadians/Land of Heart's Desire. The Flight Commander. The Glad Eye.

Quinneys. Bright Young Things. 1928: *Mademoiselle Parley-Voo. What Money Can Buy. Palais de Danse. The Last Post. The Flying Squad.* 1929: **Memories. Blackmail. Atlantic. Juno and the Paycock* (US: *The Shame of Mary Boyle*). 1930: *Elstree Calling. The Flame of Love. Children of Chance. Two Worlds.* 1931: *The Skin Game. The Singer. Two Crowded Hours. *Healthy, Wealthy and Why. Rynox. The Wickham Mystery. Murder on the Second Floor.* 1932: *A Lucky Sweep. Born Lucky.* 1934: *The Silence of Dean Maitland.* 1936: *It Isn't Done. Thoroughbred.* 1937: *French Leave. Little Miss Somebody. Jenifer Hale. Young and Innocent* (US: *The Girl Was Young*). *Dial 999.* 1938: *Bad Boy. The Gaunt Stranger* (US: *The Phantom Strikes*). 1939: *Q Planes* (US: *Clouds over Europe*). *Goodbye Mr Chips! Jamaica Inn. The Lion Has Wings.* 1940: *Branded. Contraband* (US: *Blackout*). 1941: *The Common Touch. Old Mother Riley's Circus. *Post 23. The Tower of Terror.* 1942: *Unpublished Story. Rose of Tralee.* 1943: *The Silver Fleet. *Death by Design. The Yellow Canary.* 1947: *Dusty Bates* (serial). *The Ghosts of Berkeley Square.* 1948: *Anna Karenina. The Last Load. Bonnie Prince Charlie.* 1949: *Trapped by the Terror.* 1950: *The Lady Craved Excitement. The Elusive Pimpernel* (US: *The Fighting Pimpernel*). *Pool of London.* 1951: *The Dark Light. The Man with the Twisted Lip. Trek to Mashomba. The Magic Box. Black Widow.* 1952: *The Wallet/ Blueprint for Danger.* 1954: *Dangerous Cargo. Meet Mr Callaghan.* 1955: *The Ship That Died of Shame* (US: *PT Raiders*). 1956: *The Final Column. Alias John Preston. Raiders of the River* (serial). *Count of Twelve.* 1957: *Quatermass II* (US: *Enemy from Space*). *Three Sundays to Live.* 1958: *The Silent Enemy.* 1959: *A Woman's Temptation. *Broad Waterways* (narrator only). 1960: *An Honourable Murder.* 1961: *So Evil, So Young.* 1963: *Lancelot and Guinevere* (US: *Sword of Lancelot*). 1964: *Frozen Alive.*

As director: 1932: *Come into My Parlour.*

LORD, Jack (John Ryan) 1922–
Strapping, square-faced, intent-looking American actor whose film career surprisingly stuttered and stammered without taking off. He was always more successful in television, and in 1968 found a practically permanent niche there as the immaculately-clad, per-

ennially fortyish chief of *Hawaii Five-O*, a crime series which ran for 12 years. Once an artist whose works were exhibited, he has now returned to that passion in semi-retirement.
1949: *Project X. Cry Murder.* 1955: *The Court Martial of Billy Mitchell* (GB: *One Man Mutiny*). 1956: *The Williamsburg Story. The Vagabond King.* 1957: *Tip on a Dead Jockey* (GB: *Time for Action*). *The True Story of Lynn Stuart. Pattern for Violence* (TV. GB: cinemas). 1958: *Man of the West. God's Little Acre. Reunion* (TV). 1959: *The Hangman.* 1960: *Walk Like a Dragon.* 1962: *Dr No.* 1965: *The Crime* (TV). 1966: *The Ride to Hangman's Tree. The Doomsday Flight* (TV. GB: cinemas). 1967: *The Counterfeit Killer.* 1968: *The Name of the Game is Kill!* 1980: *M Station: Hawaii* (TV).

LOREN, Sophia (Sofia Scicolone) 1934–
Stunningly beautiful, rich-lipped, full-bosomed, dark-haired Italian star with peasant-style sex appeal. At first in Italian films, but her looks, attractive English, evident sense of humour and willingness to do her best in almost any genre soon made her a big international name, as popular with women as with men. Retained her following on the continent, especially when teamed with Marcello Mastronianni (*qv*). Academy Award for *Two Women* (1961).
1950: †*Cuori sul mare.* †*Il voto.* †*Io sono il capatch.* †*Anna.* †*Bluebeard's Seven Wives.* 1951: †*Milano miliardia.* †*Il mago per forza.* †*The Dream of Zorro.* †*Quo Vadis?* ‡*E' arrivato l'accordatore.* ‡*Era lui ... si,si.* 1952: *La favorita. La tratta delle bianche* (GB: *Girls*

Marked Danger). *Africa sotto i mari* (GB: *Woman of the Red Sea*). 1953: *Carosello Napoletano. Aïda. Ci troviamo in galleria. Tempi nostri* (US: *Anatomy of Love*). *Il paese dei campanelli. La Domenica della buona gente. Un giorno in pretura. Two Nights with Cleopatra. Attila the Hun.* 1954: *Peccato che sia una canaglia* (GB: *Too Bad She's Bad*). *Gold of Naples. Woman of the River. Miseria e nobilta.* 1955: *Pellegrini d'amore. Il segno di Venere/ The Sign of Venus. La bella mugnaia. La fortuna di essera donna* (GB and US: *Lucky to be a Woman*). *Pane, amore e . . .* (GB: *Scandal in Sorrento*). 1956: *The Pride and the Passion.* 1957: *Boy on a Dolphin. Legend of the Lost.* 1958: *Desire Under the Elms. Houseboat. The Key.* 1959: *Black Orchid. That Kind of Woman.* 1960: *Heller in Pink Tights. It Started in Naples. A Breath of Scandal. The Millionairess.* 1961: *Madame. El Cid. Two Women. *Captive Islands.* 1962: *Five Miles to Midnight. Boccaccio 70. The Condemned of Altona.* 1963: *Yesterday, Today and Tomorrow. The Fall of the Roman Empire.* 1964: *Marriage Italian Style.* 1965: *Operation Crossbow* (US: *The Great Spy Mission*). *Judith. Lady L.* 1966: *Arabesque. A Countess from Hong Kong* 1967: *Cinderella Italian Style* (US: *More Than a Miracle*). 1968: *Ghosts Italian Style.* 1969: *Sunflower.* 1970: *The Priest's Wife.* 1971: *La mortadella/Lady Liberty. Bianco, rosso e . . .* (GB and US: *White Sister*). 1972: *Man of La Mancha.* 1974: *Il viaggio/The Voyage. Verdict.* 1975: *Brief Encounter* (TV). 1976: *The Cassandra Crossing.* 1977: *Una giornata particolare* (GB and US: *A Special Day*). *Angela* (released 1984). 1978: *Vengeance. Brass Target.* 1979: *Blood Feud. Shimmy Lugano e tarantelle e tarallucci e vino. Firepower.* 1980: *Sophia Loren: Her Own Story* (TV). *Tieta d'agreste.* 1984: *Aurora.*

†As Sophia Scicolone ‡As Sophia Lazzaro

LORRE, Peter (Laszlo Löwenstein) 1904–1964
Dark, squat, furtive-looking Hungarian-born actor who made an indelible impression in the German film *M* as the child murderer. But his wheedling tones and uniquely comic-sinister personality are best remembered from his Hollywood days, as one of life's victims, scuttling from its shadier corners, forever being

seized by the lapels by his oft-time cohort, huge Sydney Greenstreet (*qv*), with whom he became very popular as a sort of unholy Laurel and Hardy. Married (second of three) actress Kaaren Verne (1918–1967) from 1945 to 1952. Died after a stroke.

1928: Pioniere in Ingolstadt. 1929: Frühlings Erwachen. 1931: Bomben auf Monte Carlo. M. Die Koffer des Hern O.F. 1932: Der weisse Dämon. FP1 antwortet nicht (and French version). Fünf von der Jazzband. Schuss im Morgengrauen. 1933: Was Frauen träumen. Unsichtbare Gegner. Du haut en bas. 1934: The Man Who Knew Too Much. 1935: Mad Love (GB: Hands of Orlac). Crime and Punishment. 1936: Secret Agent. Crack-Up. 1937: Lancer Spy. Nancy Steele is Missing. Think Fast, Mr Moto. Thank You, Mr Moto. 1938: Mysterious Mr Moto. I'll Give a Million. Mr Moto's Gamble. Mr Moto Takes a Chance. 1939: Mr Moto Takes a Vacation. Mr Moto's Last Warning. Mr Moto in Danger Island (GB: Mr Moto on Danger Island). 1940: Island of Doomed Men. I Was an Adventuress. Strange Cargo. You'll Find Out. Stranger on the Third Floor. 1941: Mr District Attorney. The Maltese Falcon. The Face Behind the Mask. They Met in Bombay. 1942: Invisible Agent. All Through the Night. The Boogie Man Will Get You. Casablanca. In This Our Life. 1943: Background to Danger. The Constant Nymph. The Cross of Lorraine. Arsenic and Old Lace. 1944: Passage to Marseille. Hollywood Canteen. The Mask of Dimitrios. The Conspirators. 1945: Hotel Berlin. Confidential Agent. 1946: Three Strangers. The Chase. Black Angel. The Verdict. The Beast with Five Fingers. 1947: My Favorite Brunette. 1948: Casbah. 1949: Rope of Sand. 1950: Double Confession. Quicksand. 1951: †Die Verlorene. 1953: Beat the Devil. 1954: 20,000 Leagues under the Sea. 1956: Seidman and Son (TV). Congo Crossing. Meet Me in Las Vegas (GB: Viva Las Vegas!). Around the World in 80 Days. Operation Cicero (TV). 1957: The Story of Mankind. The Buster Keaton Story. Silk Stockings. The Last Tycoon (TV). The Jet-Propelled Couch (TV). Hell Ship Mutiny. The Sad Sack. 1959: The Big Circus. 1960: The Cruel Day (TV). Scent of Mystery (GB: Holiday in Spain). 1961: Voyage to the Bottom of the Sea. 1962: Tales of Terror. The Raven. Five Weeks in a Balloon. 1963: Comedy of Terrors. 1964: The Patsy. Muscle Beach.

†And directed

LOUISE, Anita (A.L. Fremault) 1915–1970

Fluffily blonde, delicately beautiful American actress, in leading roles as a teenager, perhaps most notable as Titania in the 1935 *A Midsummer Night's Dream*. Her vehicles grew less interesting after 1940, but she continued acting, mostly on TV, until the late fifties. Died from a cerebral stroke.

*1922: †Down to the Sea in Ships. 1924: †The Sixth Commandment. †Lend Me Your Husband. 1927: †*The Life of Franz Schubert. †The Music Master. 1928: †Four Devils. †A*

Woman of Affairs. 1929: †The Spirit of Youth. †Wonder of Women. The Marriage Playground. Square Shoulders. 1930: The Florodora Girl (GB: The Gay Nineties). What a Man! (GB: The Gentleman Chauffeur). The Third Alarm. Just Like Heaven. 1931: Millie. The Woman Between. Heaven on Earth. Everything's Rosie. The Great Meadow. 1932: The Phantom of Crestwood. 1933: Our Betters. 1934: Most Precious Thing in Life. I Give My Love. Judge Priest. The Firebird. Bachelor of Arts. Are We Civilized? Cross Streets. Madame Du Barry. 1935: Lady Tubbs (GB: The Gay Lady). A Midsummer Night's Dream. Personal Maid's Secret. Apple Sauce. Here's to Romance. 1936: The Story of Louis Pasteur. Anthony Adverse. Brides Are Like That. 1937: Call It a Day. The Go-Getter. That Certain Woman. First Lady. Green Light. Tovarich. 1938: Going Places. My Bill. The Sisters. Marie Antoinette. 1939: Reno. The Gorilla. The Little Princess. Hero for a Day. Main Street Lawyer (GB: Small Town Lawyer). These Glamour Girls. 1940: Glamour for Sale. The Villain Still Pursued Her. Wagons Westward. 1941: Two in a Taxi. Harmon of Michigan. The Phantom Submarine. 1943: Dangerous Blondes. 1944: Nine Girls. Casanova Brown. 1945: The Fighting Guardsman. Love Letters. 1946: The Devil's Mask. The Bandit of Sherwood Forest. Shadowed. Personality Kid. 1947: Blondie's Holiday. Bulldog Drummond at Bay. Blondie's Big Moment. 1952: Retreat, Hell! 1957: The Greer Case (TV).

†As Anita Fremault

LOUISE, Tina (T.L. Blacker) 1934–

Statuesque, titian-haired, whistle-worthy American leading lady who made her first impact on television before being signed up for a notable film-starring debut as Erskine Caldwell's Grizelda in *God's Little Acre*. Her career did not progress as it might have done, although she has stuck around, kept her figure and developed into a useful supporting actress.

1955: Kismet. 1958: God's Little Acre. The Trap (GB: The Baited Trap). 1959: Day of the Outlaw. The Hangman. Siege of Syracuse. 1960: Garibaldi. Sappho (GB: The Warrior Empress). 1961: Il mantenuto. Armored Command. 1964: For Those Who Think Young. 1966: Il fischio del naso. 1968: The Wrecking Crew. 1969: House of Seven Joys. The Happy Ending. The Good Guys and the Bad Guys. How to Commit Marriage. 1970: But I Don't Want to Get Married (TV). 1972: Call to Danger (TV). 1974: The Stepford Wives. 1975: Death Scream (TV). 1976: Nightmare in Badham County (TV). 1977: Look What's Happened to Rosemary's Baby (TV). SST – Disaster in the Sky/SST – Death Flight (TV). 1978: Mean Dog Blues. 1979: Friendships, Secrets and Lies (TV). 1980: The Day the Women Got Even (TV). 1981: Advice to the Lovelorn (TV). 1983: Evils of the Night. 1984: The Utterly Monstrous Mind-Roasting Summer of O.C. and Stiggs. 1985: Hellriders (completed 1983).

LOVE, Bessie (Juanita Horton) 1898–1986

One of the cinema's most indomitable ladies: a tiny blonde American actress with sweet smile, and a long nose that gave her an old-young face. Started as a teenager with D.W. Griffith in 1916, then became one of the silent screen's great beauties before working hard to make the transition to sound. Came to Britain in the early thirties and stayed, no longer pursuing her career with such single-mindedness, but playing cameo roles as she chose. In her seventies began a new and successful career as a writer. Nominated for an Academy Award in *The Broadway Melody*.

*1916: Intolerance. Reggie Mixes In (GB: Mysteries in New York). The Aryan. The Flying Torpedo. The Good Bad Man. Hell-to-Pay Austin (GB: Love in the West). A Sister of Six. Acquitted. *The Mystery of Leaping Fish. Stranded. The Heiress at Coffee Dan's. 1917: Wee Lady Betty. Nina, the Flower Girl. Cheerful Givers. Pernickety Polly Ann. A Daughter* of the Poor. The Sawdust Ring. 1918: How Could You, Caroline? The Great Adventure. Carolyn of the Corners. A Little Sister of Everybody. The Dawn of Understanding. 1919: Over the Garden Wall. The Enchanted Barn. A Yankee Princess. Cupid Forecloses. A Fighting Colleen. The Wishing Ring Man. The Little Boss. Pegeen. 1920: Bonnie May. The Midlanders. 1921: The Spirit of the Lake. Penny of Top Hill Trail. The Sea Lion. The Swamp. The Honor of Ramirez. 1922: Bulldog Courage. Deserted at the Altar. Forget-Me-Not. The Vermilion Pencil. Night Life in Hollywood. 1923: Three Who Paid. The Village Blacksmith. Souls for Sale. Mary of the Movies. St Elmo. The Adventures of Prince Courageous. Ghost Patrol. Purple Dawn. Human Wreckage. The Eternal Three. Gentle Julia. Slave of Desire. 1924: Those Who Dance. A Woman on the Jury. Dynamite Smith. Sundown. The Silent Watcher. Tongues of Flame. 1925: A Son of His Father. Soul-Fire. The Sea World. New Brooms. The King on Main Street. 1926: Going Crooked. Lovey Mary. The Song and Dance Man. Young April. 1927: Rubber Tires (GB: Ten Thousand Reward). *Life in Hollywood No. 4. Dress Parade. The American/The Flag Maker. A Harp in Hock (GB: The Samaritan). *Amateur Night. 1928: The Matinee Idol. Sally of the Scandals. Anybody Here Seen Kelly? The Swell Head. 1929: The Broadway Melody. Hollywood Revue of 1929. The Girl in the Show. The Idle Rich. 1930: Chasing Rainbows. See America Thirst. Good News. They Learned About Women. 1931: Morals for Women (GB: Farewell Party). Conspiracy. *Screen Snapshots No. 8. 1936: I Live Again. 1941: Atlantic Ferry (US: Sons of the Sea). 1942: *London Scrapbook. 1945: Journey Together. 1951: The Magic Box. No Highway (US: No Highway in the Sky). 1953: The Weak and the Wicked (US: Young and Willing). 1954: The Barefoot Contessa. Beau Brummell. 1955: Touch and Go (US: The Light Touch). 1957: The Story of Esther Costello (US: Golden Virgin). 1958: Nowhere to Go. Next to No Time! 1959: Too Young to Love. 1961: The Greengage Summer (US: Loss of Innocence). 1962: The Roman Spring of Mrs Stone. 1963: The Wild Affair. Children of the Damned. 1964: *I Think They Call Him John (narrator only). 1965: Promise Her Anything. 1967: Battle Beneath the Earth. I'll Never Forget What's 'is Name. 1969: Isadora. On Her Majesty's Secret Service. 1971: Sunday, Bloody Sunday. Catlow. 1974: Mousey (TV. GB: cinemas as Cat and Mouse). Vampyres. 1976: Gulliver's Travels (voice only). The Ritz. 1981: Ragtime. Reds. Lady Chatterley's Lover. 1983: The Hunger.

LOVEJOY, Frank 1914–1962

Tough but agreeable-looking, solidly-built American actor with dark curly hair. Acted on radio until his mid-thirties, then quickly rose to third place on film cast lists and stayed there, apart from an occasional, usually unsympathetic leading role in fairly minor films. He had left films again for theatre, TV and radio when he died from a heart attack. 1948: Black Bart (GB: Black Bart – High-

wayman). 1949: Home of the Brave. South Sea Sinner (GB: East of Java). 1950: In a Lonely Place. Breakthrough. Three Secrets. Try and Get Me (GB: The Sound of Fury). 1951: I Was a Communist for the FBI. Starlift. Goodbye, My Fancy. I'll See You in My Dreams. 1952: The Winning Team. *Screen Snapshots No. 205. Retreat, Hell! 1953: She's Back on Broadway. The Hitch Hiker. The System. House of Wax. The Charge at Feather River. 1954: Beachhead. Men of the Fighting Lady. The Americano. 1955: Mad at the World. Top of the World. Strategic Air Command. Finger Man. The Crooked Web. Shack Out on 101. 1956: Julie. The Country Husband(TV. GB: cinemas). 1957: Three Brave Men. 1958: Cole Younger, Gunfighter. 1959: The Raider (TV).

LOWE, Edmund 1890–1971

Suave, debonair, latterly moustachioed American actor with sharp, near-Barrymore profile. Mainly on stage until the twenties; then film stardom claimed him, and he enjoyed his best period in the last few years of silents, especially opposite Victor McLaglen in the 'Flagg and Quirt' comedies. Later declined to routine leading roles in crime thrillers, and made several visits to Britain. Died from a lung ailment. First wife, film actress Lilyan Tashman (1899–1934), died young: subsequently Lowe married and divorced twice. 1917: The Spreading Dawn. 1918: The Reason Why. Vive La France. 1919: Eyes of Youth (GB: The Love of Sunya). 1920: The Woman Gives. Madonnas and Men. A Woman's Business. Someone in the House. Devil. 1921: Chicken in the Case. My Lady's Latchkey. 1922: Living Lies. Peacock Alley. 1923: The Silent Command. In the Palace of the King.

The White Flower. Wife in Name Only. 1924: Honor among Men. Barbara Frietchie. The Brass Bowl. The Beautiful Cloak Model. Nellie. 1925: Soul Mates. The Winding Stair. Marriage in Transit. The Kiss Barrier. Greater than a Crown. Ports of Call. East Lynne. The Fool. Champion of Lost Causes. East of Suez. 1926: Black Paradise. What Price Glory? Siberia. The Palace of Pleasure. 1927: Iz Zat So? Baloo. One Increasing Purpose. The Wizard. Publicity Madness. 1928: Happiness Ahead. Outcast. Dressed to Kill. 1929: The Cock-Eyed World. In Old Arizona. Making the Grade. Thru Different Eyes. This Thing Called Love. 1930: Good Intentions. The Painted Angel. Happy Days. More than a Kiss. Part Time Wife. The Squealer. Born Reckless. The Bad One. Man on Call. Scotland Yard (GB: 'Detective Clive', Bart). 1931: Women of All Nations. The Cisco Kid. *Screen Snapshots No. 8. Transatlantic. Don't Bet on Women. 1932: Attorney for the Defense. *The Stolen Jools (GB: The Slippery Pearls). Guilty As Hell (GB: Guilty as Charged). American Madness. Chandu, the Magician. The Devil is Driving. The Misleading Lady. 1933: Hot Pepper. Her Bodyguard. Dinner at Eight. I Love That Man. 1934: Let's Fall in Love. Gift of Gab. Bombay Mail. No More Women. 1935: Under Pressure. The Great Hotel Murder. Mr Dynamite. Thunder in the Night. *La Fiesta De Santa Barbara. King Solomon of Broadway. Black Sheep. The Great Impersonation. 1936: Seven Sinners (US: Doomed Cargo). The Garden Murder Case. Mad Holiday. The Grand Exit. The Wrecker. The Girl on the Front Page. 1937: Under Cover of Night. The Squeaker (US: Murder on Diamond Row). Espionage. Every Day's a Holiday. 1938: Secrets of a Nurse. 1939: Our Neighbors, the Carters. Newsboys' Home. The Witness Vanishes. 1940: Honeymoon Deferred. The Crooked Road. I Love You Again. Wolf of New York. Men against the Sky. 1941: Flying Cadets. Double Date. 1942: Call Out the Marines. Klondike Fury. 1943: Murder in Times Square. Dangerous Blonde. Oh! What a Night. 1944: The Girl in the Case (GB: The Silver Key). Dillinger. 1945: The Great Mystic. The Enchanted Forest. 1946: The Strange Mr Gregory. 1948: Good Sam. 1955: *The Devil's Bible. 1956: Around the World in 80 Days. 1957: The Wings of Eagles. Execution Night (TV. GB: cinemas). 1958: Plunderers of Painted Flats. The Last Hurrah. 1960: Heller in Pink Tights.

LOWERY, Robert (R. L. Hanke) 1914–1971

Singer, juvenile lead, minor-league star, character player, serial hero and bit parts – this genial-looking American actor, with his mop of light-brown curly hair, did it all. Originally a dance-band singer, he took up acting in his early twenties and became the hero of dozens of second-features in the 1940s. After playing Batman in a serial his film career gradually drifted away, even though, as his features thickened, he donned a moustache and played a few villains. Married to Jean Parker (qv) from 1951 to 1957, third of three wives. Died from a heart attack.

1936: Come and Get It. Great Guy (GB: Pluck of the Irish). 1937: You Can't Have Everything. Wife, Doctor and Nurse. Second Honeymoon. Life Begins in College (GB: The Joy Parade). Wake Up and Live. 1938: Passport Husband. Submarine Patrol. Tail Spin. Always Goodbye. Alexander's Ragtime Band. Kentucky Moonshine (GB: Three Men and a Girl). Four Men and a Prayer. Josette. 1939: Wife, Husband and Friend. Day-Time Wife. Second Fiddle. Charlie Chan in Reno. Young Mr Lincoln. Hollywood Cavalcade. Drums along the Mohawk. Mr Moto in Danger Island (GB: Mr Moto on Danger Island). 1940: City of Chance. Free, Blonde and Twenty-One. Shooting High. Four Sons. Maryland. The Mark of Zorro. Star Dust. Charlie Chan's Murder Cruise. Murder Over New York. 1941: Private Nurse. Ride On, Vaquero! Cadet Girls. Great Guns. 1942: Dawn on the Great Divide. My Gal Sal. Criminal Investigator. Who is Hope Schuyler? She's in the Army. Lure of the Islands. Rhythm Parade. 1943: The Immortal Sergeant. Tarzan's Desert Mystery. So's Your Uncle. The North Star (later Armored Attack). Campus Rhythm. Revenge of the Zombies (GB: The Corpse Vanished). 1944: The Navy Way. Hot Rhythm. A Scream in the Dark (GB: Scream in the Night). Dark Mountain. Dangerous Passage. The Mummy's Ghost. Mystery of the River Boat (serial). 1945: Homesick Angel. Thunderbolt. Road to Alcatraz. Fashion Model. High Powered. Prison Ship. The Monster and the Ape (serial). 1946: Sensation Hunters. They Made Me a Killer. House of Horrors (GB: Joan Medford is Missing). God's Country. The Lady Chaser. Gas House Kids. 1947: Big Town. Danger Street. I Cover Big Town. Killer at Large. Queen of the Amazons. Jungle Flight. Big Town After Dark. 1948: Death Valley. Heart of Virginia. Mary Lou. Big Town Scandal. Highway 13. 1949: Shep Comes Home. Batman and Robin (serial). Arson Inc. The Dalton Gang. Call of the Forest. 1950: Gunfire. Border Rangers. Western Pacific Agent. Train to Tombstone. Everybody's Dancing. 1951: Crosswinds. 1953: Jalopy. Cow Country. The Homesteaders. 1955: Lay That Rifle Down. 1956: Two-Gun Lady. 1957: The Parson and the Outlaw. 1959: The Rise and Fall of Legs Diamond. 1962: Deadly Duo. When the Girls Take Over. Young Guns of Texas. 1963: McLintock! 1964: Stage to Thunder Rock. 1965: Zebra in the Kitchen. Johnny Reno. 1966: Waco. 1967: The Undertaker (and His Pals). The Ballad of Josie.

LOY, Myrna (M. Williams) 1905–
Red-headed Hollywood star of Welsh ancestry who moved from bit parts and oriental vamps to become the 'Queen of Hollywood' by the late 1930s (Clark Gable was voted King). Queen of sophisticated comedy she certainly was, in a dazzling period of success that ran from 1934 to 1941. Her war work for the Red Cross took the sting out of her career and she has worked only sporadically since. Four times married and divorced. Amazingly, she was never even nominated for an Academy Award.
1925: Ben-Hur. Satan in Sables. Pretty Ladies. Sporting Life. 1926: Cave Man. The Gilded Highway. Across the Pacific. Don Juan. Why Girls Go Back Home. The Love Toy. The Third Degree. Millionaires. The Exquisite Sinner. So This is Paris. Finger Prints. 1927: Ham and Eggs at the Front (GB: Ham and Eggs). Bitter Apples. The Heart of Maryland. The Jazz Singer. If I Were Single. The Climbers. The Girl from Chicago. Simple Sis. A Sailor's Sweetheart. 1928: What Price Beauty? Turn Back the Hours. Crimson City. State Street Sadie (GB: The Girl from State Street). Beware of Married Men. Midnight Taxi. Pay as You Enter. 1929: Noah's Ark. The Desert Song. Fancy Baggage. The Black Watch (GB: King of the Khyber Rifles). Hardboiled Rose. Evidence. The Show of Shows. The Squall. 1930: Cameo Kirby. Isle of Escape. The Bad Man. The Great Divide. Cock o' the Walk. Bride of the Regiment (GB: Lady of the Rose). Last of the Duanes. Under a Texas Moon. Rogue of the Rio Grande. The Truth About Youth. Renegades. The Devil to Pay. 1931: A Connecticut Yankee (GB: The Yankee at King Authur's Court). Naughty Flirt. Arrowsmith. Consolation Marriage (GB: Married in Haste). Skyline. Rebound. Transatlantic. Hush Money. Body and Soul. 1932: The Wet Parade. The Woman in Room 13. Emma. Love Me Tonight. Thirteen Women. The Animal Kingdom (GB: The Woman in His House). The Mask of Fu Manchu. Vanity Fair. New Morals for Old. 1933: Topaze. Penthouse (GB: Crooks in Clover). The Barbarian (GB: A Night in Cairo). The Prizefighter and the Lady (GB: Everywoman's Man). Night Flight. Scarlet River. When Ladies Meet. 1934: Men in White. Stamboul Quest. Manhattan Melodrama. The Thin Man. Evelyn Prentice. Broadway Bill (GB: Strictly Confidential). 1935: Wings in the Dark. Whipsaw. 1936: Wife vs Secretary. Libeled Lady. After the Thin Man. The Great Ziegfeld. Petticoat Fever. To Mary – with Love. 1937: Parnell. Double Wedding. Man-Proof. 1938: Test Pilot. Too Hot to Handle. 1939: Lucky Night. Another Thin Man. The Rains Came. 1940: Third Finger, Left Hand. I Love You Again. 1941: Shadow of the Thin Man. Love Crazy. 1943: *Show Business at War. 1944: The Thin Man Goes Home. 1946: The Best Years of Our Lives. So Goes My Love (GB: A Genius in the Family). 1947: The Senator Was Indiscreet (GB: Mr Ashton Was Indiscreet). Song of the Thin Man. The Bachelor and the Bobby Soxer (GB: Bachelor Knight). 1948: Mr Blandings Builds His Dream House. 1949: That Dangerous Age (GB: If This Be Sin). The Red Pony. 1950: Cheaper by the Dozen. 1952: Belles on Their Toes. 1956: The Ambassador's Daughter. 1958: Lonelyhearts. 1960: From the Terrace. Midnight Lace. 1969: The April Fools. 1971: Death Takes a Holiday (TV). Do Not Fold, Spindle or Mutilate (TV). 1972: The Couple Takes a Wife (TV). 1974: Indict and Convict (TV). Airport 1975. 1975: The Elevator (TV). 1977: It Happened at Lakewood Manor (TV. GB: Panic at Lakewood Manor). 1978: The End. 1979: Just Tell Me What You Want. 1981: Summer Solstice (TV).

LUCAN, Arthur (A. Towle) 1887–1954
Wry-faced British music-hall comedian who made his name with the creation of Old Mother Riley, a sentimental old harridan of an Irish washerwoman. He subsequently paraded the character through 15 barnstorming comedies and became one of Britain's most popular stars in the wartime years. His daughter on film was played by his real-life wife Kitty McShane (1898–1964). They married in 1913 and their off-stage rows were legendary. Lucan died from a heart attack.
1935: Stars on Parade. 1937: Kathleen Mavourneen (US: Kathleen). Old Mother Riley. 1938: Old Mother Riley in Paris. 1939: Old Mother Riley MP. Old Mother Riley Joins Up. 1940: Old Mother Riley in Society. Old Mother Riley in Business. 1941: Old Mother Riley's Ghosts. Old Mother Riley's Circus. 1942: Old Mother Riley Detective. 1943: Old

Mother Riley Overseas. 1945: Old Mother Riley at Home. 1949: Old Mother Riley's New Venture. 1950: Old Mother Riley Headmistress. 1951: Old Mother Riley's Jungle Treasure. 1952: Mother Riley Meets the Vampire (US: Vampire over London).

LUGOSI, Bela (B. Blasko) 1882–1956
Transylvanian-born actor of dominant and rather forbidding personality. After becoming a romantic idol of the Hungarian stage, he fled the country in the face of an oppressive regime and ended in Hollywood, where his performance as Dracula type-cast him in horror for the rest of his career. His later years were dogged by a (finally victorious) battle against drug addiction.
1917: Álarscobál. Az Elet Királya. The Leopard. A Nászdal. Tavaszi Vihar. Az Ezredes. 1918: Casanova. Lulu. 99. 1919: Sklaven Fremdes Willens. 1920: Der Fluch der Menschheit. The Head of Janus (GB: Dr Jekyll and Mr Hyde). Die Frau im Delphin. Die Todeskarawane (US: Caravan of Death). Lederstrumpf. Die Teufelsanbeter (US: The Devil Worshippers). 1921: Johann Hopkins III. Der Tanz auf dem Vulkan. 1922: The Last of the Mohicans. 1923: Silent Command. 1924: The Rejected Woman. 1925: The Midnight Girl. Daughters Who Pay. 1928: How to Handle Women. The Veiled Woman. 1929: Prisoners. The Thirteenth Chair. The Last Performance. Such Men Are Dangerous. 1930: Wild Company. Renegades. Viennese Nights. Oh, For a Man. Dracula. 1931: Fifty Million Frenchmen. Women of All Nations. The Black Camel. Broadminded. 1932: The Murders in the Rue Morgue. White Zombie. Chandu, The Magician. The Death Kiss. Island of Lost Souls. 1933: Whispering Shadows (serial). International House. Night of Terror. The Devil's In Love. 1934: The Black Cat (GB: The House of Doom). Gift of Gab. The Return of Chandu. Best Man Wins. Chandu on the Magic Isle. *Screen Snapshots No. 11. 1935: The Mysterious Mr Wong. Murder by Television. Mark of the Vampire. The Raven. The Mystery of the Marie Celeste (US: Phantom Ship). The Invisible Ray. 1936: Shadow of Chinatown (serial. GB: The Yellow Phantom). The Postal Inspector. 1937: SOS. Coastguard (serial). 1939: The Phantom Creeps (serial). Son of Frankenstein. Ninotchka. The Gorilla. Dark Eyes of London (US: Human Monster). 1940:

The Saint's Double Trouble. Black Friday. You'll Find Out. The Devil Bat. 1941: The Invisible Ghost. The Black Cat. Spooks Run Wild. The Wolf Man. 1942: The Ghost of Frankenstein. Black Dragons. The Corpse Vanishes. Night Monster. Bowery at Midnight. 1943: Frankenstein Meets the Wolf-Man. The Ape Man. Ghosts on the Loose. The Return of the Vampire. 1944: Voodoo Man. Return of the Ape Man. One Body Too Many. 1945: The Body Snatcher. Zombies on Broadway (GB: Loonies on Broadway). 1946: Genius at Work. Devil Bat's Daughter. 1947: Scared to Death. 1948: Abbott and Costello Meet Frankenstein (GB: Abbott and Costello Meet the Ghosts). 1952: Mother Riley Meets the Vampire (US: Vampire over London). Bela Lugosi Meets a Brooklyn Gorilla (GB: Monster Meets the Gorilla). 1953: Glen or Glenda? 1954: Bride of the Monster. 1956: The Black Sleep. 1958: Plan 9 from Outer Space.

LUKAS, Paul (Pál Lukács) 1887–1971
Smooth, urbane, moustachioed, Hungarian-born leading man, in Hollywood from the late twenties. Seen mostly as villains or continental Romeos at first, but later – after filming in England from 1937 to 1939 – in a more interesting variety of roles, winning an Academy Award in 1943 for Watch on the Rhine. It's hard to believe that this most civilized of men was once a wrestler – but he was. Died from a heart attack.
1915: A Man of the Earth. 1917: Heartsong. 1918: Udvari Lovegö. Sphynx. Vorrei Morir. 1920: Olavi. Névtelen Vár. Masamód. A szürkeruhás Hölgy. The Milliner. Sárga Árnyék. Little Fox. Színesnö. 1921: Hétszázeves Szerelem. A Telegram from New York/New York Expresz Kábel. 1922: Lady Violetta. Samson and Delilah. Eine versunkene Welt. 1923: Derumberkanute Morgen. Az Egyhuszasos Lány. Diadalmas Élet. 1924: Egy Fiunak a Fele. 1928: Woman from Moscow. Two Lovers. Manhattan Cocktail. Three Sinners. Hot News. The Night Watch. Loves of an Actress. 1929: The Wolf of Wall Street. Half Way to Heaven. Illusion. The Shopworn Angel. 1930: Slightly Scarlet. Young Eagles. The Benson Murder Case. Anybody's Woman. Grumpy. The Devil's Holiday. Behind the Make-Up. The Right to Love. 1931: City Streets. The Vice Squad. Strictly Dishonorable. Working Girls. Women Love Once. The Beloved Bachelor. Unfaithful.

1932: No One Man. Tomorrow and Tomorrow. A Passport to Hell. Downstairs. Rockabye. Thunder Below. 1933: Grand Slam. Sing Sinner Sing. Secret of the Blue Room. Nagana. Little Women. The Kiss before the Mirror. Captured! 1934: By Candlelight. Glamour. Affairs of a Gentleman. Gift of Gab. The Fountain. The Countess of Monte Cristo. I Give My Love. 1935: Age of Indiscretion. Father Brown – Detective. The Three Musketeers. I Found Stella Parish. The Casino Murder Case. 1936: Dodsworth. Ladies in Love. 1937: Espionage. Brief Ecstasy. The Mutiny of the Elsinore. Dinner at the Ritz. 1938: The Lady Vanishes. Dangerous Secrets. 1939: A Window in London (US: Lady in Distress). The Chinese Bungalow (US: Chinese Den). Confessions of a Nazi Spy. Captain Fury. 1940: Strange Cargo. The Ghost Breakers. 1941: They Dare Not Love. The Monster and the Girl. 1943: Watch on the Rhine. Hostages. 1944: Uncertain Glory. Address Unknown. Experiment Perilous. 1946: Temptation. Deadline at Dawn. 1947: Whispering City. 1948: Berlin Express. 1950: Kim. 1954: 20,000 Leagues Under the Sea. 1958: The Roots of Heaven. 1959: Judgment at Nuremberg (TV). 1960: Tender is the Night. Scent of Mystery (GB: Holiday in Spain). 1962: The Four Horsemen of the Apocalypse. 55 Days at Peking. 1963: Fun in Acapulco. 1964: Lord Jim. 1967: Sol Madrid (GB: The Heroin Gang). 1970: The Challenge (TV).

LUND, John 1913–
The fair-haired, blue-eyed son of a Norwegian glass-blower who had emigrated to New York, Lund only took up acting in his late twenties. After a good start in films his flair for zany comedy was swiftly shunted aside in favour of stodgy drama, and he soon slid into the almost-permanent role of the slightly dull 'other man' who never got the girl.
1946: To Each His Own. 1947: The Perils of Pauline. Variety Girl. 1948: Miss Tatlock's Millions. A Foreign Affair. Night Has a Thousand Eyes. 1949: Bride of Vengeance. My Friend Irma. 1950: No Man of Her Own. Duchess of Idaho. My Friend Irma Goes West. 1951: The Mating Season. Darling, How Could You? (GB: Rendezvous). 1952: Steel Town. Bronco Buster. Just Across the Street. The Battle at Apache Pass. 1953: The Woman They Almost Lynched. Latin Lovers. 1955: Chief Crazy Horse (GB: Valley of Fury). White

Feather. Five Guns West. 1956: Dakota Incident. High Society. Battle Stations! 1957: Affair in Reno. 1960: The Wackiest Ship in the Army. 1962: If a Man Answers.

LUNDIGAN, William 1914–1975
Tall, fair-haired American actor, similar in looks to Richard Denning. Started as a radio announcer, then turned to acting and developed slowly into a second-line leading man. Briefly in more showy lead roles with Fox in the early fifties, but his career virtually collapsed with the end of the studio system. Died from heart and lung congestion.
1937: Armored Car. Prescription for Romance. The Lady Fights Back. A Girl with Ideas. 1938: State Police. Freshman Year. Reckless Living. Wives under Suspicion. The Missing Guest. The Black Doll. That's My Story. Danger on the Air. 1939: Dodge City. Legion of Lost Flyers. *Young America Flies. Three Smart Girls Grow Up. The Old Maid. They Asked for It. Forgotten Woman. 1940: The Fighting 69th. The Man Who Talked Too Much. Three Cheers for the Irish. Santa Fé Trail. East of the River. The Sea Hawk. The Case of the Black Parrot. 1941: The Great Mr Nobody. International Squadron. A Shot in the Dark. Sailors on Leave. Highway West. The Bugle Sounds. 1942: The Courtship of Andy Hardy. Sunday Punch. Apache Trail. Northwest Rangers. Andy Hardy's Double Life. 1943: Salute to the Marines. Dr Gillespie's Criminal Case (GB: Crazy to Kill). Headin' for God's Country. 1945: What Next, Corporal Hargrove? 1947: Dishonored Lady. The Fabulous Dorseys. 1948: Inside Story. Mystery in Mexico. 1949: State Department – File 649 (GB: Assignment in China). Follow Me Quietly. Pinky. 1950: Mother Didn't Tell Me. I'll Get By. 1951: The House on Telegraph Hill. I'd Climb the Highest Mountain. Love Nest. Elopement. 1953: Down Among the Sheltering Palms. Inferno. Serpent of the Nile. 1954: Riders to the Stars. Dangerous Voyage (GB: Terror Ship). The White Orchid. 1962: Underwater City. 1967: The Way West. Where Angels Go . . . Trouble Follows.

LUPINO, Ida 1914–
Greasepaint ran in these veins all right. The daughter of popular comedian Stanley Lupino (1893–1942), who made a few films in the thirties, and pretty well all her cousins and

uncles were music-hall stars. Strangely, the pretty, impish, dark-haired (blonde for a while in the thirties) Ida was not much seen in comedy, starting off as ingenues and frightened ladies, and moving to Hollywood in this mould in 1934. From the early forties she excelled in hard-bitten roles. Has also directed a few films, some with controversial themes. Married Louis Hayward (1938–1945) and Howard Duff (1951–1968), first and third of three.
1932: The Love Race. Her First Affaire. 1933: Money for Speed. High Finance. I Lived with You. Prince of Arcadia. The Ghost Camera. 1934: Search for Beauty. Ready for Love. Come on Marines. 1935: Paris in Spring (GB: Paris Love Song). Peter Ibbetson. *La Fiesta de Santa Barbara. Smart Girl. 1936: Anything Goes. The Gay Desperado. One Rainy Afternoon. Yours for the Asking. 1937: Sea Devils. Artists and Models. Let's Get Married. Fight for Your Lady. 1939: The Lone Wolf Spy Hunt (GB: The Lone Wolf's Daughter). The Adventures of Sherlock Holmes (GB: Sherlock Holmes). The Lady and the Mob. 1940: The Light That Failed. They Drive by Night (GB: The Road to Frisco). 1941: The Sea Wolf. High Sierra. Out of the Fog. Ladies in Retirement. 1942: Moontide. Life Begins at 8.30 (GB: The Light of Heart). The Hard Way. 1943: Forever and a Day. Thank Your Lucky Stars. Devotion (released 1946). 1944: Hollywood Canteen. In Our Time. 1945: Pillow to Post. 1946: The Man I Love. 1947: Deep Valley. Escape Me Never. 1948: Road House. 1949: Lust for Gold. 1950: Woman in Hiding. 1951: On Dangerous Ground. 1952: Beware My Lovely. 1953: Jennifer. The Bigamist. 1954: Private Hell 36. 1955: The Big Knife. Women's Prison. 1956: While the City Sleeps. Strange Intruder. 1967: I Love a Mystery (TV). 1968: Backtrack (TV). 1971: Women in Chains (TV). 1972: Female Artillery (TV). Deadhead Miles. Junior Bonner. My Boys Are Good Boys. The Letters (TV). The Strangers in 7A (TV). 1975: The Devil's Rain. 1976: The Food of the Gods.

As director: 1949: Not Wanted (uncredited co-director). 1950: Outrage. Never Fear. 1951: Hard, Fast and Beautiful. 1953: The Bigamist. The Hitch-Hiker. 1966: The Trouble With Angels.

LUPINO, Stanley 1893–1942
Dapper, dark-haired, thin-mouthed, wry-

faced, London-born farceur, light singer and dancer and confident all-round entertainer. A member of a family who were pretty well all in show business, he was on stage at 17 and a star of revue soon after. His film career, though popular enough, was entirely confined to the 1930s and much restricted by his stage work. Customarily in films he would appear as a breezy young man of faintly working-class origins who got the girl of his dreams after various chicanery from other interested parties. Father of Ida Lupino (qv).
1931: Love Lies. The Love Race. 1932: Sleepless Nights. 1933: King of the Ritz. Facing the Music. You Made Me Love You. Happy. 1935: Honeymoon for Three. 1936: Cheer Up. Sporting Love. 1937: Over She Goes. 1938: Hold My Hand. 1939: Lucky To Me.

LYDON, James 'Jimmy' 1923–
If it weren't for Henry Aldrich, Jimmy Lydon probably wouldn't qualify for this book. But, under the guidance of this red-haired, gangling, dumb-looking young American actor, Henry became the world's second favourite wartime teenager after Andy Hardy. Most of Lydon's other roles have been small and his starring films seem so long ago it's hard to believe he's not long past 60.
1939: Back Door to Heaven. Two Thoroughbreds. Racing Luck. 1940: Tom Brown's Schooldays. Little Men. 1941: Naval Academy. Bowery Boy. Henry Aldrich for President. 1942: Cadets on Parade. The Mad Martindales. *A Letter from Bataan. Star Spangled Rhythm. Henry Aldrich, Editor. 1943: Henry Aldrich Gets Glamour (GB: Henry Gets Glamour). Henry Aldrich Swings It (GB: Henry

Swings It). Henry Aldrich Haunts a House (GB: Henry Haunts a House). Henry Aldrich Plays Cupid (GB: Henry Plays Cupid). Aerial Gunner. *The Aldrich Family Gets in the Scrap. 1944: Henry Aldrich Boy Scout (GB: Henry – Boy Scout). My Best Gal. The Town Went Wild. Henry Aldrich's Little Secret (GB: Henry's Little Secret). When the Lights Go On Again. 1945: Out of the Night (GB: Strange Illusion). Twice Blessed. 1946: The Affairs of Geraldine. 1947: Cynthia (GB: The Rich, Full Life). Sweet Genevieve. Life with Father. 1948: The Time of Your Life. Out of the Storm. Joan of Arc. An Old-Fashioned Girl. 1949: Bad Boy. Miss Mink of 1949. Tucson. 1950: Tarnished. When Willie Comes Marching Home. Destination Big House. Hot Rod. September Affair. The Magnificent Yankee (GB: The Man with 30 Sons). Gasoline Alley. 1951: O, Susanna. Corky of Gasoline Alley (GB: Corky). 1953: Island in the Sky. 1954: The Desperado. 1956: Battle Stations. 1957: Chain of Evidence. 1960: The Hypnotic Eye. I Passed for White. 1961: The Last Time I Saw Archie. 1965: Brainstorm. 1969: Death of a Gunfighter. 1971: Scandalous John. 1972: Bonnie's Kids. 1975: Vigilante Force. Ellery Queen (TV). 1976: The New Daughters of Joshua Cabe (TV). 1977: Peter Lundy and the Medicine Hat Stallion (TV).

LYNCH, Alfred 1933–
Fair-haired, shortish British actor whose honest, cheerful face and cultivated tones seemed to fit him for the 1960s. Indeed, he starred in his first few films, then vanished disappointingly from the screen, to reappear only occasionally in ensuing years in supporting roles. Like Tom Courtenay, he has preferred the stage, with some TV from time to time.
1961: On the Fiddle (US: Operation Snafu). 1962: Two and Two Make Six. The Password is Courage. 55 Days at Peking. 1963: West 11. 1965: The Hill. 1966: The Taming of the Shrew. 1968: Come l'amore. 1969: The Sea Gull. 1973: The Blockhouse. 1976: Joseph Andrews.

LYNLEY, Carol (Carolyn Lee) 1942–
Baby-faced American blonde, in films as a teenager. Like the similar Yvette Mimieux, also trapped in childlike roles, she was a more than competent actress who found herself in progressively less worthy parts. More prom-

ising ventures were sunk by inferior scripts and after a slough of 'Z' movies and TV films it seems as though her chance of big-time stardom may have slipped away.
1958: The Light in the Forest. 1959: Blue Denim (GB: Blue Jeans). Holiday for Lovers. 1960: Hound Dog Man. 1961: Return to Peyton Place. The Last Sunset. 1962: The Stripper (GB: Woman of Summer). 1963: Under the Yum Yum Tree. The Cardinal. 1964: Shock Treatment. The Pleasure Seekers. 1965: Harlow (TV). Bunny Lake is Missing. 1967: The Helicopter Spies (TV. GB: cinemas). The Shuttered Room. Danger Route. 1968: The Smugglers (TV). Shadow on the Land (TV). 1969: The Maltese Bippy. The Immortal (TV). Norwood. 1970: Once You Kiss a Stranger. Weekend of Terror (TV). 1971: The Cable Car Mystery (TV. GB: Crosscurrent). The Night Stalker (TV). 1972: The Poseidon Adventure. 1973: Cotter (GB: TV). 1974: Beware! the Blob (GB: Son of Blob). Death Stalk (TV). The Elevator (TV). 1975: The Four Deuces. 1976: Flood! (TV). Godzilla vs the Cosmic Monster (GB: Godzilla vs the Bionic Monster). Out of Control. 1977: Bad Georgia Road. Having Babies II (TV). 1978: The Cops and Robin (TV). The Cat and the Canary. The Beasts Are in the Streets. 1979: The Shape of Things to Come. Todos los Dias un Dia. 1980: Lady Doctor (TV). 1982: Vigilante. 1985: Balboa.

LYNN, Ann 1937–
Fair-haired, narrow-faced British actress, granddaughter of Ralph Lynn. Her rather mournful looks got her cast as downtrodden

daughters or conniving bitches. She was often the best thing in her films (and was seen in some fairly obscure ones, too), but her unpretty countenance may have given her little chance of becoming a star in the British cinema at the time. Married/divorced Anthony Newley (qv).
1955: Johnny, You're Wanted. 1958: Moment of Indiscretion. 1959: Naked Fury. 1960: Piccadilly Third Stop. 1961: Strip Tease Murder. Flame in the Streets. The Wind of Change. 1962: Strongroom. HMS Defiant (US: Damn the Defiant!). *A Woman's Privilege. 1963: The Party's Over. Doctor in Distress. 1964: The Black Torment. The System (US: The Girl Getters). A Shot in the Dark. The Uncle. 1965: Four in the Morning. 1967: Separation. I'll Never Forget What's' Is Name. 1968: Baby Love. 1971: *The Spy's Wife. 1973: Hitler: the Last Ten Days. 1983: Screamtime (video).

LYNN, Diana (Dolores Loehr) 1924–1971
As a teenager, light-haired American piano-playing prodigy Diana Lynn was as pretty as any picture. She also had a zany sense of humour and was quite delightful as a series of sassy young sisters in forties' comedies which occasionally used her musical talents as well. In maturity she remained sweet but became a shade dull. Died from a brain haemorrhage.
1939: †They Shall Have Music (GB: Melody of Youth). 1941: †There's Magic in Music. 1942: The Major and the Minor. Star-Spangled Rhythm. 1943: Henry Aldrich Gets Glamour (GB: Henry Gets Glamour). Henry Aldrich Plays Cupid (GB: Henry Plays Cupid). *The Aldrich Family Gets in the Scrap. 1944: And the Angels Sing. The Miracle of Morgan's Creek. Our Hearts Were Young and Gay. 1945: Out of This World. Duffy's Tavern. *Hollywood Victory Caravan. 1946: Our Hearts Were Growing Up. The Bride Wore Boots. 1947: Easy Come, Easy Go. Variety Girl. 1948: Every Girl Should Be Married. Ruthless. Texas, Brooklyn and Heaven (GB: The Girl From Texas). 1949: My Friend Irma. 1950: Paid in Full. My Friend Irma Goes West. Rogues of Sherwood Forest. Peggy. 1951: The People Against O'Hara. Bedtime for Bonzo. 1952: Meet Me at the Fair. 1953: Plunder of the Sun. 1954: Track of the Cat. 1955: Annapolis Story (GB: The Blue and the Gold). You're Never Too Young. The Kentuckian. 1956: Forbidden Area (TV). 1957: The Star

Wagon (TV). A Sound of Different Drummers (TV). 1958: The Return of Ansel Gibbs (TV). 1959: Marriage of Strangers (TV). 1970: Company of Killers.

†As Dolly Loehr

LYNN, Ralph 1881–1962
Dark-haired, monocled, toothy, owl-faced British farceur with idiot grin, a member of the famous trio (with Tom Walls and Robertson Hare) that convulsed audiences at the Aldwych Theatre in Ben Travers farces of the twenties and thirties, and transferred most of their best work on to screen. The archetypal English 'silly ass'.
1929: *Peace and Quiet. 1930: Tons of Money. Plunder. Rookery Nook (US: One Embarrassing Night). 1931: Chance of a Night Time. Mischief. 1932: A Night Like This. Thark. Just My Luck. 1933: Summer Lightning. Up to the Neck. Turkey Time. 1934: A Cup of Kindness. Dirty Work. 1935: Fighting Stock. Foreign

Affaires. Stormy Weather. 1936: In the Soup. All In. Pot Luck. 1937: For Valour. 1959: The Adventures of Rex (serial).

LYON, Ben 1901–1979
Genial, avuncular, dark-haired, round-faced American actor, a popular middle-range star for 15 years in the 1920s and 1930s, best recalled for Hell's Angels, a role which became the subject of a running gag in his popular wartime radio show Hi Gang! after he and his first wife Bebe Daniels (married 1931 to her death in 1971) had come to Britain in the late 1930s and scored an instant personal success. A second radio series, Life with the Lyons, was equally popular. He married his second wife, ex-actress Marian Nixon (1904–), in 1972. Died from a heart attack.
1919: Open Your Eyes. 1921: The Heart of Maryland. 1922: The Custard Cup. Ashes. 1923: Potash and Perlmutter (GB: Dr Sunshine). Flaming Youth. 1924: The White Moth.

Painted People. The Wine of Youth. Lily of the Dust. The Wages of Virtue. So Big. 1925: One Way Street. Winds of Chance. The Necessary Evil. The New Commandment. The Pace That Thrills. Bluebeard's Seven Wives. 1926: The Great Deception. The Savage. The Prince of Tempters. The Reckless Lady. 1927: For the Love of Mike. The Perfect Sap (GB: The Marriage of Marcia). Dance Magic. The Tender Hour. High Hat. Das tanzende Wien. 1928: The Air Legion. 1929: Quitter. The Flying Marine. 1930: Alias French Gertie (GB: Love Finds a Way). A Soldier's Plaything (GB: A Soldier's Pay). What Men Want. Hell's Angels. Lummox. 1931: Night Nurse. Aloha (GB: No Greater Love). Hot Heiress. My Past. Misbehaving Ladies. Compromised (GB: We Three). Bought. Her Majesty Love. *Screen Snapshots No. 7. 1932: Lady with a Past (GB: My Reputation). Week-Ends Only. Hat Check Girl (GB: Embassy Girl). By Whose Hand. *Hollywood on Parade No 3. Big Time. The Crooked Circle. *The Stolen Jools (GB: The Slippery Pearls). 1933: I Cover the Waterfront. Girl Missing. The Women in His Life. I Spy (GB: The Morning After). 1934: Crimson Romance. Lightning Strikes Twice. 1935: Frisco Waterfront (GB: When We Look Back). Beauty's Daughter (later Navy Wife). Together We Live. 1936: Dancing Feet. Down to the Sea. 1937: Not Wanted on Voyage. Mad About Money (US: He Loved an Actress). 1939: I Killed the Count (US: Who is Guilty?). Confidential Lady. 1941: Hi Gang! This Was Paris. 1943: The Dark Tower. 1953: Life With the Lyons (US: Family Affair). 1954: Adventures with the Lyons (serial). The Lyons in Paris. 1965: The March of the Movies (narrator only).

Lethal Ls. Alan Ladd and Veronica Lake find time to give the cameraman a smile that won't appear in the film *This Gun for Hire* (1942). Robert Preston's the interloper on the right.

Mmm. Tasty combination of Marilyn Monroe and Robert Mitchum in the 1952 western *River of No Return*.

N is for nominees. Patricia Neal clinched the best actress Oscar for *Hud* (1963). Co-star Paul Newman lost (somewhat improbably) to Sidney Poitier in *Lilies of the Field*.

O is for Oscar – won by Tatum O'Neal in *Paper Moon* (1973) as a mini-con artist, here with admiring father and co-star Ryan O'Neal.

1929: The Love Parade. 1930: The Vagabond King. Let's Go Native. Oh, for a Man. Monte Carlo. The Lottery Bride. 1931: Annabelle's Affairs. Don't Bet on Women. 1932: One Hour with You. Love Me Tonight. 1933: *Hollywood on Parade No. 7. 1934: The Cat and the Fiddle. The Merry Widow. 1935: Naughty Marietta. 1936: Rose Marie. San Francisco. 1937: The Firefly. Maytime. 1938: Girl of the Golden West. Sweethearts. 1939: Broadway Serenade. 1940: New Moon. Bitter Sweet. 1941: Smilin' Through. 1942: I Married an Angel. Cairo. 1944: Follow the Boys. 1948: Three Daring Daughters (GB: The Birds and the Bees). The Sun Comes Up. 1957: Charley's Aunt (TV).

which period is *Son of Kong*. Later became a successful radio producer and writer.
1923: Under the Red Robe. Grit. Zaza. Little Red School House (GB: The Greater Law). 1924: Pied Piper Malone. 1931: The Struggle. 1932: Silent Witness. While Pain Sleeps. Fargo Express. 1933: Sweepings. Melody Cruise. California Trail. Christopher Bean (GB: The Late Christopher Bean). Blind Adventure. Son of Kong. 1934: All of Me. Kiss and Make Up. You Belong to Me. The Lemon Drop Kid. College Rhythm. 1935: Four Hours to Kill. Captain Hurricane. The Return of Peter Grimm. She. 1936: The Milky Way. 1937: You Can't Buy Luck. Last Train from Madrid. Fit for a King. The Wrong Road. 1938: King of the Newsboys. Gambling Ship. I Stand Accused. Secrets of a Nurse. 1939: The Mystery of the White Room. Calling all Marines. 1940: His Girl Friday. Girls of the Road. 1941: Power Drive. 1944: And Now Tomorrow. 1945: Divorce. 1946: Strange Holiday.

MacARTHUR, James 1937–

Eager-looking American leading man with fair curly hair, and romantic air, the adopted son of Helen Hayes. Played leading roles in some bland entertainments, but his career was faltering when he became involved with the long-running TV series *Hawaii Five-O*. After ten years he was visibly tiring of the show and taking more interest in his work as explorer and geographer. He left Hawaii and the series in 1979.
1957: The Young Stranger. 1958: The Light in the Forest. 1959: Third Man on the Mountain. 1960: Kidnapped. Swiss Family Robinson. 1962: The Interns. 1963: Cry of Battle. Spencer's Mountain. 1964: The Truth about Spring. 1965: Battle of the Bulge. The Bedford Incident. 1966: Ride Beyond Vengeance. Willie and the Yank (TV. GB: cinemas as Mosby's Marauders). 1967: The Love-Ins. Hang 'Em High. 1968: The Angry Breed. Lassiter (TV). 1979: The Night the Bridge Fell Down (TV). 1980: Alcatraz: the Whole Shocking Story (TV).

MacDONALD, Jeanette 1901–1965

Pretty if slightly pasty blonde American operetta singer with a lovely sense of comedy all too rarely put to proper use in the cinema. Her early films, with Maurice Chevalier, show her flair for impishly saucy fun to quite good advantage, but it was her musicals with Nelson Eddy – all eight of them – that put her right at the top of the cinema tree. Died from a heart attack after a long battle with a heart ailment. Married Gene Raymond in 1937.

MacGRAW, Ali (Alice MacGraw) 1938–

Impassive-looking, dark-haired, olive-complexioned American leading lady. Certainly one of the Beautiful People, but her acting range on the screen has so far been limited. Has always looked (and played) younger than her age, but has filmed infrequently. Married to Steve McQueen (third) from 1973 to 1978. Received an Oscar nomination for *Love Story*. 1968: A Lovely Way to Die (GB: A Lovely Way to Go). 1969: Goodbye Columbus. 1971: Love Story. 1972: The Getaway. 1978: Convoy. Players. 1979: Just Tell Me What You Want. 1983 China Rose (TV). 1985: Murder Elite.

MACK, Helen (H. McDougall) 1913–

Personable, attractive, dark-haired American leading actress, in a couple of films when ten, and vaudeville at 13. Started her adult career in earnest at 18, keeping fairly busy through the thirties, her best-remembered film from

MacLAINE, Shirley (S. Mclean Beaty) 1934–

Gamine American star with pixieish face, wide clown's smile and short red-brown hair that one critic said 'looks as if it has been combed with an egg-beater'. The sister of actor Warren Beatty (qv), she was originally a dancer, but showed a wide range of talents in an enchanting run of successes from 1955 to 1963. After that, things went wrong for her (she was often required to do too much) and she became less of a draw at the box-office. An outspoken champion of feminist rights. Academy Award 1984 for *Terms of Endear-*

ment. Previously Oscar-nominated in *Some Came Running, The Apartment, Irma La Douce* and *The Turning Point.*

1955: The Trouble with Harry. Artists and Models. 1956: Around the World in 80 Days. 1958: Hot Spell. The Sheepman. The Matchmaker. Some Came Running. 1959: Ask Any Girl. Career. 1960: Can-Can. Ocean's Eleven. The Apartment. 1961: All in a Night's Work. Two Loves (GB: Spinster). 1962: The Children's Hour (GB: The Loudest Whisper). My Geisha. Two for the Seesaw. 1963: Irma La Douce. 1964: What a Way to Go! John Goldfarb, Please Come Home. The Yellow Rolls-Royce. 1966: Gambit. 1967: Woman Times Seven. 1968: The Bliss of Mrs Blossom. 1969: Sweet Charity. Two Mules for Sister Sara. 1971: Desperate Characters. The Possession of Joel Delaney. 1977: The Turning Point. 1979: Being There. 1980: Loving Couples. A Change of Seasons. 1983: Terms of Endearment. Cannonball Run II.

MacLANE, Barton 1900–1969
Big, burly, pudgy-faced, red-haired American actor who played tough guys with gruff voices at Warners from 1935 to 1942, a time when he was quite near the top of the tree. Insufficient variety in characterizations eventually sent him further down the cast list, although he continued to be busy. Born on Christmas Day, died on New Year's Day (of double pneumonia).

*1926: The Quarterback. 1929: The Cocoanuts. 1931: His Woman. 1933: To the Last Man. The Thundering Herd. *Let's Dance. Man of the Forest. The Torch Singer. Tillie and Gus. Hell and High Water (GB: Cap'n Jericho). Big Executive. 1934: The Last Round-Up. Lone Cowboy. 1935: The Case of the Curious Bride. Page Miss Glory. I Found Stella Parish. G-Men. Man of Iron. The Case of the Lucky Legs. Go into Your Dance (GB: Casino de Paree). Black Fury. Stranded. Dr Socrates. Ceiling Zero. The Frisco Kid. 1936: The Walking Dead. Jail Break (GB: Murder in the Big House). Bengal Tiger. God's Country and the Woman. Times Square Playboy (GB: His Best Man). Bullets or Ballots. Smart Blonde. Draegerman Courage (GB: The Cave-In). 1937: Wine, Women and Horses. You Only Live Once. San Quentin. Born Reckless. Fly-Away Baby (GB: Crime in the Clouds). The Adventurous Blonde/ Torchy Blane, the Adventurous*

Blonde. The Prince and the Pauper. Ever Since Eve. The Kid Comes Back (GB: Don't Pull Your Punches). 1938: Torchy Gets Her Man. Gold Is Where You Find It. Prison Break. You and Me. Blondes at Work. The Storm. 1939: Stand Up and Fight. Big Town Czar. Mutiny in the Big House. Torchy Blane in Chinatown. I Was a Convict. Torchy Runs for Mayor. 1940: The Secret Seven. Men without Souls. Melody Ranch. Gangs of Chicago. 1941: Western Union. Come Live with Me. Barnacle Bill. The Maltese Falcon. Hit the Road. High Sierra. Manpower. Dr Jekyll and Mr Hyde. Wild Geese Calling. 1942: All Through the Night. Highways by Night. The Big Street. In This Our Life. 1943: Song of Texas. Man of Courage. Crime Doctor's Strangest Case (GB: The Strangest Case). The Underdog. Bombardier. 1944: Cry of the Werewolf. The Mummy's Ghost. Gentle Annie. Secret Command. Marine Raiders. Nabonga (GB: The Jungle Woman). 1945: Scared Stiff. The Spanish Main. Tarzan and the Amazons. 1946: The Mysterious Intruder. Santa Fé Uprising. San Quentin. 1947: Tarzan and the Huntress. Cheyenne. Jungle Flight. 1948: Treasure of the Sierra Madre. Relentless. The Dude Goes West. Unknown Island. Silver River. Angel in Exile. The Walls of Jericho. 1949: Red Light. 1950: Kiss Tomorrow Goodbye. The Bandit Queen. Let's Dance. Rookie Fireman. 1951: Best of the Badmen. Drums in the Deep South. 1952: Bugles in the Afternoon. The Half Breed. Thunderbirds. 1953: Cow Country. Kansas Pacific. Sea of Lost Ships. Jack Slade (GB: Slade). Captain Scarface. 1954: The Glenn Miller Story. Jubilee Trail. Rails into Laramie. 1955: Foxfire. The Silver Star. Jail Busters. Hell's Outpost. Last of the Desperadoes. The Treasure of Ruby Hills. 1956: Backlash. Jaguar. The Man is Armed. Three Violent People. The Naked Gun. Wetbacks. 1957: Sierra Stranger. The Storm Rider. Hell's Crossroads. Naked in the Sun. 1958: The Girl in the Woods. Frontier Gun. The Geisha Boy. 1960: Noose for a Gunman. Gunfighters of Abilene. 1961: Pocketful of Miracles. 1963: Law of the Lawless. 1965: The Rounders. Town Tamer. 1968: Buckskin. Arizona Bushwhackers.

MacMURRAY, Fred 1907–
Bland, agreeable, well-built American actor with dark, wavy hair whose easy grin cruised its way through dozens of light romantic com-

edies and colourful action films. A former saxophonist, MacMurray got a start in Hollywood at his second attempt, and at one time became its highest-paid actor. He did his best work as plausible guys with feet of clay. Later, he was in some good low-budget westerns in the fifties and a series of gleeful romps for Disney. First wife died in 1953. Married June Haver (*qv*) the following year.

*1929: Girls Gone Wild. Tiger Rose. Glad Rag Doll. 1934: Friends of Mr Sweeney. 1935: Grand Old Girl. Car 99. Alice Adams. Men without Names. Hands Across the Table. The Bride Comes Home. The Gilded Lily. 1936: The Trail of the Lonesome Pine. The Princess Comes Across. The Texas Rangers. 13 Hours by Air. 1937: Swing High – Swing Low. Maid of Salem. True Confession. Exclusive. Champagne Waltz. 1938: Cocoanut Grove. Men with Wings. Sing, You Sinners. 1939: Café Society. Honeymoon in Bali (GB: Husbands or Lovers). Invitation to Happiness. 1940: Little Old New York. Too Many Husbands. Rangers of Fortune. Remember the Night. 1941: Virginia. New York Town. Dive Bomber. One Night in Lisbon. 1942: Star Spangled Rhythm. The Lady is Willing. The Forest Rangers. Take a Letter, Darling (GB: The Green-Eyed Woman). 1943: Above Suspicion. *Show Business at War. No Time for Love. Flight for Freedom. 1944: Standing Room Only. Double Indemnity. And the Angels Sing. 1945: Murder, He Says. Where Do We Go from Here? Practically Yours. Captain Eddie. 1947: Singapore. Suddenly It's Spring. The Egg and I. 1948: A Miracle Can Happen (later On Our Merry Way). The Miracle of the Bells. Family Honeymoon. Don't Trust your Husband. 1949: Father Was a Fullback. Borderline. 1950: Never a Dull Moment. 1951: Callaway Went Thataway (GB: The Star Said No). A Millionaire for Christy. 1953: Fair Wind to Java. The Moonlighter. 1954: The Caine Mutiny. Pushover. Woman's World. 1955: The Far Horizons. There's Always Tomorrow. The Rains of Ranchipur. At Gunpoint (GB: Gunpoint!). 1956: Gun for a Coward. 1957: False Witness (TV). 1958: Quantez. Day of the Bad Man. Good Day for a Hanging. 1959: The Shaggy Dog. Face of a Fugitive. The Oregon Trail. 1960: The Apartment. 1961: The Absent Minded Professor. 1962: Bon Voyage! 1963: Son of Flubber. 1964: Kisses for My President. 1966: Follow Me, Boys! 1967: The Happiest Millionaire. 1973: Charley and the Angel. 1974: The Chadwick Family (TV). 1975: Beyond the Bermuda Triangle (TV). 1978: The Swarm.*

MACNEE, Patrick 1922–
British leading man with round face and dark wavy hair who found his forte in middle age (notably in the TV series *The Avengers*) as superior, affable coves with military bearing who looked as though they were always thinking of some witticism to crack. Film career patchy.

1943: The Life and Death of Colonel Blimp (GB: Colonel Blimp). 1948: The Fatal Night. Hamlet. All Over the Town. 1950: The Girl is Mine. Dick Barton at Bay. The Elusive Pim-

pernel (US: The Fighting Pimpernel). 1951: Scrooge. Flesh and Blood. 1954: Three Cases of Murder. 1956: The Battle of the River Plate (US: Pursuit of the Graf Spee). 1957: Until They Sail. Les Girls. 1959: Mission of Danger. 1969: Mister Jerico (TV. GB: cinemas). 1970: Incense for the Damned. 1975: Matt Helm (TV). 1976: Sherlock Holmes in New York (TV). 1977: Dead of Night (TV). 1978: Fantastic Seven (later TV as Stunt Seven). King Solomon's Treasure. 1979: The Billion Dollar Threat (TV. GB: cinemas). 1980: The Sea Wolves. The Howling. Dick Turpin (GB: TV). 1981: Hot Touch. The Creature Wasn't Nice. Sweet Sixteen. 1982: Young Doctors in Love. For the Term of His Natural Life (TV). Rehearsal for Murder (TV). 1983: The Return of the Man from UNCLE (TV). This is Spinal Tap. 1985: A View to a Kill. Shadey. Lime Street (TV).

MacRAE, Gordon 1921–1986
Brown-haired, chubby-cheeked, ingenuous-looking American singer who played bright-eyed young hopefuls opposite Doris Day in some sparkling family musicals during a five-year Warner contract, then won the leading roles in two big musicals from stage successes. Left films for night-club work when the demand for musicals vanished. Died from cancer.
1948: The Big Punch. 1949: Look for the Silver Lining. Backfire. 1950: The Daughter of Rosie O'Grady. Tea for Two. Return of the Frontiersman. The West Point Story (GB: Fine and Dandy). 1951: *The Screen Director. Starlift. On Moonlight Bay. 1952: About Face. *Screen

Snapshots No. 205. 1953: By the Light of the Silvery Moon. *So You Want a Television Set. The Desert Song. Three Sailors and a Girl. 1955: Carousel. 1956: Oklahoma! The Best Things in Life Are Free. 1979: The Pilot.

MADISON, Guy (Robert Mosely) 1922–
Boyishly handsome, fair-haired, ski-slope nosed American actor who began in romantic roles but, in an oddly spasmodic film career, was seen from 1949 almost entirely in westerns, most of them big-budget colour productions, if not quite in the Gary Cooper class. He became popular on TV in the 1950s' series Wild Bill Hickok (many episodes of which were shown as second-feature films outside America) and very busy during the 1960s in continental westerns and action films. Married to Gail Russell (qv) from 1949 to 1954, first of two.
1944: Since You Went Away. 1946: Till the End of Time. 1947: Honeymoon (GB: Two Men and a Girl). 1948: Texas, Brooklyn and Heaven (GB: The Girl from Texas). 1949: Massacre River. 1951: Drums in the Deep South. 1952: Red Snow. †Behind Southern Lines (TV). †The Ghost of Crossbones Canyon (TV). †Border City Rustlers (TV). †Two Gun Marshal (TV). †Six Gun Decision (TV). †Arrow in the Dust (TV). 1953: †The Yellow Haired Kid (TV). †Secret of Outlaw Flats (TV). The Charge at Feather River. 1954: The Command. †Titled Tenderfoot (TV). †Timber County Trouble (TV). †Two Gun Teacher (TV). †Danger on the Trail (TV). †Marshals in Disguise (TV). †Outlaw's Son (TV). †Phantom Trails (TV). 1955: †The Matchmaking Marshal (TV). Five Against the House. The Last Frontier. 1956: Hilda Crane. Reprisal! On the Threshold of Space. The Beast of Hollow Mountain. 1957: The Hard Man. 1958: Bullwhip! 1959: Jet Over the Atlantic. 1960: La schiava di Roma (GB: Blood of the Warriors. US: Slaves of Rome). 1961: Rosamunda el Alboino (GB and US: Sword of the Conqueror). La prigioniere dell'isola del Diavolo (GB: Women of Devil's Island). 1963: Sandokan the Great. I piombi di Venezia (US: Dungeons of Venice). Il boia di Venezia (GB: Blood of the Executioner. US: Hangman of Venice). 1964: Sandokan alla riscossa (GB: Sandokan Fights Back. US: Sandokan Strikes Back). Sandokan contro il leopardo di Sarawak (GB: The Return of Sandokan. US: Tiger of

Terror). I misteri della giungla nera (GB: The Mystery of Thug Island. US: Mysteries of the Black Jungle). Old Shatterhand (GB: Apaches' Last Battle. US: Shatterhand). 1965: Adventurer from Tortuga. Sfida a Rio Bravo (GB: Duel at Rio Bravo. US: Gunmen of the Rio Grande). 1966: I cinque della vendetta (GB and US: Five Giants from Texas). LSD – Flesh of the Devil. 1967: Sette Winchester per un massacro (GB: Payment in Blood. US: Winchester for Hire). The Son of Django. The Devil's Man/War Devils. Testa di sbarco per otto implacabili (GB: Hell in Normandy). 1968: Il re dei Criminali (GB: Superargo. US: Superargo and the Faceless Giants). I lunghi giorni dell'odio. The Bang Bang Kid. 1969: Un posto all'inferno. La batalla del ultimo Panzer. Commando all'inferno. 1970: Retroguardia. 1971: Reverendo Colt. This Man Can't Die. 1975: Hatcher Bodine. Won Ton Ton, the Dog Who Saved Hollywood. The Pacific Connection. 1978: Where's Willie?

† Played as films in some countries

MAGNANI, Anna 1907–1973
Dark-haired, tempestuous, wild-eyed, angry-looking, Egyptian-born actress who became Italy's top star in post-war years. Despite a matronly figure, she took Hollywood by storm with the gale-force strength of her impassioned performances. She won an Oscar for The Rose Tattoo, and Paramount invited her back twice more. She was Oscar-nominated again for Wild is the Wind. Died, amid national mourning in Italy, from complications following a gall-bladder operation.
1927: Scampolo. 1934: La cieca di Sorrento. 1936: Tempo massimo. Cavalleria. Trenta secondi d'amore. 1937: La Principessa Tarakanova. 1939: Una lampada alla finestra. 1940: Finalmente soli. 1941: La fuggitiva. Teresa Venerdì (US: Doctor Beware). 1942: La fortuna viena dal cielo. 1943: L'ultima carrozzella. Campo de fiori (US: The Peddler and the Lady). T'amero sempre. La vita è bella. Abbasso la miseria. 1944: Il fiore sotto gli occhi. Rome – Open City/Open City. 1945: Un uomo ritorna. Abbasso la ricchezza. 1946: Il bandito. Davanti a lui tremava tutta Roma/Tosca. 1947: La sconosciuto di San Marino. Quartetto pazzo. L'onorevole Angelina (US: Angelina). 1948: Assunto Spina (US: Scarred). Molti sogni per le strade (GB: Woman Trouble). Amore (GB:

Ways of Love. US: The Miracle). 1949: Volcano. 1951: Bellissima. 1952: Camicie Rosse/ Anita Garibaldi. La carrozza d'oro (GB and US: The Golden Coach). 1953: Siamo donne (GB and US: We the Women). 1955: The Rose Tattoo. 1956: Suor Letizia. 1957: Wild is the Wind. 1958: Nella città l'inferno (GB: Caged. US: And the Wild, Wild Women). 1959: The Fugitive Kind. 1960: Risate di gioia (GB and US: The Passionate Thief). 1962: Mamma Roma. 1963: La magot de Joséfa. 1964: Volles Herz und leere Taschen. 1965: Made in Italy. 1969: The Secret of Santa Vittoria. 1972: 1870 (originally TV). Fellini's Roma.

MAHARIS, George 1928–
Dark, taciturn, plastic-looking American actor who had to wait years for his first big success, in the long-running television series Route 66. This took him into movies, but these lit no fires, and he has continued to be most busy on television. A graduate of the Actors' Studio, though you'd hardly notice if you didn't know.
1960: A Death of Princes (TV. GB: cinemas). Exodus. 1964: The Satan Bug. 1965: Sylvia. Quick Before It Melts. 1966: A Covenant with Death. 1967: The Happening. 1968: Escape to Mindanao (TV). The Desperados. 1969: Land Raiders. The Monk (TV). The Last Day of the War. 1972: The Victim (TV). 1974: Of Men and Women (TV). Come Die with Me (TV). Death in Space (TV). 1975: Murder on Flight 502 (TV). 1977: Look What's Happened to Rosemary's Baby (TV). SST – Death Flight (TV). 1978: Crash (TV). Return to Fantasy Island (TV). 1982: The Sword and the Sorcerer.

MAHONEY, Jock (Jacques O'Mahoney) 1919–
Tall, lean, whippy, fair-haired, jut-jawed American actor who gave up a military career to become a film stuntman. Became a featured player in second-feature westerns, and starred in a rip-roaring TV series, The Range Rider; then was gradually taken up by bigger studios, notably Universal-International. Played Tarzan in two films, but it seemed the role was his undoing and he faded from the scene. Stepfather of Sally Field (qv). Survived a severe stroke in the seventies.
1946: ‡South of the Chisholm Trail. ‡The Fighting Frontiersman. 1947: ‡Stranger from

Ponca City. ‡Golden Lady. ‡*Out West. 1948: ‡Smoky Mountain Melody. ‡*Squareheads of the Round Table. ‡Blazing Across the Pecos (GB: Under Arrest). 1949: ‡*Fuelin' Around. ‡*Punchy Cowpunchers.†The Doolins of Oklahoma (GB: The Great Manhunt).†Bandits of El Dorado (GB: Tricked). †The Blazing Trail. †Renegades of the Sage (GB: The Fort). Horsemen of the Sierras (GB: Remember Me). †Rim of the Canyon. †Frontier Marshal. †Strange Disappearance. 1950: †The Nevadan (GB: The Man from Nevada). †David Harding – Counterspy. †Cow Town (GB: Barbed Wire). †Texas Dynamo (GB: Suspected). †Jolson Sings Again. †Pecos River (GB: Without Risk). †Hoedown. †Lightning Guns (GB: Taking Sides). †Frontier Outpost. †Cody of the Pony Express (serial). 1951: †The Kangaroo Kid. †Santa Fé. †The Texas Rangers. †Rough Riders of Durango. †Roar of the Iron Horse (serial). 1952: **The Rough, Tough West. **Smoky Canyon. **Junction City. **The Kid from Broken Gun. **The Hawk of Wild River. **Laramie Mountains (GB: Mountain Desperadoes). 1953: **Gunfighters of the Northwest (serial). 1954: **Overland Pacific. *Knutzy Knights. 1955: A Day of Fury. 1956: Away All Boats. I've Lived Before. Battle Hymn. Showdown at Abilene. 1957: Joe Dakota. Slim Carter. The Land Unknown. 1958: Last of the Fast Guns. A Time to Live and a Time to Die. 1959: Money, Women and Guns. 1960: Three Blondes in His Life. Tarzan the Magnificent. 1962: Tarzan Goes to India. 1963: Tarzan's Three Challenges. California. 1964: The Walls of Hell. 1965: Marine Battleground. 1966: Moro Witch Doctor. Runaway Girl. 1967: The Glory Stompers. 1968: Bandolero! 1975: Tom. The Bad Bunch. 1978: The End.

‡As Jacques J. O'Mahoney †As Jock O'Mahoney **As Jack Mahoney

MAJORS, Lee (L. Yeary) 1942–
Husky, fair-haired American actor in the Hollywood beefcake tradition. His career has paralleled that of David Janssen, in that he had several hit TV series in a row (The Big Valley, Owen Marshall – Counselor at Law, The Six Million Dollar Man and The Fall Guy), while his feature films, though sometimes backed by big budgets, revealed his limited acting and were less successful. Married/ divorced Farrah Fawcett (qv), his second wife.

1964: †Strait-Jacket. 1967: Will Penny. 1969: The Ballad of Andy Crocker (TV). The Liberation of L.B. Jones. 1970: Weekend of Terror (TV). 1977: Gary Francis Powers – the True Story of the U2 Incident (TV). Just a Little Inconvenience (TV. GB: cinemas). 1978: Killer Fish. The Norseman. 1979: Steel. Ladyfingers. 1980: Agency. Sharks! The Last Chase. Circle of Two. High Noon: Part II (TV). The Fall Guy (TV). 1982: Starflight One (TV. GB: cinemas).

†As Lee Yeary

MALDEN, Karl (K. Mladen Sekulovich) 1913–
Plum-nosed, rasp-voiced, distinctive and likeable American actor whose receding dark hair was sometimes in latter years covered by a toupé. Used in supporting roles by Fox in their realist thrillers of the late 1940s, but in a variety of leading roles after an Academy Award (best supporting actor) for A Streetcar Named Desire. From 1972 to 1977 he became entrenched in a very popular TV crime series The Streets of San Francisco. Additional Oscar nomination for On the Waterfront.
1940: They Knew What They Wanted. 1944: Winged Victory. 1946: 13 Rue Madeleine. 1947: Boomerang. Kiss of Death. 1950: Where the Sidewalk Ends. The Gunfighter. Halls of Montezuma. 1951: The Sellout. A Streetcar Named Desire. Decision before Dawn. 1952: Diplomatic Courier. Ruby Gentry. Operation Secret. 1953: Take the High Ground. I Confess. 1954: Phantom of the Rue Morgue. On the Waterfront. 1956: Baby Doll. 1957: Fear Strikes Out. Bombers B-52 (GB: No Sleep

Till Dawn). 1958: The Hanging Tree. 1960: Pollyanna. One Eyed Jacks. The Great Imposter. 1961: Parrish. All Fall Down. 1962: Bird Man of Alcatraz. Gypsy. How the West Was Won. Come Fly with Me. 1964: Dead Ringer (GB: Dead Image). Cheyenne Autumn. 1965: The Cincinnati Kid. The Adventures of Bullwhip Griffin. 1966: Nevada Smith. Murderers' Row. 1967: Hotel. Billion Dollar Brain. 1968: Blue. Hot Millions. 1969: Patton (GB: Patton – Lust for Glory). Cat o' Nine Tails. 1971: Wild Rovers. The Summertime Killer. 1978: Captains Courageous (TV). 1979: Beyond the Poseidon Adventure. Meteor. 1980: The Wildcatters/Skag (TV). 1981: Word of Honor (TV). Miracle on Ice (TV). 1982: Twilight Time. 1983: The Sting II. 1984: Intent to Kill (TV). 1986: Billy Galvin.

MALONE, Dorothy (D. Maloney) 1925–
Tall, pretty, soulful-looking American leading lady. After 12 years of honest, professional but hardly inspired performances as brunette nice girls she turned to blonde floozies and immediately won an Oscar for one such lady in Written on the Wind. But now she was typed in another sort of role and 'instead of getting better, my parts just got worse'. Married to actor Jacques Bergerac (1927–) – first of three – from 1959 to 1964.
1943: †The Falcon and the Co-Eds. †Gildersleeve on Broadway. †Higher and Higher. 1944: †Youth Runs Wild. †Show Business. †One Mysterious Night (GB: Behind Closed Doors). †Hollywood Canteen. †Seven Days Ashore. 1945: *Frontier Days. Too Young to Know. 1946: Janie Gets Married. Night and Day. The Big Sleep. 1948: Two Guys from Texas (GB: Two Texas Knights). To the Victor. One Sunday Afternoon. 1949: Flaxy Martin. South of St. Louis. Colorado Territory. 1950: The Nevadan (GB: The Man from Nevada). Mrs O'Malley and Mr Malone. The Killer That Stalked New York (GB: Frightened City). Convicted. 1951: Saddle Legion. The Bushwhackers (GB: The Rebel). 1952: Torpedo Alley. 1953: Scared Stiff. Law and Order. Jack Slade (GB: Slade). 1954: Pushover. Loophole. Security Risk. The Lone Gun. Private Hell 36. The Fast and the Furious. Young at Heart. 1955: Five Guns West. Tall Man Riding. Sincerely Yours. Artists and Models. Battle Cry. At Gunpoint (GB: Gunpoint!). 1956: Pillars of the Sky (GB: The

Tomahawk and the Cross). Tension at Table Rock. Written on the Wind. 1957: Quantez. Man of a Thousand Faces. Tip on a Dead Jockey (GB: Time for Action). The Tarnished Angels. 1958: Too Much, Too Soon. 1959: Warlock. 1960: The Last Voyage. 1961: The Last Sunset. 1963: Beach Party. 1964: Fate is the Hunter. 1969: The Pigeon (TV). Femmine insaziabili (GB: The Insatiables. US: Carnal Circuit). 1970: Exzess. 1975: The Man Who Would Not Die (GB: TV). Abduction. 1976: The November Plan. 1977: Golden Rendezvous. Winter Kills (released 1979). Little Ladies of the Night (TV). 1978: Murder in Peyton Place (TV). Katie: Portrait of a Centerfold (TV). Good Luck, Miss Wyckoff. 1979: The Day Time Ended. 1980: Easter Sunday. 1983: The Being. 1984: He's Not Your Son! (TV). 1985: Peyton Place: The Next Generation (TV).

† As Dorothy Maloney

MANGANO, Silvana 1930–
This red-headed Italian sexpot, still best remembered for her busty, pouty, thigh-booted paddy-field girl in Bitter Rice, stayed in third place behind Loren and Lollobrigida in a hot league, but remained in films (and married top Italian producer Dino de Laurentiis). A beauty contest winner of English-Sicilian parentage, she eventually proved her ability with some strong performances in later years.
1946: L'elisir d'amore (GB: Elixir of Love. US: This Wine of Love). 1947: Il delitto di Giovanni Episcopo (US: Flesh Will Surrender). 1948: Le carrefour de passion. 1949: Black Magic. Riso amaro/Bitter Rice. 1950: Il lupo della Sila (GB: The Wolf of Sila. US: Lure of the Sila). Il Brigante Musolino (GB: Fugitive). 1951: Anna. 1953: Ulysses. 1954: Mambo. 1955: L'oro di Napoli (GB: Gold of Naples. US: Every Day's a Holiday). 1956: Uomini e lupi/Men and Wolves. 1958: La diga sul Pacifico (GB: The Sea Wall. US: This Angry Age). Tempest. 1959: La grande guerra (US: The Great War). Five Branded Women. 1960: Crimen (GB: Killing in Monte Carlo. US: . . . And Suddenly It's Murder). 1961: Il giudizio universale (US: The Last Judgment). Barabbas. 1962: Il processo di Verona. 1963: La mia signora. 1965: Il disco volante. 1966: Io, io, io . . . e gli altri. Le streghe/The Witches. 1967: Oedipus Rex. Scusi, lei è favorevole o

contrario? 1968: Teorema/Theorem. Viaggio di Lavoro. Capriccio all'Italiana. 1971: Morte a Venezia/Death in Venice. The Decameron. Scipione detto anche l'Africano. 1972: Ludwig/Ludwig II. 1973: The Scientific Cardplayer. D'amor si muore. 1975: Gruppo di famiglia in un interno (GB and US: Conversation Piece). 1983: Dune. 1986: The Good Ship Ulysses.

MANNHEIM, Lucie 1895–1976
Sharp-faced, dark-haired, rather anguished-looking German actress. Came to Britain in the mid-1930s, and not only stayed to avoid the Nazis, but married Marius Goring (qv). The best-recalled of her film roles is the mysterious victim at the beginning of Hitchcock's The 39 Steps, but her film appearances were generally so wide apart that her cinema career is almost a chart of her life at various ages.
1922: Der sternende Reiter. 1923: Die Austreibung. Die Prinzessin Suwarin. Der Puppenmacher von Kiang-Ning. Der Schatz. 1929: Atlantik. 1930: Der Ball. 1931: Danton. 1933: Madame wünscht keine Kinder. 1935: The 39 Steps. 1936: East Meets West. 1937: The High Command. 1943: Yellow Canary. 1944: Tawny Pipit. Hotel Reserve. *The True Story of Lilli Marlene. 1952: So Little Time. The Man Who Watched Trains Go By (US: Paris Express). Nachts auf der Strassen. 1953: Ich und Du. 1954: Das ideale Brautpaar. 1955: Du darfst nicht länger schweigen. Die Stadt ist voller Geheimnisse. 1957: Erauenarzt Dr Betram. 1958: Gestehen Sire, Dr Corda (GB: Confess, Dr Corda). Ihr 106. Geburtstag. Der eiserne Gustav. 1959: Arzt aus Leidenschaft. 1960: Der letzte Zeuge. Erste Liebe. Beyond the Curtain. 1965: Bunny Lake is Missing.

MANSFIELD, Jayne (Vera Jane Palmer) 1932–1967
Pneumatic American blonde star with little to offer beyond outsize breasts, a cute face and a little-girl voice – enough to propel her to stardom in a few major films at that home of busty blondes through the years, Twentieth Century-Fox. The seemingly inevitable downward spiral through men, drink, drugs and semi-nude appearances in night-clubs has been graphically depicted in a thousand newspaper stories. Died in a car crash.
1950: Prehistoric Women. The Big Hangover. 1954: Underwater. Female Jungle. 1955: Pete

Kelly's Blues. Illegal. The Burglar. 1956: Hell on Frisco Bay. The Girl Can't Help It. 1957: Will Success Spoil Rock Hunter? (GB: Oh! For a Man). The Wayward Bus. Kiss Them for Me. 1958: The Sheriff of Fractured Jaw. 1960: The Loves of Hercules. The Challenge. Too Hot to Handle (US: Playgirl after Dark). 1961: The George Raft Story (GB: Spin of a Coin). 1962: It Happened in Athens. 1963: Promises! Promises! Homesick for St Paul/Heimweh nach St Pauli. Panic Button. 1964: When Strangers Meet (US: Dog Eat Dog). L'amore primitivo (GB: Primitive Love). 1965: Single Room Furnished (released 1967). 1966: The Fat Spy. Las Vegas Hillbillys (GB: Country Music USA). 1967: A Guide for the Married Man. The Wild, Wild World of Jayne Mansfield. Spree. Mondo Hollywood.

MARA, Adele (Adelaida Delgado) 1923–
Slinky, brown-eyed blonde dancer, singer and actress who moved from Columbia to Republic in 1943 and was immediately worked overtime by that studio as the heroine – occasionally bad girl – of numerous second-features throughout the decade. She worked her way slowly up to bigger things by 1948, but disappointed her legions of admirers by drifting out of films and concentrating on marriage to writer-producer Roy Huggins. Still occasionally seen on TV.
*1941: *The Great Glover. Navy Blues. 1942: Shut My Big Mouth. Alias Boston Blackie. You Were Never Lovelier. Blondie Goes to College. Lucky Legs. Vengeance of the West. 1943: Reveille with Beverly. Riders of the Northwest Mounted. Redhead from Manhattan. Good Luck, Mr Yates. 1944: The Fighting Seabees. Atlantic City. Faces in the Fog.*

Thoroughbreds. 1945: The Vampire's Ghost. Flame of the Barbary Coast. Bells of Rosarita. Song of Mexico. The Tiger Woman. Girls of the Big House. Grissly's Millions. A Guy Could Change. 1946: The Invisible Informer. The Inner Circle. I've Always Loved You. Passkey to Danger. The Last Crooked Mile. Night Train to Memphis. The Catman of Paris. Traffic in Crime. The Pilgrim Lady. 1947: The Magnificent Rogue. Exposed. Web of Danger. Campus Honeymoon. Twilight on the Rio Grande. Robin Hood of Texas. Blackmail. The Trespasser. 1948: Nighttime in Nevada. I, Jane Doe (US: Diary of a Bride). Angel in Exile. The Gallant Legion. Wake of the Red Witch. The Main Street Kid. 1949: Sands of Iwo Jima. 1950: Rock Island Trail. California Passage. The Avengers. 1951: The Sea Hornet. 1953: Count the Hours (GB: Every Minute Counts). 1956: The Black Whip. Border Showdown (TV. GB: cinemas). Back from Eternity. 1958: Curse of the Faceless Man. 1959: The Big Circus.

MARCH, Fredric (Ernest Frederick Bickel) 1897–1975
Dark, stocky American leading man who settled in Hollywood with the coming of sound and remained in top roles for over 20 years, especially in the period between his two Oscars (for *Dr Jekyll and Mr Hyde* and *The Best Years of Our Lives*) when his mellifluous voice and clever, self-effacing style won him a wide variety of roles, and he proved unexpectedly adept at sophisticated comedy. Always, in fact, rather more an actor than a star personality. Married (second of two) Florence Eldridge (F. McKechnie: 1901–) in 1927. He also received Oscar nominations for *A Star is Born*, *The Royal Family of Broadway* and *Death of a Salesman*.
1921: The Glorious Adventure. Paying the Piper. 1929: Footlights and Fools. The Dummy. The Studio Murder Mystery. Jealousy. The Wild Party. Paris Bound. The Marriage Playground. 1930: Paramount on Parade. Sarah and Son. Manslaughter. The Royal Family of Broadway. Ladies Love Brutes. True to the Navy. Laughter. 1931: My Sin. Honor among Lovers. The Night Angel. Dr Jekyll and Mr Hyde. 1932: Strangers in Love. Merrily We Go to Hell (GB: Merrily We Go to —). Make Me a Star. Smilin' Through. The Sign of the Cross. 1933: The Eagle and the Hawk. Tonight

*is Ours. Design for Living. 1934: Good Dame (GB: Good Girl). All of Me. The Barretts of Wimpole Street. We Live Again. Death Takes a Holiday. The Affairs of Cellini. 1935: Les Miserables. Anna Karenina. The Dark Angel. 1936: Mary of Scotland. The Road to Glory. Anthony Adverse. 1937: Nothing Sacred. A Star is Born. 1938: The Buccaneer. Trade Winds. There Goes My Heart. 1939: The 400 Million (narrator only). 1940: Victory. Susan and God (GB: The Gay Mrs Trexel). *Lights Out in Europe. 1941: So Ends Our Night. One Foot in Heaven. Bedtime Story. *Cavalcade of the Academy Awards. 1942: I Married a Witch. *Lake Carrier. 1944: Tomorrow the World. The Adventures of Mark Twain. *Salute to France. 1946: The Best Years of Our Lives. 1948: An Act of Murder. Another Part of the Forest. 1949: Christopher Columbus. 1950: The Titan – the Story of Michelangelo (and narrator). 1951: Death of a Salesman. It's a Big Country. 1953: Man on a Tightrope. 1954: Executive Suite. The Bridges at Toko-Ri. 1955: The Desperate Hours. 1956: Alexander the Great. The Man in the Gray Flannel Suit. 1957: Albert Schweitzer (narrator only). 1959: Middle of the Night. 1960: Inherit the Wind. 1962: The Condemned of Altona. 1964: Seven Days in May. 1966: Hombre. 1969: ... tick ... tick ... tick. 1973: The Iceman Cometh.*

MARSH, Joan (Nancy Ann Rosher) 1913–
Cute, button-nosed, fresh-looking platinum blonde American actress of the 1930s. The daughter of ace cameraman Charles Rosher, she appeared as a young child in several of the films on which he worked, before reappearing at Universal at 17 under the name of Joan Marsh. She never really got a chance to excel at her forte – singing and dancing – and played a number of ingenues, second-leads and leads in minor films before drifting away from Hollywood after World War II.
1915: † The Mad Maid of the Forest. 1917: †A Little Princess. 1918: †One Hundred Per Cent American. †Johanna Enlists. 1919: †Daddy Long Legs. †Captain Kidd Junior. †The Heart o' the Hills. 1920: †Pollyanna. †Suds. 1921: †Little Lord Fauntleroy. †The Love Light. †Through the Back Door. † Young Mrs Winthrop. 1922: †Tess of the Storm Country. †Hearts Aflame. 1930: The King of Jazz. Little Accident. Eyes of the World. All Quiet on the Western Front. Shipmates. 1931: Inspi-

ration. Meet the Wife. Three Girls Lost. A Tailor Made Man. Dance Fools Dance. Politics. Maker of Men. 1932: Are You Listening? The Wet Parade. Bachelor's Affairs. That's My Boy. The Speed Demon. 1933: Daring Daughters (GB: Behind the Counter). It's Great To Be Alive. The Man Who Dared. High Gear (GB: The Big Thrill). Three-Cornered Moon. Rainbow Over Broadway. 1934: You're Telling Me. Many Happy Returns. We're Rich Again. 1935: Anna Karenina. 1936: Champagne for Breakfast. Dancing Feet. 1937: Charlie Chan on Broadway. Hot Water. Life Begins in College (GB: The Joy Parade). 1938: Brilliant Marriage. The Lady Objects. 1939: Fast and Loose. Idiot's Delight. 1941: The Road to Zanzibar. 1942: Police Bullets. Keep 'Em Slugging. The Man in the Trunk. 1943: Mr Muggs Steps Out. 1944: Follow the Leader. 1945: Mr Muggs Rides Again.

† As Nancy Ann Rosher (when billed)

MARSH, Mae (Mary Marsh) 1895–1968
Round-faced, auburn-haired American star with Irish colouring – she would have been perfect for an early Technicolor test – Mae Marsh was one of the foremost actresses of the early silent era (particularly in films by D. W. Griffith), mostly in deglamourized or anguished roles. Retired in 1926 to start a family, but came back in 1931 to play off-and-on character roles in the cinema (frequently for director John Ford) for the rest of her life. Died from a heart attack.
1911: Fighting Blood. *Home Folks. 1912: *The Old Actor. A Siren of Impulse. *The Lesser Evil. *Lena and the Geese. The New York Hat. Man's Genesis. *One is Business. *The Other Crime. *The Sands of Dee. *Brutality. *An Adventure in the Autumn Woods. *When Kings Were Law. *Just Like a Woman. *The Parasite. *Oil and Water. *The Telephone Girl and the Lady. Indian Uprising at Santa Fé. A Temporary Truce. *The Spirit Awakening/*The Spirit Awakened. *The Kentucky Girl. 1913: *Fate. *Love in an Apartment Hotel. *The Perfidy of Mary. *The Little Tease. *The Wanderer. *His Mother's Son. *The Reformers. Judith of Bethulia. The Battle of Elderberry Gulch. In Prehistoric Days. *Broken Ways. *The Tender-Hearted Boy. Brothers. Near to Earth. The Lady and the Mouse. By Man's Law. *Influence of the

Unknown. *Two Men of the Desert. *The Primitive Man. One Exciting Night. 1914: The Escape. The Avenging Conscience (GB: Thou Shalt Not Kill). The Great Leap. The Swindlers. Moonshine Molly. The Genius. Paid with Interest. Home Sweet Home. Down by the Sounding Sea. Big James' Heart. *Brute Force. 1915: The Birth of a Nation. The Outcast. The Victim. The Shattered Idol. 1916: Intolerance. Hoodoo Ann. The Wharf Rat. A Child of the Paris Street. The Little Liar. The Marriage of Molly-O. The Wild Girl. 1917: Polly of the Circus. Sunshine Alley. The Cinderella Man. 1918: The Beloved Traitor. All Woman. Spotlight Sadie. The Face in the Dark. Money Mad. Hidden Fires. The Racing Strain. Fields of Honor. The Glorious Adventure. 1919: The Mother and the Law (extended version of episode from Intolerance). The Bondage of Barbara. 1920: The Little 'Fraid Lady. 1921: Nobody's Kid. 1922: Flames of Passion. Till We Meet Again. 1923: The White Rose. Paddy-the-Next-Best-Thing. 1924: Daddies. A Woman's Secret. Arabella. 1925: The Rat. 1926: Tides of Passion. 1928: Racing Through. 1931: Over the Hill. 1932: That's My Boy. Rebecca of Sunnybrook Farm. 1933: Alice in Wonderland. 1934: Little Man, What Now? Bachelor of Arts. 1935: Black Fury. 1936: Hollywood Boulevard. 1939: Drums Along the Mohawk. 1940: The Man Who Wouldn't Talk. The Grapes of Wrath. Young People. 1941: Remember the Day. How Green Was My Valley. Tobacco Road. Belle Starr. Swamp Water (GB: The Man Who Came Back). Great Guns. Blue, White and Perfect. 1942: The Loves of Edgar Allan Poe. Son of Fury. Quiet Please, Murder. Tales of Manhattan. 1943: Dixie Dugan. The Song of Bernadette. Jane Eyre. 1944: The Sullivans. In the Meantime, Darling. 1945: Leave Her to Heaven. A Tree Grows in Brooklyn. The Dolly Sisters. 1946: My Darling Clementine. The Late George Apley. 1947: Thunder in the Valley (GB: Bob, Son of Battle). 1948: Apartment for Peggy. The Snake Pit. Three Godfathers. Fort Apache. Deep Waters. 1949: Impact. Everybody Does It. It Happens Every Spring. The Fighting Kentuckian. 1950: When Willie Comes Marching Home. My Blue Heaven. The Gunfighter. The Model and the Marriage Broker. 1952: The Quiet Man. Night without Sleep. 1953: The Sun Shines Bright. Titanic. A Blueprint for Murder. The Robe. 1955: Prince of Players. The Tall Men. Good Morning, Miss Dove. Hell on Frisco Bay. 1956: While the City Sleeps. Julie. The Searchers. Girls in Prison. 1957: The Wings of Eagles. 1958: Cry Terror! 1960: From the Terrace. Sergeant Rutledge. 1961: Two Rode Together. 1963: Donovan's Reef. 1964: Cheyenne Autumn. 1967: Arabella (and 1924 film of same title).

MARSH, Marian (Violet Krauth) 1913–
Sweet-faced, blonde, petite leading lady of 1930s' Hollywood films who usually played wilting violets or girls in danger. Born in Trinidad of mixed descent, she came to Hollywood at 17 and was almost immediately chosen by John Barrymore to star with him

in Svengali (as Trilby) and The Mad Genius. Her last good leading roles came in 1935 and she retired at 30.
1930: †Whoopee. 1931: Svengali. Five Star Final. The Road to Singapore. The Mad Genius. Under Eighteen. 1932: Beauty and the Boss. Alias the Doctor. Strange Justice. The Sport Parade. 1933: Daring Daughters (GB: Behind the Counter). The Eleventh Commandment. Notorious But Nice. 1934: A Man of Sentiment. I Like It That Way. Love at Second Sight. Over the Garden Wall. 1935: In Spite of Danger. A Girl of the Limberlost. Unknown Woman. Crime and Punishment. The Black Room. 1936: Lady of Secrets. Counterfeit. The Man Who Lived Twice. 1937: Come Closer Folks. When's Your Birthday? The Great Gambini. Saturday's Heroes. 1938: Youth on Parade. Prison Nurse. 1939: It Happened in Paris. Missing Daughters. 1940: Fugitive from a Prison Camp. 1941: Murder by Invitation. 1942: Gentleman from Dixie. House of Errors.

† As Marilyn Morgan

MARSHALL, Brenda (Ardis Gaines) 1915–
Lovely brunette American actress (actually born in the Philippines) who was a rival to Gene Tierney for sheer facial beauty, and mostly played ladies in danger in colourful adventure stories. She seemed to lose some degree of interest in her film career after marrying William Holden (qv) in 1941, but it eventually ended in divorce 30 years later.
1939: Espionage Agent. 1940: The Man Who Talked Too Much. The Sea Hawk. Money and

MASTROIANNI, Marcello 1923–

Dark-haired, bright-eyed, charming Italian star, not unlike Louis Jourdan, but with more hints of both mischief and melancholy about the eyes. Thus he has been equally at home over the years with comedy, romance and emotional torment. Since the 1960s he has formed something of a latter-day romantic team with Sophia Loren (*qv*): they have made several films together. Nominated for Academy Awards in *Divorzio all' Italiana/Divorce Italian Style* and *Una giornata particolare/A Special Day*.

1947: I miserabili. 1949: Cuori sul mare. Vent'anni. Domenica d'Agosto (GB: Sunday in August). 1950: Vita da cane. 1951: Atto di accusa. A Tale of Five Cities. Contro la legge. Parigi e' sempre Parigi. Sensualita'. Le ragazze di piazza di Spagna (GB: Girls of the Spanish Steps. US: Three Girls from Rome). 1952: L'eterna Catena. Tragico ritorno. Lulu. Gli eroi della Domenica. Penne nere. 1953: Il viale della speranza. La valigia dei sogni. Non e' mai troppo tardi. Siamo donne (GB and US: We the Women). Cronache di poveri amanti. 1954: Tempi nostri (US: The Anatomy of Love). Casa Ricordi. Peccato che sia una canaglia (GB and US: Too Bad She's Bad). Tam-Tam Mayumba. Giorni d'amore. La schiava del peccato. Febbre di vivere. 1955: La fortuna di essere donna (GB and US: Lucky to be a Woman). Le bella mugnaia (GB: The Miller's Wife. US: The Miller's Beautiful Wife). La principessa della Canarie. 1956: Il bigamo/The Bigamist. 1957: Un ettaro di cielo. Padre e figli (US: A Tailor's Maid). La ragazza della-salina. Il momento più bello. Le notti bianche (GB and US: White Nights). Il medico e lo stregone. 1958: La loi (GB and US: Where the Hot Wind Blows). Racconti d'estate (GB: Girls for the Summer. US: Love on the Riviera). I soliti ignoti (US: Big Deal on Madonna Street). 1959: Tutti innamorati. Il nemico di mia moglie. Ferdinand of Naples. La dolce vita. 1960: La notte. Fantasmi a Roma (GB: Phantom Lovers. US: Ghosts of Rome). Il bell' Antonio. Adua e la compagne (US: Love à la Carte). 1961: L'assassino (US: The Lady Killer from Rome). Vie privée (GB and US: A Very Private Affair). Divorzio all'Italia/Divorce Italian Style. 1962: Cronaca familiare (GB and US: Family Diary). 8½. I compagni (US: The Organizer). Il giorno più corto (US: The Shortest Day). Yesterday,

Today and Tomorrow. 1964: Marriage, Italian Style. 1965: Io, io, io ... e gli altri. Paranoia (US: Kiss the Other Sheik). The 10th Victim. Casanova 70. The Organiser. 1966: The Poppy is Also a Flower (TV. GB: cinemas, as Danger Grows Wild). Shoot Loud ... Louder, I Don't Understand. 1967: Lo straniero/The Stranger. 1968: Diamonds for Breakfast. Amanti (GB and US: A Place for Lovers). Questi fantasmi (GB and US: Ghosts Italian Style). 1969: Sunflower. 1970: Dramma della gelosia (US: Jealousy Italian Style. US: The Pizza Triangle). Leo the Last. Scipione, detto anche 'l' Africano'. The Priest's Wife. 1971: Permette? Rocco Papaleo (US: Rocco Papaleo). 1972: Liza. Mordi e fuggi (US: Bite and Run). What? Ça n'arrive qu'aux autres. 1870. Melampo. 1973: La grande bouffe (GB and US: Blow-Out). Rappresaglia (GB and US: Massacre in Rome). Salut l'artiste (US: The Bit Player). L'événement le plus important depuis que l'homme a marché sur la lune (GB: The Slightly Pregnant Man. US: A Slightly Pregnant Man). 1974: Touchez pas la femme blanche. C'eravamo tanto amati (GB: We All Loved Each Other So Much). Allosanfàn. 1975: Culastrisce, nobile veneziano. Down the Ancient Stairs. La divine creatura (US: The Divine Nymph). La donna delle Domenica/The Sunday Woman. 1976: La fantasie amorose di Luca Maria nobile Veneto. Signore e signori, buonanotte. 1977: Una giornata particolare/A Special Day. Mogliamante (GB and US: Wifemistress). Ciao male/Bye Bye Monkey!/The Monkey's Uncle. Doppo delitto/Double Murders. 1978: L'ingorgo (US: Traffic Jam). Vengeance (US: Revenge). 1979: Shimmy Lugano e tarantelle e tarallucci e vino. Blood Feud. Le citta delle donne. Cosi come sei (US: Stay As You Are). L'embouteillage. Giallo Napoletano. 1980: Atti atrocissimi di amore e di vendetta. Todo mondo. La terrazza. 1981: La pelle. Fantôme d'amour. 1982: Revolution. Oltre la porta (GB: Beyond the Door). The New World. 1983: Il generale dell' armata morta. Gabriela. Enrico IV. 1984: Il fu Mattia Pascal (US: The Two Lives of Mattia Pascal). 1985: Ginger and Fred. Macaroni. The Legend of the Holy Drinker. I soliti ignoti 20 anni doppo (US: Big Deal on Madonna Street – Update). 1986: The Good Ship Ulysses. Death of a Beekeeper.

MATHEWS, Carole 1920–

This Hollywood actress with the cynical smile (no wonder) and the piled-high head of golden hair at least deserves ten out of ten for trying. She played tiny, sometimes even bit parts, on stage and screen from the early forties right through to the fifties. By 1950 she had at least clawed her way up to leading lady in second-features, a position she held on to until the end of the decade. Her performances were almost always better than her roles.

1944: Together Again. Girl in the Case (GB: The Silver Key). Swing in the Saddle (GB: Swing and Sway). The Missing Juror. She's a Sweetheart. Strange Affair. Tahiti Nights. 1945: Outlaws of the Rockies (GB: A Roving Rogue). Blazing the Western Trail (GB: Who Killed Waring?). I Love a Mystery. Over 21. A Thousand and One Nights. Sing Me a Song of Texas (GB: Fortune Hunter). Ten Cents a Dance (GB: Dancing Ladies). The Monster and the Ape (serial). 1946: Stars over Texas. 1948: Sealed Verdict. The Accused. 1949: Massacre River. Special Agent. Chicago Deadline. The Great Gatsby. Amazon Quest (GB: Amazon). Cry Murder. 1950: No Man of Her Own. Paid in Full. 1951: The Man with My Face. 1952: Red Snow. Meet Me at the Fair. 1953: Two Gun Marshal (TV. GB: cinemas). City of Bad Men. Shark River. 1954: Port of Hell. Treasure of Ruby Hills. 1955: Betrayed Women. 1956: Assignment Redhead (US Requirement for a Redhead). Swamp Women. 1957: Showdown at Boot Hill. 1958: Strange Awakening (US: Female Fiends). 1960: 13 Fighting Men. 1961: Tender is the Night. Look in Any Window. 1970: Rabbit, Run.

MATHEWS, Kerwin 1926–

Tall, leanly handsome, clean-cut, quietly spoken American leading man with light wavy hair. He switched from teaching to acting in his late twenties, and unexpectedly became the dashing star of several Dynamation/Arabian Nights adventure tales. Still crops up occasionally, usually in oddball adventure yarns.

1955: Five Against the House. 1956: The Country Husband (TV. GB: cinemas). 1957: The Garment Jungle. 1958: Tarawa Beachhead. The Last Blitzkrieg. The Seventh Voyage of Sinbad. 1960: The Three Worlds of Gulliver. Sappho (GB: The Warrior Empress). Man on a String (GB: Confessions of a Counterspy). 1961: Jack the Giant Killer. The Devil at Four O'Clock. The Pirates of Blood River. 1962:

Maniac. 1963: OSS 117 se dechaine. The Waltz King. 1964: Banco à Bangkok pour OSS 117 (GB: Shadow of Evil). 1967: Battle beneath the Earth. The Viscount. Ghostbreaker (TV). 1968: Faccia D'Angelo/Zucker für den Mörder (GB: The Killer Likes Candy). 1969: Barquero. 1971: Octaman. Death Takes a Holiday (TV). 1973: The Boy Who Cried Werewolf. 1978: Nightmare in Blood.

MATTHAU, Walter (W. Matuschanskayasky) 1920–

Growly, dark-haired, bloodhound-faced, phlegmatic American actor whose mastery of comic timing and crumpled features were at first hidden behind conventional villain roles. From 1962 to 1965 he stole too many films from the stars to be denied leading parts, and an Oscar for *The Fortune Cookie* clinched his position as an unconventional superstar. Received further Oscar nominations for *Kotch* and *The Sunshine Boys*.

1955: The Kentuckian. The Indian Fighter. 1956: Bigger Than Life. 1957: Slaughter on 10th Avenue. Voice in the Mirror. A Face in the Crowd. 1958: Onionhead. King Creole. Ride a Crooked Trail. 1960: ‡The Gangster Story. Strangers When We Meet. 1962: Lonely Are the Brave. Who's Got the Action? 1963: Island of Love. Charade. 1964: Ensign Pulver. Goodbye Charlie. Fail Safe. 1965: Mirage. 1966: The Fortune Cookie (GB: Meet Whiplash Willie). 1967: A Guide for the Married Man. The Odd Couple. 1968: The Secret Life of an American Wife. Candy. 1969: Hello! Dolly. Cactus Flower. 1970: A New Leaf. 1971: Plaza Suite. Kotch. 1972: Pete 'n' Tillie. 1973: Charley Varrick. The Laughing Policeman (GB: An Investigation of Murder). 1974: †Earthquake. The Taking of Pelham 1-2-3. The Front Page. 1975: The Sunshine Boys. The Gentleman Tramp (narrator only). 1976: The Bad News Bears. 1977: Casey's Shadow. 1978: House Calls. California Suite. 1979: Funny Business (narrator only). Little Miss Marker. 1980: Hopscotch. Portrait of a 60% Perfect Man. 1981: Buddy Buddy. First Monday in October. 1982: I Ought to be in Pictures. 1983: The Survivors. 1985: Pirates. Movers and Shakers (Dreamers). 1986: Born Yesterday.

† *as Walter Matuschanskayasky*
‡ *Also directed*

MATTHEWS, Jessie 1907–1981

Dark-haired, sylph-like, big-eyed British singer and dancer with round-faced, little-girl looks and bell-like voice. She wore sizzling costumes in her musical numbers without losing her winsome appeal and became Britain's only home-grown world star of the thirties. Missed the opportunity of Hollywood stardom in the early thirties, choosing to remain in England for the sake of a (second of three) marriage to Sonnie Hale (in 1931) that would end in 1944.

*1923: The Beloved Vagabond. This England. 1924: Straws in the Wind. 1931: Out of the Blue. 1932: There Goes the Bride. The Midshipmaid. The Man from Toronto. 1933: The Good Companions. Friday the Thirteenth. 1934: Waltzes from Vienna (US: Strauss's Great Waltz). Evergreen. 1935: First a Girl. 1936: It's Love Again. 1937: *Secrets of the Stars. Head over Heels (US: Head over Heels in Love). Gangway. 1938: Sailing Along. Climbing High. 1943: Forever and a Day. 1944: Candles at Nine. Life is Nothing without Music. 1947: Making the Grade. 1958: Tom Thumb. 1977: The Hound of the Baskervilles. 1980: †Second to the Right and On till Morning. Never Never Land.*

As director: *1944: †Victory Wedding.*
† *Scenes deleted from final release print.*

MATURE, Victor 1915–

Big, craggy, black-haired, open-mouthed American star, the forerunner of a new, muscular kind of leading man, who would take over from the lounge lizards of the thirties and be dubbed 'beefcake' by the Press. His Greek-type good looks were mostly seen in open-air action yarns, and he drifted away from films after passing 45.

1939: The Housekeeper's Daughter. 1940: One Million BC (GB: Man and His Mate). Captain Caution. No, No, Nanette. 1941: The Shanghai Gesture. I Wake Up Screaming (GB: Hot Spot). 1942: Song of the Islands. My Gal Sal. Footlight Serenade. Seven Days' Leave. 1946: My Darling Clementine. 1947: Kiss of Death. Moss Rose. 1948: Fury at Furnace Creek. Cry of the City. 1949: Red, Hot and Blue. Easy Living. Samson and Delilah. 1950: Wabash Avenue. I'll Get By. Gambling House. Stella. 1952: The Las Vegas Story. Androcles and the Lion. Something for the Birds. Million Dollar Mermaid (GB: The One Piece Bathing suit). 1953: The Glory Brigade. Affair with a Stranger. The Robe. Veils of Bagdad. 1954: Demetrius and the Gladiators. Betrayed. Dangerous Mission. The Egyptian. 1955: Chief Crazy Horse (GB: Valley of Fury). Violent Saturday. The Last Frontier. 1956: Zarak. Safari. The Sharkfighters. 1957: Interpol (US: Pick-Up Alley). The Long Haul. 1958: No Time to Die! (US: Tank Force). China Doll. 1959: The Bandit of Zhobe. Escort West. Timbuktu. The Big Circus. 1960: Hannibal. The Tartars. 1966: After the Fox. 1968: Head. 1972: Every Little Crook and Nanny. 1975: Won Ton Ton, the Dog Who Saved Hollywood. 1978: Firepower. 1984: Samson and Delilah (TV).

MAUREY, Nicole 1925–

Auburn-haired, square-jawed French actress who had a middling career in her own country before her selection to co-star with Bing Crosby led to Hollywood. She left Paramount after a couple of films, and she made most of her remaining movies in England.

1944: Le cavalier noir. 1948: Les joyeux conscrits. 1949: Blondine. 1950: Le journal d'un curé de campagne (GB and US: Diary of a Country Priest). 1951: Le dernier robin des bois (GB: Smugglers at the Castle). 1952: Opération Magali. Rendez-vous à Grenade. 1953: Les compagnes de la nuit (GB: Companions of the Night). L'ennemi public No. 1. L'oeil en coulisses. Little Boy Lost. Si Versailles m'était conté. 1954: Secret of the Incas. L'aiglon. 1955: The Constant Husband. 1956: The Weapon. The Bold and the Brave. 1957: Rogue's Yarn. To Catch a Spy. 1958: Me and the Colonel.

Paris Streetwalker. 1959: The House of the Seven Hawks. The Scapegoat. The Jayhawkers. 1960: His and Hers. High Time. 1961: Don't Bother to Knock (US: Why Bother to Knock?). 1962: The Day of the Triffids. 1963: The Very Edge. 1965: Pleins feux sur Stanislaus. 1977: Gloria. 1981: Chanel Solitaire.

MAXWELL, Lois (L. Hooker) 1927–
This durable, much-travelled, tall Canadian actress with light auburn hair and sunny features has had spells in Hollywood and Italy, but spent the majority of her film career in England. Here her pleasant personality was always welcome, if somewhat wasted in playing Miss Moneypenny in the James Bond films for 24 years.
1946: Spring Song (US: Springtime). 1948: Corridor of Mirrors. The Big Punch. That Hagen Girl. The Dark Past. The Decision of Christopher Blake. 1949: The Crime Doctor's Diary. Kazan. 1950: Amore e venene. Domani è troppo tardi (GB: Tomorrow is Too Late). 1951: The Woman's Angle. 1952: Lady in the Fog (US: Scotland Yard Inspector). Women of Twilight (US: Twilight Women). Il filo d'erba. Labra bianca. 1953: Mantrap (US: Woman in Hiding). Aida. 1954: La grande speranza (GB: Torpedo Zone. US: Submarine Attack). The Blue Camellia. 1956: Passport to Treason. The High Terrace. Satellite in the Sky. 1957: Time without Pity. Kill Me Tomorrow. 1959: Face of Fire. 1960: The Unstoppable Man. 1962: Lolita. Dr No. Come Fly with Me. 1963: The Haunting. From Russia with Love. 1964: Goldfinger. 1965: Thunderball. 1967: Operation Kid Brother. You Only Live Twice. 1969: On Her Majesty's Secret Service. 1970: The Adventurers. 1971: Diamonds Are Forever. Endless Night. 1973: Live and Let Die. 1974: The Man with the Golden Gun. 1977: Age of Innocence. The Spy Who Loved Me. 1979: Lost and Found. Moonraker. 1980: Mr Patman. 1983: Octopussy. 1985: A View to a Kill. 1986: The Blue Man.

MAXWELL, Marilyn (Marvel M. Maxwell) 1921–1972
Blonde American actress and singer, usually in worldly roles. Was a dance-band vocalist at 16, but never really made her mark at M-G-M, where she was under contract for eight years, and her career faded from the early fifties. By the late sixties she was playing in burlesque

doing a singing striptease. Died from a pulmonary ailment.
1942: Stand By for Action (GB: Cargo of Innocents). 1943: Dubarry Was a Lady. Swing Fever. Thousands Cheer. Presenting Lily Mars. Dr Gillespie's Criminal Case (GB: Crazy to Kill). Pilot No. 5. Salute to the Marines. Best Foot Forward. 1944: Three Men in White. Lost in a Harem. Music for Millions. Ziegfeld Follies (released 1946). 1945: Between Two Women. 1946: The Show-Off. Summer Holiday (released 1948). 1947: High Barbaree. 1948: Race Street. 1949: Champion. 1950: Outside the Wall. Key to the City. 1951: The Lemon Drop Kid. New Mexico. 1952: Off Limits (GB: Military Policeman). 1953: East of Sumatra. Paris Model. 1955: New York Confidential. 1956: Forever, Darling. Snow Shoes (TV). 1958: Rock-a-Bye Baby. 1963: Critic's Choice. 1964: Stage to Thunder Rock. The Lively Set. 1968: Arizona Bushwhackers. 1969: From Nashville with Music. The Phynx. 1970: Wild Women (TV).

Vulture. 1925: The Haunted Ranch. Fighting Courage. The Demon Rider. The Range Fighter (serial: compilation of earlier films). 1926: The Unknown Cavalier. The North Star. Señor Daredevil. 1927: Overland Stage. Land Beyond the Law. The Red Raiders. Gun Gospel. Devil's Saddle. Somewhere in Sonora. 1928: The Upland Rider. Canyon of Adventure. The Glorious Trail. The Wagon Show. The Code of the Scarlet. 1929: Cheyenne. Señor Americano. California Mail. Wagon Master. *The Voice of Hollywood. The Phantom City. The Lawless Legion. The Royal Rider. 1930: Lucky Larkin. Parade of the West. Song of the Caballero. Sons of the Saddle. Fighting Thru. The Fighting Legion. Mountain Justice. 1931: The Pocatello Kid. Two Gun Man. Arizona Terror. Branded Men. Range Law. Alias – The Bad Man. 1932: Texas Gunfighter. Whistlin' Dan. Trail Blazers (serial). Sunset Trail. Hell Fire Austin. Dynamite Ranch. 1933: Phantom Thunderbolt. Drum Taps. Strawberry Roan (GB: Flying Fury). The Lone Avenger. Between Fighting Men. Tombstone Canyon. Fargo Express. Come On Tarzan. King of the Arena. The Fiddlin' Buckaroo. 1934: Wheels of Destiny. In Old Santa Fé. Gun Justice. Mystery Mountain (serial). Trail Drive. Smoking Guns (GB: Doomed to Die). Honor of the Range. 1935: Lawless Riders. Western Courage. Western Frontier. Heir to Trouble. 1936: The Cattle Thief. Heroes of the Range. The Fugitive Sheriff. Avenging Waters. 1937: Boots of Destiny. Trailing Trouble. 1938: Whirlwind Horseman. Six Shootin' Trouble. 1939: Flaming Lead. 1940: Death Rides the Range. Phantom Rancher. Lightning Strikes West. 1943: Wild Horse Stampede. Blazing Guns. Death Valley Rangers. The Law Rides Again. 1944: Westward Bound. Arizona Whirlwind. 1945: Blazing Frontier. Harmony Trail (GB: White Stallion). 1969: Bigfoot.

MAYNARD, Ken 1895–1973
Dark, handsome, solidly-built American cowboy star of the 1920s and 1930s, a former circus rider and rodeo champion who broke into films as a stuntman and continued to do all his own feats of derring-do in and out of the saddle. Always wore an enormous white stetson – and could carry a song as well. Died alone in his trailer home from malnutrition.
1923: The Man Who Won. *Somebody Lied. Brass Commandments. The Gunfighter. Cameo Kirby. 1924: Janice Meredith (GB: The Beautiful Rebel). $50,000 Reward. The Grey

MAYO, Virginia (V. Jones) 1920–
Blonde American dancer and actress of cream-puff complexion who rose quickly from small parts to star roles in Technicolor extravaganzas of every kind. She always gave the impression that there was earthiness lurking beneath the surface of the demurest of her ladies fayre and kept her stardom (and her perfect figure) for a full 15 years. Married to Michael O'Shea (qv) from 1947 to his death in 1973.
1942: Stand by for Action (GB: Cargo of

Innocents). 1943: *Follies Girl. The Adventures of Jack London. Sweet Rosie O'Grady. Salute to the Marines. Swing Fever. Dr Gillespie's Criminal Case* (GB: *Crazy to Kill*). 1944: *Seven Days Ashore. Pin-Up Girl. Tonight and Every Night. Three Men in White. Lady in the Death House. Up in Arms. The Princess and the Pirate.* 1945: *Wonder Man.* 1946: *The Best Years of Our Lives. The Kid from Brooklyn.* 1947: *Out of the Blue. The Secret Life of Walter Mitty.* 1948: *A Song is Born. Smart Girls Don't Talk.* 1949: *The Girl from Jones Beach. Colorado Territory. Flaxy Martin. White Heat. Always Leave Them Laughing. Red Light.* 1950: *Backfire. The West Point Story* (GB: *Fine and Dandy*). *The Flame and the Arrow.* 1951: *Along the Great Divide. Captain Horatio Hornblower RN. Starlift. Painting the Clouds with Sunshine.* 1952: *The Iron Mistress. She's Working Her Way Through College.* *Screen Snapshots No. 206.* 1953: *She's Back on Broadway. South Sea Woman. Devil's Canyon.* 1954: *The Silver Chalice. King Richard and the Crusaders.* 1955: *Pearl of the South Pacific.* 1956: *Great Day in the Morning. Congo Crossing. The Proud Ones.* 1957: *The Big Land* (GB: *Stampeded!*). *The Story of Mankind. The Tall Stranger. Fort Dobbs.* 1959: *Westbound. Jet over the Atlantic.* 1960: *Revolt of the Mercenaries.* 1964: *Young Fury.* 1966: *Castle of Evil.* 1967: *Fort Utah.* 1969: *The Haunted.* 1975: *Won Ton Ton, the Dog Who Saved Hollywood.* 1976: *The Glass Cage.* 1977: *French Quarter.*

McCALLISTER, Lon (Herbert Alonzo McCallister) 1923–
Dark-haired, earnest, rosy-cheeked, stocky American actor, in films from childhood and boyish-looking to the end of his cinema career. It seems in retrospect that McCallister was always dressed in checked shirt, grooming his horse against some Technicolor background of mountains and pines. But most of his best roles *were* in outdoor dramas and, unable to widen his range, he left show business in the fifties – a pity after working so long to gain a foothold there.

1936: *Romeo and Juliet. Let's Sing Again.* 1937: *Internes Can't Take Money* (GB: *You Can't Take Money*). *Stella Dallas. Make a Wish. Souls at Sea.* 1938: *Adventures of Tom Sawyer. Lord Jeff* (GB: *The Boy from Barnado's*). *Little Tough Guys in Society. That*

Certain Age. Judge Hardy's Children. 1939: *Babes in Arms. First Love. Spirit of Culver* (GB: *Man's Heritage*). *Angels Wash Their Faces. Confessions of a Nazi Spy.* 1940: *High School. Joe and Ethel Turp Call on the President. Susan and God* (GB: *The Gay Mrs Trexel*). 1941: †*Henry Aldrich for President.* 1942: †*That Other Woman.* †*Quiet Please, Murder.* †*Over My Dead Body. Dangerously They Live. Yankee Doodle Dandy. Gentleman Jim. The Hard Way. Always in My Heart.* 1943: *The Meanest Man in the World. Stage Door Canteen.* 1944: *Winged Victory. Home in Indiana.* 1947: *The Red House. Thunder in the Valley* (GB: *Bob, Son of Battle*). 1948: *Scudda-Hoo! Scudda-Hay!* (GB: *Summer Lighting*). 1949: *The Big Cat.* 1950: *Boy from Indiana* (GB: *Blaze of Glory*). *The Story of Seabiscuit* (GB: *Pride of Kentucky*). 1951: *A Yank in Korea* (GB: *Letter from Korea*). 1952: *Montana Territory.* 1953: *Combat Squad.*

†*as Bud McCallister*

McCALLUM, David 1933–
Blond, youthful-looking, flop-haired Scottish actor in British films, mostly as tearaways and braggarts. Went to America in 1963, and scored a big hit on television as the quietly-spoken Russian agent, Illya, in *The Man from U.N.C.L.E.*, several double-episodes of which went abroad as feature films. He proved surprisingly colourless in later leading roles, and has only occasionally been effective since. Married (first of two) to Jill Ireland, 1957–1967.

1957: *The Secret Place. Hell Drivers. Robbery Under Arms. Violent Playground.* 1958: *A Night to Remember.* 1960: *The Long and the Short and the Tall. Carolina.* 1961: *Jungle Street.* 1962: *Billy Budd. Freud* (GB: *Freud – the Secret Passion*). 1963: *The Great Escape.* 1964: *To Trap a Spy* (TV. GB: cinemas). *The Spy with My Face.* 1965: *Around the World under the Sea. The Greatest Story Ever Told. One Spy too Many* (TV. GB: cinemas). 1966: *The Spy in the Green Hat* (TV. GB: cinemas). *Three Bites of the Apple. One of Our Spies is Missing!* (TV. GB: cinemas). 1967: *The Karate Killers* (TV. GB: cinemas). *The Helicopter Spies* (TV. GB: cinemas). *Sol Madrid* (GB: *The Heroin Gang*). 1968: *How to Steal the World* (TV. GB: cinemas). *Mosquito*

Squadron. 1969: *La cattura/The Ravine. Teacher, Teacher* (TV). 1970: *Hauser's Memory* (TV). 1971: *She Waits* (TV). 1973: *The Screaming Skull* (TV). *Frankenstein: the True Story* (TV. GB: cinemas). 1975: *The Invisible Man* (TV). *The Diamond Hunters* (US: *The Kingfisher Caper*). 1976: *Dogs.* 1978: *King Solomon's Treasure.* 1981: *The Watcher in the Woods.* 1982: *Critical List.* 1983: *The Return of the Man from U.N.C.L.E.* (TV). 1985: *Terminal Choice. OSS* (TV). 1986: *Behind Enemy Lines* (TV).

McCALLUM, John 1917–
Handsome, dark-haired Australian leading man who seemed to come to Britain at just the right time (1947), looking as he did like a cross between Stewart Granger and Michael Rennie. He met and married Googie Withers (in 1948) and eight years later returned to Australia with his wife for a long period, having used his casual charm in a variety of British films.

1935: *Heritage.* 1936: *South West Pacific. Joe Came Back.* 1946: *A Son is Born. Australia is Like This.* 1947: *Bush Christmas* (narrator only). *The Root of All Evil. The Loves of Joanna Godden. It Always Rains on Sunday.* 1948: *The Calendar. Miranda.* 1949: *A Boy, a Girl and a Bike. Traveller's Joy.* 1950: *The Woman in Question* (US: *Five Angles on Murder*). 1951: *Valley of the Eagles. The Magic Box. Lady Godiva Rides Again.* 1952: *Derby Day* (US: *Four Against Fate*). *Trent's Last Case. The Long Memory.* 1953: *Melba.* 1954: *Devil on Horseback. Trouble in the Glen.* 1956: *Port of Escape. Smiley.*

As director:
1956: *Three In One.* 1971: *Nickel Queen.*

McCAMBRIDGE, Mercedes (Carlotta M. McCambridge) 1918–
Dark, heavy-set, gloweringly menacing American actress, usually in unpleasant roles. After an Academy Award in her first film, *All the King's Men*, she proved difficult to cast and was seen only now and again when the right part could be found. Her power diminished somewhat in the sixties, and she accepted lesser roles.

1949: *All the King's Men.* 1951: *Inside Straight. Lightning Strikes Twice. The Scarf.* 1954: *Johnny Guitar.* 1956: *Giant.* 1957: *A Farewell to Arms.* 1958: *Touch of Evil.* 1959:

Suddenly Last Summer. 1960: Cimarron.
Angel Baby. 1966: Run Home Slow. 1968:
Justine and Juliet. 99 Women (US: Island of
Despair). The Counterfeit Killer (TV. GB:
cinemas). 1969: Der heisse Tod. 1971: A Capi-
tol Affair (TV). Killer by Night (TV). Two
for the Money (TV). The Last Generation.
The President's Plane is Missing (TV). 1973:
Sixteen. The Girls of Huntingdon House (TV).
The Exorcist (voice only). 1974: Like a Crow
on a June Bug. 1975: Who is the Black Dahlia?
(TV). 1976: Thieves. 1979: The Sacketts
(TV). The Concorde – Airport '79 (GB: Air-
port '80 . . . the Concorde). 1980: Echoes.

McCARTHY, Kevin 1914–
Big, dark-haired, good-looking (in a slightly
shifty, predatory way) American actor, equally
convincing as hero or villain. On stage from
1938, TV from 1949, but slow to get into his
stride as a film personality. Only had a few
years as a leading man, but these included
Invasion of the Body Snatchers, from whose
aliens he was still on the run in the 1978
remake. He received an Oscar nomination for
Death of a Salesman.
1951: Death of a Salesman. 1954: Drive a
Crooked Road. The Gambler from Natchez.
1955: Stranger on Horseback. Annapolis Story
(GB: The Blue and the Gold). 1956: Night-
mare. Invasion of the Body Snatchers. 1957:
City in Flames (TV. GB: cinemas). Diamond
Safari. 1961: The Misfits. 1962: 40 Pounds of
Trouble. 1963: A Gathering of Eagles. The
Prize. 1964: The Best Man. An Affair of the
Skin. 1965: Mirage. 1966: Hotel. The Three
Sisters. A Big Hand for the Little Lady (GB:

Big Deal at Dodge City). 1968: The Hell with
Heroes. If He Hollers, Let Him Go! Shadow
on the Land (TV). I quattro dell' Ave Maria
(GB: Revenge in El Paso). 1969: Operation
Heartbeat (TV). Ace High. 1972: Richard.
Kansas City Bomber. A Great American Tra-
gedy (TV. GB: Man at the Crossroads). 1973:
Alien Thunder (later Dan Candy's Law). El
Clan de los Inmorales/Order to Kill. 1976:
Buffalo Bill and the Indians. 1977: Mary Jane
Harper Cried Last Night (TV). Exo-Man
(TV). 1978: Invasion of the Body Snatchers
(remake). Piranha. 1979: Hero at Large. 1980:
The Howling. Those Lips, Those Eyes. Portrait
of an Escort (TV). 1982: Rosie: The Rosemary
Clooney Story (TV). My Tutor. 1983: The
Twilight Zone (GB: Twilight Zone The
Movie). The Making of a Male Model (TV).
1985: The Midnight Hour (TV). 1986:
Hostage. A Masterpiece of Murder (TV).

McCLURE, Doug 1934–
Muscular, fair-haired, blue-eyed American
star of action films, equally familiar on TV
where he has appeared in several successful
series, notably the long-running *The Virginian*. Alleges that his drinking habits have him
known as 'Dean Martin on Horseback' and is
four times married and divorced. 'My wives
were good housekeepers,' he admits. 'They
all kept the house.' Second (1961–1963) was
actress Barbara Luna (1937–).
1957: The Enemy Below. 1958: South Pacific.
1959: Gidget. The Unforgiven. 1960: Because
They're Young. 1962: The Brazen Bell (TV.
GB: cinemas). 1964: The Lively Set. 1965:
Shenandoah. Beau Geste. The Longest
Hundred Miles (TV). 1967: The King's
Pirate. Nobody's Perfect. 1968: Backtrack
(TV). 1971: Terror in the Sky (TV). The
Birdmen (TV. GB: cinemas as Escape of the
Birdmen). The Death of Me Yet (TV). 1972:
Judge and Jake Wyler
(TV). Playmates (TV). 1973: Shirts/Skins
(TV). Die blutigen Geier von Alaska. 1974:
Adventure in Ventana (narrator only). What
Changed Charley Farthing? 1975: Satan's Tri-
angle (TV). The Land That Time Forgot.
1976: At the Earth's Core. 1977: SST Disaster
in the Sky/SST Death Flight (TV). The
People That Time Forgot. 1978: Wild and
Wooly (TV). Warlords of Atlantis. 1980:
Humanoids from the Deep (GB: Monster). The
Firebird. Nightside (TV). 1981: The House

Where Evil Dwells. 1983: Cannonball Run II.
1985: Half Nelson (TV). 1986: 52 Pick-Up.

McCREA, Joel 1905–
Tight-lipped but benign, square-faced and
snub-nosed, Joel McCrea was nobody's idea
of the all-American boy, but his warmth and
cheerful personality radiated from the screen,
and he was surprisingly good at light or even
zany romantic comedy. After World War II
he pursued a grimmer course as an upright
western star before retiring to his ranch in the
sixties. Married to Frances Dee (*qv*) since
1933. It has now been established that
McCrea did *not* appear as an extra in films of
1923 and 1924 previously listed.
1927: The Fair Co-Ed (GB: The Varsity
Girl). 1928: Freedom of the Press. The Enemy.
The Jazz Age. 1929: So This is College. The
Five O'Clock Girl. The Single Standard.
Dynamite. 1930: The Silver Horde. Lightnin'.
Once a Sinner. 1931: Born to Love. Kept Hus-
bands. Girls about Town. 1932: Business and
Pleasure. Bird of Paradise. Rockabye. The Lost
Squadron. The Sport Parade. The Most
Dangerous Game (GB: The Hounds of Zaroff).
1933: The Silver Cord. One Man's Journey.
Bed of Roses. Chance at Heaven. Scarlet River.
1934: Half a Sinner. Gambling Lady. The
Richest Girl in the World. 1935: Splendor.
Barbary Coast. Woman Wanted. 1936: Adven-
ture in Manhattan (GB: Manhattan
Madness). Come and Get It. Banjo on My
Knee. These Three. Two in a Crowd. 1937:
Internes Can't Take Money (GB: You Can't
Take Money). Woman Chases Man. Wells
Fargo. Dead End. 1938: Three Blind Mice.
Youth Takes a Fling. 1939: They Shall Have
Music. He Married His Wife. Espionage Agent.
Union Pacific. 1940: The Primrose Path. Fore-
ign Correspondent. 1941: Reaching for The
Sun. Sullivan's Travels. 1942: The Palm Beach
Story. The Great Man's Lady. 1943: The More
the Merrier. *Stars on Horseback. 1944: The
Great Moment. Buffalo Bill. 1945: The
Unseen. 1946: The Virginian. 1947: Ramrod.
1948: Four Faces West (GB: They Passed This
Way). 1949: Colorado Territory. South of St
Louis. 1950: Saddle Tramp. The Outriders.
Stars in My Crown. Frenchie. 1951: The Hol-
lywood Story. Cattle Drive. 1952: The San
Francisco Story. 1953: Lone Hand. Rough
Shoot (US: Shoot First). 1954: Border River.
Black Horse Canyon. 1955: Wichita. Stranger

on Horseback. 1956: The First Texan. 1957: The Oklahoman. Trooper Hook. Gunsight Ridge. The Tall Stranger. 1958: Fort Massacre. Cattle Empire. The Gunfight at Dodge City. 1961: Ride the High Country (GB: Guns in the Afternoon). 1971: Cry Blood, Apache. 1974: The Great American Cowboy (narrator only). 1976: Mustang Country.

McDERMOTT, Hugh 1908–1972

Husky, cheerful-looking Scottish-born actor with ruddy complexion and dark hair. In British films from the mid-1930s, often as Americans, he had his best role as one of Ann Todd's beaux in The Seventh Veil. His career varied from leading parts in minor thrillers to featured or small roles in major films. Later made movies abroad.

1936: David Livingstone. The Captain's Table. Well Done, Henry. 1937: The Wife of General Ling. The Divorce of Lady X. 1939: The Saint in London. Where's That Fire? 1940: Neutral Port. For Freedom. Spring Meeting. 1941: Pimpernel Smith (US: Mister V). 1942: The Young Mr Pitt. 1945: The Seventh Veil. 1946: This Man is Mine. 1948: Good Time Girl. No Orchids for Miss Blandish. 1949: The Huggetts Abroad. 1950: Lilli Marlene. 1951: Two on the Tiles. Four Days. 1952: Trent's Last Case. 1953: The Wedding of Lilli Marlene. The Love Lottery. 1954: Night People. Malaga (US: Fire over Africa). Johnny on the Spot. Devil Girl from Mars. 1955: As Long as They're Happy. 1956: You Pay Your Money. 1957: A King in New York. 1958: The Man Who Wouldn't Talk. 1964: First Men in the Moon. 1966: Bindle (One of Them Days). Delayed Flight. 1968: The Games. The File of the Golden Goose. 1969: Guns in the Heather. The Adding Machine. 1970: Lawman. 1971: Chato's Land. Captain Apache.

McDOWALL, Roddy (Andrew Roderick McDowall) 1928–

Clever and resourceful light-haired British-born child actor, in Hollywood from 1940, and popular as the star of boy-and-animal films. Proved ineffectual as a young adult star but after ten years learning his craft in the theatre came back as an astringent and interesting character actor who frequently stole scenes from those billed above him. Won great

personal popularity as star of the Apes films. Also a photographer.

1938: Murder in the Family. Scruffy. Hey! Hey! USA! I See Ice. Convict 99. Yellow Sands. John Halifax, Gentleman. Sarah Siddons. 1939: Just William. Dead Men's Shoes. Poison Pen. Murder Will Out. His Brother's Keeper. The Outsider. 1940: You Will Remember. Saloon Bar. 1941: This England. Man Hunt. How Green Was My Valley. Confirm or Deny. 1942: The Pied Piper. Son of Fury. On the Sunny Side. 1943: My Friend Flicka. Lassie Come Home. 1944: The Keys of the Kingdom. The White Cliffs of Dover. 1945: Thunderhead, Son of Flicka. Hangover Square (voice only). Molly and Me. 1946: Holiday in Mexico. 1948: Macbeth. Rocky. Kidnapped. 1949: Tuna Clipper. Black Midnight. 1950: Killer Shark. Big Timber. Everybody's Dancin'. 1951: The Steel Fist. 1958: Heart of Darkness (TV). 1960: The Subterraneans. Midnight Lace. 1961: The Power and the Glory (TV. GB: cinemas). 1962: The Longest Day. 1963: Cleopatra. 1964: Shock Treatment. 1965: The Adventures of Bullwhip Griffin. The Greatest Story Ever Told. The Third Day. That Darn Cat! The Loved One. Inside Daisy Clover. Is Paris Burning? 1966: The Defector. Lord Love a Duck. It (US: Return of the Golem). 1967: The Cool Ones. Planet of the Apes. 1968: The Fatal Mistake (TV). Five Card Stud. Hello Down There. 1969: Night Gallery (TV). Midas Run (GB: A Run on Gold). Angel, Angel, Down We Go (US: Cult of the Damned). 1971: Escape from the Planet of the Apes. Terror in the Sky (TV). A Taste of Evil (TV). Corky. Bedknobs and Broomsticks. Pretty Maids All in a Row. 1972: The Poseidon Adventure. The Life and Times of Judge Roy Bean. Conquest of the Planet of the Apes. What's a Nice Girl Like You . . .? (TV). 1973: Battle for the Planet of the Apes. Arnold. The Legend of Hell House. 1974: Dirty Mary, Crazy Larry. The Elevator (TV). Miracle on 34th Street (TV). 1975: Funny Lady. Mean Johnny Barrows. Embryo. 1976: Flood! (TV. GB: cinemas). 1977: Sixth and Main. Laser Blast. Circle of Iron/The Silent Flute. 1978: Rabbit Test. The Cat from Outer Space. 1979: The Thief of Bagdad. The Martian Chronicles (TV). Hart to Hart (TV). Nutcracker Fantasy (voice only). Scavenger Hunt. 1980: Charlie Chan and the Curse of the Dragon Queen. The Memory of Eva Ryker (TV). 1981: Kiss of Gold. The Million Dollar Face

(TV). Evil Under the Sun. 1982: Class of 1984. Mae West (TV). 1983: Robin Hood (TV). This Girl for Hire (TV). 1985: Deceptions (TV). Fright Night. 1986: Go Bats: Battle of The Rock Lords (voice only). Dead of Winter.

As director: 1971: Tam Lin.

McDOWELL, Malcolm 1943–

Slightly-built British actor whose thoughtful features adapted just as easily to cocky grin or worried frown. Starred in a number of controversial commercial successes in his twenties and became a hot property. But his films since then have seemed too few and have not proved box-office, with his own interpretations sometimes seeming wilfully eccentric. Also, like his contemporary David Hemmings (qv), he has aged quite quickly. Married Mary Steenburgen (qv) in 1980.

1967: †Poor Cow. 1968: If . . . 1970: Figures in a Landscape. The Raging Moon (US: Long Ago Tomorrow). 1971: A Clockwork Orange. 1973: O Lucky Man! 1975: Royal Flash. 1976: Aces High. Voyage of the Damned. 1977: Caligula (released 1979). 1978: She Fell Among Thieves (TV). The Passage. 1979: Time After Time. *Tigers Are Better Looking. 1982: Cat People. Britannia Hospital. Blue Thunder. 1983: Flip Out. Arthur the King (TV. Released 1985). Cross Creek. Get Crazy. 1985: Gulag.

† Scenes deleted from final release print

McENERY, Peter 1940–

Slim, light-haired, boyish British actor who seemed anxious not to get type-cast as clean-cut heroes. But his characters varied too wildly, from the innocuous to the weird, to set him up for a consistent star career. Not much seen on the screen since 1970.

*1959: 'Beat' Girl (US: Wild for Kicks). 1960: Tunes of Glory. 1961: Victim. 1963: The Moon-Spinners. 1966: The Fighting Prince of Donegal. La curée (GB: The Game is Over). 1967: I Killed Rasputin. 1968: Meglio vedova (GB: Better a Widow). Negatives. The Other People. 1969: The Adventures of Gérard. 1970: Entertaining Mr Sloane. Le mur de l'Atlantique. 1972: *Today Mexico – Tomorrow the World. 1973: Tales That Witness Madness. 1978: The Cat and the Canary. 1985: Florence Nightingale (TV).*

McGAVIN, Darren 1922–

Fair-haired American actor in tough-guy roles, adept at dog-eared heroes, slightly corrupt policemen and the occasional smiling villain. Has always shown a preference for theatre and television over films. As early as 1951 was starring in a TV series called *Crime Photographer*, the type of role that foreshadowed many of his later assignments. Became as familiar on TV in leading roles in his late forties and early fifties as did Gene Hackman (*qv*) in films.

1945: A Song to Remember. Kiss and Tell. She Wouldn't Say Yes. Counter-Attack (GB: One against Seven). 1946: Fear. 1951: Queen for a Day. 1955: Summer Madness (US: Summertime). The Court Martial of Billy Mitchell (GB: One Man Mutiny). The Man with the Golden Arm. 1957: Beau James. The Delicate Delinquent. 1958: The Case against Brooklyn. 1964: Bullet for a Badman. 1965: The Great Sioux Massacre. Ride the High Wind. 1967: The Outsider (TV). 1968: The Challengers (TV. GB: cinemas). Mission Mars. 1969: Anatomy of a Crime. 1970: The Challenge (TV). Mrs. Pollifax – Spy. Berlin Affair (TV). Battle at Gannon's Bridge (TV). Tribes (TV. GB cinemas as The Soldier Who Declared Peace). The 48 Hour Mile (TV). 1971: The Birdmen (TV. GB cinemas as Escape of the Birdmen). Banyon (TV). The Death of Me Yet (TV). The Night Stalker (TV). 1972: Something Evil (TV). The Rookies (TV). Say Goodbye, Maggie Cole (TV). The Night Strangler (TV). High Flying Spy (TV). 1973: Smash-Up Alley (TV). 'B' Must Die. †Happy Mother's Day ... Love George/Run, Stranger, Run. The Petty Story (TV). 1976: No Deposit, No Return. Law and Order (TV).

Brink's: the Great Robbery(TV). 1977: Airport 77. 1978: Zero to Sixty. The Users (TV). Donovan's Kid (TV). Hot Lead and Cold Feet. 1979: The Martian Chronicles (TV). Love for Rent (TV). 1980: Waikiki (TV). Hangar 18. 1981: The Firebird. 1983: A Christmas Story. 1984: The Natural. The Return of Marcus Welby MD (TV). The Baron and the Kid (TV). Turk 182! 1985: My Wicked, Wicked Ways: The Legend of Errol Flynn (TV). 1986: Raw Deal.

† *Also directed*

McGOOHAN, Patrick 1928–

American-born, light-haired leading man with cynical smile, laughing eyes and soft, transatlantic voice. Played some interesting roles in the British cinema from 1955 to 1963, often as sadistic villains in the early James Mason mould. Later career engulfed by two TV series, *Danger Man* and *The Prisoner*, the latter a commercial flop but great cult success. As a director rather disappointing.

1955: Passage Home. I Am a Camera. The Dam Busters. 1956: Zarak. 1957: High Tide at Noon. Hell Drivers. The Gypsy and the Gentleman. 1958: Nor the Moon by Night (US: Elephant Gun). 1961: Two Living One Dead. 1962: Life for Ruth (US: Walk in the Shadow). All Night Long. The Quare Fellow. 1963: Dr Syn – Alias the Scarecrow (US: TV). The Three Lives of Thomasina. 1968: Ice Station Zebra. 1970: The Moonshine War. 1971: Mary, Queen of Scots. 1975: The Genius. Porgi d'altra guancia/Nobody's the Greatest. 1976: Silver Streak. Un genio, due compari e un pollo. The Man in the Iron Mask (TV). 1978: Brass Target. 1979: The Hard Way (TV). Escape from Alcatraz. 1980: Scanners. 1981: Kings and Desperate Man. 1983: Jamaica Inn (TV). Finding Katie. 1984: Baby. 1985: Three Sovereigns for Sarah (TV).

As director: *1973: Catch My Soul.*

McGRAW, Charles 1914–1980

Hefty, light-haired American actor with rough-hewn, aggressive features and steely blue eyes. Two first-rate portrayals as leading man in a couple of good low-budget thrillers, *Road Block* and *The Narrow Margin*, surprisingly failed to clinch film stardom, and he moved into television, where he was constantly busy from 1955 to 1973. Later played a variety

of tough veterans. Bled to death after falling through a glass shower door.

1938: Angels with Dirty Faces. 1942: The Undying Monster/The Hammond Mystery. The Moon is Down. 1943: They Came to Blow Up America. The Mad Ghoul. Corvette K-225 (GB: The Nelson Touch). Destroyer. 1944: The Imposter. 1946: The Killers. The Big Fix. 1947: The Long Night. Brute Force. The Farmer's Daughter. The Gangster. Roses Are Red. T-Men. On the Old Spanish Trail. 1948: Hazard. The Hunted. Blood on the Moon. Berlin Express. 1949: Reign of Terror/The Black Book. Border Incident. Once More, My Darling. The Story of Molly X. Side Street. Ma and Pa Kettle Go to Town (GB: Going to Town). The Threat. 1950: Armored Car Robbery. Double Crossbones. 1951: His Kind of Woman. Road Block. The Narrow Margin. 1952: One Minute to Zero. 1953: Thunder over the Plains. Loophole. War Paint. 1954: The Bridges at Toko-Ri. 1956: Away All Boats. Toward the Unknown (GB: Brink of Hell). The Cruel Tower. Hand of Fate (TV. GB: cinemas). 1957: Joe Dakota. Joe Butterfly. Slaughter on 10th Avenue. 1958: Saddle the Wind. The Defiant Ones. Twilight for the Gods. 1959: The Man in the Net. The Wonderful Country. 1960: Spartacus. Cimarron. 1962: The Horizontal Lieutenant. 1963: It's a Mad, Mad, Mad, Mad World. The Birds. 1965: Nightmare in Chicago. 1966: The Busy Body. 1967: Hang 'em High. In Cold Blood. 1968: Pendulum. 1969: Perilous Voyage (TV). Tell Them Willie Boy is Here. 1971: Operation Cobra (TV). Johnny Got His Gun. The Devil and Miss Sarah (TV). The Night Stalker (TV). Chandler. 1972: The Longest Night (TV). 1973: Money to Burn (TV). Death and the Maiden (TV). 1974: A Boy and His Dog. 1975: The Killer Inside Me. 1976: Perilous Voyage (TV). 1977: Twilight's Last Gleaming.

McGUIRE, Dorothy 1918–

Light-haired (she describes it as 'burnt blonde') pretty, appealing American actress, mostly in gentle, often down-trodden roles and skilful at manipulating her audience's emotions. Made fewer films as a star than most people think, and moved too swiftly (in 1956) into 'mother' roles, her film career lasting only a few more years. Mother of actress Topo Swope. Nominated for an Academy Award in *Gentleman's Agreement*.

1943: Claudia. 1944: A Tree Grows in Brooklyn. 1945: The Enchanted Cottage. The Spiral Staircase. 1946: Claudia and David. Till the End of Time. 1947: Gentleman's Agreement. 1950: Mother Didn't Tell Me. Mister 880. 1951: Callaway Went Thataway (GB: The Star Said No). I Want You. Invitation. 1954: Make Haste to Live. Three Coins in the Fountain. 1955: Trial. 1956: Friendly Persuasion. 1957: Old Yeller. 1959: This Earth is Mine. The Remarkable Mr Pennypacker. A Summer Place. 1960: The Dark at the Top of the Stairs. Swiss Family Robinson. 1961: Susan Slade. 1962: Summer Magic. 1965: The Greatest Story Ever Told. 1971: Flight of the Doves. She Waits (TV). 1975: The Runaways (TV). 1978: Little Women (TV). 1979: The Incredible Journey of Dr Meg Laurel (TV). 1983: Ghost Dancing (TV). 1985: Amos (TV).

McKENNA, Virginia 1931–

English-rose-type blonde British beauty with super complexion. She had a short but showy star career in British films of the fifties and belied her delicate looks by playing a couple of gutsy war heroines with great spirit and depth of emotion. Married to Denholm Elliott (1954–1956) and Bill Travers (1957 on): her subservience to her husband's career was admirable but something of a loss to the British cinema.

1952: Father's Doing Fine. The Second Mrs Tanqueray. The Oracle (US: The Horse's Mouth). 1953: The Cruel Sea. 1954: Simba. 1955: The Ship That Died of Shame (US: PT Raiders). 1956: A Town Like Alice (US: The Rape of Malaya). 1957: The Barretts of Wimpole Street. The Smallest Show on Earth (US:

Big Time Operators). 1958: Passionate Summer. Carve Her Name with Pride. 1959: The Wreck of the Mary Deare. 1961: Two Living One Dead. 1965: Born Free. 1967: The Lions Are Free (TV). 1969: An Elephant Called Slowly. Ring of Bright Water. 1970: Waterloo. 1971: The Lion at World's End (US: Christian the Lion). 1974: Swallows and Amazons. 1976: Beauty and the Beast. 1977: Holocaust 2000 (US: The Chosen). 1978: The Disappearance. 1982: Blood Link.

McLAGLEN, Victor 1883–1959

A British-born Wallace Beery. A great cheerful hulk of a man with tousled hair, McLaglen was soldier, farmer, prospector, boxer (his battered features testified to that) and vaudeville performer before coming to the British cinema and quickly becoming popular by riding roughshod through action roles. Went to Hollywood in 1925, winning an Academy Award ten years later in *The Informer*, but being largely used as aggressive, Irish-biased comedy relief. Also received an Oscar nomination for *The Quiet Man*. Died from a heart attack.

1920: The Call of the Road. 1921: Carnival. The Prey of the Dragon. The Sport of Kings. Corinthian Jack. The Glorious Adventure. 1922: A Romance of Old Bagdad. A Sailor Tramp. Little Brother of God. The Crimson Circle. The Romany. 1923: M'Lord of the White Road. Heartstrings. In the Blood. The Beloved Brute. 1924: *The Boatswain's Mate. Women and Diamonds. The Gay Corinthian. The Passionate Adventure. 1925: The Fighting Heart. The Hunted Woman. Winds of Chance. Percy. The Unholy Three. 1926: Beau Geste. What Price Glory? Isle of Retribution. Men of Steel. 1927: Captain Lash. The Loves of Carmen. 1928: Mother Machree. Hangman's House. A Girl in Every Port. The River Pirate. 1929: Strong Boy. Sez You – Sez Me. The Cock-Eyed World. The Black Watch (GB: King of the Khyber Rifles). Hot for Paris. 1930: On the Level. Dust and Sun. Happy Days. Devil with Women. 1931: Dishonored. Annabelle's Affairs. Wicked. Women of All Nations. Not Exactly Gentlemen. 1932: Devil's Lottery. Guilty As Hell (GB: Guilty As Charged). While Paris Sleeps. Rackety Rax. *The Stolen Jools (GB: The Slippery Pearls). 1933: Dick Turpin. Laughing at Life. Hot Pepper. 1934: The Lost Patrol. No More Women.

Wharf Angel. The Captain Hates the Sea. Murder at the Vanities. 1935: The Informer. Under Pressure. Professional Soldier. The Great Hotel Murder. 1936: Mary of Scotland. Klondike Annie. Under Two Flags. The Magnificent Brute. 1937: This is My Affair (GB: His Affair). Nancy Steele is Missing. Wee Willie Winkie. Sea Devils. 1938: We're Going to be Rich. Battle of Broadway. The Devil's Party. 1939: Captain Fury. Pacific Liner. Full Confession. The Big Guy. Ex-Champ (GB: Golden Gloves). Let Freedom Ring. Rio. 1940: Diamond Frontier. South of Pago Pago. 1941: Broadway Limited. 1942: Call Out the Marines. China Girl. Powder Town. 1943: Forever and a Day. 1944: Tampico. The Princess and the Pirate. Roger Touhy, Gangster (GB: The Last Gangster). 1945: Love, Honor and Goodbye. Rough, Tough and Ready (GB: Men of the Deep). 1946: Whistle Stop. 1947: The Michigan Kid. Calendar Girl. The Foxes of Harrow. 1948: Fort Apache. 1949: She Wore a Yellow Ribbon. 1950: Rio Grande. 1952: The Quiet Man. 1953: Fair Wind to Java. 1954: Trouble in the Glen. Prince Valiant. 1955: Lady Godiva (GB: Lady Godiva of Coventry). Many Rivers to Cross. City of Shadows. Bengazi. 1957: The Abductors. 1958: Sea Fury. The Italians Are Crazy.

McNALLY, Stephen (Horace McNally)
1913–

Dark, confident, slightly oriental-looking American actor, a former lawyer who turned to the theatre in the late thirties, then Hollywood, where he began as earnest clean-cut juveniles. In post-war years he was just as likely to crop up on either side of the law and hovered on the fringe of stardom for ten years. Later on he turned up on TV, bigger, balding and blustery, in character roles.

1942: †*For the Common Defense. †*The Magic Alphabet. †*Rover's Big Chance. †Grand Central Murder. †The War Against Mrs Hadley. †Eyes in the Night. † For Me and My Gal (GB: For Me and My Girl). †Dr Gillespie's New Assistant. †Keeper of the Flame. 1943: †Air Raid Wardens. †The Man from Down Under. 1944: †An American Romance. †Thirty Seconds over Tokyo. 1945: †Bewitched. †Up Goes Maisie (GB: Up She Goes). †Dangerous Partners. †The Harvey Girls. 1946: †Magnificent Doll. 1948: Johnny Belinda. Rogues' Regiment. 1949: City across the River. Criss Cross. The Lady Gambles. Sword in the Desert. Woman in Hiding. 1950: Winchester 73. No Way Out. Wyoming Mail. 1951: Air Cadet (GB: Jet Men of the Air). Apache Drums. The Iron Man. The Raging Tide. The Lady Pays Off. 1952: Diplomatic Courier. The Duel at Silver Creek. The Black Castle. Battle Zone. 1953: Split Second. The Stand at Apache River. Devil's Canyon. 1954: Make Haste to Live. A Bullet is Waiting. 1955: The Man from Bitter Ridge. Violent Saturday. 1956: Tribute to a Bad Man. 1957: Hell's Crossroads. 1958: The Fiend Who Walked the West. Johnny Rocco. Hell's Five Hours. 1959: Hell Bent for Leather. Stampede at Bitter Creek (TV. GB: cinemas). 1965: Requiem for a Gunfighter. 1967: Panic in the City. 1969: The Lonely Profession (TV). The Whole World is Watching (TV). 1970: Once You Kiss a Stranger. Vanished (TV). 1972: Black Gunn. Call to Danger (TV). 1974: Nakla (TV). 1975: The Lives of Jenny Dolan (TV). 1976: Most Wanted (TV). 1977: Hi-Riders. Kino, the Padre on Horseback. 1979: Dear Detective (TV).

McNICHOL, Kristy 1962–
Here's the girl you *would* have put your money on five years ago to become America's next Jane Fonda. A child star on TV, an Emmy winner as a teenager in the TV series *Family*, and simply tremendous with deeply-felt performances in the TV film *Summer of My German Soldier* and the movie *Little Darlings*. Then, a series of flops and half-realised projects, films hardly seen outside preview screens and a period off for 'nervous exhaustion'. Small wonder the Fonda-style voice of this engagingly warm, petite American actress and part-time singer has been so little heard in recent years. There's still time of course. But one does now wonder about superstardom.
1976: Black Sunday. 1977: The Love Boat II (TV). 1978: Avalanche. Like Mom, Like Me (TV). The End. Summer of My German Soldier (TV). 1980: Blinded by the Light (TV). Little Darlings. 1981: Only When I Laugh (GB: It Hurts Only When I Laugh). The Night the Lights Went Out in Georgia. 1982: White Dog. My Old Man (TV). The Pirate Movie. 1983: I Won't Dance (unfinished). 1984: Just the Way You Are. Dream Lover. 1986: Love, Mary (TV).

McQUEEN, Steve (Terence S. McQueen) 1930–1980
Whippy, dynamic American star with close-cropped fair hair and pale blue eyes. Reform school in youth gave background before he took up acting in his mid-twenties. In leading roles from his third film, he became one of Hollywood's hottest box-office bets, in roles of lean, confident, sometimes even psychopathic masculinity, from 1963 through to 1972. After that, he seemed to press the self-destruct button on his career. Married to actress Neile Adams from 1955 to 1971 and Ali MacGraw from 1973 to 1978. Received an Oscar nomination for *The Sand Pebbles*. Died from a heart attack following surgery for mesothelioma (a cancer of the chest).
1956: †Somebody Up There Likes Me. †Beyond a Reasonable Doubt. 1958: †Never Love a Stranger. †The Blob. 1959: The Great St Louis Bank Robbery. Never So Few. 1960: The Magnificent Seven. 1961: The Honeymoon Machine. 1962: Hell is for Heroes! The War Lover. 1963: The Great Escape. Soldier in the Rain. 1964: Love with the Proper Stranger. 1965: Baby, the Rain Must Fall. 1966: The Cincinnati Kid. Nevada Smith. The Sand Pebbles. 1968: The Thomas Crown Affair. Bullitt. 1969: The Reivers. 1971: Le Mans. On Any Sunday. 1972: The Getaway. Junior Bonner. 1973: Papillon. 1974: The Towering Inferno. 1976: Dixie Dynamite. 1977: An Enemy of the People. 1980: Tom Horn. The Hunter.

† As Steven McQueen

McSHANE, Ian 1942–
Alert British leading man with dark, brooding, gipsy-like good looks. Started in leading roles,

and made an effective Heathcliff for television. Had made himself into a minor international name by the seventies. Married to Suzan Farmer (qv) from 1965 to 1968.
1962: The Wild and the Willing. 1965: The Pleasure Girls. Sky West and Crooked (GB: Gipsy Girl). 1968: If It's Tuesday, This Must Be Belgium. 1969: Battle of Britain. 1970: Freelance. Pussycat, Pussycat, I Love You. 1971: Tam Lin (GB: The Devil's Widow). Villain. 1972: Sitting Target. The Left Hand of Gemini. 1973: The Last of Sheila. 1974: Ransom. 1975: The Loves of Jenny Dolan (TV). 1976: Journey into Fear. 1977: Behind the Iron Mask (GB: The Fifth Musketeer). Code Name: Diamond Head (TV). 1978: The Pirate (TV). 1979: Yesterday's Hero. Dirty Money (TV). 1980: Cheaper to Keep Her. 1981: The Letter (TV). 1983: Exposed. Grace Kelly (TV). Torch Light. 1984: Ordeal by Innocence. Too Scared to Scream.

MEDINA, Patricia 1920–
Flashing-eyed British actress with a mass of very dark hair and picture-book beauty. Followed then-husband Richard Greene to Hollywood and became everyone's idea of the swashbuckler's lady fayre. Married to Greene from 1941 to 1951 and Joseph Cotten in 1960, after which she devoted less time to films.
1937: Dinner at the Ritz. 1938: Simply Terrific. Double or Quits. 1939: Secret Journey (US: Among Human Wolves). 1942: The First of the Few (US: Spitfire). The Day Will Dawn (US: The Avengers). 1943: They Met in the Dark. 1944: Hotel Reserve. Kiss the Bride Goodbye. Don't Take It to Heart. 1945: Waltz Time. 1946: The Secret Heart. 1947: Moss Rose. The Foxes of Harrow. The Beginning or the End? 1948: The Three Musketeers. 1949: The Fighting O'Flynn. Francis. OK Agostina. Children of Chance. 1950: Fortunes of Captain Blood. The Jackpot. Abbott and Costello in the Foreign Legion. 1951: The Lady and the Bandit (GB: Dick Turpin's Ride). The Magic Carpet. Valentino. 1952: Aladdin and His Lamp. Captain Pirate (GB: Captain Blood, Fugitive). Lady in the Iron Mask. Desperate Search. 1953: Siren of Bagdad. Botany Bay. Sangaree. Plunder of the Sun. 1954: Drums of Tahiti. Phantom of the Rue Morgue. The Black Knight. 1955: Pirates of Tripoli. Duel on the Mississippi. Confidential Report (US: Mr Arkadin). 1956: Stranger at My Door. Miami Exposé.

Uranium Boom. The Beast of Hollow Mountain. The Red Cloak. 1957: Buckskin Lady. 1958: Battle of the V1 (US: V1/Unseen Heroes/Missiles from Hell). 1959: Count Your Blessings. 1961: Snow White and the Three Stooges (GB: Snow White and the Three Clowns). 1968: The Killing of Sister George. 1969: Latitude Zero. 1973: The Timber Tramp.

MEEKER, Ralph (R. Rathgeber) 1920–
Fair-haired, heavily-built American actor often seen as loud-mouthed men of violence. Took over from Marlon Brando in the stage production of A Streetcar Named Desire and was much in the same mould, although never in such prestigious films. Grew heavier, like Brando, as the years wore on, and took to playing bragging cowards.
1950: Four in a Jeep. 1951: Teresa. Shadow in the Sky. 1952: Glory Alley. Somebody Loves Me. 1953: Code Two. Jeopardy. The Naked Spur. 1955: Big House USA. Desert Sands. Kiss Me Deadly. 1956: A Woman's Devotion (GB: War Shock). 1957: Run of the Arrow. The Fuzzy Pink Nightgown. Paths of Glory. Four Women in Black (TV). Deep Water (TV). 1961: Ada. Something Wild. 1963: Wall of Noise. 1967: The Saint Valentine's Day Massacre. The Dirty Dozen. Gentle Giant. 1968: The Devil's 8. The Detective. 1969: Lost Flight (TV). 1970: I Walk the Line. 1971: Incident of October 20th. The Anderson Tapes. The Reluctant Heroes (TV. GB: The Reluctant Heroes of Hill 656). The Night Stalker (TV). 1972: My Boys Are Good Boys. 1973: Birds of Prey (TV. GB: cinemas). Police Story (TV. GB: cinemas. Later on TV as Stakeout). You'll Never See Me Again (TV). The Happiness Cage. 1974: Cry Panic (TV). The Girl on the Late, Late Show (TV). Night Games (TV). The Dead Don't Die (TV). 1975: Johnny Firecloud. Brannigan. 1976: Love Comes Quietly. The Food of the Gods. 1977: Hi-Riders. Winter Kills (released 1979). 1980: Without Warning (GB: The Warning).

MENJOU, Adolphe (Adolph Menjou)1890–1963
Dark-haired, moustachioed, superciliouslooking Hollywood charmer, popular as a ladies' man though he always looked older than his years. Later a useful, if not especially biting, character actor in more avuncular roles. Married to Verree Teasdale (1904–)

third of three – from 1934 to his death from hepatitis. He received an Oscar nomination for The Front Page.
1916: A Parisian Romance. The Habit of Happiness. Manhattan Madness. The Blue Envelope. The Kiss. 1917: The Amazons. The Moth. The Valentine Girl. 1921: The Sheik. The Three Musketeers. Through the Back Door. The Faith Healer. Courage. Queenie. 1922: The Fast Mail. Clarence. Is Matrimony a Failure? Singed Wings. The Eternal Flame. Head over Heels. Pink Gods. 1923: A Woman of Paris. The World's Applause. The Spanish Dancer. Bella Donna. Rupert of Hentzau. 1924: The Fast Set. Broadway after Dark. For Sale. The Marriage Cheat. Shadows of Paris. Broken Barriers. Forbidden Paradise. The Marriage Circle. Open All Night. Sinners in Silk. 1925: Are Parents People? A Kiss in the Dark. The King on Main Street. Lost – a Wife. The Swan. 1926: A Social Celebrity. The Grand Duchess and the Waiter. Fascinating Youth. The Sorrows of Satan. The Ace of Cads. 1927: Service for Ladies. A Gentleman of Paris. Blonde or Brunette. Serenade. Evening Clothes. 1928: The Tiger Lady. His Private Life. A Night of Mystery. 1929: Bachelor Girl. Marquis Preferred. The Kiss (and earlier version). Fashions in Love. 1930: Mon gosse de père. L'enigmatique Monsieur Parkes. New Moon. Morocco. 1931: The Front Page. Men Call It Love. Friends and Lovers. The Great Lover. The Easiest Way. 1932: Two White Arms. Prestige. Bachelor's Affairs. A Farewell to Arms. Forbidden. The Man from Yesterday. Night Club Lady. Blame the Woman. 1933: Worst Woman in Paris? The Circus Queen Murder. Morning Glory. Convention City. 1934: The Trumpet Blows. Journal of a Crime. Little Miss Marker (GB: Girl in Pawn). The Mighty Barnum. The Human Side. The Great Flirtation. Easy to Love. 1935: Gold Diggers of 1935. Broadway Gondolier. 1936: Sing, Baby, Sing. Wives Never Know. One in a Million. The Milky Way. 1937: Café Metropole. A Star is Born. Stage Door. 100 Men and a Girl. 1938: Thanks for Everything. The Goldwyn Follies. Letter of Introduction. 1939: That's Right – You're Wrong. King of the Turf. Golden Boy. 1940: The Housekeeper's Daughter. A Bill of Divorcement. Turnabout. Road Show. 1941: Father Takes a Wife. 1942: Roxie Hart. Syncopation. You Were Never Lovelier. 1943: Sweet Rosie O'Grady. Hi Diddle Diddle. 1944:

Step Lively. 1945: Man Alive. 1946: Heartbeat. The Bachelor's Daughters (GB: Bachelor Girls). I'll Be Yours. 1947: The Hucksters. Mr District Attorney. 1948: State of the Union (GB: The World and His Wife). 1949: My Dream is Yours. Dancing in the Dark. 1950: To Please a Lady. 1951: The Tall Target. Across the Wide Missouri. 1952: The Sniper. 1953: Man on a Tightrope. 1955: Timberjack. 1956: Bundle of Joy. The Ambassador's Daughter. 1957: The Fuzzy Pink Nightgown. Paths of Glory. 1958: I Married a Woman. 1960: Pollyanna.

MERCOURI, Melina 1923–
The female equivalent of Anthony Quinn (qv): a barnstorming, scene-chewing, throatyvoiced, dominant blonde Greek actress who married director Jules Dassin, achieved world fame in Never on Sunday (a performance that won her an Oscar nomination) and swallowed the opposition whole in a number of international films. Later became the Jane Fonda of Greek politics, winning a seat in parliament in 1977.
1954: Stella. 1956: Celui qui doit mourir. 1957: The Gypsy and the Gentleman. 1958: La loi (GB: Where the Hot Wind Blows). 1960: Never on Sunday. 1961: Il giudizio universale (US: The Last Judgment). Phaedra. Vive Henry IV, vive l'amour! 1962: Canzoni nel mondo (US 38-24-36). 1963: The Victors. 1964: Topkapi. 1965: Les pianos mécaniques (US: The Uninhibited). 1966: A Man Could Get Killed. 10.30 pm Summer. 1969: Gaily Gaily (GB: Chicago Chicago). 1971: Promise at Dawn. 1974: Once is Not Enough/Jacqueline Susann's Once is Not Enough. †The Rehearsal. 1976: Nasty Habits. 1977: A Dream of Passion. 1983: Keine zufällige Geschichte (US: Not By Coincidence).

† Unreleased

MEREDITH, Burgess 1908–
For a man who made virtually nothing for the cinema between 1949 and 1962, this mercurial, tousle-haired American actor must be one of the most difficult tasks for any filmographer: fresh Meredith films, sometimes from the most unlikely places, seem to turn up everywhere one looks. A first-class talent who continually upset Hollywood in his earlier days, he did, and still does, attack his

parts like a terrier. Four times married, including Paulette Goddard (third) from 1944 to 1949. Long-delayed Academy Award nominations finally came for *Day of the Locust* and *Rocky*.

1936: *Winterset*. 1937: *There Goes the Groom*. 1938: *Spring Madness*. 1939: *Idiot's Delight*. *Of Mice and Men*. 1940: *San Francisco Docks*. *Castle on the Hudson* (GB: *Years without Days*). *Second Chorus*. 1941: *That Uncertain Feeling*. *The Forgotten Village* (narrator only). *Tom, Dick and Harry*. 1942: *Street of Chance*. 1943: *†Welcome to Britain*. 1944: *†Salute to France*. 1945: *The Story of GI Joe/War Correspondent*. 1946: *Magnificent Doll*. *The Diary of a Chambermaid*. 1947: *Mine Own Executioner*. *A Yank Comes Back*. 1948: *A Miracle Can Happen* (later *On Our Merry Way*). 1949: *The Man on the Eiffel Tower*. *Jigsaw*. *Golden Arrow* (US: *The Gay Adventure*). 1954: *Screen Snapshots No. 224*. 1957: *Joe Butterfly*. 1961: *Universe* (narrator only). 1962: *Advise and Consent*. 1963: *The Cardinal*. 1964: *Man on the Run/The Kidnappers*. 1965: *In Harm's Way*. 1966: *Crazy Quilt* (narrator only). *A Big Hand for the Little Lady* (GB: *Big Deal at Dodge City*). *Batman*. *Madame X*. 1967: *Torture Garden*. *Hurry Sundown*. 1968: *Mackenna's Gold*. *Stay Away, Joe*. *Skidoo*. *Hard Contract*. 1969: *The Reivers* (narrator only). 1970: *†The Yin and the Yang of Dr Go*. *There Was a Crooked Man*. *Lock, Stock and Barrel* (TV). 1971: *Getting Away from it All* (TV). *Clay Pigeon* (GB: *Trip to Kill*). *Blind Terror* (US: *See No Evil*). 1972: *The New Healers* (TV). *Probe* (TV). *The Man*. *A Fan's Notes*. *Such Good Friends*. 1973: *'B' Must Die*. 1974: *Of Men and Women* (TV). *The Day of the Locust*. *Golden Needles*. *Beware! the Blob* (GB: *Son of Blob*). 1975: *92 in the Shade*. *The Master Gunfighter* (narrator only). 1976: *The Hindenberg*. *The Sentinel*. *Burnt Offerings*. *Tail Gunner Joe* (TV). *Rocky*. 1977: *SST Death Flight* (TV). *The Wandering Muse of Artemus Flagg*. *Golden Rendezvous*. *Remember Those Poker-Playing Monkeys?* *The Manitou*. *Johnny, We Hardly Knew Ye* (TV). 1978: *The Amazing Captain Nemo*. *Shenanigans* (later *The Great Georgia Bank Hoax*). *Foul Play*. *Magic*. *Kate Bliss and the Ticker Tape Kid* (TV). *The Last Hurrah* (TV). 1979: *Puff the Magic Dragon* (voice only). *Rocky II*. 1980: *When Time Ran Out ... The Last Chase*. *Final Assignment*. 1981:

Clash of the Titans. True Confessions. Prince of the City. 1982: *Rocky III*. 1983: *The Twilight Zone* (GB: *Twilight Zone The Movie*. Narrator only). 1984: *Wet Gold* (TV). 1985: *Santa Claus*. 1986: *Outrage!* (TV). *Mr Corbett's Ghost*.

† Also directed

MERMAN, Ethel (E. Zimmerman) 1908–1984
Big, bold, brassy American brunette, a successful singer in her early twenties, with pencilled eyebrows, thin, determined lips, a shock of cotton-wool hair and a voice that would still be travelling when it hit the back of the opera house. Hollywood had as little idea of how to cope with her as it did later with Mary Martin (qv), but it did give her a couple of rampaging musical successes in middle age. Married/divorced Ernest Borgnine (fourth husband) in 1964.

1930: *Follow the Leader*. 1931: *Devil Sea*. *Roaming*. 1932: *Time on My Hands* (voice only). *Ireno*. *The Big Broadcast*. 1933: *Be Like Me*. 1934: *We're Not Dressing*. *Kid Millions*. *Shoot the Works*. 1935: *The Big Broadcast of 1936*. 1936: *Anything Goes*. *Strike Me Pink*. 1938: *Happy Landing*. *Alexander's Ragtime Band*. *Straight, Place and Show* (GB: *They're Off*). 1943: *Stage Door Canteen*. 1953: *Call Me Madam*. 1954: *There's No Business Like Show Business*. 1963: *The Art of Love*. *It's a Mad, Mad, Mad, Mad World*. 1971: *Journey Back to Oz* (voice only). 1975: *Won Ton Ton, the Dog Who Saved Hollywood*. 1979: *Rudolph and Frosty's Christmas in July* (TV. Voice Only). 1980: *Airplane!*

MERRILL, Gary 1914–
Dark-haired, morose-looking American tough-guy actor who often looked as though he needed a shave. At first as unsmiling heroes, not above using dirty methods to get results, later as weary-looking villains. Married to Bette Davis from 1950 to 1960.

1944: *Winged Victory*. 1948: *The Quiet One* (narrator only). 1949: *Slattery's Hurricane*. *Twelve O'Clock High*. 1950: *Mother Didn't Tell Me*. *Where the Sidewalk Ends*. *All About Eve*. 1951: *The Frogmen*. *Decision before Dawn*. *Another Man's Poison*. 1952: *The Girl in White* (GB: *So Bright the Flame*). *Night without Sleep*. *Phone Call from a Stranger*. 1953: *A Blueprint for Murder*. 1954: *Witness

to Murder. The Black Dakotas. The Human Jungle*. 1955: *Yacht on the High Sea* (TV. GB: cinemas). 1956: *Navy Wife* (GB: *Mother – Sir!*). *Bermuda Affair*. 1957: *Crash Landing*. *If You Knew Elizabeth* (TV). 1958: *The Missouri Traveler*. 1959: *The Wonderful Country*. *A Quiet Game of Cards* (TV). *A Corner of the Garden* (TV). *The Savage Eye*. 1960: *The Great Imposter*. 1961: *Mysterious Island*. *The Pleasure of His Company*. 1962: *A Girl Named Tamiko*. *Hong Kong Farewell/Hong Kong, un addio*. 1963: *Catacombs* (US: *The Woman Who Wouldn't Die*). 1965: *Run, Psycho, Run*. *Around the World under the Sea*. *The Last Challenge* (GB: *The Pistolero of Red River*). 1966: *Ride Beyond Vengeance*. *Cast a Giant Shadow*. *The Dangerous Days of Kiowa Jones* (TV. GB: cinemas). *Hondo and the Apaches*. *Destination Inner Space*. 1967: *The Power*. *Clambake*. *New York chiama Superdrago*. *The Incident*. 1969: *Amarsi male*. 1970: *Then Came Bronson* (TV. GB: cinemas). 1971: *Earth II* (TV). 1972: *The Murderers* (TV). 1973: *Pueblo* (TV). *Murder and the Computer* (TV). 1974: *Huckleberry Finn*. 1976: *Thieves*. 1979: *The Seekers* (TV).

MICHAEL, Gertrude 1911–1964
Bright, vivacious, platinum blonde American star of the 1930s, with wide toothpaste smile and high cheekbones. She was trained for a career as a pianist, but acting successes on stage led to offers from Hollywood, where she remained a second-line lead, although notable as the hazard-prone heroine of the Sophie Lang adventure films. After that series ended in 1937, she moved increasingly into hard-

in the Streets. Rock, Pretty Baby. 1957: Dino
(GB: Killer Dino). The Young Don't Cry.
1958: Tonka. 1959: A Private's Affair. 1960:
The Gene Krupa Story (GB: Drum Crazy).
Exodus. 1961: Escape from Zahrain. Cry Ven-
geance (TV). 1962: The Longest Day. 1964:
Cheyenne Autumn. 1965: The Greatest Story
Ever Told. 1966: Who Killed Teddy Bear? The
Dangerous Days of Kiowa Jones (TV. GB:
cinemas). 1967: Stranger on the Run (TV).
1968: The Challengers (TV. GB: cinemas).
Krakatoa – East of Java. 1969: 80 Steps to
Jonah. 1970: One Day Left Before Tomorrow
(TV). In Search of America (TV). 1971:
Escape from the Planet of the Apes. 1972: The
Family Rico (TV). 1973: Harry O (TV).
1974: The Hunters (TV). 1975: James Dean –
the First American Teenager.

MINNELLI, Liza 1946–
Explosive, exhibitionist American singer and
actress (the daughter of Judy Garland and
director Vincente Minnelli) whose singing
voice throbs with the nervous energy she scat-
ters in all directions. Her striking 'Pierette'
looks – black hair, big, dark eyes, full lips and
small, rounded face – were seen now and again
in films with varying success. After being
nominated for an Oscar in The Sterile Cuckoo,
she won the award for Cabaret. She is credited
with an appearance in The King of Comedy,
but seems to appear only as a cardboard cut-
out.
1949: In the Good Old Summertime. 1967:
Charlie Bubbles. 1969: The Sterile Cuckoo
(GB: Pookie). Tell Me That You Love Me,
Junie Moon. 1971: Journey Back to Oz (voice
only). 1972: Cabaret. 1974: That's Enter-

tainment! 1975: Lucky Lady. 1976: A Matter
of Time. Silent Movie. 1977: New York, New
York. 1980: Arthur. 1982: The King of
Comedy. 1984: The Muppets Take Manhattan.
1985: That's Dancing! A Time to Live (TV).
1986: Intensive Care (TV).

MIRANDA, Carmen (Maria Do Carmo
M. Da Cunha) 1904–1955
Extravagantly made-up, with eyebrows that
reached nearly to her black hair, and the widest mouth since Martha Raye, Carmen
Miranda could have been made of wood – but
when she danced, and sang, you knew she
wasn't. Known as 'The Brazilian Bombshell'
(although born in Portugal) she stormed to
immense popularity in wartime Hollywood
musicals – and was said to have been fired by
Fox when they found she wore no knickers
beneath her swirling dresses! Died from a
heart attack.
1933: A voz do Carnaval. 1934: Estudiantes.
1935: Alô, Alô, Brazil. 1936: Alô, Alô, Carnaval. 1938: Banana La Terra. 1940: Down
Argentine Way. 1941: That Night in Rio.
Week-End in Havana. 1942: Springtime in the
Rockies. 1943: The Gang's All Here (GB: The
Girls He Left Behind). 1944: Four Jills in a
Jeep. Greenwich Village. Something for the
Boys. 1945: *Hollywood on Parade. *All Star
Bond Rally. 1946: Doll Face (GB: Come Back
to Me). If I'm Lucky. 1947: Copacabana.
1948: A Date with Judy. 1950: Nancy Goes to
Rio. 1953: Scared Stiff.

MIRREN, Helen (Ilyena Mironoff) 1945–
Forceful blonde British actress with determined features, spectacular figure and class-

less image. She forsook a possible career as an
international sex symbol of the cinema for
the calmer waters of the Royal Shakespeare
Company, for whom she made a memorable
Lady Macbeth. In the late 1970s she returned
to films in little clusters, as tarts-with-hearts
and allied roles.
1967: Herostratus. 1968: A Midsummer
Night's Dream. 1969: Age of Consent. 1972:
Savage Messiah. 1973: O Lucky Man! 1976:
Hamlet. 1977: Caligula (released 1979). 1979:
SOS Titanic (TV. GB: cinemas). Hussy. The
Long Good Friday. 1980: The Fiendish Plot of
Dr Fu Manchu. 1981: Excalibur. 1984: Cal.
2010. 1985: White Nights. 1986: Heavenly
Pursuits, The Mosquito Coast.

MITCHELL, Cameron (C. Mizell) 1918–
Tough-talking, whippy, curly-haired, bullet-
headed American actor. At first he played
honest Joes but after coming back to films in
1951 was seen in more aggressive roles.
Abroad in the sixties making violent continental thrillers and action yarns and later, as
rough-edged as ever, a regular in the TV series
The High Chaparral. Never quite a top star,
but never far away.
1945: *The Last Instalment. What Next, Cor-
poral Hargrove? They Were Expendable. The
Hidden Eye. 1946: The Mighty McGurk. 1947:
High Barbaree. Cass Timberlane. Tenth
Avenue Angel. 1948: Homecoming. Adventures
of Gallant Bess. Leather Gloves (GB: Loser
Take All). Command Decision. 1951: Smug-
gler's Gold. The Man in the Saddle (GB: The
Outcast). The Sellout. Death of a Salesman.
Flight to Mars. Japanese War Bride. 1952:
Okinawa. The Outcasts of Poker Flat. Pony
Soldier (GB: MacDonald of the Canadian
Mounties). Les Misérables. 1953: Man on a
Tightrope. How to Marry a Millionaire. Pow-
der River. The Robe (narrator only). 1954:
Hell and High Water. Gorilla at Large. Garden
of Evil. Désirée. 1955: Strange Lady in Town.
Love Me or Leave Me. House of Bamboo. The
Tall Men. The View from Pompey's Head.
(GB: Secret Interlude). Man on the Ledge
(TV. GB: cinemas). The Ox-Bow Incident
(TV. GB: cinemas). 1956: Carousel. Tension
at Table Rock. All Mine to Give (US: The
Day They Gave Babies Away). 1957: Monkey
on My Back. No Down Payment. Escapade in
Japan. 1959: Pier 5 Havana. Three Came to
Kill. Inside the Mafia. Face of Fire. Raubfischer

in Hellas (GB and US: As the Sea Rages). 1960: The Unstoppable Man. The House on Airport Drive. The Last of the Vikings (GB: Fury of the Vikings). 1962: Invasion of the Normans/ I Normanni. Caesar the Conqueror. 1963: Girl from La Mancha. 1964: Minnesota Clay. Sei donne per l'assassino (GB and US: Blood and Black Lace). When Strangers Meet (US: Dog Eat Dog). Jim il primo (GB: Killer's Canyon). 1965: Raffica di coltelli. The Treasure of Macuba. 1966: Monster of the Wax Museum (GB: Nightmare in Wax). La Isla de la Muerte (GB: Bloodsuckers. US: Maneater of Hydra). 1967: Autopsy of a Ghost. Ride the Whirlwind. Knives of the Avenger. 1969: Rebel Rousers. 1970: The Taste of the Savage. 1971: Thief (TV). The Reluctant Heroes (TV. GB: The Reluctant Heroes of Hill 656). Buck and the Preacher. 1972: Cutter (TV). Political Asylum. The Delphi Bureau (TV). The Rookies (TV). The Big Game. The Stranger (TV). 1974: The Klansman. The Midnight Man. The Hanged Man (TV). The Girl on the Late, Late Show (TV). Hitchhike! (TV). Death in Space (TV). 1975: The Swiss Family Robinson (TV). 1976: Flood! (TV). The Taste of the Savage. 1977: Slavers. The Tool Box Murders. Haunts/The Veil. Viva Knievel! Stigma (TV). 1978: The Fish Men. Texas Detour. The Swarm. The Last Reunion. The Scalp Merchant (TV). The Hostage Heart (TV). 1979: Supersonic Man. Wild Times (TV). The Silent Scream. 1980: The Boys. Without Warning (GB: The Warning). 1981: The Demon. Raw Force. The Guns and the Fury. 1982: Texas Lightning. Blood Link. My Favorite Year. Cataclysm. Screamers (The Fish Men with added footage). Kill Squad. 1983: Murder, Baby. 1984: Prince Jack. Go for Gold. Killpoint. 1985: Savage Sunday/Mission Kill. Night Train to Terror. The Tomb. 1986: Low Blow. From a Whisper to a Scream.

MITCHELL, Yvonne (Y. Joseph) 1925–1979
Dark-haired, palely attractive British actress, largely in anguished roles. Popular both on television and in films in the fifties (she had made her stage debut at 14) she also wrote books and plays. Died from cancer.
1948: The Queen of Spades. 1949: Children of Chance. 1953: Turn the Key Softly. 1954: The Divided Heart. 1955: Escapade. 1956: Yield to the Night (US: Blonde Sinner). 1957:

Woman in a Dressing Gown. 1958: Passionate Summer. 1959: Tiger Bay. Sapphire. 1960: Conspiracy of Hearts. The Trials of Oscar Wilde (US: The Man with the Green Carnation). 1961: Johnny Nobody. 1962: The Main Attraction. 1965: Genghis Khan. 1970: The Corpse (US: Crucible of Horror). 1971: Demons of the Mind. 1972: The Great Waltz. 1976: The Incredible Sarah. 1977: Widow's Nest.

MITCHUM, Robert 1917–
Dark-haired, full-faced, lazy-lidded Hollywood star of powerful build and slow, distinctive speech. He survived the grind of 19 films in his first cinema year (and the narcotics bust that sent him to jail in 1948) to become the star of firstly RKO noir thrillers, then bigger-budget movies of varying quality, and has remained at the top of the tree. Despite a casual acting style that looks more so in rubbish, he has proved himself capable, in the right circumstances, of sensitive and haunting performances. Billed as Bob Mitchum until mid-1945. Nominated for an Academy Award in The Story of GI Joe.
1943: Follow the Band. Bar 20. Hoppy Serves a Writ. Border Patrol. Colt Comrades. We've Never Been Licked (GB: Texas to Tokyo). The Lone Star Trail. False Colors. Corvette K-225 (GB: The Nelson Touch). Riders of the Deadline. Gung Ho! The Leather Burners. The Human Comedy. Beyond the Last Frontier. Doughboys in Ireland. Aerial Gunner. The Dancing Masters. Cry Havoc. Minesweeper. 1944: Mr Winkle Goes to War (GB: Arms and the Woman). When Strangers Marry. Girl Rush. Johnny Doesn't Live Here Any More. Thirty Seconds over Tokyo. Nevada. 1945: West of the Pecos. The Story of GI Joe/War Correspondent. 1946: Till the End of Time. The Locket. Undercurrent. 1947: Pursued. Desire Me. Crossfire. Out of the Past (GB: Build My Gallows High). 1948: Blood on the Moon. Rachel and the Stranger. 1949: Holiday Affair. The Red Pony. The Big Steal. 1950: Where Danger Lives. 1951: My Forbidden Past. The Racket. His Kind of Woman. 1952: The Lusty Men. One Minute to Zero. Macao. Angel Face. 1953: Second Chance. White Witch Doctor. She Couldn't Say No (GB: Beautiful but Dangerous). 1954: Track of the Cat. River of No Return. 1955: The Man with the Gun (GB: The Trouble Shooter). Not As a Stranger. The

Night of the Hunter. 1956: Foreign Intrigue. Bandido! 1957: Heaven Knows, Mr Allison. The Enemy Below. Fire Down Below. 1958: Thunder Road. The Hunters. 1959: The Angry Hills. The Wonderful Country. 1960: A Terrible Beauty (US: The Night Fighters). The Sundowners. Home from the Hill. The Grass is Greener. 1961: The Last Time I Saw Archie. 1962: Cape Fear. Two for the Seesaw. The Longest Day. Rampage! 1963: The List of Adrian Messenger. 1964: What a Way to Go! Man in the Middle. 1965: Mr Moses. 1967: Anzio (GB:The Battle for Anzio). The Way West. El Dorado. 1968: Villa Rides! Five Card Stud. Secret Ceremony. 1969: Young Billy Young. The Good Guys and the Bad Guys. 1970: Ryan's Daughter. 1971: Going Home. 1972: The Wrath of God. 1973: The Friends of Eddie Coyle. 1974: The Yakuza. 1975: Farewell, My Lovely. 1976: Midway (GB: Battle of Midway). The Last Tycoon. 1977: The Amsterdam Kill. 1978: Matilda. The Big Sleep. 1979: Breakthrough. 1980: Agency. Nightkill. 1982: That Championship Season. One Shoe Makes It Murder. 1983: A Killer in the Family (TV). 1984: Maria's Lovers. The Ambassador. 1985: Reunion at Fairborough (TV). The Hearst and Davies Affair (TV). Blood Hunt. 1986: Thompson's Last Run (TV). Promises to Keep (TV). The Conspiracy.

MIX, Tom 1880–1940
Dark, hawk-faced American star of silent cowboy films, a former deputy sheriff and rodeo rider who liked to dress flamboyantly in films at his peak, but also to do all his own stunts. His famous horse, Tony, which outlived him by two years, was almost as popular as his master. In later years he was said to have lost a million dollars backing a circus, and was trying for a comeback as a character actor when he was killed in a car crash.
1909: On the Little Big Horn. 1910: Ranch Life in the Great South-West. Briton and Boer. An Indian Wife's Devotion. Up San Juan Hill. The Millionaire Cowboy. The Range Rider. The Long Trail. 1911: Back to the Primitive. 1912: Days of Daring. The Wagon Trail. Weary Goes Wooing. Single Shot Parker. The Sheriff's Girl. Sagebrush Tom. 1913: An Apache's Gratitude. Child of the Prairie. The Escape of Jim Dolan. The Stagecoach-Driver and the Girl. The Law and the Outlaw. Wilderness Mail. The Range Law. 1914: In the Days of The Thundering

Herd. Moving Picture Cowboy. Ranger's Romance. The Scapegoat. The Tell-Tale Knife. Why the Sheriff is a Bachelor. The Rival Stage Lines. Cactus Jake, Heartbreaker. The Real Thing in Cowboys. The Man from the East. Saved by a Watch. The Sheriff's Reward. The Way of the Red Man. The Defiance of the Law. Chip of the Flying U. An Arizona Wooing. On the Eagle Trail. The Mexican. 1915: Foreman of the Bar Z. Cactus Jim's Shop Girl. The Parson Who Fled West. Mr Bill Haywood, Producer. Getting a Start in Life. The Brave Deserve the Fair. Heart of the Sheriff. The Man from Texas. Mrs Murphy's Cooks. Pals in Blue. Sagebrush Tom. Stagecoach Guard. Badman Bobbs. The Chef at Circle G. The Conversion of Smiling Tom. Forked Trails. The Grizzly Gulch Chariot Race. The Impersonation of Tom. A Matrimonial Boomerang. Roping a Bride. The Tenderfoot's Triumph. The Outlaw's Bride. Saved by Her Horse. Athletic Ambitions. Child of the Prairie (remake). Lucky Deal. Ma's Girls. Never Again. The Range Girl and the Cowboy. Slim Higgins. The Auction Sale of a Run-Down Ranch. The Girl in the Mail-Bag. The Child, the Dog and the Villain. The Foreman's Choice. The Gold Dust and the Squaw. Her Slight Mistake. The Legal Light. The Race for a Gold Mine. The Taking of Mustang Pete. 1916: Along the Border. Making an Impression. The Canby Hill Outlaws. Comer in Water. The Cowpuncher's Peril. Going West to Make Good. Local Color. Mistakes in Rustlers. The Passing of Pete. The Raiders. The Sheriff's Blunder. Shooting Up the Movies. Taking a Chance. Tom's Sacrifice. Too Many Chefs. Western Masquerade. An Eventful Evening. The Golden Thought. Mistakes Will Happen. Starring in Western Stuff. A $5,000 Elopement. A Bear of a Story. A Close Call. The Drifter. Crooked Trails. Legal Advice. Making Good. Mix Up in Movies. The Pony Express Rider. Roping a Sweetheart. A Sheriff's Duty. Some Duel. The Taming of Grouchy Bill. Tom's Strategy. Trilby's Love Disaster. The Desert Circle Calls Its Own. 1917: The Girl of Gold Gulch. The Man Within. Roman Cowboy. Soft Tenderfoot. Twisted Trails. Six Shooter Andy. Hearts and Saddles. Six Cylinder Love. Tom and Jerry Mix. The Heart of Texas Ryan. 1918: Ace High. Cupid's Round-Up. Durand of the Badlands. Western Blood. The Rainbow Trail. 1919: Hell-Roarin' Reform. Fame and Fortune. The Coming of the Law. The Wilderness Trail. Fighting for Gold. 1920: The Cyclone. Desert Love. The Terror. Three Gold Coins. Mr Logan USA. Treat 'Em Rough. The Dare-Devil. The Speed Maniac. The Feud. The Untamed. Rough Riding Romance. 1921: Prairie Trails. The Rough Diamond. A Ridin' Romeo. The Texan. The Night Horsemen. Trailin'! Hands Off! The Queen of Sheba. The Road Demon. Big Town Round-Up. After Your Own Heart. 1922: For Big Stakes. Up and Going. Chasing the Moon. Just Tony. Catch My Smoke. Sky High. The Fighting Streak. Do and Dare. Tom Mix in Arabia. 1923: Softboiled. The Lone Star Ranger. Three Jumps Ahead. Romance Land. Stepping Fast. Mile-a-Minute Romeo. 1924: A Golden Thought. Oh, You Tony. Ladies to

Board. Eyes of the Forest. The Heart Buster. North of Hudson Bay. The Last of the Duanes. Teeth. The Trouble Shooter. The Foreman of Bar Z Ranch. 1925: Law and the Outlaw (remake). Everlasting Whisper. Riders of the Purple Sage. Dick Turpin. A Child of the Prairie. The Lucky Horseshoe. The Best Bad Man. The Rainbow Trail. The Deadwood Coach. 1926: No Man's Gold. The Great K and A Train Robbery. The Canyon of Light. Tony Runs Wild. Hardboiled. The Yankee Senor. My Own Pal. 1927: The Last Trail. Tumbling River. *Life in Hollywood No. 4. Outlaws of Red River. The Circus Ace. Silver Valley. The Bronco Twister. 1928: Hello Cheyenne. The Painted Post. Arizona Wildcat. Daredevil's Reward. King Cowboy. A Horseman of the Plains. Son of the Golden West. 1929: Outlawed. Drifter. The Big Diamond Robbery. 1930: *Voice of Hollywood No. 1. Under a Texas Moon. *Voice of Hollywood No. 2. 1931: Six Cylinder Love (remake). The Dude Ranch. The Galloping Ghost (serial). 1932: *Hollywood on Parade No. 3. My Pal, the King. The Fourth Horseman. *Hollywood on Parade No 4. Destry Rides Again. Riders of Death Valley. Texas Bad Man (GB: Defiance). The Cohens and Kellys in Hollywood. 1933: Terror Trail. Flaming Guns (GB: Rough Ridin' Romeo). Hidden Gold. Rustlers' Roundup. 1935: The Miracle Rider (serial).

MONLAUR, Yvonne 1935–
Pretty, innocent-looking, brunette French actress, originally a dancer, picked up by Britain's Hammer films for two or three menaced-sweet-young-thing roles at the beginning of the 1960s. Also appeared in French, German and Italian films, but in smaller roles and with less success.
1956: Mannequins de Paris. Honoré de Marseille. 1957: Les lavandières de Portugal. 1958: Amore a prima vista. Tre straniere a Roma. Avventura a Capri. 1959: La cento chilometri. 1960: Gerarchi si muoiri. Inn for Trouble. Circus of Horrors. The Brides of Dracula. 1961: The Terror of the Tongs. Lemmy pour les dames. 1962: Time to Remember. A cause, à cause d'une femme. Les temps de copains. 1963: La drogue du vice. 1964: Le ciel sur la tête. L'éparvier des Caraïbes. Nick Carter va tout casser (US: License to Kill). 1965: Die Rechnung – eiskalt serviert.

MONROE, Marilyn (Norma Jean Baker) 1926–1962
Blonde sex symbol who became one of the great tragic figures of American cinema. She was sure about her effect on men, but extremely unsure of her talent, which meant that directors had to be increasingly patient with her insecurities in later years. But she could be touching as fading belles (notably in Bus Stop and The Misfits) and winning in musical comedy (especially Gentlemen Prefer Blondes). Fired from her last film because of temperament and impossible timekeeping, she died from a drug overdose, probably a suicide. 1946: The Shocking Miss Pilgrim. 1947: Dangerous Years. 1948: Scudda-Hoo! Scudda-Hay! (GB: Summer Lightning). Ladies of the Chorus. 1949: Love Happy (later Kleptomaniacs). 1950: The Fireball. Right Cross. A Ticket to Tomahawk. The Asphalt Jungle. All About Eve. 1951: The Hometown Story. Love Nest. Let's Make It Legal. As Young As You Feel. 1952: We're Not Married. Clash by Night. O. Henry's Full House (GB: Full House). Monkey Business. Don't Bother to Knock. 1953: Niagara. Gentlemen Prefer Blondes. How to Marry a Millionaire. 1954: River of No Return. There's No Business Like Show Business. 1955: The Seven Year Itch. 1956: Bus Stop. 1957: The Prince and the Showgirl. 1959: Some Like It Hot. 1960: Let's Make Love. 1961: The Misfits. 1962: †Something's Gotta Give.

† Uncompleted

MONTALBAN, Ricardo 1920–
Smooth Mexican actor with dark hair, oval face and flashing smile. He could sing a bit, dance a little and project dramatic sincerity, qualities that kept him at M-G-M, several times opposite Esther Williams, for seven years. Since then has kept busy in a wide variety of roles, playing, among others, Japanese, Italians, Frenchmen and even Red Indians.
1941: *He's a Latin from Staten Island. 1942: Cinco Fueron Escogidos. El Verdugo de Sevilla. La Razon de la Culpa. 1943: La Fuga. Santa. Fantasia Ranchera. La Casa de la Zorro. 1944: Cadetes de la Naval. La Hora de la Verdad. Nosotros. 1945: Pepita Jimenez. 1947: Fiesta. 1948: The Kissing Bandit. On an Island with You. 1949: Border Incident. Neptune's

Daughter. Battleground. 1950: Mystery Street. Right Cross. Two Weeks with Love. 1951: Across the Wide Missouri. Mark of the Renegade. 1952: My Man and I. 1953: Sombrero. Latin Lovers. 1954: The Saracen Blade. The Courtesan of Babylon (GB: The Slave Woman. US: Queen of Babylon). 1955: Sombra Verde. A Life in the Balance. Operation Cicero (TV). 1956: Untouched. The Son of the Sheik. Three for Jamie Dawn. Broken Arrow (TV). 1957: Child of Trouble (TV). Sayonara. 1959: Target for Three (TV). 1960: Let No Man Write My Epitaph. 1961: Gordon il pirata nero (GB: The Black Buccaneer). 1962: The Reluctant Saint. Hemingway's Adventures of a Young Man (GB: Adventures of a Young Man). 1963: Love is a Ball (GB: All This and Money Too). 1964: Cheyenne Autumn. 1965: The Money Trap. 1966: Madame X. The Longest Hundred Miles (TV). The Singing Nun. 1967: Code Name: Heraclitus (TV). Sol Madrid (GB: The Heroin Gang). 1968: Desperate Mission (TV: released 1975). 1969: Black Water Gold (TV). The Pigeon (TV). Blue. Sweet Charity. 1970: The Aquarians (TV). La spina dorsale del Diavolo (GB and US: The Deserter). 1971: The Badge or the Cross (TV). The Face of Fear (TV). Escape from the Planet of the Apes. Taxi to Terror. 1972: Conquest of the Planet of the Apes. The Scorpio Scarab. Fireball Forward (TV). 1973: The Last Three Days of Pancho Villa. The Train Robbers. 1974: The Mark of Zorro (TV). Wonder Woman (TV). 1975: Won Ton Ton, the Dog Who Saved Hollywood. 1976: Joe Panther (GB: TV). 1977: Fantasy Island (TV). Kino, the Padre on Horseback. 1978: Captains Courageous (TV). Return to Fantasy Island (TV). 1982: Star Trek II: The Wrath of Khan. 1983: Cannonball Run II.

MONTAND, Yves (Ivo Levi) 1921–
Italian-born actor and singer in French films, usually exuding cynicism and shifty charm, with a perennial cigarette hanging from the corner of the mouth. Not a film regular until the mid-fifties, after *The Wages of Fear* had made his name. Briefly in Hollywood in the early sixties, now a respected senior citizen of the French cinema. Long married (since 1951) to the late Simone Signoret (*qv*).
1945: Etoile sans lumière. 1946: Les portes de la nuit. 1947: L'idole. 1950: Souvenirs perdus

(GB and US: Lost Property). 1951: Paris chante toujours. 1953: Le salaire de la peur (GB and US: The Wages of Fear). Tempi nostri. 1954: Napoléon. Une tranche de la vie. 1955: Les héros sont fatigués (GB and US: The Heroes Are Tired). Marguerite de la nuit. 1956: Uomini e lupi/Men and Wolves. Die vind Rose. 1957: Les sorcières de Salem (GB and US: The Witches of Salem). Premier Mai. La grande strada azzurra. 1958: La loi (GB and US: Where the Hot Wind Blows). 1959: Yves Montand chante... 1960: Let's Make Love. 1961: Sanctuary. Goodbye Again. 1962: My Geisha. 1965: The Sleeping Car Murders. Is Paris Burning? 1966: La guerre est finie. 1967: Vivre pour vivre. Grand Prix. 1968: Z. Mr Freedom. Un soir ... un train. Le diable par le queue. 1969: Le joli mai (narrator). 1970: Le cercle rouge. L'aveu. On a Clear Day You Can See Forever. 1971: La folie des grandeurs. 1972: Tout va bien. Le fils. César et Rosalie. Die Dummen streiche der Reichen. 1973: Etat de siège/State of Siege. 1974: Le hasard et le violence (GB: The Scarlet Room). 1975: Vincent, François, Paul et les autres. Le sauvage (US: Lovers Like Us). 1976: Police Python 357. 1977: Le grand escogriffe. Flashback. La menace. 1978: Les routes du sud. 1979: Clair de femme. 1980: I comme Icare. 1981: Le choix des armes. 1982: Tout feu, tout flamme (US: All Fired Up). 1983: Garçon! 1985: Jean de Florette. Manon des sources.

MONTEZ, Maria (M. Silas) 1918–1951
Exotic brunette leading lady in Hollywood films. Born in the Dominican Republic, she became the staple ingredient of Universal's

Technicolor 'easterns' of the war years until overtaken in popularity by Yvonne De Carlo. married to Jean-Pierre Aumont from 1943. Drowned in her bath, possibly after a heart attack.
1940: Boss of Bullion City. 1941: Raiders of the Desert. Lucky Devils. The Invisible Woman. That Night in Rio. South of Tahiti (GB: White Savage). Moonlight in Hawaii. 1942: The Mystery of Marie Roget. Bombay Clipper. Arabian Nights. 1943: White Savage (GB: White Captive). Ali Baba and the Forty Thieves. 1944: Cobra Woman. Gypsy Wildcat. Follow the Boys. Bowery to Broadway. 1945: Sudan. 1946: Tangier. 1947: Pirates of Monterey. The Exile. 1948: Siren of Atlantis. Hans le marin (US: The Wicked City). 1949: Portrait d'un assassin. 1950: The Thief of Venice (released 1953). Amore e sangue (US: Sensuality). The Pirate's Revenge.

MONTGOMERY, Douglass (Robert D. Montgomery) 1907–1966
Fair-haired American actor of sensitive but cheerful and outgoing personality. Began his career as Kent Douglass to avoid confusion with an already famous Robert Montgomery, but played lacklustre roles largely unworthy of his talents. Became popular in Britain on radio in World War II while serving with the Canadian army, and made several films there but was little seen, even on TV, after the mid-fifties.
1930: †Paid (GB: Within the Law). 1931: †Daybreak. †Five and Ten (GB: Daughter of Luxury). †A House Divided. †Waterloo Bridge. 1933: Little Women. 1934: Eight Girls in a Boat. Little Man, What Now? Music in the Air. 1935: The Mystery of Edwin Drood. Harmony Lane. Lady Tubbs (GB: The Gay Lady). 1936: Tropical Trouble. Everything is Thunder. 1937: Counsel for Crime. Life Begins with Love. 1939: The Cat and the Canary. 1945: The Way to the Stars (US: Johnny in the Clouds). 1946: Woman to Woman. 1947: Sinfonia fatale (GB: When in Rome). 1948: Forbidden. 1949: Back to Sorrento (narrator only).

† *As Kent Douglass*

MONTGOMERY, George (G. M. Letz) 1916–
Few Hollywood heroes were more virile than

MONTGOMERY, Robert (Henry Montgomery) 1904–1981

Dark, debonair American leading man, kept in snappy light comedy roles and romantic leads by M-G-M, although he clearly had a yen for stronger stuff and proved chillingly effective as the killer in *Night Must Fall*. This got him away from the upper-society-bracket characters with which he had become identified, but he drifted out of show business after the forties and seems little remembered today. Father of actress Elizabeth Montgomery (1933–). Received Oscar nominations for *Night Must Fall* and *Here Comes Mr Jordan*. Died from cancer.

1929: The Single Standard. So This is College. Untamed. Three Live Ghosts. 1930: Sins of the Children (GB: The Richest Man in the World). The Divorcee. Their Own Desire. Our Blushing Brides. Love in the Rough. Free and Easy. The Big House. War Nurse. 1931: Inspiration. The Easiest Way. Man in Possession. Shipmates. Private Lives. Strangers May Kiss. 1932: But the Flesh is Weak. Letty Lynton. Lovers Courageous. Faithless. Blondie of the Follies. 1933: Another Language. Hell Below. Night Flight. When Ladies Meet. Made on Broadway (GB: The Girl I Made). 1934: The Mystery of Mr X. Fugitive Lovers. Hideout. Riptide. 1935: Biography of a Bachelor Girl. Forsaking All Others. No More Ladies. Vanessa, Her Love Story. 1936: Piccadilly Jim. Petticoat Fever. Trouble for Two (GB: The Suicide Club). 1937: Ever Since Eve. Night Must Fall. The Last of Mrs Cheyney. Live, Love and Learn. 1938: Three Loves Has Nancy. The First Hundred Years. Yellow Jack. 1939: Fast and Loose. 1940: Busman's Honeymoon (US: Haunted Honeymoon). The Earl of Chicago. 1941: Rage in Heaven. Mr and Mrs Smith. Unfinished Business. Here Comes Mr Jordan. 1945: They Were Expendable. 1946: The Lady in the Lake. 1947: Ride the Pink Horse. 1948: The Secret Land (narrator only). The Saxon Charm. June Bride. 1949: Once More, My Darling. 1950: Your Witness (US: Eye Witness). 1960: The Gallant Hours.

As director: *1946: The Lady in the Lake. 1949: Once More, My Darling. 1950: Your Witness (US: Eye Witness). 1960: The Gallant Hours.*

MOORE, Cleo 1928–1973

Statuesque American actress, a minor-league blonde bombshell with handsome, open face.

She looked as though she belonged in mink and was alleged to have been discovered by an agent who saw her just that way on someone's arm at a boxing match. Became identified with brassy broads in the seamy melodramas of Hugo Haas, which never rose above B-feature status. Once ran for Governor of Louisiana.

1948: Congo Bill (serial). 1950: Dynamite Pass. This Side of the Law. Rio Grande Patrol. Hunt the Man Down. Gambling House. 1951: On Dangerous Ground. 1952: The Pace That Thrills. Strange Fascination. 1953: One Girl's Confession. Thy Neighbor's Wife. 1954: Bait. The Other Woman. 1955: Hold Back Tomorrow. Women's Prison. 1956: Over-Exposed. 1957: Hit and Run.

MOORE, Colleen (Kathleen Morrison) 1900–

Cute, chirpy American actress with dark, bobbed hair. Her appeal was somewhat akin to that of Mary Pickford, although she was often to be seen as madcap flappers in frothy comedies. Did not adapt well to sound and, after drifting on for a few years, retired on her second marriage in 1937.

*1917: Bad Boy. An Old Fashioned Young Man. The Savage. Hands Up! 1918: A Hoosier Romance. Little Orphan Annie. 1919: The Busher. The Man in the Moonlight. The Wilderness Trail. The Egg-Crate Wallop. Common Property. The Cyclone. 1920: *Her Bridal Nightmare. *A Roman Scandal. So Long Letty. The Devil's Claim. When Dawn Came. 1921: The Lotus Eater. His Nibs. Sky Pilot. Broken Hearts of Broadway. 1922: Affinities. Come on Over. Broken Chains. The Wallflower. The*

---

husky six-footer George Montgomery, who rode the upper-bracket western range (beginning as a stunt man) for more than 20 years, before becoming a star-writer-director of some very presentable action yarns filmed mostly in the Philippines. Married to Dinah Shore 1943–1960: has never remarried. Once a champion heavyweight boxer.

*1935: †Singing Vagabond. 1937: †Conquest (GB: Marie Walewska). †Springtime in the Rockies. 1938: †The Lone Ranger (serial). †Gold Mine in the Sky. †Come on, Rangers. †Billy the Kid Returns. †Hawk of the Wilderness (serial). †Shine on, Harvest Moon. 1939: †Man of Conquest. †Rough Riders' Round-Up. †Frontier Pony Express. †Wall Street Cowboy. †Hi-Yo Silver (feature version of serial The Lone Ranger). 1940: Cisco Kid and the Lady. Jennie. Charter Pilot. Young People. Star Dust. 1941: The Cowboy and the Blonde. Last of the Duanes. Riders of the Purple Sage. Cadet Girl. Accent on Love. 1942: Orchestra Wives. Ten Gentlemen from West Point. China Girl. Roxie Hart. 1943: Bombers' Moon. Coney Island. 1946: Three Little Girls in Blue. 1947: The Brasher Doubloon (GB: The High Window). 1948: The Girl from Manhattan. Lulu Belle. Belle Starr's Daughter. 1949: Dakota Lil. 1950: Davy Crockett, Indian Scout (GB: Indian Scout). Iroquois Trail (GB: The Tomahawk Trail). 1951: The Sword of Monte Cristo. The Texas Rangers. 1952: Indian Uprising. Cripple Creek. 1953: Jack McCall, Desperado. The Pathfinder. Fort Ti. Gun Belt. *Hollywood Stuntmen. 1954: The Lone Gun. Battle of Rogue River. 1955: Masterson of Kansas. Robber's Roost. Seminole Uprising. 1956: Huk! Canyon River. 1957: Last of the Badmen. Street of Sinners. Gun Duel at Durango. Pawnee (GB: Pale Arrow). Man from God's Country. 1958: Black Patch. Badman's Country. Toughest Gun in Tombstone. 1959: Watusi. King of the Wild Stallions. 1961: ‡The Steel Claw. 1962: ‡Samar! 1964: ‡From Hell to Borneo. ‡Guerillas in Pink Lace. 1965: Battle of the Bulge. Satan's Harvest. 1966: Outlaw of Red River. 1967: Hostile Guns/Huntsville. Bomb at 10:10. Warkill. 1968: Hallucination Generation. Strangers at Sunrise. 1970: ‡Ride the Tiger. 1971: Daredevil. 1972: The Leo Chronicles.*

‡ *Also directed* † *As George Letz*

Ninety and Nine. Forsaking All Others. 1923: Slippy McGee. Look Your Best. April Showers. The Nth Commandment. Through the Dark. The Huntress. Flaming Youth. 1924: Painted People. The Perfect Flapper. Flirting with Love. So Big. 1925: Sally. The Desert Flower. We Moderns. 1926: Irene. Ella Cinders. It Must Be Love. 1927: Twinkletoes. Orchids and Ermine. Naughty But Nice. Her Wild Oat. 1928: Happiness Ahead. Oh Kay! Lilac Time. Synthetic Sin. Why Be Good? 1929: Smiling Irish Eyes. Footlights and Fools. 1933: The Power and the Glory. 1934: Success at Any Price. Social Register. The Scarlet Letter.

MOORE, Dudley 1935—
Tiny, dark-haired, crumple-faced British revue comedian and jazz pianist with ingratiating smile. In partnership with long, lugubrious Peter Cook, he gained great popularity in television in the early sixties, proving adept at comic voices and funny little men, and even singing soprano. Later, he married and divorced actresses Suzy Kendall and Tuesday Weld (both qv). His popular appeal seemed to have waned when he suddenly hit the big time in Hollywood in his mid-forties, as a lightly comic leading man. Nominated for an Academy Award in Arthur.
1964: *The Hat (narrator only). 1966: The Wrong Box. 1967: 30 is a Dangerous Age, Cynthia. Bedazzled. 1969: The Bed Sitting Room. Monte Carlo or Bust (US: Those Daring Young Men in their Jaunty Jalopies). 1972: Alice's Adventures in Wonderland. 1977: The Hound of the Baskervilles. 1978: Foul Play. 1979: '10'. To Russia with Elton (narrator only). 1980: Wholly Moses! Arthur. 1981: Derek and Clive Get the Horn. 1982: Six Weeks. 1983: Lovesick. Unfaithfully Yours. Romantic Comedy! 1984: Best Defence. Micki + Maude. 1985: Santa Claus.

MOORE, Kieron (K. O'Hanrahan) 1925—
Dark, brooding, good-looking Irish actor who made a good start in British films, but whose later performances lacked animation. In the late sixties he became very interested in overseas aid development, and made two documentary films about emergent nations.
1945: †The Voice Within. 1947: A Man About the House. Mine Own Executioner. 1948: Anna Karenina. 1949: Saints and Sinners. Maria Chapdelaine (GB: The Naked Heart). 1951:

Honeymoon Deferred. David and Bathsheba. Ten Tall Men. 1953: Mantrap (US: Woman in Hiding). Recoil. 1954: Conflict of Wings. The Green Scarf. 1955: The Blue Peter (US: Navy Heroes). 1956: Satellite in the Sky. 1957: The Steel Bayonet. Three Sundays to Live. 1958: The Key. Darby O'Gill and the Little People. 1959: The Angry Hills. 1960: The League of Gentlemen. The Day They Robbed the Bank of England. The Siege of Sidney Street. 1961: Dr Blood's Coffin. 1962: The Day of the Triffids. I Thank a Fool. The Main Attraction. The 300 Spartans. 1963: Hide and Seek. Girl in the Headlines (US: The Model Murder Case). The Thin Red Line. 1964: Son of a Gunfighter. Bikini Paradise. 1965: Crack in the World. 1966: Arabesque. Run Like a Thief. Custer of the West.

As director: 1975: The Progress of Peoples (and narrator). 1979: The Parched Land (and narrator).
‡As Kieron O'Hanrahan

MOORE, Roger 1927—
Boyishly-handsome, athletic, well-built British leading man with smooth manner, and suavely cultured voice. Although palpably no great actor, he has an easy presence which disarms most criticism. After years of struggle, both in Britain and Hollywood, he hit pay dirt with the TV series The Saint; later took over from Sean Connery as James Bond. Has occasionally proved himself capable of above-par performances when pushed by a determined director.
1945: Caesar and Cleopatra. Perfect Strangers

(US: Vacation from Marriage). 1946: Gaiety George (GB: Showtime). Piccadilly Incident. 1949: Paper Orchid. Trottie True (US: Gay Lady). 1954: The Last Time I Saw Paris. 1955: Interrupted Melody. The King's Thief. Diane. 1959: The Miracle. 1960: The Sins of Rachel Cade. 1961: Gold of the Seven Saints. Il ratto delle sabine/Rape of the Sabines (US: Romulus and the Sabines). 1962: Un branco di vigliacchi/No Man's Land. 1969: Crossplot. 1970: The Man Who Haunted Himself. 1973: Live and Let Die. 1974: Gold. The Man with the Golden Gun. 1975: That Lucky Touch. 1976: Shout at the Devil. The Sicilian Cross. Sherlock Holmes in New York (TV). 1977: The Spy Who Loved Me. 1978: The Wild Geese. Escape to Athena. 1979: Moonraker. North Sea Hijack (US: ffolkes). 1980: The Sea Wolves. Les seducteurs/Sunday Lovers. 1981: The Cannonball Run. For Your Eyes Only. 1983: Octopussy. Curse of the Pink Panther. 1984: The Naked Face. 1985: A View to a Kill.

MOORE, Terry (Helen Koford) 1929—
Bright, bubbly, petite, light-haired American actress, a former child model who played several teenage roles before catching the public eye as the girl in Mighty Joe Young. She enjoyed a few years of stardom after this before beginning to slip. Received an Oscar nomination for Come Back, Little Sheba.
1940: ‡Maryland. ‡The Howards of Virginia (GB: The Tree of Liberty). 1942: †On the Sunny Side. **A-Haunting We Will Go. **My Gal Sal. 1943: **True to Life. **A Date with Destiny. 1944: **Gaslight. ‡Since You Went Away. ‡Sweet and Lowdown. 1945: ‡Son of Lassie. 1946: ‡Shadowed. †Summer Holiday (released 1948). 1947: †Devil on Wheels. 1948: The Return of October (GB: A Date with Destiny). 1949: Mighty Joe Young. 1950: The Great Rupert. He's a Cockeyed Wonder. Gambling House. 1951: Two of a Kind. Sunny Side of the Street. The Barefoot Mailman. 1952: Come Back, Little Sheba. 1953: Man on a Tightrope. Beneath the 12-Mile Reef. King of the Khyber Rifles. 1955: Portrait of Alison (US: Postmark for Danger). Shack Out on 101. Daddy Long Legs. 1956: Between Heaven and Hell. The Moneymaker (TV). 1957: The Clouded Image (TV). Bernardine. Peyton Place. 1959: A Private's Affair. Cast a Long Shadow. 1960: Platinum High School (GB:

Rich, Young and Deadly). Why Must I Die? (GB: 13 Steps to Death). 1965: Black Spurs. Town Tamer. City of Fear. 1966: Waco. 1967: A Man Called Dagger. 1970: Quarantined (TV). 1971: Daredevil. 1976: Smash Up on Interstate Five (TV). 1977: Death Dimension. 1984: Hellhole.
‡As Helen Koford **As Judy Ford
† As Jan Ford

MORE, Kenneth 1914–1982
Square-faced, cheerful British actor with a mop of light wavy hair. A revue artist at 21, he took to films in the late 1940s, at first in quiet supporting roles, but gradually coming to the fore as good-hearted, devil-may-care, ultra-British types with an eye for the ladies. He burst through to stardom in *Genevieve*, and remained one of Britain's most popular stars until the failure of the underrated *The Comedy Man*. Married (second) to Angela Douglas. Died from Parkinson's Disease.
1935: Look Up and Laugh. 1936: Carry on London. Windmill Revels. 1946: School for Secrets. 1948: Scott of the Antarctic. 1949: Man on the Run. Now Barabbas ... was a robber. Stop Press Girl. 1950: Morning Departure (US: Operation Disaster). The Clouded Yellow. Chance of a Lifetime. 1951: No Highway (US: No Highway in the Sky). The Franchise Affair. Appointment with Venus (US: Island Rescue). Brandy for the Parson. 1952: The Yellow Balloon. 1953: Never Let Me Go. Genevieve. Our Girl Friday (US: The Adventures of Sadie). 1954: Doctor in the House. 1955: Raising a Riot. The Deep Blue Sea. 1956: Reach for the Sky. 1957: The Admirable Crichton (US: Paradise Lagoon). 1958: A Night to Remember. Next to No Time! The Sheriff of Fractured Jaw. 1959: The 39 Steps. Northwest Frontier (US: Flame over India). Sink the Bismarck! 1960: Man in the Moon. The Greengage Summer (US: Loss of Innocence). 1962: Some People. We Joined the Navy. The Longest Day. 1963: The Comedy Man. 1966: †The Collector. 1967: The Mercenaries (US: Dark of the Sun). 1968: Fraulein Doktor. 1969: Oh! What a Lovely War. Battle of Britain. 1970: Scrooge. 1976: The Slipper and the Rose. Where Time Began. 1977: Leopard in the Snow. 1978: The Silent Witness (narrator only). 1979: The Spaceman and King Arthur (US: Unidentified Flying Odd-

ball). The Delessi Affair. 1981: a Tale of Two Cities (TV).
† Scenes deleted from final release print

MOREAU, Jeanne 1928–
Tight-lipped, sharp-looking brunette French actress, a magnetic screen personality and mistress of high drama. Once the youngest student at the French National Conservatory of Dramatic Art. Latterly has shown an inclination to direct. The physical resemblance to Bette Davis cannot be, one feels, entirely insignificant.
1948: Dernier amour. 1950: Pigalle-Saint-Germain-des-Prés. Meurtres. 1951: L'homme de ma vie. 1952. Docteur Schweitzer. Il es minuit. 1953: Julietta. Dortoir des grandes. Secrets d'alcove (GB and US: The Bed). 1954: Touchez pas au grisbi (GB: Grisbi. US: Honor Among Thieves). Les intrigantes. La Reine Margot. 1955: Les hommes en blanc. M'sieur la Caille (GB: The Parasites). Gas-Oil. 1956: Le salaire du péché (US: Wages of Sin). Les louves (GB and US: The She-Wolves). 1957: Jusqu'au dernier. L'étrange Monsieur Stève. Trois jours à vivre. 1958: Ascenseur pour l'echafaud (GB: Lift to the Scaffold. US: Frantic). Le dos au mur (GB and US: Evidence in Concrete). Echec au porteur. Les amants. 1959: Les quatre cents coups (GB and US: The 400 Blows). Les liaisons dangereuses. Five Branded Women. 1960: The Carmelites. Moderato cantabile. 1961: Une femme est une femme. La notte. Jules et Jim. 1962: Eve/Eva. La baie des anges. 1963: Le feu follet (GB: A Time to Live and a Time to Die. US: The Fire Within). The Trial. The Victors. Peau de banane/Banana Peel. 1964: Diary of a Chambermaid. Mata Hari Agent H 21 (GB: Mata Hari). The Yellow Rolls Royce. La peau douce (GB: Silken Skin. Voice only). 1965: The Train. Viva Maria! 1966: Chimes at Midnight (US: Falstaff). Mademoiselle. Sailor from Gibraltar. 1967: The Oldest Profession. 1968: La mariée était en noir/The Bride Wore Black. Great Catherine. The Immortal Story. 1969: Le corps de Diane. 1970: Monte Walsh. Compte à rebours. 1971: Alex in Wonderland. Cannibales en Sicile. Dead Reckoning. L'humeur vagabonde. Mille baisers de Florence. 1972: Chére Louise. 1973: Le petit théâtre de Jean Renoir (TV. GB and US: cinemas). 1974: Nathalie Granger. Les valseuses (GB: Making It). La race des 'Seigneurs'. Je t'aime. Hu-Man. 1975: Le jardin qui bascule. Souvenirs

d'en France (US: French Provincial). 1976: Mr Klein. Lumière. The Last Tycoon. 1980: Your Ticket is No Longer Valid. Les uns et les autres. 1981: La débandade. Plein Sud/Southbound. Mille milliards de dollars. La truite/The Trout. 1982: Querelle. 1983: Der Bauer von Babylon. 1986: Le paltoquet.

As director: 1976: Lumière. 1978: L'adolescente.

MORELL, André (A. Mesritz) 1909–1978
Staunch, light-haired British actor, in leading roles on stage from the thirties, and on the fringe of cinema stardom for many years without ever becoming a box-office name. In later years, mixed small roles as judges and other figures of authority with leading parts in horror films. Married to Joan Greenwood (qv) from 1960.
1938: Many Tanks Mr Atkins. *The Murdered Constable. *Confidence Trickers. *Criminals Always Blunder. *Receivers. *The Kite Mob. 13 Men and a Gun. 1939: Ten Days in Paris (US: Missing Ten Days). 1940: Three Silent Men. 1942: Unpublished Story. 1948: Against the Wind. 1949: No Place for Jennifer. 1950: Madeleine. So Long at the Fair. Stage Fright. Seven Days to Noon. The Clouded Yellow. Trio. 1951: Flesh and Blood. High Treason. 1952: Tall Headlines. Stolen Face. 1953: His Majesty O'Keefe. 1954: The Golden Link. The Black Knight. 1955: Summer Madness (US: Summertime). Three Cases of Murder. The Secret. They Can't Hang Me. 1956: The Man Who Never Was. The Black Tent. The Baby and the Battleship. Zarak. 1957: Interpol (US: Pickup Alley). Paris Holiday. The Bridge on the River Kwai. Diamond Safari. 1958: The Camp on Blood Island. 1959: The Hound of the Baskervilles. Behemoth the Sea Monster (US: The Giant Behemoth). Ben-Hur. 1960: Cone of Silence (US: Trouble in the Sky). 1961: The Shadow of the Cat. Cash on Demand. 1963: Woman of Straw. 1964: The Moon-Spinners. 1965: Judith. She. The Plague of the Zombies. 1966: The Wrong Box. 1967: The Mummy's Shroud. The Mercenaries (US: Dark of the Sun). 1968: Vengeance of She. 1970: Julius Caesar. 10 Rillington Place. 1972: Pope Joan. *The Man and the Snake. 1974: QB VII (TV). 1975: Barry Lyndon. 1976: The Slipper and the Rose. The Message. 1978: The Lord of the Rings (voice only). The First Great Train Robbery.

MORENO, Antonio (A. Monteagudo)
1886–1967
Dark, Spanish-born Hollywood star of distinguished bearing, a popular leading man in silents for 15 years. The coming of sound coincided naturally with a move into character roles, and he roamed the world in search of interesting material. Later appeared as priests, judges and aristocrats. Died from a stroke.
1912: *The Voice of the Million. *So Near, Yet So Far. *Two Daughters of Eve. *The Musketeers of Pig Alley. 1913: *No Place for Father. *The House of Discord. *By Man's Law. Judith of Bethulia. 1914: *His Father's House. *Our Mutual Girl. *Too Many Husbands. *The Ladies' War. *The Song of the Ghetto. *The Memories in Men's Souls. *Politics and the Press. *Under False Colors. *The Old Flute Player. *Classmates. *Strongheart. *The Accomplished Mrs Thompson. *The Persistent Mr Prince. *John Rance, Gentleman. *The Hidden Letters. *The Loan Shark King. *The Peacemaker. *Goodbye Summer. 1915: *In the Latin Quarter. *The Quality of Mercy. *The Park Honeymooners. *Love's Way. *The Island of Regeneration. Dust of Egypt. On Her Wedding Night. *Anselo Lee. *Youth. *The Gypsy Trail. *A 'Model' Wife. A Price for Folly. 1916: The Supreme Temptation. Kennedy Square. *Susie, the Sleuth. *She Won the Prize. The Shop Girl. The Tarantula. Rose of the South. The Devil's Prize. 1917: Her Right to Live. Aladdin from Broadway. The Magnificent Meddler. By Right of Possession. The Mark of Cain. Money Magic. The Captain of the Gray Horse Troop. A Son of the Hills. The Angel Factory. 1918: The First Law. The Naulahka. The Iron Test (serial). The House of Hate. 1919: The Perils of Thunder Mountain (serial). 1920: The Invisible Hand (serial). The Veiled Mystery (serial). 1921: The Secret of the Hills. Three Sevens. 1922: A Guilty Conscience. 1923: My American Wife. Look Your Best. The Trail of the Lonesome Pine. The Spanish Dancer. The Exciter. Lost and Found on a South Sea Island (GB: Lost and Found). 1924: Tiger Love. Flaming Barriers. The Border Legion. The Story without a Name (GB: Without Warning). Bluff. 1925: Her Husband's Secret. Learning to Love. One Year to Live. 1926: Mare Nostrum. Beverly of Graustark. The Flaming Forest. The Temptress. Love's Blindness. 1927: Madame Pompadour. It. Venus of

Venice. En la Tierra del Sol. 1928: Nameless Men. Come to My House. The Air Legion. Synthetic Sin. The Whip Woman. Midnight Taxi. Adoration. 1929: *Voice of Hollywood. Careers. Romance of the Rio Grande. El Cuerpo del Delita. 1930: Rough Romance. One Mad Kiss. El Hombre Malo. La Voluntad de Muerto. 1931: Los que Danzan. Fin de Fiesta. 1932: *The Wide Open Spaces. Primavera en Otono. La Ciudad de Carton. 1933: Rosa de Francia. Senora Casada. Necesita Marido. 1935: Storm over the Andes. 1936: Maria de la O. The Bohemian Girl. 1938: Rose of the Rio Grande. 1939: Ambush. 1940: Seven Sinners. 1941: Two Latins from Manhattan. They Met in Argentina. The Kid from Kansas. 1942: Valley of the Sun. Undercover Man. Fiesta. 1944: Tampico. 1945: The Spanish Main. Sol y Sombra. 1946: Notorious. 1947: Captain from Castile. 1949: Lust for Gold. 1950: Dallas. Crisis. Saddle Tramp. 1951: Mark of the Renegade. 1952: Untamed Frontier. 1953: Thunder Bay. Wings of the Hawk. 1954: The Creature from the Black Lagoon. Saskatchewan (GB: O'Rourke of the Royal Mounted). 1956: The Searchers. 1958: Mr Pharaoh and Cleopatra (US: Catch Me If You Can).

As director: 1931: Santa. 1932: Aguilas Frente al Sol.

MORENO, Rita (Rosita Alverio) 1931–
Flashing-eyed, fiery, petite brunette Puerto Rican actress and dancer, in show business from childhood and stealing scenes from stars from the early fifties. Did not become a star cinema attraction, even after an Oscar for West Side Story, but has continued to delight TV and nightclub audiences with her whirling dance routines.
1935: ‡The Scoundrel. 1936: ‡Silk Legs. 1945: †A Medal for Benny. 1950: †So Young, So Bad. The Toast of New Orleans. Pagan Love Song. 1952: The Fabulous Senorita. The Ring. Singin' in the Rain. Cattle Town. Ma and Pa Kettle on Vacation (GB: Ma and Pa Kettle Go to Paris). 1953: Fort Vengeance. Latin Lovers. Jivaro (GB: Lost Treasure of the Amazon). El Alamein (GB: Desert Patrol). 1954: Garden of Evil. The Yellow Tomahawk. 1955: Untamed. Seven Cities of Gold. 1956: The Vagabond King. The King and I. The Lieutenant Wore Skirts. Broken Arrow (TV). 1957: The Deerslayer. 1960: This Rebel Breed. Alas, Babylon (TV). 1961: West Side Story. Sum-

mer and Smoke. 1962: Samar! 1963: Cry of Battle. 1968: The Night of the Following Day. 1969: Popi. 1971: Carnal Knowledge. Taxi to Terror. 1972: The Voice of La Raza. 1976: The Ritz. 1978: The Boss's Son. 1979: Anatomy of a Seduction (TV). 1980: Happy Birthday Gemini. 1981: The Four Seasons.

‡ As Rosita Alverio † As Rosita Moreno

MORGAN, Dennis (Stanley Morner) 1910–
Fresh-faced, shy-seeming American actor and tenor singer, of Irish parentage. Joined Warners under his new name, and became a likeable part of their product from late 1938 until mid-1952, often in musical tandem with big, brash Jack Carson. Although he played a few action-man roles after this, his rich singing voice ensured that his future would lie in night clubs.
1935: †I Conquer the Sea. 1936: †Piccadilly Jim. †Suzy. †Old Hutch. †The Great Ziegfeld. †Down the Stretch. 1937: †Song of the City. †Navy Blue and Gold. †Mama Steps Out. 1938: †Men with Wings. †King of Alcatraz (GB: King of the Alcatraz). ‡Persons in Hiding. Waterfront. 1939: *Ride, Cowboy, Ride. *The Singing Dude. The Return of Dr X. No Place to Go. 1940: Three Cheers for the Irish. Tear Gas Squad. River's End. The Fighting 69th. Kitty Foyle. Flight Angels. 1941: Bad Men of Missouri. Affectionately Yours. 1942: Wings for the Eagle. Captains of the Clouds. In This Our Life. The Hard Way. 1943: Thank Your Lucky Stars. The Desert Song. 1944: Hollywood Canteen. *The Shining Future. Shine on Harvest Moon. The Very Thought of You. 1945: God is My Co-Pilot. Christmas in Connecticut (GB: Indiscretion). 1946: Two Guys from Milwaukee (GB: Royal Flush). One More Tomorrow. The Time, the Place and the Girl. 1947: Cheyenne. My Wild Irish Rose. 1948: Always Together. To the Victor. Two Guys from Texas (GB: Two Texas Knights). One Sunday Afternoon. 1949: It's a Great Feeling. The Lady Takes a Sailor. 1950: Perfect Strangers (GB: Too Dangerous to Love). Raton Pass (GB: Canyon Pass). Pretty Baby. 1951: Painting the Clouds with Sunshine. 1952: This Woman is Dangerous. Cattle Town. 1955: Pearl of the South Pacific. The Gun That Won the West. 1956: Uranium Boom. 1968: Rogue's Gallery. 1975: Won Ton Ton, the Dog Who Saved Hollywood.

†As Stanley Morner ‡ As Richard Stanley

MORGAN, Michele (Simone Roussel) 1920–

Narrow-faced, golden-haired, green-eyed, sulkily beautiful French actress who has also been a success in British and American films. One of the most sought-after international stars from the early forties to the mid-fifties: the darker the drama, the more haunting her performances became. Still active on the French film and theatre scene. Married to actors William Marshall and Henri Vidal, the latter leaving her a widow in 1959.

1935: †Mademoiselle Mozart. 1936: †Une fille a Papa. †Le mioche. †Mes tantes et moi. †La belle équipe. 1937: Gribouille (US: The Lady in Question). Orage. 1938: Quai des brumes. L'entraîneuse. 1939: Le récif de corail. Les musiciens du ciel. La loi du nord. Remorques. 1940: Untel, père et fils. 1942: Joan of Paris. 1943: Two Tickets to London. Higher and Higher. 1944: Passage to Marseille. 1946: The Chase. La symphonie pastorale. 1948: The Fallen Idol. Fabiola. Aux yeux du souvenir. 1949: La belle que violà. Maria Chapdelaine (GB: The Naked Heart). 1950: Madame X/L'étrange Madame X. Le château de verre. 1951: The Seven Deadly Sins. 1952: La minute de verité/The Moment of Truth. 1953: Destinées (GB: Love and the Frenchwoman. US: Daughters of Destiny). Les orgueilleux (GB: The Proud Ones). 1954: Obsession. Napoléon. 1955: Oasis. Les grandes manoeuvres (GB: Summer Manoeuvres). Marguerite de la Nuit. 1956: Si Paris nous était conté. Marie Antoinette. Les vendangés. 1957: Maxime. The Vintage. Retour de Manivelle (GB and US: There's Always a Price Tag). 1958: Le miroir a deux faces (GB and US: The Mirror Has Two Faces). Pourquoi viens-tu si tard? Racconti d'estate (GB: Girls for the Summer). 1959: Vacanze inverno. Grand Hotel/Menschen im Hotel. 1960: Fortunat. Les scélérats. 1961: Le puits aux trois vérités. Les lions sont lâchés. Rencontres. 1962: Le crime ne paie pas. Landru. The Gentle Art of Murder. 1963: Il fornaretto di Venezia. Méfiez-vous mesdames? 1964: Constance aux enfers. Les pas perdus. Les yeux cernés. Dis-moi qui tuer. 1966: Lost Command. 1968: Benjamin. 1972: Les amis de mon fils. 1975: Le chat et le souris (GB: Seven Suspects to Murder. US: Cat and Mouse). 1978: Robert et Robert.

† As Simone Roussel.

MORGAN, Terence 1921–

Darkly sleek British leading man, usually cast as handsome rats. A certain screen charisma helped mask his limited acting ability, and he enjoyed a good variety of leading roles in British films throughout the fifties.

1948: Hamlet. 1950: Shadow of the Past. 1951: Captain Horatio Hornblower RN. Encore. 1952: Mandy (US: Crash of Silence). It Started in Paradise. 1953: Street Corner (US: Both Sides of the Law). The Steel Key. Always a Bride. Turn the Key Softly. 1954: L'amante di Paridi/Eterna femmina (GB and US: The Face That Launched a Thousand Ships). Dance Little Lady. Forbidden Cargo. Svengali. 1955: They Can't Hang Me. 1956: It's a Wonderful World. The March Hare. 1957: The Scamp. 1958: Tread Softly, Stranger. 1959: The Shakedown. 1960: Piccadilly Third Stop. 1964: The Curse of the Mummy's Tomb. 1966: Tiger of the Seven Seas (GB: The Fighting Corsair). 1967: The Penthouse. 1972: Hide and Seek. 1975: The Lifetaker. 1979: Yesterday's Warriors.

MORISON, Patricia 1914–

Dark-haired, pencil-browed, exotic-looking American singer and actress of rather haughty demeanour. Although largely wasted by Hollywood in silly decorative roles, she later achieved great success in Broadway musicals.

1938: Persons in Hiding . 1939: I'm from Missouri. The Magnificent Fraud. 1940: Rangers of Fortune. Untamed. 1941: Romance of the Rio Grande. The Roundup. One Night in Lisbon. 1942: Beyond the Blue Horizon. Are Husbands Necessary? A Night in New Orleans.

1943: Silver Skates. The Song of Bernadette. Hitler's Madman. The Fallen Sparrow. Calling Doctor Death. Where Are Your Children? 1945: Without Love. Lady on a Train. 1946: Dressed to Kill (GB: Sherlock Holmes and the Secret Code). Danger Woman. 1947: Tarzan and the Huntress. Queen of the Amazons. Song of the Thin Man. Kiss of Death. 1948: The Prince of Thieves. The Return of Wildfire. Sofia. 1953: Eddie Drake Investigates (TV. GB: cinemas). 1960: Song without End. 1975: Won Ton Ton, the Dog Who Saved Hollywood.

MORLEY, Robert 1908–

Large British stage star, film character actor, writer and wit. He often looked as though he had just detected a bad smell (the script, perhaps, in many of his later films) and huffed and puffed to great effect as a comic Sydney Greenstreet. His characters were almost always larger than life and he dominated his films (the earlier ones, especially), often to the stars' discomfort. Memorable as W.S. Gilbert, Oscar Wilde and King George III. Nominated for a Best Supporting Actor Oscar in his first film.

*1938: Marie Antoinette. 1940: You Will Remember. 1941: Major Barbara. The Big Blockade. This Was Paris. 1942: The Young Mr Pitt. The Foreman Went to France (US: Somewhere in France). *Partners in Crime. 1945: I live in Grosvenor Square (US: A Yank in London). 1947: The Ghosts of Berkeley Square. 1948: The Small Back Room. 1951: Outcast of the Islands. The African Queen. 1952: Curtain Up. 1953: The Story of Gilbert and Sullivan (US: The Great Gilbert and Sullivan). The Final Test. Beat the Devil. 1954: Beau Brummell. The Good Die Young. The Rainbow Jacket. 1955: The Adventures of Quentin Durward. 1956: Around the World in 80 Days. Loser Takes All. 1958: Law and Disorder. The Sheriff of Fractured Jaw. The Journey. 1959: The Doctor's Dilemma. Misalliance (TV). Libel. The Battle of the Sexes. 1960: Giuseppe venduto dei fratelli (GB: Sold into Egypt. US: Joseph and his Brethren). Oscar Wilde. 1961: The Young Ones. Go to Blazes. 1962: The Road to Hong Kong. Nine Hours to Rama. The Boys. The Old Dark House. 1963: Murder at the Gallop. Ladies Who Do. Hot Enough for June (US: Agent 8¾). Take Her, She's Mine. 1964: Topkapi. *Rhythm 'n' Greens (narrator only). Of*

Human Bondage. 1965: Those Magnificent Men in Their Flying Machines. The Alphabet Murders. Genghis Khan. The Loved One. A Study in Terror (US: Fog). Life at the Top. 1966: Hotel Paradiso. Tendre voyou. Way ... Way Out. Finders Keepers. 1967: Woman Times Seven. The Trygon Factor. 1968: Hot Millions. 1969: Some Girls Do. Sinful Davey. Twinky (US: Lola). 1970: Cromwell. Doctor in Trouble. Song of Norway. 1971: When Eight Bells Toll. 1973: Many Moons (narrator only). Theatre of Blood. 1975: Hugo the Hippo (voice only). Great Expectations (TV. GB: cinemas). 1976: The Blue Bird. 1978: Who is Killing the Great Chefs of Europe? (GB: Too Many Chefs). 1979: The Human Factor. Scavenger Hunt. 1980: Oh Heavenly Dog. 1981: The Great Muppet Caper. 1983: High Road to China. 1985: Trouble at the Royal Rose/Trouble with Spys. Second Time Lucky. 1986: Little Dorrit I. Little Dorrit II. The Wind.

MORRIS, Chester (John C. Morris) 1901–1970
Grim-faced, square-jawed American actor with long, narrow mouth (almost a serious Joe E. Brown) and liquid eyes. Made a great impact in two dramatic early sound films, Alibi and The Big House, but declined to 'B' features and played the series character Boston Blackie, a resourceful and likeable small-time crook, from 1941 to 1949. Later successful on stage and TV, both as actor and magician. Suffered from ill-health in later years, and was found dead from a drug overdose. Academy Award nominee for Alibi.
1917: An Amateur Orphan. 1918: The Beloved Traitor. 1923: Loyal Lives. 1925: The Road to Yesterday. 1929: Fast Life. Woman Trap. The Show of Shows. Alibi. 1930: The Big House. Second Choice. She Couldn't Say No. Playing Around. The Case of Sergeant Grischa. The Divorcee. 1931: Corsair. The Bat Whispers. 1932: Sinners in the Sun. Cock of the Air. Red-Headed Woman. Breach of Promise. The Miracle Man. 1933: Tomorrow at Seven. The Infernal Machine. King for a Night. Blondie Johnson. Golden Harvest. 1934: *Hollywood Cavalcade. Gift of Gab. Embarrassing Moments. The Gay Bride. Let's Talk It Over. 1935: Public Hero Number One. Princess O'Hara. Society Doctor. I've Been Around. Frankie and Johnny. Pursuit. 1936: *Pirate Party on Catalina Isle. Counterfeit. Moonlight

Murder. They Met in a Taxi. Three Godfathers. 1937: Flight to Glory. I Promise to Pay. The Devil's Playground. 1938: Smashing the Rackets. Sky Giant. Law of the Underworld. 1939: Five Came Back. Pacific Liner. Thunder Afloat. Blind Alley. 1940: Wagons Westward. The Marines Fly High. The Girl from God's Country. 1941: Meet Boston Blackie. No Hands on the Clock. 1942: Alias Boston Blackie. Canal Zone. Confessions of Boston Blackie (GB: Confessions). Wrecking Crew. Boston Blackie Goes to Hollywood (GB: Blackie Goes Hollywood). I Live on Danger. 1943: Aerial Gunner. Tornado. After Midnight with Boston Blackie (GB: After Midnight). High Explosive. The Chance of a Lifetime. 1944: One Mysterious Night (GB: Behind Closed Doors). Gambler's Choice. Double Exposure. Secret Command. 1945: Boston Blackie Booked on Suspicion (GB: Booked on Suspicion). Rough, Tough and Ready (GB: Men of the Deep). Boston Blackie's Rendezvous (GB: Blackie's Rendezvous). 1946: One Way to Love. A Close Call for Boston Blackie (GB: Lady of Mystery). The Phantom Thief. Boston Blackie and the Law (GB: Blackie and the Law). 1947: Blind Spot. 1948: Trapped by Boston Blackie. 1949: Boston Blackie's Chinese Venture (GB: Chinese Adventure). 1955: Unchained. 1956: The She-Creature. 1957: Child of Trouble (TV). 1970: The Great White Hope.

MORRIS, Lana (Pamela Matthews) 1930–
Striking British actress whose vivid, slightly old-fashioned looks – black hair, dark eyes and a minxish mouth for her deep red lipstick – always suggested that she was capable of interpreting roles with more bite than the milk-and-water misses she actually got from the British cinema of the fifties. A junior-league Margaret Lockwood, perhaps, but her career never veered in that direction. Later a TV panellist.
1946: †School for Secrets (US: Secret Flight). 1947: The Weaker Sex. 1948: Spring in Park Lane. It's Hard to be Good. 1949: The Chiltern Hundreds (US: The Amazing Mr Beecham). Trottie True (GB: Gay Lady). 1950: Morning Departure (US: Operation Disaster). Guilt is My Shadow. The Reluctant Widow. Trio. The Woman in Question (GB: Five Angles on Murder). 1951: A Tale of Five Cities (US: A Tale of Five Women). 1953: The Red Beret (US:

Paratrooper). The Good Beginning. The Straw Man. Trouble in Store. Thought to Kill. Black 13. 1954: Radio Cab Murder. 1955: Man of the Moment. 1956: Home and Away. 1958: Moment of Indiscretion. 1959: Passport to Shame (US: Room 43). Jet Storm. No Trees in the Street. 1960: October Moth. 1969: I Start Counting.

† As Pamela Matthews

MORRIS, Mary 1915–
Wide-eyed brunette British actress with small, square, distinctive, faintly oriental features and forceful personality. Prominent in British films from 1937 to 1941, but increasingly thereafter committed to the stage, where she made a spitfire Cleopatra and a moving Saint Joan. Born in Fiji, she made her stage debut in Barbados, before education and dramatic studies in England.
1937: Victoria the Great. 1938: Prison without Bars. 1939: At the Villa Rose (US: House of Mystery). The Spy in Black (US: U-Boat 29). 1940: The Thief of Bagdad. 1941: Major Barbara. Pimpernel Smith (US: Mister V). 1943: Undercover (US: Underground Guerillas). 1944: The Agitator. 1945: The Man from Morocco. 1949: Train of Events. 1951: High Treason. Painter and Poet (narrator only). 1976: Full Circle.

MORRIS, Wayne (Bert de Wayne Morris) 1914–1959
Big, blond, open-faced American actor who played action heroes, boxers and kind-hearted tough guys. He was prominent

in Warners films of the late thirties, but absence on war service – although he was an air force hero who flew 57 combat missions, shot down seven enemy planes and won many medals – badly hit his career, the rest of which was spent in second-features. Died from a heart attack.

1936: China Clipper. Here Comes Carter (GB: The Voice of Scandal). King of Hockey (GB: King of the Ice Rink). Polo Joe. Smart Blonde. 1937: Once a Doctor. Land Beyond the Law. Submarine D-1. Kid Galahad. The Kid Comes Back (GB: Don't Pull Your Punches). 1938: Men Are Such Fools. Love, Honor and Behave. Valley of the Giants. Brother Rat. 1939: The Kid from Kokomo (GB: The Orphan of the Ring). The Return of Dr X. 1940: Brother Rat and a Baby (GB: Baby Be Good). The Quarterback. An Angel from Texas. Ladies Must Live. Gambling on the High Seas. Double Alibi. Flight Angels. 1941: Bad Men of Missouri. Three Sons o' Guns. The Smiling Ghost. I Wanted Wings. 1947: Deep Valley. The Voice of the Turtle. 1948: The Big Punch. The Time of Your Life. 1949: The Younger Brothers. A Kiss in the Dark. Task Force. John Loves Mary. The House across the Street. 1950: Stage to Tucson (GB: Lost Stage Valley). Johnny One-Eye. The Tougher They Come. 1951: Yellowfin (GB: Yellow Fin). Sierra Passage. The Big Gusher. The Bushwhackers (GB: The Rebel). 1952: Arctic Flight. Desert Pursuit. 1953: Star of Texas. The Marksman. The Master Plan. The Fighting Lawman. Texas Bad Man. 1954: The Green Buddha. Riding Shotgun. The Desperado. Port of Hell. Two Guns and a Badge. 1955: Cross Channel. Lord of the Jungle. Lonesome Trail. 1956: The Gelignite Gang (US: The Dynamiters). 1957: The Crooked Sky. Plunder Road. Paths of Glory. 1958: Buffalo Gun.

MORROW, Vic 1932–1982
Fair-haired American actor usually cast as characters with a vicious streak. Evidently tired of such aggression by 1961, he devoted himself to directing, on stage, television (where he also played in the series *Combat*) and the occasional film, before returning to acting in 1969, becoming especially prolific in TV movies. In July 1982 a helicopter, filming Morrow for an action scene, was accidentally hit by a 'firebomb' and crashed, killing him instantly.

1955: Blackboard Jungle. 1956: Tribute to a Bad Man. 1957: Men in War. 1958: God's Little Acre. Hell's Five Hours. King Creole. 1960: Cimarron. 1961: Portrait of a Mobster. Posse from Hell. 1969: How to Make It (GB: Target: Harry). River of Mystery (TV). 1970: Travis Logan DA. A Step Out of Line. 1972: The Glass House (TV. GB: cinemas). The Weekend Nun (TV). 1973: Police Story (TV. GB: cinemas). Nightmare (TV). 1974: The Take. The California Kid (TV). Death Stalk (TV). Dirty Mary, Crazy Larry. 1975: Wanted: Babysitter. Tom Sawyer (TV). The Night That Panicked America (TV). 1976: The Treasure of Matecumbe. The Bad News Bears. Funeral for an Assassin. 1977: The Man with the Power (TV). The Ghost of Cypress Swamp (TV). Curse of the Black Widow (TV). Message from Space. 1978: Wild and Wooly (TV). The Hostage Heart (TV). 1979: The Evictors. Supertrain (TV). Paris (TV). Stone/The Killing Stone (TV). BAD Cats (TV). 1980: Plutonium Incident (TV). Humanoids from the Deep (GB: Monster). 1981: L'ultimo Squalo/ Great White (GB: Shark). 1982: The Bronx Warriors. 1983: The Twilight Zone (GB: Twilight Zone The Movie).

As director: 1962: *Last Year at Malibu. 1966: Deathwatch. 1969: Sledge/A Man Called Sledge. 1979: The Evictors.

MORSE, Robert 1931–
Chirpy, rubber-faced American comic actor. Most of his work has been done on Broadway, but he was briefly in vogue in the cinema of the sixties as a kind of thinking Jerry Lewis – like Lewis, mugging gamely and sometimes singing and dancing as well.

1955: The Proud and Profane. 1958: The Matchmaker. 1963: The Cardinal. 1964: Honeymoon Hotel. 1965: Quick Before It Melts. The Loved One. 1966: Oh Dad, Poor Dad, Mama's Hung You in the Closet and I'm Feeling So Sad. 1967: How to Succeed in Business without Really Trying. A Guide for the Married Man. 1968: Where Were You When the Lights Went Out? 1970: The Boatniks. 1985: Calendar Girl Murders (TV).

MOSTEL, Zero (Samuel Mostel) 1915–1977
Dark-haired, roly-poly American comic actor

with football-shaped face. At first seen in serious roles as swarthy, sweaty, ethnic types, this part of his career was halted by blacklisting at the hands of the McCarthy Committee in 1951. After a long sojourn performing on Broadway and in nightclubs and building a reputation as a painter, he returned as a leading comic character actor, firing on all cylinders if you liked that sort of thing. Died from cardiac arrest.

1943: DuBarry Was a Lady. 1950: Panic in the Streets. The Enforcer (GB: Murder Inc). 1951: Sirocco. The Guy Who Came Back. Mr Belvedere Rings the Bell. The Model and the Marriage Broker. 1959: *Zero. 1966: A Funny Thing Happened on the Way to the Forum. 1967: The Producers. Great Catherine. *The Ride of the Valkyrie. 1968: Monsieur Lecoq (unfinished). 1969: The Great Bank Robbery. The Angel Levine. 1972: The Hot Rock (GB: How to Steal a Diamond in Four Uneasy Lessons). 1973: Rhinoceros. Marco (made for cinemas but shown only on TV). 1974: Foreplay. 1976: Mastermind (filmed 1969). Journey into Fear. The Front. 1977: Once Upon a Scoundrel. 1978: The Little Drummer Boy (TV. Voice only). Watership Down (voice only). 1979: Best Boy.

MOULDER-BROWN, John 1951–
Light-haired British child actor of cherubic countenance. He progressed well to leading juvenile roles, appearing as innocents at large in various guises at the beginning of the 1970s. But his did not become a popular name with the general public, and his film career soon seemed to have lost a firm direction.

1958: A Cry from the Streets. 1959: Night

Train for Inverness. 1961: The Missing Note. Two Living, One Dead. 1962: Night without Pity. 1963: Beware of the Dog (serial). Go Kart Go! 1964: The Uncle. 1965: Runaway Railway. 1966: Operation Third Form. 1967: Calamity the Cow. Heidi (TV). 1969: The Boys of Paul Street. The House That Screamed. 1970: The Breaking of Bumbo. Deep End. First Love. 1971: Vampire Circus. 1972: King, Queen, Knave. Ludwig. 1973: Say It with Flowers. 1979: Confessions from the David Galaxy Affair. 1981: The Grass is Singing. 1984: L'etincelle (US: Tug of Love). 1985: Dinner Date. 1986: Claudia's Story. Rumpelstiltskin.

MOUNT, Peggy 1916–

Plain-faced British actress (from 14 years old) whose long stage experience in Yorkshire must have prepared her for all those down-to-earth roles, culminating in her fearsome, stentorian-voiced mother-in-law, Mrs Hornett, in *Sailor Beware!* which she created on stage and which became her biggest film hit.

1954: The Embezzler. 1956: Sailor Beware! (US: Panic in the Parlor). Dry Rot. 1957: The Naked Truth (US: Your Past is Showing). 1960: Inn for Trouble. 1963: Ladies Who Do. 1964: One Way Pendulum. 1966: Hotel Paradiso. Finders Keepers. 1968: Oliver! 1976: The Chiffy Kids (serial).

MULLEN, Barbara 1914–1979

Tiny blue-eyed blonde purveyor of fey Irish charm, actually born in America and a dancer and variety artist for 17 years before coming to the screen in *Jeannie*, a role she repeated on stage and television. Also a writer, but best remembered as the doctors' housekeeper,

Janet, in the long-running British television (and later radio) series, *Dr Finlay's Casebook*. *1941: Jeannie. 1942: Thunder Rock. 1944: Welcome Mr Washington. 1945: A Place of One's Own. The Trojan Brothers. 1948: Corridor of Mirrors. My Sister and I. 1951: Talk of a Million (US: You Can't Beat the Irish). 1952: So Little Time. The Gentle Gunman. 1953: *The Bosun's Mate. *World of Life (narrator only). 1954: Destination Milan. The Death of Michael Turbin. The Last Moment. *Fool Notions. 1958: Innocent Sinners. 1959: The Siege of Pinchgut. 1960: The Challenge. 1963: The Very Edge. 1966: *Miss Mactaggart Won't Lie Down.*

MUNI, Paul (M. Weisenfreund) 1895–1967

Forceful, mannered, dark-haired, stockily-built Hollywood character star, born in Poland. Came to the fore in Warners' social conscience thrillers of the early thirties, then found his niche playing figures of history, usually under masses of make-up. Many of his performances look artificial by today's standards, but in 1936 he collected an Oscar for *The Story of Louis Pasteur*. Died from heart trouble. Also nominated for Oscars in *The Valiant*, *I Am a Fugitive from a Chain Gang*, *The Life of Emile Zola* and *The Last Angry Man*.

*1929: The Valiant. Seven Faces. 1932: I Am a Fugitive from a Chain Gang. Scarface (the Shame of a Nation). 1933: The World Changes. 1934: Hi Nellie! 1935: Bordertown. Dr Socrates. Black Fury. The Story of Louis Pasteur. 1937: The Good Earth. The Life of Emile Zola. The Woman I Love. 1938: *For Auld Lang Syne. 1939: Juarez. We Are Not Alone. 1940: Hudson's Bay. 1942: Commandos Strike at Dawn. 1943: Stage Door Canteen. 1945: Counter-Attack (GB: One Against Seven). A Song to Remember. 1946: Angel on My Shoulder. 1953: Stranger on the Prowl. 1958: Last Clear Chance (TV). 1959: The Last Angry Man.*

MUNRO, Caroline 1948–

Stunning, dark-haired, dark-eyed, apple-cheeked British actress with whistle-worthy figure. A throwback to the Yvonne de Carlo era, she got into films via eye-catching commercials – then seemed content to appear as slave girls, space maidens, vampires' victims and similar decoration. Male audiences cer-

tainly weren't complaining, and it's sad that so few films have found room for her. By the mid-1980s she was hostess on a TV game show.

1969: Where's Jack? 1971: The Abominable Dr Phibes. 1972: Captain Kronos – Vampire Hunter. Dracula AD 1972. 1973: The Golden Voyage of Sinbad. 1975: I Don't Want to Be Born. 1976: At the Earth's Core. 1977: The Spy Who Loved Me. 1979: Starcrash. 1980: Maniac. 1982: The Last Horror Film. 1984: Don't Open until Christmas. 1985: April Fool's Day.

MUNRO, Janet 1934–1972

Dark-haired, baby-faced, cuddly British actress who made several films for Walt Disney, but seemed to seek earthier roles back home in Britain. Later appearances restricted by an alcohol problem. Married to Tony Wright, 1956–1961, and Ian Hendry, 1963–1971. Choked to death while drinking tea.

1957: Small Hotel. 1958: The Young and the Guilty. Darby O'Gill and the Little People. The Trollenberg Terror (US: The Crawling Eye). 1959: Third Man on the Mountain. Tommy the Toreador. 1960: Swiss Family Robinson. 1961: The Horsemasters. The Day the Earth Caught Fire. 1962: Life for Ruth (US: Walk in the Shadow). 1963: Bitter Harvest. Hide and Seek. A Jolly Bad Fellow. 1964: Daylight Robbery. 1967: Sebastian. 1968: Cry Wolf.

MURDOCH, Richard 1907–

Long-faced, ever-smiling British comedian and light comic actor, with uniquely light, acidulous, upper-class tones. Proved enor-

315 MURPHY

mously successful on radio when in harness with other comedians, notably Arthur Askey in *Band Waggon* and Kenneth Horne in *Much-Binding-in-the-Marsh*, but his long, slim figure, like an elegant caricature on stilts, never really hit its stride in British films. Later, though, he had a third long-running radio success with *The Men from the Ministry*. 1934: *Evergreen*. 1937: *Over She Goes*. 1938: *The Terror*. 1939: *Band Waggon*. 1940: *Charley's (Big-Hearted) Aunt*. 1941: *The Ghost Train*. *I Thank You*. 1944: *One Exciting Night (US: You Can't Do without Love)*. 1948: *It Happened in Soho*. 1949: *Golden Arrow (US: The Gay Adventure/Three Men and a Girl*. Released 1952). 1950: *Lilli Marlene*. 1951: *The Magic Box*. 1959: *Strictly Confidential*. 1960: *Not a Hope in Hell*. 1969: *Under the Table You Must Go*. 1986: *Whoops Apocalypse*.

MURPHY, Audie 1924–1972
Baby-faced, slightly-built American actor with red-brown hair. America's most-decorated soldier of World War II with 28 medals (an experience from which he never recovered: he always kept a gun under his pillow), he took his light Texan voice and boyish appeal into movies, becoming a prolific star of 80-minute Technicolor westerns in which, he said, 'the scripts were the same – only the horses were changed'. Briefly in 'A' films after the success of the film of his autobiography, *To Hell and Back*. Married to Wanda Hendrix 1949–1950, first of two. Died in a private plane crash.
1948: *Beyond Glory*. *Texas, Brooklyn and Heaven (GB: The Girl from Texas)*. 1949:

Bad Boy. *The Kid from Texas (GB: Texas Kid – Outlaw)*. 1950: *Sierra*. *Kansas Raiders*. 1951: *The Red Badge of Courage*. *The Cimarron Kid*. 1952: *The Duel at Silver Creek*. 1953: *Gunsmoke! Column South*. *Tumbleweed*. 1954: *Ride Clear of Diablo*. *Drums Across the River*. *Destry*. *Queens of Beauty*. 1955: *To Hell and Back*. 1956: *Walk the Proud Land*. *World in My Corner*. 1957: *Joe Butterfly*. *Night Passage*. *Rock 'Em Cowboy*. *The Guns of Fort Petticoat*. 1958: *The Quiet American*. *The Gun Runners*. *Ride a Crooked Trail*. 1959: *No Name on the Bullet*. *The Wild and the Innocent*. *The Unforgiven*. *Cast a Long Shadow*. 1960: *Hell Bent for Leather*. *Seven Ways from Sundown*. 1961: *Battle at Bloody Beach (GB: Battle on the Beach)*. *Posse from Hell*. 1962: *Six Black Horses*. 1963: *Showdown*. *Gunfight at Comanche Creek*. 1964: *Bullet for a Badman*. *The Quick Gun*. *Apache Rifles*. 1965: *Arizona Raiders*. 1966: *Gunpoint*. *The Texican*. *Trunk to Cairo*. 1967: *40 Guns to Apache Pass*. 1969: *A Time for Dying*.

MURPHY, Eddie 1961–
Whippy, catlike, black American comedian and actor with slightly menacing air. After hosting a talent show at 15, he was performing in nightclubs as a stand-up comic a year later and a supremely confident star of TV's satirical *Saturday Night Live* before he was 20. Films so far have comprised one miss and three immense personal hits. Now the non-drinking, non-smoking, single-minded Murphy aims to write and direct his own films and looks set for lasting stardom.
1982: *48 Hrs*. 1983: *Trading Places*. 1984: *Best Defense*. *Beverly Hills Cop*. 1986: *The Golden Child*.

MURPHY, George 1902–
American dancer with snub nose, dark, wavy hair and light, pleasant speaking/singing voice. A vigorous hoofer with years of Broadway experience before coming to Hollywood, he soon settled down in films around the top of the second rank of stars. Played a few tough-guy roles after World War II, but left the movies in 1952 for a political career on the Republican side (Congressman for California from 1965 to 1969). Special Oscar 1950.
1934: *Kid Millions*. *Jealousy*. 1935: *Public Menace*. *I'll Love You Always*. *After the Dance*. 1936: *Woman Trap*. 1937: *London by*

Night. *Top of the Town*. *You're a Sweetheart*. *Women Men Marry*. *Broadway Melody of 1938*. 1938: *Hold That Co-Ed (GB: Hold That Girl)*. *Little Miss Broadway*. *Letter of Introduction*. 1939: *Risky Business*. *Broadway Melody of 1940*. 1940: *Little Nellie Kelly*. *Two Girls on Broadway (GB: Choose Your Partner)*. *Public Deb No. 1*. 1941: *Ringside Maisie (GB: Cash and Carry)*. *A Girl, a Guy and a Gob (GB: The Navy Steps Out)*. *Tom, Dick and Harry*. *Rise and Shine*. 1942: *For Me and My Gal (GB: For Me and My Girl)*. *Mayor of 44th Street*. *The Navy Comes Through*. 1943: *Show Business at War*. *The Powers Girl (GB: Hello! Beautiful)*. *Bataan*. *This is the Army*. 1944: *Show Business*. *Step Lively*. *Broadway Rhythm*. 1945: *Having Wonderful Crime*. *Up Goes Maisie (GB: Up She Goes)*. 1947: *The Arnelo Affair*. *Cynthia (GB: The Rich, Full Life)*. 1948: *The Big City*. *Tenth Avenue Angel*. 1949: *Border Incident*. *Battleground*. 1951: *No Questions Asked*. *It's a Big Country*. 1952: *Talk About a Stranger*. *Walk East on Beacon! (GB: The Crime of the Century)*.

MURPHY, Mary 1931–
Full-faced, sad-looking brunette American actress who played several small roles before becoming Marlon Brando's leading lady in *The Wild One*. Stardom surprisingly lasted only a few years for her, but she can still be seen, mostly on television, in character roles.
1951: *The Lemon Drop Kid*. *Darling, How Could You? (GB: Rendezvous)*. *When Worlds Collide*. *Sailor Beware*. 1952: *Carrie*. *The Turning Point*. *Come Back, Little Sheba*. *Plymouth Adventure*. *Off Limits (GB: Military*

Policemen). 1953: Houdini. Main Street to Broadway. The Wild One. 1954: Make Haste to Live. The Mad Magician. Sitting Bull. Beachhead. 1955: Hell's Island. The Desperate Hours. A Man Alone. 1956: The Intimate Stranger (US: Finger of Guilt). The Maverick Queen. 1958: Escapement (later Zex. US: The Electronic Monster). Live Fast, Die Young. 1959: Crime and Punishment USA. 1962: Red Hell. 40 Pounds of Trouble. 1965: Harlow. 1972: Footsteps (TV). Junior Bonner. 1974: I Love You ... Goodbye (TV). The Stranger Who Looks Like Me (TV). Born Innocent (TV). 1975: Katherine (TV).

MURRAY, Barbara 1929–

Sophisticated, very British brunette actress, in revue at 17, and, as one of the J. Arthur Rank Charm School, mainly starred in comedies and comedy-thrillers. Ran along Kay Kendall lines but without quite the Kendall glow. Married to John Justin (first of two) from 1952 to 1964.

1947: To the Public Danger. 1948: Saraband for Dead Lovers (US: Saraband). Anna Karenina. Badger's Green. 1949: Don't Ever Leave Me. A Boy, a Girl and a Bike. Poet's Pub. Passport to Pimlico. Boys in Brown. 1950: Tony Draws a Horse. 1951: The Dark Man. Another Man's Poison. Mystery Junction. The Frightened Man. 1952: Hot Ice. 1953: Street Corner (US: Both Sides of the Law). Meet Mr Lucifer. Death Goes to School. 1954: The Teckman Mystery. 1957: Campbell's Kingdom. Doctor at Large. 1958: A Cry from the Streets. 1959: Operation Bullshine. 1963: Doctor in Distress. 1968: A Dandy in Aspic. 1970: Some Will, Some Won't. 1971: Up Pompeii. 1972: Tales from the Crypt.

MURRAY, Bill 1950–

Bedraggled-looking American comedy actor with a practical joker's face and a scruff of dark hair. He studied to become a doctor, but graduated instead to the cult TV comedy show, *Saturday Night Live*, along with John Belushi, Chevy Chase, Dan Aykroyd (all *qv*) and others. His laconic sense of humour has been effectively used in films; attempts to go 'straight' as a dramatic actor have been less successful.

1975: La honte de la jungle (GB: Jungle Burger. US: Shame of the Jungle. Voice only). 1979: Meatballs. 1980: Where the Buffalo

Roam. Caddyshack. 1981: Stripes. Loose Shoes. 1982: Tootsie. 1984: The Razor's Edge. Ghost Busters. 1985: Nothing Lasts Forever.

MURRAY, Don 1929–

Quiet, self-effacing American actor who was a conscientious objector at the time of the Korean War (something that slowed his career) and has often associated himself with films that expressed noble ideals. His performances are always earnest and sincere, although it is hard to imagine him in comedy. Nominated for a Best Supporting Actor Oscar in *Bus Stop*.

1955: The Skin of Our Teeth (TV). 1956: Bus Stop. 1957: The Bachelor Party. A Hatful of Rain. For I Have Loved Strangers (TV). 1958: From Hell to Texas (GB: Manhunt). 1959: Shake Hands with the Devil. These Thousand Hills. 1960: One Foot in Hell. Alas, Babylon (TV). 1961: The Hoodlum Priest. 1962: Advise and Consent. Tunnel 28 (GB and US: Escape from East Berlin). 1964: One Man's Way. 1965: Baby, the Rain Must Fall. Kid Rodelo. 1966: The Plainsman. Sweet Love Bitter. 1967: The Borgia Stick (TV). The Viking Queen. Tale of the Cock. 1969: Daughter of the Mind (TV). Childish Things. 1970: The Intruders (TV). 1972: Conquest of the Planet of the Apes. Happy Birthday Wanda June. Confessions of Tom Harris (TV). 1973: Call Me by My Rightful Name. Cotter (GB: TV.). 1974: The Girl on the Late, Late Show (TV). The Sex Symbol (TV. GB: cinemas). A Girl Named Sooner (GB: TV). 1976: Hero. 1978: Rainbow (TV). 1979: The Far Turn (TV). The Boy Who Drank Too Much (TV). Confessions of a Lady Cop/The Other Side

of Fear (TV). 1980: Fugitive Family (TV). 1981: Endless Love. Return of the Rebels (TV). 1983: Thursday's Child (TV). Quarterback Princess (TV). I Am the Cheese. License to Kill (TV). 1984: A Touch of Scandal (TV). Radioactive Dreams. 1986: Peggy Sue Got Married. The Summons.

MURRAY, Peter 'Pete' 1925–

Fair-haired, long-faced, bland-looking British actor, sporadically in films from 1944, mostly in sensitive juvenile roles. Success as a toothily cheerful disc-jockey, panellist and all-round radio personality in the mid 1950s led him to essay a few minor light comedy leads in films again. But his personality remained best projected in sound rather than vision.

1944: Time Flies. 1946: Caravan. Hungry Hill. 1947: Captain Boycott. My Brother Jonathan. 1948: Portrait from Life (US: The Girl in the Painting). 1951: No Highway (US: No Highway in the Sky). 1958: Six-Five Special. 1960: A Taste of Money. Escort for Hire. 1961: Transatlantic. 1962: Behave Yourself. Design for Loving. It's Trad, Dad! 1968: Otley. 1969: Under the Table You Must Go. 1970: Cool It Carol! (US: The Dirtiest Girl I Ever Met).

MURRAY, Stephen 1912–1983

Serious-looking British actor with dark hair and high forehead. Shakespeare-trained, he moved into leading roles in British films from the early forties, without ever becoming an established star. But he became probably radio's best-known actor, with over 400 plays to his credit and, in that medium, became the unlikely star of the long-running comedy series *The Navy Lark*: did not appear in the film version.

1938: Pygmalion. 1941: The Prime Minister. 1942: The Next of Kin. 1943: Undercover (US: Underground Guerillas). 1947: Master of Bankdam. 1948: My Brother Jonathan. London Belongs to Me (US: Dulcimer Street). Alice in Wonderland (voice only). 1949: *The People Next Door (narrator only). For Them That Trespass. Now Barabbas was a robber ... Silent Dust. 1950: The Magnet. *Scrapbook for 1933 (narrator only). 1952: 24 Hours in a Woman's Life (US: Affair in Monte Carlo). 1953: Four-Sided Triangle. 1954: *The Heart of England (narrator only). The Stranger's Hand. 1955: The End of the Affair. 1956: *Across Great Waters (narrator only). Guilty? *The Door in the Wall. 1957: At the Stroke of Nine. Any Man's Kingdom (narrator only). 1958: A Tale of Two Cities. The Nun's Story. 1960: Sea Sanctuary (narrator only). The River of Life (narrator only). 1961: *Wild Highlands (narrator only). 1963: Master Spy.

MUTI, Ornella (Francesca Rivelli) 1955–
Dark-haired Italian actress, stunningly beautiful in a slightly pouty way, with a sex-symbol figure that took her into erotic roles

at 16 and often saw her cast as slightly off-centre *femmes fatales*. More often seen in semi-international ventures than most present-day Italian stars, she proved a slightly limited actress, but popular enough to run up nearly 50 films before reaching 30.

1969: La moglie più bella. 1970: Un posto ideale per uccidere. 1971: Un solo grande amore. Il sola nella pelle (GB and US: Sun on the Skin). 1972: Fiorina la vacca. La casa de las palomas. 1973: Le monache di Saint'Arcangelo (GB: The Nun and the Devil). Tutti figli di 'mamma santissima' (US: Italian Graffiti). Paolo il caldo/The Sensual Man. La seduzione (GB: Seduction). Cebo para una adolescente. Cronace di altre tempe. L'altra faccia del padrino. Amore a morte. 1974: Appassionata. Romanzo popolare (US: Come Home and Meet My Wife). Experienze prematrimoniali. Una chica y un señor. 1975: Leonor. La jeune mariée/La joven casada. Mio dio, come sono caduta in basso. 1976: L'ultima donna (GB and US: The Last Woman). Come una rosa al naso (GB: TV, as Virginity). L'agnese va a morire. L'amante adolescente. 1977: La stanza del vescovo. Morte di una carogna. I nuovi mostri. Mort d'un pourri. 1978: Primo amore. Ritra ho di Borghesia in nero (US: Nest of Vipers). Eutanasia di un amore. 1979: Giallo Napoletano. La vita è bella/Freedom to Love. 1980: Flash Gordon. Il bribetico domato. Love and Money. 1981: Tales of Ordinary Madness. Nessuno è perfetto. 1982: Bonnie è Clyde all'Italiana/Bonnie and Clyde Italian Style. 1983: The Girl from Trieste. Un amour de Swann (GB and US: Swann in Love). 1984: Firebrand – the Story of Cellini. 1985: Tutta colpa di paradiso. 1986: Stregati. Chronicle of a Death Foretold.

House of a Thousand Dolls. Sumuru (US: The Million Eyes of Sumuru). 1968: Radhapura – Endstation der Verdammten. Der Tod im roten Jaguar. Dynamit in grüner Seide. 1969: Todes-schüsse am Broadway. 1973: Beyond Atlantis. 1974: Nakia (TV).

NAGEL, Anne (Ann Dolan) 1912–1966

Strawberry-blonde American actress with wide blue eyes who played light leading roles, frightened heroines and heroines' friends in Hollywood films of the 1930s and 1940s. Also in serials, notably as the intrepid Miss Case in the *Green Hornet* adventures. In post-war years she was gradually seen in smaller roles. Married (first of two) to Ross Alexander (*qv*) from 1933 to his death in 1937. Died from cancer.

1932: Redheads on Parade. 1933: Sitting Pretty. I Loved You Wednesday. College Humor. 1934: Stand Up and Cheer. George White's Scandals. 1936: King of Hockey (GB: King of the Ice Rink). Bullets or Ballots. Polo Joe. Hot Money. Here Comes Carter (GB: The Voice of Scandal). China Clipper. Love Begins at 20 (GB: All One Night). 1937: Footloose Heiress. Guns of the Pecos. The Hoosier School-boy (GB: Yesterday's Hero). The Three Legionnaires. The Case of the Stuttering Bishop. Escape by Night. A Bride for Henry. She Loved a Fireman. The Adventurous Blonde/Torchy Blane the Adventurous Blonde. 1938: Saleslady. Gang Bullets (GB: The Crooked Way). Mystery House. Under the Big Top (GB: The Circus Comes to Town). 1939: Call a Messenger. Convicts' Code. Legion of Lost Flyers. Should a Girl Marry? The Girl from Nowhere. Unexpected Father (GB: Sandy Takes a Bow). 1940: The Green Hornet (serial). Winners of the West (serial). My Lit-tle Chickadee. Argentine Nights. Ma, He's Making Eyes at Me. Black Friday. The Green Hornet Strikes Again! (serial). Hot Steel. Dia-mond Frontier. 1941: Meet the Chump. Road Agent. Mutiny in the Arctic. Don Winslow of the Navy (serial). Man-Made Monster. Never Give a Sucker an Even Break. The Invisible Woman. Sealed Lips. 1942: The Secret Code (serial). Dawn Express. Stagecoach Buckaroo. The Mad Doctor of Market Street. Nazi Spy Ring. The Mad Monster. 1943: Women in Bondage. 1946: Murder in the Music Hall. Traffic in Crime. The Trap (GB: Murder at Malibu Beach). 1947: Blondie's Holiday. The

Hucksters. Spirit of West Point. 1948: Don't Trust Your Husband. Prejudice. Every Girl Should Be Married. Homecoming. One Touch of Venus. Family Honeymoon. 1949: The Stratton Story. 1950: Armored Car Robbery.

NAGEL, Conrad 1896–1970

Tall, fair-haired, long-faced American actor with piercing blue eyes, mostly in very serious roles. A much-respected figure on stage, he never quite achieved the same distinction in films, although busy from 1920 to 1935. Made a few avuncular appearances in post-war years, in between running an acting school.

1918: Little Women. 1919: Redhead. The Lion and the Mouse. 1920: Midsummer Madness. The Fighting Chance. Unseen Forces. 1921: Fool's Paradise. What Every Woman Knows. Sacred and Profane Love. The Lost Romance. 1922: Hate. The Impossible Mrs Bellew. Satur-day Night. Nice People. The Ordeal. Singed Wings. Pink Gods. 1923: Bella Donna. The Rendezvous. Grumpy. Lawful Larceny. The Eternal Three. 1924: The Snob. Three Weeks. Name the Man. Tess of the d'Urbervilles. Mar-ried Flirts. Sinners in Silk. The Rejected Woman. So This is Marriage. 1925: Cheaper to Marry. Sun-Up. Lights of Old Broadway (GB: Merry Wives of Gotham). The Only Thing (GB: Four Flaming Days). Pretty Ladies. Excuse Me. 1926: The Exquisite Sinner. The Waning Sex. Dance Madness. Tin Hats. There You Are. Memory Lane. 1927: Slightly Used. Quality Street. Heaven on Earth. London After Midnight. The Jazz Singer. The Hyp-notist. The Girl from Chicago. 1928: Glorious Betsy. The Mysterious Lady. The Terror. Dia-mond Handcuffs. State Street Sadie (GB: The Girl from State Street). If I Were Single. Caught in the Fog. Tenderloin. The Michigan Kid. The Divine Woman. 1929: The Idle Rich. Dynamite. The Kiss. The Sacred Flame. The Redeeming Sin. Hollywood Revue of 1929. Red Wine. Kid Gloves. Thirteenth Chair. 1930: Numbered Men. DuBarry, Woman of Passion (GB: DuBarry). Redemption. A Lady Sur-renders (GB: Blind Wives). The Divorcee. Ship from Shanghai. Second Wife. One Roman-tic Night. Free Love. Today. 1931: The Right of Way. Son of India. Bad Sister. Hell Drivers. East Lynne. The Reckless Hour. Three Who Loved. The Pagan Lady. 1932: Kongo. The Man Called Back. Divorce in the Family. Fast Life. 1933: Ann Vickers. The Constant

NADER, George 1921–

Handsome dark-haired American leading man with slow but winning smile and small, well-defined features. Struggled in show business for years before Universal-International gave him a contract, and boosted him to star roles: he was the last of their 'beefcake boys'. Nader hadn't the personality to stay at the top in Hollywood – but pursued his career with some determination in overseas movies, becoming popular in Germany as FBI man Jerry Cotton in a series of colourful thrillers.

1949: Memory of Love. 1950: Rustlers on Horseback. 1951: Two Tickets to Broadway. Han Glomde Henne Aldrig. Overland Tele-graph. Take Care of My Little Girl. 1952: Phone Call from a Stranger. Monsoon. 1953: Down Among the Sheltering Palms. Sins of Jezebel. Miss Robin Crusoe. 1954: Robot Mon-ster. Carnival Story. Four Guns to the Border. 1955: Six Bridges to Cross. The Second Greatest Sex. Lady Godiva (GB: Lady Godiva of Coventry). 1956: Away All Boats. Congo Crossing. The Unguarded Moment. Four Girls in Town. 1957: Man Afraid. Joe Butterfly. Flood Tide (GB: Above All Things). 1958: Appointment with a Shadow (GB: The Big Story). The Female Animal. Nowhere to Go. 1962: The Secret Mark of d'Artagnan. 1963: A Walk by the Sea (also directed). Zigzag. 1964: The Great Space Adventure. Alarm on 83rd Street. 1965: The Human Duplicators. Die Rechnung – eiskalt serviert. Der Mörderclub von Brooklyn. Schüsse aus dem Geigenkasten (GB: Tread Softly). Mordnacht in Manhat-tan. Um null uhr schnappt die Falle zu. 1966: Mi Hag Freitag/Operation Hurricane. 1967:

Woman. 1934: The Marines Are Coming. Dangerous Corner. 1935: One New York Night (GB: The Trunk Mystery). One Hour Late. Death Flies East. Ball at Savoy. 1936: Yellow Cargo. The Girl from Mandalay. Wedding Present. 1937: The Gold Racket. Navy Spy. 1939: The Mad Empress (GB: Carlotta, the Mad Empress). 1940: I Want a Divorce. One Million BC (GB: Man and His Mate) (narrator only). 1944: Dangerous Money (narrator only). They Shall Have Faith (later Forever Yours. GB: The Right to Live). 1945: The Adventures of Rusty. 1946: The Vicious Circle. 1948: Stage Struck. The Woman in Brown. 1949: Dynamite. 1955: All That Heaven Allows. 1956: The Swan. 1957: The Great American Hoax (TV). Hidden Fear. 1959: Stranger in My Arms. The Man Who Understood Women.

NARES, Owen (O. Ramsay) 1888–1943
Dark, saturnine, charismatic British leading man and matinee idol, who probably prolonged his leading man status beyond what was good for his career, and failed to mature into the character actor he might have become. 1913: *His Choice. 1914: *Dandy Donovan, the Gentleman Cracksman. 1916: The Real Thing at Last. Milestones. Just a Girl. 1917: The Sorrows of Satan. One Summer's Day. The Labour Leader. Flames. 1918: The Elder Miss Blossom. Tinker, Tailor, Soldier, Sailor. God Bless Our Red, White and Blue. Onward Christian Soldiers. The Man Who Won. 1919: Edge o' Beyond. Gamblers All. 1920: A Temporary Gentleman. The Last Rose of Summer. All the Winners. 1921: For Her Father's Sake. 1922: Brown Sugar. The Faithful Heart. 1923: Young Lochinvar. The Indian Love Lyrics. 1924: Miriam Rozella. 1927: His Great Moment (US: Sentence of Death). This Marriage Business. 1930: The Middle Watch. Loose Ends. The Woman Between (US: The Woman Decides). 1931: Sunshine Susie (US: The Office Girl). Frail Women. 1932: Aren't We All?/Women Who Play. The Love Contract. The Impassive Footman (US: Woman in Bondage). There Goes the Bride. Where is This Lady? Discord. *His Great Night. 1933: One Precious Year. 1934: The Private Life of Don Juan. *After Eight. 1935: I Give My Heart. Royal Cavalcade (US: Regal Cavalcade). 1936: Head Office. *The Story of Papworth. 1937: The Show Goes On. 1941: The Prime Minister.

NEAGLE, Dame Anna (Marjorie Robertson) 1904–1986
Blonde British singer, dancer and actress who rose from chorus-girl to star in thirties' musicals (1932–1941), as historical heroines (1937–1950) and in a series of frothy post-war comedy-romances with Michael Wilding. Long associated with director Herbert Wilcox, whom she married in 1943. Her career turned full circle in the sixties when she returned to musicals on the London stage. Created Dame in 1969.
1930: The Chinese Bungalow. The School for Scandal. Should a Doctor Tell? 1932: Goodnight Vienna (US: Magic Night). The Flag Lieutenant. 1933: Bitter Sweet. The Little Damozel. 1934: The Queen's Affair (US: Runaway Queen). Nell Gwyn. 1935: Peg of Old Drury. Limelight (US: Backstage). 1936: The Three Maxims (US: The Show Goes On). 1937: London Melody (US: Girls in the Street). Victoria the Great. 1938: Sixty Glorious Years (US: Queen of Destiny). 1939: Nurse Edith Cavell. 1940: Irene. No, No, Nanette. 1941: Sunny. They Flew Alone (US: Wings and the Woman). 1943: Forever and a Day. The Yellow Canary. 1945: I Live in Grosvenor Square (US: A Yank in London). 1946: Piccadilly Incident. 1947: The Courtneys of Curzon Street. Royal Wedding (narrator only). 1948: Spring in Park Lane. Elizabeth of Ladymead. 1949: Maytime in Mayfair. 1950: Odette. 1951: The Lady with a Lamp. 1952: Derby Day (US: Four Against Fate). 1954: Lilacs in the Spring (US: Let's Make Up). 1955: King's Rhapsody. 1956: My Teenage Daughter. 1957: No Time for Tears. 1958: The Man Who Wouldn't Talk. 1959: The Lady is a Square.

NEAL, Patricia (Patsy Neal) 1926–
Anxious-looking brunette American actress who brought a fresh, sharp approach to roles of *angst* and was seen in too few films, and even fewer decent ones, before her marriage to writer Roald Dahl in 1953; she won an Academy Award for *Hud* in 1963, but soon afterwards suffered a paralysing stroke. She made a slow but admirable recovery and returned to acting in the late sixties. She divorced Dahl in 1983. Also received an Oscar nomination for *The Subject Was Roses.*
1949: John Loves Mary. The Fountainhead. It's a Great Feeling. The Hasty Heart. 1950:

Bright Leaf. Three Secrets. The Breaking Point. Raton Pass (GB: Canyon Pass). 1951: Operation Pacific. The Day the Earth Stood Still. Weekend with Father. 1952: Diplomatic Courier. Washington Story (GB: Target for Scandal). Something for the Birds. 1954: Stranger from Venus (US: Immediate Decision). La tua donna. 1957: A Face in the Crowd. The Playroom (TV). 1958: The Gentleman from Seventh Avenue (TV) 1961: Breakfast at Tiffany's. 1963: Hud. 1964: Psyche 59. †The Third Secret. 1965: In Harm's Way. 1968: The Subject Was Roses. 1971: The Homecoming (TV). The Night Digger. 1972: Baxter! 1973: Happy Mother's Day ... Love George/Run, Stranger, Run. 'B' Must Die. 1974: Things in Their Season (TV). 1975: Eric (TV). 1976: Tail Gunner Joe (TV). 1977: A Love Affair – the Eleanor and Lou Gehrig Story (TV). Widows' Nest. 1978: The Passage. 1980: All Quiet on the Western Front (TV. GB: cinemas). 1981: Ghost Story. The Patricia Neal Story (TV). 1984: Shattered Vows (TV). Love Leads the Way.

† Scenes deleted from release print

NEAL, Tom 1914–1972
Shortish, but powerfully-built, dark-haired American actor, moustachioed from 1944. His leading roles were mostly in second-features, although some of them quite highly rated. His spectacular lifestyle – he was several times a headliner in brawls over women, most notably a violent one with Franchot Tone – finally broke his career when he was arrested for the shooting of his third wife, and sentenced to 10 years' jail. He was found dead in bed eight

months after release from prison, apparently from natural causes.
1938: *The Great Heart. Out West with the Hardys. 1939: Stronger than Desire. Burn 'em up O'Connor. Another Thin Man. Joe and Ethel Turp Call on the President. Within the Law. Honolulu. *Prophet without Honor. Four Girls in White. 6,000 Enemies. They All Came Out. *Help Wanted. *Money to Loan. 1940: *Jack Pot. *Rodeo Dough. Andy Hardy Meets Debutante. The Courageous Dr Christian. Sky Murder. 1941: Jungle Girl (serial). Top Sergeant Mulligan. Under Age. The Miracle Kid. 1942: Pride of the Yankees. Bowery at Midnight. Ten Gentlemen from West Point. China Girl. Flying Tigers. One Thrilling Night. 1943: Behind the Rising Sun. Air Force. She Has What It Takes. No Time for Love. Klondike Kate. *Rear Gunner. There's Something about a Soldier. Good Luck, Mr Yates. 1944: The Unwritten Code. Two-Man Submarine. Thoroughbreds. The Racket Man. 1945: Club Havana. Crime, Inc. First Yank into Tokyo (GB: Mask of Fury). Detour. 1946: The Unknown. The Brute Man. My Dog Shep. Blonde Alibi. 1947: The Case of the Baby Sitter. The Hat Box Mystery. 1948: Beyond Glory. 1949: Bruce Gentry, Daredevil of the Skies (serial). Amazon Quest (GB: Amazon). Red Desert. Apache Chief. 1950: Radar Secret Service. Joe Palooka in Humphrey Takes a Chance (GB: Humphrey Takes a Chance). Call of the Klondike. Train to Tombstone. Everybody's Dancing. I Shot Billy the Kid. King of the Bullwhip. 1951: Varieties on Parade. Danger Zone. Navy Bound. GI Jane. Let's Go Navy. Fingerprints Don't Lie. Stop That Cab! 1952: The Dupont Story. The Daltons' Women. 1953: The Great Jesse James Raid.

NEFF, Hildegarde
See KNEF, Hildegarde

NEGRI, Pola (Apollonia Chalupec) 1894–
Chunky, dark-haired Polish actress who came to Hollywood in 1922, and became one of its most flamboyant but likeable stars. Paraded down Sunset Boulevard with a tiger on a leash, enjoyed tempestuous affairs with Charlie Chaplin and Rudolph Valentino among others, and played vamps whole-heartedly. An unconscious Mae West of the silent screen.
1914: Niewolnicá Zomyslow. 1915: Czarná Ksiazeczka. Pokoj 13. 1916: Jego Ostátú Czyn.

Zona. Studenci. Arabella. Die Bestie. 1917: Die toten Augen. Küsse, die man stiehlt im Dunketh. Nicht lange tauschte mich das Glück. Rosen, die der Sturm entblättert. Zügelloses Blut (GB and US: Gypsy Blood). 1918: Carmen (US: Gypsy Blood). Der gelbe Schein (GB and US: The Yellow Ticket). Die Augen der Mumie Mâ (GB and US: The Eyes of the Mummy). Camille (US: The Red Peacock). Mania (GB and US: Mad Love). Wenn das Herz in Hass erglüht. 1919: Comptesse Daddy. Karussel des Lebens. Kreuziget sie! Madame Dubarry (US: Passion). 1920: Vendetta. Arme Violetta. Das Martyrium. Die geschlossene Kette. Die Marchesa d'Arminiani. Sumurun (GB and US: One Arabian Night). Medea. 1921: Die Bergkatze. Sappho. Die Dame im Glashave. 1922: Die Flamme (GB and US: Montmartre). 1923: Bella Donna. The Cheat. The Spanish Dancer. 1924: Shadows of Paris. Men. Lily of the Dust. Forbidden Paradise. 1925: East of Suez. The Charmer. Flower of the Night. A Woman of the World. 1926: The Crown of Lies. Good and Naughty. Hotel Imperial. 1927: Barbed Wire. The Woman on Trial. 1928: The Secret Hour. Three Sinners. Loves of an Actress. The Woman from Moscow. Are Women to Blame? 1929: The Woman He Scorned. Forbidden Paradise. 1932: A Woman Commands. 1934: Fanatisme. 1935: Mazurka. 1936: Moskau – Shanghai. 1937: Madame Bovary. Tango notturno. 1938: Die fromme Lüge. Die Nacht der Entscheidung. *Rudolph Valentino. 1943: Hi Diddle Diddle. 1963: The Moon-Spinners.

NEILL, Sam (Nigel Neill) 1947–
Dark and sharply handsome Irish-born, New Zealand-raised actor who had a hard struggle to reach international stardom after a distinguished start in Australian films. He has always seemed to make most impact, however, in roles slightly secondary to another star and, after his seemingly foolproof role in the TV series Reilly Ace of Spies failed to make him a national figure, he came back strongly in films in which he could steal scenes from those billed above him.
1975: Ashes. Landfall. 1977: Sleeping Dogs. 1979: The Journalist. Out of Reach. My Brilliant Career. 1980: Attack Force Z. 1981: From a Far Country: Pope John Paul II. The Final Conflict (later Omen III The Final Conflict). Possession. 1982: Ivanhoe (TV).

Enigma. 1983: The Country Girls (TV). 1984: Le sang des autres. 1985: Plenty. Robbery Under Arms. 1986: The Umbrella Woman. The Good Wife. For Love Alone.

NELLIGAN, Kate 1951–
Dark-haired, moist-eyed, full-lipped Canadian-born actress who plays independent women and usually gives appealingly emotional performances. In the 1970s and 1980s, she attempted to establish film careers in Britain and then America with only moderate success, considering her talent. Her greatest achievements to date have almost all been on stage. In the cinema, she has been choosy – but not always to her advantage.
1974: The Count of Monte Cristo (TV. GB: cinemas, in 1976). 1975: The Romantic Englishwoman. 1979: Dracula. 1980: Midnight Matinee. Mr Patman. 1981: Eye of the Needle. Victims (TV). 1983: Without a Trace. 1985: Eleni.

NELSON, Gene (G. Berg) 1920–
Yellow-haired, long-legged American dancer with ready grin, also a talented swimmer and skater. Became the male equivalent of Ann Miller in his five years with Warners – although a popular musical star, with a good, light singing voice to match his twinkling feet, and usually billed above the title, he was never given a vehicle of his own. Later made some good low-budget thrillers in Britain, and became a competent director of routine films.
1943: This is the Army. 1947: I Wonder Who's Kissing Her Now. 1948: Gentleman's Agreement. Apartment for Peggy. The Walls of

*Jericho. 1950: The West Point Story (GB: Fine and Dandy). The Daughter of Rosie O'Grady). Tea for Two. 1951: Lullaby of Broadway. Starlift. Painting the Clouds with Sunshine. 1952: She's Working Her Way through College. 1953: Three Sailors and a Girl. She's Back on Broadway. Crime Wave (GB: The City is Dark). *Hollywood's Great Entertainers. 1954: So This is Paris. 1955: Oklahoma! Timeslip (US: The Atomic Man). Dial 999 (US: The Way Out). 1961: The Purple Hills. 1962: 20,000 Eyes. 1963: Thunder Island. 1972: Family Flight (TV). A Brand New Life (TV). 1981: S.O.B.*

As director: 1962: The Hand of Death. 1963: Hootenanny Hoot. 1964: Kissin' Cousins. Your Cheatin' Heart. 1965: Harum Scarum (GB: Harem Holiday). 1967: The Cool Ones. The Perils of Pauline.

NERO, Franco (F. Spartanero) 1941–
Dark, glowering Italian actor with striking light blue eyes – for a long time associated in private life with Vanessa Redgrave (*qv*). He has not quite become an international star, despite several attempts in that direction. His English is not as attractive as that of some continental stars, and he is more interesting in less-than-straightforward roles. Now in his forties, he continues to be busy in films from assorted countries.
1964: Celestina/Maid at Your Service. 1965: No Tears for a Killer. I criminali della galassia (GB: Wild, Wild Planet. US: War of the Planets). Il terzo occhio. The Deadly Diaphanoids. Io la conoscevo bene. 1966: The Tramplers. Django. The Bible ... in the beginning. Texas addio (GB: The Avenger). Tecnica di un omicidio (US: Hired Killer). Tempo di massacro (US: The Brute and the Beast). 1967: Il giorno della civetta (US: Mafia). L'uomo, l'orgoglio, la vendetta. Camelot. La morta viene dal pianeta Aytin. 1968: Il mercenario (GB: A Professional Gun. US: The Mercenary). Sequestro di persona (GB: Island of Crime). The Day of the Owl. A Quiet Place in the Country. Mit Django kam der Tod. The Battle for Neretva/The Battle of Neretva. 1969: Un detective/Detective Belli. Gott mit uns. Sardinia: Ransom! 1970: Compañeros! The Virgin and the Gypsy. Drop Out! Tristana. 1971: Confessions of a Police Commissioner. Giornata nera per i Ariete. L'istruttoria è

chiusa: dimentichi. Killer from Yuma/Los guerilleros. 1972: Senza ragione/Redneck. The Monk. Pope Joan. The Fifth Day of Peace. The Aquarian. Viva la muerte tua. La vacanza. 1973: Los amigos (GB and US: Deaf Smith and Johnny Ears). Il delitto Matteotti. High Crime/La polizia incrimina, la legge assolve. 1974: White Fang. I guappi. Il cittadino si ribella. Perchè si uccide un magistrato? Corruzione al Palazzo di Giustizia. 1975: The Legend of Valentino (TV). The Flower in His Mouth). Marcia trionfale. Profezia per un delitto. Scandalo. Cry Onion. The Anonymous Avenger. I quattro dell'apocalisse. Challenge to White Fang. 1976: Un altimo di vita. Il cipollaro. L'ispettore. Autostop rosso sangue (GB: Death Drive). Keoma (GB: The Violent Breed). 21 Hours at Munich (TV. GB: cinemas). 1977: Submission. Django – il grande ritorno. Mussolini: The Last Four Days (completed 1974). 1978: Force Ten from Navarone. The Pirate (TV). 1979: Il grande respiro. The Man with Bogart's Face. The Visitor. Un dramma borghese. 1980: I contrabbandieri. Shark Hunter. Blue-Eyed Bandit. The Day of the Cobra. Danzig Roses. The Falcon. 1981: The Salamander. Sahara Cross. Enter the Ninja. The Day of the Cobra. 1982: Il fioretto. Mexico in Flames/Red Bells. Wagner. Querelle. Grog. 1983: Der Bauer von Babylon. 1984: The Last Days of Pompeii (TV). Un solitaro e mezzo. 1985: Sweet Country. Il pentito. Die Förstenbuben. Garibaldi the General. The Girl.

NESBITT, Derren 1935–
British actor with thick lips, fair, curly hair and square face. Usually cast in aggressive roles, as small-time crook, smiling two-timer or sadistic villain. Married to Anne Aubrey (*qv*) from 1961 to 1973; the violent repercussions of their subsequent break-up probably harmed his career. Also directs.
1958: A Night to Remember. Room at the Top. The Silent Enemy. 1959: Life in Danger. Behemoth the Sea Monster (US: The Giant Behemoth). In the Nick. 1960: Sword of Sherwood Forest. Carolina. 1961: The Man in the Back Seat. Victim. 1962: Strongroom. Kill or Cure. Term of Trial. 1963: The Informers. 1965: The Amorous Adventures of Moll Flanders. 1966: Operation Third Form. The Blue Max. 1967: The Naked Runner. 1968: Nobody Runs Forever. Where Eagles Dare. 1969:

Monte Carlo or Bust! (US: Those Daring Young Men in Their Jaunty Jalopies). 1970: Berlin Affair (TV). 1971: Burke and Hare. 1972: Innocent Bystanders. Ooh ... You Are Awful (US: Get Charlie Tully). Not Now Darling. 1974: †The Amorous Milkman. 1976: Spy Story. 1978: Give Us Tomorrow. The Playbirds. 1979: The House on Garibaldi Street (TV. GB: cinemas). 1981: The Guns and the Fury. 1982: Funny Money.

† And directed

NETTLETON, Lois 1931–
Light-haired American actress of sunny features and warm personality, on the tall side perhaps for romantic roles, but very effective in the earlier part of her career before too many film misfires put a stopper on her Hollywood upsurge. Not the kind of actress that the present-day cinema knows what to do with, she has recently been stealing scenes in character roles. Also very busy on TV from 1955.
1956: Rendezvous (TV). 1959: Meet Me in St Louis (TV). 1962: Period of Adjustment. Come Fly with Me. 1963: Mail Order Bride (GB: West of Montana). 1967: Valley of Mystery. 1968: The Bamboo Saucer/Collision Course. 1969: The Good Guys and the Bad Guys. Any Second Now (TV). 1970: Weekend of Terror (TV). Dirty Dingus Magee. The Sidelong Glances of a Pigeon Kicker. 1971: The Forgotten Man (TV). Terror in the Sky (TV). 1972: The Honkers. 1975: Fear on Trial (TV). Echoes of a Summer. 1979: Tourist (TV). 1980: Soggy Bottom USA. 1981: Butterfly. Deadly Blessing. 1982: The Best Little Whorehouse in Texas. 1985: Brass (TV).

NEWLEY, Anthony 1931–
Dark, jaunty, often crop-haired British actor, singer, composer and director from London's East End. He was a memorable teenage Artful Dodger before settling down as a character actor, mostly playing cocky cockneys. Unexpectedly became a pop star after *Idle on Parade* and enjoyed great success writing stage musicals. He seemed to overreach himself after the late 1960s, and faded to some extent from public favour. Married/divorced Ann Lynn and Joan Collins (both *qv*).
1947: Dusty Bates (serial). The Little Ballerina. Vice Versa. 1948: Here Come the Huggetts.

Oliver Twist. The Guinea Pig. Vote for Huggett. 1949: A Boy, a Girl and a Bike. Don't Ever Leave Me. Madeleine. 1950: Highly Dangerous. 1952: Those People Next Door. Top of the Form. 1954: Up to His Neck. The Case of the Bogus Count. 1955: Above Us the Waves. The Blue Peter (US: Navy Heroes). The Battle of the River Plate (US: Pursuit of the Graf Spee). Cockleshell Heroes. Port Afrique. 1956: X the Unknown. The Last Man to Hang? 1957: The Good Companions. Fire Down Below. How to Murder a Rich Uncle. High Flight. 1958: No Time to Die! (US: Tank Force). The Man Inside. The Lady is a Square. 1959: The Bandit of Zhobe. Idle on Parade (US: Idol on Parade). The Heart of a Man. Killers of Kilimanjaro. Jazzboat. In the Nick. 1960: Let's Get Married. 1963: The Small World of Sammy Lee. Image of Love (narrator only). 1967: Doctor Dolittle. 1968: Sweet November. Can Hieronymous Merkin Ever Forget Mercy Humppe and Find True Happiness? 1974: Mister Quilp. 1976: It Seemed Like a Good Idea at the Time. 1983: Malibu (TV). 1985: Blade in Hong Kong (TV).

As director: *1968: Can Hieronymous Merkin ...? 1971: Summertree.*

NEWMAN, Barry 1940–
Slim-but-craggy, aggressive American actor with dark, curly hair, winning smile and distinctive facial scar. He seemed headed for big things in the early 1970s, but a couple of very routine action films knocked his career off course. He enjoyed a burst of popularity as television's *Petrocelli*, but has only rarely tried again in the cinema.

1959: Pretty Boy Floyd. 1963: The Moving Finger. 1969: The Lawyer. 1971: Vanishing Point. 1972: The Salzburg Connection. Fear is the Key. 1974: Night Games (TV). 1977: Sex and the Married Woman (TV). 1978: Blue Orchids. City on Fire. Studio Murders/Fantasies (TV). 1980: King Crab (TV). 1981: Shadow Effects (TV). Amy. Deadline. 1982: Having It All. 1984: Second Sight: a Love Story (TV). 1986: Outrage (TV). My Two Loves (TV).

NEWMAN, Nanette 1934–
Dark, striking, gentle British leading lady who might have had Jean Simmons-style success had she not chosen to put family before career. Despite a British Oscar in 1971 for *The Raging Moon*, she has only flirted with films over the years, mainly in husband Bryan Forbes' productions. One applauds the decision, but regrets the waste of talent, especially as she has managed to make enough films to emphasize the point. Also writes on cookery and for children.

1945: Here We Come Gathering. 1953: Personal Affair. 1955: Triple Blackmail. 1960: Faces in the Dark. The League of Gentlemen. 1961: The Rebel (US: Call Me Genius). Pit of Darkness. House of Mystery. The Painted Smile. 1962: Twice round the Daffodils. The L-Shaped Room. †Raiders of the Spanish Main. The Wrong Arm of the Law. 1963: Seance on a Wet Afternoon. 1964: Of Human Bondage. 1966: The Whisperers. The Wrong Box. 1967: Deadfall. 1968: Captain Nemo and the Underwater City, 1969: Oh! What a Lovely War. The Madwoman of Chaillot. Journey into Darkness (TV). 1970: The Raging Moon (US: Long Ago Tomorrow). 1972: The Love Ban. 1973: Man at the Top. 1974: The Stepford Wives. 1978: International Velvet. 1981: Jessie (TV). 1985: Restless Natives.

† *US cinema release of GB TV material*

NEWMAN, Paul 1925–
Fair-haired American actor with prominent lips, luminous blue eyes and a boxer's handsomeness who stayed near the top of world popularity polls despite the occasional disaster – his first film notable among them – for 25 years before his appeal began to fall away. Never less than watchable, he has also been associated with several of Hollywood's big-

gest-ever box-office hits. Married to Joanne Woodward (second) since 1958, he has directed her three times to good effect. Nominated for an Oscar on five occasions – for *Cat on a Hot Tin Roof, The Hustler, Hud, Cool Hand Luke* and *The Verdict*, Newman has yet to win.

1954: The Silver Chalice. 1956: The Rack. Somebody Up There Likes Me. 1957: Until They Sail. The Helen Morgan Story (GB: Both Ends of the Candle). The 80 Yard Run (TV). 1958: Cat on a Hot Tin Roof. Rally 'Round the Flag, Boys! The Long, Hot Summer. The Left-Handed Gun. 1959: The Young Philadelphians (GB: The City Jungle). 1960: From the Terrace. Exodus. 1961: Paris Blues. The Hustler. 1962: Hemingway's Adventures of a Young Man (GB: Adventures of a Young Man). Sweet Bird of Youth. 1963: Hud. A New Kind of Love. The Prize. 1964: What a Way to Go! The Outrage. 1965: Lady L. 1966: Harper (GB: The Moving Target). Torn Curtain. Hombre. 1967: Cool Hand Luke. The Secret War of Harry Frigg. 1969: Winning. Butch Cassidy and the Sundance Kid. 1970: W.U.S.A. King: a Filmed Record ... Montgomery to Memphis. 1971: Sometimes a Great Notion (GB: Never Give an Inch). Pocket Money. 1972: The Life and Times of Judge Roy Bean. 1973: The Sting. The Mackintosh Man. 1974: The Towering Inferno. 1975: The Drowning Pool. 1976: Silent Movie. Buffalo Bill and the Indians, or: Sitting Bull's History Lesson. 1977: Slap Shot. Stand On It! 1979: Angel Death (narrator only). Quintet. 1980: Madonna Red. When Time Ran Out ... 1981: Fort Apache the Bronx. Absence of Malice. 1982: The Verdict. 1984: Harry and Son. 1986: The Color of Money.

As director: *1968: Rachel, Rachel. 1971: Sometimes a Great Notion (GB: Never Give an Inch. Co-directed). 1972: The Effect of Gamma Rays on Man-in-the-Moon Marigolds. 1980: The Shadow Box (TV). 1984: Harry and Son.*

NEWTON, Robert 1905–1956
Dark, scowling, attention-grabbing British actor of ruddy complexion who mixed rich characterizations with quieter roles – and was effective at both – for the British cinema of the thirties and forties. Despite bouts of alcoholism in later years, his performances remained good value. In 1950 he found his niche as the screen's most memorable Long

John Silver and played the role, with variations, for the rest of his career. Died from a heart attack.

*1932: Reunion. 1936: Fire over England. 1937: Dark Journey. Farewell Again (US: Troopship). The Squeaker (US: Murder on Diamond Row). The Green Cockatoo. 21 Days (US: 21 Days Together). 1938: Vessel of Wrath (US: The Beachcomber). †I, Claudius. Yellow Sands. 1939: Poison Pen. Dead Men Are Dangerous. Jamaica Inn. Hell's Cargo (US: Dangerous Cargo). 1940: Bulldog Sees It Through. Busman's Honeymoon (US: Haunted Honeymoon). Gaslight (US: Angel Street). *Channel Incident. 1941: Major Barbara. Hatter's Castle. 1942: They Flew Alone (US: Wings and the Woman). 1944: This Happy Breed. Henry V. 1945: Night Boat to Dublin. 1946: Odd Man Out. 1947: Temptation Harbour. 1948: Snowbound. Oliver Twist. Kiss the Blood Off My Hands (GB: Blood on My Hands). Obsession (US: The Hidden Room). 1950: Treasure Island. Waterfront (US: Waterfront Women). 1951: Tom Brown's Schooldays. Soldiers Three. 1952: Blackbeard the Pirate. Les Miserables. 1953: Androcles and the Lion. The Desert Rats. 1954: Long John Silver. The High and the Mighty. The Beachcomber. 1955: Under the Black Flag (TV. GB: cinemas). 1956: Around the World in 80 Days.*

† Uncompleted

NICHOLSON, Jack 1937–
Dry-voiced, dark, dynamic American actor with cynical smile. Despite receding hair (and an early career spent in teenage-rebel and horror roles until he was 30) he moved

forward, via an Oscar nomination for *Easy Rider*, to become one of America's best actors by the 1970s, winning Academy Awards for *One Flew Over the Cuckoo's Nest* and *Terms of Endearment*, plus five further nominations. He has also written screenplays, and occasionally directs.

1958: Cry Baby Killer. 1959: Too Soon to Love (GB: Teenage Lovers). 1960: Studs Lonigan. The Wild Ride. The Little Shop of Horrors. 1961: The Broken Land. 1962: The Raven. 1963: The Terror. 1964: Back Door to Hell. Ensign Pulver. 1966: The Shooting. 1967: Ride the Whirlwind. The St Valentine's Day Massacre. Hell's Angels on Wheels. 1968: Head. Psych-Out. 1969: Rebel Rousers. Easy Rider. 1970: On a Clear Day You Can See Forever. Five Easy Pieces. 1971: A Safe Place. Carnal Knowledge. 1972: The King of Marvin Gardens. 1973: The Last Detail. 1974: The Fortune. Chinatown. 1975: Tommy. Professione: reporter/The Passenger. One Flew Over the Cuckoo's Nest. 1976: The Last Tycoon. The Missouri Breaks. 1978: Goin' South. 1980: The Shining. 1981: The Border. The Postman Always Rings Twice. Reds. 1983: Terms of Endearment. 1984: Roadshow. 1985: Prizzi's Honor. 1986: Heartburn.

As director: *1971: Drive, He Said. 1978: Goin' South.*

NICOL, Alex 1919–
Fair-haired, coldly handsome American actor, who was usually most effective as vicious, almost sexless villains, although he played a few more routine leading roles in Britain. In acting since 1938, but only signed for films at 31. Later travelled widely, and directed one or two off-beat subjects.

1950: The Sleeping City. Tomahawk (GB: Battle of Powder River). 1951: Target Unknown. Meet Danny Wilson. The Raging Tide. Air Cadet (GB: Jet Men of the Air). 1952: Because of You. Red Ball Express. The Redhead from Wyoming. 1953: Champ for a Day. Law and Order. The Lone Hand. 1954: About Mrs Leslie. Dawn at Socorro. Face the Music (US: The Black Glove). The House Across the Lake (US: Heatwave). 1955: The Gilded Cage. The Man from Laramie. Strategic Air Command. Sincerely Yours. 1956: Great Day in the Morning. 1957: Stranger in Town. 1958: The Screaming Skull. 1959: Five Branded Women. 1960: Then There Were

Three (GB: *Three Came Back). Under Ten Flags. Tutti a casa. Run with the Devil/Via Margutta/La rue des amours faciles. Il gobbo. 1961: Look in Any Window. A Matter of WHO. 1962: The Savage Guns. 1964: Cavalca e uccidi (GB and US: Ride and Kill). Gunfighters of Casa Grande. 1969: Bloody Mama. 1970: Homer. 1971: The Night God Screamed (GB: Scream). 1973: The Clones (GB: Clones). 1975: Winner Take All (TV). 1976: Woman in the Rain. A*P*E.*

As director: *1958: The Screaming Skull. 1960: Then There Were Three (GB: Three Came Back). 1971: Point of Terror. 1985: Striker's Mountain (TV).*

NIELSEN, Leslie 1925–
Tall, blond-haired Canadian actor, at his best as treacherous charmers, becoming merely bland when asked to play the hero. After a TV debut in 1949, he became one of the medium's most prolific performers, and has done extremely well to sustain a career that has never really gone anywhere.

1955: The Vagabond King. 1956: Forbidden Planet. Ransom! The Opposite Sex. 1957: Hot Summer Night. Tammy and the Bachelor (GB: Tammy). 1958: The Sheepman. The Right Hand Man (TV). 1959: The Velvet Alley (TV). 1964: Night Train to Paris. See How They Run (TV). 1965: Harlow. Dark Intruder. 1966: Beau Geste. The Plainsman. 1967: Gunfight in Abilene. Rosie! The Reluctant Astronaut. Counterpoint. Code Name: Heraclitus (TV). Companions in Nightmare (TV). 1968: Shadow over Elveron (TV). Dayton's Devils. 1969: Four Rode Out. How to Commit Marriage. Deadlock (TV). Trial Run (TV). 1970: The Aquarians (TV). Hauser's Memory. Incident in San Francisco. Night Slaves (TV). 1971: They Call It Murder (TV). 1972: The Poseidon Adventure. The Letters (TV). Snatched (TV). 1973: And Millions Will Die. The Resurrection of Zachary Wheeler (GB: TV). 1974: Can Ellen Be Saved? (TV). Guadalcanal Odyssey (narrator only). 1975: King of the Underwater World (narrator only). 1976: Day of the Animals. Project: Kill. Brink's: the Great Robbery (TV). The Siege (TV). 1977: Viva Knievel! The Amsterdam Kill. Sixth and Main. Grand Jury (TV). 1978: Institute for Revenge (TV). Little Mo (TV). City on Fire. 1979: The Mad

Trapper. RIEL. Cave In! (TV). 1980: Prom Night. Airplane! 1981: The Creature Wasn't Nice. 1982: Creepshow. Wrong is Right (GB: The Man with the Deadly Lens). 1985: Reckless Disregard (TV). The Homefront (narrator only). Blade in Hong Kong (TV). Striker's Mountain (TV). 1986: Foxfire Light. The Patriot. Soulman. Home is Where the Hart Is.

NIGH, Jane (Bonnie Nigh) 1926–
Hollywood's red-haired Queen of Cinecolor – a favourite for low-budget outdoors adventures of the late forties and early fifties after she had worked her way up from small roles. Lost to the television series *Big Town* from 1952–1956, after which her film career never got going again.

1944: Something for the Boys. Laura. 1945: State Fair. Whistle Stop. 1946: Dragonwyck. 1947: Unconquered. 1948: Leather Gloves (GB: Loser Take All). Sitting Pretty. Blue Grass of Kentucky. Give My Regards to Broadway. Cry of the City. 1949: Red Hot and Blue. Captain Carey, USA (GB: After Midnight). Zamba (GB: Zamba the Gorilla). Fighting Man of the Plains. 1950: Border Treasure. Rio Grande Patrol. Operation Haylift. Motor Patrol. County Fair. 1951: Blue Blood. Disc Jockey. 1952: Fort Osage. Rodeo. 1956: Hold That Hypnotist.

NIVEN, David (James D. Nevins) 1909–1983
Dark-haired, suave Scottish-born actor with impeccable diction, and figure as pencil-slim as his moustache. A witty comedy player, he also showed up well as a stiff-upper-lip Briton

in Hollywood epics (having gone there in 1935) and got some meaty dramatic roles on his frequent returns to Britain. Won an Academy Award for his fake major in *Separate Tables* and later wrote two extremely popular volumes of light-hearted autobiography. Died from amyotrophic lateral sclerosis, a motor neurone (wasting) disease.

1935: Mutiny on the Bounty. Splendor. Without Regret. A Feather in Her Hat. Barbary Coast. 1936: Palm Springs (GB: Palm Springs Affair). Rose Marie. Dodsworth. Thank You, Jeeves. The Charge of the Light Brigade. Beloved Enemy. 1937: Dinner at the Ritz. We Have Our Moments. The Prisoner of Zenda. 1938: Three Blind Mice. Four Men and a Prayer. The Dawn Patrol. Bluebeard's Eighth Wife. 1939: The Real Glory. Wuthering Heights. Bachelor Mother. Eternally Yours. 1940: Raffles. 1942: The First of the Few (US: Spitfire). 1944: The Way Ahead. 1946: A Matter of Life and Death (US: Stairway to Heaven). Magnificent Doll. The Perfect Marriage. 1947: The Other Love. The Bishop's Wife. 1948: Bonnie Prince Charlie. Enchantment. 1949: A Kiss for Corliss. A Kiss in the Dark. 1950: The Elusive Pimpernel (US: The Fighting Pimpernel). The Toast of New Orleans. 1951: Happy-Go-Lovely. Appointment with Venus (US: Island Rescue). Soldiers Three. The Lady Says No. 1953: The Moon is Blue. 1954: The Love Lottery. Happy Ever After (US: Tonight's the Night). Carrington VC (US: Court-Martial). 1955: The King's Thief. 1956: The Silken Affair. The Birds and the Bees. Around the World in 80 Days. 1957: Oh, Men! Oh, Women! The Little Hut. My Man Godfrey. 1958: Bonjour Tristesse. *Glamorous Hollywood. Separate Tables. 1959: Happy Anniversary. Ask Any Girl. 1960: Please Don't Eat the Daisies. 1961: The Guns of Navarone. The Best of Enemies. 1962: Guns of Darkness. Road to Hong Kong. La citta prigioniera (GB: The Captive City. US: The Conquered City). 55 Days at Peking. 1963: The Pink Panther. 1964: Bedtime Story. 1965: Where the Spies Are. Lady L. 1966: Eye of the Devil. 1967: Casino Royale. 1968: Prudence and the Pill. The Extraordinary Seaman. The Impossible Years. 1969: Before Winter Comes. The Brain. 1970: The Statue. 1972: King, Queen, Knave. 1974: Paper Tiger. Vampira (US: Old Dracula). 1976: No Deposit, No Return. Murder by Death. 1977: Candleshoe. 1978: Escape to Athena. Death on the Nile. The Billion Dollar Movies (TV. Narrator only). 1979: A Man Called Intrepid (TV). 1980: The Sea Wolves. The Biggest Bank Robbery (TV). 1982: The Great Question. Ménage à trois/Better Late Than Never. Trail of the Pink Panther. 1983: Curse of the Pink Panther.

NOLAN, Lloyd 1902–1985
Skilful and likeable American actor of tough-guy parts, facially not unlike George Raft. Usually billed above the title but behind the stars, but quite capable of carrying a film on his own during his peak period (1935–1949), Nolan was also the star of a presentable little series of crime thrillers about detective Michael Shayne. Remained in occasional

character roles until his death from lung cancer.

1935: Stolen Harmony. Atlantic Adventure. One-Way Ticket. She Couldn't Take It (GB: Woman Tamer). G-Men. 1936: You May Be Next! (GB: Panic on the Air). Lady of Secrets. Counterfeit. 15 Maiden Lane. Big Brown Eyes. The Devil's Squadron. The Texas Rangers. 1937: Exclusive. Internes Can't Take Money (GB: You Can't Take Money). Wells Fargo. King of Gamblers. Ebb Tide. Every Day's a Holiday. 1938: Hunted Men. Dangerous to Know. Tip-Off Girls. King of Alcatraz (GB: King of the Alcatraz). Prison Farm. 1939: Undercover Doctor. St Louis Blues. The Magnificent Fraud. Ambush. 1940: Johnny Apollo. The Man Who Wouldn't Talk. The Man I Married. The Golden Fleecing. Charter Pilot. Michael Shayne, Private Detective. The House across the Bay. Gangs of Chicago. Pier 13. Behind the News. 1941: Dressed to Kill. Sleepers West. Blues in the Night. Blue, White and Perfect. Steel against the Sky. Mr Dynamite. Buy Me That Town. 1942: Just Off Broadway. It Happened in Flatbush. Time to Kill. Apache Trail. Manila Calling. The Man Who Wouldn't Die. 1943: Bataan. Guadalcanal Diary. 1944: A Tree Grows in Brooklyn. 1945: The House on 92nd Street. Circumstantial Evidence. Captain Eddie. 1946: Two Smart People. The Lady in the Lake. Somewhere in the Night. 1947: Wild Harvest. 1948: The Street with No Name. Green Grass of Wyoming. 1949: The Sun Comes Up. Bad Boy. Easy Living. 1951: The Lemon Drop Kid. 1953: Island in the Sky. Crazylegs. 1956: Santiago (GB: The Gun Runner). The Last Hunt. Toward the Unknown (GB: Brink of Hell). 1957: Galvanized Yankee (TV). Seven Waves Away (US: Abandon Ship!). Peyton Place. A Hatful of Rain. 1960: Girl of the Night. Portrait in Black. 1961: Susan Slade. 1962: We Joined the Navy. 1963: The Girl Hunters. The Case against Paul Ryker (TV. Released 1968 to cinemas as Sergeant Ryker). 1964: Circus World (GB: The Magnificent Showman). 1965: Never Too Late. 1966: An American Dream (GB: See You in Hell, Darling). 1967: The Double Man. Wings of Fire. 1968: Ice Station Zebra. 1969: Airport. 1972: My Boys Are Good Boys. 1973: Isn't It Shocking? (TV). 1974: The Abduction of Saint Anne (TV). Earthquake. 1976: The November Plan. Flight to Holocaust (TV). 1977: The Mask of Alex-

ander Cross (TV). Fire! (TV. GB: cinemas). J. Edgar Hoover, Godfather of the FBI (Later and GB: The Private Files of J. Edgar Hoover). 1979: Valentine (TV). 1980: Galyon. 1984: Prince Jack. It Came Upon the Midnight Clear (TV). 1986: Hannah and Her Sisters.

NOLTE, Nick 1941–
Fair-haired, square-jawed, huskily muscular American leading man of the 1970s who came belatedly to the fore in a TV mini-series, *Rich Man, Poor Man*, one of the most popular of its kind. Following that he showed an interest in tackling film roles that allowed him more depth and width of characterization, although occasionally he overreached himself in choosing parts for which he was not entirely suited. Seems to become progressively more gravel-voiced.
1974: Death Sentence (TV). 1975: Adams of Eagle Lake (TV). The Runaway Barge (TV). Return to Macon County (GB: Highway Girl). 1977: The Deep. 1978: Who'll Stop the Rain? (GB: Dog Soldiers). 1979: Heart Beat. North Dallas Forty. 1982: 48 Hrs. Cannery Row. 1983: Under Fire. 1984: Teachers. The Ultimate Solution of Grace Quigley (GB: Grace Quigley). 1985: Down and Out in Beverly Hills. 1986: Extreme Prejudice.

NOONAN, Tommy (T. Noon) 1921–1968
Dark-haired, breezy, bespectacled American comedian, usually as the young man shy about girls. A former teenage player, he broke through from small parts to top featured roles in *Gentlemen Prefer Blondes*. Later, there were two or three comedies in harness with Peter Marshall, with whom Noonan had already appeared in *Starlift*, before Noonan revealed the voyeur beneath the glasses by directing two sexploitation comedies. Half-brother of John Ireland (qv). Died from a brain tumour.
1938: Boys' Town. 1945: *The Big Beef. *Beware of Redheads. *What, No Cigarettes? George White's Scandals. Ding Dong Williams (GB: Melody Maker). Dick Tracy (GB: Split Face). 1946: The Bamboo Blonde. Criminal Court. The Truth About Murder (GB: The Lie Detector). The Big Fix. Crack-Up. From This Day Forward. 1947: Riff Raff. Born to Kill (GB: Lady of Deceit). A Likely Story. 1948: Open Secret. Jungle Patrol. 1949: Trapped. I Shot Jesse James. I Cheated the Law. Adam's Rib. Battleground. The Set Up. 1950: Holiday Rhythm. The Return of Jesse James. 1951: FBI Girl. Starlift. The Model and the Marriage Broker. 1953: Gentlemen Prefer Blondes. 1954: A Star is Born. 1955: Violent Saturday. How to be Very, Very Popular. 1956: The Ambassador's Daughter. The Best Things in Life Are Free. Bundle of Joy. 1957: The Girl Most Likely. 1959: The Rookie. 1960: The Schnook (GB: Double Trouble). 1962: Swingin' Along (revised version of The Schnook). 1963: †Promises! Promises! 1964: †Three Nuts in Search of a Bolt. 1967: Cotton Pickin' Chickenpickers.

† Also directed

NORMAND, Mabel (M. Fortescue) 1894–1930
Bright, bubbling brunette, the most talented of America's silent screen comediennes, with a great and deservedly devoted public following from pre-World War I times to the early twenties. Also directed, or co-directed, often without credit, many of her two-reelers. Died from tuberculosis, her career already ended by alleged involvement in a murder. Married actor Lew Cody (Louis Coté 1884–1934).
1911: Betty Becomes a Maid. The Subduing of Mrs Nag. Her Awakening. Saved by Herself. The Squaw's Love. The Unveiling. The Diving Girl. 1912: The Engagement Ring. The Brave Hunter. The Furs. Help! Help! The Interrupted Elopement. A Dash thru the Clouds. The Fickle Spaniard. Helen's Marriage. Hot Stuff. Katchem Kate. †Neighbors. Oh, Those Eyes. Tomboy Bessie. The Tourists. The Tragedy of a Dress Suit. What the Doctor Ordered. The Water Nymph. The New Neighbor. Pedro's Dilemma. Stolen Glory. The Ambitious Butler. The Flirting Husband. The Grocery Clerk's Romance. Cohen at Coney Island. At It Again. Mabel's Lovers. The Deacon's Trouble. A Temperamental Husband. The Rivals. Mr Fix-It. A Desperate Lover. Brown's Seance. A Family Mix-Up. A Midnight Elopement. Mabel's Adventures. The Duel. Mabel's Stratagem. 1913: Mabel's Dad. The Cure That Failed. The Mistaken Masher. The Deacon Outwitted. Just Brown's Luck. The Battle of Who Run. Heinze's Resurrection. Mabel's Heroes. The Professor's Daughter. Red-Hot Romance. A Tangled Affair. The Sleuths at the Floral Parade. The Rural Third Degree. A Strong Revenge. Foiling Fickle Father. A Doctored Affair. The Rube and the Baron. Those Good Old Days. Father's Choice. The Ragtime Band. At 12 O'Clock. Her New Boy. A Little Hero. Mabel's Awful Mistake. Hubby's Job. The Foreman of the Jury. Barney Oldfield's Race for Life. The Hansom Driver. The Speed Queen. The Waiters' Picnic. For the Love of Mabel. The Telltale Light. A Noise from the Deep. Love and Courage. Professor Bean's Removal. The Riot. Baby Day. Mabel's New Hero. The Gypsy Queen. Mabel's Dramatic Career. The Faithful Taxicab. The Bowling Match. Speed Kings. Love Sickness at Sea. A Muddy Romance. Cohen Saves the Day. The Gusher. Zuzu the Band Leader. The Champion. Fatty's Flirtation. 1914: A Misplaced Foot. Mabel's Stormy Love Affair. Won in a Closet. Mabel's Bare Escape. Mabel's Strange Predicament. Love and Gasoline. Mack At It Again. Mabel at the Wheel. Caught in a Cabaret. Mabel's Nerve. The Alarm. The Fatal Market. Her Friend the Bandit. Mabel's Busy Day. Mabel's Married Life. Mabel's New Job. Those Country Kids. Mabel's Latest Prank. Mabel's Blunder. Hello, Mabel! Gentlemen of Nerve. Lovers' Post Office. His Trysting Place. How Heroes Are Made. Fatty's Jonah Day. Fatty's Wine Party. The Sea Nymphs. Getting Acquainted. †Tillie's Punctured Romance. 1915: Mabel and Fatty's Washing Day. Mabel and Fatty's Single Life. Fatty and Mabel at the San Diego Exposition. Mabel, Fatty and the Law. Fatty and Mabel's Married Life. That Little Band of Gold. Wished on Mabel. Mabel and Fatty Viewing the World's Fair at San Francisco. Their Social Splash. Mabel's Wilful Way. Mabel Lost and Won. The Little Teacher. My Valet. Stolen Magic. 1916: Fatty and Mabel Adrift. He Did and He Didn't. The Bright Lights. 1918: †Mickey. †Joan of Plattsburgh. †Dodging a Million. †The Floor Below. †The Venus Model. †Peck's Bad Girl. †A Perfect 36. 1919: †Sis Hopkins. †The Rest. When Doctors Disagree. †Upstairs. †Jinx. †Pinto. 1920: †The Slim Princess. †What Happened to Rosa. 1921: †The Last Chance. †Arabella Flynn. †Molly O. 1922: †Head over Heels. 1923: †Suzanna. 1924: †The Extra Girl. 1926: †Raggedy Rose. †The Nickel Hopper. One Hour Married. Anything Once. 1927: Should Men Walk Home?

All shorts except †features

NORRIS, Chuck (Carlos Ray) 1939–
Stocky, fair-haired, unsmiling, unhandsome American action hero of few words whose shortness of stature proved no bar to becoming world middleweight karate champion from 1968 to 1974. During this time he taught action stunts to the stars and began a tentative film career, initially purely in kung-fu roles, but later in general action films whose titles spoke for themselves and whose often incredible plots paralleled those of films made by Charles Bronson (like Norris, a late starter). He became a serviceable actor and a major box-office force in America, while not quite repeating his popularity on the international market. Bearded since 1983.
1968: *The Wrecking Crew. 1972: Meng lung kuo chiang (GB: Way of the Dragon. US: Return of the Dragon). 1973: The Student Teachers (GB: Intimate Confessions of the Student Teachers). Slaughter in San Francisco (released 1981). 1977: Breaker! Breaker! Good Guys Wear Black. 1978: Game of Death (GB: Bruce Lee's Game of Death). A Force of One. 1980: The Octagon. 1981: An Eye for an Eye. 1982: Silent Rage. 1983: Forced Vengeance. Lone Wolf McQuade. 1984: Missing in Action. 1985: Code of Silence. Mission in Action 2 – The Beginning. Invasion USA. 1986: Battlerage. The Delta Force. Night Hunter. Firewalker. Delta Force II.*

NORTH, Sheree (Dawn Bethel) 1933–
Angie Dickinson, Dorothy Malone and Stella Stevens all have their supporters; but for me Sheree North is the gamest of all Hollywood's durable blondes. A leggy, curvaceous dancer with well-scrubbed looks, she was dancing professionally at 12, then struggled for ten years before Fox took her up as bait to get Marilyn Monroe back to work. They dropped her after four years, but she came back in the sixties with a series of vivid, gutsy portrayals of ladies just a little past their prime, but not their pride.
1945: An Angel Comes to Brooklyn. 1951: Excuse My Dust. 1953: Here Come the Girls. 1954: Living It Up. 1955: How to Be Very, Very Popular. The Lieutenant Wore Skirts. 1956: The Best Things in Life Are Free. 1957: The Way to the Gold. No Down Payment. Topaz (TV). 1958: Mardi Gras. In Love and War. 1966: Destination Inner Space. 1967: Code Name: Heraclitus (TV). 1968: Madigan. The Crime (TV). 1969: The Trouble with Girls. The Gypsy Moths. Survival. Then Came Bronson (TV). 1970: Vanished (TV). 1971: Lawman. The Organization. 1972: Key West (TV). Snatched (TV). Trouble Comes to Town (TV). Rolling Man (TV). 1973: Charley Varrick. The Outfit. Maneater (TV). 1974: Winter Kill (TV). The Cloning of Clifford Swimmer (TV). 1975: Shadow in the Streets (TV). Breakout. 1976: The Shootist. Survival. Most Wanted (TV). 1977: Telefon. 1978: Rabbit Test. The Night They Took Miss Beautiful (TV). Amateur Night at the Dixie Bar and Grill (TV). A Real American Hero (TV). 1979: Only Once in a Lifetime. Portrait of a Stripper (TV). 1980: Marilyn: The Untold Story (TV. GB: cinemas). 1983: Hard Hat and Legs (TV). 1984: Scorned and Swindled (TV).

NOVAK, Kim (Marilyn Novak) 1933–
There was something more to Kim Novak than a chrysanthemum head of blonde hair and a substantial bust. For a few years in the fifties she was remarkably magnetic with her combination of shyness and sexuality, especially given the right director, such as Hitchcock in *Vertigo*. Fresh in from Chicago to Hollywood with her broad, country-girl build, she played a couple of harem girls before being picked up by Columbia as a sex symbol and continued with them until the sixties, going rather too quickly then into blowsy roles. Married to Richard Johnson 1965–1966 (first of two).
1953: The Veils of Bagdad. 1954: Son of Sinbad. The French Line. Pushover. Phffft!
1955: Five Against the House. Picnic. 1956: The Eddy Duchin Story. The Man with the Golden Arm. 1957: Jeanne Eagels. 1958: Pal Joey. Bell, Book and Candle. Vertigo. 1959: Middle of the Night. 1960: Strangers When We Meet. Pepe. 1962: Boys' Night Out. The Notorious Landlady. 1964: Kiss Me, Stupid. Of Human Bondage. 1965: The Amorous Adventures of Moll Flanders. 1968: The Legend of Lylah Clare. 1969: The Great Bank Robbery. 1973: Third Girl from the Left (TV). Tales That Witness Madness. 1975: Satan's Triangle (TV). 1976: Massacre at Blood Bath Drive-In/Drive-In Massacre. 1977: The White Buffalo. 1979: Just a Gigolo. 1980: The Mirror Crack'd. 1983: Malibu (TV). 1985: Alfred Hitchcock Presents (TV).

NOVARRO, Ramon (R. Samaniegos) 1899–1968
Dark-haired, dark-eyed, ultra-handsome Mexican-born leading man, a heart-throb of the silent screen, probably second only in that department to Rudolph Valentino. His biggest hit came with the title role in *Ben-Hur*, but then sound erased much of his appeal. In later years he became an alcoholic and in 1968 was murdered by two brothers trying to find out where he kept his money. They were subsequently jailed for life.
1916: †Joan the Woman. 1917: †The Little American. †The Hostage. 1919: †The Goat. 1921: A Small Town Idol. The Four Horsemen of the Apocalypse. 1922: Mr Barnes of New York. The Prisoner of Zenda. Trifling Women. 1923: Where the Pavement Ends. Scaramouche. 1924: The Red Lily. Thy Name is Woman. The Arab. 1925: A Lover's Oath. The Midshipman. 1926: Ben-Hur. 1927: The Student Prince. Lovers? The Road to Romance. 1928: Forbidden Hours. Across to Singapore. A Certain Young Man. 1929: Devil May Care. The Flying Fleet. The Pagan. 1930: In Gay Madrid. Call of the Flesh (and Spanish and French versions). 1931: Son of India. Daybreak. 1932: Mata Hari. Huddle (GB: Impossible Lover). The Son-Daughter. 1933: The Barbarian (GB: A Night in Cairo). 1934: The Cat and the Fiddle. Laughing Boy. 1935: The Night is Young. 1937: The Sheik Steps Out. 1938: A Desperate Adventure (GB: It Happened in Paris). 1940: La comedie de bonheur. 1942: La Virgen que Forjo una Patria. 1949: We Were Strangers. The Big Steal. 1950: The Outriders. Crisis. 1960: Heller in Pink Tights.

As director: *1930: La Sevillana (Spanish-language version of Call of the Flesh). 1936: Contra la Corriente.*

† *As Ramon Samaniegos*

NOVELLO, Ivor (David I. Davies) 1893–1951
Dark, soulful-looking Welsh actor, playwright and composer with matinee idol-looks, one of the most popular figures in the British theatre over several decades. Also a popular leading man in British (also Hollywood, French and German) films for 15 years, but most fondly remembered for such romantic stage musicals as *The Dancing Years* and *Perchance to Dream*.

Died from a coronary thrombosis a few hours after appearing on stage.
1919: Call of the Blood (US: Gypsy Passion). 1920: Miarka. 1921: The Bohemian Girl. Carnival. 1923: The White Rose. Bonnie Prince Charlie. The Man without Desire. 1925: The Rat. 1926: The Lodger, a Story of the London Fog (US: The Case of Jonathan Drew). The Triumph of the Rat. 1927: The Constant Nymph. Downhill (US: Why Boys Leave Home). The Vortex. 1928: A South Sea Bubble. Der fesche Husar (GB: The Gallant Hussar). 1929: The Return of the Rat. 1930: Symphony in Two Flats. 1931: Once a Lady. 1932: The Lodger (remake) (US: The Phantom Fiend). 1933: Sleeping Car. I Lived with You. 1934: Autumn Crocus.

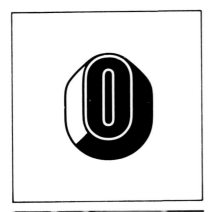

OAKIE, Jack (Lewis Offield) 1903–1978
Chubby, dark-haired, fast-talking American comedian, short of stature but long on energy. Noted for his facial grimaces, and usually cast as sunny-natured, easy-going guys. At the height of his popularity from 1929 to 1938. When he decided to take a long holiday in 1938 his studio dropped him, Hollywood cold-shouldered him, and his film career never completely recovered. Suffered from deafness in later years. Nominated for an Academy Award in *The Great Dictator*.
1928: Finders Keepers. The Fleet's In. Sin Town. Road House. Someone to Love. 1929: Close Harmony. Chinatown Nights. The Man I Love. Street Girl. Sweetie. The Wild Party. The Dummy. Fast Company. Hard to Get. 1930: The Social Lion. Paramount on Parade. The Sap from Syracuse (GB: The Sap Abroad). Hit the Deck. Let's Go Native. Sea Legs. 1931: Dude Ranch. The Gang Buster. Touchdown (GB: Playing the Game). June Moon. 1932: *The Stolen Jools (GB: the Slippery Pearls). *Cricket Flickers. Make Me a Star. Dancers in the Dark. Madison Square Garden. Once in a Lifetime. Sky Bride. Million Dollar Legs. If I Had a Million. Uptown New York. 1933: The Eagle and the Hawk. Too Much Harmony. From Hell to Heaven. Alice in Wonderland. Sailor Be Good. College Humor. Sitting Pretty. 1934: Shoot the Works. Looking for Trouble. College Rhythm. Murder at the Vanities. 1935: King of Burlesque. Call of the Wild. The Big Broadcast of 1936. 1936: The Texas Rangers. Collegiate (GB: Charm School). Colleen. That Girl from Paris. Florida Special. 1937: The Toast of New York. Cham-

pagne Waltz. Hitting a New High. Super Sleuth. Fight for Your Lady. 1938: The Affairs of Annabel. Radio City Revels. Thanks for Everything. Annabel Takes a Tour. 1940: Young People. The Great Dictator. Little Men. Tin Pan Alley. 1941: The Great American Broadcast. *Screen Snapshots No. 87. Rise and Shine. Navy Blues. 1942: Song of the Islands. 1943: Wintertime. Hello, Frisco, Hello. Something to Shout About. 1944: Sweet and Lowdown. It Happened Tomorrow. The Merry Monahans. Bowery to Broadway. 1945: On Stage, Everybody. That's the Spirit. 1946: She Wrote the Book. 1948: Northwest Stampede. When My Baby Smiles at Me. 1949: Thieves' Highway. 1950: Last of the Buccaneers. Tomahawk (GB: Battle of Powder River). 1956: Around the World in Eighty Days. 1959: The Wonderful Country. 1960: The Rat Race. 1961: Lover Come Back.

OATES, Warren 1928–1982
Kentucky-born actor with dark, curly hair, who played loutish, countrified villains in his early screen days, but was soon singled out by critics and moved into better roles. When stardom came, he proved distinctly unconventional, mixing such commercial leading roles as *Dillinger* with unshowy secondary parts in other films: he was associated with some quite weird projects in his time. Died from a heart attack.
1958: Up Periscope! 1959: Yellowstone Kelly. Private Property. Seven Against the Wall (TV). 1960: The Rise and Fall of Legs Diamond. 1961: Ride the High Country (GB: Guns in the Afternoon). 1962: Hero's Island. 1963: Mail Order Bride (GB: West of Montana). 1965: The Rounders. †Shenandoah. Major Dundee. 1966: Return of the Seven. The Shooting (released 1971). 1967: Welcome to Hard Times (GB: Killer on a Horse). In the Heat of the Night. 1968: The Split. Something for a Lonely Man (GB: TV). Crooks and Coronets (US: Sophie's Place). 1969: The Wild Bunch. Smith! Barquero. 1970: There Was a Crooked Man. The Movie Murderer (TV). 1971: Chandler. Two-Lane Blacktop. The Reluctant Heroes (TV. GB: The Reluctant Heroes of Hill 656). The Hired Hand. The Showdown (TV). 1973: The Thief Who Came to Dinner. Tom Sawyer. Kid Blue. Dillinger. Badlands. 1974: The White Dawn. Born to Kill (GB: Cockfighter). Bring Me the Head of

Alfredo Garcia. 1975: 92 in the Shade. Race with the Devil. Glass Houses. 1976: Drum. Dixie Dynamite. 1977: Prime Time (GB: American Raspberry). Sleeping Dogs. 1978: The Brink's Job. True Grit, a Further Adventure (TV). Day of Terror, Night of Fear (TV). China 9, Liberty 37/Gunfighters (US: Clayton and Catherine). 1979: And Baby Makes Six (TV). 1941. 1980: Baby Comes Home (TV). 1981: Escape from New York. The Border. Stripes. 1982: Tough Enough. Blue Thunder. My Old Man (TV).

† Scenes deleted from final release print

OBERON, Merle (Estelle M. O'Brien Thompson) 1911–1979
Cold-looking, India-born brunette beauty of regal bearing who won the heart of British film tycoon Alexander Korda (they married in 1939 and divorced in 1945) and built up a considerable career in his productions, at first in exotic roles. Widened her range in Hollywood (where she married cameraman Lucien Ballard in 1945; divorced 1949), but her looks faded at 40 and later roles were unworthy of her. Nominated for an Academy Award on *The Dark Angel*. Died from a stroke.
1929: The Three Passions. 1930: A Warm Corner. Alf's Button. 1931: Fascination. Never Trouble Trouble. Service for Ladies (US: Reserved for Ladies). 1932: Ebbtide. For the Love of Mike. Aren't We All? Wedding Rehearsal. Strange Evidence. Men of Tomorrow. 1933: The Private Life of Henry VIII. 1934: The Battle (US: Thunder in the East). The Broken Melody. The Private Life of Don Juan. The Scarlet Pimpernel. 1935: The Dark Angel. Folies Bergère. 1936: These Three. Beloved Enemy. 1937: Over the Moon. The Divorce of Lady X. I Claudius (unfinished). 1938: The Cowboy and the Lady. The Lion Has Wings. 1940: Till We Meet Again. 1941: Lydia. Affectionately Yours. That Uncertain Feeling. 1943: Forever and a Day. Stage Door Canteen. First Comes Courage. 1944: The Lodger. Dark Waters. 1945: A Song to Remember. This Love of Ours. 1946: A Night in Paradise. Temptation. 1947: Night Song. 1948: Berlin Express. 1949: Dans la vie tout s'arrange. 1951: Pardon My French (GB: The Lady from Boston). 1952: 24 Hours of a Woman's Life (US: Affair in Monte Carlo). 1954: Todo es possible en Grenada.

Desiree. Deep in My Heart. 1955: Cavalcade (TV. GB: cinemas). 1956: The Price of Fear. 1963: Of Love and Desire. 1966: The Oscar. Hotel. 1973: Interval.

O'BRIAN, Hugh (H. Krampke) 1925–

Tall, dark American actor with crooked smile, good-looking in a leathery sort of way. Played mostly lean, grim-faced villains until television success in the title role of *Wyatt Earp* pushed him towards the front rank, a position he has never quite consolidated.

1949: DOA. 1950: Never Fear. Rocketship XM. Kansas Raiders. Beyond the Purple Hills. The Return of Jesse James. 1951: On the Loose. Buckaroo Sheriff of Texas. Vengeance Valley. Fighting Coast Guard. Cave of Outlaws. Little Big Horn (GB: The Fighting Seventh). The Cimarron Kid. 1952: Red Ball Express. Battle at Apache Pass. Sally and Saint Anne. Son of Ali Baba. The Raiders. The Lawless Breed. Meet Me at the Fair. 1953: Seminole. The Man from the Alamo. The Stand at Apache River. Back to God's Country. 1954: Fireman, Save My Child. Saskatchewan (GB: O'Rourke of the Royal Mounted). Drums Across the River. There's No Business Like Show Business. Broken Lance. 1955: White Feather. The Twinkle in God's Eye. 1956: The Brass Legend. 1958: The Fiend Who Walked the West. 1959: Alias Jesse James. 1962: Come Fly With Me. 1963: Assassin...Made in Italy/Assassination in Rome. Il segreto del vestito rosso. 1964: Love Has Many Faces. Strategy of Terror. 1965: In Harm's Way. 10 Little Indians. 1966: Ambush Bay. 1967: Africa – Texas Style! 1970: Wild Women (TV). 1971: Harpy (TV). 1972: Probe (TV). 1975: Killer Force/The Diamond Mercenaries. Murder on Flight 502 (TV). 1976: The Shootist. 1977: Fantasy Island (TV). Murder at the World Series (TV). Benny and Barney: Las Vegas Undercover (TV). 1978: Game of Death. Cruise into Terror (TV).

O'BRIEN, Edmond 1915–1985

Heavy-cheeked, burly, careworn-looking American actor, in leading parts almost from the beginning of his career, who gave everything, and sometimes a little more, to his roles. His career ran in phases: comedy and drama until war service; thrillers from 1946 to 1950; westerns from 1950 to 1953, then more thrillers and a natural sidestep into leading charac-

ter parts when weight tipped him from the top of the cast. Oscar for *The Barefoot Contessa* (best supporting actor). Also a nomination for *Seven Days in May.* Married to Nancy Kelly (1941–2) and Olga San Juan (from 1948; later divorced after many years). Died from Alzheimer's Disease.

1938: Prison Break. 1939: The Hunchback of Notre Dame. 1941: The Obliging Young Lady. A Girl, a Guy and a Gob (GB: The Navy Steps Out). Parachute Battalion. 1942: Powder Town. 1943: The Amazing Mrs Holliday. 1944: Winged Victory. 1946: The Killers. 1947: The Web. 1948: Another Part of the Forest. An Act of Murder. A Double Life. Fighter Squadron. For the Love of Mary. 1949: DOA. White Heat. 1950: Backfire. 711 Ocean Drive. Between Midnight and Dawn. The Admiral Was a Lady. The Redhead and the Cowboy. 1951: Two of a Kind. Warpath. Silver City (GB: High Vermilion). 1953: Denver and Rio Grande. The Greatest Show on Earth. The Turning Point. 1953: Cow Country. China Venture. Man in the Dark. Julius Caesar. The Hitch-Hiker. The Bigamist. 1954: The Shanghai Story. Shield for Murder. The Barefoot Contessa. 1955: Pete Kelly's Blues. 1984. 1956: A Cry in the Night. D-Day the Sixth of June. The Rack. The Girl Can't Help It. 1957: The Big Land (GB: Stampeded!) The Comedian (TV). Stopover Tokyo. 1958: The World Was His Jury. The Male Animal (TV). Sing, Boy, Sing. Up Periscope! 1959: The Restless and the Damned (GB: The Climbers. US: The Ambitious Ones). The Third Voice. The Blue Men (TV). 1960: The Last Voyage. 1961: The Great Imposter. 1962: The Man Who Shot Liberty Valance. Moon Pilot. Bird Man of Alcatraz. The Longest Day. 1964: Rio Conchos. Seven Days in May. The Hanged Man (TV. GB: cinemas). 1965: Sylvia. Synanon (GB: Get Off My Back). 1966: Fantastic Voyage. 1967: Peau d'espion (GB: To Commit a Murder). The Viscount. The Doomsday Flight (TV. GB: cinemas). The Outsider (TV). 1969: The Wild Bunch. The Love God? 1970: The Intruders (TV). River of Mystery (TV). 1971: What's a Nice Girl Like You? (TV). 1972: They Only Kill Their Masters. Jigsaw (TV). 1973: Isn't It Shocking? (TV). Lucky Luciano. 1974: 99 and 44/100% Dead (GB: Call Harry Crown). 1975: The Other Side of the Wind (uncompleted).

As director: *1954: Shield for Murder (co-directed). 1961: Man-Trap.*

O'BRIEN, George 1900–1985

Rugged, rough-hewn American cowboy star. Entered films as a stunt-man, then featured in some of John Ford's earliest westerns. Settled down into the second-feature corral with the coming of sound, and later played a few character roles for Ford in post-war years. Married to Marguerite Churchill (1910-) 1933–1949: never remarried. Died following a stroke.

*1922: White Hands. Moran of the Lady Letty. 1923: Ne'er do Well. Woman Proof. Shadows of Paris/Streets of Paris. The Ghost Breakers. 1924: Painted Lady. The Iron Horse. The Man Who Came Back. The Roughneck. The Sea Hawk. 1925: Fighting Heart. The Dancers. Thank You. 1926: Fig Leaves. Havoc. The Johnstown Flood (GB: The Flood). The Blue Eagle. Three Bad Men. Silver Treasure. Rustlin' for Cupid. 1927: Paid to Love. Is Zat So? The Romantic Age. East Side, West Side. Sunrise. 1928: Sharpshooters. Honor Bound. The Case of Mary Brown. Blindfold. False Colors. 1929: Salute. Noah's Ark. Masked Emotions. True Heaven. *Graduation Daze. 1930: Last of the Duanes. The Lone Star Ranger. Rough Romance. The Man Who Came Back (remake). 1931: A Holy Terror. Fair Warning. Riders of the Purple Sage. The Seas Beneath. 1932: Mystery Ranch. The Rainbow Trail. The Gay Caballero. The Golden West. 1933: Life in the Raw. Robbers' Roost. Smoke Lightning. The Last Trail. 1934: The Dude Ranger. Frontier Marshal. Ever Since Eve. 1935: Hard Rock Harrigan. When a Man's a Man. Thunder Mountain. Whispering Smith Speaks. The Cowboy Millionaire. 1936: Daniel Boone. O'Malley of the Mounted. Border Patrolman. 1937: Windjammer. Hollywood Cowboy. Park Avenue Logger (GB: Millionaire Playboy). 1938: The Painted Desert. Gun Law. Border G-Man. Lawless Valley. 1939: The Renegade Ranger. Arizona Legion. Racketeers of the Range. Trouble in Sundown. The Fighting Gringo. Timber Stampede. 1940: Bullet Code. Marshal of Mesa City. Stage to Chino. Legion of the Lawless. Prairie Law. Triple Justice. 1947: My Wild Irish Rose. 1948: Fort Apache. 1949: She Wore a Yellow Ribbon. 1951: Gold Raiders (GB: Stooges Go West). 1964: Cheyenne Autumn.*

O'BRIEN, Margaret (Angela Maxine O'Brien) 1937–

Dark-haired, appealing and very natural American child star, with big brown eyes and long pigtails, capable of more heart-felt conviction in her performances than most adults. Received a special Oscar in 1944, but when her studio (M-G-M) suspended her in 1950 for refusing to do a planned live-action film of *Alice in Wonderland* (ironically, never made), her star career was virtually finished. Several comebacks over the years have failed.
*1941: †Babes on Broadway. 1942: Journey for Margaret. 1943: Dr Gillespie's Criminal Case (GB: Crazy to Kill). Lost Angel. *You, John Jones. Thousands Cheer. Madame Curie. Jane Eyre. 1944: The Canterville Ghost. Meet Me in St Louis. Music for Millions. 1945: Our Vines Have Tender Grapes. 1946: Three Wise Fools. Bad Bascomb. 1947: Tenth Avenue Angel. The Unfinished Dance. 1948: The Big City. 1949: Little Women. The Secret Garden. 1951: Her First Romance (GB: Girls Never Tell). 1956: Glory. 1957: The Mystery of Thirteen (TV). 1958: Little Women (TV). 1959: Second Happiest Day (TV). 1960: Heller in Pink Tights. 1964: The Turncoat (TV). 1971: Diabolical Wedding. 1972: Annabelle Lee. 1974: Death in Space (TV). 1981: Amy.*

† As Maxine O'Brien

O'BRIEN, Pat (William P. O'Brien) 1899–1983

Round-faced, dark-haired, solidly-built Hollywood star of the thirties and forties. Pat O'Brien was so Irish that one could hardly believe he actually spoke with an American accent, even if there were a hint of soft Irishness in it. A boyhood friend of Spencer Tracy, he chose acting in preference to the priesthood, but made up for it at Warners by playing priests several times, when he wasn't being fast-talking reporters or happy-go-lucky adventurers. He seemed heavy by the mid-forties and his standing gradually declined, but he kept acting, latterly in character roles. Died from a heart attack.
*1919: Married in Haste. 1921: Shadows of the West. 1922: Determination. 1929: Fury of the Wild. Freckled Rascal. 1930: *The Nightingale. 1931: The Front Page. Flying High (GB: Happy Landing). Consolation Marriage (GB: Married in Haste). Honor Among Lovers. Personal Maid. 1932: The Strange Case of Clara Deane. The Final Edition. American Madness. Virtue. Laughter in Hell. Hell's House. Scandal for Sale. Hollywood Speaks. Air Mail. 1933: Bombshell (GB: Blonde Bombshell). The World Gone Mad (GB: The Public Be Hanged). Destination Unknown. Bureau of Missing Persons. College Coach (GB: Football Coach). 1934: I've Got Your Number. Flaming Gold. Here Comes the Navy. I Sell Anything. Gambling Lady. Twenty Million Sweethearts. Personality Kid. Flirtation Walk. 1935: Oil for the Lamps of China. Devil Dogs of the Air. *A Trip thru a Hollywood Studio. Ceiling Zero. The Irish in Us. In Caliente. Page Miss Glory. Stars over Broadway/Stars on Parade. 1936: China Clipper. I Married a Doctor. Public Enemy's Wife (GB: G-Man's Wife). 1937: San Quentin. The Great O'Malley. Submarine D-1. Slim. Back in Circulation. 1938: Boy Meets Girl. Women Are Like That. The Cowboy from Brooklyn (GB: Romance and Rhythm). *For Auld Lang Syne. Garden of the Moon. Angels With Dirty Faces. 1939: The Kid from Kokomo (GB: The Orphan of the Ring). Indianapolis Speedway (GB: Devil on Wheels). Off the Record. The Night of Nights. 1940: Castle on the Hudson (GB: Years without Days). Knute Rockne – All American (GB: A Modern Hero). The Fighting 69th. Torrid Zone. Slightly Honorable. Till We Meet Again. Flowing Gold. 1941: Submarine Zone. 1942: Two Yanks in Trinidad. Broadway. The Navy Comes Through. Flight Lieutenant. 1943: The Iron Major. Bombardier. His Butler's Sister. 1944: Marine Raiders. Secret Command. 1945: Man Alive. Having Wonderful Crime. 1946: Perilous Holiday. Crack-up. 1947: Riffraff. 1948: Fighting Father Dunne. The Boy with Green Hair. *Screen Snapshots No. 166. 1949: A Dangerous Profession. 1950: The Fireball. Johnny One-Eye. 1951: The People Against O'Hara. Criminal Lawyer. 1952: Okinawa. *Screen Snapshots No. 205. 1954: Jubilee Trail. Ring of Fear. 1955: Inside Detroit. *Hollywood Fathers. 1957: Kill Me Tomorrow. Invitation to a Gunfighter (TV). 1958: The Last Hurrah. 1959: Some Like It Hot. 1965: Town Tamer. The Crime (TV). 1969: The Over-the-Hill Gang (TV). The Phynx. 1971: Welcome Home, Johnny Bristol (TV). 1972: The Adventures of Nick Carter (TV). 1976: Kiss Me, Kill Me (TV). 1977: Billy Jack Goes to Washington. 1978: The End. 1980: Scout's Honor (TV). 1981: Ragtime.*

O'CONNOR, Donald 1925–

Cheerful, slimly-built, non-stop American dancing star and light comedian with a thick brush of brown hair. A child actor of the late 1930s (the offspring of a family vaudeville act), he blossomed in medium-budget musicals at Universal, and later proved a more-than-useful foil for Hollywood's leading musical lights, without quite being able to carry a big film on his own. Was also for many years the master of Francis the talking mule, but his film career faded in the 1950s as musicals fell from fashion, and he embarked on a fresh career as a composer of light symphonic music.
1937: Melody for Two. 1938: Men with Wings. Sing, You Sinners. Tom Sawyer – Detective. Sons of the Legion. 1939: Million Dollar Legs. Unmarried (GB: Night Club Hostess). Boy Trouble. Death of a Champion. Night Work. On Your Toes. Beau Geste. 1941: What's Cookin' (GB: Wake Up and Dream). 1942: Get Hep to Love (GB: She's My Lovely). Give Out, Sisters. It Comes Up Love (GB: A Date with an Angel). When Johnny Comes Marching Home. Private Buckaroo. 1943: Strictly in the Groove. Mister Big. Top Man. 1944: Follow the Boys. This Is the Life. The Merry Monahans. Chip Off the Old Block. Bowery to Broadway. 1945: Patrick the Great. 1947: Something in the Wind. 1948: Feudin', Fussin' and a-Fightin'. Are You With It? 1949: Yes, Sir, That's My Baby. Francis. Curtain Call at Cactus Creek (GB: Take the Stage). 1950: The Milkman. Double Crossbones. 1951: Francis Goes to the Races. 1952: Singin' in the Rain. Francis Goes to West Point. I Love Melvin. 1953: Call Me Madam. Walking My Baby Back Home. Francis Covers the Big Town. 1954: There's No Business Like Show Business. Francis Joins the WACs. 1955: Francis in the Navy. 1956: Anything Goes. 1957: The Buster Keaton Story. The Jet-Propelled Couch (TV). 1961: The Wonders of Aladdin. Cry for Happy. 1965: That Funny Feeling. 1974: That's Entertainment! 1981: Ragtime. 1984: Miracle in a Manger.

O'DONNELL, Cathy (Ann Steely) 1923–1970

Lovely dark-haired American actress of gentle manner, usually in vulnerable roles. Made a

tremendous start in *The Best Years of Our Lives*, but was never a dominant actress, and had to be content thereafter with what came her way. Died from a cerebral haemorrhage.
1946: *The Best Years of Our Lives.* 1947: *Bury Me Dead.* 1948: *The Amazing Mr X/The Spiritualist. They Live by Night.* 1950: *Side Street. The Miniver Story.* 1951: *Detective Story. Never Trust a Gambler. The Woman's Angle.* 1953: *Eight O'Clock Walk.* 1954: *L'amante di Paride (GB: The Face That Launched a Thousand Ships).* 1955: *Mad at the World. The Man from Laramie.* 1957: *The Deerslayer. The Story of Mankind.* 1958: *My World Dies Screaming (GB: Terror in the Haunted House).* 1959: *Ben-Hur.*

O'HARA, Maureen (M. Fitzsimons) 1920–
Hollywood's favourite red-haired, hazel-eyed Irish colleen. A strange combination of gentleness and high spirits, she was memorable as staunch wives or spitfire village girls in several John Ford films, but also showed a penchant for action in her many swashbucklers, easterns and westerns, in which her spectacular figure showed to advantage. The story goes that, in one sword-flashing film, as Maureen fought her way to the battlements, jumped down 15 feet from them and carried on fighting without a quiver, the entire unit's stunt team fell to its knees.
1938: †*Kicking the Moon Around (US: The Playboy, later Millionaire Merry-Go-Round).* †*My Irish Molly (US: Little Miss Molly)* 1939: *Jamaica Inn. The Hunchback of Notre Dame.* 1940: *Bill of Divorcement. Dance, Girl, Dance.* 1941: *They Met in Argentina. How*

Green Was My Valley. 1942: *Ten Gentlemen from West Point. The Black Swan. To the Shores of Tripoli.* 1943: *The Immortal Sergeant. The Fallen Sparrow. This Land is Mine.* 1944: *Buffalo Bill.* 1945: *The Spanish Main.* 1946: *Sentimental Journey. Do You Love Me?* 1947: *Sinbad the Sailor. Miracle on 34th Street (GB: The Big Heart). The Foxes of Harrow. The Homestretch.* 1948: *Sitting Pretty.* 1949: *Britannia Mews (US: Forbidden Street). Father Was a Fullback. A Woman's Secret. Bagdad.* 1950: *Comanche Territory. Rio Grande. Tripoli.* 1951: *Flame of Araby. At Sword's Point (GB: Sons of the Musketeers. Completed 1949).* **Australian Diary 144/145.* 1952: *Kangaroo. The Quiet Man. Against All Flags. The Redhead from Wyoming.* 1953: *War Arrow.* 1954: *Malaga (US: Fire over Africa). The Long Gray Line.* 1955: *Lady Godiva (GB: Lady Godiva of Coventry). The Magnificent Matador (GB: The Brave and the Beautiful).* 1956: *Everything But the Truth. Lisbon.* 1957: *The Wings of Eagles.* 1959: *Mrs Miniver (TV). Our Man in Havana.* 1961: *The Deadly Companions. The Parent Trap.* 1962: *Mr Hobbs Takes a Vacation.* 1963: *Spencer's Mountain. McLintock!* 1965: *The Battle of the Villa Fiorita. The Rare Breed.* 1969: *How to Commit Marriage.* 1970: *How Do I Love Thee?* 1971: *Big Jake.* 1973: *The Red Pony (TV. GB: cinemas).*

† *As Maureen Fitzsimmons*

O'HERLIHY, Dan 1919–
Tall, taciturn, soft-spoken Irish actor, not unlike Louis Hayward in features. Began in British films, but unexpectedly got his breakthrough to more prominent roles in Mexico, from his leading performance in Bunuel's Robinson Crusoe film. Hollywood seemed to see him mainly as a smiling villain in costume adventures and after a series of unworthy roles he has worked principally for American television. Oscar nomination for *The Adventures of Robinson Crusoe.*
1946: *Odd Man Out. Hungry Hill.* 1948: *Macbeth. Kidnapped. Larceny.* 1950: *Iroquois Trail (GB: The Tomahawk Trail).* 1951: *The Desert Fox (GB: Rommel – Desert Fox). Soldiers Three. The Highwayman. At Sword's Point (GB: Sons of the Musketeers. Completed 1949). The Blue Veil.* 1952: *Actors and Sin. Operation Secret. Sword of Venus (GB: Island*

of Monte Cristo). *The Adventures of Robinson Crusoe.* 1953: *Invasion USA.* 1954: *Bengal Brigade (GB: Bengal Rifles). The Black Shield of Falworth.* 1955: *The Purple Mask. The Virgin Queen.* 1957: *The Blackwell Story (TV. GB: cinemas). That Woman Opposite (US: City After Midnight).* 1958: *Home Before Dark.* 1959: *Imitation of Life. The Young Land.* 1960: *One Foot in Hell. A Terrible Beauty (US: The Night Fighters). To the Sounds of Trumpets (TV).* 1961: *King of the Roaring Twenties (GB: The Big Bankroll). Port of Revenge.* 1962: *The Cabinet of Caligari.* 1964: *Fail Safe.* 1968: *How to Steal the World (TV. GB: cinemas).* 1969: *100 Rifles. The Big Cube.* 1970: *Waterloo.* 1971: *The People (TV).* 1972: *The Carey Treatment.* 1974: *QB VII (TV). The Tamarind Seed.* 1976: *Banjo Hackett – Roamin' Free (TV).* 1977: *Good Against Evil (TV).* 1978: *MacArthur (GB: MacArthur the Rebel General). Deadly Game (TV). The Girl in the Empty Grave (TV).* 1979: *TR Sloane of the Secret Service (TV).* 1983: *Halloween III: Season of the Witch.* 1984: *The Last Starfighter.*

O'KEEFE, Dennis (Edward 'Bud' Flanagan) 1908–1968
Cheery, fast-talking, solidly-built, light-haired American actor of Irish vaudevillian parents. He laboured for years in tiny roles as Bud Flanagan before making the breakthrough to second-grade stardom. He then moved confidently through a wide range of roles, proving equally at home in light comedy or tough-guy thrillers – occasionally taking a hand in the scripts himself. Married (second) to Hungarian actress Steffi Duna (Stephanie Berindey 1913–) from 1940. Died from lung cancer.
1931: †*Cimarron.* †*Reaching for the Moon.* 1932: †*Scarface.* †*Hat Check Girl (GB: Embassy Girl).* †*Cabin in the Cotton.* †*Crooner.* †*Big City Blues.* †*Night After Night.* †*The Man from Yesterday.* †*Two Against the World.* †*I Am a Fugitive from a Chain Gang.* †*A Bill of Divorcement.* †*Merrily We Go to Hell (GB: Merrily We Go to —).* †*Central Park.* 1933: †*Broadway thru a Keyhole.* †*Hello Everybody!* †*From Hell to Heaven.* †*Gold Diggers of 1933.* †*I'm No Angel.* †*The House on 56th Street.* †*Torch Singer.* †*Blood Money.* †*Girl Missing.* †*The Eagle and the Hawk.* †*Too Much Harmony.* †*Duck Soup.* †*Lady Killer.* 1934:

†*The Meanest Gal in Town*. †*The Red Rider* (serial). †*Jimmy the Gent*. †*Upper World*. †*Wonder Bar*. †*Death on the Diamond*. †*Desirable*. †*The Girl from Missouri* (GB: *100 Per Cent Pure*). †*Registered Nurse*. †*Man with Two Faces*. †*Lady by Choice*. †*Transatlantic Merry-Go-Round*. †*Smarty* (GB: *Hit Me Again*). †*He Was Her Man*. †*Coming Out Party*. †*Fog over Frisco*. †*Madame Du Barry*. †*College Rhythm*. †*Imitation of Life*. †**Everything's Ducky*. †*Broadway Bill* (GB: *Strictly Confidential*). 1935: †**A Night at the Biltmore Bowl*. †*Dante's Inferno*. †*Devil Dogs of the Air*. †*The Daring Young Man*. †*Top Hat*. †*Burning Gold*. †*Gold Diggers of 1935*. †*Anna Karenina*. †*Let 'em Have It* (GB: *False Faces*). †*It's in the Air*. †*Broadway Hostess*. †*Doubting Thomas*. †*Rumba*. †*The Man Who Broke the Bank at Monte Carlo*. †*Mary Burns, Fugitive*. †*Biography of a Bachelor Girl*. †*Mississippi*. †*Every Night at Eight*. †*Personal Maid's Secret*. †*Shipmates Forever*. 1936: †*Love Before Breakfast*. †*Anything Goes*. †*Till We Meet Again*. †*Three Smart Girls*. †*13 Hours by Air*. †*Nobody's Fool*. †*Rhythm on the Range*. †*Libeled Lady*. †*The Accusing Finger*. †*The Plainsman*. †*San Francisco*. †*The Last Outlaw*. †*Mr Deeds Goes to Town*. †*And So They Were Married*. †*Sworn Enemy*. †*Yours for the Asking*. †*Theodora Goes Wild*. †*Born to Dance*. †*Great Guy* (GB: *Pluck of the Irish*). 1937: †*The Great Gambini*. †*Married Before Breakfast*. †*One Mile from Heaven*. †*When's Your Birthday?* †*Swing High, Swing Low*. †*A Star is Born*. †*The Girl from Scotland Yard*. †*The Firefly*. †*Hats Off*. †*Saratoga*. †*The Big City*. †*The Lady Escapes*. †*Top of the Town*. †*Captains Courageous*. †*Parole Racket*. †*Riding on Air*. †*Easy Living*. †*Blazing Barriers*. 1938: †*Vivacious Lady*. *Bad Man of Brimstone*. *The Chaser*. *Hold That Kiss*. *Vacation from Love*. 1939: *The Kid from Texas*. *Unexpected Father* (GB: *Sandy Takes a Bow*). *Burn 'em up O'Connor*. *That's Right – You're Wrong*. 1940: *Pop Always Pays*. *Alias the Deacon*. *La Conga Nights*. *I'm Nobody's Sweetheart Now*. *The Girl from Havana*. *You'll Find Out*. *Bowery Boy*. *Arise, My Love*. 1941: *Mr District Attorney*. *Broadway Limited*. *Week-End for Three*. *Topper Returns*. *Lady Scarface*. 1942: *The Affairs of Jimmy Valentine*. *Moonlight Masquerade*. 1943: *Hangmen Also Die*. *Good Morning, Judge*. *Tahiti Honey*. *The Leopard Man*. *Hi Diddle Diddle*. 1944: *The Fighting Seabees*. *Abroad with Two Yanks*. *The Story of Dr Wassell*. *Up in Mabel's Room*. *Sensations of 1945*. 1945: *Earl Carroll Vanities*. *The Affairs of Susan*. *Getting Gertie's Garter*. *Brewster's Millions*. 1946: *Doll Face* (GB: *Come Back to Me*). *Her Adventurous Night*. 1947: *Mr District Attorney* (remake). *Dishonored Lady*. *T-Men*. 1948: *Raw Deal*. *Siren of Atlantis*. *Walk a Crooked Mile*. 1949: *Cover Up*. *Abandoned*. *The Great Dan Patch*. 1950: *Woman on the Run*. *The Company She Keeps*. *The Eagle and the Hawk*. 1951: *Follow the Sun*. *Passage West* (GB: *High Venture*). 1952: *One Big Affair*. *Everything I Have is Yours*. 1953: *The Lady Wants Mink*. *The Fake*. 1954: *The Diamond* (US: *Diamond Wizard*). *Drums of Tahiti*. ‡*Angela*. 1955: *Chicago Syndicate*.

Las Vegas Shakedown. 1956: *Inside Detroit*. 1957: *Dragoon Wells Massacre*. *Sail Into Danger*. *Lady of Vengeance*. *Confession* (TV). 1958: *Graft and Corruption*. 1961: *All Hands on Deck*. 1963: *The Flame/The Naked Flame*.

† *As Bud Flanagan* ‡*Also directed*

OLAND, Warner (Werner Ölund) 1880–1938

Big, dark, bluff, moustachioed Swedish actor, in Hollywood from the early days. Was seen as shifty foreigners in silent films – notably in serials – but came into his own when cast in 1931 as the painstaking oriental detective Charlie Chan. Died in his native Sweden from bronchial pneumonia.

1909: *Jewels of the Madonna*. 1912: *The Life of John Bunyan*. *The Pilgrim's Progress*. 1915: *Sin*. 1916: *Patria* (serial). *The Eternal Question/The Eternal Sapho*. *The Serpent*. *Destruction*. *The Fool's Revenge*. *The Reapers*. *The Rise of Susan*. 1917: *The Fatal Ring* (serial). *The Cigarette Girl*. *The Mysterious Client*. *Convict 993*. 1918: *The Naulahka*. *The Yellow Ticket*. 1919: *The Lightning Raider* (serial). *Witness for the Defense*. *Avalanche*. *Mandarin's Gold*. *Twin Pawns* (GB: *The Curse of Greed*). *The Mad Talon*. *Roaring Oaks*. 1920: *The Third Eye*. *The Phantom Foe*. 1921: *The Yellow Arm*. *Hurricane Hutch*. 1922: *East is West*. *The Pride of Palomar*. 1923: *His Children's Children*. 1924: *Curlytop*. *One Night in Rome*. *So This is Marriage*. *The Fighting American*. *The Throwback*. 1925: *Flower of Night*. *Don Q, Son of Zorro*. *The Winding Stair*. *Riders of the Purple Sage*. 1926: *Tell It to the Marines*. *Infatuation*. *Don Juan*. *The Marriage Clause*. *The Mystery Club*. *Twinkletoes*. *Man of the Forest*. 1927: *A Million Bid*. *The Jazz Singer*. *Sailor Izzy Murphy*. *When a Man Loves* (GB: *His Lady*). *Good Time Charley*. *Old San Francisco*. *What Happened to Father*. 1928: *The Scarlet Lady*. *Wheel of Chance*. *Stand and Deliver*. *Dream of Love*. *Tong War*. 1929: *The Mysterious Dr Fu Manchu*. *Chinatown Nights*. *The Mighty*. *The Studio Murder Mystery*. *The Faker*. 1930: *The Return of Dr Fu Manchu*. *Dangerous Paradise*. *The Vagabond King*. *Paramount on Parade*. 1931: *The Black Camel*. *Drums of Jeopardy*. *The Big Gamble*. *Dishonored*. *Daughter of the Dragon*. *Charlie Chan Carries On*. 1932: *A Passport to Hell* (GB: *Burnt Offering*). *Shanghai Express*. *Charlie Chan's Chance*. *The Son-*

Daughter. 1933: *Charlie Chan's Greatest Case*. *Before Dawn*. *As Husbands Go*. 1934: *Charlie Chan in London*. *Mandalay*. *Bulldog Drummond Strikes Back*. *The Painted Veil*. *Charlie Chan's Courage*. 1935: *Shanghai*. *The Werewolf of London*. *Charlie Chan in Paris*. *Charlie Chan in Egypt*. *Charlie Chan in Shanghai*. 1936: *Charlie Chan at the Circus*. *Charlie Chan at the Race Track*. *Charlie Chan's Secret*. *Charlie Chan at the Opera*. 1937: *Charlie Chan on Broadway*. *Charlie Chan at the Olympics*. *Charlie Chan at Monte Carlo*.

OLIVER, Anthony 1923–

Tall Welsh actor with fair, wavy hair, vaguely soulful looks and gentle, soothing voice. After post-war stage successes (a medium he never entirely deserted) he essayed occasional leading roles in minor British films of the early 1960s following years as a character player, often of police sergeants. But he is perhaps best known for his talents as a storyteller on radio and television.

1948: *Once a Jolly Swagman* (US: *Maniacs on Wheels*). *All over the Town*. 1950: *Waterfront* (GB: *Waterfront Women*). *The Magnet*. *The Clouded Yellow*. 1952: *The Happy Family* (US: *Mr Lord Says No*). *Penny Princess*. *Emergency Call* (US: *Hundred Hour Hunt*). *Gift Horse* (US: *Glory at Sea*). *Cosh Boy* (US: *The Slasher*). 1953: *Street Corner* (US: *Both Sides of the Law*). *The Runaway Bus*. 1954: *Mad about Men*. *To Dorothy a Son* (US: *Cash on Delivery*). 1955: *They Can't Hang Me*. *Lost* (US: *Tears for Simon*). 1956: *Checkpoint*. 1959: *The Nudist Story*. 1960: *Sink the Bismarck!* *The Entertainer*. *Crossroads to Crime*. 1961: *Transatlantic*. 1962: *HMS Defiant* (US: *Damn the Defiant!*). *Out of the Fog*. *Danger by My Side*. 1964: **Peter Studies Form* (narrator only). 1966: *Money-Go-Round*.

OLIVIER, Sir Laurence (Lord Olivier) 1907–

Dark, dominant, exciting and extremely handsome, Olivier was generally acclaimed as the finest British actor of his generation. Certainly few could be as magnetic when he so chose. Played dashing young characters in the thirties, then slightly wild but intriguing men of mystery in Hollywood, before his Shakespearian triumphs, which won him a special Oscar (1946) for *Henry V* and a best actor Oscar in 1948 for *Hamlet*, although neither

was as impressive as his Richard III. Tackled offbeat leading roles in the sixties and character roles in recent years, when he has sadly tended to substitute overacting for characterization. Married to Vivien Leigh from 1940 to 1960 (second). Now married to actress Joan Plowright. Further Special Oscar 1979. Knighted in 1947. Created Lord Olivier in 1970. Has received nine Oscar nominations.
*1930: Too Many Crooks. The Temporary Widow. 1931: Potiphar's Wife (US: The Strange Desire). The Yellow Ticket (GB: The Yellow Passport). Friends and Lovers. Westward Passage. 1932: Perfect Understanding. 1933: No Funny Business. 1935: Moscow Nights (US: I Stand Condemned). Conquest of the Air. 1936: As You Like It. Fire Over England. 1937: 21 Days (US: 21 Days Together). The Divorce of Lady X. 1939: Q Planes (US: Clouds over Europe). Wuthering Heights. 1940: Rebecca. Pride and Prejudice. 1941: That Hamilton Woman (GB: Lady Hamilton). 49th Parallel (US: The Invaders). *Words for Battle (narrator only). 1942: *George Cross Island (narrator only). 1943: The Demi-Paradise (US: Adventure for Two). *Malta GC (narrator only). 1944 ‡Henry V. This Happy Breed (narrator only). 1945: *Fighting Pilgrims (narrator only). 1948: †Hamlet. 1951: The Magic Box. 1952: Carrie. 1953: The Beggar's Opera. A Queen is Crowned (narrator only). 1955: ‡Richard III. 1957: †The Prince and the Showgirl. 1959: The Devil's Disciple. 1960: Spartacus. The Entertainer. 1961: The Power and the Glory (TV. GB: cinemas). 1962: Term of Trial. 1963: Uncle Vanya. 1965: Bunny Lake is Missing. Othello. 1966: Khartoum. 1968: The Shoes of the Fisherman. Romeo and Juliet (narrator only). 1969: Oh! What a Lovely War. Battle of Britain. The Dance of Death. David Copperfield (TV. GB: cinemas). 1970: †Three Sisters. 1971: Nicholas and Alexandra. 1972: Lady Caroline Lamb. Sleuth. 1974: Love Among the Ruins (TV). 1975: The Gentleman Tramp (narrator only). 1976: Marathon Man. The Seven-Per-Cent Solution. 1977: A Bridge Too Far. 1978: The Betsy. The Boys from Brazil. 1979: Dracula. A Little Romance. 1980: Inchon! The Jazz Singer. 1981: Clash of the Titans. 1983: The Jigsaw Man. 1984: The Bounty. The Last Days of Pompeii. 1985: Wild Geese II.*

† Also directed ‡ Also co-directed

OLSEN and JOHNSON
OLSEN, Ole
(John Olsen) 1892–1965
JOHNSON, Chic
(Harold Johnson) 1891–1962
Vaudeville comics who, after several false starts, took Hollywood by storm in *Hellzapoppin* with their flair for fast-moving, lunatic comedy with guest stars galore, running gags, a sublime sense of the ridiculous and some hilariously wacky visuals. Olsen was the sad-looking son of Norwegian immigrants and almost always wore smart suits; roly-poly Johnson was a kind of American Bud Flanagan (qv) who looked as though he'd slept in his clothes. The 'Chic' was short for Chicago, where he was born. Both men died from kidney ailments.
*1930: Oh Sailor Behave! 1931: Fifty Million Frenchmen. Gold Dust Gertie (GB: Why Change Your Husband?). 1932: *Hollywood on Parade (A-2). 1934: *Hollywood on Parade (B-13). 1937: All Over Town. Country Gentlemen. 1941: Hellzapoppin. 1943: Crazy House. 1944: Ghost Catchers. 1945: See My Lawyer.*

OLSON, Nancy 1928–
Pretty, very personable, light-haired American actress with round, fresh-looking face. Came to films straight from college and although soon nominated for an Oscar (in *Sunset Boulevard*) was mostly typed as sensible sorts and waiting wives. In consequence, has made far too few films.
1949: Canadian Pacific. 1950: Sunset Boulevard. Union Station. Mr Music. 1951: Sub-

marine Command. Force of Arms. 1952: Big Jim McLain. 1953: So Big. 1954: The Boy from Oklahoma. 1955: Battle Cry. 1960: Pollyanna. 1961: The Absent-Minded Professor. 1963: Son of Flubber. 1969: Smith! 1973: Snowball Express. 1974: Airport 1975. 1982: Making Love.

ONDRA, Anny (Aenny Ondráková) 1903–
Bubbly, baby-faced Czech actress with long golden curls. Much adored in her native country (in a similar fashion to Mary Pickford in America), where she started her screen career. Became popular in both German and English comedy films of the late twenties before sound put an end to her English-speaking career (she was dubbed in Hitchcock's *Blackmail*). Married boxer Max Schmeling (second: Czech director Karel Lamač was her first) and stayed in Germany during World War II and after.
1919: †Zmizele Pismo. †Dáma s Malou Nožkou. 1920: †Zpěv Zlata/The Song of Gold. †Setrele Pismo. †Gilly po Prevé v Praze. †Dráteniček. 1921: †Príchozí z Temnot. †Melenky Stareho Kriminalika. †Otravene Svetlo. 1922: †Drvoštěp. †Tam na Horach. 1923: †Der Mann ohne Herz. †Únos Bankeře Fuxe. †Muž bez Srdce. †Tu-Ten-Kamen. 1924: †Bílý Ráj. †Hricky v Manželství. †Chytte Ho! 1925: †Lucerne. †Hraběnka z Podskalí. †Karel Havlíček Borovsky. †Šest Mušketýrů. Ich liebe Dich. Do Panskeho Stavu. 1926: †Pantáta Bezoušek. Pisně Vězněného. Velbloud uchem Jehly. Trude, die Sechszehnjährige. 1927: Sladka Josefinka. Kvet ze Sumavy. A Chorus Girl's Romance. 1928: Dcery Eviny. Der erste Küss. Evas Töchter/Eve's Daughters. Saxsophon Susi. God's Clay. Eileen of the Trees/Glorious Youth. 1929: The Manxman. Blackmail. Die Kaviarprinzessin. Das Mädel mit der Peitsche. Sundig und Süss. 1930: Das Mädel aus USA. Sehnsucht. Die vom Rummelplatz. Eine Freundin so goldig wie Du. Die grosse Sehnsucht. 1931: On a Jeho Sestra/Er und seine Schwester. Die Fledermaus. 1932: Mamsell Nitouche. Baby. Die grausame Freundin. Eine Nacht im Paradies. Kiki. Kantor Idéal. 1933: Die Regimentstochter. Fräulein Hoffmans Erzählungen. Das verliebte Hotel. Die vertauschte Braut. 1934: Little Dorrit. Polská krev/Polenblut. 1935: Der junge Graf. Grossreinemachen. Knock Out. 1936: Donogoo Tonga. Ein Mädel vom Ballet. Flitterwochen.

1937: Důvod k Rozvodu. Der Scheidungsgrund. Der Unwiderstehliche. Vor Liebe wird gewarnt. 1938: Narren im Schnee. 1941: Der Gasmann. 1942: Himmel, wir erben ein Schloss. 1950: Schön müss man sein. 1957: Die zürcher Verlorung.

† As Aenny/Anny Ondráková

O'NEAL, Patrick 1927–
Cruel-looking, lithe American actor with equine features and prematurely grey hair. Looked as though he would follow a familiar route from villains to tough heroes, but he did not assert himself at the head of star casts, and has remained most interesting in top supporting roles, or evil leading characters, such as his maniac killer in *Chamber of Horrors*.
*1954: The Mad Magician. The Black Shield of Falworth. 1960: From the Terrace. De Sista Stegen (GB and US: A Matter of Morals). 1963: The Cardinal. 1965: King Rat. In Harm's Way. 1966: Alvarez Kelly. A Fine Madness. Matchless. Chamber of Horrors. A Big Hand for the Little Lady (GB: Big Deal at Dodge City). 1967: Assignment to Kill. 1968: Companions in Nightmare (TV). Where Were You When the Lights Went Out? The Secret Life of an American Wife. 1969: Stiletto. Castle Keep. The Kremlin Letter. 1970: El Condor. 1971: Corky. Zora. 1973: The Other Man (TV). Silent Night Bloody Night. The Way We Were. 1974: The Stepford Wives. 1975: Crossfire (TV). 1976: *Independence. The Killer Who Wouldn't Die (TV). Twin Detectives (TV). 1977: The Deadliest Season (TV). 1978: Sharon: Portrait of a Mistress (TV). To Kill the King (TV). Streets of Fear (TV). The Last Hurrah (TV). Like Mom, Like Me (TV). 1980: Make Me an Offer (TV). Studio Murders (TV). 1985: Perry Mason Returns (TV).*

O'NEAL, Ryan (Patrick R. O'Neal) 1941–
Handsome, if slightly cynical-looking, well-built American leading man with wavy fair hair. Busy in television from 1960, after beginnings as a stuntman, he soon became a favourite pin-up, especially during his run with the series *Peyton Place*. In the 1970s he became one of the world's top superstars, but he attempted some roles outside his range and his films were less successful in the early 1980s. Nominated for an Oscar in *Love Story*, he was formerly married (second) to actress Leigh Taylor-Young, but has for some years now been a steady twosome with actress Farrah Fawcett (*qv*). Father of Tatum O'Neal.
1962: This Rugged Land (TV. GB: cinemas). 1968: The Games. The Big Bounce. 1970: Love Story. Love Hate Love (TV). 1971: Wild Rovers. 1972: What's Up, Doc? 1973: The Thief Who Came to Dinner. Paper Moon. 1975: Barry Lyndon. 1976: Nickelodeon. 1977: A Bridge Too Far. 1978: Oliver's Story. The Driver (GB: Driver). 1979: The Main Event. 1980: Circle of Two. 1981: Green Ice. Partners. So Fine. 1984: Irreconcilable Differences. 1985: The Fever.

O'NEAL, Tatum 1962–
Daughter of Ryan O'Neal, nicknamed 'Tantrum' by fellow-workers and the Press, but so full of abrasive personality that she collected an Oscar at 11 in her first film. Alas, few films followed and in the later ones, though still worth watching, her performances have shown disturbing signs of becoming insipid.
1973: Paper Moon. 1976: The Bad News Bears. Nickelodeon. 1978: International Velvet. 1980: Little Darlings. Circle of Two. 1981: Captured!/Split Image. 1985: Certain Fury.

O'NEILL, Jennifer 1947–
Dark-haired American leading lady coming to prominence in the seventies, so forthright and personable that one sometimes wished there were a greater range of acting talent to go with those finely-structured features. Usually plays independent women in a man's world. Born in Brazil.
1968: For Love of Ivy. 1969: Futz. 1970: Rio Lobo. 1971: Summer of 42. 1972: Such Good Friends. The Carey Treatment. Glass Houses (released 1975). 1973: Lady Ice. 1974: The Reincarnation of Peter Proud. 1975: Whiffs (GB: C*A*S*H). Gente di rispetto (US: The Flower in His Mouth). 1976: L'innocente/The Innocent. 1977: Sette note in nero (US: The Psychic). 1978: A Force of One. Caravans. 1979: Cloud Dancer. Love's Savage Fury (TV). Steel. 1980: Scanners. 1981: The Other Victim (TV). 1985: Chase (TV).

O'SHEA, Michael (Edward M. O'Shea) 1906–1973
Smiling, red-haired Hollywood actor who played right guys in the forties after achieving popularity on radio with a crackling voice that held a hint of Irish brogue in its American accent. Once a 'straight man' in circus and vaudeville. Married to Virginia Mayo (second) from 1947. Died from a heart attack.
1943: Jack London. Lady of Burlesque (GB: Striptease Lady). 1944: The Eve of St Mark. Something for the Boys. The Man from Frisco. 1945: Circumstantial Evidence. It's a Pleasure. Where Do We Go from Here? 1947: Mr District Attorney. Violence. Last of the Redmen (GB: Last of the Redskins). 1948: Smart Woman. Parole Inc. 1949: The Big Wheel. The Threat. Captain China. 1950: The Underworld Story. 1951: Fixed Bayonets. Disc Jockey. The Model and the Marriage Broker. 1952: Bloodhounds of Broadway. 1954: It Should Happen to You.

O'SULLIVAN, Maureen 1911–
Demure, wistful, dark-haired Irish actress, most often in quiet roles, but carving her

special niche in film history as Tarzan's Jane in the thirties. Married to director John Farrow from 1936 to his death in 1963. Mother of Mia Farrow. In Hollywood from 1930. Still to be seen in the occasional character role.
*1930: Song o' My Heart. Just Imagine. So This is London. The Princess and the Plumber. 1931: Skyline. A Connecticut Yankee (GB: The Yankee at King Arthur's Court). The Big Shot (GB: The Optimist). 1932: The Silver Lining. Tarzan the Ape Man. Information Kid. Fast Companions. Skyscraper Souls. Okay America (GB: Penalty of Fame). Payment Deferred. Strange Interlude (GB: Strange Interval). 1933: Tugboat Annie. Robbers' Roost. Stage Mother. The Cohens and Kellys in Trouble. 1934: Hideout. *Screen Snapshots No. 11. Tarzan and His Mate. The Barretts of Wimpole Street. The Thin Man. 1935: Cardinal Richelieu. West Point of the Air. Anna Karenina. The Bishop Misbehaves (GB: The Bishop's Misadventures). The Flame Within. Woman Wanted. David Copperfield. 1936: The Voice of Bugle Ann. Tarzan Escapes! The Devil Doll. 1937: The Emperor's Candlesticks. A Day at the Races. My Dear Miss Aldrich. Between Two Women. A Yank at Oxford. 1938: Port of Seven Seas. The Crowd Roars. Spring Madness. Hold That Kiss. 1939: Let Us Live. Tarzan Finds a Son! 1940: Sporting Blood. Pride and Prejudice. 1941: Tarzan's Secret Treasure. Maisie Was a Lady. 1942: Tarzan's New York Adventure. 1948: The Big Clock. 1950: Where Danger Lives. 1952: Bonzo Goes to College. 1953: All I Desire. Mission over Korea (GB: Eyes of the Skies). 1954: Duffy of San Quentin (GB: Men Behind Bars). The Steel Cage. 1957: The Tall T. Edge of Innocence (TV). 1958: Wild Heritage. 1965: Never Too Late. 1969: The Phynx. 1972: The Crooked Hearts (TV). 1977: The Great Houdinis (TV). 1983: The Doorman. 1985: Too Scared to Scream. 1986: Hannah and Her Sisters. Peggy Sue Got Married.*

O'SULLIVAN, Richard 1943–
Cherubic British boy actor, able to keep in juvenile roles into his late teens because of his small stature, and often a scene stealer. Became part of the Cliff Richard musicals, then sexploitation comedies, before becoming popular in several TV series, mainly situation comedy, in the late seventies.
1954: Dance Little Lady. The Stranger's Hand.

The Green Scarf. Make Me an Offer. 1955: The Dark Avenger (GB: The Warriors). The Secret. 1956: It's Great to be Young. Raiders of the River (serial). Jacqueline. 1957: Dangerous Exile. 1959: Carry on Teacher. Witness in the Dark. And Women Shall Weep. 1960: A Story of David. 1961: Spare the Rod. The Young Ones. 1962: The Webster Boy. 1963: Dr Syn – Alias the Scarecrow. Cleopatra. 1964: Wonderful Life (US: Swingers' Paradise). Every Day's a Holiday (US: Seaside Swingers). 1968: A Dandy in Aspic. 1969: The Haunted House of Horror. 1970: Futtock's End. 1972: Au Pair Girls. Father Dear Father. 1974: Can You Keep It Up for a Week? Man About the House. 1980: Dick Turpin (GB: TV).

O'TOOLE, Peter 1932–
Charismatic, blue-eyed, fair-haired Irish-born actor, typed as idealists or philanderers (occasionally both). Popular in the sixties, when some of his films were enormous commercial successes, but has had no luck at the box-office since 1970. Noted as one of the British 'hell-raising' group in private life: married/divorced actress Sian Phillips. Six times nominated for an Academy Award (for *Lawrence of Arabia, Becket, The Lion in Winter, Goodbye Mr Chips, The Ruling Class* and *The Stuntman*), he has yet to win.
1959: The Savage Innocents. 1960: Kidnapped. The Day They Robbed the Bank of England. 1962: Lawrence of Arabia. 1963: Becket. 1964: Lord Jim. 1965: What's New Pussycat? 1966: The Bible … in the beginning. The Night of the Generals. How to Steal a Million. 1967: Casino Royale. Great Catherine. 1968: The Lion in

Winter. 1969: Goodbye Mr Chips. Country Dance (US: Brotherly Love). 1970: Murphy's War. 1971: Under Milk Wood. The Ruling Class. 1972: Man of La Mancha. 1974: Rosebud. 1975: Man Friday. Foxtrot (later The Other Side of Paradise). 1976: Rogue Male (TV). 1977: Caligula/Gore Vidal's Caligula (released 1979). The Stuntman (released 1980). 1978: Power Play. 1979: Zulu Dawn. 1980: Masada (TV. Shortened for cinemas as The Antagonists). The Markebah Passion. 1982: My Favorite Year. 1983: Svengali (TV). The World of James Joyce (TV). 1984: Kim (TV). Supergirl. 1985: Creator. Club Paradise. Hidden Talent.

OWEN, Reginald (John R. Owen) 1887–1972
Tall, upright, fair-haired British actor with owlish good looks, one of Hollywood's typical Englishmen in self-controlled roles from 1931. The only actor to have played Sherlock Holmes *and* Dr Watson in separate films, but recalled by many for his Scrooge in the 1938 *A Christmas Carol*. Still acting to within a year of his death from a heart attack. Also a writer.
*1911: Henry VIII. 1916: Sally in Our Alley. A Place in the Sun. 1922: The Grass Orphan. 1923: Phroso. 1928: *Pusher-in-the-Face. 1929: The Letter. 1931: The Man in Possession. Platinum Blonde. 1932: Sherlock Holmes. A Woman Commands. Downstairs. Lovers Courageous. The Man Called Back. 1933: Double Harness. A Study in Scarlet. The Narrow Corner. The Big Brain (GB: Enemies of Society). Voltaire. Queen Christina. 1934: The House of Rothschild. Fashions/Fashions of 1934. Mandalay. Where Sinners Meet (GB: The Dover Road). Here Is My Heart. Stingaree. Madame du Barry. The Countess of Monte Cristo. Nana. Of Human Bondage. The Human Side. Music in the Air. The Good Fairy. 1935: Anna Karenina. A Tale of Two Cities. Enchanted April. Escapade. Call of the Wild. The Bishop Misbehaves (GB: The Bishop's Misadventures). 1936: Yours for the Asking. Petticoat Fever. The Girl on the Front Page. Trouble for Two (GB: The Suicide Club). Rose Marie. Adventure in Manhattan (GB: Manhattan Madness). Love on the Run. The Great Ziegfeld. 1937: Madame X. Dangerous Number. The Bride Wore Red. Conquest (GB: Marie Walewska). Personal Property (GB:*

The Man in Possession). Rosalie. 1938: A
Christmas Carol. Kidnapped. Paradise for
Three (GB: Romance for Three). Vacation
from Love. The Girl Downstairs. Everybody
Sing. Three Loves Has Nancy. Sweethearts.
1939: Bridal Suite. Fast and Loose. Remember?
The Real Glory. Hotel Imperial. Bad Little
Angel. Balalaika. 1940: The Earl of Chicago.
Hullabaloo. Florian. Pride and Prejudice. The
Ghost Comes Home. 1941: Tarzan's Secret
Treasure. Free and Easy. They Met in Bombay.
Charley's Aunt (GB: Charley's American
Aunt). Blonde Inspiration. A Woman's Face.
Lady Be Good. Woman of the Year. 1942: I
Married an Angel. Random Harvest. Pierre of
the Plains. Cairo. Reunion/Reunion in France
(GB: Mademoiselle France). Mrs Miniver. We
Were Dancing. Crossroads. Somewhere I'll
Find You. White Cargo. 1943: Forever and a
Day. Above Suspicion. Assignment in Brittany.
Three Hearts for Julia. Salute to the Marines.
Madame Curie. Lassie Come Home. The Can-
terville Ghost. 1944: National Velvet. 1945:
The Valley of Decision. Captain Kidd. Kitty.
She Went to the Races. The Sailor Takes a
Wife. 1946: Monsieur Beaucaire. The Diary
of a Chambermaid. Cluny Brown. Piccadilly
Incident. The Imperfect Lady (GB: Mrs
Loring's Secret). 1947: Thunder in the Valley
(GB: Bob, Son of Battle). Green Dolphin
Street. If Winter Comes. 1948: Hills of Home
(GB: Master of Lassie). The Three
Musketeers. Julia Misbehaves. The Pirate.
1949: Challenge to Lassie. The Secret Garden.
1950: Grounds for Marriage. The Miniver
Story. Kim. 1953: The Great Diamond
Robbery. 1954: Red Garters. 1957: Darby's
Rangers (GB: The Young Invaders). 1962:
Five Weeks in a Balloon. 1963: Tammy and
the Doctor. The Thrill of It All. 1964: Mary
Poppins. The Voice of the Hurricane. 1967:
Rosie! 1971: Bedknobs and Broomsticks.

OWENS, Patricia 1925–

It seems improbable that a tall, dark, serious-
looking Canadian girl could struggle for 14
years in the British film industry without making barely a dent, and then land a Hollywood
contract at 32, star in several big films and
become a well-known name. But pretty Pat
Owens did it, and all power to her. She was a
capable actress who certainly deserved better
than she got in Britain.

1943: Miss London Ltd. 1944: Give Us the
Moon. Bees in Paradise. English without Tears
(US: Her Man Gilbey). One Exciting Night
(US: You Can't Do without Love). 1946:
While the Sun Shines. 1948: Panic at Madam
Tussaud's. Things Happen at Night. 1949:
Bait. I Was a Dancer. Paper Orchid. 1950:
Old Mother Riley Headmistress. The Happiest
Days of Your Life. 1951: Mystery Junction.
1952: Crow Hollow. Ghost Ship. 1953: House
of Blackmail. Colonel March Investigates.
1954: The Good Die Young. Knights of the
Round Table. The Stranger Came Home (US:
The Unholy Four). A Tale of Three Women.
Alive on Saturday (released 1957). 1955:
Windfall. 1957: Island in the Sun. No Down
Payment. Sayonara. 1958: The Law and Jake
Wade. The Fly. The Gun Runners. 1959: These
Thousand Hills. Five Gates to Hell. 1960: Hell
to Eternity. 1961: Seven Women from Hell. X-
15. 1963: Walk a Tight Rope. 1964: Black
Spurs. 1966: The Destructors.

of the Nile. The Gambler from Natchez. 1955: White Feather. Seven Angry Men. 1956: The Last Hunt. The 10 Commandments. Love Me Tender. Gun in His Hand (TV. GB: cinemas). 1957: The River's Edge. Omar Khayyam. 1958: From the Earth to the Moon. Der Tiger von Eshnapur. Das Indische Grabmal. 1960: Why Must I Die? (GB: 13 Steps to Death). The Highwaymen. Il sepolcro dei re. †Journey to the Lost City. 1961: The Most Dangerous Man Alive. 1962: Tales of Terror. Rome 1585. 1963: The Haunted Palace.

†*Abridged American version (in one film) of Der Tiger von Eshnapur and Das Indische Grabmal.*

PACINO, Al (Alfredo Pacino) 1939–
Small, dark, dynamic American leading man of Italian background who gives explosive, high-decibel performances and has already been nominated for an Academy Award five times – for *The Godfather, Serpico, The Godfather – Part II, Dog Day Afternoon* and *...And Justice for All.* He came late to prominence, but always looked and played younger than his years, and became a superstar of the 1970s and 1980s on the strength of only a few film performances.
1969: Me Natalie. 1971: Panic in Needle Park. 1972: The Godfather. 1973: Scarecrow. Serpico. 1974: The Godfather – Part II. 1975: Dog Day Afternoon. 1977: Bobby Deerfield. 1979: ...And Justice for All. 1980: Cruising. 1982: Author! Author! 1983: Scarface. 1985: Revolution. 1986: Investigation.

PAGE, Geraldine 1924–
This light-haired American lady of the theatre has perhaps been unfortunate, as far as her cinema career was concerned, to have the tag 'great actress' pinned on her from the start. Following her stage successes in the works of Tennessee Williams, she has tended to be typed as fading southern belles, although eight Oscar nominations to date testify to the depth of feeling that goes into her work. A personality of her own, however, has not come across on screen. Married (second) to Rip Torn (qv) since 1963. Finally won the Academy Award in 1986 for *The Trip to Bountiful. 1947: Out of the Night. 1953: Taxi. Hondo. 1958: Portrait of a Murderer (TV). Old Man (TV). 1961: Summer and Smoke. 1962: Sweet Bird of Youth. 1963: Toys in the Attic. 1964:*

Dear Heart. 1966: Three Sisters. You're a Big Boy Now. 1967: La Chica del Lunes/Monday's Child. The Happiest Millionaire. 1969: Whatever Happened to Aunt Alice? Trilogy/Truman Capote's Trilogy. 1971: The Beguiled. J.W. Coop. 1972: Pete 'n' Tillie. 1974: The Day of the Locust. Happy As the Grass Was Green. 1976: The Three Sisters (remake). Nasty Habits. 1977: The Rescuers (voice only). Something for Joey (TV). 1978: Interiors. Hazel's People. 1980: Harry's War. 1981: Honky Tonk Freeway. 1982: I'm Dancing As Fast As I Can. 1984: The Pope of Greenwich Village. The Parade (TV). The Dollmaker (TV). 1985: Flanagan. The Bride. White Nights. The Trip to Bountiful. 1986: My Little Girl. Native Son. Walls of Glass.

PAGET, Debra (Debralee Griffin) 1933–
Although (or perhaps because) copper-haired Debra Paget had the kind of figure that makes men walk into lamp-posts, Twentieth Century-Fox, who signed her at 15, cast her in demure roles. She lacked the animation to make much of these, apart from her Indian girl in *Broken Arrow*, but director Fritz Lang saw her come to life in a harem dance or two, and took her to Germany to play the Indian princess in his two-film saga of 1958, in which she was remarkably effective.
1948: Cry of the City. 1949: It Happens Every Spring. Mother is a Freshman (GB: Mother Knows Best). House of Strangers. 1950: Broken Arrow. 1951: Fourteen Hours. Bird of Paradise. Anne of the Indies. 1952: Belles on Their Toes. Les Miserables. Stars and Stripes Forever (GB: Marching Along). 1954: Prince Valiant. Demetrius and the Gladiators. Princess

PAIGE, Janis (Donna Tjaden) 1922–
Red-headed Hollywood musical star with spectacular vocal range. She really needed a vehicle of her own to showcase her talents, but mostly played second fiddle to Dennis Morgan and Jack Carson during her seven-year tenure at Warners. Enjoyed spectacular stage success in the fifties in *The Pajama Game* and had her best film role in *Silk Stockings.*
*1944: Bathing Beauty. Hollywood Canteen. 1945: *I Won't Play. 1946: Of Human Bondage. Her Kind of Man. Two Guys from Milwaukee (GB: Royal Flush). The Time, the Place and the Girl. 1947: Love and Learn. Cheyenne. Always Together. 1948: Wallflower. Winter Meeting. Romance on the High Seas (GB: It's Magic). One Sunday Afternoon. 1949: The House across the Street. The Younger Brothers. 1950: This Side of the Law. 1951: Fugitive Lady. Mr Universe. Two Gals and a Guy. 1957: Silk Stockings. 1960: Please Don't Eat the Daisies. 1961: Bachelor in Paradise. 1963: Follow the Boys. The Caretakers (GB: Borderlines). 1967: Welcome to Hard Times (GB: Killer on a Horse). 1975: The Return of Joe Forrester (TV). 1976: Lanigan's Rabbi (TV). 1980: Angel on My Shoulder (TV). Valentine Magic on Love Island (TV). 1983: The Other Woman (TV). 1984: No Man's Land (TV).*

PAIGE, Robert (John Paige) 1910–
Good-natured American leading man, who had a pleasant baritone singing voice, and is now remembered as the rather stiff, ever-smiling young man who backed up Olsen and Johnson, Abbott and Costello, Deanna Dur-

bin and Universal's other top stars in middle-budget comedies and musicals of the war years. Had a talent for zany comedy that was never properly exploited. Became a TV newscaster in the mid-sixties.

1935: †*Annapolis Farewell (GB: Gentlemen of the Navy). 1936:* †*Smart Blonde.* †*Hearts in Bondage.* †*Cain and Mabel. 1937:* †*Once a Doctor.* †*Melody for Two.* *†*Murder in Swingtime.* †*Marry the Girl. Meet the Boy Friend.* †*The Cherokee Strip (GB: Strange Laws). 1938: The Lady Objects. There's Always a Woman. When G-Men Step In. The Main Event. The Last Warning. The Little Adventuress. Who Killed Gail Preston? Highway Patrol. I Stand Accused. 1939: Flying G-Men (serial). Death of a Champion. Homicide Bureau. 1940: Parole Fixer. Emergency Squad. Golden Gloves. Women without Names. Opened by Mistake. 1941: San Antonio Rose. The Monster and the Girl. Melody Lane. Hellzapoppin. Dancing on a Dime. 1942: What's Cookin'? (GB: Wake Up and Dream). You're Telling Me. Almost Married. Get Hep to Love (GB: She's My Lovely). Pardon My Sarong. Don't Get Personal. Jailhouse Blues. Hi Ya, Chum! (GB: Everything Happens to Us). 1943: Frontier Badmen. Fired Wife. Crazy House. Cowboy in Manhattan. Son of Dracula. Get Going. Hi Buddy! How's About It? Mr Big. Sherlock Holmes in Washington. 1944: Her Primitive Man. Follow the Boys. Can't Help Singing. 1945: Shady Lady. 1946: Tangier. 1947: The Flame. Red Stallion. 1948: Blonde Ice. 1949: The Green Promise (GB: Raging Waters). 1953: Abbott and Costello Go to Mars. Split Second. 1959: It Happened to Jane. 1960: The Marriage-Go-Round. 1963: Bye Bye Birdie.*

†*As David Carlyle*

PALANCE, Jack (Vladimir, later changed to Walter, Palanuik) 1920–
Trying to build a Jack Palance filmography is like tracking down a whirlwind. Like some workaholic Jack the Ripper, this American actor of massive physical presence has travelled half the world in search of audiences on whom to impose his fearsome personality. With a face rebuilt by plastic surgery after war burns, and a ferocious acting style, this son of Russian immigrants could hardly fail to dominate his films, and has continued to

do so, violence smouldering beneath a surface calm, for 35 years. Received Oscar nominations for *Sudden Fear* and *Shane*. The actress Holly Palance is his daughter.
1950: †*Panic in the Streets.* †*Halls of Montezuma. 1952:* †*Sudden Fear. 1953:* †*Shane. Second Chance. Flight to Tangier. Arrowhead. Man in the Attic. 1954: Sign of the Pagan. The Silver Chalice. 1955: Kiss of Fire. The Big Knife. I Died a Thousand Times. 1956: Attack! Requiem for a Heavyweight (TV). 1957: The Last Tycoon (TV). The Lonely Man. House of Numbers. The Death of Manolete (TV). Flor de Mayo (GB: A Mexican Affair). US: Beyond All Limits). 1958: The Man Inside. Ten Seconds to Hell. 1959: Austerlitz (GB: The Battle of Austerlitz). 1960: Revak the Rebel (US TV: Rivak the Barbarian/The Barbarians). Treno di natale. 1961: Il giudizio universale (US: The Last Judgment). Rosmundo e Alboino/Sword of the Conquereor. The Mongols. La dernière attaque/La guerra continua. Barabbas. Warriors Five. 1963: Le mépris (GB: Contempt. US: A Ghost at Noon). Il criminale. 1965: Once a Thief. Night Train to Milan. 1966: The Spy in the Green Hat (TV. GB: cinemas). The Professionals. 1967: Torture Garden. Kill a Dragon/To Kill a Dragon. 1968: Dr Jekyll and Mr Hyde (TV). Il mercenario (GB and US: A Professional Gun). They Came to Rob Las Vegas/Las Vegas 500 milliones. L'urlo dei giganti (GB: A Bullet for Rommel). 1969: Ché! The Desperados. Marquis de Sade: Justine/Justine/Justine: le disavventure della virtu. Una ragazza di Eraga. La legione dei dannati (US: Legion of the Damned). The McMasters ... tougher than the west itself! 1970: Compañeros! Monte Walsh. The Horsemen. 1971: Chato's Land. Si puo fare...amigo (US: It Can Be Done, Amigo). 1972: Operation: Catastrophe. 1973: The Blu Gang (US: Brothers Blue). Dracula (TV. GB: cinemas). Oklahoma Crude. Craze. Te Deum (GB: The Con Men). 1974: The Godchild (TV). 1975: Africa Express. Bronk (TV). Il richiamo del lupo. L'infermiera (GB: I Will If You Will). The Hatfields and the McCoys (TV). The Four Deuces. 1976: Godzilla vs the Cosmic Monster (GB: Godzilla v the Bionic Monster). Eva nera (GB: Erotic Eva). Squadra antiscippo (GB: The Cop in Blue Jeans). God's Gun (US: The Cop Who Played God). The Great Adventure. 1977: Sangue di Sbirro. Il padrone della città . Mister*

Scarface. Welcome to Blood City. Jimbuck. 1978: Seven from Heaven/Angels Brigade. Dead on Arrival. 1979: The Shape of Things to Come. Cocaine Cowboys. The Ivory Ape. The Last Ride of the Dalton Gang (TV). 1980: Hawk the Slayer. One Man Jury. Without Warning (GB: The Warning). Ladyfingers. 1982: Alone in the Dark. 1983: Portrait of a Hitman. Evil Stalks the House (TV). The Golden Moment (TV).

†*As Walter (Jack) Palance*

PALMER, Lilli (L. Peiser) 1914–1986
Beautiful, full-lipped, dark-haired German actress who began her film career in Britain, offering appealing, emotional performances that usually had more depth than those around her. Went to Hollywood for some years during an eventful marriage (1943–1957) to first husband Rex Harrison (*qv*). After it was over, she made films in Britain, Germany, France and Spain. Her beauty wore well, and she remained in leading roles into her late forties. Later became a best-selling authoress. Married Argentinian-born actor Carlos Thompson (Juan C. Mundanschaffer, 1916–) in 1957. Died from cancer.
1935: Crime Unlimited. 1936: First Offence/ Bad Blood. Wolf's Clothing. Secret Agent. Good Morning, Boys. 1937: The Great Barrier (US: Silent Barriers). **Secrets of the Stars. Sunset in Vienna (US: Suicide Legion). Command Performance. 1938: Crackerjack (US: The Man with a Hundred Faces). 1939: A Girl Must Live. Blind Folly. 1940: The Door with Seven Locks (US: Chamber of Horrors). 1942: Thunder Rock. 1943: The Gentle Sex. 1944: English without Tears (US: Her Man Gilbey). 1945: The Rake's Progress (US: Notorious Gentleman). 1946: Beware of Pity. Cloak and Dagger. 1947: Body and Soul. 1948: My Girl Tisa. No Minor Vices. Hans le marin (US: The Wicked City). 1951: The Long Dark Hall. 1952: The Four Poster. 1953: Main Street to Broadway. Feuerwerk (GB: Oh! My Papa). 1955: Teufel in Seide/The Devil in Silk. 1956: Anastasia die letzte Zarentochter/Is Anna Anderson Anastasia? Zwischen Zeit und Ewigkeit/Between Time and Eternity. Wie ein Sturmwind/The Night of the Storm. 1957: Der gläserne Turm/The Glass Tower. Montparnasse 19/The Lovers of Montparnasse. 1958: Eine Frau die weiss, was sie will. Mädchen in Uniform. La vie à deux (GB: Life Together).*

1959: But Not for Me. 1960: Frau Warren's Profession. Conspiracy of Hearts. 1961: The Pleasure of His Company. The Last of Mrs Cheyney. Leviathan. Le rendezvous de minuit. Dark Journey. The Counterfeit Traitor. 1962: The Seduction of Julia/Adorable Julia. Torpedo Bay/Finche dura la tempesta. L'amore difficile (GB: Sex Can be Difficult). Finden sie, dass Constanze sich richtig verhält? Erotica. Beta som. The Miracle of the White Stallions (GB: Flight of the White Stallions). 1963: And So to Bed/Das grosse Liebesspiel. 1964: Monsieur. Le grain de sable. The Circular Triangle. 1965: Le tonnerre du Dieu. The Amorous Adventures of Moll Flanders. Operation Crossbow (GB: The Great Spy Mission). Der Kongress amüsiert sich. Die Unmoralischen. 1966: An Affair of State. Zwei Girls vom roten Stern. 1967: Paarungen. Oedipus the King. Jack of Diamonds. Danse Macabre. Sebastian. 1968: Nobody Runs Forever. The Dance of Death. 1969: Le peau de torpédo (GB: Pill of Death. US: Only the Cool). De Sade. Hard Contract. The House That Screamed. 1970: Hauser's Memory (TV). 1971: Night Hair Child. Murders in the Rue Morgue. 1976: Lotte in Weimar. 1978: The Boys from Brazil. 1981: Society Limited. 1985: The Holcroft Covenant.

PARKER, Cecil (C. Schwabe) 1897–1971
Aloof British actor who used his upper-class personality, snooty air, piggy eyes and husky voice which had an inborn note of disapproval to good effect in the British cinema for over 40 years. Cast as butlers, aristocrats, statesmen, headmasters and even killers, he propelled himself into star roles by the late forties and never let his supporters down. Largely (at home) in portly comedy roles from 1953.
1928: The Woman in White. 1933: The Golden Cage. The Silver Spoon. A Cuckoo in the Nest. Flat No. 3. 1934: Nine Forty-Five. Little Friend. Lady in Danger. Dirty Work. The Blue Squadron. The Office Wife. 1935: Foreign Affaires. Me and Marlborough. Crime Unlimited. Her Last Affaire. 1936: Jack of All Trades (US: The Two of Us). Men of Yesterday. Dishonour Bright. The Man Who Changed His Mind (US: The Man Who Lived Again). 1937: Storm in a Teacup. Dark Journey. Bank Holiday (US: Three on a Weekend). 1938: Housemaster. The Lady Vanishes. The Citadel. Old Iron. 1939: She Couldn't Say No. Sons of the Sea. The Stars Look Down. The Spider.

1940: Two for Danger. Under Your Hat. 1941: Dangerous Moonlight (US: Suicide Squadron). The Saint's Vacation. Ships with Wings. 1945: Caesar and Cleopatra. 1946: The Magic Bow. Hungry Hill. 1947: Captain Boycott. The Woman in the Hall. 1948: The First Gentleman (US: Affairs of a Rogue). Quartet. The Weaker Sex. 1949: Dear Mr Prohack. The Chiltern Hundreds (US: The Amazing Mr Beecham). Under Capricorn. 1950: Tony Draws a Horse. 1951: The Man in the White Suit. The Magic Box. His Excellency. 1952: I Believe in You. 1953: Isn't Life Wonderful! 1954: For Better, for Worse (US: Cocktails in the Kitchen). Father Brown (US: The Detective). 1955: The Constant Husband. The Lady-killers. The Court Jester. 1956: 23 Paces to Baker Street. True As a Turtle. It's Great to be Young. 1957: The Admirable Crichton (US: Paradise Lagoon). 1958: Happy is the Bride! Indiscreet. I Was Monty's Double (US: Monty's Double). The Wreck of the Mary Deare. A Tale of Two Cities. 1959: The Night We Dropped a Clanger. The Navy Lark. 1960: Follow That Horse! Under 10 Flags. A French Mistress. The Pure Hell of St Trinian's. Swiss Family Robinson. 1961: On the Fiddle (US: Operation Snafu). Petticoat Pirates. 1962: The Amorous Prawn. 1962: The Iron Maiden (US: The Swingin' Maiden). Vengeance (US: The Brain). 1963: Heavens Above! The Comedy Man. Carry on Jack. 1964: Guns at Batasi. 1965: The Amorous Adventures of Moll Flanders. A Study in Terror (US: Fog). Circus of Fear (US: Psycho-Circus). Lady L. 1966: A Man Could Get Killed. 1967: The Magnificent Two. 1969: Oh! What a Lovely War.

PARKER, Eleanor 1922–
Warmly upper-bracket American actress with red-gold hair, at her best in films where she had the dominant role or played a strong-willed woman. Less effective as straight-forward heroines. In substantial leading roles from 1946 to 1957, surprisingly declining before she was 40. Just the sort of actress one would expect to have won an Oscar, although in fact she hasn't, having been unsuccessfully nominated three times (for Caged, Detective Story and Interrupted Melody).
1941: They Died with Their Boots On. 1942: *Men of the Sky. Busses Roar. 1943: The Mysterious Doctor. Mission to Moscow. 1944: The Last Ride. Between Two Worlds. Crime by Night. The Very Thought of You. Hollywood

Canteen. 1945: Pride of the Marines. 1946: Never Say Goodbye. Of Human Bondage. 1947: The Voice of the Turtle. Escape Me Never. Always Together. The Woman in White. 1949: It's a Great Feeling. 1950: Chain Lightning. Caged. Three Secrets. 1951: Detective Story. Valentino. A Millionaire for Christy. 1952: Scaramouche. Above and Beyond. 1953: Escape from Fort Bravo. 1954: The Naked Jungle. Valley of the Kings. 1955: Many Rivers to Cross. Interrupted Melody. The Man with the Golden Arm. 1956: The King and Four Queens. 1957: Lizzie. 1959: A Hole in the Head. 1960: Home from the Hill. 1961: Return to Peyton Place. 1962: Madison Avenue. 1963: Panic Button. 1965: The Sound of Music. 1966: An American Dream (GB: See You in Hell, Darling). The Oscar. 1967: Il tigre (GB and US: The Tiger and the Pussycat). Warning Shot. 1968: How to Steal the World (TV. GB: cinemas). 1969: Eye of the Cat. 1970: Maybe I'll Come Home Again in the Spring (TV). Vanished (TV). 1972: Home for the Holidays (TV). The Great American Beauty Contest (TV). 1977: Fantasy Island (TV). 1979: She's Dressed to Kill (TV. GB: Someone's Killing the World's Greatest Models). Sunburn. 1980: Once upon a Spy (TV). Madame X (TV).

PARKER, Fess 1925–
Big, shambling, soft-spoken Texan, in small film roles until put under contract by Walt Disney in 1954. As the famous Indian fighter Davy Crockett (whose adventures were first shown on television, then released, with great success, to cinemas), Parker became a national figure, and had a few good years starring in films, before going back to TV in a long-running series as another historic westerner – Daniel Boone.
1952: Springfield Rifle. No Room for the Groom. Untamed Frontier. 1953: Thunder over the Plains. Island in the Sky. The Kid from Left Field. Take Me to Town. 1954: Them! The Bounty Hunter. Davy Crockett – King of the Wild Frontier. 1955: Battle Cry. Davy Crockett and the River Pirates. 1956: The Great Locomotive Chase. Westward Ho! The Wagons. 1957: Old Yeller. 1958: Turn Left at Mount Everest (TV). The Light in the Forest. 1959: The Hangman. Alias Jesse James. The Jayhawkers. 1960: *Saturday Matinee. 1962: Hell is for Heroes! 1966: Smoky. Daniel

Boone – Frontier Trail Rider (TV. GB: cinemas). 1972: Climb an Angry Mountain (TV).

PARKER, Jean (Luise-Stephanie Zelinska) 1912–

One of the most dramatic career turnabouts in Hollywood history. In the thirties brown-haired Jean was the cinema's sweet-tempered backwoods girl, at one with nature and radiant in such offerings as *Sequoia* and *Romance of the Redwoods*. She was also Beth in 1933's *Little Women*. After 1940 she suddenly appeared as hard-boiled broads, and became just as typed in this mould as the other. Married to actor Robert Lowery (*qv*) from 1951–1957 – fourth of four husbands.

*1932: Divorce in the Family. 1933: Rasputin and the Empress (GB: Rasputin the Mad Monk). Made on Broadway (GB: The Girl I Made). The Secret of Madame Blanche. What Price Innocence? (GB: Shall the Children Pay?). Gabriel over the White House. Little Women. Storm at Daybreak. Lady for a Day. 1934: Two Alone. A Wicked Woman. Lazy River. Sequoia. Have a Heart. Caravan. You Can't Buy Everything. Operator 13 (GB: Spy 13). Limehouse Blues. 1935: Princess O'Hara. Murder in the Fleet. The Ghost Goes West. 1936: The Farmer in the Dell. The Texas Rangers. 1937: The Barrier. Life Begins with Love. 1938: Romance of the Limberlost. The Arkansas Traveler. Penitentiary. 1939: Flight at Midnight. Romance of the Redwoods. Zenobia (GB: Elephants Never Forget). Parents on Trial. *Young America Flies. She Married a Cop. The Flying Deuces. 1940: Beyond Tomorrow. Sons of the Navy. Knights of the Range. 1941: Flying Blind. The Roar of the Press. Power Dive. No Hands on the Clock. The Pittsburgh Kid. 1942: Hi, Neighbor. Torpedo Boat. The Girl from Alaska. I Live on Danger. The Wrecking Crew. Tomorrow We Live. The Traitor Within. 1943: The Deerslayer. Alaska Highway. Minesweeper. High Explosive. 1944: Oh! What a Night! Detective Kitty O'Day. Bluebeard. One Body Too Many. Lady in the Death House. The Navy Way. Dead Man's Eyes. 1945: The Adventures of Kitty O'Day. 1950: The Gunfighter. 1952: Toughest Man in Arizona. 1953: Those Redheads from Seattle. 1954: Black Tuesday. 1955: A Lawless Street. 1957: The Parson and the Outlaw. 1966: Apache Uprising. 1972: Stigma.*

PARKER, Willard (Worster Van Eps) 1912–

Tall, craggy, sandy-haired American actor whose career was severely disrupted by war service. Took small leading roles thereafter, but never really settled as a star, moving into star-billed supporting roles by the early fifties. He was too stiff to gain a real following, although there were a few more minor leads for him at the beginning of the sixties. Married to actress Virginia Field (Margaret Field (1917–)) since 1951.

1937: Over the Goal. That Certain Woman. Back in Circulation. China Passage. The Devil's Saddle Legion. Love is on the Air. 1938: Accidents Will Happen. Invisible Menace. A Slight Case of Murder. 1939: Zero Hour. 1943: The Fighting Guardsman. What a Woman! 1946: One Way to Love. Renegades. 1948: The Mating of Millie. Relentless. The Wreck of the Hesperus. You Gotta Stay Happy. 1949: Slightly French. Calamity Jane and Sam Bass. 1950: David Harding Counterspy. Bodyhold. The Secret Fury. Emergency Wedding (GB: Jealousy). Bandit Queen. 1951: Hunt the Man Down. Apache Drums. 1952: Caribbean (GB: Caribbean Gold). 1953: The Vanquished. Sangaree. Kiss Me Kate. 1954: The Great Jesse James Raid. 1956: The Naked Gun. Lure of the Swamp. 1959: The Lone Texan. 1960: Walk Tall. 13 Fighting Men. The High-Powered Rifle. Young Jesse James. 1962: Air Patrol. 1964: The Earth Dies Screaming. 1966: Waco.

PARKS, Larry (Samuel L. Parks) 1914–1975

Black-haired American actor with open, slightly mischievous looks who, despite a weak heart (from a severe childhood attack of rheumatic fever) maintained a hectic film schedule once signed by Columbia in 1941. His eye-catching performance in *Renegades* came at just the right time and he was chosen for the title role in *The Jolson Story*, which proved a personal triumph (and a box-office gold mine). In 1951, however, he was virtually forced out of films after testifying to the Un-American Activities Committee. Married to Betty Garrett (*qv*) from 1944 to his death from a heart attack. He received an Oscar nomination for *The Jolson Story*.

1941: Honolulu Lu. Mystery Ship. You Belong to Me (GB: Good Morning, Doctor). Harmon

of Michigan. Harvard Here I Come (GB: Here I Come). Three Girls About Town. Sing for Your Supper. 1942: Alias Boston Blackie. North of the Rockies. Hello Annapolis (GB: Personal Honour). Blondie Goes to College (GB: The Boss Said 'No'). A Man's World. Flight Lieutenant. Atlantic Convoy. You Were Never Lovelier. The Boogie Man Will Get You. They All Kissed the Bride. Submarine Raider. Canal Zone. 1943: Is Everybody Happy? Redhead from Manhattan. Destroyer. That Bedside Manner. The Deerslayer. Power of the Press. Reveille with Beverly. First Comes Courage. 1944: Hey, Rookie. Stars on Parade. The Racket Man. Sergeant Mike. She's a Sweetheart. The Black Parachute. 1945: Counter-Attack (GB: One Against Seven). 1946: Renegades. The Jolson Story. 1947: Down to Earth. The Swordsman. Her Husband's Affairs. 1948: The Gallant Blade. 1949: Jolson Sings Again. 1950: Emergency Wedding (GB: Jealousy). 1951: Love is Better Than Ever (GB: The Light Fantastic). 1955: Tiger by the Tail (US: Crossup). 1962: Freud (GB: Freud: the Secret Passion).

PARRY, Natasha 1930–

Outstandingly pretty brunette British leading lady, in show business from childhood, the daughter of film director Gordon Parry (1908–1981) and a 'Cochran young lady' at 15. Not the world's most wonderful actress, perhaps, but so stunning to look at that one can only regret the paucity of her film output in her peak years: later she appeared in occasional character roles in continental pictures. Married to stage (and occasionally film) director Sir Peter Brook (1925–) since 1951. Actress Irina Brook is their daughter.

1935: Joy Ride. 1949: Trottie True (US: Gay Lady). Golden Arrow (US: Three Men and a Girl. Released 1952). 1950: Midnight Episode. Dance Hall. 1951: The Dark Man. 1952: Crow Hollow. 1954: Knave of Hearts (US: Lovers, Happy Lovers). 1957: Windom's Way. 1959: The Rough and the Smooth (US: Portrait of a Sinner). 1960: Midnight Lace. 1961: The Fourth Square. 1963: Girl in the Headlines (US: The Model Murder Case). 1968: Romeo and Juliet. 1969: Oh! What a Lovely War. 1978: Meetings with Remarkable Men. 1981: La chambre voisine. La fille prodigue. 1982: Le lit/The Bed.

PARTON, Dolly 1945–

Diminutive (well, in height at least), flamboyant, brightly blonde American country and western singer with amazing, Victorian eggtimer-type figure, a sort of Hollywood Barbara Windsor (*qv*) with vibrantly twangy, powerful singing voice thrown in. Not surprisingly, films paused before casting her in anything, but she has proved she can hold her own as an actress in light comedies and musicals. An obvious contender for a roadshow of *Hello, Dolly!* in a few years' time.

1970: The Nashville Sound. 1980: Nine to Five. 1982: The Best Little Whorehouse in Texas. 1984: Rhinestone.

PATRICK, Gail (Margaret Fitzpatrick) 1911–1980

Tall, straight-faced brunette American actress with honeyed voice, often cast in aristocratic or bitchy roles, but also able to project warmth and sincerity in the right role. Her assignments after 1940 were disappointing, and she later moved into production: her most noteworthy success was the long-running TV series *Perry Mason*. Died from leukaemia.

1932: If I Had a Million. 1933: The Phantom Broadcast (GB: Phantom of the Air). Pick-Up. The Mysterious Rider. Murder in the Zoo. Cradle Song. Mama Loves Papa. To the Last Man. 1934: Death Takes a Holiday. Wagon Wheels. Take the Stand (GB: The Great Radio Mystery). Murder at the Vanities. The Crime of Helen Stanley. One Hour Late. 1935: Doubting Thomas. Rumba. Smart Girl. Wanderer of the Wasteland. Two Fisted. Mississippi. No More Ladies. The Big Broadcast of 1936. 1936: The Preview Murder Mystery. Two in the Dark. My Man Godfrey. Murder with Pictures. The Lone Wolf Returns. Early to Bed. White Hunter. 1937: John Meade's Woman. Her Husband Lies. Artists and Models. Stage Door. 1938: Wives under Suspicion. Mad about Music. King of Alcatraz (GB: King of the Alcatraz). Dangerous to Know. 1939: Grand Jury Secrets. Disbarred. Reno. 1940. My Favorite Wife. Gallant Sons. The Doctor Takes a Wife. 1941: Kathleen. Love Crazy. 1942: We Were Dancing. Tales of Manhattan. Quiet Please, Murder. 1943: Hit Parade of 1943. Women in Bondage. 1944: Up in Mabel's Room. 1945: Twice Blessed. Brewster's Millions. 1946: Claudia and David. The Madonna's Secret. Rendezvous with Annie. The Plainsman and the Lady. 1947: Calendar Girl. King of the Wild Horses. 1948: The Inside Story.

PATRICK, Nigel (N. Wemyss) 1913–1981

Suave, brown-haired British leading man with distinctive receding hairline. Usually cast as men about town and shady smoothies, he was a better actor than most of his contemporaries, but never quite became a big star of the British cinema, and was seen mostly on stage (where he also directed) after 1961. Married to Beatrice Campbell (*qv*) from 1951 to her death in 1980. Died from lung cancer.

1939: Mrs Pym of Scotland Yard. 1948: Spring in Park Lane. Noose (US: The Silk Noose). Uneasy Terms. 1949: Silent Dust. The Jack of Diamonds. The Perfect Woman. 1950: Morning Departure (US: Operation Disaster). Trio. 1951: The Browning Version. Pandora

*and the Flying Dutchman. Encore. Young Wives' Tale. 1952: The Sound Barrier (US: Breaking the Sound Barrier). Who Goes There? (US: The Passionate Sentry). The Pickwick Papers. Meet Me Tonight. 1953: Grand National Night (US: Wicked Woman). 1954: Forbidden Cargo. The Sea Shall Not Have Them. 1955: A Prize of Gold. All for Mary. 1956: Raintree County. 1957: Count Five and Die. *Arrivederci Roma! (narrator only). How to Murder a Rich Uncle. 1958: The Man Inside. 1959: Sapphire. 1960: The League of Gentlemen. The Trials of Oscar Wilde (US: The Man with the Green Carnation). 1961: †Johnny Nobody. 1963: The Informers. 1966: Goal! World Cup 1966 (narrator only). 1969: Battle of Britain. The Virgin Soldiers. 1970: The Executioner. 1972: Tales from the Crypt. The Great Waltz. 1973: The Mackintosh Man. 1977: Silver Bears.*

†Also directed

PATTERSON, Lee 1929–

Well-muscled, dark-haired Canadian actor with husky, pop star looks who carved out a busy career for himself as the star of British 'B' film thrillers of the 1950s, some of them well above average. He went to America as the star of a TV series, *Surfside Six*, in the early 1960s, but his film career subsequently fizzled out, and he has appeared mainly on stage in latter years.

1953: Malta Story. 1954: The Good Die Young. The Passing Stranger. 36 Hours (US: Terror Street). 1955: The Diamond Expert. Above Us the Waves. 1956: Reach for the Sky. Soho Incident (US: Spin a Dark Web). Checkpoint. Dry Rot. The Counterfeit Plan. 1957: The Key Man. Time Lock. The Story of Esther Costello (US: Golden Virgin). The Flying Scot (US: Mailbag Robbery). 1958: Bed without Breakfast. The Golden Disc (US: The Inbetween Age). The Spaniard's Curse. Cat and Mouse. The Desperate Ones. Man with a Gun. 1959: Please Turn Over. Breakout. Deadly Record. The White Trap. Jack the Ripper. Third Man on the Mountain. 1960: October Moth. The Three Worlds of Gulliver. 1963: The Ceremony. 1967: Valley of Mystery. Search for the Evil One. 1971: Chato's Land. 1976: Star Street. 1982: Airplane II The Sequel. 1984: Hunter (TV). 1985: Death Wish 3.

PAVLOW, Muriel 1921–

Petite, light-haired British actress whose clean, girlish good looks enabled her to stay in youthful, albeit fairly tame leading roles for 20 years: a trim, sexy figure and cool, capable acting style certainly helped. Married to Derek Farr from 1947 to his death. Still acting, latterly on TV.

1934: Sing As We Go. 1937: A Romance in Flanders (US: Lost on the Western Front). 1941: Quiet Wedding. 1945: Night Boat to Dublin. 1946: The Shop at Sly Corner (US: The Code of Scotland Yard). 1951: Out of True. 1952: It Started in Paradise. The Net (US: Project M7). 1953: Malta Story. 1954: Doctor in the House. Conflict of Wings. Forever My Heart. 1955: Simon and Laura. 1956: Reach for the Sky. Eyewitness. Tiger in the Smoke. 1957: Doctor at Large. 1958: Rooney. 1959: Whirlpool. 1961: Murder She Said.

PAYNE, John 1912–

Dark-haired, tough-looking American actor with fretful expression and slightly husky voice. Always good value as a man of action, his career traced a faintly similar pattern to that of Dick Powell, in that it followed light musicals (especially opposite Alice Faye and Sonja Henie) with a string of tough-guy roles. Very prolific from 1949 to 1956 when he appeared in a series of thrillers and colourful outdoors action films that were sometimes of quite high quality. Married Anne Shirley (1937–1943) and Gloria De Haven (1944–1950), first and second of three.

*1936: Dodsworth. 1937: Hats Off. Fair Warning. 1938: College Swing (GB: Swing, Teacher, Swing). Garden of the Moon. Love on Toast. 1939: Indianapolis Speedway (GB: Devil on Wheels). Bad Lands. Wings of the Navy. Kid Nightingale. *Royal Rodeo. 1940: The Great Profile. Tear Gas Squad. Star Dust. Maryland. King of the Lumberjacks. Tin Pan Alley. 1941: Remember the Day. The Great American Broadcast. Week-end in Havana. Sun Valley Serenade. 1942: Iceland (GB: Katina). Springtime in the Rockies. To the Shores of Tripoli. Footlight Serenade. 1943: Hello, Frisco, Hello. 1945: The Dolly Sisters. 1946: Wake Up and Dream. Sentimental Journey. The Razor's Edge. 1947: Miracle on 34th Street (GB: The Big Heart). 1948: Larceny. The Saxon Charm. 1949: The Crooked Way. El Paso. Captain China. 1950: The Eagle and the Hawk. Tripoli. 1951: Passage West (GB: High Venture). Crosswinds. 1952: The Blazing Forest. Caribbean (GB: Caribbean Gold). Kansas City Confidential (GB: The Secret Four). 1953: Raiders of the Seven Seas. The Vanquished. 99 River Street. 1954: Rails into Laramie. Silver Lode. 1955: Hell's Island. Santa Fé Passage. The Road to Denver. Tennessee's Partner. 1956: Slightly Scarlet. The Boss. Rebel in Town. Hold Back the Night. 1957: Bail Out at 43,000 (GB: Bale Out at 43,000). 1958: Hidden Fear. 1965: †They Ran for Their Lives. 1968: Gift of the Nile. 1970: The Savage Wild. 1978: Go West, Young Girl (TV).*

†*Also directed*

PECK, Gregory (Eldred G. Peck) 1916–

Upright, immensely good-looking, dark-haired, soft-spoken American actor who rose to stardom in his first film and more than almost anyone else suggested (despite his own sporadic attempts to break the pattern) nobility and incorruptibility just by being on screen. He might have won an Oscar for his cracking-up colonel in *12 O'Clock High* (one of four unsuccessful nominations), but Hollywood typically gave him one instead for his tricksy performance under a mound of padding in *To Kill a Mockingbird*. Suddenly looking his age for the first time, Peck drifted out of films into production in the early 1970s. It was a surprise when he returned in big-budget pot-boilers at the end of the decade.

*1943: Days of Glory. 1944: The Keys of the Kingdom. 1945: The Valley of Decision. Spell-*bound. *1946: Duel in the Sun. The Yearling. 1947: Gentlemen's Agreement. The Macomber Affair. The Paradine Case. 1948: Yellow Sky. 1949: The Great Sinner. 12 O'Clock High. 1950: The Gunfighter. 1951: Captain Horatio Hornblower RN. David and Bathsheba. Only the Valiant. 1952: The Snows of Kilimanjaro. The World in His Arms. 1953: Roman Holiday. The Million Pound Note (US: Man with a Million). 1954: Night People. The Purple Plain. 1956: The Man in the Gray Flannel Suit. Moby Dick. 1957: Designing Woman. 1958: The Bravados. The Big Country. 1959: Beloved Infidel. On the Beach. Pork Chop Hill. 1961: The Guns of Navarone. 1962: Cape Fear. How the West Was Won. 1963: To Kill a Mockingbird. Captain Newman MD. 1964: Behold a Pale Horse. 1965: Mirage. 1966: Arabesque. 1968: Mackenna's Gold. The Stalking Moon. 1969: The Chairman (GB: The Most Dangerous Man in the World). Marooned. 1970: I Walk the Line. 1971: Shoot Out. 1973: Billy Two Hats. 1974: John F. Kennedy: Years of Lightning, Day of Drums (narrator only). 1976: The Omen. 1977: MacArthur (GB: MacArthur the Rebel General). 1978: The Boys from Brazil. 1979: Ken Murray's Shooting Stars. 1980: The Sea Wolves. 1982: The Blue and the Gray (TV). 1983: The Scarlet and the Black (TV).*

PENHALIGON, Susan 1950–

Philippines-born, baby-faced blonde in British films of the 1970s. Although she projected bubbling warmth and intelligence as well as sex appeal, her type was not ideally suited to 1970s' stardom, and her struggle to establish herself as a star of the cinema now seems to have ended. She was, however, more successful on television, where she admirably extended her range to playing bitches, most notably in the series *Bouquet of Barbed Wire*.

1971: Private Road. Under Milk Wood. 1973: No Sex, Please – We're British. 1974: The Land That Time Forgot. Miracles Still Happen. 1975: House of Mortal Sin. 1976: Nasty Habits. 1977: The Uncanny. Leopard in the Snow. 1978: Patrick. Soldier of Orange/Survival Run.

PENN, Sean 1960–

Slim, dark, intense, strong-jawed, seldom-smiling American actor who has so far played rebels against the system. Son of director Leo

To Victory). 1980: Battle Beyond the Stars. Your Ticket is No Longer Valid. 1981: Helicopter. Race for the Yankee Zephyr. 1982: Target Eagle. 1983: The A-Team (TV).

Penn, brother of actor Christopher Penn. Married singer-actress Madonna in 1985.
1980: The Killing of Randy Webster (TV). 1981: Taps. 1982: Fast Times at Ridgemont High (GB: Fast Times). Bad Boys. 1983: Crackers. 1984: Racing with the Moon. The Falcon and the Snowman. 1985: At Close Range. 1986: Shanghai Surprise.

PEPPARD, George 1928–
Fair-haired, blue-eyed, hard-headed American actor who looked to be a real find in the early sixties but proved disappointing in the leading roles of several big films (perhaps the wrong kind?) and was shunted into routine action thrillers and westerns. Found belated popularity as leader of TV's *The A-Team*.
1957: The Strange One (GB: End As a Man). 1959: Pork Chop Hill. 1960: Home from the Hill. The Subterraneans. 1961: Breakfast at Tiffany's. 1962: How the West Was Won. 1963: The Victors. 1964: The Carpetbaggers. 1965: Operation Crossbow (US: The Great Spy Mission). The Third Day. 1966: The Blue Max. 1967: Rough Night in Jericho. Tobruk. 1968: P.J. (GB: New Face in Hell). House of Cards. Pendulum. What's So Bad About Feeling Good? 1970: The Executioner. Cannon for Cordoba. 1971: One More Train to Rob. The Bravos (TV). 1972: The Groundstar Conspiracy. 1974: Newman's Law. 1975: Guilty or Innocent: the Sam Sheppard Case (TV). One of Our Own (TV). Doctors' Secrets (TV). 1977: Damnation Alley. 1978: †Five Days From Home. 1979: Crisis in Mid-Air (TV). Torn Between Two Lovers (TV. GB: cinemas). Da Dunkerque alla vittoria. (US: From Hell

PERKINS, Anthony 1932–
Tall, dark, frail-looking American actor with soft voice, shy smile and coat-hanger shoulders. A teenage pin-up of his time, he proved a useful portrayer of young men defying odds to succeed. *Psycho* brought him a new image, but it proved a hard trick to follow, and the ensuing years were full of oddball projects and unsuitable roles before he made two further *Psycho* films in the 1980s, directing one himself. The son of character actor Osgood Perkins (1892–1937), he was in 1984 ordained a minister of the Universal Life Church of America. Oscar nominee for *Friendly Persuasion*.
1953: The Actress. 1956: Friendly Persuasion. 1957: The Lonely Man. Fear Strikes Out. The Tin Star. 1958: Desire under the Elms. This Angry Age (GB: The Sea Wall). The Matchmaker. 1959: Green Mansions. On the Beach. 1960: Tall Story. Psycho. 1961: Phaedra. Goodbye Again/Aimez-vous Brahms? 1962: Five Miles to Midnight. The Trial. Le glaive et la balance (GB: Two are Guilty). 1963: Une ravissante idiote (GB: A Ravishing Idiot). 1965: The Fool Killer. Is Paris Burning? 1967: Le scandale (GB and US: The Champagne Murders). 1968: Pretty Poison. 1970: How Awful about Allan (TV). WUSA. Catch 22. 1971: Ten Days' Wonder. Quelqu'un derrière la porte (GB: Two Minds for Murder). 1972: The Life and Times of Judge Roy Bean. Play It As It Lays. 1973: Lovin' Molly. 1974: Murder on the Orient Express. 1975: Mahogany. 1977: Winter Kills (released 1979). 1978: First, You Cry (TV). Remember My Name. Les Miserables (TV). 1979: Twee Vrouwen/ Twice a Woman. North Sea Hijack (US: ffolkes). Double Negative. The Horror Show. The Black Hole. 1982: For the Term of His Natural Life (TV). The Sins of Dorian Gray (TV). 1983: Psycho II. 1984: Crimes of Passion/China Blue. 1986: †Psycho 3.

†*And directed*

PERKINS, Millie 1938–
Dark-haired American actress (a former cover-girl model) with dewy-eyed, waif-like appeal. Like the similar Maggie McNamara

(1928–1978) a few years earlier, she never came anywhere near matching the success of her first film, *The Diary of Anne Frank*, once her teenage appeal had faded. Married to Dean Stockwell (*qv*) from 1960 to 1964, she continues to crop up in occasional mature roles.
1959: The Story of Anne Frank. 1961: Wild in the Country. 1963: Girl from La Mancha. 1964: Ensign Pulver. 1966: The Shooting. 1967: Ride the Whirlwind. 1968: Wild in the Streets. 1974: Cockfighter/Born to Kill. 1975: Lady Cocoa. The Witch Who Came from the Sea. 1982: Table for Five. 1983: The Haunting Passion. Licence to Kill (TV). 1985: At Close Range. 1986: The Other Lover (TV).

PERREAU, Gigi (Ghislaine Perreau-Saussine) 1941–
Along with Natalie Wood, this pigtailed charmer with the fresh-faced, well-scrubbed looks was the busiest of non-star child actresses in the 1940s, actually appearing in Hollywood films for 10 years before finishing her schooling and returning in ingenue roles which, like those of Margaret O'Brien (*qv*) and despite her undoubted talent, were comparatively unsuccessful. Born in America soon after the arrival there of her French parents, who had fled from the Nazis.
1943: Madame Curie. Dear Heart. Abigail. 1944: Death in a Doll's House. Dark Waters. San Diego, I Love You. Two Girls and a Sailor. The Master Race. The Seventh Cross. Mr Skeffington. 1945: Yolanda and the Thief. Voice of the Whistler. God is My Co-Pilot. 1946: Alias Mr Twilight. To Each His Own.

1947: Song of Love. High Barbaree. Green Dolphin Street. 1948: Family Honeymoon, Enchantment. The Sainted Sisters. 1949: Roseanna McCoy. My Foolish Heart. Song of Surrender. 1950: Shadow on the Wall. Never a Dull Moment. For Heaven's Sake. 1951: A Weekend with Father. The Lady Pays Off. Reunion in Reno. 1952: Has Anybody Seen My Gal. Bonzo Goes to College. 1956: The Man in the Gray Flannel Suit. There's Always Tomorrow. Dance with Me, Henry. 1958: Wild Heritage. The Cool and the Crazy. 1959: Girls' Town. 1961: Tammy Tell Me True. Look in Any Window. 1967: Hell in the Streets/Hell on Wheels. Journey to the Center of Time.

PERRINE, Valerie 1944–
Tall, statuesque, fair-haired, seemingly permanently tanned American leading lady who sprang from showgirl to star at the ripe old age of 28 and almost immediately displayed a talent for affecting seemingly unforced emotion on screen. But producers have subsequently concentrated on showcasing her physical attributes rather than her acting ability. Nominated for an Academy Award in Lenny.
1972: Slaughterhouse-Five. The Couple Takes a Wife (TV). 1973: The Last American Hero. 1974: Lenny. 1976: W.C. Fields and Me. 1977: Mr Billion. 1978: Superman. Ziegfeld – the Man and His Women (TV). 1979: The Magician of Lublin. The Electric Horseman. 1980: Can't Stop the Music. Agency. Superman II. 1981: The Border. 1982: Marian Rose White (TV). 1985: Water.

PETERS, Jean (Elizabeth J. Peters) 1926–
Dark-haired Hollywood actress with prettily petulant looks. A star in her first film, she played mostly untamed girls and minxes – including a Mexican girl, an Indian and a spitfire pirate – before marriage to film magnate Howard Hughes disappointingly put an end to her career. The marriage, her second, ended in divorce in 1971 after 15 years, and she has since remarried and resumed acting without making any great impact.
1947: Captain from Castile. 1948: Deep Waters. 1949: It Happens Every Spring. 1950: Love That Brute. 1951: As Young As You Feel. Anne of the Indies. Take Care of My Little Girl. 1952: Viva Zapata! Wait 'Til the Sun Shines, Nellie. O.Henry's Full House

(GB: Full House). Lure of the Wilderness. 1953: Pickup on South Street. Vicki. Niagara. A Blueprint for Murder. 1954: Apache. Three Coins in the Fountain. Broken Lance. 1955: A Man Called Peter.

PETERS, Susan (Suzanne Carnahan) 1921–1952
Delicate but determined-looking brunette American actress, capable of projecting great sincerity even from a poor script. M-G-M were building her up into a star when she was paralysed from the waist down in a hunting accident. Appeared in one further film (and a TV series) from a wheelchair before her death from a chronic kidney infection. Married to actor – later director – Richard Quine from 1943 to 1948. She received an Academy Award nomination for Random Harvest.

1939: †*Sockaroo. †*Young America Flies. 1940: †Susan and God (GB: The Gay Mrs Trexel). †River's End. †The Man Who Talked Too Much. †Santa Fé Trail. †Money and the Woman. 1941: †Here Comes Happiness. †Strawberry Blonde. †Scattergood Pulls the Strings. †Meet John Doe. †Three Sons o' Guns. 1942: †Escape from Crime. Dr Gillespie's New Assistant. The Big Shot. Andy Hardy's Double Life. Tish. Random Harvest. 1943: Young Ideas. Assignment in Brittany. Song of Russia. Keep Your Powder Dry (released 1945). 1948: The Sign of the Ram.

†As Suzanne Carnahan

PETTET, Joanna 1944–
Fair-haired British-born actress, raised in Canada, who created some glowingly real

characters and rose to stardom in Hollywood films. The seventies have seen her mainly on TV. Married actor Alex Cord (A. Viespi, 1931–) in 1973, but by 1980 the couple had separated.
1966: The Group. The Night of the Generals. 1967: Casino Royale. Robbery. 1968: Blue. The Best House in London. 1972: Footsteps (TV). The Delphi Bureau (TV). The Weekend Nun (TV). 1973: Pioneer Woman (TV). Welcome to Arrow Beach (US: Tender Flesh). 1974: A Cry in the Wilderness (TV). 1975: The Desperate Miles (TV). 1976: The Hancocks (TV). The Dark Side of Innocence (TV). 1977: Sex and the Married Woman (TV). 1978: Cry of the Innocent (TV). The Evil. 1979: An Eye for an Eye. 1980: The Return of Frank Cannon (TV). 1982: Double Exposure. Othello the Black Commando. 1985: Sweet Country.

PHILIPE, Gérard 1922–1959
Dark, dashing, romantic French actor with sensitively handsome features, the foremost young leading man of the post-war French theatre and cinema. Although he generated warmth from the screen, and could turn his hand as easily to soulful, sometimes tragic heroes as to swashbuckling amorous adventurers, Philipe had still not quite reached international stardom at the time of his early death from a heart attack.
1943: Les petites du Quai aux Fleurs. 1945: La boîte aux rêves. Le pays sans étoiles. 1946: L'Idiot. Ouvert pour cause d'inventaire. 1947: Le diable au corps (US: Devil in the Flesh). 1948: La chartreuse de Parme. 1949: Une si

jolie petite plage (*US: Riptide*). *Tous les chemins mènent à Rome* (*GB and US: All Roads Lead to Rome*). 1950: *Juliette, ou la clé des songes. La beauté du diable* (*GB: Beauty and the Beast. US: Beauty and the Devil*). *La ronde. Souvenirs perdus* (*GB: Lost Property*). 1951: *Fanfan la tulipe.* 1952: *Les belles de nuit* (*US: Beauties of the Night. Les sept péchés capitaux* (*GB and US: The Seven Deadly Sins*). 1953: *Villa Borghese* (*US: It Happened in the Park*). *Les orgueilleux* (*GB: The Proud Ones. US: The Proud and the Beautiful*). *Si Versailles m'était conté* (*GB: Versailles. US: Royal Affairs in Versailles*). 1954: *Knave of Hearts* (*France: Monsieur Ripois. US: Lovers, Happy Lovers*). *Le rouge et le noir.* 1955: *Si Paris nous était conté. La meilleure part. Les grandes manoeuvres/Summer Manoeuvres.* 1956: *Les aventures de Till l'espiègle* (*GB: Till Eulenspiegel. US: Bold Adventure*). 1957: *Pot-bouille. Montparnasse 19* (*GB: Lovers of Montparnasse. US: Modigliani of Montparnasse*). 1958: *La vie à deux. Le joueur/The Gambler.* 1959: *Les liaisons dangereuses. Los ambiciosos* (*US: Republic of Sin*).

PHILLIPS, Conrad 1927–
Dark, bequiffed British actor of whippy build and earnest manner. After a few small roles in the early years of his film career, he became probably the last steadily-employed star of British second features from 1957 to 1966, also making a successful TV series, *William Tell.*
1948: *The Gentlemen Go By. A Song for Tomorrow.* 1949: *The Temptress.* 1950: *Lilli Marlene.* 1952: *The Last Page* (*US: Manbait*). *It Started in Paradise.* 1953: *Mantrap* (*US: Woman in Hiding*). *The Case of Express Delivery.* 1954: *Johnny on the Spot.* 1955: *Triple Blackmail.* 1956: *The Secret Tent.* 1957: *Strangers' Meeting.* 1958: *A Question of Adultery.* 1959: *The White Trap. The Desperate Man. Witness in the Dark.* 1960: *Circus of Horrors. Sons and Lovers. No Love for Johnnie.* 1961: *The Shadow of the Cat. The Secret Partner. The Fourth Square. Murder She Said.* 1962: *The Durant Affair. Dead Man's Evidence. Don't Talk to Strange Men. A Guy Called Caesar.* 1963: *Impact. Heavens Above! The Switch.* 1964: *Stopover Forever.* 1965: *The Murder Game. Dateline Diamonds.* 1966: *Who Killed the Cat?* 1967: *The Ghost of Monk's Island* (*serial*).

PHILLIPS, Leslie 1924–
Blond British actor with military voice and foxy laugh, in show business from childhood, but not at all well known in films until he brought his successful impersonation of the moustachioed sheep in wolf's clothing (nurtured in radio's very successful *The Navy Lark*) to the screen in the late fifties. Then enjoyed a very popular run of star parts until 1966 when a cropper with a dramatic role in *Maroc 7* temporarily slowed his career.
1935: *A Lassie from Lancashire.* 1938: *The Citadel.* 1949: *Train of Events.* 1950: *The Woman with No Name* (*US: Her Panelled Door*). 1951: *Pool of London. The Galloping Major.* 1952: *The Sound Barrier* (*US: Breaking the Sound Barrier*). 1953: *The Fake. The Limping Man. Time Bomb* (*US: Terror on a Train*). 1955: *Value for Money. The Gamma People. As Long As They're Happy.* 1956: *The Big Money.* 1957: *The Barretts of Wimpole Street. The Smallest Show on Earth. Brothers in Law. Just My Luck. Les Girls. High Flight.* 1958: *I Was Monty's Double. The Man Who Liked Funerals.* 1959: *Carry on Nurse. Ferdinand of Naples. The Angry Hills. This Other Eden. Carry on Teacher. Please Turn Over. The Night We Dropped a Clanger. The Navy Lark.* 1960: *Inn for Trouble. Watch Your Stern. Carry on Constable. Doctor in Love. No Kidding* (*US: Beware of Children*). 1961: *Raising the Wind. A Weekend with Lulu. In the Doghouse. Very Important Person.* 1962: *Crooks Anonymous. The Longest Day. The Fast Lady.* 1963: *Father Came Too.* 1965: *You Must Be Joking!* 1966: *Doctor in Clover.* *Zabaglione. Maroc 7.* 1970: *Some Will, Some Won't. Doctor in Trouble.* 1971: *The Magnificent Seven Deadly Sins.* 1972: *Not Now Darling.* 1973: *Don't Just Lie There, Say Something!* 1975: *Spanish Fly.* 1976: *Not Now, Comrade.* 1979: *The Lion, the Witch and the Wardrobe* (*TV. Voice only*). 1985: *Out of Africa.*

PICKFORD, Mary (Gladys Smith) 1893–1979
Canadian-born star with fluffy fair hair who became Hollywood's most famous silent screen actress and 'America's sweetheart'. Wildly popular in little-girl roles, which she was still playing when past 30. Formed United Artists with Chaplin and Douglas Fairbanks Snr. in 1919, and revealed herself as a for-

midable businesswoman, retiring in 1933 (after an Oscar for *Coquette* in 1929) to concentrate on being a production executive. Married to Owen Moore (1886–1939) from 1909 to 1915, Fairbanks from 1920 to 1936 and Charles 'Buddy' Rogers (1904–) from 1937 on. Became a recluse in later years. Special Oscar 1975. Died after a stroke.
1909: *Her First Biscuits. The Violin Maker of Cremona. The Son's Return. The Peach Basket Hat. The Necklace. The Country Doctor. The Lonely Villa. The Faded Lilies. The Way of Man. The Mexican Sweethearts. The Cardinal's Conspiracy. The Seventh Day. Sweet and Twenty. They Would Elope. His Wife's Visitor. The Sealed Room. The Little Darling. The Renunciation. A Strange Meeting. The Slave. The Indian Runner's Romance. Oh! Uncle. 1776. In Old Kentucky. The Broken Locket. The Awakening. The Gibson Goddess. His Lost Love. The Light That Came. The Mountaineer's Honor. The Test. Getting Even. What's Your Hurry? The Little Teacher. In the Watches of the Night. The Restoration. A Midnight Adventure. The Trick That Failed. To Save Her Soul.* 1910: *All on Account of the Mille. The Englishman and the Girl. The Thread of Destiny. The Smoker. A Rich Revenge. May and December. The Unchanging Sea. The Woman from Mellon's. The Newlyweds. The Twisted Tail. As It Is in Life. A Romance of the Western Hills. Never Again! Love among the Roses. Ramona. A Victim of Jealousy. Muggsy's First Sweetheart. The Call to Arms. The Two Brothers. In the Season of Buds. A Child's Impulse. What the Daisy Said. An Arcadian Maid. Muggsy Becomes a Hero. The Sorrows of the Unfaithful. When We Were in Our Teens. Wilful Peggy. Examination Day at School. A Gold Necklace. Waiter No. 5. A Lucky Toothache. Simple Charity. The Masher. The Song of the Wildwood Flute. A Plain Story.* 1911: *White Roses. The Italian Barber. A Decree of Destiny. The Dream. At the Duke's Command. While the Cat's Away. Artful Kate. The Message in the Bottle. When a Man Loves. Three Sisters. The First Misunderstanding. Maid or Man. The Mirror. Her Darkest Hour. A Manly Man. The Fishermaid. In Old Madrid. The Stampede. The Fair Dentist. Back to the Soil. The Master and the Man. For the Queen's Honor. Sweet Memories of Yesterday. Second Sight. For Her Brother's Sake. In the Sultan's Garden. The Lighthouse Keeper. A Gasoline Engagement. At a Quarter*

of Two (GB: At a Quarter to Two). Science. The Skating Bug. The Call of the Song. The Toss of a Coin. The Sentinel Asleep. The Better Way. His Dress Shirt. 'Tween Two Loves. The Rose's Story. From the Bottom of the Sea. The Courting of Mary. Love Heeds Not the Showers. Little Red Riding Hood. The Caddy's Dream. 1912: Honor Thy Father. The Female of the Species. Won by a Fish. A Lodging for the Night. Home Folks. The Schoolteacher and the Waif. A Pueblo Legend. The Inner Circle. Friends. A Feud in the Kentucky Hills. My Baby. The Unwelcome Guest. The Mender of Nets. Ida's Promise. Fate's Interception. Just Like a Woman. The Old Actor. A Beast at Bay. Lena and the Geese. An Indian Summer. The Narrow Road. With the Enemy's Help. So Near, Yet So Far. The One She Loved. The Informer. The New York Hat. 1913: †In the Bishop's Carriage. †Caprice. 1914: †A Good Little Devil. †Tess of the Storm Country. †Hearts Adrift. †The Eagle's Mate. †Such a Little Queen. †Behind the Scenes. †Cinderella. 1915: †Fanchon the Cricket. †Mistress Nell. †The Dawn of Tomorrow. †Little Pal. †Rags. †Esmeralda. †A Girl Yesterday. †Madam Butterfly. 1916: †The Foundling. †Poor Little Peppina. †Hulda from Holland. †The Eternal Grind. †Less Than the Dust. 1917: †The Pride of the Clan. †Poor Little Rich Girl. †A Romance of the Redwoods. †The Little American. †Rebecca of Sunnybrook Farm. †A Little Princess. 1918: †Stella Maris. †Amarilly of Clothes Line Alley. †M'Liss. †How Could You, Jean? One Hundred Per Cent American. †Johanna Enlists. 1919: †Daddy Long Legs. †Captain Kidd Junior. †The Hoodlum (GB: The Ragamuffin). †The Heart o' the Hills. 1920: †Pollyanna. †Suds. 1921: †Little Lord Fauntleroy. †The Love Light. †Through the Back Door. 1922: †Tess of the Storm Country (remake). 1923: †Rosita. 1924: †Dorothy Vernon of Haddon Hall. 1925: †Little Annie Rooney. 1926: †Sparrows (GB: Human Sparrows). 1927: †My Best Girl. †The Gaucho. †The Kiss of Mary Pickford (US: Mary Pickford's Kiss). 1929: †The Voice of Hollywood. †Coquette. †The Taming of the Shrew. 1931: Screen Snapshots No 4. †Kiki. 1932: Hollywood on Parade No 4. 1933: †Secrets. Hollywood on Parade No 12. 1935: Star Night at the Cocoanut Grove.

All shorts except † features

PIDGEON, Walter 1897–1984

Very tall, dark, conservative-looking Canadian-born actor who started as a singer (and played in some early musicals). His career was going nowhere when he signed an M-G-M contract at 40, and stayed with them for exactly 20 years, his pipe-and-slippers image boosting him to stardom in the war years when he starred opposite Greer Garson (qv) in a series of artfully-contrived box-office smashes. His deep voice stayed with us in character roles until 1977, when he retired at 80 after 53 filming years. Died after a series of strokes. Received Academy Award nominations for Mrs Miniver and Madame Curie. 1925: Mannequin. 1926: Old Loves and New.

The Outsider. Miss Nobody. Marriage License. 1927: The Gorilla. Heart of Salome. The Girl from Rio (GB: Lola). The Thirteenth Juror. 1928: Turn Back the Hours. The Gateway of the Moon. Woman Wise. Melody of Love. Clothes Make the Woman. 1929: A Most Immoral Lady. Her Private Life. 1930: Sweet Kitty Bellairs. Bride of the Regiment (GB: Lady of the Rose). Viennese Nights. Show Girl in Hollywood. 1931: Kiss Me Again (GB: The Toast of the Legion). Hot Heiress. Going Wild. The Gorilla (remake). 1932: Rockabye. 1933: The Kiss before the Mirror. 1934: Journal of a Crime. 1935: *Good Badminton. 1936: Big Brown Eyes. Fatal Lady. 1937: As Good As Married. Girl Overboard. A Girl with Ideas. She's Dangerous. Saratoga. My Dear Miss Aldrich. 1938: The Shopworn Angel. Man-Proof. Listen, Darling. Girl of the Golden West. Too Hot to Handle. 1939: Society Lawyer. Stronger Than Desire. 6,000 Enemies. My Dear Miss Aldrich. Nick Carter, Master Detective. 1940: Sky Murder. The Dark Command. It's a Date. The House across the Bay. Phantom Raiders. 1941: How Green Was My Valley. Man Hunt. Blossoms in the Dust. Flight Command. Design for Scandal. 1942: Mrs Miniver. White Cargo. 1943: The Youngest Profession. Madame Curie. 1944: Mrs Parkington. 1945: Weekend at the Waldorf. 1946: Holiday in Mexico. The Secret Heart. 1947: If Winter Comes. Cass Timberlane. 1948: Julia Misbehaves. Command Decision. 1949: The Red Danube. That Forsyte Woman (GB: The Forsyte Saga). 1950: The Miniver Story. 1951: Soldiers Three. The Unknown Man. Calling Bulldog Drummond. Quo Vadis? (narrator only). 1952: The Sellout. Million Dollar Mermaid (GB: The One Piece Bathing Suit). The Bad and the Beautiful. 1953: Scandal at Scourie. 1954: The Last Time I Saw Paris. Men of the Fighting Lady. Executive Suite. 1955: Hit the Deck. The Glass Slipper (narrator only). 1956: Forbidden Planet. The Rack. These Wilder Years. 1959: Meet Me in St Louis (TV). 1961: Voyage to the Bottom of the Sea. 1962: Advise and Consent. Big Red. The Two Colonels. 1963: Il giorno piu corto commedia umaristica (US: The Shortest Day). 1966: How I Spent My Summer Vacation (TV. GB: cinemas as Deadly Roulette). 1967: Cosa Nostra: an Arch Enemy of the FBI (TV. GB: cinemas). Warning Shot. 1968: Funny Girl. 1969: Rascal (narrator only). The Vatican

Affair. 1970: The House on Greenapple Road (TV). The Mask of Sheba (TV). 1971: The Screaming Woman (TV). 1972: Skyjacked. 1973: Harry Never Holds (GB: Harry in Your Pocket). The Neptune Factor. 1974: The Girl on the Late, Late Show (TV). The Yellow Headed Summer. Live Again, Die Again (TV). 1975: You Lie So Deep, My Love (TV). Won Ton Ton, the Dog Who Saved Hollywood. Murder on Flight 502 (TV). 1976: The Lindbergh Kidnapping Case (TV). Mayday at 40,000 Feet (TV. GB: cinemas). Two-Minute Warning. 1977: Sextette.

PILBEAM, Nova (Margery Pilbeam) 1919–

Yet another example of an immensely talented child/teenage actress who never quite made it as an adult star. This silky-haired petite blonde girl's first three performances were her best; after that, her upper-class personality (and marriage to young director Pen Tennyson, tragically killed in 1941) seemed to prevent her acting style moving with the times. 1934: Little Friend. The Man Who Knew Too Much. 1936: Tudor Rose (US: Nine Days a Queen). 1937: Young and Innocent (US: The Girl Was Young). 1939: Cheer Boys Cheer. 1940: Pastor Hall. Spring Meeting. 1941: Banana Ridge. 1942: The Next of Kin. 1943: The Yellow Canary. 1944: Out of Chaos. *Men of Science. 1946: This Man is Mine. 1947: Green Fingers. 1948: The Three Weird Sisters. Counterblast.

PISIER, Marie-France (Claudia Chauchat) 1944–

Born in Indochina (now Vietnam) and raised in New Caledonia, this small, pretty French brunette actress hardly caused a ripple on the international scene until she was past 30. Then the worldwide exposure of Celine et Julie vont en bateau and Cousin cousine (she won a French Oscar for the latter) took her to Hollywood to make (the, as it turned out, disastrous) The Other Side of Midnight. Although that more or less concluded the American connection, her standing in France remained intact, and that is where she has made the greater part of her career. 1961: Qui ose nous accuser? 1962: Les saints nitouches (GB: Wild Living). L'amour à vingt ans (GB and US: Love at Twenty). Les amoureux de France. 1963: La mort d'un tueur.

Young Girls of Good Families. 1964: Les yeux cernés. Le vampire de Dusseldorf. 1966: Trans-Europ-Express. No sta bene rubare il tesoro. 1967: Baisers volés (GB and US: Stolen Kisses). L'écume des jours. 1968: Nous n'irons plus au bois. 1969: Paulina s'en va. 1971: Le journal d'un suicide. Féminin, féminin. 1974: Céline et Julie vont en bateau (GB and US: Celine and Julie Go Boating). Souvenirs d'en France (GB and US: French Provincial). 1975: Cousin cousine. Sérail. 1976: Barocco. Le corps de mon ennemi. 1977: The Other Side of Midnight. Les apprentis sorciers. 1978: L'amour en fuite (GB and US: Love on the Run). The Brontë Sisters. 1979: French Postcards. 1980: Miss Right (originally begun in 1978). Le banquière. 44, ou les récits de la nuit (released 1985). 1981: The Hot Touch. Chanel solitaire. 1982: Der Zauberberg (US: The Magic Mountain). Meurtres sous protection. Boulevard des assassins. L'as des as. 1983: Le prix du danger (GB and US: The Prize of Peril). Der stille Ozean (US: The Silent Ocean). L'ami de Vincent. 1985: Les nanas/ The Chicks. Parking.

PITT, Ingrid (Ingoushka Petrov) 1944–
Tawny-haired Polish actress who made her film debut in Spain (where she was appearing at the National Theatre) before popping in and out of British films with a trio of lady vampires. She made a name for herself with her ferocious interpretations of these roles, which were heavily laced with sexual content. After a lull she returned in the 1980s with character roles, typically in plunging necklines

and subcutaneous trousers, and certainly as sexy as ever. Also writes novels.
1964: El sonido prehistorico/Sound of Horror. 1968: The Omegans. Where Eagles Dare. 1970: The Vampire Lovers. The House That Dripped Blood. Countess Dracula. 1971: Nobody Ordered Love. 1973: The Wicker Man. 1975: Where the Action Is (TV). 1982: Who Dares Wins. 1984: Bones (later: Parker). The House (TV). 1985: Wild Geese II. Underworld.

PITTS, ZaSu (Eliza Pitts) 1898–1963
Bird-like, dark-haired, slender American actress with large, dark, darting eyes. At first in vulnerable roles, most notably in Von Stroheim's *Greed*, she later took to comedy in early sound two-reelers, then played spinsterish character parts. Died from cancer.
*1917: *Why They Left Home. *His Fatal Beauty. *Uneasy Money. The Little Princess. A Modern Musketeer. Rebecca of Sunnybrook Farm. 1918: How Could You, Jean? As the Sun Went Down. A Society Sensation. 1919: Better Times. The Other Half. Men, Women and Money. 1920: Poor Relations. Bright Skies. Seeing It Through. Heart of Twenty. 1921: Patsy. 1922: Youth to Youth. For the Defense. Is Matrimony a Failure? A Daughter of Luxury. 1923: Poor Men's Wives. The Girl Who Came Back. Tea with a Kick. West of the Water Tower. Mary of the Movies. Souls for Sale. Three Wise Fools. 1924: Triumph. Daughters of Today. The Legend of Hollywood. The Fast Set. Greed. The Goldfish. Changing Husbands. Wine of Youth. 1925: The Great Love. The Business of Love. Old Shoes. The Re-Creation of Brian Kent. Thunder Mountain. A Woman's Faith. What Happened to Jones? The Great Divide. Lazybones. Pretty Ladies. Secrets of the Night. Wages for Wives. Mannequin. 1926: Monte Carlo (GB: Dreams of Monte Carlo). Early to Wed. Risky Business. Sunny Side Up. Her Big Night. 1927: Casey at the Bat. 1928: 13 Washington Square. Buck Privates. The Wedding March. Wife Savers. Sins of the Fathers. 1929: Her Private Life. The Argyle Case. The Dummy. Oh, Yeah! (GB: No Brakes). The Locked Door. Paris. This Thing Called Love. The Squall. Twin Beds. 1930: †All Quiet on the Western Front. Honey. The Lottery Bride. No, No, Nanette. River's End. The Squealer. The Devil's Holiday. Little Accident. Monte Carlo. Passion Flower. Sin Takes a Holiday. War Nurse.*

*1931: Finn and Hattie. Beyond Victory. Their Mad Moment. Bad Sister. The Big Gamble. Seed. A Woman of Experience. Penrod and Sam. The Guardsman. The Secret Witness. *Let's Do Things. *Catch As Catch Can. *The Pajama Party. *War Mamas. 1932: *Seal Skins. *On the Loose. *Red Noses. *The Old Bull. *Strictly Unreliable. *Show Business. *Alum and Eve. *The Soilers. Shopworn. Steady Company. The Trial of Vivienne Ware. Unexpected Father. Westward Passage. Blondie of the Follies. Make Me a Star. The Crooked Circle. Once in a Lifetime. Broken Lullaby (GB: The Man I Killed). Destry Rides Again. Strangers of the Evening. Speak Easily. Is My Face Red? Roar of the Dragon. Vanishing Frontier. Madison Square Gardens. Back Street. They Just Had to Get Married. 1933: Hello, Sister! Professional Sweetheart (GB: Imaginary Sweetheart). Love, Honor and Oh, Baby! *Sneak Easily. *Asleep in the Fleet. *Maids a la Mode. *One Track Minds. *The Bargain of the Century. Aggie Appleby, Maker of Men (GB: Cupid in the Rough). Mr Skitch. Out All Night. Her First Mate. Meet the Baron. 1934: Two Alone. The Meanest Gal in Town. Three on a Honeymoon. Mrs Wiggs of the Cabbage Patch. Their Big Moment (GB: Afterwards). Sing and Like It. Love Birds. Private Scandal. The Gay Bride. Dames. 1935: Hot Tip. Ruggles of Red Gap. The Affairs of Susan. Going Highbrow. She Gets Her Man. Spring Tonic. 1936: Thirteen Hours by Air. The Plot Thickens (GB: The Swinging Pearl Mystery). Sing Me a Love Song. Mad Holiday. 1937: Forty Naughty Girls. 52nd Street. Wanted. Merry Comes to Town. 1938: So's Your Aunt Emma (later Meet the Mob). 1939: Naughty But Nice. The Lady's from Kentucky. Mickey the Kid. Nurse Edith Cavell. Eternally Yours. 1940: No, No, Nanette (remake). It All Came True. 1941: Niagara Falls. Broadway Limited. The Mexican Spitfire's Baby. Week-End for Three. Miss Polly. 1942: Tish. Mexican Spitfire at Sea. The Bashful Bachelor. 1943: Let's Face It. 1946: The Perfect Marriage. Breakfast in Hollywood (GB: The Mad Hatter). 1947: Life with Father. *A Film Goes to Market. 1949: Francis. Denver and Rio Grande. 1954: Francis Joins the WACs. 1956: Mr Belvedere (TV. GB: cinemas). 1957: This Could Be the Night. 1959: The Gazebo. 1961: Teenage Millionaire. 1963: It's a Mad, Mad, Mad, Mad World.*

†silent version only

PLEASENCE, Donald 1919–
Initially distinctive, later eccentric bald-headed British character star whose pale blue eyes shone psychotically at many a harassed hero in the years following his portrayal of the murderous Dr Crippen. One of filmdom's hardest workers, especially in the early 1960s and from the late 1970s onwards, when he took to playing scientists and detectives compelled by circumstances to believe in the supernatural.
1954: The Beachcomber. Orders Are Orders. 1955: Value for Money. 1984. The Black Tent. 1956: The Man in the Sky (US: Decision Against Time). 1957: Manuela (US: Stow-

away Girl). Barnacle Bill (US: All at Sea).
1958: Heart of a Child. A Tale of Two Cities.
The Two-Headed Spy. The Man Inside. 1959:
Killers of Kilimanjaro. Look Back in Anger.
The Battle of the Sexes. The Shakedown. 1960:
Hell is a City. Circus of Horrors. The Flesh and
the Fiends. The Big Day. Suspect. Sons and
Lovers. The Hands of Orlac. A Story of David.
No Love for Johnnie. 1961: The Wind of
Change. Spare the Rod. The Horsemasters.
What a Carve-Up! (US: Home Sweet Homi-
cide). 1962: Dr Crippen. The Inspector (US:
Lisa). 1963: The Caretaker. The Great Escape.
1965: The Greatest Story Ever Told. The Hal-
lelujah Trail. 1966: Fantastic Voyage. Match-
less. Cul-de-Sac. Eye of the Devil. The Night
of the Generals. 1967: You Only Live Twice.
Will Penny. 1968: Mr Freedom. 1969: The
Madwoman of Chaillot. Arthur Arthur. 1970:
Outback. Soldier Blue. 1971: The Jerusalem
File. Kidnapped. The Pied Piper. THX 1138.
1972: Henry VIII and His Six Wives. Innocent
Bystanders. Death Line. 1973: Wedding in
White. The Rainbow Boys. The Seaweed Chil-
dren. Tales That Witness Madness. From
Beyond the Grave. 1974: The Mutations. The
Black Windmill. Escape to Witch Mountain.
The Count of Monte Cristo (TV. GB:
cinemas). Altrimenti ci arrabiamo (GB: Watch
Out, We're Mad). Barry McKenzie Holds His
Own. 1975: Hearts of the West (GB: Hol-
lywood Cowboy). I Don't Want to be Born.
1976: The Devil's Men (US: Land of the
Minotaur). Journey into Fear. The Eagle Has
Landed. The Last Tycoon. Passover Plot. Trial
by Combat (US: Dirty Knight's Work). 1977:
The Final Eye (TV). The Uncanny. Golden-
rod. Blood Relatives. Oh, God! Telefon. Tomor-
row Never Comes. 1978: The Dark Secret of
Harvest Home (TV. Voice only). Devil Cat
(US: Night Creature). The Defection of Simas
Kudirka. Jaguar Lives. Power Play. L'ordre et
la sécurité du monde. Good Luck, Miss Wyckoff.
Halloween. Sergeant Pepper's Lonely Hearts
Club Band. 1979: Gold of the Amazon Women
(TV). Dracula. Labyrinth. L'homme en colère.
Out of the Darkness (TV). All Quiet on the
Western Front (TV. GB: cinemas). Better
Late than Never (TV). 1980: The Puma Man.
Final Eye. Blade on the Feather (TV). The
Monster Club. Witch-hunt. 1981: Dick Turpin
(GB: TV). Halloween II. Race for the Yankee
Zephyr. Escape from New York. 1982: Alone
in the Dark. Witness for the Prosecution (TV).

The Devonsville Terror. 1983: Warrior of the
Lost World (released 1985). Frankenstein's
Great Aunt Tillie (released 1985). A Breed
Apart. Where is Parsifal? 1984: To Kill a
Stranger. The Treasure of the Amazon/
Treasure of Doom. Arch of Triumph (TV).
Terror in the Aisles. The Black Arrow (cable
TV). The Ambassador. Master of the Game
(TV). 1985: Reel Horror. Phenomena (GB:
Creepers). The Corsican Brothers (TV). Sotto
il vestito niente (US: Nothing Underneath).
1986: Pompeii. Honor Thy Father (TV).
Rainbow Four. I Love N.Y.

PLESHETTE, Suzanne 1937–
Tremendously talented, dark-haired American actress with bedroom smile, sad eyes
and sub-surface smoulder. She made it in the
movies at her second attempt, but later made
some unfortunate choices of script, mainly in
rampant melodrama. She was more successful
in roles that revealed her zany sense of
comedy. Married to Troy Donahue (qv) for a
few months in 1964. Since remarried, she also
now designs sheets and bedwear.
1958: Marjorie Morningstar. The Geisha Boy.
1962: 40 Pounds of Trouble. Rome Adventure
(GB: Lovers Must Learn). 1963: Wall of
Noise. The Birds. 1964: A Distant Trumpet.
Fate is the Hunter. Youngblood Hawke. 1965:
A Rage to Live. The Adventures of Bullwhip
Griffin (released 1967). Mr Buddwing (GB:
Woman Without a Face). 1966: Nevada
Smith. The Ugly Dachshund. 1967: Wings of
Fire (TV). The Power. 1968: Blackbeard's
Ghost. 1969: If It's Tuesday, This Must Be
Belgium. How To Make It (GB: Target:
Harry). Along Came a Spider (TV). 1970:
River of Gold (TV). Hunters Are for Killing
(TV). Suppose They Gave a War and Nobody
Came. 1971: Support Your Local Gunfighter.
In Broad Daylight (TV). A Capitol Affair
(TV). 1975: The Legend of Valentino (TV).
Beyond the Bermuda Triangle (TV). 1976:
The Shaggy DA. Law and Order (TV). 1978:
Kate Bliss and the Ticker Tape Kid (TV).
1979: Hot Stuff. Flesh and Blood (TV). 1980:
Oh, God! Book II. If Things Were Different
(TV). Studio Murders/Fantasies (TV). 1982:
Help Wanted: Male (TV). 1983: DIXIE:
Changing Habits (TV). One Cooks, the Other
Doesn't (TV). 1984: For Love or Money
(TV). 1985: Kojak: The Belarus File (TV).

PLUMMER, Christopher 1927–
Finely-boned Canadian actor, a more hand-
some version of Peter Cushing (qv). His sharp
features proved equally adaptable to kind-
liness, literacy, nobility and psychotic villainy.
Married to English actress Elaine Taylor.
Came late to films, although a regular per-
former on American TV from 1953.
1958: Wind Across the Everglades. Stage
Struck. 1962: The Fall of the Roman Empire.
*Trans-Canada Journey (narrator only).
1965: The Sound of Music. Inside Daisy
Clover. 1966: The Night of the Generals. Triple
Cross. 1967: Oedipus the King. 1968: Nobody
Runs Forever. 1969: Lock Up Your Daughters!
Battle of Britain. The Royal Hunt of the Sun.
1970: Waterloo. 1973: The Pyx. 1974: The
Return of the Pink Panther. 1975: Conduct
Unbecoming. The Man Who Would Be King.
The Spiral Staircase. 1976: Assassination!
(US: The Day That Shook the World). Aces
High. 1977: Uppdraget (GB: The Assign-
ment). 1978: The Silent Partner. Sherlock
Holmes: Murder by Decree (GB: Murder by
Decree). International Velvet. The Dis-
appearance. 1979: Hanover Street. Arthur
Miller – on Home Ground. Starcrash. RIEL.
1980: Highpoint. Eyewitness (GB: The Jani-
tor). Desperate Voyage (TV). Somewhere in
Time. The Shadow Box (TV). 1981: Being
Different (narrator only). Dial M for Murder
(TV). When the Circus Came to Town (TV).
1982: The Amateur. Little Gloria – Happy at
Last (TV). 1983: The Scarlet and the Black
(TV). Játszani kell/Lily in Love/Fitz and Lily.
Dreamscape. Prototype (TV). 1984: Ordeal by
Innocence. 1985: The Boy in Blue.

PLUNKETT, Patricia 1926–
While Rank starlets all around her were
changing their plain-Jane names to something
more glamorous, pretty, dark-haired, full-
lipped Patricia Plunkett stuck to hers – and
perhaps unwisely. She didn't get the parts to
project her into a star career and, although
very good in Landfall, found that it led
nowhere. Struggled on for several years in
British films before disappearing.
1947: It Always Rains on Sunday. 1948: Bond
Street. 1949: For Them That Trespass. Landfall. Man on the Run. 1950: Murder without
Crime. 1952: Mandy (US: Crash of Silence).
1954: The Crowded Day. 1957: The Flesh is
Weak. 1958: Dunkirk. 1960: Identity

Unknown. Escort for Hire. 1961: Two Living, One Dead.

POITIER, Sidney 1924–

Imposingly good-looking black American actor – the first to attract international audiences as a leading man. Although he broke down few actual barriers, he brought dignity to the portrayal of the black man on screen and, more important, played several roles that might have easily been portrayed by a white man. As an actor, most interesting when being less than saintly; as a director, rather dull. Academy Award for *Lilies of the Field*. Married actress Joanna Shimkus (1943–) in 1976 after the couple had lived together for six years: his second marriage. Also Oscarnominated for *The Defiant Ones*.

1949: From Whence Cometh My Help. 1950: No Way Out. 1951: Cry the Beloved Country. 1952: Red Ball Express. 1954: Go Man Go! 1955: Blackboard Jungle. 1956: Goodbye My Lady. Edge of the City (GB: A Man is Ten Feet Tall). 1957: Band of Angels. 1958: Something of Value. Mark of the Hawk. The Defiant Ones. Virgin Island/Our Virgin Island. 1959: Porgy and Bess. 1960: All the Young Men. 1961: A Raisin in the Sun. Paris Blues. 1962: Pressure Point. 1963: Lilies of the Field. The Long Ships. 1965: The Greatest Story Ever Told. The Bedford Incident. The Slender Thread. A Patch of Blue. 1966: Duel at Diablo. To Sir, with Love. 1967: In the Heat of the Night. Guess Who's Coming to Dinner. 1968: For Love of Ivy. 1969: The Lost Man. 1970: Brother John. They Call Me Mister Tibbs! King: a Filmed Record... Montgomery to

Memphis. 1971: The Organisation. Buck and the Preacher. 1973: A Warm December. 1974: Uptown Saturday Night. The Wilby Conspiracy. 1975: Let's Do It Again. 1977: A Piece of the Action.

As director: 1971: Buck and the Preacher. 1973: A Warm December. 1974: Uptown Saturday Night. 1975: Let's Do It Again. 1977: A Piece of the Action. 1980: Stir Crazy. 1982: Hanky Panky. 1984: Shootout. 1985: Fast Forward.

PORTMAN, Eric 1903-1969

Light-haired British actor with incisive, slightly reedy voice. Rose to stardom in the forties as forthright, hard-headed, occasionally vindictive characters which reflected some of his own Yorkshire bluntness. His image mellowed as he grew into a character actor, but in his last film he was back to his calculating best.

1933: The Girl from Maxim's. 1935: Abdul the Damned. Old Roses. Maria Marten, or: Murder in the Red Barn. Hyde Park Corner. 1936: The Cardinal. The Crimes of Stephen Hawke. Hearts of Humanity. The Prince and the Pauper. 1937: Moonlight Sonata. 1941: 49th Parallel. 1942: Uncensored. One of Our Aircraft is Missing. Squadron Leader X. 1943: We Dive at Dawn. Millions Like Us. Escape to Danger. 1944: A Canterbury Tale. 1945: *The Air Plan (narrator only). Great Day. 1946: Wanted for Murder. Men of Two Worlds. Daybreak (released 1948). 1947: Dear Murderer. The Mark of Cain. 1948: Say it with Flowers (narrator only). Corridor of Mirrors. The Blind Goddess. 1949: The Spider and the Fly. 1950: Cairo Road. 1951: The Magic Box. His Excellency. Painter and Poet (narrator only). 1952: South of Algiers (US: The Golden Mask). 1954: The Colditz Story. 1955: The Deep Blue Sea. 1956: Child in the House. 1957: The Good Companions. 1961: The Naked Edge. 1962: Freud (GB: Freud – the Secret Passion). The Man Who Finally Died. 1963: West 11. 1965: The Bedford Incident. 1966: The Spy with a Cold Nose. The Whisperers. 1967: Assignment to Kill. Deadfall.

POWELL, Dick 1904–1963

American actor with dimpled smile and light, frizzy hair who spent most of the thirties as the baby-faced crooner (most notably teamed

with Ruby Keeler) in Warner Brothers musicals. Seemed washed up in the early forties but then came back (thanks to RKO) as the hero of some tough, hard-hitting and well-made thrillers. A TV regular from 1952 to 1962 in his own drama series. Married to Joan Blondell (second of three) from 1936 to 1945 and June Allyson (both *qv*) from 1945 on. Died from cancer.

1931: Street Scene. 1932: Big City Blues (voice only). Too Busy to Work. Blessed Event. 1933: The King's Vacation. Convention City. 42nd Street. Gold Diggers of 1933. College Coach (GB: Football Coach). Footlight Parade. 1934: Twenty Million Sweethearts. Dames. Flirtation Walk. Happiness Ahead. Wonder Bar. 1935: Gold Diggers of 1935. Broadway Gondolier. Shipmates Forever. Page Miss Glory. A Midsummer Night's Dream. 1936: Stage Struck. Colleen. Hearts Divided. Gold Diggers of 1937. 1937: On the Avenue. Varsity Show. The Singing Marine. Hollywood Hotel. 1938: Cowboy from Brooklyn (GB: Romance and Rhythm). *For Auld Lang Syne. Going Places. Hard to Get. 1939: Naughty But Nice. 1940: Christmas in July. I Want a Divorce. 1941: In the Navy. Model Wife. 1942: Star Spangled Rhythm. Happy Go Lucky. 1943: Riding High (GB: Melody Inn). True to Life. 1944: It Happened Tomorrow. Meet the People. 1945: Murder, My Sweet (GB: Farewell, My Lovely). Cornered. 1947: Johnny O'Clock. 1948: Pitfall. To the Ends of the Earth. Station West. Rogues' Regiment. 1949: Mrs Mike. 1950: The Reformer and the Redhead. Right Cross. 1951: Cry Danger. The Tall Target. You Never Can Tell (GB: You Never Know). Callaway Went Thataway (GB: The Star Said No). 1952: The Bad and the Beautiful. 1954: Susan Slept Here.

As director: 1953: Split Second. 1956: The Conqueror. You Can't Run Away from It. 1957: The Enemy Below. 1958: The Hunters.

POWELL, Eleanor 1910–1982

Dark-haired American musical star with a happy face. Eleanor Powell was the only female dancer, according to Fred Astaire, who 'put 'em down like a man'. Billed at the time as 'the world's greatest tap dancer', her fast and gutsy dancing looked relaxed and effortless, and she had a run of eight years at M-G-M. Religion later took over her life, and

she became an ordained minister of the Unity Church. Married to Glenn Ford from 1943 to 1959. Died from cancer.

1934: George White's Scandals. 1935: Broadway Melody of 1936. 1936: Born to Dance. 1937: Rosalie. Broadway Melody of 1938. 1939: Honolulu. Broadway Melody of 1940. 1941: Lady Be Good. 1942: Ship Ahoy. 1943: I Dood It (GB: By Hook or By Crook). Thousands Cheer. 1944: Sensations of 1945. 1950: Duchess of Idaho.

POWELL, Jane (Suzanne Burce) 1929–
Sweet-faced American singing star with bubbly blonde hair, the refreshing teenager who gazed at the hero from afar but eventually got him, in M-G-M musicals of the forties and fifties. Her film career suffered with the demise of the original screen musical.

1944: Song of the Open Road. 1945: Delightfully Dangerous. 1946: Holiday in Mexico. 1948: Three Daring Daughters (GB: The Birds and the Bees). A Date with Judy. Luxury Liner. 1950: Two Weeks with Love. Nancy Goes to Rio. Royal Wedding (GB: Wedding Bells). 1951: Rich, Young and Pretty. 1953: Small Town Girl. Three Sailors and a Girl. 1954: Seven Brides for Seven Brothers. Athena. Deep in My Heart. 1955: Hit the Deck. 1957: The Girl Most Likely. 1958: The Female Animal. Enchanted Island. 1970: Wheeler and Murdoch (TV). 1972: The Letters (TV). 1976: Mayday at 40,000 Feet (TV. GB: cinemas). 1977: Tubby the Tuba (TV. Voice only).

POWELL, Robert 1945–
Charismatic British leading man with striking blue–green eyes and beguilingly modulated

voice, who sprang to prominence in his early twenties (in a TV series, *Doomwatch*) and promised to be one of the few international stars produced by the British cinema of the 1970s. Films cashed in on his other-worldly qualities to cast him in several mystical roles while, for a television epic series, Franco Zeffirelli made him *Jesus of Nazareth*. As for many another actor, the part seems to have cast something of a hoodoo on his career, for there were few box-office successes for him after that.

*1969: The Italian Job. Walk a Crooked Path. 1971: Secrets. 1972: Running Scared. Asylum. The Asphyx (US: Horror of Death). 1974: Mahler. 1975: Tommy. 1977: Beyond Good and Evil. 1978: The Four Feathers (TV. GB: cinemas). Cocktails for Three. The Thirty-Nine Steps. 1979: The Dilessi Affair. Harlequin. 1980: *A Fair Way to Play. Jane Austen in Manhattan (TV). 1981: The Survivor. 1982: The Hunchback of Notre Dame (TV). The Imperative. 1984: The Jigsaw Man. Secrets of the Phantom Caverns.*

POWELL, William 1892–1984
Suave, moustachioed, droop-eyed American leading man who really hit his stride when joining M-G-M in 1934, and became the epitome of the sophisticate with a cigarette in one hand and a cocktail in the other, in a series of smartly scripted detective stories and screwball comedies, most notably the *Thin Man* series opposite oft-time screen vis-a-vis Myrna Loy. Illness unfortunately curtailed his appearances after 1940. Married Carole Lombard 1931–1933, second of three. Was

going to marry Jean Harlow at the time of her death in 1937. He received Academy Award nominations for *The Thin Man*, *My Man Godfrey* and *Life with Father*. Died from respiratory failure.

1922: When Knighthood Was in Flower. Sherlock Holmes (GB: Moriarty). Outcast. 1923: The Bright Shawl. 1924: Romola. Under the Red Robe. Dangerous Money. 1925: White Mice. Too Many Kisses. The Beautiful City. Faint Perfume. My Lady's Lips. 1926: The Runaway. Sea Horses. Beau Geste. The Great Gatsby. Desert Gold. Aloma of the South Seas. Tin Gods. 1927: Special Delivery. New York. Paid to Love. Nevada. She's a Sheik. Time for Love. Senorita. Love's Greatest Mistake. 1928: Partners in Crime. Beau Sabreur. The Dragnet. Forgotten Faces. The Last Command. Feel My Pulse. The Vanishing Pioneer. 1929: The Greene Murder Case. Interference. The Four Feathers. The Canary Murder Case. Charming Sinners. Pointed Heels. 1930: Shadow of the Law. The Benson Murder Case. Street of Chance. Paramount on Parade. Behind the Makeup. For the Defense. 1931: The Road to Singapore. Man of the World. Ladies' Man. 1932: Jewel Robbery. Lawyer Man. High Pressure. One Way Passage. 1933: Private Detective 62. The Kennel Murder Case. Double Harness. 1934: The Key. Fashions of 1934. Manhattan Melodrama. The Thin Man. Evelyn Prentice. 1935: Escapade. Star of Midnight. Reckless. Rendezvous. 1936: My Man Godfrey. The Great Ziegfeld. The Ex Mrs Bradford. After the Thin Man. Libeled Lady. 1937: Double Wedding. The Last of Mrs Cheyney. The Emperor's Candlesticks. 1938: The Baroness and the Butler. 1939: Another Thin Man. 1940: I Love You Again. 1941: Shadow of the Thin Man. Love Crazy. 1942: Crossroads. 1943: The Youngest Profession. 1944: The Thin Man Goes Home. Ziegfeld Follies (released 1946). 1946: The Hoodlum Saint. 1947: Song of the Thin Man. Life with Father. 1948: Mr Peabody and the Mermaid. The Senator Was Indiscreet (GB: Mr Ashton Was Indiscreet). 1949: Take One False Step. Dancing in the Dark. 1951: The Treasure of Lost Canyon. It's a Big Country. 1953: The Girl Who Had Everything. How to Marry a Millionaire. 1955: Mister Roberts.

POWER, Tyrone 1913–1958
One of those seemingly-doomed, Adonis-like

leading men that Hollywood has thrown up from time to time, in a long line from Valentino to Christopher Jones. Dark hair, a flashing smile and boyish handsomeness were enough to send a *frisson* up most pre-war female spines, when Power was equally effective as ne'er-do-wells and dashing heroes. When he returned from war service, his face had hardened into earnestness and gravity and he gradually declined, dying of a heart attack on set – just like his actor father. Married to actresses Annabella (*qv*), from 1939 to 1948, and Linda Christian (Bianca Welter 1932–), from 1949 to 1955 – first and second of three.

1932: Tom Brown of Culver. 1934: Flirtation Walk. 1935: Northern Frontier. 1936: Girls' Dormitory. Ladies in Love. Lloyds of London. 1937: Thin Ice (GB: Lovely to Look At). Love is News. Café Metropole. Second Honeymoon. Ali Baba Goes to Town. 1938: Marie Antoinette. In Old Chicago. Alexander's Ragtime Band. Suez. 1939: Jesse James. The Rains Came. Rose of Washington Square. Daytime Wife. Second Fiddle. 1940: Brigham Young – Frontiersman (GB: Brigham Young). The Mark of Zorro. Johnny Apollo. 1941: Blood and Sand. A Yank in the R.A.F. 1942: This Above All. Son of Fury. The Black Swan. Crash Dive. 1943: *Screen Snapshots No 108. 1946: The Razor's Edge. 1947: Nightmare Alley. Captain from Castile. 1948: That Wonderful Urge. The Luck of the Irish. 1949: Prince of Foxes. 1950: The Black Rose. An American Guerilla in the Philippines (GB: I Shall Return). 1951: Rawhide. The House in the Square (US: I'll Never Forget You). 1952: Diplomatic Courier. Pony Soldier (GB: McDonald of the Canadian Mounties). 1953: King of the Khyber Rifles. *Memories in Uniform. Mississippi Gambler. 1954: The Long Gray Line. 1955: Untamed. 1956: The Eddy Duchin Story. 1957: Seven Waves Away (US: Abandon Ship!). The Rising of the Moon (narrator only). Witness for the Prosecution. The Sun Also Rises.

POWERS, Mala (Mary Ellen Powers) 1931–
Small, solid, petulant-looking American actress with red-brown hair, a sultry star in her first major film, and best employed as strong-willed central characters. Hollywood never made the most of this forte, and, forced into come-hither decoration, her career

declined. A former child player.

1942: Tough As They Come. 1950: Outrage. Edge of Doom (GB: Stronger Than Fear). Cyrano de Bergerac. 1952: Rose of Cimarron. City Beneath the Sea. 1953: City That Never Sleeps. Geraldine. 1954: The Yellow Mountain. 1955: Bengazi. Rage at Dawn. 1957: The Storm Rider. Tammy and the Bachelor (GB: Tammy). Death in Small Doses. The Unknown Terror. Man on the Prowl. 1958: Sierra Baron. Colossus of New York. 1960: Flight of the Lost Balloon. The Warrior's Path (TV). Fear No More. 1967: Rogue's Gallery. Doomsday. 1969: Daddy's Gone a-Hunting. 1975: Six Tickets to Hell. 1976: The Siege (TV).

POWERS, Stefanie (Stefania Federkiewicz) 1942–
Buoyant brunette Hollywood actress with typically American features. She looked to be a rare find in her early days, but went off the boil after marriage and a flop TV series (*The Girl from UNCLE*) came all in one year. Still shows flashes of that original talent, but nowadays much lost to TV rubbish. Married to actor Gary Lockwood (John G. Yusolfsky 1937–) from 1966 to 1974. Later was associated for some years with the late William Holden (*qv*).

1961: Tammy Tell Me True. 1962: The Young Sinner. Experiment in Terror (GB: The Grip of Fear). The Interns. If a Man Answers. 1963: McLintock! Palm Springs Weekend. 1964: The New Interns. Love Has Many Faces. 1965: Fanatic (US: Die, Die, My Darling). 1966: Stagecoach. 1967: Warning Shot. 1969: Crescendo. Man Without Mercy (later Gone With the West). Lancer (TV). 1970: The Boatniks. 1971: Ellery Queen: Don't Look Behind You (TV). Five Desperate Women (TV). Sweet Sweet Rachel (TV). Paper Man (TV). 1972: The Magnificent Seven Ride! No Place to Run (TV). Hardcase (TV). 1973: Herbie Rides Again. Shoot-Out in a One-Dog Town (TV). 1974: Manhunter (TV). Night Games (TV). 1975: Sky Heist (TV). 1976: The Feather and Father Gang (TV). Return to Earth (TV). The Man Inside. It Seemed Like a Good Idea at the Time. 1977: The Astral Factor. 1978: Escape to Athena. Death in Canaan (TV). Nowhere to Run (TV). 1979: Hart to Hart (TV). 1984: Mistral's Daughter (Video). Family Secrets (TV). Invisible Strangler (revised version of The Astral Factor). 1985: Deceptions (TV).

PRENTISS, Paula (P. Ragusa) 1939–
Gorgeous, tall, gurgle-voiced, dark-haired American actress, adept from an early age at sophisticated comedy. She seemed quite the best thing to have hit Hollywood screens in the early sixties, but unfortunately subordinated her career to that of her husband Richard Benjamin (married 1960) and has not succeeded in re-establishing herself.

1960: Where the Boys Are. 1961: The Honeymoon Machine. Bachelor in Paradise. 1962: The Horizontal Lieutenant. 1963: Follow the Boys. 1964: Looking for Love. Man's Favorite Sport? The World of Henry Orient. 1965: What's New Pussycat? In Harm's Way. 1970: Catch 22. Move. 1972: Last of the Red Hot Lovers. The Couple Takes a Wife (TV). 1974: Crazy Joe. The Parallax View. The Stepford Wives. 1977: Having Babies II (TV). 1978: No Room to Run. 1979: Top of the Hill (TV). Friendships, Secrets and Lies (TV). 1980: The Black Marble. Lady Doctor (TV). 1981: Buddy Buddy. Saturday the 14th. 1982: El orgasmo y el extasis. 1983: Packin' It In (TV). MADD: Mothers Against Drunk Drivers (TV).

PRESLE, Micheline (M. Chassagne) 1922–
Light-haired French actress with Claudette Colbert-style personality, in films as a teenager. Briefly but unhappily in Hollywood in post-war years, she has shown up best as older women and is still busy in the French cinema more than 40 years after her debut. Billed as 'Prelle' on her three Hollywood films.

1938: †Je Chante. †Vous seule que j'aime.

†*Petite peste. 1939: Jeunes filles en détresse. Paradis perdu. Fausse alerte. 1940: Lé comedie du bonheur. Elles étaient douze femmes. 1941: Parade en sept nuits. Le soleil a toujours raison. Histoire de rire. 1942: La nuit fantastique. Félicie Nanteuil. La belle aventure. 1943: Un seul amour. 1944: Falbalas. 1945: Boule de suif. 1946: Le diable au corps. 1947: Les jeux sont faits. The Last Days of Pompeii. 1948: Tous les chemins mènent à Rome. 1949: Under My Skin. 1950: An American Guerilla in the Philippines (GB: I Shall Return). The Adventures of Captain Fabian. 1952: La dame aux camélias. 1953: Si Versailles m'était conté (US: Royal Affairs at Versailles). L'amour d'une femme. 1954: Casa Ricordi. Napoléon. Les amants de la Villa Borghese. Les impures. Camille. 1955: Treize à table. Béatrice Cenci. 1956: La mariée est trop belle (GB and US: The Bride is Too Beautiful). 1957: Les louves. Les femmes sont marrantes. Le château des amants. 1958: Bobosse. Christine. 1959: Une fille pour l'été (US: A Mistress for the Summer). Blind Date (US: Chance Meeting). 1960: Mistress of the World/Il mistero dei tre continenti. Le baron de l'écluse. 1961: L'amant de cinq jours. Les grandes personnes. L'assassino. I briganti Italiani (GB: Seduction of the South). The Seven Deadly Sins. Infidelity. La loi des hommes. 1962: The Devil and the 10 Commandments. If a Man Answers. Coup de bambou. 1963: The Prize. Imperial Venus. Dark Purpose. 1964: Les pieds nickelés. 1965: La religieuse. Je vous salue Mafia (US: Hail Mafia). La chasse à l'homme. 1966: King of Hearts. 1968: To Be a Crook. 1969: Le bal du compte d'orgei. Le clair de terre. 1970: Peau d'âne (GB: Once Upon a Time. US: The Magic Donkey). 1971: The Legend of Frenchie King/Les pétroleuses. Il diavolo nel cervello. L'événement le plus important depuis que l'homme a marché sur la lune (GB: The Slightly Pregnant Man). 1973: L'oiseau rare. Eulalie quitte les champs (US: The Star, the Orphan and the Butcher). Mords pas, on t'aime. 1974: La preda. Deux grandes filles danse un pyjama. 1975: Trompe l'oeil. 1976: Le diable dans la boîte. Néa (GB: A Young Emmanuelle). 1978: Va voir, Maman, Papa travaille. La couleur du temps. On efface tout. 1979: S'il vous plaît la mer. Je tetiens, tu me tiens par La Barbichette. 1980: La tête à ça. 1983: Thieves After Dark. 1984: Le chien. Les fausses confidences. 1986: Poulet roti.

PRESLEY, Elvis 1935–1977

Dark, insolent-looking American idol who took the world, especially the teenage public, by storm in the mid-fifties and remained the world's top-selling record star for well over a decade. Nicknamed 'Elvis the Pelvis' because of his hip-swivelling gyrations on stage – but films only rarely caught the electric arrogance that set audiences alight. At first he revealed some talent for wacky comedy, but as the sixties progessed, both man and films got duller and duller. The end came from drugs and a heart attack.

1956: Love Me Tender. 1957: Loving You. Jailhouse Rock. 1958: King Creole. 1960: Flaming Star. GI Blues. 1961: Wild in the

Country. Blue Hawaii. Follow That Dream. 1962: Kid Galahad. Girls! Girls! Girls! 1963: Fun in Acapulco. It Happened at the World's Fair. 1964: Kissin' Cousins. Roustabout. Viva Las Vegas (GB: Love in Las Vegas). 1965: Girl Happy. Tickle Me. Harum Scarum (GB: Harem Holiday). 1966: Frankie and Johnny. Spinout (GB: California Holiday). Paradise – Hawaiian Style. 1967: Easy Come, Easy Go. Double Trouble. Clambake. 1968: Stay Away, Joe. Speedway. Live a Little, Love a Little. 1969: Charro. Change of Habit. The Trouble with Girls – and How to Get into It. 1970: Elvis – That's the Way It is. 1972: Elvis on Tour. 1981: This is Elvis.

PRESTON, Robert (R.P. Meservey) 1917– Handsome, dark, often moustachioed, solidly-built American actor, much confused with Preston Foster in his earlier days, when he was with Paramount for 12 useful years without quite becoming a big star, getting the girl in B features, and losing her in As. He always looked about 35, and still did when he returned to films in triumph in the sixties after phenomenal musical success as star of Broadway's *The Music Man*. Married to actress Catherine Craig (Kay Feltus 1918–) since 1940.

1938: King of Alcatraz (GB: King of the Alcatraz). Illegal Traffic. 1939: Union Pacific. Disbarred. Beau Geste. 1940: North West Mounted Police. Moon over Burma. Typhoon. 1941: The Lady from Cheyenne. New York Town. The Night of January 16th. Parachute Battalion. 1942: Wake Island. This Gun for Hire. Pacific Blackout. Star Spangled Rhythm. Reap the Wild Wind. 1943: Night Plane from

Chungking. 1947: Variety Girl. The Macomber Affair. Wild Harvest. 1948: Blood on the Moon. Big City. 1949: Whispering Smith. The Lady Gambles. Tulsa. The Sundowners (GB: Thunder in the Dust). 1951: My Outlaw Brother. When I Grow Up. Cloudburst. Best of the Badmen. 1952: Face to Face. 1955: The Last Frontier. 1956: Made in Heaven (TV). Sentinels in the Air (narrator only). 1960: The Dark at the Top of the Stairs. 1961: The Music Man. 1962: How the West Was Won. 1963: Island of Love. All the Way Home. 1972: Junior Bonner. Child's Play. 1974: Mame. 1975: My Father's House (TV). 1977: Semi-Tough. 1979: The Chisholms (TV). 1981: SOB. 1982: Victor/Victoria. Rehearsal for Murder (TV). 1983: September Gun (TV). 1984: Finnegan Begin Again (GB: TV). The Last Starfighter. 1986: Outrage! (TV).

PRICE, Dennis (Dennistoun Rose-Price) 1915–1973
Smooth, devious-looking British actor whose aristocratic charmers were often rotten to the core. When his leading-man career fell away in the fifties, there was a failed suicide bid, but he came back to play a series of sometimes dramatic, sometimes comic characters whose credentials were usually as fake as their smile and old school tie. Died from heart failure.

*1944: A Canterbury Tale. 1945: A Place of One's Own. The Echo Murders. 1946: Caravan. Hungry Hill. The Magic Bow. 1947: Jassy. Holiday Camp. Master of Bankdam. Dear Murderer. Easy Money. The White Unicorn (US: Bad Sister). 1948: Snowbound. Good Time Girl. The Bad Lord Byron. 1949: Kind Hearts and Coronets. Helter Skelter. The Lost People. 1950: The Dancing Years. Murder without Crime. The Adventurers (US: The Great Adventure). 1951: The Magic Box. The House in the Square (US: I'll Never Forget You). Lady Godiva Rides Again. 1952: Song of Paris (US: Bachelor in Paris). Tall Headlines. 1953: Noose for a Lady. Murder at 3 a.m. The Intruder. 1954: Time is My Enemy. For Better, For Worse (US: Cocktails in the Kitchen). 1955: Oh Rosalinda!! *Account Closed. That Lady. 1956: Private's Progress. Charley Moon. Port Afrique. A Touch of the Sun. 1957: Fortune is a Woman (US: She Played with Fire). The Naked Truth (US: Your Past is Showing). 1958: Hello London. 1959: Danger Within (US: Breakout). Don't Panic Chaps! I'm All Right, Jack. 1960: Piccadilly Third*

Stop. The Millionairess. The Pure Hell of St Trinian's. School for Scoundrels. Oscar Wilde. Tunes of Glory. No Love for Johnnie. 1961: Five Golden Hours. The Rebel (US: Call Me Genius). Watch It Sailor! Double Bunk. What a Carve Up! (US: No Place like Homicide). Victim. 1962: The Amorous Prawn. Go to Blazes. Play It Cool. The Pot Carriers. *Behave Yourself. Kill or Cure. The Cool Mikado. The Wrong Arm of the Law. 1963: Doctor in Distress. Tamahine. The Comedy Man. The VIPs. A Jolly Bad Fellow. The Horror of It All. The Cracksman. 1964: The Earth Dies Screaming. Murder Most Foul. Curse of Simba (US: Curse of the Voodoo). 1965: Ten Little Indians. A High Wind in Jamaica. 1966: Just Like a Woman. 1967: Rocket to the Moon (US: Those Fantastic Flying Fools). 1969: The Magic Christian. The Haunted House of Horror (US: Horror House). 1970: Some Will, Some Won't. †Count Downe. Venus in Furs. The Horror of Frankenstein. The Rise and Rise of Michael Rimmer. 1971: Vampyros Lesbos. Twins of Evil. 1972: Pulp. Tower of Evil (US: Horror of Snape Island). Alice's Adventures in Wonderland. That's Your Funeral. Go for a Take. The Adventures of Barry McKenzie. 1973: Horror Hospital. Theatre of Blood.

† unreleased

PRICE, Vincent 1911–

Tall, handsome but faintly shifty-looking American actor. That slight sneer got him cast in some good forties roles as untrustworthy associates, with a couple of rich accounts of ham actors thrown in. But he was never quite a top-of-the-cast man until he settled into horror films, and became known as the Master of Menace, although in truth he rarely seemed in earnest and one was sure there was just a big old softie behind the demonic scowl. Also a cookery and art expert. Married (third) Coral Browne (1913–   ).

1938: Service De Luxe. 1939: The Private Lives of Elizabeth and Essex. Tower of London. The Invisible Man Returns. 1940: The House of Seven Gables. Green Hell. Brigham Young–Frontiersman (GB: Brigham Young). Hudson's Bay. 1943: The Song of Bernadette. 1944: Wilson. The Eve of St Mark. Laura. The Keys of the Kingdom. 1945: A Royal Scandal (GB: Czarina). Leave Her to Heaven. 1946:

Dragonwyck. Shock. 1947: Moss Rose. The Long Night. The Web. 1948: Abbott and Costello Meet Frankenstein (Voice only. GB: Abbott and Costello Meet the Ghosts). Up in Central Park. Rogues' Regiment. The Three Musketeers. 1949: Bagdad. The Bribe. Curtain Call at Cactus Creek (GB: Take the Stage). 1950: Baron of Arizona. Champagne for Caesar. The Adventures of Captain Fabian. 1951: His Kind of Woman. Pictura: An Adventure in Art. 1952: The Las Vegas Story. 1953: House of Wax. Casanova's Big Night. 1954: The Mad Magician. Dangerous Mission. 1955: Son of Sinbad. *The Story of Colonel Drake. 1956: Serenade. The Ten Commandments. While the City Sleeps. Forbidden Area (TV). 1957: The Story of Mankind. Lone Woman (TV). The Clouded Image (TV). 1958: The Fly. The House on Haunted Hill. 1959: The Bat. The Big Circus. The Tingler. Return of the Fly. 1960: House of Usher (GB: The Fall of the House of Usher). 1961: Master of the World. The Pit and the Pendulum. Nefertite, regina del Nilo (GB and US: Queen of the Nile). Gordon il pirata nero (GB: The Black Buccaneer. US: Rage of the Buccaneer). The Last Man on Earth. Naked Terror (narrator only). 1962: Convicts Four (GB: Reprieve!). Tales of Terror. Tower of London (remake). Confessions of an Opium Eater (GB: Evils of Chinatown). The Raven. 1963: Comedy of Terrors. Twice Told Tales. Diary of a Madman. *Chagall (narrator only). Beach Party. Taboos of the World (narrator only. GB: Tabu). The Haunted Palace. 1964: The Masque of the Red Death. 1965: City under the Sea (US: War Gods of the Deep). Dr Goldfoot and the Bikini Machine (GB: Dr G and the Bikini Machine). The Tomb of Ligeia. 1966: Dr Goldfoot and the Girl Bombs (GB: Dr G and the Love Bomb). 1967: House of 1,000 Dolls. The Jackals. 1968: Witchfinder General (US: The Conqueror Worm). More Dead Than Alive. 1969: The Trouble with Girls . . . and How to Get into It. The Oblong Box. Scream and Scream Again. Cry of the Banshee. 1971: The Abominable Dr Phibes. What's a Nice Girl Like You. . . .? 1972: The Aries Computer. Dr Phibes Rises Again. 1973: Theatre of Blood. 1974: Percy's Progress. Madhouse. 1976: The Butterfly Ball (narrator only). Journey into Fear. 1978: Days of Fury (narrator only). 1979: Scavenger Hunt. 1980: The Monster Club. 1981: The Thief and the Cobbler (voice only). 1982: House of the Long Shadows. 1983: Blood Bath at the House of Death. *Michael Jackson's Thriller (V). Praying Mantis (TV. American prologue only). 1986: From a Whisper to a Scream.

PROVINE, Dorothy 1937–

Fizzy, impish, pinch-cheeked Hollywood blonde (originally from Deadwood City of Calamity Jane fame), who started in leading roles and enjoyed great success as the Charleston-dancing nightclub entertainer in the television series The Roaring Twenties. She seemed to grow more subdued and less interesting in the 1960s, and her career did not progress. Little seen after 1970.

1958: The Bonnie Parker Story. Live Fast, Die Young. 1959: Riot in Juvenile Prison. The 30-

Foot Bride of Candy Rock. 1963: It's a Mad, Mad, Mad, Mad World. Wall of Noise. 1964: Good Neighbor Sam. 1965: That Darn Cat! The Great Race. One Spy Too Many (TV. GB: cinemas). 1966: Kiss the Girls and Make Them Die. 1967: Who's Minding the Mint? Never a Dull Moment. 1968: The Sound of Anger (TV).

PRYCE, Jonathan 1947–

Offbeat British leading man with a scruff of dark hair; his long face can be mournful or menacing at a rearrangement of the mouth and his handful of film appearances to date have been an extraordinary assortment of leads in big films, guest spots and bad guys of one kind or another. His preference for the stage has kept him from being internationally well known on the big screen, but the man has such unusual presence that it could still happen.

1976: Voyage of the Damned. 1979: Breaking Glass. Loophole. 1982: Murder is Easy/Agatha Christie's Murder is Easy (TV). Something Wicked This Way Comes. 1983: The Ploughman's Lunch. 1984: Brazil. 1985: The Doctor and the Devils. 1986: Haunted Honeymoon.

PRYOR, Richard 1940–

American night-club comedian, a black Lenny Bruce, who toned down his style to find success in commercial Hollywood films, tried drama without too much effect and showed the world his old scathing and scatological self in films of his night-club material. Hasn't yet realized his full potential for the cinema.

1966: The Busy Body. 1968: ‡The Green

Berets. Wild in the Streets. 1969: The Phynx. The Young Lawyers (TV). 1970: Carter's Army (TV). 1971: Dynamite Chicken. You've Got to Walk It Like You Talk It Or You'll Lose That Beat. Richard Pryor – Live and Smokin'. 1972: Lady Sings the Blues. 1973: Hit! The Mack. Wattstax. Some Call It Loving. 1974: Uptown Saturday Night. 1975: Adios Amigo. 1976: The Bingo Long Traveling All-Stars and Motor Kings. Car Wash. Silver Streak. 1977: Greased Lightning. Which Way Is Up? 1978: The Wiz. The Muppet Movie. Blue Collar. California Suite. 1979: Richard Pryor Live in Concert. In God We Trust. 1980: Wholly Moses! Stir Crazy. 1981: Bustin' Loose. Some Kind of Hero. 1982: Richard Pryor Live on The Sunset Strip. The Toy. 1983: Superman III. †Richard Pryor Here and Now. 1984: Brewster's Millions. 1985: †Jo Jo Dancer. 1986: Critical Condition.

‡ As Richard 'Cactus' Pryor
† And directed

PURDOM, Edmund 1924–

No more handsome leading man came to Hollywood than this tall, dark Briton, but his rather stiff personality was all at sea in the silly costume epics they gave him, after a much-publicized leap to stardom when Mario Lanza walked out on The Student Prince. He offered his best performances later on, in modern dress, as characters of dubious ethics, but

there were more frivolities both before and after. Later lived and worked in Italy.

1953: Titanic. Julius Caesar. 1954: The Student Prince. Athena. The Egyptian. 1955: The Prodigal. The King's Thief. 1956: Strange Intruder. 1957: Agguato in Tangeri (GB: Ambush in Tangiers. US: Trapped in Tangiers). 1959: Herod the Great. The Cossacks. Salambò (US: The Loves of Salambo). 1960: Nights of Rasputin. Moment of Danger (US: Malaga). The Last of the Vikings (GB: Fury of the Vikings). 1961: La Fayette. L'ammutinamento (GB and US: White Slave Ship). Nefertite, regina del Nilo (GB and US: Queen of the Nile). Suleiman the Conqueror. 1963: The Comedy Man. 1964: The Beauty Jungle (US: Contest Girl). Last Ride to Santa Cruz. The Charge of the 7th. The Yellow Rolls Royce. 1965: L'uomo che ride (GB: The Man with the Golden Mask). 1967: The Black Corsair. 1968: Crisantemi per un branco di carogne. Piluk il Timido. 1969: The Queer ... the Erotic (narrator only). GB: The Satanists). Naked England (narrator only). 1970: Naked and Violent (narrator only). 1971: Evil Fingers. 1973: L'onorata famiglia (uccidere è cosa nostra). Frankenstein's Castle of Freaks. 1975: Night Child. The Cursed Medallion. 1977: Il padrone della città/Mister Scarface. 1978: The New Godfathers. 1980: Sophia Loren: Her Own Story (TV). 1981: Greed. Absurd. L'altra donna. 1982: Ator the Fighting Eagle. Pieces. 1983: The Mystery of Gaudo and Mata-

pan. The Scarlet and the Black (TV). 1984: †Don't Open Until Christmas. After the Fall of New York. The Assisi Underground. 1985: Killer vs Killer. Fracchio contro Dracula.

† And directed

PURVIANCE, Edna 1894–1958

Girlish, happy-looking, fair-haired American actress, plump by today's standards, who was discovered by Charlie Chaplin and appeared exclusively in his films. His attempt to make her a world star with the 1923 A Woman of Paris was a disaster.

1915: A Night Out. The Champion. In the Park. A Jitney Elopement. The Tramp. By the Sea. Work. A Woman. The Bank. Carmen/Charlie Chaplin's Burlesque on Carmen. A Night in the Show. Shanghaied. 1916: Police. The Fireman. The Floorwalker. The Vagabond. The Count. The Pawn Shop. The Rink. Behind the Screen. 1917: Easy Street. The Cure. The Immigrant. The Adventurer. 1918: Triple Trouble. A Dog's Life. *How To Make Movies. †Shoulder Arms. Liberty Loan Appeal/Charles Chaplin in a Liberty Loan Appeal. 1919: Sunnyside. A Day's Pleasure. 1920: †The Kid. 1921: The Idle Class. 1922: Pay Day. 1923: †The Pilgrim. †A Woman of Paris. 1926: ‡A Woman of the Sea. †The Seagull. L'education du prince. 1947: †Monsieur Verdoux. 1952: †Limelight.

All shorts except †features
‡ Unreleased

QUAID, Dennis 1954–

Dark-haired, young-looking American actor with jaunty smile and breezy, relaxed personality. The brother of character star Randy Quaid (1948–), he came slowly through to leading roles, but his portrayal of the cocky Gordon Cooper in *The Right Stuff* made his features more familiar, and he was an above-the-title star by the mid-1980s.
1975: Crazy Mama. 1977: 9/30/55 (GB: TV, as 30 September, 1955). 1978: Amateur Night at the Dixie Bar and Grill (TV). Seniors. Our Winning Season. 1979: GORP. Breaking Away. 1980: The Long Riders. 1981: All Night Long. Caveman. The Night the Lights Went Out in Georgia. Bill (TV). 1982: Johnny Belinda (TV). Tough Enough/Tough Dreams. 1983: Jaws 3-D. The Right Stuff. Dreamscape (released 1985). Bill: On His Own (TV). 1985: Enemy Mine. Nothing But the Truth. 1986: The Big Easy.

QUAYLE, Sir Anthony 1913–

Distinguished British stage actor with rounded cheeks, friendly smile, light, curly hair and determined gaze. At 42 he quite unexpectedly became a star of the cinema as well, revealing a pleasing personality that was most seen within men of action, but was adaptable to any kind of role. Character roles in the 1970s were less successful, but he won renewed plaudits on stage. Married to actress Dorothy Hyson (1915–), his second wife. Won an Emmy for 1974's *QB VII*. Nominated for an Oscar for *Anne of the 1,000 Days*. Knighted in 1985.
*1935: Moscow Nights (US: I Stand Con-demned). 1938: Pygmalion. 1948: Hamlet. Saraband for Dead Lovers (US: Saraband). 1955: Oh Rosalinda!! 1956: The Battle of the River Plate (US: Pursuit of the Graft Spee). The Wrong Man. 1957: Woman in a Dressing Gown. No Time for Tears. 1958: The Man Who Wouldn't Talk. Ice Cold in Alex (US: Desert Attack). 1959: Tarzan's Greatest Adventure. Serious Charge (US: A Touch of Hell). 1960: The Challenge. 1961: The Guns of Navarone. *Drums for a Queen (narrator only). 1962: HMS Defiant (US: Damn the Defiant!). *This is Lloyd's (narrator only). Lawrence of Arabia. 1963: The Fall of the Roman Empire. 1964: East of Sudan. 1965: Operation Crossbow (US: The Great Spy Mission). A Study in Terror (US: Fog). 1966: The Poppy is Also a Flower (TV. GB: cinemas as Danger Grows Wild). 1967: Incompreso (GB and US: Misunderstood). 1968: Mackenna's Gold. 1969: Destiny of a Spy (TV). *Island Unknown (narrator only). Before Winter Comes. 1970: Anne of the 1,000 Days. 1972: Everything You Always Wanted to Know About Sex **But Were Afraid to Ask. 1973: Bequest to the Nation. Jarrett (TV). 1974: The Tamarind Seed. QB VII (TV). 1975: Moses. Great Expectations (TV. GB: cinemas). 1976: The Eagle Has Landed. 21 Hours at Munich (TV. GB: cinemas). 1977: Holocaust 2000 (US: The Chosen). 1978: Sherlock Holmes: Murder by Decree (GB: Murder by Decree). 1980: The Antagonists. 1981: Dial M for Murder (TV). The Manions of America (TV). 1984: The Last Days of Pompeii (TV).*

QUINLAN, Kathleen 1952–

Well, how could I leave out Kathleen (no relation, alas)? This young-looking, dark-haired American actress's moist-eyed appeal got her cast as religious figures and girls in peril of the mind, body and spirit. Her all-stops-out emotional performances won her critical praise in the late 1970s, but she has not become a box-office bet. An all-round athlete, her earliest ambition was to compete in the Olympic Games … but acting intervened.
1972: †One is a Lonely Number. 1973: †American Graffiti. 1974: The Abduction of St Anne/They've Kidnapped Anne Benedict (TV). Lucas Tanner (TV). Where Have All the People Gone? (TV). The Missing Are Deadly (TV). Can Ellen Be Saved? (TV). Judgment Day (TV). 1976: Lifeguard. 1977: Little Ladies of the Night (TV). Airport 77. I Never Promised You a Rose Garden. 1978: The Promise. 1979: The Runner Stumbles. 1980: Les séducteurs/Sunday Lovers. 1981: She's in the Army Now (TV). 1982: Hanky Panky. 1983: Restless/Independence Day. The Twilight Zone (GB: Twilight Zone The Movie). Hakkoref ha' acharon (US: The Last Winter). 1984: When She Says No (TV). 1985: Blackout. Warning Sign. Children of the Night (TV). 1986: The Tuscaloosan.

†As Kathy Quinlan

QUINN, Anthony 1915–

Flamboyant, dark-haired Mexican-born actor, who played Indians and scowling Dago bad guys until his second Oscar, for *Lust for Life* (the first was for *Viva Zapata!*), since when he has lived that title to the hilt playing any number of earth-loving characters of widely varying nationalities. Married (first of two) to actress Katherine DeMille (K. Lester 1911–) from 1937 to 1965. Additional Oscar nominations for *Wild Is the Wind* and *Zorba the Greek*.
1936: The Milky Way. Parole! Sworn Enemy. Night Waitress. The Plainsman. 1937: Swing High, Swing Low. Waikiki Wedding. Daughter of Shanghai (GB: Daughter of the Orient). Last Train from Madrid. Partners in Crime. 1938: The Buccaneer. Tip Off Girls. Dangerous to Know. Bulldog Drummond in Africa. Hunted Men. King of Alcatraz (GB: King of the Alcatraz). 1939: Island of Lost Men. King of Chinatown. Union Pacific. Television Spy.

1940: Road to Singapore. Parole Fixer. Emergency Squad. City for Conquest. The Ghost Breakers. 1941: Thieves Fall Out. Knockout. Texas Rangers Ride Again. Blood and Sand. Bullets for O'Hara. They Died with Their Boots On. The Perfect Snob. 1942: The Black Swan. Road to Morocco. The Ox-Bow Incident (GB: Strange Incident). Larceny Inc. 1943: Guadalcanal Diary. 1944: Buffalo Bill. Roger Touhy, Gangster (GB: The Last Gangster). Ladies of Washington. Irish Eyes Are Smiling. 1945: Where Do We Go from Here? China Sky. Back to Bataan. 1946: California. The Imperfect Lady (GB: Mrs Loring's Secret). 1947: Sinbad the Sailor. Black Gold. Tycoon. 1951: The Brave Bulls. Mask of the Avenger. 1952: Viva Zapata! The World in His Arms. The Brigand. Against All Flags. 1953: City beneath the Sea. Seminole. Ride, Vaquero! East of Sumatra. Blowing Wild. Ulysses. Donne proibite (GB: Forbidden Women. US: Angels of Darkness). Cavalleria Rusticana. Attila the Hun. 1954: La strada. The Long Wait. 1955. The Magnificent Matador (GB: The Brave and the Beautiful). The Naked Street. Seven Cities of Gold. 1956: The Man from Del Rio. Lust for Life. The Wild Party. 1957: The River's Edge. The Ride Back. The Hunchback of Notre Dame. Wild is the Wind. 1958: Hot Spell. 1959: The Black Orchid. Last Train from Gun Hill. Warlock. The Savage Innocents. 1960: Heller in Pink Tights. Portrait in Black. 1961: The Guns of Navarone. Barabbas. 1962: Requiem for a Heavyweight (GB: Blood Money). Lawrence of Arabia. 1964: The Fabulous Adventures of Marco Polo (GB: Marco the Magnificent). Behold a Pale Horse. The Visit. Zorba the Greek. 1965: A High Wind in Jamaica. 1966: Lost Command. 1967: The Rover. The 25th Hour. The Happening. 1968: Guns for San Sebastian. The Shoes of the Fisherman. The Magus. 1969: The Secret of Santa Vittoria. A Dream of Kings. A Walk in the Spring Rain. 1970: RPM. Flap (GB: The Last Warrior). King: a Filmed Record ... Montgomery to Memphis. 1971: Arruza (narrator only). The City (TV). Forbidden Knowledge (TV). 1972: Across 110th Street. The Voice of La Raza (and narrator). 1973: Los amigos (GB and US: Deaf Smith and Johnny Ears). The Don is Dead. 1974: The Marseilles Contract (US: The Destructors). 1975: Bluff. L'eredità Ferramonti (GB: The Inheritance). 1976: Tigers Don't Cry. The Message. 1978: The Greek Tycoon. Caravans. The Children of Sanchez. The Passage. 1980: Lion of of Sanchez. The Passage. 1980: Lion of Desert/Omar Mukhtar – Lion of the Desert. The Contender. 1981: High Risk. The Salamander. Bon Appetit. The Dream of Tangier. 1982: Roma Regina. Valentina. 1984: The Last Days of Pompeii. 1986: Zorba The Musical.

As director: 1958: The Buccaneer.

Mind these Ps and Qs ... Gregory Peck, Anthony Quinn and Anthony Quayle line up for action as Allied saboteurs in 1961's *The Guns of Navarone*.

Reptilian rogues. Edward G. Robinson and George Raft, two of Hollywood's biggest gangster stars, are here on opposite sides of the law (past their prime but as ruthless as ever) in *A Bullet for Joey* (1955).

Ss in the snow. Sylvester Stallone and Talia
Shire in their familiar roles of Rocky and
Adrian, here in *Rocky II* (1979).

Few heroes had a ladye as fayre as Elizabeth
Taylor. Here namesake Robert Taylor looks
set to do battle for her honour in *Ivanhoe*
(1952).

RADFORD, Basil 1897–1952

Amiable, avuncular, moustachioed British actor who looked (and was) a cricket fanatic, a facet of his personality that he put to good use from the late 1930s on, as he and Naunton Wayne (qv) gained great popularity in a series of comedy-thrillers in which they played Charters and Caldicot, Englishmen at large more interested in the Test score than in bodies falling all about them. Died from a heart attack.

*1929: Barnum Was Right. 1932: There Goes the Bride. 1933: A Southern Maid. Just Smith (US: Leave It to Smith). 1936: Broken Blossoms. Dishonour Bright. 1937: Jump for Glory (US: When Thief Meets Thief). Captain's Orders. Young and Innocent (US: The Girl Was Young). 1938: Climbing High. Convict 99. The Lady Vanishes. 1939: Trouble Brewing. Let's Be Famous. The Four Just Men (US: The Secret Four). Spies of the Air. Jamaica Inn. Just William. She Couldn't Say No. Secret Journey (US: Among Human Wolves). The Girl Who Forgot. 1940: Room for Two. The Flying Squad. Night Train to Munich (US: Night Train). Crooks' Tour. The Girl in the News. 1941: *Save Rubber. 1942: *London Scrapbook. Next of Kin. Unpublished Story. Flying Fortress. *Partners in Crime. 1943: Dear Octopus (US: The Randolph Family). Millions Like Us. 1944: Twilight Hour. 1945: The Way to the Stars (US: Johnny in the Clouds). Dead of Night. 1946: Captive Heart. A Girl in a Million. 1948: Quartet. The Winslow Boy. It's Not Cricket. 1949: Helter Skelter. Stop Press Girl. Whisky Galore! (US: Tight Little Island). The Blue*

Lamp. 1950: Chance of a Lifetime. 1951: White Corridors. The Galloping Major.

RAFFERTY, Chips (John Goffage) 1909–1971

Tall, lanky, tanned, light-hearted, hook-nosed Australian actor, no great looker, but for many years a stalwart, and indeed the epitome of the Australian cinema. Made some British and international films, but always returned to Australia, where he ultimately died from a heart attack.

*1939: Ants in His Pants. 1940: Dad Rudd MP. 40,000 Horsemen. 1944: Rats of Tobruk (US: The Fighting Rats of Tobruk). 1946: The Overlanders. 1947: Bush Christmas. The Loves of Joanna Godden. 1948: Eureka Stockade (US: Massacre Hill). 1950: Bitter Springs. 1951: *Australian Diary. 1952: Kangaroo. The Desert Rats. 1953: The Phantom Stockman. 1954: Cattle Station. King of the Coral Sea. 1956: Smiley. Walk into Paradise. 1958: Smiley Gets a Gun. 1959: *Power with Precision (narrator only). 1960: The Sundowners. The Wackiest Ship in the Army. 1962: Mutiny on the Bounty. 1966: They're a Weird Mob. 1967: Double Trouble. Kona Coast. 1969: Skullduggery. 1970: Outback.*

RAFFIN, Deborah 1953–

Tall, fair-haired American actress of 'innocent' looks. The daughter of minor 1940s' star Trudy Marshall (1922–), she leapt from fashion model to film star at 20 and was immediately cast as virginal daughters. She has tried hard to find interesting roles over the years (and once or twice succeeded),

although her acceptance of a role in TV's *Lace 2* made it look as though she might have given up the struggle. Certainly she has led a sporadic acting career to date.

1973: Forty Carats. 1974: The Dove. Once is Not Enough/Jacqueline Susann's Once is Not Enough. 1976: Nightmare in Badham County (TV). The Sentinel. 1977: Deadly Encounters. Demon/God Told Me To. Maniac/Assault on Paradise. 1978: Ski-Lift to Death (TV). How to Pick Up Girls! (TV). 1979: Willa (TV). 1980: Touched by Love. 1981: Haywire (TV). Mind Over Murder (TV). 1982: Dance of the Dwarfs. 1983: Sparkling Cyanide/Agatha Christie's Sparkling Cyanide (TV). 1984: The Predator. 1985: Death Wish 3.

RAFT, George (G. Rauft) 1895–1980

Silken-smooth, narrow-eyed, rather menacing American actor who slipped from a somewhat dubious background as consort of criminals and night-club dancers to portray criminals and dancers on screen. Dark hair slicked down, he glided lizard-like through both guises, but it was gangster roles that won him most public favour and he played thriller leads until he was 60. Died from leukaemia.

1929: Queen of the Night Clubs. 1931: Goldie. Quick Millions. Hush Money. Palmy Days. 1932: Night World. Dancers in the Dark. Night After Night. Scarface. Madame Racketeer (GB: The Sporting Widow). If I Had a Million. Undercover Man. Taxi. Love is a Racket. 1933: The Bowery. Pick Up. Midnight Club. 1934: The Trumpet Blows. All of Me. Bolero. Limehouse Blues. 1935: Rumba. The Glass Key. She Couldn't Take It. Every Night at Eight. Stolen Harmony. 1936: It Had to Happen. Yours for the Asking. 1937: Souls at Sea. 1938: You and Me. Spawn of the North. The Lady's from Kentucky. 1939: Each Dawn I Die. I Stole a Million. Invisible Stripes. 1940: The House Across the Bay. They Drive by Night (GB: The Road to Frisco). 1941: Manpower. 1942: Broadway. 1943: Background to Danger. Stage Door Canteen. 1944: Follow the Boys. 1945: Nob Hill. Johnny Angel. 1946: Whistle Stop. Mr Ace. Nocturne. 1947: Christmas Eve. Intrigue. 1948: Race Street. 1949: Outpost in Morocco. Johnny Allegro (GB: Hounded). Nous irons à Paris (GB: Let's Go to Paris). A Dangerous Profession. Red Light. 1951: Lucky Nick Cain (GB: I'll Get You for This). 1952: Loan Shark. Adventure in Algiers/Secret of the

Casbah (released 1954). Escape Route (US: I'll Get You). 1953: Man from Cairo (GB: Crime Squad). 1954: Rogue Cop. Black Widow. 1955: A Bullet for Joey. 1956: Around the World in 80 Days. 1959: Jet over the Atlantic. Some Like It Hot. 1960: Ocean's Eleven. 1961: The Ladies' Man. 1964: The Patsy. For Those Who Think Young. 1965: Du rififi à Paname (GB: Rififi in Paris). 1967: Five Golden Dragons. Casino Royale. Madigan's Millions. 1968: Skidoo. †The Silent Treatment. 1972: Hammersmith is Out. Deadhead Miles. 1977: Sextette. 1979: The Man with Bogart's Face.

†*Unreleased*

RAINER, Luise 1909–
Pretty, doll-like brunette Austrian actress with appealingly expressive face and finely pencilled eyebrows. She won two Oscars in consecutive years after coming to America for *The Great Ziegfeld* and *The Good Earth*, after which too much seemed to be expected of her. M-G-M dropped her after only one more year, and one forties' film was her only remaining screen appearance.
1930: Ja, der Himmel über Wien. 1931: Sehnsucht 202. 1933: Heut' kommt's Drauf an. 1935: Escapade. 1936: The Great Ziegfeld. 1937: The Good Earth. The Big City. The Emperor's Candlesticks. 1938: The Great Waltz. The Toy Wife (GB: Frou Frou). Dramatic School. 1943: Hostages.

RAINES, Ella (E. Raubes) 1921–
Beautiful, strong-looking American actress with silky brunette hair, just as adept at resourceful heroines as bitchy mistresses, but not well treated by Hollywood who, after a few interesting roles, only offered her nice girls in dull, mediocre films.
1943: Corvette K-225 (GB: The Nelson Touch). Cry Havoc. 1944: Hail the Conquering Hero. Tall in the Saddle. Phantom Lady. Enter Arsène Lupin. 1945: The Strange Affair of Uncle Harry/Uncle Harry. The Suspect. 1946: The Runaround. White Tie and Tails. 1947: The Web. Time Out of Mind. Brute Force. 1948: The Senator Was Indiscreet (GB: Mr Ashton Was Indiscreet). 1949: A Dangerous Profession. The Walking Hills. Impact. 1950: Singing Guns. The Second Face. 1951: Fighting Coast Guard. 1952: Ride the Man Down. 1956: The Man in the Road.

RAINS, Claude (William C. Rains) 1889–1967
Grey-haired (originally dark), stocky British character star who came to Hollywood in young middle age but stayed to become for more than 15 years one of its very best actors. His smooth, relaxed sophistication could just as easily seem chilly or kindly, his clipped tones were inimitable and he was an unselfish and integral part of some very fine films. Four times nominated for the best supporting actor Oscar, he did not win one. Five times married including (first) actress Isabel Jeans (1892–1985). Died after an intestinal haemorrhage.
*1920: Build Thy House. 1933: The Invisible Man. 1934: Crime without Passion. 1935: The Man Who Reclaimed His Head. The Mystery of Edwin Drood. The Clairvoyant. The Last Outpost. 1936: Hearts Divided. Anthony Adverse. The Prince and the Pauper. Stolen Holiday. 1937: They Won't Forget. 1938: The Adventures of Robin Hood. Gold is Where You Find It. Four Daughters. White Banners. 1939: Daughters Courageous. They Made Me a Criminal. Juarez. Mr Smith Goes to Washington. *Sons of Liberty. Four Wives. 1940: The Sea Hawk. Lady with Red Hair. Saturday's Children. 1941: Four Mothers. The Wolf Man. Here Comes Mr Jordan. Kings Row. 1942: Now, Voyager. Moontide. Casablanca. 1943: Forever and a Day. Phantom of the Opera. 1944: Passage to Marseille. Mr Skeffington. 1945: Caesar and Cleopatra. This Love of Ours. Strange Holiday (GB: The Day After Tomorrow). 1946: Angel on My Shoulder. Deception. Notorious. 1947: The*

Unsuspected. 1949: Rope of Sand. Song of Surrender. The Passionate Friends (US: One Woman's Story). 1950: The White Tower. Where Danger Lives. 1951: Sealed Cargo. 1952: The Man Who Watched Trains Go By (US: Paris Express). 1956: Lisbon. 1957: The Pied Piper of Hamelin (TV. GB: cinemas). 1959: Judgement at Nuremberg (TV). This Earth is Mine. 1960: The Lost World. 1961: Battle of the Worlds. 1962: Lawrence of Arabia. 1963: Twilight of Honor (GB: The Charge is Murder). 1965: The Greatest Story Ever Told.

RALSTON, Vera (V. Hruba) 1919–
Fair-haired (later dark) champion ice-skater from Czechoslovakia, with very Slavic looks – thick lips and even thicker accent – who became an actress and might have done well in sinister roles had she not fallen under the influence of Republic chief Herbert J. Yates, who was determined to groom her as a leading lady (very much a W.R. Hearst–Marion Davies parallel) and eventually married her in 1952. Thus, she was frequently miscast and the public never really took to her.
1941: ‡Ice-Capades. 1942: ‡Ice-Capades Revue (GB: Rhythm Hits the Ice). 1944: †Storm over Lisbon. †Lake Placid Serenade. †The Lady and the Monster (GB: The Lady and the Doctor). 1945: †Dakota. 1946: †Murder in the Music Hall. The Plainsman and the Lady. 1947: The Flame. Wyoming. 1948: I, Jane Doe (GB: Diary of a Bride). Angel on the Amazon (GB: Drums Along the Amazon). 1949: The Fighting Kentuckian. 1950: Surrender. 1951: Belle le Grand. The Wild Blue Yonder (GB: Thunder Across the Pacific). Hoodlum Empire. 1953: A Perilous Journey. Fair Wind to Java. 1954: Jubilee Trail. 1955: Timberjack. 1956: Accused of Murder. 1957: Spoilers of the Forest. Gunfire at Indian Gap. 1958: The Notorious Mr Monks. The Man Who Died Twice.

‡*As Vera Hruba* †*As Vera Hruba Ralston*

RAMPLING, Charlotte 1945–
Tall, rangy British actress, noted in her early career for portraits of passionate decadence and rich bitches. From the mid-seventies, however, her rather harsh features began to project a more sympathic image.
1965: The Knack ... and how to get it. Rotten

to the Core. 1966: Georgy Girl. 1967: The Long Duel. 1968: Sequestro di persona (GB: Island of Crime). Gotterdämmerung/The Damned. 1969: How to Make It (GB: Target: Harry). Three. 1970: †Zabriskie Point. 1971: The Ski Bum. 'Tis Pity She's a Whore. Corky. 1972: Henry VIII and His Six Wives. Asylum. 1973: Zardoz. The Night Porter. 1974: Caravan to Vaccares. La chair de l'orchidée. 1975: Farewell, My Lovely. Foxtrot (later The Other Side of Paradise). 1976: Sherlock Holmes in New York (TV). 1977: Taxi mauve. Orca . . . Killer Whale. 1979: Bugsy. 1980: Stardust Memories. 1982: The Verdict. 1984: Viva la vie. 1985: Tristesse et beauté. On ne meurt que deux fois (GB and US: He Died with His Eyes Open). 1986: Angel Heart.

†Scenes deleted from final release print

RANDALL, Tony (Leonard Rosenberg) 1920–

Dark-haired American comic actor with smooth face and sour mouth. He made no films until his late thirties, then was riotously successful as the lead in satirical comedies at Fox, and as the hero's droll friend in Doris Day fol-de-rols at Universal. After several mediocre mid-sixties films, he disappointingly returned to television.

1957: Will Success Spoil Rock Hunter? (GB: Oh! For a Man!). No Down Payment. Oh, Men! Oh, Women! The Playroom (TV). 1959. The Mating Game. Second Happiest Day (TV). Pillow Talk. 1960: The Adventures of Huckleberry Finn. Let's Make Love. 1961: Lover Come Back. 1962: Boys' Night Out. 1963: Island of Love. 1964: The Seven Faces of Dr Lao. The Brass Bottle. Send Me No

Flowers. 1965: Fluffy. The Alphabet Murders. 1966: Our Man in Marrakesh (US: Bang Bang You're Dead). 1968: Hello Down There. 1972: Everything You Always Wanted to Know About Sex* *But Were Afraid to Ask. 1978: Kate Bliss and the Ticker Tape Kid (TV). Foolin' Around (released 1980). 1979: Scavenger Hunt. 1981: A Girl's Best Friend/Sidney Shorr: A Girl's Best Friend (TV). 1982: The King of Comedy (released 1983). 1985: Hitler's SS: Portrait in Evil (TV. GB: cinemas). 1986: That's Adequate! My Little Pony (voice only).

RANDELL, Ron 1918–

Cheerful-looking Australian leading man with dark, wavy hair who made a strong impression in post-war Australian films before going to Hollywood in 1947 and playing leads in minor features, including such series detectives as Bulldog Drummond and the Lone Wolf. Made his home in Britain for a while, gaining notoriety as a TV panellist who winked at the ladies, before returning to America and small film roles.

1946: Smithy (GB: Southern Cross. US: Pacific Adventure). A Son is Born. 1947: It Had to be You. Bulldog Drummond at Bay. Bulldog Drummond Strikes Back. 1948: The Sign of the Ram. The Loves of Carmen. The Mating of Mille. 1949: Omoo-Omoo (GB: The Shark God). The Lone Wolf and His Lady. Make Believe Ballroom. 1950: Counterspy Meets Scotland Yard. Tyrant of the Sea. 1951: China Corsair. Lorna Doone. 1952: The Brigand. Captive Women. 1953: The Girl on the Pier. 3000 AD. Mississippi Gambler. Kiss Me Kate. 1954: The Triangle. One Just Man. The Yellow Robe. Three Cornered Fate. The Blue Camellia. 1955: Triple Blackmail. Desert Sands. I Am a Camera. 1956: Bermuda Affair. Beyond Mombasa. Count of Twelve. The Hostage. The She-Creature. Quincannon, Frontier Scout (GB: Frontier Scout). 1957: The Story of Esther Costello (US: Golden Virgin). Morning Call (US: The Strange Case of Dr Manning). The Girl in Black Stockings. Davy. Man of the Law (TV. GB: cinemas). 1961: King of Kings. The Most Dangerous Man Alive. The Phoney American (GB: It's a Great Life). 1962: Come Fly with Me. The Longest Day. Gold for the Caesars. 1963: Follow the Boys. 1966: Legend of a Gunfighter. Savage Pampas. 1971: The Seven Minutes. Whity. 1983: Exposed.

RANDLE, Frank (Arthur McEvoy) 1901–1957

Big-nosed, light-haired, abrasive music-hall comedian, fond of disguises and (for their time) rude jokes. Made several low-budget comedies in which one could almost see the cracks in the scenery – but they were immensely popular in his native Lancashire, and didn't do badly elsewhere.

1940: Somewhere in England. 1941: Somewhere in Camp. 1942: Somewhere on Leave. 1943: Somewhere in Civvies. 1945: Home Sweet Home. 1946: *Randle and All That. 1947: When You Come Home. 1948: Holidays with Pay. 1949: Somewhere in Politics. School for Randle. 1953: It's a Grand Life.

RATHBONE, Basil (Philip B. Rathbone) 1892–1967

Suave, sharp-featured, dark-haired, sophisticated British actor, in Hollywood from the late twenties, who proved equally at home with a sword or a witty remark. A sneering dominant villain in thirties' costume pieces, and the screen's best Sherlock Holmes, he spent his latter days in a weird variety of horror films. Died from a heart attack. Nominated for Academy Awards in Romeo and Juliet and If I Were King.

1921: Innocent. The Fruitful Vine. 1923: The Loves of Mary, Queen of Scots. The School for Scandal. 1924: Trouping with Ellen. 1925: The Masked Bride. 1926: The Great Deception. 1929: The Last of Mrs Cheyney. Barnum Was Right. 1930: The Bishop Murder Case. A Notorious Affair. The Lady of Scandal (GB: The High Road). This Mad World. The Flirting Widow. A Lady Surrenders (GB: Blind Wives). Sin Takes a Holiday. 1931: Once a Lady. 1932: A Woman Commands. After the Ball. 1933: One Precious Year. Loyalties. 1935: David Copperfield. Anna Karenina. The Last Days of Pompeii. A Feather in Her Hat. Captain Blood. A Tale of Two Cities. 1936: Kind Lady (GB: House of Menace). Private Number (GB: Secret Interlude). Romeo and Juliet. The Garden of Allah. 1937: Confession. Love from a Stranger. Make a Wish. Tovarich. 1938: The Adventures of Marco Polo. The Adventures of Robin Hood. If I Were King. The Dawn Patrol. 1939: Son of Frankenstein. The Hound of the Baskervilles. The Sun Never Sets. The Adventures of Sherlock Holmes (GB: Sherlock Holmes). Rio. Tower of London. 1940: Rhythm on the River. The Mark of Zorro. The Mad Doctor (GB: A Date with Destiny). 1941: The Black Cat. *Screen Snapshots No. 87. International Lady. Paris Calling. 1942: Fingers at the Window. Crossroads. Sherlock Holmes and the Voice of Terror. Sherlock Holmes and the Secret Weapon. 1943: Sherlock Holmes in Washington. Crazy House. Above Suspicion. Sherlock Holmes Faces Death. Sherlock Holmes and the Spider Woman (GB: Spider Woman). 1944: The Scarlet Claw. Bathing Beauty. The Pearl of Death. Frenchman's Creek. 1945: The House of Fear. The Woman in Green. Pursuit to Algiers. 1946: Terror by Night. Heartbeat. Dressed to Kill (GB: Sherlock Holmes and the Secret Code). 1949: The Adventures of Ichabod and Mr Toad (narrator only). 1953: Casanova's Big Night. 1955: We're No Angels. The Court Jester. 1956: The Black Sleep. 1958: The Last Hurrah. 1961: The Magic Sword. Pontius Pilate. 1962: Red Hell. Two Before Zero (narrator only). Tales of Terror. 1963: The Comedy of Terrors. 1966: Planet of Blood/Queen of Blood. Ghost in the Invisible Bikini. 1967: Voyage to a Prehistoric Planet (GB: Prehistoric Planet Women). Dr Rock and Mr Roll. Autopsy of a Ghost. 1968: Hillbillys in a Haunted House.

international roles, then returned to Hollywood in the mid-1960s in co-starring parts. Still a busy actor, albeit in lesser films – often as men of violence. Once married (1954–6) to Jeff Donnell (1921–).
1951: Saturday's Hero (GB: Idols in the Dust). My True Story. 1951: Pat and Mike. The Marrying Kind. 1953: Let's Do It Again. Miss Sadie Thompson. 1955: We're No Angels. Battle Cry. Three Stripes in the Sun (GB: The Gentle Sergeant). 1956: Nightfall. 1957: Men in War. 1958: The Naked and the Dead. God's Little Acre. 1959: The Siege of Pinchgut (US: Four Desperate Men). 1960: Musketeers of the Sea. The Day They Robbed the Bank of England. 1961: Johnny Nobody. 1963: Nightmare in the Sun. 1965: Sylvia. 1966: What Did You Do in the War, Daddy? Dead Heat on a Merry-Go-Round. Welcome to Hard Times (GB: Killer on a Horse). 1967: Riot on Sunset Strip. Kill a Dragon/To Kill a Dragon. The Power. The Violent Ones. 1968: The Green Berets. The Silent Treatment. Suicide Commandos. 1969: Man Without Mercy (later Gone with the West). Deadlock (TV). The Haunted. 1970: Angel Unchained. 1972: La course du lièvre à travers les champs (GB and US: And Hope to Die). 1974: Seven Alone. Centerfold Girls. Stud Brown (GB: The Dynamite Brothers). 1975: Tom. Promise Him Anything. Inside Out. The Man Who Would Not Die. Won Ton Ton, the Dog Who Saved Hollywood. Psychic Killer. 1976: The Bad Bunch. 1977: Haunts/The Veil. Kino, the Padre on Horseback. Death Dimension. 1978: Shy Dove. Bog. 1979: Just Not the Same without You. Human Experiments. Sanctuary for Evil. When I Am King. The Glove (released 1981). 1980: Skycopter Summer. Box Office. 1981: Jayne Mansfield – an American Tragedy. Don't Go Near the Park. 1982: The Secret of NIMH (voice only). Sweet Sexy Savage. 1983: Evils of the Night. Frankenstein's Great Aunt Tillie (released 1985). Vultures in Paradise/Flesh and Bullets. 1984: To Kill a Stranger. The Executioner Part II. 1985: Biohazard (completed 1983). Prison Ship 2005. 1986: Red Nights.

ingly, she didn't settle as a big star. Went to Hollywood after World War II (after a one-film visit in 1938) for a lengthy stay. But it was too late: she only got one film part. Later became a successful novelist.
1928: Palais de Danse. 1929: Varsity. High Treason. Atlantic. 1930: Young Woodley. 1931: Keepers of Youth. Peace and Quiet. The Mystery of Marriage. Tonight's the Night. 1932: When London Sleeps. Dance Pretty Lady. Born Lucky. *The Changing Year. Two White Arms (US: Wives Beware). Here's George. Smilin' Along. The King's Cup. 1933: Excess Baggage. Tiger Bay. 1934: Easy Money. Rolling in Money. Nine Forty-Five. Once in a New Moon. 1935: Full Circle. Street Song. Royal Cavalcade (US: Regal Cavalcade). The Passing of the Third Floor Back. 1936: His Lordship (US: Man of Affaires). Beloved Imposter. Crime over London. 1937: Jenifer Hale. Farewell Again (US: Troopship). The Green Cockatoo. The Rat. Bank Holiday (US: Three on a Weekend). Please Teacher. 1938: Housemaster. Mountains o' Mourne. That Certain Age. Weddings Are Wonderful. The Return of the Frog. 1939: Home from Home. 1940: *The Call for Arms. Old Bill and Son. 1947: They Made Me a Fugitive (US: I Became a Criminal). If Winter Comes. *Pathe Pictorial No. 132. 1951: The Galloping Major. 1952: Women of Twilight (US: Twilight Women). 1954: The Good Die Young. 1957: The Vicious Circle (US: The Circle).

RAY, Ted (Charles Olden) 1909–1977
Ever-smiling, dark-haired, square-faced, bark-voiced, wisecracking British comedian who, like Jack Benny and Vic Oliver, played the violin at the end of his act. His great success in post-war years with the radio show Ray's a Laugh led him to make a few films, in one of which he was perfectly cast as a seedy schoolmaster in the Will Hay (qv) tradition. Father of actor Andrew Ray (1939–) and TV and radio personality Robin Ray. Died from a heart attack.
1930: Elstree Calling. 1934: Radio Parade of 1935 (US: Radio Follies). 1950: A Ray of Sunshine. 1952: Meet Me Tonight. 1953: Escape by Night. 1956: My Wife's Family. 1959: The Crowning Touch. Please Turn Over. Carry On Teacher.

RAY, Aldo (A. da Re) 1926–
Bullet-headed, thick-necked, crew-cut, fair-haired American actor who was a local sheriff before taking up a movie career. At first, amusingly, he was seen in ingenuous roles, later played sometimes tender-hearted tough guys. A star until 1961, he drifted into some

RAY, René (Irene Creese) 1912–
Sharply pretty brunette British actress, on stage from childhood, in films as a teenager. In the thirties her film roles varied bewilderingly from leads to quite small parts: not surpris-

RAYE, Martha (Margaret Reed) 1908–
Chasm-mouthed, strawberry blonde, power-

house American vocalist and comedienne with the energy of Betty Hutton and a voice that made Ethel Merman sound like Peggy Lee. Mostly on stage, but popular for a while in vigorous screen musicals of the late thirties and early forties. Much later reappeared, dyspeptically personable, as a housekeeper in the TV series *McMillan*.

1934: *A Nite in a Nite Club. *1936:* Rhythm on the Range. College Holiday. The Big Broadcast of 1937. *1937:* Mountain Music. Hideaway Girl. Artists and Models. Waikiki Wedding. Double or Nothing. *1938:* College Swing (*GB:* Swing, Teacher, Swing). The Big Broadcast of 1938. Tropic Holiday. Give Me a Sailor. *1939:* Never Say Die. $1,000 a Touchdown. *1940:* The Boys from Syracuse. The Farmer's Daughter. *1941:* Navy Blues. Hellzapoppin. Keep 'em Flying *1944:* Pin-Up Girl. Four Jills in a Jeep. *1947:* Monsieur Verdoux. *1952:* *Hollywood Night at 21 Club. *1962:* Billy Rose's Jumbo (*GB:* Jumbo). *1969:* The Phynx. *1970:* Pufnstuf. *1979:* The Concorde – Airport '79 (*GB:* Airport '80 . . . the Concorde). The Gossip Columnist (*TV*).

RAYMOND, Gene (R. Guion) 1908–
Fair-haired, strong-looking American leading man, former child actor, who won some quite decent leading roles in the Hollywood of the thirties, but is mostly remembered for being married to Jeanette MacDonald (*qv*) from 1937 to her death in 1965.

1931: Personal Maid. Ladies of the Big House. *1932:* Forgotten Commandments. If I Had a Million. Red Dust. The Night of June 13th. *1933:* Ann Carver's Profession. Ex-Lady. Brief

Moment. Zoo in Budapest. Flying Down to Rio. The House on 56th Street. *1934:* Transatlantic Merry-Go-Round. Coming Out Party. I Am Suzanne! Behold My Wife. Sadie McKee. *1935:* Transient Lady (*GB:* False Witness). The Woman in Red. Seven Keys to Baldpate. Hooray for Love. *1936:* Walking on Air. Love on a Bet. That Girl from Paris. The Smartest Girl in Town. The Bride Walks Out. *1937:* There Goes My Girl. The Life of the Party. *1938:* Stolen Heaven. *Hollywood Personalities. She's Got Everything. *1940:* Cross-Country Romance. *1941:* Mr and Mrs Smith. Smilin' Through. *1946:* The Locket. *1948:* Assigned to Danger. †Million Dollar Week-End. Sofia. *1955:* Hit the Deck. *1957:* Plunder Road. *1964:* The Best Man. I'd Rather Be Rich. The Hanged Man (*TV. GB: cinemas*). *1970:* Five Bloody Graves (narrator only).

†*Also directed*

RAYMOND, Paula (P. Ramona Wright) 1923–
Tall, slim, glamorous, dark-haired American actress, a model who decided to try a film career in 1948. M-G-M picked her up and gave her some quite good roles but once she left them in 1952 her career slid into second-features and, much later, cheap horror films. Her acting-by-numbers technique did not improve with the years and, while easy on the eye, she never seemed entirely at her ease on screen.

1948: Racing Luck. Rusty Leads the Way. Blondie's Secret. *1949:* Challenge of the Range. Adam's Rib. *1950:* Devil's Doorway. Sons of New Mexico (*GB:* The Brat). Duchess of Idaho. Crisis. Grounds for Marriage. *1951:* Inside Straight. The Tall Target. The Sellout. Texas Carnival. *1952:* Bandits of Corsica (*GB:* Return of the Corsican Brothers). *1953:* The Beast from 20,000 Fathoms. City That Never Sleeps. *1954:* The Human Jungle. King Richard and the Crusaders. *1955:* The Gun That Won the West. *1961:* Hand of Death. *1962:* The Flight That Disappeared. *1964:* The Spy with My Face. *1967:* Blood of Dracula's Castle. *1969:* Five Bloody Graves.

REAGAN, Ronald 1911–
The film career of this brown-haired, friendly-looking American actor bore no hint of his lofty ambition to be US President. He was a loyal servant to Warners for 13 years as

easy-going types, without quite getting into the mainstream of their product. When his features hardened with middle age, he played tough westerns for a while before going into politics, becoming Governor of California from 1966 to 1974, and being elected President in 1980. He was re-elected for a further term in 1984. Married to Jane Wyman (*qv*) from 1940 to 1948 and to Nancy Davis (1924–   ) from 1952 onwards.

1937: Love is on the Air (*GB:* The Radio Murder Mystery). †Submarine D-1. Hollywood Hotel. Swing Your Lady. *1938:* Cowboy from Brooklyn. Sergeant Murphy. Brother Rat. Girls on Probation. Boy Meets Girl. Going Places. Accidents Will Happen. *1939:* Code of the Secret Service. Dark Victory. Hell's Kitchen. Smashing the Money Ring. Angels Wash Their Faces. Naughty But Nice. Secret Service of the Air. *1940:* Brother Rat and a Baby (*GB:* Baby Be Good). Murder in the Air. Tugboat Annie Sails Again. Knute Rockne – All American (*GB:* A Modern Hero). Sante Fé Trail. An Angel from Texas. *1941:* Nine Lives Are Not Enough. The Bad Man (*GB:* Two Gun Cupid). Kings Row. International Squadron. Million Dollar Baby. *1942:* Juke Girl. Desperate Journey. *1943:* This is the Army. *1947:* That Hagen Girl. Stallion Road. The Voice of the Turtle. Night unto Night (released 1949). *1949:* John Loves Mary. The Girl from Jones Beach. It's a Great Feeling. The Hasty Heart. *1950:* Louisa. Storm Warning. *1951:* The Last Outpost. Bedtime for Bonzo. Hong Kong. *1952:* The Winning Team. She's Working Her Way Through College. *1953:* Law and Order. Tropic Zone. *1954:* Prisoner-of-War. Cattle Queen of Montana. Beneath These Waters (*TV. GB: cinemas*). *1955:* Tennessee's Partner. *1957:* Hellcats of the Navy. *1961:* The Young Doctors (narrator only). *1963:* The Truth about Communism (narrator only). *1964:* The Killers.

†*Scenes deleted from final release print*

REDFORD, Robert (Charles R. Redford) 1936–
Tall, blond, athletic, hawk-nosed, honest-looking and very handsome American leading man who became one of the great superstar pin-ups of the seventies. His interests – skiing, the American west, climbing, riding – and opinions have often reflected themselves in his acting and writing. Won 1981 Best Director

Oscar for *Ordinary People*. Nominated for an acting Academy Award in *The Sting*.
1960: *In the Presence of Mine Enemies (TV)*. 1961: *War Hunt*. 1965: *Situation Hopeless – but not Serious*. *Inside Daisy Clover*. 1966: *The Chase*. *This Property is Condemned*. 1967: *Barefoot in the Park*. 1969: *Tell Them Willie Boy is Here*. *Butch Cassidy and the Sundance Kid*. *The Making of Butch Cassidy and the Sundance Kid*. *Downhill Racer*. 1970: *Little Fauss and Big Halsy*. 1972: *Jeremiah Johnson*. *The Candidate*. *The Hot Rock (GB: How to Steal a Diamond in Four Uneasy Lessons)*. 1973: *The Way We Were*. *The Sting*. 1974: *The Great Gatsby*. 1975: *The Great Waldo Pepper*. *Three Days of the Condor*. 1976: *All the President's Men*. 1977: *A Bridge Too Far*. 1979: *The Electric Horseman*. 1980: *Brubaker*. 1984: *The Natural*. 1985: *Out of Africa*. 1986: *Legal Eagles*. 1987: *Springs (project)*.

As director: 1980: *Ordinary People*.

REDGRAVE, Lynn 1943–
Warm, bouncy, extrovert, tawny-haired British comedy actress, daughter of Sir Michael Redgrave. Her appeal was somewhere between Joyce Grenfell and TV actress Pauline Collins, and her *Georgy Girl*, which won her an Academy Award nomination, was a tragi-comic *tour-de-force*. But after that the cinema seemed to see her as tarts-with-hearts, and she has seldom received roles in films that emphasized her individual appeal.
1963: *Tom Jones*. *Girl with Green Eyes*. 1966: *The Deadly Affair*. *Georgy Girl*. 1967: *Smashing Time*. 1969: *The Virgin Soldiers*. *Last of the Mobile Hot-Shots (later Blood Kin)*. 1971:

Los guerilleros (US: Killer from Yuma). 1972: *Viva la muerte-tua!* *Everything You Always Wanted to Know about Sex** **But Were Afraid to Ask*. *Every Little Crook and Nanny*. 1973: *The National Health*. 1975: *The Happy Hooker*. *Don't Turn the Other Cheek*. 1976: *The Big Bus*. 1978: *Sooner or Later (TV)*. 1979: *Gauguin – the Savage*. 1980: *Sunday Lovers*. *The Seduction of Miss Leona (TV)*. 1982: *The Bad Seed (TV)*. *Rehearsal for Murder (TV)*. 1985: *Home Front*. 1986: *My Two Loves (TV)*.

REDGRAVE, Sir Michael 1908–1985
Tall, scholarly-looking British actor with light-brown hair. He switched from teaching to acting in the 1930s, and proved a stalwart servant of the British cinema, often in ideological roles, although also capable of raising a chill. Mainly in guest roles from the late 1950s, he was in very poor health in his last few years. Married to actress Rachel Kempson (1910–), he was the father of actors Lynn, Vanessa (both *qv*) and Corin Redgrave. Son of British actor Roy Redgrave (1872–1922), who starred in Australian silent films. Nominated for an Oscar in *Mourning Becomes Electra*, he was knighted in 1959. Died from Parkinson's Disease.
1936: *Secret Agent*. 1938: *The Lady Vanishes*. *Stolen Life*. *Climbing High*. 1939: *A Window in London (US: Lady in Distress)*. *The Stars Look Down*. 1941: *Kipps (US: The Remarkable Mr Kipps)*. *Jeannie*. *Atlantic Ferry (US: Sons of the Sea)*. *The Big Blockade*. 1942: *Thunder Rock*. 1945: *The Way to the Stars (US: Johnny in the Clouds)*. *Dead of Night*. *A Diary for Timothy (narrator only)*. 1946: *The Captive Heart*. *The Years Between*. 1947: *The Man Within (US: The Smugglers)*. *Fame is the Spur*. *Mourning Becomes Electra*. 1948: *Secret Beyond the Door*. 1949: **Her Fighting Chance (narrator only)*. 1951: *The Browning Version*. *Painter and Poet (narrator only)*. **Winter Garden (narrator only)*. *The Magic Box*. 1952: *The Importance of Being Earnest*. 1954: *The Sea Shall Not Have Them*. *The Green Scarf*. *The Dam Busters*. 1955: **The Lake District (narrator only)*. *The Night My Number Came Up*. *Oh Rosalinda!!* 1984. *Confidential Report (US: Mr Arkadin)*. 1956: **Kings and Queens (narrator only)*. *The Happy Road*. 1957: *Time without Pity*. 1958: *The Quiet American*. *Law and Disorder*. *Behind*

the Mask. **The Immortal Land (narrator only)*. 1959: *Shake Hands with the Devil*. *The Wreck of the Mary Deare*. 1960: **May Wedding (narrator only)*.**The Questioning City (narrator only)*. 1961: *No, My Darling Daughter*. *The Innocents*. 1962: *The Loneliness of the Long Distance Runner*. 1963: *Uncle Vanya*. 1964: *Young Cassidy*. 1965: *The Hill*. *The Heroes of Telemark*. 1966: *Palaces of a Queen (narrator only)*. 1967: *The 25th Hour*. *Assignment K*. *October Revolution (narrator only)*. 1968: *Heidi Comes Home (US: Heidi)*. 1969: *Oh! What a Lovely War*. *Battle of Britain*. *Goodbye, Mr Chips*. *Connecting Rooms*. *David Copperfield (TV. GB: cinemas)*. 1970: *Goodbye Gemini*. *The Go-Between*. 1971: *Nicholas and Alexandra*.

REDGRAVE, Vanessa 1937–
Gaunt, fair-haired British actress, daughter of Sir Michael Redgrave. Generally well liked by the critics, she has never become a box-office force, despite her liberated lifestyle and well-publicized espousal of left-wing causes. After unsuccessful Oscar nominations for *Morgan – a Suitable Case for Treatment*, *Isadora* and *Mary, Queen of Scots*, she won a best supporting actress Academy Award (and deservedly so) for *Julia*. Married/divorced director Tony Richardson; her long association with actor Franco Nero (*qv*) also came to an end.
1958: *Behind the Mask*. 1961: **The Circus at Clopton Hall (narrator only)*. 1965: *Morgan – a Suitable Case for Treatment*. 1966. *A Man for All Seasons*. *Blow-Up*. 1967: *Tonite Let's All Make Love in London*. *Red and Blue*. *Sailor from Gibraltar*. *Camelot*. 1968: *The Charge of the Light Brigade*. 1969: *Isadora*. *A Quiet Place in the Country*. *Oh! What a Lovely War*. *The Sea Gull*. 1970: *Drop Out!* *The Body (narrator only)*. *La vacanza*. 1971: *The Devils*. *The Trojan Women*. *Mary, Queen of Scots*. 1974: *Murder on the Orient Express*. 1975: *Out of Season*. 1976: *The Seven-Per-Cent Solution*. 1977: *Julia*. 1978: *Agatha*. *Yanks*. 1979: *Bear Island*. 1980: *Playing for Time (TV)*. 1982: *Wagner*. *My Body, My Child (TV)*. 1983: *Sing Sing*. 1984: *The Bostonians*. *Steaming*. 1985: *Wetherby*. *Three Sovereigns for Sarah (TV)*. 1986: *Second Serve (TV)*.

REED, Donna (D. Mullenger) 1921–1986
Lovely, dark-haired actress who enjoyed the quietest of Hollywood careers, mainly in nice-

girl roles, while gaining a reputation on the other side of the camera as an outspoken critic of directors. Perhaps, in view of the routine nature of her films, it's not surprising. Nor does it say too much for M-G-M, where she spent half her career, that all her best roles (with the possible exception of the later *Ransom!*) were for other studios, including *From Here to Eternity*, for which she won a best supporting actress Oscar. Died from cancer of the pancreas.
1941: †*Babes on Broadway*. †*The Get-Away*. *The Bugle Sounds*. *Shadow of the Thin Man*. 1942: *Mokey*. *Calling Dr Gillespie*. *Apache Trail*. *The Courtship of Andy Hardy*. *Eyes in the Night*. 1943: *Thousands Cheer*. *The Human Comedy*. *Dr Gillespie's Criminal Case* (*GB: Crazy to Kill*). *The Man from Down Under*. 1944: *Gentle Annie*. *See Here, Private Hargrove*. *Mrs Parkington*. 1945: *The Picture of Dorian Gray*. *They Were Expendable*. 1946: *Faithful in My Fashion*. *It's a Wonderful Life*. 1947: *Green Dolphin Street*. 1948: *Beyond Glory*. 1949: *Chicago Deadline*. 1951: *Scandal Sheet* (*GB: The Dark Page*). *Saturday's Hero* (*GB: Idols in the Dust*). 1952: *Hangman's Knot*. 1953: **Hollywood Laugh Parade*. *Raiders of the Seven Seas*. *Trouble Along the Way*. *The Caddy*. *From Here to Eternity*. *Gun Fury*. 1954: *Three Hours to Kill*. *The Last Time I Saw Paris*. *They Rode West*. 1955: *The Far Horizons*. 1956: *Ransom!* *The Benny Goodman Story*. *Backlash*. *Beyond Mombasa*. 1958: *The Whole Truth*. 1960: *Pepe*. 1974: *The Yellow Headed Summer* (*TV*). 1979: *The Best Place to Be* (*TV*). 1983: *Deadly Lessons* (*TV*).

†*As Donna Adams*

REED, Maxwell 1919–1974
Tall, dark, glowering Irish-born leading man who gained something of a reputation as the wild man of British films before marriage to Joan Collins (*qv*) in 1952 (they were subsequently divorced). His career ran downhill after the mid-fifties as he looked around for international roles.
1946: *No Ladies Please*. *The Years Between*. *Gaiety George* (*US: Showtime*). *Daybreak*. 1947: *The Brothers*. *Dear Murderer*. *Daughter of Darkness*. 1948: *Night Beat*. 1949: *Madness of the Heart*. *The Lost People*. 1950: *Blackout*. *The Clouded Yellow*. 1951: *The Dark Man*. *There is Another Sun* (*US: Wall of Death*).

Flame of Araby. 1953: *Sea Devils*. *The Square Ring*. *Marilyn* (later *Roadhouse Girl*). *Le corsaire des Caraibes*. 1954: *The Brain Machine*. *Helen of Troy*. 1955: *Before I Wake* (*US: Shadow of Fear*). 1959: *Captain Phantom*. 1961: *Pirates of Tortuga*. 1962: *The Notorious Landlady*. *Advise and Consent*. 1966: *Picture Mommy Dead*.

REED, Oliver 1937.
Brutish-looking, powerful, heftily-built British actor, much given to sullenness and melodramatics, but also capable of interesting, sometimes touching performances (*The Trap, Hannibal Brooks, Women in Love, Tommy*). The nephew of director Sir Carol Reed, he started as bullies and sneering villains, but powered his way into leading roles by the early sixties and had many female fans breathing heavily before he himself became rather too heavy for romantic roles.
1955: *Value for Money*. 1958: *Hello London*. *The Square Peg*. *The Captain's Table*. 1959: '*Beat Girl*' (*US: Wild for Kicks*). 1960: *The League of Gentlemen*. *The Angry Silence*. *Sword of Sherwood Forest*. *His and Hers*. *No Love for Johnnie*. 1961: *The Rebel* (*US: Call Me Genius*). *The Bulldog Breed*. *The Curse of the Werewolf*. *The Pirates of Blood River*. 1962: *Captain Clegg* (*US: Night Creatures*). *The Damned* (*US: These Are the Damned*). *Paranoiac*. *The Party's Over*. 1963: *The Scarlet Blade*. 1964: *The System* (*US: The Girl Getters*). 1965: *The Brigand of Kandahar*. 1966: *The Trap*. *The Jokers*. 1967: *The Shuttered Room*. *I'll Never Forget What's 'is Name*. 1968: *Oliver!* *Hannibal Brooks*. *The Assassin-*

ation Bureau. 1969: *Women in Love*. *Take a Girl Like You*. 1970: *The Lady in the Car with Glasses and a Gun*. 1971: *The Devils*. *The Hunting Party*. 1972: *Sitting Target*. *Z.P.G.* (*GB: Zero Population Growth*). *The Age of Pisces*. *The Triple Echo*. 1973: *Mordi e fuggi/Bite and Run*. *Un Uomo* (*GB and US: Fury*). *The Three Musketeers – the Queen's Diamonds*. *Blue Blood*. *Revolver*. 1974: *And Then There Were None*. *The Four Musketeers – the Revenge of Milady*. 1975: *Tommy*. *Lisztomania*. *Royal Flash*. *The Sellout*. *Blood in the Streets*. 1976: *The Great Scout and Cathouse Thursday*. *Burnt Offerings*. 1977: *The Prince and the Pauper* (*US: Crossed Swords*). *Tomorrow Never Comes*. *Assault on Paradise* (*US: Maniac*. *GB: TV. as Ransom*). 1978: *The Big Sleep*. *The Class of Miss MacMichael*. *Touch of the Sun*. 1979: *The Brood*. *The Mad Trapper* (*unfinished*). 1980: *Lion of the Desert/Omar Mukhtar – Lion of the Desert*. *Dr Heckyl and Mr Hype*. 1981: *Condorman*. *Death Bite* (later *Spasms*). *Venom*. 1982: *The Great Question* (*Al Mas à la Al Kubra*). *Clash of Loyalties*. *Masquerade* (*TV*). 1983: *The Sting II*. *99 Women*. *Frank and I*. *Fanny Hill*. *Two of a Kind*. 1984: *The Black Arrow* (*cable TV*). 1986: *Captive*. *Last of the Templars*.

REEVE, Christopher 1952–
Strapping young American actor who landed the title role in *Superman,* and surprised many by sustaining the stardom it brought him. Reeve's subtle differentiation between the shy reporter and his alter ego, the Man of Steel, together with subsequent performances in other leading roles, confirmed his talent as being distinctly above the average for portrayers of comic-strip heroes.
1977: *Gray Lady Down*. 1978: *Superman*. 1979: *Somewhere in Time*. 1980: *Superman II*. 1981: *Deathtrap*. 1982: *Street Smart*. *Monsignor*. 1983: *Superman III*. 1984: *The Bostonians*. 1985: *Aviator*. 1986: *Superman IV*.

REEVES, Steve 1926–
Dark-haired American muscleman who took up acting after winning 'Mr World' and 'Mr Universe' titles and achieved enormous success in Italian sword-and-sandal spectacles, attracting the same kind of queues as would Clint Eastwood with his spaghetti westerns the following decade. Tried without much

luck to extend his range and eventually returned to America to become a rancher.
1954: Athena. The Hidden Face. Jail Bait. 1957: The Labours of Hercules (GB: Hercules). 1958: Hercules and the Queen of Sheba (GB: Hercules Unchained). 1959: Il terrore dei barbari (GB and US: Goliath and the Barbarians). The White Devil (GB: The White Warrior). The Giant of Marathon. 1960: The Thief of Baghdad. Morgan the Pirate. 1961: Romulus and Remus (GB: Duel of the Titans). The Trojan War (GB: The Wooden Horse of Troy). The Last Days of Pompeii. 1962: The Legend of Aeneas. Son of Spartacus. 1963: Sandokan the Great. Il giorno piu corto commedia umaristica (US: The Shortest Day). 1964: I pirati della Malesia/Sandokan and the Pirates of Malaya. 1968: Vivo per la tua morte/A Long Ride from Hell.

REMICK, Lee 1935–
Cool, blonde American actress with prettily thin features and pale blue eyes. Started her film career playing southern states sexpots, but progressed to more level-headed women, often very much in control of their own fortunes. Lived in Britain for some time in the seventies and can now turn on an impeccable English accent. Nominated for an Academy Award in Days of Wine and Roses.
1957: A Face in the Crowd. The Last Tycoon (TV). 1958: Last Clear Chance (TV). The Long, Hot Summer. 1959: These Thousand Hills. Anatomy of a Murder. 1960: Wild River. 1961: Sanctuary. 1962: Experiment in Terror (GB: The Grip of Fear). Days of Wine and Roses. 1963: The Running Man. The Wheeler

Dealers (GB: Separate Beds). 1965: Baby, the Rain Must Fall. The Hallelujah Trail. 1967: No Way to Treat a Lady. 1968: The Detective. Hard Contract. 1970: A Severed Head. Loot. 1971: Sometimes a Great Notion (GB: Never Give an Inch). 1972: Of Men and Women (TV). And No One Could Save Her (TV). 1973: The Blue Knight (TV. GB: cinemas). Touch Me Not. 1974: A Delicate Balance. A Girl Named Sooner (TV). QB VII (TV). 1975: Hustling (TV). Hennessy. The Hunted. 1976: The Omen. 1977: Telefon. 1978: The Medusa Touch. Breaking Up (TV). 1979: The Europeans. Torn Between Two Lovers (TV. GB: cinemas). 1980: Tribute. The Women's Room (TV). The Competition. 1981: The Letter (TV). Haywire (TV). 1983: The Gift of Love: A Christmas Story (TV). 1984: Mistral's Daughter (Video). Rearview Mirror (TV). 1985: Toughlove (TV). 1986: Emma's War.

RENNIE, Michael 1909–1971
Tall, dark British actor, good-looking in a lean-and-hungry sort of way (at times uncannily like John Justin) who supplemented his earnings as a salesman in the mid-thirties by doing film extra and action stand-in work and had drifted into sufficiently big parts just before World War II service to make acting a full-time career when he returned to civilian life. Became a big star in Britain and went to America in 1951 with some success. Died from heart failure.
1935: Conquest of the Air (released 1940). 1936: The Man Who Could Work Miracles. Gipsy. Secret Agent. 1937: Gangway. Bank Holiday (US: Three on a Week-End). 1938: The Divorce of Lady X. 1939: This Man in Paris. 1941: The Patient Vanishes (later This Man is Dangerous). Turned Out Nice Again. Pimpernel Smith (US: Mister V). Dangerous Moonlight (US: Suicide Squadron). Ships with Wings. The Tower of Terror. The Big Blockade. 1945: I'll Be Your Sweetheart. The Wicked Lady. Caesar and Cleopatra. 1947: The Root of All Evil. White Cradle Inn (US: High Fury). 1948: Idol of Paris. Uneasy Terms. 1949: Miss Pilgrim's Progress. The Golden Madonna. 1950: Trio. The Black Rose. The Body Said No! 1951: The House in the Square (US: I'll Never Forget You). The Thirteenth Letter. The Day the Earth Stood Still. 1952: Phone Call from a Stranger. Five

Fingers. Les Misérables. 1953: Single-Handed (US: Sailor of the King). The Robe. King of the Khyber Rifles. Dangerous Crossing. 1954: Demetrius and the Gladiators. Princess of the Nile. Desirée. 1955: Mambo. Soldier of Fortune. Seven Cities of Gold. The Rains of Ranchipur. 1956: Teenage Rebel. 1957: Circle of the Day (TV). Island in the Sun. Omar Khayyam. 1958: Battle of the V1 (US: V1/Unseen Heroes). 1959: Third Man on the Mountain. 1960: The Lost World. 1963: Mary, Mary. 1966: Ride Beyond Vengeance. Hondo and the Apaches (TV. GB: cinemas). Hotel. 1967: The Power. Cyborg 2087 (GB: Man from Tomorrow). Sette vergine per il diavolo (US: The Young, the Evil and the Savage). Bersaglio mobile (GB and US: Death on the Run). 1968: Subterfuge. The Search (TV). El Alamein (GB: Desert Tanks). The Devil's Brigade. Scaccio internazionale. 1969: Operation Terror/Assignment Terror. 1970: Gold Seekers. Dracula versus Frankenstein. 1971: The Last Generation.

REYNOLDS, Burt (Burton Reynolds) 1936–
Round-faced, dark-haired, latterly moustachioed, panther-like American leading man, a superstar of the 1970s and 1980s who, like McQueen and Belmondo, insisted on doing much of his action stunt-work. The sense of fun which has added a great deal to his appeal lay submerged for years in a slew of poker-faced macho heroes. Later, the relaxed cockiness could turn to alarm with amusing results, which were occasionally overdone. Also a director with ideas. Married (1963–1966) actress Judy Carne (1939–); later relationships with Dinah Shore and Sally Field (both qv) were long-lasting but ultimately broke up. Like his famous centre-spread, he has perhaps been over-exposed in recent times, but despite health scares in the 1980s has only marginally eased up on a prodigious work rate.
1960: Angel Baby. Alas, Babylon (TV). 1961: Armored Command. 1965: Last Message from Saigon (GB: Operation CIA). 1966: Un dollaro a testa (GB and US: Navajo Joe). 1967: Shark! (released 1970). 1968: Impasse. 100 Rifles. Fade In. 1969: Skullduggery. Sam Whiskey. 1970: Run Simon Run (TV). Hunters Are for Killing (TV). 1972: Everything You Always Wanted to Know About Sex**But

Were Afraid to Ask. Deliverance. Fuzz. Shamus. 1973: White Lightning. The Man Who Loved Cat Dancing. 1974: The Longest Yard (GB: The Mean Machine). 1975: WW and the Dixie Dancekings. At Long Last Love. Hustle. Lucky Lady. 1976: Nickelodeon. Silent Movie. †Gator. 1977: Smokey and the Bandit. Semi-Tough. 1978: Hooper. †The End. 1979: Starting Over. 1980: Smokey and the Bandit II (GB: Smokey and the Bandit Ride Again). Roughcut. The Cannonball Run. 1981: †Sharky's Machine. Paternity. 1982: The Best Little Whorehouse in Texas. Best Friends. 1983: Stroker Ace. Cannonball Run II. The Man Who Loved Women. Smokey and the Bandit – Part 3. 1984: †Stick. City Heat. 1985: Uphill All the Way. 1986: Heat.

† *Also directed*

REYNOLDS, Debbie (Mary Reynolds) 1932–
Energetic, exuberant, jack-in-the-box, tiny, cute-looking, brown-haired American dancer and light singer, who played refreshingly in several M-G-M musicals (most notably *Singin' in the Rain*) and comedies of the fifties. She also plays several musical instruments (probably all at once, if she could). Later, there were some appealing acting performances and one tour-de-force (in *The Unsinkable Molly Brown*) before her luck ran out in the mid-sixties. Married to Eddie Fisher 1955–1959, first of three; Carrie Fisher (*qv*) is their daughter. Nominated for an Academy Award in *The Unsinkable Molly Brown*. *1948: June Bride. 1950: The Daughter of Rosie O'Grady. Mr Imperium (GB: You Belong to My Heart). Three Little Words. Two Weeks with Love. 1952: Skirts Ahoy. Singin' in the Rain. I Love Melvin. 1953: The Affairs of Dobie Gillis. Give a Girl a Break. 1954: Athena. Susan Slept Here. 1955: The Tender Trap. Hit the Deck. 1956: Bundle of Joy. The Catered Affair (GB: Wedding Breakfast). Meet Me in Las Vegas (GB: Viva Las Vegas!). 1957: Tammy and the Bachelor (GB: Tammy). 1958: This Happy Feeling. 1959: The Mating Game. Say One for Me. The Gazebo. 1960: Pepe. The Rat Race. 1961: The Second Time Around. The Pleasure of His Company. 1962: How the West Was Won. 1963: My Six Loves. Mary, Mary. 1964: Goodbye Charlie. The Unsinkable Molly Brown. 1966:*

The Singing Nun. 1967. Divorce American Style. 1968: How Sweet It Is! 1971: What's the Matter with Helen? 1972: Charlotte's Web (voice only). 1974: That's Entertainment!

REYNOLDS, Marjorie (née Goodspeed) 1921–
Blonde American actress with pert face, who started young and played perky girl-scout types, most notably the intrepid reporter in the *Mr Wong* series, before Paramount picked her up in 1942 and gave her a more glamorous image – if, *Ministry of Fear* excepted, few decent roles. Played leads in second-features for some years before becoming popular on TV in the mid-fifties as William Bendix's wife in *The Life of Riley*. *1923: Scaramouche. 1924: Revelation. 1933: †College Humor. †Wine, Women and Song. 1935: †The Big Broadcast of 1936. 1936: †Collegiate (GB: The Charm School). College Holiday. 1937: Tex Rides with the Boy Scouts. Murder in Greenwich Village. Champagne Waltz. 1938: The Black Bandit. Man's Country. Guilty Trails. Western Trails. Overland Express. Rebellious Daughters. Six-Shootin' Sheriff. 1939: Streets of New York. Tailspin Tommy. Racketeers of the Range. Mr Wong in Chinatown. Gone with the Wind. Mystery Plane. The Phantom Stage. Stunt Pilot. Danger Flight (GB: Scouts of the Air). Timber Stampede. Sky Patrol. 1940: Doomed to Die (GB: The Mystery of the Wentworth Castle). The Fatal Hour (GB: Mr Wong at Headquarters). Midnight Limited. Chasing Trouble. Enemy Agent (GB: Secret Enemy). 1941: Secret Evidence. Robin Hood of the Pecos. Dude Cowboy. Cyclone on Horseback. Up in the Air. The Great Swindle. Tillie the Toiler. Top Sergeant Mulligan. 1942: Holiday Inn. Star Spangled Rhythm. 1943: Dixie. Ministry of Fear. 1944: Up in Mabel's Room. Three is a Family. 1945: Bring on the Girls. Duffy's Tavern. 1946: Monsieur Beaucaire. Meet Me on Broadway. The Time of Their Lives. 1947: Heaven Only Knows. 1948: Bad Men of Tombstone. 1949: That Midnight Kiss. 1950: The Great Jewel Robbery. Customs Agent. Rookie Fireman. 1951: The Home Town Story. His Kind of Woman. 1952: Models Inc./Call Girl (later and GB: That Kind of Girl). No Holds Barred. 1955: Mobs Inc. 1959: Juke Box Rhythm. 1964: The Silent Witness.*

†*As Marjorie Moore*

REYNOLDS, Peter (P. Horrocks) 1925–1975
A rarity in British films of the fifties: a leading man who played villains. Though Reynolds was tall, blond and good looking, there was something shifty about the blue-eyed gaze and untrustworthy about the set of the mouth, and he played callous small-time crooks and scheming wastrels, much given to dark shirts and light ties. Also did well as fast-talking reporters busting crime rings. Went to Australia in the sixties, and died while acting there.
*1946: The Captive Heart. 1947: The Dark Road. 1948: The Guinea Pig. Things Happen at Night. 1949: Adam and Evelyne. 1950: Guilt is My Shadow. 1951: Smart Alec. Four Days. The Magic Box. The Woman's Angle. 1952: The Last Page (US: Manbait). 24 Hours in a Woman's Life (US: Affair in Monte Carlo). I vinti. I nostri figli. 1953: The Good Beginning. Black 13. 1954: The Delavine Affair. The Accused. Destination Milan. *Little Brother. Devil Girl from Mars. One Just Man. 1955: You Can't Escape. Born for Trouble. 1957: The Long Haul. 1958: The Bank Raiders. 1959: Wrong Number. Shake Hands with the Devil. Your Money or Your Wife. 1960: The Challenge. The Man Who Couldn't Walk. 1961: Spare the Rod. The Breaking Point. A Question of Suspense. Highway to Battle. The Painted Smile. 1962: Gaolbreak. 1963: West 11. 1968: Nobody Runs Forever.*

RICE, Joan 1930–
With so pretty a face and so sumptuous a figure, small wonder this petite brunette

beauty contest winner was whisked from waiting at tables to starring in films. She wasn't a terribly strong actress, but few red-blooded males minded that, and it was a pity her bigger films asked too much of her, hastening her decline. She was certainly as pretty and spirited a Maid Marian as ever graced the screen.
1950: Blackmailed. 1951: One Wild Oat. 1952: Curtain Up. The Story of Robin Hood and His Merrie Men. Gift Horse (US: Glory at Sea). 1953: His Majesty O'Keefe. The Steel Key. A Day to Remember. 1954: The Crowded Day. One Good Turn. 1955: Police Dog. 1956: Women without Men (US: Blonde Bait). 1958: The Long Knife. 1959: Operation Bullshine. 1961: Payroll. 1970: The Horror of Frankenstein.

RICHARD, Cliff (Harold Webb) 1940–
British singer who began his days as a hip-wiggling teen idol in white jacket and drain-pipes, dark hair dripping with grease. By 1961 he was projecting an image as Mr Clean in a series of musicals that started well, but tailed away. A hard-working spokesman for Christianity.
1959: Serious Charge (US: A Touch of Hell). 1960: Expresso Bongo. 1961: The Young Ones. 1962: Summer Holiday. 1964: Wonderful Life (US: Swingers' Paradise). 1966: Finders Keepers. 1967: Two a Penny. 1973: Take Me High (US: Hot Property).

RICHARDSON, John 1934–
Impressively-built, fair-haired, idyllically handsome, globe-trotting British leading man who proved an effectively muscular foil for

some of Hammer's busty leading ladies of the 1960s, but whose film career before and since has been spotty, to say the least, not helped by too often getting into films whose leading ladies were their raisons d'être.
1952: Ivanhoe. 1958: Bachelor of Hearts. Operation Amsterdam. 1959: The 39 Steps. 1960: Mask of the Demon/Black Sunday. 1961: Pirates of Tortuga. 1965: She. 1966: One Million Years BC. 1967: La cintura di castità (GB: The Chastity Belt. US: A Funny Thing Happened to Me on the Way to the Crusades). John il bastardo. 1968: The Vengeance of She. Execution. 1969: Candidate for a Killing. 1970: On a Clear Day You Can See Forever. 1972: Frankenstein Mosaic 1980. 1973: Torso. 1974: Anna quel particolare Piacere (GB: Secrets of a Call Girl). 1975: Duck à l'Orange. 1978: Battle of the Stars. Death by Reservation. Cosmos. 1980: La notte dei passi felpati. Unconscious. 1981: Happy Birthday Harry!

RICHARDSON, Sir Ralph 1902–1983
Solemn-looking, round-faced, beady-eyed British character star with a slick of dark hair that would gradually vanish as he passed through middle age. His careful, well-modulated speech could lend character to men from all walks of life, and he could just as easily be pompous as down-to-earth. At his (considerable) peak from 1937 to 1952, during which time he produced some memorable film performances – for one, in The Heiress – he was nominated for an Oscar. First wife died; married actress Meriel Forbes (1913–) in 1944. Knighted in 1947. Died from a virus infection.
1933: The Ghoul. Friday the Thirteenth. 1934: The King of Paris. Thunder in the Air. The Return of Bulldog Drummond. Java Head. 1935: Bulldog Jack (US: Alias Bulldog Drummond). 1936: Things to Come. The Man Who Could Work Miracles. Thunder in the City. The Amazing Quest of Ernest Bliss (US: Romance and Riches). 1937: South Riding. The Divorce of Lady X. 1938: *Smith. The Citadel. 1939: Q Planes (US: Clouds Over Europe). The Four Feathers. The Lion Has Wings. On the Night of the Fire (US: The Fugitive). 1940: *Health for the Nation (narrator only). *Forty Million People (narrator only). 1942: The Day Will Dawn (US: The Avengers). 1943: The Silver Fleet. The Biter Bit (narrator only). The Volunteer. 1946: School for Secrets

(US: Secret Flight), 1947: Anna Karenina. 1948: The Fallen Idol. 1949: *Faster Than Sound (narrator only). The Heiress. Come Saturday (narrator only). *Rome and Vatican City (narrator only). 1950: *Eagles of the Fleet (narrator only). 1951: *Cricket (narrator only). Outcast of the Islands. 1952: †Home at Seven (US: Murder on Monday). The Sound Barrier (US: Breaking the Sound Barrier). The Holly and the Ivy. 1955: Richard III. 1956: Smiley. 1957: The Passionate Stranger (US: A Novel Affair). 1959: Our Man in Havana. 1960: Exodus. Oscar Wilde. 1962: The 300 Spartans. Long Day's Journey into Night. 1963: Woman of Straw. 1965: Doctor Zhivago. 1966: Khartoum. The Wrong Box. 1969: Oh! What a Lovely War. Battle of Britain. The Looking Glass War. Midas Run (GB: A Run on Gold). The Bed Sitting Room. David Copperfield (TV. GB: cinemas). 1970: Eagle in a Cage. 1971: Whoever Slew Auntie Roo? (US: Who Slew Auntie Roo?). 1972: Tales from the Crypt. Alice's Adventures in Wonderland. Lady Caroline Lamb. 1973: A Doll's House (Garland). O Lucky Man! Frankenstein – the True Story (TV. GB: cinemas, in abridged version). 1975: Rollerball. 1976: The Man in the Iron Mask (TV). Jesus of Nazareth (TV). 1978: Watership Down (voice only). 1979: Charlie Muffin (TV). 1981: Time Bandits. Dragonslayer. 1982: Wagner. Witness for the Prosecution (TV). 1983: Invitation to the Wedding. 1984: Greystoke: The Legend of Tarzan, Lord of the Apes. Give My Regards to Broad Street.

†Also directed

RIGG, Diana 1938–
Brisk, businesslike, brown-haired British actress with impish smile who came to the cinema via success in theatre and television (especially in the TV series The Avengers), media to which she has, after a few cinematic forays, by and large returned. Hopes that the renewed demand for resourceful heroines in the late 1970s might herald a permanent return to films did not materialize.
1968: A Midsummer Night's Dream. The Assassination Bureau. 1969: On Her Majesty's Secret Service. 1970: Julius Caesar. 1971: The Hospital. 1973: Theatre of Blood. 1975: In This House of Brede (TV). 1976: A Little Night Music. 1981: The Great Muppet Caper. Evil Under the Sun.

THE RITZ BROTHERS
(The Joachim Brothers) Al 1901–1965 Jimmy 1903–1985 Harry 1906–1986
Family trio of raucous, long-faced, big-nosed American comedians/comic dancers who provided fun interludes in big-budget musicals, headed up lesser vehicles of their own, were almost as zany as the Marxes and could always be depended on for the unexpected. Al died from a heart attack: Jimmy from heart failure, Harry died from cancer.
1934: *Hotel Anchovy. 1936: Sing Baby Sing. 1937: Life Begins in College (GB: The Joy Parade). One in a Million. On the Avenue. You Can't Have Everything. 1938: Kentucky Moonshine (GB: Three Men and a Girl). The Goldwyn Follies. Straight, Place and Show (GB: They're Off). 1939: The Three Musketeers (GB: The Singing Musketeer). The Gorilla. Pack Up Your Troubles (GB: We're in the Army Now). 1940: Argentine Nights. 1942: Behind the Eight Ball (GB: Off the Beaten Track). Hi Ya, Chum (GB: Everything Happens to Us). 1943: *Screen Snapshots, series 2: No. 3. Never a Dull Moment. *Screen Snapshots, series 2: No. 8. Al alone: 1918: The Avenging Trail. Harry and Jimmy: 1975: Won Ton Ton, the Dog Who Saved Hollywood. Blazing Stewardesses. Harry alone: 1976: Silent Movie.

RIX, Sir Brian 1924–
Dark-haired British farceur who played gormless idiots in film comedies with Ronald Shiner, gradually becoming the more popular of the two, although not for long. After the early sixties devoted himself to running, and playing in famous farces at London's White-hall Theatre for more than a decade. In real life the most urbane of men, the very opposite of his film and stage self. Married to actress Elspet Gray (1928–   ) since 1949. Left show business in 1980 to work full-time for the mentally handicapped. Knighted in 1986.
1951: Reluctant Heroes. 1954: Up to His Neck. What Every Woman Wants. 1956: Dry Rot. 1957: Not Wanted on Voyage. 1959: The Night We Dropped a Clanger. 1960: The Night We Got the Bird. And the Same to You. 1961: Nothing Barred. 1973: Don't Just Lie There, Say Something!

ROBARDS, Jason Jnr 1920–
Wry, laconic, rasp-voiced American actor with hangdog expression. In semi-star roles for the cinema (after a distinguished stage career) from early middle age. The standard of his performance could vary infuriatingly, but he won two best supporting actor Oscars (for All the President's Men and Julia) in the 1970s, and was nominated again for Melvin and Howard. Married (third of four) to Lauren Bacall from 1961 to 1973. His father was silent-screen lead and sound character actor Jason Robards Snr (1892–1963).
1958: The Journey. 1959: For Whom the Bell Tolls (TV). 1961: By Love Possessed. Tender is the Night. 1962: Long Day's Journey into Night. 1963: Act One. 1965: A Thousand Clowns. 1966: Any Wednesday (GB: abridged as Bachelor Girl Apartment). A Big Hand for the Little Lady (GB: Big Deal at Dodge City). 1967: Divorce American Style. Hour of the Gun. The St Valentine's Day Massacre. 1968: The Night They Raided Minsky's. Once Upon a Time . . . in the West. 1969: Isadora. Rosolino Paternò, soldato (US: Operation Snafu). 1970: Tora! Tora! Tora! Julius Caesar. The Ballad of Cable Hogue. Fools. 1971: Murders in the Rue Morgue. Johnny Got His Gun. 1972: The House without a Christmas (TV). Tod eines Fremden (GB: The Execution. US: Death of a Stranger). The War Between Men and Women. 1973: Play It As It Lays. Pat Garrett and Billy the Kid. A Boy and His Dog. 1974: Mr Sycamore. 1976: All the President's Men. 1977: Julia. L'imprécateur. 1978: Comes a Horseman. A Christmas to Remember (TV). 1979: Hurricane. Cabo Blanco. 1980: Melvin and Howard. Raise the Titanic! Ghosts of Cape Horn (narrator only). 1981: The Legend of the Lone Ranger. FDR: The Last Year (TV).
1982: Burden of Dreams. Something Wicked This Way Comes. 1983: Max Dugan Returns. The Day After (TV). 1984: America and Lewis Hine (voice only). Sakharov (TV). 1985: The Atlanta Child Murders (TV).

ROBERTS, Lynne (Mary Hart) 1919–
Most film buffs seem agreed that this resolute, sweet-faced, blue-eyed, auburn-haired American star was probably the best actress never to get out of 'B' pictures. There were frequent name changes, and 17 years of sterling service to low-budget westerns and thrillers. After ending in the arms of a man-eating crab in Port Sinister, she finally gave up. Who could blame her?
1937: ‡Love is On the Air. †Mama Runs Wild. †Stella Dallas. †Dangerous Holiday. 1938: †Call the Mesquiteers (GB: Outlaws of the Wild). †The Hollywood Stadium Mystery. †The Higgins Family. †The Lone Ranger (serial). †Billy the Kid Returns. ‡Come on Rangers. ‡Shine On, Harvest Moon. ‡Dick Tracy Returns (serial). ‡Heart of the Rockies. 1939: ‡Rough Riders' Roundup. ‡Should Husbands Work? ‡Frontier Pony Express. ‡Southward Ho. ‡In Old Caliente. ‡The Stadium Murders. ‡The Mysterious Miss X. ‡My Wife's Relatives. ‡Everything's on Ice. 1940: ‡Hi-Yo Silver (feature version of serial The Lone Ranger). †Street of Memories. †High School. ‡Parole Fixer. †Star Dust. †Romance of the Rio Grande. 1941: †Ride on, Vaquero! †The Bride Wore Crutches. †Riders of the Purple Sage. †Last of the Duanes. †Moon over Miami. 1942: †Young America. †Dr Renault's Secret. †The Man in the Trunk. †Quiet Please, Murder. 1943: †The Ghost That Walks Alone. 1944: Port of 40 Thieves. My Buddy. The Chicago Kid. The Big Bonanza. 1945: Behind City Lights. The Phantom Speaks. Girls of the Big House. 1946: The Inner Circle. Sioux City Sue. 1947: The Pilgrim Lady. That's My Gal. The Magnificent Rogue. Robin Hood of Texas. Saddle Pals. Winter Wonderland. 1948: Lightnin' in the Forest. The Timber Trail. Eyes of Texas. Madonna of the Desert. Secret Service Investigator. Trouble Preferred. 1950: Dynamite Pass. Call of the Klondike. The Blazing Sun. The Great Plane Robbery. Hunt the Man Down. 1951: Murder Ad Lib (TV. GB: cinemas). 1952: Because of You. The Blazing Forest. 1953: Pattern for Murder. Port Sinister.

‡As Mary Hart †As Lynn Roberts

ROBERTS, Rachel 1927–1980
Mature-looking, dark-haired Welsh actress, mostly on stage until hitting the film big-time as a randy housewife in *Saturday Night and Sunday Morning*. Despite some quieter parts, she found herself typed as blowsy widows and sexy landladies, to which she gave a strong erotic charge. Later on she was seen in harsher, broader roles. Married/divorced actors Alan Dobie (1932–) and Rex Harrison. Received an Academy Award nomination for *This Sporting Life*. Poisoned herself.
1953: *Valley of Song (US: Men Are Children Twice). The Limping Man. The Weak and the Wicked. 1954: The Crowded Day. 1957: The Good Companions. Davy. 1959: Our Man in Havana. 1960: Saturday Night and Sunday Morning. 1962: Girl on Approval. 1963: This Sporting Life. 1968: A Flea in Her Ear. 1969: Destiny of a Spy/The Gaunt Woman (TV). The Reckoning. 1970: Doctors' Wives. 1971: Wild Rovers. Baffled! 1973: O Lucky Man! The Belstone Fox. 1974: Murder on the Orient Express. 1975: Great Expectations (TV. GB: cinemas). Alpha Beta. Picnic at Hanging Rock. 1977: A Circle of Children (TV). 1978: Foul Play. Yanks. 1979: A Man Called Intrepid (TV). When a Stranger Calls. 1980: Charlie Chan and the Curse of the Dragon Queen. The Hostage Tower. 1981: The Wall.*

ROBERTSON, Cliff 1925–
Dark, curly-haired American actor with attractive speaking voice (it's surprising he hasn't been used more for narrations) whose film career had barely got started before he volunteered for service as a merchant seaman. He made a reputation on stage before returning to Hollywood and success as a leading man. After winning an Oscar for *Charly*, he set up a number of his own projects, but these proved largely uncommercial, and he has been most successful with roles that reveal the shadier side to his all-American looks. Married (second) to actress Dina Merrill (1925–) from 1966 to 1986.
1943: *Corvette K-225 (GB: The Nelson Touch). We've Never Been Licked (GB: Texas to Tokyo). 1955: Picnic. 1956: Autumn Leaves. 1957: The Girl Most Likely. 1958: The Naked and the Dead. Natchez (TV). Days of Wine and Roses (TV). 1959: Gidget. Battle of the Coral Sea. As the Sea Rages. 1961: Underworld USA. All in a Night's Work. The Big Show. The Cruel Day (TV). 1962: The Interns. PT 109. 1963: My Six Loves. Sunday in New York. 1964: 633 Squadron. The Best Man. Love Has Many Faces. 1965: Masquerade. Up from the Beach. 1967: The Honey Pot. 1968: The Devil's Brigade. Charly. The Sunshine Patriot (TV). 1969: Too Late the Hero. 1971: †J.W. Coop. 1972: The Great Northfield Minnesota Raid. 1973: Ace Eli and Rodger of the Skies. The Man without a Country (TV). 1974: A Tree Grows in Brooklyn (TV). Man on a Swing. 1975: My Father's House (TV). Three Days of the Condor. Out of Season. 1976: Midway (GB: Battle of Midway). Return to Earth (TV). Obsession. Shoot. 1977: Fraternity Row (narrator only). 1978: Overboard (TV). Dominique. 1979: †The Pilot. 1981: Brainstorm (released 1983). 1983: Class. Two of a Kind (TV). Star 80. 1985: Shaker One.*

†*Also directed*

ROBERTSON, Dale (Dayle Robertson) 1923–
Tall, dark, rugged, he-man American actor who quit schoolteaching for Hollywood in the late forties and was soon in leading roles. Did not quite survive a big star build-up from his studio, Fox, as a romantic lead, but remained a respected western star, in regular TV series from 1957. Also sings. Married/divorced Mary Murphy (*qv*).
1948: *The Boy with Green Hair. Johnny Belinda. 1949: The Girl from Jones Beach. Fighting Man of the Plains. Flamingo Road.* 1950: *The Cariboo Trail. Two Flags West. 1951: Call Me Mister. Take Care of My Little Girl. Golden Girl. 1952: Lydia Bailey. Return of the Texan. The Outcasts of Poker Flat. O. Henry's Full House (GB: Full House). 1953: The Silver Whip. The Farmer Takes a Wife. City of Bad Men. Devil's Canyon. 1954: The Gambler from Natchez. Sitting Bull. 1955: Top of the World. Son of Sinbad. 1956: The High Terrace. A Day of Fury. Dakota Incident. 1957: Hell Canyon Outlaws (GB: The Tall Trouble). Anna of Brooklyn/Fast and Sexy. The Still Trumpet (TV). 1963: Law of the Lawless. 1964: Blood on the Arrow. Coast of Skeletons. The Man from Button Willow (voice only). 1966: The One-Eyed Soldiers. Scalplock (TV). 1974: Melvin Purvis G-Man (GB: cinemas as The Legend of Machine Gun Kelly). 1975: Kansas City Massacre (TV). 1979: The Last Ride of the Dalton Gang (TV).*

ROBESON, Paul 1898–1976
Black American singer and actor with magnificent bass-baritone voice that seemed to come from somewhere near his boots. Made a number of indelible film appearances in the 1930s, mostly as labourers becoming kings of far-off lands, and became famous for his rendition of *Ol' Man River*, but his Communist-influenced political views hampered his later career. Died following a stroke (and a long period of ill-health).
1924: *Body and Soul. 1930: Borderline. 1933: The Emperor Jones. 1935: Sanders of the River. 1936: Show Boat. My Song Goes Forth/Africa Looks Up. Song of Freedom. 1937: Jericho (US: Dark Sands). Big Fella. King Solomon's Mines. 1939: The Proud Valley. 1942: Tales of Manhattan. Native Land (and narrator). 1955: Il canto dei grandi fiumi. 1979: Paul Robeson: Portrait of an Artist.*

ROBEY, Sir George (G. Wade) 1869–1954
For many years Britain's most famous and best-liked music-hall comedian, this bowler-hatted, bescarfed, beetle-browed laughter-maker was dubbed 'The Prime Minister of Mirth'. Made occasional silent comedies in between a hectic stage schedule; later proved a very respectable character actor.
1900: **The Rats 1913: *Good Queen Bess. *And Very Nice Too. 1914: *George Robey Turns Anarchist. 1916: £66 13s 9¾d for Every*

Man, Woman and Child. Blood Tells or: the Anti-Frivolity League. 1917: Doing His Bit. 1918: George Robey's Day Off. 1923: The Rest Cure. Widow Twan-Kee/One Arabian Night. Don Quixote. 1924: The Prehistoric Man. 1926: *Hints and Hobbies. No. 1. 1928: *Safety First. *The Barrister. 1929: *The Bride. *Mrs Mephistopheles. 1931: The Temperance Fete. 1932: Marry Me. 1933: Don Quixote (remake). 1934: Chu Chin Chow. 1935: Birds of a Feather. Royal Cavalcade (US: Regal Cavalcade). 1936: Men of Yesterday. Southern Roses. Calling the Tune. 1938: *Cavalcade of Stars. 1939: A Girl Must Live. 1942: Variety Jubilee. Salute John Citizen. 1943: They Met in the Dark. 1944: *Highlights of Variety No. 27. Henry V. 1945. The Trojan Brothers. Waltz Time. 1952: The Pickwick Papers. 1953: Ali Baba Nights.

ROBIN, Dany 1927–
Charming light-haired French actress. as pretty as her name. Boosted as a new international star in Act of Love in the early fifties, she gave an appealing performance, but preferred to remain in French films, with the occasional overseas venture.
1946: Lunegarde. Le destin s'amuse. Les portes de la nuit. Six heures à perdre. 1947: Une jeune fille savait. L'eventail. Le silence est d'or. Les amoureux sont seuls au monde. 1948: La passagère. 1949: Au p'tit zouave. Le soif des hommes. La voyage inattendue. 1951: Deux sous de violettes. Le plus joli péché du monde. Une histoire d'amour. 1952: Douze heures de bonheur. La fête à Henriette. 1953: Julietta. Les revoltés de Lomanach. Act of Love. Tempi

nostri. 1954: Napoléon. Cadet-Rouselle. 1955: Escale à Orly/Un soir à Orly. Frou-Frou. Paris coquin. 1956: C'est arrivé à Aden. Bonsoir Paris, bonjour l'amour. Le coin tranquille. 1957: C'est la faute d'Adam. Quand sonnera midi. 1958: L'école des cocottes. Mimi Pinson. Les dragueurs (GB: The Young Have No Morals). Suivez-moi, jeune homme. 1959: Le secret du chevalier d'Éon. 1960: Love and the Frenchwoman. Scheldungsgrund Liebe. 1961: Amours célèbres. Les Parisiennes. 1962: Waltz of the Toreadors. Mysteries of Paris. Conduite à gauche. Mandrin, bandit gentilhomme. 1963: Follow the Boys. Comment trouvez-vous ma soeur? 1964: Sursis pour un espion. La corde au cou. 1966: Don't Lose Your Head. 1968: The Best House in London. 1969: Topaz.

ROBINSON, Edward G. (Emmanuel Goldenberg) 1893–1973
Squat, wide-mouthed, toad-faced, dark-haired, totally magnetic, Romanian-born Hollywood star who made his name in gangster films and spat out his dialogue like bullets from a machine-gun. Also brought great power to quieter roles. Career somewhat harmed by the McCarthy witch-hunts. Special Academy Award 1972. In later life an acknowledged art expert (and avid collector). Died from cancer.
1916: Arms and the Woman. 1923: The Bright Shawl. 1929: The Hole in the Wall. 1930: Outside the Law. Night Ride. The Widow from Chicago. A Lady to Love. East is West. Little Caesar. 1931: Five Star Final. Smart Money. 1932: Tiger Shark. *The Stolen Jools (GB: The Slippery Pearls). Silver Dollar. The Hatchet Man (GB: The Honourable Mr Wong). Two Seconds. 1933: Little Giant. I Loved a Woman. 1934: The Man with Two Faces. Dark Hazard. The Whole Town's Talking (GB: Passport to Fame). 1935: Barbary Coast. 1936: Bullets or Ballots. *A Day at Santa Anita. Thunder in the City. 1937: The Last Gangster. Kid Galahad. 1938: I Am the Law. The Amazing Dr Clitterhouse. A Slight Case of Murder. 1939: Confessions of a Nazi Spy. Blackmail. 1940: Dr Ehrlich's Magic Bullet (GB: The Story of Dr Ehrlich's Magic Bullet). A Dispatch from Reuter's (GB: This Man Reuter). Brother Orchid. 1941: Manpower. The Sea Wolf. Unholy Partners. 1942: Larceny Inc. Tales of Manhattan. 1943: Flesh and Fantasy. Destroyer. 1944: Mr Winkle Goes to War

(GB: Arms and the Woman). Tampico. The Woman in the Window. Double Indemnity. 1945: Scarlet Street. Our Vines Have Tender Grapes. Journey Together. 1946: The Stranger. 1947: The Red House. 1948: All My Sons. Night Has a Thousand Eyes. Key Largo. 1949: House of Strangers. It's a Great Feeling. 1950: My Daughter Joy (US: Operation X). 1951: *Hollywood Memories (narrator only). 1952: Actors and Sin. 1953: The Big Leaguer. Vice Squad (GB: The Girl in Room 17). The Glass Web. 1954: Black Tuesday. The Violent Men (GB: Rough Company). 1955: A Bullet for Joey. Illegal. Hell on Frisco Bay. Tight Spot. 1956: Nightmare. The Ten Commandments. 1958: Shadows Tremble (TV). 1959: A Hole in the Head. Israel (narrator only). 1960: Seven Thieves. Pepe. 1962: My Geisha. Two Weeks in Another Town. Sammy Going South (US: A Boy Ten Feet Tall). 1963: The Prize. 1964: The Outrage. Good Neighbor Sam. Robin and the Seven Hoods. Cheyenne Autumn. 1965: The Cincinnati Kid. Who Has Seen the Wind? (TV). 1966: The Biggest Bundle of Them All. 1967: La blonde de Pékin. Never a Dull Moment. Grand Slam. Operation St Peter's. 1968: Uno scacco tutto matto (GB: It's Your Move. US: Mad Checkmate). Mackenna's Gold. 1969: UMC (TV. GB: Operation Heartbeat). 1970: Song of Norway. The Old Man Who Cried Wolf (TV). 1972: Neither by Day or by Night. 1973: Soylent Green.

ROBSON, Dame Flora 1902–1984
Distinguished British stage actress with dark, tightly-bunched hair and plain, Anne Revere-type looks that often got her cast as (sometimes frustrated) spinsters, but also enabled her to tackle an enviable range of character studies, from queens to killers. In Hollywood 1939–1942. Created Dame in 1960. Nominated for an Academy Award in Saratoga Trunk.
1931: Gentleman of Paris. 1932: Dance Pretty Lady. 1933: One Precious Year. Catherine the Great. 1936: Fire over England. 1937: Farewell Again (US: Troopship). †I Claudius. 1939: Poison Pen. *Smith. Wuthering Heights. Invisible Stripes. We Are Not Alone. 1940: The Sea Hawk. 1941: Bahama Passage. 1944: 2,000 Women. 1945: Saratoga Trunk. Great Day. Caesar and Cleopatra. 1946: The Years Between. 1947: Frieda. Black Narcissus. Holiday Camp. 1948: Good Time Girl. Saraband

for Dead Lovers (US: Saraband). 1952: Tall Headlines. 1953: Malta Story. *She Shall Be Called Woman (narrator only). 1954: Romeo and Juliet. 1957: High Tide at Noon. The Gypsy and the Gentleman. No Time for Tears. 1958: Innocent Sinners. 1962: 55 Days at Peking. 1963: Murder at the Gallop. 1964: Young Cassidy. Guns at Batasi. 1965: Those Magnificent Men in Their Flying Machines. A King's Story (voice only). Seven Women. 1966: Eye of the Devil. Cry in the Wind. 1967: The Shuttered Room. 1970: The Beast in the Cellar. The Beloved (GB: TV, as Sin). Fragment of Fear. 1971: La grande scrofa nera. 1972: Alice's Adventures in Wonderland. 1978.: Les Miserables (TV). Dominique. 1979: Gauguin – the Savage. A Man Called Intrepid (TV). 1981: A Tale of Two Cities (TV). Clash of the Titans.

†Unfinished

ROC, Patricia (Felicia Riese) 1918–
Glamorous brown-haired (sometimes blonde) British actress, one of the famous Gainsborough (Studios) ladies of the forties, who continually sought to further her career, travelling to France, Italy and Hollywood in search of top star roles, but always returning to Britain. Her fresh looks enabled her to stay in youthful roles until well into her thirties. An actress called Felicia Roc appears in the 1966 Spanish-made film Savage Pampas. It seems an extraordinary coincidence, but I have not yet seen a print of this film.
1938: The Rebel Son/Taras Bulba. The Gaunt Stranger (US: The Phantom Strikes). 1939: The Mind of Mr Reeder (US: The Mysterious Mr. Reeder). The Missing People. A Window in London (US: Lady in Distress). Dr O'Dowd. 1940: Pack Up Your Troubles. Three Silent Men. Gentleman of Venture (US: It Happened to One Man). 1941: The Farmer's Wife. My Wife's Family. 1942: Let the People Sing. We'll Meet Again. Suspected Person. 1943: Millions Like Us. 1944: 2,000 Women. Madonna of the Seven Moons. Love Story (US: A Lady Surrenders). 1945: The Wicked Lady. Johnny Frenchman. 1946: Canyon Passage. 1947: So Well Remembered. Jassy. The Brothers. Holiday Camp. When the Bough Breaks. 1948: One Night with You. 1949: Retour à la vie. The Perfect Woman. The Man on the Eiffel Tower. 1950: Blackjack (US: Captain Blackjack). L'inconnue de Montréal/Fugitive from

Montreal. 1951: Circle of Danger. 1952: Something Money Can't Buy. 1953: La Mia vita e' tua/My Life is Yours. 1954: Cartouche. 1955: La vedova (GB: The Widow). 1957: The Hypnotist (US: Scotland Yard Dragnet). The House in the Woods. 1960: Bluebeard's 10 Honeymoons.

ROGERS, Ginger (Virginia McMath) 1911–
Bright, vivacious, likeable blonde American dancer who, after a memorable series of thirties musicals with Fred Astaire, carved herself out a second career as an actress, winning an Oscar for Kitty Foyle. Her no-nonsense approach reflected itself in her (still very feminine) dancing, as well as her acting, and most of her heroines were self-reliant working girls. Married Lew Ayres 1934–1941 and Jacques Bergerac (1927–) 1953–1957, second and fourth of five.
1929: *Campus Sweethearts. *A Night in a Dormitory. *A Day of a Man of Affairs. 1930: *Office Blues. Queen High. Young Man of Manhattan. The Sap from Syracuse (GB: The Sap Abroad). Follow the Leader. 1931: Honor Among Lovers. The Tip Off (GB: Looking for Trouble). Suicide Fleet. 1932: The Tenderfoot. Carnival Boat. Hat Check Girl (GB: Embassy Girl). You Said a Mouthful. The Thirteenth Guest. *Hollywood on Parade No. 1. *Screen Snapshots No. 12. 1933: Broadway Bad (GB: Her Reputation). Professional Sweetheart (GB: Imaginary Sweetheart). A Shriek in the Night. 42nd Street. *Hollywood on Parade No. 3. Gold Diggers of 1933. Don't Bet on Love. Sitting Pretty. Flying Down to Rio. Chance at Heaven. 1934: Rafter Romance. Finishing School. Change of Heart. 20 Million Sweethearts. Upperworld. *Hollywood on Parade No. 13. The Gay Divorcee (GB: The Gay Divorce). Romance in Manhattan. 1935: Star of Midnight. Top Hat. In Person. Roberta. 1936: Follow the Fleet. Swing Time. 1937: *Holiday Greetings. Shall We Dance? Stage Door. 1938: Vivacious Lady. Having Wonderful Time. Carefree. 1939: Bachelor Mother. The Story of Vernon and Irene Castle. 1940: Lucky Partners. The Primrose Path. Kitty Foyle. 1941: Tom, Dick and Harry. 1942: Tales of Manhattan. Once Upon a Honeymoon. Roxie Hart. The Major and the Minor. 1943: *Show Business at War. Tender Comrade. *Safeguarding Mili-

tary Information. 1944: *Battle Stations (narrator only). Lady in the Dark. I'll Be Seeing You. *Ginger Rogers Finds a Bargain. 1945: Weekend at the Waldorf. 1946: Heartbeat. Magnificent Doll. 1947: It Had to Be You. 1949: The Barkleys of Broadway. 1950: Storm Warning. Perfect Strangers (GB: Too Dangerous to Love). 1951: The Groom Wore Spurs. 1952: We're Not Married. Dreamboat. Monkey Business. 1953: Forever Female. *Hollywood's Great Entertainers. 1954: Black Widow. Beautiful Stranger (US: Twist of Fate). 1955: Tight Spot. 1956: The First Travelling Saleslady. Teenage Rebel. 1957: Oh, Men! Oh, Women! 1964: The Confession (GB: TV as Quick! Let's Get Married). 1965: Harlow (TV).

ROGERS, Roy (Leonard Slye, later legally changed) 1911–
Light-haired, slight, faintly oriental-looking American singing cowboy who became for many years the world's number one money-making western star. His medium-budget westerns at Republic were longer (around 75 minutes) than the average and actually burst into colour for a while in the late forties. Also a popular recording star. His horse Trigger (1932–1965) was almost as famous. Married (second; first wife died) to Dale Evans (qv), his oft-time leading lady, since 1947. Still around, singing at carefully-constructed camp-fires and signing autographs, as ever, 'Happy Trails'.
1935: ‡*Slighty Static. †Way Up Thar. ‡The Old Homestead. **‡Tumbling Tumbleweeds. ‡Gallant Defender. 1936: ‡*Lonesome Trailer. ‡The Big Show. ‡Rhythm on the Range. ‡The Mysterious Avenger. ‡The Old Corral (GB: Texas Serenade). 1937: ‡The Old Wyoming Trail. †Wild Horse Rodeo. 1938: †The Old Barn Dance. Under Western Stars. Come on Rangers. Shine on, Harvest Moon. Billy the Kid Returns. 1939: Rough Raiders' Roundup. Frontier Pony Express. Southward Ho. In Old Caliente. The Arizona Kid. Wall Street Cowboy. Saga of Death Valley. Days of Jesse James. Jeepers Creepers (GB: Money Isn't Everything). 1940: The Dark Command. The Carson City Kid. The Ranger and the Lady. Colorado. Young Buffalo Bill. *Rodeo Dough. Young Bill Hickok. Border Legion. 1941: Robin Hood of the Pecos. *Meet Roy Rogers. In Old Cheyenne. Arkansas Judge (GB: False

Witness). Nevada City. Sheriff of Tombstone. Bad Man of Deadwood. Jesse James at Bay. Red River Valley. 1942: Man from Cheyenne. South of Santa Fé. Sunset on the Desert. Romance on the Range. Sons of the Pioneers. Sunset Serenade. Heart of the Golden West. Ridin' down the Canyon. 1943: King of the Cowboys. Idaho. Song of Texas. Silver Spurs. Man from Music Mountain. Hands across the Border. 1944: The Cowboy and the Senorita. The Yellow Rose of Texas. Song of Nevada. San Fernando Valley. Lights of Old Santa Fé. Brazil. Hollywood Canteen. Lake Placid Serenade. 1945: Bells of Rosarita. Utah. Sunset in El Dorado. The Man from Oklahoma. Don't Fence Me In. Along the Navajo Trail. 1946: Song of Arizona. Rainbow over Texas. My Pal Trigger. Under Nevada Skies. Roll on Texas Moon. Home in Oklahoma. Out California Way. 1947: Heldorado. 1947: Hit Parade of 1947. Apache Rose. Bells of San Angelo. Springtime in the Sierras. On the Old Spanish Trail. The Gay Ranchero. Under California Skies. Eyes of Texas. Nighttime in Nevada. Grand Canyon Trail. The Far Frontier. 1949: Susanna Pass. Down Dakota Way. The Golden Stallion. Bells of Coronado. 1950: Twilight in the Sierras. Trigger Jr. Sunset in the West. North of the Great Divide. Trail of Robin Hood. 1951: Spoilers of the Plains. Heart of the Rockies. In Old Amarillo. South of Caliente. Pals of the Golden West. 1952: *Screen Snapshots No. 205. Son of Paleface. 1954: *Screen Snapshots No. 224. 1959: Alias Jesse James. 1972: Outdoor Rambling. 1975: MacKintosh and T.J. (GB: TV).

‡As Leonard Slye (when billed) †As Dick Weston
**Scene deleted from final release print

ROGERS, Will 1879–1935
Drawling, straw-haired American comedian and entertainer with sagging lower lip, who won the hearts of the nation with his folksy humour, rope-twirling tricks and homespun philosophy. His became a guiding voice during the Depression. His films, once sound came along, were hugely popular, and he was much mourned when killed in a plane crash. 1918: Laughing Bill Hyde. 1919: Jubilo. Almost a Husband. Water Water Everywhere. 1920: Jes' Call Me Jim. Cupid the Cowpuncher. The Strange Boarder. 1921: Boys Will Be Boys. Honest Hutch. Guide of Women. Doubling

for Romeo. An Unwilling Hero. 1922: One Glorious Day. The Headless Horseman. A Poor Relation. Hustling Hank. The Ropin' Fool. One Day in 365. Uncensored Movies. 1923: Fruits of Faith. Hollywood. Gee Whiz, Genevieve. Family Fits. Highbrow Stuff. 1924: Don't Park There. The Cake Eater. Going to Congress. A Truthful Liar. Big Moments From Little Pictures. The Cowboy Sheik. Our Congressman. Two Wagons. 1927: Tiptoes. A Texas Steer. *Winging 'round Europe. *With Will Rogers in Dublin. *With Will Rogers in London. *With Will Rogers in Paris. *Reeling down the Rhine. 1928: *Over the Bounding Blue. 1929: They Had to See Paris. 1930: So This is London. Happy Days. Lightnin'. 1931: A Connecticut Yankee (GB: The Yankee at King Arthur's Court). Ambassador Bill. As Young As You Feel. 1932: Down to Earth. Too Busy to Work. Business and Pleasure. The Plutocrat. 1933: State Fair. Doctor Bull. Mr Skitch. 1934: David Harum. Handy Andy. Judge Priest. *Hollywood on Parade No. 13. 1935: The County Chairman. Life Begins at 40. Steamboat 'Round the Bend. Doubting Thomas. In Old Kentucky.

ROLAND, Gilbert (Luis de Alonso) 1905–
Stunningly handsome, moustachioed, black-haired Mexican leading man (from the same town as Anthony Quinn) who kept his good looks until well into middle age, and surprised many by becoming one of Hollywood's most efficient actors in the latter stages of his career. Married (first of two) to Constance Bennett from 1941 to 1946. 1925: The Lady Who Lied. The Plastic Age. 1926: The Blonde Saint. The Midshipman. The Campus Flirt. 1927: The Love Mart. Camille. The Dove. Rose of the Golden West. 1928: The Woman Disputed. 1929: New York Nights. 1930: Men of the North (and Spanish-language version). 1931: Resurrección. Hombres en mi Vida. 1932: Call Her Savage. Life Begins (GB: The Dawn of Life). No Living Witness. The Passionate Plumber. A Parisian Romance. The Woman in Room 13. 1933: Our Betters. She Done Him Wrong. Yo, tu y Ella. Una Viuda Romantica. Gigolettes of Paris. Tarnished Youth. After Tonight (GB: Sealed Lips). 1934: Elinor Norton. 1935: Ladies Love Danger. Mystery Woman. *La Fiesta de Santa Barbara. 1936: Julieta Compra un Hijo. 1937: Thunder Trail. Midnight Taxi. Last Train

from Madrid. 1938: Gateway. 1939: La Vida Bohemia. Juarez. 1940: The Sea Hawk. Isle of Destiny. Gambling on the High Seas. Rangers of Fortune. 1941: My Life with Caroline. Angels with Broken Wings. 1942: Enemy Agents Meet Ellery Queen (GB: The Lido Mystery). Isle of Missing Men. 1944: The Desert Hawk (serial). 1945: Captain Kidd. 1946: The Gay Cavalier. South of Monterey. Beauty and the Bandit. Le Rebellión de los Fantasmas. 1947: Riding the California Trail. The Other Love. Robin Hood of Monterey. High Conquest. King of the Bandits. Pirates of Monterey. 1948: The Dude Goes West. 1949: Malaya (GB: East of the Rising Sun). We Were Strangers. 1950: The Torch (GB: Bandit General). Crisis. The Furies. 1951: The Bullfighter and the Lady. Ten Tall Men. Mark of the Renegade. 1952: Glory Alley. Apache War Smoke. The Bad and the Beautiful. My Six Convicts. The Miracle of Our Lady of Fatima (GB: The Miracle of Fatima). 1953: Beneath the 12-Mile Reef. The Diamond Queen. Thunder Bay. 1954: The French Line. 1955: Underwater! The Racers (GB: Such Men Are Dangerous). The Treasure of Pancho Villa. That Lady. 1956: Around the World in 80 Days. Bandido! Three Violent People. 1957: The Midnight Story (GB: Appointment with a Shadow). Invitation to a Gunfighter (TV). 1958: Last of the Fast Guns. Mr Pharaoh and Cleopatra (US: Catch Me If You Can). 1959: The Wild and the Innocent. The Big Circus. Guns of the Timberland. 1962: Samar! 1964: Cheyenne Autumn. 1965: The Reward. 1966: The Poppy is Also a Flower (TV. GB: cinemas as Danger Grows Wild). 1968: Ognimo per se (GB and US: The Ruthless Four). Vado l'ammazzo e torno (GB and US: Any Gun Can Play). Anche nel West, c'era una volta Dio. Quella sporca storia del West. 1969: Entre Dios y El Diablo. Johnny Hamlet. 1971: The Christian Licorice Store. 1972: Incident on a Dark Street (TV). 1973: Running Wild. 1974: The Mark of Zorro (TV). Deliver Us from Evil. 1975: The Black Pearl. The Pacific Connection. The Deadly Tower (TV. Narrator only). 1976: Islands in the Stream. 1979: The Sacketts (TV). CaboBlanco. 1982: Barbarosa (filmed 1979).

ROLFE, Guy 1915–
Very tall, dark, gaunt, spidery British leading man, popular in serious roles between 1946

and 1960. One was surprised that such skull-like handsomeness was not more often found in horror films of the sixties and seventies than it was. A trip to Hollywood in the early fifties brought scant reward.

1937: Knight Without Armour. 1938: The Drum (US: Drums). 1946: Odd Man Out. Hungry Hill. 1947: Nicholas Nickleby. Meet Me at Dawn. Easy Money. Uncle Silas (US: The Inheritance). Broken Journey. 1948: Saraband for Dead Lovers (US: Saraband). Portrait from Life (US: The Girl in the Painting). 1949: Fools Rush In. The Spider and the Fly. 1950: The Reluctant Widow. Prelude to Fame. 1951: Home to Danger. 1952: Ivanhoe. 1953: Young Bess. The Veils of Bagdad. King of the Khyber Rifles. Operation Diplomat. 1954: Dance Little Lady. 1955: You Can't Escape. 1956: It's Never Too Late. 1958: Girls at Sea. 1959: Yesterday's Enemy. The Stranglers of Bombay. 1960: Revak the Rebel (US: The Barbarian). 1961: King of Kings. Snow White and the Three Stooges (GB: Snow White and the Three Clowns). 1962: Mr Sardonicus (GB: Sardonicus). Taras Bulba. 1963: The Fall of the Roman Empire. 1965: The Alphabet Murders. 1969: Land Raiders. 1971: Nicholas and Alexandra. 1973: And Now the Screaming Starts. 1979: Bloodline/Sidney Sheldon's Bloodline. 1983: The Case of Marcel Duchamp. 1986: The Doll/Dolls.

ROMAIN, Yvonne (Y. Warren) 1938–
Breathtakingly beautiful brunette London-born, French-raised actress, a former photographer's-model and in British films as a teenager. Her liquid eyes and stunning figure proved just the ticket for Hammer horror heroines, and she played them with spirit. After the horror vogue waned in the mid 1960s she was, alas, seldom seen. Long married to composer Leslie Bricusse.

1956: The Baby and the Battleship. 1957: Interpol (US: Pick Up Alley). Action of the Tiger. Portrait of a Matador. Seven Thunders (US: The Beasts of Marseilles). 1958: The Silent Enemy. Murder Reported. Corridors of Blood. 1960: Circus of Horrors. 1961: The Curse of the Werewolf. The Frightened City. Village of Daughters. 1962: Captain Clegg (US: Night Creatures). 1963: Return to Sender. The Devil Doll. 1964: Smokescreen. 1965: The Brigand of Kandahar. 1966: The

Swinger. Double Trouble. 1973: The Last of Sheila.

ROMAN, Ruth 1924–
Dark, curvaceous, vividly attractive, if slightly cold-looking American actress who struggled up to stardom through small roles and serials. Her peak starring time was quite short, but she has since come back as a mature, but still glamorous, character actress. Daughter of a circus barker.

*1943: Stage Door Canteen. 1944: Ladies Courageous. White Stallion/Harmony Trail. Since You Went Away. Storm over Lisbon. 1945: See My Lawyer. Jungle Queen (serial). The Affairs of Susan. Incendiary Blonde. You Came Along. She Gets Her Man. 1946: Without Reservations. A Night in Casablanca. Gilda. 1947: The Web. 1948: Belle Starr's Daughter. The Big Clock. Night Has a Thousand Eyes. Good Sam. 1949: Beyond the Forest. Always Leave Them Laughing. The Window. Champion. 1950: Barricade. Dallas. Three Secrets. Colt 45. 1951: Starlift. Lightning Strikes Twice. Strangers on a Train. Tomorrow is Another Day. *The Screen Director. 1952: Young Man with Ideas. Invitation. Mara Maru. 1953: Blowing Wild. 1954: Tanganyika. The Shanghai Story. The Far Country. Down Three Dark Streets. 1955: Joe Macbeth. La peccatrice del deserto. 1956: The Bottom of the Bottle (GB: Beyond the River). Great Day in the Morning. Rebel in Town. The Sinners. 1957: Five Steps to Danger. 1958: Bitter Victory. 1959: Desert Desperados. 1961: Look in Any Window. Miraglo a los Cobardes. 1964: Love Has Many Faces. 1970: The Old Man Who Cried Wolf (TV). Incident in San Francisco (TV). 1972: The Baby. 1973: The Killing Kind. Go Ask Alice (TV). 1974: Punch and Jody (TV). Impulse. A Knife for the Ladies. 1975: Dead of Night. 1976: Day of the Animals. 1979: The Sacketts (TV). 1980: Echoes. 1983: Silent Sentence.*

ROME, Stewart (Septimus Ryott) 1886–1965
Tall, dark, airily handsome British leading man of military bearing, one of the first great fan pin-ups of the silent screen. Immensely popular from 1914 to 1924, he soldiered on afterwards as a kind of father-figure to the British cinema, in character roles mainly as

stern and well bred as had been his intrepid early heroes.

*1913: *A Throw of the Dice. 1914: *The Price of Fame. *The Whirr of the Spinning Wheel. *Thou Shalt Not Steal. *What the Firelight Showed. *The Girl Who Played the Game. *The Girl Who Lived in Straight Street. *The Guest of the Evening. *The Stress of Circumstance. *Only a Flower Girl. *The Schemers. *Unfit. *The Bronze Idol. *His Country's Bidding. *The Awakening of Nora. *So Much Good in the Worst of Us. *The Quarry Mystery. *Tommy's Money Scheme. *The Double Event. *The Man from India. *They Say – Let Them Say. *John Linworth's Atonement. *The Lie. Justice. The Heart of Midlothian. The Great Poison Mystery. Creatures of Clay. *The Breaking Point. The Terror of the Air. Dr Fenton's Ordeal. The Grip of Ambition. The Chimes. The Brothers. Time, the Great Healer. Despised and Rejected. Life's Dark Road. The Cry of the Captive. The Strength of the Weak. 1915: *The Shepherd of Souls. *The Man with the Scar. *They Called Him Coward. *Schoolgirl Rebels. *The Confession. *Spies. *A Moment of Darkness. *One Good Turn. *Jill and the Old Fiddle. *The Recalling of John Gray. The Canker of Jealousy. Barnaby Rudge. A Lancashire Lass. The Incorruptible Crown. The Curtain's Secret. Court-Martialled. The Bottle. The Baby on the Barge. The Second String. The Sweater. Her Boy. Sweet Lavender. The Golden Pavement. The White Hope. The Nightbirds of London. As the Sun Went Down. Iris. Face to Face. 1916: Sowing the Wind. Trelawney of the Wells. Annie Laurie. The White Boys. Grand Babylon Hotel. Partners. The Marriage of William Ashe. Comin' Thro' the Rye. Molly Bawn. Her Marriage Lines. The House of Fortescue. Love in a Mist. 1917: The Cobweb. The American Heiress. The Man Behind 'The Times'. A Grain of Sand. The Eternal Triangle. 1918: The Touch of a Child. 1919: The Gentleman Rider (US: Hearts and Saddles). A Daughter of Eve. A Great Coup. Snow in the Desert. 1920: The Great Gay Road. The Case of Lady Camber. Her Son. The Romance of a Movie Star. 1921: The Penalty/Her Penalty. Christie Johnstone. The Penniless Millionaire. The Imperfect Lover. In Full Cry. 1922: Son of Kissing Cup. Dicky Monteith. When Greek Meets Greek. The White Hope (remake). 1923: Fires of Fate. The Prodigal Son. The Uninvited*

Guest. The Woman Who Obeyed. 1924: The Desert Sheik. The Colleen Bawn. The Eleventh Commandment. The Stirrup Cup Sensation. Nets of Destiny. The Shadow of the Morgue. Reveille. 1925: The Silver Treasure. 1926: Thou Fool. 1927: Somehow Good. 1928: The Ware Case. The Passing of Mr Quin. The Man Who Changed His Name. Zero. 1929: The Crimson Circle. Dark Red Roses. 1930: The Last Hour. The Price of Things. Kissing Cup's Race. 1931: The Great Gay Road (remake). Other People's Sins. Deadlock. Rynox. *Sound Cinemagazine No. 273. 1932: Reunion. Betrayal. The Marriage Bond. 1933: Song of the Plough. 1934: The Girl in the Flat. Important People. Lest We Forget. Designing Woman. Temptation. 1936: Men of Yesterday. Debt of Honour. 1937: The Squeaker (US: Murder on Diamond Row). Dinner at the Ritz. Wings of the Morning. 1938: The Dance of Death. 1939: Confidential Lady. The Warning. Shadowed Eyes. 1941: Banana Ridge. 1942: Salute John Citizen. One of Our Aircraft is Missing. 1944: *Tom's Ride. The World Owes Me a Living. 1946: The Magic Bow. 1947: The White Unicorn (US: Bad Sister). Jassy. 1948: My Sister and I. Woman Hater. 1950: Let's Have a Murder.

ROME, Sydne 1946–
So what's a nice Jewish girl from Ohio doing in films like these? At least this bubbly blonde American-born star provided lively decoration to French and Italian films of the seventies, most noticeably as the seldom-clothed Alice-in-Black-Wonderland heroine of Polanski's What! Her name really is Sydne Rome.
1969: Vivi, o preferibilimente morti. Some Girls Do. 1970: Ciao, Gulliver. La ragazza di latta. 1971: Un doppio a metà. 1972: Cosi sia. 1973: What! Order to Kill/El Clan de los Inmorales. Le ultimo ore di une vergine. L'ospite della notte. Reigen (GB: Dance of Love. US: Merry-Go-Round). La sculacciata. 1974: La race des 'Seigneurs'. Nel corpo e nell' anima. Il ragno. Nastro nero in casae Nichols. 1975: Wanted: Babysitter. Sex with a Smile. That Lucky Touch. Il faut vivre dangereusement. Creezy. 1976: L'immenso è rosso. Shadow of a Killer. The Twist/Folies Bourgeoises. 1977: Pour le corps d'une femme. Moi, fleur bleue (US: Stop Calling Me Baby! The Fiend/Il mostro. 1978: Just a Gigolo. Speed Fever/Formula 1. 1980: The Puma Man. Los locos vecinos del segundo.

1981: The Couples. Looping. 1982: Red Bells/Ten Days That Shook the World. Crazy Family/Arrivano i miei. 1986: The Final Romance.

ROMERO, Cesar 1907–
Handsome, strong-chinned, black-haired moustachioed American actor of Italian–Mexican parentage, typed as a Latin Lover from his earliest Hollywood days, although he had made his reputation as a dancer. For many years the film capital's most eligible bachelor, Romero has never married.
1933: The Shadow Laughs. 1934: Cheating Cheaters. The Thin Man. British Agent. 1935: The Good Fairy. Clive of India. Hold 'Em Yale (GB: Uniform Lovers). Diamond Jim. Rendezvous. Strange Wives. Cardinal Richelieu. The Devil is a Woman. Metropolitan. Show Them No Mercy (GB: Tainted Money). 1936: Nobody's Fool. Fifteen Maiden Lane. Love Before Breakfast. Public Enemy's Wife (GB: G-Man's Wife). 1937: Wee Willie Winkie. She's Dangerous. Dangerously Yours. Armored Car. 1938: Always Goodbye. Happy Landing. My Lucky Star. Five of a Kind. 1939: Return of the Cisco Kid. Charlie Chan at Treasure Island. Wife, Husband and Friend. The Little Princess. Frontier Marshal. 1940: Lucky Cisco Kid. He Married His Wife. Viva Cisco Kid. The Gay Caballero. The Cisco Kid and the Lady. 1941: Ride on, Vaquero! Tall, Dark and Handsome. Dance Hall. The Great American Broadcast. Romance of the Rio Grande. Week-End in Havana. 1941: Tales of Manhattan. Orchestra Wives. A Gentleman at Heart. Springtime in the Rockies. 1943: *Screen Snapshots No. 105. Coney Island. Wintertime. 1947: Carnival in Costa Rica. Captain from Castile. 1948: Deep Waters. Julia Misbehaves. That Lady in Ermine. 1949: The Beautiful Blonde from Bashful Bend. 1950: Once a Thief. Love That Brute. 1951: Happy-Go-Lovely. FBI Girl. The Lost Continent. 1952: The Jungle. Lady in the Fog (US: Scotland Yard Inspector). 1953: Prisoners of the Casbah. Street of Shadows (US: Shadow Man). 1954: El Corazon y la Espada (US: The Sword of Granada). Vera Cruz. 1955: *Hollywood Shower of Stars. The Americano. The Racers (GB: Such Man Are Dangerous). 1956: Around the World in 80 Days. Manhattan Tower (TV). *Screen Snapshots No. 235. The Leather Saint. *All's Fair in Love

(TV. GB: cinemas). 1957: The Story of Mankind. 1958: Villa! 1960: Ocean's Eleven. Pepe. 1961: Seven Women from Hell. 1962: If a Man Answers. The Castilian. 1963: We Shall Return. Donovan's Reef. 1964: A House is Not a Home. Two on a Guillotine. 1965: Sergeant Deadhead. Marriage on the Rocks. Broken Sabre (TV. GB: cinemas). 1966: Batman. 1967: Madigan's Millions. 1968: Hot Millions. A Talent for Loving. Crooks and Coronets (US: Sophie's Place). Skidoo. 1969: Don't Push, I'll Charge When I'm Ready (TV). Latitude Zero. How to Make It (GB: Target: Harry). Midas Run (GB: A Run on Gold). 1970: The Computer Wore Tennis Shoes. 1971: Soul Soldier (GB: Men of the Tenth). The Last Generation. 1972: Now You See Him, Now You Don't. The Specter of Edgar Allen Poe. The Proud and the Damned (GB: TV). 1973: Timber Tramp. 1974: The Strongest Man in the World. 1975: Won Ton Ton, the Dog Who Saved Hollywood. 1977: Kino, the Padre on Horseback. 1979: Monster. 1983: Vultures in Paradise/Flesh and Bullets. 1984: Lust in the Dust.

ROONEY, Mickey (Joseph Yule) 1920–
Dynamic, light-haired, pocket-sized American star, in films from childhood, after a stage debut at two in his parents' vaudeville act. Rooney could sing, dance, play piano and drums and act in such an engagingly chirpy way that he was soon the favourite of millions. After a career in comedy shorts from the late twenties he joined M-G-M and, whether making The Hardy Family series or teen-swing musicals with Judy Garland, became the world's number one box-office star for three years from 1939. After war service his star exploded, but he clawed his way back with some gritty acting performances, and still pops up in featured roles. Special Oscars 1938 and 1983. Nominated for Academy Awards in Babes in Arms, The Human Comedy, The Bold and the Brave and The Black Stallion. Eight times married. First wife (1942–1943) was Ava Gardner, third (1949–1951) Martha Vickers.
1926: *Not to be Trusted. 1927: †*Mickey's Pals. †*Mickey's Circus. †*Mickey's Eleven. Orchids and Ermine. †*Mickey's Battle. 1928: †*Mickey's Parade. †*Mickey's Little Eva. †*Mickey's Nine. †*Fillum Frolics. †*Mickey's Athletes. †*Mickey's Rivals. †*Mickey's Triumph. †*Mickey's Movies. †*Mickey's Big

Game Hunt. †*Mickey the Detective. †*Mickey's Babies (GB: Baby Show). †*Mickey's Wild West. 1929: †*Rattling Racers. †*Mickey's Surprise. •†*Mickey's Big Moment. †*Mickey's Brown Derby. †*Mickey's Explorers. †*Mickey's Great Idea. †*Mickey's Initiation. †*Mickey's Last Chance. †*Mickey's Menagerie. †*Mickey's Northwest Mounted. †*Mickey's Mix-Up. †*Birthday Squeakings. †*Mickey's Midnight Follies. 1930: †*Mickey's Strategy. †*Mickey's Champs. †*Mickey's Luck. †*Mickey's Master Mind. †*Mickey's Musketeers. †*Mickey's Whirlwinds. †*Mickey's Winners. †*Mickey's Warriors. †*Mickey the Romeo. †*Mickey's Merry Men. †*Mickey's Bargain. 1931: †*Mickey's Rebellion. †*Mickey's Diplomacy. †*Mickey's Thrill Hunters. †*Mickey's Helping Hand †*Mickey's Stampede. †*Mickey's Crusaders. †*Mickey's Sideline. †*Mickey's Big Business. †*Mickey's Wildcats. 1932. †*Mickey's Travels. †*Mickey's Holiday. †*Mickey's Golden Rule. †*Mickey's Busy Day. †*Mickey's Charity. Information Kid/ Fast Companions. My Pal the King. Sin's Pay Day. Beast of the City. 1933: †*Mickey's Ape Man. †*Mickey's Race. †*Mickey's Big Broadcast. †*Mickey's Covered Wagon. †*Mickey's Disguises. †*Mickey's Touchdown. †*Mickey's Tent Show. Broadway to Hollywood (GB: Ring Up the Curtain). The Big Cage. The Chief (GB: My Old Man's a Fireman). The World Changes. The Life of Jimmy Dolan (GB: The Kid's Last Fight). The Big Chance. 1934: The Lost Jungle (serial). †*Mickey's Minstrels. †*Mickey's Rescue. †*Mickey's Medicine Men. Love Birds. Beloved. I Like It That Way. Manhattan Melodrama. Hide-Out. Half a Sinner. Death on the Diamond. Chained. Upper World. Blind Date. 1935: The County Chairman. A Midsummer Night's Dream. The Healer. Reckless. Riff Raff. Ah, Wilderness! 1936: Down the Stretch. *Pirate Party on Catalina Isle. Little Lord Fauntleroy. The Devil is a Sissy (GB: The Devil Takes the Count). 1937: The Hoosier Schoolboy (GB: Yesterday's Hero). Thoroughbreds Don't Cry. Captains Courageous. A Family Affair. Slave Ship. Live, Love and Learn. 1938: Judge Hardy's Children. Hold That Kiss. Love is a Headache. Lord Jeff (GB: The Boy from Barnardo's). Love Finds Andy Hardy. Boys' Town. Out West with the Hardys. Stablemates. 1939: The Adventures of Huckleberry Finn. The Hardys Ride High. Babes in Arms. Judge Hardy and Son. Andy Hardy Gets Spring Fever. 1940. *Rodeo Dough. Andy Hardy Meets Debutante. Young Tom Edison. Strike Up the Band. Andy Hardy's Private Secretary. 1941: Men of Boys' Town. *Cavalcade of the Academy Awards. Life Begins for Andy Hardy. Babes on Broadway. *Meet the Stars No. 4. 1942: The Courtship of Andy Hardy. A Yank at Eton. Andy Hardy's Double Life. 1943: Girl Crazy. Thousands Cheer. The Human Comedy. 1944: National Velvet. Andy Hardy's Blonde Trouble. 1946: Love Laughs at Andy Hardy. Summer Holiday (released 1948). 1947: Killer McCoy. 1948: Words and Music. *Rough but Hopeful. 1949: The Big Wheel. 1950: He's a Cockeyed Wonder. The Fireball. 1951: My

Outlaw Brother. The Strip. 1952: *Screen Snapshots No. 205. Sound Off. Off Limits (GB: Military Policemen). 1953: A Slight Case of Larceny. *Mickey Rooney – Then and Now. 1954: Drive a Crooked Road. The Bridges at Toko-Ri. The Atomic Kid. 1955: The Twinkle in God's Eye. 1956: The Bold and the Brave. Magnificent Roughnecks. Francis in the Haunted House. 1957: The Comedian (TV). Operation Mad Ball. Baby Face Nelson. *Playtime in Hollywood. 1958: Andy Hardy Comes Home. *Glamorous Hollywood. 1959: A Nice Little Bank That Should Be Robbed. The Last Mile. The Big Operator. 1960: Platinum High School (GB: Rich, Young and Deadly). The Private Lives of Adam and Eve. 1961: King of the Roaring Twenties (GB: The Big Bankroll). Everything's Ducky. Breakfast at Tiffany's. 1962: Requiem for a Heavyweight (GB: Blood Money). 1963: It's a Mad, Mad, Mad, Mad World. 1964: The Secret Invasion. 1965: How to Stuff a Wild Bikini. The Devil in Love. 24 Hours to Kill. 1966: Ambush Bay. 1968: The Extraordinary Seaman. Skidoo. 1969: 80 Steps to Jonah. The Comic. The Cock-eyed Cowboys of Calico County (GB: TV as A Woman for Charlie). 1970: Hollywood Blue. 1971: Evil Roy Slade (TV). Journey Back to Oz (voice only). B.J. Lang Presents. 1972: Pulp. Richard. 1974: That's Entertainment! Ace of Hearts. Bon Baisers de Hong Kong. 1975: Rachel's Man. 1976: The Domino Killings. 1977: Pete's Dragon. 1978: The Magic of Lassie. Donovan's Kid (TV). 1979: Rudolph and Frosty's Christmas in July (voice only). Arabian Adventure. The Black Stallion. 1980: Find the Lady. My Kidnapper, My Love (TV). Odyssey of the Pacific. 1981: Leave 'Em Laughing (TV). The Fox and the Hound (voice only). Bill (TV). Senior Trip (TV). 1983: Bill: On His Own (TV). 1984: It Came Upon the Midnight Clear (TV). 1985: The Care Bears Movie (voice only). 1986: The White Stallion. The Return of Mike Hammer (TV).

ROSAY, Françoise (F. de Nalèche) 1891–1974

For many years the grande dame of French cinema. Sang at the Paris Opera as a young girl, then married director Jacques Feyder in 1917, but her film career did not really get under way until the coming of sound. After fleeing to England in 1943, and making a number of films there, she became a character actress greatly in demand on the international

scene. Also a writer.

1913: Falstaff. 1915: Les vampires. 1916: Tête de femme, femme de tête. 1922: Crainquebille. 1925: Gribiche. 1927: Les deux timides. 1928: Madame Recamier. Le bâteau de verre. 1929: The One Woman Idea. Soyons gais. Echec au roi. Si l'empereur savait ça. The Trial of Mary Dugan (French version). Buster se marie (French version of Spite Marriage). Le petit café. 1930: A Lady's Morals (GB: Jenny Lind). The Magnificent Lie. 1931: Casanova wider willen (German version of Parlor, Bedroom and Bath. GB: Romeo in Pyjamas). Quand on est belle. La chance. La femme en homme. 1932: Papa sans le savoir. Le rosier de Madame Husson (GB: The Virtuous Isadore US: He). Tambour battant. Le pouponnière. 1933: Le billet de mille. Hé! 1934: L'abbé Constantin. Le grand jeu. Coralie et compagnie. Vers l'abime. Pension Mimosas. Remous. Gangster malgré lui. Tout pour rien. Die Insel. 1935: Maternité. Marchand d'amour. Marie des Angoisses. La kermesse heroïque (GB and US: Carnival in Flanders). 1936: Le secret de polichinelle. Jenny. La porteuse de pain. Die letzten vier von Santa Cruz/Die letzten vier von St. Paul. 1937: Drôle de drame. Mein Sohn, der Herr Minister. Un carnet de bal (GB: A Dance Programme. US: Christine). Le fauteuil. 1938: Paix sur le Rhin. Ramuntcho. Le joueur d'échecs. Le ruisseau. Fahrendes Volk/Les gens du voyage. La symphonie des brigands. 1939: Die Hochzeitreise (US: Wedding Journey). Bizarre Bizarre. Serge Panine. 1940: Elles étaient douze femmes. 1941: Une femme disparait. 1943: Le père Chopin. 1944: Halfway House. 1945: Johnny Frenchman. 1946: Macadam. La dame de Haut-le-Bois. 1948: The Barton Mystery. Saraband for Dead Lovers (US: Saraband). Quartet. 1949: Maria Chapdelaine (GB: The Naked Heart). 1950: On n'aime qu'un fois. September Affair. Les vagabonds du rêve. Femmes sans nom. Le banquet de frandeurs. 1951: The Thirteenth Letter. The Seven Deadly Sins. The Red Inn/L'auberge rouge. Fils de personne (GB: Nobody's Child). L'orgeuil. 1952: Sur le point des soupirs. Wanda la pécheresse. Tempo di Charleston. 1953: Qui est sans péché? La princesse d'Eboli. 1954: La reine Margot. 1955: La chasse aux maris. That Lady. Raggazze d'oggi. Le long des trottoirs. 1957: Interlude. The Seventh Sin. 1958: Du rififi chez les femmes (US: Riff Raff Girls). Le joueur. Me and the Colonel. The Sound and the Fury. 1959: Sans tambour ni trompette. Les yeux de l'amour. Une fleur au fusil. 1960: Stefanie in Rio. Le bois des amants (GB: Between Love and Duty). 1961: The Full Treatment (US: Stop Me Before I Kill!). Le cave se rebiffe (US: The Sucker Strikes Back). The Last of Mrs Cheyney/La mystérieuse Madame Cheyney. 1962: The Longest Day. Pourquoi Paris? 1963: Volles Hertz und leere Taschen. 1965: Up from the Beach. La metamorphose des cloportes. 1967: The 25th Hour. 1968: Léontine/Operation Léontine. Faut pas prendre les enfants du bon Dieu pour des canards sauvages. 1969: Un merveilleux parfum d'oseille. 1972: Trois milliards sans ascenseur. Pas folle la guêpe. 1973: Le piéton/ The Pedestrian.

ROSMER, Milton (Arthur M. Lunt) 1881–1971

Dark, forbidding British stage actor (since 1899) with voice to match. Barnstormed his way through many early British silent features, but later preferred to concentrate on direction with the odd meaty character role.
1915: *The Mystery of a Hansom Cab.* 1916: *Cynthia in the Wilderness. Whoso is without Sin. Lady Windermere's Fan. Still Waters Run Deep. The Man without a Soul (US: I Believe). The Greater Need.* 1917: *Little Women.* 1919: *The Odds Against Her. The Chinese Puzzle.* 1920: *Wuthering Heights. With All Her Heart. The Golden Web. Col. Newcome the Perfect Gentleman. The Twelve Pound Look. Torn Sails.* 1921: *Demos (US: Why Men Forget). A Woman of No Importance. A Romance of Wastdale. The Amazing Partnership. Belphegor the Mountebank. The Diamond Necklace. General John Regan. The Will.* 1922: **David Garrick. The Passionate Friends. The Pointing Finger.* 1923: *A Gamble with Hearts.* 1924: *The Shadow of Egypt.* 1929: *High Treason.* 1930: *The 'W' Plan.* 1934: *Grand Prix. The Phantom Light.* 1937: *South Riding.* 1939: *Let's Be Famous. *Beyond Our Horizons. Goodbye Mr Chips! The Lion Has Wings. Return to Yesterday. The Stars Look Down.* 1940: **Dangerous Comment.* 1941: *Atlantic Ferry (US: Sons of the Sea). *You're Telling Me. Hatter's Castle.* 1946: *Daybreak.* 1947: *Frieda. Fame is the Spur. The End of the River.* 1948: *Who Killed Van Loon? The Monkey's Paw. The Small Back Room.*

As director: 1926: **Cash on Delivery. *The Woman Juror.* 1930: *P.C. Josser.* 1931: *Many Waters.* 1932: *After the Ball.* 1933: *Channel Crossing.* 1934: *The Secret of the Loch. What Happened to Harkness.* 1935: *The Guv'nor (US: Mister Hobo). Emil and the Detectives (US: Emil). Maria Marten, or: Murder in the Red Barn.* 1936: *Everything is Thunder.*
As co-director: 1929: *Balaclava.* 1931: *Dreyfus (US: The Dreyfus Case).* 1937: *The Great Barrier (US: Silent Barriers).* 1938: *The Challenge.*

ROSS, Katharine 1942–
Attractive, very dark, tart-voiced American actress whose career did not race on at quite the pace expected after three big hits in the late 1960s. Tried (perhaps too hard) to be choosy, but has been in routine roles now for the past decade. Her third husband (since 1984) is actor Sam Elliott (*qv*). Nominated for an Academy Award in *The Graduate*.
1965: *Mr Buddwing (GB: Woman Without a Face). The Singing Nun. Shenandoah.* 1966: *The Longest Hundred Miles (TV).* 1967: *The Graduate. Games.* 1968: *Hellfighters.* 1969: *Butch Cassidy and the Sundance Kid. Tell Them Willie Boy is Here.* 1970: *Get to Know Your Rabbit. Fools.* 1972: *They Only Kill Their Masters.* 1974: *Le hasard et le violence (GB: The Scarlet Room). The Stepford Wives.* 1976: *Wanted: The Sundance Woman (TV). Voyage of the Damned.* 1978: *The Betsy. The Swarm. The Legacy.* 1979: *Murder by Natural Causes (TV).* 1980: *The Final Countdown. Rodeo Girl (TV).* 1981: *Murder in Texas (TV).* 1982: *Wrong Is Right (GB: The Man with the Deadly Lens). Pigs (later Daddy's Deadly Darling. Filmed 1972). Travis McGee (TV). The Shadow Riders (TV). Marian Rose White (TV).* 1983: *Secrets of a Mother and Daughter (TV).*

ROUNDTREE, Richard 1937–
Tree-like black American actor who came to the fore with his powerhouse portrayal of detective John Shaft in a violent thriller series – James Bond for adults only. Unfortunately, a subsequent *Shaft* television series and secondary roles in pot-boiler adventures seem to have tamed his explosive style.
1969: *What do you say to a Naked Lady?* 1971: *Shaft.* 1977: *Embassy. Shaft's Big Score. Charley One Eye.* 1973: *Shaft in Africa. Firehouse (TV).* 1974: *Earthquake.* 1975: *Man*

Friday. Diamonds. 1977: *Jimbuck.* 1978: *Escape to Athena.* 1979: *Game for Vultures.* 1980: *Inchon!* 1981: *Day of the Assassin. An Eye for an Eye.* 1982: *'Q' The Winged Serpent. The Graduates of Malibu High. One Down Two to Go. Portrait of a Hitman.* 1983: *The Big Score. Young Warriors.* 1984: *Killpoint. City Heat.* 1985: *The Baron and the Kid. Road Trip. Clay Pigeons.* 1986: *The Fifth Missile (TV).*

ROURKE, Mickey (Philip Rourke) 1955–
Dark-haired, strong-jawed American actor whose 'Bowery Boy'-style good looks and rough-edged tones have often qualified him for rebels from the wrong side of the tracks. A former boxer, he quickly attracted attention when breaking through to featured roles in his late twenties. Can seize a film by the scruff of its neck and dominate it totally, rather more than most of his contemporaries in the Hollywood 'young lions' brigade. Married to actress Debra Feuer.
1979: *Panic on Page One (TV. Later: City in Fear). 1941.* 1980: *Act of Love (TV). Heaven's Gate. Fade to Black.* 1981: *Body Heat.* 1982: *Diner. Eureka.* 1983: *Rumble Fish. Rape and Marriage: The Rideout Case (TV).* 1984: *The Pope of Greenwich Village. 9½ Weeks.* 1985: *Year of the Dragon. †Homeboy.* 1986: *Angel Heart.* 1987: *Barfly.*

†*And directed*

ROWLANDS, Gena (Virginia Rowlands) 1934–

Cool, blonde American leading lady, mainly on stage and television, and most effective for the cinema in films directed by her husband, actor-director John Cassavetes (qv; married 1954). Increasingly appeared in bravura roles in his films, and has been twice nominated for Academy Awards, for *A Woman under the Influence* and *Gloria*.

1958: *The High Cost of Loving*. 1962: *A Child is Waiting*. *Lonely Are the Brave*. *The Spiral Road*. 1967: *Tony Rome*. 1968: *Faces*. *Gli intoccabili/Machine Gun McCain*. 1969: *The Happy Ending*. 1971: *Minnie and Moscowitz*. 1974: *A Woman under the Influence*. 1976: *Two-Minute Warning*. 1977: *Opening Night*. 1978: *The Brink's Job*. *A Question of Love (TV)*. 1979: *Strangers: the Story of a Mother and Daughter (TV)*. 1980: *Gloria*. 1982: *Tempest*. 1983: *Thursday's Child (TV)*. *Love Streams*. 1984: *I'm Almost Not Crazy …* 1986: *The Third Day Comes*. *An Early Frost (TV)*. *Light of Day*.

RUGGLES, Charles 1886–1970
Small, sandy-haired, moustachioed American comic actor, all huffle and snuffle and an amusingly off-hand style: a likeable asset to a film whether as support or star, and especially popular as the dapper but henpecked husband in a very successful series of comedies with big Mary Boland as his wife. Brother of director Wesley Ruggles. Died from cancer.

1915: *Peer Gynt*. *The Reform Candidate*. *The Majesty of the Law*. 1923: *The Heart Raider*. 1928: **Wives Etc*. 1929: *The Lady Lies*. *Gentlemen of the Press*. *The Battle of Paris*. 1930: **The Hot Air Merchant*. **The Family Next Door*. *Queen High*. *Roadhouse Nights*. *Young Man of Manhattan*. *Charley's Aunt*. 1931: *The Girl Habit*. *Honor Among Lovers*. *Beloved Bachelor*. *The Smiling Lieutenant*. *This is the Night*. 1932: *Husband's Holiday*. *Make Me a Star*. *One Hour with You*. *70,000 Witnesses*. *Evenings for Sale*. *Madame Butterfly*. *Love Me Tonight*. *This Reckless Age*. *The Night of June 13*. *Trouble in Paradise*. *If I Had a Million*. 1933: *Mama Loves Papa*. *Murders in the Zoo*. *Alice in Wonderland*. *Melody Cruise*. *Girl without a Room*. *Goodbye Love*. *Terror Aboard*. 1934: *Murder in the Private Car (GB: Murder on the Runaway Train)*. *Six of a Kind*. *The Pursuit of Happiness*. *Friends of Mr Sweeney*. *Melody in Spring*. 1935: *No More Ladies*. *People Will Talk*. *Ruggles of Red Gap*. *The Big Broadcast of 1936*. 1936: *Wives Never Know*. *Early to Bed*. *Anything Goes*. *Mind Your Own Business*. *The Preview Murder Mystery*. *Hearts Divided*. 1937: *Exclusive*. *Turn off the Moon*.

1938: *Service De Luxe*. *Bringing Up Baby*. *His Exciting Night*. *Breaking the Ice*. 1939: *Sudden Money*. *Yes, My Darling Daughter*. *Invitation to Happiness*. *Boy Trouble*. *Balalaika*. *Night Work*. 1940: *Maryland*. *The Farmer's Daughter*. *Opened by Mistake*. *Public Deb. No. 1*. *No Time for Comedy*. 1941: *Model Wife*. *The Invisible Woman*. *The Parson of Panamint*. *The Perfect Snob*. *Go West, Young Lady*. 1942: *Friendly Enemies*. 1943: *Dixie Dugan*. 1944: *Our Hearts Were Young and Gay*. **The Shining Future*. *The Doughgirls*. *Three is a Family*. 1945: *Bedside Manner*. *Incendiary Blonde*. 1946: *The Perfect Marriage*. *A Stolen Life*. *Gallant Journey*. 1947: *It Happened on Fifth Avenue*. *Ramrod*. 1948: *Give My Regards to Broadway*. 1949: *The Loveable Cheat*. *Look for the Silver Lining*. 1958: *The Male Animal (TV)*. *Girl on the Subway (TV. GB: cinemas)*. 1961: *All in a Night's Work*. *The Pleasure of His Company*. *The Parent Trap*. 1963: *Son of Flubber*. *Papa's Delicate Condition*. 1964: *I'd Rather Be Rich*. 1966: *The Ugly Dachshund*. *Follow Me, Boys!*

RULE, Janice 1931–
Tall, tawny-haired American actress in quiet, well-bred roles. In a spasmodic film career (although she never missed a year on television until 1973) magazines always appeared to be referring to her latest 'comeback'. Yet, even when it gave her sexier roles, the cinema seemed to miss out on her latent warmth. Married to Ben Gazzara (qv) from 1961 to 1979.

1951: *Goodbye My Fancy*. *Starlift*. 1952: *Holiday for Sinners*. *Rogue's March*. 1956: *A Woman's Devotion (GB: War Shock)*. *Gun for a Coward*. 1957: *Four Women in Black (TV)*. 1958: *Bell, Book and Candle*. 1960: *Journey to the Day (TV)*. *The Subterraneans*. 1964: *Invitation to a Gunfighter*. 1966: *The Chase*. *Alvarez Kelly*. *Welcome to Hard Times (GB: Killer on a Horse)*. 1967: *The Swimmer*. *The Ambushers*. 1968: *Shadow on the Land (TV)*. 1969: *Trial Run (TV)*. 1970: *Doctors' Wives*. 1971: *The Devil and Miss Sarah (TV)*. *Gumshoe*. 1973: *Kid Blue/Dime Box*. 1977: *Three Women*. 1982: *Missing*. 1984: *Rainy Day Friends*. 1985: *American Flyers*.

RUSH, Barbara 1927–
There wasn't a prettier actress in the movies in the early fifties than dark-haired, dark-eyed

Miss Rush. She had a trim figure, a lovely smile and talent too. As with so many of their latently-talented lovelies, Universal-International didn't treat her too well, keeping her in ingenue roles. She gave her best performance (in *Bigger Than Life*) just after leaving them, and, although not quite a strong enough actress to hold her place at the top, has stayed in there slugging. Married to Jeffrey Hunter (1950–1955), first of two.

1950: *Molly*. 1951: *The First Legion*. *Quebec*. *When Worlds Collide*. *Flaming Feather*. 1953: *Prince of Pirates*. *It Came from Outer Space*. 1954: *Taza, Son of Cochise*. *The Black Shield of Falworth*. *Magnificent Obsession*. *Captain Lightfoot*. 1955: *Kiss of Fire*. 1956: *World in My Corner*. *Bigger Than Life*. *Flight to Hong Kong*. 1957: *Oh Men! Oh Women!* *No Down Payment*. *The Troublemakers (TV)*. 1958: *The Young Lions*. *Harry Black and the Tiger (GB: Harry Black)*. 1959: *The Young Philadelphians (GB: The City Jungle)*. 1960: *The Bramble Bush*. *Strangers When We Meet*. *Alas, Babylon (TV)*. 1963: *Come Blow Your Horn*. 1964: *Robin and the Seven Hoods*. *Strategy of Terror (TV. GB: cinemas)*. 1966: *Hombre*. 1971: *Suddenly Single (TV)*. *The Man*. 1972: *The Eyes of Charles Sand (TV)*. *Moon of the Wolf (TV)*. *Crime Club (TV)*. 1973: *Cutter (TV)*. 1974: *Superdad*. *Of Men and Women II (TV)*. *Fools, Females and Fun (TV)*. 1975: *The Last Day (TV)*. 1976: *The Siege (TV)*. 1979: *The Night the Bridge Fell Down (TV. Released 1983)*. *Death Car on the Freeway (TV)*. 1980: *Can't Stop the Music*. 1982: *Summer Lovers*.

RUSSELL, Gail 1924–1961
Another of Hollywood's great tragedies: a haunting, beautiful, limpid-eyed, gentle-seeming brunette who played helpless heroines beset by problems. In real life she was indeed beset, by the alcoholism that started at an early stage of her career and had ruined it by the early fifties. Found dead on the floor of her apartment 'of natural causes'. Married to Guy Madison 1949–1954.

1943: *Henry Aldrich Gets Glamour (GB: Henry Gets Glamour)*. 1944: *Lady in the Dark*. *Our Hearts Were Young and Gay*. *The Uninvited*. 1945: *Duffy's Tavern*. *The Unseen*. *Salty O'Rourke*. 1946: *Our Hearts Were Growing Up*. *The Bachelor's Daughters (GB: Bachelor Girls)*. 1947: *Variety Girl*. *Angel and the Badman*. *Calcutta*. 1948: *Moonrise*. *Night Has a*

Thousand Eyes. Wake of the Red Witch. 1949: Song of India. Captain China. El Paso. The Great Dan Patch. 1950: The Lawless (GB: The Dividing Line). 1951: Air Cadet (GB: Jet Men of the Air). 1956: Seven Men from Now. 1957: The Tattered Dress. 1958: No Place to Land (GB: Man Mad). 1961: The Silent Call.

RUSSELL, Jane (Ernestine J. Russell) 1921–

A rarity: not only a brunette sex symbol but one who became more fondly regarded by the public as time wore on. She looked as though she liked the cinema to be fun, and her sense of humour and acceptance of her own limited ability lifted more than one of her films. A big, raw-boned lady, she is most enjoyable in her roles opposite Robert Mitchum and Bob Hope – two leading men to whom she obviously responded.

1943: The Outlaw. 1946: Young Widow. 1948: The Paleface. Montana Belle (released 1952). 1950: Double Dynamite. *Hollywood Goes to Bat. 1951: His Kind of Woman. 1952: Road to Bali. Macao. Son of Paleface. The Las Vegas Story. *Screen Snapshots No. 205. 1953: Gentlemen Prefer Blondes. 1954: The French Line. *Hollywood Cowboy Stars. 1955: Gentlemen Marry Brunettes. Foxfire. Underwater. The Tall Men. 1956: Hot Blood. The Revolt of Mamie Stover. 1957: *Playtime in Hollywood. The Fuzzy Pink Nightgown. 1964: Fate is the Hunter. 1966: Johnny Reno. Waco. †The Honorable Frauds. 1967: Born Losers. 1970: Darker Than Amber. 1973: Cauliflower Cupids. 1981: The Jackass Trail.

†*Unreleased.*

RUSSELL, John 1921–

Handsome heavies are not exactly a dime-a-dozen, so it's surprising that clean-looking, very tall, brown-haired American actor John Russell, with his quiet menace and sharkish smile, did not become a bigger name, especially during his period with 20th Century-Fox. He had some success on TV, especially in the *Lawman* series, but has been seen only sporadically in films and TV since 1960, often in films starring Clint Eastwood. Films previously credited to Russell between 1937 and 1940 are almost certainly the work of a younger actor, also known as Johnny Russell.

1945: A Royal Scandal (GB: Czarina). Don Juan Quilligan. A Bell for Adano. Within These Walls. 1946: Somewhere in the Night. The Dark Corner. Wake Up and Live. 1947: Forever Amber. 1948: Sitting Pretty. Yellow Sky. 1949: Slattery's Hurricane. The Gal Who Took the West. The Story of Molly X. Undertow. 1950: Saddle Tramp. Frenchie. 1951: The Fat Man. Fighting Coast Guard. The Barefoot Mailman. Man in the Saddle (GB: The Outcast). Hoodlum Empire. 1952: Oklahoma Annie. 1953: The Sun Shines Bright. Fair Wind to Java. 1954: Jubilee Trail. 1955: Hell's Outpost. The Last Command. 1957: Untamed Youth. The Dalton Girls. Hell Bound. 1958: Fort Massacre. 1959: Rio Bravo. Yellowstone Kelly. 1965: Apache Uprising. 1966: Fort Utah. 1967: Hostile Guns. 1968: If He Hollers, Let Him Go! Buckskin. 1970: Cannon for Cordoba. 1971: Smoke in the Wind. Noon Sunday. Legacy of Blood. 1976: The Outlaw Josey Wales. Six Tickets to Hell. 1977: Kino, the Padre on Horseback. 1981: Uncle Scam. 1982: Honkytonk Man. 1985: Pale Rider.

RUSSELL, Kurt 1951–

Light-haired, chubby-faced American actor, of medium height but thickly built, in bouncy roles as a teenager, then in juvenile leads for the Disney Studio. He also became a minor league baseball star in the 1970s and at one time almost quit acting altogether. But after his striking impersonation of Elvis Presley in a TV movie, he appeared in tougher, more rugged roles and, if not quite in the superstar class, has become a major leading man in the 1980s. The son of character actor Bing Russell, he is divorced from actress Season Hubley. Married Goldie Hawn (*qv*) in 1986.

1963: It Happened at the World's Fair. 1965: Guns of Diablo (TV. GB: cinemas). 1966: Follow Me Boys! Willie and the Yank (TV. GB: cinemas, as Mosby's Marauders). 1968: The One and Only, Genuine, Original Family Band. The Horse in the Gray Flannel Suit. Guns in the Heather. 1969: The Computer Wore Tennis Shoes. 1970: *Dad, Can I Borrow the Car? (narrator only). 1971: Fools' Parade (GB: Dynamite Man from Glory Jail). 1972: Now You See Him, Now You Don't. 1973: Charley and the Angel. 1974: Superdad. 1975: The Strongest Man in the World. Search for the Gods (TV). The Deadly Tower (TV). 1976: The Quest (TV). 1977: Christmas Miracle in Caulfield USA (GB: The Christmas Coal Mine Miracle). 1979: Elvis! (TV. GB: cinemas, as Elvis – The Movie). 1980: Amber Waves (TV). Used Cars. 1981: The Fox and the Hound (voice only). Escape from New York. 1982: The Thing. 1983: Silkwood. Swing Shift. 1985: The Mean Season. The Best of Times. 1986: Big Trouble in Little China.

RUSSELL, Rosalind 1908–1976

Regal American brunette actress who always seemed most at home in tweeds or silk evening gowns, and was often cast as a brisk businesswoman. After her success as the reporter in *His Girl Friday*, she was able to exercise her own (sometimes strange) choice of dominant leading roles, and did not pull out another real plum for herself until her stage mother in *Gypsy*. Four times nominated for an Oscar (in *My Sister Eileen, Sister Kenny, Mourning Becomes Electra* and *Auntie Mame*), she was given a special Academy Award in 1972 for her charity work. Died from cancer.

1934: *Forsaking All Others. Evelyn Prentice.* 1935: *West Point of the Air. The President Vanishes* (GB: *Strange Conspiracy*). *The Casino Murder Case. China Seas. The Night is Young. Reckless. Rendezvous.* 1936: *Trouble for Two* (GB: *The Suicide Club*). *It Had to Happen. Under Two Flags. Craig's Wife.* 1937: *Live, Love and Learn. Night Must Fall.* 1938: *Man-Proof. The Citadel. Four's a Crowd.* 1939: *The Women. Fast and Loose. His Girl Friday.* 1940: *Hired Wife. No Time for Comedy.* 1941: *Design for Scandal. This Thing Called Love* (GB: *Married But Single*). *They Met in Bombay. The Feminine Touch.* 1942: *Take a Letter, Darling* (GB: *The Green-Eyed Woman*). *My Sister Eileen.* 1943: *Flight for Freedom. What a Woman!* (GB: *The Beautiful Cheat*). 1945: *Roughly Speaking. She Wouldn't Say Yes.* 1946: *Sister Kenny.* 1947: *The Guilt of Janet Ames. Mourning Becomes Electra.* 1948: *The Velvet Touch.* 1949: *Tell It to the Judge.* 1950: *A Woman of Distinction.* 1952: *Never Wave at a WAC* (GB: *The Private Wore Skirts*). 1954: **Screen Snapshots No. 222.* 1955: *The Girl Rush. Picnic.* 1958: *Auntie Mame.* 1961: *A Majority of One.* 1962: *Five Finger Exercise. Gypsy.* 1965: *The Trouble with Angels.* 1966: *Oh Dad, Poor Dad, Mama's Hung You in the Closet and I'm Feeling So Sad.* 1967: *Rosie!* 1968: *Where Angels Go ... Trouble Follows!* 1971: *Mrs Pollifax – Spy.* 1972: *The Crooked Hearts* (*TV*).

RUTHERFORD, Ann 1917–
Zippy, plumply pretty brunette American actress, in leading roles as a teenager in low-budget westerns with John Wayne and Gene Autry. Later won a small slice of screen immortality as Polly, the perennial girl-friend of M-G-M's Andy Hardy series. Mainly in supporting roles after leaving M-G-M in the early forties.

1935: *Waterfront Lady. Melody Trail. The Fighting Marines* (serial). *The Singing Vagabond.* 1936: *The Harvester. The Lawless Nineties. Down to the Sea. The Lonely Trail. Doughnuts and Society* (GB: *Stepping into Society*). *Comin' round the Mountain. The Oregon Trail.* 1937: **Annie Laurie. Public Cowboy No. One. Espionage. The Bride Wore Red. Live, Love and Learn.* 1938: *Judge Hardy's Children. Of Human Hearts. A Christmas Carol. Love Finds*

Andy Hardy. You're Only Young Once. Dramatic School. Out West with the Hardys. 1939: *The Hardys Ride High. *Angel of Mercy. Four Girls in White. Dancing Co-Ed* (GB: *Every Other Inch a Lady*). *Gone with the Wind. Andy Hardy Gets Spring Fever. These Glamour Girls. Judge Hardy and Son.* 1940: *Wyoming* (GB: *Bad Man of Wyoming*). *Pride and Prejudice. The Ghost Comes Home. Andy Hardy Meets Debutante.* 1941: *Washington Melodrama. Keeping Company. Life Begins for Andy Hardy. Badlands of Dakota. Andy Hardy's Private Secretary. Whistling in the Dark.* 1942: *Orchestra Wives. The Courtship of Andy Hardy. Whistling in Dixie. Andy Hardy's Double Life. This Time for Keeps.* 1943: *Happy Land. Whistling in Brooklyn.* 1944: *Bermuda Mystery.* 1945: *Bedside Manner. Two O'Clock Courage.* 1946: *The Madonna's Secret. Murder in the Music Hall. Inside Job.* 1947: *The Secret Life of Walter Mitty.* 1949: *Adventures of Don Juan* (GB: *The New Adventures of Don Juan*). 1950: *Operation Haylift.* 1972: *They Only Kill Their Masters.* 1975: *Won Ton Ton, the Dog Who Saved Hollywood.*

RUTHERFORD, Dame Margaret 1892–1972
There couldn't have been an actor who didn't tremble in his boots at the thought of having plump, querulous, owl-eyed, round-mouthed, multi-chinned Margaret Rutherford in the same film, knowing that her breathlessly-relaxed delivery and inimitable booming tones would steal every scene. British films used this most British of actresses mostly in comedy as endearing eccentrics; over the years only Alastair Sim and Dame Edith Evans even gave her a run for her money, and she finally won an Academy Award for *The VIPs*. A glorious Miss Marple. Created Dame in 1967. Married to actor Stringer Davis (1896–1973) from 1954. Died after breaking a hip in a fall.

1936: *Dusty Ermine* (US: *Hideout in the Alps*). *Troubled Waters. Talk of the Devil.* 1937: *Missing, Believed Married. Beauty and the Barge. Big Fella. Catch As Catch Can.* 1940: *Spring Meeting.* 1941: *Quiet Wedding.* 1943: *The Yellow Canary. The Demi-Paradise* (US: *Adventure for Two*). 1944: *English without Tears* (US: *Her Man Gilbey*). 1945: *Blithe Spirit.* 1946: *While the Sun Shines.* 1947: *Meet Me at Dawn.* 1948: *Miranda.* 1949: *Passport to Pimlico.* 1950: *The Happiest Days of Your*

Life. Her Favourite Husband (US: *The Taming of Dorothy*). 1951: *The Magic Box.* 1952: *Curtain Up. The Importance of Being Earnest. Castle in the Air. Miss Robin Hood.* 1953: *Innocents in Paris. Trouble in Store.* 1954: *Aunt Clara. The Runaway Bus. Mad about Men.* 1955: *An Alligator Named Daisy.* 1957: *Just My Luck. The Smallest Show on Earth.* 1959: *I'm All Right, Jack.* 1961: *On the Double. Murder She Said.* 1963: *The Mouse on the Moon. Murder at the Gallop. The VIPs.* 1964: *Murder Most Foul.* 1965: *The Alphabet Murders. Murder Ahoy.* 1966: *Chimes at Midnight* (US: *Falstaff*). *A Countess from Hong Kong. The Wacky World of Mother Goose* (voice only). 1967: *Arabella.*

RYAN, Kathleen 1922–1985
Tall, copper-haired Irish actress with lovely complexion and attractive soft speaking voice. Mostly typed as flowing-haired colleens after starring in her first film. Consequently made too few films and, despite a couple of invitations to Hollywood, her career petered out.

1946: *Odd Man Out.* 1947: *Captain Boycott.* 1948: *Esther Waters.* 1949: *Christopher Columbus. Give Us This Day* (US: *Salt to the Devil*). 1950: *Prelude to Fame. Try and Get Me* (GB: *The Sound of Fury*). 1952: *The Yellow Balloon.* 1953: *Laxdale Hall* (US: *Scotch on the Rocks*). 1954: *Captain Lightfoot.* 1955: **The Clock.* 1956: *Jacqueline.* 1957: *Sail into Danger.*

RYAN, Peggy (Margaret Ryan) 1924–
Peppy, bow-lipped American dancer and comedienne with attractive dark red-brown hair, usually piled high, in show business from infancy with her Irish parents, 'The Merry Dancing Ryans'. An electric dancer, she fizzed through a mass of minor musicals for Universal in the forties. Married (second of three) to actor-dancer Ray McDonald (1921–1959) from 1953 to 1957. Popped up in the late sixties as Jack Lord's secretary in TV's *Hawaii Five-O*.

1930: **The Wedding of Jack and Jill.* 1937: *The Women Men Marry. Top of the Town.* 1939: *She Married a Cop. The Flying Irishman.* 1940: *The Grapes of Wrath.* 1941: *Sailor's Lady.* 1942: *What's Cookin'* (GB: *Wake Up and Dream*). *Private Buckaroo. Miss Annie Rooney. Get Hep to Love* (GB: *She's*

My Lovely). Give Out, Sisters! Girls' Town. When Johnny Comes Marching Home. 1943: Top Man. Mr Big. 1944: Follow the Boys. The Merry Monahans. Bowery to Broadway. Chip Off the Old Block. This is the Life. Babes on Swing Street. 1945: Here Come the Co-Eds. On Stage, Everybody! Patrick the Great. That's the Spirit. Men in Her Diary. 1949: Shamrock Hill. There's a Girl in My Heart. 1953: All Ashore.

RYAN, Robert 1909–1973

Tall, lean, dark-haired American actor who, after a spotty early career interrupted by war service, found that his whippy, gritty per-

formances earned him some good leading roles at RKO from 1947 to 1952. After that, often cast as embittered men, he was mostly second or third on the cast list of largely unworthy films, although working steadily. He received an Oscar nomination for his performance in *Crossfire.* Died from cancer.

1940: The Ghost Breakers. Queen of the Mob. Golden Gloves. Northwest Mounted Police. Texas Rangers Ride Again. 1941: The Feminine Touch. 1943: Gangway for Tomorrow. The Sky's the Limit. Behind the Rising Sun. Bombardier. The Iron Major. Tender Comrade. 1944: Marine Raiders. 1947: Johnny O'Clock. The Woman on the Beach. Trail Street. Crossfire. 1948: Return of the Bad Men. Berlin Express. The Boy with Green Hair. Act of Violence. 1949: Caught. The Set-Up. The Woman on Pier 13. 1950: The Secret Fury. Born to be Bad. 1951: The Racket. Best of the Badmen. Flying Leathernecks. On Dangerous Ground. 1952: Clash by Night. Horizons West. Beware My Lovely. 1953: The Naked Spur. City beneath the Sea. Inferno. 1954: Alaska Seas. About Mrs Leslie. Her Twelve Men. Bad Day at Black Rock. 1955: Escape to Burma. House of Bamboo. The Tall Men. 1956: The Proud Ones. Back from Eternity. 1957: Men in War. 1958: The Great Gatsby (TV). God's Little Acre. Lonelyhearts. 1959: Day of the Outlaw. Odds Against Tomorrow. 1960: Ice Palace. 1961: The Canadians. King of Kings. 1962: Billy Budd. The Longest Day. 1964: The Inheritance (narrator only). The Crooked Road. 1965: La guerre secrète (GB and US: The Dirty Game). Battle of the Bulge. 1966: The Busy Body. The Professionals. Custer of the West. 1967: Hour of the Gun. Anzio (GB: The Battle for Anzio). The Dirty Dozen. 1968: A Minute to Pray, a Second to Die (GB: Dead or Alive). Captain Nemo and the Underwater City. 1969: The Wild Bunch. 1971: Lawman. The Love Machine. 1972: And Hope to Die. La course du lièvre à travers les champs. 1973: The Iceman Cometh. Executive Action. Lolly Madonna XXX (GB: The Lolly Madonna War). Man without a Country (TV). The Outfit.

RYAN, Sheila (Katherine McLaughlin)
1921–1975

Lovely dark-haired American actress with large, open face and Irish colouring, the resourceful heroine of numerous second features in the forties. Ended up in Gene Autry westerns – not surprising as she was married to Autry's comic sidekick, Pat Buttram (1915–   ). Died from a lung ailment.

1940: The Gay Caballero. 1941: Golden Hoofs. We Go Fast. Dead Men Tell. Sun Valley Serenade. Great Guns. Dressed to Kill. 1942: The Lone Star Ranger. Pardon My Stripes. Footlight Serenade. Who is Hope Schuyler? A-Haunting We Will Go. Careful, Soft Shoulders. 1943: The Gang's All Here (GB: The Girls He Left Behind). Song of Texas. 1944: Something for the Boys. Ladies of Washington. 1945: The Caribbean Mystery. Getting Gertie's Garter. 1946: The Lone Wolf in London. Slightly Scandalous. Deadline for Murder. The Big Fix. 1947: Philo Vance's Secret Mission. Railroaded! Heartaches. 1948: Caged Fury. The Cobra Strikes. 1949: Ringside. Joe Palooka in the Counterpunch. Hideout. The Cowboy and the Indians. 1950: Square Dance Katy. Western Pacific Agent. Mule Train. 1951: Jungle Manhunt. Gold Raiders (GB: The Stooges Go West). Mask of the Dragon. Fingerprints Don't Lie. 1953: Pack Train. On Top of Old Smoky. 1954: Crime Squad. 1958: Street of Darkness.

Exodus. 1962: All Fall Down. 1964: 36 Hours. Carol for Another Christmas (TV). 1965: The Sandpiper. 1966: The Russians Are Coming, the Russians Are Coming. Grand Prix. 1968: The Stalking Moon. 1969: A Talent for Loving. 1970: Loving. 1972: Cancel My Reservation. 1975: The McAhans – How the West Was Won (TV). 1978: A Christmas to Remember (TV). 1979: When Hell Was in Session (TV). 1981: Splendor in the Grass (TV). The Best Little Girl in the World (TV). 1983: Jane Doe (TV). 1984: Love Leads the Way. 1986: The Last Days of Patton (TV). Nothing in Common.

SABU (S. Dastagir) 1924–1963

Impish, loveable, slightly-built son of an Indian elephant-driver, snatched from the elephant stables of Mysore by a British film unit in 1936 for his first film, in which his natural charm won the hearts of millions. Made his home in Hollywood after 1940 and appeared entirely in fantasies and jungle films, some of which he journeyed to Europe to make. A war hero with a cluster of medals, he died from a heart attack.

*1937: Elephant Boy. 1938: The Drum (US: Drums). 1940: The Thief of Bagdad. 1942: Jungle Book. Arabian Nights. 1943: White Savage (GB: White Captive). Cobra Woman. *Screen Snapshots No. 103. *Screen Snapshots No. 105. 1946: Tangier. 1947: Black Narcissus. The End of the River. 1948: Man-Eater of Kumaon. 1949: Song of India. 1951: Savage Drums. 1952: Hello Elephant! 1954: The Treasure of Bengal (US: Jungle Hell). 1955: The Black Panther. 1956: Jaguar. 1957: Sabu and the Magic Ring. 1960: Mistress of the World/Il mistero dei tre continenti. 1962: Rampage! 1963: A Tiger Walks.*

SAINT, Eva Marie 1924–

Slender, waif-like blonde American actress seen as harried heroines, or in sympathetic roles. Made her first film at the age of 30 (fortunately she looked very young for her age) and won an Academy Award for it. But proper casting for her has proved elusive, and she has not always made the impact she might.

1954: On the Waterfront. 1956: That Certain Feeling. 1957: Raintree County. A Hatful of Rain. 1959: North by Northwest. 1960:

SANDERS, George 1906–1972

Suave, civilized, cynical, sophisticated, sometimes sinister: Russian-born Sanders, with his heavy head like some huge uncoiled snake, was all of these sibilants. One could almost see the sins beneath the skin. He started in British films, but Hollywood soon seized his rakish charm and gave him an Oscar for *All About Eve*, but few decent parts after that, although no-one was more suited to the voice of Sheré-Khan the tiger. Married to Zsa Zsa Gabor 1949–1957 and Benita Hume 1958 to her death in 1967, third and fourth of five. Committed suicide with barbiturates, leaving behind an aggrieved note complaining of boredom.

1934: Love, Life and Laughter. 1936: Find the Lady. Strange Cargo. The Man Who Could Work Miracles. Dishonour Bright. Things to Come. My Second Wife. Lloyd's of London. 1937: The Lady Escapes. Love is News. Slave Ship. Lancer Spy. 1938: International Settlement. Four Men and a Prayer. 1939: Allegheny

*Uprising (GB: The First Rebel). Mr Moto's Last Warning. So This is London. The Saint Strikes Back. The Outsider. Nurse Edith Cavell. The Saint in London. Confessions of a Nazi Spy. 1940: The Saint Takes Over. Green Hell. Bitter Sweet. Foreign Correspondent. Son of Monte Cristo. The Saint's Double Trouble. Rebecca. The House of Seven Gables. 1941: Man Hunt. The Saint in Palm Springs. Rage in Heaven. A Date with the Falcon. Sundown. The Gay Falcon. 1942: Her Cardboard Lover. The Black Swan. The Falcon Takes Over. Quiet Please, Murder. The Moon and Sixpence. Tales of Manhattan. Son of Fury. The Falcon's Brother. 1943: Appointment in Berlin. This Land is Mine. Paris After Dark. They Came to Blow Up America. 1944: Action in Arabia. The Lodger. Summer Storm. 1945: Hangover Square. The Picture of Dorian Gray. Uncle Harry/The Strange Affair of Uncle Harry. 1946: A Scandal in Paris. The Strange Woman. 1947: The Private Affairs of Bel Ami. Lured (GB: Personal Column). The Ghost and Mrs Muir. Forever Amber. 1949: The Fan (GB: Lady Windermere's Fan). Samson and Delilah. 1950: All About Eve. Blackjack (US: Captain Blackjack). 1951: I Can Get It For You Wholesale/Only the Best (GB: This is My Affair). The Light Touch. 1952: Ivanhoe. *Screen Snapshots No. 205. Assignment – Paris! 1953: Call Me Madam. Viaggio in Italia (GB: Voyage to Italy. US: The Strangers). 1954: Witness to Murder. King Richard and the Crusaders. 1955: Jupiter's Darling. Laura (TV. GB: cinemas). Moonfleet. The Scarlet Coat. The King's Thief. 1956: Death of a Scoundrel. While the City Sleeps. Never Say Goodbye. That Certain Feeling. 1957: The Seventh Sin. 1958: The Whole Truth. From the Earth to the Moon. 1959: A Touch of Larceny. Solomon and Sheba. That Kind of Woman. 1960: Bluebeard's 10 Honeymoons. Cone of Silence (US: Trouble in the Sky). Village of the Damned. The Last Voyage. 1961: The Rebel (US: Call Me Genius). Five Golden Hours. 1962: Le Rendez-vous. Operation Snatch. In Search of the Castaways. 1963: Cairo. The Cracksman. Dark Purpose/L'intrigo. Un aereo per Baalbeck. 1964: A Shot in the Dark. The Golden Head. 1965: World By Night (narrator only). The Amorous Adventures of Moll Flanders. Trunk to Cairo. 1966: The Quiller Memorandum. 1967: Warning Shot. Good Times. The Jungle Book (voice only). Laura (TV. Remake). One Step to Hell (US: King of Africa). 1968: The Best House in London. The Candy Man. 1969: The Body Stealers. The Seven Men of Sumuru. The Kremlin Letter. 1971: Endless Night. The Night of the Assassin. 1972: Doomwatch. Psychomania.*

SARANDON, Susan (S. Tomaling) 1946–

Light-haired, rosy-cheeked, piquant American actress, pretty in a stringy sort of way, who looked born to play women trodden down by the land, but in fact has played a bright variety of roles. Trained for ballet, she turned to acting instead, married/divorced actor Chris Sarandon and has won critical approval for her performances without quite becoming a major star. An enthusiastic amateur racing

driver, she also likes to do her own stunts when there are any going.

1970: Joe. 1971: Lady Liberty/La mortadella. 1972: Walk Away Madden. 1973: Lovin' Molly. 1974: The Front Page. 1975: The Great Waldo Pepper. The Rocky Horror Picture Show. 1976: The Other Side of Midnight. Crash. Dragonfly/One Summer's Love. 1977: The Last of the Cowboys (later The Great Smokey Roadblock). 1978: Pretty Baby. King of the Gypsies. 1979: Something Short of Paradise. 1980: Loving Couples. Atlantic City USA (GB and US: Atlantic City). 1981: Who Am I This Time? (TV). 1982: The Hunger. Tempest. 1983: The Buddy System. 1984: Eyes. Io e il duce (US: Mussolini and I). 1985: Compromising Positions.

SARRAZIN, Michael (Jacques Sarrazin) 1940–
Good-looking, dark-haired Canadian-born actor with deep-set eyes, lined lips and guileless look. Often cast as younger men undergoing initiation at the hands of older men. Despite leading roles opposite Jane Fonda, Barbra Streisand and Julie Christie (or perhaps because of them) he has not quite held his place at the front of things.

1966: Gunfight in Abilene. The Doomsday Flight (TV. GB: cinemas). 1967: The Flim Flam Man (GB: One Born Every Minute). The Sweet Ride. Journey to Shiloh. 1968: A Man Called Gannon. 1969: In Search of Gregory. They Shoot Horses Don't They? Eye of the Cat. The Pursuit of Happiness. 1971: Believe in Me. Sometimes a Great Notion (GB: Never Give an Inch). 1972: The Groundstar

Conspiracy. 1973: Frankenstein: the True Story (TV. GB: cinemas). Harry Never Holds (GB: Harry in Your Pocket). 1974: The Reincarnation of Peter Proud. For Pete's Sake. 1976: The Gumball Rally. Scaramouche. 1978: Caravans. 1979: Double Negative. 1981: The Seduction. 1982: Fighting Back (GB: Death Vengeance). 1983: The Train Killer. 1985: Joshua Then and Now. Keeping Track.

SAVALAS, Telly (Aristotle Savalas) 1924–
Shaven-headed, strong-faced, grinning American character star of Greek parentage. He switched from being a TV executive to an actor in the late 1950s. His slightly unbalanced features got him cast as psychopathic villains, and it was only with his great personal success as the tough detective in the TV series *Kojak* that he managed to break the mould. His attempts at direction on that series were very promising, but his one film as director proved disappointing. Nominated for an Academy Award in *Birdman of Alcatraz*.

1961: The Young Savages. Mad Dog Coll. The Young Doctors. 1962: Birdman of Alcatraz. Cape Fear. The Interns. 1963: Love is a Ball (GB: All This and Money Too). The Man from the Diners' Club. Johnny Cool. 1964: The New Interns. 1965: The Greatest Story Ever Told. Battle of the Bulge. The Slender Thread. Genghis Khan. 1966: Beau Geste. 1967: The Dirty Dozen. The Karate Killers (TV. GB: cinemas). Cosa Nostra, an Arch Enemy of the FBI (TV. GB: cinemas). Sol Madrid (GB: The Heroin Gang). 1968: The Scalphunters. Buona Sera, Mrs Campbell. The Assassination Bureau. Mackenna's Gold. Crooks and Coronets (US: Sophie's Place). 1969: Land Raiders. On Her Majesty's Secret Service. 1970: Violent City. Kelly's Heroes. 1971: A Town Called Bastard. Mongo's Back in Town (TV). Pretty Maids All in a Row. Pancho Villa. Clay Pigeon (GB: Trip to Kill). 1972: The Lost World of Libra. A Reason to Live, a Reason to Die. Assassino . . . è al telefono (GB: The Killer Is on the Phone). Panico en al Transiberio (GB: Horror Express). Red Neck. Visions (TV). I familiari delle vittime non saranno avvertiti. 1973: She Cried Murder (TV). J and S, a Criminal Story of the Far West (US: Sonny and Jed). The Marcus-Nelson Murders (TV). 1975: The Diamond Mercenaries. Inside Out. House of Exorcism (US: Lisa and the Devil). 1976: Crime Boss.

†Mati (released 1985 as Beyond Reason). 1977: Capricorn One. 1978: The Muppet Movie. Escape to Athena. 1979: Beyond the Poseidon Adventure. 1980: Alcatraz: The Whole Shocking Story (TV). The Border. Hellinger's Law (TV). 1981: *Telly Savalas Looks at Birmingham. *Telly Savalas Looks at Portsmouth. *Telly Savalas Looks at Aberdeen. 1982: Fake-Out. 1983: Cannonball Run II. 1984: The Ambassador. The Cartier Affair (TV). 1985: Kojak: The Belarus Field (TV).

† And directed

SAXON, John (Carmen Orrico) 1935–
Very dark-haired American actor of baby-faced handsomeness. Of Italian parentage, he started his career as a teenage rave, but soon veered into off-centre roles. Spent some time in Italy in the sixties, and re-emerged on the international scene with hair receding, but as a much harder actor with terse delivery who frequently played nasty customers.

1953: It Should Happen to You. 1955: Running Wild. 1956: The Unguarded Moment. Rock, Pretty Baby. 1957: Summer Love. 1958: The Reluctant Debutante. The Restless Years. This Happy Feeling. 1959: Portrait in Black. The Unforgiven. Cry Tough. The Big Fisherman. 1960: The Plunderers. 1961: Posse from Hell. War Hunt. 1962: La ragazza che sapeva troppo/The Girl Who Knew Too Much (GB: The Evil Eye). Agostino. Mr Hobbs Takes a Vacation. 1963: The Cardinal. 1964: The Cavern. 1965: The Ravagers. The Night Caller (US: Blood Beast from Outer Space). 1966: The Appaloosa (GB: Southwest to Sonora). The Doomsday Flight (TV. GB: cinemas). Planet of Blood/Queen of Blood. 1967: The Magnificent Thief (TV). Winchester 73 (TV). 1968: For Singles Only. Istanbul Express (TV. GB: cinemas). Vado, vedo e sparo. 1969: Death of a Gunfighter. 1970: Company of Killers. The Intruders (TV). 1972: Joe Kidd. Snatched (TV). 1973: Mr Kingstreet's War (GB: TV). Linda (TV). Enter the Dragon. Baciamo le mani (US: Mafia War). 1974: Black Christmas. Can Ellen be Saved? (TV). Planet Earth (TV). 1975: The Swiss Conspiracy. Mitchell. Strange New World (TV). Crossfire (TV). 1976: Family Killer. Moonshine County Express. Raid on Entebbe (TV. GB: cinemas). Blazing Magnum (US: Strange Shadows in an Empty Room). Napoli Violenta (GB: Death

Dealers). *Italia a mano armata (GB: Special Cop in Action)*. 1977: *House Made of Dawn. Tre soldi e la donna di classe*. 1978: *The Bees. Fast Company. Shalimar*. 1979: *The Glove. The Electric Horseman*. 1980: *Savage Apocalypse (US: Cannibals in the Streets). Battle Beyond the Stars. Blood Beach (filmed 1978). Golden Gate (TV)*. 1981: *Beyond Evil*. 1982: *Wrong is Right/The Man with the Deadly Lens. Tenebrae*. 1983: *Desire. Prisoners of the Lost Universe. Hardcastle and McCormick (TV). The Big Score*. 1984: *A Nightmare on Elm Street*. 1985: *Brothers-in-Law (TV). Fever Pitch*.

SCHEIDER, Roy 1934–

Dark, thin-faced American leading man with hard-driving acting style that was chiefly employed in thrillers, but ultimately proved adaptable to other genres. Has made the most of his late chance at film stardom after coming to prominence in his late thirties. Nominated for Academy Awards in *The French Connection* and *All That Jazz*.

1963: †*The Curse of the Living Corpse*. 1968: *Paper Lion*. 1969: *Stiletto*. 1970: *Puzzle of a Downfall Child. Loving*. 1971: *Klute. The French Connection*. 1972: *L'attentat (GB: Plot. US: The French Conspiracy). Un homme est mort (GB and US: The Outside Man). Assignment Munich (TV)*. 1973: *The Seven-Ups*. 1975: *Jaws. Sheila Levene is Dead and Living in New York*. 1976: *Marathon Man*. 1977: *Sorcerer (GB: Wages of Fear)*. 1978: *Jaws 2*. 1979: *Last Embrace. All That Jazz*. 1982: *Still of the Night. Blue Thunder*. 1983: *Tiger Town. Jacobo Timmerman/Prisoner Without a Name, Cell Without a Number (TV)*. 1984: *2010*. 1985: *Mishima (narrator only)*. 1986: *The Men's Club. 52 Pick-Up*.

† *As Roy R. Scheider*

SCHELL, Maria 1926–

Wispily-blonde, Austrian-born leading lady (of Swiss nationality), who rarely smiled in mostly red-eyed roles across Europe, Britain and Hollywood. Could give very touching performances, but did not quite have the stamp of an international star. Sister of Maximilian Schell.

1941: *Quarry/Steinbruch*. 1943: *Maturareise*. 1948: *Nach dem Sturm. Wiener Kavalkade*. 1949: *Der Engel mit der Posaune/The Angel with the Trumpet. Ser Angeklagte hat das Wort. Marosi*. 1950: *Es kommt ein Tag. The Affairs of Dr Holl*. 1951: *The Magic Box*. 1952: *So Little Time. The Heart of the Matter. Der träumende Mund (US: Dreaming Lips). Bis wir uns wiedersehen*. 1953: *Tagebuch einer Verliebten. Die letzte Brücke/The Last Bridge. Solange Du da Bist*. 1954: *Angelika. Napoléon*. 1955: *Uragano sul Po. Gervaise. Die Ratten. Herr über Leben und Tod*. 1956: *Liebe/Love*. 1957: *Rose Bernd. White Nights/Le notti bianchi. Ungarn in Flammen (narrator only)*. 1958: *Une vie. The Brothers Karamazov. The Hanging Tree. Word from a Sealed-Off Box (TV). Der Schinderhannes (US: Duel in the Forest)*. 1959: *Raubfischer in Hellas (GB and US: As the Sea Rages). For Whom the Bells Toll (TV)*. 1960: *Cimarron*. 1961: *Das Riesenrad. The Mark*. 1962: *Ich bin auch nur eine Frau (US: Only a Woman)*. 1963: *L'assassin connait la musique. Zwei Whisky und ein Sofa (US: Rendezvous in Trieste)*. 1965: *Who Has Seen the Wind?* 1968: *99 Women. Heidi Comes Home (US: Heidi)*. 1969: *Le diable par le queue. La provocation*. 1970: *Der Hexentoter von Blackmoor (US: The Bloody Judge)*. 1971: *Such a Pretty Cloud. Dans la poussière du soleil/Lust in the Sun*. 1972: *Chamsin. Die Pfarrhauskomodie*. 1974: *The Odessa File. Change*. 1975: *The Quack. So oder so ist das Leben*. 1976: *Voyage of the Damned. Folies Bourgeoises/The Twist*. 1978: *Just a Gigolo. Die erste Polka. Superman*. 1979: *Christmas Lilies of the Field (TV)*. 1984: *Samson and Delilah (TV)*. 1919.

SCHELL, Maximilian 1930–

Dark-haired, long-faced Austrian actor, brother of Maria Schell. His features adapted equally well to kindliness and fanaticism, and it was with a mixture of both that he won his reputation in TV and film versions of *Judgment at Nuremberg*, the film of which won him an Oscar. But his roles gradually deteriorated to the point where he started directing his own films.

1955: *Kinder, Mütter und ein General. Ein Mädchen aus Flandern*. 1956: *Der 20 Juli. Reifende Jügend. Ein Herz kehrt Heim*. 1957: *Taxi-Chauffeur Bartz. Die Letzten werden die Ersten sein*. 1958: *Ein wunderbaren Sommer. The Young Lions*. 1959: *Judgment at Nuremberg (TV). Child of Our Time (TV)*. 1960: *The Fifth Column (TV)*. 1961: *Judgment at Nuremberg*. 1962: *Five Finger Exercise. The Reluctant Saint*. 1963: *The Condemned of Altona*. 1964: *Topkapi*. 1965: *Return from the Ashes*. 1966: *The Deadly Affair*. 1967: *Counterpoint*. 1968: *The Desperate Ones. Krakatoa – East of Java. Heidi Comes Home (US: Heidi)*. 1969: *The Castle. Simon Bolivár*. 1970: *First Love*. 1971: *Trotta*. 1972: *Pope Joan*. 1973: *Paulina 1880. Der Fussgänger/Le piéton*. 1974: *The Odessa File*. 1975: *The Man in the Glass Booth*. 1976: *Assassination! (US: The Day That Shook the World)*. St Ives. 1977: *Julia. Cross of Iron. A Bridge Too Far*. 1978: *Avalanche Express*. 1979: *The Black Hole. Together/I Love You, I Love You Not. Players*. 1980: *Diary of Anne Frank (TV)*. 1981: *The Chosen. Les isles*. 1983: *Phantom of The Opera (TV)*. 1984: *Morgen in Alabama (US: A German Lawyer). The Assisi Underground*. 1986: *Laughter in the Dark*.

As director: 1969: *The Castle*. 1970: *First Love*. 1973: *Der Fussgänger/Le pieton*. 1976: *End of the Game*. 1979: *Tales from the Vienna Woods*. 1980: *Diary of Anne Frank (TV)*.

SCHNEIDER, Romy (Rosemarie Albach-Retty) 1938–1982

Tartly attractive brunette Austrian actress, in films as a teenager at first, as pretty apple dumplings in frothily empty fifties' concoctions; but when she came back to films in 1961 after two years away there was much more bite to her work and she quickly became an international star in demand. Died from a heart attack.

1953: *Wenn der weisse Flieder blüht*. 1954: *Feuerwerk (GB: Oh! My Papa). Der Zigeuner-*

baron. *Mädchenjahre einer Königin. 1955: Die Deutschmeister. Der letzte Mann. Sissi. 1956: Kitty. Sissi die junge Kaiserin. 1957: Robinson soll nicht sterben. Monpti. Scampolo. Sissi – Schicksalsjahre einer Kaiserin. 1958: Mädchen in Uniform. Christine. Die Halbzarte. †Forever My Love. 1959: Mademoiselle Ange (US: Angel on Earth). Die schöne Lugnerin. Katia. Plein soleil. 1961: Le combat dans l'île. Die Sendung der Lysistrata. 1962: Boccaccio 70. The Legend of Robinson Crusoe. The Trial. 1963: The Victors. The Cardinal. 1964: Good Neighbor Sam. 1965: What's New, Pussycat? 1966: 10.30 p.m. Summer. La volense. Triple Cross. Schornstein No. 4. 1968: Otley. La piscine (GB: The Sinners). 1969: Les choses de la vie (GB: The Things of Life. US: These Things Happen). My Lover, My Son. Bloomfield. 1970: Qui? (GB, TV: Who Are You? US: The Sensuous Assassin). Don't You Cry. 1971: La califfa. Max et les ferailleurs. The Assassination of Trotsky. 1972: Ludwig. César et Rosalie. 1973: Le train. Un amour de pluie. Le mouton enragé (GB: The French Way). 1974: Le trio infernal. L'important c'est d'aimer (US: That Most Important Thing: Love!). Innocents with Dirty Hands. 1975: Le vieux fusil (GB: The Hidden Gun). 1976: Une femme à sa fenêtre. Macho/Mado. Portrait de groupe avec dame/Gruppenbild mit Dame. 1978: Une histoire simple. 1979: Clair de femme. Mort en direct/Deathwatch. Bloodline/Sidney Sheldon's Bloodline. 1980: La banquière. 1981: Fantôme d'amour. Garde à vue (GB: The Inquisitor. US: The Grilling). La passante du Sans Souci.*

†*Combined GB version of The Three 'Sissi' films*

SCHWARZENEGGER, Arnold 1947–
Austrian muscleman, bodybuilder and, latterly, actor, with solid features, gap-toothed smile and a surprisingly subtle sense of humour. A five-times Mr Universe, Schwarzenegger's boyhood idol was Steve Reeves (qv); after a stop-go start in movies, he now looks set to revive the Reeves genre films almost single-handed. In the 1980s the scale of the action in his violent adventure movies rapidly pushed him up towards the top of the league of Hollywood's most bankable stars. For the record, he's six-feet-two, weighs 240 pounds and has a 57-inch chest!
1969: †Hercules Goes Bananas (later: Hercules in New York). 1973: †The Long Goodbye.

1976: Stay Hungry. 1977: Pumping Iron. 1979: Scavenger Hunt. The Villain (GB: Cactus Jack). 1981: Conan the Barbarian. The Jayne Mansfield Story (TV). 1984: Conan the Destroyer. The Terminator. 1985: Red Sonja. Commando. 1986: Outpost. Raw Deal.

† *As Arnold Strong*

SCHYGULLA, Hanna 1943–
Polish-born, Bavarian-raised, sultry-looking, square-built blonde actress with faintly mysterious air. Studied to be a teacher, but instead joined Munich's offbeat 'action theatre' where she met director Rainer Werner Fassbinder (together with others they founded the city's famous 'anti-theatre'), in whose films she would rise to stardom. She gained international prominence belatedly with *Lili Marleen*, but after Fassbinder's death in 1982 her career faltered.
*1968: *Der Bräutigam, die Komödiantin und der Zuhälter (GB: The Bridegroom, the Comedienne and the Pimp). 1969: Liebe ist kälter als der Tod. Katzelmacher. Götter der Pest (GB and US: Gods of the Plague). Jagdzenen aus Niederbayern. Baal (TV). 1970: Rio das Mortes (TV). Niklaushaüsener Fahrt. Pioniere in Ingolstadt (TV). Das Kaffeehaus (TV). Kuckucksei im Gangsternest. 1971: Whity. Warnung vor einer heiligen Nutte (GB: Warning of a Holy Whore. US: Beware the Holy Whore). Der Händler der vier Jahreszeiten (GB and US: The Merchant of Four Seasons). Jacob Von Gunten. 1972: Die bitteren Tränen der Petra von Kant (GB and US: The Bitter Tears of Petra von Kant). Wildwechsel (GB: Wild Game. US: Jail Bait). Das Haus am Meer. 1974: Fontane: Effi Brest (GB and US: Effi Brest). 1975: Falsche Bewegung (GB: Wrong Movement. US: The Wrong Move). Ansichten eines Clowns. Der Stumme. 1977: Die Dämonen. Die Heimkehr des alten Herrn. 1978: Aussagen nach einer Verhaftung (TV). Die grosse Flatter. Die Ehe der Maria Braun (GB and US: The Marriage of Maria Braun). 1979: Berlin–Alexanderplatz (originally series for TV). 1980: Lili Marleen. 1981: Die Fälschung (GB and US: Circle of Deceit). 1982: Passion. Revolution. La nuit de Varennes. La storia di Piera. Antonieta. 1983: Heller Wahn (GB: Friends and Husbands. US: A Labor of Love). 1984: The Future is Woman. Eine Liebe in Deutschland (GB and US: A Love in Germany). 1986: Storm over Venice/Storm in Venice. The Delta Force. Forever Lulu.*

SCOFIELD, Paul 1922–
Light-haired, intelligent-looking, quietly-spoken British actor who has been little seen in films. Acclaimed for his performance as Sir Thomas More in *A Man for All Seasons*, which won him an Academy Award, he still preferred to return to the theatre.
1955: That Lady. 1958: Carve Her Name with Pride. 1965: The Train. 1966: A Man for All Seasons. The Other World of Winston Churchill (narrator only). 1967: Tell Me Lies. 1970: King Lear. Bartleby. 1972: Scorpio. 1974: A Delicate Balance. 1983: Ill Fares the Land (TV. Voice only, uncredited). 1984: 1919. 1985: Summer Lightning (TV). 1986: The Conspiracy. Mr Corbett's Ghost.

SCOTT, George C 1926–
Craggy, rasp-voiced American whose earthy arrogance dominated his films but rarely over-balanced them. He won notoriety as the first actor to refuse to accept an Oscar (awarded for *Patton*), but by and large his roles have not been worthy of his larger-than-life talents. Married (fourth) to Trish Van Devere (Patricia Dressel, 1943–) from 1972 to 1983. Also Oscar-nominated for *Anatomy of a Murder*, *The Hustler* and *The Hospital*. Lately bogged down in Dickensian roles.
1958: The Hanging Tree. 1959: Anatomy of a Murder. Target for Three (TV). 1961: The Power and the Glory (TV. GB: cinemas). The Hustler. 1962: The Brazen Bell (TV. GB: cinemas). 1963: The List of Adrian Messenger. Dr. Strangelove, or: How I Learned to Stop Worrying and Love the Bomb. 1964: The Yellow Rolls Royce. 1966: The Bible ... in the

beginning. Not with My Wife, You Don't! Shadow on the Land (TV). 1967: The Flim Flam Man (GB: One Born Every Minute). 1968: Petulia. 1969: Patton (GB: Patton – Lust for Glory). 1970: Jane Eyre (TV. GB: cinemas). 1971: They Might Be Giants. The Hospital. The Last Run. 1972: The New Centurions (GB: Precinct 45: Los Angeles Police). Rage. 1973: Oklahoma Crude. The Day of the Dolphin. 1974: Bank Shot. The Savage is Loose. 1975: The Hindenberg. Fear on Trial (TV). 1976: Islands in the Stream. Beauty and the Beast. 1977: The Prince and the Pauper (GB: Crossed Swords). 1978: Movie Movie. Hardcore (GB: The Hardcore Life). 1979: Arthur Miller – on Home Ground. The Changeling. 1980: The Formula. 1981: Taps. 1982: Oliver Twist (TV. GB: cinemas). 1983: China Rose (TV). 1984: Firestarter. A Christmas Carol (TV. GB: cinemas). 1986: The Last Days of Patton (TV). Choices (TV).

As director: 1972: Rage. 1974: The Savage is Loose

SCOTT, Gordon (G. Werschkul) 1927–
Muscular, fair-haired American leading man whisked from his job as a lifeguard to become the screen's new Tarzan in 1955. Unwisely gave up the role five years (and several above-average Tarzan films) later, and went into Italian muscleman epics. Not heard from since the mid-sixties. Married to Vera Miles (1955–1959), first of two.
1955: Tarzan's Hidden Jungle. 1957: Tarzan and the Lost Safari. 1958: Tarzan's Fight for Life. Tarzan and the Trappers. 1959: Tarzan's Greatest Adventure. 1960: Tarzan the Magnificent. 1961: Romulus and Remus (GB: Duel of the Titans). Maciste against the Vampires (GB: Goliath against the Vampires). Maciste alla corte del Gran Kan (GB: Samson and the Seven Miracles). 1962: A Queen for Caesar. The Gladiator of Rome (GB: Battles of the Gladiators). Son of the Sheik. Hero of Babylon (GB: Goliath – King of the Slaves). Coriolanus. 1963: Zorro and the Three Musketeers. Hercules against Moloch (GB: Hercules Attacks). The Lion of St Mark. Il giorno piu corto commedia umaristica (US: The Shortest Day). Thunder of Battle (US: Hero of Rome). Arrow of the Avenger. Conquest of Mycene. Goliath and the Black Hercules. 1964: Buffalo Bill, Hero of the Far West. Arm of Fire. The Tyrant of Lydia against the Son of Hercules.

The Colossus of Rome. 1966: The Tramplers. Segretissimo (US: Top Secret). 1967: Nest of Spies.

SCOTT, Janette (Thora J. Scott) 1938–
Talented brown-haired, pigtailed British child star who broke a million hearts in No Place for Jennifer. Tried hard to make a go of an adult career, but never seemed completely at ease. Daughter of actress Thora Hird (1913–). Married to Mel Tormé (1923–), second of two, from 1966–1977.
1942: Went the Day Well? (US: 48 Hours). 1943: The Lamp Still Burns. 1944: 2,000 Women. Medal for the General. 1949: Conspirator. No Place for Jennifer. 1951: The Magic Box. The Galloping Major. No Highway (US: No Highway in the Sky). 1953: Background (US: Edge of Divorce). 1954: Helen of Troy. 1955: As Long As They're Happy. 1956: Now and Forever. 1957: The Good Companions. 1958: Happy is the Bride. 1959: The Lady is a Square. The Devil's Disciple. 1960: School for Scoundrels. His and Hers. 1961: Double Bunk. 1962: Two and Two Make Six. The Day of the Triffids. Paranoiac. The Old Dark House. 1963: Siege of the Saxons. 1964: The Beauty Jungle (US: Contest Girl). Bikini Paradise. 1965: Crack in the World.

SCOTT, Lizabeth (Emma Matzo) 1922–
Sultry blonde American actress of husky voice and strong personality, initially billed as 'The Threat'. Usually played tough babes who ended up with no more than they deserved. Has never married.
1945: You Came Along. 1946: The Strange

Love of Martha Ivers. Dead Reckoning. 1947: Desert Fury. I Walk Alone. Variety Girl. 1948: Pitfall. 1949: Too Late for Tears. Easy Living. 1950: Dark City. Paid in Full. 1951: Two of a Kind. The Company She Keeps. The Racket. Red Mountain. 1952: Stolen Face. 1953: Scared Stiff. 1954: Bad for Each Other. Silver Lode. 1956: Overnight Haul (TV. GB: cinemas). The Weapon. 1957: Loving You. 1972: Pulp.

SCOTT, Margaretta 1911–
Forceful, dark-haired, austere-looking but attractive British actress who made films in between engagements for the theatre – a medium in which she was constantly busy after her debut at 15 as a pageboy in Romeo and Juliet. In films she often played 'other women', later domineering mothers.
1934: Dirty Work. The Private Lives of Don Juan. 1935: Conquest of the Air (released 1940). Peg of Old Drury. 1936: Things to Come. 1937: Action for Slander. The Return of the Scarlet Pimpernel. 1940: The Girl in the News. 1941: Quiet Wedding. Atlantic Ferry (US: Sons of the Sea). 1942: Sabotage at Sea. 1944: Fanny by Gaslight (US: Man of Evil). 1945: The Man from Morocco. 1947: Mrs Fitzherbert. 1948: Idol of Paris. The First Gentleman (US: Affairs of a Rogue). Calling Paul Temple. Counterblast. The Story of Shirley Yorke. 1949: Landfall. 1952: Where's Charley? 1956: The Last Man to Hang? Town on Trial! 1957: The Scamp. 1958: A Woman Possessed. 1960: An Honourable Murder. 1969: Crescendo. 1970: Percy.

SCOTT, Martha 1914–
Appealing strawberry blonde American actress who always seemed to be required to age in her films: ironically, her youthful looks faded fast and she had a very short star career, although she has continued to crop up through the years in mother roles. She received an Academy Award nomination for Our Town.
1940: The Howards of Virginia (GB: The Tree of Liberty). Our Town. 1941: Cheers for Miss Bishop. One Foot in Heaven. They Dare Not Love. 1943: Hi Diddle Diddle. In Old Oklahoma/War of the Wildcats. Stage Door Canteen. 1947: So Well Remembered. 1949: Strange Bargain. 1951: When I Grow Up. 1955: The Desperate Hours. 1956: The Ten Commandments. 1957: Sayonara. Eighteen and Anxious. 1959: Ben-Hur. A Trip to Paradise

(TV). 1972: Charlotte's Web (voice only). 1973: Sorority Kill (TV). 1974: Airport 1975. The Devil's Daughter (TV). Thursday's Game (TV). The Abduction of Saint Anne/They've Kidnapped Anne Benedict (TV). 1975: Medical Story (TV). 1977: The Turning Point. 1979: Charleston (TV). 1980: Father Figure (TV). 1983: Adam (TV). Summer Girl (TV).

SCOTT, Randolph (R. Crane) 1903–
Sandy-haired light leading man of the twenties and thirties who developed in post-war years into Hollywood's number one westerner. Grim faced, quietly spoken and two-fisted, he played men of rigid integrity who pursued single-minded courses for what they thought was right. Always looked around 45, and appeared consistently in high-budget colour westerns while almost every other cowboy star was in black-and-white 'Bs'.
1928: Sharp Shooters. 1929: The Far Call. The Black Watch. The Virginian. Dynamite. 1931: The Women Men Marry. Sky Bride. 1932: Hot Saturday. Island of Lost Souls. Heritage of the Desert. A Successful Calamity. 1933: Supernatural. When the West Was Young. Murders in the Zoo. Wild Horse Mesa. Cocktail Hour. To the Last Man. The Thundering Herd. Hello, Everybody! Sunset Pass. Man of the Forest. Broken Dreams. 1934: Wagon Wheels. The Last Round-Up. The Lone Cowboy. 1935: Home on the Range. The Rocky Mountain Mystery. She. Roberta. Village Tale. So Red the Rose. 1936: And Sudden Death. Follow the Fleet. The Last of the Mohicans. Go West, Young Man. *Pirate Party on Catalina

Isle. 1937: High, Wide and Handsome. 1938: The Texans. Rebecca of Sunnybrook Farm. Road to Reno. 1939: Jesse James. Susannah of the Mounties. Frontier Marshal. 20,000 Men a Year. Coast Guard. 1940: When the Daltons Rode. Virginia City. My Favorite Wife. 1941: Paris Calling. Western Union. Belle Starr. 1942: Pittsburgh. To the Shores of Tripoli. The Spoilers. 1943: Bombardier. Gung Ho! The Desperadoes. Corvette K-225 (GB: The Nelson Touch). 1944: Follow the Boys. Belle of the Yukon. 1945: China Sky. Captain Kidd. 1946: Home Sweet Homicide. Abilene Town. Badman's Territory. 1947: Gunfighters (GB: The Assassin). Christmas Eve. Trail Street. 1948: Coroner Creek. Albuquerque (GB: Silver City). Return of the Bad Men. 1949: The Doolins of Oklahoma (US: The Great Manhunt). The Walking Hills. Canadian Pacific. Fighting Man of the Plains. 1950: The Nevadan (GB: The Man from Nevada). The Cariboo Trail. Colt .45. 1951: Sugarfoot. Santa Fé. Starlift. Fort Worth. Man in the Saddle (GB: The Outcast). 1952: Carson City. Hangman's Knot. The Man Behind the Gun. 1953: Thunder over the Plains. The Stranger Wore a Gun. 1954: Riding Shotgun. The Bounty Hunter. 1955: Ten Wanted Men. Tall Man Riding. Rage at Dawn. A Lawless Street. 1956: Seventh Cavalry. Seven Men from Now. 1957: The Tall T. Shoot Out at Medicine Bend. Decision at Sundown. 1958: Buchanan Rides Alone. 1959: Ride Lonesome. Westbound. 1960: Comanche Station. 1961: Ride the High Country (GB: Guns in the Afternoon).

SCOTT, Zachary 1914–1965
Treachery was Zachary Scott's stock-in-trade: this dark-haired, moustachioed American actor with a way of looking sideways at his fellow-players was almost exclusively cast as scoundrels or powerful criminals, all of them used to a high standard of living. He was capable of a good range – as The Southerner showed – but sneers and hollow laughter prevailed. Died from a brain tumour.
1944: The Mask of Dimitrios. Hollywood Canteen. 1945: The Southerner. Mildred Pierce. Danger Signal. 1946: Her Kind of Man. 1947: Cass Timberlane. Stallion Road. The Unfaithful. 1948: Whiplash. Ruthless. Flaxy Martin. 1949: South of St Louis. Flamingo Road. One Last Fling. 1950: Guilty Bystander. Shadow on the Wall. Born to be Bad. Colt .45. Pretty

Baby. 1951: Let's Make It Legal. The Secret of Convict Lake. Lightning Strikes Twice. 1952: Wings of Danger. 1953: Appointment in Honduras. 1954: The Treasure of Ruby Hills. 1955: Shotgun. Flame of the Islands. 1956: Bandido. The Counterfeit Plan. 1957: Man in the Shadow. Flight into Danger. 1960: Natchez Trace. 1961: The Young One (GB: Island of Shame). 1962: It's Only Money.

SEBERG, Jean 1938–1979
Blonde American actress who brought warmth, vitality and emotional appeal to French films of the early sixties after a shaky start in her own country in Saint Joan. Later films never trained her abilities along the right line and, although she continued to look better in French films than those of Hollywood, her film career had ground to a halt some years before she committed suicide with barbiturates. Married to writer-director Romain Gary (b.1914) from 1963 to 1970. He shot himself in 1980.
1957: Saint Joan. 1958: Bonjour tristesse. 1959: The Mouse That Roared. A bout de souffle/Breathless. 1960: Let No Man Write My Epitaph. La recréation (GB and US: Playtime). Les grandes personnes (GB: A Taste of Love). L'amant de cinq jours (GB: Infidelity). 1961: Congo vivo (GB: Eruption). 1962: In the French Style. 1963: Les plus belles escroqueries du monde. 1964: Lilith. Echappement libre (US: Backfire). 1965: Un milliard dans un billard (GB: Diamonds Are Brittle). Moment to Moment. 1966: Estouffade à la Caraïbe (GB: The Looters). A Fine Madness. La ligne de démarcation. 1967: The Road to Corinth. 1968: Pendulum. Birds in Peru/Birds Come to Die in Peru. 1969: Paint Your Wagon. Airport. A Bullet for Rommel. Ondata di calore. 1970: Macho Callahan. 1971: Questa specie d'amore. Kill. 1972: L'attentat (GB: Plot). The Corruption of Chris Miller (US: Behind the Shutters). Camorra. 1973: Mousey (TV. GB: cinemas as Cat and Mouse). 1975: Le grand delire. 1976: The Wild Duck.

SECOMBE, Sir Harry 1921–
Explosive, ebullient, crinkly-haired Welsh zany comedian and singer, forever giggling between singing operatic arias, and an integral part of the success of the innovative British 1950s' radio comedy programme The Goon Show. His plumpness increased with the

years – he should have played Tweedledum and Tweedledee – until a peritonitis attack caused the emergence of a new slimline Secombe. Films featuring him as star have by and large not been popular successes. Knighted in 1981.

1948: Hocus Pocus. 1949: Helter Skelter. 1950: Fake's Progress (narrator only). 1951: London Entertains. Penny Points to Paradise. 1952: Down Among the Z Men. 1953: Forces' Sweetheart. 1954: Svengali. 1957: Davy. 1959: Jet Storm. 1968: Oliver! 1969: The Bed Sitting Room. 1970: Song of Norway. Rhubarb. Doctor in Trouble. 1971: The Magnificent Seven Deadly Sins. 1972: Sunstruck. 1980: *A Fair Way to Play.

SEGAL, George 1934–
American leading man with fair hair and lived-in face; his wry, sly sense of fun permeated most of his best work and, coupled with a naturalistic acting style, allowed him to be cast as an assortment of dog-eared heroes, frayed charmers and potential losers destined to win by sheer, dogged persistence. A star of the cinema until 1980 – he made rather too many comedies in the late 1970s – he reappeared from 1983 in a variety of out-of-the-way roles. Oscar nominee for Who's Afraid of Virginia Woolf?
1961: The Young Doctors. 1962: The Longest Day. 1963: Act One. 1964: Invitation to a Gunfighter. The New Interns. 1965: King Rat. Ship of Fools. 1966: Lost Command. Who's Afraid of Virginia Woolf? The Quiller Memorandum. 1967: The St Valentine's Day Massacre. No Way to Treat a Lady. 1968: Bye Bye Braverman. Tenderly/The Girl Who Couldn't

Say No. 1969: The Southern Star. The Bridge at Remagen. 1970: Loving. Where's Poppa? The Owl and the Pussycat. 1971: Born to Win. 1972: A Touch of Class. The Hot Rock (GB: How to Steal a Diamond in Four Uneasy Lessons). 1973: Blume in Love. 1974: The Terminal Man. California Split. 1975: The Black Bird. Russian Roulette. 1976: The Duchess and the Dirtwater Fox. Fun with Dick and Jane. 1977: Rollercoaster. 1978: Who is Killing the Great Chefs of Europe? (GB: Too Many Chefs). 1979: Lost and Found. Arthur Miller – on Home Ground. 1980: The Last Married Couple in America. Carbon Copy. 1983: The Cold Room. Robin Hood (TV). Trackdown: Finding the Goodbar Killer (TV). 1984: Stick. 1985: Not My Kid (Video). Who's in the Closet? Killing 'Em Softly (filmed 1982 as The Man in 5A).

SELLARS, Elizabeth 1923–
Cool, elegant, brunette British actress who was cast as a neurotic young girl in her first film, and thereafter often found herself in roles of anguish, latterly as unsympathetic wives. Built up a wider range on stage and TV.
1949: Floodtide. 1950: Madeleine. Guilt is My Shadow. 1951: Cloudburst. Night Was Our Friend. 1952: Hunted (US: The Stranger in Between). The Gentle Gunman. The Long Memory. 1953: Three's Company. The Broken Horseshoe. Recoil. 1954: Forbidden Cargo. Desiree. *Conscience. The Barefoot Contessa. 1955: Three Cases of Murder. Prince of Players. 1956: The Last Man to Hang? The Man in the Sky (US: Decision against Time). 1957: The Shiralee. 1958: Law and Disorder. 1959: Jet Storm. 1960: The Day They Robbed the Bank of England. Never Let Go. 1962: 55 Days at Peking. The Webster Boy. 1963: The Chalk Garden. 1967: The Mummy's Shroud. 1973: The Hireling.

SELLECK, Tom 1945–
Big, dark, heavily-moustached, bearlike American actor of seemingly gentle disposition. In minor leading roles in his twenties, his career seemed to go backwards after that until it took off again with his casting as the detective in the TV series Magnum PI; to do the series he had to turn down the leading role in Raiders of the Lost Ark. Hasn't shown too much personality as yet, but his bulk, all

6' 4" of it, and good looks will undoubtedly keep him going as tough action heroes for some time to come.
1969: Judd for the Defense: The Holy Ground (TV). 1970: Myra Breckinridge. The Movie Murderer (TV). 1971: The Seven Minutes. 1972: Daughters of Satan. 1973: Terminal Island (GB: Knuckle-Men). 1974: Washington Affair. 1975: Returning Home (TV). 1976: Most Wanted (TV. Later: Killer). Midway (GB: Battle of Midway). 1977: Coma. 1978: Superdome (TV). 1979: The Sacketts (TV). Concrete Cowboys (TV). 1982: Divorce Wars (TV). The Shadow Riders (TV). The Chinese Typewriter (TV). 1983: High Road to China. Lassiter. 1984: Runaway. 1986: Sullivan's Travels (TV).

SELLERS, Peter (Richard Sellers) 1925–1980
Plump-faced, dark-haired, apprehensive-looking British comic actor who sprang to fame as a man of many funny voices on radio, then hit his stride in an hilarious series of comedies from 1957 to 1963, before his talent began to overreach itself. Recovered from a serious heart attack in 1964, but only occasionally regained his old brilliance. Married to Britt Ekland 1963–1968 and Lynne Frederick (1954–) from 1977, second and fourth wives, and suffered several minor heart attacks before another major one killed him. Nominated for an Academy Award in Being There.
1951: Penny Points to Paradise. Let's Go Crazy. London Entertains. Burlesque on Carmen (sound reissue, narrator only). 1952: Down Among the Z Men. 1953: *The Super Secret

Service. Our Girl Friday (US: The Adventures of Sadie: voice only). 1954: Orders Are Orders. 1955: John and Julie. The Ladykillers. *The Case of the Mukkinese Battlehorn. 1956: The Man Who Never Was (voice only). 1957: *Insomnia is Good for You. *Cold Comfort. The Smallest Show on Earth. *Death of a Salesman. The Naked Truth (US: Your Past is Showing). 1958: Up the Creek. tom thumb. 1959: Carlton-Browne of the FO. (US: Man in a Cocked Hat). The Battle of the Sexes. I'm All Right, Jack. The Mouse That Roared. Two-Way Stretch. 1960: Climb Up the Wall. *The Running, Jumping and Standing Still Film. Never Let Go. 1961: Only Two Can Play. †Mr Topaze (US: I Like Money). Lolita. 1962: The Waltz of the Toreadors. The Road to Hong Kong. The Dock Brief (US: Trial and Error). The Wrong Arm of the Law. 1963: Heavens Above! Dr Strangelove, or: How I Learned to Stop Worrying and Love the Bomb. The Pink Panther. 1964: A Shot in the Dark. A Carol for Another Christmas (TV). The World of Henry Orient. 1965: What's New, Pussycat? 1966: After the Fox. The Wrong Box. *Birds, Bees and Storks (narrator only). 1967: Woman Times Seven. The Bobo. Casino Royale. 1968: The Party. I Love You, Alice B Toklas. 1969: The Magic Christian. 1970: Hoffman. *Simon, Simon. There's a Girl in My Soup. A Day at the Beach. 1971: Where Does It Hurt? 1972: Alice's Adventures in Wonderland. 1973: Soft Beds, Hard Battles. The Optimists of Nine Elms. The Blockhouse. 1974: The Return of the Pink Panther. Ghost in the Noonday Sun. The Great McGonagall. 1976: Murder by Death. The Pink Panther Strikes Again. 1978: Revenge of the Pink Panther. The Prisoner of Zenda. 1979: Being There. 1980: The Fiendish Plot of Dr Fu Manchu. 1982: Trail of the Pink Panther. The Great Pram Race (voice only).

† Also directed

SEYMOUR, Jane (Joyce Frankenberger) 1951–
Strikingly lovely British brunette actress whose career faltered after she was cast as the heroine in a James Bond film. She later seemed typed as high-born ladies and painted dolls but, right at the end of the 1970s and in between cosmetics commercials, signs of real talent began to emerge and she gave notable

performances in Somewhere in Time and the TV mini-series and movie East of Eden and Dark Mirror.
1969: Oh! What a Lovely War. 1970: Oktober-Dage (GB: The Only Way). 1972: Young Winston. 1973: Frankenstein – the True Story (TV. GB: cinemas in abridged version). Live and Let Die. 1974: The Hanged Man (TV). 1977: Sinbad and the Eye of the Tiger. Benny and Barney: Las Vegas Undercover (TV). Killer on Board (TV). 1978: Battlestar Galactica (TV. GB: cinemas). The Four Feathers (TV. GB: cinemas). Matilda. Dallas Cowboy Cheerleaders (TV). Love's Dark Ride (TV). 1979: The Pirate (TV). 1980: Oh Heavenly Dog. Somewhere in Time. 1981: East of Eden (TV). 1983: Lassiter. Jamaica Inn (TV). Phantom of the Opera (TV). The Haunting Passion. 1984: The Scarlet Pimpernel (TV). Dark Mirror (TV). 1985: Obsessed with a Married Woman. The Sun Also Rises (TV). Head Office.

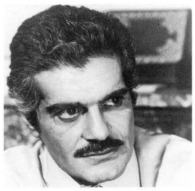

SHARIF, Omar (Michel Shalhoub) 1932–
Black-haired Egyptian actor with flashing dark eyes and faintly bogus smile. Built up a reputation as the number one male pin-up of the Egyptian cinema from 1954 to 1961 before venturing into international films. Was cast almost entirely in blockbuster epics, and found, in the seventies, that the public were less willing to accept him in smaller-scale dramas. Now in co-starring roles, and concentrating on his first love – bridge. Nominated for an Academy Award in Lawrence of Arabia.
1954: ‡The Blazing Sun. ‡Our Happy Days. ‡Devil of the Sahara. 1955: ‡Struggle on the Pier. ‡Land of Peace. 1956: ‡No Sleep. †La chatelaine du Liban. 1957: †Shore of Secrets. †My Lover's Mistake. †Goha. 1958: †For the Sake of a Woman. †The Lady of the Castle. †Rendezvous with a Stranger. ‡Scandal at Zamalek. 1959: †We the Students. †Struggle on the Nile. 1960: †Love Rumour. †The Beginning and the End. †The Agony of Love. †River of Love. †The Mamelukes (GB: Revolt of the Mamelukes). †I Love My Boss. †My Only Love. 1961: †A Man in Our House. 1962: Lawrence of Arabia. 1963: The Fall of the Roman Empire. 1964: The Fabulous Adventures of Marco Polo (GB: Marco the Magnificent). Behold a Pale Horse. The Yellow Rolls Royce. 1965: Genghis Khan. Doctor Zhi-

vago. 1966: The Night of the Generals. The Poppy is Also a Flower (TV. GB: cinemas as Danger Grows Wild). 1967: C'era una volta/ Once Upon a Time (GB: Cinderella Italian Style. US: More Than a Miracle). 1968: Funny Girl. Mayerling. Mackenna's Gold. 1969: The Appointment. Che! 1970: *Simon, Simon. The Horsemen. The Last Valley. 1971: Le casse (GB and US: The Burglars). 1972: Elle lui chrait dans l'île. 1973: The Mysterious Island of Captain Nemo. 1974: Juggernaut. The Tamarind Seed. 1975: Funny Lady. Crime and Passion. 1976: The Pink Panther Strikes Again. The Right to Love. 1979: Ashanti. Bloodline/Sidney Sheldon's Bloodline. S*H*E. The Baltimore Bullet. 1980: Oh Heavenly Dog. Pleasure Palace (TV). 1981: Chanel solitaire. Green Ice. 1984: Ayoub (TV). Top Secret!

‡ As Omar el Cherif   † As Omar Cherif

SHATNER, William 1931–
Solidly-built Canadian actor with dark, curly hair and easy smile. After a start in repertory in his native Montreal, he broke into American television in 1956, films from 1958. Despite a promising start in The Brothers Karamazov, Shatner's film career faltered during the 1960s and it took the successful TV series Star Trek to make his name and face familiar. Film assignments, however, continued to be largely outside the mainstream, but he had another hit television series in the 1980s with T J Hooker.
1957: The Defenders (TV). No Deadly Medicine (TV). 1958: A Town Has Turned to Dust (TV). The Brothers Karamazov. 1961: Judgment at Nuremberg. The Intruder (GB: The Stranger). The Explosive Generation. 1964: The Outrage. 1968: Hour of Vengeance. 1969: Sole Survivor. 1971: Vanished (TV). Owen Marshall, Counsellor at Law (TV). 1972: The People (TV). The Hound of the Baskervilles (TV). 1973: Incident on a Dark Street (TV). Go Ask Alice (TV). The Horror at 37,000 Feet (TV). Pioneer Woman (TV). 1974: Dead of Night. Indict and Convict (TV). Big Bad Mama. Pray for the Wildcats (TV). 1975: Impulse. Barbary Coast (TV. GB: Incident in San Francisco). The Devil's Rain. 1976: Perilous Voyage (TV). A Whale of a Tale. 1977: Kingdom of the Spiders. 1978: Land of No Return (released 1981). Little Women (TV). The Third Walker. Crash (TV). 1979: Riel. Star Trek The Motion Picture. The Kid-

napping of the President. 1980: The Babysitter (TV). 1981: Visiting Hours. 1982: Star Trek The Wrath of Khan. Airplane II The Sequel. 1984: Secrets of a Married Man (TV). Star Trek III: The Search for Spock. 1985: North Beach and Rawhide (TV). 1986: Star Trek IV The Voyage Home.

SHAW, Robert 1927–1978
Wide-faced, forceful British actor who made his name as a man of action in a fifties' TV series, The Buccaneers, moved into more thoughtful roles, then eventually returned to adventurers. Powered his way into world stardom by the seventies, but was killed by a heart attack. Married to Mary Ure (second of three) from 1963 to her death in 1975. Also a best-selling writer. Nominated for an Academy Award in A Man for All Seasons.
1951: The Lavender Hill Mob. 1954: The Dam Busters. 1956: Doublecross. A Hill in Korea (US: Hell in Korea). 1958: Sea Fury. 1959: Libel. 1961: The Valiant. 1962: Tomorrow at Ten. 1963: The Cracksman. The Caretaker. From Russia with Love. *North to the Dales (narrator only). 1964: The Luck of Ginger Coffey. Carol for Another Christmas (TV). 1965: Battle of the Bulge. 1966: A Man for All Seasons. Custer of the West. 1969: Battle of Britain. The Royal Hunt of the Sun. The Birthday Party. 1970: Figures in a Landscape. 1971: A Town Called Bastard. Young Winston. A Reflection of Fear. 1973: The Hireling. The Sting. 1974: The Taking of Pelham 1-2-3. 1975: Diamonds. Jaws. The Judge and His Hangman (US: End of the Game. Later: Deception). 1976: Robin and Marian. Swashbuckler (GB: The Scarlet Buccaneer). Black Sunday. 1977: The Deep. 1978: Force Ten from Navarone. 1979: Avalanche Express.

SHAW, Susan (Patsy Sloots) 1929–1978
Lovely British blonde actress, on stage as a teenager, who came up through the Rank 'Charm School' of the forties, and played working-class glamour girls. Married to Albert Lieven 1949–1953 and Bonar Colleano 1954 to his death in 1958, first and second of three. Later fell on hard times, and died in poverty from cirrhosis of the liver, her funeral being paid for by Rank.
1946: London Town (US: My Heart Goes Crazy). Walking on Air. 1947: The Upturned Glass. Jassy. Holiday Camp. It Always Rains

on Sunday. 1948: To the Public Danger. My Brother's Keeper. London Belongs to Me (US: Dulcimer Street). Quartet. Here Come the Huggetts. 1949: It's Not Cricket. Vote for Huggett. Marry Me. The Huggetts Abroad. Train of Events. 1950: Waterfront (US: Waterfront Women). The Woman in Question (US: Five Angels on Murder). Pool of London. 1951: There is Another Sun (US: Wall of Death). 1952: Wide Boy. A Killer Walks. 1953: Small Town Story. The Large Rope. The Intruder. 1954: The Good Die Young. Devil's Point (US: Devil's Harbor). Time is My Enemy. 1955: Stolen Time (US: Blonde Blackmailer). Stock Car. 1956: Fire Maidens from Outer Space. 1957: Davy. 1958: Diplomatic Corpse. Girls at Sea. Chain of Events. 1959: Carry on Nurse. 1960: The Big Day. 1962: Stranglehold. 1963: The Switch.

SHEARER, Norma (Edith N. Fisher) 1900–1983
Brown-haired Canadian actress who married M-G-M's top producer of the twenties and thirties, Irving Thalberg, and became the studio's first lady until his death in 1936. Her well-bred looks and ultra-smart wardrobe made her a byword for chic sophistication, although she sometimes could not stay away from roles for which she was too old. Academy Award for The Divorcee. Also nominated for Academy Awards on Their Own Desire, The Barretts of Wimpole Street, Romeo and Juliet and Marie Antoinette. Died from bronchial pneumonia.
1920: Way Down East. The Flapper. The Stealers. The Restless Sex. 1921: The Sign on the Door. Torchy's Millions. 1922: The Boot-

leggers. The Devil's Partner. Channing of the Northwest. The Man Who Paid. The Leather Pushers (serial). 1923: Pleasure Mad. A Clouded Name. Man and Wife. The Wanters. Lucretia Lombard. 1924: Blue Waters. Broadway After Dark. Empty Hands. He Who Gets Slapped. Married Flirts. Trail of the Law. The Wolf Man. Broken Barriers. The Snob. 1925: Pretty Ladies. Lady of the Night. The Tower of Lies. His Secretary. A Slave of Fashion. Excuse Me. Waking Up the Town. 1926: Upstage (GB: The Mask of Comedy). The Devil's Circus. The Waning Sex. 1927: The Student Prince. The Demi-Bride. After Midnight. 1928: Lady of Chance. The Latest from Paris. The Actress (GB: Trelawny of the Wells). 1929: Hollywood Revue of 1929. The Trial of Mary Dugan. The Last of Mrs Cheyney. 1930: Let Us Be Gay. The Divorcee. Their Own Desire. 1931: Private Lives. Strangers May Kiss. A Free Soul. *Jackie Cooper's Christmas (GB: The Christmas Party). 1932: Smilin' Through. *The Stolen Jools (GB: The Slippery Pearls). Strange Interlude (GB: Strange Interval). 1934: Riptide. *Hollywood on Parade No.13. The Barretts of Wimpole Street. 1936: Romeo and Juliet. 1938: Marie Antoinette. 1939: The Women. Idiot's Delight. 1940: Escape. 1941: *Cavalcade of the Academy Awards. 1942: We Were Dancing. Her Cardboard Lover.

SHEEDY, Ally (Alexandra Sheedy) 1962–
Dark-haired American actress, dancer and all-round child prodigy who somehow contrives to look quite different in every film in which she appears. She had a children's book published at 12 and reviewed children's literature for The New York Times the following year. At 15 she was acting in TV commercials and had a leading role in a TV movie at 18. Filmwise she has become part of the current 'youth ensemble' pictures and has already demonstrated the ability to touch the emotions.
1980: The Best Little Girl in the World (TV). 1981: The Day the Loving Stopped (TV). Splendor in the Grass (TV). 1982: Deadly Lessons (TV). 1983: Bad Boys. War Games. 1984: Oxford Blues. The Breakfast Club. 1985: St Elmo's Fire. Twice in a Lifetime. 1986: Blue City. Short Circuit.

SHEEN, Martin (Ramon Estevez) 1940–
Good-looking, brooding, tight-lipped, dark-haired American actor, perhaps the first star

of the seventies to be made by TV work. In the theatre since 1960, but it was 10 years before films and TV caught up with his talent, and then his youthful looks enabled him to play men in their early twenties. He has been in two or three of the best TV movies ever made, but his film work – apart from *Badlands* – has been disappointingly routine. Two sons, Emilio Estevez (*qv*) and Charlie Sheen, are also film actors.

1967: *The Incident.* 1968: *The Subject Was Roses. Then Came Bronson* (*TV. GB: cinemas*). 1970: †*When the Line Goes Through. Catch 22.* 1971: †*The Forests Are Nearly All Gone. Welcome Home, Johnny Bristol* (*TV*). *Mongo's Back in Town* (*TV*). *Goodbye, Raggedy Ann* (*TV*). *No Drums, No Bugles.* 1972: *Rage. Crime Club* (*TV*). *Pursuit* (*TV*). *That Certain Summer* (*TV*). *Pick Up on 101* (*GB: Echoes of the Road*). 1973: *Message to My Daughter* (*TV*). *Letters from Three Lovers* (*TV*). *Catholics* (*TV*). *Harry O* (*TV*). *A Prowler in the Heart* (*TV*). *The Execution of Private Slovik* (*TV*). *Badlands.* 1974: *Pretty Boy Floyd* (*TV*). *The Missiles of October* (*TV*). *The California Kid* (*TV*). 1975: *The Legend of Earl Durand. Roman Gray* (*TV. GB: The Art of Crime*). *Sweet Hostage* (*TV*). *The Last Survivors* (*TV*). 1976: *The Cassandra Crossing. The Little Girl Who Lives Down the Lane.* 1978: *Eagle's Wing.* 1979: *Apocalypse Now.* 1980: *The Final Countdown. Loophole.* 1981: *Blind Ambition* (*TV*). 1982: *Gandhi. In the Custody of Strangers* (*TV*). *Enigma. That Championship Season.* *No Place to Hide (narrator only). In The King of Prussia. Man, Woman and Child.* 1983: *Kennedy* (*TV*). *The Dead Zone. Choices of the Heart* (*TV*). 1984: *Firestarter. The Atlanta Child Murders.* ‡*Listen to the City. The Guardian* (*TV*). 1985: *Consenting Adults* (*TV*). *In the Name of the People (narrator only). Shattered Spirits. Out of Darkness* (*TV*). *A State of Emergency.* 1986: *Judgement in Berlin. News at Eleven* (*TV*). *Samaritan: The Mitch Snyder Story* (*TV*).

† *Unreleased*
‡ *Scene deleted from final release print*

SHEFFIELD, Johnny 1931–
A freckle-faced American boy actor with fair, curly hair who played Tarzan's son, and then, when he grew up, Bomba the Jungle Boy. Sheffield quit films at the age of 25, and, for

many years, has made his career in real estate. Son of Reginald Sheffield (1901–1957), a child star of the silents in his native Britain, who came to America in the 1920s and, after taking the lead in *David Copperfield* (1923), played mainly character roles until his death.

1939: *Tarzan Finds a Son! Babes in Arms.* 1940: *Little Orvie. Lucky Cisco Kid. Knute Rockne – All American* (*GB: A Modern Hero*). 1941: *Million Dollar Baby. Tarzan's Secret Treasure.* 1942: *Tarzan's New York Adventure.* 1943: *Tarzan Triumphs. Tarzan's Desert Mystery.* 1944: *The Great Manhunt. Our Hearts Were Young and Gay. The Man in Half Moon Street. Wilson.* 1945: *Roughly Speaking. Tarzan and the Amazons.* 1946: *Tarzan and the Leopard Woman.* 1947: *Tarzan and the Huntress.* 1949: *Bomba the Jungle Boy. Bomba on Panther Island.* 1950: *The Lost Volcano. Bomba and the Hidden City.* 1951: *The Lion Hunters* (*GB: Bomba and the Lion Hunters*). *Bomba and the Elephant Stampede.* 1952: *African Treasure* (*GB: Bomba and the African Treasure*). *Bomba and the Jungle Girl.* 1953: *Safari Drums* (*GB: Bomba and the Safari Drums*). 1954: *The Golden Idol. Killer Leopard.* 1955: *Lord of the Jungle.* 1956: *The Black Sleep.* 1960: *Midnight Lace.*

SHEFFIELD, Reginald
See Sheffield, Johnny

SHELLEY, Barbara (B. Kowin) 1933–
Lovely brunette British leading lady of porcelain beauty who spent the first three years of her career in Italian films, then came home to become the first lady of British horror films, proving a match for, and sometimes even

turning into, things that went bump in the House of Hammer.

1953: †*Mantrap* (*US: Woman in Hiding*). 1954: *Ballata tragica/Love without Tomorrow. The Barefoot Contessa.* 1955: *La crime di spora. Luna nuova. Motivo in maschera. I quattro del getto tonante/ Four in a Thunderjet.* 1956: *Destinazione Piovarolo. Suprema confessione. The Little Hut. Mio figlio Nerone/Nero's Weekend.* 1957: *Cat Girl. The End of the Line.* 1958: *The Camp on Blood Island. The Solitary Child. Blood of the Vampire.* 1959: *Deadly Record. Bobbikins. Murder at Site Three.* 1960: *A Story of David. Village of the Damned.* 1961: *The Shadow of the Cat.* 1962: *Death Trap. Postman's Knock. Stranglehold.* 1963: *Blind Corner.* 1964: *The Secret of Blood Island. The Gorgon.* 1965: *Dracula – Prince of Darkness. Rasputin the Mad Monk.* 1967: *Quatermass and the Pit* (*US: 5,000,000 Miles to Earth*). 1969: *The Spy Killer* (*TV*). 1974: *Ghost Story.*

† *As Barbara Kowin*

SHELTON, Joy (Joyce Shelton) 1922–
Dark-haired British actress with gentle, refined features and faintly old-fashioned looks, a RADA scholarship winner at 15. Played a good variety of wives, waifs and (not always willingly) waiting women in films, and became much loved on radio as the girlfriend of the bungling PC 49 in a long-running comedy-thriller series, a role she later repeated on film. From the mid-1950s she worked mostly in the theatre. Married to actor Sydney Tafler (b 1916) from 1944 to his death in 1979.

1943: *Millions Like Us.* 1944: *Bees in Paradise. Waterloo Road.* 1946: *Send for Paul Temple.* 1948: *Uneasy Terms.* *Designing Women. No Room at the Inn.* 1950: *The Golden Age (narrator only). Midnight Episode. Once a Sinner.* 1951: *A Case for PC 49.* 1952: *Emergency Call* (*US: Hundred Hour Hunt*). 1953: *Park Plaza 605* (*US: Norman Conquest*). 1955: *Impulse.* 1960: *No Kidding* (*US: Beware of Children*). 1961: *The Greengage Summer* (*US: Loss of Innocence*). *Five Golden Hours.* 1962: *HMS Defiant* (*US: Damn the Defiant!*).

SHEPARD, Sam (S. S. Rogers) 1943–
Lean-faced (it seems somehow permanently in shadow), dark-haired, soft-spoken American Pulitzer Prize-winning playwright and

on-off actor and singer. The son of an Air Force man who retired to be a farmer, Shepard is a country-loving man recently reclaimed by acting (in which he made his show-business start) after big writing successes off and on Broadway. Now combines the two careers. Has lived for some years with actress Jessica Lange (*qv*). Nominated for an Academy Award for his performance in *The Right Stuff*, his characters exude quiet charisma and authority.

1969: *Easy Rider (voice only)*. 1977: *Renaldo and Clara*. 1978: *Days of Heaven*. 1980: *Resurrection*. 1981: *Raggedy Man*. 1982: *Frances*. 1983: *The Right Stuff*. 1984: *Country*. 1985: *Fool for Love*. 1986: *Crimes of the Heart*.

SHEPHERD, Cybill 1949–
Blonde, forties-style Hollywood beauty, who plays characters who cock a snook at conventions. Was for several years associated with director Peter Bogdanovich, and appeared in a number of his films. Her career faltered when the relationship broke up. But she has the talent to survive, and hopefully will do so. She certainly scored a big personal success in the mid 1980s with the TV series *Moonlighting*.

1971: *The Last Picture Show*. 1972: *The Heartbreak Kid*. 1974: *Daisy Miller*. 1975: *At Long Last Love*. 1976: *Taxi Driver*. *Special Delivery*. 1977: *Silver Bears*. 1978: *A Guide for the Married Woman (TV)*. 1979: *The Lady Vanishes*. 1981: *The Return*. 1984: *Secrets of a Married Man (Video)*. 1985: *Moonlighting (TV)*.

SHERIDAN, Ann (Clara Lou Sheridan) 1915–1967
Tough but hopeful: those were the characters that this fair-haired American actress played in her heyday, even before she became world famous as the 'oomph girl'. She'd been kicked around, but was still an optimist: the mould suited the wartime years, and the wide-faced, mockingly-smiling star herself, who had appeared in numerous small roles before hitting the big time. Married to Edward Norris (1910–) from 1936–1939 and George Brent (*qv*) from 1942–1943, first and second of three. Died from cancer.

1933: †*Search for Beauty*. 1934: †*One Hour Late*. †*Ready for Love*. †*Ladies Should Listen*. †*Murder at the Vanities*. †*Bolero*. †*Shoot the Works (GB: Thank Your Stars)*. †*Mrs Wiggs of the Cabbage Patch*. †*You Belong to Me*. †*Come on, Marines!* †*Kiss and Make Up*. †*The Notorious Sophie Lang*. †*College Rhythm*. †*Wagon Wheels*. †*Limehouse Blues*. 1935: †*Rumba*. †*Enter Madame*. †*Home on the Range*. *Rocky Mountain Mystery*. *Behold My Wife*. *The Glass Key*. *Fighting Youth*. **Star Night at the Cocoanut Grove*. *Mississippi*. *Car 99*. *The Crusades*. *Red Blood of Courage*. 1936: *Black Legion*. *Sing Me a Love Song*. 1937: *Wine, Women and Horses*. *The Great O'Malley*. *Footloose Heiress*. *San Quentin*. 1938: *The Patient in Room 18*. *Alcatraz Island*. *Cowboy from Brooklyn (GB: Romance and Rhythm)*. *She Loved a Fireman*. *Mystery House*. *Little Miss Thoroughbred*. *Broadway Musketeers*. *Letter of Introduction*. *Angels with Dirty Faces*. 1939: *Naughty But Nice*. *They Made Me a Criminal*. *Indianapolis Speedway (GB: Devil on Wheels)*. *Winter Carnival*. *Dodge City*. 1940: *Torrid Zone*. *Castle on the Hudson (GB: Years without Days)*. *City for Conquest*. *It All Came True*. *They Drive by Night (GB: The Road to Frisco)*. 1941: *Honeymoon for Three*. *Kings Row*. *Navy Blues*. *The Man Who Came to Dinner*. 1942: *George Washington Slept Here*. *Juke Girl*. *Wings for the Eagle*. 1943: *Thank Your Lucky Stars*. *Edge of Darkness*. 1944: *The Doughgirls*. *Shine on, Harvest Moon*. 1946: *One More Tomorrow*. 1947: *Nora Prentiss*. *The Unfaithful*. 1948: *The Treasure of the Sierra Madre*. *Silver River*. *Good Sam*. 1949: *I Was a Male War Bride (GB: You Can't Sleep Here)*. 1950: *Stella*. *Woman on the Run*. 1952: *Steel Town*. *Just across the Street*. 1953: *Take Me to Town*. *Appointment

in Honduras. 1956: *Come Next Spring*. *The Opposite Sex*. 1957: *Triangle on Safari (US: Woman and the Hunter)*. *Without Incident (TV)*.

† *As Clara Lou Sheridan*

SHERIDAN, Dinah (D. Mec) 1920–
Although fondly remembered from *Genevieve*, this fair-haired, grey-eyed, very lovely British actress with smiling mouth and high cheekbones made only 25 films in nearly 20 years, and enjoyed just a few years as a star before retiring (too early) to marry her second husband (actor Jimmy Hanley was the first). A lone appearance in the seventies showed that she had lost none of her grace and charm.

1935: *I Give My Heart*. 1936: *Irish and Proud of It*. *Landslide*. 1937: *Father Steps Out*. *Behind Your Back*. 1938: *Merely Mr Hawkins*. 1939: *Full Speed Ahead*. 1942: *Salute John Citizen*. 1943: *Get Cracking*. 1945: *29 Acacia Avenue (US: The Facts of Life)*. *For You Alone*. *Murder in Reverse*. 1947: *The Hills of Donegal*. 1948: *Calling Paul Temple*. 1949: *The Story of Shirley Yorke*. *The Huggetts Abroad*. *Dark Secret*. 1950: *No Trace*. *Paul Temple's Triumph*. *Blackout*. 1951: *Where No Vultures Fly (US: Ivory Hunter)*. 1952: *The Sound Barrier (US: Breaking the Sound Barrier)*. 1953: *Appointment in London*. *The Story of Gilbert and Sullivan (US: The Great Gilbert and Sullivan)*. *Genevieve*. 1970: *The Railway Children*. 1980: *The Mirror Crack'd*.

SHIELDS, Brooke 1965–
Leggy, dark-haired, striking American actress with heavy eyebrows and lips. A child model,

she started a whole new look in fashion modelling, as well as launching an acting career, principally with her role as a child prostitute in *Pretty Baby*. But she seemed unprepared or unable to offer more than a surface performance in later films, and the scripts were little help.

1976: *Communion/Alice Sweet Alice*. 1977: †*Morning, Winter and Night*. *The Prince of Central Park* (*TV*). 1978: *Pretty Baby*. *Wanda Nevada*. *King of the Gypsies*. 1979: *Just You and Me Kid*. *An Almost Perfect Affair*. 1980: *Tilt*. *The Blue Lagoon*. 1981: *Endless Love*. 1983: *Sahara*. 1984: *Wet Gold* (*TV*). *The Muppets Take Manhattan*.

† *Unfinished*

SHINER, Ronald 1903–1966
Raucous-voiced, beady-eyed, dark-haired British comedy actor who played dozens of cockney character parts before a repeat of a successful stage role (in *Worm's Eye View*) catapulted him to stardom. Once he reached the top, he insured his substantial nose for £20,000. The 1950s saw him in a series of broad but at first very popular comedies (several of them remakes of 1930s' successes), before his popularity faded again late in the decade. He was a Mountie in his twenties.

1934: *My Old Dutch*. *Doctor's Orders*. 1935: *Gentleman's Agreement*. *It's a Bet*. *Limelight* (*US: Backstage*). *Squibs*. *Royal Cavalcade* (*US: Regal Cavalcade*). *Once a Thief*. *Line Engaged*. 1936: *Excuse My Glove*. *King of Hearts*. 1937: *Dreaming Lips*. *The Black Tulip*. *Farewell Again* (*US: Troopship*). *Dinner at the Ritz*. *Beauty and the Barge*. *A Yank at Oxford*. 1938: *Prison Without Bars*. *They Drive By Night*. *St Martin's Lane* (*US: Sidewalks of London*). 1939: *Flying Fifty Five*. *The Mind of Mr Reeder* (*US: The Mysterious Mr Reeder*). *I Killed the Count* (*US: Who is Guilty?*). *Discoveries*. *The Middle Watch*. *Trouble Brewing*. *The Missing People*. *The Gang's All Here* (*US: The Amazing Mr Forrest*). *The Lion Has Wings*. *Come On George*. 1940: '*Bulldog*' *Sees It Through*. *Salvage with a Smile*. *Spare a Copper*. *Let George Do It*. *The Case of the Frightened Lady* (*US: The Frightened Lady*). *Old Bill and Son*. 1941: *The Black Sheep of Whitehall*. *South American George*. *The Seventh Survivor*. *Major Barbara*. *The Big Blockade*. *They Flew Alone* (*US: Wings and the Woman*). 1942: *The Young Mr*

Pitt. *Sabotage at Sea*. *The Balloon Goes Up*. *Those Kids from Town*. *King Arthur Was a Gentleman*. *The Night Invader*. *Unpublished Story*. *Squadron Leader X*. 1943: *The Gentle Sex*. *Get Cracking*. *Thursday's Child*. *Miss London Ltd*. *My Learned Friend*. *The Butler's Dilemma*. 1944: *Bees in Paradise*. 1945: *I Live in Grosvenor Square* (*US: A Yank in London*). *Caesar and Cleopatra*. *The Way to the Stars* (*US: Johnny in the Clouds*). 1946: *George in Civvy Street*. 1947: *Dusty Bates* (*serial*). *The Man Within* (*US: The Smugglers*). *The Ghosts of Berkeley Square*. *Brighton Rock* (*US: Young Scarface*). 1948: *Forbidden*. *Rise and Shiner*. 1951: *The Magic Box*. *Worm's Eye View*. *Reluctant Heroes*. 1952: *Little Big Shot*. *Top of the Form*. 1953: *Innocents in Paris*. *Laughing Anne*. 1954: *Aunt Clara*. *Up to His Neck*. 1955: *See How They Run*. 1956: *Keep It Clean*. *Dry Rot*. *My Wife's Family*. 1957: *Carry On Admiral* (*US: The Ship Was Loaded*). *Not Wanted on Voyage*. 1958: *Girls at Sea*. 1959: *Operation Bullshine*. *The Navy Lark*. 1960: *The Night We Got the Bird*.

SHIRE, Talia (née Coppola) 1945–
Petite, toothily pretty American actress with very dark hair, the sister of director Francis (Ford) Coppola. Usually plays 'ordinary' girls. After a few minor roles she had her first part of consequence in her brother's *The Godfather*, but has become best known as Sylvester Stallone's girl-friend/wife in the *Rocky* films. Nominated for Academy Awards on *The Godfather Pt II* and *Rocky*. Turned producer in 1985.

1963: †'*X*' (*GB: The Man with the X-Ray Eyes*). 1966: †*You're a Big Boy Now*. 1968: †*The Wild Racers*. 1969: †*Don't Push, I'll Charge When I'm Ready* (*TV*). 1970: †*The Dunwich Horror*. †*Gas-s-s-s – or – It Became Necessary to Destroy the World in Order to Save It*. 1971: †*The Christian Licorice Store*. *The Godfather*. 1972: *Un homme est mort* (*GB and US: The Outside Man*). 1974: *The Godfather Pt II*. 1975: *Foster and Laurie* (*TV*). *Doctors' Secrets* (*TV*). 1976: *Rocky*. 1977: *Kill Me If You Can/The Caryl Chessman Story* (*TV*). 1978: *Old Boyfriends*. *Daddy, I Don't Like It Like This* (*TV*). 1979: *Rocky II*. *Corky*. *Prophecy*. 1980: *Windows*. 1982: *Rocky III*, 1983: *The Butcher*. 1985: *Rocky IV*. *Reel Horror*. 1986: *Rad*. *Hyper Sapien*.

† *As Talia Coppola*

SHIRLEY, Anne (Dawn Paris) 1918–
Pretty-as-a-picture auburn-haired child actress of the twenties (under the name Dawn O'Day) who, when she grew into a teenager, proved perfect casting for *Anne of Green Gables*, legally changing her name to that of the heroine in that film. Her films were too lachrymose for her to last, though she was a charming purveyor of sweetness-and-light through the tears. Married to John Payne 1937–1943, first of three. Nominated for an Academy Award on *Stella Dallas*.

1922: †*The Hidden Woman*. †*Moonshine Valley*. 1923: †*The Spanish Dancer*. †*The Rustle of Silk*. 1924: †*The Fast Set*. †*The Man Who Fights Alone*. 1925: †*Riders of the Purple Sage*. 1926: †**Alice's Mysterious Mystery* (*and subsequent series*). 1927: †*The Callahans and the Murphys*. †*Night Life*. 1928: †*Mother Knows Best*. †*Sins of the Father*. 1929: †*Four Devils*. 1930: †*City Girl*. †*Liliom*. 1931: †*Rich Man's Folly*. 1932: †*Young America* (*GB: We Humans*). †*Emma*. †*So Big*. †*The Purchase Price*. †*Three on a Match*. 1933: †*The Life of Jimmy Dolan* (*GB: The Kid's Last Fight*). †*Rasputin and the Empress* (*GB: Rasputin – the Mad Monk*). 1934: †*The Key*. †*Picture Palace. †*This Side of Heaven*. †*Private Lessons. †*Finishing School*. †*School for Girls*. *Anne of Green Gables*. 1935: *Steamboat 'Round the Bend*. **A Night at the Biltmore Bowl*. *Chasing Yesterday*. 1936: *Make Way for a Lady*. *Chatterbox*. *M'Liss*. 1937: *Meet the Missus*. *Too Many Wives*. *Stella Dallas*. 1938: *Law of the Underworld*. *Condemned Women*. *Mother Carey's Chickens*. *Girls' School*. *A Man to Remember*. 1939: *Sorority House* (*GB: That Girl from College*). *Career*. *Boy Slaves*. 1940: *Anne of Windy Poplars* (*GB: Anne of Windy Willows*). *Vigil in the Night*. *Saturday's Children*. 1941: *Unexpected Uncle*. *West Point Widow*. *All That Money Can Buy/The Devil and Daniel Webster*. *Four Jacks and a Jill*. 1942: *Mayor of 44th Street*. 1943: *Lady Bodyguard*. *The Powers Girl* (*GB: Hi! Beautiful*). *Bombardier*. *Government Girl*. 1944: *Man from Frisco*. *Music in Manhattan*. 1945: *Murder, My Sweet* (*GB: Farewell, My Lovely*).

† *as Dawn O'Day*

SHORE, Dinah (Frances Shore) 1917–
Sweet-faced, strawberry-blonde, healthy-looking American singing star (a child enter-

tainer, as Fanny Rose), whose rich, melodious adult voice captivated record buyers and radio audiences in the early 1940s. Her special appeal never came across in her few films. Married to George Montgomery (*qv*) from 1943 to 1960. A long association with Burt Reynolds (also *qv*) a decade later was eventually broken off.

1943: Thank Your Lucky Stars. 1944: Up in Arms. Follow the Boys. Belle of the Yukon. 1946: Make Mine Music (voice only). Till the Clouds Roll By. 1947: Fun and Fancy Free. 1952: Aaron Slick from Punkin Crick (GB: Marshmallow Moon). 1977: Oh, God! 1979: Health.

(GB: Merrily We Go to –). Madame Butterfly. Make Me a Star. 1933: Jennie Gerhardt. Pick-Up. 1934: Behold My Wife. Good Dame (GB: Good Girl). Thirty Day Princess. 1935: Accent on Youth. Mary Burns, Fugitive. 1936: Sabotage (US: The Woman Alone). Fury. Trail of the Lonesome Pine. 1937: Dead End. You Only Live Once. 1938: You and Me. 1939: . . . One Third of a Nation. 1941: The Wagons Roll at Night. 1945: Blood on the Sun. 1946: The Searching Wind. Mr Ace. 1947: Love from a Stranger (GB: A Stranger Walked In). 1952: Les Miserables. 1955: Man on the Ledge (TV. GB: cinemas). Violent Saturday. 1956: Behind the High Wall. 1957: Helen Morgan (TV). 1958: The Gentleman from Seventh Avenue (TV). 1971: Do Not Fold, Spindle or Mutilate (TV). 1973: Summer Wishes, Winter Dreams. 1975: Winner Take All (TV). The Secret Night Caller (TV). 1976: Raid on Entebbe (TV. GB: cinemas). Demon/God Told Me To. Death at Love House (TV). 1977: I never Promised You a Rose Garden. Snowbeast (TV). 1978: Damien – Omen II. Siege (TV). 1979: The Gossip Columnist (TV). 1980: Hammett (shown and later copyrighted 1982). The Shadow Box (TV). 1981: A Small Killing (TV). FDR: The Last Year (TV). 1982: Having It All. 1983: Order of Death. 1984: Finnegan Begin Again (GB: TV). 1986: An Early Frost (TV).

Manège. 1950: Four Days' Leave. Le Traqué/ Gunman in the Streets. La ronde. 1951: Ombre et lumière. 1952: Casque d'or. 1953: Thérèse Raquin. 1954: Les diaboliques/The Fiends. 1956: La muerte en este jardin (GB: Evil Eden. US: Death in the Garden). Die Windrose. 1957: The Witches of Salem. 1958: Room at the Top. 1959: Yves Montand chante. . . . 1960: Le joli mai (narrator only). Les mauvais coups. Adua e la compagne (GB: Hungry for Love). 1961: Les amours célebres. 1962: Le jour et l'heure. Term of Trial. 1963: Dragées au poivre (GB: Sweet and Sour). Il giorno piu corto commedia umaristica (US: The Shortest Day). 1965: Ship of Fools. Is Paris Burning? Compartiment tueurs/the Sleeping Car Murders. 1966: The Deadly Affair. 1967: Games. 1968: The Seagull. Mr Freedom. 1969: † Américain. L'armée des ombres. 1970: Le rose et le noir. L'aveu. Compte à rebours. 1971: Le chât. La veuve Couderc. 1973: Les granges brûlées (GB: TV, as The Investigator). 1974: Rude journée pour la reine. La chair de l'orchidée. Défense de savoir. 1975: Madame le juge (TV). And ensuing series). 1976: Police Python 357. 1977: La vie devant soi (GB: Madame Rosa). 1978: Une femme dangereuse. L'adolescente. 1979: Judith Therpauve. Je t'ai écrit une lettre d'amour/Chère inconnue (US: I Sent a Letter to My Love). 1980: L'étoile du nord. 1981: Gina. 1982: Guy de Maupassant. 1983: Des 'Terroristes' à la retraite (narrator only).

SIDNEY, Sylvia (Sophia Kosow) 1910–
Pretty, plaintive-looking, dark-haired American actress who played plucky working girls battling against environmental odds, and only sometimes winning. Her naturalistic acting style made her one of Paramount's biggest stars of the thirties, but her decision to do stage work in 1939 came at the wrong time in her career, and a film comeback in the mid-forties failed. In the seventies she unexpectedly returned, playing elderly character roles. Has written a book on needlepoint. Married to Luther Adler (1903–1984) from 1938 to 1946, second of three. Nominated for an Academy Award on *Summer Wishes, Winter Dreams*.

*1927: Broadway Nights. 1929: Thru Different Eyes. 1930: *Five Minutes from the Station. 1931: Confessions of a Co-Ed (GB: Her Dilemma). An American Tragedy. Ladies of the Big House. City Streets. Street Scene. 1932: The Miracle Man. Merrily We Go to Hell*

SIGNORET, Simone (S. Kaminker) 1921–1985
Blonde French actress (born in Germany), mostly in moody roles. In her youth she was prettily comely and sensual but even in early middle age her features had turned heavier and this led to some fairly gloomy film roles. Academy Award for *Room at the Top* (she also won three British Academy Awards, plus an Oscar nomination for *Ship of Fools*). Married/divorced director Yves Allégret. Married to Yves Montand (*qv*) from 1951 to her death from cancer. Failing sight put an end to her acting career in the early 1980s, but she found new success as a writer.

1942: Le prince charmant. Boléro. Les visiteurs du soir. 1943: La boîte aux rêves. Adieu Léonard. 1944: Béatrice devant le désir. 1945: Les démons de l'aube. Le couple idéal. 1946: Macadam. 1947: Dédée d'Anvers (GB and US: Dédée). Fântomas. 1948: Against the Wind. L'impasse aux deux anges. 1949:

SILVERS, Phil (P. Silver) 1912–1985
Explosive, bespectacled American comedian whose vigorous shirkers entertained wartime film audiences before he returned to vaudeville and stage shows. In the mid-1950s he re-emerged on television as one of the world's most popular comedians, playing the bald, scheming army sergeant Bilko in the long-running *You'll Never Get Rich*. Film appearances since then did not repeat that success, and he was in poor health for some years before his death.

1940: Hit Parade of 1941. Strike Up the Band. †Pride and Prejudice. 1941: †Ball of Fire. The Penalty. The Wild Man of Borneo. Ice-Capades. Tom, Dick and Harry. Lady Be Good. You're in the Army Now. 1942: Roxie Hart. All Through the Night. My Gal Sal. Footlight Serenade. Just Off Broadway. 1943: Coney Island. A Lady Takes a Chance. 1944: Cover Girl. Four Jills in a Jeep. Something for the

Boys. Take It or Leave It. 1945: Billy Rose's Diamond Horseshoe (GB: Diamond Horseshoe). A Thousand and One Nights. 1946: If I'm Lucky. 1950: Summer Stock (GB: If You Feel Like Singing). 1952: Top Banana. 1954: Lucky Me. 1962: 40 Pounds of Trouble. 1963: It's a Mad, Mad, Mad, Mad World. 1966: A Funny Thing Happened on the Way to the Forum. 1967: Follow That Camel. 1968: Buona Sera, Mrs Campbell. 1970: The Boatniks. 1975: The Deadly Tide (TV). The Strongest Man in the World. Won Ton Ton, the Dog Who Saved Hollywood. All Trails Lead to Las Vegas (TV). 1976: Murder by Death. 1977: The Chicken Chronicles. The New Love Boat (TV). 1978: Racquet. The Night They Took Miss Beautiful (TV). The Cheap Detective. 1979: 'Hey Abbott!' (TV). Goldie and the Boxer (TV). 1980: The Happy Hooker Goes to Hollywood. Hollywood Blue.

† Scene deleted from final release print

SIM, Alastair 1900–1976
Long-faced, tombstone-toothed Scottish-born character star, bald from an early age, whose expressions of ghoulish glee, doleful dithering and agonized anguish, coupled with uniquely gurgling diction, were associated with much that was best in British comedies and comedy-thrillers from the late 1930s to the mid-1950s. The cinema let him go too early at 60. An incomparable Scrooge. Died from cancer.
1935: The Case of Gabriel Perry. The Riverside Murder. A Fire Has Been Arranged. The Private Secretary. Late Extra. 1936: Wedding Group (US: Wrath of Jealousy). Troubled Waters. Keep Your Seats Please. The Mysterious Mr Davis (US: My Partner Mr Davis). The Big Noise. The Man in the Mirror. She Knew What She Wanted. Strange Experiment. 1937: The Squeaker (US: Murder on Diamond Row). Clothes and the Woman. Melody and Romance. Gangway. A Romance in Flanders (US: Lost on the Western Front). 1938: Alf's Button Afloat. Sailing Along. The Terror. Climbing High. This Man is News. Inspector Hornleigh. 1939: This Man in Paris. Inspector Hornleigh on Holiday. 1940: Law and Disorder. *Her Father's Daughter. 1941: Cottage to Let (US: Bombsight Stolen). Inspector Hornleigh Goes to It (US: Mail Train). 1942: Let the People Sing. 1943: *Fid-

dling Fuel. 1944: Waterloo Road. 1945: Journey Together. 1946: Green for Danger. 1947: Hue and Cry. Captain Boycott. 1948: London Belongs to Me (US: Dulcimer Street). 1950: The Happiest Days of Your Life. Stage Fright. 1951: Laughter in Paradise. Lady Godiva Rides Again. Scrooge (US: A Christmas Carol). 1952: Folly to be Wise. 1953: Innocents in Paris. 1954: The Belles of St Trinian's. An Inspector Calls. 1955: Escapade. *Festival in Edinburgh (narrator only). Geordie (US: Wee Geordie). 1956: The Green Man. 1957: Blue Murder at St Trinian's. 1959: The Doctor's Dilemma. Left, Right and Centre. 1960: The Millionairess. School for Scoundrels. 1971: The Ruling Class. 1975: Royal Flash. 1976: Rogue Male (TV). Escape from the Dark (US: The Littlest Horse Thieves).

SIM, Sheila 1922–
Fresh-faced, light-haired British actress with chubbily pretty features and piquant personality. A stage performer at 16, she has been married to Sir Richard Attenborough since 1945. She made a few films (although not as many as one remembers), mainly as nice girls subservient to the plot, but has been seen mainly on stage.
1944: A Canterbury Tale. 1945: Great Day. †Journey Together. 1947: Dancing with Crime. 1948: The Guinea Pig. 1949: Dear Mr Prohack. 1950: Pandora and the Flying Dutchman. 1951: The Magic Box. 1954: West of Zanzibar. 1955: The Night My Number Came Up.

† Scenes deleted from final release print

SIMMONS, Jean 1929–
Britain never sent a prettier actress to Hollywood (and few more talented): all the more pity the film capital did so little with her. The demure-looking brunette with oval face and stunning figure had done rather well in Britain, but had to wait 10 years for comparable American roles. In leading roles as a teenager. Married to Stewart Granger (qv) 1950–1960. A later marriage to director Richard Brooks also ended in divorce. Nominated for Academy Awards on Hamlet and The Happy Ending.
1944: Give Us the Moon. Mr Emmanuel. Kiss the Bride Goodbye. Meet Sexton Blake. 1945: *Sports Day. The Way to the Stars (US:

Johnny in the Clouds). Caesar and Cleopatra. 1946: Great Expectations. Hungry Hill. 1947: Black Narcissus. Uncle Silas (US: The Inheritance). The Woman in the Hall. 1948: Hamlet. The Blue Lagoon. 1949: Adam and Evelyne. Trio. So Long at the Fair. Cage of Gold. The Clouded Yellow. 1952: Androcles and the Lion. Angel Face. 1953: She Couldn't Say No (GB: Beautiful But Dangerous). Young Bess. Affair with a Stranger. The Actress. The Robe. 1954: The Egyptian. Desiree. A Bullet is Waiting. 1955: Footsteps in the Fog. Guys and Dolls. 1956: Hilda Crane. 1957: This Could Be the Night. Until They Sail. 1958: Home Before Dark. The Big Country. 1959: This Earth is Mine. 1960: Elmer Gantry. Spartacus. 1961: The Grass is Greener. 1963: All the Way Home. 1965: Life at the Top. Mr Buddwing (GB: Woman without a Face). 1967: Rough Night in Jericho. Divorce American Style. 1968: Heidi Comes Home (US: Heidi). 1969: The Happy Ending. 1970: Decisions! Decisions! (TV). Say Hello to Yesterday. 1975: Mr Sycamore. The Easter Promise (TV). 1978: The Dain Curse (TV). Dominique. 1981: A Small Killing (TV). Golden Gate (TV). 1983: Robin Hood (TV). 1984: Midas Valley (TV). 1985: Yellow Pages.

SIMON, Simone 1910–
Pert, mercurial, dark-haired French actress with child-like face (and voice to match). Producer Darryl F. Zanuck brought her to Hollywood in 1935, but only one or two films – Seventh Heaven, Cat People – capitalized on her special appeal, and her best work was done in her native France, where she now lives.

1941: Nice Girl? Badlands of Dakota. 1942: Men of Texas. To Be or Not To Be. *Keeping Fit. Eagle Squadron. 1948: Miss Tatlock's Millions. Fighter Squadron. A Date with Judy. 1950: Mr Music. 1951: My Outlaw Brother. The Bullfighter and the Lady. 1953: Bwana Devil. Sabre Jet. Conquest of Cochise. War Paint. 1954: The High and the Mighty. The Iron Glove. 1955: Good Morning, Miss Dove. House of Bamboo. Laura (TV. GB: cinemas). 1956: Great Day in the Morning. Written on the Wind. 1957: The Tarnished Angels. Panic Button (TV). 1958: The Gift of Love. 1959: John Paul Jones. The Scarface Mob (TV. GB: cinemas). 1960: The Last Voyage. 1963: The Caretakers (GB: Borderlines). 1965: Is Paris Burning? 1966: The Peking Medallion (US: The Corrupt Ones). 1967: Le soleil de voyous (GB and US: Action Man). Asylum for a Spy (TV). The Pill Caper (TV). 1969: Storia di una donna (GB and US: The Story of a Woman). 1970: Battle at Gannon's Bridge (TV). 1975: Adventures of the Queen (TV). Murder on Flight 502 (TV). The Strange and Deadly Occurrence (TV). 1976: Most Wanted (TV). 1978: Un second souffle. Check Up. 1979: 1941. 1980: My Kidnapper, My Love (TV). 1983: Uncommon Valor. 1984: Big Trouble. Lusitano (narrator only).

STAMP, Terence 1940–

Pale-eyed, clear-faced, unsmiling British leading man. A sensation in his first two films, but a star career has gradually drifted away from him. Most recently seen as men of mystery and menace, he still remains one of filmland's most eligible bachelors. Oscar nominee for *Billy Budd.*

1962: Term of Trial. Billy Budd. 1965: The Collector. 1966: Modesty Blaise. 1967: Far from the Madding Crowd. Poor Cow. Histoires extraordinaires (GB: Tales of Mystery). 1968: Theorem/Teorema. Blue. 1969: The Mind of Mr Soames. 1971: Una stagione all' inferno. 1974: Hu-man. 1975: La divina creatura (US: The Divine Nymph). 1976: Striptease. 1978: Meetings with Remarkable Men. The Thief of Bagdad. Superman. 1979: Amo non amo/I Love You I Love You Not/Together. 1980: Superman II. Monster Island. 1981: Morte in Vaticano. 1984: The Hit. The Company of Wolves. 1985: Link. 1986: Under the Cherry Moon. Legal Eagles.

STALLONE, Sylvester 1946–

Muscular, surly-looking, dark-haired American actor with big ambitions who, after early struggles, shot into the superstar bracket with *Rocky*, an old-fashioned entertainment movie which he wrote himself. The film won an Oscar as best picture (Stallone received a best actor nomination), but its star has had to work hard to stay at the top. The characters of Rocky and, later, Vietnam veteran Rambo, have enabled him to brush aside failures in other directions and stay in the superstar class. Known to his friends as 'Sly'.

1970: Party at Kitty and Studs (later re-released as The Italian Stallion). 1971: Bananas. 1974: No Place to Hide. The Prisoner of Second Avenue. The Lords of Flatbush. 1975: Farewell, My Lovely. Capone. Death Race 2000. 1976: Rocky. Carquake (GB: Cannonball). 1978: F.I.S.T. †Paradise Alley. 1979: †Rocky II. 1980: Nighthawks. 1981: Escape to Victory (US: Victory). 1982: First Blood. †Rocky III. 1983: Rebel. †Staying Alive. 1984: Rhinestone. 1985: Rambo: First

STAMP-TAYLOR, Enid 1904–1946

British blonde actress with finely-boned features, a beauty contest winner who, after a shaky transition to sound, moved on to be a busy minor leading lady of the thirties, mostly in comedy. She was playing character roles as 'other women' deserted by the hero for someone younger, when she died at 41 from injuries sustained in a fall.

Blood Part II. †Rocky IV. 1986: Over the Top. Cobra.

†And directed.

1927: Land of Hope and Glory. Easy Virtue. Remembrance. 1928: A Little Bit of Fluff (US: Skirts). Yellow Stockings. Cocktails. 1929: Broken Melody. 1933: Meet My Sister. A Political Party. 1934: The Feathered Serpent. Virginia's Husband. Gay Love. 1935: Mr What's-His-Name. Radio Pirates. While Parents Sleep. So You Won't Talk? Jimmy Boy. Two Hearts in Harmony. 1936: Queen of Hearts. Blind Man's Bluff. House Broken. 1937: Underneath the Arches. Take a Chance. Talking Feet. Feather Your Nest. Okay for Sound. Action for Slander. 1938: Old Iron. Blondes for Danger. Stepping Toes. Climbing High. 1939: The Lambeth Walk. The Girl Who Forgot. 1940: The Farmer's Wife. Spring Meeting. 1941: Hatter's Castle. South American George. 1942: Alibi. 1943: Candlelight. 1945: The Wicked Lady. 1946: Caravan.

STANWYCK, Barbara (Ruby Stevens, later legally changed) 1907–

Although it has been made before, the comparison between the real and assumed names of this tough, well-liked Hollywood lady (perhaps the best actress never to win an Oscar) is inescapable. So many of her characters were women, good or bad, struggling to escape the Ruby Stevens image and cross to Barbara Stanwyck on the glamorous side of the tracks. Often, their efforts ended in violence and tragedy. But whatever else, Stanwyck (who was also nifty in comedy) grabbed her films by the scruff of their necks, and left an indelible imprint. Married (second) to Robert Taylor 1939–1952. Never remarried. Special Academy Award 1982, following four unsuccessful nominations (*Stella Dallas, Ball of Fire, Double Indemnity, Sorry, Wrong Number*). Still stealing scenes, now in TV supersoaps.

1927: Broadway Nights. 1929: The Locked Door. Mexicali Rose. *The Voice of Hollywood. 1930: Ladies of Leisure. 1931: Illicit. Ten Cents a Dance. Miracle Woman. *Screen Snapshots No. 4. Night Nurse. 1932: Forbidden. Shopworn. So Big. The Purchase Price. 1933: Baby Face/Baby Face Harrington. The Bitter Tea of General Yen. Ladies They Talk About. Ever in My Heart. 1934: A Lost Lady (GB: Courageous). Gambling Lady. The Secret Bride (GB: Concealment). 1935: Red Salute (GB: Arms and the Girl). The Woman in Red. Annie Oakley. 1936: The Bride Walks Out. A Message to Garcia. The Plough and the Stars. His Brother's Wife. Banjo on My Knee. 1937:

Internes Can't Take Money (GB: You Can't Take Money). This is My Affair (GB: His Affair). Stella Dallas. Breakfast for Two. 1938: The Mad Miss Manton. Always Goodbye. 1939: Union Pacific. Golden Boy. 1940: Remember the Night. 1941: You Belong to Me. Ball of Fire. The Lady Eve. Meet John Doe. 1942: The Gay Sisters. The Great Man's Lady. 1943: Lady of Burlesque (GB: Striptease Lady). Flesh and Fantasy. 1944: Hollywood Canteen. Double Indemnity. My Reputation (released 1946). 1945: *Hollywood Victory Caravan. Christmas in Connecticut (GB: Indiscretion). 1946: The Bride Wore Boots. California. The Strange Love of Martha Ivers. 1947: The Two Mrs Carrolls. Variety Girl. The Other Love. Cry Wolf. 1948: BF's Daughter (GB: Polly Fulton). Sorry, Wrong Number. 1949: Thelma Jordon (GB: The File on Thelma Jordon). East Side, West Side. The Lady Gambles. *Eyes of Hollywood. 1950: To Please a Lady. The Furies. No Man of Her Own. 1951: The Man with a Cloak. 1952: Clash by Night. 1953: All I Desire. Titanic. Jeopardy. The Moonlighter. Blowing Wild. 1954: Witness to Murder. Executive Suite. Cattle Queen of Montana. The Violent Men (GB: Rough Company). 1955: Escape to Burma. 1956: The Maverick Queen. These Wilder Years. There's Always Tomorrow. 1957: Crime of Passion. Forty Guns. Trooper Hook. 1962: A Walk on the Wild Side. 1964: Roustabout. 1965: The Night Walker. 1970: The House That Wouldn't Die (TV). 1971: A Taste of Evil (TV) 1972: The Letters (TV).

STARRETT, Charles 1904–1986
Well-built, dark-haired, square-jawed American leading man (a former star footballer) who played handsome, rocklike juvenile leads until he started making westerns in 1936. The rugged Starrett quickly became one of America's most popular 'B' Western stars, especially in those dust-rousers which featured him as the Durango Kid. Some of the title changes in this list are quite extraordinary. He died from cancer.
1926: The Quarterback. 1930: The Royal Family of Broadway. Fast and Loose. 1931: Touchdown (GB: Playing the Game). The Viking. Silence. The Age for Love. Damaged Love. Sky Bride. 1932: Lady and Gent. The Mask of Fu Manchu. 1933: The Return of Casey Jones (GB: Train 2419). Our Betters. The Jungle

Bride. The Sweetheart of Sigma Chi (GB: Girl of My Dreams). 1934: Murder on the Campus (GB: On the Stroke of Nine). This Man is Mine. Desirable. Gentlemen Are Born. Call It Luck. Green Eyes. The Silver Streak. One in a Million. Three on a Honeymoon. Stolen Sweets. 1935: What Price Crime? Sons of Steel. Make a Million. The Gallant Defender. A Shot in the Dark. One New York Night (GB: The Trunk Mystery). So Red the Rose. 1936: Stampede. Along Came Love. Code of the Range. Dodge City Trail. The Mysterious Avenger. The Cowboy Star. Secret Patrol. 1937: Westbound Mail. Two-Gun Law. One Man Justice. Outlaws of the Prairie. Old Wyoming Trail. Two-Fisted Sheriff. Trapped. 1938: Law of the Plains. Start Cheering. Colorado Trail. South of Arizona. West of the Santa Fé. Cattle Raiders. West of Cheyenne. Call of the Rockies. Rio Grande. 1939: The Man from Sundown (GB: A Woman's Vengeance). Spoilers of the Range. Texas Stampede. The Stranger from Texas (GB: The Stranger). North of the Yukon. Western Caravans (GB: Silver Sands). Riders of Black River. Outpost of the Mounties (GB: On Guard). The Thundering West. 1940: Two-Fisted Rangers. Bullets for Rustlers (GB: On Special Duty). West of Abilene (GB: The Showdown). Thundering Frontier. Blazing Six-Shooters (GB: Stolen Wealth). Texas Stagecoach (GB: Two Roads). The Durango Kid (GB: The Masked Stranger). 1941: The Medico of Painted Springs (GB: Doctor's Alibi). Outlaws of the Panhandle (GB: Faro Jack). Thunder over the Prairie. Royal Mounted Patrol (GB: Giants A'Fire). The Pinto Kid (GB: All Square). The Prairie Stranger (GB: The Marked Bullet). Riders of the Badlands. 1942: Down Rio Grande Way (GB: The Double Punch). West of Tombstone. Bad Men of the Hills (GB: Wrongly Accused). Riding through Nevada. Lawless Plainsmen. Riders of the Northland (GB: Next in Line). Overland to Deadwood (GB: Falling Stones). Pardon My Gun. 1943: Robin Hood of the Range. The Fighting Buckaroo. Hail to the Rangers (GB: Illegal Rights). Cowboy in the Clouds. Frontier Fury. Law of the Northwest. 1944: Sundown Valley. Riding West (GB: Fugitive from Time). Cyclone Prairie Rangers. Cowboy Canteen (GB: Close Harmony). Cowboy from Lonesome River (GB: Signed Judgment). Saddle Leather Law (GB: The Poisoner). 1945: Both Barrels Blazing (GB: The Yellow Streak). Rough Ridin' Justice (GB: Decoy). Rustlers of the Badlands (GB: By Whose Hand?) Outlaws of the Rockies (GB: A Roving Rogue). Sagebrush Heroes. Return of the Durango Kid (GB: Stolen Time). Blazing the Western Trail (GB: Who Killed Waring?). Lawless Empire (GB: Power of Possession). Texas Panhandle. 1946: Roaring Rangers (GB: False Hero). Frontier Gun Law (GB: Menacing Shadows). Two-Fisted Stranger. Heading West (GB: The Cheat's Last Throw). Terror Trail (GB: Hands of Menace). Gunning for Vengeance (GB: Jail Break). Galloping Thunder (GB: On Boot Hill). The Desert Horseman (GB: Checkmate). Landrush (GB: The Claw Strikes). The Fighting Frontiersman (GB: Golden Lady).

South of the Chisholm Trail. 1947: The Lone Hand Texan (GB: The Cheat). Prairie Raiders (GB: The Forger). The Buckaroo from Powder River. Riders of the Lone Star. West of Dodge City (GB: the Sea Wall). Law of the Canyon (GB: The Price of Crime). The Stranger from Ponca City. The Last Days of Boot Hill. 1948: Whirlwind Raiders (GB: State Police). Phantom Valley. Blazing across the Pecos (GB: Under Arrest). El Dorado Pass (GB: Desperate Men). West of Sonora. Six Gun Law. Trail to Laredo (GB: Sign of the Dagger). Quick on the Trigger (GB: Condemned in Error). 1949: Desert Vigilante. Challenge of the Range (GB: Moonlight Raid). Horsemen of the Sierras (GB: Remember Me). Bandits of El Dorado (GB: Tricked). The Blazing Trail (GB: The Forged Will). South of Death Valley (GB: River of Poison). Laramie. Renegades of the Sage (GB: The Fort). 1950: Trail of the Rustlers (GB: Lost River). Outcasts of Black Mesa (GB: The Clue). Across the Badlands (GB: The Challenge). Raiders of Tomahawk Creek (GB: Circle of Fear). Texas Dynamo (GB: Suspected). Streets of Ghost Town. Lightning Guns (GB: Taking Sides). Frontier Outpost. 1951: Fort Savage Raiders. Prairie Roundup. Bonanza Town (GB: Two-Fisted Agent). The Kid from Amarillo (GB: Silver Chains). Riding the Outlaw Trail. Snake River Desperadoes. Cyclone Fury. Pecos River (GB: Without Risk). 1952: Junction City. Smoky Canyon. The Hawk of Wild River. The Rough, Tough West. Laramie Mountains (GB: Mountain Desperadoes). The Kid from Broken Gun.

STEEL, Anthony 1920–
Strongly-built, smilingly boyish, light-haired British leading man, trained for stardom by the Rank Organization, and the number one 'beefcake' pin-up of the British cinema from 1951 to 1956. Broke with Rank after marrying (1956–1962) Anita Ekberg, and resumed his career in Italy, but did not regain his former eminence with the British public. Recently playing elder statesmen in sexploitation movies.
1948: Quartet. Saraband for Dead Lovers (US: Saraband). Portrait from Life (US: The Girl in the Painting). A Piece of Cake. 1949: The Blue Lamp. Once Upon a Dream. Marry Me. Helter Skelter. Poet's Pub. Don't Ever Leave Me. The Chiltern Hundreds (US: The Amazing Mr Beecham). Trottie True (US:

Gay Lady). Christopher Columbus. 1950: Trio. The Wooden Horse. The Mudlark. 1951: Another Man's Poison. Laughter in Paradise. Where No Vultures Fly (US: Ivory Hunter). Emergency Call (US: Hundred Hour Hunt). 1952: Something Money Can't Buy. The Planter's Wife (US: Outpost in Malaya). 1953: Malta Story. Albert RN (US: Break to Freedom). The Master of Ballantrae. 1954: West of Zanzibar. The Sea Shall Not Have Them. 1955: Out of the Clouds. Passage Home. Storm over the Nile. 1956: Checkpoint. The Black Tent. 1957: Valerie. 1958: Harry Black (US: Harry Black and the Tiger). A Question of Adultery. 1959: The Man in the Middle. Honeymoon. Forty Eight Hours to Live. 1960: Revenge of the Barbarians. 1961: Vacanze alla baia d'argento. 1962: Tiger of the Seven Seas. 1963: The Switch. A Matter of Choice. Hell is Empty (released 1967). 1965: Winnetou II (GB: Last of the Renegades). 1966: Le fate (GB: Sex Quartet). Zwei Girls vom Roten Stern. 1967: Anzio (GB: The Battle for Anzio). War Devils/The Devil's Man. 1968: A Case for Inspector Blomfeld. 1969: Funkstreife XY. Häschen in der Grube. 1973: Massacre in Rome. 1975: Run, Rabbit, Run. 1976: The Night of the High Tide. The Story of O. 1977: Hardcore. Let's Get Laid. 1979: The World is Full of Married Men. 1980: The Mirror Crack'd.

STEELE, Barbara 1937–
Hauntingly beautiful, black-haired British actress with startlingly large brown eyes and unsettling presence. She went to Italy in 1960 (after a variety of small roles in Britain and Hollywood), where her strong, chilling performances in tales of fright earned her the title 'queen of horror films'. Disappeared in the late 1960s, before re-emerging for a while in Canadian and American films, older but still disturbingly watchable. Married playwright/screenwriter James Poe.
1958: Bachelor of Hearts. Houseboat. 1959: Sapphire. The 39 Steps. Upstairs and Downstairs. Your Money or Your Wife. 1960: Mask of the Demon (GB: Black Sunday). 1961: The Iron Captain. The Pit and the Pendulum. 1962: Revenge of the Mercenaries. 8½. L'orribile segreto del Dr Hichcock (GB: The Terror of Dr Hichcock. US: The Horrible Dr Hitchcock). Le coup. Amour sans landemain. Danse macabre (GB and US: Castle of Blood). 1963: The Spectre (US: The Ghost). Hours of Love. Un

tentativo sentimentale. Le voci bianche. Les baisers. 1964: Le sexe des anges. I maniaci (US: The Maniacs). The Long Hair of Death. Amore facile. Le monocle rit jaune. El ataco (US: The Road to Violence). 1965: I soldi. L'armata Brancaleone. Cinque tombe per un medium (GB and US: Terror-Creatures from the Grave). Gli amanti d'oltre tomba (GB: The Faceless Monster. US: Nightmare Castle). La sorella di Satana (GB: Revenge of the Blood Beast. US: The She Beast). 1966: Young Törless. Un angelo per Satan/An Angel for Satan. For Love and Gold. 1967: Fermato il mondo ... voglio scendere. 1968: Handicap. Curse of the Crimson Altar (US: Crimson Cult). 1969: Honeymoon with a Stranger (TV). 1974: The Parasite Murders (GB: Shivers. US: They Came from Within). Caged Heat. 1977: I Never Promised You a Rose Garden. 1978: Piranha. Pretty Baby. La clé sur la porte. The Space Watch Murders (TV). 1979: The Silent Scream.

STEELE, Tommy (T. Hicks) 1936–
Cheerful, energetic, fair-haired, eager-to-please British entertainer who began as a rock 'n' roll star but soon enlarged his range, becoming a dancer and comedy actor, and brought his chirpy cockney personality and engaging grin to several films. Entirely a stage star in the seventies and eighties.
1957: Kill Me Tomorrow. The Shiralee (voice only). The Tommy Steele Story (US: Rock Around the World). 1958: Europe by Night. The Duke Wore Jeans. 1959: Tommy the Toreador. 1960: Light Up the Sky. 1963: It's All Happening (US: The Dream Maker). 1967: The Happiest Millionaire. Half a Sixpence. 1968: Finian's Rainbow. 1969: Where's Jack?

STEENBURGEN, Mary 1952–
Vivacious, wide-smiling American actress with dark, curly hair, warm, slightly offbeat personality, and deliberate speaking voice. A late arrival on the movie scene, she has somehow seemed difficult to cast and therefore made too few films, despite an Academy Award for her performance in Melvin and Howard. Married to Malcolm McDowell (qv) since 1980.
1978: Goin' South. 1979: Time After Time. 1980: Melvin and Howard. 1981: Ragtime. 1982: A Midsummer Night's Sex Comedy. 1983: Cross Creek. Romantic Comedy! 1985: One Magic Christmas. 1986: Dead of Winter.

STEIGER, Rod (Rodney Steiger) 1925–
Stocky, intense American actor whose ranting, raving, chew-up-the-scenery style made him one of the few modern-day acting targets for impressionists. In time, his performance grew less mannered and more enjoyable. Won an Oscar in 1967 for In the Heat of the Night. Married (second) to Claire Bloom from 1959 to 1971. Additional Oscar nominations for On the Waterfront and The Pawnbroker.

1951: Teresa. 1954: On the Waterfront. 1955: The Big Knife. Oklahoma! The Court-Martial of Billy Mitchell (GB: One Man Mutiny). 1956: The Harder They Fall. Back from Eternity. Jubal. 1957: The Unholy Wife. Run of the Arrow. Across the Bridge. 1958: A Town Has Turned to Dust (TV). Cry Terror! 1959: Al Capone. 1960: Seven Thieves. 1961: The Mark. On Friday at 11. 1962: Convicts Four (GB: Reprieve!). 13 West Street. The Longest Day. 1963: Gli indifferenti (GB and US: Time of Indifference). Hands across the City. 1964: E venne un uomo/A Man Named John. 1965: The Pawnbroker. The Loved One. Doctor Zhivago. 1967: In the Heat of the Night. The Girl and the General. The Movie Maker (TV). No Way to Treat a Lady. 1968: The Sergeant. The Illustrated Man. Three into Two Won't Go. 1970: Waterloo. 1971: A Fistful of Dynamite/Duck You Sucker. Happy Birthday Wanda June. 1972: The Heroes. 1973: Lucky Luciano. Lolly Madonna XXX (GB: The Lolly Madonna War). 1974: Innocents with Dirty Hands. 1975: Hennessy. 1976: W. C. Fields and Me. 1977: Jimbuck. Mussolini: the Last Four Days. 1978: Love and Bullets. Wolf Lake (released 1984). F.I.S.T. 1979: Breakthrough/Sergeant Steiner. The Amityville Horror. Cattle Annie and Little Britches. 1980: Klondike Fever. Lion of the Desert/Omar Mukhtar Lion of the Desert. The Lucky Star. 1981: The Chosen. 1982: Der Zauerberg (US: The Magic Mountain). 1983: Mafia Kingpin. Portrait of a Hitman. Cook and Peary: The Race to the Pole (TV). 1984: The Naked Face.

STEN, Anna (Anjuschka Stenski Sujakevich) 1908–

Attractive, sympathetic blonde Russian actress imported by Samuel Goldwyn to Hollywood in 1933, but not a hit with the public. Best as portraying earth-rooted girls doomed to tragic romance. Stayed in America, and became a painter in the sixties: has held several exhibitions.

1927: Zluta Knizka/The Yellow Ticket. Devushka a Korobkoi. 1928: Potomok Chingis-Khana (GB and US: Storm over Asia). Moskva v Oktjabre (GB: Moscow Laughs and Cries. US: When Moscow Laughs). Belyi Orel (GB: The White Eagle. US: The Lash of the Czar). The House on Trubnaya Square. 1929: Moj Syn. Zolotoj Kljuv. 1930: Lohnbuchhalter Kremke. 1931: Bomben auf Monte Carlo. Der Mörder Dimitri Karamasoff/The Brothers Karamozov. Salto Mortale (US: Trapeze). Stürme der Leidenschaft. 1934: Nana. We Live Again. 1935: The Wedding Night. 1936: A Woman Alone (US: Two Who Dared). 1939: Exile Express. 1940: The Man I Married. 1941: So Ends Our Night. 1943: They Came to Blow Up America. Chetniks. 1944: Three Russian Girls (GB: She Who Dares). 1948: Let's Live a Little. 1955: Soldier of Fortune. 1956: Runaway Daughters. 1957: Heaven Knows, Mr Allison. 1962: The Nun and the Sergeant.

STEPHEN, Susan 1931–

Demurely pretty British actress, her fair hair usually cropped short, with pin-up figure and attractively semi-husky speaking voice, in appealing leading roles within months of leaving RADA. Her roles after 1956 were disappointing. Married (second) to cinematographer (later director) Nicolas Roeg.

1951: His Excellency. 1952: Stolen Face. Treasure Hunt. Fanciulle di lusso/Luxury Girls. Father's Doing Fine. 1953: The Red Beret (US: Paratrooper). The Case of the Studio Payroll. 1954: The House across the Lake (US: Heatwave). For Better, For Worse (US: Cock-

tails in the Kitchen). Dangerous Cargo. Golden Ivory (US: White Huntress). 1955: As Long As They're Happy. Value for Money. 1956: It's Never Too Late. Pacific Destiny. 1957: The Barretts of Wimpole Street. 1959: Carry on Nurse. 1960: Operation Stogie. 1961: The Court Martial of Major Keller. Return of a Stranger. 1962: Three Spare Wives.

STEPHENSON, James 1888–1941

One of the cinema's more extraordinary figures. A dark, moustachioed, tautly handsome British stage actor who made no films until he was nearly 50. He went to Hollywood in 1938, and, at Warners, advanced slowly to leading roles, revealing a talent and presence that had not been evident in his British films. Then, after only a handful of star parts, he dropped dead from a heart attack. Nominated for an Academy Award on The Letter.

1937: The Man Who Made Diamonds. Dangerous Fingers (US: Wanted by Scotland Yard). The Perfect Crime. Take It from Me. You Live and Learn. 1938: The Dark Stairway. It's in the Blood. Mr Satan. Cowboy from Brooklyn (GB: Romance and Rhythm). Heart of the North. When Were You Born? White Banners. Nancy Drew, Detective. Boy Meets Girl. 1939: The Private Lives of Elizabeth and Essex. The Old Maid. On Trial. Torchy Blane in Chinatown. *Sons of Liberty. Espionage Agent. Secret Service of the Air. We Are Not Alone. Adventures of Jane Arden. Confessions of a Nazi Spy. Beau Geste. King of the Underworld. 1940: *The Monroe Doctrine. Wolf of New York. Devil's Island. Murder in the Air. Calling Philo Vance. A Dispatch from Reuter's (GB: This

Man Reuter). The Letter. The Sea Hawk. South of Suez. River's End. 1941: Shining Victory. Flight from Destiny. International Squadron.

STERLING, Jan (Jane S. Adriance) 1923–

Thin-faced, pencil-slim blonde American actress. Her looks got her cast as bitches, but her warm personality sometimes saw her through to more sympathetic roles. A solid dramatic performer whose considerable comedy talents were under-used. Married (second) to Paul Douglas from 1950 to his death in 1959. Nominated for an Academy Award on The High and the Mighty.

1947: †Tycoon. 1948: Johnny Belinda. 1950: The Skipper Surprised His Wife. Mystery Street. Caged. Union Station. 1951: Appointment with Danger. The Big Carnival (GB: Ace in the Hole). The Mating Season. Rhubarb. 1952: Flesh and Fury. Sky Full of Moon. 1953: Pony Express. Split Second. The Vanquished. 1954: Alaska Seas. The High and the Mighty. The Human Jungle. Return from the Sea. 1955: The Man with the Gun (GB: The Trouble Shooter). Women's Prison. Female on the Beach. 1984. 1956: The Harder They Fall. Requiem for a Heavyweight (TV). 1957: Slaughter on Tenth Avenue. Clipper Ship (TV. GB: cinemas). 1958: Kathy O'. The Female Animal. High School Confidential. 1961: Love in a Goldfish Bowl. 1967: The Incident. 1968: The Angry Breed. 1969: The Minx. 1976: Sammy Somebody. Having Babies (TV). 1981: First Monday in October. 1982: Dangerous Company (TV).

† As Jane Adrian

STERLING, Robert (William Hart) 1917–

Brown-haired, boyish, blandly handsome American leading man; busy in the early war years, he rose slowly to co-star status, but found rewarding roles difficult to come by after returning from war service as an army pilot instructor. Chiefly noteworthy for marrying two glamorous actresses – Ann Sothern (1943–1949) and Anne Jeffreys (1923–) from 1951 on. With Jeffreys he had some success in the TV series Topper, but eventually quit show business to go into computer software.

1939: Blondie Brings Up Baby. Blondie Meets the Boss. *Charles Goodyear. Golden Boy. The Man They Could Not Hang. Mr Smith Goes

to Washington. *My Son is Guilty (GB: Crime's End)*. *Those High Gray Walls (GB: The Gates of Alcatraz)*. *Beware Spooks! Only Angels Have Wings*. *First Offenders*. *Good Girls Go to Paris*. *Missing Daughters*. *Outside These Walls*. *A Woman is the Judge*. *Romance of the Redwoods*. 1940: *Yesterday's Heroes*. *Scandal Sheet*. *The Gay Caballero*. *Manhattan Heartbeat*. 1941: *The Getaway*. *The Penalty*. *Two-Faced Woman*. *Ringside Maisie*. *Johnny Eager*. *Dr Kildare's Victory (GB: The Doctor and the Debutante)*. *I'll Wait for You*. 1942: *This Time for Keeps*. *Somewhere I'll Find You*. 1946: *The Secret Heart*. 1949: *The Sundowners (GB: Thunder in the Dust)*. *Roughshod*. 1950: *Bunco Squad*. 1951: *Show Boat*. 1953: *Column South*. 1961: *Return to Peyton Place*. *Voyage to the Bottom of the Sea*. 1963: *A Global Affair*. 1973: *Letters from Three Lovers (TV)*.

STEVENS, Connie (Concetta Ingolia) 1938–
Bright, busty American leading lady who flourished briefly in the cinema as a kind of cross between Sandra Dee and Connie Francis. Usually in innocent roles that belied her looks. Only very sporadically seen in the cinemas after the mid-sixties. Married to actor James Stacy and singer Eddie Fisher (both divorced).
1957: *Eighteen and Anxious*. *Young and Dangerous*. 1958: *Rock-a-Bye Baby*. *Dragstrip Riot*. *The Party Crashers*. 1961: *Susan Slade*. *Parrish*. 1963: *Palm Springs Weekend*. 1964: *Two on a Guillotine*. 1965: *Never Too Late*. 1967: *Way . . . Way Out*. 1969: *Mr Jerico*. 1971: *The Grissom Gang*. *The Last Generation*.

STEVENS, Craig (Gail Shikles) 1918–
Tall, broad-shouldered American leading man with wavy, brown hair who played solid, reliable types in largely undistinguished films and was much more successful on television, especially from 1958 in the series *Peter Gunn*, a private eye he later recreated on screen. Married to Alexis Smith since 1944.
1941: *Law of the Tropics*. *Affectionately Yours*. *Dive Bomber*. *Steel against the Sky*. 1942: *Secret Enemies*. *Now, Voyager*. *Spy Ship*. *The Hidden Hand*. 1943: *This is the Army*. 1944: *Resisting Enemy Interrogation*. *Hollywood Canteen*. *The Doughgirls*. *Since You Went Away*. 1945: *God is My Co-Pilot*. *Roughly Speaking*. *Too Young to Know*. 1946: *The Man I Love*. *Humoresque*. 1947: *That Way with Women*. *Love and Learn*. 1948: **Melodies of Memory Lane*. 1949: *The Lady Takes a Sailor*. *Night unto Night*. 1950: *Where the Sidewalk Ends*. *Blues Busters*. 1951: *The Lady from Texas*. *Drums in the Deep South*. 1952: *Phone Call from a Stranger*. 1953: *Murder without Tears*. *Abbott and Costello Meet Dr Jekyll and Mr Hyde*. 1954: *The French Line*. 1955: *Duel on the Mississippi*. 1957: *The Deadly Mantis*. 1958: *Buchanan Rides Alone*. 1967: *Gunn*. 1968: *The Limbo Line*. 1972: *The Female Instinct (TV. GB: The Snoop Sisters)*. 1974: *The Killer Bees (TV)*. 1975: *The Elevator (TV)*. *Nick and Nora (TV)*. 1977: *The Cabot Connection (TV)*. 1978: *Secrets of Three Hungry Wives (TV)*. 1981: *SOB*.

STEVENS, Inger (I. Stensland) 1934–1970
Swedish-born actress in Hollywood, whose smooth, enigmatic, high-cheekboned prettiness somehow gave hints of great sex appeal smouldering below the surface. Had a tough time in the mid-sixties when many would-be employers apparently ostracized her after it was discovered she had married a coloured man. Committed suicide with sleeping pills.
1957: *Man on Fire*. 1958: *Cry Terror! The Buccaneer*. 1959: *The World, the Flesh and the Devil*. *Diary of a Nurse (TV)*. 1964: *The New*

Interns. 1967: *A Guide for the Married Man*. *The Borgia Stick (TV)*. *A Time for Killing (GB: The Long Ride Home)*. *Firecreek*. 1968: *Madigan*. *Hang 'Em High*. *House of Cards*. *Five Card Stud*. 1969: *A Dream of Kings*. 1970: *Run, Simon, Run (TV)*. *The Mask of Sheba (TV)*.

STEVENS, Mark (Richard Stevens) 1915–
Dark-haired American actor of serious personality who began his career in Canada, then came to Hollywood in 1941 to play small roles as Stephen Richards. Did his best work as fatalistic heroes in *noir* thrillers; later directed a few of his own films, proving quite efficient at manipulating suspense.
1941: †*Two-faced Woman*. 1943: †*Destination Tokyo*. †*Background to Danger*. †*Northern Pursuit*. 1944: †*Passage to Marseille*. †*The Doughgirls*. †*Hollywood Canteen*. 1945: †*Objective Burma*. †*Pride of the Marines (GB: Forever in Love)*. †*Roarin' Guns*. †*Rhapsody in Blue*. †*God is My Co-Pilot*. *Within These Walls*. 1946: *From This Day Forward*. *The Dark Corner*. 1947: *I Wonder Who's Kissing Her Now?* 1948: *The Street with No Name*. *The Snake Pit*. 1949: *Will James' Sand (GB: Sand)*. *Oh, You Beautiful Doll*. *Dancing in the Dark*. 1950: *Please Believe Me*. *Between Midnight and Dawn*. 1951: *Target Unknown*. *Katie Did It*. *Reunion in Reno*. *Little Egypt (GB: Chicago Masquerade)*. 1953: *Mutiny*. *Torpedo Alley*. *The Lost Hours (US: The Big Frame)*. 1953: *Jack Slade (GB: Slade)*. 1954: ‡*Cry Vengeance*. 1955: ‡*Timetable*. 1957: *Gunsight Ridge*. ‡*Gun Fever*. 1958: *Gunsmoke in Tucson*. 1960: *September Storm*. 1964:

‡*Escape from Hell Island. Fate is the Hunter. Frozen Alive.* ‡*Vergeltung in Catano (GB and US: Sunscorched).*

† *As Stephen Richards*
‡ *Also directed*

STEVENS, Stella (Estelle Eggleston) 1936–
Another of Hollywood's gutsy blondes, still in there slugging as she pushes on towards her fifties. With rosebud lips, turned-up nose and a figure that would look good in a sack, Stella found herself mostly used in films as lightweight decoration. But she also has lots of personality, spirit and too-rarely-tapped acting ability, only *Too Late Blues* and *The Ballad of Cable Hogue* bringing out anything like the best in her. The thoughtfulness behind the ingenuously sexy surface appeal was underlined when she directed a feature documentary in 1980. Mother of actor Andrew Stevens (1955–).
1959: Say One for Me. The Blue Angel. Li'l Abner. 1961: Mantrap. Too Late Blues. 1962: Girls! Girls! Girls! 1963: The Courtship of Eddie's Father. The Nutty Professor. Advance to the Rear (GB: Company of Cowards). 1965: Synanon (GB: Get Off My Back). The Secret of My Success. 1966: The Silencers. Rage (Glenn Ford). 1967: How to Save a Marriage ... and Ruin Your Life. Sol Madrid (GB: The Heroin Gang). 1968: Where Angels Go ... Trouble Follows. The Mad Room. 1970: The Ballad of Cable Hogue. 1971: A Town Called Bastard. Stand Up and Be Counted. In Broad Daylight (TV). 1972: The Poseidon Adventure. Rage (George C. Scott). Climb an Angry Mountain (TV). Slaughter. 1973: Arnold. Linda (TV). 1974: The Day the Earth Moved (TV). Honky Tonk (TV). 1975: Cleopatra Jones and the Casino of Gold. The New Original Wonder Woman (TV). 1976: Las Vegas Lady. Wanted: the Sundance Woman (TV). Nickelodeon. Kiss Me, Kill Me (TV). 1977: Charlie Cobb: Nice Night for a Hanging (TV). The Manitou. The New Love Boat (TV). 1978: The Jordan Chance (TV). The Hostage Heart (TV). Cruise into Terror (TV). The Deadly Price of Paradise (TV. GB: Nightmare at Pendragon's Castle). Murder in Peyton Place (TV). 1979: Supertrain (TV. Later: Express to Terror). Hart to Hart (TV). Friendships, Secrets and Lies (TV). The Night They Took

Miss Beautiful (TV). 1980: Make Me an Offer (TV). 1981: Twirl (TV). Mister Deathman. 1982: Children of Divorce (TV). Wacko. 1983: Women of San Quentin (TV). 1984: Amazons (TV). No Man's Land (TV). 1985: The Long Shot. 1986: Monster in the Closet. A Masterpiece of Murder (TV).

As director: *1980: The American Heroine.*

STEWART, Alexandra 1939–
Tall, cool, sandy-haired Canadian actress who began her career in France, and has filmed all over the world without quite becoming an international star. Tackled all kinds of cinema, but (perhaps because of this) there was little consistency to her work: Truffaut one moment, Emmanuelle the next.
1958: Le bel âge (GB: Love is Where You Find It). 1959: L'eau à la bouche (GB: The Game of Love). Les motards. Deux hommes dans Manhattan. Liaisons dangereuses. 1960. Merci natercia (released 1962). 1960: La mort de belle. The Season for Love. Les distractions (GB: Trapped by Fear). Tarzan the Magnificent. Exodus. 1961: Une grosse tête. Naked Autumn. Les Mauvais coups. Rendez-vous de minuit. 1962: Humenaje a la hora de la siesta (US: Four Women for One Hero). Violenza secreta. Die Bekenntnisse eines möblierten Herrn. Climats. Rogopag. 1963: And So to Bed/Das grosse Liebesspiel. Dragées au poivre (GB and US: Sweet and Sour). Le feu follet (GB: A Time to Live and a Time to Die. US: Will o' the Wisp). The Passion of Slow Fire. 1964: Die endlose Nacht. The Man Called Gringo/Sie nannten ihn, Gringo. Volles Herz und leere Taschen. 1965: Thrilling. Wedding March. Mickey One. La Ley del Forastero. 1966: Maroc 7. 1967: La loi du survivant. L'écume des jours. 1968: Waiting for Caroline. Only When I Larf. La mariée était en noir/The Bride Wore Black. Besessen – das Lock in der Wand. 1969: Ohrfeigen. Bye Bye Barbara. Umano o umano. 1970: The Man Who Had Power over Women. Le ciel est bleu. Ils. 1971: Valparaiso, Valparaiso. Zeppelin. Ou est passé, Tom? 1972: Les soleils de l'île de Pâques. The Rape. 1973: La nuit Américaine (GB and US: Day for Night). 1974: The Marseilles Contract (US: The Destructors). 1975: Black Moon. Un animal odue de déraison. 1977: Goodbye Emmanuelle. Julie Pot-de-Cole/The Chains of Pity. The Uncanny. In Praise of Older Women. 1978: The Little Girl in Blue Velvet. 1980:

Agency. The Last Chase. Le soleil en face. Final Assignment. 1981: Chanel solitaire. Madame Claude 2 (later and US: Intimate Moments). GB: The Girls of Madame Claude). Aiutami e sognare. 1983: Sans soleil (narrator only). Le sang des autres/The Blood of Others. Femmes. 1984: Kusameikyu (narrator of English version only). Mistral's Daughter (cable TV). 1985: Le matou (US: The Alley Cat). 1986: Under the Cherry Moon. Peau d'ange (filmed 1983).

STEWART, James 1908–
Tall, slim, long-faced, dark-haired, much-loved American leading man with a slow bumbling drawl which reflected those qualities of thoughtfulness and honesty which he projected in so many of his roles and made him the target for a million drawing-room impressionists. His best roles (pre-war) cast him as one man against the system, or (post-war) one man against the odds in westerns and suspense thrillers. Only his later comedies are consistently less successful: but even in films as late as *Firecreek* and *The Magic of Lassie*, his sincerity is still capable of raising a lump in the throat. Oscar for *The Philadelphia Story.* Also nominated for Academy Awards on *Mr Smith Goes to Washington, It's a Wonderful Life!, Harvey* and *Anatomy of a Murder.*
*1935: *Important News. The Murder Man. 1936: Next Time We Love (GB: Next Time We Live). Rose Marie. Wife vs. Secretary. Small Town Girl. Speed. Born to Dance. The Gorgeous Hussy. After the Thin Man. 1937: Seventh Heaven. The Last Gangster. Navy Blue and Gold. 1938: Of Human Hearts. The Shopworn Angel. Vivacious Lady. You Can't Take It with You. 1939: Ice Follies of 1939. It's a Wonderful World. Made for Each Other. Destry Rides Again. Mr Smith Goes to Washington. 1940: No Time for Comedy. The Shop Around the Corner. The Mortal Storm. The Philadelphia Story. 1941: Ziegfeld Girl. Come Live with Me. Pot o' Gold (GB: The Golden Hour). 1942: *Screen Snapshots No.103. *Fellow Americans. *Winning Your Wings. 1946: *American Brotherhood Week. It's a Wonderful Life! 1947: Thunderbolt (narrator only). Magic Town. Call Northside 777. 1948: A Miracle Can Happen (later: On Our Merry Way). Rope. You Gotta Stay Happy. *10,000 Kids and a Cop. 1949: The Stratton Story. Malaya (GB: East of the Rising Sun). 1950: *And Then There Were Four (narrator only).*

The Jackpot. Winchester '73. Broken Arrow. Harvey. 1951: *No Highway (US: No Highway in the Sky).* 1952: *The Greatest Show on Earth. Bend of the River (GB: Where the River Bends). Carbine Williams.* 1953: *Thunder Bay.* **Hollywood Laugh Parade. The Naked Spur. The Glenn Miller Story.* 1954: *Rear Window. The Far Country.* 1955: *Strategic Air Command. The Man from Laramie.* 1956: *The Man Who Knew Too Much.* 1957: *Night Passage. The Spirit of St Louis.* 1958: *Bell, Book and Candle. Vertigo.* 1959: *The FBI Story. Anatomy of a Murder.* 1960: *The Mountain Road.* 1961: *Two Rode Together. X-15 (narrator only).* 1962: *The Man Who Shot Liberty Valance. Mr Hobbs Takes a Vacation. How the West Was Won.* 1963: *Take Her, She's Mine.* 1964: *Cheyenne Autumn.* 1965: *Dear Brigitte... The Flight of the Phoenix. Shenandoah. The Rare Breed.* 1967: *Firecreek.* 1968: *Bandolero!* 1970: *The Cheyenne Social Club.* 1971: *Fools' Parade (GB: Dynamite Man from Glory Jail).* 1974: *That's Entertainment!* 1976: *The Shootist.* 1977: *Airport 77.* 1978: *The Big Sleep. The Magic of Lassie. Mr Krueger's Christmas (TV).* 1981: *The Green Horizon/A Tale of Africa.* 1983: *Right of Way (TV).*

STING (Gordon Sumner) 1951–
Tall, slim, fair-haired, waspish-looking British singer and, latterly, actor. Rising to fame as lead singer with the pop group Police (after beginning his career as a teacher), Sting moved into movies, but soon showed he needed casting with care to get the most out of his unusual and faintly unsettling personality. Brilliantly effective in *Brimstone and Treacle*, he sounded far less happy in *The Bride*, and is now wisely hunting for more suitable projects which he hopes to adapt himself. Married (first of two) to actress Frances Tomelty.
1979: *Quadrophenia. Radio On.* 1982: *The Secret Policeman's Other Ball. Brimstone and Treacle.* 1984: *Dune.* 1985: *The Bride. Plenty. Bring On the Night.*

ST JOHN, Jill (J. Oppenheim) 1940–
Red-headed American actress with sumptuous figure and headline-hitting private life. Had a surprised sort of face and usually played slightly daffy but likeable heroines. Whatever her merits as an actress, she was a performer of some spirit, notably in her intrepid heroine

of *Diamonds Are Forever* and swashbuckling spitfire of *The King's Pirate*, the latter proving she could have filled Maureen O'Hara's boots had not the time for the genre long passed.
1957: *Summer Love.* 1959: *The Remarkable Mr Pennypacker. Holiday for Lovers.* 1960: *The Lost World.* 1961: *The Roman Spring of Mrs Stone. Tender is the Night.* 1963: *Who's Been Sleeping in My Bed? Who's Minding the Store? Come Blow Your Horn.* 1964: *Honeymoon Hotel.* 1965: *The Liquidator.* 1966: *The Oscar. Fame is the Name of the Game (TV). How I Spent My Summer Vacation (TV. GB: cinemas as Deadly Roulette).* 1967: *Banning. Eight on the Lam (GB: Eight on the Run). The King's Pirate. Tony Rome.* 1969: *Foreign Exchange (TV). The Spy Killer (TV).* 1971: *Decisions, Decisions! (TV). Diamonds Are Forever.* 1972: *Sitting Target.* 1974: *Brenda Starr, Girl Reporter (TV).* 1978: *Telethon (TV).* 1979: *Hart to Hart (TV).* 1982: *The Concrete Jungle. The Act.* 1983: *99 Women.*

STOCKFELD, Betty 1905–1966
This blonde Australian actress with square chin and friendly eyes wasn't exactly pretty. But she had a forthright personality that endeared her to British audiences of the 1930s and she made the majority of her screen career in that country, mostly as girls of strong character. There was also a debut film in Hollywood and a few forays to France. In billing, her surname was sometimes (erroneously) spelt Stockfield. She died from cancer.
1926: *What Price Glory?* 1930: *City of Song (US: Farewell to Love).* 1931: *Captivation. 77*

Park Lane. 1932: *Life Goes On/Sorry You've Been Troubled. Money for Nothing. The Impassive Footman (US: Woman in Bondage). The Maid of the Mountains. Women in Chains.* 1933: *King of the Ritz. Lord of the Manor. Anne One Hundred.* 1934: *The Man Who Changed His Name. The Battle (US: Thunder in the East). Brides To Be.* 1935: *The Lad. Runaway Ladies.* 1936: *Under Proof. Beloved Vagabond. Dishonour Bright.* 1937: *Who's Your Lady Friend? L'ange du foyer. Club des femmes (US: Girls' Club).* 1938: *I See Ice. The Slipper Episode.* 1939: *Ils etaient neuf célibataires (US: Nine Bachelors).* 1940: *Elles etaient douze femmes. Derrière la façade.* 1942: *Hard Steel. Flying Fortress.* 1950: *Edouard et Caroline. The Girl Who Couldn't Quite.* 1955: *The Lovers of Lisbon.* 1956: *Guilty? True As a Turtle.* 1957: *Le désir interdit.*

STOCKWELL, Dean (Robert D. Stockwell) 1936–
Appealing American boy actor with dark, curly hair. As a young adult, he offered two excellent performances, in *Compulsion* and *Sons and Lovers*, but his career drifted away from him in the sixties: some said he was too choosy. Maybe he is just a clever actor who lacks the strength and stature of a superstar. Married to Millie Perkins 1960–1964.
1945: *The Valley of Decision. Abbott and Costello in Hollywood. Anchors Aweigh.* 1946: *Home Sweet Homicide. The Green Years.* **A Really Important Person.* 1947: *Song of the Thin Man. The Mighty McGurk. The Arnelo Affair. The Romance of Rosy Ridge. Gentleman's Agreement.* 1948: *Deep Waters. The Boy with Green Hair.* 1949: *Down to the Sea in Ships. The Secret Garden.* 1950: *The Happy Years. Stars in My Crown. Kim.* 1951: *Cattle Drive.* 1956: *Gun for a Coward.* 1957: *Horsepower (TV). The Careless Years.* 1959: *Made in Japan (TV). Compulsion.* 1960: *Sons and Lovers.* 1962: *Long Day's Journey into Night.* 1965: *Rapture.* 1968: *Psych-Out.* 1970: †*Ecstasy 70. The Dunwich Horror.* 1971: *The Last Movie. The Failing of Raymond (TV).* 1972: *Paper Man (TV).* 1972: *The Loners. The Adventures of Nick Carter (TV).* 1973: *The Werewolf of Washington.* 1974: *Another Day at the Races (GB: Win, Place or Steal). Edweard Muybridge, Zoopraxographer (narrator only).* 1975: *Won Ton Ton, the Dog Who Saved Hollywood. The Pacific Connection. The Return*

of Joe Forrester (TV). 1976: Tracks. 1977: The Killing Affair (TV). 1979: She Came to the Valley (uncompleted). 1981: Born to be Sold (TV. GB: The Baby Brokers). 1982: Wrong is Right/The Man with the Deadly Lens. Human Highway. 1983: Alsino y El Condor. 1984: To Kill a Stranger. Dune. Paris, Texas. 1985: The Legend of Billie Jean. Papa Was a Preacher. To Live and Die in LA.

† Unreleased

STONE, Lewis 1879–1953

Lean, straight-backed American actor, a leading man of silents with occasional forays into silky villainy. His slightly sinister personality became concerned as the sound years wore on, and he became totally identified with his running role as the wise *paterfamilias*, Judge Hardy, in the Andy Hardy series. Nominated for an Academy Award on *The Patriot*. Died from a heart attack when trying to chase vandals from his property.

1915: The Man Who Found Out. 1916: Honor's Altar. According to the Code. The Havoc. 1918: Inside the Lines. 1919: Man of Bronze. Man's Desire. Johnny Get Your Gun. 1920: Held by the Enemy. Milestones. Nomads of the North. The River's End. The Concert. 1921. The Golden Snare. The Child Thou Gavest Me. Beau Revel. Pilgrims of the Night. Don't Neglect Your Wife. 1922: A Fool There Was. The Dangerous Age. Trifling Women. The Rosary. The Prisoner of Zenda. 1923: Scaramouche. You Can't Fool Your Wife. The World's Applause. 1924: Why Men Leave Home. The Stranger. Cytherea. Inez from Hollywood. Husbands and Lovers. 1925: The Lost World. Confessions of a Queen. Cheaper to Marry. The Lady Who Lied. What Fools Men. The Talker. Fine Clothes. 1926: Old Loves and New. The Girl from Montmartre. Don Juan's Three Nights. Midnight Lovers. Too Much Money. The Blonde Saint. 1927: The Notorious Lady. An Affair of the Follies. The Prince of Head Waiters. Lonesome Ladies. The Private Life of Helen of Troy. 1928: Freedom of the Press. Foreign Legion. The Patriot. Inspiration. 1929: The Trial of Mary Dugan. A Woman of Affairs. Madame X. Wild Orchids. The Circle. 1930: Romance. Strictly Unconventional. Their Own Desire. The Office Wife. The Big House. Passion Flower. Father's Son. 1931: Inspiration. My Past. The Sin of Madelon Claudet

(GB: The Lullaby). Always Goodbye. Phantom of Paris. The Bargain. The Secret Six. Mata Hari. Stolen Heaven. 1932: Night Court (GB: Justice for Sale). Grand Hotel. The Wet Parade. Letty Lynton. Divorce in the Family. Unashamed. New Morals for Old. Red-Headed Woman. The Mask of Fu Manchu. The Son-Daughter. Strange Interlude. 1933: Looking Forward (GB: Service). The White Sister. Queen Christina. Bureau of Missing Persons. Men Must Fight. 1934: Treasure Island. The Mystery of Mr X. You Can't Buy Everything. The Girl from Missouri (GB: 100 Per Cent Pure). 1935: David Copperfield. Vanessa, Her Love Story. China Seas. Shipmates Forever. West Point of the Air. Public Hero Number One. Woman Wanted. 1936: The Unguarded Hour. Small Town Girl. Suzy. Three Godfathers. Sworn Enemy. Don't Turn 'Em Loose. 1937: The Man Who Cried Wolf. Outcast. The Thirteenth Chair. You're Only Young Once. 1938: Stolen Heaven. Bad Man of Brimstone. Judge Hardy's Children. The Chaser. Out West with the Hardys. Yellow Jack. Love Finds Andy Hardy. 1939: Joe and Ethel Turp Call on the President. The Hardys Ride High. Ice Follies of 1939. Andy Hardy Gets Spring Fever. Judge Hardy and Son. 1940: Sporting Blood. Andy Hardy Meets Debutante. 1941: Andy Hardy's Private Secretary. The Bugle Sounds. Life Begins for Andy Hardy. 1942: The Courtship of Andy Hardy. Andy Hardy's Double Life. 1943: *Plan for Destruction (narrator only). 1944: Andy Hardy's Blonde Trouble. 1946: The Hoodlum Saint. Love Laughs at Andy Hardy. Three Wise Fools. 1948: State of the Union (GB: The World and His Wife). 1949: Any Number Can Play. 1950: Key to the City. Stars in My Crown. Grounds for Marriage. 1951: Angels in the Outfield (GB: Angels and the Pirates). Bannerline. The Unknown Man. It's a Big Country. Night into Morning. 1952: Just This Once. Talk about a Stranger. Scaramouche (remake). The Prisoner of Zenda (remake). 1953: All the Brothers Were Valiant.

STOOGES, The Three

FINE, Larry 1911–1974
HOWARD, Curly (Jerome Horowitz) 1906–1952
HOWARD, Moe (Moses Horowitz) 1895–1975
HOWARD, Shemp (Samuel Horowitz) 1891–1955

Pie-in-the-face group of American comedians whose humour was very basic, but who made millions of children laugh in scores of shorts throughout the 1930s, 1940s and 1950s. They whacked each other on the head, kicked each other's ankles and poked their fingers in each other's eyes; the soundtracks of their films seemed very noisy. Larry, Curly and Moe were the Stooges from 1933 to 1946. Shemp, who had left in 1933, rejoined in 1946, replacing an ailing Curly. Vaudeville comedians Joe Besser and Joe de Rita were later Stooges. Curly died from a stroke, Shemp from a coronary occlusion, Larry (the one with the wild hair) from a stroke and Moe (the leader, the one with the pudding-basin haircut) from can-

cer. One of their early two-reelers, *Men in Black*, was nominated for an Academy Award. 1930: *‡Hollywood on Parade. ‡Soup to Nuts. 1933: †Dancing Lady. †Turn Back the Clock. †Meet the Baron. †Fugitive Lovers. †Myrt and Marge (GB: Laughter in the Air). 1934: †Hollywood Party. †The Captain Hates the Sea. †Gift of Gab. Hello Pop. Plane Nuts. The Big Idea. Beer and Pretzels. Woman Haters. Punch Drunks. Men in Black. Three Little Pigskins. 1935: Pop Goes the Easel. Horses' Collars. Restless Knights. Hoi Polloi. Uncivil Warriors. Screen Snapshots No 6. Pardon My Scotch. Three Little Beers. 1936: Half-Shot Shooters. A Pain in the Pullman. Whoops I'm an Indian. Ants in the Pantry. Movie Maniacs. Disorder in the Court. False Alarms. Slippery Silks. 1937: Three Dumb Clucks. Grips, Grunts and Groans. Back to the Woods. Playing the Ponies. Dizzy Doctors. Goofs and Saddles. Cash and Carry. The Sitter-Downers. 1938: †Start Cheering. Termites of 1938. Tassels in the Air. Three Missing Links. Mutts to You. Wee Wee Monsieur. Healthy, Wealthy and Dumb. Violent is the Word for Curly. Flat Foot Stooges. 1939: A Ducking They Did Go. Three Little Sew and Sews. Saved by the Belle. Oily to Bed, Oily to Rise. We Want Our Mummy. Yes We Have No Bonanza. Calling All Curs. Three Sappy People. 1940: A-Plumbing We Will Go. You Natzy Spy! Nutty But Nice. No Census No Feeling. Boobs in Arms. How High is Up? Cuckoo Cavaliers. Rockin' Through the Rockies. 1941: †Time Out for Rhythm. All the World's a Stooge. So Long, Mr Chumps. An Ache in Every Stake. Some More of Samoa. In the Sweet Pie and Pie. Dutiful But Dumb. I'll Never Heil Again! Loco Boy Makes Good. 1942: †My Sister Eileen. Matri-Phony. Cactus Makes Perfect. Even as IOU. Sock-a-Bye Baby. What's the Matador? Three Smart Saps. 1943: Spook Louder. They Came to Conga. Three Little Twerps. I Can Hardly Wait. Phony Express. Dizzy Detectives. Back from the Front. Higher Than a Kite. Dizzy Pilots. A Gem of a Jam. 1944: The Yoke's on Me. Crash Goes the Hash. Gents without Cents. Busy Buddies. Idle Roomers. No Dough, Boys. 1945: †Rockin' in the Rockies (and 1940 short with similar title). Idiots Deluxe. Three Pests in a Mess. Micro Phonies. If a Body Meets a Body. Booby Dupes. 1946: †Swing Parade of 1946. Uncivil Warbirds: Beer Barrel Polecats.

Monkey Businessmen. G I Wanna Go Home. Three Little Pirates. A Bird in the Head. The Three Troubledoers. Three Loan Wolves. Rhythm and Weep. 1947: Out West. Half Wits' Holiday. Brideless Groom. All Gummed Up. Fright Night. Hold That Lion. Sing Me a Song of Six Pants. 1948: Squareheads of the Round Table. Shivering Sherlocks. Heavenly Daze. I'm a Monkey's Uncle. Crime on Their Hands. Pardon My Clutch. Fiddlers Three. Hot Scots. Mummy's Dummies. 1949: The Ghost Talks. Hocus Pokus. Who Done It? Fuelin' Around. Vagabond Loafers. Malice in the Palace. Dunked in the Deep. 1950: Dopey Dicks. Punchy Cowpunchers. Love at First Bite. Three Hams on Rye. Slap Happy Sleuths. Hugs and Mugs. Self Made Maids. Studio Stoops. A Snitch in Time. 1951: †Gold Raiders (GB: Stooges Go West). Don't Throw That Knife. Three Arabian Nuts. Merry Mavericks. Hula La-La. Baby Sitters' Jitters. Scrambled Brains. The Tooth Will Out. The Pest Man Wins. 1952: Corny Casanovas. Gents in a Jam. Cuckoo on a Choo-Choo. Three Dark Horses. He Cooked His Goose. Listen, Judge. A Missed Fortune. 1953: Loose Loot. Up in Daisy's Penthouse. Spooks. Rip, Sew and Stitch. Goof on the Roof. Booty and the Beast. Tricky Dicks. Pardon My Backfire. Bubble Trouble. 1954: Pals and Gals. Income Tax Sappy. Shot in the Frontier. Knutzy Knights. Scotched in Scotland. Musty Musketeers. 1955: Gypped in the Penthouse. Fling in the Ring. Stone Age Romeos. Hot Ice. Of Cash and Hash. Bedlam in Paradise. Wham-Bam-Slam. Blunder Boys. 1956: Flagpole Sitters. Husbands Beware. Rumpus in the Harem. Scheming Schemers. Creeps. For Crimin' Out Loud. Hot Stuff. Commotion on the Ocean. 1957: A Merry Mix-Up. Hoofs and Goofs. Space Ship Sappy. Horsing Around. Outer Space Jitters. Muscle Up a Little Closer. Gun a-Poppin'. Rusty Romeos. 1958: Pies and Guys. Quiz Whiz. Flying Saucer Daffy. Fifi Blows Her Top. Sweet and Hot. Oil's Well That Ends Well. 1959: †Have Rocket, Will Travel. Triple Crossed. Sappy Bullfighters. 1960: †Three Stooges Scrapbook. †Stop! Look! And Laugh! 1961: †Snow White and the Three Stooges (GB: Snow White and the Three Clowns). 1962: †The Three Stooges in Orbit. †The Three Stooges Meet Hercules. 1963: †It's a Mad, Mad, Mad, Mad World. †The Three Stooges Go Around the World in a Daze. †Four for Texas. 1964: †The Outlaws is Coming.

Moe alone:

1958: †Space Master X-7. 1966: Don't Worry, We'll Think of a Title. 1973: †Dr Death – Seeker of Souls.

Shemp alone:

1937: †Hollywood Round-Up. †Headin' East. 1938: Home on the Range. 1940: Boobs in the Woods. Money Squawks. †Millionaires in Prison. †Give Us Wings. †The Bank Dick (GB: The Bank Detective). †Buck Privates (GB: Rookies). †The Leather Pushers. 1941: †The Invisible Woman. †Meet the Chump. †Mr Dynamite. †Tight Shoes. †Hold That Ghost. †Too Many Blondes. †Hellzapoppin. †Six Lessons from Madame La Zonga. †In The Navy.

†San Antonio Rose. †Hit the Road. 1942: †Mississippi Gambler. †The Strange Case of Dr RX. †Private Buckaroo. †Arabian Nights. †Butch Minds the Baby. †Pittsburgh. 1943: †It Ain't Hay (GB: Money for Jam). Farmer for a Day. †How's About It? †Crazy House. †Strictly in the Groove. †Keep 'em Sluggin'. 1944: †Three of a Kind. †Strange Affair. †Moonlight and Cactus. 1946: †The Gentleman Misbehaves. †Blondie Knows Best. †Swing Parade of 1946. †Dangerous Business. †One Exciting Week. 1949: †Africa Screams.

All shorts except † features
‡ As The Racketeers

STORM, Gale (Josephine Cottle) 1922–
Small, sturdy, resilient American actress with lovely, round face and light auburn hair who was also a lively singer. Her pert peppiness presumably helped her maintain her popularity through a host of minor films until television swallowed her up in 1952 for her own show, which ran, under various titles, for the remainder of the fifties.
1940: Tom Brown's School Days. One Crowded Hour. 1941: Saddlemates. Jesse James at Bay. Let's Go Collegiate (GB: Farewell to Fame). Gambling Daughters. City of Missing Girls. Red River Valley. 1942: Rhythm Parade. Smart Alecks. Lure of the Islands. Foreign Agent. The Man from Cheyenne. Freckles Come Home. 1943: Cosmo Jones – Crime Smasher (GB: Crime Smasher). Where Are Your Children? Nearly Eighteen. Campus Rhythm. Revenge of the Zombies (GB: The Corpse Vanished). 1944: They Shall Have Faith/Forever Yours (GB: The Right to Live). 1945: GI Honeymoon. Sunbonnet Sue. 1946: Swing Parade of 1946. 1947: It Happened on Fifth Avenue. 1948: The Dude Goes West. 1949: Stampede. The Kid from Texas (GB: Texas Kid – Outlaw). Abandoned. Curtain Call at Cactus Creek (GB: Take the Stage). 1950: The Underworld Story. Between Midnight and Dawn. 1951: Al Jennings of Oklahoma. The Texas Rangers. 1952: Woman of the North Country.

STRASBERG, Susan 1938–
Tiny dark-haired American actress who, after an auspicious debut, was looked on as a great star in the making in the late fifties. Alas, her career followed a similar pattern to that of

Dean Stockwell: she did not seem to come to terms with mainstream American cinema and was soon in continental dramas and American-International youth movies. Daughter of acting teacher/actor Lee Strasberg, who founded The Method. Married/divorced actor Christopher Jones (1941–).
1955: Picnic. The Cobweb. 1957: Stage Struck. 1960: Kapo. 1961: Taste of Fear (US: Scream of Fear). 1962: Désordre/Disorder. Hemingway's Adventures of a Young Man (GB: Adventures of a Young Man). 1963: Il giorno più corto commedia unmaristica (US: The Shortest Day). 1964: The High Bright Sun (US: McGuire Go Home!). 1967: The Trip. Cosa Nostra, an Arch Enemy of the FBI (TV. GB: cinemas). 1968: Chubasco. Psych-Out. The Name of the Game is Kill! The Brotherhood. 1969: Le sorelle. Sweet Hunters. 1970: Hauser's Memory (TV). 1971: Mr and Mrs Bo Jo Jones (TV). 1972: Toma (TV. GB: Man of Many Faces). 1973: And Millions Will Die. Frankenstein (TV). 1974: Who Fears the Devil? Best of All the Safecrackers (TV). 1976: Sammy Somebody. 1977: SST Disaster in the Sky/SST Death Flight (TV). The Manitou. Tre soldi e la donna di classe. Rollercoaster. In Praise of Older Women. 1980: Bloody Birthday. 1981: Sweet Sixteen. Lee Strasberg and the Actors' Studio. 1982: Mazes and Monsters/Rona Jaffe's Mazes and Monsters (TV). 1983: The Returning. 1986: The Delta Force.

STREEP, Meryl (Mary Louise Streep) 1949–
Fair-haired, freckle-faced American actress whose determined features and naturalistic

style initially took her into fairly unsympathetic roles as ambitious bitches. Later she played tormented women. An Academy Award for *Kramer vs Kramer* pushed her forward towards superstar status, which she consolidated with another Oscar for *Sophie's Choice*. Also nominated for Oscars on *The Deer Hunter*, *The French Lieutenant's Woman*, *Silkwood* and *Out of Africa*.

1976: *Julia*. 1977: *The Deadliest Season (TV)*. 1978: *The Deer Hunter*. 1979: *Manhattan*. *The Seduction of Joe Tynan*. *Kramer vs Kramer*. 1981: *The French Lieutenant's Woman*. 1982: *Still of the Night*. *Sophie's Choice*. *Alice at the Palace (TV)*. 1983: *Silkwood*. 1984: *In Our Hands*. *Falling in Love*. 1985: *Plenty*. *Out of Africa*. 1986: *Heartburn*.

STREISAND, Barbra (Barbara Streisand) 1942–

Dark-haired (although it seems to be getting lighter), sexy, aggressive American singer and actress whose prominent nose and clown's smile sit well with her talent for comedy. Her larger-than-life personality and magical singing voice – all throb and passion – grabbed her an Oscar for *Funny Girl*. She was further nominated for *The Way We Were*. Her sense of throwaway comedy remains pleasing, but she can over-dominate a film and after a series of dispiriting misfires, proved in 1983 with *Yentl* that she was in her element when producing, directing and starring all at once.

1968: *Funny Girl*. 1969: *Hello, Dolly!* 1970: *On a Clear Day You Can See Forever*. *The Owl and the Pussycat*. 1972: *What's Up Doc?* *Up the Sandbox*. 1973: *The Way We Were*. 1974: *For Pete's Sake*. 1975: *Funny Lady*. 1976: *A Star is Born*. 1979: *The Main Event*. 1981: *All Night Long*. 1983: †*Yentl*. 1986: *Nuts*.

† *And directed*

STRIBLING, Melissa 1928–

Blonde, blue-eyed Scottish actress whose calculating looks suggested that she would make a good villainess along the lines of Kathleen Byron (*qv*). But producers only rarely gave her a chance, and she remains best remembered as the frightened heroine in Hammer's *Dracula*, a role for which she was not ideally cast. Started as an assistant in the cutting room at Ealing Studios.

1948: *The First Gentleman (US: Affairs of a Rogue)*. 1952: *Wide Boy*. *Crow Hollow*. *Decameron Nights*. *Ghost Ship*. 1953: *Noose for a Lady*. *Thought to Kill*. 1954: *Out of the Clouds*. 1956: **Destination Death*. 1957: *Murder Reported*. *The Safecracker*. 1958: *Dracula (US: The Horror of Dracula)*. **The Changing Years*. 1960: *The League of Gentlemen*. 1961: *The Secret Partner*. 1966: **Road to St Tropez*. 1968: *Only When I Larf*. 1971: *Crucible of Terror*. 1974: *Confessions of a Window Cleaner*. 1975: *Feelings*.

STUART, Gloria (G. S. Finch) 1909–

Delicate, poised, blonde beauty resident firstly at Universal, then Fox throughout the thirties. Remembered best as the frightened heroine of *The Old, Dark House*, she later became active in Screen Actors' Guild Work and in the art world. Made a surprising comeback to acting in the mid-seventies.

1932: *The All American (GB: Sport of a Nation)*. *Street of Women*. *Laughter in Hell*. *Airmail*. *The Old, Dark House*. 1933: *Private Jones*. *Roman Scandals*. *It's Great to be Alive*. *Secret of the Blue Room*. *The Kiss before the Mirror*. *The Girl in 419*. *The Invisible Man*. *Sweepings*. 1934: *I'll Tell the World*. *Beloved*. *The Love Captive*. *Gift of Gab*. *I Like It That Way*. *Here Comes the Navy*. 1935: *Laddie*. *Maybe It's Love*. *Gold Diggers of 1935*. 1936: *Poor Little Rich Girl*. *The Prisoner of Shark Island*. *The Girl on the Front Page*. *The Crime of Dr Forbes*. *Professional Soldier*. *36 Hours to Kill*. *Wanted: Jane Turner*. 1937: *Life Begins in College (GB: The Joy Parade)*. *The Lady Escapes*. *Girl Overboard*. 1938: *Island in the*

Sky. *Rebecca of Sunnybrook Farm*. *Time Out for Murder*. *Keep Smiling*. *Change of Heart*. *The Lady Objects*. 1939: *Winner Take All*. *The Three Musketeers (GB: The Singing Musketeer)*. *It Could Happen to You*. 1943: *Here Comes Elmer*. 1944: *Enemy of Women*. *The Whistler*. 1946: *She Wrote the Book*. 1975: *Adventures of the Queen (TV)*. *The Legend of Lizzie Borden (TV)*. 1976: *Flood! (TV. GB: cinemas)*. 1979: *The Best Place to Be (TV)*. 1982: *My Favorite Year*.

STUART, John (J. Croall) 1898–1979

The British cinema's longest career (59 years) belongs to this tall, dark, sharp-featured Scottish-born actor, enormously popular (and prolific) in the twenties and thirties, who slipped into supporting roles in the wartime period, as police inspectors and the like. Later turned to writing, while still playing tiny parts in the sixties and seventies. Married/divorced actress Muriel Angelus (M. A. Findlay 1909–   ), first of two.

1920: *Her Son*. *The Lights of Home*. *The Great Gay Road*. 1921: *Land of My Fathers*. **Eileen Alannah*. **Home Sweet Home*. *Sally in Our Alley*. *Leaves from My Life*. 1922: **A Sporting Double*. *Sinister Street*. **The Extra Knot*. *If Four Walls Told*. *The Little Mother*. 1923: **The Mistletoe Bough*. **The Reverse of the Medal*. *This Freedom*. *Little Miss Nobody*. **Constant Hot Water*. *The School for Scandal*. *The Loves of Mary Queen of Scots*. 1924: *A Daughter of Love*. *His Grace Gives Notice*. *Claude Duval*. *The Alley of Golden Hearts*. *The Gayest of the Gay*. *Her Redemption*. 1925: *We Women*. *Die Frauen zweier Junggesellen*. *Irrgarten der Leidenschaft/The Pleasure Garden*. *Venezianische Liebesabenteuer (GB: Venetian Lovers)*. **Parted*. **The Phantom Gambler*. **Kenilworth Castle and Amy Robsart*. **The Tower of London*. 1926: *Bachelor Wives*. *London Love*. *Mademoiselle from Armentières*. **Curfew Shall Not Ring Tonight*. **Back to the Trees*. **The Woman Juror*. **Baddesley Manor*. 1927: *The Glad Eye*. *Hindle Wakes (silent)*. *A Woman in Pawn*. *Sailors Don't Care*. *Roses of Picardy*. *The Flight Commander*. 1928: *Die Jacht der sieben Sünden*. *Mademoiselle Parley-Voo*. *Kitty (silent)*. *Smashing Through*. 1929: **Memories*. *High Seas*. *Taxi for Two*. *Atlantic*. *Kitty (sound)*. 1930: *No Exit*. *Eve's Fall*. *Kissing Cup's Race*. *The Nipper/The Brat*. *Children of Chance*.

1931: Hindle Wakes (sound). Midnight. The Hound of the Baskervilles. 1932: Men of Steel. In a Monastery Garden. Number Seventeen. Verdict of the Sea. Atlantide. *Women Are That Way. Little Fella. 1933: This Week of Grace. Mr Quincey of Monte Carlo. Head of the Family. Enemy of the Police. Mayfair Girl. The Lost Chord. Love's Old Sweet Song. Home Sweet Home. The Wandering Jew. The House of Trent. The Black Abbot. The Pointing Finger. Naughty Cinderella. 1934: Bella Donna. Four Masked Men. Blind Justice. D'Ye Ken John Peel? (US: Captain Moonlight). Grand Prix. The Blue Squadron. The Green Pack. 1935: Lend Me Your Husband. Abdul the Damned. Royal Cavalcade (US: Regal Cavalcade). Once a Thief. 1936: The Secret Voice. Reasonable Doubt. 1937: The Show Goes On. The Elder Brother. Pearls Bring Tears. Talking Feet. 1938: The Claydon Treasure Mystery. 1940: Old Mother Riley in Society. 1941: Old Mother Riley's Ghosts. The Seventh Survivor. Penn of Pennsylvania (US: The Courageous Mr Penn). Ships With Wings. Banana Ridge. Hard Steel. The Big Blockade. 1942: Women Aren't Angels. The Missing Million. 1943: Headline. 1944: Candles at Nine. Welcome Mr Washington. Madonna of the Seven Moons. 1945: Camera Reflections (narrator only). 1947: The Phantom Shot. Mrs Fitzherbert. Mine Own Executioner. 1948: House of Darkness. Escape from Broadmoor. Third Time Lucky. 1949: The Man from Yesterday. The Temptress. Man on the Run. 1951: The Magic Box. Mr Denning Drives North. The Blonde Informer. 1952: Hounded. The Ringer. *To the Rescue. 1953: Street Corner (US: Both Sides of the Law). Four-Sided Triangle. Mantrap (US: Woman in Hiding). Front Page Story. 1954: Men of Sherwood Forest. Three Cornered Fate. 1955: The Gilded Cage. *The Mysterious Bullet. It's a Great Day. *The Secret Place. *Missing from Home. The Quatermass Xperiment (US: The Creeping Unknown). Johnny You're Wanted. John and Julie. 1956: Tons of Trouble. Alias John Preston. Reach for the Sky. Raiders of the River (serial). Eyewitness. The Last Man to Hang? 1957: The Naked Truth (US: Your Past is Showing). Quatermass 2 (US: Enemy from Space). 1958: The Revenge of Frankenstein. Further Up the Creek. Blood of the Vampire. The Betrayal. Chain of Events. The Secret Man. 1959: Too Many Crooks. *The Unseeing Eye. The Mummy. 1960: Sink the Bismarck! Compelled. Bottoms Up! Village of the Damned. 1961: Pit of Darkness. 1962: Danger by My Side. Paranoiac. 1963: The Scarlet Blade. 1966: Son of the Sahara (serial). 1971: Young Winston. 1975: Royal Flash. 1978: Superman.

SULLAVAN, Margaret (M. Brooke) 1911–1960

Light-haired, sweet-faced, petite American actress of high stage reputation who became the June Allyson of the thirties in a succession of high-class weepies. Like Allyson, she was touching and beguiling on-screen, and hot-tempered off. Married Henry Fonda (first of four) from 1931–1932, but in later days her stage career was less successful than it had

been and, in 1956, she committed herself to a sanatorium. Deaf in the last years of her life, she died from an overdose of sleeping pills. She received an Academy Award nomination for *Three Comrades*.

1933: Only Yesterday. 1934: Little Man, What Now? 1935: The Good Fairy. So Red the Rose. 1936: The Moon's Our Home. Next Time We Love (GB: Next Time We Live). 1938: The Shining Hour. Three Comrades. The Shopworn Angel. 1940: The Shop Around the Corner. The Mortal Storm. 1941: Appointment for Love. So Ends Our Night. Back Street. 1943: Cry Havoc. 1950: No Sad Songs for Me.

SULLIVAN, Barry (Patrick Barry) 1912–

Tall, very dark and serious-looking American actor – an open-mouthed Sullivan smile is rare indeed – who started his film career late and must have thought his chance had gone after working years at Paramount without much effect. But a couple of successes in low-budget crime stories and a switch to M-G-M did the trick. Within a couple of years he had achieved a solid second-grade stardom which lasted a decade. Best playing characters whose affable exterior hid a ruthless streak.

1942: *We Refuse to Die. 1943: The Woman of the Town. High Explosive. 1944: Lady in the Dark. And Now Tomorrow. Rainbow Island. 1945: Getting Gertie's Garter. Duffy's Tavern. 1946: Two Years before the Mast. Suspense. 1947: Framed (GB: Paula). The Gangster. 1948: Smart Woman. Bad Men of Tombstone. 1949: The Great Gatsby. Any Number Can Play. Tension. Nancy Goes to Rio. 1950: A Life of Her Own. The Outriders. Grounds for

Marriage. Mr Imperium (GB: You Belong to My Heart). 1951: Three Guys Named Mike. Inside Straight. Payment on Demand. No Questions Asked. The Unknown Man. I Was a Communist for the FBI. 1952: Skirts Ahoy. The Bad and the Beautiful. 1953: Jeopardy. Cry of the Hunted. China Venture. 1954: Playgirl. The Miami Story. Loophole. Her 12 Men. 1955: Strategic Air Command. Queen Bee. Texas Lady. 1956: The Maverick Queen. Julie. Snow Shoes (TV). 1957: The Way to the Gold. Dragoon Wells Massacre. Ain't No Time for Glory (TV). Forty Guns. 1958: Wolf Larsen. Nightmare at Ground Zero (TV). Another Time, Another Place. 1959: A Quiet Game of Cards (TV). Dark December (TV). 1960: Seven Ways from Sundown. The Purple Gang. 1961: The Light in the Piazza. 1963: A Gathering of Eagles. 1964: Pyro (GB: Wheel of Fire). Stage to Thunder Rock. My Blood Runs Cold. Man in the Middle. 1965: Harlow (TV). Terrore nello spazio (GB: Planet of the Vampires. US: The Demon Planet). 1966: Intimacy. An American Dream (GB: See You in Hell Darling). The Poppy is Also a Flower (TV. GB: Danger Grows Wild). 1967: Shark! (released 1970). 1968: This Savage Land (TV). How to Steal the World (TV. GB: cinemas). Buckskin. The Silent Treatment. 1969: Night Gallery (TV). The Immortal (TV). Tell Them Willie Boy is Here. It Takes All Kinds. 1970: The House on Greenapple Road (TV). 1971: Yuma (TV). 1972: Savage (TV). The Candidate (voice only). 1973: Letters from Three Lovers (TV). ‡Pat Garrett and Billy the Kid. The Magician (TV). 1974: Earthquake. Hurricane (TV). 1975: The 'Human' Factor. Take a Hard Ride. 1976: Survival. Collision Course (TV). Napoli violenta (GB: Death Dealers). 1977: Grand Jury (TV). Oh, God! 1978: No Room to Run. Caravans. 1979: Casino/SS Casino (TV).

‡ *Scenes deleted from final release print, but seen in some TV versions*

SUTHERLAND, Donald 1935–

Hollow-cheeked, wild-eyed Canadian actor with distinct deep, bumbling speech, long on British TV. Unenviably became the only one of *The Dirty Dozen* not to get star billing on the posters; but more extravagant portrayals brought a belated star status. His choice of roles, however, continues to be as erratic as it

is idiosyncratic. So do his performances. His son, Kiefer Sutherland, is also an actor.
1963: The World 10 Times Over (US: Pussycat Alley). 1964: Castle of the Living Dead. Dr Terror's House of Horrors. 1965: The Bedford Incident. Fanatic (US: Die, Die, My Darling). Morgan – a Suitable Case for Treatment (voice only). Promise Her Anything. 1967: The Dirty Dozen. Billion Dollar Brain. Interlude. Oedipus the King. 1968: Sebastian. The Sunshine Patriot (TV). Joanna. The Split. 1969: Start the Revolution without Me/Two Times Two. 1970: M*A*S*H. Kelly's Heroes. Act of the Heart. 1971: Little Murders. Alex in Wonderland. Johnny Got His Gun. Klute. 1972: Steelyard Blues. Don't Look Now. 1973: Lady Ice. FTA. Alien Thunder (later Dan Candy's Law). 1974: S*P*Y*S. The Day of the Locust. 1975: Murder on the Bridge. La spirale (narrator only). The Judge and His Hangman (US: End of the Game. Later: Deception). 1976: The Eagle Has Landed. Fellini's Casanova. 1900. 1977: Blood Relatives. Kentucky Fried Movie. The Disappearance. National Lampoon's Animal House. Bethune (TV). 1978: Invasion of the Body Snatchers. The First Great Train Robbery. Sherlock Holmes: Murder by Decree (GB: Murder by Decree). 1979: Bear Island. Nothing Personal. 1980: Gas. A Man, a Woman and a Bank/A Very Big Withdrawal. Ordinary People. 1981: Eye of the Needle. Threshold. 1982: A War Story (narrator only). 1983: Max Dugan Returns. Hotel de la Paix. Crackers. 1984: Ordeal by Innocence. 1985: Heaven Help Us (GB: Catholic Boys). Trouble with Spys/Trouble at the Royal Rose. Revolution. 1986: Gauguin. Oviri.

SUTTON, John 1908–1963
Dark-haired, round-faced British actor (born in India) who, after early experience running ranches and plantations in British colonies, went to Hollywood in the mid-1930s, initially as technical adviser, but soon as suave, plausible, moustachioed, often swashbuckling villains. Remained in America until the early 1960s, working mostly on TV after 1953.
1936: The Last of the Mohicans. 1937: Bulldog Drummond Comes Back. Bulldog Drummond's Revenge. 1938: Four Men and a Prayer. The Adventures of Robin Hood. The Blonde Cheat. Booloo. Mad About Music. Dawn Patrol. The Affairs of Annabel. Fools for Scandal. The

Buccaneer. Kidnapped. Zaza. 1939: The Private Lives of Elizabeth and Essex. Arrest Bulldog Drummond! Susannah of the Mounties. Tower of London. Bulldog Drummond's Bride. Charlie McCarthy Detective. 1940: The Invisible Man Returns. I Can't Give You Anything But Love, Baby. South to Karanga. British Intelligence (GB: Enemy Agent). Murder Over New York. Hudson's Bay. Sandy Is a Lady. *Christabel Caine. 1941: A Very Young Lady. A Yank in the RAF. Moon Over Her Shoulder. 1942: My Gal Sal. Ten Gentlemen from West Point. Thunder Birds. 1943: Tonight We Raid Calais. Jane Eyre. 1944: The Hour Before the Dawn. 1946: Claudia and David. 1947: Captain from Castile. 1948: The Adventures of Casanova. Mickey. The Counterfeiters. The Three Musketeers. 1949: Bride of Vengeance. The Fan (GB: Lady Windermere's Fan). Bagdad. 1950: The Second Face. The Second Woman (GB: Ellen). 1951: Payment on Demand. David and Bathsheba. 1952: Captain Pirate (GB: Captain Blood, Fugitive). Thief of Damascus. The Golden Hawk. Lady in the Iron Mask. My Cousin Rachel. 1953: East of Sumatra. Sangaree. 1956: The Amazon Trader (TV. GB: cinemas). Death of a Scoundrel. 1959: Return of the Fly. Beloved Infidel. The Bat. Tom Dooley – Held der grüne Holle. 1961: The Canadians. 1962: Marizinia. 1963: Shadow of Fear. 1964: Of Human Bondage.

SVENSON, Bo 1941–
Fair-haired, tree-like, Swedish-born Hollywood leading man who crashed his way through the star roles of a number of action films in the 1970s. Has travelled widely searching for heroes who combined brain with brawn, although he looks set to follow the same sort of monolithic career as Chuck Connors (qv).
1971: The Bravos (TV). 1973: You'll Never See Me Again (TV). Maurie (later Big Mo. TV). Frankenstein (TV). 1975: The Great Waldo Pepper. Target Risk (TV). Part Two Walking Tall (GB: Legend of the Lawman). 1976: Breaking Point. Special Delivery. 1977: Snowbeast (TV). Jimbuck. Final Chapter Walking Tall. 1978: The Inglorious Bastards. Our Man in Mecca. 1979: Gold of the Amazon Women (TV). North Dallas Forty. 1980: Due nelle stelle. Virus. 1981: Thrilled to Death. 1982: Butcher, Baker, Nightmare Maker. 1983: Portrait of a Hitman. Thunder! Jealousy.

1984: Crossfire. Man Hunt Warning. 1985: Wizards of the Lost Kingdom (filmed 1983 as Wizard Wars). 1986: Brothers in Blood. On Dangerous Ground. Delta Force Kammando.

SWANSON, Gloria (G. Swenson) 1897–1983
Dark-haired, highly mannered American star and (very) dramatic actress. Moved from being a Mack Sennett bathing beauty at 18 to the silent screen's adventuress par excellence, moving chicly through a new-found sexual freedom. Never really cashed in her abilities as a comedienne, and her career foundered with the coming of sound, although she made one remarkable comeback appearance in Sunset Boulevard. Married to Wallace Beery (qv) 1916–1918, first of six. Oscar nominee for Sadie Thompson, The Trespasser and Sunset Boulevard. Died following heart surgery.
1915: *The Romance of an American Duchess. *At the End of a Perfect Day. *Broken Pledge. *The Ambition of the Baron. *The Fable of Elvira and Farina and the Meal Ticket. *His New Job. 1916: *Sweedie Goes to College. *A Dash of Courage. *Girls' Dormitory. *Hearts and Sparks. *A Social Club. *Haystacks and Steeples. *Danger Girl. *The Nick-of-Time Baby. *Teddy at the Throttle. 1917: *Baseball Madness. *The Pullman Bride. *The Sultan's Wife. *Dangers of a Bride. 1918: Her Decision. You Can't Believe Everything. Society for Sale. Station Content. Shifting Sands. The Secret Code. Everywoman's Husband. Wife or Country. 1919: Don't Change Your Husband. Male and Female (GB: The Admirable Crichton). For Better, For Worse. 1920: Why Change Your Wife? Something to Think About. 1921: The Affairs of Anatol (GB: A Prodigal Knight). The Great Moment. Under the Lash (GB: The Shulamite). Don't Tell Everything. 1922: Her Husband's Trademark. Beyond the Rock. The Gilded Cage. The Impossible Mrs Bellew. My American Wife. 1923: Bluebeard's Eighth Wife. Prodigal Daughters. Hollywood. Zaza. 1924: Manhandled. The Humming Bird. The Wages of Virtue. A Society Scandal. Her Love Story. 1925: Madame Sans Gêne. The Coast of Folly. Stage Struck. 1926: The Untamed Lady. Fine Manners. 1927: The Loves of Sunya. 1928: Queen Kelly. Sadie Thompson. 1929: The Trespasser. 1930: What a Widow! 1931: Indiscreet. Tonight or Never. *Screen Snapshots No 4. 1932: Perfect Under-

standing. *1934: Music in the Air. 1941: Father Takes a Wife. 1950: Sunset Boulevard. 1952: Three for Bedroom C. 1956: Mio figlio Nerone (GB: Nero's Weekend. US: Nero's Mistress). 1974: The Killer Bees (TV). Airport 1975.*

SWINBURNE, Nora (Elinore S. Johnson) 1902–
Cool, pretty, blonde English actress, a former dancer, of faintly genteel personality, who filmed fairly regularly from 1920, and continued in character roles from 1942. Long married to Esmond Knight (*qv*), her third husband.
*1920: Saved from the Sea. Branded. 1921: The Fortune of Christina McNab. The Autumn of Pride. 1922: The Wee McGregor's Sweetheart. 1923: Hornet's Nest. 1924: The Unwanted. His Grace Gives Notice. 1925: One Colombo Night. A Girl of London. 1930: Caste. Alf's Button. 1931: Potiphar's Wife (US: Her Strange Desire). Alibi. *Sound Cinemagazine No. 273. Man of Mayfair. These Charming People. 1932: White Face. A Voice Said Goodnight. Mr Bill the Conqueror (US: The Man Who Won). Perfect Understanding. 1933: Too Many Wives. 1934: The Office Wife. Boomerang. 1935: Lend Me Your Husband. Jury's Evidence. 1936: The Gay Adventure. The Lonely Road (US: Scotland Yard Commands). 1937: Dinner at the Ritz. Lily of Laguna. 1938: The Citadel. 1940: Gentleman of Venture (US: It Happened to One Man). The Farmer's Wife. 1941: They Flew Alone (US: Wings and the Woman). 1943: The Man in Grey. Dear Octopus (US: The Randolph Family). 1944: Fanny by Gaslight (US: Man of Evil). 1945: They Knew Mr Knight. 1947: Jassy. 1948: Good Time Girl. The Blind Goddess. Saraband for Dead Lovers (US: Saraband). Quartet. 1949: The Bad Lord Byron. Fools Rush In. Marry Me. Christopher Columbus. Landfall. 1950: My Daughter Joy (US: Operation X). 1951: The River. Quo Vadis? 1954: Betrayed. Helen of Troy. 1955: The End of the Affair. 1958: Strange Awakening (US: Female Fiends). 1959: Third Man on the Mountain. 1960: Conspiracy of Hearts. 1963: Decision at Midnight. 1967: Interlude. 1970: Anne of the Thousand Days. 1971: Up the Chastity Belt.*

SYDNEY, Basil (B. S. Nugent) 1894–1968
Heavily-built, testy-looking British actor, seen as narrow-eyed villains, senior civil ser-

vants, domineering fathers and the like, with a few leading roles thrown in, especially in the early thirties.
1920: Romance. (US: Red-Hot Romance. 1932: The Midshipmaid (US: Midshipmaid Gob). 1934: The Third Clue. Dirty Work. 1935: The Tunnel (US: Transatlantic Tunnel). The Riverside Murder. White Lilac. The Amateur Gentleman. 1936: Accused. Blind Man's Bluff. Talk of the Devil. Crime over London. Rhodes of Africa (US: Rhodes). 1939: The Four Just Men (US: The Secret Four). Shadowed Eyes (US: Dr Zander). 1940: The Farmer's Wife. Spring Meeting. 1941: Ships with Wings. The Big Blockade. The Black Sheep of Whitehall. 1942: The Next of Kin. Went the Day Well? (US: 48 Hours). 1945: Caesar and Cleopatra. 1947: Meet Me at Dawn. The Man Within (US: The Smugglers). Jassy. 1948: Hamlet. 1950: The Angel with the Trumpet. Treasure Island. 1951: The Magic Box. 1952: Ivanhoe. 1953: Salome. Three's Company. Hell Below Zero. Star of India. 1954: Simba. The Dam Busters. 1956: Around the World in 80 Days. 1957: Seawife. Island in the Sun. Man from Tangier (US: Thunder over Tangier). 1958: A Question of Adultery. 1959: John Paul Jones. The Devil's Disciple. The Three Worlds of Gulliver. 1960: The Hands of Orlac. A Story of David.

SYKES, Eric 1923–
Long, lean, dark, mournful-looking British comedian and comic actor who began as a scriptwriter for radio comedy programmes, had some interesting leading roles at the beginning of the sixties, then settled down to

stealing scenes in all-star comedies, and to working on his own long-running television show in partnership with Hattie Jacques.
1954: Orders Are Orders. 1956: Charley Moon. 1959: Tommy the Toreador. 1960: Watch Your Stern. 1961: Very Important Person. Invasion Quartet. Village of Daughters. 1962: Kill or Cure. 1963: Heavens Above! 1964: One Way Pendulum. The Bargee. 1965: Those Magnificent Men in their Flying Machines. Rotten to the Core. The Liquidator. 1966: The Spy with a Cold Nose. 1967: †*The Plank. 1968: Shalako. 1969: Monte Carlo or Bust! (US: Those Daring Young Men in Their Jaunty Jalopies). 1970: †Rhubarb. 1972: The Alf Garnett Saga. 1973: Theatre of Blood. 1983: The Boys in Blue. 1986: Absolute Beginners.

† *Also directed*

SYLVESTER, William 1922–
American actor with dark, curly hair, resident in Britain since coming to study at RADA in 1946. In the fifties became familiar as the resolute hero of some intelligently-constructed and above-average second-features. Returned to America in 1968, but has rarely been seen on screen since. Married (second) to Veronica Hurst from 1954 to 1970.
1949: Give Us This Day/Salt to the Devil. 1950: They Were Not Divided. 1952: The Yellow Balloon. 1953: Appointment in London. House of Blackmail. Albert RN (US: Break to Freedom). 1954: What Every Woman Wants. The Stranger Came Home (US: The Unholy Four). 1955: Portrait of Alison (US: Postmark for Danger). 1957: High Tide at Noon. 1958: Dublin Nightmare. 1959: Whirlpool. 1960: Offbeat. Gorgo. 1961: Information Received. 1962: Incident at Midnight. 1963: The Devil Doll. Blind Corner. Ring of Spies. 1964: Devils of Darkness. 1966: The Hand of Night. 1967: The Last Safari. Red and Blue. 1968: 2001: a Space Odyssey. The Syndicate. The Challengers (TV. GB: cinemas). The Lawyer. 1973: Busting. Don't Be Afraid of the Dark (TV). 1975: The Hindenburg. Guilty or Innocent: The Sam Sheppard Murder Case (TV). 1978: Heaven Can Wait. 1979: Sharks!

SYMS, Sylvia 1934–
Blonde British actress with long face and sexy mouth, good at expressing emotions, a star in her first film and 'hot' in the British cinema

from 1956 to 1963, tackling a wide variety of roles. Seemed to become more ordinary after 1964 and has been mostly seen recently in repertory.

1956: My Teenage Daughter (US: Teenage Bad Girl). 1957: The Birthday Present. No Time for Tears. Woman in a Dressing Gown. 1958: Bachelor of Hearts. The Moonraker. Ice Cold in Alex (US: Desert Attack). 1959: No Trees in the Street. Ferry to Hong Kong. Expresso Bongo. 1960: Conspiracy of Hearts. Les vierges de Rome/The Virgins of Rome. The World of Suzie Wong. 1961: Flame in the Streets. Victim. 1962: The Quare Fellow. The Punch and Judy Man. 1963: The World Ten Times Over (US: Pussycat Alley). 1964: East of Sudan. 1965: Operation Crossbow (US: The Great Spy Mission). The Big Job. 1967: Danger Route. 1968: Hostile Witness. 1969: Run Wild, Run Free. 1972: Asylum. 1974: The Tamarind Seed. 1978: Give Us Tomorrow. 1979: There Goes the Bride. 1986: Absolute Beginners.

TALBOT, Lyle (Lysle Henderson) 1902–
Square-faced, wide-mouthed, heavy-set, dark-haired American actor, a second-rank leading man of the 1930s who later appeared as villains in mostly minor westerns and thrillers. He seems to have been content to play anything; certainly he kept very busy for three decades. Began his career as a teenage magician; later founded his own repertory company before heading for Hollywood when sound came in. A cross between Lon Chaney Jr and Richard Arlen (both *qv*).
1930: *The Nightingale. 1931: *The Clyde Mystery. 1932: The Purchase Price. Big City Blues. Three on a Match. Miss Pinkerton. Stranger in Town. Klondike. Love is a Racket. No More Orchids. Unholy Love (GB: Deceit). The Thirteenth Guest. 20,000 Years in Sing Sing. 1933: Ladies They Talk About. 42nd Street. College Coach (GB: Football Coach). The Life of Jimmy Dolan (GB: The Kid's Last Fight). Parachute Jumper. A Shriek in the Night. Girl Missing. Mary Stevens MD. She Had to Say Yes. Havana Widows. 1934: The Dragon Murder Case. Mandalay. A Lost Lady. Fog Over Frisco. One Night of Love. Registered Nurse. Return of the Terror. Murder in the Clouds. Heat Lightning. 1935: While the Patient Slept. Party Wire. Page Miss Glory. Chinatown Squad. The Case of the Lucky Legs. Red Hot Tires (GB: Racing Luck). Oil for the Lamps of China. It Happened in New York. Our Little Girl. Broadway Hostess. 1936: Murder by an Aristocrat. Trapped by Television (GB: Caught by Television). The Law in Her Hands. Mind Your Own Business. The Singing Kid. Boulder Dam. Go West, Young Man.

1937: Second Honeymoon. Three Legionnaires. The Affairs of Cappy Ricks. Westbound Limited. What Price Vengeance? (GB: Vengeance). 1938 Get-a-Way. Change of Heart. I Stand Accused. Call of the Yukon. One Wild Night. The Arkansas Traveler. 1939: They Asked for It. Forged Passport. Second Fiddle. Torture Ship. 1940: A Miracle on Main Street. He Married His Wife. Parole Fixer. 1941: A Night for Crime. 1942: They Raid by Night. She's in the Army. Mexican Spitfire's Elephant. 1943: Man of Courage. 1944: One Body Too Many. Dixie Jamboree. Are These Our Parents? (GB: They Are Guilty). Up in Arms. The Falcon Out West. Mystery of the River Boat (serial). Gambler's Choice. Sensations of 1945. 1945: Trail to Gunsight. 1946: Murder is My Business. Strange Impersonation. Gun Town. Song of Arizona. Chick Carter, Detective (serial). Shep Comes Home. 1947: Danger Street. The Vigilante (serial). 1948: Appointment with Murder. Joe Palooka in Winner Take All (GB: Winner Take All). Quick on the Trigger (GB: Condemned in Error). The Vicious Circle. Parole Inc. The Devil's Cargo. Highway 13. Thunder in the Pines. 1949: Sky Dragon. Fighting Fools. Mississippi Rhythm. Batman and Robin (serial). Joe Palooka in the Big Fight. The Mutineers. Ringside. 1950: Border Rangers. Atom Man versus Superman (serial). Cherokee Uprising. Revenue Agent. Lucky Losers. Federal Man. Tall Timber (GB: Big Timber). The Jackpot. Champagne for Caesar. 1951: Abilene Trail. The Man from Sonora. Jungle Manhunt. Purple Heart Diary (GB: No Time for Tears). Colorado Ambush. Oklahoma Justice. Fury of the Congo. Fingerprints Don't Lie. Texas Lawman. Hurricane Island. Gold Raiders (GB: Stooges Go West). Varieties on Parade. Blue Blood. 1952: The Old West. Sea Tiger. With a Song in My Heart. Son of Geronimo (serial). Kansas Territory. Montana Incident. Outlaw Women. Desperadoes' Outpost. The Daltons' Women. Six-Gun Decision (TV. GB: cinemas). Feudin' Fools. African Treasure (GB: Bomba and the African Treasure). Texas City. Untamed Women. 1953: Down Among the Sheltering Palms (completed 1951). White Lightning. Trail Blazers. Star of Texas. Commander Cody, Sky Marshal of the Universe (serial). 1954: Tobor the Great. Captain Kidd and the Slave Girl. There's No Business Like Show Business. Jail Bait. *So You Want to Be Your Own Boss. The Hidden Face. The Steel Cage. Trader Tom of the China Seas (serial). Gunfighters of the Northwest (serial). 1955: Jail Busters. Stories of the Century No 1 – Quantrill and His Raiders. Sudden Danger. 1956: Calling Homicide. The Great Man. 1957: She Shoulda Said No. 1958: Hot Angel. The Notorious Mr Monks. Plan 9 From Outer Space. High School Confidential. 1959: City of Fear. 1960: Sunrise at Campobello.

TALBOTT, Gloria 1933–
Snub-nosed, dark-haired, slightly-built American actress of waif-like appeal. She could project determination well, but usually played girls in need of protection, especially the one who married a monster from outer space! After experience in high school plays

and repertory, she was a television regular at 18 (often in the *Wild Bill Hickok* series, some episodes of which were pasted together to make films for overseas). But she never quite got into the class of film which would have made her a name with the public.
1951: ‡Hollywood Barn Dance. 1952: Border City Rustlers. 1953: Desert Pursuit. Northern Patrol. 1954: We're No Angels. 1955: Crashout. Lucy Gallant. All That Heaven Allows. 1956: The Cyclops. The Young Guns. Strange Intruder. The Oklahoman. 1957: Daughter of Dr Jekyll. The Kettles on Old MacDonald's Farm. Taming Sutton's Gal. 1958: Cattle Empire. I Married a Monster from Outer Space. 1959: Alias Jesse James. Girls' Town. The Oregon Trail. The Leech Woman. 1960: Oklahoma Territory. 1961: The Crimebusters. 1965: Arizona Raiders. 1966: An Eye for an Eye.

‡ As Lori Talbott

TALMADGE, Norma 1893–1957
There were few prettier silent screen actresses than this dark-haired, dark-eyed charmer, popular in romance but with a keen sense of comedy. But her Brooklyn accent was not able to survive the coming of sound. Her sisters Constance (1898–1973) and Natalie (1898–1969) were also silent screen players. Died from a cerebral stroke after contracting pneumonia.
1910: Uncle Tom's Cabin. Heart o' the Hill. A Dixie Mother. The Love of the Chrysanthemums. Murder by Proxy. The Household Pest (GB: The Four-Footed Pest). 1911: Mrs 'Enery 'Awkins. A Tale of Two Cities. Nellie

the Model. The Four Poster Pest. Forgotten. The Wildcat. Her Sister's Children. Sky Pilot. Paola and Francesca. In Neighboring Kingdoms. Her Hero. The Convict's Child. The Child Crusoes. The Thumb Print. A Broken Spell. The General's Daughter. 1912: Mr Butler Buttles. The First Violin. Fortunes of a Composer. Mrs Carter's Necklace. Mr Bolter's Sweetheart. The Extension Table. Captain Barnacle's Messmate. The Troublesome Stepdaughter. Captain Barnacle's Reformer. Omens and Oracles. The Midget's Revenge. O'Hara Helps Cupid. Squatter and Philosopher. Captain Barnacle's Waif. 1913: The Blue Rose. The Other Woman. Under the Daisies. Counsel for the Defense. The Silver Cigarette Case. Fanny's Conspiracy. Plot and Counterplot. Sleuthing. Officer John Donovan. Country Barber. An Old Man's Love Story. Solitaires. His Official Appointment. His Silver Bachelorhood. Casey at the Bat. Wanted – a Strong Hand. He Fell in Love with his Mother-in-Law. 'Arriet's Baby. The Doctor's Secret. Father's Hatband. A Lady and Her Maid. The Sacrifice of Kathleen. His Little Page. O'Hara as a Guardian Angel. The Tables Turned. Just Show People. The Varasour Ball. O'Hara's Godchild. The Honorable Algernon. An Elopement at Home. 1914: Sawdust and Salome. The Hero. Cupid vs. Money. John Rance, Gentleman. The Loan Shark King. Goodbye Summer. Memories in Men's Souls. The Peacemaker. The Curing of Myra May. The Mill of Life. A Wayward Daughter. Old Reliable. The Helpful Sisterhood. Mr Murphy's Wedding Present. Politics and the Press. A Question of Clothes. Sunshine and Shadows. The Hidden Letters. A Daughter of Israel. Fogg's Millions. Etta of the Footlights. Dorothy Danebridge, Militant. 1915: Elsa's Brother. The Barrier of Faith. The Criminal. The Battle Cry of Peace. Janet of the Chorus. A Daughter's Strange Inheritance. The Pillar of Flame. The Captivating Mary Carstairs. 1916: Martha's Vindication. The Missing Links. The Honorable Algy. The Devil's Needle. Fifty-Fifty. The Crown Prince's Double. The Children in the House. Going Straight. The Social Secretary. 1917: The Secret of Storm Country. Panthea. The Moth. Under False Colors. Poppy. The Law of Compensation. The Lone Wolf. 1918: The Ghost of Yesterday. The Forbidden City. De Luxe Annie. The Heart of Wetona. The Safety Curtain. By Right of Purchase. Her Only Way. Salome. 1919: The New Moon. The Probation Wife. The Way of a Woman. The Isle of Conquest. 1920: A Daughter of Two Worlds. The Right of Way. Yes or No. The Loves and Lies. The Branded Woman. The Woman Gives. 1921: Love's Redemption. The Passion Flower. The Sign on the Door. The Wonderful Thing. 1922: Smilin' Through. Foolish Wives. The Eternal Flame. Branded! 1923: Ashes of Vengeance. The Song of Love. Dust of Desire. The Voice from the Minaret. Within the Law. Sawdust. 1924: Secrets. The Only Woman. In Hollywood with Potash and Perlmutter. 1925: Graustark. The Lady. 1926: Kiki. 1927: Camille. The Dove. 1928: The Woman Disputed. Show People. 1929: New York Nights. 1930: Du Barry, Woman of Passion (GB: Du Barry).

TAMBLYN, Russ (Russell Tamblyn) 1934–
Slight, springy, ginger-haired American star with winning smile – first a boy actor, then a dancing star with spectacular high leaps, just about M-G-M's last such animal before their musicals dwindled to a halt. Tamblyn's career dwindled, too, without the electric spark he gave to dancing, and he has been little seen in recent years. Nominated for an Oscar in Peyton Place. Lately combining cabaret work with a painting career.
1948: †The Boy with Green Hair. 1949: †Reign of Terror/The Black Book. †Deadly is the Female (later Gun Crazy). †The Kid from Cleveland. †Captain Carey USA (GB: After Midnight). †Samson and Delilah. 1950: †The Vicious Years. †Father of the Bride. 1951: †Father's Little Dividend. †As Young As You Feel. 1952: The Winning Team. Retreat Hell! 1953: Take the High Ground. 1954: Seven Brides for Seven Brothers. Deep in My Heart. 1955: Many Rivers to Cross. Hit the Deck. 1956: The Last Hunt. The Fastest Gun Alive. The Young Guns. 1957: Don't Go Near the Water. Peyton Place. 1958: High School Confidental. tom thumb. 1960: Cimarron. 1961: West Side Story. 1962: The Wonderful World of the Brothers Grimm. How the West Was Won. 1963: Follow the Boys. The Haunting. The Long Ships. 1964: Son of a Gunfighter. 1966: War of the Gargantuas. 1970: Dracula vs. Frankenstein (GB: Blood of Frankenstein). Satan's Sadists. 1971: Scream Free! The Last Movie. 1974: Another Day at the Races (GB: Win, Place or Steal). 1976: Black Heat. 1982: Human Highway.

† As Rusty Tamblyn

TANI, Yoko 1932–
Very pretty, full-lipped, petite, Paris-born Japanese leading lady whose father was attached to the Japanese embassy in Paris. Completing her education in Japan, she returned to Paris to train as a dancer, but began playing small acting roles in films from the mid-1950s. Quickly breaking through to leading roles, she showed herself capable of very touching performances (especially in The Wind Cannot Read and The Savage Innocents), but was too often caught up in international hotch-potches about secret agents.
1956: Mannequins de Paris. 1957: Les oeufs de l'autriche. La fille de feu (GB: Fire in the

Flesh). The Quiet American. 1958: The Wind Cannot Read. 1959: The Savage Innocents. 1960: Piccadilly Third Stop. First Spaceship on Venus. 1961: Samson and the Seven Miracles of the World/Maciste alla corte del Gran Kan/Samson and the Seven Miracles. Ursus e la ragazza tartara (GB: The Savage Hordes. US: Tartar Invasion). 1962: My Geisha. Marco Polo. The Sweet and the Bitter. 1963: Who's Been Sleeping in My Bed? Un aereo per Baalbeck. 1964: Agent 225 – Desperate Mission. Bianco, rosso, giallo, rosa. 1965: OSS 77, Operation Lotus Flower. Die Todesstrahlen des Dr Mabuse. 1966: Goldsnake. Invasion. Le spie amano i fiori. 1967: Seven Golden Chinamen. The Power. 1978: Tilt.

TATI, Jacques (J. Tatischeff) 1908–1982
Tall, gangling French pantomimist, writer, comic actor and director who invented the great, hulking, mournful Monsieur Hulot, a continual catalyst of disaster, and played him in several very successful post-war comedies whose gentle humour, visual invention and explosive belly-laughs sometimes reduced audiences to tears. Unfortunately he was (as a film-maker) almost as disorganized as his creation. His last announced project, Confusion, in 1977, was all too aptly titled and did not materialize. Died from a pulmonary embolism.
1932: *Oscar, champion de tennis. 1934: *On demande une brute. 1935: *Gai Dimanche. 1936: *Soigné ton gauche. 1938: Retour à la terre. 1945: Sylvie et le fantôme (US: Sylvia and the Ghost). 1946: Le diable au corps (GB and US: Devil in the Flesh). 1947: *L'école

des facteurs. 1949: Jour de fête. 1951: Monsieur Hulot's Holiday. 1956: Mon oncle/My Uncle. 1967: Playtime. *Cours du soir. 1971: Traffic. 1974: Parade (TV).

As director: 1947: *L'école des facteurs (co-directed). 1949: Jour de fête. 1951: Monsieur Hulot's Holiday. 1956: Mon oncle/My Uncle. 1967: Playtime. 1971: Traffic. 1974: Parade (TV).

TAYLOR, Alma 1895–1974

Brown-haired, blue-eyed, round-faced British actress of great charm who started as a child in early silents, and continued in child-like roles into her late teens. Best remembered for her roles in the long-running 'Tilly the Tomboy' series. Her output and popularity began to fall away in the twenties (she first lost star billing in 1928), but she kept working, most often, in later times, on TV.

1907: His Daughter's Voice. 1908: The Little Flower Girl. 1909: The Little Milliner and the Thief. The Story of a Picture. 1910: Tilly the Tomboy Goes Boating. The Burglar and Little Phyllis. Tilly the Tomboy Buys Linoleum. A New Hat for Nothing. Tilly the Tomboy Visits the Poor. Tilly at the Election. 1911: Evicted. Tilly's Party. Tilly's Unsympathetic Uncle. When Tilly's Uncle Flirted. Tilly – Matchmaker. Tilly and the Mormon Missionary. Tilly and the Fire Engines. A Wilful Maid. Envy, Hatred and Malice. For a Baby's Sake. Tilly at the Seaside. The Veteran's Pension. A Fight with Fire. The Smuggler's Stepdaughter. A Seaside Introduction. Tilly and the Smugglers. 1912: Bill's Reformation. The Curfew Must Not Ring Tonight. †Oliver Twist. King Robert of Sicily. The Curate's Bride. Winning His Stripes. Tilly and the Dogs. Tilly Works for a Living. Tilly in a Boarding House. The Dear Little Teacher. For Love and Life. The Real Thing. The Tailor's Revenge. 1913: The Lover Who Took the Cake. The Mill Girl. Petticoat Perfidy. Partners in Crime. Adrift on Life's Tide. A Little Widow is a Dangerous Thing. A Midnight Adventure. †The Old Curiosity Shop. Blind Fate. The Whirr of the Spinning Wheel. Tried in the Fire. Paying the Penalty. Tilly's Breaking Up Party. Her Little Pet. The Girl at Lancing Mill. †David Copperfield. †The Cloister and the Hearth. The Broken Oath. Justice. The Price of Fame. 1914: †The Heart of Midlothian. An Engagement of Convenience.

Over the Garden Wall. The Kleptomaniac. The Hills Are Calling. His Country's Bidding. The Awakening of Nora. Time, The Great Healer. His Great Opportunity. Oh My Aunt! The Canker of Jealousy. Tilly at the Football Match. By Whose Hand? The Girl Who Lived in Straight Street. The Schemers, or: The Jewels of Hate. The Basilisk. In the Shadow of Big Ben. Aladdin, or: a Lad Out. Morphia the Death Drug. The Double Event. 1915: Spies. The Painted Lady Betty. A Moment of Darkness. Tilly and the Nut. The Passing of a Soul. †The Man Who Stayed at Home. The Outrage. Love in a Mist. A Lancashire Lass. Alma Taylor. Jill and the Old Violin/Jill and the Old Fiddle. Court-Martialled! The Baby on the Barge. †Sweet Lavender. †The Golden Pavement. †Iris. The Man at the Wheel. 1916: †Annie Laurie. †Trelawney of the Wells. †The Grand Babylon Hotel. †Molly Bawn. †Sowing the Wind. †The Marriage of William Ashe. †Comin' Through the Rye. †The Cobweb. 1917: †Nearer My God to Thee. The American Heiress. †Merely Mrs Stubbs. 1918: The W.L.A. Girl. †The Touch of a Child. The Refugee. †Boundary House. A New Version. The Leopard's Spots. Tares. Broken in the Wars. 1919: †Sheba. †The Nature of the Beast. †The Forest on the Hill. †Sunken Rocks. 1920: †Helen of Four Gates. †Anna the Adventuress. †Alf's Button. †Mrs Erricker's Reputation. 1921: †Dollars in Surrey. †The Tinted Venus. †Tansy. †The Narrow Valley. 1923: †Strangling Threads. †The Pipes of Pan. †Comin' thro' the Rye (remake). †Mist in the Valley. 1924: †The Shadow of Egypt. 1926: †The House of Marney. 1927: †Quinneys. 1928: †Two Little Drummer Boys. †The South Sea Bubble. 1931: †Deadlock. 1932: †Bachelor's Baby. 1933: †House of Dreams. 1934: †Things Are Looking Up. 1936: †Everybody Dance. 1954: †Lilacs in the Spring (US: Let's Make Up). 1955: †Stock Car. †Lost (US: Tears for Simon). 1957: †Blue Murder at St Trinian's.

* All shorts except † Features.

TAYLOR, Don 1920–

Genial, red-haired American leading man who displayed some warmth in playing pleasant fellows for ten years or so, but turned to direction in the late fifties, and has made some very competent features without setting the screen on fire. Married (third) to Hazel Court (qv) since 1964.

1943: The Human Comedy. Thousands Cheer. Girl Crazy. Swing Shift Maisie (GB: The Girl in Overalls). Salute to the Marines. 1944: Winged Victory. 1945: The Red Dragon. 1947: Song of the Thin Man. 1948: The Naked City. For the Love of Mary. 1949: Battleground. Ambush. 1950: Father of the Bride. 1951: Flying Leathernecks. Target Unknown. Father's Little Dividend. Submarine Command. The Blue Veil. 1952: Japanese War Bride. 1953: The Girls of Pleasure Island. Destination Gobi. Stalag 17. 1954: Johnny Dark. Men of Sherwood Forest. 1955: I'll Cry Tomorrow. 1956: The Bold and the Brave. 1957: Love Slaves of the Amazon/Lost Slaves of the Amazon. Ride the High Iron. 1962: The Savage Guns. 1973: Tom Sawyer.

As director: 1961: Everything's Ducky. 1964: Ride the Wild Surf. 1967: Jack of Diamonds. 1968: Something for a Lonely Man (TV). 1969: The Five Man Army. The Man Hunter (TV). 1970: Wild Women (TV). 1971: Escape from the Planet of the Apes. 1972: Heat of Anger (TV). 1973: Tom Sawyer. 1974: Honky Tonk (TV). Night Games (TV). 1975: Echoes of a Summer (US: The Last Castle). 1976: The Great Scout and Cathouse Thursday. 1977: A Circle of Children (TV). The Island of Dr Moreau. 1978: Damien – Omen II. 1979: The Gift (TV). 1980: The Final Countdown. 1981: Broken Promise (TV). The Red Flag. 1982: A Change of Heart (TV). Listen to Your Heart (TV). 1983: September Gun (TV). 1984: He's Not Your Son (TV). 1985: Going for the Gold: The Bill Johnson Story (TV). 1986: Classified Love (TV).

TAYLOR, Elizabeth 1932–

Raven-haired child star who developed into a breathtaking beauty and highly professional actress, if with a limited range. However, she did win Academy Awards for Butterfield 8 and Who's Afraid of Virginia Woolf?, and was further Oscar-nominated for Raintree County, Cat on a Hot Tin Roof and Suddenly Last Summer. Seven times married (six divorces and once widowed), including (second) Michael Wilding (qv) 1952–1957; (fourth) singer Eddie Fisher (1928–) 1959–1964, and (fifth and sixth) Richard Burton (qv) 1964–1974 and briefly remarried 1976.

1942: *Man or Mouse. One Born Every Minute. 1943: Lassie Come Home. Jane Eyre.

1944: *The White Cliffs of Dover. National Velvet.* 1946: *Courage of Lassie.* 1947: *Cynthia (GB: The Rich, Full Life). Life with Father.* 1948: *A Date with Judy. Julia Misbehaves.* 1949: *Little Women. Conspirator.* 1950: *The Big Hangover. Father of the Bride.* 1951: *Love is Better than Ever (GB: The Light Fantastic). A Place in the Sun. Father's Little Dividend. Quo Vadis? Callaway Went Thataway (GB: The Star Said No).* 1952: *Ivanhoe.* 1953: *The Girl Who Had Everything.* 1954: *The Last Time I Saw Paris. Rhapsody. Beau Brummell. Elephant Walk.* 1956: *Giant.* 1957: *Raintree County.* 1958: *Cat on a Hot Tin Roof.* 1959: *Suddenly Last Summer.* 1960: *Butterfield 8. Scent of Mystery (GB: Holiday in Spain).* 1963: *Cleopatra. The VIPs.* 1965: *The Sandpiper.* 1966: *Who's Afraid of Virginia Woolf?* 1967: *The Taming of the Shrew. The Comedians. Reflections in a Golden Eye.* 1968: *Dr Faustus. Boom. Secret Ceremony.* 1969: *Anne of the Thousand Days. The Only Game in Town.* 1971: *Zee and Co (US: X, Y and Zee).* 1972: *Under Milk Wood.* 1972: *Hammersmith is Out.* 1973: *Night Watch. Ash Wednesday.* 1974: *The Driver's Seat/Identikit. That's Entertainment!* 1976: *Victory at Entebbe (TV. GB: cinemas). The Blue Bird.* 1977: *A Little Night Music. Winter Kills (released 1979).* 1978: *Return Engagement (TV).* 1980: *The Mirror Crack'd.* 1981: *Genocide (narrator only).* 1983: *Nobody Makes Me Cry.* 1985: *Malice in Wonderland (TV).* 1986: *Poker Alice (TV).*

TAYLOR, Kent (Louis Weiss) 1907–
Perhaps this smooth, dark-haired, moustachioed American actor lacked the variety of expression to become a top star, but he deserves some kind of award for his longevity as a second-feature hero, keeping his ranking in the genre from 1932 to 1963.
1931: *Road to Reno.* 1932: *Dancers in the Dark. Forgotten Commandments. Two Kinds of Women. Husband's Holiday. The Devil and the Deep. Merrily We Go to Hell (GB: Merrily We Go to —). The Sign of the Cross. Make Me a Star. If I Had a Million. Sinners in the Sun. Blonde Venus.* 1933: *Mysterious Rider. A Lady's Profession. The Story of Temple Drake. Sunset Pass. I'm No Angel. White Woman. Cradle Song. Under the Tonto Rim.* 1934: *Death Takes a Holiday. Many Happy Returns. David Harum. Double Door. Mrs Wiggs of the*

Cabbage Patch. Limehouse Blues. 1935: *The County Chairman. College Scandal (GB: The Clock Strikes Eight). Smart Girl. Without Regret. Two-Fisted. My Marriage.* 1936: *The Sky Parade. Florida Special. Ramona. The Accusing Finger.* 1937: *When Love is Young. Wings over Honolulu. The Lady Fights Back. A Girl with Ideas. Prescription for Romance. Love in a Bungalow.* 1938: *The Jury's Secret. The Last Express.* 1939: *Four Girls in White. Pirates of the Skies. The Gracie Allen Murder Case. Five Came Back. Three Sons. Escape to Paradise. I Take This Woman.* 1940: *Sued for Libel. Two Girls on Broadway (GB: Choose Your Partner). The Girl in 313. Men Against the Sky. I'm Still Alive. The Girls from Avenue A.* 1941: *Washington Melodrama. Repent at Leisure.* 1942: *Mississippi Gambler. Tombstone, The Town Too Tough to Die. Army Surgeon. Half Way to Shanghai. Frisco Lil. Gang Busters (serial).* 1943: *Bombers' Moon.* 1944: *Roger Touhy, Gangster (GB: The Last Gangster). Alaska.* 1945: *The Daltons Ride Again.* 1946: *Smooth as Silk. Young Widow. Tangier. Deadline for Murder. Dangerous Millions (GB: The House of Tao Ling).* 1947: *Second Chance. The Crimson Key.* 1948: *Half Past Midnight.* 1950: *Federal Agent at Large. Western Pacific Agent. Trial without Jury.* 1951: *Payment on Demand.* 1954: *Playgirl. Track the Man Down.* 1955: *Secret Venture. Ghost Town. The Phantom from 10,000 Leagues.* 1956: *Slightly Scarlet. Frontier Gambler.* 1957: *The Iron Sheriff.* 1958: *Fort Bowie. Gang War.* 1960: *Walk Tall.* 1961: *The Purple Hills.* 1962: *The Broken Land. The Firebrand.* 1963: *The Day Mars Invaded Earth. Harbor Lights. Law of the Lawless. The Crawling Hand.* 1968: *Brides of Blood.* 1969: *Smashing the Crime Syndicate (released 1973).* 1970: *Satan's Sadists.* 1971: *The Mighty Gorga.* 1974: *Girls for Rent. The Phantom of Hollywood (TV).*

TAYLOR, Robert (Spangler Brugh) 1911–1969

Tall, dark and, in his twenties, idyllically handsome American star who grew a moustache to escape the 'pretty-boy' image and stayed at or near the top for 25 years. Although his features hardened quickly after return from war service, his career was prolonged by several first-class slices of historical adventure in the early fifties. Married to Barbara Stanwyck from 1939 to 1952 and Ursula

Thiess (1929–) from 1954 on. Died from lung cancer.
1934: *Handy Andy. A Wicked Woman. There's Always Tomorrow.* *Buried Loot.* 1935: *Society Doctor. Lest We Forget. Murder in the Fleet. West Point of the Air. Times Square Lady. Magnificent Obsession.* *La Fiesta de Santa Barbara. Broadway Melody of 1936. Only Eight Hours.* 1936: *His Brother's Wife. Small Town Girl. Private Number (GB: Secret Interlude). The Gorgeous Hussy. Camille.* 1937: *Personal Property (GB: The Man in Possession). This is My Affair (GB: His Affair). Broadway Melody of 1938.* *Lest We Forget. A Yank at Oxford.* 1938: *The Crowd Roars. Three Comrades.* 1939: *Lady of the Tropics. Remember? Stand Up and Fight. Lucky Night.* 1940: *Escape. Waterloo Bridge. Flight Command.* 1941: *Billy the Kid. When Ladies Meet.* 1942: *Her Cardboard Lover. Johnny Eager. Stand by for Action! (GB: Cargo of Innocents).* 1943: *The Youngest Profession. Bataan. Song of Russia.* 1945: *The Fighting Lady (narrator only).* 1946: *Undercurrent.* 1947: *The High Wall.* 1948: *The Secret Land (narrator only). The Bribe.* 1949: *Ambush. Conspirator.* 1950: *Devil's Doorway.* 1951: **Challenge in the Wilderness. Quo Vadis? Westward the Women.* 1952: *Above and Beyond. Ivanhoe. I Love Melvin.* 1953: *All the Brothers Were Valiant. Ride, Vaquero!* 1954: *Knights of the Round Table. Rogue Cop. Valley of the Kings.* 1955: *The Adventures of Quentin Durward (US: Quentin Durward). Many Rivers to Cross.* 1956: *The Last Hunt. The Power and the Prize. D-Day the Sixth of June.* 1957: *Tip on a Dead Jockey (GB: Time for Action).* 1958: *Party Girl. Saddle the Wind. The Law and Jake Wade.* 1959: *The House of the Seven Hawks. The Hangman. Killers of Kilimanjaro.* 1962: *Recoil (TV. GB: cinemas). Miracle of the White Stallions (GB: Flight of the White Stallions).* 1963: *Cattle King (GB: Guns of Wyoming).* 1964: *A House is Not a Home.* 1965: *The Night Walker.* 1966: *Savage Pampas. Johnny Tiger. Return of the Gunfighter. Hondo and the Apaches (TV. GB: cinemas).* 1967: *The Glass Sphinx. Where Angels Go ... Trouble Follows.* 1968: *The Day the Hot Line Got Hot. Devil May Care.*

TAYLOR, Rod (Robert Taylor) 1929–
Chunky, jut-jawed, fair-haired Australian actor who came to Hollywood in 1954 and had

a hard struggle to establish himself. Once in leading roles, he showed genuine warmth, charm and forcefulness, although only a top star from 1963–1968; producing his own films at this stage proved rather a mistake in terms of his box-office popularity, which should have solidified, but instead ebbed away.

1951: †*The Sturt Expedition*. 1954: †*Long John Silver*. 1955: *The Virgin Queen*. *Hell on Frisco Bay*. *Top Gun*. 1956: *The Rack*. *The Catered Affair* (*GB: Wedding Breakfast*). *Giant*. *World without End*. 1957: *Raintree County*. 1958: *Step Down to Terror* (*GB: The Silent Stranger*). *Separate Tables*. *Verdict of Three* (*TV*). *The Great Gatsby* (*TV*). *The Long March* (*TV*). 1959: *The Raider* (*TV*). *Ask Any Girl*. *Misalliance* (*TV*). *Queen of the Amazons* (*GB: Colossus and the Amazon Queen*). 1960: *The Time Machine*. 1961: *One Hundred and One Dalmatians* (*voice only*). *Seven Seas to Calais*. 1963: *Sunday in New York*. *A Gathering of Eagles*. *The Birds*. *The V.I.P.s*. 1964: *Fate is the Hunter*. *Thirty-Six Hours*. *Young Cassidy*. 1965: *Do Not Disturb*. *The Liquidator*. 1966: *The Glass Bottom Boat*. *Hotel*. 1967: *The Mercenaries* (*US: Dark of the Sun*). *Chuka*. 1968: *The Hell with Heroes*. *Nobody Runs Forever*. 1969: *Zabriskie Point*. 1970: *The Man Who Had Power over Women*. *Darker than Amber*. 1971: *Powderkeg* (*TV. GB: cinemas*). 1972: *Family Flight* (*TV*). *The Heroes*. 1973: *The Train Robbers*. *Trader Horn* (*GB: TV*). *The Deadly Trackers*. 1974: *Partizan* (*US: Hell River*). 1975: *Blondy* (*US: Vortex*). *Shamus* (*TV. GB: A Matter of Wife and Death*). 1976: *The Oregon Trail* (*TV*). 1977: *The Picture Show Man*. *The Thoroughbreds* (later *Treasure Seekers*). 1978: *Cry of the Innocent* (*TV*). *An Eye for an Eye*. 1980: *Seven Graves for Rogan*. *Hellinger's Law* (*TV*). 1982: *Jacqueline Bouvier Kennedy* (*TV*). *Charles and Diana – a Royal Love Story* (*TV*). *On the Run*. 1983: *Masquerade* (*TV*). 1985: *Marbella*. *Half Nelson* (*TV*). *Mask of Murder*.

† *As Rodney Taylor*

beguiling. The combination of these factors was irresistible, and she was an above-the-title star at six. She couldn't really sing, but did, delightfully; and danced with the confidence of a Kelly. She was America's top star from 1935 to 1938, having taken a special Oscar in 1934. One could wish she had persevered a little more with her adult career: instead she became a diplomat. Married John Agar (*qv*) 1945–1949, first of two.

1932: **War Babies*. **Glad Rags to Riches*. **Pie Covered Wagon*. **The Runt Page*. *Red-Haired Alibi*. 1933: **Polly-Tix in Washington*. **Kid 'n' Hollywood*. **Kid 'n' Africa*. *To the Last Man*. **Kid's Last Fight*. **Merrily Yours*. **Dora's Dunkin' Donuts*. *Out All Night*. 1934: **Pardon My Pups*. **Managed Money*. *Mandalay*. *New Deal Rhythm*. *Carolina*. *Stand Up and Cheer*. *Now I'll Tell* (*GB: When New York Sleeps*). *Change of Heart*. *Little Miss Marker* (*GB: Girl in Pawn*). *Baby, Take a Bow*. *Now and Forever*. *Bright Eyes*. **Hollywood Cavalcade*. 1935: *Curly Top*. *The Little Colonel*. *Our Little Girl*. *The Littlest Rebel*. 1936: *Captain January*. *Dimples*. *Poor Little Rich Girl*. *Stowaway*. 1937: *Wee Willie Winkie*. *Heidi*. *Ali Baba Goes to Town*. 1938: *Rebecca of Sunnybrook Farm*. *Little Miss Broadway*. *Just Around the Corner*. 1939: *The Little Princess*. *Susannah of the Mounties*. 1940: *The Blue Bird*. *Young People*. 1941: *Kathleen*. 1942: *Miss Annie Rooney*. 1944: *Since You Went Away*. *I'll Be Seeing You*. 1945: *Kiss and Tell*. 1947: *Honeymoon* (*GB: Two Men and a Girl*). *The Bachelor and the Bobby-Soxer* (*GB: Bachelor Knight*). *That Hagen Girl*. 1948: *Fort Apache*. 1949: *Mr Belvedere Goes to College*. *A Kiss for Corliss*. *Adventure in Baltimore* (*GB: Bachelor Bait*). *The Story of Seabiscuit* (*GB: Pride of Kentucky*).

1948: *A Date with a Dream*. *The Brass Monkey*/*Lucky Mascot*. 1949: *Helter Skelter*. *Melody Club*. 1951: **Cookery Nook*. **The Queen Steps Out*. 1956: *Private's Progress*. *The Green Man*. 1957: *Blue Murder at St Trinian's*. *Brothers in Law*. *Lucky Jim*. *The Naked Truth* (*US: Your Past is Showing*). 1958: *Happy is the Bride*. *tom thumb*. 1959: *Too Many Crooks*. *Carlton-Browne of the F.O.* (*US: Man in a Cocked Hat*). *I'm All Right, Jack*. 1960: *School for Scoundrels*. *Make Mine Mink*. *His and Hers*. 1961: *A Matter of WHO*. 1962: *Operation Snatch*. *Bachelor Flat*. *Kill or Cure*. *The Wonderful World of the Brothers Grimm*. 1963: *It's a Mad, Mad, Mad, Mad World*. *Mouse on the Moon*. 1964: *The Wild Affair*. 1965: *Strange Bedfellows*. *Those Magnificent Men in Their Flying Machines*. *How to Murder Your Wife*. *You Must Be Joking!* 1966: *The Daydreamer* (*voice only*). *Our Man in Marrakesh* (*US: Bang Bang You're Dead*). *Operation Paradise*. *The Sandwich Man*. *Munster Go Home*. *Kiss the Girls and Make Them Die*. *La grande vadrouille* (*GB: Don't Look Now, We're Being Shot At*). 1967: *Rocket to the Moon* (*US: Those Fantastic Flying Fools*). *Arabella*. *Bandidos*. *I Love a Mystery* (*TV*). *The Karate Killers* (*TV. GB: cinemas*). *The Perils of Pauline*. *A Guide for the Married Man*. *Top Crack*. *Diabolik* (*GB: Danger: Diabolik*). 1968: *Don't Raise the Bridge, Lower the River*. *Uno scacco tutto matto* (*US: Mad Checkmate*). *Sette volte sette*/*Seven Times Seven*. *How Sweet It Is!* *Where Were You When The Lights Went Out?* 1969: †*Arthur, Arthur*. *2,000 Years Later*. *Monte Carlo or Bust!* (*US: Those Daring Young Men in their Jaunty Jalopies*). *Twelve Plus One*/*Una su Zradici*. 1970: *Le mur de l'Atlantique*. *The Abominable Dr Phibes*. 1972: *The Cherrypicker*. *The Heroes*. *Dr Phibes Rises Again*. 1973: *Vault of Horror*. *Robin Hood* (*voice only*). 1974: *Who Stole the Shah's Jewels?* 1975: *Side by Side*. *The Bawdy Adventures of Tom Jones*. *Spanish Fly*. 1977: *The Hound of the Baskervilles*. *The Last Remake of Beau Geste*. 1979: *The Tempest*. 1981: *Happy Birthday Harry!*

† *Unreleased*

TEMPLE, Shirley 1928–
There never has been a child star to compare with Shirley Temple. An adorable golden-haired child, with the timing, reactions, know-how and sly wit of an adult, she appeared completely natural on screen, and quite

TERRY-THOMAS (Thomas Terry Hoar-Stevens) 1911–
Gap-toothed, dark-haired, moustachioed British comedian whose exaggerated upper-crust accent, benign but foxy expression and long cigarette holder were all part of the act. Gained reputation as a stand-up comic (always prefacing his act with 'How do you *do*') before successfully tackling character comedy on film, alternately playing blustering idiots and wily rogues. In poor health in recent years.

THAXTER, Phyllis 1921–
Pretty, brown-haired American actress who tended to play nice girls and women who

wrung their hands and waited, but her performances were spirited enough to bring an extra dimension to such roles. The impetus of her career was badly hit by an attack of infantile paralysis in 1952, but she has continued to act, latterly in character roles. Mother of actress Skye Aubrey (Schuyler Aubrey. 1945–).

1944: Thirty Seconds over Tokyo. 1945: Bewitched. Weekend at the Waldorf. 1947: Sea of Grass. Living in a Big Way. 1948: The Sign of the Ram. Act of Violence. Tenth Avenue Angel. Blood on the Moon. 1950: No Man of Her Own. The Breaking Point. 1951: Come Fill the Cup. Fort Worth. Jim Thorpe – All American (GB: Man of Bronze). 1952: She's Working Her Way Through College. Springfield Rifle. Operation Secret. 1955: Women's Prison. 1957: Man Afraid. 1960: The Cruel Day (TV). 1964: The World of Henry Orient. 1971: Incident in San Francisco (TV). 1972: The Longest Night (TV). 1978: Superman. 1985: Three Sovereigns for Sarah (TV).

THOMAS, Jameson 1889–1939

Dark, dominant, moustachioed, somewhat severe-looking, smoothly-groomed British actor who looked born to play nasty pieces of work, but was equally adept as heroes and became a big star of British films in the years immediately preceding sound, which revealed his crackling tones. He went to America as early as 1930 but after a couple of leading roles gradually regressed to handsome lotharios and 'other men'. Increasingly ill in his later years, he died at 49 from tuberculosis.

*1923: Chu Chin Chow. 1924: *The Drum. *The Cavern Spider. Decameron Nights. The Sins Ye Do. *Chester Forgets Himself. 1925: Daughter of Love. The Apache. Afraid of Love. The Gold Cure. 1926: *The Brotherhood. Jungle Woman. Pearl of the South Seas. 1927: Blighty. *As We Lie. Roses of Picardy. Poppies of Flanders. 1928: The White Sheik (US: King's Mate). The Farmer's Wife. Tesha (US: A Woman in the Night). The Rising Generation. Weekend Wives. 1929: Piccadilly. Power Over Men. The Feather. *Memories. High Treason. The Hate Ship. 1930: Night Birds. Elstree Calling. Extravagance. 1931: Lover Come Back. Convicted. Night Life in Reno. 1932: Three Wise Girls. The Trial of Vivienne Ware. The Phantom President. No More Orchids. Escapade. 1933: Brief Moment. The Invisible Man. Bombay Mail. Self Defense. 1934: A Lost Lady (GB: Courageous). The Scarlet Empress. It Happened One Night. Now and Forever. The Man Who Reclaimed His Head. Beggars in Ermine. Sing Sing Nights (GB: Reprieved). Stolen Sweets. The Moonstone. Jane Eyre. A Woman's Man. A Successful Failure. 1935: Lives of a Bengal Lancer. The World Accuses. Rumba. Mr Dynamite. Coronado. The Lady in Scarlet. Charlie Chan in Egypt. Crimson Romance. The Last Outpost. 1936: Mr Deeds Goes to Town. Lady Luck. 1937: House of Secrets. The League of Frightened Men. The Man Who Cried Wolf. 100 Men and a Girl. 1938: Death Goes North.*

THOMAS, Richard 1951–

Young-looking, light-haired American actor who became immensely popular on TV as John Boy in the long-running series *The Waltons*. In films as a teenager, he has played several sensitive roles and (rather more effectively) one or two nasty ones. But he has, on the whole, not made the strides that one might have hoped for and, although still in leading roles, has been seen mostly in TV movies in recent times.

1969: †Winning. Last Summer. 1970: Cactus in the Snow. The Todd Killings. You Can't Have Everything. 1971: The Homecoming (TV). Red Sky at Morning. 1972: You'll Like My Mother. 1974: The Red Badge of Courage (TV). 1975: The Silence (TV). 1977: Getting Married (TV). 9–30–55 (GB: TV, as 9 September, 1955). 1979: No Other Love (TV). 1980: All Quiet on the Western Front (TV. GB: cinemas). Battle Beyond the Stars. To Find My Son (TV). 1981: Berlin Tunnel 28 (TV). 1982: Johnny Belinda (TV). 1983: Living Proof: The Hank Williams Jr Story (TV). Hobson's Choice (TV). 1985: Final Jeopardy (TV). 1986: Welcome to Our Night (TV).

† As Richard Thomas Jr

THOMPSON, Marshall (James M. Thompson) 1925–

Tall, unassuming, sandy-haired American actor who played quiet juvenile roles at M-G-M for eight years before carrying on his career as a third-line leading man in equally unspectacular fashion. But his most successful period was yet to come, starting with the film *Clarence the Cross-Eyed Lion*, which led to the long-running TV animal-clinic series *Daktari*.

He continued his association with wild-life producer Ivan Tors into the seventies.

1944: The Purple Heart. Reckless Age. Blonde Fever. 1945: The Valley of Decision. The Clock. Twice Blessed. They Were Expendable. 1946: The Cockeyed Miracle (GB: Mr. Griggs Returns). Bad Bascomb. The Show Off. Gallant Bess. The Secret Heart. 1947: The Romance of Rosy Ridge. 1948: Homecoming. B.F.'s Daughter (GB: Polly Fulton). Words and Music. Command Decision. 1949: Battleground. Roseanna McCoy. 1950: Mystery Street. Devil's Doorway. Dial 1119 (GB: The Violent Hour). 1951: The Tall Target. The Basketball Fix (GB: The Big Decision). 1952: My Six Convicts. The Rose Bowl Story. 1953: The Caddy. 1954: Port of Hell. Battle Taxi. 1955: Cult of the Cobra. Crashout. Good Morning, Miss Dove. To Hell and Back. 1956: La grande caccia. 1957: Lure of the Swamp. Young Man from Kentucky (TV. GB: cinemas). The Blackwell Story (TV). 1958: Fiend without a Face. It! The Terror from Beyond Space. The Secret Man. 1959: First Man into Space. 1961: Flight of the Lost Balloon. 1962: No Man is an Island (GB: Island Rescue). East of Kilimanjaro/The Big Search. 1964. †A Yank in Viet-Nam. The Mighty Jungle. 1965: Clarence the Cross-Eyed Lion. 1966: To the Shores of Hell. Around the World Under the Sea. 1970: George! 1977: The Turning Point. 1978: Cruise into Terror (TV). Bog. 1980: ‡The Formula. 1981: White Dog. 1986: Dallas: The Early Years (TV).

† Also directed   ‡Scenes deleted from final release print

THORBURN, June 1931–1967

Pretty, rose-cheeked, fair-haired British actress, born in Kashmir. A former junior skiing champion, her cinema course was from second-features into major films – and back again. She retired to concentrate on married life in 1964, but was killed in a plane crash.

1952: The Pickwick Papers. 1953: The Cruel Sea. The Triangle. 1954: Fast and Loose. Delayed Action. Orders Are Orders. Children Galore. The Death of Michael Turbin. 1955: The Hornet's Nest. Touch and Go (US: The Light-Touch). 1956: True as a Turtle. 1958: Rooney. tom thumb. 1959: Broth of a Boy. 1960: The Price of Silence. The Three Worlds of Gulliver. Escort for Hire. 1961: Fury at Smuggler's Bay. Don't Bother to Knock! (US:

Why Bother to Knock?). Transatlantic. The Spanish Sword. 1962: Design for Loving. 1963: The Scarlet Blade. Master Spy.

THORNDIKE, Dame Sybil 1882–1976
Distinguished British stage actress of upright bearing – a memorable St Joan in her late youth. Made a few film appearances in between a string of stage triumphs – mostly in old age. Married to equally distinguished stage actor Sir Lewis Casson (1876–1969). Made a Dame in 1931. Died from a heart attack.

*1921: Moth and Rust. 1922: *Nancy. Bleak House. *Macbeth: extract. *Jane Shore. *The Lady of the Camellias: extract. *The Merchant of Venice: extract. *Esmeralda. *The Scarlet Letter: Extract. 1927: *Saint Joan: extract. 1928: Dawn. 1929: To What Red Hell. 1931: Hindle Wakes. A Gentleman of Paris. 1936: Tudor Rose (US: Nine Days a Queen). 1941: Major Barbara. 1947: Nicholas Nickleby. 1949: Britannia Mews (US: Forbidden Street). 1950: Stage Fright. Gone to Earth (US: The Wild Heart). 1951: The Magic Box. The Lady with a Lamp. 1953: Melba. The Weak and the Wicked. 1957: *Bernard Shaw. The Prince and the Showgirl. 1958: Smiley Gets a Gun. Alive and Kicking. 1959: Shake Hands with the Devil. Jet Storm. 1960: Hand in Hand. The Big Gamble. 1963: Uncle Vanya.*

THULIN, Ingrid 1929–
Cool, long-necked Swedish actress whose bleak blonde beauty has been best used in the films of Ingmar Bergman. Elsewhere she has made some strange movies that sometimes

border on sexploitation, but proved herself a formidable stage actress in her native country.
*1948: Känn dej som Hemma. Dit Vindarna Bär. 1949: Havets Son. Kärlekan Segrar. 1950: Hajarter Knekt. När Kärlekan Kom till Byn. 1951: Leva pa 'Hoppet'. 1952: Möte med Livet. Kalle Karlsson fran Jularbo. 1953: En Skärgardsnatt. Goingehovdingen. 1954: Tva Sköna Juveler. I Rök och Dans. 1955: Hoppsan! Danssalongen. 1956: Foreign Intrigue. 1957: Smultronstället/Wild Straw-berries. Aldrig i Livet. 1958: Nära Livet/So Close to Life. Ansiktet/The Face. 1960: Domaren. 1961: The Four Horsemen of the Apocalypse. 1962: Agostino. 1963: Nattvardsgästerna/Winter Light. Tystna-den/The Silence. 1964: Die Lady (GB: Frus-tration). Der Film den Niemand sieht. Sekstet. 1965: †*Hängivelse. Return from the Ashes. La guerre est finie. 1966: Night Games. 1967: Domani non siamo più qui. 1968: Varg-timmen/Hour of the Wolf. Adelaide (GB: The Depraved). Badarna (GB and US: I, a Virgin). 1969: Ritten/The Rite. Un Diablo bajo la Almohada. La caduta degli dei (GB and US: The Damned). 1970: Deux affreux sur le sable. 1971: N.P. il segreto. 1972: La sainte famille. Cries and Whispers/Viskingar och Rop. 1973: En Handfull Kärlek (GB TV: A Handful of Love). 1974: Monismanien. 1975: La cage (GB: TV). Moses. 1976: The Cassandra Crossing. 1977: En och En. Il viaggio nella vertigini. 1981: Brustel Himmel (GB: Broken Sky. Directed only).*

† *Also directed*

TIERNEY, Gene 1920–
Dark-haired, glowingly beautiful American star, probably the most strikingly lovely Hol-lywood actress of the forties. She enjoyed a good variety of attractive star roles, before her beauty, health, career and marriage all began to fade in the late forties. There was a nervous breakdown and a rather half-hearted come-back in the early sixties. She received an Acad-emy Award nomination for *Leave Her to Heaven.*
1940: The Return of Frank James. Hudson's Bay. 1941: Sundown. Tobacco Road. The Shanghai Gesture. Belle Starr. 1942: Thunder Birds. Rings on Her Fingers. Son of Fury. China Girl. 1943: Heaven Can Wait. 1944: Laura. 1945: Leave Her to Heaven. A Bell for

Adano. 1946: Dragonwyck. The Razor's Edge. 1947: The Ghost and Mrs Muir. 1948: The Iron Curtain. That Wonderful Urge. 1949: Whirlpool. 1950: Night and the City. Where the Sidewalk Ends. 1951: On the Riviera. The Mating Season. Close to My Heart. The Secret of Convict Lake. 1952: Plymouth Adventure. Way of a Gaucho. 1953: Never Let Me Go. Personal Affair. 1954: The Egyptian. Black Widow. 1955: The Left Hand of God. 1962: Advise and Consent. 1963: Toys in the Attic. 1964: The Pleasure Seekers. 1969: Daughter of the Mind (TV).

TIERNEY, Lawrence 1919–
Grim-looking, square-faced, light-haired American 'tough-guy' actor, brother of Scott Brady (qv). The title role in *Dillinger* was his biggest break, and he infused it with menace and sub-surface violence. But Tierney was unable to follow through to all-round stardom. He worked for minor studios, and still plays small parts.
*1943: Government Girl. The Ghost Ship. Gil-dersleeve on Broadway. 1944: Youth Runs Wild. The Falcon Out West. 1945: Mama Loves Papa. *Birthday Blues. Dillinger. Those Endearing Young Charms. Back to Bataan. 1946: San Quentin. Badman's Territory. Step by Step. 1947: The Devil Thumbs a Ride. Born to Kill (GB: Lady of Deceit). 1948: Bodyguard. 1950: Kill or Be Killed. Shake-down. 1951: The Hoodlum. Best of the Badmen. The Bushwhackers (GB: The Rebel). 1952: The Greatest Show on Earth. 1954: The Steel Cage. 1956: Female Jungle. 1962: A Child is*

Waiting. 1966: Custer of the West. 1971: Such Good Friends. 1975: Abduction. 1976: Bad/Andy Warhol's Bad. 1978: The Kirlian Witness. 1980: Never Pick Up a Stranger/Bloodrage. Gloria. Arthur. 1981: Rosemary's Killer. 1982: Midnight. 1985: Prizzi's Honor. 1986: Silver Bullet.

TOBIN, Genevieve 1901–

Sophisticated, blue-eyed, effervescent, platinum blonde American actress with bee-stung lips. Coming to Hollywood at 29 with a formidable stage reputation, she found herself all too often cast as the 'other woman' and entrapped many a hapless hero with her terrific figure and low-lidded gaze. In real life she proved a hard girl to catch, but eventually married director William Keighley in 1938. A sort of high-class Gloria Grahame (*qv*) in her film characters, though their cynicism was often sugared with her personal charm.

1923: No Mother to Guide Her. 1930: Free Love. A Lady Surrenders (GB: Blind Wives). 1931: Seed. Up for Murder. The Gay Diplomat. 1932: One Hour with You. Hollywood Speaks. The Cohens and Kellys in Hollywood. Perfect Understanding. 1933: Infernal Machine. Pleasure Cruise. The Wrecker. Golden Harvest. Goodbye Again. I Loved a Woman. 1934: Ninth Guest. Easy to Love. Dark Hazard. Uncertain Lady. Success at Any Price. Kiss and Make Up. 1935: The Woman in Red. The Goose and the Gander. Here's to Romance. The Case of the Lucky Legs. Broadway Hostess. The Petrified Forest. 1936: Snowed Under. The Man in the Mirror. 1937: The Great Gambini. The Duke Comes Back (GB: The Call of the Ring). 1938: Kate Plus Ten (US: The Queen of Crime). Dramatic School. Zaza. 1939: Yes, My Darling Daughter. Our Neighbors, The Carters. 1940: No Time for Comedy.

TODD, Ann 1909–

Glacial British blonde actress whose porcelain features and set expression helped keep her in leading roles for a long time. Her career was severely disrupted in the early thirties by a car accident, but in the mid-forties she became one of Britain's most popular stars, married (third) director David Lean and appeared in several of his films. Later made a few critically-praised documentary films.

1931: Keepers of Youth. The Ghost Train. These Charming People. 1932: The Water

Gipsies. 1934: The Return of Bulldog Drummond. 1936: Men of Yesterday. Things to Come. 1937: Action for Slander. The Squeaker (US: Murder on Diamond Row). South Riding. 1939: Poison Pen. 1941: Danny Boy. Ships with Wings. 1945: Perfect Strangers (US: Vacation from Marriage). The Seventh Veil. 1946: Gaiety George (US: Showtime). Daybreak. 1947: The Paradine Case. 1948: So Evil My Love. 1949: The Passionate Friends (US: One Woman's Story). 1950: Madeleine. 1952: The Sound Barrier (US: Breaking the Sound Barrier). 1954: The Green Scarf. 1957: Time without Pity. 1961: Taste of Fear (US: Scream of Fear). 1963: The Son of Captain Blood. 1965: Ninety Degrees in the Shade. 1971: The Fiend. 1979: The Human Factor. 1985: The McGuffin (TV).

As director: *1965: *Thunder in Heaven. 1966: *Thunder of the Gods. 1967: *Thunder of the Kings.*

TODD, Richard (R. Palethorpe-Todd) 1919–

Dark-haired, boyish-looking Irish-born actor who, despite a lack of stature, was plucked from repertory work at 30, and became a major star of the British cinema almost at once. His performance as the dying Scot in *The Hasty Heart* made him an international name and, with varying success, he appeared in several films for Warners, Fox and Disney. His standing slipped away in the sixties and in the following decade he was back appearing regularly in repertory, one of the first big names in the British cinema to do so. Oscar-nominated for *The Hasty Heart*.

1949: For Them That Trespass. The Inter-

*rupted Journey. The Hasty Heart. 1950: Portrait of Clare. Stage Fright. 1951: Lightning Strikes Twice. Flesh and Blood. 1952: Elstree Story. The Story of Robin Hood and his Merrie Men. 24 Hours of a Woman's Life (US: Affair in Monte Carlo). Venetian Bird (US: The Assassin). 1953: The Sword and the Rose. Rob Roy the Highland Rogue. Secrets d'alcove (GB and US: The Bed). 1954: A Man Called Peter. 1955: *People and Places. The Dam Busters. The Virgin Queen. 1956: D-Day the Sixth of June. Marie Antoinette. 1957: Yangtse Incident (US: Battle Hell). Saint Joan. 1958: Chase a Crooked Shadow. The Naked Earth. Intent to Kill. 1959: Danger Within (US: Breakout). 1960: Never Let Go. The Long and the Short and the Tall (US: Jungle Fighters). 1961: Don't Bother to Knock! (US: Why Bother to Knock?). The Hellions. 1962: Le crime ne paie pas (GB: The Gentle Art of Murder). The Boys. The Longest Day. 1963: The Very Edge. Death Drums Along the River. 1964: Coast of Skeletons. 1965: Operation Crossbow (US: The Great Spy Mission). The Battle of the Villa Fiorita. 1967: The Love-Ins. 1968: Subterfuge. The Last of the Long-Haired Boys. 1970: Dorian Gray. 1972: Asylum. The Aquarian. 1977: No. 1 of the Secret Service. 1978: The Big Sleep. Home Before Midnight. 1982: House of the Long Shadows.*

TODD, Thelma 1905–1935

Tall, funny, blonde American character comedienne with pencilled eyebrows and happy, expressive face. A former beauty contest winner, she stooged for almost all the great early thirties comedians, including the Marx Brothers and Laurel and Hardy, and proved herself a funny lady in her own right in a long series of two-reelers with ZaSu Pitts (*qv*) and Patsy Kelly. Died from carbon monoxide poisoning, in her garaged car. The subsequent enquiry never determined whether it was murder, suicide or accident.

*1926: God Gave Me Twenty Cents. Fascinating Youth. 1927: Rubber Heels. Nevada. The Shield of Honor. The Gay Defender. 1928: The Haunted House. Vamping Venus. Seven Footprints to Satan. The Crash. Heart to Heart. The Noose. Naughty Baby (GB: Reckless Rosie). 1929: Trial Marriage. Bachelor Girl. Careers. House of Horror. Her Private Life. *Look Out Below. *Snappy Sneezer.*

*Crazy Feet. *Stepping Out. *Unaccustomed As We Are. *Hurdy Gurdy. *Hotter Than Hot. *Shy Boy. *The Head Guy. *The Real McCoy. 1930: Command Performance. Follow Through. Swanee River. No Limit. Hell's Angels. Her Man. *Whispering Whoopee. *Another Fine Mess. *All Teed Up. *Dollar Dizzy. *Looser than Loose. *High Cs. *The Fighting Parson. *The Shrimp. *The King. 1931: Aloha (GB: No Greater Love). The Hot Heiress. Broad-Minded. Corsair. Monkey Business. The Maltese Falcon. Beyond Victory. This is the Night. *Catch as Catch Can. *Love Fever. *Let's Do Things. *Chickens Come Home. *Rough Seas. *The Pip from Pittsburgh. *The Pajama Party. *War Mamas. 1932: Klondike. Speak Easily. Call Her Savage. Horse Feathers. Big Timer. No Greater Love. *The Nickel Nurser. *Seal Skins. *On the Loose. *Cauliflower Alley. *Strictly Unreliable. *Red Noses. *Alum and Eve. *The Old Bull. *Show Business. *The Soilers. 1933: The Devil's Brother (GB: Fra Diavolo). Air Hostess. Mary Stevens M.D. Sitting Pretty. Deception. Cheating Blondes (GB: House of Chance). Counsellor at Law. Son of a Sailor. *Maids à la Mode. *Sneak Easily. *One Track Minds. *Asleep on the Feet. *Bargain of the Century. *Air Fright. *Beauty and the Bus. *Backs to Nature. You Made Me Love You. 1934: Palooka (GB: The Great Schnozzle). Bottoms Up. Hips, Hips, Hooray. Cockeyed Cavaliers. The Poor Rich. Take the Stand. *Maid in Hollywood. *Babes in the Goods. *Three Chumps Ahead. *Opened by Mistake. *Bum Voyage. *Soup and Fish. *I'll Be Suing You. *One Horse Farmers. *Done in Oil. 1935: Two for Tonight. Lightning Strikes Twice. After the Dance. *The Tin Man. *Treasure Blues. *Slightly Static. *Twin Triplets. *Top Flat. *Sing, Sister, Sing. *The Misses Stooge. *Hot Money. *All American Toothache. 1936: The Bohemian Girl.

Strictly Dishonorable. 1931: White Shoulders. *The Devil's Parade. 1932: Speak Easily. *Over the Counter. Tom Brown of Culver. Strangers in Love. Is My Face Red? Blondie of the Follies. The Phantom President. Blonde Venus. Radio Patrol. 1933: The Way to Love. He Learned about Women. Billion Dollar Scandal. King of the Jungle. The World Changes. The Narrow Corner. 1934: Registered Nurse. Dark Hazard. Romance in Manhattan. Upper World. Operator 13 (GB: Spy 13). Massacre. Spitfire. The Trumpet Blows. Here Comes the Groom. 1935: Orchids to You. Call of the Wild. This is the Life. The Daring Young Man. Champagne for Breakfast. 1936: The Longest Night. Three Godfathers. Give Us This Night. Our Relations. The Gorgeous Hussy. 1937: Double Wedding. That Certain Woman. Quality Street. 1938: Up the River. Gold is Where You Find It. If I Were King. Three Comrades. One Wild Night. The Mysterious Rider. Charlie Chan in Honolulu. Wide Open Faces. 1939: The Kid from Kokomo (GB: The Orphan of the Ring). Charlie Chan in Reno. Disbarred. Law of the Pampas. Charlie Chan at Treasure Island. King of Chinatown. Charlie Chan in City in Darkness. Heritage of the Desert. Broadway Cavalier. 1940: Charlie Chan in Panama. Charlie Chan's Murder Cruise. Murder over New York. Charlie Chan at the Wax Museum. 1941: Dead Men Tell. Charlie Chan in Rio. 1942: Castle in the Desert. The Adventures of Smilin' Jack (serial). A Night to Remember. 1943: Isle of Forgotten Sins. White Savage (GB: White Captive). Charlie Chan in the Secret Service. 1944: Black Magic. Charlie Chan in the Chinese Cat. The Scarlet Clue. It's in the Bag (GB: The Fifth Chair). 1945: The Jade Mask. The Shanghai Cobra. The Red Dragon. 1946: Shadows over Chinatown. Dark Alibi. Dangerous Money. The Trap (GB: Murder at Malibu Beach).

Family. Pimpernel Smith (US: Mister V). 1945: The Way to the Stars (US: Johnny in the Clouds). Journey Together. 1946: I See a Dark Stranger (US: The Adventuress). School for Secrets. 1947: Master of Bankdam. Easy Money. Fame is the Spur. Broken Journey. 1948: Love in Waiting. Miranda. Here Come the Huggetts. My Brother's Keeper. Sleeping Car to Trieste. Warning to Wantons. 1949: Helter Skelter. Vote for Huggett. Landfall. Marry Me. The Chiltern Hundreds (US: The Amazing Mr. Beecham). 1950: So Long at the Fair. The Wooden Horse. 1951: The Magic Box. Hotel Sahara. Calling Bulldog Drummond. 1952: Castle in the Air. Made in Heaven. 1953: Is Your Honeymoon Really Necessary? 1955: All for Mary. 1956: Three Men in a Boat. 1957: Carry on Admiral (US: The Ship Was Loaded). 1958: Up the Creek. Further Up the Creek. 1960: Follow That Horse! 1963: Tom Jones. 1964: Mary Poppins. The Truth about Spring. 1965: City under the Sea (US: War Gods of the Deep). The Liquidator. 1969: The Love Bug. 1971: Bedknobs and Broomsticks. 1974: Bon Baisers de Hong Kong. 1977: Wombling Free. 1978: Dominique. The Water Babies. 1980: The Fiendish Plot of Dr Fu Manchu.

TONE, Franchot (Stanislas F. Tone) 1905–1968
Smooth, brown-haired American actor, adept at callow charmers, and too often employed in that mould, or as lounge lizards, or best friends not strong enough to get the girl. When handed unusual assignments he became much more interesting, and did some good character work in his later years. Married/divorced Joan Crawford (1935–1939) and three blonde starlets: Jean Wallace from 1941 to 1948, Barbara Payton (1927–1967) from 1951 to 1952, and Dolores Dorn (1935–) from 1956 to 1959. Oscar-nominated in the best actor category in Mutiny on The Bounty, Tone might well have won an Academy Award had the category of best supporting actor been brought in a year earlier. Died from lung cancer.
1932: The Wiser Sex. 1933: Today We Live. Gabriel over the White House. Bombshell (GB: Blonde Bombshell). Midnight Mary. Dancing Lady. Stage Mother. The Stranger's Return. 1934: Straight is the Way. Moulin Rouge. The Girl from Missouri (GB: 100 Per Cent Pure).

TOLER, Sidney 1874–1947
Dark-haired, heavy-set American character actor who staked his claim to a niche in the Hollywood Hall of Fame when he took over the role of Charlie Chan, the wily oriental detective, from Warner Oland (qv), when the latter died in 1938. Toler played the role for nine years (he never looked his age) before he too died, and Roland Winters (1904–) took over the declining series.
1929: *In the Nick of Time. Madame X. 1930:

TOMLINSON, David 1917–
Dark-haired, crumple-faced British comic actor, the archetypal 'silly-ass' of his day. Because of the variety of roles he played in post-war years, it took him a while to come into his own, but he enjoyed a good star run in scatty comedies from 1951–1960, later registering well in character roles for the Disney studio.
1940: *Name, Rank and Number. Garrison Follies. 1941: Quiet Wedding. My Wife's

The World Moves On. Gentlemen Are Born. Sadie McKee. 1935: Reckless. Lives of a Bengal Lancer. Dangerous. Mutiny on the Bounty. No More Ladies. One New York Night (GB: The Trunk Mystery). 1936: The Unguarded Hour. Exclusive Story. The King Steps Out. The Gorgeous Hussy. Suzy. Love on the Run. 1937: They Gave Him a Gun. Between Two Women. Quality Street. The Bride Wore Red. 1938: Man-Proof. Three Comrades. Love is a Headache. Three Loves Has Nancy. 1939: Thunder Afloat. Fast and Furious. 1940: Trail of the Vigilantes. 1941: Nice Girl? She Knew All the Answers. This Woman is Mine. 1942: Star Spangled Rhythm. The Wife Takes a Flyer. 1943: True to Life. His Butler's Sister. Pilot No. 5. Five Graves to Cairo. 1944: Phantom Lady. The Hour before the Dawn. Dark Waters. 1945: That Night with You. 1946: Because of Him. 1947: Honeymoon (GB: Two Men and a Girl). Her Husband's Affairs. Lost Honeymoon. 1948: Every Girl Should Be Married. I Love Trouble. 1949: Jigsaw. Without Honor. The Man on the Eiffel Tower. 1951: Here Comes the Groom. 1957: The Thundering Wave (TV). 1958: †Uncle Vanya. 1959: A Quiet Game of Cards (TV). Hidden Image (TV). 1960: The Shape of the River (TV). 1962: Advise and Consent. 1963: La bonne soupe. 1964: See How They Run (TV). 1965: In Harm's Way. Mickey One. 1968: Nobody Runs Forever. Shadow over Elveron (TV).

† *Also co-directed*

TOOMEY, Regis 1902–
Slight, pleasant, pale-eyed, light-haired, fast-talking American actor, in on sound films from the outset, and popular in minor leads in the 1930s, usually as breezy, clean-cut juveniles. Later played reporters, tail-gunners, cab-drivers and other eager-beaver types, sometimes the second-line good guy who bit the dust, but only rarely on the wrong side of the law. Enjoyed new popularity in the 1960s as one of Gene Barry's sidekicks in the long-running TV show *Burke's Law.*
1929: Rich People. Wheel of Life. Alibi. Illusion. 1930: The Light of Western Stars. Crazy That Way. Framed. A Man from Wyoming. Good Intentions. Street of Chance. Shadow of the Law. 1931: Finn and Hattie. Perfect Alibi. Graft. Scandal Sheet. 24 Hours (GB: The Hours Between). Touchdown (GB: Playing the Game). Murder by the Clock. The

*Finger Points. Kick In. Other Men's Women. Under 18. Sky Bride. 1932: Shopworn. They Never Come Back. The Crowd Roars. A Strange Adventure. The Midnight Patrol. The Penal Code. 1933: Laughing at Life. State Trooper. Picture Brides. Soldiers of the Storm. She Had to Say Yes. Big Time or Bust (GB: Heaven Bound). 1934: Red Morning. What's Your Racket? Redhead. She Had to Choose. Murder on the Blackboard. 1935: One Frightened Night. G Men. Reckless Roads. Shadow of Doubt. Skull and Crown. Manhattan Moon (GB: Sing Me a Love Song). The Great God Gold. 1936: Bulldog Edition (GB: Lady Reporter). *Sweethearts and Flowers. Shadows of the Orient. 1937: The Big City. Midnight Taxi. Back in Circulation. Submarine D-1. 1938: His Exciting Night. Hunted Men. Illegal Traffic. The Invisible Menace. 1939: Smashing the Spy Ring. Street of Missing Men. Wings of the Navy. Indianapolis Speedway (GB: Devil on Wheels). Hidden Power. The Phantom Creeps (serial). Society Smugglers. Pirates of the Skies. The Mysterious Miss X. Confessions of a Nazi Spy. Trapped in the Sky. Union Pacific. Thunder Afloat. His Girl Friday. 1940: Northwest Passage. Till We Meet Again. Northwest Mounted Police. Arizona. 1941: A Shot in the Dark. Law of the Tropics. Meet John Doe. The Lone Wolf Takes a Chance. They Died with Their Boots On. Reaching for the Sun. The Nurse's Secret. Dive Bomber. You're in the Army Now. 1942: The Forest Rangers. Bullet Scars. Tennessee Johnson (GB: The Man on America's Conscience). I Was Framed. 1943: Adventures of the Flying Cadets (serial). Jack London. Destroyer. Phantom Lady. 1944: Song of the Open Road. The Doughgirls. Dark Mountain. Follow the Boys. Raiders of Ghost City (serial). When the Lights Go On Again. Murder in the Blue Room. 1945: Follow That Woman. Spellbound. Betrayal from the East. Out of the Night (GB: Strange Illusion). 1946: Mysterious Intruder. Her Sister's Secret. The Big Sleep. Child of Divorce. Sister Kenny. The Big Fix. 1947: High Tide. The Guilty. The Thirteenth Hour. Magic Town. The Bishop's Wife. 1948: I Wouldn't Be in Your Shoes. Raw Deal. Station West. The Boy with Green Hair. 1949: The Devil's Henchman. Mighty Joe Young. Come to the Stable. Beyond the Forest. 1950: Undercover Girl. Again, Pioneers. Mrs O'Malley and Mr Malone. Tomahawk (GB: Battle of Powder River). Dynamite Pass. Frenchie. 1951: The Tall Target. Navy Bound. Show Boat. Cause for Alarm. The People Against O'Hara. Cry Danger. 1952: Just For You. My Six Convicts. My Pal Gus. The Battle at Apache Pass. Never Wave at a WAC (GB: The Private Wore Skirts). Take the High Ground. 1953: The Nebraskan. Island in the Sky. It Happens Every Thursday. Son of Belle Starr. 1954: Drums Across the River. The High and the Mighty. The Human Jungle. 1955: Top Gun. Guys and Dolls. 1956: Great Day in the Morning. Dakota Incident. Three for Jamie Dawn. Men Against Speed (TV. GB: cinemas). 1957: The Still Trumpet (TV). 1958: Sing, Boy, Sing. Joy Ride. 1959: Warlock. The Hangman. Guns of the Timberland. 1961: The Last Sunset. Voyage*

to the Bottom of the Sea. King of the Roaring Twenties (GB: The Big Bankroll). 1963: Man's Favorite Sport? 1966: Night of the Grizzly. 1967: Gunn. 1969: Change of Habit. 1970: Cover Me Babe. 1972: The Carey Treatment. 1974: The Phantom of Hollywood (TV). God Damn Dr Shagetz/God Bless Dr Shagetz. 1975: Won Ton Ton, the Dog Who Saved Hollywood. 1979: Chomps.

TOREN, Marta (Märta Torén) 1925–1957
Tall, dark, sultry Swedish actress who always seemed to pose with her eyes half-closed, and her full lips in a semi-pout. Hollywood liked what it saw and signed her up even though she had made only one film in Sweden. She returned from America in 1952, but seemed to be losing her appetite for films when she was killed by a rare brain disease.
1947: Eviga Länkar. 1948: Casbah. Rogues' Regiment. 1949: Illegal Entry. Sword in the Desert. 1950: One-Way Street. Spy Hunt (GB: Panther's Moon). Deported. Mystery Submarine. 1951: Sirocco. 1952: The Man Who Watched Trains Go By (US: Paris Express). Assignment – Paris! Puccini, une vie de l'amour. 1953: Maddalena. 1954: Casa Ricordi. L'ombra. 1955: La vena d'oro. 1956: Carta a Sara. L'ultima notte d'amore (GB: Femme Fatale. US: Fatal Rendezvous). Tormento d'amore. 1957: La puerta abierta.

TORN, Rip (Elmore Torn) 1931–
Mean-looking, dynamic, dark-haired, thin-faced American actor who has made the stage the major part of his career, but appeared spasmodically in films, mainly in unsym-

pathetic but eye-catching roles. Married Geraldine Page (1963).
1956: Baby Doll. 1957: Time Limit. A Face in the Crowd. 1958: Cat on a Hot Rin Roof. Bomber's Moon (TV). Face of a Hero (TV). 1959: The Tunnel (TV). Pork Chop Hill. 1961: King of Kings. 1962: Sweet Bird of Youth. Hero's Island. 1963: Critic's Choice. 1965: One Spy Too Many (TV. GB: cinemas). The Cincinnati Kid. 1966: You're a Big Boy Now. 1967: Beach Red. Sol Madrid (GB: The Heroin Gang). 1968: Beyond the Law. Coming Apart. 1969: The Rain People. Tropic of Cancer. One PM. 1970: Maidstone. 1971: The President's Plane is Missing (TV). 1972: Slaughter. 1973: Payday. Cotter (TV). 1974: Crazy Joe. 1975: Attack on Terror (TV). The Man Who Fell to Earth. 1976: Birch Interval. Nasty Habits. 1977: J. Edgar Hoover, Godfather of the F.B.I. (Later and GB: The Private Files of J. Edgar Hoover). Coma. 1978: Betrayal (TV). Steel Cowboy (TV). 1979: A Shining Season (TV). The Wobblies (voice only). The Seduction of Joe Tynan. Heartland. 1980: Sophia Loren – Her Own Story (TV). One Trick Pony. Rape and Marriage: The Rideout Case (TV). First Family. 1981: Blind Ambition (TV). A Stranger is Waiting. 1982: Jinxed! Airplane II The Sequel. The Beast-Master. Scarab. 1983: Cross Creek. Misunderstood. 1984: When She Says No (TV). Flashpoint. City Heat. Songwriter. 1985: The Execution (TV). The Atlanta Child Murders (TV). Summer Rental. Beer. 1986: Extreme Prejudice.

TOTTER, Audrey 1918–
American actress with narrow features, reddish-blonde hair and petite sexy figure. Well known on radio as 'the girl with a thousand voices' before being whisked off by M-G-M who made use of her talent for accents. Later her looks got her cast as hard-boiled, flint-hearted types. Tended to play leads in co-features and top supporting roles in big productions.
1944: Ziegfeld Follies (released 1946). Main Street After Dark. 1945: Bewitched (voice only). The Sailor Takes a Wife. The Hidden Eye. Her Highness and the Bellboy. Adventure. Dangerous Partners. 1946: The Postman Always Rings Twice. The Cockeyed Miracle (GB: Mr Griggs Returns). The Secret Heart. The Lady in the Lake. 1947: The Beginning or

the End? The High Wall. The Unsuspected. 1948: Tenth Avenue Angel. The Saxon Charm. Alias Nick Beal (GB: The Contact Man). 1949: The Set-Up. Any Number Can Play. Tension. 1950: Under the Gun. 1951: The Blue Veil. The Sellout. FBI Girl. 1952: My Pal Gus. Assignment – Paris! 1953: Man in the Dark. The Woman They Almost Lynched. Cruisin' down the River. Mission over Korea (GB: Eyes of the Skies). Champ for a Day. 1954: Massacre Canyon. 1955: Women's Prison. A Bullet for Joey. One Life (TV. GB: cinemas). The Vanishing American. 1957: Ghost Diver. 1958: Jet Attack (GB: Through Hell to Glory). Man or Gun. 1963: The Carpetbaggers. 1965: Harlow (TV). 1967: The Outsider (TV). 1968: Chubasco. 1975: The Fourth Sex (TV. Formerly episodes of Medical Center series). 1978: The Magnificent Hustle (TV). 1979: The Apple Dumpling Gang Rides Again. 1984: City Killer (TV).

TRACY, Lee (William L. Tracy) 1898–1968
Stocky, bouncy, light-haired American actor, possibly the screen's fastest talker. Very popular in the early thirties as a wisecracking reporter, but became so stereotyped in the image that eventually it was used as light relief in serious stuff. His appeal dated and faded quickly (he had also upset Louis B. Mayer), and he was little seen when the thirties were through. Died from cancer of the liver. Oscar nominee for The Best Man.
1929: Big Time. 1930: Liliom. She Got What She Wanted. Born Reckless. 1931: On the Level. 1932: Blessed Event. The Strange Love of Molly Louvain. Night Mayor. The Half-Naked Truth. Love is a Racket. Doctor X. Washington Merry-Go-Round (GB: Invisible Power). 1933: The Nuisance (GB: Accidents Wanted). Clear All Wires. Turn Back the Clock. Advice to the Lovelorn. Private Jones. Dinner at Eight. Bombshell (GB: Blonde Bombshell). Phantom Fame. 1934: The Lemon Drop Kid. I'll Tell the World. You Belong to Me. 1935: Carnival. Two-Fisted. 1936: Sutter's Gold. Wanted – Jane Turner. 1937: Behind the Headlines. Criminal Lawyer. 1938: Crashing Hollywood. 1939: Fixer Dugan (GB: Double Daring). Spellbinder. 1940: Millionaires in Prison. 1942: The Payoff. 1943: Power of the Press. 1945: Betrayal from the East. I'll Tell the World (remake). 1947: High Tide. 1964: The Best Man.

TRACY, Spencer 1900–1967
Rugged, thick-set, brown-haired American star with un-handsome but determined and sympathetic features, now generally acknowledged to have been Hollywood's best actor from the early thirties to the early fifties. Certainly, few were more successful at compelling total audience belief, thanks to a naturalistic approach to acting that always made him seem sincere. Two Academy Awards (for Captains Courageous and Boys' Town) and seven nominations. Also noted for a series of salty battle-of-the-sexes comedies opposite Katharine Hepburn, with whom he was long professionally and privately associated. Died from a heart attack.
1930: *Taxi Talks. *The Strong Arm. *The Hard Guy. Up the River. 1931: Quick Millions. Six Cylinder Love. Goldie. 1932: She Wanted a Millionaire. Sky Devils. Disorderly Conduct. Young America (GB: We Humans). Society Girl. The Painted Woman. Me and My Gal (GB: Pier 13). 20,000 Years in Sing Sing. 1933: The Face in the Sky. Shanghai Madness. The Power and the Glory. The Mad Game. Man's Castle. 1934: Bottoms Up! The Show-Off. Looking for Trouble. Now I'll Tell (GB: When New York Sleeps). Marie Galante. 1935: It's a Small World. Dante's Inferno. The Murder Man. Whipsaw. Riffraff. 1936: San Francisco. Fury. Libeled Lady. 1937: They Gave Him a Gun. Captains Courageous. The Big City. Mannequin. 1938: Boys' Town. Test Pilot. 1939: Stanley and Livingstone. I Take This Woman. 1940: Northwest Passage. Edison the Man. Boom Town. 1941: Men of Boys' Town. Dr Jekyll and Mr Hyde. 1942: Woman of the Year. Tortilla Flat. Ring of Steel (narrator only). Keeper of the Flame. 1943: A Guy Named Joe. *US War Bonds Trailer. 1944: The Seventh Cross. Thirty Seconds over Tokyo. *Battle Stations (narrator only). 1945: Without Love. 1947: The Sea of Grass. Cass Timberlane. 1948: State of the Union (GB: The World and His Wife). 1949: Edward My Son. Adam's Rib. Malaya (GB: East of the Rising Sun). 1950: Father of the Bride. 1951: The People Against O'Hara. Father's Little Dividend. 1952: Pat and Mike. Plymouth Adventure. 1953: The Actress. 1954: Broken Lance. Bad Day at Black Rock. 1956: The Mountain. 1957: Desk Set (GB: His Other Woman). 1958: The Last Hurrah. The Old Man and the Sea. 1960: Inherit the Wind. 1961: The Devil

at Four O'Clock. Judgment at Nuremberg. 1962: How the West Was Won (narrator only). 1963: It's a Mad, Mad, Mad, Mad World. 1967: Guess Who's Coming to Dinner.

TRAVERS, Bill (William Lindon-Travers) 1921–

Dark, tall, taciturn British actor, quietly-spoken brother of Linden Travers. Took up acting after war service, and progressed very gradually to leading roles by 1955: studio handouts often chopped several years off his age at the time. However, after the early sixties he became much more interested in animals and nature films than commercial stardom. Married (second) to Virginia McKenna (qv) since 1957: they appeared in several wildlife movies together.

1949: Conspirator. 1950: Trio. The Wooden Horse. 1951: The Browning Version. 1952: Hindle Wakes (US: Holiday Week). It Started in Paradise. The Planter's Wife (US: Outpost in Malaya). 1953: Mantrap (US: Woman in Hiding). Street of Shadows (US: Shadow Man). The Genie. Counterspy (US: Undercover Agent). The Square Ring. 1954: Romeo and Juliet. 1955: Footsteps in the Fog. Geordie (US: Wee Geordie). 1956: Bhowani Junction. 1957: The Barretts of Wimpole Street. The Seventh Sin. The Smallest Show on Earth (US: Big Time Operators). 1958: Passionate Summer. 1959: The Bridal Path. 1960: Gorgo. 1961: Two Living One Dead. The Green Helmet. Invasion Quartet. 1965: Born Free. 1966: Duel at Diablo. 1967: The Lions Are Free (TV). 1968: A Midsummer Night's Dream. 1969: Ring of Bright Water. An Elephant Called Slowly. 1970: Boulevard du rhum (US: Rum Runner). 1971: The Lion at World's End (US: Christian the Lion). 1973: The Belstone Fox.

TRAVERS, Linden (Florence Lindon-Travers) 1913–

Florid, sharp-faced British brunette actress (occasionally blonde), sister of Bill Travers. Usually seen in vivid, brittle portrayals, often as women whose mental makeup rendered them not to be trusted.

1935: Children of the Fog. 1936: Wednesday's Luck. 1937: Brief Ecstasy. Double Alibi. The Last Adventurers. Against the Tide. Bank Holiday (US: Three on a Week-End). 1938: The Terror. Almost a Honeymoon. The Lady Van-

*ishes. 1939: The Stars Look Down. Inspector Hornleigh on Holiday. 1941: The Ghost Train. South American George. The Seventh Survivor. 1942: The Missing Million. 1946: Beware of Pity. 1947: Jassy. Master of Bankdam. 1948: No Orchids for Miss Blandish. Quartet. 1949: The Bad Lord Byron. Christopher Columbus. Don't Ever Leave Me. 1955: *The Schemer.*

TRAVOLTA, John 1954–

Black-haired American actor, dancer and singer whose rather surly and aggressive looks could break into arrogant, charismatic smiles and, coupled with his dynamic, loose-limbed dancing, made him a teenage favourite in the late 1970s, when he was nominated for an Academy Award for his performance in the abrasive *Saturday Night Fever*. His films since then have been surprisingly lukewarm performers at the box-office, but he has remained a star.

1975: The Devil's Rain. 1976: Carrie. The Boy in the Plastic Bubble (TV). 1977: Saturday Night Fever. 1978: Grease. Moment by Moment. 1980: Urban Cowboy. 1981: Blow Out. 1983: Staying Alive. Two of a Kind. 1985: Perfect. 1986: Public Enemies.

TREVOR, Claire (C. Wemlinger) 1909–

This blonde American actress with the direct stare certainly looked in films as though she had knocked about a bit (or even been knocked about a bit). Small wonder, then, that this quality saw her spending half a lifetime as molls, broads, floozies, showgirls and whores: for 25 years if there was a saloon in town, the

odds were that Claire Trevor had a hand in running it. Stayed in leading roles to her late forties. Oscar for *Key Largo*. Also Oscar-nominated in *Dead End* and *The High and the Mighty*.

1933: Life in the Raw. Jimmy and Sally. The Last Trail. The Mad Game. 1934: Hold That Girl. Baby Take a Bow. Elinore Norton. Wild Gold. 1935: Dante's Inferno. Spring Tonic. Navy Wife. Black Sheep. 1936: Human Cargo. My Marriage. The Song and Dance Man. To Mary – with Love. 15 Maiden Lane. Career Woman. Star for a Night. 1937: One Mile from Heaven. Time Out for Romance. Second Honeymoon. Big Town Girl. Dead End. King of Gamblers. 1938: The Amazing Dr Clitterhouse. Walking Down Broadway. Valley of the Giants. Two of a Kind. 1939: I Stole a Million. Stagecoach. Allegheny Uprising (GB: The First Rebel). 1940: The Dark Command. 1941: Texas. Honky Tonk. 1942: Street of Chance. The Adventures of Martin Eden. Crossroads. 1943: Woman of the Town. The Desperadoes. Good Luck, Mr Yates. 1945: Murder, My Sweet (GB: Farewell, My Lovely). Johnny Angel. 1946: Crack-Up. The Bachelor's Daughters (GB: Bachelor Girls). 1947: Born to Kill (GB: Lady of Deceit). 1948: The Velvet Touch. Raw Deal. Key Largo. The Babe Ruth Story. 1949: The Lucky Stiff. 1950: Borderline. 1951: Hard, Fast and Beautiful. Best of the Badmen. Hoodlum Empire. 1952: My Man and I. Stop, You're Killing Me. 1953: The Stranger Wore a Gun. 1954: The High and the Mighty. 1955: Man without a Star. Lucy Gallant. 1956: The Mountain. 1957: If You Knew Elizabeth (TV). 1958: Marjorie Morningstar. 1962: Two Weeks in Another Town. The Stripper (GB: Woman of Summer). 1965: How to Murder Your Wife. 1967: The Cape Town Affair. 1982: Kiss Me Goodbye.

TRINDER, Tommy 1909–

Long-chinned, slyly smiling, dark-haired (often hidden under pork-pie hat) British music-hall comedian, very popular in film comedies from 1938 to the end of the war, later equally successful as a master of ceremonies in TV variety shows. Catchphrase: 'You Lucky People.'

*1938: Almost a Honeymoon. Save a Little Sunshine. 1939: She Couldn't Say No. Laugh It Off. 1940: Sailors Three (US: Three Cockeyed Sailors). 1941: *Eating Out with Tommy.*

1942: The Foreman Went to France (US: Somewhere in France). 1943: The Bells Go Down. 1944: Fiddlers Three. Champagne Charlie. 1946: *Staggered Holidays. 1947: *Family Guide. 1950: Bitter Springs. 1955: You Lucky People. 1959: Make Mine a Million. 1964: The Beauty Jungle (US: Contest Girl). 1969: Under the Table You Must Go. 1974: Barry McKenzie Holds His Own.

TRINTIGNANT, Jean-Louis 1930–
Quiet, introspective, dark-haired, slightly fretful-looking French actor. A romantic figure in his wryly Gallic way, Trintignant, who threw up a legal career to take up acting, became a star in his first year in French films, and has since enjoyed international hits too, none more so than *Un homme et une femme*, to which he made a sequel 20 years later. He has also had some famous romances of his own, including a much-publicized liaison with Brigitte Bardot. His first wife was actress Stephane Audran (1932–), his second is director Nadine Trintignant. The son of motor-racing ace Maurice Trintignant, Jean-Louis himself escaped a 200 mph crash in the 1980 Le Mans endurance race.
1955: *Pechinef. Si tous les gars du monde (GB: Race for Life). La loi des rues. 1956: Et Dieu créa la femme (GB: And Woman … Was Created. US: And God Created Woman). Club des femmes. 1959: Les liaisons dangereuses. L'estate violente. Austerlitz (GB: The Battle of Austerlitz). La millième fenêtre. 1960: Pleins feux sur l'assassin. Le coeur battant (US: The French Game). 1961: L'Atlantide (GB: Atlantis, The Lost Continent/The Lost Kingdom.

US: Journey Beneath the Desert). Le jeu de la verité. Le combat dans l'île. Horace '62. Les sept péchés capitaux (GB: The Seven Deadly Sins. US: Seven Capital Sins). 1962: Il successo. Il sorpasso (US: The Easy Life). 1963: Château en Suède (US: Naughty, Nutty Chateau). 1964: Les pas perdus. La bonne occase. Mata Hari – Agent H 21. Angélique, Marquise des Anges (GB and US: Angélique). Io uccido, tu uccidi. 1965: *Un jour à Paris. Merveilleuse Angélique (GB: Angelique: The Road to Versailles). Compartiment tueurs (GB and US: The Sleeping Car Murder). Is Paris Burning? 1966: Meurtre à l'Italienne (US: Murder Italian Style). La longue marche. Le dix-septième ciel. Un homme et une femme (GB and US: A Man and a Woman). Safari-diamants. 1967: Trans-Europ Express. Enigma. Col cuoror al gola (US: Deadly Sweet). L'homme qui ment. Mon amour … mon amour. La morte ha fatto l'uovo (GB: A Curious Way to Love. US: Plucked). *Fragilité ton nom est femme. Les biches (US: The Does). 1968: La matriarcha (US: The Libertine). Il grande silenzio. Le voleur des crimes. 1969: Z. Ma nuit chez Maud (GB: My Night with Maud. US: My Night at Maud's). Metti una sera a cena (US: The Love Circle). Cosi dolce, cosi perversa/So Sweet … So Perverse. L'Américain. Il conformista (GB and US: The Conformist). Las secretas intenciones. L'opium et le baton. 1970: Le voyou (GB: Simon the Swiss. US: The Crook/The Criminal). Par le sang versé. Le bâteau. 1971: La course du lièvre à travers les champs (GB and US: And Hope to Die). Sans mobile apparent (GB and US: Without Apparent Motive). 1972: L'homme aux cerveaux greffés. L'attentat (GB: Plot. US: The French Conspiracy). Un homme est mort (GB and US: The Outside Man). 1973: †Une journée bien remplie (GB: TV, as A Full Day's Work). Defense de savoir (US: Forbidden to Know). Le train. 1974: Les violons du bal. Glissements progressifs du plaisir. Le mouton enragé (GB: The French Way. US: Love at the Top). Le secret. L'escapade. Le jeu avec le feu (US: Playing with Fire). 1975: La donna della domenica. L'agression. Flic Story. Il pleut sur Santiago. Le voyage de noces. 1976‛ L'ordinateur des pompes funèbres. Le desert des Tartares. Les passagers (GB: Shattered). 1977: Repérages (US: Faces of Love). L'affaire. 1978: †Le maître-nageur (GB and US: The Lifeguard). L'argent des autres. 1979: Melancholy Baby. La terrazza. 1980: La banquière. Je vous aime. Malville/Malevil. 1981: Un assassin qui passe. Passione d'amore. Une affaire d'homme. Eaux profondes. Le gran pardon. Boulevard des assassins. La nuit de Varennes. 1982: Colpire al cuore. Under Fire. Meurtres sous protection. 1983: Vivement dimanche (GB: Finally Sunday! US: The Long Saturday Night). Le bon plaisir. La crime (US: Cover-Up). Credo (TV). 1984: Femmes de personne. Viva la vie. 1985: Partir, revenir. David, Thomas, et les autres. Rendezvous. L'homme aux yeux d'argent. 1986: Vingt ans déjà (Un homme et une femme II).

† And directed

TRYON, Tom 1925–
Tall, brooding American leading man, a handsomer version of John Travolta. Boosted as a new star in his first film (at 31, after an eventful early life), he played rugged roles in westerns and other action films, but was a little too unbending for top stardom. In any case he didn't need it, forsaking acting to become the best-selling author of epic novels, a couple of which have been filmed.
1956: The Scarlet Hour. Screaming Eagles. Three Violent People. 1957: The Unholy Wife. Young Man from Kentucky (TV. GB: cinemas). Charley's Aunt (TV). 1958: I Married a Monster from Outer Space. Texas John Slaughter (TV. GB: cinemas). 1959: Gunfight at Sandoval (TV. GB: cinemas). 1960: Geronimo's Revenge (TV. GB: cinemas). The Story of Ruth. 1961: Showdown at Bitter Creek (TV. GB: cinemas). Marines, Let's Go. 1962: Moon Pilot. The Longest Day. 1963: The Cardinal. 1965: In Harm's Way. The Glory Guys. 1967: The Narco Men. Winchester '73 (TV). 1969: Color Me Dead.

TUCKER, Forrest 1915–
Very tall, rugged American actor with pugnacious good looks and wavy blond hair, persuaded to try his luck in films in 1940 while on holiday in California. He started well but war service came along, and his career never quite retained its drive thereafter, although he remained in leading roles until the late fifties.
1940: The Westerner. The Howards of Virginia (GB: The Tree of Liberty). 1941: Emergency Landing. New Wine. Honolulu Lu. Canal Zone. Camp Nuts. 1942: Tramp, Tramp, Tramp.

Shut My Big Mouth. Parachute Nurse. The
Spirit of Stanford. Keeper of the Flame. Boston
Blackie Goes Hollywood (GB: Blackie Goes
Hollywood). My Sister Eileen. Submarine
Raider. Counter Espionage. 1946: The Man
Who Dared. Talk about a Lady. Renegades.
Dangerous Business. Never Say Goodbye. The
Yearling. 1947: Gunfighters (GB: The
Assassin). 1948: Adventures in Silverado (GB:
Above All Laws). The Plunderers. Montana
Belle (released 1952). Coroner Creek. Two
Guys from Texas (GB: Two Texas Knights).
1949: The Big Cat. Brimstone. The Last
Bandit. Sands of Iwo Jima. Hellfire. 1950: The
Nevadan (GB: The Man from Nevada). Rock
Island Trail (GB: Transcontinent Express).
California Passage. 1951: Fighting Coast
Guard. O, Susanna. Crosswinds. Hoodlum
Empire. The Wild Blue Yonder (GB: Thunder
Across the Pacific). Flaming Feather. Warpath.
1952: Bugles in the Afternoon. Hurricane
Smith. Ride the Man Down. 1953: Pony
Express. San Antone. Flight Nurse. 1954: Jubi-
lee Trail. Laughing Anne. Trouble in the Glen.
1955: Rage at Dawn. Finger Man. The Van-
ishing American. Night Freight. Break in the
Circle. Paris Follies of 1956. 1956: Stagecoach
to Fury. Three Violent People. The Quiet Gun.
1957: The Deerslayer. The Abominable Snow-
man. Girl in the Woods. 1958: The Strange
World of Planet X (US: Cosmic Monsters).
The Trollenberg Terror (US: The Crawling
Eye). Auntie Mame. Gunsmoke in Tucson. Fort
Massacre. 1959: Counterplot. 1966: Don't
Worry, We'll Think of a Title. 1968: The Silent
Treatment. The Night They Raided Minsky's.
1969: Barquero. 1970: Chisum. 1971: Welcome
Home, Johnny Bristol (TV). 1972: Footsteps
(TV). The Incredible Rocky Mountain Race
(TV). Cancel My Reservation. 1973: Jarrett
(TV). 1975: The Wild McCullochs. 1976: The
Wackiest Wagon Train in the West. 1977: Final
Chapter Walking Tall. 1978: The Adventures
of Huckleberry Finn (TV). A Real American
Hero (TV). 1981: Carnauba. 1983: Blood
Feud (TV). 1985: Thunder Run. Outtakes.

TUFTS, Sonny (Bowen Tufts III) 1911–
1970
Strapping blond American actor and light
singer, a success at Paramount in the war
years. His high-spirited, hell-raising, heavy-
drinking lifestyle put an end to his marriage
and, after 1950, his career, although there

were periodic comeback roles in the best of
which (Gift Horse, Come Next Spring) he was
almost back to his old, likeably buoyant self.
Died from pneumonia.
1939: Ambush. 1943: So Proudly We Hail!
Government Girl. 1944: I Love a Soldier. Here
Come the Waves. In the Meantime, Darling.
Miss Susie Slagle's (released 1946). 1945:
Bring on the Girls. Duffy's Tavern. 1946: The
Virginian. The Well-Groomed Bride. Swell
Guy. 1947: Easy Come, Easy Go. Variety Girl.
Blaze of Noon. Cross My Heart. 1948: The
Untamed Breed. 1949: The Crooked Way. Easy
Living. 1950: *Hollywood Goes to Bat. 1952:
Gift Horse (US: Glory at Sea). 1953: No
Escape. Run for the Hills. Cat Women of the
Moon. 1954: Serpent Island. 1955: The Seven
Year Itch. 1956: Come Next Spring. *Hol-
lywood Goes a-Fishing. 1957: The Parson and
the Outlaw. 1965: Town Tamer. 1967: Cotton-
pickin' Chickenpickers.

TURNER, Kathleen 1956–
Tall, tawny-haired, smooth-moving American actress with purring voice and challenging eyes, slightly reminiscent of Lauren
Bacall. Although physically no great beauty,
she was often cast in steamy roles calling for
great erotic charge. She was more than
adequate at supplying that, although she has
also been very effective in frenetic comedy
roles. Currently one of Hollywood's hottest
female leads.
1982: Body Heat. 1983: The Man with Two
Brains. 1984: Romancing the Stone. A Breed
Apart. Crimes of Passion/China Blue. 1985:
Prizzi's Honor. The Jewel of the Nile. 1986:
Peggy Sue Got Married.

TURNER, Lana (Julia 'Judy' Turner)
1920–
Blonde (originally auburn) American actress
and sex symbol, dubbed 'The Sweater Girl'
and later a shimmering platinum queen of
melodrama, who lived the film star image to
the hilt and has been married seven times,
including (fourth) Lex Barker from 1953 to
1957. Weathered various unpalatable headline
stories to extend her star run to 25 years.
Oscar-nominated for Peyton Place.
1937: A Star is Born. Topper. The Great Garrick. They Won't Forget. 1938: †The Chaser.
Four's a Crowd. The Adventures of Marco Polo.
Dramatic School. Love Finds Andy Hardy.

Rich Man, Poor Girl. 1939: Dancing Co-Ed
(GB: Every Other Inch a Lady). Calling Dr
Kildare. These Glamour Girls. 1940: Two Girls
on Broadway (GB: Change Your Partners).
We Who Are Young. 1941: Dr Jekyll and
My Hyde. Ziegfeld Girl. Johnny Eager. Honky
Tonk. 1942: Somewhere I'll Find You. 1943:
*Show Business At War. Slightly Dangerous.
DuBarry Was a Lady. The Youngest
Profession. 1944: Marriage is a Private Affair.
1945: Weekend at the Waldorf. Keep Your
Powder Dry. 1946: The Postman Always Rings
Twice. 1947: Green Dolphin Street. Cass Tim-
berlane. 1948: Homecoming. The Three Mus-
keteers. 1950: A Life of Her Own. Mr Imperium
(GB: You Belong to My Heart). 1952: The
Merry Widow. The Bad and the Beautiful.
1953: Latin Lovers. 1954: Flame and the Flesh.
Betrayed. 1955: The Prodigal. The Sea Chase.
Diane. The Rains of Ranchipur. 1957: Peyton
Place. 1958: The Lady Takes a Flyer. Another
Time, Another Place. 1959: Imitation of Life.
1960: Portrait in Black. 1961: Bachelor in
Paradise. By Love Possessed. 1962: Who's Got
the Action? 1964: Love Has Many Faces. 1966:
Madame X. 1969: The Big Cube. 1974: Per-
secution. 1976: Bittersweet Love. 1978: Wit-
ches' Brew (released 1985).

† Most scenes deleted from final release print

TUSHINGHAM, Rita 1940–
Dark-haired, big-eyed, waif-like British
actress with appealing 'ugly duckling' looks.
Has given several very affecting performances,
if her output has been a little disappointing –
only just over one film a year. Took a British
Academy Award for her very first film role.

1961: A Taste of Honey. 1963: The Leather Boys. A Place to Go. Girl with Green Eyes. 1965: The Knack ... and how to get it. Doctor Zhivago. 1966: The Trap. 1967: Smashing Time. 1968: Diamonds for Breakfast. The Guru. 1969: The Bed Sitting Room. 1972: Straight on Till Morning. The Case of Laura C. Where Do You Go from Here? 1974: Instant Coffee. 1975: Rachel's Man. The 'Human' Factor. Ragazzo di borgata. 1976: The Search for Green Eyes (TV). 1977: Slaughter Day. Gran bollito. 1978: Sotto choc. Mysteries/Knut Hamsum's Mysteries. 1982: Spaghetti House. 1985: Flying. 1986: A Judgement in Stone.

TWELVETREES, Helen (nee Jurgens)
1907–1958

This blonde American weepie queen of the Depression era with the swooping pencilled eyebrows never looked far from tears. In films she played fallen women and long-suffering girlfriends. Millions wept with her through

the early 1930s, but the popularity of her image faded with more prosperous times and she was out of films by the end of the decade. Her personal life had its traumas too: her first husband, an alcoholic, died young, and there

were violent repercussions to the break-up of her second marriage. Her third seemed happy enough and she played the lead in *A Streetcar Named Desire* on stage in the early 1950s. But in February 1958 she died from an overdose of sleeping pills at the age of 50.

1929: The Ghost Talks. Blue Skies. Words and Music. 1930: The Grand Parade. The Cat Creeps. Swing High. Her Man. 1931: The Painted Desert. A Woman of Experience. Millie. Bad Company. 1932: Young Bride. Panama Flo. State's Attorney (GB: Cardigan's Last Case). Is My Face Red? Unashamed. 1933: A Bedtime Story. Disgraced! My Woman. King for a Night. 1934: All Men Are Enemies. Now I'll Tell (GB: When New York Sleeps). She Was a Lady. One Hour Late. 1935: Times Square Lady. She Gets Her Man. The Spanish Cape Mystery. Frisco Waterfront (GB: When We Look Back). 1936: Thoroughbred. 1937: Hollywood Round-Up. 1939: Persons in Hiding. Unmarried (GB: Night Club Waitress).

ULLMANN, Liv 1939–

Sandy-haired, Japan-born, Norwegian-raised star actress whose strained expression seems made for anguish. All her best roles have so far been for director Ingmar Bergman (with whom she was associated for many years, and by whom she has a child). Her international ventures have been sad misfires, and one doubts that she will try Hollywood again after such daunting failures. Received Academy Award nominations for *The Emigrants* and *Face to Face*.

*1957: Fjols til Fjells. 1959: Ung Flukt (GB: The Wayward Girl). 1962: Tonny. Kort är Sommaren. 1965: De Kalte Ham Skarven. 1966: Persona. 1968: Skammen/The Shame. Vargtimmen/Hour of the Wolf. 1969: An-Magritt. En Passion/A Passion (US: The Passion of Anna). Cold Sweat. 1971: The Night Visitor. The Emigrants. 1972: Pope Joan. The New Land. Cries and Whispers. 1973: *Foto: Sven Nykvist. Lost Horizon. Forty Carats. 1974: Scenes from a Marriage (TV). The Abdication. Zandy's Bride. 1975: Face to Face. 1976: Leonor. 1977: The Serpent's Egg. A Bridge Too Far. 1978: Autumn Sonata. Couleur chair. 1979: Players. 1980: The Gates of the Forest. 1981: Richard's Things (TV). 1983: The Wild Duck. Jacobo Timmerman/Prisoner Without a Name, Cell Without a Number (TV). 1984: The Bay Boy (TV). 1985: La diagonale du fou (US: Dangerous Moves). 1986: Let's Hope It's a Girl.*

UNDERDOWN, Edward 1908–

Tall, erect, stick-like British actor who also pursued a successful career as a steeplechase jockey. Came to prominence in films when in his 40s, but his dour mien and diffident acting style (and some dull roles) pushed him back down the cast list. Subsequently, he was often seen in quite small roles.

1934: The Warren Case. Girls Please! 1935: Annie, Leave the Room! 1937: Wings of the Morning. 1938: The Drum (US: Drums). Inspector Hornleigh. 1940: Inspector Hornleigh Goes To It (US: Mail Train). 1947: The October Man. The Woman in the Hall. 1948: The Brass Monkey/Lucky Mascot. 1949: Man on the Run. 1950: They Were Not Divided. The Woman with No Name (US: Her Panelled Door). 1951: The Dark Man. The Woman's Angle. 1952: The Voice of Merrill (US: Murder Will Out). 1953: Street of Shadows (US: Shadow Man). Recoil. Beat the Devil. 1954: The Rainbow Jacket. 1958: The Camp on Blood Island. The Two-Headed Spy. Heart of a Child. 1961: The Day the Earth Caught Fire. The Third Alibi. Information Received. 1962: Locker 69. Dr Crippen. 1963: The Bay of Saint Michel (US: Pattern for Plunder). Man in the Middle. Woman of Straw. 1964: Dr Terror's House of Horrors. Traitor's Gate. 1965: Thunderball. 1966: Khartoum. The Hand of Night. 1968: The Great Pony Raid. 1969: The Magic Christian. 1971: The Last Valley. 1972: Running Scared. 1973: Digby – the Biggest Dog in the World. 1974: The Abdication. 1978: Tarka the Otter.

URE, Mary 1933–1975

Slim, cool, sleek, blonde Scottish-born actress who was acting at 17 and on the London stage at 21. The major part of her career, in fact, was for the theatre, although the cinema was lucky enough to get her in the occasional leading role, often in projects which involved her first husband, playwright John Osborne, or her second (married 1963), film actor Robert Shaw (*qv*). She died tragically, from an accidental mixture of champagne and barbiturates, after celebrating her successful opening in a new play.

1955: Storm Over the Nile. 1957: Windom's Way. 1959: Look Back in Anger. 1960: Sons and Lovers. 1962: The Mind Benders. 1964: The Luck of Ginger Coffey. 1966: Custer of the West. 1968: Where Eagles Dare. 1973: A Reflection of Fear.

URQUHART, Robert 1922–

Fresh-faced, dark-haired, frail-looking Scottish actor. Briefly popular in leading roles in the British cinema around 1953–1958, but seemed to age quickly. Perhaps it was being nearly throttled by the Frankenstein monster that did it.

*1952: You're Only Young Twice. Tread Softly (US: Tread Softly, Stranger). Paul Temple Returns. 1953: The House of the Arrow. Isn't Life Wonderful! 1954: Happy Ever After (US: Tonight's The Night/O'Leary Night). Knights of the Round Table. Golden Ivory (US: White Huntress). 1955: The Dark Avenger (US: The Warriors). You Can't Escape. 1956: The Curse of Frankenstein. 1957: Yangtse Incident (US: Battle Hell). 1958: Dunkirk. 1960: Trouble with Eve. Foxhole in Cairo. Danger Tomorrow. Murder in Mind. The Bulldog Breed. 1962: The Break. 55 Days at Peking. 1963: Murder at the Gallop. 1968: The Syndicate. The Limbo Line. Mosquito Squadron. 1969: The Looking Glass War. Country Dance (US: Brotherly Love). 1980: The Dogs of War. 1981: A Tale of Two Cities (TV). *The Dollar Bottom. 1982: P'Tang Yang Kipperbang (TV. Later shown in cinemas.) 1984: Sharma and Beyond (TV). 1985: Restless Natives. Hitler's SS: Portrait in Evil (TV. GB: cinemas).*

USTINOV, Peter 1921–

Heavily-built, shambling British actor-writer-director-raconteur with mop of hair and mellifluous, drawling voice, a treasured after-dinner speaker and sometimes hilarious supporting player in his own films. Something of a juvenile prodigy, he wrote his first screen-

play at 23 and directed his first film at 25. Two Academy Awards as best supporting actor – for *Spartacus* and *Topkapi*. Also nominated for an Oscar in *Quo Vadis?*

*1940: Hullo Fame! Mein Kampf, My Crimes. 1942: The Goose Steps Out. One of Our Aircraft is Missing. 1944: The Way Ahead (US: Dig That Juliet). 1949: Private Angelo. 1950: Odette. 1951: Hotel Sahara. The Magic Box. Quo Vadis? 1954: Beau Brummell. The Egyptian. We're No Angels. 1955: I girovaghi/The Wanderers. Lola Montès. 1957: Les espions. Un angelo è sceso a Brooklyn/The Man Who Wagged His Tail. 1959: Adventures of Mr Wonderbird (voice only). 1960: Spartacus. The Sundowners. 1961: Romanoff and Juliet (US: Immortal Battalion). 1962: Billy Budd. 1964: *The Peaches (narrator only). John Goldfarb, Please Come Home. Topkapi. 1965: Lady L. 1967: The Comedians. Blackbeard's Ghost. 1968: Hot Millions. 1970: Viva Max! A Storm in Summer (TV). 1972: Hammersmith is Out. Big Mack and Poor Clare. 1973: Robin Hood (voice only). 1975: One of Our Dinosaurs is Missing. 1976: Logan's Run. Treasure of Mate-*

cumbe. 1977: Doppio delitto/Double Murders. Taxi mauve/Purple Taxi. The Last Remake of Beau Geste. The Mouse and His Child (voice only). 1978: The Thief of Bagdad. Death on the Nile. Tarka the Otter (narrator only). 1979: Ashanti. Players. Winds of Change (narrator only). 1980: Charlie Chan and the Curse of the Dragon Queen. Short Cut to Haifa. 1981: Grendel Grendel Grendel (voice only). The Great Muppet Caper. Evil Under the Sun. 1983: Memed My Hawk. 1985: Thirteen at Dinner (TV). 1986: Dead Man's Folly.

As director:

1946: School for Secrets (US: Secret Flight). 1947: Vice Versa. 1949: Private Angelo (co-directed). 1961: Romanoff and Juliet (US: Dig That Juliet). 1962: Billy Budd. 1965: Lady L. 1972: Hammersmith is Out. 1983: Memed My Hawk.

Very cold-looking shot, as Brenda Vaccaro and Jon Voight keep warm with furs, in this scene from 1969's *Midnight Cowboy*.

Frequent co-stars Jean Wallace and Cornel Wilde had little trouble putting passion into their love scenes. They were (and still are) man and wife in real life.

. . . as were Natalie Wood and Robert Wagner. Twice over, in fact, since they divorced and then remarried before her early death. Here they are together in *The Affair* (1973).

VACCARO, Brenda 1939–

Dark-haired, chubby-faced, personable American actress with throaty voice, mostly in toughly independent roles, but hot on the wisecracks when needed. She was acting busily on TV from the early 1960s; Hollywood obviously missed out on a good thing (and anyone who can get nominated for an Oscar from a film like *Once is Not Enough* has to be a class act), before John Schlesinger found her for *Midnight Cowboy*. Although she has not become a box-office star, she can often be an oasis of talent amid scriptual wastes.
1969: Midnight Cowboy. Where It's At. 1970: I Love My Wife. Travis Logan DA (TV). 1971: Summertree. What's a Nice Girl Like You...? (TV). Going Home. 1973: Honor Thy Father (TV. GB: cinemas). Sunshine (TV. GB: cinemas). 1974: Once is Not Enough/Jacqueline Susann's Once is Not Enough. 1976: The House by the Lake (GB and US: Death Weekend). 1977: Airport 77. Capricorn One. 1978: Fast Charlie ... the Moonbeam Rider. 1979: Dear Detective (TV). 1980: Oh, God! Oh, God! The First Deadly Sin. Guyana Tragedy: The Story of Jim Jones (TV). 1981: Chanel Solitaire. A Long Way Home (TV). Zorro the Gay Blade. The Pride of Jesse Hallam (TV). 1984: Supergirl. 1985: Water. Deceptions (TV). 1986: The White Stallion.

VALENTINO, Rudolph (Rodolpho di Valentino d'Antonguolla) 1895–1926

Dark-eyed Italian dancer and actor with slicked-back dark hair who became the great lover of Hollywood's silent screen and the idol of worshipping female millions. He played mysterious, dominant men, usually from other, far-flung parts of the world, who swept the heroine off to their tent/temple/palace. He died from peritonitis brought on by a perforated ulcer and was mourned by vast crowds amid a lying-in-state.
1914: My Official Wife. 1916: Patria. Isle of Love. Ambition. 1918: Alimony. All Night. A Society Sensation (GB: The Little Duchess). 1919: The Delicious Little Devil. A Rogue's Romance. The Homebreaker. The Big Little Person. Out of Luck. Virtuous Sinners. Eyes of Youth (GB: The Love of Sunya). 1920: The Cheater. The Married Virgin (later Frivolous Wives). Once to Every Woman. Passion's Playground. An Adventuress (later The Isle of Love). Stolen Moments. The Wonderful Chance. 1921: The Conquering Power. The Four Horsemen of the Apocalypse. Uncharted Seas. Camille. The Sheik. 1922: Moran of the Lady Letty. Beyond the Rocks. Blood and Sand. The Young Rajah. 1924: Monsieur Beaucaire. A Sainted Devil. 1925: Cobra. The Eagle. 1926: Son of the Sheik.

VALLEE, Rudy (Hubert Vallee) 1901–86

Before Presley there was Sinatra; before Sinatra there was Crosby; and before Crosby there was Rudy Vallee – and his megaphone. With round face, brown hair parted just left of centre and appealing blue eyes, Vallee was the crooning idol of thousands of flappers as he led his band, the Connecticut Yankees, through the jazz era. In the late thirties he became a useful comic character actor, usually as the ineffectual suitor who didn't get the girl. Married Jane Greer (second of three) 1943–1945.
1929: *Radio Rhythm. *Rudy Vallee and his Connecticut Yankees. Vagabond Lover. Glorifying the American Girl. 1930: *Campus Sweethearts. 1931: *Musical Justice. 1932: *Rudy Vallee Melodies. 1933: International House. George White's Scandals of 1934. 1935: Sweet Music. *A Trip thru a Hollywood Studio. 1938: *For Auld Lang Syne. Gold Diggers in Paris (GB: The Gay Imposters). 1939: Second Fiddle. 1941: Time Out for Rhythm. Too Many Blondes. 1942: The Palm Beach Story. 1943: Happy Go Lucky. 1944: It's in the Bag! 1945: Man Alive. 1946: People Are Funny. The Fabulous Suzanne. The Sin of Harold Diddlebock (later/(GB: Mad Wednesday). 1947: The Bachelor and the Bobby-Soxer (GB: Bachelor Knight). 1948: I Remember Mama. So This is New York. My Dear Secretary. Unfaithfully Yours. 1949: Mother is a Freshman (GB: Mother Knows Best). The Beautiful Blonde from Bashful Bend. Father Was a Fullback. 1950: The Admiral was a Lady. 1954: Ricochet Romance. 1955: Gentlemen Marry Brunettes. 1957: The Helen Morgan Story (GB: Both Ends of the Candle). 1967: How to Succeed in Business Without Really Trying. The Night They Raided Minsky's (narrator only). 1968: The Silent Treatment. Live a Little, Love a Little. 1969: The Phynx. 1974: Sunburst. 1975: Won Ton Ton, the Dog Who Saved Hollywood.

VALLI, Alida (A. Altenburger) 1921–

It's hard to reconcile the Valli (as she was known in her English-speaking films of the forties and fifties) of today – the hardened, square face looks type-cast for a prison governess and indeed is usually seen in severe roles – with the lovely, soulful, shiningly dark-haired creature of *The Third Man*. How green was our Valli then. Still, the facial structure was always there, emphasizing the enigma of *The Paradine Case*, too, and at least this talented and gentle Italian actress has kept very busy, even if in decreasingly worthwhile roles.
1935: Il capello a tre punte. 1936: I due sergenti. 1937: Il feroce Saladino. L'ultima nemica. Sono stato io! 1938: Ma l'amor mio non muore. L'ha fatto una signore. La casa del peccato. Mille lire al mese. 1939: Assenza ingiustificata. Manon Lescaut. Ballo al castello. Taverna rossa/The

Red Inn. 1940: Oltre l'amore. La prima donna che passa. Piccolo mondo antico. Luce nelle tenebre. 1941: L'amante segreta. Ore nove lezione di chimica. 1942: Catene invisibili. Noi vivi. Addio Kira! Le due orfanelle. I Pagliacci. Stasera niente di nuovo. 1943: Apparizione. T'amero' sempre. 1945: Circo equestre za bum. La vita ricomincia (US: Life Begins Anew). Giovanna. Il canto della vita. 1946: La vita continua. Eugénie Grandet. 1947: †The Paradine Case. 1948: †The Miracle of the Bells. 1949: †The Third Man. Les miracles n'ont lieu qu'une fois. 1950: Ultimo incontro. †Walk Softly Stranger. †The White Tower. 1952: †The Lovers of Toledo. 1953: Siamo donne (GB and US: We the Women). Senso (GB and US: The Wanton Countess). Il mondo le condanna. 1954: †The Stranger's Hand. 1957: Les bijoutiers du clair de lune (GB: Heaven Fell That Night. US: The Night Heaven Fell). Il grido. La grande strada azzurra. 1958: †This Angry Age (GB: The Sea Wall). Tal Vez. L'uomo dai Calzoni Corti. 1959: L'assegno. Le dialogue des Carmélites. Arsène Lupin et la toison d'or. Les yeux sans visage/Eyes without a Face. 1960: Le gigolo. Treno di natale. 1961: Il peccato degli Anni Verdi. Une aussi longue absence. 1962: The Happy Thieves. La fille du torrent. Homenaje a la Hora de la Siesta/Four Women for One Hero. Al otro lado de la ciudad. Il disordine (GB: Disorder). The Castilian. Ophélia. 1963: El Hombre de Papel. 1964: L'autre femme. 1965: Umorismo nero. 1967: Oedipus Rex. 1970: Le champignon. The Spider's Strategem (TV. GB and US: cinemas). 1971: Concerto per pistola solista. L'occhio nel labirinto (GB: Blood). 1972: La prima notte di quiete. Diario di un Italiano. 1974: Tendre Dracula. No es nada Mama, solo un Juego. La chair de l'orchidée. 1975: House of Exorcism (US: Lisa and the Devil). Ce cher Victor (US: Cher Victor). Il caso Raoul. 1976: The Antichrist (GB: The Tempter). Suspiria. Le jeu de solitaire. 1900. The Cassandra Crossing. 1977: Berlinguer, ti voglio bene. Cuore semplice. 1978: Zoo/Zéro. 1979: Porco momdo. La Luna. Suor omicida (GB: The Killer Nun). 1980: Inferno. Aquella casa en las Afueras. Puppenspiel mit toten Augen. 1981: La caduta degli angeli ribelli. 1985: Segreti, segreti.

†As Valli

VALLONE, Raf 1916–
Good-natured, dark-haired, thick-set Italian actor, persuaded to give up a career as a

reporter in the late forties in favour of acting. Usually seen in sweaty, earthy roles, he got his best parts in the late fifties and early sixties. After this he went international, only to be handed increasingly silly assignments from which he has not re-emerged as the powerful actor he can be.

1948: Bitter Rice/Riso amaro. 1949: Non c'è pace fra gli ulvi. Vendetta. 1950: Cuori senza frontiere. Il cammino della speranza. Il bivio. 1951: Anna. Cristo proibito. 1952: Camicie rosa. Roma ore 11. Mandrin. Carne inquieta/Restless. Uomini senza pace. Gli eroi della Domenica. Perdonami. 1953: Domanda di grazia. Los Ojos dejan Huellas. Delirio. La spiaggia. Thérèse Raquin. 1954: Human Torpedoes. Destinies. The Sign of Venus. 1955: Uragano sul Po. Andrea Chenier. Obsession. Siluri umani. 1956: Les possédés. Le secret de Soeur Angèle. Liebe. Guendalina. 1957: Rose Bernd. 1958: La venganza. Le piège. La violetera. 1960: Recours en grâce. La garçonnière. 1961: Two Women/La ciociara. El Cid. Phaedra. A View from the Bridge. 1963: The Cardinal. 1964: The Secret Invasion. Una voglia da morire. La scoperta dell' America. 1965: Harlow. 1966: Nevada Smith. Volver a vivir. Kiss the Girls and Make Them Die. 1968: The Desperate Ones. 1969: The Italian Job. The Kremlin Letter. 1970: La morte risale a ieri sera. Cannon for Cordoba. A Gunfight. 1971: Summertime Killer. Perchè non ci lasciate in pace?/Why Don't You Leave Us in Peace?La villa. 1973: Honor Thy Father (TV. GB: cinemas). Small Miracle (TV). Catholics (TV). Grazie, amore mio. 1974: Rosebud. L'histoire de l'oeil. 1975: That Lucky Touch. The 'Human' Factor. 1977: The Other Side of Midnight. The Devil's Advocate. 1978: The Greek Tycoon. 1979: Retour à Marseille. An Almost Perfect Affair. 1980: Seven Graves for Rogan. Lion of the Desert/Omar Mukhtar Lion of the Desert. 1985: Power of Evil/Le pouvoir du mal.

VAN CLEEF, Lee 1925–
Lean, mean-looking, dark-haired, narrow-eyed American actor of faintly oriental aspect, almost entirely confined to westerns. Spent more than a decade as ugly villains (with the occasional Red Indian thrown in) with itchy trigger fingers. Then lost his hair, grew a moustache, and pleasantly surprised us all by becoming a star of spaghetti westerns in the wake of Clint Eastwood. Still around, as ruthless as ever on either side of the law.

1950: The Showdown. 1952: Untamed Frontier. High Noon. Kansas City Confidential (GB: The Secret Four). The Lawless Breed. 1953: Arena. The Bandits of Corsica (GB: The Return of the Corsican Brothers). Tumbleweed. The Beast from 20,000 Fathoms. Vice Squad (GB: The Girl in Room 17). The Nebraskan. Private Eyes. White Lightning. Jack Slade (GB: Slade). 1954: Arrow in the Dust. Gypsy Colt. Dawn at Socorro. Princess of the Nile. The Desperado. The Yellow Tomahawk. Rails into Laramie. 1955: Ten Wanted Men. I Cover the Underworld. Man without a Star. The Naked Street. The Road to Denver. The Big Combo. The Vanishing American. A Man Alone. The Treasure of Ruby Hills. The Kentuckian. 1956: The Conqueror. Tribute to a Bad Man. Red Sundown. Pardners. Accused of Murder. It Conquered the World. Backlash. The Quiet Gun. Gunfight at the OK Corral. 1957: Last Stagecoach West. The Lonely Man. Joe Dakota. Gun Battle at Monterey. The Badge of Marshal Brennan. The Tin Star. 1958: Raiders of Old California. China Gate. The Bravados. Day of the Bad Man. Machete. The Young Lions. 1959: Ride Lonesome. Guns, Girls and Gangsters. 1961: Posse from Hell. 1962: The Man Who Shot Liberty Valance. How the West Was Won. 1965: For a Few Dollars More. 1966: Call to Glory. The Good, the Bad and the Ugly. 1967: The Big Gundown. Death Rides a Horse. Day of Anger. 1968: Above the Law. Commandos (US: Sullivan's Marauders). Die letzte Rechnung zählst du selbst. Der Tod ritt Dienstags. A Mercenary for Any War. 1969: Sabata! A Professional Gun. Creed of Violence. Bite the Dust. Barquero. 1970: El Condor. 1971: Captain Apache. Bad Man's River. Return of Sabata. 1972: The Grand Duel. The Magnificent Seven Ride! Drei Vaterunser für vier Halunken. 1973: The Gun. Mean Frank and Crazy Tony. 1974: Blood Money. 1975: Take a Hard Ride. Power Kill. The Stranger and the Gunfighter. Power Boss. 1976: Vendetta. Dio sei proprio un padveterno/Gangster Story. 1977: The Perfect Killer. Nowhere to Hide. Kid Vengeance. 1978: The Big Rip-Off (US: The Squeeze). 1979: The Hard Way (TV). 1980: The Octagon. Trieste File. 1981: Escape from New York. 1984: Codename Wildgeese. 1985: Captain Yankee and the Jungle Raiders. 1986: Killing Machine (made 1983). The Jade Jungle.

VAN DOREN, Mamie (Joan Olander) 1932–
Petite, voluptuous platinum blonde American actress with moon-shaped face and come-hither dark eyes. She failed in her first attempt to break into films, as a teenager, then, after she had become a dance band vocalist, Universal signed her up, but never did more than make her the sex-bomb of the double-feature, a niche in which she found herself stuck. Later followed Jayne Mansfield's route by taking her clothes off in one of producer-star Tommy Noonan's exploitation comedies. Made a surprise comeback to acting in the 1980s.
1950: †Jet Pilot (released 1957). 1951: †His Kind of Woman. 1953: Forbidden. The All-

American (GB: The Winning Way). 1954: Yankee Pasha. Francis Joins the WACs. 1955: Ain't Misbehavin. The Second Greatest Sex. Running Wild. 1956: Star in the Dust. 1957: Untamed Youth. The Girl in Black Stockings. 1958: High School Confidential. Teacher's Pet. Guns, Girls and Gangsters. Le bellissime gambe di Sabrina. 1959: Born Reckless. The Beat Generation. Girls' Town. The Big Operator. 1960: Vice Raid. The Beauty and the Robot. College Confidential. Sex Kittens Go to College. The Private Lives of Adam and Eve. 1964: The Sheriff Was a Lady/Freddy und das Lied der Prairie. Three Nuts in Search of a Bolt. 1965: The Navy vs. the Night Monsters (GB: Monsters of the Night). 1966: Women of the Prehistoric Planet/Voyage to the Planet of Prehistoric Women. Las Vegas Hillbillies. 1967: You've Got to be Smart. 1985: The Tomb. 1986: Boarding School (later Free Ride).

† *as Joan Olander*

VAN DYKE, Dick 1925–
Long-jawed, gangling, widely-smiling, fair-haired American funny-man of great visual comic talents. His television show was enormously popular from 1961 to 1966; the brightest of the films that sprang from it were those that appealed to juvenile audiences. His much-publicized but finally triumphant battle with alcohol may have damaged his career in the seventies, when he seemed to feel the need to prove his worth as a serious actor.
1963: Bye Bye Birdie. 1964: What a Way to Go! Mary Poppins. 1965: The Art of Love. 1966: Lt Robin Crusoe USN. 1967: Divorce American Style. Fitzwilly (GB: Fitzwilly

Strikes Back). Never a Dull Moment. 1968: Chitty Chitty Bang Bang. 1969: The Comic. 1970: Some Kind of Nut. 1971: Cold Turkey. 1974: The Morning After (TV). 1977: Tubby the Tuba (TV. Voice only). 1979: The Runner Stumbles. 1982: Dropout Father (TV). 1983: Found Money (TV).

VAN EYCK, Peter (Götz von Eyck) 1911–1969
If there had been a competition for the title 'The Devil's Imp', German-born Van Eyck would almost certainly have won. Very blond, brown-eyed, square-faced and Teutonic looking, he went to America in the mid-thirties as a musician, but his features so eminently qualified him for playing Nazis that it was not surprising he broke into Hollywood films in the early forties. In post-war years he was busy in America, Germany and Britain, without ever becoming a star, usually as a cold-eyed, tight-lipped but plausible menace.
1942: The Moon is Down. 1943: Edge of Darkness. Action in the North Atlantic. Hitler's Children. Five Graves to Cairo. 1944: Address Unknown. The Imposter. The Hitler Gang. 1949: Hello, Fräulein. 1950: Opfer des Herzens. Export in Blond. Königskinder. Epilog. Furioso. 1951: The Desert Fox (GB: Rommel – Desert Fox). Die Dritte von rechts. Au coeur de la Casbah. 1953: Alerte au sud. Le salaire de la peur (GB and US: The Wages of Fear). Single-Handed (US: Sailor of the King). Die letzte Etappe. Das unsichtbare Netz. La chair et le diable/Flesh and the Devil. 1954: Night People. The Blue Camellia. Le grand jeu. 1955: A Bullet for Joey. Sophie et le crime (US: The Girl on the Third Floor). Tarzan's Hidden Jungle. Jump into Hell. Confidential Report (US: Mr Arkadin). Der Cornet. 1956: Le feu au poudre. Fric-Frac en dentelles. Attack! The Rawhide Years. Run for the Sun. 1957: Der sechste Mann. Der gläserne Turm/The Glass Tower. Retour de manivelle (GB and US: There's Always a Price-Tag). Tous peuvent me tuer/Anyone Can Kill Me. Dr Crippen Lives. 1958: The Snorkel. The Girl Rosemarie. Schmutziger Engel (GB: Dirty Angel). Du gehörst mir. Schwarze Nylons – heisse Nächte (US: Indecent). 1959: The Rest is Silence. Rommel ruft Kairo. Verbrechen nach Schulschuss (US: The Young Go Wild). Sweetheart of the Gods. Labyrinth. Abschied von den Wolken (GB: Rebel Flight to Cuba).

Geheimaktion schwartze Kapelle (GB and US: Black Chapel). 1960: The 1,000 Eyes of Dr Mabuse. Foxhole in Cairo. 1961: Legge di guerra. Die Stunde, die du glücklich bist. La fête espagnole (US: No Time for Ecstasy). On Friday at 11 (US: World in My Pocket). Unter Ausschluss der Öffentlichkeit. 1962: Finden sie, dass Constanze sich richtig verhält? Kriegsgesetz. Vengeance (US: The Brain). The Devil's Agent. The Longest Day. Station Six – Sahara. 1963: And So to Bed. Scotland Yard jagt Dr Mabuse. Verführung am Meer (GB: Island of Desire. US: Seduction by the Sea). The River Line. 1964: I misteri della giungla nera (GB: The Mystery of Thug Island. US: Mysteries of the Black Jungle). Kennwort: Reiher. 1965: La guerre secrète (GB and US: The Dirty Game). Duell vor Sonnenuntergang. Die Herren. Spione unter sich. Die Todesstrahlen des Dr Mabuse. The Spy Who Came in from the Cold. 1966: Der Chef schickt seinen besten Mann (GB and US: Requiem for a Secret Agent). 1967: Assignment to Kill. Million Dollar Man. Karriere. Sechs Pistolen jagen Professor Z. 1968: Shalako. The Bridge at Remagen. Heidi Comes Home (US: Heidi). 1969: Tevye and His Seven Daughters. Code Name Red Roses.

VARNEY, Reg 1922–
Stocky, relentlessly cheerful British comedian, usually with a foot of grease on his dark hair. He was over 40 when success came to the jolly, bustling bungler, usually led astray by his friends and half-afraid of girls, that he portrayed. Then he cashed in with five feature films in three years, three of them based on his hit television series *On the Buses*.
1952: Miss Robin Hood. 1965: Joey Boy. 1966: The Great St Trinian's Train Robbery. 1971: On the Buses. 1972: Mutiny on the Buses. Go for a Take. The Best Pair of Legs in the Business. 1973: Holiday on the Buses.

VARSI, Diane 1938–
Sweet-faced American actress with light brown hair, one of Fox's big new young stars of the late fifties. However, she left the studio after only four films, and she has been seen infrequently since, although one would have thought she had sufficient talent to survive. Oscar-nominated for *Peyton Place*.
1957: Peyton Place. 1958: Ten North Frederick. From Hell to Texas (GB: Manhunt).

*1959: Compulsion. The Dingaling Girl (TV).
1966: Sweet Love Bitter. 1967: Roseanna.
1968: Wild in the Streets. Killers Three. 1969:
Bloody Mama. 1971: Johnny Got His Gun.
The People (TV). 1977: I Never Promised
You a Rose Garden.*

VAUGHAN, Frankie (F. Abelsohn) 1928–
Handsome, black-haired, thick-lipped British
singer, a great showman. Seemed to be
everybody's favourite – even Hollywood's –
in the late fifties and early sixties, and even
co-starred with Monroe. But the bubble
burst, and suddenly he was back on the stage,
wowing the mums with the high kicks, winks
and waves of the straw hat and cane.
*1956: Escape in the Sun (singing commentary
only). Ramsbottom Rides Again. 1957: These
Dangerous Years (US: Dangerous Youth).
1958: Wonderful Things! 1959: The Lady is a
Square. The Heart of a Man. 1960: Let's Make
Love. 1961: The Right Approach. 1963: It's
All Over Town.*

VAUGHN, Robert 1932–
Dark-haired, cold-eyed, superior-looking
American actor with metallic, calculating
voice. He had already caught the eye as shifty,
upper-class villains (typically the gone-to-the-
bad scion of a good family) before sensational
success in the James Bond-style TV series
The Man from UNCLE – several double-
episodes of which were released as films outside America – as the smooth-as-silk agent
Napoleon Solo. Alas, he got rather better film
roles before the series than after it, and has
recently been seen happily playing thoroughly
nasty, conniving villains. One of Hollywood's

more politically-minded actors; nominated for
an Oscar on *The Young Philadelphians.*
*1956: The Ten Commandments. 1957: Hell's
Crossroads. The Troublemakers (TV). No
Time To Be Young (GB: Teenage Delinquents). 1958: Teenage Caveman (GB: Out of
the Darkness). Unwed Mother. A Good Day
for a Hanging. 1959: The Young Philadelphians
(GB: The City Jungle). Made in Japan (TV).
1960: The Magnificent Seven. 1961: The Big
Show. 1963: The Caretakers (GB: Border-
lines). 1964: To Trap a Spy (TV. GB:
cinemas). Honeymoon Hotel. The Spy with My
Face. 1965: One Spy Too Many (TV. GB:
cinemas). 1966: One of Our Spies is Missing!
(TV. GB: cinemas). The Venetian Affair. The
Spy in the Green Hat (TV. GB: cinemas). The
Glass Bottom Boat. 1967: The Karate Killers
(TV. GB: cinemas). The Helicopter Spies
(TV. GB: cinemas). 1968: Bullitt. How to
Steal the World (TV. GB: cinemas). The
Bridge at Remagen. If It's Tuesday, This Must
Be Belgium. 1969: The Mind of Mr Soames.
1970: Julius Caesar. 1971: Clay Pigeon (GB:
Trip to Kill). The Statue. 1972: The Woman
Hunter (TV). 1974: The Towering Inferno.
1975: Wanted: Babysitter. 1976: Kiss Me, Kill
Me (TV). 1977: Demon Seed (voice only).
Starship Invasions. 1978: Good Luck, Miss
Wyckoff. The Islander (TV). Brass Target.
The Deadly Price of Paradise (TV. GB: Night-
mare at Pendragon's Castle). 1979: Panic on
Page One/City in Fear (TV). The Gossip
Columnist (TV). 1980: Cuba Crossing. Virus.
Battle Beyond the Stars. Hangar 18. The
Franken Project (TV). Mirror, Mirror (TV).
Studio Murders/Fantasies (TV). 1981: SOB.
A Question of Honor (TV). 1982: The Cour-
ageous. The Day the Bubble Burst (TV). 1983:
Superman III. The Return of the Man from
UNCLE (TV). Intimate Agony(TV). 1984:
Atraco en la jungla (completed 1978). 1985:
The Hitchhiker. Black Moon Rising. Private
Sessions (TV). International Airport (TV).
Murrow (TV). 1986: The Delta Force. That's
Adequate. Prince of Bel Air (TV).*

VEIDT, Conrad (C. Weidt) 1893–1943
Dark, fine-boned German actor with piercing
gaze and considerable presence. Handsome in
a slightly sinister way, he was a key figure in
the early German cinema, seeming to be in on
many of its most striking and/or innovative
films. Left Germany in 1934 (after a visit

to Hollywood in the late twenties), and his
remaining roles in Britain and America were
mostly as clever enemy agents that you more
or less loved to hate. Died from a heart attack.
*1916: Der Spion. Der Weg des Todes. 1917:
Das Rätsel von Bangalor. Wenn Tote sprechen.
Die Seeschlacht. Es werde Licht. Die Claudi
von Geiserhot. Furcht. 1918: Colomba. Das
Dreimäderlhaus. Das Tagebuch einer Verlorenen (parts 1 and 2). Henriette Jacoby.
Jettchen gebert. Dida Ibsens Geschichte. Noc-
turno der Liebe. Opfer der Gesellschaft. Peer
Gynt. Opium. Die Serenyi. Die Japanerin.
1919: Anders als die Andern. Chopin. Die Pros-
titution (parts 1 and 2). The Cabinet of Dr
Caligari. Around the World in 80 Days. Die
Nacht auf Goldenhall. Die Okarina. Die Mexi-
kanerin. Unheimliche Geschichten. Die sich ver-
kaufen. Prinz Kuckuck. Satanas. Wahnsinn.
Gewitter im Mai. 1920: Abend-Nacht-Morgen.
Das Geheimnis von Bombay. Der Gang in die
Nacht. Der Graf von Cagliostro. Der Janus-
kopf/Dr Jekyll and Mr Hyde. Der Reigen/
Merry-Go-Round. Die Augen der Welt. Kün-
sterlaunen. Kurfürstendam. Menschen im
Rausch. Liebestaumel. Manolescus Memoiren
(GB: The Memoirs of Manolescu). Moriturus.
Nachtsgestalten. Patience. Sehnsucht. Welt-
brand. 1921: Christian Wahnschaffe/Die Flucht
aus dem goldenen Kerker. Das Indische Grabmal
(parts 1 and 2). Der Leidensweg der Inge
Krafft. Die Liebschaffen des Hektor Dalmore.
Lady Hamilton. Landstrasse und Grossstadt.
Sündige Mütter. 1922: Lukrezia Borgia.
Danton. 1923: Glanz gegen Glück. Paganini.
Wilhelm Tell. 1924: Carlos und Elisabeth. Nju
(GB and US: Husbands or Lovers). Orlacs
Hände (GB and US: The Hands of Orlac).
Schicksal/Fate. Das Wachsfigurenkabinett
(GB: Waxworks. US: Three Wax Men).
1925: Graf Kostja/Le comte Kostja. Liebe
macht blind. Ingmarsarvet (GB: In Dalarna
and Jerusalem). 1926: Die Brüder Schel-
lenberg. Durfen wir schweigen? Die Fluch in die
Nacht. Der Geiger von Florenz (GB: Impetu-
ous Youth). Kreuzzug des Weibes. Der Student
von Prag (GB: The Student of Prague. US:
The Man Who Cheated Life). 1927: Enrico
IV. Jerusalem. Les maudits. The Beloved
Rogue. The Man Who Laughs. A Man's Past.
The Last Performance (GB: Erik the Great).
Husbands or Lovers. 1928: Two Brothers.
1929: Das Land ohne Frauen. 1930: Die grosse
Sehnsucht. Die letzte Compagnie (and English*

version. US: 13 Men and a Girl). Menschen im Käfig/Cape Forlorn. Bride 68. 1931: Der Mann, der den Mord beging. Nachte am Bosporus. Die ändere Seite. Die Nacht der Entscheidung. Congress Dances. 1932: Rome Express. Rasputin. Ich und die Kaiserin. Der schwarze Husar. 1933: Wilhelm Tell (remake). FP.1. I Was a Spy. The Wandering Jew. 1934: Bella Donna. Jew Süss. 1935: The Passing of the Third Floor Back. King of the Damned. 1937: Dark Journey. Under the Red Robe. 1938: Tempête sur l'Asie/Storm over Asia. Joueur d'echecs (GB: The Chess Player. US: The Devil is an Empress). 1939: The Spy in Black (US: U-Boat 29). 1940: Contraband (US: Blackout). The Thief of Bagdad. Escape. 1941: A Woman's Face. Whistling in the Dark. The Men in Her Life. 1942: Nazi Agent. All through the Night. Casablanca. 1943: Above Suspicion.

As director: 1919: Die Nacht auf Goldenhall. 1922: Lord Byron.

VELEZ, Lupe (Guadelupe V. de Villalobos) 1908–1944
Tiny, curvaceous, dark-haired, tempestuous Mexican actress who lived life to the full and seemingly had enough energy for a dozen of her kind. As volatile in life as on the screen – where she is best remembered from the Mexican Spitfire comedies – she was married to Johnny Weissmuller (qv) from 1933 to 1938. Committed suicide with sleeping pills.
1927: *What Women Did for Me. *Sailors, Beware! 1928: The Gaucho. Stand and Deliver. 1929: Lady of the Pavements (GB: Lady of the Night). Wolf Song. Tiger Rose. Where East is East. 1930: †East is West. Hell Harbor. *Voice of Hollywood No. 1. The Storm. 1931: †Resurrection. Cuban Love Song. The Squaw Man (GB: The White Man). Hombres en mi Vida. 1932: The Half-Naked Truth. The Broken Wing. Kongo. 1933: Hot Pepper. Mr Broadway. 1934: Palooka (GB: The Great Schnozzle). Hollywood Party. Strictly Dynamite. 1935: The Morals of Marcus. 1936: Gypsy Melody (US: Under Your Spell). 1937: High Flyers. La Zandunga. Mad about Money (US: He Loved an Actress). 1939: The Girl from Mexico. Mexican Spitfire. 1940: Mexican Spitfire Out West. 1941: Six Lessons from Madame La Zonga. Honolulu Lu. Mexican Spitfire's Baby. Playmates. 1942: Mexican

Spitfire at Sea. Mexican Spitfire Sees a Ghost. Mexican Spitfire's Elephant. 1943: Mexican Spitfire's Blessed Event. Ladies' Day. Redhead from Manhattan. 1944: Nana.

† and Spanish version

VERA-ELLEN (Vera-Ellen Rohe) 1920–1981
Peppy, pert, petite blonde American dancing star with cute figure, engaging smile and rosy cheeks. Usually played the little girl from the sticks who somehow kept the wolves at bay while becoming a star. Retired too soon, even though studio publicity for years hid her real age. Died from cancer.
1945: Wonder Man. 1946: The Kid from Brooklyn. Three Little Girls in Blue. 1947: Carnival in Costa Rica. 1948: Words and Music. 1949: Love Happy (later Kleptomaniacs). On the Town. 1950: Three Little Words. 1951: Happy-Go-Lovely. The Belle of New York. 1953: Call Me Madam. Big Leaguer. 1954: White Christmas. 1956: Let's Be Happy.

VERSOIS, Odile (Katiana de Poliakoff-Baidarov) 1930–1980
Gentle blonde French star, a ballet dancer-turned-actress and a far cry from her sultry sister Marina Vlady (qv). Won acting awards at two festivals for her first film, and scored a big hit in Britain (where she filmed several times) in The Young Lovers. Her fragile beauty did not wear too well, and she was much beset by illness in her later years.
1947: Les dernières vacances. 1948: Fantômas contre Fantômas. 1949: Orage d'été. 1950:

Francesca di Rimini. Bel amour. Les anciens de Saint-Loup. Mademoiselle Josette, ma femme. *Désordre. Into the Blue (US: The Man in the Dinghy). 1951: Domenica. 1953: A Day to Remember. 1954: The Young Lovers (US: Chance Meeting). To Paris with Love. 1955: Les insoumises. 1956: Checkpoint. 1957: Herrscher ohne Krone. 1958: Night is Not for Sleep. 1959: Passport to Shame (US: Room 43). Toi, le venin (GB and US: Nude in a White Car). 1960: La dragée haute. 1961: Le rendez-vous. Le trésor des hommes bleus. Cartouche (GB: Swords of Blood). 1962: A cause, à cause d'une femme. Transit à Saigon. 1964: Le dernier tiercé. 1968: Benjamin. 1972: Eglantine. 1977: Le crabe-tambour.

VICKERS, Martha (M. MacVicar) 1925–1971
Minxish brunette American actress, a good bad girl (especially when playing sulky and spoiled) who could also sing and dance a little. Her biggest success came early – as the nymphomaniac Carmen Sternwood in the 1946 version of The Big Sleep. Marriage to Mickey Rooney (second of three) from 1949 to 1951 virtually finished her big-screen career, and she died young after a lengthy illness.
1943: †Frankenstein Meets the Wolf Man. †Hi' Ya Sailor. †Captive Wild Woman. †Top Man. 1944: †Marine Raiders. †The Mummy's Ghost. †This is the Life. †The Falcon in Mexico. 1946: The Big Sleep. The Time, the Place and the Girl. 1947: That Way with Women. Love and Learn. 1948: Ruthless. 1949: Alimony. Bad Boy. Daughter of the West. 1955: The Big Bluff. The Burglar. 1959: Four Fast Guns.

† as Martha MacVicar

VINCENT, Jan-Michael 1944–
Fresh-faced, youthful, strongly-built, fair-haired American actor in leading roles from 1970. Despite being photogenic and personable, and continuing to star in action films, he has not quite made the big-budget film and superstar bracket. But he scored major personal successes on television in the 1980s both in the mini-series The Winds of War and the action series Airwolf.
1967: †Journey to Shiloh. 1969: †The Undefeated. 1970: Tribes (TV. GB: cinemas, as The Soldier Who Declared Peace). 1971: The

Catcher (TV). 1972: Sandcastles. The Mechanic (later Killer of Killers). 1973: The World's Greatest Athlete. Deliver Us from Evil (TV). 1974: Buster and Billie. 1975: Bite the Bullet. White Line Fever. Vigilante Force. 1976: Baby Blue Marine. Shadow of the Hawk. 1977: Damnation Alley. Big Wednesday. 1978: Hooper. 1979: Defiance. 1980: Hard Country. 1981: The Return. 1983: Last Plane Out. Airwolf (TV).

† as Michael Vincent

VITTI, Monica (M. Ceciarelli) 1933–
Wispily delicate blonde Italian actress, at her haunting best in films by Antonioni, four in all. Subsequent international ventures have leaned too heavily on her physical attractions and alleged gift for comedy and have been less than successful. She continues, however, to prosper in Italian films.
1955: Ridere, ridere, ridere. 1956: Una pelliccia di visone. 1957: Il grido/The Cry (voice only). 1958: Le dritte (US: Smart Girls). 1960: L'avventura. La notte. 1962: L'eclisse (GB and US: Eclipse). 1963: Les quatres vérités (GB and US: Three Fables of Love). Château en Suède (US: Naughty, Nutty Chateau). Dragées au poivre (GB: Sweet and Sour). 1964: The Red Desert. Alta infedeltà (GB and US: High Infidelity). Il disco volante. Le bambole (GB: Four Kinds of Love. US: The Dolls). 1966: Le fate (GB: Sex Quartet. US: The Queens). Modesty Blaise. Fai in fretta ad uccidermi ... ho freddo! 1967: The Chastity Belt (US: On My Way to the Crusades, I Met a Girl Who .../A Funny Thing Happened on the Way to the Crusades). 1968: La femme

écarlate. Le ragazza con la pistola. 1969: Amore mio, aiutami (US: Help Me, Darling). Vedo nudo. 1970: Le coppie/The Couples. Nini Tirabuscio, la donna che inventò la mossa. Dramma della gelosia (GB: Jealousy Italian Style. US: The Pizza Triangle). 1971: La pacifista. Lei. La supertestimone. Noi donne siamo fatte così. 1972: Gli ordini sono ordini. Teresa la ladra. 1973: Tosca. 1974: The Phantom of Liberté. Polvere di Stelle. 1975: Qui comincia l'avventura (US: Lucky Girls). A mezzanotte va la ronda del piacere (GB and US: Midnight Pleasures). Canard à l'orange. 1976: L'anitra all'arancia. Mimi Bluette. La goduria. Basta che non si sappia in giro. 1977: L'altra meta del cielo. 1978: La raison d'état. Amori miei/My Loves. Per vivere meglio/The Good Life. 1979: The Mystery of Krantz. An Almost Perfect Affair. Take Two. Letti selvaggi/Tigers in Lipstick (released 1985). 1980: The Mystery of Oberwald. Camera d'albergo. 1981: Appuntamento d'amore. Tango della gelosia. 1982: Infedelmente tua. I Know That You Know That I Know. 1983: When Veronica Calls.

VLADY, Marina (M. de Poliakoff-Baidarov) 1937–
Seemingly doomed throughout her career to playing tawny temptresses, this light-haired French actress of brooding nature, sister of Odile Versois (qv), was a sex-kitten (of a more tigerish variety) second only to Bardot, after tremendous international impact in The Wicked Go To Hell. Her name continued to have marquee value outside the continent, although she never really made an international career. She did, however, develop into a stronger actress than many of her contemporaries. Married/divorced French actor Robert Hossein. Became very busy in movie roles in the mid 1980s.
1949: Orage d'été. Due sorelle amano. 1952: Franciulle di lusso (GB and US: Luxury Girls). Grand gala. Penne nere. Le infedeli. La figlia del diavolo. 1953: Canzoni, canzoni, canzoni (US: Cavalcade of Song). L'âge de l'amour. Avant le déluge. Des gosses de riches. L'età dell'amore. 1954: Le avventure di Giacomo Casanova/Casanova (GB: The Adventures of Casanova. US: Sins of Casanova). Le crâneur. Musoduro. Giorno d'amore. Sinfonia d'amore – Schubert. 1955: Les salauds vont en

enfer (GB and US: The Wicked Go To Hell). Sie/Her. Sophie et le crime (US: The Girl on the Third Floor). La sorcière (GB and US: The Sorceress). 1956: Crime and Punishment. Pardonnez nos offences. 1957: Symphonie inachevée. La Liberté surveillée. 1958: Toi, le venin (GB and US: Nude in a White Car). 1959: La sentence. La nuit des espions (US: Night Encounter). Les canailles. 1960: La fille dans la vitrine. La princesse de Clèves. 1961: Adorable menteuse. La steppa. Les sept péchés capitaux (GB: The Seven Deadly Sins. US: Seven Capital Sins). 1962: Climats (US: Climates of Love). La cage. Le meutrier (GB and US: Enough Rope). 1963: Les bonnes causes (GB and US: Don't Tempt the Devil). Dragée au poivre (GB and US: Sweet and Sour). Ape Regina (GB: Queen Bee. US: The Congjual Bed). 1964: On a volé La Joconde. 1965: Run for Your Wife. 1966: Chimes at Midnight (US: Falstaff). Mona, pour une étoile sans nom. 1967: Deux ou trois choses que je sais d'elle/One or Two Things I Know About Her. A tout coeur à Tokyo pour OSS 117 (US: Terror in Tokyo). 1968: Le temps à vivre. 1969: Sirokko (GB: Winter Sirocco. US: Winter Wind). Siuzhet dlya nebolshova rass kaza (US: Theme for a Short Story). Le temps des loups (US: The Last Shot). 1970: La nuit Bulgare. Contestazione generale. Sapho/Sappho/Sex is My Game. 1972: Tout le monde il est beau, tout le monde il est gentil. 1973: Le complot. 1974: Que la fête commence (US: Let Joy Reign Supreme). 1975: Sept morts sur ordonnance. 1977: Ok ketten (GB and US: The Two of Them). The Bermuda Triangle. 1978: The Thief of Baghdad (TV. GB: cinemas). 1979: Il malato immaginario (US: The Hypochondriac). 1980: L'oeil du maître. 1981: Les jeux de la comtesse Dolingen de Gratz/Styrie. L'ogre de Barbarie. 1985: Tangos – L'exil de Gardel. Bordello. 1986: Il sapore del grano. An Island Boogie Woogie. Twist Again à Moscou. Laughter in the Dark.

VOIGHT, Jon 1938–
Fair-haired, flush-cheeked, boyish-looking American leading man who, after early struggles, broke through to stardom in Midnight Cowboy. He has since chosen his roles carefully, with the accent on painful realism, both mental and physical: thus only 16 films in nearly 20 years. As he approached 50 his output came dangerously close to drying up.

Academy Award for *Coming Home*; also nominated in *Midnight Cowboy* and *Runaway Train*.
1967: *The Hour of the Gun*. 1968: *Fearless Frank*. 1969: *Out Of It*. *Midnight Cowboy*. 1970: *Catch 22*. *The Revolutionary*. *The All-American Boy (released 1973)*. 1972: *Deliverance*. 1974: *The Odessa File*. *Conrack*. 1975: *The Judge and His Hangman (US: End of the Game*. Later: *Deception*). 1978: *Coming Home*. *The Champ*. 1980: *Lookin' to Get Out*. 1982: *Table for Five*. 1985: *Runaway Train*. 1986: *Desert Bloom*.

VON STROHEIM, Erich (Hans E.S. von Nordenwall, or E. Oswald Stroheim) 1885–1957
Egocentric Austrian actor and director with a death's head countenance and aristocratic manner, qualifying him for villainous ladies' men. As a director he proved impossibly extravagant, a quality which led to several projects being taken out of his hands by studios, and the eventual cessation of his directing career. Acting in sound films, he built up a new reputation as 'The Man You Love to Hate'. Oscar-nominated as an actor for *Sunset Boulevard*. Died from a spinal ailment.
1914: *Captain McLean*. 1915: *The Birth of a Nation*. *Old Heidelberg*. *A Bold Impersonation*. *The Failure*. *Ghosts*. 1916: *Intolerance*. *His Picture in the Papers*. *Macbeth*. *The Social Secretary*. *Less than the Dust*. 1917: *For France*. *Reaching for the Moon*. *In Again, Out Again*. *Sylvia of the Secret Service*. *Panthea*. 1918: *Hearts of the World*. *Hearts of Humanity*. *The Unbeliever*. *The Hun Within*. 1919: *Blind Husbands*. 1921: *Foolish Wives*. 1928: *The Wedding March*. 1929: *The Great*

Gabbo. 1930: *Three Faces East*. 1931: *Friends and Lovers*. 1932: *The Lost Squadron*. *As You Desire Me*. 1934: *Crimson Romance*. *House of Strangers*. *The Fugitive Road*. 1935: *The Crime of Dr Crespi*. 1936: *Marthe Richard au service de la France*. 1937: *Mademoiselle docteur*. *La grande illusion*. *Between Two Women*. *Les pirates du rail*. *L'alibi*. 1938: *L'affaire Lafarge*. *Les disparus de Saint-Agil*. *Gibraltar*. 1939: *Boys' School*. *Tempête sur Paris/Thunder over Paris*. *Derrière la façade*. *Rappel immédiat/Instant Recall*. *Macao — l'enfer du jeu (GB and US: Gambling Hell)*. *Paris–New York*. *Pièges*. *Le monde tremblera*. 1940: *I Was an Adventuress*. *Ultimatum*. 1941: *So Ends Our Night*. *Personal Column*. 1943: *Storm over Lisbon*. *Five Graves to Cairo*. *North Star*. 1944: *Armored Attack*. *The Lady and the Monster (GB: The Lady and the Doctor)*. *32 Rue de Montmartre*. 1945: *Scotland Yard Investigator*. *The Great Flamarion*. 1946: *The Mask of Diijon*. *La foire aux chimères (GB: The Fair Angel. US: The Devil and the Angel)*. *On ne meurt pas comme ça*. *La danse de mort*. 1948: *Le signal rouge*. 1949: *Portrait d'un assassin*. *Le diable et l'ange*. 1950: *Sunset Boulevard*. 1952: *La maison du crime*. *Alraune*. 1953: *Alert au sud*. *L'envers du paradis*. *Minuit – Quai de Bercy*. 1954: *Napoléon*. *Série noire*. 1955: *La modone des sleepings*. 1956: *L'homme aux cent visages/Man of 100 Faces*.

As director: 1919: *Blind Husbands*. 1920: *The Devil's Pass Key*. 1921: *Foolish Wives*. 1923: †*Merry-Go-Round*. 1924: †*Greed*. 1925: *The Merry Widow*. 1927: *The Wedding March*. 1928: †*Mariage du prince*. †*Queen Kelly*. 1933: †*Hello Sister/Walking Down Broadway*.

†*Taken out of director's hands before issue of release print*

VON SYDOW, Max (Carl Von Sydow) 1929–
Tall, blond Swedish actor of austere countenance, ideal for the gloom of Ingmar Bergman's films (he has been in ten to date) and seized on as an international utility player from the mid-sixties, in which capacity his sombre expression and tones – although initially seen as Christ, and as the missionary in *Hawaii* (his best English-speaking performance) – have mostly loomed up as double agents and master spies.
1949: *Bara en Mor*. 1951: *Miss Julie*. 1953: *Ingen Mans Kvinna*. 1956: *Rätten att Älska*. 1957: *Det Sjunde Inseglet (GB and US: The Seventh Seal)*. *Prästen i Uddarbo*. *Smul-*

tronstället (GB and US: Wild Strawberries). 1958: *Nära Livet (GB: So Close to Life. US: Brink of Life)*. *Spion 503*: *Ansiktet (GB and US: The Face)*. 1960: *Jungfrukällen (GB and US: The Virgin Spring)*. *Bröllopsdagen*. 1961: *Såsom i en Spegel (GB and US: Through a Glass Darkly)*. 1962: *Nils Holgerssons Underbara Resa*. *Älskarinnen*. 1963: *Nattvardsgästerna (GB and US: Winter Light)*. 1965: *4 × 4/Uppehåll i Myrlandet*. *The Greatest Story Ever Told*. *The Reward*. 1966: *Hawaii*. *The Quiller Memorandum*. 1968: *Vargtimmen (GB and US: Hour of the Wolf)*. *Här Här Du Ditt Liv (GB: Here is Your Life)*. *Svarta Palmkronor*. *Skammen (GB and US: The Shame)*. 1969: *Made in Sweden*. *A Passion/En Passion (US: The Passion of Anna)*. *The Kremlin Letter*. 1971: *The Night Visitor*. *The Touch*. *The Emigrants*. *Äppelkriget*. *I hausbandet*. 1972: *Embassy*. *The New Land*. 1973: *The Exorcist*. 1974: *Steppenwolf*. *Ägget är löst (GB: Egg! Egg! A Hardboiled Story)*. 1975: *Foxtrot (later The Other Side of Paradise)*. *Illustrious Corpses*. *Three Days of the Condor*. *The Ultimate Warrior*. *Cuore di cane*. 1976: *Voyage of the Damned*. 1977: *Le désert des Tartares*. *Exorcist II: The Heretic*. *March or Die*. *La signora della orrori (US: Black Journal)*. 1978: *Brass Target*. *Gran bollito*. 1979: *Hurricane*. *Deathwatch/Le mort en direct*. *Footloose/Venetian Lies*. 1980: *Flash Gordon*. 1981: *Flight of the Eagle*. *Escape to Victory (US: Victory)*. *Conan the Barbarian*. 1982: *Target Eagle*. *She Dances Alone*. 1983: *Strange Brew*. *Never Say Never Again*. *Dreamscape*. 1984: *Dune*. *Samson and Delilah (TV)*. 1985: *Kojak: The Belarus File (TV)*. *Il pentito*. *Code Name: Emerald*. 1986: *The Second Victory*. *Gift of the Heart (Duet for One)*. *Hannah and Her Sisters*.

day). *Killer by Night* (*TV*). *The Cable Car Mystery* (*TV. GB: Crosscurrent*). *Madame Sin* (*TV. GB cinemas*). 1972: *The Streets of San Francisco* (*TV*). 1973: *The Affair* (*TV. GB: cinemas*). 1974: *The Towering Inferno. The Abduction of St Anne* (*TV*). 1976: *Death at Love House* (*TV*). *Midway* (*GB: Battle of Midway*). 1978: *The Critical List* (*TV*). 1979: *The Concorde – Airport '79* (*GB: Airport '80 . . . the Concorde*). *Hart to Hart* (*TV*). 1983: *Curse of the Pink Panther. I Am the Cheese.* 1984: *To Catch a King.* 1985: *Lime Street* (*TV*).

WALKEN, Christopher (Ronald Walken) 1943–

Tall, blond, handsome American actor, reminiscent of the late 1920s and early 1930s in looks and often cast in unsmiling roles. He had one or two showy parts before a supporting Oscar for *The Deer Hunter* made him a star at 35, a position he has not quite consolidated.

1968: *Me and My Brother.* 1971: *The Anderson Tapes.* 1972: *The Happiness Cage.* 1975: *Next Stop, Greenwich Village.* 1976: *The Sentinel.* 1977: *Annie Hall. Roseland.* 1979: *The Deer Hunter.* 1979: *Last Embrace.* 1980: *Heaven's Gate. The Dogs of War. Shoot the Sun Down.* 1981: *Brainstorm* (released 1983). *Pennies from Heaven. Who Am I This Time?* (*TV*). 1983: *The Dead Zone.* 1985: *A View to a Kill.* 1986: *At Close Range. The Conspiracy. River of Death. War Zone.*

WAGNER, Robert 1930–

Boyish, cherubically handsome, dark-haired American actor, a good bet at the box-office for Fox in the fifties, when he was one of the prime targets for teenage fan-mail. He tried to improve his range after 1960, but the end product did not always match his ambition, and he wisely became one of the first big stars to move positively into TV, where he has exuded bland masculinity for the last 15 years. Married to Natalie Wood (*qv*) 1957–1963; remarried her 1972, with another marriage in between. Widowed in 1981.

1950: *The Happy Years. Halls of Montezuma.* 1951: *Let's Make It Legal. The Frogmen.* 1952: *With a Song in My Heart. What Price Glory? Stars and Stripes Forever* (*GB: Marching Along*). 1953: *Titanic. The Silver Whip. Beneath the 12-Mile Reef.* 1954: *Prince Valiant. Broken Lance.* 1955: *White Feather. The Ox-Bow Incident* (*TV. GB: cinemas*). 1956: *A Kiss before Dying. Gun in His Hand* (*TV. GB: cinemas*). *The Mountain. Between Heaven and Hell.* 1957: *The True Story of Jesse James* (*GB: The James Brothers*). *Stopover Tokyo.* 1958: *The Hunters. In Love and War.* 1959: *Say One for Me.* 1960: *All the Fine Young Cannibals.* 1961: *Sail a Crooked Ship.* 1962: *The Longest Day. The War Lover. The Condemned of Altona.* 1963: *The Pink Panther.* 1966: *How I Spent My Summer Vacation* (*GB: cinemas, as Deadly Roulette*). *Harper* (*GB: The Moving Target*). 1967: *The Magnificent Thief* (*TV*). *Banning.* 1968: *Don't Just Stand There. The Biggest Bundle of Them All.* 1969: *Winning.* 1971: *City Beneath the Sea* (*TV. GB: cinemas, as One Hour to Dooms-*

WALBROOK, Anton (Adolf A. Wohlbrück) 1900–1967

Stylish, dark-haired, moustachioed, dashing Austrian actor. From a family of circus clowns, he rose to fame in German operettas of the early thirties, but leaving Germany in 1936 soon revealed himself to be a sound dramatic actor (notably in the British *Gaslight* and in *The Queen of Spades*) in both British and American films. Died from a heart attack.

1915: *Marionetten.* 1922: *Mater Dolorosa.* 1925: *Der Fluch der bösen Tat. Das Geheimnis auf Schloss Elmshoh.* 1931: *Der Stolz der dreiter Kompanie. Salto Mortale.* 1932: *Baby. Cinq gentilhommes maudits. Drei von der Stempenstelle. Melodie der Liebe.* 1933: *Keine Angst vor Liebe. Viktor und Viktoria. Walzerkrieg. Mond über Marokko.* 1934: *Die englische Heirat. Die vertauschte Braut. Eine Frau, die weiss, was sie will. Maskerade* (*GB: Masquerade in Vienna*). *Regina.* 1935: *Der Student von Prag/The Student of Prague. Ich war Jack Mortimer. Zigeunerbaron.* 1936: *Allotria. Der Kurier des Zaren. Port Arthur* (and English, French and Czech versions). 1937: *Victoria the Great. The Rat. The Soldier and the Lady* (*GB: Michael Strogoff*). 1938: *Sixty Glorious Years* (*US: Queen of Destiny*). 1940: *Gaslight* (*US: Angel Street*). *Dangerous Moonlight* (*US: Suicide Squadron*). 1941: *49th Parallel.* 1943: *The Life and Death of Colonel Blimp* (*US: Colonel Blimp*). 1945: *The Man from Morocco.* 1948: *The Red Shoes.* 1949: *The Queen of Spades.* 1950: *La ronde.* 1951: *Wien tanzt* (*US: Vienna Waltzes*). 1953: *L'affaire Maurizius* (*GB: On Trial*). 1955: *Oh Rosalinda !! Lola Montès.* 1956: *König für eine Nacht.* 1957: *Saint Joan. I Accuse!*

WALKER, Clint (Norman Walker) 1927–

Big, husky, dark-haired, deep-voiced American actor, a major part of whose career was taken up by a television western series called *Cheyenne*, which ran from 1955 to 1963. In the cinema he had a few leading roles in colourful adventure dramas, and one or two interesting supporting parts that guyed his own giant he-man image.

1954: †*Jungle Gents.* 1956: *The Ten Commandments. Border Showdown* (*TV. GB: cinemas*). *The Storm Riders* (*TV. GB: cinemas*). *Julesburg* (*TV. GB: cinemas*). *Mountain Fortress* (*TV. GB: cinemas*). *The Argonauts* (*TV. GB: cinemas*). *The Outlander* (*TV. GB: cinemas*). *Decision* (*TV. GB: cinemas*). *Last*

Train West (TV. GB: cinemas). 1957: Fort
Dobbs. 1959: Yellowstone Kelly. 1961: Gold of
the Seven Saints. 1964: Send Me No Flowers.
1965: None But the Brave. 1966: Night of the
Grizzly. Maya. 1967: The Dirty Dozen. 1968:
Sam Whiskey. More Dead Than Alive. 1969:
The Great Bank Robbery. The Phynx. 1971:
Yuma (TV). Pancho Villa. 1972: Hardcase
(TV). The Bounty Man (TV). 1974:
Killdozer (TV). Scream of the Wolf (TV).
1975: Death Harvest. 1976: Baker's Hawk.
1977: Snowbeast (TV). The White Buffalo.
1979: Island of Sister Teresa/Mysterious Island
of Beautiful Women (TV). 1982: Hysterical.
1983: The Golden Viper. 1985: The Serpent
Warriors.

† As Jett Norman

WALKER, Robert 1914–1951

Solidly-built, brown-haired American actor
with clear-cut features. The turmoil in this
unhappy man's private life finally reflected
itself in his roles, as he moved from sensitivity
and sincerity to mania lurking beneath an
over-bright surface – brilliantly effective
though this was in Strangers on a Train. Married Jennifer Jones in 1939, but lost her to
David O. Selznick by 1945; a second marriage
was disastrous. There was a period in a psy-
chiatric clinic and a conviction for drunken
driving. Death came from respiratory failure
after a dose of sedatives.
1939: Dancing Co-Ed (GB: Every Other Inch
a Lady). These Glamour Girls. Winter Carnival. 1940: Pioneer Days. 1941: I'll Sell My
Life. 1943: Bataan. Madame Curie. 1944: See
Here, Private Hargrove. Thirty Seconds over
Tokyo. Since You Went Away. 1945: What
Next, Corporal Hargrove? Her Highness and
the Bellboy. The Sailor Takes a Wife. The
Clock. 1946: Till the Clouds Roll By. 1947:
The Sea of Grass. The Beginning or the End?
Song of Love. 1948: One Touch of Venus. 1950:
Please Believe Me. The Skipper Surprised His
Wife. 1951: Vengeance Valley. Strangers on a
Train. 1952: My Son John.

WALKER, Robert Jr 1940–

Underfed-looking, light-haired, pale-eyed
American actor, son of Robert Walker. After
a bright start he was often seen in dreamy,
moody, introspective or even mystic roles,
almost always the oppressed rather than
oppressor. Performed steadily on TV from

1961, but has never entered the Hollywood
mainstream.
1963: The Hook. The Ceremony. 1964: Ensign
Pulver. 1966: The Happening. 1967: The War
Wagon. 1968: The Savage Seven. Killers
Three. The Face of Eve (US: Eve). 1969:
Easy Rider. Young Billy Young. Man without
Mercy (later Gone with the West). Agilok and
Blubbo. 1970: The Road to Salina. The Man
from ORGY. 1971: Beware! The Blob (GB:
Son of Blob). 1972: The Specter of Edgar Allan
Poe. Prelude to Taurus. 1973: Hex. Don Juan,
or: If Don Juan Were a Woman. 1974: God
Bless Dr Shagetz/God Damn Dr Shagetz.
1976: The Passover Plot. 1978: The Deadly
Price of Paradise (TV. GB: Nightmare at Pen-
dragon's Castle). 1981: Double Jeopardy.
Angkor. Olivia (later A Taste of Sin). 1983:
Hambone and Hillie (GB: The Adventures of
Hambone). 1984: The Jungle. 1985: Heated
Vengeance.

WALLACE, Jean (J. Walasek) 1923–

Platinum blonde American actress of clear
complexion and slinky looks. At first she
played femmes fatale in comedies, but later
revealed herself capable of stronger and more
sensitive portrayals. Stormily married (1941–
1948) to Franchot Tone, then from 1951 to
Cornel Wilde (both qv), and from that time
appeared exclusively in his films.
1941: Louisiana Purchase. Ziegfeld Girl. 1944:
You Can't Ration Love. 1946: It Shouldn't
Happen to a Dog. 1947: Blaze of Noon. 1948:
When My Baby Smiles at Me. 1949: Jigsaw.
The Man on the Eiffel Tower. 1950: The Good
Humor Man. 1951: Native Son. 1953: Star of
India. 1955: The Big Combo. Storm Fear.

1957: The Devil's Hairpin. 1958: Maracaibo.
1963: Lancelot and Guinevere (US: The
Sword of Lancelot). 1967: Beach Red. 1970:
No Blade of Grass.

WALLACH, Eli 1915–

Dark-haired, plum-nosed American actor
who always looked about to say something
forceful, even when he wasn't. Started sensationally in Baby Doll (after nearly 20 years
as a stage actor), then played extrovert villains,
with some nicely-played light comedy roles
thrown in, sometimes opposite his wife, Anne
Jackson (married 1948). The rasping voice is
redolent of his native Brooklyn.
1956: Baby Doll. 1958: The Plot to Kill Stalin
(TV). The Line Up. 1959: For Whom the Bells
Toll (TV). Seven Thieves. 1960: A Death of
Princes (TV. GB: cinemas). The Magnificent
Seven. 1961: The Misfits. 1962: Hemingway's
Adventures of a Young Man (GB: Adventures
of a Young Man). How the West Was Won.
1963: Act One. The Victors. The Moon-Spinners. 1964: Kisses for My President. Lord Jim.
1965: Genghis Khan. 1966: The Poppy is Also
a Flower (TV. GB: cinemas, as Danger Grows
Wild). The Good, the Bad and the Ugly. How
to Steal a Million. 1967: The Tiger Makes Out.
How to Save a Marriage ... and Ruin Your
Life. 1968: Mackenna's Gold. A Lovely Way
to Go. I quattro dell' Ave Maria (GB: Revenge
in El Paso). 1969: The Brain. Ace High. 1970:
Zigzag (GB: False Witness). The Angel
Levine. The People Next Door. The Adventures
of Gerard. 1971: Romance of a Horsethief. Los
Guerilleros (US: Killer from Yuma). 1973: A
Cold Night's Death (TV). The Last Chance
(US: Stateline Hotel). 1974: Indict and Con-
vict (TV). Crazy Joe. Cinderella Liberty.
Samurai. 1975: Don't Turn the Other Cheek.
1976: The Domino Killings (released 1978).
Nasty Habits. Twenty Shades of Pink (TV).
The Sentinel. 1977: The Deep. Winter Kills
(released 1979). The Silent Flute/Circle of
Iron. 1978: Girl Friends. Movie Movie. Squa-
dra antimafia (US: Little Italy). 1979: Fire-
power. 1980: The Hunter. Fugitive Family
(TV). 1981: The Salamander. The Wall
(TV). The Pride of Jesse Hallam (TV). Sko-
kie (TV. GB: Once They Marched Through
a Thousand Towns). 1982: The Executioner's
Song. Alby and Elizabeth. 1984: Anatomy of
an Illness (TV). Sam's Son. 1985: Our Family
Honor (TV). 1986: Murder: by Reason of
Insanity (TV). Tough Guys.

WALLS, Tom 1883–1949
Bluff, dark-haired, dark-complexioned British farceur, a guiding light behind London's famous Aldwych Theatre farces, most of which he transferred to the screen. During the war years found a new career as a forceful dramatic character star.
1930: Rookery Nook (US: One Embarrassing Night). †Canaries Sometimes Sing. On Approval. †Plunder. 1932: †Thark. †A Night Like This. †Leap Year. 1933: †Turkey Time. †Just Smith. †The Blarney Stone (US: The Blarney Kiss). †A Cuckoo in the Nest. 1934: †A Cup of Kindness. †Lady in Danger. 1935: †Fighting Stock. Me and Marlborough. †Stormy Weather. †Foreign Affaires. 1936: †Dishonour Bright. †Pot Luck. 1937: †Second Best Bed. †For Valour. 1938: †Old Iron. Strange Boarders. Crackerjack (US: Man with a Hundred Faces). 1943: Undercover (US: Underground Guerillas). They Met in the Dark. 1944: Halfway House. Love Story (US: A Lady Surrenders). 1945: Johnny Frenchman. 1946: This Man is Mine. 1947: Master of Bankdam. While I Live. 1948: Spring in Park Lane. 1949: Maytime in Mayfair. The Interrupted Journey.

† Also directed
Also as director: 1930: Tons of Money. 1934: Dirty Work.

WALSH, Dermot 1924–
Handsome dark-haired Irish actor with grey streak in his hair, quickly in leading roles in the British cinema after the war, then lost to the theatre for a few years. Returned to become one of Britain's busiest B-feature leads, belted raincoat at the ready, with occasional small parts in major films. Later on television. Married to Hazel Court (qv) from 1949–1963; they appeared a number of times together in low-budget thrillers. Busy on the stage since 1963, where he has stayed in leading roles.
1946: Bedelia. Hungry Hill. 1947: Jassy. The Mark of Cain. 1948: My Sister and I. To the Public Danger. Third Time Lucky. 1949: Torment (US: Paper Gallows). 1952: The Frightened Man. Ghost Ship. 1953: Counterspy (US: Undercover Agent). The Blue Parrot. The Straw Man. The Floating Dutchman. 1954: The Night of the Full Moon (released 1956). 1956: Bond of Fear. The Hideout. 1957: At the Stroke of Nine. 1958: Chain of Events. A Woman of Mystery. Sea Fury. Sea of Sand. 1959: Crash Drive. Make Mine a Million. The Bandit of Zhobe. The Crowning Touch. The Witness. 1960: The Flesh and the Fiends (US: Mania). The Clock Struck Three. The Challenge. The Tell-Tale Heart. The Trunk. 1961: Shoot to Kill. The Breaking Point. Tarnished Heroes. Out of the Shadow. 1962: Emergency. The Cool Mikado. 1963: The Switch. 1966: *Infamous Conduct. 1983: The Wicked Lady.

WALSH, Kay 1914–
Fair-haired British leading lady with the common touch. A former dancer, she proved bright and popular in the thirties, although her later career was marred by ill-health. But she has made useful contributions as a character actress. Also a writer. Married director David Lean, later divorced.
1934: How's Chances? Get Your Man. 1935: The Luck of the Irish. Smith's Wives. 1936: All That Glitters. If I Were Rich. The Secret of Stamboul. 1937: Keep Fit. The Last Adventurers. 1938: I See Ice. Meet Mr Penny. 1939: The Mind of Mr Reeder (US: The Mysterious Mr Reeder). All at Sea. Sons of the Sea. The Missing People. The Middle Watch. The Chinese Bungalow (US: Chinese Den). 1940: The Second Mr Bush. 1942: In Which We Serve. 1944: This Happy Breed. 1947: Vice Versa. The October Man. 1948: Oliver Twist. 1950: Last Holiday. Stage Fright. The Magnet. 1951: The Magic Box. Encore. 1952: Hunted (US: The Stranger in Between). Meet Me Tonight. 1953: Young Bess. Gilbert Harding Speaking of Murder. 1954: The Rainbow Jacket. Lease of Life. 1955: Cast a Dark

Shadow. 1956: Now and Forever. 1958: The Horse's Mouth. 1960: Tunes of Glory. 1961: Greyfriars Bobby. 1962: Lunch Hour. Reach for Glory. 1963: 80,000 Suspects. Dr Syn – Alias the Scarecrow. 1964: Circus World (GB: The Magnificent Showman). The Beauty Jungle (US: Contest Girl). Bikini Paradise. 1965: A Study in Terror (US: Fog). He Who Rides a Tiger. 1966: The Witches (US: The Devil's Own). 1969: Taste of Excitement. Connecting Rooms. 1970: The Virgin and the Gypsy. Scrooge. 1971: The Ruling Class. 1982: Night Crossing.

WALTER, Jessica 1940–
Striking, dark-haired American leading lady, usually in strong roles. Despite one or two vividly effective performances for the cinema – notably her psychopath in Play 'Misty' for Me – her talents have mostly been consigned to television in less interesting roles.
1964: Lilith. 1966: Grand Prix. The Group. 1968: Bye Bye Braverman. 1969: Number One. The Immortal (TV). Three's a Crowd (TV). 1971: Women in Chains (TV). The Showdown (TV). They Call It Murder (TV). Play 'Misty' for Me. 1972: Home for the Holidays (TV). 1974: Hurricane (TV). 1976: Having Babies (TV). Victory at Entebbe (TV. GB: cinemas). Amy Prentiss (TV). 1977: Black Market Baby (TV). 1978: Wild and Wooly (TV). Secrets of Three Hungry Wives (TV). Dr Strange (TV). 1979: Vampire (TV). She's Dressed to Kill (TV). Goldengirl (TV version only). 1984: The Flamingo Kid.

WALTERS, Julie 1950–
Bubbly, extrovert British actress and com-

edienne with a mass of light-brown hair who, after years as a cabaret entertainer providing faintly risqué jokes and songs with long-time partner Victoria Wood, burst upon the acting scene with her stage and film performances in *Educating Rita*. Somewhat typecast as sex-minded scatterbrains, she projects the image of someone who refuses to take life seriously. Also popular in the TV series *The Secret Diary of Adrian Mole*. Oscar-nominated for *Educating Rita*.

1976: Occupy! 1983: Educating Rita. 1984: Unfair Exchanges. She'll Be Wearing Pink Pyjamas. 1985: Car Trouble. Dreamchild (voice only). 1986: Personal Services (Madame Cyn).

WARD, Fred 1949–

Stockily-built, dark, taciturn, squatly good-looking American actor, usually in tough roles. After throwing over an Air Force career to study acting, Ward roamed the world in search of decent chances. But it was a Hollywood role, as Clint Eastwood's partner in *Escape from Alcatraz*, that gave him the breakthrough. By 1985 he was in leading roles, although it remains to be seen whether he has the versatility to remain at the top.

1971: No Available Witness. 1973: L'eta di Cosimo de' Medici (originally for TV). 1974: Descartes (originally for TV). 1979: Escape from Alcatraz. 1980: Carny. Tilt. Belle Starr (TV). 1981: Cardiac Arrest. Southern Comfort. 1982: Timerider: The Adventure of Lyle Swann. 1983: Uncommon Valor. The Right Stuff. Silkwood. Swing Shift. 1984: Secret Admirer. Uforia 84 (filmed 1980). 1985: Remo Williams: The Adventure Begins (GB: Remo: Unarmed and Dangerous). 1986: Florida Straits.

WARD, Rachel 1957–

Brown-haired British beauty, model and actress of aristocratic background. A classic looker somewhere between Elizabeth Taylor and Brigitte Bardot, she has plenty of room to expand a limited acting talent (although the agent who rated the early Ward as 'looks, 9 out of 10; acting 4½' underestimated her on both counts) but made great public impact in the early 1980s – especially in the TV series *The Thorn Birds* – before a year off screen to have a baby, following marriage to Australian actor Bryan Brown *(qv)* in 1983.

1980: Night School (GB: Terror Eyes). 1981: Campsite Massacre/Three Blind Mice/Carnivore. Sharky's Machine. Dead Men Don't Wear Plaid. 1984: Against All Odds. 1985: Fortress (TV). 1986: Umbrella Woman. The Good Wife. Hotel Colonial.

WARD, Simon 1941–

Boyish, diffident, fair-haired British actor who, after a few small roles, was thrust into the limelight as Winston Churchill. Not surprisingly, that proved a hard act to follow, and Ward was not exactly charismatic. But, to his credit, he has continued to graft away in top supporting and minor leading roles.

1968: If ... 1969: Frankenstein Must Be Destroyed. I Start Counting. 1971: Quest for Love. Young Winston. 1973: Hitler: the Last Ten Days. The Three Musketeers: the Queen's Diamonds. Dracula (TV. GB: cinemas). 1974: All Creatures Great and Small. Deadly Strangers. The Four Musketeers: the Revenge of Milady. 1975: Valley Forge (TV). 1976: Aces High. 1977: Die Standarte/Battle Flag. Holocaust 2000 (US: The Chosen). Children of Rage. 1978: The Four Feathers (TV. GB: cinemas). Dominique. 1979: Raising Daisy Rothschild (US: TV, as The Last Giraffe). Zulu Dawn. The Sabina. 1980: The Monster Club. 1981: The Bomber. 1984: Supergirl. L'etincelle (US: Tug of Love). 1985: The Corsican Brothers (TV). Leave All Fair.

WARNER, David 1941–

Tall, fair-haired, raw-boned, harassed-looking British actor. Made his name in Shakespeare on stage, but started in mournful comedies in the cinema. Later played men desperate in one way or another and does not

seem to have realized his full potential as a film star. His success as Heydrich in the TV series *Holocaust* (1978) saw him cast in a succession of 'evil' roles.

1962: *The King's Breakfast. 1963: Tom Jones. 1965: A King's Story (voice only). Morgan – a Suitable Case for Treatment (US: Morgan). 1966: The Deadly Affair. 1967: Work is a Four-Letter Word. 1968: A Midsummer Night's Dream. The Fixer. The Bofors Gun. 1969: The Sea Gull. Michael Kohlhaas. 1970: The Engagement. Perfect Friday. The Ballad of Cable Hogue. 1971: Straw Dogs. 1973: A Doll's House (Losey). From Beyond the Grave. 1974: Mister Quilp. Little Malcolm and his Struggle against the Eunuchs. 1976: The Omen. 1977: The Disappearance. Cross of Iron. Age of Innocence. Silver Bears. Providence. 1978: The Thirty Nine Steps. 1979: S.O.S. Titanic (TV. GB: cinemas). Time After Time. Nightwing. The Concorde – Airport '79 (GB: Airport '80 ... the Concorde). 1980: The Island. †William and Dorothy. Masada (TV. GB: cinemas, in abridged version, as The Antagonists). 1981: Time Bandits. The French Lieutenant's Woman. 1982: Tron. 1983: The Man with Two Brains. 1984: Charlie (TV). The Company of Wolves. A Christmas Carol (TV. GB: cinemas). 1985: Hitler's SS: Portrait in Evil (TV. GB: cinemas).

†Unreleased

WARNER, Jack (John Waters) 1894–1981

Good-natured, square-faced, brown-haired brother of comediennes Elsie and Doris Waters, and on stage from the twenties as monologuist and comedian (best-known

catchphrase 'Mind my bike!'). Quite unexpectedly became a film character star in the immediate post-war years, portraying more successfully than anyone else the common man and, although never a romantic figure, remaining a major star of the British cinema throughout his fifties. Later popular on TV as 'the world's oldest copper' in the long-running *Dixon of Dock Green*, based on a character he himself created in *The Blue Lamp*. Died from pneumonia after a stroke.
1943: *The Dummy Talks*. 1946: *The Captive Heart*. 1947: *Hue and Cry*. *Easy Money*. *It Always Rains on Sunday*. *Holiday Camp*. *Dear Murderer*. 1948: *Against the Wind*. *Here Come the Huggetts*. *My Brother's Keeper*. 1949: *Vote for Huggett*. *Train of Events*. *The Huggetts Abroad*. *The Blue Lamp*. *Boys in Brown*. 1951: *Talk of a Million* (US: *You Can't Beat the Irish*). *Valley of the Eagles*. *Scrooge*. 1952: *Emergency Call* (US: *Hundred Hour Hunt*). *Le dernier robin des bois* (GB: *Smugglers at the Castle*. *Narrator English version only*). *Meet Me Tonight*. *Those People Next Door*. 1953: *Albert RN* (US: *Break to Freedom*). *The Final Test*. *The Square Ring*. 1954: *Bang! You're Dead* (US: *Game of Danger*). *Forbidden Cargo*. 1955: *The Quatermass Xperiment* (US: *The Creeping Unknown*). *The Ladykillers*. 1956: *Home and Away*. *Now and Forever*. 1958: *Carve Her Name with Pride*. 1962: *Jigsaw*. 1978: *Dominique*.

WASSON, Craig 1952–
Stocky American actor with homely face and fair, wavy, flowing hair, especially good at worried, desperate or small-town characters. On his way to accept a drama scholarship, he auditioned for the national touring company of *Hair* and landed a leading role. He never took up the scholarship, but made his Broadway debut in 1975 and started playing leading roles in films (after one bit part) from 1977. His roles are nearly always sympathetic, often as men trapped in circumstances beyond their control.
1977: *Rollercoaster*. *The Boys in Company C*. *Go Tell the Spartans*. 1979: *The Outsider*. 1980: *Thornwell* (TV). *Carny*. *Schizoid*. 1981: *Ghost Story*. *Skag/The Wildcatters* (TV). *Four Friends* (GB: *Georgia's Friends*). 1982: *Second Thoughts*. 1983: *The Innocents Abroad* (TV). 1984: *Body Double*. *Why Me?* (TV). 1986: *The Men's Club*.

WATERMAN, Dennis 1948–
Pugnacious, fair-haired British actor, who started by playing cheeky kids, notably television's *Just William*, then moved on to adult roles that by and large reflected his own South London background. Career seemed to be faltering in the early seventies, when he had an enormous hit with the TV series *The Sweeney*, following it with the equally successful *Minder*. Also a singer and composer.
1959: *Night Train for Inverness*. 1960: *Ali and the Camel* (serial. Voice only). *Snowball*. 1961: *The Pirates of Blood River*. 1963: *Go Kart Go!* 1967: *Up the Junction*. 1969: *The Smashing Bird I Used to Know*. *A Promise of Bed*. *I Can't...I Can't* (GB: *Wedding Night*). 1970: *My Lover, My Son*. *The Scars of Dracula*. 1971: *Fright*. *Man in the Wilderness*. 1972: *Alice's Adventures in Wonderland*. 1973: *The Belstone Fox*. 1976: *Sweeney!* 1978: *Sweeney 2*. 1985: *Minder on The Orient Express* (TV). 1986: **A Dog's Day Out*.

WATERSTON, Sam 1940–
Dark-haired, slightly-built, languid American actor who, like so many of his generation, only came to film prominence in his thirties. He has tackled a good range of parts, but seems to lack that inner drive that creates charisma, and his Anthony Perkins-like personality did not settle into a star niche. His Academy Award nomination for *The Killing Fields* may have come too late to make him a box-office force, but was a welcome recognition of consistent talent, intelligently applied.
1967: *Fitzwilly* (GB: *Fitzwilly Strikes Back*). 1969: *Three*. *Generation* (GB: *A Time for Giving*). 1970: *Cover Me Babe*. †*The Plastic Dome of Norma Jean*. 1971: *Who Killed Mary What's Her Name?* 1972: *Savages*. 1973: *A Delicate Balance*. *The Glass Menagerie*. 1974: *The Great Gatsby*. *Reflections of Murder* (TV). *Rancho de Luxe*. 1976: *Dandy, the All American Girl* (GB: *Sweet Revenge*). *Journey into Fear*. 1977: *Coup de foudre*. *Capricorn One*. 1978: *Interiors*. *Eagle's Wing*. 1979: *Sweet William*. *Friendly Fire* (TV). 1980: *Hopscotch*. *Heaven's Gate*. 1981: *QED* (TV). 1982: *Games Mother Never Taught You* (TV). 1983: *In Defense of Kids* (TV). *Dempsey* (TV). 1984: *Finnegan Begin Again* (GB: TV). *The Killing Fields*. 1985: *Love Lives On* (TV). *Something in Common*. *Flagrant Desire*. *Warning Sign*. 1986: *Just Between Friends*. *Hannah and Her Sisters*. *The Fifth Missile* (TV).

† *Unreleased*

WATLING, Jack 1923–
Fair-haired, round-faced, boyish-looking British actor, in films as a teenager. Despite experience on the Shakespeare stage, he found himself cast in post-war years as slightly shady, trilby-tilted types from working-class backgrounds. From 1952 to 1964 he was the hero of many low-budget light thrillers and comedies. Several of his children later took up acting careers, although none with quite the same success.
1938: *Sixty Glorious Years* (US: *Queen of Destiny*). *The Housemaster*. 1939: *Goodbye Mr Chips!* 1942: *The Young Mr Pitt*. *The Day Will Dawn* (US: *The Avengers*). 1943: *The Demi-Paradise* (US: *Adventure for Two*). *We Dive at Dawn*. 1944: *The Way Ahead*. 1945: *Journey Together*. 1947: *The Courtneys of Curzon Street* (US: *The Courtney Affair*). *Easy Money*. 1948: *The Winslow Boy*. *Quartet*. 1949: *Maria Chapdelaine/The Naked Heart*. *Under Capricorn*. 1950: *Once a Sinner*. 1951: *White Corridors*. 1952: *Private Information*. *Father's Doing Fine*. 1953: *Flannelfoot*. *Meet Mr Lucifer*. 1954: *A Tale of Three Women*. *Dangerous Cargo*. *Trouble in the Glen*. *The Golden Link*. *The Sea Shall Not Have Them*. 1955: **The Imperfect Gentleman*. *Windfall*. *A Time to Kill*. *Confidential Report* (US: *Mr Arkadin*). 1956: *Reach for the Sky*. 1957: *The Birthday Present*. *The Admirable Crichton* (US: *Paradise Lagoon*). *That Woman*

Opposite (US: City After Midnight). 1958: Gideon's Day (US: Gideon of Scotland Yard). A Night to Remember. Chain of Events. The Solitary Child. Links of Justice. 1960: Sink the Bismarck! 1961: Nearly a Nasty Accident. Three on a Spree. Mary Had a Little. Nothing Barred. The Queen's Guards. 1962: Flat Two. 1964: Who Was Maddox? 1965: The Nanny. 1971: Follow Me. 1972: Father Dear Father. 1974: 11 Harrowhouse.

WAYNE, David (W. D. McMeekan) 1914–
Despite an oddball face, a slight build and a lack of stature, Wayne had so much talent that he almost made it as a star, after coming to Hollywood from the theatre in the late forties. Three of his performances, in *M, Tonight We Sing* and the underrated *Wait 'Til the Sun Shines, Nellie*, are among the best early fifties acting from Hollywood. But the fair-haired, close-cropped American actor slipped back into top supporting roles, and rightly judged he would be more gainfully employed in the theatre.
1948: Portrait of Jennie (GB: Jennie). 1949: Adam's Rib. 1950: The Reformer and the Redhead. My Blue Heaven. Stella. 1951: M. Up Front. As Young As You Feel. 1952: With a Song in My Heart. O. Henry's Full House (GB: Full House). We're Not Married. Wait 'Til the Sun Shines, Nellie. 1953: Down Among the Sheltering Palms. The 'I Don't Care' Girl. Tonight We Sing. How to Marry a Millionaire. 1954: Hell and High Water. 1955: The Tender Trap. 1956: The Naked Hills. 1957: The Sad Sack. The Three Faces of Eve. 1959: The Last Angry Man. 1960: The Big Gamble. 1968: Holloway's Daughters (TV). 1970: The Andromeda Strain. The Boy Who Stole the Elephants (TV). 1971: The Catcher. King Elephant (narrator only). 1974: The Front Page. Huckleberry Finn. Return of the Big Cat. The Apple Dumpling Gang. The FBI versus Alvin Karpis (TV). 1975: Ellery Queen (TV). 1977: In the Glitter Palace (TV). Tubby the Tuba (TV. Voice only). 1978: Murder at the Mardi Gras (TV). The Girls in the Office (TV). The Gift of Love (TV). It's a Bird, It's a Plane, It's Superman (TV). 1979: The Prize Fighter. An American Christmas Carol (TV). Lassie: The New Beginning (TV). 1984: Finders Keepers.

WAYNE, John (Marion Morrison) 1907–
1979
Giant-sized, slow-spoken, brown-haired American star with twinkling smile, whom one could always depend upon to be himself on screen. Started as a football player turned actor and had some good leading roles in the early thirties, notably in *The Big Trail* and *Baby Face*. Slipped into low-budget and singing-cowboy westerns until rescued by *Stagecoach* in 1939, after which he rode increasingly tall in the saddle, gradually becoming an American institution, as the solitary, basically friendless, almost allegorical man of action. His last performance is possibly his best. Died from complications arising from the treatment of cancer. Academy Award for *True Grit*. Also Oscar-nominated in *Sands of Iwo Jima*.
*1926: Brown of Harvard. 1927: The Drop Kick (GB: Glitter). Mother Machree. 1928: Hangman's House. Four Sons. 1929: Salute. Words and Music. 1930: Cheer Up and Smile. Men without Women. The Big Trail. Born Reckless. Rough Romance. 1931: Arizona (GB: The Virtuous Wife). Men Are Like That. Girls Demand Excitement. Range Feud. Three Girls Lost. 1932: The Hurricane Express (serial). Maker of Men. *The Hollywood Handicap. Texas Cyclone. Ride Him Cowboy (GB: The Hawk). The Big Stampede. Shadow of the Eagle (serial). Two Fisted Law. Lady and Gent/The Challenger. *Station S.T.A.R. Haunted Gold. 1933: The Telegraph Trail. The Three Musketeers (serial). Central Airport. The Sagebrush Trail. The Life of Jimmy Dolan (GB: The Kid's Last Fight). The Man from Monterey. College Coach (GB: Football Coach). His Private Secretary. Baby Face. Somewhere in Sonora. Riders of Destiny. 1934: Lucky Texan. West of the Divide. Randy Rides Alone. The Trail Beyond. Blue Steel. The Man from Utah. The Star Packer. Neath Arizona Skies. 1935: Lawless Range. Texas Terror. Paradise Canyon. Westward Ho!. The Lawless Frontier. Rainbow Valley. The Dawn Rider. Desert Trail. New Frontier. 1936: The Lawless Nineties. King of the Pecos. The Oregon Trail. Winds of the Wasteland. The Sea Spoilers. The Lonely Trail. Conflict. 1937: California Straight Ahead. I Cover the War. Idol of the Crowds. Adventure's End. Born to the West/ Hell Town. 1938: Pals of the Saddle. Overland Stage Raiders. Red River Range. Santa Fé Stampede. 1939: The Night Riders. Three*

*Texas Steers (GB: Danger Rides the Range). Wyoming Outlaw. Stagecoach. The New Frontier/Frontier Horizon. Allegheny Uprising (GB: The First Rebel). 1940: Dark Command. Three Faces West. Seven Sinners. The Long Voyage Home. 1941: Lady for a Night. The Shepherd of the Hills. The Lady from Louisiana. A Man Betrayed (GB: Citadel of Crime). 1942: Reunion/Reunion in France (GB: Mademoiselle France). In Old California. Pittsburgh. Reap the Wild Wind. The Spoilers. Flying Tigers. 1943: In Old Oklahoma (GB: War of the Wildcats). A Lady Takes a Chance. 1944: The Fighting Seabees. Tall in the Saddle. 1945: Flame of the Barbary Coast. They Were Expendable. Back to Bataan. Dakota. 1946: Without Reservations. 1947: Angel and the Badman. Tycoon. 1948: Wake of the Red Witch. Three Godfathers. Red River. Fort Apache. 1949: *Hollywood Rodeo. Sands of Iwo Jima. She Wore a Yellow Ribbon. The Fighting Kentuckian. 1950: Rio Grande. *Reno's Silver Spurs Award. Jet Pilot (released 1957). 1951: Flying Leathernecks. Operation Pacific. 1952: The Quiet Man. Big Jim McLain. 1953: Island in the Sky. Trouble along the Way. Hondo. 1954: The High and the Mighty. *Hollywood Cowboy Stars. 1955: Blood Alley. The Sea Chase. 1956: The Searchers. The Conqueror. 1957: The Wings of Eagles. Legend of the Lost. I Married a Woman. 1958: The Barbarian and the Geisha. 1959: Rio Bravo. The Horse Soldiers. 1960: North to Alaska. †The Alamo. 1961: The Comancheros. 1962: The Man Who Shot Liberty Valance. Hatari! The Longest Day. How the West Was Won. 1963: Donovan's Reef. McLintock! 1964: Circus World (GB: The Magnificent Showman). 1965: In Harm's Way. The Sons of Katie Elder. The Greatest Story Ever Told. 1966: Cast a Giant Shadow. *The Artist and the American West. 1967: El Dorado. The War Wagon. 1968: ‡The Green Berets. Hellfighters. 1969: The Undefeated. True Grit. 1970: Rio Lobo. Chisum. 1971: Big Jake. The Cowboys. No Substitute for Victory (narrator only). 1972: Cancel My Reservation. 1973: The Train Robbers. Cahill: United States Marshal (GB: Cahill). 1974: McQ. Brannigan. 1975: Rooster Cogburn. 1976: The Shootist.*
†Also directed ‡Also co-directed

WAYNE, Naunton (N. Davies) 1901–1970
Dapper, round-faced, Welsh-born light actor in British films, with dark, boot-polish hair and a casual way with a funny line. Most successful in company with Basil Radford, with whom he was felicitously teamed in *The Lady Vanishes*. They became the archetypal cricket-loving Englishmen abroad, and made several more engaging films together before Radford's early death broke the partnership.
*1932: The First Mrs Fraser. 1933: Going Gay (US: Kiss Me Goodbye). For Love of You. 1938: The Lady Vanishes. 1939: A Girl Must Live. 1940: Night Train to Munich (US: Night Train). Crooks' Tour. 1942: *Partners in Crime. Next of Kin. 1943: Millions Like Us. 1945: Dead of Night. 1946: A Girl in a Million. 1948: Quartet. 1949: It's Not Cricket. Passport*

A Man Called Sledge). 1971: The Great Man's Whiskers (TV). The Forgotten Man (TV). What's the Matter with Helen? 1972: Duel (TV. GB: cinemas). Rolling Man (TV). Female Artillery (TV). 1973: Terror on the Beach (TV). 1977: Ishi: the Last of His Tribe (TV). 1978: A Cry for Justice (TV). Battered! (TV). The Islander (TV). 1979: The Ordeal of Patty Hearst (TV). Stone/The Killing Stone (TV). 1980: Amber Waves (TV). The Ordeal of Dr Mudd (TV). 1981: The Day the Loving Stopped (TV). 1982: Cocaine: One Man's Poison (TV). Don't Go to Sleep (TV). 1985: Going for the Gold: The Bill Johnson Story (TV).

to Pimlico. Obsession (US: The Hidden Room). Stop Press Girl. Helter Skelter. 1950: Trio. Double Confession. Highly Dangerous. 1951: Circle of Danger. 1952: Tall Headlines. Treasure Hunt. The Happy Family (US: Mr Lord Says No). 1953: The Titfield Thunderbolt. 1954: You Know What Sailors Are. 1959: Operation Bullshine. 1961: Double Bunk. Nothing Barred.

WAYNE, Patricia
see CUTTS, Patricia

WEAVER, Dennis 1924–
Laconic, slant-faced, brown-haired, twangily-spoken American actor who, after an apprenticeship with Universal-International, mostly as villains, was involved in several hit series on TV from 1955, most notably as the limping deputy Chester in *Gunsmoke*, and the bulldozing marshal at large in city life in *McCloud*. Has also starred in some above-average TV movies.
1952: The Raiders. Horizons West. The Lawless Breed. 1953: The Redhead from Wyoming. Mississippi Gambler. Law and Order. Column South. It Happens Every Thursday. The Man from the Alamo. The Golden Blade. The Nebraskan. 1954: War Arrow. Dangerous Mission. Dragnet. 1955: Ten Wanted Men. The Bridges at Toko-Ri. Seven Angry Men. Chief Crazy Horse (GB: Valley of Fury). Storm Fear. 1958: Touch of Evil. The Dungeon (TV). 1960: The Gallant Hours. 1966: Duel at Diablo. Way ... Way Out. 1967: Gentle Giant. 1968: Mission Batangas. 1970: Sledge (GB:

WEAVER, Sigourney (Susan Weaver) 1949–
Energetic, lithe American actress with mass of dark-brown hair and wide-eyed, challenging gaze. She has always looked younger than her age, yet naturally brought a maturity to her roles that often set her above her fellow-players, most notably in *Alien*, in which her forthright astronaut landed her on the front covers of many magazines. But her films to follow this were surprisingly less than smash-hits and by 1986, in need of a career boost, she was back fighting aliens in outer-space in her old role. Niece of character actor Doodles Weaver (Winstead Weaver; 1911–1983).
1977: Annie Hall. Tribute to a Madman. 1978: Camp 708. 1979: Alien. 1981: Eyewitness (GB: The Janitor). 1982: The Year of Living Dangerously. 1983: Deal of the Century. 1984: Ghost Busters. 1985: Une femme ou deux. 1986: Half Moon Street. Aliens.

WEBB, Clifton (W. Hollenbeck) 1893–1966
Tall, thin, light-haired, moustachioed American star with superior expression, a former exhibition dancer and Broadway musical star who came back to films in the forties, and played punctilious, aesthetic narcissists who hated women and children. This pose was equally successful in drama and comedy, and Webb became a highly-rated star with Fox for the next 15 years, appearing in some beguiling entertainments. Died from a heart attack. The date of birth given seems the most probable. Other sources give 1889, 1891 and 1896. Three times Oscar-nominated, for *Laura*, *The Razor's Edge* and *Sitting Pretty*.

*1920: Polly with a Past. 1924: Let Not Man Put Asunder. New Toys. 1925: The Heart of a Siren. 1926: *Still Alarm. 1944: Laura. 1946: The Razor's Edge. The Dark Corner. 1948: Sitting Pretty. 1949: Mr Belvedere Goes to College. 1950: Cheaper by the Dozen. For Heaven's Sake. 1951: Mr Belvedere Rings the Bell. Elopement. 1952: Dreamboat. Stars and Stripes Forever (GB: Marching Along). 1953: Titanic. Mr Scoutmaster. 1954: Woman's World. Three Coins in the Fountain. 1956: The Man Who Never Was. 1957: Boy on a Dolphin. 1959: The Remarkable Mr Pennypacker. Holiday for Lovers. 1962: Satan Never Sleeps.*

WEBB, Jack 1920–1982
Dark-haired American actor with 'honest Joe' face who, after a few variable supporting roles in films, moved into TV in 1951 and became one of the most successful of early television stars with his series *Dragnet* and the catchphrase: 'My name's Friday, I'm a cop'. When later careers as film actor-director and head of Warner TV did not open out as he had hoped, he returned, in 1967, to a new series of *Dragnet*. Directed his last six films. Married (first of three) to Julie London (*qv*) from 1945 to 1953. Died from a heart attack.
1948: He Walked by Night. Hollow Triumph (GB: The Scar). 1950: Halls of Montezuma. The Men. Dark City. Sunset Boulevard. USS Teakettle (later You're in the Navy Now). 1951: Appointment with Danger. 1954: Dragnet. 1955: Pete Kelly's Blues. 1957: The D.I. 1959: –30– (GB: Deadline Midnight). 1961: The Last Time I Saw Archie. 1969: Dragnet (TV. GB: The Big Dragnet).

Lord Love a Duck. 1968: Pretty Poison. 1970: I Walk the Line. 1971: A Safe Place. 1973: Play It As It Lays. 1974: Reflections of Murder (TV). 1976: F. Scott Fitzgerald in Hollywood (TV). 1977: Looking for Mr Goodbar. 1978: Who'll Stop the Rain? (GB: Dog Soldiers). A Question of Guilt (TV). 1980: Serial. Madame X (TV). 1981: Thief (later and GB: Violent Streets). Mother and Daughter – a Loving Pair (TV). 1982: Author! Author! 1983: Once Upon a Time in America. 1984: Scorned and Swindled (TV).

WEISSMULLER, Johnny (Peter J. Weissmuller) 1904–1984

Tall, powerfully-built, light-haired American actor, a former Olympic swimming champion (he won five gold medals at the 1924 and 1928 games) who became the screen's best-known and longest-serving Tarzan, bringing a human touch to the jungle adventures, the earlier of which, at M-G-M, were extremely well made. When his features hardened and his waist thickened he played another long-running character, Jungle Jim. In poor health in later years. Married Lupe Velez (qv; 3rd of six).

1929: Glorifying the American Girl. 1930: *Grantland Rice's Swim Shorts (series). 1931: Tarzan the Ape-Man. 1934: Tarzan and His Mate. Hollywood Party. 1936: Tarzan Escapes! 1939: Tarzan Finds a Son! 1940: *Rodeo Dough. 1941: Tarzan's Secret Treasure. 1942: Tarzan's New York Adventure. 1943: Stage Door Canteen. Tarzan Triumphs. Tarzan's Desert Mystery. 1945: Tarzan and the Amazons. 1946: Swamp Fire. Tarzan and the Leopard Woman. 1947: Tarzan and the Huntress. 1948: Tarzan and the Mermaids. Jungle Jim. 1949: *Sports Serenade. The Lost Tribe. 1950: Captive Girl. Mark of the Gorilla. Pigmy Island. 1951: Fury of the Congo. Jungle Manhunt. 1952: Voodoo Tiger. Jungle Jim in the Forbidden Land. 1953: Savage Mutiny. Valley of the Headhunters. Killer Ape. 1954: Jungle Man-Eaters. Cannibal Attack. 1955: Jungle Moon Men. Devil Goddess. 1969: The Phynx. 1975: Won Ton Ton, the Dog Who Saved Hollywood.

WELCH, Raquel (R. Tejada) 1940–

Chestnut-haired, open-mouthed, big-busted American actress, the sex symbol of the late 1960s, with a personality that was winning or irritating, according to taste. Later she showed a talent for warm comedy, but it was insufficiently exploited. Unexpectedly faded from (or turned her back on) the cinema scene in the late 1970s, even though she had more ability than her critics allowed. She proved her durability in the 1980s when she became a Broadway musical star, nightclub attraction and best-selling author of fitness courses.

1964: Roustabout. A House is Not a Home. 1965: Do Not Disturb. A Swinging Summer. 1966: One Million Years BC. Fantastic Voyage. The Biggest Bundle of Them All. Le

fate (GB: Sex Quartet. US: The Queens). Shoot Loud . . . Louder, I Don't Understand. 1967: Fathom. The Oldest Profession. Bedazzled. 1968: Bandolero! Lady in Cement. 100 Rifles. 1969: Flareup. The Magic Christian. 1970: Myra Breckinridge. The Beloved (GB: TV, as Sin). 1971: Hannie Caulder. 1972: Kansas City Bomber. Bluebeard. Fuzz. 1973: The Last of Sheila. The Three Musketeers: the Queen's Diamonds. 1974: The Four Musketeers: the Revenge of Milady. The Wild Party. Mother, Jugs and Speed (released 1976). 1977: The Prince and the Pauper (US: Crossed Swords). L'animal. 1979: You and Me Together. The Legend of Walks Far Woman (TV).

WELD, Tuesday (Susan Weld) 1943–

Dark-eyed, fair-haired, baby-faced American actress, in show business from childhood (once described by Danny Kaye as '14 going on 27'), who moved from knowing blonde nymphets to the darker side of emotional disturbance. But she did not seem fashionable in the seventies and, considering the depth of which she is capable, the cinema has made remarkably little of her. An Academy Award nominee for her performance in Looking for Mr Goodbar.

1956: The Wrong Man. Rock, Rock, Rock. 1958: Rally Round the Flag, Boys! 1959: The Five Pennies. 1960: Because They're Young. High Time. Sex Kittens Go to College. The Private Lives of Adam and Eve. 1961: Return to Peyton Place. Wild in the Country. 1962: Bachelor Flat. 1963: Soldier in the Rain. 1965: I'll Take Sweden. The Cincinnati Kid. 1966:

WELLES, Orson (George O. Welles) 1915–1985

Tall, brooding, intense, dark-haired American actor-director with uniquely soft, resonant voice. Came to Hollywood after building a formidable reputation as a maverick genius with his Mercury Theatre company, and opened more than a few critical eyes with his memorably innovative Citizen Kane. After this, Welles proved an elusive wanderer, forever in search of another masterpiece and, although there were directorial highspots, he was more impressive as an actor, lending his dominant, larger-than-life and increasingly overweight style to projects which he often seemed to mock. Academy Award 1941 for co-writing script of Citizen Kane. Special Oscar 1970. Collapsed and died at home after a long battle with heart trouble and diabetes.

1934: *The Hearts of Age. 1938: †Too Much Johnson. 1940: Swiss Family Robinson (narrator only). 1941: Citizen Kane. 1942: The Magnificent Ambersons (narrator only). Journey into Fear. 1943: *Show Business at War. Jane Eyre. 1944: Follow the Boys. 1945: Tomorrow is Forever. 1946: Duel in the Sun (narrator only). The Stranger. 1948: The Lady from Shanghai. Macbeth. 1949: The Third Man. Black Magic. Prince of Foxes. *Désordre. The Black Rose. 1951: Othello. *Return to Glennauscaul. 1952: Trent's Last Case. Man, Beast and Virtue. 1953: Si Versailles m'était conté. 1954: Napoléon. Trouble in the Glen. 1955: Three Cases of Murder. Confidential Report (US: Mr. Arkadin). 1956: Moby Dick. 1957: Man in the Shadow (GB: Pay the Devil). 1958: The Vikings (narrator only). South Seas Adventure (narrator only). Lords of the Forest (narrator only). Touch of Evil. The Long, Hot Summer. The Roots of Heaven. 1959: Ferry to Hong Kong. High Journey (narrator only). Compulsion.

Crack in the Mirror. Austerlitz (GB: The Battle of Austerlitz). 1960: The Mongols. The Tartars. David and Goliath. Masters of the Congo Jungle (narrator only). 1961: La Fayette. King of Kings (narrator only). 1962: The Trial. River of the Ocean (narrator only). RoGoPaG. 1963: The VIPs. 1964: The Finest Hours (narrator only). The Fabulous Adventures of Marco Polo (GB: Marco the Magnificent). 1965: Is Paris Burning? 1966: A Man for All Seasons. Chimes at Midnight (US: Falstaff). 1967: Casino Royale. Sailor from Gibraltar. I'll Never Forget What's 'is Name. Oedipus the King. 1968: House of Cards. Kampf um Rom. The Immortal Story. Tepepa. 1969: Twelve Plus One/Una su tradici. The Southern Star. Kampf um Rom II. The Battle of Neretva. Start the Revolution without Me. The Kremlin Letter. Barbed Water (narrator only). 1970: Get to Know Your Rabbit. Waterloo. Catch 22. A Horse Called Nijinsky (narrator only). 1971: La décade prodigieuse (GB and US: Ten Days' Wonder). Malpertuis. Happiness in 20 Years (narrator only). Treasure Island. A Safe Place. 1972: Necromancy. Kelly Country (narrator only). 1973: F for Fake. 1974: And Then There Were None (voice only). 1975: Bugs Bunny, Superstar (narrator only). 1976: Voyage of the Damned. 1977: It Happened One Christmas (TV). 1978: The Muppet Movie. Filming Othello. A Woman Called Moses (narrator only). The Late, Great Planet Earth. Future Shock (TV. And narrator). 1980: Never Trust an Honest Thief. The Secret of Nikola Tesla. Shogun (narrator only). The Man Who Saw Tomorrow (and narrator). 1981: History of the World Part I. Butterfly. Genocide (narrator only). 1982: Slapstick (voice only. US Slapstick of Another Kind). 1983: Where is Parsifal? 1984: Almonds and Raisins (narrator only).

As director: _1934: *The Hearts of Age (co-directed). 1938: †Too Much Johnson. 1941: Citizen Kane. 1942: The Magnificent Ambersons. Journey into Fear (co-directed). ‡It's All True. 1946: The Stranger. 1948: The Lady from Shanghai. Macbeth. 1951: Othello. 1955: Confidential Report (US: Mr Arkadin). 1958: Touch of Evil. The Fountain of Youth. 1959: ‡Don Quixote. 1962: The Trial. 1966: Chimes at Midnight (US: Falstaff). 1968: Immortal Story. 1973: F for Fake._

Welles had also been working on the unfinished film 'The Other Side of the Wind' on and off from 1975.

†_Unreleased_ ‡_Uncompleted_

WELLS, Jacqueline
See BISHOP, Julie

WERNER, Oskar (Josef Bschliessmayer)
1922–1984
Baby-faced, fair-haired, blue-eyed, innocent-looking Austrian actor who always appeared years younger than his real age. Despite a memorable performance in his first Hollywood film, _Decision Before Dawn_, he did not break through to international stardom. It found him in the mid-sixties, but somehow slipped through his fingers, and he went back

to the theatre. An Oscar nominee for _Ship of Fools_, he died from a heart attack.
1949: The Angel with the Trumpet. 1950: Eroica. 1951: The Wonder Kid. Ruf aus dem Aether. Ein Lächeln in Sturm. Das gesothlene Jahr. Decision before Dawn. 1955: Der letzte Akt (GB: Ten Days to Die. US: The Life of Hitler). Spionage. Lola Montès. 1956: The Life of Mozart. 1961: Jules et Jim. 1965: Ship of Fools. The Spy Who Came in from the Cold. 1966: Fahrenheit 451. 1967: Interlude. 1968: The Shoes of the Fisherman. 1972: Ludwig. 1976: Voyage of the Damned.

WEST, Mae 1892–1980
Plumply sexy, stylish, fruity and scandalous blonde American entertainer who sidled along like a predatory costumed lobster casting her eyes (and antennae) over the men most likely to. Wrote most of her own material – a stream of clever _double-entendre_ one-liners with the accent on sex – and took Hollywood by storm after successful stage excesses, proving conclusively that 'When women go wrong, men go right after 'em'. The Hays Office's censors put an end to the best of her badinage, and latter-day appearances were sadly unnecessary. Died from complications following a stroke.
1932: Night after Night. 1933: She Done Him Wrong. I'm No Angel. 1934: Belle of the Nineties. 1935: Goin' to Town. 1936: Klondike Annie. Go West, Young Man. 1938: Every Day's a Holiday. 1940: My Little Chickadee. 1943: The Heat's On (GB: Tropicana). 1970: Myra Breckinridge. 1977: Sextette.

WHALEN, Michael (Joseph Shovlin)
1902–1974
Genial, tall, dark-haired, well-built American leading man who came to Hollywood after becoming a well-known voice in radio drama series (occasionally he sang too). A useful second-line star with his husky charm and solid presence, he played heroes in second-features (or second fiddle to Shirley Temple). War service disrupted his career, and he was too old to regain his place in the line-up of things on his return – although there were one or two more leads in 'B' thrillers. Died from bronchial pneumonia.
1935: Professional Soldier. 1936: The Man I Marry. The Song and Dance Man. Poor Little Rich Girl. Career Woman. The Country Doctor. Sing, Baby, Sing. White Fang. 1937: The Lady Escapes. Woman Wise. Time Out for Romance. Wee Willie Winkie. 1938: Time Out for Murder. Walking Down Broadway. Speed to Burn. Inside Story. Meridian 7–1212. Change of Heart. Island in the Sky. While New York Sleeps. Pardon Our Nerve. 1939: The Mysterious Miss X. They Asked for It. Outside These Walls. 1940: Ellery Queen, Master Detective. 1941: Sign of the Wolf. I'll Sell My Life. 1942: Nazi Spy Ring. Tahiti Honey. 1947: Gas House Kids in Hollywood. 1948: Blonde Ice. Highway 13. Thunder in the Pines. 1949: Omoo Omoo (GB: The Shark God). Sky Liner. Son of a Badman. Treasure of Monte Cristo. Shep Comes Home. Tough Assignment. Parole Inc. 1950: Sarumba. 1951: Mask of the Dragon. According to Mrs Hoyle. Kentucky Jubilee. Fingerprints Don't Lie. GI Jane. 1952: Waco (GB: The Outlaw and the Lady). King of the Bullwhip. 1955: The Silver Star. The Phantom from 10,000 Leagues. 1957: She Shoulda Said No. 1958: Missile to the Moon. 1960: Elmer Gantry.

WHEELER and WOOLSEY
WHEELER, Bert 1895–1968
WOOLSEY, Robert 1889–1938
American knockabout vaudeville comedy team whose slap-happy minor comedies proved popular with audiences (if not critics) in the thirties: their run was broken by Woolsey's early death from a kidney disease. He was the one who looked a bit like George Burns, and sported large spectacles and a stream of cigars. Wheeler had dark, wavy hair, a fresh face and seemingly endless teeth. He died from an emphysema.

*1929: Rio Rita. 1930: The Cuckoos. Half-Shot at Sunrise. Hook, Line and Sinker. Dixiana. 1931: *Oh! Oh! Cleopatra. Cracked Nuts. Caught Plastered. Peach O'Reno. 1932: *The Stolen Jools (GB: The Slippery Pearls). *Hollywood on Parade No. 3. Girl Crazy. Hold 'Em Jail. 1933: So This is Africa. Diplomaniacs. 1934: Hips! Hips! Hooray! Cockeyed Cavaliers. Kentucky Kernels (GB: Triple Trouble). 1935: The Nitwits. The Rainmakers. 1936: Silly Billies. Mummy's Boys. 1937: On Again, Off Again. High Flyers.*
Wheeler alone: *1929: *Small Timers. *The Voice of Hollywood. 1931: Too Many Cooks. 1932: *Hollywood Handicap. 1935: *A Night at the Biltmore Bowl. 1939: Cowboy Quarterback. 1941: Las Vegas Nights (GB: The Gay City). 1951: *The Awful Sleuth.*
Woolsey alone: *1922: Captain Fly-by-Night. 1930: *The Voice of Hollywood (2nd series). 1931: Everything's Rosie. 1933: Hollywood on Parade (B-7).*

WHITE, Carol 1941–
Impish child actress who grew up into a big, busty blonde. Had some promising ingenue roles in the early sixties, but her career seemed to have faded away when she made a sensational comeback in a television play, *Cathy Come Home,* and proved very effective in a few films as working-class girls whose bodies ruled their destinies. Less successful outside this mould.
1956: Circus Friends. 1959: Web of Suspicion. Carry on Teacher. 1960: Beat Girl. Surprise Package. Never Let Go. Linda. 1961: The Man in the Back Seat. A Matter of WHO. Village

of Daughters. 1962: The Boys. Gaolbreak. Bon Voyage! 1963: Ladies Who Do. 1965: The Playground (GB: Take Me When I'm Warm). 1966: Slave Girls (US: Prehistoric Women). 1967: Poor Cow. I'll Never Forget What's 'is Name. 1968: The Fixer. 1969: Daddy's Gone a-Hunting. 1970: The Man Who Had Power over Women. 1971: Something Big. Dulcima. 1972: Made. 1973: Some Call It Loving. 1977: The Squeeze. 1982: Nutcracker.

WHITE, Chrissie 1894–
Light-haired teenage actress from the early days of the British cinema, with which, at time of writing, she is the sole surviving link. The peak of her popularity came with Alma Taylor (*qv*) in the 'Tilly the Tomboy' series. She grew into a delicately pretty adult star, but disappointed her admirers by retiring in the early 1920s, with only a couple of appearances thereafter. Married her co-star and sometime director, Henry Edwards (*qv*).
1908: For the Little Lady's Sake. 1909: The Jewel Thieves. The Little Milliner and the Thief. The Cabman's Good Fairy. The Girl Who Joined the Bushrangers. 1910: The Sheriff's Daughter. Over the Garden Wall. Tilly the Tomboy Goes Boating. Tilly the Tomboy Buys Linoleum. 1911: A Sprained Ankle. Gipsy/Nan. When Tilly's Uncle Flirted. Tilly's Party. Tilly at the Seaside. Tilly Matchmaker. Tilly and the Mormon Missionary. Janet's Flirtation. Wealthy Brother John (US: Our Wealthy Nephew John). Tilly and the Fire Engine. The Greatest of These. The Reclamation of Sharky. In Jest and Earnest. The Fireman's Daughter. Tilly and the Smugglers. 1912: Love in a Laundry. Her Only Pal. A Curate's Love Story. The Mermaid. The Lieutenant's Bride. Tilly and the Dogs. The Deception. Tilly Works for a Living. Her 'Mail' Parent. A Man and a Serving Maid. Tilly in a Boarding House. The Unmasking of Maud. A Harlequinade Let Loose. Plot and Pash. 1913: Held for Ransom. The Curate's Bride. The Real Thing. At the Foot of the Scaffold. Love and a Burglar. The Defecting Detective. Blood and Bosh. Drake's Love Story. The Mysterious Philanthropist. All's Fair. The Man or His Money. Her Crowning Glory. Tilly's Breaking Up Party. Captain Jack VC. The Dogs and the Desperado. The Inevitable. Peter's Little Picnic. The Promise. The Old Nuisance. Kissing Cup. Look Before You Leap. Dr Trimball's Verdict. The Red

Light. Lt Pie's Love Story. The Gift. †The Vicar of Wakefield. For the Honour of the House. One Fair Daughter. A Damp Deed. For Marion's Sake. †Shadows of a Great City. For Love of Him. †David Garrick. Deceivers Both. †The Lady of Lyons. 1914: The Sneeze. The Curtain. Misleading Miss. Judged by Appearances. The Jealous Count. The Girl Who Played the Game. Two of a Kind. The Girl Who Lived in Straight Street. The Breaking Point. Only a Flower Girl. Dr Fenton's Ideal. A Knight of the Road. Rhubarb and Rascals. Lucky Jim. Simpkins Gets the War Scare. The Basilisk. The Unseen Witness. Wildflower. Pals. Time the Great Healer. Getting His Own Back. The Lie. Despised and Rejected. Tilly at the Football Match. John Linworth's Atonement. 1915: A Losing Game. †Barnaby Rudge. The Little Mother. The Man with the Scar. Coward! (US: They Called Him Coward). One Good Turn. Tilly and the Nut. Sister Susie's Sewing Shirts for Soldiers. Phyllis and the Foreigner. Behind the Curtain. †The Incorruptible Crown. The Sweater. The Second String. †The Man Who Stayed at Home. †Her Boy. †Sweet Lavender. Wife, the Weaker Vessel. †The Nightbirds of London. The Recalling of John Grey. †As the Sun Went Down. The Painted Lady Betty. Schoolgirl Rebels. The Confession. Marmaduke and His Angel. 1916: Who's Your Friend? Miggles' Maid. Face to Face. †A Bunch of Violets. †The White Boys. †Sowing the Wind. Partners. Tubby's Spanish Girls. Tubby's Bungle-Oh! Tubby's Good Work. †Comin' thro' the Rye. †Molly Bawn. 1917: †Her Marriage Lines. †The Man Behind 'The Times'. †Carrots. †The Eternal Triangle. †The Failure. A Grain of Sand. The Countess of Summacount. Lollipops and Poses. Neighbours. The Joke That Failed. †The Blindness of Fortune. †The Failure. †Broken Threads. †Dick Carson wins Through. 1918: †The Hanging Judge. The Message. Against the Grain. Anna. Her Savings Saved. The Poet's Windfall. What's the Use of Grumbling? The Secret. The Refugee. †Towards the Light. 1919: Broken in the Wars. †His Dearest Possession. †The Kinsman. †Possession. †The City of Beautiful Nonsense. 1920: †A Temporary Vagabond. † Aylwin. †The Amazing Quest of Ernest Bliss. †John Forrest Finds Himself. 1921: †The Lunatic at Large. †Wild Heather. †The Bargain. 1922: †Simple Simon. †Tit for Tat. 1923: †Lily of the Alley. †Boden's Boy. †The Naked Man. 1924: †The World of Wonderful Reality. 1930: †The Call of the Sea. 1933: †General John Regan.

All shorts except †features

WHITE, Pearl 1889–1938
Round-faced, resolute-looking, auburn-haired American star who began as a stunt girl, then became the queen of the silent serials, in a series of hair-raising chapter plays, at the end of each episode of which she would be left in some quite inextricable predicament. Her name survives in memory more than many of her more distinguished contemporaries. She quit Hollywood in the 1920s

and went to live in France, but died there from a liver ailment at 49.

1910: The Life of Buffalo Bill. The New Magdalene. The Hoodoo. The Girl from Arizona. A Summer Flirtation. The Maid of Niagara. The Woman Hater. 1911: The Power of Love. The Lost Necklace. Helping Him Out. Through the Window. Angel of the Slums. Home Sweet Home. For the Honor of the Name. 1912: Mayblossom. The Gypsy Flirt. A Tangled Marriage. The Girl in the Next Room. Her Dressmaker's Bills. Locked Out. His Birthday. Bella's Beau. The Chorus Girl. The Mind Cure. Oh Such a Night! 1913: Pearl's Mistake. Where Charity Begins. Pearl's Hero. The Women and the Law. Girls Will Be Boys. Hubby's New Coat. The Convict's Daughter. Hearts Entangled. Dress Reform. Robert's Lesson. His Rich Uncle. A Woman's Revenge. The Cabaret Singer. A Dip into Society. Heroic Harold. That Other Girl. Pearl as a Detective. The Girl Reporter. Pearl and the Tramp. Pearl and the Poet. Oh, You Pearl! Accident Insurance. 1914: Shadowed. The Perils of Pauline (serial). The Exploits of Elaine (serial). The Ring. Lizzie and the Ice Man. Willie's Disguise. 1915: The New Exploits of Elaine (serial). The Romance of Elaine (serial). New York Lights. 1916: Pearl of the Army (serial). The Iron Claw (serial). Hazel Kirke. The King's Game. 1917: The Fatal Ring (serial). 1918: The House of Hate (serial). 1919: The Black Secret (serial). The Lightning Raider (serial). 1920: The White Moll. Black is White. The Dark Mirror. 1921: A Virgin Paradise. Know Your Men. The Thief. Beyond Price. Tiger's Cub. The Mountain Woman. 1922: Any Wife. Without Fear. The Broadway Peacock. 1923: Plunder (serial). 1924: Parisian Nights. 1925: Perils of Paris/Terreur (serial).

WHITELAW, Billie 1932–

Tawny, tigerish British actress, often in strong-willed roles: can play tough, sexy or friendly. A familiar radio voice from an early age, notably as 'Henry' in the long-running Norman and Henry Bones series for children, she has since made shamefully few films, and it is some mystery why she did not make the front rank in the British cinema. Married/divorced Peter Vaughan (P. Ohm 1923–   ).

1953: The Fake. 1954: Companions in Crime. The Sleeping Tiger. 1955: Room in the House.

1957: Small Hotel. Miracle in Soho. 1958: Gideon's Day (US: Gideon of Scotland Yard). Carve Her Name with Pride. 1959: Bobbikins. 1960: The Flesh and the Fiends (US: Mania). Hell is a City. Make Mine Mink. No Love for Johnnie. 1961: Mr Topaze (US: I Like Money). Payroll. 1962: The Devil's Agent. 1963: The Comedy Man. Becket. 1967: Charlie Bubbles. 1968: Dr Jekyll and Mr Hyde (TV). Twisted Nerve. 1969: The Adding Machine. Start the Revolution without Me. 1970: Leo the Last. Eagle in a Cage. 1971: Gumshoe. 1972: Frenzy. 1973: Night Watch. 1976: The Omen. 1977: Leopard in the Snow. 1978: The Water Babies. 1981: A Tale of Two Cities (TV). An Unsuitable Job for a Woman. 1982: The Dark Crystal (voice only). 1983: Tangier. Slayground. 1984: Camille (TV). 1985: The Chain. Shady. Murder Elite.

WHITMAN, Stuart 1926–

Black-haired, craggy-faced American leading man who played a lot of very small roles before breaking into the big time via a Fox contract. These years at the studio (1958–1965) were his only ones as a top Hollywood star, and contain his best performances. Since then he has remained a regular, if somewhat immobile, second-line leading man. Won an Oscar nomination for The Mark.

1951: When Worlds Collide. The Day the Earth Stood Still. 1952: Barbed Wire (GB: False News). One Minute to Zero. 1953: The All-American (GB: The Winning Way). All I Desire. The Veils of Bagdad. 1954: Rhapsody. Silver Lode. Brigadoon. Passion. 1955: King of the Carnival (serial). Diane. 1956: Seven Men

from Now. Crime of Passion. 1957: Bombers B-52 (GB: No Sleep Till Dawn). Johnny Trouble. Hell Bound. The Girl in Black Stockings. War Drums. Darby's Rangers (GB: The Young Invaders). 1958: Ten North Frederick. The Decks Ran Red. China Doll. 1959: These Thousand Hills. The Sound and the Fury. Hound Dog Man. 1960: Murder Inc. The Story of Ruth. 1961: The Mark. The Fiercest Heart. Francis of Assisi. The Comancheros. 1962: Convicts Four (GB: Reprieve!). The Longest Day. Le jour et l'heure. 1964: Signpost to Murder. Shock Treatment. Rio Conchos. 1965: Those Magnificent Men in Their Flying Machines. Sands of the Kalahari. 1966: An American Dream (GB: See You in Hell, Darling). 1968: The Last Escape. The Invincible Six. 1969: Sweet Hunters. Four Rode Out. The Only Way Out is Dead (US: TV, as The Man Who Wanted to Live Forever). 1970: The Man Who Died Twice (TV). 1971: City Beneath the Sea (TV. GB: cinemas, as One Hour to Doomsday). Captain Apache. Revenge! (TV). The Last Generation. Breakout. 1972: The Woman Hunter (TV). Seeta the Mountain Lion (GB: Run Cougar Run). Night of the Lepus. The Lost World of Libra. The Heroes. 1973: The Cat Creature (TV). Welcome to Arrow Beach (US: Tender Flesh). 1974: Shatter (US: Call Him Mr Shatter). 1975: Las Vegas Lady. Mean Johnny Barrows. Oil: The Billion Dollar Fire. Crazy Mama. 1976: Blazing Magnum/Strange Shadows in an Empty Room. Delta Fox. On a Dead Man's Chest. Eaten Alive (GB: Death Trap). Tony Saitta/Tough Tony. 1977: The White Buffalo. Assault on Paradise (GB: Maniac. Later on TV, as Ransom). Ruby. The Thoroughbreds (later Treasure Seekers). 1978: Go West Young Girl (TV). Woman from the Torrid Land. Run for the Roses. 1979: Guyana: The Crime of the Century. When I Am King. The Seekers (TV). 1980: Cuba Crossing. Macabra (US: Demonoid). Hostages. The Monster Club. 1981: Greed. Butterfly. Magnum Thrust. High Country Pursuit. 1982: Sweet Dirty Tony. 1983: Vultures in Paradise/Flesh and Bullets. 1984: Treasure of the Amazon/Treasure of Doom. 1985: First Strike. Deadly Thunder.

WIDMARK, Richard 1914–

Fair-haired, pale-faced, grey-eyed American actor with distinctive metallic voice. Began his career as a teacher, and Hollywood failed to

another decade in big-budget laughter-and-tears stuff. Received two Oscar nominations, for *The Pied Piper* and *Since You Went Away*. Died from a kidney ailment.

*1936: Ladies in Love. 1937: Live, Love and Learn. Nothing Sacred. 1938: Arsene Lupin Returns. Everybody Sing. Girl of the Golden West. Lord Jeff (GB: The Boy from Barnardo's). Artists and Models Abroad (GB: Stranded in Paris). Three Comrades. Young Dr Kildare. Vacation from Love. Zaza. 1939: Midnight. Never Say Die. Man About Town. *See Your Doctor. Honeymoon in Bali (GB: Husbands or Lovers). Dancing Co-Ed (GB: Every Other Inch a Lady). 1941: The Man Who Came to Dinner. 1942: Tonight at 8:30 (GB: The Light of Heart). The Pied Piper. 1943: Holy Matrimony. 1944: Irish Eyes Are Smiling. Since You Went Away. 1945: Molly and Me. 1946: Night and Day. 1947: The Bishop's Wife. 1948: Miss Tatlock's Millions. Paris 1900 (narrator only). 1951: As Young As You Feel. 1955: Kismet. 1956: Eloise (TV).*

WOOLSEY, Robert
See WHEELER and WOOLSEY

WORTH, Brian 1914–1978
Dark-haired, heftily-built, smoothly good-looking British romantic leading man of

upper-crust appeal. He looked to have all the qualities for stardom, but drifted into second-features and then supporting roles. A trip to Hollywood might have helped, but in Britain he proved more successful on television, especially in the 1950s. War service undoubtedly damaged the flow of his film career.

1939: The Lion Has Wings. The Arsenal Stadium Mystery. 1940: Pastor Hall. Gentleman of Venture (US: It Happened to One Man). 1948: One Night with You. Cardboard Cavalier. 1950: Last Holiday. 1951: Tom Brown's Schooldays. The Man in the White Suit. Scrooge (US: A Christmas Carol). 1952: Song of Paris (US: Bachelor in Paris). Treasure Hunt. Hindle Wakes (US: Holiday Week). It Started in Paradise. Father's Doing Fine. 1953: Operation Diplomat. Thought to Kill. 1954: An Inspector Calls. 1955: Barbados Quest (US: Murder on Approval). Windfall. The Final Column. 1956: Breakaway. Assignment Redhead (US: Requirement for a Redhead). Battle of the River Plate (US: Pursuit of the Graf

Spee). 1957: Ill-Met by Moonlight (US: Night Ambush). 1958: The Square Peg. Room at the Top. 1959: Northwest Frontier (US: Flame over India). Peeping Tom. 1960: Sink the Bismarck! Moment of Danger (US: Malaga). Dead Lucky. 1961: The Terror of the Tongs. 1969: On Her Majesty's Secret Service. 1972: The Boy Who Turned Yellow.

WRAY, Fay (Vina F. Wray) 1907–
Canadian actress with red-brown hair and attractive almond eyes, a great beauty adrift in westerns when whisked to stardom by Erich von Stroheim in *The Wedding March*; immortalized a few years later as the girl admired by *King Kong*. She gained a reputation as the great screaming heroine of thirties' horror films. Retired on marrying her second husband, writer-producer Robert Riskin, in 1942, but he died in 1955.

*1923: *Gasoline Love. 1925: *What Price Goofy? *No Father to Guide Her. The Coast Patrol. A Cinch for the Gander. 1926: Wild Horse Stampede. Lazy Lightning. *Don't Shoot. The Man in the Saddle. A One-Man Game. Loco Luck. 1927: Spurs and Saddles. 1928: The Wedding March. Legion of the Condemned. The First Kiss. The Streets of Sin. The Four Feathers. 1929: Pointed Heels. Thunderbolt. 1930: Captain Thunder. Behind the Make-Up. The Sea God. The Border Legion. Paramount on Parade. The Texan (GB: The Big Race). 1931: Not Exactly Gentlemen (GB: The Three Rogues). The Finger Points. The Lawyer's Secret. The Conquering Horde. *The Stolen Jools (GB: The Slippery Pearls). Dirigible. The Unholy Garden. 1932: The Most Dangerous Game (GB: The Hounds of Zaroff). Stowaway. Doctor X. 1933: Below the Sea. King Kong. The Woman I Stole. The Vampire Bat. Ann Carver's Profession. The Big Brain (GB: Enemies of Society). The Mystery of the Wax Museum. One Sunday Afternoon. The Bowery. Master of Men. Shanghai Madness. 1934: The Countess of Monte Cristo. Madame Spy. The Affairs of Cellini. The Richest Girl in the World. Woman in the Dark. Once to Every Woman. Viva Villa! Black Moon. Cheating Cheaters. White Lies. 1935: Bulldog Jack (US: Alias Bulldog Drummond). Come Out of the Pantry. The Clairvoyant. Mills of the Gods. 1936: When Knights Were Bold. They Met in a Taxi. Roaming Lady. 1937: Murder in Greenwich Village. It Happened in*

Hollywood (GB: Once a Hero). 1938: The Jury's Secret. Smashing the Spy Ring. 1939: Navy Secrets. 1940: Wildcat Bus. 1941: Adam Had Four Sons. Melody for Three. 1942: Not a Ladies' Man. 1953: Small Town Girl. Treasure of the Golden Condor. 1955: The Cobweb. Queen Bee. Hell on Frisco Bay. 1956: In Times Like These (TV. GB: cinemas). 1957: Rock Pretty Baby. Crime of Passion. Tammy and the Bachelor (GB: Tammy). Dragstrip Riot (GB: The Reckless Age). Summer Love. 1959: Second Happiest Day (TV). 1980: Gideon's Trumpet (TV).

WRIGHT, Teresa (Muriel T. Wright) 1918–
Small, slight, gentle-mannered American actress with reddish-brown hair, an Oscar-winner in her second film (*Mrs Miniver*) but, seen far too early in mother roles (the first in 1953), she faded from the film scene and has spent most of her later years on stage. Married (second) to playwright Robert Anderson in 1959. Also received Oscar nominations for *The Little Foxes* and *Pride of the Yankees*.

1941: The Little Foxes. 1942: Pride of the Yankees. Mrs Miniver. 1943: Shadow of a Doubt. 1944: Casanova Brown. 1945: The Trouble with Women (released 1947). 1946: The Best Years of Our Lives. The Imperfect Lady (GB: Mrs Loring's Secret). 1947: Pursued. 1948: Enchantment. 1950: The Capture. The Men. 1952: Something to Live For. California Conquest. The Steel Trap. 1953: The Actress. Count the Hours. 1954. Track of the Cat. 1955: Miracle on 34th Street (TV. GB: cinemas). 1956: The Search for Bridey Murphy. 1957: The Miracle Worker (TV). Escapade in Japan. Edge of Innocence (TV). 1958: The Restless Years (GB: The Wonderful Years). 1969: Hail Hero! The Happy Ending. 1972: Crawlspace (TV). 1974: The Elevator (TV). 1975: Flood! (TV). 1977: Roseland. 1980: Somewhere in Time. 1983: Bill: On His Own (TV).

WRIGHT, Tony 1925–1986
Fair-haired British actor who had his first success in French films (after varied early career including whaling in the Antarctic, and repertory in South Africa), then, for a few brief years, became the 'beefcake boy' of British films. Hadn't quite the acting range required for permanent stardom, but he

remained a working actor, latterly in small parts on television. Died from multiple injuries after a fall.

1953: *The Flanagan Boy* (US: *Bad Blonde*). 1954: *A toi de jouer, Callaghan* (GB: *The Amazing Mr Callaghan*). 1955: *Plus de whisky pour Callaghan*. 1956: *Et par ici la sortie. Jumping for Joy. Jacqueline. Tiger in the Smoke*. 1957: *Seven Thunders* (US: *The Beasts of Marseilles*). *The Stars Don't Shine*. 1958: *The Spaniard's Curse*. 1959: *Broth of a Boy. In the Wake of a Stranger. The Rough and the Smooth* (US: *Portrait of a Sinner*). 1960: *Faces in the Dark. And the Same to You. The House in Marsh Road* (US: *The Invisible Creature*). 1961: *Attempt to Kill. Callaghan remet ça*. 1962: *Journey to Nowhere*. 1965: *The Liquidator*. 1970: *The Man Who Haunted Himself*. 1971: *All Coppers Are...Clinic Xclusive. The Magnificent Six and a Half (third series). Kidnapped*. 1972: *The Creeping Flesh*. 1975: *Hostages*. 1979: *Can I Come Too?*

WYATT, Jane 1912–
It rhymes with 'quiet' and that's just the impression one gets from this small, pretty, brown-haired American actress capable on occasions of such glowing warmth that it was a shame her film career was largely limited to waiting women. Still, she did rather better on stage, and won three Emmys for the long-running TV series *Father Knows Best* in the fifties.

1934: *One More River* (GB: *Over the River*). *Great Expectations*. 1936: *We're Only Human. The Luckiest Girl in the World*. 1937: *Lost Horizon*. 1940: *The Girl from God's Country*. 1941: *Kisses for Breakfast. Hurricane Smith.*

Week-End for Three. 1942: *Army Surgeon. The Navy Comes Through*. 1943: *Buckskin Frontier* (GB: *The Iron Road*). *The Kansan* (GB: *Wagon Wheels*). 1944: *None But the Lonely Heart*. 1946: *Strange Conquest. The Bachelor's Daughters* (GB: *Bachelor Girls*). 1947: *Gentleman's Agreement. Boomerang*. 1948: *Pitfall. No Minor Vices*. 1949: *Task Force. Bad Boy. Canadian Pacific*. 1950: *Our Very Own. House by the River. My Blue Heaven. The Man Who Cheated Himself*. 1951: *Criminal Lawyer*. 1957: *Interlude*. 1961: *The Two Little Bears*. 1964: *See How They Run* (TV). 1965: *Never Too Late*. 1970: *Weekend of Terror* (TV). 1973: *You'll Never See Me Again* (TV). 1975: *Tom Sawyer* (TV). *Katherine* (TV). 1976: *The Treasure of Matecumbe. Amelia Earhart* (TV). 1977: *The Father Knows Best Christmas Reunion* (TV). *A Love Affair: the Eleanor and Lou Gehrig Story* (TV). 1978: *Superdome* (TV). *The Millionaire* (TV). *The Nativity* (TV). 1982: *Missing Children: a Mother's Story* (TV). 1986: *Star Trek IV: The Voyage Home*.

WYMAN, Jane (Sarah J. Fulks) 1914–
Brunette (earlier blonde) American actress, singer, dancer, painter and designer who served ten years as girl-friends in routine thrillers and comedies before getting a reward for perseverance with the lead in *The Lost Weekend*. That led to *Johnny Belinda* (an Oscar as a deaf mute) and a lushly-mounted series of films known as Wyman weepies, in which she plucked at the heartstrings of the world as she suffered in poverty and luxury alike. Married (second of four) to Ronald Reagan (*qv*), 1940 to 1948. Also nominated for Academy Awards on *The Yearling, The Blue Veil* and *Magnificent Obsession*.

1932: †*The Kid from Spain*. 1933: †*Elmer the Great*. 1934: †*College Rhythm*. 1935: †*Rumba*. †*All the King's Horses*. †*Stolen Harmony*. †*King of Burlesque*. 1936: †*Polo Joe*. †*Anything Goes. Cain and Mabel. Gold Diggers of 1937. My Man Godfrey. Smart Blonde. Stage Struck*. 1937: *Slim. The King and the Chorus Girl* (GB: *Romance is Sacred*). *Public Wedding. Ready, Willing and Able. The Singing Marine. Mr Dodd Takes the Air*. 1938: *Wide Open Faces. The Spy Ring Brother Rat. The Crowd Roars. He Couldn't Say No. Fools for Scandal. Tailspin*. 1939: *The Kid from*

Kokomo (GB: *Orphan of the Ring*). *Private Detective. Torchy Plays with Dynamite. Kid Nightingale*. 1940: *Brother Rat and a Baby* (GB: *Baby Be Good*). *Flight Angels. Tugboat Annie Sails Again*. *The Sunday Round-Up. An Angel from Texas. My Love Came Back. Gambling on the High Seas*. 1941: *The Body Disapppears. Bad Men of Missouri. You're in the Army Now*. 1942: *Footlight Serenade. Larceny Inc. My Favorite Spy*. 1943: *Princess O'Rourke*. 1944: *The Doughgirls. Make Your Own Bed. Hollywood Canteen. Crime By Night*. 1945: *The Lost Weekend*. 1946: *One More Tomorrow. Night and Day. The Yearling*. 1947: *Magic Town. Cheyenne*. 1948: *Johnny Belinda*. 1949: *The Lady Takes a Sailor. A Kiss in the Dark. It's a Great Feeling. Stage Fright*. 1950: *The Glass Menagerie*. 1951: *The Blue Veil. Three Guys Named Mike. Starlift. Here Comes the Groom*. 1952: *Just for You. The Will Rogers Story* (GB: *The Story of Will Rogers*). 1953: *Let's Do It Again. So Big*. 1954: *Magnificent Obsession*. 1955: *All That Heaven Allows. Lucy Gallant. Miracle in the Rain*. 1959: *Holiday for Lovers*. 1960: *Pollyanna*. 1962: *Bon Voyage!* 1969: *How to Commit Marriage*. 1971: *The Failing of Raymond* (TV). 1979: *The Incredible Journey of Dr Meg Laurel* (TV).

† *As Sarah Jane Fulks (when billed)*

WYNTER, Dana (Dagmar Spencer-Marcus) 1930–
Raven-haired, pale-faced, coolly glamorous, British-born, South African-raised leading lady, at first in small roles in British films, but then enjoying a few years of Hollywood stardom (she stayed in America) as a Fox contractee.

1951: †*White Corridors*. †*Lady Godiva Rides Again*. †*The Woman's Angle*. 1952: †*The Crimson Pirate*. †*Something Money Can't Buy*. †*It Started in Paradise*. 1953: †*Colonel March Investigates. Knights of the Round Table*. 1955: *Laura* (TV. GB: *cinemas*). *The View from Pompey's Head* (GB: *Secret Interlude*). 1956: *Invasion of the Body Snatchers. D-Day the Sixth of June*. 1957: *Winter Dreams* (TV). *Something of Value. Diamond Safari*. 1958: *The Violent Heart* (TV). *Fraulein. In Love and War. Wings of the Dove* (TV). 1959: *Shake Hands with the Devil*. 1960: *Sink the Bismarck!* 1961: *On the Double*. 1963: *The*

List of Adrian Messenger. 1966: Danger Has Two Faces (TV). 1968: If He Hollers, Let Him Go! Companions in Nightmare (TV). The Crime (TV). 1969: Airport. Any Second Now (TV). 1971: Triangle. Owen Marshall—Counsellor at Law (TV). 1972: Santee. 1973: The Connection (TV). The Questor Tapes (TV). 1975: The Lives of Jenny Dolan (TV). Le sauvage (US: Lovers Like Us). 1980: M Station: Hawaii (TV). 1984: The Royal Romance of Charles and Diana (TV).
† as Dagmar Wynter.

WYNYARD, Diana (Dorothy Cox) 1906–1964

Fair-haired, personably attractive British actress who went to Hollywood in 1932, but returned after only seven feature films there and went back to the stage. Fortunately, the

British cinema persuaded her to try another little burst of films, including the brilliant

Gaslight, before her star days were over. Married/divorced director Carol Reed. Received an Academy Award nomination for *Cavalcade*. Died from a kidney ailment.

*1933: Rasputin and the Empress (GB: Rasputin the Mad Monk). Cavalcade. Men Must Fight. Reunion in Vienna. 1934: Where Sinners Meet (GB: The Dover Road). *Hollywood on Parade No. 13. One More River (GB: Over the River). Let's Try Again (GB: Marriage Symphony). 1939: On the Night of the Fire (US: The Fugitive). 1940: Gaslight (US: Angel Street). 1941: Freedom Radio (US: A Voice in the Night). The Prime Minister. Kipps (US: The Remarkable Mr Kipps). 1947: An Ideal Husband. 1951: Tom Brown's Schooldays. 1956: The Feminine Touch (US: The Gentle Touch). 1957: Island in the Sun. 1959: The Second Man (TV).*

YORK, Michael 1942–

Fair-haired British actor with gentle, refined voice whose almost impossibly boyish good looks are fortunately tempered and toughened by a broken nose. Usually seen as callow aristocrats, but has hinted that he could also play comedy better than most. One of Britain's busiest actors in the 1970s, but his box-office success faltered after 1978 and it may take him some time to mature into character roles.

1962: *The Mind Benders.* 1966: *The Taming of the Shrew.* 1967: *Smashing Time. Confessions of a Loving Couple. Accident. Red and Blue.* 1968: *The Guru. Romeo and Juliet. The Strange Affair.* 1969: *Justine. Alfred the Great.* 1970: *Something for Everyone (GB: Black Flowers for the Bride).* 1971: *Zeppelin.* 1972: *Cabaret. England Made Me. Lost Horizon.* 1973: *The Three Musketeers: the Queen's Diamonds.* 1974: *Murder on the Orient Express. The Four Musketeers: the Revenge of Milady.* 1975: *Great Expectations (TV. GB: cinemas). Conduct Unbecoming. Touch and Go.* 1976: *Seven Nights in Japan. Logan's Run.* 1977: *The Island of Dr Moreau. The Last Remake of Beau Geste.* 1978: *Death on the Nile. The Riddle of the Sands. Fedora.* 1979: *A Man Called Intrepid (made for cinemas but shown only on TV).* 1980: *Final Assignment.* 1981: *The White Lions (released 1983).* 1983: *For Those I Loved/Au nom de tous les miens. Phantom of the Opera (TV). Le sang des autres.* 1984: *Success is the Best Revenge.* 1985: *L'aube.*

YORK, Susannah (S. Fletcher) 1939–

Beguiling, baby-faced, charismatic star actress, another in the long line of plummy-voiced British blondes. At first in appealing ingenue roles, she then played anything from English roses to boldly sexual roles, without compromising her popularity, which lasted until near the end of the 1970s. Also a writer of children's books, she won an Academy Award nomination for *They Shoot Horses, Don't They?*

1960: *Tunes of Glory. There Was a Crooked Man.* 1961: *The Greengage Summer.* 1962: *Freud (GB: Freud – the Secret Passion).* 1963: *Tom Jones.* 1964: *The Seventh Dawn. *Scene Nun, Take One.* 1965: **Scruggs. Sands of the Kalahari.* 1966: *Kaleidoscope. A Man for All Seasons.* 1967: *Sebastian.* 1968: *Duffy. The Killing of Sister George.* 1969: *They Shoot Horses, Don't They? Lock Up Your Daughters! Oh! What a Lovely War. Battle of Britain. Country Dance (US: Brotherly Love).* 1970: *Jane Eyre (TV. GB: cinemas).* 1971: *Zee and Co. (US: X, Y and Zee). Happy Birthday. Wanda June.* 1972: *Images.* 1974: *Gold. The Maids.* 1975: *Conduct Unbecoming. Sky Riders. That Lucky Touch.* 1977: *Eliza Fraser (GB: TV, as The Rollicking Adventures of Eliza Fraser).* 1978: *The Shout. Long Shot. The Silent Partner. Superman.* 1979: *The Specter on the Bridge/The Golden Gate Murders (TV). Falling in Love Again (released 1981).* 1980: *The Awakening. Alice. Loophole. *Late Flowering Love.* 1983: *Yellowbeard. 99 Women.* 1984: *A Christmas Carol (TV. GB: cinemas).*

YOUNG, Gig (Byron Barr) 1913–1978

Sardonically-smiling, dark-haired American leading man, mainly in comedy in his latter days, although an Academy Award winner in 1969 in a dramatic role (*They Shoot Horses, Don't They?*). Started as a moustachioed romantic lead, but soon became known as the amiable guy who didn't get the girl, notably in Doris Day comedies of the late fifties and early sixties. He didn't get the girl in real life, either: of his five marriages, four ended in divorce (his second wife died), including the third, to actress Elizabeth Montgomery (1933–). He received additional Oscar nominations for *Come Fill the Cup* and *Teacher's Pet*. Committed suicide (shot himself).

1940: †*Misbehaving Husbands.* 1941: †*One Foot in Heaven. *†Here Come the Cavalry.* †*Dive Bomber.* †*The Man Who Came to Dinner.* †*You're in the Army Now.* †*Sergeant York.* †*They Died with Their Boots On.* †*Navy Blues.* 1942: †*The Male Animal.* †*Captains of the Clouds.* †*The Gay Sisters.* 1943: *Old Acquaintance. Air Force.* 1947: *Escape Me Never. The Woman in White.* 1948: *Wake of the Red Witch. The Three Musketeers.* 1949: *Tell It to the Judge. Lust for Gold.* 1950: *Hunt the Man Down.* 1951: *Target Unknown. Too Young to Kiss. Come Fill the Cup. Only the Valiant. Slaughter Trail.* 1952: *Holiday for Sinners. You for Me.* 1953: *City That Never Sleeps. The Girl Who Had Everything. Arena. Torch Song.* 1954: *Young at Heart.* 1955: *The Desperate Hours.* 1957: *Desk Set (GB: His Other Woman).* 1958: *Teacher's Pet. The Tunnel of Love.* 1959: *Ask Any Girl. The Story on Page One.* 1962: *That Touch of Mink. Kid Galahad. Five Miles to Midnight.* 1963: *For Love or Money. A Ticklish Affair.* 1965: *Strange Bedfellows.* 1966: *The Shuttered Room.* 1968: *Companions in Nightmare (TV).* 1969: *They Shoot Horses, Don't They?* 1970: *Lovers and Other Strangers.* 1971: *The Neon Ceiling (TV).* 1974: *The Great Ice Rip-Off (TV). Bring Me the Head of Alfredo Garcia. Deborah/A Black Ribbon for Deborah.* 1975: *The Hindenberg. Michèle. The Killer Elite.* 1976: *Sherlock Holmes in New York (TV).* 1977: *Spectre (TV).* 1978: *Game of Death.*

YOUNG, Loretta (Gretchen Belzer) 1913– Blue-eyed brunette (sometimes blonde in earlier days) American actress with liquid lips who was both pretty and glamorous and stayed at the top (admittedly in mostly mediocre films) for more than 20 years before calling it a day. Best roles came in the early thirties and late forties (during which latter period she won an Oscar for *The Farmer's Daughter*). Married Grant Withers (1904–1959) from 1930 to 1931, first of two. Also nominated for an Academy Award on *Come to the Stable*.

1917: †The Only Way. 1921: †The Sheik. 1927: Naughty But Nice. 1928: The Magnificent Flirt. Whip Woman. Scarlet Seas. Laugh, Clown, Laugh. The Head Man. 1929: The Fast Life. The Squall. The Show of Shows. The Girl in the Glass Cage. The Careless Age. The Forward Pass. 1930: Show Girl in Hollywood. The Man from Blankley's. The Second Floor Mystery. Loose Ankles. Kismet. The Devil to Pay. Road to Paradise. The Truth about Youth. 1931: Three Girls Lost. Beau Ideal. Big Business Girl. Platinum Blonde. The Right of Way. Too Young to Marry. I Like Your Nerve. The Ruling Voice. 1932: Play Girl. Taxi. Life Begins (GB: The Dawn of Life). The Hatchet Man (GB: The Honourable Mr Wong). Week-End Marriage (GB: Working Wives). They Call It Sin (GB: The Way of Life). 1933: Employees' Entrance. The Life of Jimmy Dolan (GB: The Kid's Last Fight). Grand Slam. Zoo in Budapest. Midnight Mary. The Devil's in Love. Man's Castle. Heroes for Sale. She Had to Say Yes. 1934: Bulldog Drummond Strikes Back. The House of Rothschild. The White Parade. Born to be Bad. Caravan. 1935: Call of the Wild. Clive of India. Shanghai. The Crusades. 1936: Ramona. The Unguarded Hour. Private Number (GB: Secret Interlude). Ladies in Love. 1937: Love under Fire. Love is News. Second Honeymoon. Café Metropole. Wife, Doctor and Nurse. 1938: Suez. Four Men and a Prayer. Kentucky. Three Blind Mice. 1939: Eternally Yours. The Story of Alexander Graham Bell (GB: The Modern Miracle). Wife, Husband and Friend. 1940: The Doctor Takes a Wife. He Stayed for Breakfast. 1941: Bedtime Story. The Lady from Cheyenne. The Men in Her Life. 1942: A Night to Remember. 1943: China. 1944: And Now Tomorrow. Ladies Courageous. 1945: Along Came Jones. 1946: The Stranger. The Perfect Marriage. 1947: The Farmer's Daughter. The Bishop's Wife. 1948: Rachel and the Stranger. The Accused. 1949: Mother is a Freshman (GB: Mother Knows Best). Come to the Stable. 1950: Key to the City. 1951: Half Angel. Cause for Alarm. 1952: Paula (GB: The Silent Voice). Because of You. 1953: It Happens Every Thursday. 1960: The Immaculate Road (TV. GB: cinemas).

†*as Gretchen Young*

YOUNG, Robert 1907–

Quiet, round-faced, dark-haired, well-groomed American star with ready faint smile. After many years of charming blandness (he once described himself in Hollywood in the early sound days as 'an introvert in a field of extroverts'), he surprisingly developed into a solid actor, defeated alcoholism, and made

almost all his best films in a very good run from 1941 to 1948. From 1949 to 1961, first on radio, then on TV, starred in the phenomenally successful series *Father Knows Best*, winning two Emmys along the way. Another successful TV series, *Marcus Welby MD*, followed from 1969 to 1975.

1931: The Sin of Madelon Claudet (GB: The Lullaby). The Black Camel. Hell Divers. Guilty Generation. 1932: New Morals for Old. The Wet Parade. The Kid from Spain. Strange Interlude (GB: Strange Interval). Unashamed. 1933: Men Must Fight. Today We Live. Saturday's Millions. Tugboat Annie. Right to Romance. Hell Below. 1934: Cardboard City. The House of Rothschild. Spitfire. Hollywood Party. Paris Interlude. The Band Plays On. Carolina (GB: The House of Connelly). Lazy River. Whom the Gods Destroy. Death on the Diamond. 1935: Calm Yourself. West Point of the Air. The Bride Comes Home. Vagabond Lady. Red Salute (GB: Arms and the Girl). Remember Last Night? 1936: It's Love Again. Secret Agent. Sworn Enemy. The Longest Night. Three Wise Guys. The Bride Walks Out. Stowaway. 1937: The Emperor's Candlesticks. Dangerous Number. The Bride Wore Red. I Met Him in Paris. Married Before Breakfast. 1938: The Toy Wife (GB: Frou-Frou). Paradise for Three (GB: Romance for Three). Rich Man, Poor Girl. Josette. Three Comrades. The Shining Hour. 1939: Maisie. Honolulu. Miracles for Sale. Bridal Suite. 1940: The Mortal Storm. Florian. Sporting Blood. Dr Kildare's Crisis. Northwest Passage. 1941: Lady Be Good. The Trial of Mary Dugan. Married Bachelor. Western Union. H.M. Pulham Esq. 1942: Joe Smith, American (GB: Highway to Freedom). Cairo. Journey for Margaret. 1943: Sweet Rosie O'Grady. Slightly Dangerous. Claudia. 1944: The Canterville Ghost. 1945: Those Endearing Young Charms. The Enchanted Cottage. 1946: Lady Luck. Claudia and David. The Searching Wind. 1947: Crossfire. They Won't Believe Me. 1948: Relentless. Sitting Pretty. 1949: Bride for Sale. Adventure in Baltimore (GB: Bachelor Bait). That Forsyte Woman (GB: The Forsyte Saga). 1950: And Baby Makes Three. The Second Woman (GB: Ellen). 1951: Goodbye, My Fancy. 1952: The Half-Breed. 1954: The Secret of the Incas. 1968: Holloway's

Daughters (TV). 1970: Vanished (TV). 1972: All My Darling Daughters (TV). 1973: My Darling Daughters' Anniversary (TV). 1977: The Father Knows Best Christmas Reunion (TV). 1978: Little Women (TV). 1984: The Return of Marcus Welby MD (TV).

YOUNG, Roland 1887–1953

Huffly-snuffly, apologetic, moustachioed British-born actor with a wisp of brown hair, who was almost always beautifully bewildered, and deservedly became a star character actor, his best run coming from 1935 to 1941, years in which he played the ghost-beset banker Topper three times. For the first of the series, Young was nominated for an Academy Award.

1922: Sherlock Holmes (GB: Moriarty). 1923: Fog Bound. Grit. 1929: The Unholy Night. Her Private Life. 1930: Madam Satan. Wise Girl. New Moon. The Bishop Murder Case. 1931: The Squaw Man (GB: The White Man). The Prodigal. The Sin of Madelon Claudet (GB: The Lullaby). The Guardsman. Don't Bet on Women. Annabelle's Affairs. Pagan Lady. This is the Night. 1932: Wedding Rehearsal. A Woman Commands. Street of Women. Lovers Courageous. One Hour with You. 1933: Pleasure Cruise. They Just Had to Get Married. His Double Life. A Lady's Profession. Blind Adventure. 1934: Here is My Heart. 1935: David Copperfield. Ruggles of Red Gap. 1936: The Man Who Could Work Miracles. Gypsy. The Unguarded Hour. One Rainy Afternoon. Give Me Your Heart (GB: Sweet Aloes). 1937: King Solomon's Mines. Call It a Day. Ali Baba Goes to Town. Topper. 1938: Sailing Along. The Young in Heart. 1939: The Night of Nights. Topper Takes a Trip. Here I Am, a Stranger. Yes, My Darling Daughter. 1940: Star Dust. He Married His Wife. Dulcy. The Philadelphia Story. Irene. Private Affairs. No, No, Nanette. 1941: Two Faced Woman. Topper Returns. The Flame of New Orleans. 1942: Tales of Manhattan. The Lady Has Plans. They All Kissed the Bride. 1943: Forever and a Day. 1944: Standing Room Only. 1945: And Then There Were None (GB: Ten Little Niggers). 1948: Bond Street. You Gotta Stay Happy. 1949: The Great Lover. 1950: Let's Dance. 1951: St Benny the Dip (GB: Escape If You Can). 1953: That Man from Tangier.

ZETTERLING, Mai 1925—
Blonde Swedish actress with waif-like qualities but sexy sea-green eyes. Came to Britain
after the international success of *Frenzy* and
brought grace, intelligence and a sense of
humour to assignments that were often rather
dreary or mere decoration. Remained a major
star until the late fifties, then became a director for a few years, with considerable critical
success.
*1941: Lasse-Maja. 1943: Jag Dräpte. 1944:
Hets/Frenzy. Prins Gustaf. 1946: Iris och
Löjtnantshjärta (GB: Iris). Driver Dagg,
Faller Regn. 1947: Frieda. Musuk: Mörker
(GB: Night is My Future). 1948: Nu Börjar
Livet. Quartet. Portrait from Life (US: The
Girl in the Painting). 1949: The Bad Lord
Byron. The Lost People. The Romantic Age
(US: Naughty Arlette). 1950: Blackmailed.
1951: Hell is Sold Out. 1952: Tall Headlines.
The Ringer. 1953: Desperate Moment. 1954:
Knock on Wood. Dance Little Lady. 1955: A
Prize of Gold. 1956: Ent Dockhem. 1957:
Seven Waves Away (US: Abandon Ship!).
Giftas. 1958: The Truth about Women. Lek pa
Regnbågen (GB: The Rainbow Game). 1959:
Jet Storm. 1960: Faces in the Dark. Piccadilly
Third Stop. Offbeat. 1961: Only Two Can
Play. 1962: The Man Who Finally Died. The*
*Main Attraction. 1963: The Bay of Saint
Michel (US: Pattern for Plunder). 1965:
Lianbron.*

As director: *1963: The War Game. 1964:
Alskande Par/Loving Couples. 1966: Night
Games. 1967: Doktor Glas. 1968: The
Girls/Flickorna. 1972: Vincent the Dutchman.
1973: Visions of Eight (co-directed). 1982:
Scrubbers.*

ZIEMANN, Sonja 1925—
Vivaciously pretty, dark-haired German
actress who came to films as a teenager, survived working during the Nazi years, and
later made several forays into the international
market, most notably when she was recruited
by Britain's Rank Organisation to play a sexy
Hungarian maid in *Made in Heaven*. The British connection didn't last, and she was based
in Germany for the remainder of her career.
*1942: Ein Windstross. 1943: Die Jungfern vom
Bischofsberg. Geliebte Schatz. 1944: Eine kleine
Sommermelodie. Freunde. Hundstage. Spuk im
Schloss. 1945: Eine reizende Familie. Liebe
nach Noten. 1946: Sag' die Wahrheit. 1947:
Herzkönig. Wege im Zwielicht. 1948: Nichts
als Zufälle. 1949: Die Freunde meine Frau.
Nach Regen scheint Sonne. Nächte am Nil. Um
eine Nasenlänge. Eine Nacht in Séparée. 1950:
Maharadscha wider Willin. Schwarz-
waldmädel/Girl of the Black Forest. Die lustigen
Weiber von Windsor/The Merry Wives of
Windsor. Schön muss man sein. Die Frauen des
Herrn S. 1951: Grün ist die Heide. Johannes
und die 13 Schönheitsköniginnen. 1952: Die
Diebin von Bagdad. Alle kann ich nicht
heiraten. Am Brunnen vor dem Tore. Made in
Heaven. 1953: Mit 17 beginnt das Leben. Die
Privatsekretärin. Hollandmädel. 1954: Bei Dir
war es immer so schön. Die sieben Kleider der
Katrin. La tzarévitch. Meine Schwester und
Ich/My Sister and I. 1955: Liebe ohne Illusion.
Grosse Stern-Parade. Ich war ein hässliches
Mädchen. Mädchen ohne Grezen. 1956: Das
Bad auf der Tenne. Dany, bitte schreiben sie.
Opernball. Nichs als Ärger mit der Liebe. Kais-*
*erball. 1957: Die Zürcher Verlobung. Frühling
in Berlin. Tabarin. Die grosse Sünde. Frauen-
arzt Dr Bertram. 1958: Der achte Wochentag
(GB: Eighth Day of the Week). Hunde, wollt
ihr ewig leben! (GB: Battle Inferno). Gli ital-
iani sono matti. Serenade au Texas. 1959: Liebe
auf Krummen Beinen. Menschen im Hotel.
Abschied von den Wolken. Strafbataillon 999
(GB: March to the Gallows). 1960: Nacht viel
über Gotenhafen. Au voleur. 1961: The Secret
Ways. A Matter of WHO. Affaire Nabob.
Denn das Weib ist schwach. Traum von Lieschen
Müller. 1962: Journey into Nowhere. Ihr
schönster Tag. Axel Munthe, der Arzt von San
Michèle. Der Tod fahrt mit. 1964: Frühstück
mit dem Tod. 2×2 im Himmelblatt. 1965:
Murder by Proxy. 1968: The Bridge at
Remagen. 1969: De Sade.*

ZIMBALIST, Efrem Jr 1918–
Dark, well-built American actor who plays
solid, reliable (even a shade dull) types. The
son of a famous concert violinist, his early
acting career was interrupted by distinguished
war service and the death of his first wife,
as well as a period devoted to writing and
researching musicology. From the late 1950s
there were a few films as he returned to acting
full time, but much TV as leading man,
including 16 consecutive seasons on the two
crime series *77 Sunset Strip* and *The FBI*.
*1949: House of Strangers. 1957: Bombers B-
52 (GB: No Sleep Till Dawn). Band of Angels.
Execution Night (TV. GB: cinemas). The Deep
Six. 1958: Violent Road. Girl on the Run.
Hell's Highway. Home Before Dark. Too
Much, Too Soon. 1960: The Crowded Sky.
1961: A Fever in the Blood. By Love Possessed.
The Chapman Report. 1965: The Reward.
Harlow (Carol Lynley version). 1967: Cosa
Nostra: an Arch Enemy of the FBI (TV. GB:
cinemas). Wait Until Dark. 1974: Airport
1975. 1975: Who is the Black Dahlia? (TV).
1979: Terror Out of the Sky (TV). A Family
Upside Down (TV). The Gathering, Part One
(TV). 1980: The Gathering, Part Two (TV).
1983: Shooting Stars (TV).*